The Theoretical man should know 'WHY'
The Practical man should know 'HOW'
The man who would guide should know 'WHY' and 'HOW'

Lectures on

MANAGEMENT ACCOUNTANCY

AF633416

Lectures on

MANAGEMENT ACCOUNTANCY

Principles, System, and Practice

A Textbook on Management Accountancy

Prof. Dr B K Basu

MCom, PhD, DLitt, FBIM, FFA (London)

Prof. of Commerce, University of Calcutta

New Central Book Agency (P) Ltd

LONDON

HYDERABAD ERNAKULAM BHUBANESWAR

DELHI KOLKATA PUNE

NCBA

REGD OFFICE
8/1 Chintamoni Das Lane, Kolkata 700 009, India
email: ncbapvtltd@eth.net

OVERSEAS
NCBA (UK) Ltd, 149 Park Avenue North, Northampton, NN3 2HY, UK
email: ncbauk@yahoo.com

EXPORT
NCBA Exports Pvt. Ltd, 212 Shahpur Jat, New Delhi 110 049
email: ncbaexp@ncbapvtltd.com

BRANCHES

208B Peacock Lane, Shahpur Jat
New Delhi 110 049
email: ncbadel@ncbapvtltd.com

House No. 3-1-315, 1st Floor
Nimboliadda, Kachiguda, **Hyderabad** 500 027
email: ncbahydb@ncbapvtltd.com

Shop Nos. 3 & 4, Vinayak Towers
681/B Budhwar Peth, Appa Balwant Chowk
Pune 411 002
email: ncbapune@ncbapvtltd.com

GSS Shopping Complex, 1st Floor
Opposite College Post Office, Convent Road
Ernakulam 682 035
email: ncbaernk@ncbapvtltd.com

Shop No. 15, Bharati Towers, Ground Floor
Forest Park, **Bhubaneswar** 751 001
email: ncbabub@ncbapvtltd.com

LECTURES ON MANAGEMENT ACCOUNTANCY

© Copyright reserved by B K Basu

Publication, Distribution, and Promotion Rights reserved by the Publisher

All rights reserved. No part of the text in general, and the figures, diagrams, page layout, and cover design in particular, may be reproduced or transmitted in any form or by any means—electronic, mechanical, photocopying, recording, or by any information storage and retrieval system—without the prior written permission of the Publisher

First Published: October 1971
Revised and Enlarged **Central Edition**: January 2008
Reprinted: January 2012

PUBLISHER
New Central Book Agency (P) Ltd
8/1 Chintamoni Das Lane, Kolkata 700 009

TYPESETTER
Aruna Printers, Kolkata

PRINTER
New Central Book Agency (P) Ltd
Web-Offset Division, Dhulagarh, Sankrail, Howrah

COVER DESIGNER
Soumen Paul

COVER PRINTER
Biswanath Studio, Kolkata

PROOF CHECKING
Subas Maitra

PROJECT TEAM
Mithu Karmakar, Prabhat Jas and Somenath Ganguly

ISBN 978 81 7381 736 6

Price ₹ 495.00

Dedicated to
Late Professor Satyendra Nath Sen MA, PhD (London)
Vice-Chancellor (1968-1976), Calcutta University
an ardent meditator in the Vineyard of Muses

CONTENTS IN BRIEF

PART V : DECISION ACCOUNTING

PART VI : CONTROL ACCOUNTING

CONTENTS IN DETAIL

PART I
DIMENSIONS OF ACCOUNTING

PART II
FINANCIAL ACCOUNTING

PART III
COST ACCOUNTING

PART IV

FINANCIAL MANAGEMENT

PART V
DECISION ACCOUNTING

PART VI
CONTROL ACCOUNTING

N. K. Bose, BSc, DBA
FCWA, FICWA, AMBIM, ACIS, JDIP MA
Past President
Institute of Cost and Works Accountants of India

2 Fairlie Place
Kolkata

August 17, 1971

FOREWORD

Books on Management Accountancy by Indian authors have so far been few. I am glad that Dr B. K. Basu has added one to the list.

It gives me pleasure to forward his book ***"Lectures on Management Accountancy"*** and I hope that the book will be useful to those for whom it is meant.

(N. K. Bose)

PREFACE TO THE REVISED AND ENLARGED CENTRAL EDITION

A tree is not beautiful without flowers. A writer is not perfect without readers. This revised and enlarged edition of the book ensures the writer that success is the pillar of success rather than to confirm the idea that 'failure is the pillar of success'. For this success the author congratulates the readers and hopes that their inspiring patronage will continue unabated.

This text, which is thoroughly revised and enlarged, will cater to the needs of all concerned—Students, Teachers, Research Scholars, Management Consultants and even Non-Accountants. Different syllabuses of different Indian universities as well as professional courses viz. The Institute of Chartered Accountants of India, The Institute of Cost and Works Accountants of India, The Institute of Company Secretaries of India, The Indian Institute of Bankers, different IIMs etc. have been given due regards while preparing this volume.

It is important to note that even a person having no background of accounting and finance will understand the concept of accounting and finance with the aid of this epitome because of the fact that different human behavioural aspects and different examples of day-to-day life activities are given herein to make the subject understandable.

A few new chapters — Activity-Based Costing, Portfolio Management, Transfer Pricing, Responsibility Accounting and Performance Evaluation — have been incorporated in this volume to cater to the need of the readers.

Request from my ex-students motivated me to bring out the book in the market because of the inherent characteristics of this book :

(i) Presentation in the form of conversation (not in question-answer form).

(ii) A quite classroom environment can be enjoyed without attending any classes.

(iii) Human behavioural approach can be assessed through the techniques of financial management, and

(iv) Numerous problems of different examinations have been solved.

Many of my colleagues of my department inspired me to bring out this edition. I also want to mention the names of Dr Pran Gopal Bhattacharya, Dr S. Sarbadhikari, Mr Amitabha Sen, Director of New Central Book Agency (P) Ltd, Dr Pankaj Kr. Bose and Dr Abani Mukherjee. My heartiest blessing will go to Ram Prahlad Choudhary of Bankim Sarder College, Prabir Dutta of S. R. Fatepuria College and Anulekha Banerjee of St Xavier's College without whose active participation in collecting materials from different libraries, proof-reading and preparing index, the book could not see the light of the day.

Last but not least my blessings should go to my daughter Chayanika Basu, who sacrificed the presence of her father for writing this book, after the demise of her mother Suparna Basu.

I request the readers for constructive suggestions for further improvement of this book.

Prof. Dr B.K. Basu

Department of Commerce
University of Calcutta
Dewali 2007

PREFACE TO THE FIRST EDITION

The increasing complexities of modern Industrial and Commercial life has necessitated that accounting presentation should play a dynamic role in modern management. The aim of traditional accounting is to report operational result — Profit/Loss of the organisation. This does not cater to the needs of the decision-makers. That a company earns higher profit and pays higher dividend should not be the basis of assaying organisational efficiency; on the other hand, a company with lower profit margin and inability to pay higher dividend cannot be regarded as less productive. Since, payment of higher dividends and lower dividends are both equally a problem to management. Payment of higher dividends depending on inflationary profits leads to 'erosion of real capital'. Similarly, a fall in the rate of dividend, on the other hand, may sometimes indicate managerial inefficiency or tendency to plough-back sufficient profit at the cost of the shareholders' interest or a tendency to retain profit at higher doses for the future expansion programmes.

It is sometimes reported that accounting systems do not sufficiently aid management in arriving at its decision. 'If accountancy were an airplane in full flight, its location could be determined from certain facts such as longitude, latitude, altitude, compass-bearing, wind-drift, true course. The techniques of navigation are not available for orienting accounting in relation to its surroundings'. However, that accounting system do not aid management sufficiently does not mean that the system is defective—it is due to the inefficiency on the part of those who handle it.

The processes of profitability are Directing, Coordinating, Control and Motivation. These processes fail to achieve its objective if the same are not supported by plan, fact and control. It should be noted in this context that accounting systems contribute much to all the processes mentioned above. However, if the accounting systems are to be utilised for the benefits of the managerial needs, it should be designed to fit all the changing conditions of the business, as well as of the society. Because, 'Accounting is a practical commonsense discipline. However, this does not mean that a clear thinking is not required. We do, indeed, require the coolest, most clear-headed survey of our dogma'.

However, the whole system of accounting can be classified as :

(1) Custodial Accounting.

(2) Responsibility Accounting; and

(3) Decision Accounting.

Custodial Accounting is nothing but Financial Accounting which attempts to report the operating result during a year, as well as the position of assets and liabilities at a particular date. This only caters to the needs of the shareholders and not the management.

Responsibility Accounting has been introduced to avoid the possible shortcomings arising from Custodial Accounting. This is only to avoid the possible losses arising from mishandling the financial data and to boost up the performance strategy of the business. Take for an example, Financial Accounting does not stress too much emphasis on whether a particular expenditure is justifiable or not. It attempts to assist the management by reporting the results at regular intervals and at different levels of activitiy. Thus the main characteristic of Responsibility Accounting is to measure the responsibility of actual performance against planned performance.

It is a fact that 'many important data for managerial use are beyond the ability of accountancy to supply—for example, market demand, status of competition, general business conditions, engineering design, personnel informantion, legal regulations and limitations'. Decision Accounting has been originated to fulfil managerial needs by providing the said important data which normal accounting fails to supply. So it is a system of accounting which evaluates alternative course of action as to the following : Planning for Profit, Product Pricing, Inventory Policies, etc.

The term 'management accounting' implies the systems of accounting which are to be designed for the benefit of management needs. The question of 'management' arises only when there are some problems; or it may arise for the improvement and smooth running of the existing system to avoid the possible problems that may enter in the process of management. If the Management Accountants are not aware of the existing or the possible financial and management problems that may enter in the process of management the study of management accountancy and the role of the Management Accountants in their respective capacities will be useless. The book *Lectures on Management Accountancy* has been written embracing all the discussions made earlier.

However, the students of today will be 'Decision-makers' of tomorrow. If the students do not get sufficient training at the initial stage and cannot think within themselves for the subject in which they are interested, in the long run they will be crowned with 'bony' decisions. Lack of original and independent thinking makes one the 'puppet' of others. This book has been written following a long survey on the students' psychology. This book will give them some light for the innovation of new ideas and techniques. This book, first of its kind in approach, which is written in a dialogue form, will be helpful to Managers, Management Consultants, Teachers, Research Scholars and even to Non-Accountants.

The author owes his gratitude to various authors such as Professor Sitalacharan Sengupta, Dr Batty, Professors Brown and Howard, Professors Gordon and Shillinglaw, Professor Roy, Dr Bogen, Professor Anthony, Professors Broad and Carmichael, Mr Wheldon and others from whose works the author has taken so many ideas for his treatise.

The author is under a deep debt of gratitude to Mr N. K. Bose, the past President of The Institute of Cost and Works Accountants of India for his kindness to contribute a Foreword to this work.

The author wishes to acknowledge his indebtedness to Dr A. K. Sur, MA, DSc (Econ), Director, Institute of Company Affairs, for his advice for the improvement of a few chapters of this book.

The author is pleased to put on record his best wishes to Professor Goldberg of Melbourne University, Australia, Dr Johan Marsh, Director-General, British Institute of Management, London, Prof. S. C. Sengupta, Prof. S. N. Banerjee, Prof. D. K. Banerjee, Prof. K. P. Roy, Prof. A. K. Nandy, Prof. S. K. Chakraborty, Prof. B. Dey, Prof. R. Chakraborty of Calcutta University, Mr R. N. Bhaduri, and Mr D. K. Bose of the State Bank of India, Calcutta, in return of their inspiration and encouragement when the book was on the verge of completion.

Though the author sometimes felt vexation on the constant and untiring approach of Mr Manabendra Nath Dutta of N. M. Roychowdhury Co. (P) Ltd to complete the manuscript immediately, the author now recognises his sincere endeavours without which the early publication of this book would not have been possible.

It would really be unjust if the name of Mr Sukhendu Sengupta of M/s S. C. Sengupta and Company is not mentioned here who helped the author by providing so many journals of the subject from different sources.

Last but not least, the author does not like to express any formal gratitude to his wife Suparna Basu for her assistance in proof-reading and preparing indexes.

The author welcomes constructive criticisms and suggestions from all quarters for future improvement of the book.

Department of Commerce
Calcutta University
October 18, 1971
Dewali

B. K. Basu

PART I

DIMENSIONS OF ACCOUNTING

"Every fundamental inquiry, whether in the fields of science or of philosophy, starts out from at least one notion belonging uniquely to its own field which it is compelled to leave undefined...

Examples of characteristic notions of this sort include : for arithmetic number; for geometry point; for physics force; for astronomy space; for biology life; for psychology consciousness; for logic thinking; for ethics goodness; for aesthetics beauty; for music consonance; for law justice; for government equality; for economics values;" for management accounting...?

1

INTRODUCTION TO MANAGEMENT ACCOUNTANCY

• Good morning! I welcome to you all on the firstday of my lecture on **'Management Accountancy'.** Well, before I would dwell on the definition of management accountancy and its relevant aspects, let me forward the subject in a form of introduction.

Vision of Business

You see, the study of different aspects of management accountancy —such as definition, nature, scope and span of application—will not be sophisticated unless we realise the fact that accounting is a 'vision' of business. Since accounting furnishes the 'eyes' through which business and administration 'see'. Thus, accounting furnishes information which are the basis of initiating and executing the business strategy, policy and control.

Language of Business

Moreover, accounting is a language of business—language as to solvency, profitability, efficiency and health of business, i.e. Over-Capitalization, Under-Capitalization etc. which are the basis of management accounting. Unless the language is clearly explained or clarified, the basic philosophy of business, the maximisation of profit—or, in other words, maximisation of wealth of the owner of the business, as well as extending its services for the benefit of the society—may not be realised. Most important factor is the 'purpose' for which the language is used. Particular language may bring some tangible result in a particular case but not in all cases. This is because of the dynamic nature of the business world, where change in our business environment is so common-place that we take little care of it, unless spectacular or dramatic. Change may be for the better or worse.

Navigation in Accounting

To avoid worst business problems and to bring about an improvement on existing business conditions, some dynamic concept in the 'technique' of language should be imparted which should be cut to size as circumstances dictate or should be tailored to fit each circumstance. Since, the sequence of language applications may have some direct and far-reaching effects on the profitability of an enterprise, Management Accounting is a 'specific' business language designed to attain some 'specific' purpose.

Obviously, a business is controlled by the use of information collected from accounting records and reports. For this it should not be assumed that all accountings—Financial, Cost, and Responsibility Accounting, whatever sense they contain, are management accounting. Each of them has, in fact, got independent entity not exactly related to the essential character of management accounting itself. All these branches of accounting are to be 'integrated' for orienting accounting in relation to its surrounding which is composed of so many internal and external problems.

It is a fact that no accounting statement, whether it is financial or cost, has any amount of managerial value by the mere fact of its existence; it must be scrutinised, reviewed, analysed and interpreted before the information contained therein are available for managerial use. That general accounting system can not cope with the varied business problems was felt by Professor A.C. Littleton when he was found to express his view that—"the techniques of navigation are not available for orienting accounting in relation to surroundings."[1] Besides, it has been felt by the accountants[2] that meagre attention has been focused to the purposes served by accounting. Thus, to tackle adverse business problems and to navigate 'system of accounting' in relation to its surroundings, moreover, for designing accounting, the language of business, for some specific purpose, the idea of management accounting can be conceived of. And the 'navigator' of the system may be termed as 'Management Accountant'.

Accountant's Responsibility

Thus the development of management accounting arises mainly from the demand of business—to solve business and accounting problems. Here management accounting may be considered as a basis of informing and enforcing business policy and control. However, it is a fact that it is not an easy task on the part of the navigator, i.e. the Management Accountant*, to direct the accounting system. For that is needed a man of dynamic personality. This is because the management has to depend largely on the efficiency of the accountant.

Management Accountant's Meditation

The Manager formerly heavily relied upon *intuition* and *personal observations* to supplement the limited financial data available from the accounts; but now function of gathering, analysing and interpreting a broad range of economic information are extensively delegated to the accountant. For this the management accountant should be well-aware of the different types of problems related to management, control and accounting. He should have thorough knowledge about different accounting concepts such as business entity concept, money measurement concept, cost concept and going concern concept etc. He should have an ability to test the soil of business environment under which a business is likely to operate.

Moreover, the management accountant should have an analytical mind and an insight into the causes of the following queries :

- Why should change be enforced in the accounting system?
- What are the factors which necessitated the great development of accounting in modern times?
- What are the multiplicity of causes which, from practical point of view contribute to the introduction of management accounting?

---

[1] ***Structure of Accounting Theory**, P. 1.*

[2] *"Relatively little attention has been given to the purposes served by accounting" —Walter B. Mcfarland. "I have searched accounting literature and have talked to persons well-informed on this subject and cannot find in any place (1) a clear statement of the purposes and objectives of accounting. (2) a statement of the basic standards (whether they are called postulates, concepts or something else) that effect the purposes and objectives, or (3) a testing of existing principles and practices against such standards. Many well-informed lawyer, bankers and other businessmen find it difficult to comprehend the fact that this has never been done by the accounting profession" —George R. Catlett, **"A New Approach to Creative & Constructive Accounting Research"**, Arthur Anderson Chronicle, P. 463.*

* *In some cases Management Accountant is termed 'Controller'.*

Well, what should be the essential qualifications of management accountant and what part should be played by him in the dynamic nature of business world, will be discussed in the subsequent chapter. Now I would like to discuss the problems of business and the services rendered by the management accounting system to tackle it.

Need for Management Accounting

It has been stated earlier that a business has to face many problems, internal and external. The interaction of different administrative and management processes—such as organising, planning, directing, motivating, controlling etc.—has invited management with many problems and complications—problems as to planning for profit, product design, status of competition, cash management etc. Lack of proper guidance to any one of the aforesaid processes may discount the profitability of a business or enterprise. Here we may have at a glance the controlling problem arising from interaction of different process, as mentioned earlier, if we take a note of Prof. Sheldon's remark.

Professor Sheldon in his book '*Philosophy of Management*' explained the controlling problem as "organisation is the formation of an effective machine; management of an effective executive; administration of an effective direction; administration determines the organisation; management uses it. Administration defines the goal; management strives towards it. Organisation is the machine of management in its achievements of ends determined by administration".

Anyway, coordination is necessary among different processes to tackle the problems. There is no denying the fact, as pointed out earlier, that coordination among various processes through mere general accounting is quite impossible. It is a fact that "many important data for managerial use are beyond the ability of accountancy to supply—for example market demand, status of competition, general business conditions, engineering design, personnel information, legal regulations and limitations."[3]

Managerial accounting has been originated to fulfil managerial needs by providing the said important data which normal accounting fails to supply. Indeed, management or managerial accounting is a specialised course of study which attempts to solve most of the problems the business faces, and to assist the management in coordinating the various processes of management by generating needed information. The main aim of managerial accounting is either to tackle adverse business situations and problems or to overcome the possible defects which might peep through the process of management, or both.

How managerial accounting manages business problems and how it attempts to solve the business and managerial problems with the aid of different techniques, will be taken up for discussion afterwards. Before that I would like to discuss the nature of management accounting and the principal needs which accounting serves to the modern world of business.

Accounting as Man-made Art

You are well aware that management has to take day to day, hour to hour and even minute to minute management decisions, thanks to changing conditions of business environment. 'Precision' in the area of managerial decision is possible only when management is well-informed about the accounting records and reports. It should be noted that the function of accounting is to report time to time on the operating conditions of business; since accounting records and reports are the basis of any forecast which assists in formulating budgets and standard of operation. It is the means through which operations are checked and results are reported.

---

[3] *Littleton, op cit, P. 22.*

Future planning and control of any enterprise depends on how far accounting is able to identify its pupose. It is a fact that the design of accounting, i.e. information system, starts with the identification of respective problems. By the by, here I would like to mention the remarks—made by the *National Association of Accountants*—that "accounting is a man-made art, designed to aid men in achieving certain aims. It does not exist apart from human purposes and does not make sense unless viewed in the light of ends to be served"[4]. Well, what harm is there if the said man-made art is subject to change as demanded by the business as well as society?

However, I was discussing with you about accounting records and reports. What are accounting records and reports will be taken up for discussion in details in the respective chapters on 'Accounting Ratios and Interpretation of Financial Statement' and 'Reporting'. In this context I would like to mention that, in general, by accounting records and reports we mean annual records and reports needed to take some business decision. But if management takes its decision depending on annual records and reports, it would definitely be an unwise policy on its part; since change is the order of the business environment. This 'static' or a 'snapshot' of the annual records and reports would misguide the management in its formulation of plan and policy. That is why we are to depend time to time on accounting records and reports to arrive at correct decision. Here we can feel the dynamic nature of management accountancy. Here management can feel the importance of periodical Fund Flow Statement, Cash Flow Statement, Cash Forecast, Cash Budget etc. which may be considered as 'top management report'. Accordingly, management can take a decision as to a proposal—whether a particular proposal as to the replacement of existing machine or purchase of a new one—will be profitable or not. All these points will be discussed in details afterwards under the head of 'Investment Decision'.

For the time being I want to make clear one more point—if management can understand beforehand what cash is needed, say in the month of June of a year, then a number of alternatives can be chosen to face the adverse situation. This is possible only when management is well-informed about month to month, day to day reports regarding business condition and situation. Similarly, if management is able to know beforehand, with the aid of different information systems, the causes which might necessitate some changes in the capital structure or which might cause 'erosion of real capital' of the business, a suitable solution in the matter can be conceived of.

Media of Management Accounting

You see, it is not an easy job to arrive at any concrete management decision unless it is accentuated on some aids or medias. So certain medias or tools are necessary to reach the target. These are forecasting, planning for profit, standard costing, business budgets and budgetary control etc. All these aspects would be discussed when needed.

Centre of Gravity for Management Accounting

By the by, I would like to give you some ideas which are very important for your understanding of the inner thought of management accounting principles. You have already noted the name of Professor Littleton. Well, Littleton, who happens to be the pioneer in explaining the principles of accounting by the idea of 'centre of gravity for accounting', says "there must be some basic concept which makes accounting different from all other methods of quantitative analysis, there must be some central idea which expresses better than others the objectives, effects results, ends, aims that are characteristic of accounting—'a centre of gravity' so to speak"[5] are financial statement, assets, capital and income. The

[4] ***"Objectives and Methods of Research in Management Accounting"***, NNA Bulletin, P. 32.

[5] *Littleton, op cit, P. 18.*

discussions so far made resemble the concept of the 'centre of gravity for accounting'. The centres of gravity for accounting are the related concepts of management accounting. To locate the centre of gravity for accounting is not an easy task. Because, opinions regarding proper assessment and preserving the integrity of the centres as mentioned earlier, may vary from accountant to accountant. For that is needed trained accountants who should possess adequate knowledge of the computation of accounting income and statement under which business operate. To locate properly the centres is definitely a sign of efficiency on the part of the management accountant. At present there is a large demand for trained and successful accountants who are in a position to control the major operations of an enterprise. Most often operational problems relate to marketing and financial problems, that is to say purchasing, manufacturing, selling and controlling of finance. Besides the problems of marketing and finance, what more actuate is control and coordination. The proper success of any enterprise depends on how all the departments are 'integrated', 'coordinated' and'controlled'. The success of an enterprise may, to a greater extent, be assured if the techniques of 'Budgets and Budgetary Control' and standard costing are introduced in the processes of management. That is to say, co-ordination and control through Budgets and Budgetary Control. Here I like to refer you to a few of my paper and articles[6] on Budgeting. These, along with other relevant aspects of budget and budgetary control, will be discussed in subsequent chapters under respective heads.

Need for Accounting

Besides coordinating and controlling in the area of business and financial management, the Management Accountant has to play a vital role to overcome the difficulties arising from the threat of rising prices. The Management Accountant, thus, holds a key position upon whose negligence the 'integrity' of the business may be jeopardised; the lack of alertness and foresight on his part may tend the business towards 'erosion of real capital' unnoticed. This aspect of management accounting will be discussed in the chapter on "Accounting for Inflation".

Well, before explaining the different components of management accounting I would like to explain the principal needs which accounting serves in the world of business. Since, as has been stated earlier, that any attempt to study management accounting may loose its simplicity unless the services of accounting are taken care of.

The accounting serves the world of business in the following ways :

(i) Maintaining proper accounting and financial records.

(ii) Helping the top management in the application of budgets and budgetary control by providing different accounting and financial data.

(iii) Supplying pertinent information to the concerning authorities who are in charge of managerial control.

(iv) Advising management in the formulation of plan and policy on the basis of interpretation of various facts such as valuation of assets, determination of income etc.

(v) Coordinating the activities of various departments by furnishing accounting and financial reports to all heads of the department.

---

[6] ***'Business Budgets to Guide Management Decision'***
(A Paper read at XXIII *All India Commerce Conference held at Kerala).*
How Business Budget can help in Taking Management Decision—I
How Budgeting can Ensure Financial Viability of an Enterprise—II
*(Both articles appeared in **'Capital'** on 29.4.71 and 6.5.71)*

(vi) Comparing the actual performances with the set standards and its diagnosis for the cause of variance.

After reviewing all the points on how accounting serves the modern world, I once again repeat the discussions made at the outset of this chapter, that internal and external problems withhold the progress of the business. In the same context I discussed the controlling problems of management refering to the view of Prof. Sheldon. However, complacency in the study of management accounting may not be realised unless a clear idea about management problems is obtained beforehand. You perhaps remember that, I discussed earlier that management accounting has originated out of the demand of the business which has to tackle the problems of management. If you want to be well-acquainted with the 'concept' of managerial accounting it may not be realised unless you have a clear idea about management problems. Then only will your study of management accounting be concrete. The nature and extent of problems runs parallel to the purpose or objects of management. In that sense, perhaps, American Technical Society envisaged the following as being the management problems :

Management Problems

(a) Management must conduct the activities of the enterprise in such a way as to produce commodities and services that will find a ready market at a favourable price.

(b) Management must coordinate the activities of the various departments so that they will not be working at cross-purposes.

(c) Management must earn adequate profits to ensure a fair return on the Capital invested in the enterprise and to perpetuate it along normal lines of growth and expansion.

(d) Management must secure the proper division of labour in the operations so as to afford largest returns on the efforts expended; it must also secure and retain the cooperation and goodwill of the workers.

(e) Management must conduct training courses for the employees with the view of promotion, and in this manner ensure hearty cooperation from the employees and, at the same time, be assured of managerial ability when needed.

The problem before the present-day management is to earn adequate profit over and above cost of capital (both equity and debt). For this many authors have used the term of (EVA)—Economic Value Added.

However, there is no doubt that the function of accounting department is to assist management by providing needed data in the execution of plan and policy; but it has been stated earlier, from the subjective point of view, that some changes are to be introduced in the accounting system with a view to navigating the accounting system in relation to its surroundings, to design accounting for some 'specific' purpose, and to solve the management problems arising out of the execution of management objectives. It is to be noted that to overcome the above major problems of management, is needed the assistance of a few pertinent information—market demand, status of competition and legal regulations etc.—which normal accounting fails to supply.[7] So some changes in the existing accounting is called for the smooth running of the business.

Need for Change in Accounting Principles

However, from the objective point of view accounting changes appear to be arising to meet the following needs :

(i) For measuring uncertainty and risk, in all types of investment decision.

[7] *See Note 3.*

(ii) For determining and achieving the level of accuracy needed for accounting data.

(iii) For determining the work related to cost determinations and to segregate them into suitable parts.

(iv) For ascertaining important changes in the state of equality of cost so that random fluctuations in the level of cost can confidently be avoided.

(v) For planning accounting project and to revise the same whenever needed.

(vi) For implementing the concept of 'man-management', i.e. how to use the staff of the organisation as efficiently as possible.

(vii) For meeting the demand of the society.

(viii) For avoiding the conflict that exists between the tax rules and accounting principles.[8]

And the divergence of taxable income from the reported net income has set the accounting profession one of the toughest problems.[9]

You see, it has been stated earlier that accounting is a man-made art and it makes no sense unless it serves man.[10] Well, that man-made art should be subject to change as necessitated by the demand of the society. However, changes in accounting method are taking place in most of the progressive companies—both in India and abroad—with a view to reducing cost of producing accounting information and to make better use of available information. By the by, in the context of change in the method of accounting, I would like to refer to you two examples regarding 'change' 'in the principles of accounting'.

If you are interested, only then I can explain—

● Do you like to hear?

☐ "Yes, yes, sir, kindly enlighten us".

●. Well, I have something to tell you in connection with the change in accounting principles—one arising from conversion of loan capital into equity capital; and the other arising from recording of goodwill.

Regarding conversion of loan into equity, you see, an obvious dilemma was found to exist in the mid-1970s in India whether loan capital should be converted to equity capital?

Conversion of Loan into Equity

The fact was that the Industrial Finance Corporation took the decision to convert loans or overdue interests into equity of six companies which borrowed from it Rs. 4 crores. An attempt was made at that time to counteract the decision by maintaining that "in principle such conversion cannot be recommended...by arbitrarily exercising the right of conversion, the Government has shaken the confidence in equity. It is also difficult to understand how lending institutions will be benefitted from such conversions. Good companies will not agree to conversion."

---

[8] *Paton and Dixon, "Essential of Accounting", P. 494.*

[9] *Ross, "The Elusive Art of Accounting", P. 107.*

[10] *See Note 4.*

Change in Accounting Principles on the Ground of Social Needs

Well, you see, at that time I felt that no harm will be there if the man-made art, i.e. the principles of accounting, is adjusted or altered on the ground of greater benefit of the society. So, in my article entitled "Impact of Conversion of Loan into Equity on Company Finance"[11], I expressed my view that 'it is an abnormal situation where a company fails to pay interest due to the lending institutions. The objectives of financing institution is to lend money to earn a return. If a company cannot earn profit to pay interest to lending institutions and dividends to the ordinary and equity shareholders, there remains no difference between the properties of loan capital and equity capital. Besides, it is not a good company which fails to pay interest to the lending institutions regularly. The Government of India will be taking its decision against those companies which overdue their interests. In principle, the conversion of loan into equity cannot be recommended, but the principles of accounting are being changed on the grounds of social needs. There is no hard and fast rule that the principles of accounting should not be changed. For that is needed a close comparison between two situations—benefits expected to be enjoyed as a result of change and unchanged condition. For that, an expert[12] in the line held "accounting is a practical, commonsense discipline. However, this does not mean that a clear thinking is not required. We do indeed require the coolest, most clear headed survey of our dogma." So the decision taken by the Government of India is a right step towards the conservation of social capital. Because, direct government participation is a guarantee against expected liquidation of companies.

Goodwill vs Earning Ratio

Regarding 'goodwill' I am to say that a change should be brought in the existing principles of recorded goodwill, if the management accountant is to take a right step in calculating the profitability ratio such as earning per share, dividend per share ratio etc. As a matter of fact, whenever capital or aggregate of the fixed assets is the antecedent or the consequent of a ratio, the fundamental question that would arise in the mind of a management accountant or financial analyst is whether recorded goodwill would be included or excluded. The situation becomes all the more difficult when accountants are at controversy[13] as to the justification for recorded goodwill being added to, or excluded from a particular antecedent or consequent. This controversy arises as a result of basic and inherent defect of recorded goodwill—that recording to goodwill follows the overstatement of initial share capital of business. Besides, recorded goodwill, which results in the overstatement of nominal value of share capital, is invariably recognised by analysts while making ratio analysis. As for instance, as stated earlier, at the time of finding out earning ratio, goodwill and other intangibles are always deducted from the book values of share capital, proprietary capital, as the case may be. But this allowance is never made when 'yield per share' is calculated on the overstated nominal value of share capital. Naturally, the yield per share cannot be expected to be incommensurate with the corresponding earning ratio, though, in fitness of things, this should have been so. This nonuniformity in the stated ratio will misguide the investor and others who are interested in the financial

Recording of Goodwill follows overstatement of Initial Nominal Value of Share Capital

Accounting through 'Trial & Error' Method

---

[11] ***'Capital'** 17th Dec 1970, Pp. 1043-1044.*

[12] *Ross, op cit, P. 20.*

[13] *Yorston, Smyth and Brown—**Advanced Accounting**, 4th Ed. (1959), Vol. 2, P. 372.*

statement. It should be noted in this context that "since accounting has evolved over many years through trial and error, it should be continuously improved on the basis that is responsive to the requirements of those groups in our society who use the end product—financial statement"[14]. However, to avoid the adverse effect of recorded goodwill, following the overstatement of nominal value of initial share capital and to settle the controversies that exist among accountants, and to bring about an uniformity in the presentation of accounts, it is suggested that 'recorded' goodwill should be recorded against share premium* account[15]. It is strongly recommended that if the existing provision of Companies Act cannot be interpreted to allow the same, that is, recording of goodwill against share premium account, a suitable amendment in the Companies Act may very well be called for.[16] This device will definitely cure the basic and inherent defects of goodwill as stated earlier as well as controversies among accountants. As a result of it, the investor may get a true and fair view of the earning ratio and 'yield' ratio; which is calculated on the inflated value of share capital following the recording of goodwill.

Recording of Goodwill against Security Premium Account

Need for Amendment of Companies Act

I think you have followed my lecture. Is there any question please?

☐ "Sir, is there anything worth noting in regard to Goodwill?"

● Yes, there is. For that I would request you to go through my thesis "Accounting for Goodwill and its effects on Enterprise and Social Economy." There you may get details about goodwill. You may collect the same from your library.

However, the sum and substance of the discussions made earlier is that the need for changes and development of accounting literature, the language of business, arises out of the following reasons :

Causes for Development in Accountancy

(a) Changing pattern of business environment.

(b) Demand of the society and business.

(c) Protection and right direction to investor.

(d) Increase complexities of taxation for profit.

So far what we have studied is that the management accountant should understand the causes and need for change of accounting principles and system; the knowledge of which will help him to navigate the accounting system in a better way.

I think you have followed my lecture. Do you find any interest in the 'Lecture' as well as in the subject?

☐ "Very interesting indeed. Sir! This simply excites our curiosity."

● Well, what do you want me to tell you to satisfy your curiosity? Well, please be frank if you want me to satisfy your curiosity.

---

14 *G. R. Catlett, C.P.A., **"Factors that Influence Accounting Principles"**, **The Journal of Accountancy**, Oct. 1960, P. 5.*

* *Now it is known as security premium.*

15 *Dr. B. K. Basu, **"Accounting for Goodwill"**, Ghosh Dastidar Publishing Concerns. Kolkata 9.*

16 *Ibid.*

☐ "Sir, you have pointed out earlier that the Management Accountant should have an insight as to : firstly, why change should be enforced in accounting system, secondly, what are the factors which necessitated the development of accounting, and, finally, what are the multiplicity of causes, which, from practical point of view, contribute to the introduction of management accounting? You have not given us any light in regard to the third one."

Multiplicity of Causes for the Introduction of Management Accounting

● It was a sad omission, I am really very sorry for that. Well, to explain this I would like to refer you to a part of the text of the address delivered by the then President of the Institute of Cost and Works Accountants. Mr. R. Glendinning, on the occasion of the 50th Annual General Meeting of the Institute held in London on 14th June 1969. In his lecture Mr. Glendinning cited the following multiplicity of causes which lead to the introduction of Management Accounting :

(i) Firstly, there has been an expansion in the importance of industry which has come to play a predominant part in the economies of Western countries. This situation has necessitated more and better accountancy. Moreover, besides the establishment of quite new industries, themselves causing great changes in many aspects of life, scientific research has brought into being many new matérials and processes. To mention only two examples—the chemical industry has expanded rapidly, while the advent of automation, which is gradually revolutionising industrial method, is causing great changes in the structure of industry. For these and other reasons the complexity of industrial life is increasing and—both to enable correct decisions to be taken in regard to high capital expenditures and to control effectively these new industries—it has been necessary not so much to develop new techniques as to apply the established one more intensively. For both reasons much more accountancy aimed at assisting management has been needed.

(ii) Secondly, there has been emergence of strong pressure for increased productivity and efficiency in all economic spheres : in other words, a pressure for decreased cost. This factor particularly has stimulated the production of better management accountancy and, naturally, has had the greatest impact on it.

(iii) Thirdly, there has been extension of Government influence, revealing itself—so far as management accountancy is concerned—partly through the demand for better information regarding purchases made by the State and partly in order to regulate the nation's activities in various directions.

(iv) Fourthly, the increase in internal cooperation and in the extent of assistance given by the wealthier countries to those which are less wealth—endowed demands better methods of assessing assistance projects.

(v) Finally, there has been a change in social philosophy, which demands greater material output—in part for the sake of the underdeveloped countries, in part for the sake of the underprivileged at home.'

So it is clear from the above discussions that management accounting assists management in planning, decision-making and control, by way of adopting, analysing, diagnosing and interpreting the financial statements. Well, management accounting—which is vital in the context of planned economy in India—should be introduced in the public and private sector undertakings irrespective of their size.

Oh! Yes. I have overlooked one question put by you. Can you please remind me?

☐ "Sir, what is the difference between Cost Accountant and Management Accountant?"

Relationship between Cost Accountancy and Management Accountancy

- Your question is indeed very interesting. This indicates that you have taken much interest in the subject. For your proper understanding I would like to bring your attention to a welcome address delivered by Mr. N. K. Bose, the then President of the Institute of Cost and Works Accountants of India, at a two-day seminar on Cost and Management Accounting in public sector undertakings, organised by the Institute in collaboration with the Bureau of Public Enterprise, held in Vigyan Bhavan, New Delhi on 3rd May 1969. Here Mr. Bose tried to bring an interrelationship between Cost and Management Accounting. Mr. Bose said, "Cost and Management Accounting involves presentation of accounting information in a manner that facilitates prudent planning, correct decision making and effectively controlling day to day operations."

Cost Accountants vs Management Accountants

By the by, I would like to mention that some confusion may arise in the mind of the common people, whether cost accountant is management accountant? This is because the cost accountant, in most of the cases, are found reluctant to draw a bifurcation line between the two—Cost Accountant and Management Accountant. That's why they are found to express that the title "Management Accountant" is more impressive and glamourous than the title "Cost Accountant". This should not be the case in actual practice. Needless to mention that data and information furnished by cost accountants are the basis of managerial planning and decision. One of the past Presidents of The Institute of Cost and Work Accountants of England and Wales rightly said, "Cost and works accountancy, as practised by the members of the Institute with their practical experience of costing in industry and their ability to see figures in terms of real things and real happenings, is the very stuff of management accounting". So, it does not mean, that the cost accountant, who handles the 'cost and works accountancy' which is the stuff of management accounting, is management accountant. An insight is needed to draw a bifurcation line between the two. The distinction can be made with reference to the level of management services provided by the cost accountant and management accountant. So an expert in the line suggests that "a differentiation between Cost Accountant and Management Accountant can be made only with reference to the level at which management services are provided by the two".

You see, in the light of the discussions made earlier you may put me the question, 'What factor is to be added to existing accounting functions, both financial and cost, to make it management accounting"?

Well, we have seen earlier that the functions of accounting are—

- to determine cost and profit or loss of an enterprise.
- to have a 'snap-shot' of the financial position of an enterprise; that is to say, correct evaluation of the assets and liabilities position of an enterprise and correct basis of computation of cost.
- to generate information as to cost and financial accounting to a various level of management.

You see, we have seen here, in brief, three functions of accounting—both financial and cost; well, a fourth function, which is to assist management in planning and decision making process, is to be added to the above list to make it management accounting. To illustrate it an analogy with human beings may be drawn. As you are aware, man is the gift of the God; that man sometimes becomes father, uncle, son etc. Whenever one speaks about one's father the basic thing to be observed is that the 'father' is a man. Similarly, whenever one speaks about one's son the basic thing is that the 'son' is a man. The responsibility of a father, who happens to be the guardian of a family, is higher than that of his son who is assumed to be minor or dependent. Although the 'son' and 'father' both are man but their responsibility and service function to the family will differ at their respective level. So if the responsibility and service function of the father, the guardian of the family, is assigned to the son, the son becomes the guardian of the family. Similarly, if the responsibility and service function—that is planning and decision—is assigned to the existing functions of accounting, as cited above, it becomes management accounting.

Added Function to Existing Accounting Function

So the functions of management accounting can be summed up as :

Functions of Management Accounting

(i) Determination of cost and profit or loss.

(ii) Evaluation of assets and liabilities and the process of cost.

(iii) Generating needed information for proper direction of cash managements.

(iv) Assisting management in planning and decision making process.

So the distinction between 'Cost Accountant' and 'Management Accountant' from the point of view of responsibility and service function is clear and certain.

Now I would like to discuss about the introduction of management accounting in India. You see, the introduction of management accounting is a comparatively recent phase in India. Besides the demand of the business, the development of the subject in U.S.A. and U.K. has induced to the introduction of management accounting in India. The Institute of Chartered Accountants of India and the Institute of Cost and Works Accountants of India have introduced a course on 'Management Accountancy' to train up the qualified accountants in their respective areas. In England also, the Institute of Cost and Works Accountants, London has introduced a course on 'Management Accounting' following the recommendation of Management Accounting Team. Again, it should be mentioned in this context that management accounting becomes popular and fashionable both in U.K and U.S.A. as early as 1950 following a visit of Management Accounting Team to United States under the auspices of the Anglo–American Council of Productivity. In their report entitled 'Management Accounting', which was published in November 1950, the team defined the nature of management accounting as "the presentation of accounting information in such a way as to assist management in the creation of policy and in the day-to-day operation of an undertaking". To introduce the concept in its real sense and to popularise management accounting, the professional bodies and Institutes are found to convert the name of their official organ to 'Management Accounting'. Say, for an example, previously the name of the journal, that is official organ, of the Institute of Cost and Works Accountant of India was 'The Cost and Works Accountant'. Now they have converted the title of the journal and named it 'The Management Account' I hope, I have made it clear to you. Is there any question please, on this concept of the subject?

A Brief History of Management Accounting

☐ "Sir, my curiosity is whetted all the more. We shall be obliged if you kindly enlighten us with the idea of the phases of evolution of management accounting."

• Well, for that I would like to refer you to an 'observation'[17] made by the Editorial Board of the Institute of Cost and Works Accountants of India, in this regard. From this observation we may get the phases of development.

Origin of Management Accounting

'Indeed any attempt to trace the origin of Management Accounting will inevitably lead to the developments that had taken place in the realm of Cost Accounting in two decades (1960-1980). Cost Accounting has to pass through three distinct phases of evolutions before it was able to attain the status of calling itself Management Accounting. Tracing the history of growth of Cost Accounting one finds that during the early phase its chief emphasis was on finding out the actual cost of production. Various techniques were developed for identification of cost with the unit and also for allocation, apportionment and absorption of expenses—all directed towards finding out unit cost more and more scientifically. Very soon, it was discovered that cost ascertainment, though by itself important for a wide variety of reasons, was not enough to serve the needs of Management. Intense research followed, and the phase of cost control gradually came into existence. The concept of cost control was applied to industries through techniques like Budgetary Control and Standard Costing. This phase of development of Cost Accountancy marked the beginnings of associating cost accountancy intimately and on day-to-day basis with the management and in discharge of management functions. Indeed, the objectivity with the principles have been evolved for budgeting, establishing standard of performance and for reporting variations to management at different levels set in the process of management interest and participation in cost accountancy and vice-versa'. Now I think you have followed in detail the different phases of evolution of Management Accountancy. If you cannot understand please be frank.

Phases of Evolution of Management Accounting

☐ "Sir, I cannot follow the three phases."

• Well, please note :

1 1 + 0		2 1 + 1		3 1 + 1 + 1
Cost of Production	→	**Cost of Production + Cost Control**	→	**Cost of Production + Cost Control + Art of Management**

I am sure that this time I am clear to you. Do you follow?

☐ "Yes Sir".

---

[17] *The Management Accountant, Vol. 4, No. 6, June 1969.*

● Well, from the above discussions we can find out the components of Management Accountancy which are :

MA	=	CP + CC + AM	MA	=	Management Accounting
CC	=	BC + SC	CP	=	Cost of Production
MA	=	CP + BC + SC + AM	CC	=	Cost Control
			BC	=	Budgetary Control
			SC	=	Standard Cost
			AM	=	Art of Management

I think, the above interpretation is clear to you. Is there any questions?

☐ "Sir, you have not added Financial Accounting. Is it not an element of Management Accountancy?"

● Yes, it's an element.

You see, I have already stated at the outset of this chapter that any study on management accountancy will be deprived of its simplicity unless the importance of financial accounting is felt. Since, the knowledge of financial accounting is an essential prerequisite to management accounting. Is there any questions?

☐ "Sir, what do you mean by the term 'Art of Management' in this respect? Please enlighten us."

● By the 'Art of Management' I mean the art of directing and controlling the needed information in planning and decision making process.

However, in short, management accounting consists of the :

Anatomy of Management Accounting

1. **Financial Accounting**
2. **Cost Accounting**
3. **Financial Management**
4. **Decision Accounting**
5. **Control Accounting**

Well, **Financial Accounting** is concerned with the preparation, computation, presentation, analysis, interpretation and review of the financial statements. That is to say, appraisal of past activities.

Cost Accounting is concerned with computation of cost of production including standard costing.

Financial Management is concerned with the aspect that finance flows through every artery and capillary of business; and to see that flow of finance is steady.

Decision Accounting is concerned with the art of management. It includes preparation of short term and long term planning for profit, forecast, evaluation of alternative investment decision etc. following the information of market research, status of competition, product design etc.

Control Accounting is concerned with the function that all techniques of control such as standard costing, budget and budgetary control, management audit are in operation smoothly. That is to say, control of 'controlling devices'.

☐ "Sir, give us some idea about standard costing, budgets and budgetary control".

• You will get all these information in Part III and Part VI of this book. So, I do not like to take up the matter in details for the time being.

☐ "Sir, we shall be pleased if you kindly give us more *ABC* knowledge of the concept. It will help us to have a quick grasping power of the concept".

• Well, I will discuss the same in a separate chapter of this book as I told you earlier. Are you happy... pleased?

☐ "Yes Sir".

Management Accountancy vs Cost Accountancy

• Here I would like to draw your attention to the concept of 'management'. In our future discussions we shall assume the term 'management' as financial or personnel management or man-management. However, a review of all discussions made earlier says that Management Accounting constitutes a wider field into which Cost Accountancy has developed itself by natural process of evolution'. I think you have followed my last lecture—the origin and different components of Management Accountancy as well as need for the change in accounting system. In my next lecture I shall be discussing with you in details what Management Accounting is; how the term is related to the different aspects of business and process of management.

Thank you all.

QUESTIONS

1. What are the functions of Management Accounting?
2. What is the origin of Management Accounting? Answer both from subjective and objective point of view.
3. Is Management Accounting developed through 'trial and error' method? If so, support your answer with suitable examples.
4. Distinguish between Cost Accounting and Management Accounting; Cost Accountant and Management Accountant.
5. What are the multiplicity of causes which lead to the introduction of Management Accounting?
6. Explain in brief the anatomy of **Management Accounting.**

2

DEFINITION, PRINCIPLES, OPERATION AND STAGES OF MANAGEMENT ACCOUNTANCY

• Good morning to you all.

☐ "Good morning Sir."

• Well In my last lecture I explained in detail about different problems of management— the business faces; and it was observed that general accounting system, i.e. custodial accounting, cannot cope with the varied business problems. That's why some changes should be imparted to the present accounting system which is said to be a 'man-made art' and developed through 'trial and error' process. In that context the principal needs which accounting serve to the modern world were discussed. Then I discussed, in brief, the origin of management accountancy, and how it is related to the concept of cost accountancy. Besides, it was observed that accounting is a language of business which is the basis of management accounting. It was also felt that, in order to tackle the adverse business problems and to bring about an improvement on existing accounting system and to navigate the accounting system in relation to the surroundings of business; moreover, for designing accounting, the language and vision of business, the idea of management accounting can be conceived of. Now I would like to discuss with you about the definition of management accountancy and its relevant aspects.

Well, before explaining the definition of management accountancy and its relevant aspects, let us see what business philosophy is! It should be noted with caution that unless a business has some aim to be attained, the basic idea of running and managing the business is just like sailing a boat without destination. It is reasonable for the accountant to assume that the philosophy of business must, in general, conform to an acceptable realisation of standard of quality and reliability; and that a profit will be made. Otherwise the company will go out of business. The philosophy of business, in general, may be assumed as :

Business Philosophy

(i) Maximisation of profit, or better to say, maximisation of wealth of the owner; that is to say, to enhance the value of the business,

(ii) Minimisation of losses

(iii) Reduction of cost

(iv) Increase of productivity

(v) Increase of turnover

(vi) Increase of business efficiency

(vii) Expansion of market

However, the actual realisation of basic business philosophy, the maximisation of profit, is dependent on the evolution of other stages of business philosophy which had been pointed out earlier.

For the proper accomplishment of the said objectives, better to say for the realisation of the said business philosophy, special knowledge is required on the part of the management accountant.

The special knowledge can be applied through different processes of accounting :

Processes of Accounting

(a) Method of accounting
(b) System of accounting
(c) Technique of accounting
(d) Art of accounting.

Coupled with special knowledge and knowledge of different processes of accounting as stated earlier, the management accountant/controller can attempt to find out some solution to the existing business problems and tries to introduce the art of management accounting in the process of management. Thus management accounting is a specialised course of study which deals with the business and social environment. In that sense management accounting may be considered as Business Environment Accounting. So, management accounting may be defined as a method, system, technique and intuitive art of accounting through which business philosophy can be realised. Similar type of idea has been given by Dr. Batty in his book 'Management Accountancy' which I would like to discuss afterwards.

Business Environment Accounting

Method of Accounting

↑

System of Accounting ← **SPECIAL KNOWLEDGE** → **Art of Accounting**

↓

Technique of Accounting

$$\left.\begin{aligned} 5+4 &= 9\\ 6+3 &= 9\\ 8+1 &= 9\\ 7+2 &= 9\\ 9+0 &= 9 \end{aligned}\right\}\ \text{Analysis}$$

So it is clear from the analysis shown that 9 (nine) can be attained through a number of alternatives. It depends upon the nature and circumstances of each individual case. Well, if you are required to compute the internal rate of return in respect of a proposed capital expenditure project, you will have to search for a number of discounting rates before they can find the rate at which discounted cash inflows equal the cash outflows. In the example cited above, i.e. analysis

Insight into Interpretation

of nine (9), the management accountant should select a situation, out of so many, best suited to attain certain objectives. That is to say, in order to find out a suitable discounting rate which equilibrates the discounted value of cash inflows with discounted value of cash outflows, the management accountant will have to proceed with different discounting rates, say, 18%, 19%, 20%, 21%, 22%, and so on, until the equilibrium rate is attained. That's why the interpretation of Nine has been made to have an insight into the concept of Discounted Cash Flow Method. Of course, you may be eager to know what is Discounted Cash Flow Method. Well, this portion will be discussed under 'Decision Accounting' part.

Special Knowledge in Management Accounting

It is obvious that **SPECIAL KNOWLEDGE** is needed on the part of management accountant in order to interpret, diagnose and direct the situation. Now you may say "Sir, what do you understand by the term special knowledge?"

Well, by **SPECIAL KNOWLEDGE** I mean the aggregate knowledge of the following, apart from knowledge of Cost and Financial Accountancy :

(i) Art of management
(ii) Managerial economics
(iii) Managerial finance
(iv) Art of technology/Knowledge of information technology
(v) Statistical technique
(vi) Law of the business environment—Mercantile laws, Tax laws, and, finally,
(vii) Applied psychology

Area of Application of Knowledge

You see, armed with all these knowledge the management accountant can apply his efficiency with a view to providing information in the following broad areas :

- Measurement at the work point in order to monitor variations and losses.
- Measurement of the cumulative effects of gains and losses as the activity proceeds.
- Comparison of losses with the costs of preventive measures. Effects of losses on planned output.
- Measurement of yield ratios.
- Comparative efficiency of alternative methods of production.
- Assessment of alternative methods of inspection.
- Allocation of responsibility and reasons for rejections.
- Performance of suppliers and sub-contractors.
- Relation between various reports in order to assess influences not apparent from the study of isolated information.
- Comparative efficiency of alternative machinery and the assessment of future capital expenditure.

- Examination of recovery costs and the disposal of rejects and waste materials.
- After-sales servicing, including the repair and replacement costs.
- Estimating and the assessment of price levels.
- Forecasting future trends.

By supplying the needed information and by pinpointing the areas of loophole the management accountant/controller acts as a specialist and adviser to management.

I think you are following my lecture. Do you find it boring?

□ "No Sir, it's really very exciting."

● Well, what were we discussing?

Oh, yes, I was discussing the qualifications of management accountant/controller. Isn't it so?

□ "Yes Sir".

● However, it is vital to note in this context that sometimes businesses are found to go into liquidation due to inefficient operation of the controller or management accountant; although the controller has the 'know-how' of business operation. I think, this is because of a lack of adequate material knowledge on the part of the controller.

Material Knowledge of Management Accountant

We can classify the knowledge of controller/management accountant into two :

A. Academic knowledge, and

B. Material knowledge.

Although academic qualifications are prerequisite to the attainment of the position of controller/management accountant; 'material' knowledge or qualification is the 'key' which preserves the 'integrity' of his position. The material knowledge can be cultivated through experience, observation and meditation.

Qualities of Management Accountant

I think you remember it was stated in the first chapter that it is not an easy task on the part of the management accountant or controller to navigate the accounting system in relation to business surroundings and to provide the control information in specific or appropriate areas. For that is needed a man of dynamic personality who has a thorough accounting and business knowledge and an insight into business and social conditions.

Well, in order to tackle adverse business problems with the aid of management accounting techniques, the management accountant or controller should have the following qualities :

(a) Pleasing personality to unite all management groups into a cohesive whole.

(b) Grasping power of management views and capabilities of generating all types of information the management requires.

(c) Intelligent enough to assess his position and his role as an expert and adviser to management.

(d) Stable outlook about the operation of business.

(e) Feasibility in comparing and contrasting the factors which are attributable to profitability and solvency of a concern.

I hope you have understood all the above types of qualities to be possessed by the management accountant.

☐ "Sir, may I ask a question?"

• Yes, yes, You can ask me any question without any hesitation.

☐ "Sir, It is an irrelevant question".

• However, Is it relevant to this particular context?

☐ "Yes Sir".

• Then feel free to ask it.

☐ "Sir, Is it found in practical field that firms seek to get persons who are, in a sense, all-rounders for the position of controller or management accountant?"

Challenging Role of Management Accountant

Of course, it is. If you observe very minutely, you will see that advertisements are made in newspapers or professional journals for the post of Controller who should have all the qualities mentioned earlier. However, for your understanding I cite here one[1] of such advertisements :

"One of the largest public sector organisations is looking for a dynamic and progressive controller who will be willing to accept the tremendous challenge that the post offers. The successful candidate will be answerable to the Managing Director/ Chief Executive for the development and efficient operation of the financial planning and control systems of the company, including cost and management information. He will also be responsible for financial management and internal audit. Applicant should be Chartered Accountant or Cost Accountant."

You can now easily realise how challenging position the Management Accountant enjoys. The efficiency and dynamism of Management Accountant can be tested on his performances, how he is able to apply the concept of "management', which is the art and science of directing human effort in the field of accountancy.

Management Accountant as Financial Diplomat

Now you can realise what difficult task it is when Management Accountant has to direct accounting and economic information in the area of planning and decision-making process. That's why, you see, the position of Management Accountant is considered as a challenging position. So it is obvious that the "principles of cost and management accounting are applicable not only at production stages but also in planning and constructions stages." However, it should be noted that, in a sense, the role of the Management Accountant is like that of a 'diplomat'. The role of a 'diplomat' is envisaged during crisis. So the role of the Management Accountant is also envisaged during the problem of business and financial crisis. You perhaps know that the concept of 'management' originates out of 'problem'. Unless there would have arisen any problems in financial accounting, the idea of management accounting could not be conceived of. So it is obvious that the ordinary or

[1] *The Statesman Consumer Service, Vol. III, No. 7, P. 7.*

financial accountant cannot solve the existing problem. If they could, the post of the management accountant could not have been created. Now you can realise what diplomatic role is to be played by the Management Accountant when he has to tackle accounting, business, financial, economic and human problems which impair the growth of the organisation. If we interpret the expected functions of an accountant, as appeared in "Horizons for a Profession"[2] which reads as under, it will be apparent that the essential characteristics of an accountant, say Management Accountant, are alike to that of a 'diplomat':

"This, the world of affairs, is the domain of the accountant. It is his mission to perceive it, to analyse it, to bring order to it, to portray it, and the more complex this world becomes, the more demanding becomes the task of the accountant."

So it will not be unjustified if anyone considers the Management Accountant a Financial Diplomat in the organisational structure of management. I hope that you have followed details about the task of Management Accountant. Is there any question?

☐ "Sir, I could not follow the task of Management Accountant. Please enlighten me in a simpler way."

● You see, I have nothing more to say in this respect. Because, I have already explained the basic concept of the same in course of my earlier lecture. However, please note that the task of management accountant or controller is to apply all the 'Special Knowledge' in the area of accountancy. That is to say, with the aid of those knowledge, as referred earlier, we can prepare cash forecast, profit and loss forecast, forecast regarding future trend of the market and forecast about investment decision etc. The function of Management Accountant is to provide facts and figures and forecast through disciplined and analytical approach upon which decision is to be taken by the top management. Thus you see, the Management Accountant has to play a vital role in the execution of planning and decision making. In this context I would like to bring your attention to the views of the Society of Industrial Accountants of Canada as to the role of accountants of Canada. They are of opinion that involvement in the process of management decision making is an increasingly important part of the accountant's role in modern business. It is this area that is developing faster and will certainly continue to do so. But apart from being on hand for emergencies, he has the continuing responsibility to provide the organisation's information and control centre. He collects financial data on all the phases of buying, manufacturing, and selling as well as on any external economic factors that might affect the operation. This information is recorded, analysed and interpreted, with the aid of latest data processing equipment. From it are prepared the financial progress reports, analysis of cost and price factors and budgets, based on sales forecasts, comparing expected income with probable expenditure. Communicating this information in a logical and concise manner is an essential part of the management accountant's role, for on this platform will be based the plans and decisions affecting the company's future performance. The final stage of management accountant's responsibility is the implementation and control of these plans, identifying deviations from

Task of Management Accountant

Functions of Management Accountant

---

[2] *The study of "**The Common Body of Knowledge for Certified Public Accountants**", sponsored by the Carnegie Corporation of New York and the Institute of Certified Public Accountants, appeared in 1967 under the title 'Horizon for a Profession' which looks at the future of accountancy in U.S.A., P. 44.*

them and also continuing the process of recording, analysing and interpreting which is the key to this job.

Here I would like to mention for your convenience the six functions of a controller as defined by the Financial Executive Institute of U.S.A. :

(i) To establish, coordinate, and maintain through authorised management an integrated plan for the control of operations. Such a plan would provide, to the extent required in the business, cost standards, expense budgets, sales forecasts, profit-planning, and programmes for capital investment and financing, together with the necessary procedures to effectuate the plan.

(ii) To measure performance against approved operating plans and standards and to report and interpret the results of operations to all level of management. This function includes the design, installation, and maintenance of accounting and cost systems and records; the determination of accounting policy; and the compilation of statistical records as required.

(iii) To measure and report on the validity of the objectives of the business and on the effectiveness of its policy, organisation structure and procedure in attaining these objectives. This includes consulting with all levels of management responsible for policy or action, concerning any phase of the operation of the business as it relates to the performances of this function.

(iv) To report to government agencies as required, and to supervise all matters relating to taxes.

(v) To interpret and report on the effect of external influences on the attainment of the objectives of the business. This function includes the continuous appraisal of economic and social forces and of governmental influences as they affect the operation of the business.

(vi) To provide protection for the assets of the business. This function includes establishing and maintaining adequate internal control and auditing, and assuring proper insurance coverage.

Span of Management Accounting

Now you see, the functions of Management Accountant—as cited by the Financial Executive Institute—is exhaustive of all the areas where the Management Accountant has to function. So, from the above, the 'span' of management accounting can be summarised as :

(i) General Accounting.
(ii) Cost Accounting.
(iii) Forecasting and Budgeting with reference to standard cost.
(iv) Cost and Statistics.
(v) Taxes.
(vi) Audit.
(vii) Organising and Method.
(viii) Capital Expenditure (to measure profitability of the existing project and evaluation of a proposed project).
(ix) Inventory Management.

Do you follow what I want to say?

☐ "Yes Sir, we shall be glad if you kindly explain to us briefly about those concepts."

• Well, in regard to all those 'span of management accounting' I am to say that besides preparation and presentation of financial statement the **General Accounting** is concerned with receipt and disbursement of cash, recording of inventory, liabilities, reorganisation, setting up of receivable and sales.

Cost Accounting acts as a supplement to financial accounting. It strengthens the internal aspect of financial accounting. It is concerned with the application of cost to job, product, process and operation. It is concerned with the development of standard and unit cost.

Forecasting and Budgeting are concerned with the preparation of cash forecast, profit and loss forecast and budgeted balance sheet as well as preparation of budgets in keeping with the requirement of operating and other departments.

Cost Control is concerned with the preparation of the internal report in order to convert the budget into operating service. This can be done by drawing a comparison between actual and standard.

Cost and Statistics is concerned with generating statistical and analytical cost information to all departments of the organisation.

Taxation is concerned with computation, verification of income, filing tax return, making tax payment for payroll, excise, sales and personal income.

Organising and Method is concerned with improving office operations as well as accounting operation through preparation and issuance of accounting records and manuals.

Audit is concerned with the central aspect of accounting. It is concerned with accounting control. So it is clear that 'management accounting' has a vital relation with all those areas explained earlier.

I do hope that this time I am clear to you.

☐ "Yes Sir."

• Is there any question?

☐ "Sir, in the 'Span of Management Accounting', you have cited General and Cost Accounting, Forecasting and Budget and Procedure of Cost Control etc. Is it possible, Sir, from the discussion to extract a few points which may be termed as 'Faces of Management Accounting"?

• Why not? You can...yes, yes, you please try.

☐ "Sir, It may not be up to the mark."

• Well, at least you try.

☐ "Sir, in our first chapter we had seen the 'anatomy of management accounting' which are Financial Accounting, Cost Accounting, Financial Management, Decision

Accounting and Control Accounting. So, if I say these are the facets of management accounting, am I correct Sir"?

• Yes, yes, you are correct..........

However, I would like to explain the facet of management accounting in detail. Before that let me explain the meaning of 'facet'.

You know, the general meaning of 'facet' is 'one side of a many-sided body'.

Facet of Management Accounting

Regarding facet of management accounting I am to say that a facet is one particular part of many constituent parts of management accounting. These are financial accounting, cost accounting, cost control, budgetary control, reporting etc. All these points I pointed out earlier in the first chapter. However, for your better understanding I like to place before you the following facets of management accounting as emphasised by the 7th International Congress of Accountants, held in 1957 at Amsterdam, which are :

1. Cost accounting, including standard costs.
2. Material control, not limited to inventories but extending to material usage during manufacturing.
3. Budgetary control, embracing the preparation of fixed or flexible operation budgets and their use as standards of performance for interim periods.
4. Interim reporting, including monthly or quarterly profit and loss accounts, together with significant data as of the end of these periods; for example, statement of current assets and liabilities, orders on hand, etc.
5. Determination of the most efficient and economical accounting system applicable to the particular business, including the best use of mechanical and electronic devices.
6. Special cost and economic studies, such as the study of capital costs and potential profits if output is increased or additional lines are produced. This requires the study of cost-volume-profit relationships, mathematics of the break-even chart, etc.
7. Assisting management in the interpretation of financial data and rendering advice in connection with pending decision which can properly be made on the basis of such information.

Well, I think that the above discussions are sufficient to understand about the different facets of management accountancy. Do you like, further or more discussions?

☐ "No Sir".

• "Have you got any query?"

☐ "Sir, How does management accounting operate"?

• It's really very fine and interesting that you try to have an insight into the subject. I am really very glad for that. Well, it operates through rendering its different services to management in their policy and decision-making process. Its successful operation will be reflected as to how the enterprise is able to integrate the capital structure and guard against the possible adverse situation which might caúse erosion of real capital and impair the mobilisation of capital of the business, through different techniques of management accounting.

How Management Accounting Operates

Management accounting operates through :

1. **Method of operation :** To keep the method of operation running, the management accountant should be concerned with the following aspects :

   (i) To appraise special report on inspection method and standard over and above the normal operating report.

   (ii) To see that standard as per specification of product is inspected.

   (iii) To reconcile any change in specification and standard.

   (iv) To regulate 'specification' in line with change in customers' minimum requirements.

   (v) To evaluate the business circumstances and the cause and effect of change affecting the destiny of the organisation.

   (vi) To coordinate the various departments of the organisation for the smooth running of the business.

2. **Profit planning :** For effective profit planning the management accountant—besides adoption of operating budgets, capital budgets, cash budgets and control budgets etc.—should appraise the following factors as contributory to profitability :

   (i) Material planning.

   (ii) Labour planning.

   (iii) Time planning.

   (iv) Organising planning.

   (v) Method study planning.

   (vi) Product design planning.

3. **New product line :** For launching new product lines the management accountant should be concerned with :

   (i) Market research.

   (ii) Economic condition.

   (iii) Cost-volume-profit relationship.

4. **Improving communication :** For improving better communication system which is the basis of improving profitability, the management accountant should be concerned with the following :

   (i) To coordinate the employer and employee through the presentation of pertinent information to all concerned.

   (ii) To inspire the workers or employees for raising productivity higher through recommendation to management for production bonus, incentive bonus and profit bonus.

(iii) To improve presentation of information by adding other information to the existing list of information such as 'changes on design and production, production policy, measurement of the effectivenss of labour and of productivity generally, market investigation and sales policies'[3].

From the discussions made earlier, it would not be unnatural if any one searches for some guidelines for the smooth and better management accounting operation. You see...

☐ "Sir, are there any guidelines for effective management accounting?"

• Yes, yes there are...

☐ "Sir, really speaking, I was just thinking of asking this question."

• Guides to effective management accounting practice.

☐ "Sir our curiosity is whetted all the more."

• Well, for effective guide to management accounting practice, the following points are worth noting :

a. **Identification of purpose :** Accounting, financial and cost data must be relevant to specified purpose and area of problem. It should be noted in this context that management information system does not mean the collection and processing system. It should be designed in such a way as to assist management to use it in appropriate purpose.

Effectiveness in Management Accounting

b. **Diagnosis of data relevant to particular purpose :** After identification the 'use' and 'purpose' for which data is to be used, the next step is to diagnose whether the collected data is relevant or appropriate to the identification of purpose. Determination of the appropriate data and information is the basis of management information system. "Determining what kind and type of information is needed is the more basic part of establishing an adequate business information system. Unfortunately, and all too frequently, this goal has been subordinated to the second step which is the search for improved methods and more sophisticated techniques"[4]. However, it has been observed by one of the experts in the field of management accounting that a modern system of accounting "produces data for a variety of purpose and these are corresponding entities represented by responsibilities for management control; projects, products, and markets for profit planning; legal entities for ownership of assets and for tax reporting etc."

It was stated in the first chapter that the technique of navigation of accounting in relation to surroundings are not available. For example, information with regard to market demand, status of competition, general business condition, legal regulations and limitations are beyond the ability of accounting to supply. So there emerges a clear definition and concept of relevant information or entities, as cited above, or the basic guide to determine what data is to be 'admitted' or which to 'exist' from appropriate accounting records and reports.

---

[3] *H. J. Furness, **"The Accountants' Contribution to Increased Prosperity"**, The Cost Accountant, July 1954, P. 68.*

[4] *Pfenning, **"Business Information System"**, Accounting Review, April 1962, P. 236 :*

c. **Implementation of 'concept' with practical technique :** It is obvious that in selecting accounting methods for all suited purpose, a marriage between 'accounting theory' and 'practical business condition' is essential. So it has been found in actual practice to realise by the financial consultant that "in selecting accounting methods, practical compromises are usually required". National Association of Accountants has made an extensive research on the concept and they are found to insert an example in their Research Report No. 40 which reads :

'For example, theory underlying the economic order quantity and the timing of inventory replenishment sometimes employs concepts of cost which are immeasurable. Thus the familiar economic order size formula calls for unit costs of placing an order and of carrying inventory. In both cases a substantial part of the total cost of these functions is capacity cost and the unit cost is indeterminate. While an average unit cost can be calculated if the quantity is specified, this procedure does not help when the quantity to order is the unknown being sought. Other costs cannot be measured or estimated reliably enough for practical use. Thus there is no way to measure the opportunity costs of orders not received, because customers are dissatisfied with the company's ability to make delivery with acceptable promptness'.

Definitions of Management Accounting

I hope you all have understood the different aspects of management accounting and its underlying philosophy. Now I feel that you are eager to know the various definitions of management accounting given by different scholars, experts in the subject as well as different professional bodies of the world.

"Management Accounting... is concerned with accounting information that is useful to management"—Robert N. Anthony.

"Management Accounting is the term used to describe the accounting methods, system and techniques which, coupled with special knowledge and ability, assist management in its task of maximising profit or minimising losses"— Dr. J. Batty.

"Management Accounting is accounting for effective Management". — N. K. Bose.

"Management Accountancy is the adoption and analysis of accounting information, and its diagnosis and explanation in such a way as to assist management." —T. G. Rose.

"The essential aim of management accountancy should be to assist management in decision-making and control" —Brown and Howard.

'The term "Management Accounting' covers all those services by which the accounting department can assist top management and other departments in the formulation of policy, the control of its execution and appreciation of its effectiveness" —Broad & Carmichael.

"Management Accountancy is the presentation of accounting information in such a way to assist management in the creation of policy and in the day-to-day operation of an undertaking" —The Anglo-American Council on Productivity Report.

"Management Accounting includes the methods and concepts necessary for effective planning, for choosing among alternative business actions and for control through the evolution and interpretation of performances" —The American Accounting Association.

"Any form of accounting which enables a business to be conducted more efficiently can be regarded as Management Accounting" —The Institute of Chartered Accountants of England and Wales.

"The application of accounting and statistical techniques to the specified purpose of producing and interpreting information designed to assist management in the function of promoting maximum efficiency and in envisaging, formulating and co-ordinating their executions" —The Association of Certified Corporate Accountants.

I think all these definitions are sufficient to understand what management accounting is. Is there any question, please?

☐ "Sir, we are very glad to have all these definition of management accounting. We shall be obliged if you would please give us your interpretation relating to the definition of management accounting".

Art and Science Concept of Management Accounting

• You see, I have already given my interpretation about the subject in course of my earlier discussions. However, as you are interested, I have the pleasure to give you my definition relating to management accountancy which is : Management Accountancy is the art and science of directing accounting information to the concerned person in order to realise the business philosophy—the maximisation of profit.

That is to say, presenting the accounting information in a manner which aids the management in taking management decision(s).

☐ "Sir, why is it science and art?"

• I note with pleasure your curiosity. I was thinking previously that this type of question may arise in your mind. You know, I think, the meaning of science in general—special knowledge. Management Accounting possesses all the properties of special knowledge—Budgetary Control, Standard Costing etc. That's why it may be termed as science of knowledge. You know, 'presentation' is an art. Presenting all the accounting information to the concerning persons in a form suitable for analysis and interpreting is nothing but 'art of accounting'.

I think I am able to give you some idea about the 'art' and 'science' concept of accounting in management. If you are interested in more discussions on 'Management Accounting—a Science', I would request you to consult the work of T. G. Rose—'Top Management Accounting'.

Now one thing which may peep through in your mind—why adopt such system of accounting, i.e. management accounting, when financial and cost accounting are in force?

Management Accounting vs Financial Accounting

If you think over the matter you will get your own answer. Besides, it had been stated in first chapter that existing financial accounting cannot cope with the varied business problems as well as day-to-day changing condition of the society. That is to say, the limitations of financial accounting have involved wider application of management accountancy in the world of business. In other words, to over come the defects of financial accounting—which is said to be static, management accounting has been used. Because, management accounting is dynamic. Students or general readers may be misguided or may have a wrong interpretation about the concept of the two. To avoid this, I like to refer you to a remark made by Professor Anthony. He says that the terms 'Financial Accounting' and 'Management Accounting' are not precise description or descriptions they comprise. All accounting is financial in the sense that all accounting systems are in monetary terms, and management is responsible for the content of financial accounting reports.

Principles of Management Accounting

It is true that management accounting, instead of objectives aimed at, will give wrong direction unless it is designed with some basic principles. The basic principles of management accounting are accuracy, objectives and standardisation etc. In this context, I would like to draw your attention to the effective management accounting principles as suggested by J. Sandford Smith in his book "Management Control Information".

Ten principles of Management Accounting are :

(i) **Scope :** The scope of management accounting figures should not exceed the level of authority of the recipient.

(ii) **Accuracy :** Accuracy and completeness of management accounting figures need be sufficient only to enable appropriate action to be based on them.

(iii) **Punctuality :** Daily management accounting figures should be presented to all recipients in the first hour of the following working day. Weekly management accounting figures should be presented to all recipients in the first day of the following working week.

Monthly management accounting figures should be presented to all recipients in the first week of the following month.

Annual management accounting figures should be presented to all recipients in the first month of the following year.

(iv) **Scale :** The lower the recipient is in the hierarchy of management, the more direct should be the scale of measurement.

(v) **Fairness :** Management Accounts must be prepared on a fair basis with no conscious weighing of factors for or against a line of policy or point of view.

(vi) **Precision of Definition :** Every management accounting statement should define itself precisely.

(vii) **Time Span :** The length of view taken varies directly with the height in the management hierarchy.

(viii) **Comparison :** A management accounting figure is seldom of use by itself. It requires some comparative figure as a standard to give it scale; a comparison with an intention or with a similar situation or with a similar figure at a different time.

(ix) **Concordance of Standards :** A standard is only a useful management tool if it is agreed to be a fair and reasonable standard by those who are charged with achieving it.

(x) **Effectiveness :** Management Accounting figures should lead to action and a deeper penetration of the situation is demanded according to the degree of action that can be taken from the information provided.

After bearing all the points in mind as mentioned earlier, I would like to give you some idea about the fields where the management accountant can play a vital role to boost up the prestige of the enterprise. Before that let me know whether you have understood the principles of management accounting.

☐ "We don't find it at all difficult".

☐ "At all...no difficulty, Sir! Please enlighten us about the field where management accountant can show his skill and ability".

Fields of Management Accounting

• You see, following are the areas or fields where management accountant has to play a vital role in the execution of policy and decision—making process :

a. Financial and Cost accounting.

b. Development programme of the organisation, i.e. in the area of 'capital expenditure decision'.

c. Development, installing and maintaining an integrated management information system encompassing :

(i) Accounting, (ii) Inventory, (iii) Budgeting, (iv) Fund Flow & Cash Flow, (v) Production, (vi) Control.

Field of Management Accountant

(i) Dividend Policy.

(ii) Interfirm Comparison.

(iii) Productivity & Profitability.

(iv) Capital Structure & Cost of Capital.

(v) Measurement of performance through Ratio Analysis and detection of the New spots of operation efficiency.

(vi) Consideration of Investment proposals (profitability analysis), New Investment, change in product line or change in product mix through P/V analysis and where there are more than one key factor through linear programming.

Well, we have seen above that the management accountant can make his contribution in the field of accounting, budgeting, production, inventory and controlling aspect of the organisation etc.

Ways of Performance

Now one more thing which may crop up in your mind—How is it possible? That is to say, in how many ways the management accountant can make his contribution? Well, please note that a management accountant can do the same in the following manner :

(a) Establishing the minimum and maximum stock level, re-ordering the level for raw material and calculating economic reorder with the knowledge of data processing.

(b) Providing information regarding causes for machine idleness and its span of time of idleness.

(c) Generating information about change in the level of stock.

(d) Providing information as to defective work including the cost of re-working and the consequent loss of production time.

(e) Supplying information as to efficiency of labour.

(f) Consulting and discussing with personnel of different sections of the same department whether 'tolerances are too light for the purpose required, whether this causes too high a proportion of defective work'.

(g) Consulting with the other staffs as to sampling techniques when 'the size of the samples taken could be reduced with benefit, and still yield an acceptable confidence interval'.

(h) Coordinating among various departments with regard to quality control.

(i) Supplying information as to financial aspect of the business after assaying the aim in the light of changing economic and social conditions.

(j) Advising management regarding financial aspect, purchases, sales and production of the business.

Finally, I would like to emphasise more on the human aspect of management on which stands the basic structure of management accounting. Here I would like to introduce before you an article "Industrial Management and the Accountant" by A. B. Waring where he was found to emphasise more on human aspect in accounting, for the smooth operation of the business. Mr. Waring observed that 'the proper study of management is man, common man'. The task of management accountant is to bring 'home' all the people, at all levels, by the friendly channels of joint consultation, the compelling urgency of increasing productivity and lowering cost. 'The problem of permanent prosperity is as much one of permanent and tradition of technique'.

Man Management and Management Accounting

I think I am able to give you a clear idea about the different aspects of management accounting, discussed earlier. Isn't it so?

☐ "It is really very fine, Sir. The discussions made by you have given us an insight into management accounting".

● Have you got anything more to ask me?

☐ "Sir, we shall be obliged if you would kindly tell us about the different stages of management accounting?"

Stages of Management Accounting

● I cannot understand why you could not digest my last lectures. I already explained the same in course of my previous lectures. However, note below the different stages of Management Accounting :

Re-arrangement	:	Classifying the financial data.
Adoption	:	Processing of financial data.
Analysis	:	Interpreting the financial statement.
Diagnosis	:	The causes of the effects, i.e. a result of financial and cost statement.
Explanation	:	Suggestion, i.e. the result of analysis and diagnosis.
Mental Revolution	:	The concept of human psychology regarding the introduction of the art of management in the field of accountancy.

Re-arrangement → Adoption → Analysis →
Mental Revolution ← Explanation ← Diagnosis ← ↓

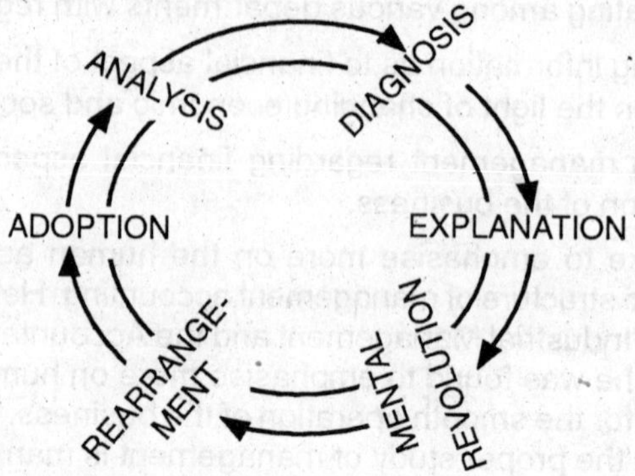

Now I think I am clear to you in this respect. I shall be glad if you please tell me any point which is not clear to you. However, I conclude my lecture with the ray of hope that you all would be able to understand my subsequent lectures which are the advanced stages of the subject. Please try to preserve all my earlier discussions in the 'secret reserve' of your brain for your future study.

Techniques of Management Accounting

In my next lectures I shall be discussing with you about the different techniques of management accounting under different parts :

1. Financial Accounting[5].
2. Cost Accounting.
3. Financial Management.
4. Decision Accounting.
5. Control Accounting.

QUESTIONS

1. What are the functions of Management Accounting?
2. What is the 'Span of Management Accounting'?
3. Explain the facets of Management Accounting.
4. As an accountant of a firm how would you operate a Management Accounting System?
5. What are the factors which should be taken into account for the effectiveness of Management Accounting?
6. Give an outline of Management Accounting Principles.

[5] *"Book-keeping is so much associated with accounting. Book-keeping is, of course, a necessary part of management accounting" —W. M. Harper, A.M.B.I.M.*

PART II

FINANCIAL ACCOUNTING

"The interdependence of accounting theory and practice suggests an interrelation like that between melody and harmony in music."

3

ACCOUNTING MECHANISM

☐ "Good morning, Sir."

• Good morning.

Well, what will be discussed this morning?

☐ "Sir, you promised to discuss about the concept of accounting."

• Yes, yes. Oh, yes, I did.

It was observed in the preceding chapter that one of the techniques of Management Accounting is Financial Accounting. I find it essential to give you some basic concepts on Financial or Custodial Accounting.

Please note that .... what are you doing there! Silence please. Please note that management needs various types of information to take decisions. Financial Accounting acts as a reliable source of information to management. This is virtually the primary source of information and provides the basis for analysis, which, in turn, facilitates decision-making functions. Thus, it is essential to have reasonable knowledge of Financial Accounting.

Satisfaction and Dissatisfaction in Accounting

As you are well aware, in day-to-day life we observe two situations—suffering and joy; satisfaction and dissatisfaction. That is to say, one's joy, other's suffering and one's satisfaction, other's dissatisfaction. Similarly, in business too, we find two types of recording—one '**Debit**', and the other '**Credit**'. That is to say, every 'Debit' should have a corresponding 'Credit' and every 'Credit' should have corresponding 'Debit'. In a restricted sense, not in general sense, all sufferings and dissatisfactions are Debit. All joy and satisfactions are Credit. Income, gains are Credit; losses, expenses are Debit. Take for an example, when a guardian, say in my own case, pays private tuition fees for his son—it constitutes expense to the guardian and income to the private tutor. That is to say, satisfaction to the private tutor and dissatisfaction on the part of the guardian. The very 'Private Tuition Fee Account' will appear to the Guardian as Debit and the same will appear to the Private tutor as Credit. Please observe very minutely the following situations :

In the Book of the Guardian	**In the Book of the Private Tutor**
Tuition Fee A/c. Dr.	Cash A/c. Dr.
To Cash A/c	To Tuition Fee A/c

So, it is clear from the above situation that every 'satisfaction' entries must have corresponding 'dissatisfaction' entries and every 'dissatisfaction' entries must have corresponding 'satisfaction' entries.

It is to be noted in this connection that it is not possible to bear up in mind all the happenings in day-to-day life. It should be recorded. Similarly, when numerous transactions and changes are taking place in the world of business and when there are several parties involved in day-to-day operations of the business, it needs recording of all business positions and events. That is to say, position of assets and liabilities, events regarding purchases, sales, expenses, income or gain and, finally, profit and loss. Here we can realise the importance of keeping of accounts, i.e. Book-keeping. Now you may put to me the question. What is Book-keeping?

Definition of Book-keeping

Well, Book-keeping may be defined as the art and science of recording business transactions and this recording facilitates ascertaining the change in the financial position of business.

So, from the above discussions, the objects of book-keeping may be summed up as :

Objects of Book-keeping

(a) To ascertain the profit or loss of an enterprise or business.

(b) To ascertain the total debt due to and from the business.

(c) To evaluate the position of assets and liabilities.

(d) To ascertain over-all financial position of the business.

(e) To exercise control for efficient financial management.

I think, you are able to understand the objects of book-keeping. Is there any question?

☐ "Sir, what is the difference between Book-keeping and Accounting?

Difference between Book-keeping and Accounting

• Though your question is very simple it is very difficult to answer. Because, often accounting is regarded as a mere 'synonym of book-keeping'[1]. However, I am to say that Accounting begins where Book-keeping ends. That is to say, book-keeping ends with collecting, sorting and recording of financial data; and accounting begins with finding out the gross and net financial and operating results. Or, in other words, the distinction can be drawn in the following manner :

---

[1] *"The nature and scope of accountancy are popularly misunderstood. Often accountancy is regarded as a mere synonym for book-keeping. Accountancy is the field of knowledge concerned with :*

(a) systematic records of the transactions of economic enterprises.

(b) the use of those records to prevent or detect fraud, relate results to responsibility, determine equities and provide information to business owners and managers, taxation and other government authorities and any other persons or groups who are legitimately interested in the activities of the enterprises.

Accounting is the process used in this field". Sir Alexander Fitzerald in the inaugural Commonwealth Institute of Accountants Annual Research Lecture in the University of Melbourne, Oct. 1940.

Book-keeping	Accounting
1. It is primary.	1. It is secondary.
2. It deals with collection, sorting and recording of business and financial transactions.	2. It deals with finding out net operating and financial results after proper checking and adjustments, out of the collected data from book-keeping.
3. The work of book-keeping is done by the book-keeper.	3. Accounting activities are performed by the accountant.
4. Book-keeping fails to provide useful information to external parties.	4. Accounting provides useful information to various interested parties after analysing the recorded facts.
5. Lower level of knowledge is required for the purpose of Book-keeping.	5. Higher level of knowledge and analytical skills are required for the purpose of Accountancy.

By the by, here I would like to draw your attention to the concept of 'Accountancy' and 'Accounting'.

You please tell the difference, yes, yes, yes, ... you.

☐ "Sir, these two words—'Accountancy' and 'Accounting' are used interchangeably. So, no difference is there".

● You see, this is not the correct approach.

Well, in this respect I like to refer to a remark made by Professor V. L. Gole. Prof. Gole is of opinion that "Accountancy could be regarded as the function; an area of knowledge, accounting could be regarded as the action or process used in this area".

Difference between Accountancy and Accounting

However, the concepts of 'book-keeping and accounting', 'accountancy and accounting' are correlated. Thus accounting may be defined as the art of recording, classifying and summarising in a significant manner and in terms of money transactions, events which are in part at least of a financial character, and interpreting the results thereof.[2]

Well, from the discussions made earlier we have come accross the following terms :

- Transaction
- Debit
- Credit
- Summarising and Classifying
- Accounts

Let us explain the above terms in the light of the accepted principles of accounting.

[2] *The American Institute of Accountants (1941).*

Transaction denotes :

Transaction

(i) Exchange of money or money worth.

(ii) Change in the financial condition of parties or business measurable in terms of money.

CHARACTERISTICS OF TRANSACTION

(i) Existence of two parties.

(ii) Existence of two situations effecting change in the financial condition of business.

Do you follow the meaning and characteristics of transactions?

☐ "Yes Sir. But Sir, what are the principles to be applied to test a transaction?"

● Well, to test a transaction the following principles are to be applied :

- **It must be related to persons or institutions :** For example, Mr. A has advanced Rs 50 to the Book-seller. Paid Rs. 335 insurance premium to L.I.C. of India.

- **It must be complete by itself :** For example, I have Rs. 30. This is not a transaction, since it is not complete. If I say, I have Rs. 30 and deposited it into bank, then it is a transaction.

- **It must be measurable in terms of money :** For example, if I say, my property has been damaged, this is not a transaction. But if I say my property has been damaged and the estimated value of damage is Rs. 5,00,000 then it is a transaction.

- **It must effect some change :**

  (i) **Change in financial condition.** For example, value of my machine for Rs. 1,000 has been depreciated @ 10%. Here my financial condition to the extent of 'depreciation' has been affected.

  (ii) **Change in structural condition.** For example, Mr. A has Rs. 300 and with that amount he has purchased a book 'Accounting for Goodwill' written by Dr. B. K. Basu. This is a structural change and it can be regarded as transaction.

Well, now I like to discuss with you about the Double Entry System of Book-keeping—that is to say, recording of two aspects. Although, I discussed this at the outset of this chapter. However, please note :

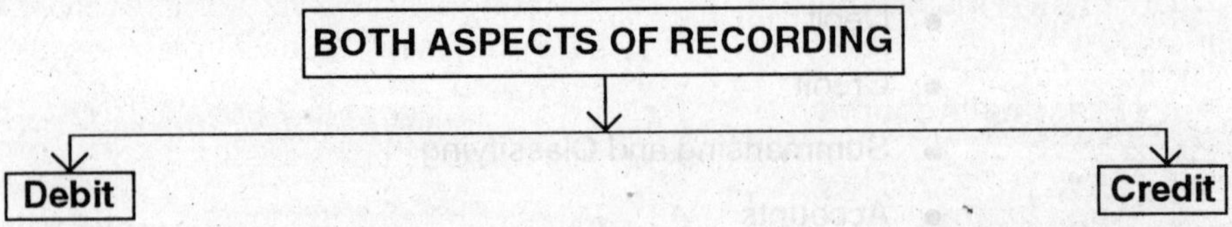

Rules for Debit and Credit

Please note that all transactions or, better to say, all components of transactions, will be placed either on the 'Debit' side or on the 'Credit' side. For that a close observation of the situation is needed. Here I would like to explain the principles of double entry system of Book-keeping for proper diagnosis of **Debit** and **Credit**.

Debit	:	All assets and properties.
Credit	:	All liabilities and obligations.
Debit	:	All values coming in.
Credit	:	All values going out.
Debit	:	All receivers of any benefit.
Credit	:	All givers of any benefit.
Debit	:	All dissatisfaction, i.e. expenses, losses etc.
Credit	:	All satisfaction, i.e. incomes, gains, profit etc.

Do you follow? Is there any question? Do you find any difficulty?

☐ "Sir, it would be very helpful if you kindly explain the terms '**Debit**' and '**Credit**' with the help of a few examples."

● Yes, I will. Before that let me explain the different types of Accounts—Personal, Real and Nominal. The concept of '**Debit**' and '**Credit**' may be explained under the respective heads of accounts. However, Accounts may be defined as a classified or summarised statement of all types of transactions under respective heads—Personal, Real and Nominal.

Now you may put to me the question : What are Personal Accounts, Real Accounts and Nominal Accounts? Well, note the following explanations :

ACCOUNTS

- **Personal Account** (Dealing with persons, firms, companies or organisations, viz. Mr. X, Mr. Ram's A/c LIC of India, and A and Co. etc.)
- **Impersonal Account** (Not dealing with persons or firms. It deals with property, real things, satisfaction & dissatisfaction)
  - **Real Account** (Dealing with property and things viz. Cash, Plant & Machinery, Stock etc.)
  - **Nominal Account** (Dealing with Satisfaction & Dissatisfaction; Suffering and Joy, viz. Rent received and paid, Incomes, Gains, Profits/Losses etc.)

Personal Account	:	Dr. The Receiver of any benefit Cr. The Giver of any benefit.
Real Account	:	Dr. What comes in, i.e. values coming in. Cr. What goes out, i.e. values going out.
Nominal Account	:	Dr. Dissatisfaction, i.e. Losses & Expenses etc. Cr. Satisfaction, i.e. Gains and Incomes, Profit.

STEPS IN BOOK-KEEPING

Journal or Books of Original Entry
(The book in which transactions are recorded as and when they occur)

Ledger or Books of Final Entry
(The book in which all transactions are recorded in a condensed and classified form)

Do you follow?

☐ "Sir, how is Journal transferred to Ledger? That is sir,...mechanism of Ledger?'

● Well, it is done by 'Posting'.

☐ "Sir, what is 'Posting"?

● You see, the act of transferring transactions from Journal to Ledger is known as 'Posting'.

☐ "Excuse me Sir! Please explain, what is Narration."

Narration ● Please jot down the meaning of the term Narration :

Narration is a brief explanation of each and every transaction given at the end of Journal(s).

By the by, for your understanding I would like to explain the term 'Narration' which should be given at the end of each journal.

Please note one more point relating to 'Debit' and 'Credit' which I have forgotten to tell you. The point is that, Ledger Account has two sides—'Debit' and 'Credit'. Every debit entry is preceded by the word **"TO"** on the Debit (Dr.) side of Ledger A/c, and every credit entry is preceded by the word **"BY"** on the Credit (Cr.) side of the Ledger A/c.

☐ "Sir, please explain this point at this moment, otherwise everything may get confused".

● Well, take an example. On 1st January 2006, Taste and Co. purchased a machine from Please and Co. of Coimbatore on credit worth Rs. 2,500. Here the transaction is a credit transaction. Whenever a credit transaction takes place we should remember the name of the party. The name of the party should be recorded. In case of cash transaction, the name of the party need not to be recorded. Thus the journal entry in the book of Taste and Co. will be as under :

in the Book of Taste & Co.

Date	Particulars		L.F.	*Dr.* Amount	*Cr.* Amount
	Machine Account To Please & Co. A/c (Being the Machine purchased on credit)	Dr.		Rs. 2,500	Rs. 2,500

Now from the said Journal Entry there will be two Ledger Accounts in the book of Taste and Co. which are :

Dr. **Machine Account** Cr.

Date	Particulars	J.F.	Amount	Date	Particulars	J.F.	Amount
2006 Jan. 1	To Please & Co. A/c		Rs. 2,500				Rs.

Dr. **Please & Co. Account** Cr.

Date	Particulars	J.F.	Amount	Date	Particulars	J.F.	Amount
			Rs.	2006 Jan. 1	By Machine A/c		Rs. 2,500

So, if we analyse the above transaction we can see that Machine is coming in. We have seen earlier that what comes in is 'Debit'. Here machine is coming in, that's why Machine Account has been Debited. And the giver is 'Credit'. Here, Please & Co. is the giver. So, Please and Co. is Credited. Had the transaction been a cash transaction, the name of the party or parties need not be recorded. Here the party is Please and Co.

In that case the Journal Entry would be :

Machine Account Dr. Rs. 2,500
 To Cash A/c Rs. 2,500

Here the 'Narration' will be read as :

Being the Machine purchased in cash.

And the Ledger Account in the book of Taste & Co. would be as :

Dr. **Machine Account** Cr.

Date	Particulars	J.F.	Amount	Date	Particulars	J.F.	Amount
Jan 1 2006	To Cash A/c		Rs. 2,500		By		Rs.

Dr. **Cash Account** Cr.

Date	Particulars	J.F.	Amount	Date	Particulars	J.F.	Amount
			Rs.	Jan 1 2006	By Machine A/c		Rs. 2,500

I think you have followed my lecture.

Is there any question? Please don't feel shy. Yes, what do you want to say?

☐ "Nothing, Sir".

☐ "Sir, I have one question. Earlier you have written **Account** under respective Ledger Accounts. Now you are writing **A/c** instead of **Account**. Is there any difference between the two writings"?

- No, No. It is all the same. 'Account' can be written in short as A/c.

☐ "Sir, I have another question from 'Posting' point of view. I mean Sir, while Posting from

Journal to Ledger how should I confirm what item(s) will go to the Debit side, i.e. Dr. side, and what item(s) will go to the Credit side, i.e. Cr. side of the Ledger Account, i.e. Ledger A/c?

● You see, watch very minutely the Journal Entry or Entries; there is a word 'To'. Have a look here. Please let us go back to our earlier discussion where we passed Journal Entries in the Book of Taste and Co.

Machine Account	Dr.	Rs. 2,500	
To Cash Account			Rs. 2,500

See, where you are standing in case of Machine A/c in this example. Machine is appearing or standing on the Dr. side. When you are preparing Machine A/c (in the Ledger), go to the Debit side (Dr. side) of the concerned A/c and post it on the Dr. side counterpart A/c after prefixing the word **To**. The word 'To' appearing in the Journal means that it will go to the Credit side (Cr. side) of the Ledger Account; and the counterpart will appear on the Cr. side of the Ledger A/c prefixing the word '**By**'.

Please go through the workings again shown earlier. Are you feeling tired?

☐ "No sir, you have explained in such a manner that even a non-accountant like me, an engineer, can understand easily".

● Thank you, I want to give you a break for 10 minutes.

By the by, I have forgotten to tell you one important point regarding Cash Book, i.e. Cash A/c; the Debit side (Dr.) of the Cash Book, i.e. Cash A/c, records all **Receipts of Cash** and Credit Side (Cr.) of the Cash Book, i.e. Cash A/c, records all **Payments of Cash**. Moreover, Cash Book, i.e. Cash A/c, may be treated as both Journal and Ledger.

Now, do you follow my lecture? I shall be happy to hear from you any point which is not clear to you.

☐ "Sir, what are Purchase Day Book and Sale Day Book"?

● Well, I will explain everything step by step.

We have seen earlier that Journal is a Prime entry in which all transactions are recorded as and when they occur. It is devised in such a way that all entries are classified into two aspects—(i) **Debit**, and (ii) **Credit**. Previously all transactions were passed through one book called Journal. But now-a-days, to minimise clerical load of work, general Journal has been sub-divided into two parts—(a) Sectional Journal, and (b) Journal Proper.

JOURNAL

Sectional Journal	**Journal Proper**
(Each Sectional Journal is intended for recording transactions of one particular type)	(Transactions which cannot be recorded in one of the Sectional Journals and passed through original journal, are meant for Journal Proper)
Examples	**Examples**
a. Cash Book	a. Opening Entries
b. Purchase Day Book	b. Transfer Entries
c. Sales Day Book	c. Rectification Entries

d. Return Outward Book
e. Return Inward Book
f. Bills Receivable Book
g. Bills Payable Book

d. Adjusting Entries
e. Closing Entries
f. Other transactions which cannot be passed through other book

Well, before explaining in details about Sectional Journal and Journal Proper, let us journalise a few transactions. I think you will appreciate my view. One thing I would like to clear to you at this stage—it will not be possible for me to journalise the transactions and post it to ledger in appropriate sketch in all the cases. This will disturb the progress of my lecture. But you will have to follow the appropriate sketch for all time to come.

However, take the following transactions for work-out :

ILLUSTRATION ONE

Journalise the following transactions with proper narration :
June 2006

1. Started a business with Capital of Rs. 10,000
2. Purchased furniture for Cash Rs. 250
3. Purchased goods worth Rs. 1,000
3. Received from A. Bros. & Co. Rs. 1,500
7. Sold goods for cash Rs. 300
10. Sold goods worth Rs. 500 to N.T. & Co. Ltd.
11. Goods worth Rs. 400 purchased from A & Co. Ltd. on credit
22. Received from N.T. & Co. Ltd. Rs. 500 on account
30. Paid electric charges Rs. 150
30. Paid rent Rs. 35
30. Paid salary and wages for Rs. 550

Before journalising all these transactions let us see what item(s) will be 'Debit' and what item(s) will be 'Credit'.

Well, please note one thing—All assets are 'debit balance' and all liabilities are 'credit balance'; whenever any asset loses its value by way of depreciation or for any other reason, it loses the character of debit to the extent of its depreciated value, and the particular asset will be placed on credit side to the extent of its depreciated or lost value.

Take for an example : Mr. X started a business with Rs. 12,000 in Cash, Rs. 3,000 worth of Goods, Rs. 10,000 worth of Plant and Machinery and Rs. 5,000 worth of Furniture.

Well, following **Situation** will be observed in light of 'depreciated or lost value' and appreciated value of Plant and Machinery :

(i) The value of Plant & Machinery has been depreciated @ 10%.
(ii) Addition to Plant & Machinery worth Rs. 5,000.
(iii) Plant & Machinery revalued at Rs. 8,000.
(iv) Plant & Machinery revalued at Rs. 13,000.
(v) Mr. X withdraws his Capital Rs. 2,000.

Please observe the above **situations** very minutely and remember our previous discussions that every 'Debit' should have corresponding 'Credit'; and every 'Credit' should have corresponding 'Debit' : All assets are 'Debit' and all liabilities are 'Credit'.

Please note the following :

Journal Entries in the book of Mr. X

Date	Particulars	L.F.	Amount	Amount
			Rs.	Rs.
	Plant & Machinery A/c Dr.		10,000	
	Furniture A/c Dr.		5,000	
	Cash A/c Dr.		12,000	
	Opening Stock A/c Dr.		3,000	
	To Capital A/c			30,000
	(Being the Plant & Machinery, Furniture, Cash and value of Goods introduced as Capital).			

Situation I

Plant & Machinery worth Rs. 10,000 has been depreciated @ 10%, i.e. Rs. 1,000. Here Plant & Machinery loses its basic character of 'Debit' to the extent of Rs. 1,000. So Plant & Machinery will be credited to the extent of the loss of its value which is Rs, 1000. Here Depreciation A/c will be debited. Since depreciation is an item of expense (dissatisfaction), it is 'Debit'.

Date	Particulars	L.F.	Amount	Amount
			Rs.	Rs.
	Depreciation A/c Dr.		1,000	
	To Plant & Machinery A/c			1,000
	(Being Plant & Machinery depreciated)			

Situation II

Addition to Plant & Machinery worth Rs. 5,000.

I told you earlier that whenever any asset increases it will be debited to the extent of its appreciated or increased value. So, it will be 'Debit'. In Situation No. I, the asset is depreciated. So, the 'Asset' was credited to the extent of its depreciated or lost value. Here in Situation No. II. the Journal entry will be :

Date	Particulars	L.F.	Amount	Amount
			Rs.	Rs.
	Plant & Machinery A/c Dr.		5,000	
	To Cash			5,000
	(Being addition in the Plant & Machinery)			

Now, you may put me the question : Why the other asset, i.e. Cash, has been reduced to make the fixed assets appreciated?

You see, a part of Cash (Asset) is used for the purchase or acquisition or addition to another asset Plant and Machinery. Here value of Cash (Asset), which bears the character of Debit, has declined. I told you earlier that when an Asset (in this case Cash) loses its character, it is to be credited to the extent of its lost or decreased value. Therefore, Cash is credited. Moreover, it can be explained in another way. Please note that one Asset (here Cash) is sacrificed to have another Asset. That is to say Old Asset (here Cash) is sacrificed for the acquisition of New Asset (here Plant & Machinery). So, sacrificed portion of the old Asset will be credited. So, cash is credited.

You see, a little thinking in the theory of Double Entry Book-keeping will suggest that every 'Debit' must have a corresponding 'Credit'.

Here the value of the asset could have been appreciated at the cost of increasing liability, say sundry creditors. So, the Journal will follow as :

Date	Particulars		L.F.	Amount	Amount
				Rs.	Rs.
	Plant & Machinery A/c	Dr.		5,000	
	To XYZ & Co.				5,000
	(here Creditor)				
	(Being the Plant & Machinery purchased from XYZ & Co. on credit)				

Situation III

Plant & Machinery has been revalued at Rs. 8,000. It means, the value of the asset has been brought down to the extent of Rs. 2,000 (Rs. 10,000 – Rs. 8,000). So, the particular asset will be credited to the extent of the loss of value. So, Machinery A/c will be credited.

☐ "Sir, here is no question of Depreciation, then what account is to be Debited to give its actual effect or what account is to be Credited to make double entry"?

● Here we have 'Credit' item, but the 'Debit' item is to be found out. Here Revaluation A/c is to be debited :

Date	Particulars		L.F.	Amount	Amount
				Rs.	Rs.
	Revaluation A/c	Dr.		2,000	
	To Plant & Machinery A/c				2,000
	(Being the value of the Plant & Machinery purchased written down)				

Situation IV

Here revaluation on existing Plant & Machinery has been made at Rs. 13,000. So, here increase in the value of assets is Rs. 3,000. So, Plant & Machinery Account will be debited to the extent of Rs. 3,000 and Revaluation Account is to be credited :

Date	Particulars		L.F.	Amount	Amount
				Rs.	Rs.
	Plant & Machinery A/c	Dr.		3,000	
	To Revaluation A/c				3,000
	(Being the appreciation in the value of Plant & Machinery)				

Situation V

Withdrawal of Capital indicates that the Capital will lose its credit character to the extent of withdrawal. That is to say, Capital Account or Drawing A/c will be debited to the extent of Rs. 2,000 :

Date	Particulars		L.F.	Amount Rs.	Amount Rs.
	Capital (Drawing) A/c	Dr.		2,000	
	To Cash				2,000
	(Being the Capital withdrawn)				

Please note that the above discussions can be reproduced in the following manner :

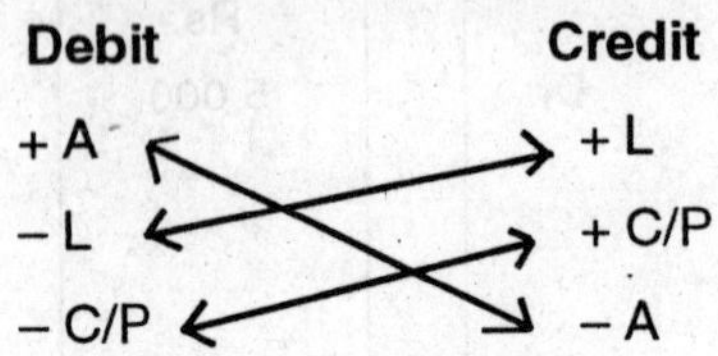

(–) = Decrease
(+) = Increase
A = Assets
L = Liabilities
C/P = Capital or Proprietorship

Dr. Assets A/c	Cr.
Plus (+)	Minus (–)

Dr. Liabilities or Capital A/c	Cr.
Minus (–)	Plus (+)

Dr. Expenses & Losses A/c	Cr.
Plus (+)	Minus (–)

Dr. Incomes & Gains A/c	Cr.
Minus (–)	Plus (+)

However, I hope you have followed the above interpretation.

☐ "Excuse me Sir, you have not worked out **Illustration One**. Please give us some guidelines on the same."

● I think, at this stage of progress, you may work out the said illustration.

Well, you please try. At least you answer which item will be debit and which item will be credit. Let me have some test checking. After that I will work it out.

Regarding transaction relating to June 1, you answer what item is debit and which one is credit.

☐ "Sir, Capital is debit and Cash is credit".

● You see, I think you could not digest my last lecture, otherwise this type of answer cannot be expected from you. Well what's your logic behind this answer?

☐ "Sir, you have said, what comes in is debit and what goes out is credit. So, capital is coming in, cash is going out. So capital has been debited and cash is credited.

● You see, a business, whatever type it may be, has a separate and legal entity of its own, and should be differentiated from the proprietor of the business. "The 'enterprise' is

Business Entity Concept

viewed as a distinct impersonal entity. This view-point is a basic feature of double entry accounting. An enterprise, as such, is always differentiated from individuals or firms with which it deals, such as employees, debtors, creditors, and even proprietors."[3]

So, business is started with the joint liabilities of creditors and proprietor[4]. And it should be noted that the rights of the creditors in most of the assets of a business are known as liabilities of an enterprise or of the business[5]. So, that's why capital account should be credited and assets account should be debited. Because, as per our principles of accountancy mentioned earlier, we had seen that all assets are debit and all liabilities are credit. Is there any question(s)?

Yes, yes. What is your question?

☐ "Sir! Suppose I have one 5 (five)-rupee coin. It is cash, that is to say, it is an asset to me. Sir, when will the said cash with me become capital? Are 'Capital' and 'Cash' two distinct aspect, or are they same?"

• Your question is really beautiful. It is rather a **brain-storming question.**

You see, people may have cash with them. For example Mr. A has Rs. 5,000 in cash. It cannot be capital. When **mental attitude is attributed to this cash—to start a business—the said cash became capital**. So, here cash and capital are same. That is to say, one side of the same coin is Cash (i.e., Asset) and other side of the same coin is Capital (i.e. Liability).

Suppose one man has Rs. 10,000 in his account, this Rs. 10,000 is to be treated as cash, i.e. Asset; it cannot be capital; but when the same man wants to start a business with the said amount of cash, the said cash is to be treated as Capital.

Please note that with the start of business, business is known by its name, not by the name of persons who owns it. Hence, the Journal Entry will be :

Cash A/c	Dr.	Rs. 10,000	
To Capital A/c			Rs. 10,000

And the Initial or Opening Position of the Balance Sheet will be :

Balance Sheet

Capital and Liabilities	Amount	Assets and Properties	Amount
	Rs.		Rs.
Capital	10,000	Cash	10,000
	10,000		10,000

What is Balance Sheet and what are its functions — all would be discussed in due course of time. Well, I am working out **Illustration One :**

[3] *C. R. Rorem and H. D. Kerrigan, "**Accounting Method**", Third Edition, P. 19.*

[4] *Liabilities and proprietorship are very similar in their basic characteristics; they both represent rights in assets. Creditors and proprietors may, broadly speaking, be regarded as joint participants in an enterprise. To be sure, the creditors invest their assets under different conditions than do the proprietors; nevertheless they provide the portions of the total assets of the enterprise; and until they withdraw their portions; they have certain definite rights over the assets of the enterprise".—**Rorem and Kerrigan**, op. cit., Pp. 22-23.*

[5] *Nobel and Niswonger, **Accounting Principle**, P. 6 and p. 23.*

Journal Entries in the book of ....

Date		Particulars	L.F.	Dr.	Cr.
2006				Rs.	Rs.
June	1	Cash A/c Dr. To Capital A/c (Being cash introduced as capital)		10,000	10,000
"	2	Furniture A/c Dr. To Cash A/c (Being furniture purchased)		250	250
"	3	Purchase A/c Dr. To Cash A/c (Being the goods purchased)		1,000	1,000
"	3	Cash A/c Dr. To A Bros. & Co. A/c (Being the amount received)		1,500	1,500
"	7	Cash A/c Dr. To Sales A/c (Being the goods sold on cash)		300	300
"	10	N.T. & Co. Ltd. A/c Dr. To Sales A/c (Being the goods sold on credit)		500	500
"	11	Purchases A/c Dr. To A & Co. Ltd. (Being the goods purchased on credit)		400	400
"	22	Cash A/c Dr. To N.T. & Co. Ltd. (Being the amount received)		500	500
"	30	Electric Charges A/c Dr. To Cash A/c (Being electric charges paid)		150	150
"	30	Rent A/c Dr. To Cash A/c (Being the rent paid)		35	35
"	30	Salary and Wages A/c Dr. To Cash A/c (Being the salary and wages paid)		550	550
		Total		15,185	15,185

I think, you have followed the above workings.

Is there any question?

☐ "Sir, you told earlier that what is coming is Debit; and what is going out is Credit. So, when goods come in it is to be debited and when goods go out it should be credited. Why, Sir, instead of goods you have used the words Purchase and Sale?"

• Please the note that when goods come in, we will call it purchase and when goods out we will call it sales. Please further note that when sales material are found defective by the customers it will be returned by them. In that case in the books of the company 'Return Inward A/c' will be debited because it is sales return. don't make sales return A/c as debit (Dr.). Similarly when are purchase material from supplier is found defective then the same will be returned to the supplier. In that case 'Return Outward A/c' will be credited. Don't say purchase return A/c credit (Cr.). It is unethical from the philosophy of accounting.

☐ "Sir, why you are considering it unethical?"

● You see, it is departure from traditional approach. An insight into the matter would reveal that the very word 'purchase' should not be allowed to appear on the credit side in any from. That is why to avoid this mental conflict it is desirable to say 'Return Outward' instead of purchase return. So, suppliers A/c to be debited and Return outward A/c should be credited.

A similar principle is to be followed in case of sales return also.

☐ "Yes Sir, very interesting indeed, Sir!"

● Now I would like to give you a few information from which I plan to work out Journal,

Steps of Balance Sheet

Ledger and Trial Balance and from the same information, i.e., from Trial Balance, I would like to work out Trading A/c, Profit and Loss A/c, and Balance Sheet. This is because I want to give you a clear understanding of the **'Chain of Accountancy'**. That is to say, I will give you details about the ***Steps of Balance Sheet***.

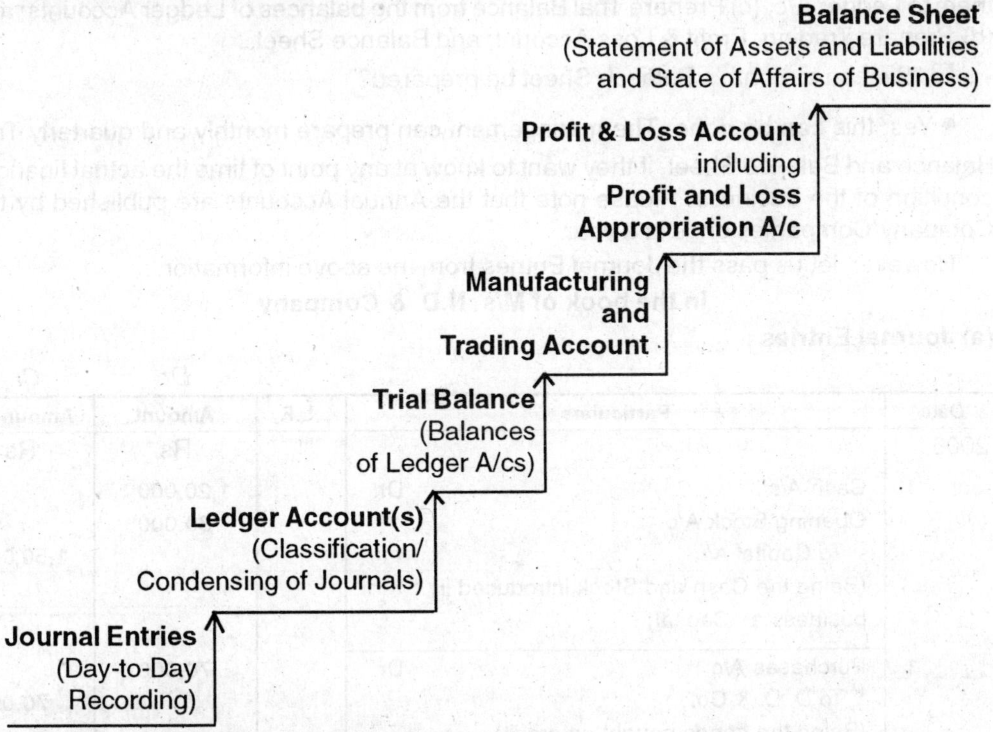

Now you may put to me the following questions :

(a) What is Trial Balance?
(b) What is Trading Account?
(c) What is Profit & Loss A/c? and, finally,
(d) What is Balance Sheet?

Well, all those queries would be satisfied in due course of time. Before that jot down the following information for reaching Balance Sheet step by step—from Journal to Ledger; from Ledger to Trial Balance, and from Trial Balance to Trading Account, Profit & Loss A/c and Balance Sheet.

ILLUSTRATION TWO

On 1st January 2006 M/s N. D. & Co. started a business with Rs. 1,20,000 in Cash and Rs. 30,000 worth of Goods.

Following are the transactions for the month of January 2006 :

Jan. 1. Bought goods from D. D. & Co. worth Rs. 70,000
3. Bought goods for cash Rs. 1,000
5. Sold goods for cash Rs. 5,000
7. Sold goods to Z & Co. for Rs. 7,400
8. Paid Rs. 70,000 to D. D. & Co.
10. Paid salaries and wages Rs. 4,000
12. Purchased fuel Rs. 1,000
15. Z & Co. returned goods Rs. 4,000
18. Purchased goods worth Rs. 7,500 from L & Co.
28. Received Commission Rs. 720
30. Sold goods to R & Co. worth Rs. 7,330
31. Received damaged goods worth Rs. 1,330 from R & Co.

From the information supplied, you are requested—(a) to pass Journal entry; (b) post them to Ledger A/c; (c) Prepare Trial Balance from the balances of Ledger Accounts; and (d) Prepare Trading, Profit & Loss Account; and Balance Sheet.

☐ "Sir, can a month's Balance Sheet be prepared?"

● Yes, this can be done. The management can prepare monthly and quarterly Trial Balance and Balance Sheet, if they want to know at any point of time the actual financial condition of the business. Please note that the Annual Accounts are published by the Company/Companies once in a year.

However, let us pass the Journal Entries from the above information :

In the book of M/s. N.D. & Company

(a) Journal Entries :

Date	Particulars		L.F.	Dr. Amount	Cr. Amount
2006				Rs.	Rs.
Jan. 1	Cash A/c	Dr.		1,20,000	
	Opening Stock A/c			30,000	
	To Capital A/c				1,50,000
	(Being the Cash and Stock introduced in business as Capital)				
1	Purchases A/c	Dr.		70,000	
	To D. D. & Co.				70,000
	(Being the goods bought on credit)				
" 3	Purchases A/c	Dr.		1,000	
	To Cash A/c				1,000
	(Being the goods purchased in cash)				

Date	Particulars		L.F.	Dr. Amount	Cr. Amount
2006				Rs.	Rs.
" 5	Cash A/c	Dr.		5,000	
	To Sales A/c				5,000
	(Being the goods sold in cash)				
" 7	Z & Co. A/c	Dr.		7,400	
	To Sales A/c				7,400
	(Being the goods sold on credit)				
Jan. 8	D. D. & Co. A/c	Dr.		70,000	
	To Cash A/c				70,000
	(Being the amount paid)				
" 10	Salaries & Wages A/c	Dr.		4,000	
	To Cash A/c				4,000
	(Being the Wages & Salaries paid)				
" 12	Fuel A/c	Dr.		1,000	
	To Cash A/c				1,000
	(Being the amount paid as cost of fuel)				
" 15	Return Inward A/c	Dr.		4,000	
	To Z & Co. A/c				4,000
	(Being the goods returned by Z & Co.)				
" 18	Purchases A/c	Dr.		7,500	
	To L & Co. A/c				7,500
	(Being the goods bought on credit)				
" 28	Cash A/c	Dr.		720	
	To Commission A/c				720
	(Being the commission received)				
" 30	R & Co. A/c	Dr.		7,330	
	To Sales A/c				7,330
	(Being the goods sold on credit)				
" 31	Return Inward A/c	Dr.		1,330	
	To R & Co. A/c				1,330
	(Being the goods returned by R & Co.)				
	Total			3,29,280	3,29,280

(b) Now let us post all those Journal entries into the Ledger. Here we will have to open the following Ledger A/cs—Cash A/c, Opening Stock A/c, Capital A/c, Purchase A/c, D. D. & Co. A/c, Sales A/c, L & Co. A/c, R & Co. A/c, Commission A/c, etc.

Cash A/c

Dr. **Recepit** | **Payment** *Cr.*

Date	Particulars	J.F.	Amount	Date	Particulars	J.F.	Amount
2006			Rs.	2006			Rs.
Jan. 1	To Capital A/c		1,20,000	Jan. 3	By Purchases A/c		1,000
" 5	" Sales A/c		5,000	" 8	" D. D. & Co. A/c		70,000
" 28	" Commission A/c		720	" 10	" Salaries & Wages A/c		4,000
				" 12	" Fuel A/c		1,000
				" 31	" Balance c/d		49,720
			1,25,720				1,25,720
Feb. 1	To Balance b/d		49,720				

Dr. **Opening Stock A/c** Cr.

Date	Particulars	J.F.	Amount	Date	Particulars	J.F.	Amount
2006			Rs.	2006			Rs.
Jan. 1	To Capital A/c		30,000	Jan. 31	By Balance c/d		30,000
			30,000				30,000
Feb. 1	To Balance b/d		30,000				

Dr. **Capital A/c** Cr.

Date	Particulars	J.F.	Amount	Date	Particulars	J.F.	Amount
2006			Rs.	2006			Rs.
Dec. 31	To Balance c/d		1,50,000	Jan. 1	By Cash A/c		1,20,000
				"	Stock A/c		30,000
			1,50,000				1,50,000
				Feb. 1	By Balance b/d		1,50,000

Dr. **Purchases A/c** Cr.

Date	Particulars	J.F.	Amount	Date	Particulars	J.F.	Amount
2006			Rs.	2006			Rs.
Jan. 1	To D.D. & Co.		70,000	Dec. 31	By Balance c/d		78,500
" 3	" Cash A/c		1,000				
" 18	" L & Co. A/c		7,500				
			78,500				78,500
Feb. 1	To Balance b/d		78,500				

Dr. **Sales A/c** Cr.

Date	Particulars	J.F.	Amount	Date	Particulars	J.F.	Amount
2006			Rs.	2006			Rs.
Jan. 31	To Balance c/d		19,730	Jan. 5	By Cash A/c		5,000
				" 7	" Z & Co.		7,400
				" 30	" R & Co.		7,330
			19,730				19,730
				Feb. 1	By Balance b/d		19,730

Dr. **D. D. & Co. A/c** Cr.

Date	Particulars	J.F.	Amount	Date	Particulars	J.F.	Amount
2006			Rs.	2006			Rs.
Jan. 8	To Cash A/c		70,000	Jan. 1	By Purchases A/c		70,000
			70,000				70,000

Dr. **Z & Co. A/c** Cr.

Date	Particulars	J.F.	Amount	Date	Particulars	J.F.	Amount
2006			Rs.	2006			Rs.
Jan. 7	To Sales A/c		7,400	Jan. 15	By Return Inward A/c		4,000
				Jan. 31	" Balance c/d		3,400
			7,400				7,400
Feb. 1	To Balance b/d		3,400				

Dr. **R & Co. A/c** Cr.

Date	Particulars	J.F.	Amount	Date	Particulars	J.F.	Amount
2006			Rs.	2006			Rs.
Jan. 30	To Sales A/c		7,330	Jan. 31	By Return Inward A/c		1,330
				31	" Balance c/d		6,000
			7,300				7,330
Feb. 1	To Balance b/d		6,000				

Dr. **L & Co. A/c** Cr.

Date	Particulars	J.F.	Amount	Date	Particulars	J.F.	Amount
2006			Rs.	2006			Rs.
Jan. 31	To Balance c/d		7,500	Jan. 1	By Purchases A/c		7,500
			7,500				7,500
				Feb. 1	By Balance b/d		7,500

Dr. **Commission A/c** Cr.

Date	Particulars	J.F.	Amount	Date	Particulars	J.F.	Amount
2006			Rs.	2006			Rs.
Jan. 31	To Balance c/d		720	Jan. 28	By Cash		720
			720				720
				Feb. 1	By Balance b/d		720

Dr. **Return Inward A/c** Cr.

Date	Particulars	J.F.	Amount	Date	Particulars	J.F.	Amount
2006			Rs.	2006			Rs.
Jan. 15	To Z & Co. A/c		4,000	Jan. 31	By Balance c/d		5,330
Jan. 31	To R & Co. A/c		1,330				
			5,330				5,330
Feb. 1	To Balance b/d		5,330				

Fuel A/c

Dr.							Cr.
Date	**Particulars**	**J.F.**	**Amount**	**Date**	**Particulars**	**J.F.**	**Amount**
2006			Rs.	2006			Rs.
Jan.12	To Cash A/c		1,000	Jan. 31	By Balance c/d		1,000
			1,000				1,000
Feb. 1	To Balance b/d		1,000				

Salary & Wages A/c

Dr.							Cr.
Date	**Particulars**	**J.F.**	**Amount**	**Date**	**Particulars**	**J.F.**	**Amount**
2006			Rs.	2006			Rs.
Jan.10	To Cash A/c		4,000	Jan. 31	By Balance c/d		4,000
			4,000				4,000
Feb. 1	To Balance b/d		4,000				

Well, from the above balances of Ledger Accounts we can now prepare Trial Balance.

☐ "Sir, what is Trial Balance?"

- You see, Trial Balance may be defined as a statement prepared from the debit and credit balances of the ledger accounts to verify the arithmetical accuracy of the books of accounts maintained by any Proprietorship Business, Partnership Business and Joint Stock Company.

Definition of Trial Balance

I think you have followed the discussions made earlier. However, here I prepare Trial Balance from the balances of ledger accounts, as shown earlier. Please take down :

Trial Balance of M/s N. D. & Co.
as at 31st January 2006

SL.	Particulars		L.F.	Dr. Amount	Cr. Amount
				Rs.	Rs.
1	Cash A/c			49,720	
2	Opening Stock A/c			30,000	
3	Capital A/c				1,50,000
4	Purchases A/c			78,500	
5	Sales A/c				19,730
6	Debtors A/c :				
7	Z & Co.	3,400			
8	R & Co.	6,000		9,400	
9	Salary and Wages A/c			4,000	
10	Fuel A/c			1,000	
11	Return Inward A/c			5,330	
12	Creditors A/c : L & Co.				7,500
13	Commission A/c				720
	Total			1,77,950	1,77,950

Now, from the above information, i.e. from Trial Balance, we can prepare Trading, Profit & Loss A/c, and Balance Sheet.

Trading and Profit & Loss A/c
for the month of January 2006

Dr. *Cr.*

Particulars	Amount Rs.	Particulars	Amount Rs.
To Opening Stock	30,000	By Sales : 19,730	
" Purchases	78,500	*Less* Return 5,330	14,400
" Fuel	1,000	By Gross Loss c/d	95,100
	1,09,500		1,09,500
To Gross Loss b/d	95,100	By Commission	720
" Salary and Wages	4,000	" Net Loss transferred to Capital A/c	98,380
	99,100		99,100

Balance Sheet of M/s N. D. & Co.
as at 31.1.2006

Capital and Liabilities	Rs.	Amount Rs.	Assets and Properties	Amount Rs.
Capital :	1,50,000		Cash	49,720
Less Net Loss	98,380	51,620	Debtors	9,400
Creditors		7,500		
		59,120		59,120

By the by, I would like to point out one thing regarding presentation of *Loss* in Balance Sheet. We have shown it as a deduction from capital. But from Companies Act point of view it should be shown on the Assets side of the Balance Sheet and should be written-off gradually from the future earned profit of the company.

However, it can be presented as under :

Balance Sheet
as at 31.1.2006

Capital and Liabilities	Amount Rs.	Assets and Properties	Amount Rs.
Capital	1,50,000	Cash	49,720
Creditors	7,500	Debtors	9,400
		Profit and Loss A/c (Dr.) Balance	98,380
	1,57,500		1,57,500

☐ "Excuse me Sir. What is Profit & Loss Account Debit balance, i.e. Profit and Loss A/c (Dr.) Balance?"

- **Please note**, Profit and Loss A/c (Dr.) Balance means Net Loss.

For your better understanding I am giving another example from which please work out Journal, Ledger A/c, Trading A/c, Profit & Loss A/c and Balance Sheet. This is your home task :

On 1st January 2006, Max Pvt. Ltd. started business as a retail trader. The following transactions took place during six months ending on 30th June 2006. All Cash received were immediately deposited into bank and payments were made by issuing cheques :

Jan.	1	Started business with Bank balance Rs. 1,00,000, Building Rs. 1,20,000 and Stock worth Rs. 50,000.
Jan.	1	Delivery van purchased for Rs. 25,000.
Jan.	13	Bought goods and issued cheque for Rs. 45,000 and Carriage Inward paid Rs. 2,000.
Jan.	22	Bought goods from New York Trader for Rs. 78,000 and Carriage Inward paid Rs. 2,300.
Feb.	5	Sold goods for Cash Rs. 60,000.
Feb.	10	Commission paid Rs. 4,000.
Feb.	20	Bought goods from Dinesh Cloth for Rs. 82,000 and Carriage Inward paid Rs. 1,500.
Feb.	28	Sold goods for Cash Rs. 58,000 and Carriage Outward paid Rs. 1,500.
March	1	Furniture purchased for Rs. 50,000.
March	17	Good returned to Dinesh Cloth worth Rs. 8,000.
March	26	Goods worth Rs. 2,000 returned to New York Trader.
April	1	Rent paid Rs. 3,000.
April	7	Sold goods to Ramesh & Co. for Rs. 55,000.
April	20	Cheque for Rs. 50,000 issued to New York trader.
April	27	Goods returned by Ramesh & Co. for Rs. 7,000.
May	10	Cash Rs. 43,000 received from Ramesh & Co.
May	25	Cheque for Rs. 62,000 issued to Dinesh Cloth.
June	1	Cash Sale Rs. 72,000.
June	9	Commission paid Rs. 5,000.
June	29	Salary and Wages paid Rs. 15,000.

Other Information :

Value of Closing Stock Rs. 85,000

Outstanding Rent Rs. 500

Outstanding Salary and Wages Rs. 1,000

Depreciation on Building @ 4% p.a., Furniture @ 3% p.a., Delivery Van @ 4% p.a.

Journalise the above transactions and post them to Ledger Accounts and prepare Trading A/c, Profit & Loss A/c for the 6 (six) months and Balance Sheet as on 30.6.2006.

☐ "Excuse me Sir! I have one question."

• What is that?

☐ "Sir, what is p.a.?"

• Well, the full form is per annum which means yearly. It is a Latin Word.

☐ "Excuse me Sir, I request you to work out the problem. From next time, I will not request you."

• Well, please note :

Solution :

Journal

Date	Particulars		L.F.	Dr. Amount	Cr. Amount
				Rs.	Rs.
2006					
Jan. 1	Bank A/c	Dr.		1,00,000	
	Building A/c	Dr.		1,20,000	
	Stock A/c	Dr.		50,000	
	To Capital A/c				2,70,000
	(Being business started with Cash at Bank, Building and Stock)				
Jan. 1	Delivery Van A/c	Dr.		25,000	
	To Bank A/c				25,000
	(Being delivery van purchased)				
Jan. 13	Purchases A/c	Dr.		45,000	
	To Bank A/c				45,000
	(Being goods purchased and issued cheque)				
Jan. 13	Carriage Inward A/c	Dr.		2,000	
	To Bank A/c				2,000
	(Being Carriage Inward paid)				
Jan. 22	Purchases A/c	Dr.		78,000	
	To New York Trader A/c				78,000
	(Being goods purchased from New York Trader)				
Jan. 22	Carriage Inward A/c	Dr.		2,300	
	To Bank A/c				2,300
	(Being Carriage Inward paid)				
Feb. 5	Bank A/c	Dr.		60,000	
	To Sales A/c				60,000
	(Being goods sold and Cash immediately deposited into bank)				

Journal

Date	Particulars		L.F.	Dr. Amount	Cr. Amount
				Rs.	Rs.
2006					
Feb. 10	Commission A/c To Bank A/c (Being commission paid)	Dr.		4,000	4,000
Feb. 20	Purchases A/c To Dinesh Cloth A/c (Being goods purchased from Dinesh Cloth)	Dr.		82,000	82,000
Feb. 20	Carriage Inward A/c To Bank A/c (Being Carriage Inward paid)	Dr.		1,500	1,500
Feb. 28	Bank A/c To Sales A/c (Being goods sold for cash and deposited into bank)	Dr.		58,000	58,000
Feb. 28	Carriage Outward A/c To Bank A/c (Being Carriage Outward paid)	Dr.		1,500	1,500
Mar. 1	Furniture A/c To Bank A/c (Being furniture purchased)	Dr.		50,000	50,000
Mar. 17	Dinesh Cloth A/c To Return Outward A/c (Being goods returned to Dinesh Cloth)	Dr.		8,000	8,000
Mar. 26	New York Trader A/c To Return Outward A/c (Being goods returned to New York Trader)	Dr.		2,000	2,000
April 1	Rent A/c To Bank A/c (Being rent paid)	Dr.		3,000	3,000
April 7	Ramesh & Co. A/c To Sales A/c (Being goods sold to Ramesh & Co.)	Dr.		55,000	55,000
April 20	New York Trader A/c To Bank A/c (Being cheque issued to New York Trader)	Dr.		50,000	50,000
April 27	Return Inward A/c To Ramesh & Co. A/c (Being goods returned by Ramesh & Co.)	Dr.		7,000	7,000
May 10	Bank A/c To Ramesh & Co. A/c (Being cash received from Ramesh & Co. and deposited into bank)	Dr.		43,000	43,000

Journal

Date	Particulars		L.F.	Dr. Amount	Cr. Amount
				Rs.	Rs.
2006					
May 25	Dinesh Cloth A/c	Dr.		62,000	
	To Bank A/c				62,000
	(Being cheque issued to Dinesh Cloth)				
June 1	Bank A/c	Dr.		72,000	
	To Sales A/c				72,000
	(Being goods sold for cash)				
June 9	Commission A/c	Dr.		5,000	
	To Bank A/c				5,000
	(Being commission paid)				
June 29	Salary and Wages A/c	Dr.		15,000	
	To Bank A/c				15,000
	(Being salary and wages paid)				
	Total			10,01,300	10,01,300

Cash Book

Dr. Cr.

Date	Particulars	J.F.	Amount	Date	Particulars	J.F.	Amount
2006			Rs.	2006			Rs.
1.1	To Capital		1,00,000	1.1	By Delivery Van A/c		25,000
5.2	" Sales A/c		60,000	13.1	" Purchases A/c		45,000
28.2	" Sales A/c		58,000	13.1	" Carriage		
10.5	" Ramesh & Co. A/c		43,000	22.1	Inward A/c		2,000
1.6	" Sales A/c		72,000		" Carriage		
					Inward A/c		2,300
				10.2	" Commission A/c		4,000
				20.2	" Carriage		
					Inward A/c		1,500
				28.2	" Carriage		
					Outward A/c		1,500
				10.3	" Furniture A/c		50,000
				1.4	" Rent A/c		3,000
				20.4	" New York		
					Trader A/c		50,000
				25.5	" Dinesh Cloth A/c.		62,000

Continued

Dr. **Cash Book** **Cr.**

Date	Particulars	J. F.	Amount	Date	Particulars	J. F.	Amount
2006			Rs.	2006			Rs.
				9.6	" Commission A/c		5,000
				29.6	" Salary & Wages A/c		15,000
				30.6	" Balance c/d		66,700
			3,33,000				3,33,000
1.7	To Balance b/d		66,700				

Dr. **Purchases A/c** **Cr.**

Date	Particulars	J. F.	Amount	Date	Particulars	J. F.	Amount
2006			Rs.	2006			Rs.
13.1	To Bank A/c		45,000				
22.1	" New York Trader		78,000				
20.2	" Dinesh Cloth		82,000				
				30.6	By Balance c/d		2,05,000
			2,05,000				2,05,000
1.7	To Balance b/d		2,05,000				

Dr. **Sales A/c** **Cr.**

Date	Particulars	J. F.	Amount	Date	Particulars	J. F.	Amount
2006			Rs.	2006			Rs.
				5.2	By Bank A/c		60,000
				28.2	" Bank A/c		58,000
30.6	To Balance c/d		2,45,000	7.4	" Ramesh & Co. A/c		55,000
				1.6	" Bank A/c		72,000
			2,45,000				2,45,000
				1.7	By Balance b/d		2,45,000

Dr. **Carriage Inward A/c** **Cr.**

Date	Particulars	J. F.	Amount	Date	Particulars	J. F.	Amount
2006			Rs.	2006			Rs.
13.1	To Bank A/c		2,000				
22.1	" Bank A/c		2,300	30.6	By Balance c/d		5,800
20.2	" Bank A/c		1,500				
			5,800				5,800
1.7	To Balance b/d		5,800				

Dr. **Carriage Outward A/c** Cr.

Date	Particulars	J.F.	Amount	Date	Particulars	J.F.	Amount
2006			Rs.	2006			Rs.
28.2	To Bank A/c		1,500	30.6	By Balance c/d		1,500
			1,500				1,500
1.7	To Balance b/d		1,500				

Dr. **Return Inward A/c** Cr.

Date	Particulars	J.F.	Amount	Date	Particulars	J.F.	Amount
2006			Rs.	2006			Rs.
27.4	To Ramesh & Co. A/c		7,000	30.6	By Balance c/d		7,000
			7,000				7,000
1.7	To Balance b/d		7,000				

Dr. **Return Outward A/c** Cr.

Date	Particulars	J.F.	Amount	Date	Particulars	J.F.	Amount
2006			Rs.	2006			Rs.
30.6	To Balance c/d		10,000	17.3	By Dinesh Cloth		8,000
				26.4	" New York Trader		2,000
			10,000				10,000
				1.7	By Balance b/d		10,000

Dr. **New York Trader A/c** Cr.

Date	Particulars	J.F.	Amount	Date	Particulars	J.F.	Amount
2006			Rs.	2006			Rs.
26.3	To Return Outward		2,000	22.1	By Purchases A/c		78,000
20.4	To Bank A/c		50,000				
30.6	To Balance c/d		26,000				
			78,000				78,000
				1.7	By Balance b/d		26,000

Dr. **Dinesh Cloth A/c** Cr.

Date	Particulars	J.F.	Amount	Date	Particulars	J.F.	Amount
2006			Rs.	2006			Rs.
17.3	To Return Outward		8,000	22.2	By Purchases A/c		82,000
25.3	" Bank A/c		62,000				
30.6	" Balance c/d		12,000				
			82,000				82,000
				1.7	By Balance b/d		12,000

Dr. Ramesh & Co. A/c Cr.

Date	Particulars	J.F.	Amount	Date	Particulars	J.F.	Amount
2006			Rs.	2006			Rs.
7.4	To Sales A/c		55,000	27.4	By Return Inward A/c		7,000
				10.5	" Bank A/c		43,000
				30.6	" Balance c/d		5,000
			55,000				55,000
1.7	To Balance b/d		5,000				

Dr. Commission A/c Cr.

Date	Particulars	J.F.	Amount	Date	Particulars	J.F.	Amount
2006			Rs.	2006			Rs.
10.2	To Bank A/c		4,000				
9.6	To Bank A/c		5,000	30.6	By Balance c/d		9,000
			9,000				9,000
1.7	To Balance b/d		9,000				

Dr. Salary & Wages A/c Cr.

Date	Particulars	J.F.	Amount	Date	Particulars	J.F.	Amount
2006			Rs.	2006			Rs.
29.6	To Bank A/c		15,000				
				30.6	By Balance c/d		15,000
			15,000				15,000
1.7	To Balance b/d		15,000				

Dr. Rent A/c Cr.

Date	Particulars	J.F.	Amount	Date	Particulars	J.F.	Amount
2006			Rs.	2006			Rs.
1.4	To Bank A/c		3,000				
				30.6	By Balance c/d		3,000
			3,000				3,000
1.7	To Balance b/d		3,000				

Dr. Building A/c Cr.

Date	Particulars	J.F.	Amount	Date	Particulars	J.F.	Amount
2006			Rs.	2006			Rs.
1.1	To Capital		1,20,000				
				30.6	By Balance c/d		1,20,000
			1,20,000				1,20,000
1.7	To Balance b/d		1,20,000				

Dr. **Capital A/c** Cr.

Date	Particulars	J.F.	Amount	Date	Particulars	J.F.	Amount
2006			Rs.	2006			Rs.
				1.1	By Bank A/c		1,00,000
					" Building A/c		1,20,000
30.6	To Balance c/d		2,70,000		" Stock A/c		50,000
			2,70,000				2,70,000
				1.7	By Balance b/d		2,70,000

Dr. **Furniture A/c** Cr.

Date	Particulars	J.F.	Amount	Date	Particulars	J.F.	Amount
2006			Rs.	2006			Rs.
1.3	To Bank A/c		50,000				
				30.6	By Balance c/d		50,000
			50,000				50,000
1.7	To Balance b/d		50,000				

Dr. **Delivery Van A/c** Cr.

Date	Particulars	J.F.	Amount	Date	Particulars	J.F.	Amount
2006			Rs.	2006			Rs.
1.1	To Bank A/c		25,000				
				30.6	By Balance c/d		25,000
			25,000				25,000
1.7	To Balance b/d		25,000				

Trial Balance as at 30.6.2006

SL No.	Particulars	L.F.	Dr. Amount	Cr. Amount
			Rs.	Rs.
1	Purchases		2,05,000	—
2	Sales		—	2,45,000
3	Carriage Inward		5,800	—
4	Carriage Outward		1,500	—
5	Return Inward		7,000	—
6	Return Outward		—	10,000
7	New York Trader (Creditor)		—	26,000
8	Dinesh Cloth (Creditor)		—	12,000
9	Ramesh & Co. (Debtor)		5,000	—
10	Commission		9,000	—

Continued

SL No.	Particulars	L.F.	Dr. Amount	Cr. Amount
			Rs.	Rs.
11	Salary & Wages		15,000	—
12	Rent		3,000	—
13	Building		1,20,000	—
14	Capital		—	2,70,000
15	Furniture		50,000	—
16	Delivery Van		25,000	—
17	Cash at Bank		66,700	—
18	Opening Stock		50,000	—
	Total		5,63,000	5,63,000

Trading & Profit and Loss A/c
for the six months ended 30.6.06

Dr. *Cr.*

Particulars	Amount Rs.	Amount Rs.	Particulars	Amount Rs.	Amount Rs.
To Opening Stock		50,000	By Sales	2,45,000	
To Purchases	2,05,000		*Less* Return	7,000	
Less Return Outward	10,000	1,95,000			2,38,000
To Carriage Inward		5,800	By Closing Stock		85,000
To Gross Profit c/d		72,200			
		3,23,000			3,23,000
To Carriage Outward		1,500	By Gross Profit b/d		72,200
To Commission		9,000			
To Salary & Wages	15,000				
Add Outstanding	1,000	16,000			
To Rent	3,000				
Add Outstanding	500	3,500			
To Depreciation					
on Building	2,400				
on Furniture	500				
on Delivery Van	500	3,400			
To Capital A/c (Net Profit transferred)		38,800			
		72,200			72,200

Workings :
Depreciation on

Building : $1{,}20{,}000 \times \frac{4}{100} \times \frac{1}{2} = 2{,}400$

Furniture : $50{,}000 \times \frac{3}{100} \times \frac{4}{12} = 500$

Delivery Van : $25{,}000 \times \frac{4}{100} \times \frac{1}{2} = 500$

Balance Sheet
as at 30.6.06

Dr. *Cr.*

Liabilities	Amount Rs.	Amount Rs.	Assets	Amount Rs.	Amount Rs.
Capital	2,70,000		Building	1,20,000	
Add Net Profit	38,800	3,08,800	*Less* Depreciation	2,400	1,17,600
New York Trader		26,000	Furniture	50,000	
Dinesh Cloth		12,000	*Less* Depreciation	500	49,500
Outstanding Rent		500	Delivery Van	25,000	
Outstanding Salary			*Less* Depreciation	500	24,500
& Wages		1,000	Stock		85,000
			Ramesh & Co.		5,000
			Cash at Bank		66,700
		3,48,300			3,48,300

I think you have followed very minutely the '**chain of accounting system**' from one set of information, i.e. the preparation of Balance Sheet from different scattered business transactions. Now I would like to give you details about the Trial Balance, Trading A/c, Profit & Loss A/c and Balance Sheet.

Is there any question?

☐ "Sir, I have one question to ask."

• What is that? Please tell me frankly what do you want to know.

☐ "Sir, in case of Journal entries you have used L.F. and in case of Ledger A/c you have used J.F. What are J.F. and L.F.?"

• You see, these are Journal Folio (J.F.) and Ledger Folio (L.F.). Folio means page(s). These refer to respective pages of Journal and Ledger where these are recorded.

Well, in our previous discussions I defined the meaning of Trial Balance which is a statement of balances of different ledger accounts. If the two sides, i.e. Debit and Credit side, of the Trial Balance agree, you may consider it as a conclusive proof of true recording of transactions. But it has been found in actual

Errors not Detected from Trial Balance

practice that often, in spite of the existence of certain types of errors, the two sides of the Trial Balance agree. That's why I am to say that '**the agreement of the Trial Balance is only an apparent but not a conclusive proof**'.

☐ "Sir, what are the different types of errors which are not disclosed in Trial Balance"?

● Well, the following errors are worthy of notice; the existence of which does not affect the agreement of Trial Balance :

(i) **Errors of Omission :** Errors of omission means when a transaction or a set of transactions has or have been omitted from recording. Take for an example :

Purchase of goods worth Rs. 500 from Mr. X. Here Purchases A/c should be debited and Mr. X A/c should be credited. This transaction will be considered as error of omission when the transaction is entirely omitted. That is to say, neither of the transactions is debited nor credited.

(ii) **Errors of Commission :** Errors of Commission results from the following two situations :

(a) When a transaction is entered for wrong amount. For example, sold goods for Rs. 789 for cash. Here the journal entry may be passed as :

Cash A/c	Dr.	Rs. 897	
To Sales A/c			Rs. 897

In this state of affair the Trial Balance will agree, since both Debit and Credit side is recorded for Rs. 897.

(b) When a transaction is posted in wrong account. For example, Mr. Z has to trade with different parties of which there are two parties—R.K. Basu & Co. and K.K. Basu & Co. Suppose, sale of goods to R.K. Basu & Co. for Rs. 250 has been recorded as under :

K.K. Basu A/c	Dr.	Rs. 250	
To Sales A/c			Rs. 250

(iii) **Errors of Principles :** When principles of accounting are violated, it is said to be errors of principle. This will not affect the Trial Balance. For example, when Furniture is purchased as an asset of a business, Furniture A/c should be debited; but if, instead of debiting Furniture we debit Purchases Account—it indicates that total omission of Furniture. You know that Purchases A/c is always debit and increase in asset will always be debit. So, the debit side of the Trial Balance is not in any way affected; similarly credit side too.

(iv) **Compensating Errors :** When one error is compensated by another error; that is to say, when a wrong debit entry is counter balanced by another or a series of wrong credit postings; similarly when a wrong credit entry is balanced by another or a series of wrong debit entries. For example, a debit balance is undercast by Rs. 100 and the credit balance is undercast by the same amount of Rs. 100.

Well, I am sure that you have understood the details of the errors not disclosed in the Trial Balance. Is there any question?

☐ "Sir, what are the different types of errors which can be detected from Trial Balance"?

I am really very happy to see that you have taken much interest in the subject.

However, please note that when the two sides of the trial balance disagree, it can be assumed that it results out of one or any one of the following errors :

- Posting from Journals to Ledgers.
- Addition in Ledger.
- Addition in Trial Balance.
- Extraction of balances, and, finally,
- Brought down of the balances in Ledger Account(s).

Well, now I like to discuss about the details of Trading, Profit & Loss Account and Balance Sheet.

☐ "Sir, if you kindly include the Manufacturing Account in the proposed lists of your discussions it would really enrich our stock of knowledge".

• Yes, yes, I will.....

Before that let us recapitulate our previous discussions. We have seen earlier that Trading, Profit and Loss Account and Balance Sheet—all are prepared from Trial Balance. Trial Balance is prepared from the balances of Ledger A/c and the Ledger A/c from the Journal. It was also seen that certain errors such as errors of principles, errors of omission etc. can't be detected from the Trial Balance. It should be noted in this context that if the correct appraisal of the financial statement is sought then all those errors should be detected and corrected at the very primary level of recording. The Accountant can get all these errors rectified by accounts clerks through personal guidance. However, we have seen, in general, that business is started for some motive—Profit or Wealth as well as Service. That a business has earned some profit (wealth) or sustained losses can be reflected through Trading and Profit & Loss A/c and Balance Sheet. And the profit so earned is added to the capital of an enterprise, and vice versa.

However, the Trading and Profit and Loss A/c and Balance Sheet can be explained in the following manner :

(Sales + Closing Stock) – (Opening Stock + Purchase + Trading Expense)

= **Gross Satisfaction** or **Gross Profit.**

or, Sales – (Cost of Goods Sold + Operating or Trading Expenses)

= **Gross Profit** or **Gross Satisfaction.**

Cost of Goods Sold = (Opening Stock + Purchase) – Closing Stock.

Gross Satisfaction – Item of Dissatisfaction = **Net Satisfaction**

or, **Gross Profit – Items of Expenses = Net Profit**

Now, by the by, I would like to show you how a part of the profit is represented by Closing Stock and how this profit is manipulated. Suppose, the Capital of a firm is represented by Land and Building Rs. 2,000; Machinery Rs. 4,000; Furniture Rs. 2,000; Cash Rs. 2,000. That is to say —

Balance Sheet
as at 31st March ...

Liabilities	Amount	Assets	Amount
	Rs.		Rs.
Capital	10,000	Land & Building	2,000
		Machinery	4,000
		Furniture	2,000
		Cash	2,000
	10,000		10,000

Well, during the operation of business, stock at end is estimated at, suppose, Rs. 5,000 and other information were—Opening Stock 8,000, Purchase Rs. 6,000, Sales Rs. 21,000. Then the position of Trading A/c will be as under without taking into account the value of Closing Stock.

☐ "Sir, how is it possible? When opening cash is Rs. 2,000."

● You see, to have an effective operation of the business, suppose the firm borrowed from a nationalised bank Rs. 14,000 to get its stock worth Rs. 8,000 and purchase of other materials worth Rs. 6,000 for trade purpose. Bank Loan was paid off. Total Sales during the year is estimated at Rs. 21,000.

Do you follow?

☐ "Yes sir".

● Please note :

Dr. **Trading A/c** *Cr.*

	Particulars	Amount	Particulars	Amount
		Rs.		Rs.
To	Opening Stock	8,000	By Sales	21,000
"	Purchase	6,000		
"	Gross Profit	7,000		
		21,000		21,000

Balance Sheet

Capital & Liabilities	Amount	Assets & Properties	Amount
	Rs.		Rs.
Capital	10,000	Land & Building	2,000
Net Profit	7,000	Machinery	4,000
		Furniture	2,000
		(Old) Cash	2,000
		(New) Cash	7,000
	17,000		17,000

Here, in the absence of other information relating to Profit & Loss Account, the Gross Profit represents the Net Profit which is Rs. 7,000. And it is represented by only Cash, considering the fact that there were no credit transactions.

Now I show you how a part of the Profit is represented by valuation of Closing Stock. For this, value of Closing Stock is estimated at Rs. 5,000 (see previous information) :

Dr. **Trading A/c** *Cr.*

Particulars	Amount	Particulars	Amount
	Rs.		Rs.
To Opening Stock	8,000	By Sales	21,000
" Purchases	6,000	" Closing	5,000
" Gross Profit	12,000		
	26,000		26,000

If we assume that there is no other expenses, or, if we assume that the proprietor himself manufacture and sells in the market, then no expenses are incurred. Then this Rs. 12,000 may be treated as Net Profit and this amount will be appearing on the Liability side of Balance Sheet. So, the position of the Balance Sheet would be :

Balance Sheet

Capital & Liabilities	Amount	Assets & Properties	Amount
	Rs.		Rs.
Capital	10,000	Land & Building	2,000
Net Profit	12,000	Machinery	4,000
		Furniture	2,000
		(Old) Cash	2,000
		(New) Cash	7,000
		Closing Stock	5,000
	22,000		22,000

Here Net Profit Rs. 12,000 is represented by Cash Rs. 7,000 and Rs. 5,000 in Stock.

Net Profit Rs. 12,000 = Cash Rs. 7,000 + Stock Rs. 5,000.

Well, in **Illustration Two** the reported financial position of the business shows a Gross Loss Rs. 95,100. This could have been avoided if artful manipulation in estimating any such amount for Closing Stock is made; and the same is inserted in the Trading A/c of the business. Please note that **Illustration Two** is not a suitable example for explanation. However, for your better understanding of this idea, I am taking the said example assuming that closing stock is estimated at Rs. 1,00,000. The artificial insertion of closing stock may offset the Net Loss of the business. The illustration will indicate you the *Principles of Operation*.

Please do not disturb me by saying that the figures presented here are abnormal.

Dr. **Trading and Profit & Loss A/c** Cr.
for the year ended ...

Particulars	Amount	Particulars	Amount
	Rs.		Rs.
To Opening Stock	30,000	By Net Sales	14,400
" Purchases	78,500	" Closing Stock	1,00,000
" Fuel	1,000		
" Gross Profit	4,900		
	1,14,400		1,14,400
To Salary & Wages	4,000	By Gross Profit	4,900
" Net Profit	1,620	" Commission	720
	5,620		5,620

Balance Sheet
as at ....

Capital & Liabilities	Amount	Assets & Properties	Amount
	Rs.		Rs.
Capital	1,50,000	Cash	49,720
Net Profit	1,620	Debtor(s)	9,400
Creditor(s)	7,500	Closing Stock	1,00,000
	1,59,120		1,59,120

Have you noticed one important point in the above discussion?

☐ "Yes Sir, you are going to speak about outside Trial Balance information. Here it is stock".

● Very nice, indeed, that you have grasped the subject. Well, I want to say that Trial Balance has been prepared after completing the process of Double Entry—Debit and Credit. So, Outside Trial Balance Information (O.T.I.) should be given double effect. Here Closing Stock is an item of Outside Trial Balance Information (O.T.I.). To give its double effect, it has been included in the Trading A/c's credit side and the same has been included in the Assets side of the Balance Sheet. Take another example, if the outside Trial Balance information states that Depreciation on Plant & Machinery, which appears in Trial Balance for Rs. 10,000, should be charged @ 10%. Then, to give its double effect, Depreciation should appear on the Debit side of Profit & Loss A/c and the same will be deducted from Plant and Machinery A/c which appears in the Assets side of the Balance Sheet :

Dr. **Profit and Loss Account** Cr.

Particulars	Amount	Particulars	Amount
	Rs.		Rs.
To Depreciation	1,000		

Balance Sheet

Capital & Liabilities	Amount	Assets & Properties		Amount
	Rs.			Rs.
		Plant & Machinery	10,000	
		Less : Depreciation	1,000	9,000

I think, you have followed the discussions made.

☐ "It's really exciting Sir! Please go on delivering lecture".

• Well, you all know that the sources of profit are :

Sources of Profit

i **Increase of Sale.**

ii **Elimination of Expenses.**

iii **Increase in Sale Price.**

iv **Decrease in Purchase Price.**

Well, as a student, or, better to say, lover of accounting literature, you should know the mechanism—how profit is inflated and how profit of the business is drained out intentionally.

We have seen earlier that the profit of the business—other expenditures remaining the same—is often represented falsely by way of :

i Artificial insertion of Closing Stock.

ii Valuation of Closing Stock at higher figure.

Manipulation of Profit

However, the profit of the business may be drained out, besides insertion of artificial expenditure, by way of willful charge of Bad Debt at excessive doses. And the mechanism of Bad Debt may be adopted to retain a part of the profit which goes out of the business by way of excessive Profit Tax. So, it should be noted in this context that erosion of real capital may result from excessive Profit Tax.[6]

However, take an example to illustrate it. A business is started with Cash Rs. 10,000. Then the journal entry will be :

Cash A/c	Dr.	Rs. 10,000	
To Capital A/c			Rs. 10,000

So, on that very moment, the position of Balnce Sheet would be :

Balance Sheet

Liabilities	Amount	Properties	Amount
	Rs.		Rs.
Capital	10,000	Cash	10,000
	10,000		10,000

After the start of the business the following events occurred :

i. Purchase of ready stock for Rs. 8,000.

[6] *United States Steel Corporation Annual Report, 1952.*

ii. Purchase of other materials needed to start production Rs. 6,000.

iii. Total sales during the year Rs. 21,000 of which Cash Sales Rs. 15,000; Credit Sales Rs. 6,000.

iv. Assume that there is no Closing Stock and other expenses incurred.

So, the position of Trading A/c from the above information would be :

Trading A/c

Dr. Particulars	Amount Rs.	Cr. Particulars		Amount Rs.
To Opening Stock	8,000	By Sales :		21,000
" Purchase	6,000	Cash	15,000	
" Profit	7,000	Credit	6,000	
	21,000			21,000

Cash Book

Dr. Particulars	Amount Rs.	Cr. Particulars	Amount Rs.
To Balance b/d	10,000	By Purchase	6,000
" Sales	15,000	" Stock	8,000
		" Balance c/d	11,000
	25,000		25,000
To Balance b/d	11,000		

Debtor A/c

Dr. Particulars	Amount Rs.	Cr. Particulars	Amount Rs.
To Sale	6,000	By Balance c/d	6,000
	6,000		6,000
To Balance b/d	6,000		

Balance Sheet

Liabilities	Amount Rs.	Assets	Amount Rs.
Capital	10,000	Cash	11,000
Profit during the year	7,000	Debtors	6,000
	17,000		17,000

Here the actual realisation of Profit depends on the collection from Debtor(s). It should be noted that one of the important areas of **dormant capital** is accounts receivable. It constitutes an item of assets with "**a strong tendency to become losses**"[7].

Well, upon the happenings of actual Bad Debt, a part of the profit is lost.

[7] *An extract of the text of the lecture "Accounting Observations and Control" delivered by Dr. B. K. Basu at the invitation of the Calcutta Management Association, July 1971.*

Dr. Profit and Loss A/c for the Next Year (assuming the same figure) Cr.

Particulars	Amount	Particulars	Amount
	Rs.		Rs.
To Bad Debt	3,000		
" Profit	4,000		

Balance Sheet

Liabilities	Amount	Assets		Amount
	Rs.			Rs.
		Debtor(s)	6,000	
		Less : Bad Debt	3,000	3,000

Well, if the Bad Debt is intentional, naturally Rs. 3,000 may be misappropriated—pretending lawfully and honestly. The general principle is that on realisation of bad debt it should be recorded. So, when bad debt has been made with some intention, the question of recording of realized bad debt money cannot arise. However, accounts receivable has been considered earlier as **dormant capital**. So, the artful handling of dormant capital may curb profit against payment of profit tax. So, one of the ways which may be adopted by unscrupulous business- man to stop capital erosion arising from profit tax is to make or create Bad Debt.

However, in the context of growing and planned economy in India, the evasion of tax should be discouraged. The above situation can be explained as under :

Example

Dr. Profit & Loss A/c Cr.

Particulars	Amount	Particulars	Amount
	Rs.		Rs.
To Expenses	5,000	By Gross Profit	15,000
" Net Profit	10,000		
	15,000		15,000

Assume Profit Tax 50%

So, Profit after Tax is Rs. 5,000

Example

Dr. Profit & Loss A/c Cr.

Particulars	Amount	Particulars	Amount
	Rs.		Rs.
To Expenses	5,000	By Gross Profit	15,000
" Bad Debt	2,500		
" Net Profit	7,500		
	15,000		15,000

Assume Profit Tax 50%

So, Profit after Tax is Rs. 3,750

Now, total amount that may remain in the hand of the company after wilful manipulation of Bad Debt is Rs. 2,500. Thus the amount retained is :

	Rs.
Profit after tax	3,750
Bad Debt	2,500
	6,250

Please note that unless the above mechanism is followed the profit may have gone out from the business. So as a result of the above process the extra profit after deduction of tax in Example 2, as compared with Example 1, is (Rs. 6,250 – 5,000) = Rs. 1,250.

You see, we have gone far ahead of our original discussions.

Yes, what is quite untouched for discussion?

☐ "Sir, we have followed your lecture. However, you have not given us any light on the Sectional Journal and Journal Proper".

● Well, now I would like to discuss the same. You see, from General Journal we have prepared Balance Sheet. However, in our earlier discussion we had seen that journal may be sub-divided into two parts—Sectional Journal and Journal Proper. In that context we had seen that sectional journals are of seven types—Cash Book, Purchase Day Book, Sales Day Book, Return Inward Book, Return Outward Book etc. And we had also seen that Journal Proper are of following types—Opening entries, Transfer entries, Rectification of Errors entries, Adjusting entries and Closing entries and credit sale and credit purchase of assets. So I would like to discuss all these aspects in order of preference.

Cash Book

All receipts and payments of cash transaction is recorded in cash book. It is classified as a Book of Original Entry. Cash Book may be considered as both journal and ledger. It is journal in the sense that it records all the transactions relating to Cash as and when they occur, followed by a suitable narration. It is a ledger in the sense that it maintains the form of an account.

There are two sides of cash book—Receipts of Cash and Payments of Cash. Debit side relates to all receipts of cash and the credit side relates to all payment of cash. However, it should be noted in this context that business transactions do not confine to receipt and payment of only liquid cash. So cheques are used in this respect. Sometimes discounts are received and paid during the process of a transaction and this should be shown in the cash book.

So Cash Book is of three types :

Different Types of Cash Book

a. Single column cash book — relates only to cash.

b. Double column cash book — relates to cash and cheque.

c. Triple column cash book — relates to cash, cheque and discount.

You see, you may come across a few transactions which have double effects. This types of transactions may be considered as '***contra entries***.' That is to say, the effects of such transactions should be given on both sides of the cash book—Debit side and Credit side.

Contra Entries : These entries are the transfer of money from Bank to Cash and contra transfer from Cash to Bank.

Rules of Contra entries :

A. When cash is paid into Bank :

Debit : Bank columm on the receipts side.
Credit : Cash columm on the payment side.

B. When cash is drawn from the Bank :

Debit : Cash column on the receipt side
Credit : Bank column on the payment side.

Examples of Contra Entries :

Drew from Bank for office cash Rs. 10.
Paid into Bank from office cash Rs. 5.

Solution :

Cash Book

Dr.	**Receipt Side**					**Payment side**			*Cr.*
Date	**Particulars**	**L. F.**	**Cash**	**Bank**	**Date**	**Particulars**	**L. F.**	**Cash**	**Bank**
	To Bank To Cash	(c) (c)	10	 5		By Cash By Bank	(c) (c)	 5	10

Cash Discount : i. **Cash discount allowed :** When cash discount is allowed, it should be entered in the Discount column of the Receipt side of the cash book which represents Debit side of cash book. The reason is that all dissatisfactions are debit. Allowing discount is an item of dissatisfaction.

ii. **Cash discount received :** When cash discount is received, it should be entered on the Payment side of the cash book which represents Credit side of cash book. The reason is that all satisfactions are credit. Receipt of discount is an item of satisfaction. So it is credited.

I hope, you have now understood the concept of cash book and the rules of contra entries. Is there any question, please?

☐ "Sir, please give us some transactions from which we can prepare a Cash Book with Cash, Bank and Discount column".

● Well, I will ....

Please take down the following information :

Illustration :

From the following information prepare three-column Cash Book :

2006			Rs.
January	1.	Cash at Bank	2,710
	"	Cash in hand	250

January		Rs.
1.	Drew cheque for petty cash payment	100
2.	Bought office furniture by cheque	200
5.	Received cheque from A. Das	870
5.	Discount allowed to A. Das	20
10.	Paid cheque to G. Basu	680
10.	Discount received from G. Basu	10
15.	Paid wages in cash	180
18.	Received cheque from R. Kundu	280
18.	Discount allowed to R. Kundu	10
19.	Paid rent by cheque	160
28.	Drew from bank for office cash	100
31.	Sold goods for cheque	110
31.	Refunded petty cash expenses by cheque	90
31.	Paid into bank from office cash	50

☐ "Sir, Is the transaction relating to 'Drew cheque for petty cash payment' a contra?"

• No. Contra will be confined in respect of withdrawal and deposit of cash between Office cash and Bank.

However, I am working out the above problem for your understanding :

Dr. **Cash Book** *Cr.*

Date	Particulars	L. F.	Dis-count	Cash	Bank	Date	Particulars	L. F.	Dis-count	Cash	Bank
			Rs.	Rs.	Rs.				Rs.	Rs.	Rs.
1.1	To Balance b/d			250	2,710	1.1	By Petty Cash				100
5.1	" A. Das		20		870	2.1	" Off. Furniture				200
18.1	" R. Kundu		10		280	10.1	" G. Basu		10		680
28.1	" Bank	(c)		100		15.1	" Wages			180	
31.1	" Sales				110	19.1	" Rent				160
31.1	" Cash	(c)			50	28.1	" Cash	(c)			100
						31.1	" Petty Exp.				90
						31.1	" Bank	(c)		50	
						31.1	" Balance c/d			120	2,690
				350	4,020					350	4,020
Feb. 1	To Balance b/d			120	2,690						

☐ "Excuse me sir, you have not shown here narration why sir?"

• I have done it intentionally to see whether you are alert or not? I am happy that you have gone into deep of the subject you prepare it yourself. Can you?

☐ "Yes Sir."

• **Purchase Day Book :** Purchase Day Book may be defined as a Sectional Journal where all credit purchases of trading goods are to be recorded.

Return Outward Book : It is also known as Purchase Return Book. It records the return of all goods to the suppliers by the purchasers. The goods may be returned by the purchaser for various reasons such as supply of below specification goods and goods may not be tallying with sample. Please note that when the question of purchase return arises the purchaser issues a Debit Note along with goods returned. So every return outward should be accompanied by a Debit Note. So Debit Note may be defined as a statement 'issued by one party to the other showing the amount for which the latter has been debited, and a brief explanation thereof'.

Sales Day Book : It is a book where all credit sales of trading goods are to be recorded.

Return Inward Book : It is also known as Sales Return Book. When any portion of goods sold is returned by the party it is recorded in Return Inward Book. Please note that when goods are returned by the customer, the seller acknowledges the receipt of the returned goods through Credit Note. So Credit Note may be defined as' a statement issued by a trader to another trader showing the amount by which the latter has been credited and a brief explanation for such credit'.

Illustration :

From the following, enter into proper Subsidiary Books :

2006

Feb. 4 Purchased from M/s B. Banerjee and Co. of Kolkata 250 yds Terry Cloth @ 40 per yd as per invoice No. CF/14. Trade Discount allowed @ 10%.

6 Purchased from M/s Wingson Trading Co. of Mumbai goods worth Rs. 40,000. Trade Discount allowed @ 10%.

8 Sold 100 yds Bombay Dyeing Cloth to M/s M. Chaudhury and Co. @ Rs. 10 per yd, less 5% discount.

10 Returned as per Debit Note No. 13 Terry Cloth, 50 yds, being below specification to M/s B. Banerjee and Co.

15 Credit Note No. CN 14 shows a receipt of 20 yds Bombay Dyeing cloth from M/s M. Chaudhury & Co. for that being defective.

15 Sold goods worth Rs. 2,000 to M/s G. Sinha and Co. as per Invoice 293.

That's all. I hope you would be able to work it out. So I do not like to work out this problem.

☐ "Sir, work it out for our guidance please".

• Well, just notice the following :

Purchase Day Book

Date	Particulars	L.F.	Invoice No.	Details	Amount
				Rs.	Rs.
4.2.06	**M/s B. Banerjee & Co., Kolkata**				
	250 yds of Terry Cloth @ Rs. 40 per yd		CF/14	10,000	
	Less : 10% Trade Discount			1,000	9,000
6.2.06	**M/s. Wingson Trading Co.**				
	Goods worth			40,000	
	Less : T.D. @ 10%			4,000	36,000
	Purchases A/c Dr.				45,000

Return Outward or Purchase Return Book

Date	Particulars	L.F.	Debit Note	Details	Amount
				Rs.	Rs.
10.2.06	**M/s B. Banerjee & Co.**				
	50 yds of cloth @ Rs. 40 per yd		13	2,000	
	Less : T.D. @ 10%			200	1,800
	Return Outward A/c Cr.				1,800

Sales Day Book

Date	Particulars	L.F.	Debit Note	Details	Amount
				Rs.	Rs.
8.2.06	**M/s M. Chaudhury & Co.**				
	100 yds Bombay Dyeing Cloth				
	@ Rs. 10 per yd			1,000	
	Less : T.D. @ 5%			50	950
15.2.06	**M/s G. Sinha & Co.**				
	Goods worth		293		2,000
	Sales A/c Cr.				2,950

Return Inward or Sales Return Book

Date	Particulars	L.F.	Debit Note	Details	Amount
				Rs.	Rs.
15.2.06	**M/s M. Chaudhury & Co.**				
	20 yds Bombay Dyeing Cloth				
	@ Rs. 10 per yd			200	
	Less : T.D. @ 5%			10	190
	Return Inward A/c Dr.				190

Bills Receivable Book : It records the transaction relating to Bills drawn by one party on the other and the same duly accepted by the latter.

Bills Receivable Book

No. of Bill	Date Recd.	Name of Acceptor	Where Payable	Date of Bill	Term	Due Date	L. F.	Amount	How disposed

Bills Payable Book : It records all bills as 'granted by customers to the creditors'.

Bills Payable Book

No. of Bill	Date of Acceptance	By whom drawn	To whom Payable	Where Payable	Date of Bill	Term	Due Date	Amount	How disposed

Now I am really very glad to see that you all have grasped the subject. Now I would like to discuss the other portion of journal—Journal Proper—which has not yet been discussed.

This portion is very simple. Whenever you have been able to understand the key principles of financial accounting, I think you would be able to understand the different divisions of journal proper—Opening Entries, Transfer Entries, Rectification of Errors, Adjusting Entries, and Closing Entries.

Opening Entries :

From the following closing balances as at 31st Dec. 2005, pass opening entries as on 1st January 2006 :

	Balance as on 31.12.2005
	Rs.
Land and Buildings A/c	4,000
Plant and Machinery A/c	8,000
Furniture & Fittings A/c	5,000
Cash at Bank A/c	6,000
Sundry Debtors A/c	2,800
Loan A/c	5,000
Creditors A/c	10,800

Solution

Journal Entries

Date	Particulars		L.F.	Dr. Amount	Cr. Amount
2006				Rs.	Rs.
Jan. 1	Land and Buildings A/c	Dr		4,000	
	Plant and Machinery A/c	Dr.		8,000	
	Furniture & Fittings A/c	Dr.		5,000	
	Sundry Debtors A/c	Dr.		2,800	
	Cash at Bank A/c	Dr.		6,000	
	To Loan A/c				5,000
	" Sundry Creditors A/c				10,800
	" Capital A/c (Bal. Fig)				10,000
	(Being the assets and liabilities brought over from previous year)				
	Total			25,800	25,800

Transfer Entries :

The drawing of Mr. X during the year 2006 is Rs. 2,500. The Capital Account represents a credit balance for Rs. 10,000. During the year Mr. X had taken goods from the business worth Rs. 1,000. It had been decided that his drawings in goods for the said amount is to transfer from his Capital A/c to Credit Sales A/c.

Pass necessary journal entries on 31st December 2006.

Date	Particulars		L.F.	Dr. Amount	Cr. Amount
2006				Rs.	Rs.
Dec. 31	Capital A/c	Dr.		2,500	
	To Drawings A/c				2,500
	(Being the amount of drawing transferred to Capital A/c)				
	Capital A/c	Dr.		1,000	
" 31	To Sales A/c				1,000
	(Being the drawings of goods adjusted against Capital A/c)				

Rectification Entries :

(a) Repairs to Buildings Rs. 250 has been debited to Building A/c :

Date	Particulars		L.F.	Dr. Amount	Cr. Amount
2006				Rs.	Rs.
	Repair A/c	Dr.		250	
	To Building A/c				250
	(Being the amount wrongly debited to Building A/c, now rectified).				

(b) A credit Sales for Rs. 5,000 to S. Bose and Co. has been wrongly debited to B. Bose and Co. :

Date	Particulars		L.F.	Dr. Amount	Cr. Amount
2006				Rs.	Rs.
	S. Bose and Co. A/c	Dr.		5,000	
	To B. Bose and Co. A/c				5,000
	(Being the amount wrongly debited to B. Bose and Co. A/c, now rectified).				

(c) An amount of Rs. 2,000 received in cash on account of commission has been credited to Interest A/c :

Date	Particulars		L.F.	Dr. Amount	Cr. Amount
2006				Rs.	Rs.
	Interest A/c	Dr.		2,000	
	To Commission A/c				2,000
	(Being the amount wrongly credited to Interest A/c, now rectified).				

(d) Sales A/c has been undercast to the extent of Rs. 500 :

Date	Particulars	L.F.	Dr. Amount	Cr. Amount
2006			Rs.	Rs.
	Suspense A/c Dr.		500	
	To Sales A/c			500
	(Being the undercast in Sales A/c, now rectified).			

(e) Purchase of Stationery for Rs. 150 has been debited to Office Typewriter A/c :

Date	Particulars	L.F.	Dr. Amount	Cr. Amount
2006			Rs.	Rs.
	Stationery A/c Dr.		150	
	To Office Typewriter A/c			150
	(Being the Stationery purchased previously debited to Typewriter A/c, now rectified).			

(f) Casting of sales day book amounting to Rs. 57,977 has been carried to the balance as Rs. 75,977 :

Date	Particulars	L.F.	Dr. Amount	Cr. Amount
2006			Rs.	Rs.
	Sales A/c Dr.		18,000	
	To Suspense A/c			18,000
	(Being the overcast in the Sales Day Book A/c, now rectified).			

(g) Return Inward amounting to Rs. 250 was not credited to the Debtors A/c :

Date	Particulars	L.F.	Dr. Amount	Cr. Amount
2006			Rs.	Rs.
	Suspense A/c Dr.		250	
	To Sundry Debtors			250
	(Being the amount of Return Inward not credited to Debtors A/c, now rectified)			

(h) Return Inward Book was undercast by Rs. 1,000 :

Date	Particulars	L.F.	Dr. Amount	Cr. Amount
2006			Rs.	Rs.
	Return Inward A/c Dr.		1,000	
	To Suspense A/c			1,000
	(Being the undercast in Return Inward, now rectified)			

(i) Purchases A/c has been overcast for Rs. 100 :

Date	Particulars		L.F.	Dr. Amount	Cr. Amount
2006				Rs.	Rs.
	Suspense A/c	Dr.		100	
	To Purchases A/c				100
	(Being the overcast in Purchases A/c, now rectified)				

(j) A Cash Discount of Rs. 50 received from a creditor was debited to Discount A/c :

Date	Particulars		L.F.	Dr. Amount	Cr. Amount
2006				Rs.	Rs.
	Suspense A/c	Dr.		100	
	To Cash Discount				100
	(Being Cash Discount for Rs. 50 received from a creditor, previously debited to Cash Discount, now rectified).				

Adjusting Entries :

(a) Rent for Rs. 200 and Salary for Rs. 300 are outstanding :

Date	Particulars		L.F.	Dr. Amount	Cr. Amount
2006				Rs.	Rs.
	Rent A/c	Dr.		200	
	Salary A/c	Dr.		300	
	To Outstanding Expenses				500
	(Being the liabilities on account of unpaid rent and salary brought into account)				

(b) Prepaid Insurance for Rs. 100 :

Date	Particulars		L.F.	Dr. Amount	Cr. Amount
2006				Rs.	Rs.
	Prepaid Insurance A/c	Dr.		100	
	To Insurance A/c				100
	(Being the prepaid insurance premium brought forward)				

(c) Value of Machine, Rs. 10,000, and Depreciation charged @ 10%

Date	Particulars		L.F.	Dr. Amount	Cr. Amount
2006				Rs.	Rs.
	Depreciation A/c	Dr.		1,000	
	To Machine A/c				1,000
	(Being the amount for depreciation adjusted against Machine A/c)				

Closing Entries :

Date	Particulars		L.F.	Dr. Amount	Cr. Amount
				Rs.	Rs.
	(a) Return Outward A/c	Dr.		**	
	To Purchase A/c				**
	(Being the Purchase Return credited to Purchase A/c)				
	(b) Sales A/c	Dr.		**	
	To Return Inward A/c				**
	(Being the Sales Return debited to Sales A/c)				
	(c) Trading A/c	Dr.		***	
	To Stock A/c				**
	" Purchases A/c				**
	" Wages A/c				**
	" Carriage on Purchases A/c				**
	(Being the transfer of various accounts)				
	(d) Sales A/c	Dr.		***	
	To Trading A/c				***
	(Being the transfer of Sales Account)				
	(e) Closing Stock A/c	Dr.		**	
	To Trading A/c				**
	(Being the value of closing stock brought into account)				
	(f) Trading A/c	Dr.		***	
	To Profit & Loss A/c				***
	(Being the transfer of gross profit to P/L A/c)				
	(g) Profit & Loss A/c	Dr.		***	
	To Carriage on Sales A/c				**
	" Trade Expenses A/c				**
	" Insurance A/c				**
	" Depreciation A/c				**
	(Being the transfer of balances of various accounts)				
	(h) Capital A/c	Dr.		**	
	To Drawing A/c				**
	(Being the transfer of Drawing A/c to Capital)				
	(i) Profit & Loss A/c	Dr.		**	
	To Capital A/c				**
	(Being the transfer of net profit to Capital A/c)				

I think, you have understood about the details of journal—Sectional Journal and Journal Proper. Well, from the above discussed closing entries we can prepare a proforma of Trading, Profit & Loss A/c and Balance Sheet.

☐ "Sir, give us also a proforma of Trading Account. Does Trading A/c differ from Manufacturing A/c?"

Well, the Trading Account is prepared to ascertain the Trading result. It tries to bring out a relationship between the Sale price and Cost of Sales :

Cost of Sale < Sale Price = Gross Profit

Cost of Sale > Sale Price = Gross Loss

Thus, from the above relationship, the Gross Loss and Profit of any enterprise is ascertained.

Manufacturing account is sometimes used as 'being synonymous with Trading Account'. In the absence of any clear indication as to drawing of a bifurcation line between the Manufacturing and Trading Account, all the items of Trading and Manufacturing Account are incorporated under the head of Trading Account. Unlike the Trading Account, Manufacturing Account—which is sometimes termed as 'Production Account'[8] —in its real sense indicate the cost of manufacture of articles. It takes into account cost of material, manufacturing wages and direct and indirect charges incidental to manufacture, viz., electric power, fuel etc. The price thus appearing exhibits work cost or factory cost. Sometimes manufacturing account is credited with the market price of the goods so manufactured. The difference will represent either profit or loss on manufacture.

Manufacturing Account

Market price of manufactured articles > Cost of Manufacture = Profit on Manufacture.

Market price of manufactured articles < Cost of Manufacture = Loss on Manufacture.

The philosophy behind this is to see the Manufacturing result separately from Trading result. From the two sets of results—Trading result and Manufacturing result—the management can take its decision 'whether it is worth while to manufacture the articles or to engage simply in trade purchasing the articles from other manufacturers'.

Trading and Profit & Loss Account

Well, by the by, I like to give you the basic idea of Profit and Loss Account. The main function of Profit and Loss Account is to ascertain the net profit resulting from trading operation of a particular period.

Balance Sheet, on the other hand, may be described as a 'snap-shot' of financial position of a business. It may be described as a Statement of Assets and Liabilities of a business at any given moment of time or on a particular date.

Now I would like to give you the proforma of Manufacturing, Trading, Profit & Loss Account and Balance Sheet from which you may have a clear idea about their components :

Dr. **Manufacturing Account** *Cr.*

Particulars		Amount	Particulars	Amount
		Rs.		Rs.
To Material consumed :			By Cost of Production	***
Opening Stock	*			
Purchases	*			
	**			
Less : Closing Stock	*	**		
Work in Progress :				
Opening	**			
Less : Closing Work in Progress	*	**		
Factory Overheads		*		
		***		***

[8] B. G. Vickery, "**Principles and Practice of Book-keeping and Accounts**", 16th Ed., P. 266.

Dr. **Trading Account** **Cr.**

Particulars	Amount	Particulars	Amount
	Rs.		Rs.
		By Sales	***
To Opening Stock of Finished Goods	***	" Closing Stock of finished goods	***
" Cost of Production	***		
" Warehouse rent	***		
" Warehouse wages	***		
" Gross Profit (balancing figure)	***		
	***		***

Well, please note that in the absence of Manufacturing Account, the Trading Account will incorporate the following items :

Dr. **Trading Account for the year ended** **Cr.**

Particulars		Amount	Particulars		Amount
		Rs.			Rs.
To Opening Stock		***	By Sales	***	
" Purchase	***	***	*Less* : Return	***	***
Less : Return	***		" Closing Stock		***
" Freight		***			
" Coal and Coke		***			
" Dock Charges		***			
" Carriage Inward		***			
" Factory Lighting & Power		***			
" Cartage		***			
" Water		***			
" Import Duty		***			
" Factory Wages		***			
" Railway Freight		***			
" Gross Profit transferred		***			
to P & L A/c		***			
(balancing figure)					
		***			***

Dr. **Profit and Loss Account for the year ended ...** **Cr.**

Particulars		Amount	Particulars		Amount
		Rs.			Rs.
To Office Salaries	***		By Gross Profit		***
Add Outstanding	***		" Discount Received	***	
(expired) (O.T.I.)		***	*Less* : Received in advance	***	
" Insurance			(O.T.I.)		
Less : Prepaid (O.T.I.)	***	***	" Interest		***
(Unexpired)			*Add* Outstanding (O.T.I.)		
" Carriage Outward		***	or		
" Commission		***	Accrued Interest but not		***
" Bad Debt		***	received		
" Bad Debt (O.T.I.)		***			
" Interest		***			
" Trade Expenses		***			

Dr. Profit and Loss Account for the year ended Cr.

Particulars	Amount	Particulars	Amount
	Rs.		Rs.
To Rent and Taxes	***		
" Depreciation	***		
" Depreciation (O.T.I.)	***		
" Discount	***		
" Interest on Capital	***		
" Net Profit transferred to Capital A/c (balancing figure)	***		
	***		***

O.T.I. = Outside Trial Balance Information.

This Outside Trial Balance Information should be given double effect. That is to say, it should appear either in Trading or Profit & Loss A/c and the same should be given effect in the Balance Sheet.

I think you have understood the proforma. Do you remember one important point for the preparation of Manufacturing Account? In earlier context I discussed that the trader wants to get the result of two types of operation—Manufacturing operation and Trading operation. This can be prepared to arrive at correct management decision :

Proformas of this type of presentation are given below for your perusal.

Dr. Manufacturing, Trading and Profit & Loss A/c for the year ended Cr.

Particulars		Amount	Particulars	Amount
		Rs.		Rs.
To Opening Stock of Raw Material		*	By Cost of Goods Manufactured c/d	*
" Purchases		*		
Less Closing Stock of Raw Material		*		
		*		
" Opening Work-in-Progress	*			
Less Closing Work in Progress	*	*		
Wages		*		
" Factory Expenses		*		
		***		***
To Cost of Goods Manufactured b/d		***	By Market Value of Goods Manufactured (c/d)	***
" Gross Profit on Manufacture transferred to Profit & Loss A/c (A)		***		
		***		***
To Opening Stock of Finished Goods		***	By Sales	***
" Market value of Goods manufactured b/d		***		
		***		
" *Less* Closing Stock of Finished Goods		***		
" Gross Profit on Trading A/c (B)		***		
		***		
		***		***

Dr. **Manufacturing, Trading and Profit & Loss A/c** Cr.

Particulars	Amount	Particulars	Amount
	Rs.		Rs.
To Rent	*	By Gross Profit on Manufacturing A/c (A)	***
" Rates and Taxes	*	" Gross Profit on Trading A/c (B)	***
" Miscellaneous Expenses	*	" Discounts	*
" Salaries	**		
" Travelling Expenses	*		
" Net Profit c/d	**		
	***		***

Now I would like to give you some idea on how the Profit & Loss Appropriation Account can be prepared. Suppose Total Profit during a year is estimated at Rs. 50,000. Now this entire amount will not be distributed to the shareholders in a form of dividend; appropriation on existing profit as well as the balance of last year's profit will be made for the following purposes :

i. Proposed Dividend.
ii. General Reserve.
iii. Sinking Fund.
iv. Provision for Taxation.
v. Any other Fund.
vi. Surplus.

Dr. **Profit & Loss Appropriation A/c** Cr.

Particulars	Amount	Particulars	Amount
	Rs.		Rs.
To Proposed Dividend	**	By Profit for the current year	**
" General Reserve	**	" Profit for the last year	**
" Sinking Fund	**		
" Provision for Taxation	**		
" Surplus	**		
	***		***

Well, do you find any interest in the above discussion?

☐ "Sir, very interesting indeed! Sir, please give us a proforma of Balance sheet".

● Well, please note below the proforma of Balance Sheet.

Balance Sheet
as at 31st Dec.

Capital and Liabilities	Amount	Assets and Properties		Amount
	Rs.			Rs.
Share Capital	**	**Fixed Assets**		
Reserve and Surplus		Goodwill		**
All types of Reserves	**	Land & Building		**
Secured Loan		Plant & Machinery	***	
Debentures and other loan	**	*Less* Dep. (O.T.I.)	***	**
Unsecured Loan	**	Furniture & Fixture		**

Capital and Liabilities	Amount	Assets and Properties		Amount
	Rs.			Rs.
Items of short term loan	**	**Investment**		**
Current Liabilities and Provisions		**Current Assets, Loans and Advance**		
Sundry Creditors	**	Interest Accrued (O.T.I.)		**
Bills Payable	**	Prepaid Insurance		**
Rent Received in Advance (O.T.I.)	**	Sundry Debtors	***	
Outstanding Liability (O.T.I.)	**	*Less* Bad Debt (O.T.I.)	***	**
Provision for Taxation	**	Bills Receivable		**
Provision for Dividend etc.	**	Stock		**
		Cash and Bank		**
		Miscellaneous Expenditure		
		Preliminary Expenses		**
		Discount on issue of shares		**
		P.L. A/c (Dr.) balance		**
	***			***

As you have taken much interest in the subject, I would like to mention here with pleasure that when you would be placed in management position then you will appreciate this lecture.

Change in Working Capital

However, for that I would like to give you some first-hand idea how the aforesaid Profit and Loss A/c & Balance Sheet would be used as an aid to managerial decision. That is to say, from Balance Sheet you can find out or you may get an idea of your actual working capital position.

☐ "Sir, How is Working Capital computed?"

● You see, Working Capital can be found out as :

Total Current Assets – Total Current Liabilities = Working Capital

Change in Cash Position

Well, by comparing the Working Capital of two consecutive periods or years, you can get an idea whether the working capital of the business—where you would be acting as Head of Management Accounting Department—is increasing or decreasing. So the change in working capital position may be found out by comparing the Balance Sheets of different years. This mechanism is known as Fund Flow Statement. Besides all these things, as a management accountant you should know the technique of 'cash' control of the business. For that you should have a general knowledge about the causes of change in cash position of two consecutive periods or years.

Take for an example, the Balance Sheet of 2005 shows a cash balance Rs. 80,000 and the Balance Sheet of 2006 shows a cash balance Rs. 60,000. This means during the year 2006, Cash for Rs. 20,000 goes out of business. That is to say, during the years the total payments of cash of the business is higher to the extent Rs. 20,000 than the total Receipts of cash. This mechanism is known as Cash Flow Statement.

Besides the knowledge of Cash Flow and Fund Flow Statement you should have a general knowledge about the financial position of the business. That is to say, whether your business is solvent and profitable. If you compare the position of current assets and current liabilities you can get an idea about the solvency position. That is to say, your current assets should be, in general, twice that of current liabilities. And you would be eager to know what profit is earned on a particular investment; whether your return on investment is higher than that of other industries of similar type. This mechanism is known as Interpretation of Financial Statement and Investment Decision.

All these aspects would be discussed under subsequent chapters on — Funds Flow Statement, Cash Flow Statement and Ratio Analysis and Interpretation of Financial Statement and Investment Decision.

If you are interested I can give you a first-hand idea about the same.

☐ "Sir, we would be highly obliged. Please give us an idea of the same".

● Well, for this I give you the following information from which I plan to work out Journal Entries, Ledger Accounts, Trial Balance, Trading Account, Profit & Loss Account, Balance Sheet, Fund Flow Statement, Cash Flow Statement and the Interpretation of Profit & Loss Account and Balance Sheet. So, I want to show you the 'chain of accounting mechanism' i.e., Integration between Financial Accounting and Management Accounting.

CHAIN OF ACCOUNTING MECHANISM

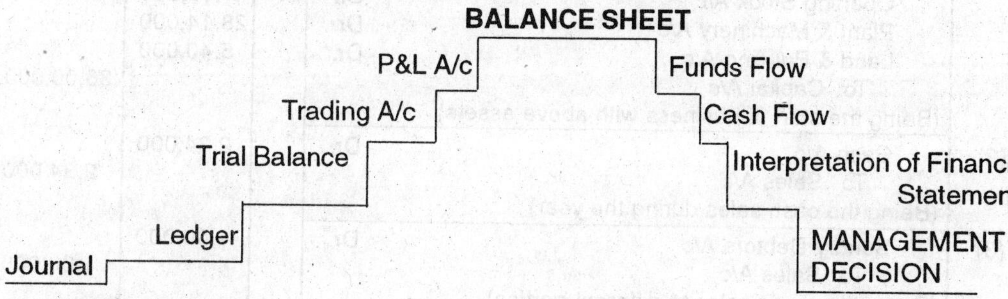

Illustration :

On 1st January 2005, Roundover Trading Co. Ltd. started a business with capital for Rs. 36,00,000 consisting of the following :

Cash	1,46,000
Opening Stock	1,00,000
Plant & Machinery	28,14,000
Land & Building	5,40,000

During the year the following transactions occurred :

The total cash sales of the company was Rs. 2,34,000 and total credit sales to different parties was Rs. 1,00,000 : Expenses incurred during the year Rs. 40,000; Purchases during the year from different parties Rs. 3,19,000; Purchase of Furniture and Fittings Rs. 2,10,000 by Cash.

Depreciation charged on Plant and Machinery to the extent Rs. 10,000. Closing Stock, as on 31st December 2005 was estimated at Rs. 2,35,000.

The total transactions of the said business during the year 2006 were :

Cash Sales Rs. 2,29,000; Issue of new shares Rs. 4,00,000, Loan from Central Bank of India Rs. 5,35,000. Total purchase of raw materials is Rs. 66,000 of which Rs. 20,000 Cash Purchase. Credit Sales during the year Rs. 60,000. Addition to Plant and Machinery Rs. 7,40,000, Land and Building Rs. 4,80,000. Expenses incurred during the year Rs. 14,000. The same amount of depreciation as was made in 2005 has been charged on Plant and Machinery. Stock at the end of year estimated at Rs. 2,55,000.

From the above information, prepare Journal entries, Ledger Accounts, Trial Balance, Trading and Profit & Loss Account and Balance Sheet for the two consecutive years. And also prepare a Cash Flow Statement, Fund Flow Statement.

From the above information you are requested to comment about the working as well as financial condition of the business.

Can you prepare it?

☐ "Quite impossible for us, yet, Sir. Please work out the problem".

● Well, observe the following workings :

Journal entires in the book of Roundover Trading Co. Ltd. during the year 2005 :

Date	Particulars		L.F.	Dr. Amount	Cr. Amount
2005				Rs.	Rs.
(1)	Cash A/c	Dr.		1,46,000	
	Opening Stock A/c	Dr.		1,00,000	
	Plant & Machinery A/c	Dr.		28,14,000	
	Land & Building A/c	Dr.		5,40,000	
	To Capital A/c				36,00,000
	(Being the start of business with above assets)				
(2)	Cash A/c	Dr.		2,34,000	
	To Sales A/c				2,34,000
	(Being the cash sales during the year)				
(3)	Sundry Debtors A/c	Dr.		1,00,000	
	To Sales A/c				1,00,000
	(Being the credit sales to different parties)				
(4)	Expenses A/c	Dr.		40,000	
	To Cash A/c				40,000
	(Being the total expenses incurred during the year)				
(5)	Purchase A/c	Dr.		3,19,000	
	To Sundry Creditors A/c				3,19,000
	(Being the total credit purchases during the year)				
(6)	Furniture & Fixture A/c	Dr.		2,10,000	
	To Cash A/c				2,10,000
	(Being the purchase of furniture)				
	Total			45,03,000	45,03,000

You see, before I proceed to work out the different ledger accounts, I want to make clear one important point—on the 1st day when the business was started, i.e. on 1st January 2005, as well as on the very moment after the start of business, the position of Balance Sheet will be :

Balance Sheet
as on1st Jan. 2005

Capital and Liabilities	Amount	Assets and Properties	Amount
	Rs.		Rs.
Share Capital	36,00,000	**Fixed Assets**	
		Plant & Machinery	28,14,000
		Land & Buildings	5,40,000
		Current Assets	
		Stock	1,00,000
		Cash	1,46,000
	36,00,000		36,00,000

Ledger Accounts in the book of Roundover Trading Co. Ltd.

Dr. **Cash Book** *Cr.*

Date	Particulars	L.F.	Amount	Date	Particulars	L.F.	Amount
2005			Rs.				Rs.
	To Balance b/f				By Expenses A/c		40,000
	(Opening balance)		1,46,000		" Furniture and Fixture A/c		2,10,000
	" Sales A/c		2,34,000		" Balance C/d		1,30,000
			3,80,000				3,80,000
	To Balance b/d		1,30,000				

Dr. **Capital Account** *Cr.*

Date	Particulars	L.F.	Amount	Date	Particulars	L.F.	Amount
2005			Rs.				Rs.
	To Balance c/d		36,00,000		By Cash A/c		1,46,000
					" Opening stock A/c		1,00,000
					" Plant and Machinery A/c		28,14,000
					" Land and Building A/c		5,40,000
			36,00,000				36,00,000
					By Balance b/d		36,00,000

Dr. **Sales A/c** *Cr.*

Date	Particulars	L.F.	Amount	Date	Particulars	L.F.	Amount
2005			Rs.				Rs.
	To Balance c/d		3,34,000		By Cash A/c		2,34,000
					" Debtors A/c		1,00,000
			3,34,000				3,34,000
					By Balance b/d		3,34,000

Dr. **Purchases A/c** *Cr.*

Date	Particulars	L.F.	Amount	Date	Particulars	L.F.	Amount
2005			Rs.				Rs.
	To Sundry Creditors A/c		3,19,000		By Balance c/d		3,19,000
			3,19,000				3,19,000
	To Balance b/d		3,19,000				

Dr. **Sundry Debtors A/c** *Cr.*

Date	Particulars	L.F.	Amount	Date	Particulars	L.F.	Amount
2006			Rs.				Rs.
	To Sales A/c		1,00,000		By Balance c/d		1,00,000
			1,00,000				1,00,000
	To Balance b/d		1,00,000				

Dr. **Sundry Creditors A/c** Cr.

Date	Particulars	L.F.	Amount	Date	Particulars	L.F.	Amount
2005			Rs.				Rs.
	To Balance c/d		3,19,000		By Purchase A/c		3,19,000
			3,19,000				3,19,000
					By Balance b/d		3,19,000

Dr. **Expenses A/c** Cr.

Date	Particulars	L.F.	Amount	Date	Particulars	L.F.	Amount
2005			Rs.				Rs.
	To Cash A/c		40,000		By Balance c/d		40,000
			40,000				40,000
	To Balance b/d		40,000				

Dr. **Furniture & Fixture A/c** Cr.

Date	Particulars	L.F.	Amount	Date	Particulars	L.F.	Amount
2005			Rs.				Rs.
	To Cash A/c		2,10,000		By Balance c/d		2,10,000
			2,10,000				2,10,000
	To Balance b/d		2,10,000				

Trial Balance of Roundover Trading Co. Ltd.
for the year 2005

Sl. No.	Heads of Accounts	L.F.	Dr. Amount	Cr. Amount
			Rs.	Rs.
1	Cash		1,30,000	
2	Capital			36,00,000
3	Sales			3,34,000
4	Stock on 1st January 2005		1,00,000	
5	Plant and Machinery		28,14,000	
6	Purchases		3,19,000	
7	Land and Buildings		5,40,000	
8	Expenses		40,000	
9	Sundry Creditors			3,19,000
10	Furniture and Fixture		2,10,000	
11	Sundry Debtors		1,00,000	
	Total		42,53,000	42,53,000

Further information :

(i) Depreciation on Plant and Machinery to be charged to the extent Rs. 10,000.

(ii) Stock as on 31st December 2,35,000.

Journal entries of Roundover Trading Co. Ltd. during the year 2006 :

Date	Particulars		L.F.	Dr. Amount	Cr. Amount
2006				Rs.	Rs.
	(1) Cash A/c	Dr.		2,29,000	
	To Sales A/c				2,29,000
	(Being cash sales during the year)				
	(2) Cash A/c	Dr.		4,00,000	
	To Share Capital A/c				4,00,000
	(Being issue of new shares)				
	(3) Cash A/c	Dr.		5,35,000	
	To Loan from Bank A/c				5,35,000
	(Being loan from Central Bank of India)				
	(4) Purchase A/c	Dr.		20,000	
	To Cash A/c				20,000
	(Being purchase of raw material by cash)				
	(5) Purchase A/c	Dr.		46,000	
	To Sundry Creditors A/c				46,000
	(Being purchase of raw material on credit)				
	(6) Sundry Debtors A/c	Dr.		60,000	
	To Sales A/c				60,000
	(Being credit sale to respective parties)				
	(7) Plant & Machinery A/c	Dr.		7,40,000	
	Land & Building A/c	Dr.		4,80,000	
	To Cash A/c				12,20,000
	(Being purchase of above assets)				
	(8) Expenses A/c	Dr.		14,000	
	To Cash A/c				14,000
	(Being amount paid for expenses)				
	Total			25,24,000	25,24,000

Ledger Accounts in the books of Roundover Trading Co. Ltd.

Cash A/c

Dr. Cr.

Date	Particulars	L.F.	Amount	Date	Particulars	L.F.	Amount
2006			Rs.				Rs.
	To Balance b/d		1,30,000		By Purchases A/c		20,000
	" Sales A/c		2,29,000		" Plant & Machinery A/c		7,40,000
	" Share Capital A/c		4,00,000		" Land & Building A/c		4,80,000
	" Loan from Bank A/c		5,35,000		" Expenses A/c		14,000
					" Balance c/d		40,000
			12,94,000				12,94,000
	To Balance b/d		40,000				

Dr. **Sales A/c** Cr.

Date	Particulars	L.F.	Amount	Date	Particulars	L.F.	Amount
2006			Rs.				Rs.
	To Balance c/d		2,89,000		By Cash A/c		2,29,000
					" Debtors A/c		60,000
			2,89,000				2,89,000
					By Balance b/d		2,89,000

Dr. **Purchases A/c** Cr.

Date	Particulars	L.F.	Amount	Date	Particulars	L.F.	Amount
2006			Rs.				Rs.
	To Cash A/c		20,000		By Balance c/d		66,000
	" Sundry Creditors A/c		46,000				
			66,000				66,000
	To Balance b/d		66,000				

Dr. **Sundry Debtors A/c** Cr.

Date	Particulars	L.F.	Amount	Date	Particulars	L.F.	Amount
2006			Rs.				Rs.
	To Balance b/d		1,00,000		By Balance c/d		1,60,000
	" Sales A/c		60,000				
			1,60,000				1,60,000
	To Balance b/d		1,60,000				

Dr. **Sundry Creditors A/c** Cr.

Date	Particulars	L.F.	Amount	Date	Particulars	L.F.	Amount
2006			Rs.				Rs.
	To Balance c/d		3,65,000		By Balance b/d		3,19,000
					" Purchases A/c		46,000
			3,65,000				3,65,000
					By Balance b/d		3,65,000

Dr. **Expenses A/c** Cr.

Date	Particulars	L.F.	Amount	Date	Particulars	L.F.	Amount
2006			Rs.				Rs.
	To Cash A/c		14,000		By Balance c/d		14,000
			14,000				14,000
	To Balance b/d		14,000				

Trial Balance of Roundover Trading Co. Ltd.
for the year 2006

Sl. No.	Heads of Accounts	L.F.	Dr. Amount	Cr. Amount
			Rs.	Rs.
1	Capital			40,00,000
2	Land and Building		10,20,000	
3	Furniture and Fixture		2,10,000	
4	Plant and Machinery		35,44,000	
5	Loan from Bank			5,35,000
6	Profit & Loss A/c			1,00,000
7	Cash		40,000	
8	Sales			2,89,000
9	Purchases		66,000	
10	Sundry Debtors		1,60,000	
11	Sundry Creditors			3,65,000
12	Stock as on 1st January 2006		2,35,000	
13	Expenses		14,000	
	Total		52,89,000	52,89,000

Further information :

(i) Closing stock valued at Rs. 2,55,000

(ii) Depreciation on Plant and Machinery to be charged Rs. 10,000.

(iii) Provision should be made for Dividend to the extent Rs. 2,00,000.

☐ "Sir, please work out the ledger accounts for Land and Building, Plant and Machinery, Furniture and Fixtures and Loan Account as well as Capital Account.

● Well, I am working out all those accounts :

Dr. **Land and Building A/c** Cr.

Date	Particulars	L.F.	Amount	Date	Particulars	L.F.	Amount
2006			Rs.				Rs.
	To Balance b/d		5,40,000		By Balance c/d		10,20,000
	" Cash A/c		4,80,000				
			10,20,000				10,20,000
	To Balance b/d		10,20,000				

Dr. **Furniture and Fixture A/c** Cr.

Date	Particulars	L.F.	Amount	Date	Particulars	L.F.	Amount
2006			Rs.				Rs.
	To Balance b/d		2,10,000		By Balance c/d		2,10,000
			2,10,000				2,10,000
	To Balance b/d		2,10,000				

Dr. **Plant and Machinery A/c** Cr.

Date	Particulars	L.F.	Amount	Date	Particulars	L.F.	Amount
2006			Rs.				Rs.
	To Balance b/d		28,04,000 *		By Balance c/d		35,44,000
	" Cash A/c		7,40,000				
			35,44,000				35,44,000
	To Balance b/d		35,44,000				

* (Rs. 28,14,000 – Rs. 10,000 for Depreciation)

Dr. **Loan from Bank A/c** Cr.

Date	Particulars	L.F.	Amount	Date	Particulars	L.F.	Amount
2006			Rs.				Rs.
	To Balance c/d		5,35,000		By Cash A/c		5,35,000
			5,35,000				5,35,000
					By Balance b/d		5,35,000

Dr. **Profit & Loss A/c** Cr.

Date	Particulars	L.F.	Amount	Date	Particulars	L.F.	Amount
2006			Rs.				Rs.
	To Balance c/d		1,00,000		By Balance b/d (Profit for the last year)		1,00,000
			1,00,000				1,00,000
					By Balance b/d		1,00,000

Dr. **Capital A/c** Cr.

Date	Particulars	L.F.	Amount	Date	Particulars	L.F.	Amount
2006			Rs.				Rs.
	To Balance c/d		40,00,000		By Balance b/d		36,00,000
					" Cash A/c		4,00,000
			40,00,000				40,00,000
					By Balance b/d		40,00,000

I think, you have understood all the above accounts. Is there any question?

Now I want to work out the comparative percentaged Trading and Profit and Loss A/c as well as comparative Balance Sheet.

☐ "Why comparative, Sir"?

● You see, in order to arrive at correct management decision you should always compare the performance of at least two years. From the study you can recommend for the betterment of the organisation or business. Do you follow?

☐ "Yes, Sir, please give us some light about the percentaged Trading and Profit and Loss A/c".

● It is really very satisfactory that you have taken much interest in the subject. I am working out all these just now :

Comparative Trading and Profit & Loss Account

Dr. *Cr.*

Particulars	Figures for previous year 2005 %	Figures for previous year 2005 Rs.	Figures for current year 2006 %	Figures for current year 2006 Rs.	Particulars	Figures for previous year 2005 %	Figures for previous year 2005 Rs.	Figures for current year 2006 %	Figures for current year 2006 Rs.
To Cost of Goods Sold *	55	1,84,000	16	46,000	By Sales	100	3,34,000	100	2,89,000
" Gross Profit	45	1,50,000	84	2,43,000					
	100	3,34,000	100	2,89,000		100	3,34,000	100	2,89,000
To Expenses	12	40,000	5	14,000	By Gross Profit	45	1,50,000	84	2,43,000
" Depreciation	3	10,000	3	10,000					
" Net Profit	30	1,00,000	76	2,19,000					
	45	1,50,000	84	2,43,000		45	1,50,000	84	2,43,000

* Here Cost of goods sold = Opening stock + Purchases (During the year) – Closing stock.

∴ Cost of goods sold for the year 2005 : 1,00,000 + 3,19,000 – 2,35,000 = 1,84,000

Again cost of goods sold for the year 2006 : 2,35,000 + 66,000 – 2,55,000 = 46,000

Profit & Loss Appropriation A/c for the year 2006

Dr. *Cr.*

Particulars	Amount Rs.	Particulars	Amount Rs.
To Provision for Dividend	2,00,000	By Profit for the current year	2,19,000
" Surplus transferred to Balance Sheet	1,19,000	" Balance of Profit for the last year	1,00,000
	3,19,000		3,19,000

Comparative Balance Sheet

Liabilities	2005 Rs.	2006 Rs.	Assets	2005 Rs.	2006 Rs.
Creditors	3,19,000	3,65,000	Cash	1,30,000	40,000
Provision for Dividend	—	2,00,000	Debtors	1,00,000	1,60,000
Loan		5,35,000	Stock & Work-in-progress	2,35,000	2,55,000
Net Worth :			Land & Building	5,40,000	10,20,000
Equity Capital	36,00,000	40,00,000	Plant and Machinery Less Depreciation	28,04,000	35,34,000
Surplus	1,00,000	1,19,000	Furniture and Fittings	2,10,000	2,10,000
	40,19,000	52,19,000		40,19,000	52,19,000

You see, from the above percentaged comparative Trading and Profit & Loss A/c we can recommend about the financial position.

Here we may get a few ratios from the above Trading and Profit and Loss A/c :

Ratio	Components	2005	2006
Gross Profit Ratio	$\frac{\text{Gross Profit}}{\text{Sales}}$	45%	84%
Net Profit Ratio	$\frac{\text{Net Profit}}{\text{Sales}}$	30%	79%
Expense Ratio	$\frac{\text{Expense}}{\text{Sales}}$	12%	5%
Operating Ratio	$\frac{\text{Cost of Goods Sold}}{\text{Sales}}$	55%	16%
Stock Turnover Ratio	$\frac{\text{Cost of Goods Sold}}{\text{Average Stock}}$	1.1 times	0.2 times
Return on Capital Employed	$\frac{\text{Profit}}{\text{Capital Employed}}$	2.79%	5.3%
Turnover of Capital	$\frac{\text{Sales}}{\text{Capital Employed}}$	.093 times	0.67 times

Check of Return on Capital Employed :

2005			2006		
Margin on Sale	=	30%	Margin on Sale	=	79%
Turnover of Capital	=	.093 times	Turnover of capital	=	0.67 times
T.C.X.M.S.			T.C.X.M.S.		
$.093 \times 30\% = 2.79\%$			$.067 \times 79\% = 5.3\%$		

From the above it is clear that increase in profit (79% – 30%) to the extent of 49% is due to the following reasons, although the turnover of capital in the year 2006 had decreased :

i. Higher Margin of Profit.
ii. Lower Operation Ratio.
iii. Decrease in Expense Ratio.

However, now I would like to give you a first hand idea of Fund Flow and Cash Flow statement. Don't worry. All these aspects—Interpretation of Accounts, Fund Flow Statement and Cash Flow Statement would be discussed in detail in the subsequent part of 'Financial Management.'

Fund Flow Statement :

Statement showing change in Working Capital

Current Assets :	**2005** Rs.	**2006** Rs.
Cash	1,30,000	40,000
Debtors	1,00,000	1,60,000
Work-in-Progress	2,35,000	2,55,000
Total Current Assets (A)	4,65,000	4,55,000

Current Liabilities :	Rs.	Rs.
Sundry Creditors	3,19,000	3,65,000
Total Current Liabilities (B)	3,19,000	3,65,000
Working Capital (A – B)	1,46,000	90,000
Decrease in Working Capital		56,000
	1,46,000	1,46,000

Fund Flow Statement

Statement showing Source & Application of Fund
for the year 2006

Source	Amount Rs.	Application	Amount Rs.
Issue of shares	4,00,000	Purchase/Addition to Plant & Machinery	7,40,000
Increase in surplus	29,000	Purchase of Land and Building	4,80,000
Long term Loan	5,35,000		
Provision for Dividend	2,00,000		
Decrease in Working Capital	56,000		
	12,20,000		12,20,000

Cash Flow Statement :

Cash Flow Statement for the year 2006

Particulars	Amount Rs.	Amount Rs.	Amount Rs.
Cash as on 31.12.2005			1,30,000
Received during the year :			
Issue of Shares	4,00,000		
Increase in Surplus	29,000		
Long Term Loan	5,35,000		
Provision for Dividend	2,00,000		
	11,64,000		
Less Increase in Debtors	60,000	11,04,000	
Payments during the year :			
Addition to Stock	20,000		
Purchase of Plant and Machinery	7,40,000		
Purchase of Land and Building	4,80,000		
	12,40,000		
Less Increase in Creditors	46,000	11,94,000	(–) 90,000
Cash as at 31.12.2006			40,000

Well, I am quite sure that you have understood the details of accounting mechanism. In my next chapter I shall be discussing with you in general about some theoretical aspects of accounting literature which would be needed in the context of management accounting study.

Good-bye.

☐ Excuse me Sir, Please give us a Flow Chart of Entire Accounting Mechanism.

● Please wait. Let me see any other question coming from your side.

I will discuss everything.

Wait for my next class please.

☐ "Sir, give us some journal entries for our study concerning Share Issued at a Premium and Share Issued at a Discount".

● You, you, please stand up. Why you are talking with each other?

☐ "I am not talking, Sir! I want to know from him what is the difference between Preference Share and Equity or Ordinary Share?"

● You clarify all your queries, not from him—I am here to clarify your queries. Please don't hesitate. Be frank with me. Don't feel shy. You see, what I feel is that students are raw materials, teachers are machines. Unless there is any cordial understanding between the raw material and machine, in this situation the teacher and the taught the development of mental and academic faculty can not be possible.

Are there any questions?

☐ "Sir I have a question to put. Please tell me the forms of Balance Sheet according to the Companies Act, 1956".

● What is your question?

Yes see, the time is over now. I will answer all your queries tomorrow.

☐ "Thank you Sir."

☐ "Sir, I have forgotten to tell you to explain the concept of Accounting Mechanism."

● You see I have explained all these already.

☐ "Please, Sir".

● Have you not attended all my previous lectures?

☐ "No Sir".

● Please note that unless you attend your classes you would be suffering from two dimensions—(a) Lack of knowledge, and (b) not to be permitted to sit for the examination for lack of adequate class attendance, i.e., short of percentage.

Bye, see you tomorrow.

****

● Good morning.

☐ "Good morning, Sir"!

● I want to discuss about .....

☐ "Sir you promised to answer our questions".

● Oh, yes, what were those questions?

The first question was perhaps on Equity Share(s), Preference Share(s). Is it so?

☐ "Yes Sir".

● Before I discuss on these shares, I feel it is essential to discuss about different types of business —Sole Proprietor, Partnership and Companies, i.e. Joint Stock Company. You see, in the Proprietary form of business the proprietor is the single owner. The profit earned in the business is added to his own capital and loss(es), if thereby any incurred during the business process, is or are deducted from his capital. The problem of this form of business is paucity of fund; this problem leads to the formation of Partnership form of business where capital is contributed by two or more partners. The profit of the partners are distributed either in capital ratio or as decided by their agreement. Here also the problem exists of adequate finance or fund for expansion of business. The problem leads to the formation of joint stock company or companies as solution to the problem —paucity of fund. Here money is contributed by the shareholders of the company.

Different forms of Business— Sole-proprietorship, Partnership and Company

Please note that shares are of two types—Equity or Ordinary Shares and Preference Shares.

By the by, I am to say that the company secures finance not only by issue of shares but also by issuing Debentures in the market. This Debenture is termed as Loan Capital.

Please note :

CLASSIFICATION OF SHARE CAPITAL

- **Ordinary Share Capital**
- **Preference Share Capital**

Please note that the other name of Ordinary Share is Equity Share; naturally Ordinary Share Capital is known as Equity Share Captial.

You see a share may be stated as a unit of measure of shareholder(s') interest in the company. Therefore, share capital is divided into equal parts comprising large number and that each part of the dividend capital is termed 'share'.

Meaning of Share

Companies Act, 1956, states that a Public Company limited by Shares is allowed to issue two types of shares — (i) Ordinary Shares (Equity Share); and

(ii) Preference Shares.

Regarding Preference Share I am to say that the term 'Preference' indicates that it enjoys some extra benefit other than ordinary share. That is to say, the holders of Preference Shares enjoy certain preferential rights and privileges :

Preference Share

Rights Enjoyed by Preference Shareholder(s)

- Right to Dividend
- Right to Participate in surplus profit
- Right to Repayment of capital

Preference shareholders are entitled to receive a fixed rate of Dividend, say 6%, Preference Share Capital amounts to Rs. 1,00,000; here the Preference Shareholders will receive Dividend on the capital invested by them, here 6% on Rs. 1,00,000 is Rs. 6,000. The fixed rate so computed above will be paid out of the net profit of the company prior to declaration of Dividend on Equity or Ordinary Shareholders.

Right to Dividend

Do you follow what I say?

☐ "Sir, I could not follow. I am in a confusion whether Preference Shareholders will get Dividend at fixed rate direct from the Net Profit".

• You are right. Amount so calculated will be paid out of the Net Profit. But, as I already told you, that fixed amount will be calculated on the capital invested by them. Take an example. 6% Preference Share Capital is Rs. 1,00,000. The Net Profit of the company is, say, 20,000. So, fixed rate will be 6% on the capital contributed by the Preference shareholders not 6% on Net Profit. As already explained that fixed rate is 6%. So, 6% on Rs. 1,00,000 = Rs. 6,000. This Rs. 6,000 will be deducted from Net Profit Rs. 20,000. The residual amount Rs. 14,000 (Rs. 20,000 – Rs. 6,000) will be available for payment to Ordinary or Equity Shareholders as Dividend.

Computation of Dividend to Preference Shareholders

I think you have followed the concept of ***Right to Dividend***.

☐ "Yes Sir, Thank you Sir"!

• Now I would like to tell you regarding ***Right to Participate*** in Surplus Profit.

You see, the holders of Participating Preference shares are entitled to a share in the surplus of profit—if there remains—after paying Dividend to the Equity or Ordinary shareholders. Please note that participating Preference shareholders get (i) Fixed rate of Dividend, plus (ii) Share in Surplus Profit.

Right to Participate in Surplus Profit

Well, regarding ***Right to Repayment of Capital***, I am to say that the repayment of Preference Capital arises in the event of winding-up of the company. This facility is not enjoyed by the Ordinary or Equity Share- holders.

Right to Repayment of Capital

By the by, I am to tell you that Preference Shareholders are not the owners of the business or company. But they enjoy the status of ownership of the company. Real ownership lies with Equity or Ordinary Shareholders. The Preference Shareholders have no ***Voting Power*** in the company. Voting Right rests with Equity or Ordinary Shareholders.

Do you follow?

☐ No sir, please explain it taking an example of normal day-to-day activities or behaviour.

• You see, difference between Preference Shareholder and Equity Shareholder may be drawn taking an example of difference between Father and Father-in-Law.

Father-in-law enjoys some preferential right as to Breakfast, Lunch and Dinner. Father-in-law is not the owner of the family but he enjoys the status of ownership in the family. Father has a voting power in his family (son) but father-in-law has no voting power in the house of son-in-law, unless otherwise ....

☐ "Sir! What does all these dots (......) mean?"

● You are to fill up these blanks as days pass.

Do you follow?

☐ "Yes Sir, you have explained it in such a way that any lay man can understand it.

● Now I am to discuss the classification of Preference Shares.

CLASSIFICATION OF PREFERENCE SHARES

- Cumulative and Non-Cumulative
- Redeemable and Irredeemable
- Participating and Non-Participating
- Convertible and Non-Convertible

You see, normally question of payment of Dividend arises when profit is there. That is to say, question of payment of Dividend does not arise when company incurs loss. But, in case of Cumulative Preference Share, unpaid Dividend, i.e., arrears, will be carried forward for future when company earns profit; in case of Non-Cumulative Preference Share question of arrear dividend does not arise. The holder of Non-Cumulative Preference Shares will get their Dividend only when company earns profit.

Regarding Redeemable and Irredeemable Preference shares I am to say that at present issue of Irredeemable Preference Shares has been prohibited. Only Redeemable Preference Shares are in use which will be redeemed (paid-off) after a few years as within the period of existing rule.

You see, I have already explained about Participating Preference Shares. This type of shareholders enjoy fixed Dividend plus share is surplus profit.

You see, Convertible Preference Share means that, after a few years, depending upon existing rules and regulations, these types of shares are converted to Equity shares. In that case these shareholders, after conversion, enjoy voting right of the company. The term non-convertible is self-explanatory, it requires no discussion.

☐ "Sir, you have not explained the journal entries taking into consideration Shares Issued at Premium and Shares Issued at a Discount. Please Sir!"

● I remember, all these I will explain step by step.

Please write down the following :

Example

A company issued 1,000 Equity Shares of Rs. 10 each at a premium of Rs. 2 per share.

Yes see shares are issued at a premium when the image of profitability and solvency is in good condition. Taking the advantage of all these the company issues shares in the market at a premium.

Please note, you say, what is coming in, also say receipt of premium is satisfaction on the part of company. What will be Debit and what will be credit?

☐ "Sir, should I answer?"

● Yes, Yes.

☐ "Sir! Cash is coming in two sources (i) as inflow of cash as capital and inflow of premium money as satisfaction; and we have learnt that capital is credit. So, Sir, journal entry will be as follows :

Date	Particulars		L.F.	Amount	Amount
2005				Rs.	Rs.
	Cash/Bank A/c	Dr.		12,000	
	To Equity Share Capital A/c				10,000
	To Securities Premium A/c				2,000
	(Being the shares issued at a Premium)				

Sir! This securities Premium money would be shown in the Liability side of the Balance Sheet under the head Reserve and Surplus".

• Thank you very much. Please note securities premium was previously known as share premium I am glad to see your performance. Well, you stand up and answer the following :

Example

A company issued 1,000 Ordinary (Equity) Shares of Rs. 10 each at a discount of Rs. 2.00 per share.

You see, unlike shares issued at a premium, shares are issued at a discount. Reasons for discount issue are low profitability, unhealthy growth of the business, no attraction of share in the capital or share market.

☐ "Sir, here is the journal entry".

Date	Particulars		L.F.	Amount	Amount
2005				Rs.	Rs.
	Cash/Bank A/c	Dr.		8,000	
	Discount on Issue of Shares A/c	Dr.		2,000	
	To Equity Share Capital A/c				10,000
	(Being the shares issued at a discount)				

• Please explain it.

☐ "Sir, cash is coming in. What comes in is Debit (Dr.). Share Capital is always credit balance. In this transaction the company is getting dissatisfaction for the loss in capital value. You told us that all loss—that is to say all dissatisfaction—is Debit."

• Thank you.

Bye, see you tomorrow.

☐ Sir! If I am excused please explain what is **Debenture** and what are the different types of Debentures.

• Thank you I will explain it tomorrow.

****

• Good morning to you all.

☐ Good morning, Sir!

• Well, I would give you some idea about **Debenture**.

First of all let us know what Debenture is.

You see, **Debenture** may be defined as a document which acknowledges loan to a company. It may be stated that it is a bond acknowledging a loan. Needless to mention that it constitute a major part of loan capital of the company.

Meaning of Debenture

☐ "Sir, can I define Debenture as follows :
It is an acknowledgement of a debt by the company."

• You are perfectly right.

Now, note the different types of Debentures :

TYPES OF DEBENTURE

Secured Debenture	Unsecured Debenture	Registered Debenture	Bearer Debenture	Redeemable Debenture	Convertible Debenture
It is known as Mortgage Debenture	It is also known as simple or Naked Debenture. Because they do not carry any security on the assets of the company	Here names of the persons are recorded in the Certificate Book of the company. They can be transferred after filling in transfer deed	Bearer Debenture can be transferred by mere delivery without any notice to the company	They can be redeemed after expiry of certain years	When Debentures are converted to equity capital

Do you follow the above chart?

☐ Yes Sir, but, I cannot understand the concept of Convertible Debenture. For easy understanding of the concept please give us an example.

• Well, just think about a situation. In a family three members are there — Father, Mother and their only daughter. A tutor was appointed to teach the daughter English and Mathematics. The tutor is an outsider; after a few years that tutor became son-in-law of the family; that is to say, Loan Capital is converted into Equity Capital. Consider the outsider as Debentureholder, i.e. loan capital. At that time he had no ownership in the family. After conversion from outsider to insider of the family he enjoys voting right in the family.

Well, you wanted me to show you the forms of Balance Sheet as per Companies Act, 1956. I am showing it. Before that, note that the contents of the Balance Sheet which I already discussed remains the same. Only point is that the Act provides for two forms of presentations of Balance Sheet —(1) *Horizontal Form, and (2) Vertical Form.* In Horizontal form there would be two columns on both sides of Assets and Liabilities — Figures for Previous Year and Figures for Current Year. This is shown below :

A. HORIZONTAL FORM

Balance Sheet of ....[Here enter the name of the company]

As at ......[Here enter the date on which the balance sheet is made out]

Instructions in accordance with which liabilities should be made out	LIABILITIES		ASSETS		*Instructions in accordance with which assets should be made out*
	Figures for the previous year Rs.	*Figures for the current year Rs.*	*Figures for the previous year Rs.*	*Figures for the current year Rs.*	

Companies Act, 1956

B. VERTICAL FORM

Name of Company ....

Balance Sheet as at ....

	Schedule No.	Figures as at the end of current financial year	Figures as at the end of previous financial year
I. Sources of funds :			
(1) *Shareholders' Fund*			
(a) Capital			
(b) Reserves and Surplus			
(2) *Loan Funds*			
(a) Secured Loans			
(b) Unsecured Loans			
TOTAL :			
II. Application of funds :			
(1) *Fixed assets*			
(a) Gross block			
(b) *Less* depreciation			
(c) Net block			
(d) Capital work-in-progress			
(2) *Investments*			
(3) *Current assets, Loans, and Advances :*			
(a) Inventories			
(b) Sundry debtors			
(c) Cash and bank balances			
(d) Other current assets			
(e) Loans and advances			
Less			
Current Liabilities and Provisions :			
(a) Liabilities			
(b) Provisions			
Net Current Assets			
(4) (a) Miscellaneous expenditure to the extent not written-off or adjusted			
(b) Profit & Loss Account			
TOTAL :			

Notes : 1. Details under each of the above items shall be given in separate Schedules. The Schedules shall incorporate all the information required.

FLOW CHART OF ACCOUNTING MECHANISM

STEPS ←	*ACCOUNTING MECHANISM*	→ FUNCTIONS
Identification of economic transactions or events	→ Through →	Appropriate voucher which means supporting evidence
Recording of Transactions or events	→ Through →	Maintenance of Day Books
Classification of transactions or events	→ Through →	Preparation of Ledger A/cs under respective heads on the basis of nature of transactions or events
Summarisation of transactions or events	→ Through →	Preparation of Trial Balance
Results of transactions or events	→ Through →	Preparation of Trading A/c, Profit & Loss A/c, Balance Sheet, Cash Flow Statement, Funds Flow Statement. These are called Financial Statements
Reporting of results	→ Through →	Preparation of Audit Report. Auditor in his report writes whether Financial Statements exhibit *true and fair* view of the state of affairs of the business or not

QUESTIONS

1. Distinguish between 'Book-keeping' and 'Accountancy'; 'Accountancy' and 'Accounting'.
2. What is Balance Sheet? What are the various types of information which can be obtained from Balance Sheet?
3. "A Company cannot pay its dividend money as well as taxes in spite of high reported profit" —Discuss.
4. What are the Mechanisms of Accounting?
5. The books of Docking and Engineering Co. Ltd. show the following Balance on 31st December 2005 :

   (a) Share Capital, authorised, issued and Paid-up 25,000 shares of Rs. 50 each;

(b) Purchases of materials and stores Rs. 40,98,459; (c) Sales and work done Rs. 67,89,734; (d) Managing Agent's commission and allowances Rs. 72,000; (e) Interest Rs. 95,390; (f) Bad Debts written-off Rs. 3,545; (g) Miscellaneous Receipts Rs. 100; (h) Loans and Advances (Dr) Rs. 7,01,529; (i) Sundry Creditors Rs. 19,64,840; (j) Sundry Debtors Rs. 10,70,686; (k) Cash and Bank balance Rs. 45,733; (l) Manufacturing Expenses Rs. 38,87,791; (m) General Reserve Rs. 20,50,000; (n) Dividend Equalisation Reserve Rs. 1,50,000; (o) Credit to Profit & Loss Account on January 1, 2005 Rs. 46,167; (p) Secured Loans Rs. 18,37,620; (q) Unsecured Loan Rs. 6,00,000; (r) Unclaimed Dividends Rs. 9,901; (s) Advance against Work in Progress (Cr) Rs. 80,75,522; (t) Directors' Fees Rs. 1,800.

Fixed Assets at written down value on January 1, 2005—Rs. 21,72,827; Materials and Stores, January 1, 2005—Rs.6,87,724, Work in Progress, January, 1, 2005—Rs. 99,36,409.

At December 31, 2005—Survey of the stock of materials and stores shows its value at Rs. 7,15,205; and work in progress value Rs. 1,15,88,817.

Provide Rs. 19,270 on account of Agent's Commission and Rs. 4,500 on account of Auditor's fees, Depreciate Fixed Assets by Rs. 1,08,057.

Proposed dividend for the year ended 31.12.05 is Rs. 1,56,250.

Prepare a Trading and Profit and Loss Account for the year ended 31st December 2005 and a Balance Sheet as at that date.

6. From the undermentioned Trial Balance of a trader as on 31st December, 2005 prepare a Trading and Profit and Loss Account for the year ended 31st December 2005 and a Balance Sheet as on that date :

Dr. **Trial Balance** *Cr.*

Particulars	Amount Rs.	Particulars	Amount Rs.
Cash in hand	1,200	Capital A/c	1,00,000
Purchases	12,000	Bills Payable	22,000
Stock (opening)	35,000	Sundry Creditors	24,000
Sundry Debtors	50,000	Sales	1,00,200
Plant & Machinery	60,000	Bad Debts Reserve	1,000
Furniture & Fixture	23,000		
Bill Receivable	20,000		
Rent & Taxes	10,000		
Wages	16,000		
Salaries	20,000		
	2,47,200		2,47,200

Additional information supplied :

(a) Closing Stock Rs. 40,000; (b) Provide Outstanding Liabilities; Rent and Taxes Rs. 2,000, Wages Rs. 3,000; Salaries Rs. 4,000; (c) Depreciation : Plant and Machinery 5%; Furniture & Fixtures 10%; (d) Bad Debts Reserve 2.5% on Sundry Debtors.

7. Prepare the Profit & Loss Account for the year ended 31st December 2005 and the Balance Sheet as at that date with the help of following Trial Balance and adjustments.

Particulars		Dr. Amount Rs.	Cr. Amount Rs.
Opening Stock		80,000	
Freehold Premises		60,000	
Plant and Machinery		50,000	
Purchase and Sales		75,000	1,90,000
Discount		350	400
Sundry Debtors		40,000	
Sundry Creditors			25,000
Carriage in		750	
Carriage out		1,200	
Furniture and Fixtures		5,000	
Wages		10,000	
Salaries		7,500	
Bad Debts		1,200	
Commission			42,500
Capital Accounts : (Fixed)			
A.	30,000		
B.	20,000		50,000
Bills Receivable		20,000	
Bills Payable			5,000
A's Loan A/c			50,000
Cash in hand		750	
Cash at Bank		5,250	
Trade Expenses		5,900	
		3,62,900	3,62,900

The following adjustments are required :

(i) Closing stock amounted to Rs. 75,000, (ii) Plant and Machinery and Furniture and Fixtures are to be depreciated at 6% and 20%, respectively. (iii) Outstanding Liabilities to be provided for : Wages Rs. 2,000; Salaries Rs. 3,000; (iv) Partnership salaries to be provided for; A Rs. 5,000; B Rs. 4,000. (v) Interest on Capital is to be paid at 5% p.a. (vi) Interest on A's loan is to be provided for the whole year. (vii) 50% of the distributable profit is to be carried to Reserve Fund. (viii) No Bad Debts Reserve is to be passed to the partners; think all debtors are good.

RECTIFICATION OF ERRORS

8. (a) Give the corrective Journal entries with full narration in the books of Shibram Sikdar, a trader :

(i) Goods sold for Rs. 575 to J. K. Sharma were debited to K. J. Sharma. (ii) A cheque for Rs. 755 paid for the purchase of an Office Typewriter was debited to Repairs Account (iii) A cheque for Rs. 500 paid to a Creditor was credited to a Debtors Account. (iv) A cash discount of Rs. 10 received from a Creditor was debited to Cash Discount Account. The Trial Balance was prepared by transferring the difference to a 'Suspense Account'.

(a) Show how the Suspense Account will then be eliminated.

(b) For what other types of entries is the Journal proper utilised?

4

HIGHLIGHTS OF BASIC ACCOUNTING CONCEPTS

● Good morning to you all.

☐ "Good morning Sir."

● In my last lecture I discussed with you about the different processes of accounting.

Accounting Doctrines

Now I like to discuss about the different accounting doctrines, viz. Objectivity, Disclosure, Consistency, Materiality and Conservatism which characterise the accounting processes.

1. **Objectivity :** The basic principle of objectivity is to underline the work of the accountant. That is to say, the recorded facts in accounting statements must be supported by 'objective evidence' of its existence or happenings. Entries in the books of accounts depending on 'whim' or 'fancy'[1] should not be recorded or recognised in accounting. To write-up[2] the value of goodwill and to write-back[3] the value of goodwill, which was previously written-off or amortized, depending on 'whim' or 'fancy' will lead to recording faked goodwill[4]. It is a fact that changes in 'account balances' must be supported by evidence. So evidence may be either in the nature of supporting documents or of events or both. For example, in the case of the former the evidences include invoices, bill of sale or a receipt, employee time card, market price and, in the case of the latter, the documents include actual happening or events. To explain it, it should be noted that recording of goodwill follows on the happening of certain events, such as admission of partner, retirement of partner, death of partner, change in the profit-sharing ratio and sale of partnership to limited company. Such events may be treated as a supporting evidence of recording. Unless the accounting entries are supported by objective evidence—examples cited above, the confidence of all parties—shareholders, creditors, investors, employees, government—who are interested in the affairs of the business may be lost. So any decision taken from accounting or financial records or reports which are not supported by objective evidence may be detrimental to the business.

Objectivity

'Whim' or 'Fancy' in Accounting

2. **Disclosure :** The financial or accounting statement should or must disclose the results of managerial 'stewardship'. If the financial statements, say, profit & loss account and balance sheet, are to present 'fairly', the full disclosure of pertinent information should be given.

Disclosure

---

[1] *Finney and Miller, **Principles of Accounting**—Introductory, P. 2*

[2] ***Accounting for Goodwill.** op. cit.*

[3] ***Stapley vs Read Bros.***

[4] ***Accounting for Goodwill.** op. cit.*

Fairness in accounting means :

Meaning of 'Fairness' in Accounting

i. Free from bias.

ii. Free from dishonesty.

iii. Free from sentiment in disclosing material information needed for evaluating or appraising the performances of the business or firm.

iv. Free from difficulties for the completeness of information.

So, nothing should be concealed or withheld and it should be transparent. For example, if any extraordinary gain resulting from the sale of fixed assets, say machinery, is included in the total of operating income, the shareholders and other interested parties would be wrongly informed about the earning power of the company. Because, most of the shareholders are not expert in studying the financial statements 'between the lines'. Generally, the doctrine of disclosure implies that the 'accounting records and statements conform to generally accepted accounting principles'.[5] Now if you think on the matter, you will find that the concept of 'true' or 'truth' in disclosure is contradictory. Take for an example : Mr. X and Mr. Y both are trading with same amount of capital and working under same social and economic set-up. They report different figures for trading or operating profit; say Mr. X Rs. 5,000 and Mr. Y Rs. 8,000. The extra reported profit Rs. 3,000 of Mr. Y results from the valuation of closing stock at *FIFO* (First in first out method); on the other hand, decrease in the reported profit to the extent of Rs. 3,000 in case of X as compared with Y may result from the valuation of closing stock either at *LIFO* (Last in first out) or *cost or market price*, whichever is lower. Besides, like valuation of stock at different methods, the reported profit may also vary—other things remaining the same—following the different methods of charging depreciation. So it is clear that the concept of 'true' is a flexible term in light of the above illustration.

Contradiction of the Concept 'True'

Can you say that the reported profit of Mr. X is wrong and that of Mr. Y is right?

I think both are correct. Because they have computed their profit depending 'on the set accounting rules of stock valuation'. So the concept of 'true' or 'truth' under the doctrine of 'disclosure' is fully dependent on 'choice approach', which varies from firm to firm and accountant to accountant. So full disclosure does not necessarily imply that 'the statement will exhibit all the facts, all truth'. That's why an expert opines that "when lack of opportunity to tell all the truths necessitates a choice from two or more methods or items, any one of which could be established as a fact and is within the accepted system, the one chosen should be the most useful for the purpose for which the report is prepared ...... if the inventory valuation choice is available of either first in first out, or last in first out, the company probably will choose the one resulting in the lower net income"[6].

Choice Approach in Accounting

So to have an uniformity in presenting accounting information, there should be some basic principles, although an expert opines that "it is difficult to discern in accounting practice any 'principles' which are universally applicable at all times and in all circumstances..... these standards or rules of good practice are derived from certain assumptions or postulates upon which accounting is based".[7]

---

[5] *Yorston and others, **Advanced Accounting**, P. 15.*

[6] *Foster, **Understanding Financial Statement and Corporate Annual Reports**, 1968, P. 43.*

[7] *Fitzgerald, **Analysis and Interpretation of Financial Statements**, P. 6.*

Please note that in spite of the existence of many difficulties it has been made possible to formulate certain principles of subject, like social sciences—Economics, Law and Government etc.—which are always subject to change and amendment. So accounting is a social science which should have certain universally accepted basic principles and should be changed depending on the requirement of the society. If certain principles in case of economics and law can be formulated there cannot be any ground why standard accounting principles should not be enforced in case of accounting. For that, extensive research should be made to identify accounting in any one group of knowledge mentioned below :

Class of Knowledge

Arts & letters	Biological Science	Physical Science	Abstract Science	Social Science
Examples	*Examples*	*Examples*	*Examples*	*Examples*
Drama,	Botany	Astronomy	Mathematics	Sociology, History
Language	Zoology	Physics	Statistics	Anthropology
Literature	Physiology	Chemistry	Logic	Philosophy
Painting	Genetics	Geology		Ethics, Psychology,
Sculpture				Law, Government,
Music				Economics

From the above classes of knowledge we can identify the character of accounting associated with economics as well as statistics. Since economics is concerned with income, value and cost, and accounting is concerned with the determination of income, value and cost. The basic function of statistics is to classify and compress the data chronologically and systematically, so does accounting by classifying the accounts under Personal, Real and Nominal account. So Professor Littleton had rightly observed that "accounts are often greatly influenced by law & government action; accounting is often considered to be mathematical; —at least arithmetical; public practice has its ethics and history. Yet none of these contacts touch the fundamental nature of accounting in the way economics and statistics do. For, the subject matter in accounting—inescapably economic and its basic

Accounting as Social Science

methodology—is unquestionably statistical in character. Accounting method is statistical in character, because its central mechanism consists of accounts, and accounts are in classification categories used for compressing and simplifying a mass of enterprise transactions. The chief functions of statistical method is to classify, compress, and simplify masses of data so that their significance may be better understood. Accounting has the same function". So from the above discussion we can observe that the nature and character of accounting partly resembles social science and partly abstract science. However, in a sense, we can consider 'accounting' as a pure social science; 'pure' in the sense that it is based on the properties of abstract science.

"Do you follow my lecture? Is there any question, please?"

☐ **"Sir, what are the difficulties which stand in the way of accounting to formulate certain principles? Please enlighten us".**

Practical Difficulties in the Formulation of Accounting Principles

• Your question is very interesting. I am really very glad to see that you want to go deep into the subject. However, for your understanding, I would like to draw your attention to the observation made by Professor Gilman[8] as to the difficulties to formulate accounting principles :

i. Difficulties due to the convention of the annual accounting period and the valuation convention.

ii. Difficulties due to the necessary application of the simple entity convention to the diverse and complex relationships of modern business.

iii. Difficulties due to limitation in accounting.

iv. Difficulties caused by the shift from the Balance Sheet to the profit and loss view point.

v. Difficulties due to the contradiction among principles.

vi. Legal difficulties.

vii. Difficulties due to self-interest.

viii. **Difficulties due to lack of definitions.**

Well, I hope you have understood all the points explained earlier. Now I like to discuss on the other portion of the accounting doctrines which are :

Consistency

3. **Consistency :** Consistency is one of the important features in accounting. This implies that same basis of stock valuation as well as depreciation charges should be maintained for current year and the years to come. There are several methods of stock valuation and depreciation charges. So the accountant should seek to apply any one of the methods best suited for the firm. So switching over from Diminishing Balance Method of depreciation to Straight Line Method of depreciation, or vice versa, would bring some confusion in the mind of the prospective investors as to reported profit—Is reported profit inflated? Is the company not doing well?

However, consistency in the system of maintaining books of accounts is the proper basis as well as a good guide for evaluating the performance of the business and it is best suited for Inter-firm comparison. In actual practice, difficulties arise, because different firms use different definitions and different valuation principles in arriving at their profit, cost and assets figures[9]. Comparison of performance of a particular company becomes all the more difficult when methods of charging depreciation is found to change.[10] So consistency plays an important role in presenting accounting and financial information 'true and fair.'

Materiality

4. **Materiality :** Materiality may be defined as a state of 'relative importance'. The state of 'relative importance' may vary from person to person and accountant to accountant. Well, you see, what is material to me may be immaterial to another. Say, is 10% of Rs. 10,000 material or is 10% of Rs. 1,000 material? Although, there is no boundary line to judge a particular item as being material or immaterial. So the judgement is dependent on time factor and exact position of the firm. So materiality is dependent on some allied factors which evaluate the particular expenditure or incident or happening as being material or immaterial.

---

8 ***Accounting Concepts of Profit**, 1939, Pp. 1-11.*

9 *H. Ingham, **Interfirm Comparison for Management**, P. 19.*

10 *Hindustan Housing Ltd., New Delhi, 16th Annual Report.*

*See **Finance and Society**, previously known as **Finance and Commerce**, for critical review of the said Balance **Sheet**. **Reviewed by Dr. B. K. Basu**, July 1970, Pp. 653-655.*

I think you are feeling bored. Well, I would like to tell you a story best suited to this particular example. You see, a man was asked by his friend, "How many sweets (rosogolla) you like to taste?" Before answering the same the man enquired "Who will bear the expenditure?" The friend asked, "How many you can, if it is in my own cost?" The man answered "One kilogram". Again the friend asked "How many at your own cost?" The man answered, "Only one gram". From the above story, you can realise that "the materiality of an item depends on its size, its nature, or a combination of both. An item should be regarded as material if there is reason to believe that knowledge of it would influence the decisions or attitude of an informed investor.[11] So it should be noted in this context that what is material in one environment may be quite immaterial in another environment. Take for example : Taxi expenditure for Rs. 500 is incurred for return to home at Bhatpara from Kolkata is material only when the train and bus services are dislocated. The same, again, would be immaterial when the train and bus services are normal. So to have a boundary line between the two, "much depends on the absolute judgement and knowledge of the environment on the part of the persons making the decision."[12]

Conditional and Environmental Factor in Materiality

5. **Conservatism :** Conservatism, in accounting, has developed an 'implication similar to pessimism or understatement'. "The doctrine of conservatism is that when two or more reasonable conclusions exist, conservatism dictates the choice of the one that results in the least favourable immediate showing". Sometimes it conflicts with the doctrine of 'disclosure'. Conservatism results in misstatement of financial statements. That is to say, it distorts the financial position of the business. Shareholders may be deprived of their legitimate dividend and the government may be deprived of getting proper tax as a result of understatement of reported profit. Modern concept of conservatism is that profit should neither be overstated nor understated. So it means a middle ground between understatement and overstatement. That is to say, liabilities and expenses should not be overstated and revenue and assets should not be understated to a point below their net realisable cash amount'.

Techniques of Conservatism

However, conservatism may be practiced in any one of the following ways :

i. Valuation of closing stock at a lower figure.
ii. Valuation of debtors through the provision of bad and doubtful debts.
iii. Valuation of Plant and Machinery through depreciation provision.
iv. Over-valuation of liabilities figure in balance sheet.

I think you have followed all the different accounting doctrines—Objectivity, Disclosure, Consistency, Materiality and Conservatism. Is there any question, please?

☐ "Sir, Give us some concept about depreciation and stock valuation".

• Yes, I will discuss all these points in due course of time. Before that I request you to recapitulate the discussions made in the first chapter where I told you that the management accountant should have some idea about different concepts such as—Going Concern Concept, Business Entity Concept, Money Measurement Concept, Cost Concept, Dual Aspect and Accrual Concept.

---

[11] ***Concepts and Standards Underlying Corporate Financial Statements**. Supplementary Statement No. 8 (American Accounting Association).*

[12] *Gole, **Accounting for Businessmen**, P. 7.*

Do you remember? At that time I simply pointed out all those concepts. Now I like to discuss all those concepts step by step. Before that I would like to tell you by way of reference that Professor Anthony in his book "Management Accounting Principles" discussed these concepts. However, I like to discuss the above concepts as follows :

1. **Going Concern Concept :** This means that, in the absence of any good evidence to the contrary, 'accounting assumes' that the business is being operated or conducted with the expectation of continuing the same indefinitely or over a reasonable period of time. The going concern may be termed as 'Continuity' concept. 'Liquidation values' 'Break-up values' and 'Market values'—all these are irrelevant to going concern concept. Since assets are acquired to start the business or for earning purpose and not for resale and not with the hope for liquidation in the foreseeable future; and also not for assessment of its market price. But the cost of product, so produced by the use of the capital of the business, should be subject to market assessment and it should be measured by comparing with the market price. Unless a business earns adequately over and above the cost of capital as well as cost of production, the going concern concept may be jeopardised. Hence, the 'continuity' or 'going concern concept' is dependent on earning capacity of the business. So, in this sense, 'going concern, attains the significance of value. It is a fact that when the business starts production and earns reasonable rate of return, as well as when the prospect of the business is unquestionable, the 'going concern value' is higher than the 'break-up' values of each and every asset used in the business. So, unlike 'market value' and 'break-up value', the going concern concept is concerned with 'use value'.

Going Concern Concept

'Value' Concept in Going Concern

2. **Entity Concept of Business :** A business has a separate entity of its own. Its separate assumed existence helps the business to expand. It is a fact, a business starts with capital contributed by the shareholders and outsiders. With the start of a business, the business is known by its name. Say, Dola Trading Corporation, Bagha Steel Company Limited, and not by the name of the respective contributors. Hence a business has a legal entity separate from the persons who own it.

Entity Concept

So an enterprise, as such, 'is always differentiated from individuals or firms with which it deals such as employees, debtors, creditors and even proprietor'.[13] The entity concept is the basic step towards the realisation of 'Dual Aspect Concept'.

The entity concept is often considered as 'an artificial man' or an 'artificial body' "which has no soul to be damned and no body to be kicked." However, I already discussed the Entity Concept in Chapter One of Part Two of the book. For that, I request you to consult the footnote 3 of the said chapter.

Entity Concept & Artificial Man

Please be frank; if you cannot understand, please say so. Do you like to have any clarification on any concept so far discussed?

☐ "Sir, we are very glad that you have explained the concepts understandably."

• 3. **Money Measurement Concept :** In my last chapter, i.e., in Accounting Mechanism, I discussed that one of the tests of transaction is money measurement. That is to say, it must be measurable in terms of money. This indicates that accounting records entertain only those facts which can be expressed in terms of money. 'The advantage of

[13] *Rorem and Kerrigan, op. cit, P. 19.*

Money Measurement Concept

expressing facts in monetary terms is that money provides a common denominator by means of which heterogeneous facts about a business can be added and subtracted. Although the common denominator concept is an essential one and 'although money is probably the only practical denominator, the use of money implies a homogeneity'.[14]

4. **Cost Concept :** If the accounting doctrines—i.e. Objectivity, Disclosure, Consistency and Conservatism—are to be realised, the basic thing would be to show all the assets at their respective cost value. If this principle is followed, uniformity in keeping accounts can be maintained. For that, assets should neither be shown in the books of accounts at current replacement values or realisation value and it should be shown as it is. Dr. Canning[15] rightly said that cost is significant at the time the transaction is entered into, thereafter it becomes merely historical and does not reflect value in exchange when carried on to subsequent balance sheets'. However, different concepts of cost would be discussed later on.

Cost Concept

5. **Dual Aspect Concept :** In my last chapter I discussed the concept of double entry where we had seen that every 'debit' should have a corresponding 'credit' and every 'credit' should have a corresponding 'debit'. When a business is started with, say, Rs. 5,000, it is concerned with two aspects —(a) the entity's (the business) possession of cash (asset) for Rs. 5,000, and (b) the owner's claim against asset (cash). Because we had seen earlier under the entity concept that a business is viewed as 'an artificial man' without having any soul and body. This point of view is the basic feature of dual aspect concept of book-keeping.[15A] Here, in the above example, the proprietorship indicates the owner's interest in the asset (cash) of the business. And the ownership right in the assets and properties of the business is known as equities[16]. So it can be expressed as :

Dual Aspect of Accounting

Equities = Assets

It is a fact that the proprietor is not the only financier of business capital and it may be financed by anyone other than the proprietor, i.e. creditors. In this situation the sources of finance for the start and for the acquisition of business come from the proprietor and the creditors. Now the moot point is whether the creditors are to be included in the group of equity.

Equities

Do you follow?

☐ "Yes, Sir. Go on speaking Sir. It's really very interesting".

● Here I can refer you to the work of Black and Champion where they suggest that the sources from which a business derives its assets are referred to as equities.[17]

So two types of Equities are there :

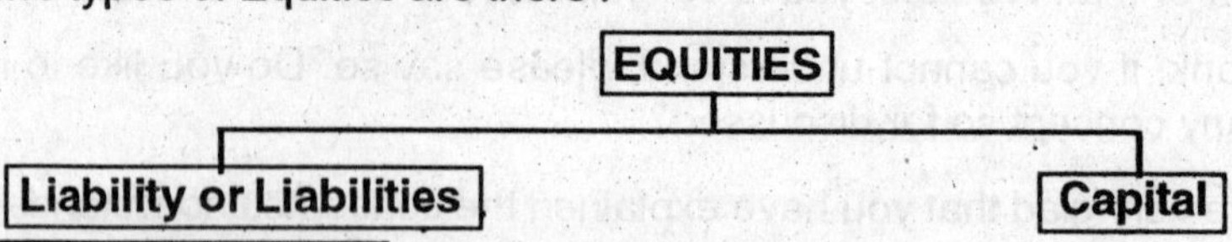

[14] *Anthony—**Management Accounting Principles**, Pp. 17-18.*

[15] ***The Economics of Accountancy**, P. 58.*

[15A] *Rorem and Kerrigan op. cit, P. 19.*

[16] *Pyle, **Fundamentals of Accounting Principles** (1955), P. 3.*

[17] *Black and Champion, **Accounting in Business Decision** (1961), P. 25.*

To revise again, liability and capital may be equal to the total assets of the business. But confusion may arise as to proper identification of the shortfall of the figures appearing on the equity or liability side of Balance Sheet. Again, the question may arise whether the figure for shortfall in the liability side of Balance Sheet represents equity or not.

The situation will be clear if the following examples are dealt with :

A business is started with capital Rs. 13,000, contributed by the proprietor Rs. 10,000 and creditors Rs. 3,000. Plant and Machinery for Rs. 5,000, Land and Building for Rs. 4,000, Furniture and Fixture for Rs. 2,000 and Materials for Rs. 2,000 were purchased with the said Rs. 13,000, contributed by two equities—the owner and outsiders or creditors.

The Balance Sheet position on the same day when production and business starts is :

Balance Sheet

Liabilities	Amount	Assets	Amount
	Rs.		Rs.
Owner's Equity	10,000	Land & Building	4,000
Outsiders' Equity	3,000	Plant & Machinery	5,000
		Furniture & Fittings	2,000
		Stock	2,000
	13,000		13,000

After one year's operation the business earns tangible cash profit Rs. 2,000 which will be added in the list of right hand members of the equity. It has been stated earlier that the sources from which a business derives its assets are referred to as equities[18]. Now the point is : What is the source of this asset (cash)? The owner of the 'profit' is the proprietor (and/or shareholders). So the shortfall in the liability side resulting from the increase in the asset side is compensated by 'insertion' of the figure for profit which may be shown under the 'caption' *Reserve* and *Surplus*. That's why perhaps a specialist [18A] is found to use the word 'proprietorship' as one of the items of equity.

No. 1 **Balance Sheet**

Liabilities	Amount	Assets	Amount
	Rs.		Rs.
Owner's Equity	10,000	Land & Building	4,000
Outsiders' Equity	3,000	Plant & Machinery	5,000
		Furniture & Fittings	2,000
	?	Stock	2,000
		Cash	2,000
	15,000		15,000

[18] *Ibid*, P. 25.

[18A] *Anthony*, ***Management Accounting Principles***, 1965, P. 22.

No. 2 **Balance Sheet**

Liabilities	Amount	Assets	Amount
	Rs.		Rs.
Owner's Equity	10,000	Land & Building	4,000
Outsiders' Equity	3,000	Plant & Machinery	5,000
Profit or Reserve &		Furniture & Fittings	2,000
Surplus	2,000	Stock	2,000
		Cash	2,000
	15,000		15,000

Well, if you look at the No. 1 Balance Sheet you may realise the cause for the source of assets. Here, the increase in asset without increase in the outsiders' equity must represent increase of proprietorship or Net Worth of the business.

Dr. Canning described proprietorship as "assets less liabilities"[19]. The proprietorship includes proprietor's capital and profit or surplus of the business. So, Profit or Reserve and Surplus is one of the items of equity which is generally included in Proprietary Fund. So, the proprietary fund may be termed as 'Net Worth'.

EQUITIES

Proprietary Capital or Proprietor's Fund or Net Worth	**Creditors or Outsider or Loan Capital**

So, the whole thing can be described under three accounting equations :

$E = A$	(i)	E = Equities
$P + L = A$	(ii)	A = Assets
$A - L = P$	(iii)	P = Proprietor's Equity
		L = Liability or Outsiders' Equity.

It should be noted in this context that assets and liabilities are the two independent variables, and the owner's equity is the dependent variable; since it is derived from the valuation given to the assets and liabilities.[20]

I think, you can understand my lecture.

☐ "Yes Sir".

● Is there any question?

☐ Would you kindly, Sir, enlighten us on the various situations which are likely to affect the three variables of accounting equations—Assets, Liabilities and Proprietorship?

---

[19] ***Economics of Accountancy**, P. 11.*

[20] *Yorston and others, **Advanced Accountancy**, P. 18.*

Mechanism for Increase in Equity

Well, shown below are the situations which will help you to understand the effects resulting from the change of an item of variables :

Situations	Results
i. Increase in asset without corresponding increase in liability or outsiders' equity.	i. Increase in owner's equity or proprietorship.
ii Increase in assets without corresponding increase in proprietor's equity.	ii. Increase in liability or outsiders' equity
iii. Increase in any assets without corresponding increase in owner's and outsiders' equity, i.e. liability and proprietorship.	iii. Decrease in the amount of other assets.
iv. Increase in any liability.	iv. Decrease in the amount of other liability.
v. Increase in outsiders' equity.	v. Decrease in owner's equity.
vi. Decrease in asset without corresponding decrease in net worth or owner's equity.	vi. Decrease in outsiders' equity or liability.

Accrual Concept of Accounting

6. **The Accrual Concept :** Sometimes the accrual concept is described as 'Matching Concept'. You see, it has been stated in Dual Aspect Concept that if assets increase, corresponding increase in the equities is inevitable. That is to say, the source of finance for the increase in cash position, as explained in dual aspect, is Profit. So, in that example, increase in the owner's equity resulting from the operation of business is called 'profit', not 'revenue'. Similarly, any decrease in the owner's equity is called 'losses', not 'expenses'.

Professor Anthony in his book explained that 'any increase in owner's equity resulting from operation of the business is called revenue. Any decrease is called expenses."[21] It is a fact that revenue and expenses are the basis of computing income or gain. All these incomes or gains are subject to adjustment[22] and alteration depending on the business situation. Revenue and income are not the final operational result. And the mere concept 'Revenue' and 'Expenses' should not be the basis of evaluating 'increase' or 'decrease' in owner's equities. So Income and Expenditure is an integral part of the 'Accrual Concept'.

Now let me discuss the different concepts which are prerequisites to the idea of matching process of Income and Expenditure.

Income : Income is prerequisite to the concept of net profit of the business. It is the money equivalent earned during the year from different revenue sources and its net figure thus enhances proprietor's equity as well as assets of the business. Thus, from accounting point of view, it may be defined that "income is generally conceived to be a residuum which emerges out of matching expired cost against revenue".[23]

21 ***Management Accounting Principles**, P. 40.*

22 *"Revenue is a gross concept, whereas income is a net or resultant amount. If revenues exceed expenses, the business earns income, the dollar amount thereof being shown in the income statement usually as "net income". If expenses exceed revenues, a loss results." Finney and Miller—**Principles of Accounting**—Introductory, Pp. 246-247.*

23 *Backer, **Handbook of Modern Accounting Theory**, P. 209.*

☐ "Sir, what is 'expired cost'?

● Wait please. I will satisfy you not only by explaining this particular concept but also different terminologies of cost.

Revenue : It represents the different sources of Income—both operating and non-operating. Examples of these sources are :

(i) Sale of goods or services; (ii) Interest from Investment; and (iii) Receipt of dividend from shares.

Net Income/Net Profit : Net Profit is the main source for strengthening the integrity of business capital. It results from the efficient business operation and can be found out by differentiating the Income/Revenue from Expenditure. That is to say, as already explained in the last chapter, it is the excess of revenue over expenses. This results in an increase in proprietary capital or proprietor's equity.

Net Income

Expense vs Expenditure : Generally, the terms 'expenditure' and 'expenses' are used by common people to denote the same thing. It results because of the fact that expenditure involves the 'cost' of capital outlay and expenses are the costs incurred in connection with the earning of revenue by the use of capital outlay in assets and materials, or it may be stated that expenses are the cost which are applied against revenue or income. So it is clear that expenditure and 'expenses' are needed for the realisation of the basic business philosophy—maximisation of profit. The expenditure incurred by the business becomes 'expense' with the passage of time. Take for an example, heavy expenditures incurred for advertisement purpose become 'expense' with the loss of its value. Thus, in the long run, after the loss of value of expenditure, expenditure becomes expense. So this leads to determine or find out what part of the cost has been expired during a particular year. So the expired cost is termed as expense. It is a fact that 'cost' expires through consumption process. How expenditure becomes expense through the consumption process may very well be illustrated by the idea of purchase of petrol. If I purchase petrol for my 'Ambassador' car for Rs. 200 and do not move here and there is no expense. The purchase is expenditure. If I consume the petrol by its use in the car to the extent of, say, Rs. 100, then it (Rs. 100) becomes expense.

Controversy of Expenses and Expenditure

I do hope that you have understood the discussions made earlier. Is there any question?

☐ "Sir, discussions made earlier are really very fine. But Sir, give us a comprehensive definition of the concept of expense".

● Well, here I like to give you a comprehensive definition of expenses as expressed by the American Accounting Association Committee in their work "Accounting and Reporting Standards for Corporate Financial Statements". So, according to the Committee, 'expense is the expired cost, directly or indirectly related to a given fiscal period, of the flow of goods or services into the market and of related operations. Recognition of cost expiration is based either on a complete or partial decline in the usefulness of assets, or on the appearance of a liability without a corresponding increase in assets'.

You see, as expense plays a vital role in matching with revenues, so recognition of expense should be given with caution. Irrelevant expenses, that is to say, expenses not related to a particular year, may distort the

Recognition of Expenses

real picture of the 'state of affairs' of the business; and thus be contrary to the 'doctrine of disclosure', one of the basic accounting doctrines. For that we can again rely on the observation made by the American Accounting Association as to the recognition of expenses. According to the Committee[24], expense is given recognition in the period in which there is

a. a direct identification or association with the revenue of the period, as in the case of merchandise delivered to customers;

b. an indirect association with the revenue of the period, as in the case of office salaries or rent; or

c. a measurable expiration of asset cost even though not associated with the production of revenue for the current period, as in the case of losses from flood or fire.

However, we have already considered under 'Conservatism' concept of accounting doctrine that accountants should follow the path that profit should neither be overstated or understated. Improper matching cost with revenue may result in overstatement or understatement of profit. So the overstatement or understatement of profit, arising from the matching process, can very well be removed if the following two rules are followed strictly :

Rules of Matching

1. 'If revenue is deferred because it is regarded as not yet earned, all elements of revenue and expense related to such deferred revenue must be deferred also, in order to achieve a proper matching and a proper determination of income for the period.

2. In case a 'future' expense is associated with current revenue, provisions for such future outlays should be made by charges to expense in the period when the related revenue is earned'.[25]

☐ "Sir, what is Capital Expenditure and what is Revenue Expenditure?"

● You see, the expenditure which is incurred for the acquisition of assets and other future advantage—that will benefit both current and future accounting period—is called Capital Expenditure. On the other hand, the portion of that expenditure which does not possess any expected service in future, and whose allocated services has already been realized for earning revenue—and which is subject to matching against revenue for the current accounting period—is called Revenue Expenditure.

Capital Expenditure and Revenue Expenditure

Now I hope you have understood the concept of Capital Expenditure and Revenue Expenditure. However, now I would like to explain the matching process problem arising from such expenses or costs which are dependent on the choice of the accountant. Depreciation is a difficult problem because the economic life of the assets on which the depreciation is calculated and which, in turn, determines the periodic amount to be charged is a matter of opinion and conjecture all along the line. So it is clear that different methods of stock valuation and methods of charging depreciation may bring many confusions in the mind of the people—saying that owing to the defective process of matching the reported profit fluctuates. You see, it is not due to the process, but due to the 'choice methods' of

[24] *Accounting Review, October 1957, P. 341.*

[25] *Finney and Miller, op. cit., P. 247.*

generating information for the process. So it may be said that the figures for stock valuation and depreciation should be subject to observation and scrutiny. Take for an example the adoption of conservative 'cost or market' basis or methods of stock valuation—this results in understatement of profit in one period and inflation of profit in the succeeding period. For that it should be assumed that matching process or accrual process is defective.

Now I would like to take up for discussion the different methods of stock valuation on which matching of cost of goods sold (cost of sales) with revenue is dependent. So :

Cost of Goods Sold = (*Opening Stock* + *Purchase*) – *Closing Stock*.

We can face three reported figures for cost of sales, better to say Cost of Goods Sold (C.G.S.) arising from different methods of stock valuation :

(i) *C.G.S.* = (Opening Stock + Purchase) – Closing Stock @ FIFO

(ii) *C.G.S.* = (Opening Stock + Purchase) – Closing Stock @ LIFO

(iii) *C.G.S.* = (Opening Stock + Purchase) – Closing Stock @ Cost or Market Price, whichever is lower

Different Methods of Stock Valuation

So from the above discussion it is clear that of the different methods of stock valuation the most important are LIFO (Last in first out), FIFO (First in first out), Cost or Market Price, whichever is lower.

Let me discuss these concepts step by step.

First-in-First-out

First in first out method (FIFO) : This method is sometimes termed original cost method. This method, as a basis of stock valuation, uses the most recent price paid for the stock (goods). It results in inflated profit, owing to inflated value of stock, during the rise in price level, and reported profit understated during the period of deflation or fall in prices. Or, in other words, this method assumes that items first purchased or received are the first to be issued and 'that requisitions are priced at the cost at which these items were placed in stock.'

Do you follow this concept?

☐ "No, Sir. Please explain it to us in a simple way."

• You see, I have already explained the concept in a very simple way. However, I will make you clear on this point again. You see, this method assumes that items taken out of the books are those which were purchased or bought first.

Well, is it clear now?

☐ "Yes, Sir."

☐ "Sir, please explain this with the help of a suitable illustration".

• Well, take down the following information :-

Illustration :

Material Purchased					**Material Issued**		
January	1	10	Units	@ Re. 1	January	4	15 Units
"	3	20	"	@ Rs. 1.50	January	8	22 Units
"	7	10	"	@ Rs. 2.00			

From the above information you will have to find out the inventory valuation under *FIFO method*:

Date	Receipt		Issued			Inventories		
	Qty	Rate	Qty	Rate	Amount	Qty	Rate	Amount
		Rs.		Rs.	Rs.		Rs.	Rs.
1.1	10	1.00	–	–	–	10	1.00	10.00
3.1	20	1.50	–	–	–	10 20	1.00 1.50	40.00
4.1	–	–	10 5	1.00 1.50	17.50	15	1.50	22.50
7.1	10	2.00	–	–	–	15 10	1.50 2.00	42.50
8.1	–	–	15 7	1.50 2.00	36.50	3	2.00	6.00

Last in first out method (LIFO) : This method is often called replacement cost method. In this method the unit sold is taken to be the one which was purchased most recently. That is to say, that item bought is the first to be used, 'the balance on hand being priced at the cost of earliest purchase.' However, this method will show least profit during the period of inflation and will show more profit during the period of deflation or fall in prices.

Now I would like to explain this method. Please note below *FIFO method*:

Date	Receipt		Issued			Inventories		
	Qty	Rate	Qty	Rate	Amount	Qty	Rate	Amount
		Rs.		Rs.	Rs.		Rs.	Rs.
Jan 1	10	1.00	–	–	–	10	1.00	10.00
" 3	20	1.50	–	–	–	10 20	1.00 1.50	40.00
" 4	–	–	15	1.50	22.50	10 5	1.00 1.50	17.50
" 7	10	2.00	–	–		10 5 10	1.00 1.50 2.00	37.50
" 8	–	–	10 5 7	2.00 1.50 1.00	34.50	3	1.00	3.00

Cost or Market Price

Cost or Market Price, whichever is lower: This method of valuation is more applicable to inventory valuation rather than valuation of issues or pricing issues. The basis on which stocks are valued definitely comes under the 'conservative' idea of accounting doctrine. Because, 'unrealised profit are not taken up in the accounts while probable losses that are still unrealised received recognition.[26] That is to say, this method is based on the 'time honoured' accounting maxim that 'provide for expected losses but do not take into account unrealised profits'. This method assumes that out of the two figures for price rates—cost price and market price—selection should be made as to one which shows least favourable financial position.

This can be explained by an illustration :

Types of stock	Cost Price (CP)	Market Price (MP)	Figures for Valuation (FV) Lower of Cost or Market Price
	Rs.	Rs.	Rs.
X	200.00	150.00	150.00 (MP)
Y	300.00	400.00	300.00 (CP)
Z	500.00	400.00	400.00 (MP)
	1000.00	950.00	850.00

You see, if you consult the above illustration you will find out how under this method the profit is underestimated. This observation can be made by comparing the CP with FV as well as MP with FV :

CP – FV

Rs. 1,000 – Rs. 850 = Rs. 150 .... (i)

MP – FV

Rs. 950 – Rs. 850 = Rs. 100 .... (ii)

So the profit of the business is underestimated in both the cases. Even if the stock had been valued at MP rather than actual cost price the profit would have been underestimated to the extent of Rs. 50.

I do hope that you have understood all the discussions made earlier. Well, before explaining the meaning and different methods of depreciation charges, I would like to make one point clear to you—the causes of depreciation is dependent on :

a. The nature of the asset concerned.

b. The use to which it is put.

This will be clear if we consider two examples—the machinery decreases its value through use and leased property for a fixed term of year loses or diminishes its value with the passage of time.

Now I would like to discuss the different methods of charging depreciation. Because 'depreciation plays a key role in matching depreciation costs or expenses with revenue'.

---

[26] *Ronem and Kerrigan, op. cit., P. 365.*

Well, it is a fact that capital assets like plant and machinery are needed for the smooth operation of business.

Depending Factors for Replacement

And, after a year's service or use, it becomes worn out and needs replacement. The replacement of machine is dependent on two factors :

(i) When its service-rendering capacity has been exhausted, or it may be that it becomes physically unusable.

(ii) When it becomes economically unusable. That is to say, the existing machines need to be replaced by modern or uptodate machine(s) to meet business competition by lowering the production cost.

So when the question of replacement or purchase of machine arises, there arises a further question for the present new replaced machine. Since, with the passage of time and with the amount of rendering its services, it will become old.

Old is replaced by new; further new is replaced by new—these processes should be given proper attention since each year a fixed or otherwise charge for depreciation is to be made in the income statement. That is to say, depreciation expenses are to be added to the list of expenses appearing on the debit side of Profit & Loss Account or Income and Expenditure Statement. And these depreciation expenses should be treated like other types of expenses such as Rent, Wages, Salaries, Interest. All these expenses are balanced either by cash or by accounts payable. But depreciation expense or expenses is or are balanced by an entry in the asset account. As depreciation expenses involve no cash transaction, it may be called a book expense—this is very important for matching process. It should be noted in this context that depreciation represents an expense for carrying on business and this depreciation expense is not dependent on profit being earned. Definitely the summation of estimated book expense for machine constitutes Depreciation Reserve Fund which is the source of finance for further replacement of machine.

So in order to visualise that financial statement should present a 'true and fair' view of the state of affairs of the business, moreover, to follow accounting doctrines—Disclosure and Consistency—some adjustments should be made both in Profit & Loss Account and Balance Sheet. For example, depreciation should be listed to debit side of P/L A/c and

True and Fair

the same should be deducted from the original figure or balance of figure which appear in the assets side of balance sheet. But, in actual practice, problems arise as to the amount to be charged as depreciation. This is because of difficulty in estimating the life of machine. Because, an asset is sometimes found to be 'alive' even when it has been declared 'dead' by the expert in the line. So let us see the different important methods of charging depreciation.

☐ "Sir, what is the definition of depreciation?"

You see, the concept of depreciation is an important consideration both to accountants and engineers. As stated earlier, with the passage of time, wear and tear is a 'must' for the Plant and Machinery and other tangible fixed assets. Before defining 'depreciation' I would

Depreciation

like to make clear two concepts (1) Depletion; and (2) Obsolescence. Depletion arises from the exhaustion of a few wasting assets; for example, Oil-well, a Tract of timber, as well as mines. Obsolescence arises from (i) the loss of asset's value as a consequence of 'being outdated' (ii) discovery of new machinery; and (iii) change of fashions. So the above three causes should not be considered as a cause for depreciation. But an expert in the line is found to use the word 'obsolescence' in the definition of depreciation : "Depreciation is the measure of the exhaustion of the effective life of a fixed asset owing to use or obsolescence during a given period".[27]

Mr. Montgomery[28] defined depreciation as 'allocation of the entire cost of depreciable assets to the operating expense of a series of fiscal periods'. However, the way in which depreciation is to be allocated is well-defined by the Third International Congress on Accounting. It refers to depreciation as the process of 'spreading the value of a fixed asset over the accounting periods comprising its service life'. So it is clear that depreciation involves matching cost with revenue.

Definition of Depreciation

Well, let us see what are the causes of depreciation. This will help us to understand the different methods of charging depreciation.

Causes for Depreciation : Causes for Depreciation of assets can be considered from two approaches :

(1) Accountant's Approach; and (2) Engineer's approach.

However, we shall concentrate here on the Accountant's approach point of view.

(a) *Accountant's Approach :*

i. Ordinary or extraordinary wear and tear from operation.

ii. Obsolescence – both normal and extraordinary.

iii. Inadequacy.

iv. Physical deterioration resulting from time and the elements.

v. Negligence.

vi. Diminution in the supply of raw material.

vii. Structural defects.

viii. Supersession.

Well, regarding different methods of depreciation, I would like to discuss only those which are in common use.

Before that, please note that the calculation of depreciation is dependent on the consideration of the following three factors :

Depreciation Calculation Consideration

i. The cost of the assets, say Plant and Machinery.

ii. The expected life of the machine or assets or, in other words, its useful life.

iii. The residual value.

All these factors are responsible for the variation in the calculation of depreciation charges; since these factors are dependent on the matter of choice and estimation of the individual concerned.

---

[27] *Spicer and Pegler's **Book-keeping and Accounts,** 15th ed, Pp. 47-48.*

[28] ***Auditing Theory and Practice.***

Different methods of charging depreciation :

Different methods of Depreciation

A. *Straight Line Method.*

B. *Diminishing Balance Method.*

C. *Composite Rate Method.*

D. *Sinking Fund Method.*

E. *Sum of the Year's Digits Method.*

A. Straight-Line Method : This is the most simple method and perhaps most widely used method of charging depreciation. It is based on the proposition that if the service life of a machine is estimated at N years, its value should be withdrawn by $\frac{1}{N}$ each year.

That is to say, the total depreciable amount is to be spread-out in equal amounts over the estimated life of the machine. This can be expressed as a percentage of cost :

$$d = \frac{C-S}{N}$$

C = Cost of machine or asset

S = Scrap value

N = Number of years the machine is expected to render service

$$r = \frac{d}{c}$$

d = Amount of annual depreciation

r = Rate of annual depreciation

Example : Asset Cost Rs. 1,500; Salvage value Rs. 300; Life 12 years.

$$d = \frac{\text{Rs. } 1{,}500 - \text{Rs. } 300}{12} = \text{Rs. } 100$$

$$r = \frac{100}{1{,}500} \times 100 = 6\frac{2}{3}\%$$

B. Diminishing-Balance Method : This method is called Declining Balance Method and, sometimes, Matheson Method. Under this method heavy depreciation is charged in the earlier period when maintenance cost is lower. This is because this method is based on the supposition that the assets wear out faster towards the latter period, whereas its economic life diminishes more rapidly in the earlier period.

$$r = 1 - \sqrt[n]{\frac{S}{C}}$$

r = Constant rate or rate of annual depreciation.

n = Number of years the machine is expected to render its service.

S = Scrap value.

C = Cost of assets.

The depreciated book value by this method will be, as such, for different years :

1st year $= C(1-r)$

2nd year $= C(1-r) - C(1-r)r = C(1-r)^2$

n-th year $= C(1-r)^n$

Example : Cost of Assets Rs. 100; service life 25 years, Scarp value Re. 1.

$$r = 1 - \sqrt[25]{\frac{1}{100}}$$

$= .168236$ or 16.82%

The depreciation for first year is Rs. 16.82%. The net book value is (100 – 16.82) = Rs. 83.18. The depreciation for the second year is Rs. 13.99 (i.e. 16.82% of Rs. 83.18) and the net book value on that particular period is Rs. 69.19.

Please note that the formula would result meaningless if scrap value is considered as 'Nil'. So, to make the formula fruitful, some figure for scrap should be assumed.

C. Composite Rate Method: This method is based on the average life of a plant. 'The composite life system contemplates depreciation as a unit, a number of mixed assets assembled to perform a particular service, but with each such unit having a different life expectancy'.

Please note, Finney and Miller in their book 'Intermediate Accounting' expressed the mechanism of Composite Rate Method of valuation. According to them the method 'permits a single rate to be applied to the total investment in all depreciable assets of varying useful lives. The average life of all depreciating assets is determined by grouping them into what may be called life classes' :

1. $$r = \frac{\frac{(C-S)_1}{N_1} + \frac{(C-S)_2}{N_2} + \frac{(C-S)_3}{N_3} + \dots\dots\dots + \frac{(C-S)_n}{N_n}}{\Sigma C}$$

2. $d = \Sigma C_x \times r$

r = Composite rate of depreciation

C = Cost of asset

S = Salvage value

ΣC = Sum of the cost

ΣC_x = Sum of the asset costs at the end of particular accounting period

d = Depreciation for a particular year

N_1, N_2, N_3, N_n = Estimated life of assets

Examples :

At the end of fiscal year, a composite rate of depreciation was computed for the following items from the following information :

Items	Cost Rs.	Salvage Rs.	Estimated life years
T	300	50	5
C	600	100	10
A	400	40	9
D	1,500	0	15
Total :	2,800		

(1) What is the composite rate of depreciation at the end of the fiscal year

(2) If the total assets in the group amounted to Rs. 3,500; what amount should be charged to depreciation expense for that year?

1. $$r = \frac{\frac{(300 - 50)}{5} + \frac{(600 - 100)}{10} + \frac{(400 - 40)}{9} + \frac{(1{,}500 - 0)}{15}}{2{,}800}$$

$$r = \frac{240}{2{,}800}$$

$$r = 0.0857$$

$$= 8.57\%$$

2. $$d = \Sigma C_x \times r$$

$$= 3{,}500 \times .0857 = \text{Rs. } 299.95$$

D. The Sinking-Fund Method : This system suggests that a fixed sum of money should be set aside from surplus and put into Compound Interest. Then the total sum of money so set aside and invested in compound interest process, together with interest, will represent the amount which is equal either to cost or cost less salvage. In this method 'Depreciation may increase in constant amounts or in constant percentages. When a constant rate of increase is applied, the annual allowance for depreciation increases at a compound interest rate for successive periods until the end of the estimated life of the asset. The amount of annual credits to the Allowance for Depreciation account are such that the total credit will equal the depreciable value at the end of the service life'.[29]

Did you follow my lecture?

☐ "No Sir, I could not follow. Please present it with the help of a simple illustration".

● What portion of the above method you could not follow?

☐ "Sir, I cannot understand the *abc* of the fund method".

● Do you follow the 'dual aspect' of accounting which was discussed earlier?

☐ "Yes Sir".

● Then, I hope, you will be able to understand the following points :

---

[29] *Rorem & Kerrigan, P. 392.*

1. Every debit should have its corresponding credit; so in this method, annual Depreciation charges* should be Debited to Profit and Loss Account and Credited to Depreciation Sinking Fund. Ordinarily we debit Profit and Loss A/c and credit Depreciation A/c.

2. Depreciation Sinking Fund represents liquid cash which can be invested in gilt-edged securities or it may be invested in Bank's Cash Certificate which offers the payment of Rs. 20,000; say, in the year 2006, if Rs. 4,000 is invested this year by way of purchase of cash 'certificate'. In case of investment in other securities the interest received from such investment may further be invested along with next instalment.

3. Under this method the assets remain at the original cost figure in the balance sheet.

Following are the five accounting entries which can be passed in connection with Depreciation Sinking Fund :

Situation	Debit Item	Credit Item
On setting aside annual Instalment	Profit & Loss A/c	Depreciation Sinking Fund A/c
On investing in outside investment	Depreciation Sinking Fund Investment	Cash A/c
On receipt of interest from Investment	Cash A/c	Depreciation Sinking Fund A/c
On reinvestment of interest	Depreciation Sinking Fund A/c	Cash A/c
On expiry of the life of machine	Depreciation Sinking Fund A/c	Machine A/c
On the purchase of new asset	(1) Bank A/c (2) New Machine A/c	(1) Depreciation Sinking Fund Investment A/c (2) Bank A/c

E. Sum of the Years Digits Method : This method is often termed as Cole Method. In 1954 this method of charging depreciation was first used[30]. It expresses depreciation rate as fraction. 'The numerator is the remaining useful life of the property at the beginning of the tax year, the denominator is the sum of the years of the useful life at acquisition'. The main characteristics of this methods is that it helps to write-off investment more quickly than the other method described earlier. This method ensures the business against the possible losses arising from obsolescence.

This method can be illustrated in the following way. Thus for an asset, say, a Truck, costing Rs. 18000 (Rs. 3000 residual salvage value) with estimated useful life for 5 years, the denominator of the fraction for each year would be 15 (1 + 2 + 3 + 4 + 5) years. The allowable depreciation for the first year is 5/15 of cost, for second year 4/15 of the cost of Truck or machine, and so on.

---

* *It should be ascertained from Interest Table.*

[30] *Walter and Raymand.* ***The Economics of Industrial Management****, P. 260.*

Year	Cost of Asset	Sum of digit	Allocating factors	Depreciation
1	15,000	1	5/15 of 15,000	= Rs. 5,000
2	15,000	3	4/15 of 15,000	= 4,000
3	15,000	6	3/15 of 15,000	= 3,000
4	15,000	10	2/15 of 15,000	= 2,000
5	15,000	15	1/15 of 15,000	= 1,000

You see, the Sum of Years Digits Method of depreciation can be calculated with the help of following formula :

$$D_p = \frac{L-N}{\sum L} \times (C-S)$$

D_p = Depreciation for particular year

L = Estimated life of asset

N = Number of years prior to depreciation (N = 1 – p)

$\sum L$ = Sum of digit (cumulative life)

C = Cost of asset

S = Salvage value

Example : Cost of Machine Rs. 1,00,000; Estimated useful life 20 yrs. Expected salvage value Rs. 10,000. Find out the amount of depreciation for the 14th year.

$$D_p = \frac{L-N}{\sum L} \times (C-S)$$

$$D_{14} = \frac{20-13}{210} \times (1,00,000 - 10,000)$$

$$D_{14} = \frac{7}{210} \times 90,000$$

$$D_{14} = \text{Rs. } 3,000$$

I think you have understood all the discussions made earlier. Before concluding this chapter I shall be happy to hear from you any concept which you want to clarify.

☐ "Excuse me Sir. Sir how the figure 210 is arrived at?"

- You see $\sum L = 210$. So $\sum L$ stants for $\frac{N(N+1)}{2}$. That means.

$$D_P = \frac{L - N}{\frac{N(N+1)}{2}} \times (C - S)$$

Is it clear to You?

☐ "Thank you Sir."

☐ "Sir, please give us some idea about the concept of Cost and the definition of different types of Cost".

• It is really a sad omission. I should have discussed it earlier. However, you know, in general, the concept of cost. It means 'sacrifice' or 'release' value. The very word 'cost' is a flexible concept. This flexibility arises out of the purposes to which the concept is used. Long ago Clark, in his work "Studies in the Economics of Overhead Costs", expressed : 'We may start with the general proposition that the terminology of costs is a state of much confusion and that it is impossible to solve this confusion by discovering and adopting the one correct usage, because there is no one correct usage, being governed by the varying needs of varying business situations and problems'.

It is a fact that the differences of opinion regarding cost do not arise from the fundamental concept of cost but it stems 'from failure to recognize that cost data prepared for one purpose may not be appropriate for other purposes'.[31] However, it is suggested that the uses of cost data should be directed towards the following purposes :

a. **Periodic determination of profit and valuation of inventory :** For determining the periodic profit, historical costs are needed. Because if 'consistency' in presenting accounting information is to be maintained, moreover, for matching cost with income on consistency basis, the process of historical cost is needed.
b. **Budgetary Planning :** It is concerned with Cost, Volume and Profit Analysis for better and future business operation(s). For that, management is concerned with expected Actual Cost 'for each set of conditions'.
c. **Control of cost :** It is concerned with actual and standard cost. This process is concerned with comparison of actual cost with predetermined cost or standard cost.
d. **Pricing Policy :** Pricing policy determines the product price in such a way as to ensure management the maximisation of profit. For that management needs 'projected product cost' which should be based on the determination of normal capacity as well as conditional cost.
e. **Current application of business policy and Plan :** It should be noted that the application and executing business plan and policy in actual field requires the concept of 'environmental cost' which does not stick to a particular type of cost. It takes the help of different types of cost including system cost which varies from firm to firm, time to time, and place to place.

In a sense it 'requires almost any combination of those and other types of costs drawn from regular cost reports or assembled to meet the needs of the moment'. However, the common type of definition of cost concept was furnished by Devine in his work "Cost Accounting and Analysis" which runs as : "The core of meaning which is common to all types of cost may be summed up by the word sacrifice. It is not by chance that accountants speak of cost as effort exerted and that political leaders talk of having cannons instead of butter'.

Well, you have requested me to give you the definitions of different types of costs. For that I would like to refer your attention to the work of the National Association of Accountants Committee on "Cost Concepts and Standards".[32]

---

[31] ***N.A.A. Research Series**, No. 7.*

[32] ***Accounting Review**, Vol. 27.*

You see, following are the **different types of cost** as defined by the Committee :

i. *Historical Cost* : It is the cost which is measured by actual cash payment or their equivalent at the time of outlay.

ii. *Replacement Cost* : It is the cost in the present market.

iii. *Future Costs* : These costs are expected to be incurred at a later date.

iv. *Standard Costs* : These costs are scientifically predetermined costs.

v. *Estimated Costs* : These costs are predetermined costs.

vi. *Product Cost* : This cost is associated with units of output.

vii. *Period Cost* : It is that cost which is associated with the income of a time period.

viii. *Direct Costs* : These costs are those costs obviously traceable to a unit of output or a segment of operation of the business.

ix. *Prime Costs* : These costs include direct labour costs and direct material costs. And these costs are traceable to a unit of output.

x. *Indirect Costs* : These are those costs which are not obviously traceable to a unit of output or to a segment of business operations.

xi. *Fixed Costs* : These costs are that part of costs which do not change or varies with the change of production.

xii. *Variable Costs* : These are those costs which change with the change of output.

xiii. *Opportunity Costs* : It is the measurable advantage as a result of rejection of alternative uses of resources, whether of material, labour or other facilities.

xiv. *Imputed Costs* : These are those costs that do not involve at any time actual cash outlay and which do not, as a consequence, appear in the financial records; nevertheless, such costs involve a foregoing on the part of the person or persons whose costs are being calculated.

xv. *Controllable Costs* : These costs are those costs which are subject to direct control at some managerial supervision level.

xvi. *Non-Controllable Costs* : These costs are those costs which are not subject to control at some managerial authority level.

xvii. *Joint Costs* : These exist when from any one unit source, materials or process, there are produced units of goods or sources which have different unit value or values.

xviii. *Sunk Costs* : These are historical costs which are irrecoverable in a given situation.

xix. *Discretionary Costs* : These costs are often termed as 'escapable' or 'avoidable' costs which are not essential to the accomplishment of managerial objective.

xx. *Postponable Costs* :	These are those costs which may be shifted to the future with little or no effect on the efficiency of current operations.
xxi. *Out-of-Pocket Cost* :	These are the costs which give rise to cash expenditure in respect of a given management decision.
xxii. *Differential Cost* :	These are the costs which are concerned with change in specific element of cost on increase or decrease in total cost as necessitated from any variation in operation.

Now, I think, you have understood the discussions made earlier. So, in my next lecture I shall be discussing with you about the different aspects of cost accounting such as definition and concept of cost accounting, its underlying principles, control of material, labour; and overhead cost, operating costing, standard costing etc.—which are the basis of management accountancy.

☐ "Sir, are you going out? I have one question more"

● Why don't not you put the question in the class? Why on the way to have. What is your question?

☐ "I am sorry Sir, my question is what is *Locked-in cost*?"

● Well you see, it is one type of *forecast cost* which may be considered as locked in cost when management decision is taken to incur any expenditure on the basis of forecast.

☐ "Thank you, Sir".

● Same to you.

QUESTIONS

1. Explain briefly how Doctrine of Accounting Principles aid Management Accountants.
2. What is Accounting? Is Accounting a Social Science?
3. What is Equity? How it is dependent on business environment?
4. What are the different methods of charging depreciation? How Sum of the Years Digits Method helps Management in long term investment policy of the business?
5. What are the different methods of valuing stock? Which one is best suited to stop Capital Erosion resulting from Inflation of Profit?
6. Discuss how Financial Accounting is related to Management Accountancy.

[M.Com. (Cal.)]

PART III

COST ACCOUNTING

"The core of meaning which is common to all types of cost may be summed up by the word sacrifice. It is not by chance that accountants speak of cost as effort exerted and that political leaders talk of having cannons instead of butter."

5

STRUCTURE OF COST ACCOUNTING

☐"Good morning Sir".

• Very good morning.

In the last part of my lecture I explained to you about the Accounting Mechanism and Highlights of Basic Accounting Concepts. In that context it was felt that costs play important role in 'Matching Concept'. It is a fact that cost determination and its application is not only useful to accountants but it may be used as a device of management decision, industrial control and business strategy. Now I think it proper to give you a basic and constructive idea about the mechanism of cost accounting principle which, I think, will aid you to understand its applicability in Management Accounting. Please note the following very minutely.

☐ "Sir, what is Cost Accounting and what are its advantages?"

Definition of Cost Accounting

• Just now I am thinking about giving you the definition of cost accounting. Well, I will try to satisfy you. For that I need your cooperation. However, please note the following ideas and concepts.

Costing & Cost Accountancy

Cost Accounting may be defined as the art and science of computing and determining the cost of production. The Institute of Costs and Works Accountants of London defined Cost Accountancy as 'the application of costing and cost accounting principles, methods and techniques to the science, art and practice of cost control and the ascertainment of profitability. It includes the presentation of information derived there from for the purpose of managerial decision making'.

The Chartered Institute of Management Accountants (CIMA), England (new name of The Institute of Cost and Management Accountants) defines Cost Accounting as :

"That part of management accounting which establishes budgets and standard costs and actual cost of operations, processes, departments or products and the analysis of variances, profitability or social use of funds."

Thus, Cost Accounting may be defined as a method of identifying, measuring and reporting information relating to the cost of acquiring and consuming resources. It also includes control of Cost through Variance Analysis.

☐ "Sir, what is the difference between 'Cost Accountancy' and 'Costing'?"

• You see, Cost Accountancy is concerned with the application of costing or cost accounting principles whereas 'Costing' is a 'term' which denotes the 'technique' or 'process' of ascertaining cost. However, the terminology of the CIMA has recommended using the word Costing with a qualifying adjective such as Operating Costing, Marginal Costing, etc.

I think, you have followed the distinction.

☐ "Yes, Sir".

• Oh Yes, what was I discussing?

☐ "Sir, you were discussing the definition of Cost Accounting."

• Yes, yes, now I like to refer you to the ***Dictionary for Accounts*** where one may get a comprehensive definition which is appropriate in all circumstances. Here Mr. Kohler defined cost accounting as :

Comprehensive Definition of Cost Accounting

'That branch of accounting dealing with the classification, recording, allocation, summarisation, and reporting of current or prospective costs. Included in the field of cost accounting are the design and operation of cost systems and procedures; the determination of costs by departments, functions, responsibilities, activities, products, territories, periods, and other units of forecasted future costs and standard or desired costs, as well as historical costs; the comparison of costs of different periods, of actual with estimated or standard costs, and of alternative costs; the presentation and interpretation of cost data as an aid to management in controlling current and future operations.'

Now I would like to enlighten you about the cost object. I have just discussed that the use of the word Costing is meaningless unless used with a qualifying adjective. The word object means anything for which separate measurement of cost is desired. Thus, object may be product, process, service, department, activity etc. For example, 'cost of Rs. 15.00' communicates nothing, but the statement 'Cost of product P is Rs. 15.00' completes the meaning. Here product 'P' is cost object.

Cost objects can be classified into two groups :
i. Cost centre; and ii. Cost unit.

Cost centre is a location, item of equipment, or activity in respect of which cost may be ascertained—machine shop, regional office etc.

On the other hand, cost unit is a quantitative unit of a product or service in relation to which costs are ascertained—cost per kg, cost per litre, cost per km etc.

Do note in this connection that sometimes the use of single unit does not serve the purpose of accurate measurement of cost. In that case, composite units are used, kilo-watt, passenger-km etc. That is, two factors are considered simultaneously.

Well, before taking up the matter for discussion such as objects, usefulness or advantages, activities or functions, methods and techniques of Cost Accounting, I, would like to give some idea about its relationship with other fields of study viz, Financial Accounting, Management Accounting, Industrial Engineering and Operation Research.

Cost Accounting and Financial Accounting

Cost Accounting and Financial Accounting : It is a fact that in computing the net operating result, cost plays an important role. The stability and future operation of business depends on its proper determination and matching with income. For example, the cost of goods sold (opening stock + purchase – closing stock), varies from time to time depending on its various methods of cost valuation. As the technique of finding out profit is too much associated with the concept of 'cost', so it is found to express[1] the view that there exists little difference between the two. So it may be stated without any hesitation that cost accounting has been introduced as a supplement to financial accounting, or it may be stated that cost accounting is an 'extension' of financial accounting.

However, how Cost Accounting differs from Financial Accounting and how they are associated with each other — can be understood from the following remarks of experts :

'Financial Accounting is concerned chiefly with the requirements of creditors, owners, the government, prospective investors, and persons outside management'—Russell (***NAA Bulletin***, Vol. 29).

'The chief characteristic of cost accounting is that phase of general accounting which informs management of the unit cost of the goods manufactured and sold. General accounting classifies, records, presents and interprets in terms of money, transactions, and events that are of a financial character, thereby providing management with the facts and figures necessary for the preparation of the periodic financial statements—the balance sheet and the income statement.

Cost Accounting, on the other hand, classifies, records, presents, and interprets in a significant manner the cost of materials, labour, and expenses necessary to manufacture and sell each product. The year-end statements of general accounting, presenting the total cost figures, can thus be supported by the details of these costs that have been collected through cost accounting methods and procedures' —Matz-Curry-Frank (***Cost Accounting***).

I hope that you have understood the relationship between Cost Accounting and Financial Accounting. Now I like to discuss Cost Accounting's relationship with Management Accounting.

Cost Accounting and Management Accounting : Cost Accounting is an integral part of Management Accounting. Because, the basis of computation, standardisation and control of cost – all are identical to Management Accountancy. All these said concepts are also the subject matter of Cost Accounting. However, please note the following opinions which will help in the operating system of Management Accountancy :

Cost Accounting and Management Accounting

'Management Accounting for profit control includes income accounting, cost accounting, and budgetary planning and control. Of these processes, cost accounting is the keystone. Actual costs must be determined and compared with those planned to guide management towards their profit objectives... Costs must be determined not only in total but also by areas of management responsibility and by products' —Keller (***Management Accounting for Profit Control***).

'Management Accounting functions largely through operating reports based upon standard costs and budgets compared with actual expenditures, through internal auditing, and through special duties and reports pertaining to the probable effect of proposed plans and programs'. —(Crossman, ***Accounting Review***; Vol. 33).

---

[1] *Mr. Devine, in his book* ***Cost Accounting and Analysis****, opines from a broad point of view 'consider general or financial accounting to be cost accounting in the sense that the determination of income requires the assembling of costs and their assignment to operating periods'.*

Cost Accounting and Industrial Engineering : There is a close inter-relationship between Cost Accounting and Industrial Engineering Department. For the smooth running of the business a close tie between Cost Department and Engineering Department is essential.

The Cost Department feeds back to Engineering Department in the following ways :

i. By informing as to spoilage and other extra costs incurred due to either engineering errors or other than engineering errors, or both.

Coordination between Cost Accounting and Industrial Engineering

ii. By informing as to cost of quality product.

iii. By informing cost of analysed by-product, major types of expenditure as well as cost of engineering functions.

iv. By informing pros and cons of product design costs.

On the other hand, the Engineering Department feedbacks to Cost Department :

i. By generating different information, such as appropriate quality and quantity of materials and labours for a specific job in the process of estimating standard cost.

ii. By estimating the life of the machine which is the basis of different aspects of machine allocation cost.

Thus, it is clear that there is a close tie between cost accounting and industrial engineering.

Cost Accounting and Operation Research : It is a fact that cost analysis and information is an essential and effective part in the application of operation research.

☐ "Sir, what is Operation Research" ?

● Regarding the general concept of operation research I would like to draw your attention to the view of Kozmetsky and Kircher. In their work ***Electronic Computers and Management Control*** they pointed out that 'as corporations have grown in size, in variety of products, and in extent of market, the need for improved systems of planning and control, and data processing, has become increasingly evident. Executives have recognized this need. They have purchased or leased office machines, analysed procedures, and encouraged attempts to raise clerical efficiency. They have studied reporting systems. They have attempted to relate the gathering and processing of information to the decision needs of the organization. In both office and factory, and for certain types of engineering and other research as well, there also has been a development of certain new scientific methods of analysis. These methods use tools which are primarily mathematical in nature although not necessarily so. One of the names given to this development is "Operation Research."

Cost Accounting and Operation Research

However, one similarity between cost accounting and management accounting may be drawn if it is considered that both are directed towards management service—decision-making process. But the degree of service performance through operation research is greater than cost accounting. As we have seen earlier, cost accounting has been introduced as a supplement to financial accounting. Here we can say that operation research may be introduced as a supplement to cost accounting. However, it has been accepted by accountants[2] that 'the use of operation research has a number of implications for the

---

[2] *T.P. Abel.* ***Operations Research and the Accountant in Understanding Operation Research.***

accountant in the area of budgeting and providing information for operating control and decision-making. The technique in assembling-line production or in a process cost operation (such as the oil refinery) where many variables can be sorted out in a mathematical model and matched up to give a least cost or optimum production solution, can aid the accountant in budgeting. For example, the effects of a proposed change in one or more variables in the process on the budgeted total production costs for a subsequent period can be determined by entering the proposed changes in a prepared or predetermined mathematical formula programmed for computer solution and by rating the effect on the other variables or total end result'.

Now I would like to take up for discussion the following aspects of Cost Accounting. Please note them very minutely :

Objects of Cost Accounting :

The objects of Cost Accounting can be grouped under two heads :

Objects of Cost Accounting

(A) Primary objectives; and

(B) Secondary objectives.

(A) Primary Objectives :

Primary Objectives

i. To ascertain the cost of producing an article or job or service rendered.

ii. To ascertain the performance of an operation as well as services rendered.

iii. To control and regulate selling price and to see that cost of production of an article or articles are recovered in selling price.

iv. To prepare tender estimate and quotation and obviate the risks of losses when preparing or estimating prices for quotations.

v. To point out and to obviate wastes and leakages or loopholes in elements of cost.

vi. To ensure 'productivity' of an organisation.

vii. To help management to take many important strategic decisions, such as launch of new product, sales-mix, make or buy.

(B) Secondary Objectives :

Secondary Objectives

i. To generate reliable 'cost' information in order to help the management to have a comparison between worker's efficiency and machine as well as tracing leakages in labour and material, maintain control over Inventory etc.

ii. To aid management in arriving at management decision on project plan and period plan.

iii. To facilitate control of cost through comparison of actual costs with budget and standard and taking corrective action with regard to any unfavourable variance.

iv. To aid in exercising social control of business.

☐ "Sir, what do you mean by Project Plan and Period Plan?"

● You see, Period Plan includes Budgeting which estimates the future cost and revenues of a coordinated plan of an enterprise activity. Whereas, Project plan includes location of plant, resource replacement, expansion of volume etc.

However, the said objectives of cost accounting can be summed up as :

Broad objects of Cost Accounting

(a) To aid management in their determination of inventory valuation and profit and loss.

(b) To aid management in planning their future operation and policy formulation.

(c) To aid management in controlling operating efficiency and cost.

☐ "Sir, what is the usefulness of cost accounting"?

● You see, the usefulness of cost accounting is more or less similar to the objectives as cited earlier. However, please note the following usefulness :

Usefulness of Cost Accounting

i. Useful in assessing the periodic income of a firm or firms.

ii. Useful in planning future growth, operation, as well as profit, through Standard Costing, Direct Costing, Cost-Volume-Profit Analysis and Comparative Cost Analysis.

iii. Useful in controlling current and future cost of the firms or organisations.

Now, please note the functions or activities of Cost Accounting.

Cost Accounting is concerned with the following functions or activities :

Functions of Cost Accounting

i. **Cost Recording :** It involves cost recording, classification and distribution in appropriate ledger accounts.

ii. **Cost Finding :** It takes into account measuring or estimating, costing and pricing of individual product, department as well as elements of cost.

iii. **Cost Analysis :** It takes into account the relationship between cost and its determinant aspect as well as it involves the determination of why costs are out of line and who is responsible.

iv. **Cost Planning :** It means the procedure planning of cost system.

v. **Cost Comparison :** This involves the comparison of cost in the area of production or distribution as to alternative method, products or activities.

vi. **Cost Control :** This involves control of cost so as to determine whether current cost 'represents what is regarded as a satisfactory performance'.

vii. **Cost Reporting :** It involves communication of different cost data to concerning persons of the organisation.

We have seen earlier that no business or firm can survive unless at least recovery of total production cost is guaranteed. So, the long term stability of a business is dependent on how it has been able to earn adequate profit. In general, profit indicates excess of selling price over cost of production.

Selling Price – Cost of Production = Profit.

So profit is dependent on two aspects — (a) Selling Price; and
(b) Cost of Production.

Profit can be maximised by controlling and regulating the above two aspects. For example, if selling price is increased, profit may be increased; and if expenses relating to material, labour and overhead are minimised, profit may be increased. So it should be the function of Management Accountant to advise the top management relating to the above aspects. So, before taking up the discussions on Material, Labour Overhead and Cost Control, let us see what are the components of total cost of production :

ELEMENTS OF COST
- Prime Cost = Direct Materials + Direct Labour + Direct Expenses
- Overhead Expenses = Summation of Indirect Cost, Indirect Wages and Indirect Expenses.

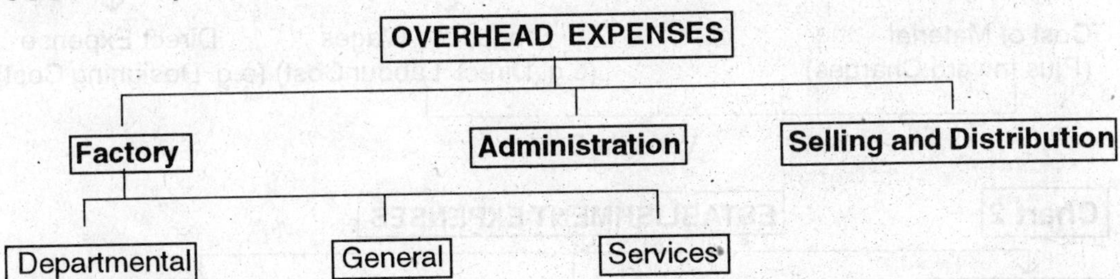

Works Cost or Factory Cost = Prime Cost + Factory Overhead expenses or Works on cost.

Production Cost = Prime Cost + Factory Overhead or Factory on cost + Administration Overhead, or Administrative or Office on Cost.

Total Cost = Production Cost + Selling and Distribution Expenses.

Selling Price = Margin of Profit + Total Cost or Cost to Sell.

Profit = Selling Price – Total Cost.

Well, the above discussions can be explained by means of two charts :

(1) Analysis of Manufacturer's Selling Price.

(2) Analysis showing how the established expenses of a firm are analysed into three main divisions and distribution of administrative expenses to the factory and selling divisions.

Chart 1

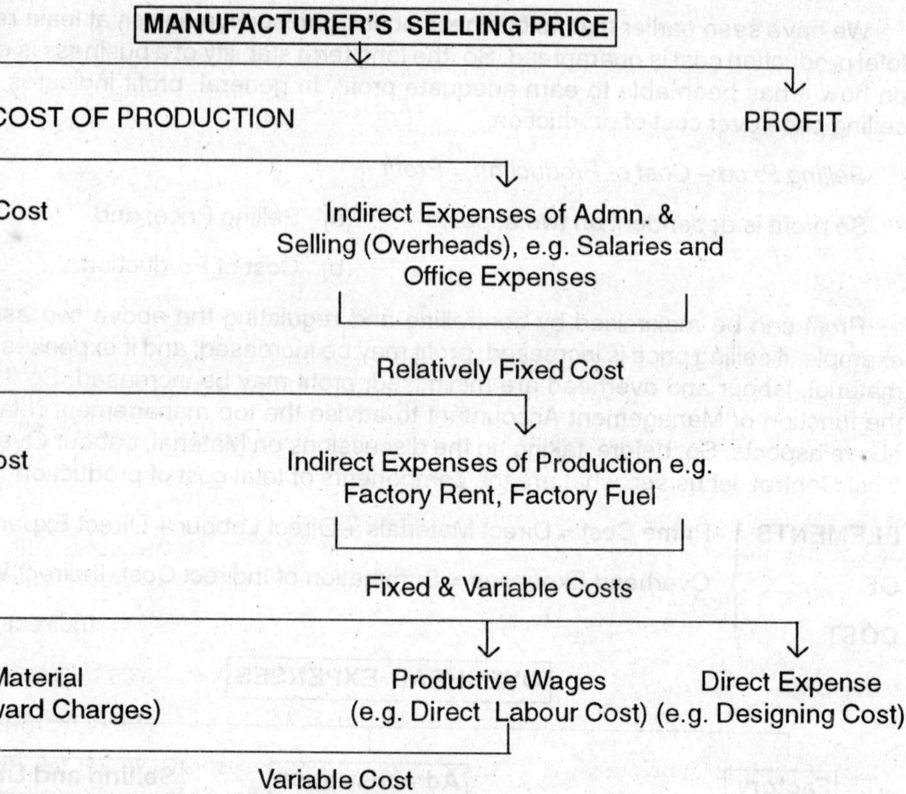

Chart 2

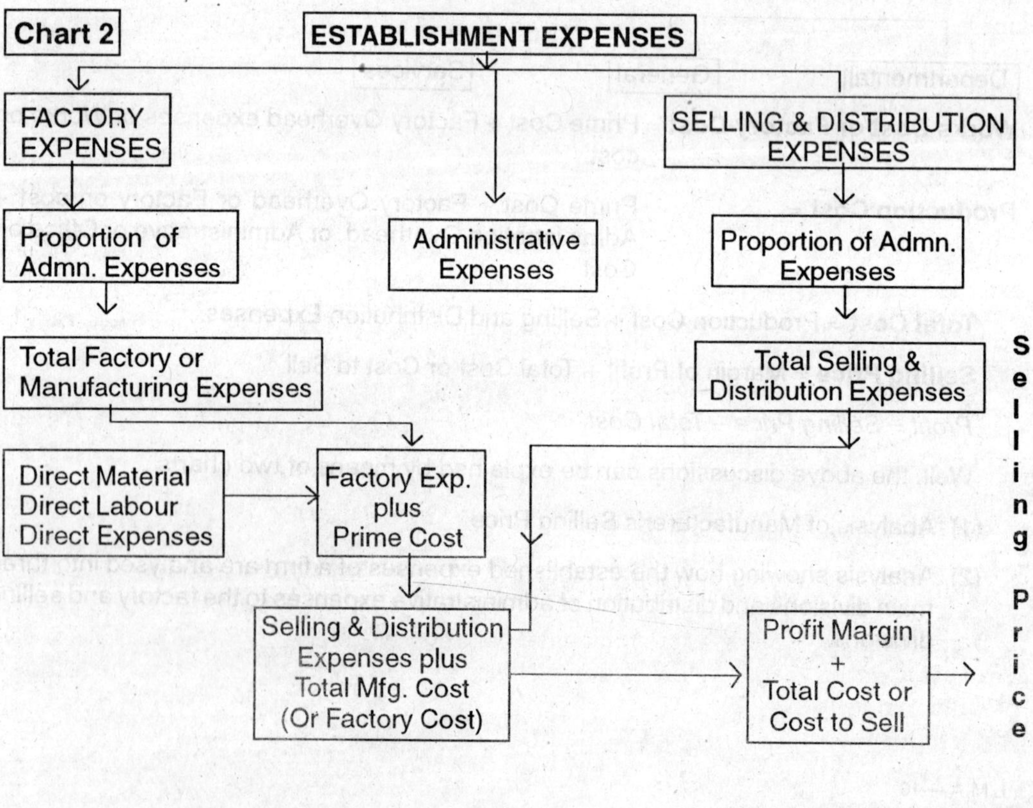

I hope that you have followed the above discussions. Is there any question?

□ "Sir, Please enlighten us in brief about the concept of Overhead."

• Well, you can put to me any other question which is not clear to you.

□ "Sir I could not follow the concept of 'Variable Cost'; and what are Semi-Fixed Costs and what are Semi-Variable costs?"

• You see I have explained the concept of 'Overhead Expense' and 'Variable Costs'. However, as you have requested I am explaining the same again :

Definition of Overhead Expenses : It incorporates all expenses other than direct expenses. It may be defined as the aggregate of indirect material, labour and expenses.

Classification of Overheads : Overheads can be classified under three heads :

(a) Fixed Overhead : It is an overhead which is unaffected by variations in the volume of output. For example, rent, insurance for factory building, salary to administrative staff, depreciation—these expenses are fixed. It should be noted in this connection that with the expansion of market and increased output no expense remains unchanged.

However, the impact of fixed overhead on unit cost would be :

Fixed Overhead

(i) If the production is low, the unit cost would be higher.

(ii) If the production is higher, the unit cost would be lower.

(b) Variable Overhead : It is that portion of total overhead which varies ('up' and 'down') proportionately with the volume of production. For example, consumable stores, loose tools, bolts, nuts, lubricant, fuel, power.

(c) Semi-variable Overhead : This is sometimes called Semi-fixed Overhead. it represents that portion of total overhead cost which is partly fixed and partly variable. So expenses 'that are neither constant nor vary in direct proportion to the volume of production are called semi-variable overhead'. For example, in case of maintenance of transport vehicles, certain expenses such as taxes, premium for vehicle insurance, garage rent, salary to conductors and drivers and depreciation—are fixed; whereas expenses of variable nature includes, lubricant, petrol etc. These expenses show 'up' and 'down' with use of transport vehicle.

Semi-variable Overhead

Now I would like to depict graphically the variable cost, fixed cost and semi-variable cost :

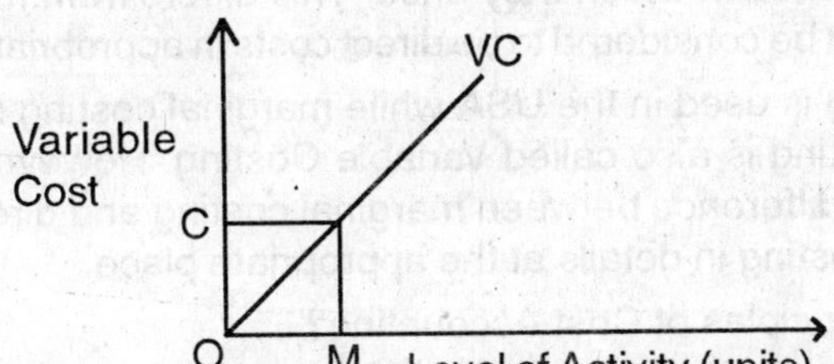

Here, Variable Cost varies proportionately with the level of activity. At 'O' level of activity, Variable Cost is also 'O'. But when activity level is 'M', Variable Cost increases proportionately to 'C' :

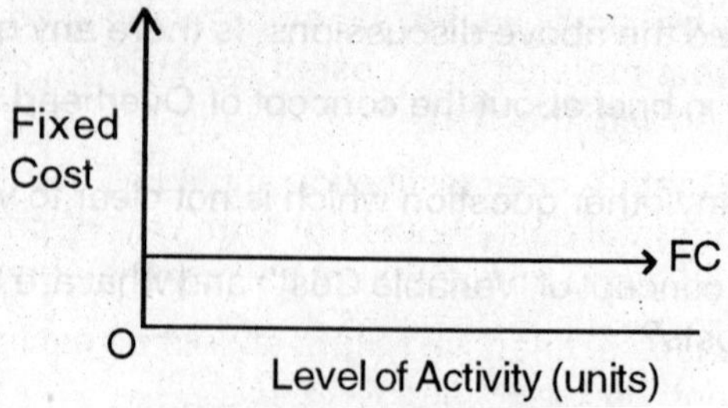

It is clear from the previous picture that fixed cost remains unaffected at different levels of activity.

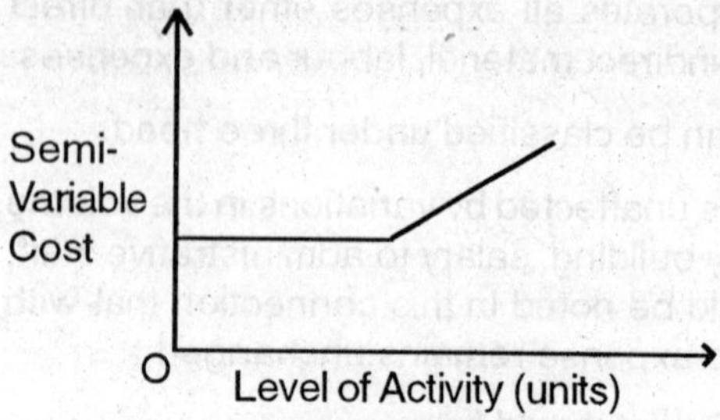

Picture A

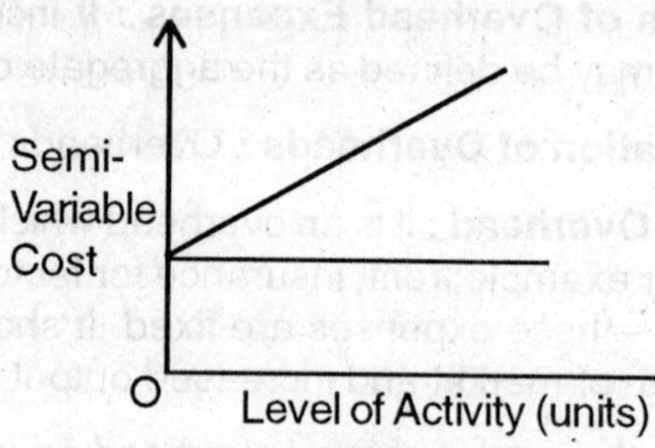

Picture B

Semi- variable cost either remains fixed up to a certain level of activity then varies with the Level of Activity (as in case of Picture 'A') or Partly remains fixed and partly begins to vary from 'O' level of activity (as in case of Picture 'B').

Well, regarding variable cost, I have told you earlier that variable cost is the cost which tends to vary proportionately with increase or decrease in production or output. Please note that in Direct Costing System, variable costs are sometimes referred to as Direct Cost. However, semi-variable cost or semi-fixed cost is referred to as cost which is partly fixed and partly variable.

I hope you have understood all these concepts.

☐ "Sir, what is Direct Costing? How does it differ from Marginal Costing?"

● Well, according to the 'Terminology of Cost Accountancy' issued by the Institute of Costs and Works Accountants of London, Direct Costing implies 'the practice of charging all direct costs to operations, processes or products, leaving all indirect costs to be written off against profits in the period in which they arise. This differs from marginal costing in that some fixed costs could be considered to be direct costs in appropriate circumstances'.

The term direct costing is used in the USA while marginal costing is used in the UK.

Direct Costing

Direct Costing is also called Variable Costing. However, there exists no significant difference between marginal costing and direct costing. I shall discuss about marginal costing in details at the appropriate place.

☐ "Sir, what are the principles of Cost Accounting?"

● Well, followings may be regarded as the basic principles of cost accounting :

(i) **Materiality :** A detailed analysis of an item of cost depends on whether it is material or not. In other words, analysis of cost must be backed by cost-benefit analysis and, of course, detailed analysis would be done only when the benefit is greater than the cost.

Otherwise, accuracy of cost may be sacrificed. For example, thread used for manufacturing a shirt may be treated as indirect material and costed accordingly for its small value, though it can be directly identified with the shirt.

(ii) **Normal and Abnormal Cost :** A clear distinction should be made between normal cost and abnormal cost. An abnormal cost should not form part of product cost so that product cost becomes comparable and management can control abnormal cost.

(iii) **Adjustment :** The expenses of financial nature should be excluded from product cost. For example, cash discount, bad debt, etc.

(iv) **Hypothesis :** Cost accounting also considers notional costs such as rent on own building, interest on own capital etc. for making correct decision.

Now I would like to point out about the different methods and techniques of cost accounting. This will help you to understand the anatomy of the cost accounting system :

Methods of Costing

i. Job Costing.
ii. Batch Costing.
iii. Contract Costing.
iv. Process Costing.
v. Operation Costing.
vi. Operating Costing.
vii. Multiple Costing.
viii. Activity-Based Costing.
ix. Farm Costing.

Techniques of Costing

i. Absorption Costing.
ii. Standard Costing.
iii. Budgetary Control.
iv. Marginal Costing.
v. Uniform Costing.
vi. Target Costing.
vii. Life Cycle Costing.

☐ "Please Sir, give us a bird's eye view of the Methods and Techniques of Costing."

• Well, please note the following :

Methods of Cost Accounting

Job Costing Concept

Under **JOB COSTING** method, cost object is taken as job. Job Costing is used to determine cost and profit & loss of each job separately. Job Costing is suitable for those industries which produce goods against order. Thus painters, printers, machine tool manufacturers, caterers etc. use job costing system.

In **BATCH COSTING** a batch of similar products is treated as a cost object. Here a batch order number is assigned for each batch and costs are accumulated according to

Batch Costing Concept

batch order number and divided by the number of units produced in that particular batch to arrive at unit cost. Batch costing is used by toy industries, bakeries, pharmaceutical industries etc.

Contract Costing Concept

The **CONTRACT COSTING** is used by constructional industries. Please note that here Cost object itself is contract. The construction work usually extends over a number of years. And the objective is to determine cost and profit or loss of each contract undertaken. It is also called **Terminal Costing**.

Process Costing Concept

PROCESS COSTING is used by those industries which convert raw materials into finished goods through continuous process. The object is to determine cost of each process and also cost of transfer. You see, Process Costing gives birth to Transfer Pricing. It is used by industries such as refineries, chemicals, flour mills, food processing, cement, mining, rubber etc.

You, please stand up. What is your problem? Why do you look blank? Any problem?

☐ "No, Sir. I feel enlightened from your lecture. It is really lucid".

- Now let me discuss in a nutshell the other concepts :

Operation Costing Concept

In **OPERATION COSTING** cost of each operation is individually distinctly costed and then cost of all operations are added to determine the total cost of finished product. Thus, here, each operation is taken as the *cost centre*. It is suitable in those industries which produce goods or services through a series of distinct operations.

Operating Costing Concept

OPERATING COSTING is used by those industries which render services instead of producing goods, such as, transport industries, hospitals, hotels, power houses etc. The total cost of rendering a service is divided by the units of service to find out the unit cost of service. In these industries, usually, composite units, such us passenger-miles/kms, per patient bed-day, kilowatt hour etc. are used.

Multiple Costing Concept

MULTIPLE COSTING is also called Composite Costing. The use of job costing and process costing simultaneously is called multiple costing. It is used in those industries which produce different components first and then assemble them to produce finished product. For example, industries producing television, radio, motor car, cycle, refrigerator, aeroplane etc.

Activity-Based Costing (ABC) Concept

ACTIVITY-BASED COSTING (ABC) is a system of overhead cost accounting under which activities performed to produce products or render services are first identified and the cost of these activities are then assigned to products or services on the basis of extent of activities consumed by these products or services. ABC is suitable in those industries which produce variety of products consuming different volume of activities and also where overhead costs are relatively high.

Farm Costing

FARM COSTING is used by agricultural farms. The agricultural farms are different from manufacturing industries. Therefore, distinct costing method should be used for agricultural farms. Farm Costing follows the Period Approach. The cost of a period is divided by the number of units of crop produced to obtain the cost per unit.

Now I would like to discuss about **Techniques of Cost Accounting.**

We know that one of the main objectives of cost accounting is to control Cost. Techniques of cost accounting are used for achieving this objective.

The followings are the different techniques of cost accounting:

Absorption Costing Concept

In **ABSORPTION COSTING** costs are ascertained after they have been incurred. Here both fixed costs and variable costs are considered as product cost. Predetermined rates are usually used for absorbing overhead cost which may result in over or under absorption of overhead. It is also called traditional or historical costing. Since costs are ascertained after they have been incurred, it has little use so far as cost control is concerned.

Marginal Costing Concept

In **MARGINAL COSTING** costs are divided into fixed and variable. Only variable costs are considered as product cost and charged to cost unit. Fixed costs, on the other hand, are considered as period cost and recovered from the contribution of that period. Marginal costing has valuable contribution in many important policy decisions such as product pricing, sales-mix, make or buy etc.

Standard Costing Concept

STANDARD COSTING refers to a technique which specifies level of excellence in respect of each element of cost. This is called standard cost. These standards are then compared with actual costs so that appropriate control can be exercised, in case there is any unfavourable variance. It aids to cost control.

A **Budget** can be defined as a financial or quantitative interpretation, prior to a defined period of time, of a policy to be pursued for that period to attain a given objective.

Budgetary Control Concept

BUDGETARY CONTROL can be defined as the establishment of Departmental Budgets relating the responsibilities of executives to the requirement of a policy and the continuous comparison of actual with budgeted results—"either to secure by individual action on the objective of that policy, or to provide a basis for its revision".

Uniform Costing Concept

UNIFORM COSTING refers to an arrangement under which several undertakings use the same costing system (i.e. the same basic costing methods, principles and techniques). Thus, uniform costing facilitates inter-firm comparisons so that real performance of firms can be judged.

Target Costing Concept

TARGET COSTING is a recently developed technique of calculating the cost at which a proposed product with specified quality and functional characteristics must be produced in order to generate target operating income while selling the product or service at the anticipated selling price which customers are willing to pay. It is reverse approach to determining cost of production. In this approach target price is determined first which the customers are willing to pay 'perceiving its want-satisfying ability'. Target operating profit is then deducted from the target price in order to determine target cost at which the product or service must be produced. Thus, here target price and target profit are independent variables and the target cost is dependent variable. That is

Target Cost = Target Price – Target Profit

In order to determine target price, a company needs information on—What do customers want? What prices are they willing to pay for it? What are the prices charged by competitors for the same type of products?

Companies generally adopt Value Engineering to achieve target cost—"Value Engineering is the systematic evaluation of all aspects of the value chain business functions with the objective of reducing cost while satisfying customer needs".[3] It results in improvement in product designs, changes in material specifications, modifications in process methods etc. Value engineering identifies non-value added costs and try to reduce it to achieve target costs.

LIFE-CYCLE COSTING is an important technique of cost accounting. It is a basis of Strategic Cost Management. It considers estimated costs of a product or service over its economic life with the object of product or service costing and pricing. In other words, Life-cycle Costing not only considers production cost, but pre-production costs, also (e.g. research & development and design cost), and post-production costs (e.g. marketing distribution and customers sales service cost) over the entire economic life of a product. The pricing of a product or service-based on Life Cycle Costing ensures the recovery of costs to be incurred over the economic life of the product. It also facilitates the control of costs of each of the value-chain activities, i.e. from research & development to final customer service.

Life-Cycle Costing Concept

One thing I would like to clear you before hand that the study of cost accounting would be worthless if the interlocking of financial and cost accounting systems is not understood. So, for that, a general concept of reconciliation of financial and cost accounting systems is essential. So, I would like to discuss this aspect when needed.

Integrated Accounts

You see, of the different methods and techniques of costing I would like to discuss in the subsequent chapters only those topics which are needed in connection with the study of Management Accountancy.

Well, these topics include:

1. Material Cost Control.
2. Labour Cost Control.
3. Overhead Cost Control and Recovery of Overheads.
4. Cost Control Accounts.
5. Reconciliation and Integrated Accounts.
6. Operating Costing.
7. Standard Costing.
8. Activity-Based Costing.

□ "Sir, will you not discuss Marginal Costing"?

● Yes, I shall. It will be discussed in the part **'Decision Accounting'** under the heading 'Cost-Volume-Profit Analysis'.

Is there any question?

□ "No, Sir."

Now I would like to give a chart which is used for analysing and determining total cost of production. The chart is popularly known as Cost Sheet. The chart can be prepared by following either Absorption Costing or Marginal Costing.

[3] Horngren, Datar & Foster, ***Cost Accounting — A Managerial Emphasis***, 11th ed., Prentice-Hall of India Pvt. Ltd., 2003, P. 417.

Statement of Cost and Profit & Loss based on Absorption Costing

	Rs.	Rs.
Direct Material	***	
Add: Direct Labour	***	
Add: Direct Expenses	***	
Prime Cost		***
Add:		
Absorbed Factory Overheads	***	
Add: Opening W-I-P	***	
	***	
Less: Closing W-I-P	***	***
Factory Cost (Works Cost)		***
Add: Administration Overhead		***
Cost of Production		***
Add: Opening stock of finished goods		***
		***
Less: Closing stock of finished goods		***
Cost of Production of Goods Sold		***
Add: Selling and Distribution Overhead		***
Cost of Sales		***
Profit		***
Sales		***

Statement of Cost and Profit & Loss based on Marginal Costing

	Rs.	Rs.
Direct Material	***	
Direct Labour	***	
Direct Expenses	***	
Prime Cost		***
Add:		
Variable Overheads :		
Production or Factory	***	
Administration	***	
Selling & Distribution	***	***
[A] Marginal Cost		***
[B] Sales		***
Contribution [B – A]		***
Less: Fixed Overheads :		
Factory	***	
Administration	***	
Selling & Distribution	***	
		***
Profit		***

Problem

Following information are supplied to you

		Rs.
Direct Material Cost		20,000
Direct Wages		12,000
Direct Expenses		400
Factory Overheads :		
Variable	5,000	
Fixed	1,000	6,000
Administration Overheads :		
Variable	400	
Fixed	1,600	2,000
Selling and Distribution Overheads :		
Variable	2,400	
Fixed	1,200	3,600
Sales		50,000

You are required to compute :

(a) Prime Cost, Works Cost, Cost of Production, Total Cost and Profit, under Full Costing.

(b) Marginal Cost and Profit, under Marginal Costing.

Solution

Statement of Cost and Profit & Loss under Absorption Costing

	Rs.	Rs.
Direct Material Cost	20,000	
Direct Wages	12,000	
Direct Expenses	400	
Prime Cost		32,400
Add: Factory Overhead		6,000
Factory Cost (Works Cost)		38,400
Add: Administrative Overhead		2,000
Cost of Production		40,400
Add: Selling and Distribution Overhead		3,600
Cost of Sales		44,000
Profit		6,000
Sales		50,000

Statement of Cost and Profit & Loss under Marginal Costing

	Rs.	Rs.
Direct Material	20,000	
Direct Wages	12,000	
Direct Expenses	400	
Prime Cost		32,400
Variable Overheads :		
Factory	5,000	
Administration	400	
Selling & Distribution	2,400	
		7,800
Marginal Cost		40,200
Sales		50,000
Contribution or Gross Profit		9,800
Less : Fixed Overhead :		
Factory	1,000	
Administration	1,600	
Selling & Distribution	1,200	
		3,800
Profit		6,000

Problem

From the following particulars relating to the production and sales for the year ended 31st December 2006, prepare a Cost Statement showing (i) Prime Cost; (ii) Works Cost; (iii) Cost of Production; (iv) Cost of Sales; and (v) Profit per unit :

Stock as on 1.1.2006	Rs.	Rs.
(a) Raw Materials		25,000
(b) Work-in-Progress—		
At Prime Cost	30,000	
Add : Manufacturing Exp.	6,000	36,000
(c) Finished goods (at cost)		1,44,000
Raw materials purchased		2,00,000
Freight on raw materials transfer		10,000
Machine-Hour Rate		3
Machine-Hours worked : 48,000		
Chargeable Expenses		50,000

Factory Wages for direct labour		2,76,000
Administration Expenses		1,00,000
Selling Expenses		54,000
Distribution Expenses		36,000
Sale proceeds of Finished Goods (30,000 units)		9,00,000
Stock as on 31st December 2006 :		
(a) Raw Materials		45,000
(b) Work-in-Progress		
At Prime Cost	45,000	
Add: Mfg. Expenses	9,000	54,000
(c) Finished Goods at Cost (10,000 units)		
Finished Goods produced 32,000 units		

Apply LIFO principle in finished goods valuation. **[C.U. B.Com. (Hons.) Adapted]**

Solution

Statement of Cost

	Rs.	Rs.
Opening Stock of Raw Materials	25,000	
Add: Purchase of Raw Materials	2,00,000	
	2,25,000	
Less: Closing Stock of Raw Materials	45,000	
		1,80,000
Freight on Raw Materials		10,000
Factory Wages for Direct Labour		2,70,000
Chargeable Expenses		50,000
		5,10,000
Add: Opening Work-in-Progress		30,000
		5,40,000
Less: Closing Work-in-Progress		45,000
(i) Prime Cost		4,95,000
Add: Production Overhead [48,000 hrs × Rs. 3.00]		1,44,000
		6,39,000
Add: Opening Work-in-Progress at manufacturing cost		6,000
		6,45,000
Less: Closing Work-in-Progress at manufacturing cost		9,000
(ii) Factory Cost (Work Cost)		6,36,000

	Rs.	Rs.
Administration Expenses		1,00,000
(iii) Cost of Production		7,36,000
Add: Opening Stock of finished goods		1,44,000
		8,80,000
Less: Closing Stock of finished goods [Working No. 1]		1,90,000
		6,90,000
Add: Selling Expenses		54,000
Distribution Expenses		36,000
(iv) Cost of Sales		7,80,000
Profit		1,20,000
Sales		9,00,000

$$\text{(v) Profit per unit} = \frac{\text{Total Profit}}{\text{Sales units}} = \frac{\text{Rs. }1{,}20{,}000}{30{,}000} = \text{Rs. } 4$$

Working No. 1

Finished Goods produced 32,000 units

Cost of Production = Rs. 7,36,000

$$\therefore \text{ Cost of Production per unit} = \frac{\text{Rs. }7{,}36{,}000}{32{,}000} = \text{Rs. } 23.00$$

Since LIFO principle is used for valuing closing stock, 2,000 units out of 32,000 units of production remain in stock.

Therefore, total value of closing stock (for 10,000 units) would be —

Value of 8,000 units = Rs.1,44,000

Value of 2,000 units = Rs. 46,000

$$\left[\frac{\text{Rs. }7{,}36{,}000}{32{,}000} \times 2{,}000\right] \qquad \text{Rs. }1{,}90{,}000$$

☐ "Thank you sir, for your valuable lecture".

☐ "Sir, what would be discussed in your next lecture"?

• I have already given the plan, cited above, according to which my lecture will follow. Say one chapter for Material Cost Control, and other for Labour Cost Control, and so on. Do you follow?

☐ "Thank you, Sir."

QUESTIONS

1. What is Cost Accounting? What are the segments of Cost Accounting?
2. How does Cost Accounting aid Management Accounting?
3. Compare and contrast Cost Accounting with other branches of study—Financial Accounting, Industrial Engineering, and Operation Research.
4. What are the objectives of Cost Accounting? Do you think that present objective of cost accounting is sufficient in the context of growing need of the society?
5. What are the functions of the Cost Accounting?
6. What are the methods of costing?
7. Do you think that techniques of cost accounting and methods of cost accounting are co-related?
8. Give a proforma of cost sheet based on absorption costing and marginal costing with imaginary figures.
9. What are the industries where marginal costing can be applied profitably?

6

MATERIAL COST CONTROL

- Good morning to you all.

□ "Good morning Sir."

- Well, what will be discussed. Well, I remember.

You see, to keep the process of production running efficiently and smoothly, control of material is needed. Because, materials are to be purchased and sold, of course, sold in the form of finished product. Thus goes the life of the business. Of the two processes—purchase and sale—a middle process is there which is known as Production Process.

Purchase → Production → Sale → Purchase → Production → Sale ...

Objects of Material Accounting

Thus we see that materials purchased feed the production process. Again, if material purchased is not of good quality, the finished product so produced will not be a marketable one. If the flow of any one of the above chains is disturbed or withheld, the basic philosophy of business—maximisation of profit, may be realised with struggle. For example, the flow of work of production department may be disturbed if the purchase department cannot feed either adequate material properly or adequate quality material in time, or both. For that, proper control of storing department is needed from where materials are sent to production department. Again, it is to be ensured that material is not stored unnecessarily in excess of requirement, because it blocks working capital unnecessarily. It is a fact that the policy of management is to purchase material from market at a 'suitable rate' and sale the same in the form of finished product at a 'suitable rate'. Thus you see, 'suitable rate' is the major decision-area which regulates the fate of the business — expansion or liquidation.

The maximisation of 'suitable rate' at the time of either purchase or sale entails the process of realisation of business philosophy — the maximisation of profit. Besides, this ensures the integrity of business and efficient production management. For that the need for Material Accounting is felt. So, the objects of Material Accounting as a part and parcel of material control are[1] :

1. To keep continuous records of goods on hand as to quantity and value of each kind of raw material.
2. To keep record of purchases and goods received at cost, as to quantity and kind of raw material.
3. To keep a record of goods issued at cost as to quantity and kind of raw material, and as to each job or process or department which receives goods from stores.

[1] Dohr. Ingram and Love, *'Cost Accounting'*

4. To correlate procurement of raw materials and production requirements by :
   a. Ensuring that proper goods will be on hand when required.
   b. Segregating goods received or reserved for specific units of production or processes or department.
   c. Showing goods available for further production.
   d. Showing actual goods on hand.
   e. Showing goods ordered but not received.
   f. Showing when additional goods should be purchased.
5. To improve purchases by indicating appropriateness of past purchases for required uses.
6. To prevent goods accumulating in excess of requirements because of cost thereof.
7. To locate goods in storeroom.
8. To assist in case of goods in storage and establish accountability for such goods on part of store-keeper.
9. To furnish basis for materials consumption in preparing statements.
10. To measure efficiency of material used through setting of standard.

Do you follow?

☐ "Yes, Sir, very interesting indeed! This simply excites my curiosity. Sir, would you kindly enlighten us about the need for control?"

Need for Material Control

• Well, just notice the following points which can be advanced in support of the need for material control :

i. To eliminate wastage in the use of materials.
ii. To eliminate or reduce the loss arising from fraud and pilferage.
iii. To ensure efficiency in the use of capital.
iv. To make easy the preparations of monthly, quarterly and yearly financial statements.
v. To furnish information promptly when needed, regarding the value of material used in different manufacturing departments.
vi. To strengthen the liquidity position of business.
vii. To prevent delay in production due to lack of proper quality and quantity supply of material in time.
viii. To locate the area of responsibility and thus to help in the introduction of 'Responsibility Accounting'.

Areas of Material Control

You see, so far we are concerned about the objects of Material Accounting as well as need for Material Cost Control. Now let us see how material cost control can be enforced. Well, material cost control involves the control of the following activities :

A. Purchasing
B. Storing and Inventory Control
C. Material Cost
D. Accounting for Material Losses.

Now I would like to discuss elaborately the above four functions involved in the process of material control.

A. PURCHASING

Functions of Purchasing Department

Functions of Purchasing Department

a. To receive or originate the purchase request.

b. To determine quantity of materials to be ordered.

c. To contact supplier— before placing purchase order in black and white—for suitable price and mode of delivery.

d. To place order for purchase with vendor.

e. To follow—up order.

f. To certify and verify the quality and quantity as well as acknowledge the receipt of ordered goods.

g. To check invoices received from vendor before payment.

Do you follow what I have discussed?

☐ "Yes Sir".

- Is there any question, please?

☐ "Sir, Does purchase of material means only purchase of direct material?"

- You see, only direct material is not enough to start production process. To mobilise the direct material the most important thing required is indirect material. Take for example, oil, grease and waste for machine which are indirect material items needed to convert raw material into finished goods. Let us see what are the meanings of direct materials and indirect materials. One point you note here that the requirement of 'direct' material is dependent upon the nature of industry and circumstances of the case. Particular material may be direct in particular industry and the same constitutes indirect material in another industry. This will be clear if we take a note of Professor Carl E. Allen's observation that in practice 'various industries are not uniform or consistent with respect to what constitutes direct material. In printing industry it consists of paper, ink, linkery materials, electors, engravings, artwork, outside machine composition, outside press work, outside ruling and binding, and miscellaneous purchases used on specific orders. In many industries a product is not finished until it has been packed or boxed. In such industries, the cost of wrapping and packing material—which becomes part of unit sold to ultimate customer—is properly treated as a direct material cost. Thus, in the hosiery industry such packing materials as ticket labels, bonds paper and boxes are classified as direct materials. In the electronics manufacturing industry the cost of cartons and pasteboard boxes in which products are packed for display purposes and for protection while in stock are treated as direct material costs'.

Direct and Indirect Material Depends on the Nature of Individual Case

So it is clear that by material purchase we should mean direct material and factory supplies or indirect material.

☐ "Sir, what do you mean by Supplies? Please give us some concept on the same".

● Well, by Supplies I mean materials which are not directly involved in production process. It may also mean material 'used for purpose other than production'.

SUPPLIES

- **Factory supplies** — **Examples**: Indirect material items such as oil, grease, cotton waste, brooms
- **Office supplies** — **Examples**: Paper, pencil, carbon paper, stencil, ink
- **Delivery, Packing and Shipping supplies** — **Examples**: Cartons, boxes, packing and crating material, tags, twine, wrapping paper, boxes

Now you may ask : How can control measure in purchasing material be made effective?

Control of Purchase Activities

For that I would like to bring to your attention the following forms and records which are used in controlling purchase activities :

i. Material and Purchase Budget.

ii. Purchase requisition.

iii. Material specification.

iv. Quotation price.

v. Purchase order.

vi. Material Receipt and Inspection.

vii. Control of payment voucher.

☐ "Sir, kindly discuss the above six points or procedures."

● You may get all these discussions from any standard book on costing. Please collect the same from that source.

☐ "Please, Sir".

● Well, take a note of the following :

i. Material and Purchase Budget : It was discussed at the outset of this chapter that there should be close integration between purchase on the one hand and sales

Factors in the Preparation of Purchase Budget

and production department on the other. Accordingly, there should be a Material or Purchase Budget which should be based on production and sales forecast of the organisation. However, in the preparation of budgets for purchase materials and inventories the following points or factors[2] are to be considered :

[2] Heckert and Wilson, ***Business Budgeting and Control***

a. Quantity or quantities of raw materials to be used.

b. Time when materials are to be required.

c. Material cost to be used.

d. Value and quantity or quantities of materials to be carried on in inventory.

e. Quantities of materials that are to be purchased and its cost.

f. Time when materials are to be purchased.

g. Value and quantity or quantities of work-in-progress and finished goods that are to be carried in inventory.

h. Control method to be employed in controlling material cost and inventory values and quantities.

Well, in the light of the above discussion, can you tell me what are the purposes of Material Budget?

☐ "Sir, I cannot answer. Please enlighten us on the concept".

• Well, the purposes of Material Budget are to provide data in the

a. determination of planning and budgeting of raw materials purchase.

b. preparation of budget for raw material cost of production.

c. determination of inventory quality and quantity standard for control of raw material inventory level.

d. determination of cash budget for the purchase of raw materials.

e. determination of the basis of material control.

Nature of Purchase Requisition

ii. Purchase Requisition : Purchase requisition may be defined as request made to purchasing department by concerned persons or departments— viz. store keeper, plant and maintenance engineer, Head of the Department and production control department— to purchase materials and supplies needed in production process and smooth running of the business. Thus purchasing department places orders for materials and supplies in accordance with the requisition received from such persons or department as mentioned earlier.

Did you follow what I discussed?

☐ "Yes Sir."

☐ "Sir, how many copies are required for such requisition?"

• I told you earlier that purchase requisitions may originate either from Store-keeper or any other persons other than Store-keeper, say, store supervisor or departmental manager. If it originates with Store-keeper at least two copies are required (1) one is to be retained by the Stores department, and (2) other to be sent to the purchase department. Again, if it originates with other than Store-keeper, purchase requisition should be made out in triplicate—(i) Original, and (ii) duplicate are to be sent to the Purchasing department and (iii) the triplicate—is to be retained by the originating department. 'When purchase order is issued, the vendor, order number, routing etc. are entered in the requisition and returned to the originating department as a notice that the purchase order has been placed. The original is retained in the purchasing department files and may be filed by the commodity or vendor. It is sometimes attached to a copy of purchase order.'

I think you have followed the discussions made earlier. Is there any question?

☐ "Sir, give us a specimen of Purchase Requisition."

● Well, note the following :

Taste and Bitter Co. Ltd.

PURCHASE REQUISITION Date ....

Please purchase for........Department No. ....

Item No.	Code No.	Description	Quantity Required	Purchase Order No.	Supplier	Remarks

Now I would like to discuss about the specification of material. In my earlier discussions I told you that to control the purchase planning, the importance of material specification is felt.

☐ "Sir, is there any distinction between specification of material and bill of material?"

● No, it is all the same. Material specification is synonymous with bill of material. However, let us see in detail what is specification of material.

iii. Material Specification : It is a complete schedule of materials which is required for a particular job or order and this material specification is prepared or formulated and issued by the Drawing Office together with 'necessary blueprints'. It would be noted that purchase requisition made by Plant and Maintenance Engineer or Production Control Department in some cases is based on the material specification, prepared by the Drawing Section. Thus, it serves various departments in different manners—purchase requisition to purchasing department; material or stores requisition to the store-keeper, works order to production department.

Well, the advantages of material requisition are manifold. Because it aids purchase department, stores department, production department and accounts department by way of minimising time and generating all needed information.

However, I am giving you a specimen or proforma of material specification. Look, here is your proforma of material specification :

Specification of Material

For Order No. BC269 E C Type. Assembly Drawing No. 93. Dt.

Part No.	Des-crip-tion	No. per set	Total No.	Material			Re-marks	For Purchase Department			
				Code No.	Descrip-tion	Quan-tity		Reqn. No.	Date	Delivery Specified	Order No.

Drawing Office Copy :	Dt. order Delivery : No. of Sheets :	Prepared by : Checked by :	Dated to Stores : Dated from Stores : Dated to Shops :

iv. Quotation Price : After the receipt of the purchase requisition, it becomes essential to determine what vendor the purchase order should be placed with. Selection of vendor or seller is an important task. Because quality, quantity, price and availability of product are the pertinent factors for the selection of vendor. Request for price quotation are to be sent to various vendors or sometimes advertisements are made inviting price quotation. Sometimes requests for price quotation are sent to vendor in duplicate, instructing the vendor to retain one copy and return the other duly filled in. Such reply forms may help the purchasing department by providing different information whether particular vendor would be able to supply quantity materials in time. So, in selecting vendor, price quotation should not be the basis of selection; other factors, as mentioned earlier, should be taken into consideration. However, the selection of vendor in some cases is dependent on the 'mood of the production' as well as the condition and status of the organisation.

Form and Purpose of Quotation Price

Schedule of Quotations

Material **Date......** **File No....**

Name of Parties	Rate Rs.	Amount	Delivery time	Terms	Delivery Free/ Not free	Remarks

Factors in connection with Purchase Order

Now I would like to discuss about the concept of Purchase Order and Receiving and Inspection Note. Well, let me first discuss purchase order.

v. Purchase Order : It is a fact that before placing order for a purchase, a suitable quotation should be accepted. And we have seen earlier that the following factors are to be scrutinised and reviewed before placing order to a particular vendor or a group of vendors :

a. Price

b. Condition(s) of delivery

c. Specification

d. Time of delivery

e. Different charges

f. Terms of payment and discount.

Well, after placing purchase order, it constitutes a contract between the purchaser and supplier or vendor.

Do you follow my lecture?

☐ "Yes Sir".

☐ Sir....

• Yes, What do you want to know. Please be frank.

☐ "Sir, how many copies of purchase order form are required? Please enlighten us"

• You see, it depends upon the nature and organisational set up of a business. However, a small firm generally requires three copies while a large firm requires five copies.

☐ "Sir, what are the routes of these five purchase order copies?"

Well, note the following routes :

i. To be sent to the supplier or vendor.
ii. To be retained in the purchasing department.
iii. To be sent to the originator of purchase requisition.
iv. To be sent to the Cost and Accounts Department.
v. To be sent to the Receiving Department.

Here is a specimen of Purchase Order form. Note it very minutely.

Purchase Order

From .... Date ....
To .... Ref. No. ......

Please supply the following items, in accordance with the instructions mentioned herein :

Descriptions	Rate	Quantity	Amount	Date of Delivery	Remarks

Delivery ....
Mark order No. .... For..... Co. Ltd.
Terms.......... (Signature)

Now I would like to discuss about the remaining part of the control measure of purchase — Receiving and Inspection. Before explaining the same please tell me whether the discussion made earlier is clear to you. Again, is there any question?

Follow-up

☐ "Sir, What is 'follow up'? Is it a related part of purchase procedure?"

• Yes, it is a related part. Follow-up is a procedure where the purchasing department takes the initiative of constant watch that the materials ordered for purchase are delivered in time by the supplier. The 'follow-up' procedure is :

i. To obtain confirmation from the vendor or suppliers.

ii. To keep watch over the arrangement made by the supplier to supply ordered material.

iii. To issue reminder as and when required.

Yes, I think, you want to say something, yes?

☐ "Sir, what is Economical Buying Quantity? Please give us some light about the concept".

● I am really very glad that you have taken much interest in the subject. Anyway, please note the following discussion on 'Economical Buying Quantity'.

Economical Buying Quantity

Economical Buying Quantity : It indicates the choice of quantity of material to order at a specified time. It is determined by balancing the acquisition cost against owning materiel cost. Many formulae have been developed in determining the purchase of most economical quantity. Now I like to present before you one[3] of such formulas which embraces all pertinent information of the concept 'Economical Buying Quantity' :

$$Q = \sqrt{\frac{2CS}{UI + A}}$$

Indications :

Q = Number of units for most economical order.

C = Cost of placing order.

S = Number of units consumed in one year.

U = Unit price of materials item.

I = Assumed annual interest rate.

A = Annual carrying cost per unit.

Illustration

Use of annual material = 1,000 units

Unit Cost = Rs. 5

Annual rate of interest = 5%

Annual carrying cost per unit = Rs. 0.30

Note : The last item assumes 12% annual carrying cost.

Per unit average investment = Rs 5.00 divided by 2 = Rs. 2.50

Annual carrying cost per unit = Rs. 2.50 x 12% = Rs. 0.30.

[3] Matz-Curry-Frank. *Cost Accounting*

Solution

Economical Buying Quantity (EBQ)

$$EBQ = \sqrt{\frac{2CS}{UI + A}}$$

$$= \sqrt{\frac{2 \times Rs.\ 8 \times 1{,}000}{Rs.\ 5 \times 5\% + 0.30}}$$

C = Rs. 8.00
S = 1,000 Units
U = Rs. 5.00
I = 5%
A = Rs. 0.30

$$= \sqrt{\frac{16{,}000}{0.55}}$$

= 171 Units (Approx)

□ "Sir, Please give us a derivation of the formula".

● All right, please jot down the following as to how EBQ is derived :

Economic Order Quantity

Let, A = Annual demand.

P = Cost of placing an order.

S = Cost of carrying one unit in stock for one year.

C = Total annual cost.

E = Order Size [or volume of order]

∴ E/2 = Average Inventory.

Mathematically, we represent the annual total cost in the following way :

$$\text{Total Cost (C)} = \text{Carrying Cost} \left(\frac{E}{2} \times S\right) + \text{Order Cost} \left(\frac{A}{E} \times P\right)$$

$$\text{Or, } C = \frac{E}{2} \times S + \frac{A}{E} \times P$$

$$\text{Or, } C = \frac{ES}{2} + \frac{AP}{E}$$

Differentiating the above equation with respect to E we get

$$\frac{dc}{dE} = \frac{S}{2} - \frac{AP}{E^2}$$

Since the target is to reduce cost to 'O', we can equate the above derivative with 'O'

$$\therefore \frac{S}{2} - \frac{AP}{E^2} = 0$$

where, E = order size.
A = Annual demand.
P = Ordering cost per order.
S = Cost of carrying one unit in stock for one year.

$$\text{Or, } \frac{SE^2 - 2AP}{2E^2} = 0$$

Or, $SE^2 - 2AP = 0$ Or, $SE^2 = 2AP$

Or, $E^2 = \frac{2AP}{S}$ Or, $E = \sqrt{\frac{2AP}{S}}$

I hope you have followed the above discussion.

□ "Yes Sir".

- Is there any question?

□ "Sir, give us some concept about the determination of purchase price which you have not discussed yet".

- I am really sorry for that.

However, please note that the determination of purchase price depends upon the agreement between the purchaser and suppliers.

While calculating the price of material the following points play important role:

i. Quality Discount.

ii. Cash Discount.

iii. Trade Discount.

iv. Transport and Storage Charges.

v. Containers.

Well, let me explain the above concepts. You see, Quality Discount implies an allowance made by the vendor or seller or supplier to the purchaser of material. This is to encourage a bulk order. The allowance of this discount is dependent on the order placed by the purchaser. So per unit price becomes lower if the quantity ordered is large.

Well, regarding trade and cash discount I am to say that trade discount is an allowance made by the suppliers to the wholesale traders or buyers who have to re-sell the article. This trade discount is always deducted from the invoice. The rate of discount varies from time to time and trade to trade. However, cash discount is an allowance made by the seller to the purchaser in consideration of prompt payment of accounts. Regarding storage and transport charge it should be noted that sometimes purchase price, as quoted by the vendor or supplier, includes the transporting cost to the purchaser and storage charges in connection with this should be included. In the absence of this the purchaser has to bear all these charges.

It should be noted in this context that the cost of the container may be charged or may not be charged in the purchase price. If it is not charged, the purchaser need not pass any accounting entry in his book. In case containers are charged separately, treatment should be made depending on situation of respective cases. For example, when container is non-returnable the cost of containers will be added to purchase and when the containers are returnable and are credited at full value on return, the cost of container would not be included in the price of material, and when the container are returnable and credited at reduced value on return the difference in value—the cost of the container minus the amount credited by the supplier—will be added to the purchase price of the materials.

Now I would like to discuss about Material Receipt and Inspection.

vi. Material Receipt and Inspection : After placing purchase order and necessary follow-up for the receipt of materials and supplies, the goods or materials are despatched to the material receipt and inspection department along with the delivery or advice note in duplicate. Sometime the supplier sends a copy of the purchase order along with the advice note. This is to ensure proper inspection and receipt of material ordered. However, after the proper inspection of the material, a copy of the advise note is being sent back to the supplier after proper receipt note is made on it. In some organisations, in the absence of Material Receipt and Inspection Department the task is solely entrusted to the Stores Department. After that the materials are binned and a bin number is given for internal reference on the goods or material received.

Purpose of Material Receipt and Inspection

Now I like to give you the proforma of Goods Received Note. Well, before that I would like to clear one point—four copies of the note are to be made and should be sent to the following departments besides a copy retained by the department:

i. Purchase Department.

ii. Accounts Department.

iii. The Department which initiated purchase requisition.

iv. Stores Department.

Goods Received Note

From : **G. R. No. ....**
Date.....................

Goods Descrp. Code	Qty.	Pack-ages	Order No.	Advice Note/ Invoice No.	Remarks	Inspection Rejected —Reason
Carrier	Received by	Bin No.	Stores Ledger	Account reference	Remarks	Initials

I hope you have followed the discussion made earlier.

Yes, I think you want to know something. What's your question?

□ "Sir, you have not yet told us about comprehensive functions of receiving and inspection department".

● Well, please note the functions of receiving and inspection department:

a. To sign on the material receipt note or receipt of material and supplies from the supplier.

b. To count and weight all in-coming raw materials and supplies.

c. To inspect the quality of material.

d. To send the material to stores department for proper custody and inventory control.

e. To inform the purchasing department as to the facts which require adjustment with vendor.

vii. Control of Payment Voucher : On receipt of the invoice by the purchasing department, the preparation of voucher begins.

Documents needed in connection with the preparation of voucher are :

Documents for Payment Voucher

a. Purchase Requisition.

b. Purchase Order.

c. Goods Received Note.

d. Inspection and Testing Report.

e. Debit Note.

I think you have some general knowledge of the above documents. Isn't it so?

☐ "Sir, you have not given us any concept about Debit Note".

● You see, I explained to you the concept of Debit Note and Credit Note in Chapter Three of this book. However, for your understanding, I am going to explain here the concept of Debit Note. Debit note is issued when entire or a part of the materials are returned to the supplier on the ground of below specification of material supplied. However, I am giving you a specimen of Debit Note:

DEBIT NOTE

No. ....

From

Date.................

Dear Sir

With reference of your Goods Received Note No................dated................your account has been debited with the value of materials for the reasons mentioned below :

Description	Specification	Price Rs.	Amount Rs.

Reasons :

Purchase Order No.	Goods Received Note No.	Debit Note No.	Invoice No.	Date of Receipt

I hope you have followed the above discussions. Is there any question please?

☐ "Sir we shall be obliged if you kindly give us a specimen of "Payment Voucher".

● Well, now I am giving you the proforma of Payment Voucher. Note minutely.

....Co.

Bhatpara

Stores Receipt

Receipt No. ....

Date..............

Order No. ....

Supplier ....

Code No. ....

Bill Verification				
Challan/R/R		Bill		Date Voucher passed for payment
No.	Date	No.	Date	

1	2	3	4	5	6	7	8	9	10	11	12
Descriptions of items	Item Code	Unit of Qty. Code	Sl. No.	Actual Qty. Recd.	Unit of Qty. inward	Qty. in term of Supplier Unit	Suppls. Unit of Qty. inward	Rate	Total cost item-wise as per Bill/Note	Additional Charges Rs.	Total (Column 10 + 11) Rs.

Prepared by	Checked by	Stores Officer	For Works Manager

Passed for Payment

.... Co. Ltd.

Now I herewith conclude my lecture on purchase control which is one of the parts of material cost control. Well, now I would like to discuss about the storing and inventory control, one of the control measures of material. However, you see......

□ "Sir, please work out at least a few problems on the discussions made earlier."

• Well, please note :

Illustration : After inviting tenders, two quotations are received :

(a) Rs. 1.20 per unit.

(b) Rs. 1.10 per unit plus Rs. 3,000 fixed charges to be added irrespective of units ordered.

Advise with your arguments on whom orders should be placed and what quantity is to be ordered.

The following additional information may be of interest :

Present stock	35,000 units
Average monthly requirement	10,000 units
Maximum level requirement	80,000 units
Minimum level	30,000 units

Sales Tax problem may be ignored. **[I.C.W.A. India]**

Solution : From the above it is clear that quotation (b) is preferable when large quantities of materials are purchased to justify fixed charges for Rs. 3,000.

But quotation (a) is preferable for lesser purchase. Here quotation (b) is cheaper than quotation (a) to the extent of Re. 0.10 (Rs.1.20 – Rs.1.10) per unit. Here, to justify fixed charge for Rs. 3,000, the quantity of minimum order should be 30,000 units.

□ "How is this possible sir?"

• This has been done by calculation in the following manner :

$$\frac{\text{Rs. } 3{,}000}{\text{Rs. } 0.10} = 30{,}000 \text{ units}$$

It is clear that a purchase order for above 30,000 units will be economic for those who are willing to accept quotation (b). From the information it is obvious that 5,000 units are consumed.

□ "How is it possible sir?"

• You see, the present stock level reaches its minimum stock level during the period when fresh supplies did not reach the store department. So, it is 5,000 units.

□ "Sir, what is the time to get fresh supplies?"

• You see, the average rate of consumption is 10,000 units per month. Hence, the time taken is 15 days:

$$\frac{5,000}{10,000} \times 30 \text{ days} = 15 \text{ days}$$

So the Economic Order Size = (80,000 units – 35,000 units) + 5,000 units = 50,000 units.

Please note, the above calculation has been made following the formula of Economic Order Size which is:

EOS = Maximum level – Ordering point + Rate of consumption during the time to get fresh supplies.

I hope you have followed.

☐ "Yes sir, please work out one more problem".

● **Illustration :** A lorry load of materials of mixed grade was purchased for Rs. 9,000. These were sorted into the following grades whose market rate is shown against each:

Grade	Units	Selling rate Per unit
Grade A	5,000	Rs. 1.20
Grade B	3,000	Rs. 1.00
Grade C	2,000	Rs. 0.50

Find the purchase rate per unit of each grade of the material assuming all grades yield the same rate of profit. **[I.C.W.A. India]**

Solution

Total sale value = Rs. 10,000*

Total purchase cost = Rs. 9,000

Therefore, Purchase Value = 9/10th of sales, i.e. $\frac{\text{Rs. } 9,000}{\text{Rs. } 10,000}$

Thus, the purchase rate of A, B, C is :

$$\text{Rs. } \frac{9}{10} \times 1.20 = \text{Rs. } \frac{10.8}{10} = \text{Rs. } 1.08$$

$$\text{Rs. } \frac{9}{10} \times 1.00 = \text{Rs. } \frac{9}{10} = \text{Rs. } 0.90$$

$$\text{Rs. } \frac{9}{10} \times 0.50 = \text{Rs. } \frac{4.5}{10} = \text{Rs. } 0.45$$

(*5,000 × 1.20 + 3,000 × 1.00 + 2,000 × 0.50

= Rs. 6,000 + Rs. 3,000 + Rs. 1,000 = Rs. 10,000.)

Illustration

A supplier quotes for material "X" as :

Lot price	100 Units	@	Rs. 5.00
	500 Units	@	Rs. 4.75
	1,000 Units	@	Rs. 4.50

T.D 20%, C.D. 5% in 7 days.

Containers charged at Rs. 10.00 each; Rs. 7.50 credited on return. 1 (one) container is required for every 100 units. The purchaser decides to purchase 600 units. Transport and Storing charges amounted to Rs. 67.50 and Rs. 12.50, respectively, which were charged by the supplier.

Solution **Calculation of Purchase Price**

		Amount Rs.	Cost per unit Rs.
Material 'X' 600 units @ Rs. 4.75		2850	4.75
Less T.D. at 20%		570	0.95
Returnable containers :		2,280	3.80
6 containers @ Rs. 10	60.00		
Less credited on Return	45.00	15	0.02
at Rs. 7.50		2,295	3.82
Transport :	67.50		
Storage	12.50	80	0.13
		2,375	3.95

Now I would like to discuss about Storing and Inventory Control as a basis of Material Cost Control.

B. INVENTORY CONTROL : This aspect of study, as one of the steps towards Material Cost Control, is very important in the sense that the store department not only keeps the material in its custody but also feedbacks entire production system in proper time. It has been sometimes held by a few authors that except the 'custody' function the stores department has no important role to play. I do not share the view. Because, the function of stores department is such that upon its proper handling and control, the existing or expected losses of the business can be avoided or minimised. The negligence of the stores department may result in the production process grinding to a standstill. So, one of the important tasks of the stores department is Inventory Control which means a system which ensures smooth running of production by providing quality and quantity material with minimum amount of capital.

Requirements in Connection with Inventory Control

Inventory Control is effective if the following aspects are properly dealt with :

1. Receipt of materials.
2. Issue of materials.
3. Return of materials to stores.
4. Transfer of materials from one job to another.
5. Keeping material records.
6. Control of stock level depending on the mode of production.
7. The perpetual inventory system.

Well, let me explain all these aspects step by step. Do you follow?

□ "Sir, how many categories of inventory can be classified?"

● Well, inventories can be classified into four different categories :

Classification of Inventory

i. Raw material.

ii. Work-in-progress.

iii. Finished goods.

iv. Engineering and Consumable stores.

You see, the above four categories of inventory can be grouped under two heads, depending on their urgency :

a. Consumption stocks.

b. Safety stocks.

Consumption and Safety Stock

Well, consumption stocks are those stocks which are required to meet consumption needs. Thus material requisition from the department concerned are made from consumption stock. Safety stock, on the other hand, ensures the production management in emergencies and uncertainties. For example, if, for any reason, despatch of materiel from supplier is delayed, say for a day or two, the production may be delayed. This may result in loss of marketability of product. So the essence of production management is to keep smooth running of production.

You see, the amount of safety stock is dependent on two crucial factors :

i. The demand for an item or group of items.

ii. Procurement lead time of an item or group of items.

□ "Sir, does the concept of 'reserve stock' bear any meaning on 'safety stock'?"

● Yes, the purpose is the same. Is there any question?

□ "Sir, what is 'lead time'?"

● You see, it is the average time between placing an order for material to the supplier and the receipt of the material.

Is there any question?

□ "Sir, how can safety stock be determined?"

● Well, we can here apply POISON's formula in determining the safety stock. It can be stated as:

$S = K\sqrt{D}$

S = Safety Stock, K = Standard Deviation of Demand.

D = Average Lead time of Demand.

Well, what was I discussing? Please remind me.

□ "Sir, you were discussing Receipt and Issue of Material."

• "Is it so?"

☐ "Yes Sir."

• Then let me first discuss about receipt of material.

1. Receipt of Material

We have seen earlier that the incoming materials—after proper examination and inspection—are sent to stores department. And thus, to keep accounting procedure uniform, Goods Received Note is passed, along with the incoming material, to the stores department. The store-keeper then places the material in actual Bin. A location code to each bin is given to ensure easy, quick and prompt despatch of material to department. A specimen of Bin Card is given for your understanding:

Nature of Material Receipt

BIN CARD

Description :
Material Code :
Location Code :
Store Ledger Folio :

Bin No. :
Code No. :
Maximum :
Minimum :
Ordering :
Danger :
Ordering Quantity :

Receipt			Issues			Bal.	Audit Notes	
Date	**G. R. No.**	**Qty.**	**Date**	**Material Req. No.**	**Qty.**	**Qty.**	**Date**	**Initial**

I think you have followed the Bin Card system.

☐ "Yes Sir."

• Well, now I want to give you some idea about the Cardex system which, in practical cases, is found to use to strengthen the efficient and smooth operation of stores department. In this cardex system, details about material requistion, material ordered, expected date of delivery of material, actual date of receipt of material and monthly consumption of material are given. However, please note the next.

Code No. :				Card No.
Description. :				
No.	VENDORS	No.		VENDORS
A		A		
B		B		
C		C		

REQUISITON			ORDERED				Effected delivery date	RECEIPTS				Monthly Consumption			
Date	No.	Qty.	Date	No.	On Supp.	Qty.		Dt.	Ref. No.	Qty.	Balance	Month	20....	20....	20....
												Jan.			
												Feb.			
												Mar.			
												Apr.			
												. . .			
												TOTAL			
												AVG			

2. Issue of Materials : It is the function of the store-keeper to issue materials to different departments on receipt of authorised documents from the department concerned. The documents, depending on which he issues materials, is known as Material Requisition. It should be noted in this context that Material Requisitions are generally made in triplicate. One copy is retained by the Stores Department for necessary entry in the Bin Card or Cardex, the other copy is sent to the Control Department, and the remaining one, after necessary entries in the stock, is to be sent to Cost Accounting Department for price fixation and this, in turn forms stock voucher for necessary accounting entry. However, I am showing you two proformas of Material Requisition and Cardex for your easy understanding :

Issue of Materials

MATERIAL REQUISITION

Material Required for... Department ... Date :
Job No. : No. :
Shop No. :

Qty.	Unit	Descriptions	Code No.	Weight	Rate	Amount (Rs.)	Notes/Remarks

Foreman/Chargeman or Supervisor	Store Ledger No.: Bin No. Store-keeper :	Cost Officer's Ref No. Priced by

CARDEX

Code No.: Card No.
Description :

IN-OUT AND BALANCE RECORD

Date	Ref No.	Recd.	Issued	Balance	Remarks	Date	Ref. No.	Recd	Issued	Balance	Remarks

3. Return of Materials to Stores : The question of return of material arises out of two basic points : (i) When materials were issued in excess of requirement; and (ii) When consumption of material is saved by efficient operation of production department.

The proforma of Material Return Note is given :

MATERIAL RETURN NOTE

Issuing Dept. : Job No. :					Date : No. :	
Qty.	Descri-ption	Code No.	Weight	Rate Rs.	Amount Rs.	Notes/Remarks
Authorised by : Received by :		Bin No. Store Ledger No.			Cost Office Ref. Priced by	

4. Transfer of Material from one Job to Another :

Material Transfer from one Job to other

Transfer of material from one job to another should not be encouraged or allowed unless the procedure or system is adequately recorded in Material Transfer Note. Such transfers are found to occur when some urgent orders have to be placed.

The proforma of Material Transfer Note is given:

MATERIAL TRANSFER NOTE

Issuing Dept. Receiving Dept : From Job No.				To Job No.	No. : Date :	
Qty.	Description	Code No.	Weight	Rate Rs.	Amount Rs.	Remarks
Authorised by :		Issued by : Received by :			Cost Office Ref. : Priced by :	

5. Material Records : Important material records includes :

(i) Bin Cards;

(ii) Stores Ledger.

(i) **Bin Card**

Bin Card

Well, I have already given you the basic idea of Bin Card. To repeat, Bin Card maintains the receipts, issues and balances of stock in a simplest form. Now let me discuss about Stores Ledger:

(ii) **Stores Ledger**

Stores Ledger

It usually appears in the form of card or loose leaf; and it maintains the record of different classes of materials. These are kept in the cost department. This stores ledger provides a great advantage for planning the future purchase(s) by providing pertinent information of actual stock position.

Stores Ledger is generally found in two forms—one for general purpose, and the other for actual control of inventory which contains the details about material ordered, material reserved, material received and issued and material in hand.

Two forms of Stores Ledger is given below for your observation.

☐ "Excuse me Sir. Please work out a few problems taking into account all the discussions made earlier."

● You mean you want a problem on 'Stores Ledger'?

Is it so?

☐ "Yes Sir".

● You see, if you have not obtained adequate knowledge on the theoretical aspect of the same, it would not be possible to work out advanced problems on the concept. So, let me show the form of two types of Stores Ledger Account. After that, at the end of this chapter, I would like to work out a few problems on the same.

☐ "Thank you Sir."

● Well, please note below two types of Stores Ledger Account :

Stores Ledger Account

Material :	Folio :
Code No :	Bin :
Unit :	Location :
Grade :	Maximum Level :
	Minimum Level :
	Re-ordering Level :

Receipt					Issues				Stock			
Date	Qty.	G. R. N. No.	Rate	Amount	Reqn. No.	Qty.	Rate	Amount	Qty.	Price	Amount	Remarks

Stores Ledger Account

Material :	Maximum Level :
Code No. :	Minimum Level :
Location :	Re-ordering Level :
Folio :	

Ordered			Reserved			Received					Issued				Stock			Check	
Dt.	Ref.	Qty.	Dt.	Ref.	Qty.	Dt.	GN. No.	Qty.	Price	Amt.	SR. No.	Qty.	Price	Amt.	Qty.	Price	Amt.	Dt.	Initial Notes

6. Control of Stock Level depending on the Mode of Production :

Stock constitutes one of the items of working capital. Any decision taken to change working capital position is dependent on the levels of stock maintained by the organisation. Different levels of stocks maintained by the stores department are :

Level of Stock

a. Maximum Stock Level.
b. Minimum Stock Level.
c. Re-ordering Level.
d. Danger Level.
e. Ordering Quantity.

Please note that, of the five aspects mentioned above, I have already given you idea about Ordering Quantity. So, I would not like to discuss the same.

☐ "Sir, is it Economic Buying Quantity?"

- "Yes, it is".

a. Maximum stock Level : It is that level of stock which should not be exceeded. Determination of such maximum level is dependent on :

i. Material consumption rate.
ii. Delivery time.
iii. Availability of needed capital.
iv. Risk factor of preserving storing qualities, i.e. evaporation or deterioration.
v. Storage cost and space.
vi. Expected or inherent price fluctuation factor.
vii. 'Mood' of the market, i.e. the possibility of obsolescence, depletion and changed specification.
viii. Economic buying quantity or quantities.
ix. Impact of incidence of insurance cost on a few materials.
x. Forecast of economic condition.

Formula of Maximum Stock Level

Maximum Level = (Re-order Level + Re-order Quantity) – (Minimum Consumption during a period × Minimum Re-order Period).

b. Minimum Stock Level : It is the level of stock below which the stock should not be allowed to fall. If it is done, there arises the possibility of stoppage of production.

The fixation of minimum stock level is dependent on two factors :

i. Average material consumption rate.
ii. Time required to obtain delivery of new materials and supplies.

Formula of Minimum Stock Level

Minimum Stock Level = Re-order level – (Normal Consumption × Normal re-order period).

c. Re-Order Level

It is a point which is settled between the maximum level of stock and minimum level of stock. It also indicates at what time it needs to initiate purchase requisition. Again, this re-order stock level point is made slightly higher than the minimum level of stock to ensure the production process which may be disturbed by delay in delivery of fresh supplies.

The re-order level is dependent on following factors :

i. Average Rate of Consumption.

ii. Lead Time,

iii. Economic Purchasing Quantity.

Formula of Re-order level is:

Re-order level = Maximum Re-order Period × Maximum Consumption rate during period.

☐ "Sir, what is Re-ordering Quantity?"

● Well, you see, when is order for material placed? — When it is required. So re-order quantity represents the quantities which are ordered each time fresh materials or supplies are required.

Following factors govern re-order quantity :

i. Storage Cost.

ii. Purchasing Cost.

iii. Average Consumption of Material, etc.

Please note, regarding Danger Level and Economic Ordering Quantity, I have discussed these earlier. I hope you have followed all the discussions made earlier. Now I would like to discuss the other part of material control which deals with Material Cost. I explained earlier the first two parts of material cost control which are (A) Purchasing, (B) Storing and Inventory Control.

Anyway, please let me discuss about Material Cost.

☐ "Sir, you have not given us any light about Perpetual Inventory".

● Is it so?

☐ "Yes Sir".

● Well, it is an omission. However, you see, it is a method used to facilitate regular and continuous checking of stock of material. It simultaneously shows at a glance the position of receipt, issue and balance of stock. This method is devised to aid material control and, for ascertaining the real accuracy of perpetual inventory method, physical checking of stock is recommended. However, perpetual inventory is some-times described by many cost accountants as 'Continuous Inventory'. I think you have understood the concept of perpetual inventory system.

Well, just take down an example to cover the above discussions.

Illustration

(i) Average delivery time = One month 10 days

(ii) Maximum Delivery time = 2 months

(iii) Minimum Delivery Time = One month

(iv) Maximum Delivery Time for emergency purchases = 10 days

(v) Average consumption rate per day = 50 units

(vi) Minimum consumption rate per day = 28 units

(vii) Maximum consumption rate per day = 70 units

(viii) Standard ordering quantity = 1,200 units

(ix) Maximum time taken to deliver emergencies purchase = 10 days.

From the above information you are requested to calculate

(a) Re-ordering Level.

(b) Minimum Level.

(c) Maximum Level.

(d) Danger Level.

☐ "Sir, you have not given us any formula for the computation of 'Danger Level'."

● Well, note below the Formula of Danger Level.

Danger Level =

Maximum delivery time from emergency purchase × Maximum Rate of Consumption.

Solution

(a) **Re-ordering Level :** Maximum Delivery Time × Maximum Consumption Rate per day.

= 2 months (60 days) × 70 units = 4,200 units

(b) **Minimum Level :** (Maximum Delivery Time × Maximum rate of Consumption) – (Average Delivery Time × Average Rate of Consumption)

= (60 days × 70 units) – (40 days × 50 units)

= 4,200 units – 2,000 units = 2,200 units

(c) Maximum Level : (Re-ordering Level) – (Minimum Delivery Time × Minimum Rate of Consumption) + Standard Ordering Quantity/Purchase.

= 4,200 – (30 × 28) + 1,200 = 4,200 – 840 + 1,200

= 5,400 – 840 = 4,560 units.

(d) Danger Level :

Maximum Delivery Time for Emergency Purchase × Maximum Rate of Consumption

= 10 days × 70 units = 700 units.

I hope you are now satisfied with the discussions made earlier.

☐ "Yes sir. Now will you please discuss about Material Cost".

● Well, now I am discussing about Material Cost.

C. MATERIAL COST

Following are the different **common methods** used in determining the cost of materials :

i. First-in-First-out (FIFO).

ii. Last-in-First-out (LIFO).

iii. Cost or Market, whichever is less.

iv. Average Methods :

(a) Simple Average.

(b) Weighted Average.

(c) Periodic Average.

(d) Moving Average.

However, I already discussed LIFO, FIFO, Cost or Market, whichever is lower, in Chapter Four. But I have not discussed average methods. Now I would like to discuss only the average methods to make the 'chain of study' complete.

a. Simple Average : It is computed or determined by way of simple arithmetical average method. In this method the total of all unit prices are divided by the number of invoices. Here the quantity on each invoice is ignored for computation. Take for an example :

Date	Units of Quantity Bought	Price Per unit	Cost (Rs.)
January 20	30	11.00	330.00
February 18	5	12.00	60.00
March 1	40	10.00	400.00
April 20	10	11.50	115.00
May 15	50	9.50	475.00
June 10	20	12.00	240.00
	155	66.00	1,620.00

Average Price Per Unit $\frac{\text{Rs. } 66}{6}$ = Rs. 11.00

Now price of 155 units is 155 × Rs. 11.00 = Rs. 1,705

Please note that, if there are 30 units on hand at the last date of June, the value of the inventory would be 30 × Rs. 11.00 = 330

155 × 11.00 = Rs. 1,705
30 × 11.00 = 330
Rs. 2,035

b. Weighted Average : The concerns which desire to spread over total cost of goods on hand, and want to have greater accuracy in the calculation of material issues, are found to employ the Weighted Average Method :

Following procedures are to be followed in computing weighted average :

i. Total quantity received is to be added to total quantity on hand.
ii. Cost of material received is to be added to cost of materials on hand.
iii. Total value is to be divided by total quantities.

Example :

Date	Received		Issued		Balance	
	Qty.	Unit Cost Rs.	Qty.	Unit Cost Rs.	Amount Cost Rs.	Qty.
Feb.5	100	1.00	—	—	—	100
7	—	—	30	1.00	30.00	70
10	200	0.90	—	—	—	270
15	—	—	110	0.92593	101.85	160
18	100	1.10	—	—	—	260
20	—	—	50	0.99288	49.64	210

Well, the value of closing inventory can be found out as :

(a) Quantity at the end = 210 units.

(b) Last average unit cost = Rs. 0.99288.

Value of ending inventory = 210 units × Rs. 0.99288 = Rs. 208.50

Please note in this connection that, until new purchases are received, average unit cost is used in pricing requisitions and ending balance.

However, this method is best suited in the conditions where fluctuation in some material prices are found to exist.

c. Periodic Average

This method of pricing is a variation of weighted average method. The essence of this method is that "instead of computing an average unit cost after each purchase, the computation is delayed until the end of some period, usually a month". Issues of material are then priced at the average unit cost, obtained by dividing the total value of the beginning inventory and purchases for the month by the total quantities available.

Formula

$$U = \frac{V + V_i}{Q + Q_i}$$

U = Periodic average unit cost.

V = Value of inventory at the beginning of the period.

V_i = Value of inventory for the period.

Q = Quantity of inventory at the beginning of the period.

Q_i = Quantity of purchases for period.

d. Moving Average : In day-to-day life we find wild fluctuation of crude oil price in the international market. Moving Average is the best suited stabilised method in a condition of constant price fluctuation. So in the case of oil refining industry, crude oil is generally charged out to operation depending on the basis of 6 months moving average. The calculation of this method runs as :

Month	Price Rs.	Moving Average
January	20.00	
February	22.00	
March	21.00	
April	23.00	
May	22.00	
June	23.00	...... 21.84
July	22.00	...... 22.17
August	24.00	...... 22.50
September	22.00	...... 22.67

The calculations run as :

$$\frac{(20 + 22 + 21 + 23 + 22 + 23)}{6} = 21.83$$

$$\frac{(22 + 21 + 23 + 22 + 23 + 22)}{6} = 22.17$$

I think you are very eager to get a few advanced problems on material cost. I would definitely work out the same afterwards. Before that I would like to discuss the last part of the discussion of material control.

□ "Excuse me Sir. Kindly give us some light on ABC Analysis".

● All right, please note the following :

ABC Analysis

The ABC Analysis is an analytical tool which is widely used across industries as a tool of inventory control. Under this technique, items of inventory are classified according to the annual consumption value. All items of inventory which occupy a substantial portion of the total consumption value are classified as 'A' category items. On the other hand, all items which occupy insignificant portion of the total consumption value are classified as 'C' category items. 'B' category items fall between 'A' category and 'C' category items. The technique is also called **Always Better Control** or **Proportional Parts Value Analysis.** However, the limits of clssification may vary from industry to industry depending upon the size of the undertaking and inventory as well as the classes of items controlled.

The limits of value usually used for classification in many industries are:

a) Items of inventory occupying almost 70% of the total consumption value are classified as 'A' category items. These items (A category) are just 10% of the total quantity of materials required for production. These are called high value/items.

b) About 70% of the total quantity of materials are classified as 'C' category materials which consume just 10% to 15% of the annual consumption value.

c) About 20% of the total quantity of materials account for 20% of the annual consumption value. These items are classified as 'B' category items.

The ABC analysis can be graphically shown as :

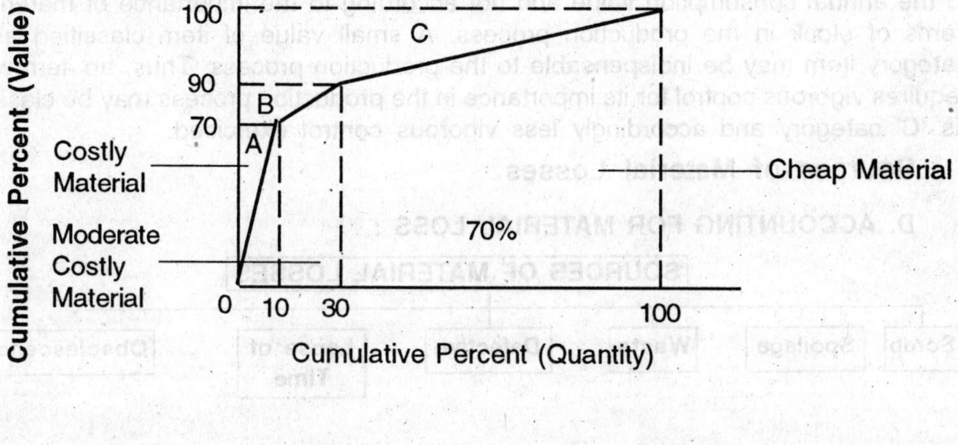

The main objective of the ABC analysis is to develop policy to guide the control functions relating to inventory. The following policy guidelines can be developed in respect of each category of inventory :

A High Consumption Value	B Moderate Consumption Value	C Low Consumption Value
1. Repeated ordering or weekly deliveries.	Less repeated ordering.	Bulk ordering.
2. Very low or no safety stock.	Low safety stock.	High safety stock.
3. Severe control by top management.	Moderate control by middle level management.	Relaxed control by lower level management.
4. Weekly control reports.	Monthly control reports.	Quarterly control statements.
5. Stern value analysis.	Moderate value analysis.	Minimum value analysis.
6. Maximum follow up and expediting.	Periodic follow up.	Follow-up and expediting in exceptional cases.
7. Centralised purchase and store.	Both centralised and decentralised buying.	Decentralised buying.
8. Maximum efforts to reduce lead time.	Moderate efforts.	Minimum efforts.
9. Fortnightly control over obsolete and surplus items.	Quarterly control over obsolete and surplus items.	Annual control.

The ABC Analysis has the following advantages :

1. The ABC analysis helps management to exercise selective control. Manager is required to concentrate only on those items which have high value.
2. It helps to optimise investment in inventory and, thus, ensures profitable use of investible funds.
3. Better control over obsolete items is possible.
4. It helps efficient utilisation of stock items and increase stock turnover rate.
5. It helps to reduce carrying costs.

But the main defects with this technique is that it classifies item of inventory according to the annual consumption value and not according to the importance of material or items of stock in the production process. A small value of item classified as 'C' category item may be indispensable to the production process. Thus, an item which requires vigorous control for its importance in the production process may be classified as 'C' category and accordingly less vigorous control exercised.

Sources of Material Losses

D. ACCOUNTING FOR MATERIAL LOSS :

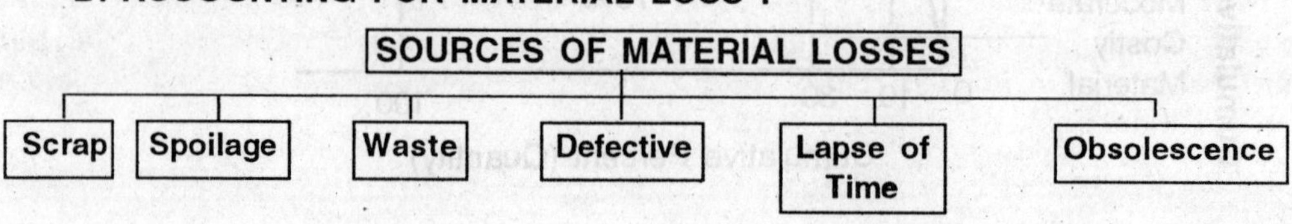

Well, above are the sources of material losses. It should be the duty of production management to have a close watch on the above sources of material losses in order to make effective material control devices. So we need not discuss the above concepts, because all those concepts are self-explanatory.

Now I would like to work-out a few problems on the discussions made earlier:

Illustration

	Material A		**Material B**		**Material C**	
	Qty.	Value Rs.	Qty.	Value Rs.	Qty.	Value Rs.
Bin Card	20	—	4	—	20	—
Stores Ledger	40	400.00	—	212.00	25	—
Perpetual Inventory (physical count)	15	—	5	—	20	—

The above comparisons have been taken from the Material Control records of a company.

You are requested to summarise the causes of these discrepancies, and state how you would investigate them. **[Adapted from I.C.W.A. London]**

Solution

It should be noted that the balance in Bin Card should agree with Stores Ledger if the same are posted from the same source, i.e. Material Receiving Note and Stores Requisition.

The disagreement between the two in general may be due to the reasons listed:

a. In the stores, department posting has been made in the Bin Card while corresponding posting has not been made in the stores ledger.

b. Clerical errors.

So it is clear that while investigating the discrepancies the balances of stores ledger and bin card are to be reconciled first. After that the physical balances are to be compared and verified.

Well, from the above illustration, say in case of Material A, it is clear that there exists a difference of 20 units between Bin Card and Stores Ledger. Here the discrepancies may be due to:

a. Excess material issue.

b. Misplacement of material.

c. Errors in counting and recording, and

d. Under-issue of materials.

Now take Material B. Here also Bin Card and Stores Ledger balances are to be reconciled first. You see, if, after proper checking with Stores Ledger, the Bin Card balance of 4 units is found correct, then it is evident that physical balance is more than book balance.

This discrepancies may be due to :

a. Misplacement of material.

b. Errors in counting and recording, and

c. Under-issue of materials.

In case of Material C, we find that Bin Card balance agrees with physical balance i.e perpetual inventory. The disagreement with Stores Ledger may be due to the fact that recording in Stores Ledger for one or two issues have been missed.

I hope you have followed the problem. Now I will take up another example.

Illustration

A manufacturing concern purchases from time to time large quantities of a commodity used in the manufacture of one of its products.

The details of purchases during six months ended June 30, 2006 are :

2006	Quantities	Cost Price per 100 Units Rs.
February 2	10,000	10.00
March 15	25,000	10.50
April 20	20,000	9.50
May 3	15,000	9.00
June 1	12,000	9.00
June 20	3,000	8.50

There were 15,000 units in stock on Jan. 1, 2006 which were valued at Rs. 9.50 per 100 units.

Quantities issued from stores during the six months were:

2006		
January 25	.....	10,000
February 28	.....	8,000
March 29	.....	25,000
April 30	.....	20,000
May 15	.....	18,000
June 29	.....	15,000

At what prices should the issues be charged and the closing stock valued?

Prepare a Stores Ledger Sheet illustrating your views.

[Adapted from I.C.W.A. London]

Solution : As materials are purchased and issued in large quantities, either LIFO or FIFO may be the basis of stock valuation.

Well, I pointed out earlier that the FIFO method of stock valuation overstates profit at the time of rising price. There results less retention of profit. Here price level shows decreasing trend. So, FIFO method would show lower profit and lower inventory value. However, the above problem is solved here depending on FIFO.

STORES LEDGER SHEET (FIFO METHOD)

	RECEIPTS				ISSUES				STOCK/BALANCE		
Date	PR No.	Qty.	Rate Rs.	Amount Rs.	SR No.	Qty. Rs.	Rate Rs.	Amount	Qty. Rs.	Price Rs.	Amount
Jan. 1		—	—	—		—	—		15,000	9.50	1,425.00
Jan. 25		—	—	—		10,000	9.50	950	5,000	9.50	475.00
Feb. 2		10.000	10.00	1,000		—	—	—	5,000 10,000	9.50 10.00	— 1,475.00
Feb. 28						5,000 3,000	9.50 10.00	775	7,000	10.00	700.00
March 15		25,000	10.50	2,625	—	—	—	—	7,000 25,000	10.00 10.50	3,325.00
March 29		—	—	—		7,000 18,000	10.00 10.50	2,590	7,000	10.50	735.00
April 20		20,000	9.50 —	1,900 —	— —	— —	— —	—	7,000 20,000	10.50 9.50	2,635.00
April 30						7,000 13,000	10.50 9.50	1,970	7,000	9.50	665.00
May 3		15,000	9.00	1,350		—	—	—	7,000 15,000	9.50 9.00	2,015.00
May 21		—	—	—		7,000 11,000	9.50 9.00	1,655	4,000	9.00	360.00
June 1		12,000	9.00	1,080		—	—	—	16,000	9.00	1440.00
June 20		3,000	8.50	255		—	—	—	16,000 3,000	9.00 8.50	1695.00
June 29		—	—	—		15,000	9.00	1,350	1,000 3,000	9.00 8.50	345.00

Illustration

From the following data, ascertain prime cost (per unit) of two products X and Y. Assume there is no regular cost accounting system in this small factory.

(a) Extracts from the financial accounts for the year 2006 :

Material :	Rs.
Balance as on 1.1.2006	15,000
Purchase during the year	2,10,000
Total	2,25,000
Balance as on 31.12.2006	7,500
Consumption during the year	2,17,500
Wages incurred	67,000
Sales proceeds of Shippings	720 (income)

(b) As per production records, total quantities of X and Y produced during the year were 5,000 and 500 units, respectively. The opening and closing balances of the work-in-progress were almost the same and, therefore, ignored.

(c) All materials purchased and the balances in stock were direct materials, meant only for product X. The raw material for the product Y was from borings recovered from the X product. Total quantity of borings recovered during the year was 20 tonnes and the entire quantity was consumed in the product Y. The rate may be estimated Rs. 100 per ton.

(d) 75 tons of chippings was recovered from production, i.e. 70 tonnes from the product X and 5 tons from the product Y, out of which 72 tons were sold at the rate of Rs. 10 per ton and the balance of 3 tons could be treated as wastages.

(e) The total wages of Rs. 67,000 should be analysed as :

	Percentage
Product X	60
Product Y	5
Overheads	35
	100

[I.C.W.A.I.]

Solution

Product X

		Rs.
Direct Material consumed		2,17,500
Less : 20 tons of borings @ Rs. 100 transferred to product Y Rs.	2,000	
Chippings sold*	672	2,672
Direct Material Cost		2,14,828
Direct Wages $\left(\frac{60 \times 67,000}{100}\right)$		40,200
		2,55,028

Prime Cost Per Unit $= \frac{2,55,028}{5,000}$ = Rs. 51 (approx)

Product Y

	Rs.
Boring Received from Product X	2,000
Less : Sale of Chippings $\left(\frac{5 \times 720}{75}\right)$	48
Direct Material Cost	1,952
Add : Direct Wages : $\left(\frac{5 \times 67,000}{100}\right)$	3,350
Prime Cost =	5,302

Prime Cost Per unit $\frac{5,302}{500}$ = Rs. 10.60 (approx)

* Chippings Sold $\frac{70 \times 720}{75}$ = Rs. 672

Illustration

Refreshing Morning Limited makes and sells Product 12 among many others. Three raw materials are used exclusively in the manufacture of the product.

You are given the following information :

Raw Material	X	Y	Z
	kg	kg	kg
Standard Quantity required per unit of Product No. 12	60	40	20
Maximum Stock Level	72,000	48,000	24,000
Stocks at 1st April 2006	62,000	38,000	24,000
Purchase orders placed but not delivered	18,000	12,000	6,000

	Product 12
Maximum stock level	1,200
On 1st April 2004, there were :	
Stock in work in progress (material—complete)	100
Stock in finished goods store	1,000
Sales orders received but not delivered	400

An order from an important export customer was received on 1st April 2006 for 1,800 units of Product 12. No other orders are expected to be received for this product during the quarter.

In addition to completing the export customer's order, the company has decided to increase the stock of this product to the maximum stock level, in anticipation of orders during the next quarter.

It is also decided to increase the Stock of materials X, Y and Z to maximum stock level.

You are required to prepare a statement showing :

(i) The production order requirements in respect of Product 12.

(ii) The standard quantity of each material X, Y and Z needed on the production programme.

(iii) The purchase order requirements for materials X, Y and Z.

[Adapted from I.C.W.A. London]

Solution

(i) Requirement of Production Order in respect of Product 12 = Level of Stock to be maintained + Orders to be supplied – Stock at the beginning – Work-in-Progress

= 1,200 + 2,200 – 1,000 – 100 = 2,300 units.

☐ "Sir, how has the figure for 2,200 units been computed?"

● Well, this figure consists of two parts = 1,800 + 400.

1,800 units represent the order received from an important export customer and 400 units represent Sales Order received but not delivered.

Do you follow?

☐ "Yes Sir".

● Well, please note below the other parts of this problem :

(ii) Standard Quantity of Material required for

Material X = 60 × 2,300 kg. = 1,38,000 kg.

Material Y = 40 × 2,300 kg. = 92,000 kg.

Material Z = 20 × 2,300 kg. = 46,000 kg.

	X kg	Y kg	Z kg
Stock Level	72,000	48,000	24,000
Requirement of product	1,38,000	92,000	46,000
	2,10,000	1,40,000	70,000
Stock at the beginning	62,000	38,000	24,000
	1,48,000	1,02,000	46,000
Material already on order	18,000	12,000	6,000
Material to be ordered	1,30,000	90,000	40,000

I hope, you have followed the above workings. Is there any question?

☐ "Sir, what is the formula of the requirement of Raw Material Purchase?"

● Well, note below. Besides, if you can really follow the above workings you can yourself find out the formula.

However, please note.

Stock Level to be maintained + Production Requirement – Opening Stock – Quantities of Materials on Order.

Well, in my next lecture I shall be discussing with you the concept of Labour Cost Control. For the time being I may be excused for taking rest for a while.

☐ "If I am excused, Sir, would you kindly outline some points to prepare a comprehensive questionnaire for Internal Audit purposes relating to Material Stores?"

● Well, note the following points relating to your question :

● You see, a questionnaire is an important tool for evaluating the system of Internal check of any types of department. Material Stores questionnaire is a schedule of different matters to assemble information for evaluating the system of Internal control system in operation. Well, here is a specimen of the questionnaire :

(i) Nature of Internal check in use?
(ii) Name of the authorised officers for Material reacquisition?
(iii) Name of the authorised officer for Material purchase order?
(iv) Basis of Material purchase?
(v) Are purchase orders followed up?
(vi) Documents for inspection of the incoming material?

(vii) Procedure for issue of material from stores?

(viii) How surplus material in shop is disposed of and accounted for?

(ix) How scrap materials are disposed of and accounted for?

(x) How often stores are checked physically and materials are compared with that shown by Bin Card or Stores Ledger?

Problem

Anil company buys its annual requirement of 36,000 units in 6 instalments. Each unit costs Re.1 and the ordering cost is Rs. 25. The inventory carrying cost is estimated at 20% of unit value.

Find the total annual cost of the existing inventory policy.

How much money can be saved by Economic Order Quantity? **[C.A. Final]**

Solution

Total Annual Cost of the existing inventory policy

	Rs.
Cost of Purchase [36,000 × Re.1]	36,000
Add : Ordering Cost [Rs. 25 × 6]	150
Add : Carrying Cost	
[@ 20% of average inventory value i.e. $\frac{36,000}{6\times2}$ × Re. 1 × 20%]	600
Total Cost	36,750

$$EOQ = \sqrt{\frac{2AO}{C}}$$

$$= \sqrt{\frac{2\times36,000\times25}{1\times20\%}}$$

$$= \sqrt{\frac{18,00,000}{0.2}} = \sqrt{90,00,000} = 3,000 \text{ units}$$

Total Cost using EOQ :

	Rs.
Purchase Cost [36,000 × Re. 1]	36,000
Add : Ordering Cost $\left[\frac{36,000}{3,000}\times \text{Rs. } 25\right]$	300
Add : Carrying Cost $\left[\frac{3,000}{2}\times \text{Re. } 1\times20\%\right]$	300
Total Cost	36,600

Saving in Cost = Rs. 36,750 – Rs. 36,600 = Rs. 150

Problem

G. Ltd. produces a product which has a monthly demand of 4,000 units. The product requires a component X which is purchased at Rs. 20. For every finished product, one unit of component is required. The ordering cost is Rs. 120 per order and the holding cost is 10% p.a.

You are required to calculate :

(i) Economic Order Quantity.

(ii) If the minimum lot size to be supplied is 4,000 units, what is the extra cost the company has to incur?

(iii) What is the minimum carrying cost the company has to incur?

[C.A. Inter]

Solution

(i) $E = \sqrt{\frac{2AO}{C}}$

where

E = Economic Order Quantity

A = Annual Consumption

O = Ordering cost per order

C = Carrying cost per unit

$$E = \sqrt{\frac{2 \times 4{,}000 \times 12 \times 120}{20 \times 10\%}}$$

$$= \sqrt{\frac{1{,}15{,}20{,}000}{2}} = \sqrt{57{,}60{,}000} = 2{,}400 \text{ units}$$

∴ Number of Order = 48,000/2,400 = 20.

(ii) For minimum lot size of 4,000 units, number of order to be placed

$$= \frac{4{,}000 \times 12}{4{,}000} = 12$$

	No. of Order	
	12 (Rs.)	20 (Rs.)
Ordering Cost (Rs. 120 per order)	1,440	2400
Add : Carrying Cost (10% of average inventory value)		
$\left[\frac{2{,}400}{2} \times \text{Rs. } 20 \times 10\%\right]$	—	2,400
$\left[\frac{4{,}000}{2} \times \text{Rs. } 20 \times 10\%\right]$	4,000	—
	5,440	4,800

∴ Extra cost incurred by the company = Rs. 5,440 − Rs. 4,800 = Rs. 640

(iii) Minimum carrying cost $\frac{2,400}{2} \times \text{Rs. } 20 \times 10\%$

= Rs. 2,400

Problem

The Purchase Department of your organisation has received an offer of quantity discounts on its orders of materials as :

Price per tonne	Tonnes
Rs.	
1,200	Less than 500
1,180	500 and less than 1,000
1,160	1,000 and less than 2,000
1,140	2,000 and less than 3,000
1,120	3,000 and above

The annual requirement for the material is 5,000 tonnes. The delivery cost per order is Rs. 1,200 and the stock holding cost is estimated at 20% of material cost per annum.

You are required to advise the Purchase Department the most economic Purchase Level. **[M.Com., Bangalore University]**

Solution

Ordering Quantity (Tonnes) Q	Price per tonne (Rs.) P	Purchasing cost of 5,000 tonnes (Rs.) 500 × P	Ordering Cost (Rs.) $\frac{5,000}{Q} \times \text{Rs. } 1,200$	Carrying Cost (Rs.) $\frac{Q}{2} \times P \times 20\%$	Total Cost (Rs.)
400	1,200	60,00,000	15,000	48,000	60,63,000
500	1,180	59,00,000	12,000	59,000	59,71,000
1,000	1,160	58,00,000	6,000	1,16,000	59,22,000
2,000	1,140	57,00,000	3,000	2,28,000	59,31,000
3,000	1,120	56,00,000	2,000	3,36,000	59,38,000

It is clear from the above table that the most economic Purchase Order is 1,000 units, since, at this level, the total cost is the minimum.

Problem

Two components X and Y are used as :

Normal usage	:	100 units per week each
Minimum usage	:	50 units per week each
Maximum usage	:	150 units per week each

Re-order quantity : X 800 units, Y 1,200 units.

Re-order period : X 4 to 6 weeks, Y 2 to 4 weeks.

Calculate for each component :

(a) Re-order Level.

(b) Minimum Level.

(c) Maximum Level, and

(d) Average Stock Level. **[B.Com., Bangalore University]**

Solution

(a) Re-order level = Maximum usage × maximum lead time.

X = 150 × 6 = 900 units

Y = 150 × 4 = 600 units

(b) Minimum level = Re-order level – (Normal usage × Average lead time)

X = 900 – (100 × 5) = 400 units.

Y = 600 – (100 × 3) = 300 units.

(c) Maximum level = Re-order level + Re-order quantity – (Minimum usage × minimum lead time)

X = 900 + 800 – (50 × 4) = 1,500 units

Y = 600 + 1,200 – (50 × 2) = 1,700 units

(d) Average Stock Level $= \frac{\text{Minimum level + Maximum level}}{2}$

X $= \frac{400 + 1,500}{2} = 950$ units

Y $= \frac{300 + 1,700}{2} = 1,000$ units

Problem

A manufacturer uses 200 units of a component every month and he buys them entirely from an outside supplier. The order placing and receiving cost is Rs 100 and annual carrying cost per unit is Rs. 12. From the given set of data, calculate the Economic Order Quantity.

P Ltd. uses three types of materials A, B and C for production of X, final product. The relevant monthly data for the components are :

	A	B	C
Normal usage (units)	200	150	180
Minimum usage (units)	100	100	90
Maximum usage (units)	300	250	270
Re-order quantity (units)	750	900	720
Re-order period (months)	2 to 3	3 to 4	2 to 3

Calculate for each component :

(i) Re-order Level,

(ii) Maximum Level,

(iii) Minimum Level, and

(iv) Average Stock Level. **[C.S. Inter]**

Solution

$$\text{Economic Order Quantity} = \sqrt{\frac{2AO}{C}}$$

$$= \sqrt{\frac{2 \times 200 \times 12 \times 100}{12}}$$

$$= \sqrt{40{,}000}$$

$$= 200 \text{ units.}$$

(i) Re-order Level = Maximum usage × Maximum lead time

A = 300 × 3 = 900 units

B = 250 × 4 = 1,000 units

C = 270 × 3 = 810 units

(ii) Maximum Level =

(Re-order level + Re-order quantity) − (Minimum usage× Minimum lead time)

A = (900 + 750) − (100 × 2)
= 1,650 − 200 = 1,450 units

B = (1,000 + 900) − (100 × 3)
= 1,900 − 300 = 1,600 units

C = (810 + 720) − (90 × 2)
= 1,530 − 180 = 1,350 units

(iii) Minimum Level = Re-order Level − (Normal usage × Average lead time)

A = 900 − (200 × 2·5)
= 900 − 500 = 400 units

B = 1,000 − (150 × 3·5)
= 1,000 − 525 = 475 units

C = 810 − (180 × 2·5)
= 810 − 450 = 360 units

(iv) Average Stock Level = Minimum Level + (1/2 re-order quantity)

A = 400 + (1/2 × 750) = 775 units

B = 475 + (1/2 × 900) = 925 units

C = 360 + (1/2 × 720) = 720 units

Problem

The following is the extract of the record of receipts and issues of sulphur in a chemical factory during February 2006 :

Feb.	1	Opening balance, 500 tonnes at Rs. 200.
	7	Issued, 250 tonnes.
	13	Received from supplier, 200 tonnes at Rs. 190.
	14	Returned from department, 15 tonnes.
	16	Issued, 180 tonnes.
	20	Received from supplier, 240 tonnes at Rs. 200.
	24	Issued, 300 tonnes.
	25	Received from supplier, 320 tonnes at Rs. 190.
	26	Issued, 115 tonnes.
	27	Returned from departments, 35 tonnes.
	28	Received from supplier 100 tonnes at Rs. 190.

Issues are to be priced on the principle FIFO. The stock verifier had found a shortage of 10 tonnes on 22nd and left a note accordingly.

Draw up a priced ledger, showing the above transactions.

[B.Com., Calicut University]

Solution

Name of Material :	Folio No. :	Max. Level :
Description :	Bin No. :	Min. Level :
Code No. :	Unit of quantity :	Re-order Level :
Location Code :		Re-order Quantity :

Date	Receipts			Issues			Balance		
	Qty.	Rate Rs.	Amount Rs.	Qty.	Rate Rs.	Amount Rs.	Qty.	Rate Rs.	Amount Rs.
2006									
Feb. 1	–	–	–	–	–	–	500	200	1,00,000
7	–	–	–	250	200	50,000	250	200	50,000
13	200	190	38,000	–	–	–	250 200	200 190	88,000
14	15	200	3,000	–	–	–	250 200 15	200 190 200	91,000
16	–	–	–	180	200	36,000	70 200 15	200 190 200	55,000

Date	Receipts			Issues			Balance		
	Qty.	Rate	Amount	Qty.	Rate	Amount	Qty.	Rate	Amount
		Rs.	Rs.		Rs.	Rs.		Rs.	Rs.
20	240	200	48,000	–	–	–	70 200 15 240	200 190 200 200	1,03,000
22	–	–	–	10	200	2,000	60 200 15 240	200 190 200 200	1,01,000
24	–	–	–	60 200 15 25	200 190 200 200	58,000	215	200	43,000
25	320	190	60,800	–	–	–	215 320	200 190	1,03,800
26	–	–	–	115	200	23,000	100 320	200 190	80,800
27	35	200	7000	–	–	–	100 320 35	200 190 200	87,800
28	100	190	19,000	–	–	–	100 320 35 100	200 190 200 190	1,06,800

Problem

On 1st March 2006 there are 1,500 units of materials at Rs 12 per unit in stock. The following transactions were made during the month :

Mar. 2 Issued 200 units.
4 Purchased 1,000 units at Rs 15 per unit.
5 Issued 1,200 units.
6 Purchased 600 units at Rs 20 per unit.
7 Issued 650 units.
7 Returned to store from issues of 2 March, 100 units.
9 Purchased 300 units at Rs 25 per unit.
13 Issued 250 units.
17 Issued 300 units.

Prepare Stores Ledger Account by LIFO method.

[B.Com., Kakatiya University, Adapted]

Solution

STORES LEDGER ACCOUNT

LIFO Method

Name of Material :	Unit of Quantity	Max. Level :
Description :	Bin No. :	Min. Level :
Code No. :	Location Code :	Re-order Level :
		Re-order Quantity :

Date	Receipts			Issues			Balance		
	Qty.	Rate	Amount	Qty.	Rate	Amount	Qty.	Rate	Amount
		Rs.	Rs.		Rs.	Rs.		Rs.	Rs.
2006									
Mar. 1	–	–	–	–	–	–	1,500	12	18,000
2	–	–	–	200	12	2,400	1,300	12	15,600
4	1,000	15	15,000	–	–	–	1,300 1,000	12 15	30,600
5	–	–	–	1,000 200	15 12	17,400	1,100	12	13,200
6	600	20	12,000	–	–	–	1,100 600	12 20	25,200
7	–	–	–	600 50	20 12	12,600	1,050	12	12,600
7	100	12	1,200	–	–	–	1,050 100	12 12	13,800
9	300	25	7,500	–	–	–	1,150 300	12 25	21,300
13	–	–	–	250	25	6,250	1,150 50	12 25	15,050
17	–	–	–	50 250	25 12	4,250	900	12	10,800

Problem

The stock of material A, as on 1st June 2006, is 500 units, at Re 1 per unit. Following purchases and issues of this item were made subsequently :

	Receipts Quantity (units)	Rate Per Unit Rs.	Issue Quantity (units)
June 6	–	–	200
10	400	1.10	–
15	300	1.20	–
20	–	–	500
21	–	–	200
24	500	1.30	–
25	–	–	300
28	–	–	200

Prepare a stores ledger account showing how the value of the above issues should be arrived at under the Base Stock Method when it operates in conjunction with LIFO. Base Stock is 200 units. **[B.Com., Annamalai University, Adapted]**

Solution

STORES LEDGER ACCOUNT

LIFO Method

Name of Material :	Unit of Quantity	Max. Level :
Description :	Folio No. :	Min. Level :
Code No. :	Location Code	Re-order Level :
		Re-order Quantity :

Date	Receipts			Issues			Balance		
	Qty.	Rate Rs.	Amount Rs.	Qty.	Rate Rs.	Amount Rs.	Qty.	Rate Rs.	Amount Rs.
2006									
June 1	–	–	–	–	–	–	500	1.00	500
6	–	–	–	200	1.00	200	300	1.00	300
10	400	1.10	440	–	–	–	300 400	1.00 1.10	740
15	300	1.20	360	–	–	–	300 400 300	1.00 1.10 1.20	1,100
20	–	–	–	300 200	1.20 1.10	580	300 200	1.00 1.10	520
21	–	–	–	200	1.10	220	300	1.00	300
24	500	1.30	650	–	–	–	300 500	1.00 1.30	950
25	–	–	–	300	1.30	390	300 200	1.00 1.30	560
28	–	–	–	200	1.30	260	300	1.00	300

QUESTIONS

1. Discuss the importance of Material Cost Control.
2. Chalk out an ideal plan for Material Cost Control for a small factory.
3. According to you, what method of stock valuation is by far the best, and why?
4. What is Material Accounting? What are its importance?
5. "Material Budget is the key to Material Cost Control."—Explain.
6. Calculate maximum level, minimum level and re-ordering level from the following data :

   Re-ordering Quantity — 1,200 units Maximum Consumption 300 units per week
   Re-ordering Period — 4 to 6 weeks Minimum Consumption 200 units per week
   Normal Consumption 250 units per week.

   [C.U. B.Com. Hons.]

7. Two components A and B are used as follows :

   Normal Usage — 50 per week each
   Maximum Usage — 75 per week each
   Minimum Usage — 25 per week each
   Reorder Quantity : A — 300; B — 500
   Reorder Period : A — 4 to 6 weeks; B — 2 to 4 weeks.

   Calculate for each element (a) Reordering Level, (b) Minimum Level, (c) Maximum Level and (d) Average Level.

   [I.C.W.A. Inter, N.B.U. B.Com. Hons. B.U. B.Com. Hons.]

8. From the following data for the twelve months, compute the average stock level for a component :

   Maximum Usage per month 300 Nos.
   Minimum Usage per month 200 Nos.
   Average Usage per month 225 Nos.
   Time Lag in procurement of Material :
   Maximum 6 months : Minimum 2 months
   Reorder Quantity 750 Nos. **[V.U. B.Com.]**

9. Compute the various stock levels from the following data :

   Normal Consumption 300 units per day
   Maximum Consumption 420 units per day
   Minimum Consumption 240 units per day
   Reorder Quantity 3,600 units
   Reorder Period 10 to 15 days
   Normal Reorder Period 12 days **[Andhra Univ., M.Com.]**

10. The following information is available in respect of a component :

Maximum stock level	8,400 units
Budgeted consumption :	Maximum 1,500 units per month
	Minimum 800 units per month
Estimated delivery period :	Maximum 4 months
	Minimum 2 months

You are required to calculate (i) reorder level and (ii) reorder quantity.

[I.C.W.A., Inter]

11. Two Components A and B are used as below :

Minimum Usage	25 units per week each
Maximum Usage	75 units per week each
Maximum Stock Levels	A = 650 units; B = 750 units
Reorder Period	A = 4 to 6 weeks; B = 2 to 4 weeks

Calculate for each component : (i) Reorder level, (ii) Minimum level and (iii) Reorder quantity. **[B.U. B.Com. Hons.]**

12. Actual Consumption—18,000 units (per annum)

Cost per unit—Rs. 1.50

Cost of placing order and processing the delivery — Rs. 12 per order

Inventory carrying cost — 20% of unit value.

Calculate Economic Order Quantity for the material. **[C.U. B.Com. Hons.]**

13. From the figures given below, calculate economic ordering quantity and number of orders to be placed per year :

Total consumption of material per year		10,000 kgs.
Buying cost per order	Rs. 50	
Unit cost of Material	Rs. 2 per kg.	

Carrying and storage cost on inventory value 8% **[Madurai Univ., B.Com.]**

14. The daily demand for an electronic machine is approximately 25 items. Everytime when an order is placed, a fixed cost of Rs. 25 is incurred. The daily holding cost per item of inventory is Re. 0.40. If the lead time is 16 days, determine the economic lot. **[I.C.W.A.]**

15. A company is trying to establish a control policy to reduce inventory costs of a Spare Part No. 033-04-177.

The Financial Manager estimates that a three-week delivery schedule can be expected. The purchase price per unit is Rs. 6 and purchase order cost is Rs. 245. The total pruchase requirement for a 50 week year is estimated to be 4,000 units and carrying costs are estimated at 20% of average inventory value. Safety stock of the company is 160 units. You are required to compute

(i) the economical order quantity; (ii) the optimum number of orders to be palced and (iii) the minimum level of inventory before reordering.

[C.U. M.Com. Adapted]

16. About 200 units are required per quarter. Rs. 100 per order is incurred for placing an order. The inventory carrying cost per unit is Rs. 4. The re-order level is 350 units. The minmum usage is 25 units per week and the re-order periods is 4-6 weeks.

Compute — (a) Economic Order Quantity; (b) Maximum Level.

[C.U. B.Com. Hons.]

17. The Ganges Pump Company uses about 75,000 valves per year and usage is fairly constant at 6,250 valves per month.

The valves cost Rs. 1.50 per unit when bought in quantites and the carrying cost is estimated to be 20% of average inventory investment on the annual basis.

The cost to place an order and process the delivery is Rs. 18.

It takes 45 days to receive delivery from the date of an order and a safety stock of 3,250 valves is desired.

You are required to determine :

(i) the most economical order quantity and frequency of orders.

(ii) the order point, and

(iii) the most economical order quantity if the valves cost Rs. 4.50 each instead of Rs. 1.50 each.

[Delhi Univ., M.Com.]

18. (a) A company uses 5,120 units of a component in a year. The purchase price per unit of the component is Rs. 5 and the carrying cost including interest is estimated at 20% of the average inventory investment on annual basis. The cost of placing an order and process the delivery is Rs. 10

Ascertain the Economic Order Quantity and the number of orders each of the Economic Order Quantity to be placed for the component in a year.

(b) Assuming that the average daily consumption of the above component is 14 units and that the normal lead time is 15 days, calculate the Ordering Level for the component where safety stock is considered to be equal to 25 days' consumption.

[C.U. B.Com. Hons.]

19. Prepare Stores Ledger from the following particulars under FIFO Method :

2001 Dec. 1	Opening Stock	1,000 units	@ Rs. 12 each
6	Received	600 units	@ Rs. 13 each
8	Issued	1,300 units	
10	Received	800 units	@ Rs. 12.50 each
16	Issued	950 units	
22	Received	550 units	@ Rs. 10.90 each
26	Received	200 units	@ Rs. 11.00 each
30	Issued	600 units	
31	Stolen from Godown	50 units	@ Rs. 11.00 each

[B.U. B.Com. Pass]

20. Using Last-In-First-Out (LIFO) basis, calculate the value of Closing Stock of January (preparation of Stores Ledger not necessary) :

January	1	Opening Stock	500 kg. @ Rs. 5 per kg.
	12	Purchased	400 kg. @ Rs. 6 per kg.
	18	Issued	600 kg.
	22	Purchased	500 kg. @ Rs. 7 per kg.
	30	Issued	300 kg.

[C.U. B.Com. Pass]

21. With the help of the following information, prepare a Stores Ledger Card based on the Weighted Average Price Method of pricing issues :

2002 September	1	Opening Balance	24,000 kgs. @ Rs. 7,500 per tonne.
	1	Purchase	44,000 kgs. @ Rs. 7,600 per tonne.
	1	Issue	10,000 kgs.
	5	Issue	16,000 kgs.
	12	Issue	24,000 kgs.
	13	Purchase	10,000 kgs. @ Rs. 7,800 per tonne.
	18	Issue	24,000 kgs.
	22	Purchase	50,000 kgs. @ Rs. 8,000 per tonne.
	28	Issue	30,000 kgs.
	30	Issue	22,000 kgs.

[I.C.W.A., Inter]

22. From the following details write Stores Ledger under Simple Average method :

2002 December	1	Opening Balance	100 kgs. @ Rs. 5.00
	5	Received	50 kgs. @ Rs. 5.20
	8	Issued	120 kgs.
	10	Issued	10 kgs.
	15	Received	80 kgs. @ Rs. 5.40
	18	Issued	50 kgs.
	20	Received	100 kgs. @ Rs. 5.60
	25	Issued	40 kgs.
	29	Issued	60 kgs.

The stock verifier found a shortage of 10 kgs. on 16.12.2002 and another shortage of 10 kgs. on 26.12.2002. **[C.U. B.Com. Hons.]**

23. Prepare a Stores Ledger Account under the LIFO Method of pricing the issue of stores, using the following information :

2002 January	1	Balance in hand @ Rs. 1.10 per unit	100 units
	2	Received @ Rs. 1.20 per unit	200 units
	10	Issued	150 units
	14	Received @ Rs. 1.30 per unit	100 units
	18	Issued	150 units

23 Returned from the issue on 10th Jan.	20 units
26 Received @ Rs. 1.20 per unit	100 units
30 Wastage	10 units
31 Issued	110 units

[C.U. B.Com. Hons.]

24. Show the year-end value of inventory under LIFO method for the following data : Opening balance : 12,000 units @ Rs. 2.00 per unit.

	Received (Units)	Issued (Units)
1st quarter	20,000 @ Rs. 2.20	16,000
2nd quarter	30,000 @ Rs. 2.40	26,000
3rd quarter	25,000 @ Rs. 2.30	32,000
4th quarter	10,000 @ Rs. 2.25	8,000

Assume that purchases were made on the first day of the quarter.

[B.Com., Andhra U.]

25. On 1st January the stock of a component in the stores was 554 units at Rs. 35 per hundred. During three months the receipts and issues were as follows :

2001	Purchased		Issued
January	434 units	@ Rs. 37.50 per hundred	400 units
February	500 units	@ Rs. 40.00 per hundred	610 units
March	750 units	@ Rs. 42.00 per hundred	950 units

When the stock was taken at 31st March a discrepancy of 49 units was revealed. Prepare a Store Ledger Card under the FIFO method and show how would you deal with the discrepancy. **[V.U. B.Com. (Hons.)]**

Value of closing stock on 31.3.1997. 299 units @ Rs. 42 per hundred = Rs. 96.18.

26. Sachin Ltd. furnishes the following information : (i) consumption — 300 units per quarter; (ii) Cost per unit Rs. 40; (iii) Cost of processing an order Rs. 600; (iv) Obsolescence 15%; (v) Insurance on inventory 25%.

Compute (a) Economic Order Quantity (b) No of Orders per year (c) Time lag between two consecutive Orders.

A supplier offers a discount of 2% on a purchase of 600 units. Should it be accepted? **[C.U. B.Com. Hons.]**

27. From the following particulars, calculate the best quantity to be ordered :

Ordering Quantity (in kg.)	Price per kg. (Rs.)
Less that 500	10.00
500 and less than 1,600	9.60
1,600 and less than 4,000	9.40

4,000 and less than 8,000	9.20
8,000 and above	9.00

The annual requirement of the material is 8,000 kg. Stock holding (carrying) costs is 20% of material cost per annum. Ordering (reordering) cost per order is Rs. 10. **[C.U. B.Com. Hons.]**

28. A firm is able to obtain quantity discount on its orders of material as follows :

Price per tonne Rs.	Forgone discount per tonne Rs.	Order size Tonnes
6.00	0.40	Less than 250
5.90	0.30	250 and less than 800
5.80	0.20	800 and less than 2,000
5.70	0.10	2,000 and less than 4,000
5.60	—	4,000 and over

The annual demand for the material is 4,000 tonnes. Stock holding costs are 20% of material cost per annum. The delivery cost per order is Rs. 6.00. **[C.I.M.A., London]**

29. From the following information, you are required to prepare a schedule showing the associated cost if 1,2,3,4,5 or 6 orders were placed during the year for a single product. From your schedule, state the number of orders to be placed each year and the economic order quantity :

Annual usage of product	600 units
Unit cost of product	Rs. 2.40
Cost of placing an order	Rs. 6.00

Stock holding cost as a % of average stock value 20%.

[C.I.M.A., London, Adapted]

30. A company uses a special bracket in the manufacture of its product which it orders from outside supplies. The appropriate date are :

Demand = 2,000 per annum.

Ordering Cost = Rs. 20 per order.

Carrying Cost = 20% of item price.

Basic item price = Rs. 10 per bracket.

The company is offered the following discounts on the basic price :

400-799	less 2%
800-1599	less 4%
1600 and over	less 5%

It is required to establish the most economical quantity to order.

[C.I.M.A., London, Adapted]

7

LABOUR COST CONTROL

● Good morning my dear students. Are you all present in the class?

☐ "Good morning Sir, yes, we all are present."

● In my last lecture I discussed in detail the different aspects of Material Cost Control. Labour cost is one of the elements of total cost of production. If the labour cost is higher, it will have a far-reaching effect on the sale price of the product. We have seen earlier that managerial decision is mainly concentrated on Profit Planning. Planning for profit may be fruitful if all the elements of cost are properly directed and controlled.

Cost of Product + Profit = Selling Price

Selling Price – Cost of Production = Profit

In a competitive market, where margin of profit seems to be lower, the management solely depends on the *Philosophy*– 'Production of quality and time-out goods at a reduced price'. In the sphere of planning for profit, labour cost plays an important role. I would like to point out at the outset of this discussion that labour cost control, in its true sense is neither payment of wages at a reduced rate, nor it should mean reduction of labour's wages. Labour cost control should mean control through increase in labour productivity.

Real Concept of Labour Cost Control

☐ "Sir, what is productivity?"

● Well, it is the ratio between 'Input' and 'Output' :

$$\textit{Productivity} = \frac{\textbf{Output}}{\textbf{Input}}$$

Here I would I like to refer to a remark made by our former Prime Minister, Sri Lal Bahadur Shastri. He defined: 'Higher productivity means more efficient use of all types of resources in employment, using them to produce as many goods and services as possible, of the kind and quality most wanted by consumers, at lower and lower cost. It is, in essence, a multi-pronged mass attack on waste on the one hand and optimum use of all instruments and tools of production, on the other.' So it is clear that labour cost control means to control the leakage areas of labour cost.

Meaning of Productivity

Oh yes! I have totally forgotten to give you the definition of productivity as given by the International Labour Office–Geneva (1966) :

Well, here is the definition :

'Higher productivity means that more is produced with the same expenditure of resources; at the same cost in terms of material, machine time or labour used up, thus releasing some of these resources for the production of other things.'

I think now you have followed the concept of 'Productivity'.

Well, before taking up different aspects of Labour Cost Control for discussion, let us see what are the different elements of labour cost:

ELEMENTS OF LABOUR COST			
Direct labour	**Indirect labour**	**Labour losses**	**Labour related cost**
Labour expended for the completion of product or products	Labour is not expended for the completion of product or products	Losses take into account the factors like waiting line, machine delays	Cost which takes into account the factors like premium pay, holiday and vacation pay, etc.

There is no denying the fact that the above elements of labour cost, from managerial and accounting point of view, can be considered an 'Integrated' area of cost. Mr. Matz and others in their book '***Cost Accounting***' defined labour cost from fundamental point of view to its extended area of meaning. They are of opinion that 'fundamentally a labour cost consists of the hourly rate, the daily or weekly wage, or the monthly salary of the employees. In addition to the base pay, generally based on a 40-hour work week, other elements enter into the labour cost. Factors such as overtime earnings, premium pay, shift bonuses, production incentives, vacation pay, apprenticeship or trainee costs, and pensions constitute other types of labour costs besides the base pay. In addition to these elements, labour cost may include paid holidays; unemployment compensation; old age and survivor's benefits; and even free lunches. The measure of cost to keep an employee at work an hour or a day must include all these elements where they exist.'

It is a fact that the management is interested in the computation and analysis of labour cost :

Purposes of Computation of Labour Cost

i) To control labour cost in the context of Productivity and profitability of the organisation.
ii) To arrive at management decision(s).
iii) To evaluate labour performance.
iv) To find out ways and means for better operation of the business.

So it is clear from the above discussions that labour cost control is inevitable and is a 'must' for maintaining sound 'integrity' of the business position and to keep high the morale of the employees.

Now let us see what are the different techniques of labour cost control. Well, you see, following are the broad techniques which can be used as a basis of labour cost control :

Techniques of Labour Cost Control

1 *LABOUR BUDGET AND STANDARD*
2 *LABOUR REPORTING*
3 *PAYROLL ACCOUNTING*

I hope you have followed the above discussion. Now I would like to discuss the above techniques one by one.

1. LABOUR BUDGET AND STANDARD

Suppose you have a plan as to how much is to be produced, and what should be the proportion of labour cost. Then it becomes easy on the part of the management to have an estimate about required labour to complete a job. Again, depending on the production, workers are either recruited or retrenched. So it is clear that the preparation of Labour Budget is dependent on estimated production, projected labour cost etc.

Labour budget is a forecast of direct labour hour of direct labour cost. However, the main purposes or objects of this budget are :

Objects of Labour Budget

a. For determining the required direct labour in terms of labour hours to meet production requirements.
b. For determining the direct labour cost of production.
c. For facilitating the personnel department in their recruitment activities.
d. For providing information for estimating cash requirements for direct labour.
e. For providing direct labour cost data for managerial control through comparison with actual labour cost.

You see, it is not an easy task in actual practice to implement the labour budget unless general and overall ideas about the following concepts are conceived of :

A. Services of Personnel Department.
B. Services of the Time Keeping Department.
C. Services of Works Department.
D. Productivity of Labour.
E. Nature and Pattern of Labour Turnover.
F. Employees' Remuneration and Incentives.

Now I would like to discuss the above six aspects one by one :

A. Services of Personnel Department : The Primary function of Personnel Department is to execute the business policies and plans regarding labours of the business. However, the other functions of the Personnel Department may be summed up as :

i. Appointment of employees or workers following the request of Labour Placement Requisition.

Functions of Personnel Department

ii. Discharge of employees or workers.
iii. Transfer of employees.
iv. Maintain Personal Record Cards of employees.
v. Maintain detailed records of overtime and shift work of workers.
vi. Appraise the process of Merit-Rating.

☐ "Sir what is 'Merit Rating' ?"

● You see, it indicates the assessment of merits or capabilities of workers or a worker in each and every time of work or job. The merit rating process helps in the selection of the right man for the right job. I think you have followed.

☐ "Yes Sir".

B. Services of The Time Keeping Department : The primary function of Time Keeping Department is to keep attendance records of the employees or workers.

The purposes of the attendance records are :

Purpose of Attendance Records

i. For disclosing the tardiness or absence.

ii. For measuring overtime.

iii. For helping the Pay-Roll Department by providing different dates viz., overtime, absence or tardiness.

I hope you have followed the above discussion. Now I would like to give you some ideas about the objects of time keeping of the workers.

Well, these are for :

i. Cost Allocation.

ii. Labour Cost Comparisons.

iii. Controlling and Checking Work Evasion and Idle Time.

iv. Overhead Apportionment.

However, the services of the Time Department can be studied under two broad heads — (i) Attendance Time; and (ii) Job Time.

Do you follow?

☐ "No Sir, I can't follow".

● I find no reason why you could not follow. However, please note :

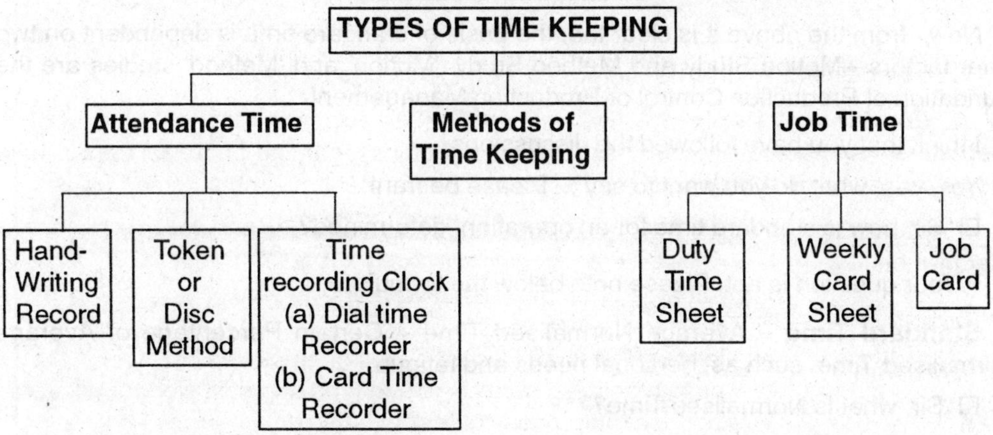

Now let me discuss the above concepts in a nutshell.

Well, attendance time indicates the recording of time which is spent by the workers or employees. It had been pointed out earlier that generally three methods are adopted in keeping time. Under the hand-writing records or register method, each employee has to sign on the register stating his/her time of arrival and departure. The check token or disc method is found to exist in most of the factories. Under this method, workers are provided with different numbered metal discs. At the time of entering into the factory the worker takes his numbered token which is placed on the board and then each drops his disc into a box. All these tokens are then collected by the time keeper for proper recording of attendance. Regarding time keeping clock it can be stated that it is a more accurate and indisputable time recording system. Time recording clocks are of two types—(a) Dial Time Recorder; and (b) Card Time Recorder. However, Card Time Recorder is universally adopted.

Job time system of time keeping is concerned with the recording of time spent on a particular process or a job. Here, generally, three methods are used as a measure of proper recording of time spent on processes or jobs. These terms are self-explanatory. So, I need not like to discuss them.

C. Services of the Works Department : Works study is the main purpose of Works Department. Works Study is the function of studying the technical aspects of production. It consists of Time Study, Motion Study and Method Study :

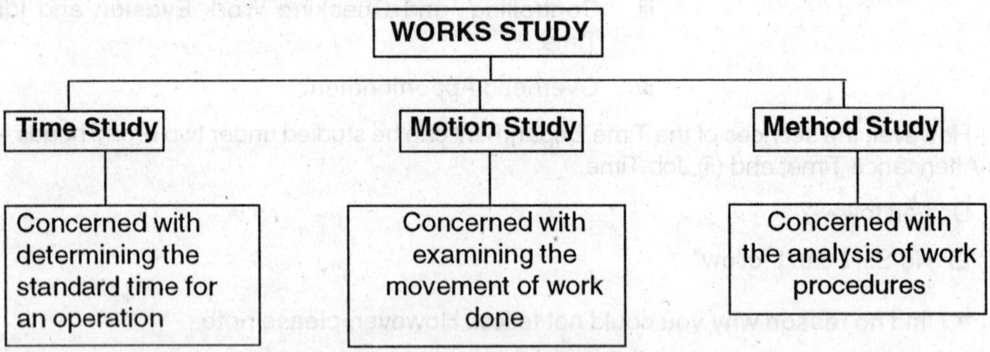

Now, from the above it is clear that the basis of standard time is dependent on two other factors—Motion Study and Method Study. 'Motion' and 'Method' studies are the foundation of Production Control or Production Management.

I think that you have followed the discussions.

Yes, yes, what do you want to say ... Please be frank.

☐ "Sir, how is standard time for an operation determined?"

• Your question is apt. Please note below the formula:

Standard Time = Average Normalised Time + Certain Percentage of Average Normalised Time, such as, personal needs and fatigue.

☐ "Sir, what is Normalised Time?"

• Well, normalised time can be computed as :

$$\textbf{Normalised Time} = \text{Time Taken} \times \frac{\text{Rating}}{\text{General Rating (Basic or Normal)}}$$

D. Productivity of Labour : I have already given you the basic concept of productivity at the outset of this chapter. As labour cost plays an important role in determining total cost of production, so the productivity of labour should be increased.

The productivity of labour can be improved through :

Improvement of Labour Productivity

i. Production Planning.
ii. Merit Rating.
iii. Training of Workers.
iv. Replacement of Workers.
v. Workers' Remuneration and Incentives.
vi. Standardisation and Simplification of work or job.
vii. Good Working Conditions and Facilities.

Well, the measurement of Labour Productivity can be studied from two approaches — (i) Effective Time; and (ii) Ineffective Time.

(i) **Effective Time :** In case of standard and uniform output, the labour productivity can be obtained from the following relationship :

$$\frac{\text{Output}}{\text{Actual Hours}}$$

Well, the computation of Labour Productivity will be, in case outputs consists of different types :

$$\frac{\text{Standard Hour Production}}{\text{Actual Hour Worked}}$$

(ii) **Ineffective Time :** Please note the relationship between two factors which entail the concept of productivity from the point of view of cost or ineffective time. If the percentage of cost time or ineffective time is found to decrease, it is definitely a step towards higher productivity :

$$\text{Lost or Ineffective Time} = \frac{\text{Man Hour Lost}}{\text{Possible or Expected Man Hour}}$$

$$\%\ \text{Lost Time} = \frac{\text{Loss of Man Hour}}{\text{Possible Man Hour}}$$

I think you have followed the concept of Labour Productivity.

Now I would like to discuss Turnover of Labour.

E. Nature and Pattern of Labour Turnover : Labour Turnover is the change in labour force during a particular year or a given period; or it may be expressed as the rate of change in the composition of labour force. It should be noted in this context that high turnover rate is one of the major causes of higher labour costs. Management should have a strong tendency to keep the labour turnover rate to the minimum.

Labour Turnover

The labour turnover rate can be measured in two ways :

$$\frac{\text{Number of Workers Replaced (or Freshly Recruited)}^{*}}{\text{Average Number of Workers on Rolls}} \times 100 \quad \text{... (i)}$$

$$\frac{\text{No. of Workers Who Leave During a Period or Year}^{**}}{\text{Average Number of Workers on Rolls}} \times 100 \quad \text{... (ii)}$$

*New recruitment due to opening of new department should not be taken into account.

** Loss of workers' job due to closure of department should not be taken for computation.

I think you have followed the above discussions.

☐ "Sir, I could not follow formula (ii). Please enlighten me in a simple manner".

• Well, take an example. Say, total number of workers in a factory are 1,000; out of which 200 workers leave and are replaced. Here Labour Turnover Rate will be

$$\frac{200}{1,000} \times 100 = 20\%$$

So Labour Turnover Rate is 20%.

Is there any question ?

☐ "Sir, what are the causes of labour turnover and how can the rate be minimised?"

• Well, the causes of labour turnover are :

i. Dismissal

ii. Retrenchment

iii. Resignation or retirement.

The labour turnover occasions loss to management in the form of (i) More Supervision (ii) High Wastage (iii) Scrap (iv) Loss of Production, and, finally (v) Cost of Recruitment and training of new workers.

Well, Labour Turnover Rate can be minimised by

i. Maintaining amicable industrial relation.

ii. Introducing proper wage and incentive policies.

iii. Removing vague management sentiment in the idea that a worker, though he is physically, academically, technically equipped, will not be allowed promotion unless he has the taste of 'Grey hair', i.e. is advanced in years!

Is there any question, please?

☐ "Sir, we are really very glad to get all those above ideas. Thank you, Sir".

• Now I would like to discuss about Employees' Remunerations and Incentives.

F. Employees' Remuneration and Incentives : Before I am to explain the different methods in determining employees' remuneration and incentives, I would like to explain first what is meant by Remuneration and Incentives.

'Remuneration' is paid as a mark of reward for performing a job and rendering services; whereas 'Incentive' is a stimulus offering workers extra monetary and non-monetary benefits over and above the present salary or wages in exchange for increased productivity or over normal production. However, workers are paid for their services in preserving the business 'integrity' and 'continuity' in the form of Remuneration and Incentives.

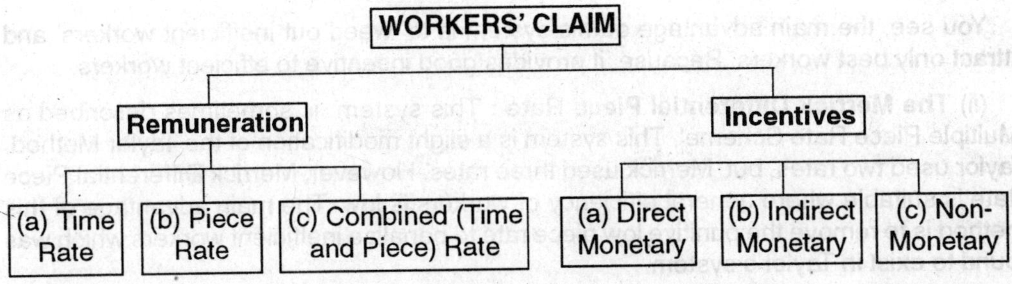

Now let me discuss the above chart step by step :

(A) Time Rate (Remuneration) : The formula under this method is :

Earnings = Agreed Time × Per Hour Rate

(B) Piece Rate (Remuneration) : Piece Rate can be studied under two heads :

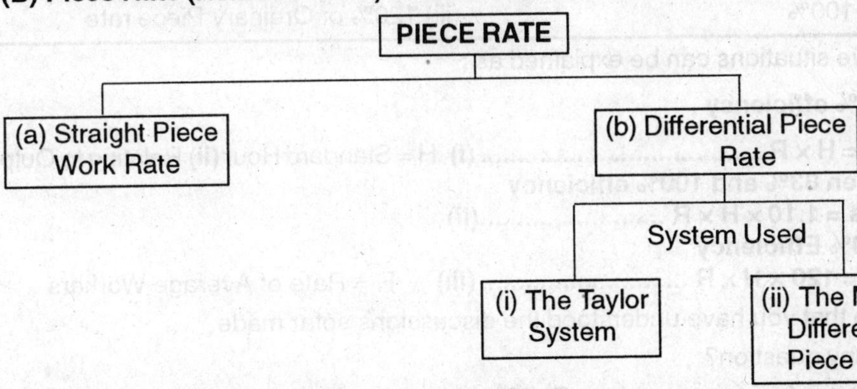

(a) **Straight Piece Work Rate :** Workers under this method are allowed a 'flat rate' pay 'per unit of output', irrespective of time taken. Here, rate of amount plays an important consideration since the worker's earning during a given period of time is dependent on the number of 'units produced at an agreed rate'.

The formula of this method is :

Earnings = Number of Unit × Rate Per Unit (i)

Earnings = Standard Hour of Produced Work × Rate Per Standard Hour (ii)

(b) **Differential Piece Work Rate :** With the rise in the level of output, the per standard hour or per piece rate of production, in this method, is bound to increase. This method takes into account any variable factors in the process of computation or remuneration.

Please note that there are two major systems in computing differential piece work-rate :

(i) **The Taylor System :** This method was introduced first in U.S.A. by F. W. Taylor. Here two types of piece are taken into account for computation. Rather, it is based on two rates and suggests different types of treatment for different types of situations:

Situation	Treatment
(i) For output below standard	(i) A low piece rate
(ii) For output above standard	(ii) A high piece rate

You see, the main advantage of this system is to 'weed out inefficient workers' and attract only best workers. Because, it provides good incentive to efficient workers.

(ii) **The Merrick Differential Piece Rate :** This system is sometimes described as 'Multiple Piece Rate Scheme'. This system is a slight modification of the Taylor Method. Taylor used two rates, but Merrick used three rates. However, Merrick Differential Piece Rate is suitable where general efficiency of workers is low. The main advantage of this method is to remove the punitive low piece rate to penalise inefficient workers which was found to exist in Taylor's system.

The rates of output percentage as suggested by Merrick are :

Situation	Treatment
(i) Up to 83%	(i) Ordinary Piece rate
(ii) 83% to 100%	(ii) 110% of Ordinary Piece rate
(iii) Over 100%	(iii) 120% of Ordinary Piece rate

The above situations can be explained as :

Up to 83% efficiency

Earning = H × R .... **(i)** H = Standard Hour **(ii)** Relating to Output

In between 83% and 100% efficiency

Earnings = 1.10 × H × R ....**(ii)**

Over 100% Efficiency

Earning = 120 × H × R .... **(iii)** R = Rate of Average Workers

I am sure that you have understood the discussions sofar made.

Is there any question?

□ "Sir, we are facing no problem. But Sir, I have one question to ask."

• What is that?

□ "Sir what is Combined Time and Piece Work Rate?"

• Well, please note that it is a mechanism or process to calculate or determine the remuneration of workers based on their normal as well as efficient performance followed by the measure of *time* and *piece* work rate system. Combination of time and piece work rate is found to exist in (i) Emerson's Efficiency System; and (ii) Gantt Task and Bonus Scheme.

Now let me explain both the methods :

(i) Emerson's Efficiency System : This is an American scheme. It combines 'ordinary fixed day wages with a differential piece rate.' This method is found useless when efficiency exceeds standard 100%. However, the salient features of this scheme are :

a. Workers, irrespective of level of efficiency, are assured for their wages for the time put in by them.
b. Ideal and fair task for the workers are established through proper detailed study of standard of performance and production details.
c. Maximum output and level of efficiency of workers are ensured.

Formula : Earnings = Worked Hours × Per Hour Rate + Bonus percentage × Worked Hour × Per Hour Rate.

(ii) Gantt Task and Bonus System : This system may be interpreted as 'Gantt Chart'. It is a system which compares the actual performance with target. Depending on careful observation of time and motion study, the standard of performance is determined. It has been stated earlier that labour efficiency is determined by comparing actual performance with that of standard. If the worker's efficiency is below 100%, only time wage is to be paid. A bonus of 20% is to be paid to the workers at 100% efficiency level. Where efficiency exceeds 100%, i.e. when workers complete a job before standard time, he is paid for the standard time plus a bonus of 20%.

Now I would like to discuss various incentives which are offered to workers.

(A) Direct Monetary Incentives : Direct monetary incentives indicate payment of bonus to the workers. There are various methods of bonus system :

a. Halsey Scheme
b. Weir Premium System
c. Rowan System
d. Barth Scheme
e. Accelerating Premium Bonus.

Well, now let me explain the above systems one by one :

a. Halsey Scheme : An American engineer, F. A. Halsey, introduced the scheme in 1891. That is why this scheme is known as Halsey Scheme. The salient feature of this scheme is that a fixed percentage bonus is paid to each worker for saving time.

The formula of this scheme is :

Earnings = Hours Worked × Per Hour Rate + 1/2 (Time Allowed – Hour Worked) × Per Hour Rate.

b. Weir Premium System : In about 1900, Weir Limited introduced the system. Since then it is known as Weir system. This is also known as 33.33 : 67.67 sharing plan. And it is similar to Halsey plan. Sometimes this system is termed Halsey-Weir Premium System.

c. Rowan System : As this scheme was introduced by David Rowan in the early part of the 20th century, it is known as Rowan system. This system differs from Halsey scheme in respect of time taken. In Halsey Scheme fixed percentage is being taken, whereas, in this method, a proportion is taken.

However, Rowan system can be explained under two methods :

i. Adjustment of per hour rate method =

$$\textbf{Earnings} = \text{Hours worked} \times \text{Per Hour Rate} + \left(\frac{\text{Time allowed} - \text{Hours Worked}}{\text{Time Allowed}}\right) \times \text{Per Hour Rate}$$

ii. Addition To Normal Time Wage :

$$\textbf{Earnings} = (\text{Hours worked} \times \text{Per Hour Rate}) + \left(\frac{\text{Time Allowed} - \text{Hours Worked}}{\text{Tme Allowed}}\right) \times \text{Hours Worked} \times \text{Per Hour Rate.}$$

d. Barth Scheme : This is suitable and applicable to beginners or apprentices.

The formula of this scheme is:

$$\textbf{Earnings} = \text{Per Hour Rate} \times \sqrt{\text{Standard Hour} \times \text{Hours worked}}$$

e. Accelerating Premium Bonus : Unlike Halsey and Rowan Method— where bonus is to be paid on fixed percentage and decreasing proportion—bonus under this scheme tends to increase at a 'faster and faster' rate. It provides greater incentives to workers. Maximisation of production is possible in this scheme with ease. Needless to mention that this method is quite unsuitable for machine operator who 'will tend to rush his work'.

Please note that there is no simple formula for such method. However, graph of $Y = 0.8X^2$ gives a general guidance of the scheme. Here X is the efficiency and Y is the wages.

% Efficiency	X =	100	120	140	160	180
	X =	1	1.2	1.4	1.6	1.8
	X^2 =	1	1.44	1.96	2.56	3.24
	$Y = 0.8X^2$ =	0.8	1.15	1.57	2.05	2.59

It should be noted in this context with care that percentage wage (%Y) against percentage efficiency (%X) can be obtained by multiplying X and Y by 100.

☐ "Sir, please give us some idea about Group Bonus Schemes".

● I am very pleased to see that you have taken much interest in the subject.

Well, note below details of Group Bonus Schemes.

Group Bonus Schemes

The schemes of remuneration discussed so far are applicable for determining incentives of individual worker. But a situation may arise where it is required to determine bonus of a group of workers instead of a single worker. Group Bonus Scheme is suitable or applicable where execution of works requires participation of a group of workers of different skill and it is difficult to measure the performance of individual labour. Under this scheme performance of a group of workers is measured and bonus is paid accordingly.

The Advantages of these schemes are that group bonus schemes :

Advantages of Group Bonus Schemes

(i) develop team spirit among workers.

(ii) help less efficient workers to learn from efficient workers.

(iii) help to increase output and quality of work.

The Disadvantages are :

Disadvantages of Group Bonus Schemes

(i) Bonus earned due to the work of efficient workers shared by all.

(ii) Inefficient workers may develop habit of evading responsibility.

(iii) It is difficult to develop method of sharing bonus among workers.

The following Group Bonus Schemes are generally used :

(i) Priestman's Production Bonus Scheme

(ii) Ruker Plan or Share of Production Plan

(iii) Scanlon Plan.

(iv) Towne Gain Sharing Plan

Let us discuss each of the schemes one by one :

(i) Priestman's Production Bonus Scheme

Under this scheme, standard output or point is fixed for a group of workers and then the actual output or point of the group is measured and compared with the standard. The group bonus is the percentage of actual output or point which is in excess of the standard output to the actual output. Let us give an example:

Suppose standard output is 30,000 units and actual output is 39,000 units. The group bonus under this scheme is $\frac{9,000}{30,000} \times 100 = 30\%$ of the wages of the group.

This plan is suitable where mass production of standard output is done.

(ii) Ruker Plan or Share of Production Plan

Under this method, value addition made to the product is ascertained first. It is the excess of realisable value of product or service over the cost of purchased material or service. Thereafter, the ratio of labour earning to value added is ascertained. Any reduction in the ratio qualifies for a bonus at a certain percentage of value added. For example, the ratio of labour cost to value added based on average past performance is 40. Suppose, in the next year, the ratio is reduced to 38%. The management decided to pay bonus of 1% on value added if there is any reduction in the ratio. Thus, workers will get bonus of 1% on value added.

(iii) Scanlon Plan

Under this method, average ratio of labour earnings to scales is taken for calculating group bonus of workers. For example :

Suppose average ratio of labour earnings to sales revenue is 25% and sales revenue and wages of labour in any particularly year are Rs. 30,00,000 and Rs. 6,60,000, respectively. Then the amount due to labour would be 25% of Rs. 30,00,000 i.e. Rs. 7,50,000. Therefore, the amount due to employees would be Rs. 90,000 (7,50,000 – 6,60,000). This amount of Rs. 90,000 would be the bonus of employees.

(iv) Towne Gain Sharing Plan

Under this method, standard labour cost is ascertained and if the actual labour cost is less than the standard cost, the workers will receive bonus at 50% of the saving in labour cost. The bonus is paid pro rata in addition to basic wages.

(B) Indirect Monetary Incentive

It includes:

(a) Profit Sharing.

(b) Co-partnership.

(a) Profit Sharing

Profit Sharing

In this scheme there is an agreement between the employer and employees for the payment of bonus to the employees at a rate as bargained by two parties. However, in India, the payment of bonus is governed by the Payment of Bonus Act, 1966. This method ensures increased productivity and reduced labour turnover.

Co-partnership

(b) Co-partnership. It is sometimes described as Co-ownership Method. Under this scheme, employees are granted loan for the purchase of company's share. After the purchase of the shares, the employees or workers become the owner of the business as has been found in case of 'shareholder rights'. By virtue of their ownership, they are entitled to get a part of the profit in the form of dividend. The main advantage of this method is to bring a sense of self-confidence in the mind of workers who will work better, assuming the company their own, for increased profitability and productivity. This method also reduces the labour turnover rate.

(C) Non-Monetary Incentives : Apparently it may be argued that what's the use of non-monetary incentives when it is not received in form of cash. An insight in the matter will reveal that these are needed for increased productivity and for maintaining 'labour integrity.' These include:

i. Health and Safety
ii. Sports
iii. Better working condition.

Now I would like to discuss about Labour Reporting. I think you have followed my earlier discussions. Is there any question?

□ "No Sir."

● Well, please note below the concept of Labour Reporting.

2. LABOUR REPORTING

Reporting is the basis of controlling activities. So, labour cost reporting is the basis of labour cost control. If management gets detailed information of different aspects of labour activities and costs, then it becomes easier on their part to have a comparison of 'actual' with 'standard' or budget. This will help them to find out ways and means for better improvement or to chalk out further plan(s) for better improvement of profitability and productivity. It is a fact that 'the varied causes and sources of variations ... call for a good reporting of labour performance. A variance in one department may be unavoidable because of failure elsewhere in the organisation. Corrective action may have to be initiated at a higher level of management than the departmental level because of the interlocking nature of interdepartmental activities ... Because of the many possible reasons for variations from standard time, the accurate reporting of them frequently is difficult but, nevertheless, important'[1]. However labour report includes – Training and Recruitment Cost, Level of Activity, Labour Efficiency, Labour Utilisation, Labour Turnover, Labour Absenteeism, Labour Accident, Labour Illness and Labour Wages etc.

Importance of Labour Reporting

Now I would like to discuss the different ratios of the above reports and components thereof for your ready reference :

DIFFERENT LABOUR RATIOS

	Ratios	Indication	Components	Periods 1	2	3	4
1.	Labour Efficiency	To compare the efficiency of different labours	Actual Production (in standard hours) / Actual worked hours	x	x	x	x
2.	Activity Level	To assess the level of performance	Actual Production (in standard hours) / Budgeted Hours	x	x	x	x
3.	Labour Utilisation	To assess the performance of Labour as well as Foreman and Works Manager.	Actual Hours / Available Hours	x	x	x	x
4.	Per Person Wage Earning	To assess the wage earning capacity of workers	Wage Earned to Date / No. of Workers to Date	x	x	x	x

[1] Heiser ***"Budgeting—Principles and Practice".***

You see, in the above way you can find out other ratios, viz. Absenteeism, Illness, and Accident Ratio.

☐ "Sir, Please show us".

● Well, please note :

$$\textbf{Absenteeism Ratio} = \frac{\text{No. of Absentees}}{\text{Average number employed}}$$

$$\textbf{Illness Ratio} = \frac{\text{Hours lost (arising from illness)}}{\text{Total man hour}}$$

$$\textbf{Accident Ratio} = \frac{\text{No. of accidents to date}}{\text{No. of weeks or months to date}}$$

I think you have followed all the discussions made earlier. Now I would like to take up for discussion the last part of labour cost control technique—i.e. Payroll Accounting.

Before that please confirm whether you have followed my earlier discussions or not?

☐ "We have followed, Sir".

● Now I would like to discuss Payroll Accounting.

3. PAYROLL ACCOUNTING

Vouching and verification of any system or method is the proper step towards control of accounting. Payroll Accounting may be defined as 'Labour Cost Control Accounting.'

Functions of Pay Roll Department

Because a major part of the revenue may be lost through payment of faked wages and manipulation in wage rate calculation. So, it is clear that payroll accounting is the 'key' to the actual labour cost control. It may be considered as a control device of other control devices of labour cost.

Important functions of payroll department are summed up as :

i. To determine and compute regular wages.
ii. To determine and compute overtime hours.
iii. To check and verify wage rates of different workers.
iv. To compute premiums and bonuses.
v. To compute payroll deduction and to calculate and enter net pay.
vi. To prepare payroll documents viz., payroll register, pay checks and payroll tax returns.
vii. To prepare necessary accounting data and send it for proper check to concerned persons.
viii. To supply employees payroll data.
ix. To report management regarding payroll accounting.

I think you have followed my discussions. Is there any question?

☐ "Sir, what documents are required by the Payroll Accounting Department for their work?"

● Well, these are the following documents :

Documents in Connection with Payroll

a. Employee's service records.

b. Clock cards and attendance registers.

c. Recorded in-out-time.

d. Performance records and notes from the respective heads of the sections or departments.

Well, in my next lecture I would like to take up for discussion ...

Yes, what do you want to say?

□ "Sir, please work out at least a few problems on Labour Cost Control".

● Well, I am working out. Please don't disturb.

Problem

From the following details calculate, for bonus entitlement, the Standard Time per Unit article with a provision for efficiency margin at 60% and 5% for defectives :

Particulars	For Batch of 400 Units (Mts.)	For A Trial Run of 180 Units (Mts.)
Reading drawings etc.	4.5	–
Obtaining tools	6.0	–
Tool fixing	16.5	–
Feeding material for 45 Nos.	–	3.5 (each time)
Setting time for jigs etc.	45.0	–
1st operation	–	145.0
2nd operation	–	112.0
Removing the setting	15.0	–
3rd operation	–	188.5

[I.C.W.A. India]

Solution

Details of Time Taken for 400 Units

Description of Respective Heads	Time Taken (minutes)
1. Reading drawing etc.	4.5
2. Obtaining tools	6.0
3. Tool fixing	16.5
4. Feeding materials	31.1 (A)
5. Setting time for jigs	45.0
6. 1st operation	322.2 (B)
7. 2nd operation	250.0 (C)
8. Removing the setting	15.0
9. 3rd operation	418.9 (D)
Total Time (in minutes) :	**1,109.2**

I think you have followed the above workings.

☐ "Sir, please explain items 4, 6, 7 and 9".

- (A) **Feeding Materials :** $\frac{3.5}{45} \times 400 = \frac{35}{450} \times 400 = 31.1$ Minutes

(B) **1st Operation :** $\frac{145 \times 400}{180} = 322.2$

(C) **2nd Operation :** $\frac{112.5 \times 400}{180} = 250.0$

(D) **3rd Opeation :** $\frac{188.5 \times 400}{180} = 418.9$

Please note, Defective allowance is 5%.

So, Output = 95% of 400 units = 380 units.

Efficiency Margin is at 60%.

So, Standard Time for 380 units = $\frac{1{,}109.2 \times 100}{6 \times 380} = 48.65$ minutes

Formula of Standard Time = $\frac{\textbf{Actual Time Taken}}{\textbf{Efficiency}}$

Problem

Ten men work as a group. When the weekly production of the group exceeds standard 200 pieces per hour, each man of the group is paid a bonus for the excess production in addition to his hourly rates. The bonus is computed thus :

The percentage of production in excess of the standard amount is found and half percentage is considered as the men's share. Each man in the group is paid as a bonus this percentage or wage of Rs. 6.66 per hour. There is no relationship between the individual workman's hourly rate and the bonus rate. The following is one week's record :

Day	Hours worked	Production
Monday	90	22,100
Tuesday	88	20,600
Wednesday	90	24,200
Thursday	84	20,100
Friday	88	20,400
Saturday	40	10,200
	480	1,17,600

(a) Compute the rate and amount of bonus for the week, and

(b) Compute the total of Mr. Joy who worked $41\frac{1}{2}$ hours and was paid Rs.4.75 per hour basic, and of Mr. Smile who worked $44\frac{1}{2}$ hours and was paid Rs.5.25 per hour basic. **[Adapted from I.C.W.A., London]**

Solution

(a) Total hours worked during the week = 480
Total production during the week = 1,17,600 units
Standard weekly production = 96,000 units
(200 units of pieces x 480)
Increase over standard of production = 21,600 units
Actual – Standard =
1,17,600 – 96,000 = 21,600 Units.

$$\% \text{ Increase in Production} = \frac{21{,}600 \times 100}{96{,}000} = 22\tfrac{1}{2}\%$$

As per information given in the problem, it is clear that percentage used in calculating bonus is half (1/2) of the percentage of the increased production.

So, percentage used in calculating bonus = $\frac{1}{2}$ of $22\frac{1}{2}\% = 11\frac{1}{4}\%$

Here bonus earned weekly for 480 hours is Rs.360.

☐ "How is it possible Sir !"

● Well, note the workings :

54 units × Rs.6.66 = Rs.360

You see, 54 units have been computed in the following manner :

$$11\tfrac{1}{4}\% \text{ of } 480 \text{ units} = \frac{45}{4} \times \frac{480}{100} = 54 \text{ units}$$

Now from the above information we can find out hourly rate of bonus for each worker.

Here hourly rate of bonus for each worker is $= \frac{\text{Rs. } 360}{480 \text{ units}} = \text{Re. } 0.75.$

(b) Total Pay of Mr. Joy

Basic hourly rate	Rs. 4.75
Hourly Bonus rate	Re. 0.75
Total rate of pay	Rs. 5.50

Hours worked during the week = $41\frac{1}{2} = \frac{83}{2}$

$$\text{Total Pay} = \frac{83 \times \text{Rs. } 5.50}{2}$$

$$= \frac{83}{2} \times \frac{11}{2} = \text{Rs. } 228.25.$$

Total pay of Mr. Smile

Basic Hourly rate	Rs. 5.25
Hourly Bonus rate	Re. 0.75
Total rate of pay	Rs. 6.00

Hours worked during the week = $44\frac{1}{2} = \frac{89}{2}$ hours

Total Pay = $\frac{89}{2} \times$ Rs. 6 = Rs. 267.

Problem

A manufacturer introduces new machinery into his factory with the result that production per worker is increased. The workers are paid by results, and it is agreed that for every 2% increase in average individual output an increase of 1% on the rate of wages will be paid. At the time the machinery is installed, the selling price of the product falls by $8^1/_3$%.

Show the net saving in production costs which would be required to offset the losses expected from reduced turnover and bonus paid to the workers.

	1st Period	2nd Period
Number of workers	175	125
Number of articles produced	1,68,000	1,40,000
Wages Paid	Rs. 33,600	
Total Sales	Rs. 75,600	

[Adapted from I.C.W.A. Final London]

Solution

	1st Period	2nd Period
Average Individual Output =	$\frac{1,68,000}{175}$	$\frac{1,40,000}{125}$
	= 960 units	1,120 units

Percentage increase of 1st Period = $\frac{160 \times 100}{960} = 16\frac{2}{3}\%$

Anyway, an increase of 1% in the rate for every 2% increase in output can be explained or interpreted in the following manner :

The increase rate is ($16\frac{2}{3}$ divided by 2) $8\frac{1}{3}\%$

Average wage per worker in the 1st Period = Rs. $\frac{33,600}{175}$ = Rs.192.

Thus Bonus Wages per worker in the 1st Period is = $8\frac{1}{3}\%$ of Rs.192 = Rs.16

You see, the basic wages paid in the Second Period is :

Rs. 192 × 125 = Rs.24,000

☐ "Sir, how is Rs.192 arrived at?"

• You see, in the absence of any information, the average rate of pay of the 1st Period has been taken into account.

Similarly, the figures for bonus paid in the First Period will be taken into account to calculate the bonus paid in the Second Period. Therefore, the Bonus paid in the Second Period is (Rs.16 × 125) Rs. 2,000.

Note very minutely that selling price per unit of article in the 1st Period is

$\frac{75,600}{1,68,000} = \frac{9}{20}$ = Re. 0.45

Selling price per article in the Second Period is $91\frac{2}{3}$% of Rs. $\frac{9}{20} = \frac{33}{80}$ = Re. 0.41

☐ "Sir, how $91\frac{2}{3}$% is calculated"?

● Please Note — $\left(100\% - 8\frac{1}{3}\%\right) = 91\frac{2}{3}\%$

Now you see, the total sales figure during the Second Period is $\left(\frac{33}{80} \times 1,40,000\right)$ = Rs. 57,750

Note that the losses in the Second Period arising out of lower sale is (Rs.75,600–57,750) Rs.17,850.

		Rs.
Thus total loss on account of Bonus paid	=	2,000
Lower Sale	=	17,850
		19,850

Saving on account of lower basic pay in the Second Period is (33,600–24,000) Rs.9,600.

It is clear that the net saving in production cost required to earn same level of profit as in the first period is

(Loss on account of bonus paid and low sales in second period) – (Saving on account of lower wage paid in the second period)

Rs.19,850 – 9,600 = Rs.10,250.

Problem

In a factory section, there are 80 workers and the average rate of wages per worker is Re.0.50 per hour. Standard working hours per week is 45; Standard performance is 6 units per hour.

During 4 weeks in February, wages paid for 40 workers were Re.0.50 per hour, for 15 workers Re.0.60 per hour, and 25 workers Re.0.40 per hour. The section did not work for 4 hours due to break-down of Machinery.

Work out the Labour Rate Variance for the section for the 4 weeks.

[C.A. Final]

Solution

Before working out this problem one important point should be noted that the workers could not work 4 hours. This is due to break-down of machinery. This should be taken into consideration while calculating Labour Rate Variance.

The Standard Wages for 80 workers for 4 weeks = Rs.7,200
(80 × Rs. 90)

		Rs.
One worker : 1 week of 45 hours @ Re.0.50	=	22.50
One worker : 4 week of 45 hours	=	90.00
Actual wages of 80 workers for 4 weeks	=	7,020
4 weeks of 45 hours each or 180 hours during the period :		
40 workers @ Re.0.50 per hour	=	3,600
15 workers @ Re.0.60 per hour	=	1,620
25 workers @ Re.0.40 per hour	=	1,800
		7,020

Standard – Actual = Variance

Rs.7,200 – Rs.7,020 = Rs.180

So, a Labour Rate Variance = Rs.180.

I think you have followed the working of the above problem. Is there any question? Well, in my next chapter I shall be discussing with you the concept of Overhead Cost Control and its Recovery.

Goodbye.

Problem

From the following data provided to you, find out Labour Turnover Rate by applying :

(a) Flux Method, (b) Replacement Method, (c) Separation Method.

Number of workers on the payroll :

At the beginning of the month 500, and at the end of the month 600.

During the month, 5 workers left, 20 persons were discharged and 75 workers were recruited. Of these, 10 workers were recruited in the vacancies of those leaving, while the rest were engaged in an expansion scheme. **[I.C.W.A. Inter]**

Solution

(a) **Flux Method :**

$$\text{Labour Turnover Rate} = \frac{\text{No. of separation + No. of replacements}}{\text{Average number of workers}}$$

$$\text{Average No. of Workers} = \frac{\text{No. at the beginning + No. at the end}}{2}$$

$$= \frac{500 + 600}{2} = 550$$

$$\text{Labour Turnover Rate} = \frac{25 + 75}{550} \times 100 = 18.18\%$$

(b) **Replacement Method :**

$$\text{Labour Turnover Rate} = \frac{\text{Number of workers replaced}}{\text{Average number of workers}} = \frac{10}{550} \times 100 = 1.818\%$$

(c) **Separation Method :**

$$\text{Labour Turnover Rate} = \frac{\text{Number of separations}}{\text{Average number of workers}} = \frac{25}{550} \times 100 = 4.54\%$$

Problem

The cost accountant of Tirupati Electronics Ltd. has computed labour turnover rates for the quarter ending 31st March 2006 as 10%, 5% and 3%, respectively, under 'Flux Method'. 'Replacement Method', and 'Separation Method'.

If the number of workers replaced during that quarter is 30, find out the number of (a) Workers recruited and joined, and (b) workers left and discharged.

[B.Com., Hons., Delhi Adapted]

Solution

We have to first find out the average (Av) number of workers on roll.

$$\text{Labour Turnover Rate under Replacement Method} = \frac{\text{No. of workers replaced}}{\text{Av. no. of workers on roll}} \times 100$$

$$\text{or, } 5\% = \frac{30}{\text{Av. no. of workers on roll}} \times 100$$

$$\text{or, Av. no. of workers on roll} = \frac{30}{5} \times 100 = 600$$

$$\text{Labour Turnover Rate under Separation Method} = \frac{\text{No. of workers separated}}{\text{Av. no. of workers on roll}} \times 100$$

$$\text{or, } 3\% = \frac{\text{No. of worker separated}}{600} \times 100$$

$$\text{or, No. of workers separated} = \frac{3 \times 600}{100} = 18$$

Labour Turnover Rate under Flux Method =

$$\frac{\text{No. of separation} + \text{No. recruited and joined}}{\text{Av. no. of workers}} \times 100$$

$$\text{or, } 10 = \frac{18 + \text{No. recruited and joined}}{600} \times 100$$

$$\text{or, } 18 + \text{No. recruited and joined} = \frac{600 \times 10}{100}$$

or, No. recruited and joined = 60 – 18 = 42

(a) Workers recruited and joined = 42

(b) Workers left and discharged = 18

Problem

The output of a worker A is 65 units in a 40-hour week. Guaranteed time rate is Rs.5.50 per hour. Ordinary piece rate is Rs.2.50 per unit.

Show the earning of worker A under Piece Rate and Time Rate systems.

[B.Com., Mysore, Adapted]

Solution

Time wages of A = 40 × Rs.5.50 = Rs.220

Piece wages of A = 65 × Rs.2.50 = Rs.162.50

Problem

Calculate the earnings of Barun, a worker, under Straight Piece Rate System and Taylor's Differential Piece Rate System from the following :

Normal rate per hour : Rs.2.50

Standard time per unit : 30 seconds

Differential to be applied :

80% of piece rate below standard and 120% of piece rate at or above standard. Worker Barun produces 850 units per day of 8 hours.

Solution

Normal rate per hour = Rs.2.50
Standard time per unit = 30 seconds.

$\therefore$ Standard output per hour = $\frac{60 \times 60}{30}$ = 120 units.

$\therefore$ Standard output for 8 hours = 120 × 8 = 960 units.
Actual Production = 850 units

$\therefore$ Earnings of Barun under Straight Piece Rate System = $\frac{\text{Rs.}2.50}{120} \times 850$ = Rs.17.71

Differential to be applied :

Below Standard : 80% of piece rate

Above Standard : 120% of piece rate.

Since actual production is 850 units below standard, piece rate will be applied.

$\therefore$ Earnings under Taylor's Differential Piece Rate System = $\frac{\text{Rs.}2.50}{120} \times 80\% \times 850$ = Rs.14.17

Problem

Calculate wages of workers A, B and C under Merrick Differential Piece Rate System from the following information :

Standard output : 10 units per hour.

Basic Wage rate : Rs.1.50 per hour.

In a day of 8 hours

A produces 40 units

B produces 75 units

C produces 90 units

Solution

Standard output per hour = 10 units

Wage rate per hour = Rs.1.50

$\therefore$ Piece rate = $\frac{1.50}{10}$ = Re 0.15

Standard output for 8 hours = 10 × 8 = 80 units

Calculation of percentage efficiency :

$A = \frac{40}{80} \times 100 = 50\%$

$B = \frac{75}{80} \times 100 = 93.75\%$

$C = \frac{90}{80} \times 100 = 112.5\%$

A will get ordinary piece rate (efficiency being less than 83%), B will get 110% of piece rate (efficiency between 83% to 100%), and C will get 120% of piece rate (efficiency being more than 100%).

$\therefore$ A will get : Re.0.15 × 40 = Rs.6.00

B will get : Re.0.15 × 110% × 75 = Rs.12.37

C will get : Re.0.15 × 120% × 90 = Rs.16.20

Problem

The guaranteed time rate is Rs.1.50 per hour. High piece rate is Re.0.25 per unit and the standard output is 12 units per hour.

In a day of 8 hours Amal produces 75 units, Bimal produces 96 units and Kamal 100 units.

Calculate the earnings of Amal, Bimal and Kamal (under Gantt's Task and Bonus Scheme).

Solution

Standard output in a day = 12 × 8 = 96 units.

Amal's output is below 96 units.

$\therefore$ Amal's earnings = 8 × Rs.1.50 = Rs.12.00

Bimal's output is equal to standard.

$\therefore$ Bimal's earning = 8 × Rs.1.50 × 120% = Rs.14.40.

Kamal's output is above standard

$\therefore$ Kamal's earning = 100 × Re.0.25 = Rs.25.

Problem

During the first week of January 2006, Mohan produced 400 articles. He received wages for a guaranteed 48 hours a week at Rs.5 per hour. The estimated time to produce one article is 12 minutes.

Calculate his wages according to (a) Halsey Premium Plan; and (b) Rowan Premium Plan. **[B.Com., Bangalore]**

Solution

Standard time to produce one article = 12 minutes.

Standard time to produce 400 articles = $\frac{12 \times 400}{60}$ = 80 hours

Standard time	=	80 hours
Actual time taken	=	48 "
Time saved	=	32 hours

Mohan's wages under

(a) **Halsey Premium Plan**		Rs.
Time wages : 48 hrs. × Rs.5 per hour	=	240
Add Bonus : 50% of 32 (time saved) × Rs.5	=	80
Total earnings	=	320
(b) **Rowan Premium Plan**		Rs.
Time Wages : 48 hrs × Rs.5.00 per hr.	=	240

Add Bonus : $\frac{\text{Time taken}}{\text{Time allowed}}$ × time saved x rate

$= \frac{48}{80} \times 32 \times \text{Rs.}5.00$	=	96
Total earnings	=	336

Problem

A worker's wage for a guaranteed 48 hour–week is Rs.8.00 per hour. The estimated time to produce one article is 35 minutes and, under the incentive scheme, time allowed is increased by 20%. During one week he manufactured 100 articles.

Calculate his total wages under the Rowan Bonus Plan.

[B.Com., Bangalore, Adapted]

Solution

Standard time to produce 1 article	=	35 minutes
Add: Additional time allowed under the Incentive Scheme (35 × 20%)	=	7 minutes
	=	42 minutes
∴ Time allowed to produce 100 articles $\left(\frac{42 \times 100}{60}\right)$ hrs.	=	70 hours
Less : Actual time taken	=	48 hours
Time saved	=	22 hours

∴ Total wages under Rowan Plan :

Time Wages (48 × Rs.8.00) = Rs. 384.00

Add: Bonus

$$(\text{time saved} \times \frac{\text{time taken}}{\text{time allowed}} \times \text{rate})\ (22 \times \frac{48}{70} \times \text{Rs.}8.00) = \text{Rs. } 120.69$$

Total earnings = Rs. 504.69

QUESTIONS

1. The Works Manager of a factory unit which produces 4 types of Standardised Automobile Parts feels that the cost figures as assembled and compared from month to month do not evaluate the production efficiency of the factory properly. The outputs for May and June 2006 (Product-wise) together with a split up of cost elements are :

	May 2006		June 2006		Cost per unit				
Product	Qty.	May '06 Value	Qty.	June '06 Value	Material	Labour Hour	Cost	Over-heads	Total
W	200	10,000	400	20,000	10	8	16	24	50
X	500	20,000	600	24,000	10	6	12	18	40
Y	700	31,500	300	13,500	25	4	8	12	45
Z	900	40,500	700	31,500	20	5	10	15	45
Total	2,300	1,02,000	2,000	89,000	–	–	–	–	–

[Adapted from C.A. India Final]

The hours of Labour (actuals) in both the months are the same.

Prepare a comparative statement of production for the two months highlighting labour efficiency with which the Works Manager is primarily concerned.

2. In an engineering works the standard time for a job is 16 hours and the basic wage is Rs.4 per hour. A bonus scheme is instituted so that the operator is to receive his normal rate for hours actually worked and for half the hours saved.

   Material for the job costs Rs.40 and the factory overhead is charged out on the basis of Rs.6 per labour hour.

   Calculate the wages and the effective rate of earnings per hour if the job is completed (i) in 12 hours; (ii) in 14 hours.

   Tabulate the total factory cost of the job on the same basis.

   [Adapted from I.C.W.A. London]

3. Describe Halsey Premium System mentioning its advantages and disadvantages.
4. What is Payroll Accounting? What are its functions?
5. Compare and contrast Time Rate and Piece Rate systems of remuneration.

6. From the following data calculate total monthly remuneration of three workers X, Y and Z :

   (i) Standard production per month per worker is 1,000 units.

   (ii) Actual production during the months : X–800 units, Y–700 units, Z–900 units.

   (iii) Piece work rate per unit of actual production – 15 paise.

   (iv) Dearness wages – Rs. 40 per month (fixed).

   (v) House rent allowance – Rs. 20 per month.

   (vi) Additional production bonus at the rate of Rs.5 for each percentage of actual production exceeding 75 percent actual production over standard.

[I.C.W.A. India]

8

OVERHEAD COST CONTROL

● Good morning to you all my dear students.

☐ "Good morning Sir."

● In my last chapter I dealt with the details of Labour Cost Control. In that context the following aspects were discussed—i.e. Real Concept of Labour Cost Control, Meaning of Productivity, Real Meaning of Labour Cost, Technique of Labour Cost Control. It is a fact that mere controlling of material cost and labour cost is not enough towards the achievement of productivity and profitability of an enterprise. Unless Overhead Costs are controlled, any attempt to control the other elements of production cost will go up in smoke. So in this chapter I would like to take up for discussion the details of overhead costs control. Before that, let us see what is the meaning of overhead cost.

Meaning of Overhead

Overhead Cost, according to the Terminology of Cost Accountancy, is 'the aggregate of indirect materials cost, indirect wages (indirect labour cost) and indirect expenses'. So it is clear that it includes all factory operating expenses other than direct material and direct labour. Please note that overhead cost is also known by other names such as Factory Burden, Manufacturing Expenses, and Indirect Factory Cost.

Components of Overhead Cost :

Components of Overhead Cost

a. **Indirect Material Cost**—It means those materials which are needed in the consumption of production process, they never form part of manufactured product.

b. **Indirect Labour**—It means the labour cost which are not needed for the direct production but are needed for the proper direction of direct labour. Examples of these types of cost include salary to Foreman, Works Manager, etc.

c. **Indirect Factory Costs**—It means the items of expenses which become 'must' with the start of business as well as production process. Examples of these types of costs include Rent, Insurance, Depreciation.

Span of Overhead Cost :

Span of Overhead Cost

i. Production Overhead.

ii. Administrative Overhead.

iii. Selling and Distribution Overhead.

It is a fact that the importance of the existence of direct cost of any factor of production cannot be realised unless variable cost of elements of production are accounted for. An insight into the concept of overhead cost will reveal that overhead costs is a 'must' whether production process operates or not. So, it is really very difficult to determine the appropriate amount of overhead to be included in the cost of a product or job. Well, before I am to explain about this aspect of the problem, let us see the nature of overhead and the purposes of overhead rates.

Nature of Overhead :

Nature of Overhead

a. Fixed Overhead.

b. Semi-fixed Overhead.

c. Variable Overhead.

You see, I have already explained in details about the nature of overhead at the outset of First Chapter of this Part. Now note below the purposes of overhead rates :

Purpose of Overhead Rates

i. For computing the required amount of production overhead for inclusion in manufacturing processes, job, lot and batches.

ii. For permitting the prompt computation on the completion of manufacture.

iii. For providing a basis for accounting entries. For example. Cost is to be transferred to work-in-progress Inventory Accounts from Manufacturing Overhead Cost Accounts.

iv. For estimating production overhead in advance of production which is applicable to a product, process job or batch.

Now regarding the problems as cited above I am to say that it arises out of two factors :

1. Mechanical.

2. Conceptual.

The mechanical problems result from the impossibility of tracing overhead to product cost with precision. And the conceptual problem arises out of the variable factors in desirability of normalising the overhead charge. So, the best way is to find out a rate which will justify equitable allocation.

However, let us see what experts in the line say about the problem of allocating the overhead cost in product cost.

'The task of charging such cost to the jobs they benefit is more difficult than is the case with direct materials and direct labour. The reacquisition for the direct material may be charged to the production order for which it was withdrawn, and the time of the direct labourer may be charged on his time ticket to the particular job or on which he worked. But the depreciation of the building or the salary of the factory superintendent or of the night watchman requires more involved handling before being charged against the production orders they benefit' —Boyd and Dickey (***Basic Accounting***).

'The problem is being made more and more actual everyday by the growing tendency to effect reductions in prime cost at the expense of increases in overhead cost. When a large, single-purpose machine tool is purchased with the objective of reducing machining time, the base used for applying overhead (whether it be direct labour cost or prime cost) is reduced, and the overhead costs of depreciation, power, and the like are increased. As a result, overhead rates are climbing rapidly, any errors contained in allocating overhead are also growing' —Franking (***N.A.A. Bulletin***, Vol. 32).

I think, you have followed the above discussion. Is there any question?

□ "Sir, what is Machine Hour Rate?"

● Wait please. I will explain every aspect of overhead cost. Before that I like to explain the different methods used in the process of overhead cost control.

Yes, yes, you, I mean you, what do you want to say? Please be frank.

□ "Sir, what are the different types of records used in computing overhead?"

● Well, the types of records are :

a. Invoices

b. Stores Requisition

c. Wages Analysis Book

d. Journal Entries.

All these concepts are self-explanatory. Besides, all these concepts were discussed in earlier chapter. Well, you wanted me to let you know about the concept of Machine Hour Rate. I am explaining the concept mentioned below. Yes, yes, what do you want to say?

□ "Sir, Is Machine Hour Rate relevant to the discussion of overhead?"

● Yes, Definitely, it is.

(a) **Standard Machine Hour Rate** is one of the three standards method used frequently to apply normal overhead in Standard Costing System.

□ "Sir, what are the other two methods? Besides, what is Standard Costing, Sir?"

Methods Used to Apply Normal Overhead

● You see, regarding Standard Costing System I am to say that it will be discussed in the subsequent chapter. Anyway, the other two methods which you wanted me to let you know are :

(b) **Standard Direct Labour Hour.**

(c) **Standard Direct Labour Rupee.**

Please note below the formulae used in computing the above three methods :

$$\textbf{Standard Percentage of Direct Labour Cost} = \frac{\text{Overhead at Normal Capacity} \times 100}{\text{Amount of Standard Direct Labour Cost}}$$

$$\textbf{Per Direct Labour Hour Standard Overhead} = \frac{\text{Overhead at Normal Capacity}}{\text{Standard Direct Labour Hour}}$$

From the above it is very easy to derive a formula for Per Direct Labour Hour Standard Rate which is

$$\frac{\text{Normal Direct Overheads}}{\text{Standard Direct Labour Hour}} + \frac{\text{Allocated General Overheads}}{\text{Standard Direct Labour Hour}}$$

$$\textbf{Per Machine Hour Standard Overhead} = \frac{\text{Overhead at Normal Capacity}}{\text{Standard Machine Hour}}$$

I think you have followed the above discussions. Now let me discuss about Machine Hour Rate.

Computation of Machine Hour Rate is very important. Since, it helps in allocating overhead to different jobs or process. It is done by multiplying the machine hour rate by number of hours, of course machine hours, involved in a particular operation or production. Machine Hour Rate can be computed by drawing a comparison between anticipated amount of overhead cost and anticipated machine hours. This can be stated as :

$$\textbf{Machine Hour Rate Ratio} = \frac{\text{Cost of Anticipated Overhead}}{\text{Expected Machine Hours}}$$

Now I would like to explain about the different types of Machine Hour Rates which are used in actual practice :

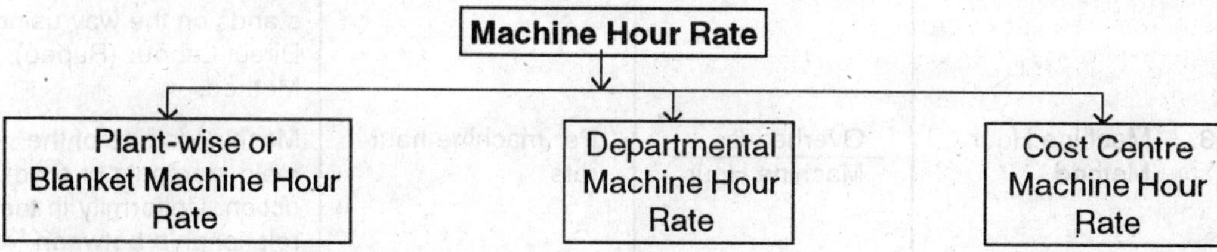

Regarding Plant-wise Machine Hour Rate it can be stated that this method is useful to those areas where only one type of machinery is used.

Take, for an example, total estimated machine hours, say, in a weaving business is 15,000 hours and the anticipated overhead cost is, say, Rs. 33,000.

Here Machine Hour Rate can be calculated as :

$$\textbf{Machine Hour Rate} = \frac{\text{Cost of Anticipated Overhead} = \text{Rs. } 33{,}000}{\text{Expected Machine Hours} = 15{,}000} = \text{Rs. } 2.20$$

This indicates that for every hour of weaving, Rs. 2.20 overhead cost is to be added. Now if it is given that Job 20 requires 30 minutes of weaving, the overhead to be added to the said job is Rs. 1.10 (2.20×30 minutes).

You see, the usefulness of Department Cost Hour Rate and Cost Centre Machine Hour Rate has been explained in the works of Professor March. Professor March, in his book '***Cost Accounting***', explained the Machine Hour Rate as : 'In a department where the machine overhead is a large factor, the use of a departmental rate per machine hour is sometimes recommended. Only in unusual circumstances, however, is the machine hour a suitable base for a departmental burden rate. It may be used satisfactorily where all the work points in a department are similar machines, but then the department is a machine (cost) centre and the departmental rate would be in effect a machine rate'.

With regard to Cost Centre Machine Hour Rate, Prof. March explained that 'a burden centre or cost centre is a segment of a plant, or in some cases an entire plant, which is treated as a functional unit for the purpose of applying process overhead. It may be a single work point smaller than a department, a processing department, or an entire plant. A burden rate is computed for each burden centre to use in applying overhead to work processed in that centre'.

I think, the above discussions are clear to you. Before ending this chapter I would like to give you a few formulas of overhead and their uses. Please note that the ideas of all these formulas have been derived from the writing of Professor A. B. Carson of California University and Professor Donald D. Kennedy of University of New York.

Please jot down these formulas :

** OVERHEAD FORMULAE AND THEIR USES

Method	Components	Indication	Usefulness
1. Direct Labour Rupee Method	$\frac{\text{Overheads}}{\text{Direct Labour (Rupees)}}$	% of Overhead per direct Labour (Rupee)	Labour is the important productive element, no other material pays rate variance.
2. Direct Labour Hour Method	$\frac{\text{Overheads}}{\text{Direct Labour Hour}}$	Per direct Labour Hour rate	Labour is the main productive element; differences in different pay rates stands on the way using Direct Labour (Rupee) Method.
3. Machine Hour Method	$\frac{\text{Overheads}}{\text{Machine Hour}}$	Per machine hour rate	Machine is one of the main elements of production. Uniformity in the relationship between man-time and machine-time is rarely found.
4. Product Unit Method	$\frac{\text{Overheads}}{\text{Product Units}}$	Per unit overhead cost of Product	One product may be mass-produced or a few products may be produced of great uniformity which may be related by a point of system or by weight.
5. Cost of Material Method or Material Cost Method	$\frac{\text{Overheads}}{\text{Direct Material}}$	Proportion of overhead per direct material (Rupee)	It is very useful to apply material burden. It can be used for special processing of material. Besides, it can be applied profitably in special departments.
6. Prime Cost Method and Direct Labour Cost	$\frac{\text{Overheads}}{\text{Direct Material and Direct Labour cost}}$	Proportion of overhead per Rupee of Prime cost	It is used in special situations only. Here material and labour is combined and follow uniform pattern.
7. Market Value Method	$\frac{\text{Market Value of Product X}}{\text{Total Market value of all products.}}$	Proportion of overhead apportioned to Product X	Used for joint product cost.

Method	Components	Indication	Usefulness
8. Supplementary Rate Method	Actual Overheads minus (–) Absorbed Overheads / Rupees, Hours, Units	Supplementary rate or rates	It is used to ascertain actual overhead cost for product in the cases where predetermined rate is used. This assists in modifying costs during a period without affecing the main rates.
9. Moving Average Rate Method	Average Monthly Overhead Cost / Estimated Direct Labour Hrs. or Rupees or Machine Hour	Monthly per productive factor rate	It is used to remove fluctuation in month-to-month cost.
10. Blanket Rate Method	Total Overhead Cost for Plant / Total Units or Hours Rupee	For Blanket Rate	This method is used in the following situations : (a) Where one product is made in continous process. (b) Where identical products are made involving equal amount of time and energy at each stage.
11. Departmental Rate Method	Direct departmental Overheads plus (+) Apportioned Overhead / Hours, Rupees, Units for Department	Department Rate	This method is used in the following situations where — (a) Difference in Processing occur, and (b) Production of diversified products.
12. Departmental Hourly Cost Rate Method	Departmental Direct Labour Cost plus (+) Departmental Overhead / Hours, Rupees or Units for Department	Hourly Cost Rate of the Department	This method is used in the following situations where (a) Direct labour as separate element of cost is not separated, and (b) Departmental rate is desired to be calculated with ease.
13. Cost Centre Rate Method	Direct Overheads for Cost Centre plus (+) Apportioned Overheads / Hours, Rupees or Units for Cost Centre	Cost centre rate	This method can be used profitably in the case where departmental rates are inaccurate.
14. Cost Centre Hourly Cost Rate Method	Direct Labour Cost for Cost Centre plus (+) Cost Centre Overhead, Direct and Apportioned / Hours, Rupees, or	Cost centre hourly rate	This method is used in the following situations : (a) When the necessity of having cost centre rate is felt. (b) When ease of calcul-

Method	Components	Indication	Usefulness
			ating unit cost is desired. (c) When direct labour as a separate element of cost is less distinct.
15. Normal Rate Method	Budgeted Overhead at Normal Capacity / Normal Production, in Hours, Rupees, or Units	Normal Rate	This method is applied in the following situations : (a) When it is wished to eliminate fixed charges applicable to excess capacity from inventory value and unit cost. (b) When leveling of overhead unit cost over certain period is desired.
16. Standard Production Hour Method	Normal Overhead, direct and apportioned + (plus) Standard Direct Labour Rupees / Standard Production Hour	Per productive hour standard rate	It may be computed for practical capacity. The main advantage of this method is that it combines cost centre hourly rates and standard rate.
17. Overhead Rates by Productive Factor Method	Overhead relating to Productive Factor (materials labour and other facilities) / Hours, Rupees, Units	To find out productive factor rate	This method can be applied in the following situations : (a) Where products or jobs differ as to comparative importance in material manufacture, labour, machine and facilities. (b) Where it is difficult to handle the above differences plant-wise or departmental labour related to overhead rate.
18. Service Department Overhead Rate Method	Department Direct Overhead +(plus) Apportioned Overhead / Hours, Rupees or Units	To find out service department's overhead rate	This method can be used where the bases of overhead rate of the producing department are not appropriate for a particular function.
19. Direct Cost Rate Method	Variable Overhead / Hours, Rupees or Units	To find out the rate of direct costing	This method can be applied where the costs of the products show marginal cost or out-of-pocket costs.
20. Practical Capacity Rate Method	Budgeted Overhead at Practical Capacity / Practical Capacity in Hours, Rupees	To find out practical capacity rate	This method can be used in the cases where it is expected that unit costs or inventories should be

Method	Components	Indication	Usefulness
	or Units		kept free from the charges not used in production. This means that all fixed charges or expenses representing capacity which is not used in production should be eliminated from unit cost and inventory.
21. Overhead Rate Method	Fixed Overhead/ and Variable / Hours, Rupees or Units	To find out fixed overhead rate & variable overhead rate	For distributing overhead to using department.
22. Supplementary Rate Method	Actual Overhead – Absorbed Overhead / Hours, Rupees or Units	To find out Supplementary Rate	This method is used for the following purposes : (a) For obtaining the actual overhead cost of the products where a predetermined rate was used. (b) for modifying cost without charging the main rate. (c) For correcting the minor miscalculated rate for overhead.
23. Standard Method	Standard Overhead Rate for Practical Capacity / Hours, Rupees or Unit for Standard Overhead at Normal Capacity	To find out Standard Overhead Rate	This method may be applied in the situation where Standard Costing Method is used.

I think, you have followed the above discussions. Is there any question? Please tell me frankly.

☐ "Sir, please work out a few practical problems on overhead cost control."

☐ "Sir, What is recovery of Overhead Cost?"

Recovery of Overheads

● You see, we have seen earlier that all expenses of service department are transferred to production departments. And it becomes a great concern to cost department as to how to recover the overhead cost. Like material and labour, the cost of overhead expenses is to be charged to product or job. So, overhead cost control means the recovery of overhead expenses from products or jobs.

☐ "Sir, what is Recovery?"

Overhead Absorption

Well, recovery means charging or applying any expenses to job or jobs. Accordingly, overhead cost recovery means the application or charging overhead expenses to jobs or products in logical and equitable manner. Please note that some writers describe the term 'overhead recovery' as 'overhead absorption'. It means overhead allotment to the cost of unit. However, the Terminology of Cost Accountancy defines overhead absorption as follows: Overhead absorption is usually achieved by the use of one or a combination of overhead rates. Such rates are often referred to as 'recovery' rates. The use of this term is somewhat confusing since it may be understood to imply ultimate recovery in selling price which is not necessarily achieved and for this reason 'absorption is recommended'.

Now I would like to discuss about the important bases of overhead absorption. Well, just notice the following important bases :

Overhead Bases

a. Direct Material Cost
b. Direct Wages
c. Direct Labour Hour
d. Machine Hour
e. Product Unit
f. Volume of Physical Output
g. Prime Cost.

It should be noted in this context that, out of the above six important bases of overhead absorption, the second one, i.e. Direct Wages basis, is most widely used. This is for its simplicity and easy computation. The product unit method may be recommended for its simplicity. And this is applied when one or more like products are manufactured and when one unit is actual representative of other. Direct Labour Hour and Machine Hour basis is to be given on time factor.

Whether labour hour rate is to be followed or not depends on working pattern. When manual labour is more than machine work, labour hour rate is to be followed. When machine work is more than the manual labour, the machine hour rate is to be followed. In case where both machine and manual labour are in existence, it is recommended that both rates are to be used.

Volume of physical output, prime cost and direct material as bases of overhead absorption rate is complicated. However, different formulas of above items as the base of overhead absorption rate are given below although I have already given you a broad idea of the computation of different rates in the middle of this chapter.

a. **In case of Direct Material Cost**

The formula of Predetermined Manufacturing Overhead Absorption Rate Per Unit of Material is :

$$\frac{\text{Predetermined total Manufacturing Overhead for the period or year}}{\text{Predetermined total Direct Material Cost for the period or year}}$$

b. **In case of Direct Wages**

The formula of Predetermined Overhead Absorption Rate per Direct Wage is :

$$\frac{\text{Predetermined total Manufacturing Overhead for a year or period}}{\text{Predetermined total Direct Wage for a year or period}}$$

c. **In case of Direct Labour Hour**

The formula of Predetermined Manufacturing Overhead Absorption Rate per Labour Hour is :

$$\frac{\text{Predetermined total Manufacturing Overhead for a year or period}}{\text{Predetermined total Direct Labour Hour for a period}}$$

d. **In case of Machine Hour**

The formula of Predetermined Manufacturing Overhead Absorption Rate per Machine Hour is :

$$\frac{\text{Predetermined total Manufacturing Overhead for a period or Year}}{\text{Predetermined total Machine Hour for a period or year}}$$

e. **In case of Product Unit**

The formula of Predetermined Manufacturing Overhead Absorption Rate per Unit is:

$$\frac{\text{Predetermined total Manufacturing Overhead for a period or year}}{\text{Predetermined total number of units for a period or year}}$$

f. **In case of Volume of Physical Output**

The formula of Predetermined Manufacturing Overhead Absorption Rate per Unit of quantity output is :

$$\frac{\text{Predetermined total Manufacturing Overhead for a period or year}}{\text{Predetermined total Quantity of Output for a period or year}}$$

g. **In case of Prime Cost**

The formula of Predetermined Manufacturing Overhead Absorption Rate as a proportion of Prime Cost is :

$$\frac{\text{Predetermined total Manufacturing Overhead for a period}}{\text{Predetermined total Prime Cost for a period}}$$

Now what do you feel about these ?

□ "Fine, Sir".

□ "Very interesting indeed, Sir. This simply excites our curiosity.

□ Please Sir, work out a few problems on the topic."

● Thank you for your interest. I am really very glad to see that you have grasped the subject. I am working out a few problems. Please note below.

□ "Excuse me, Sir."

● Yes ?

□ "Sir, you have not given us any theoretical concept about the basis of distribution of items of expenditure, viz., Rent, Rates and Taxes, Depreciation, Insurance of Stock."

● Do you know the bases used for distribution of production overhead ?

□ "Yes, Sir".

Basis of Apportionment of Expenditures

● You see, it is a nominal matter which will be observed while solving different problems in the following chapter. However, please note the basis of distribution :

Nature of Expenditures	Basis of Apportionment or Distribution
(A) Rent, Rates, Taxes, Insurance and Depreciation of Building	(A) On the basis of Area Occupied
(B) Insurance of Stock and Fire Insurance.	(B) On the basis of Stock Value or Value of Stock
(C) Insurance, Repair, Depreciation of Plant and Machinery	(C) On the basis of Capital value. For example value of plant
(D) Power	(D) On the basis of Horse Power (HP) of machines
(E) Electricity, i.e., Light etc.	(E) On the basis of light-points
(F) Employer's Liability Insurance	(F) On the basis of Number of Employees
(G) Supervision	(G) On the basis of Wages of Employees

Do you follow?

□ "Yes Sir."

● Are there any questions?

□ "Sir, you have not thrown any light on the concept of under- or, over-absorbed overhead and the mechanism of how they are disposed of".

Over- and Under-Absorption

● It is an omission. However, you see, it is very natural that there may be some differences between the amount of Absorbed Overhead and Incurred Overhead when the use of predetermined rate is found for overhead absorption purpose. You see, the predetermined rates which are applied to manufactured product during the periods or years in question were set up before the start of actual production. And here lies the difference.

Over-absorption and under-absorption can be reflected from the following observations:

Amount Absorbed or Recovered > Amount Incurred = Over-Absorption.

Amount Absorbed or Recovered < Amount Incurred = Under-Absorption.

I think you have followed. Please note that Over- or Under-Absorption may be disposed of as per below-mentioned set practices :

i. To write-off to Costing Profit and Loss Account.

ii. To carry forward to next year.

iii. To use supplementary rate.

I think you are satisfied now.

□ "Yes Sir."

● Now let me work out a few problems.

Problem

The New Enterprise Ltd. has three production departments A, B, C and two service departments D and E. Following figures are extracted from the records of the company :

	Rs.
Rent and Rates	5,000
General Lighting	600
Indirect wages	1,500
Power	1,500
Depreciation of Machinery	10,000
Sundries	10,000

The following further details are available :

	Total	A	B	C	D	E
Floor space (sq.ft.)	10,000	2,000	2,500	3,000	2,000	500
Light points	60	10	15	20	10	5
Direct wages (Rs.)	10,000	3,000	2,000	3,000	1,500	500
H. P. Machines	150	60	30	50	10	—
Value of Machinery	2,50,000	60,000	80,000	1,00,000	5,000	5,000
Working Hours	—	6,226	4,028	4,066	—	—

The expenses of D and E are allocated as :

	A	B	C	D	E
D :	20%	30%	40%	—	10%
E :	40%	20%	30%	10%	—

What is the total cost of an article if its raw material cost is Rs. 50, labour cost Rs. 30 and it passes through departments A, B and C for 4, 5 and 3 hours, respectively?

[I.C.W.A.I., Adapted]

Solution

OVERHEAD ANALYSIS AND DISTRIBUTION

Overhead Expenses	Basis of Apportionment	Total	Production Depts. A	Production Depts. B	Production Depts. C	Service Depts. D	Service Depts. E
		Rs.	Rs.	Rs.	Rs.	Rs.	Rs.
Direct wages	Actual	2,000	—	—	—	1,500	500
Rent and Rates	Floor space Re. 0.50 per sq. ft.	5,000	1,000	1,250	1,500	1,000	250
General Lighting	No. of points × Rs. 10 per pt.	600	100	150	200	100	50

Overhead Expenses	Basis of Apportionment	Total	Production Depts. A	Production Depts. B	Production Depts. C	Service Depts. D	Service Depts. E
		Rs.	Rs.	Rs.	Rs.	Rs.	Rs.
Indirect Wages	15% of Direct wages	1,500	450	300	450	225	75
Power	H. P. — Rs. 10 per H. P.	1,500	600	300	500	100	—
Depreciation	Machine valuation 4% of Machine valuation	10,000	2,400	3,200	4,000	200	200
Sundries	Direct wages — 100% of direct wages	10,000	3,000	2,000	3,000	1,500	500
Total Departmental Overhead		30,600	7,550	7,200	9,650	4,625	1,575
Overhead Distribution :							
Service Dept.	D		925	1,387	1,850	(4625)	463
Service Dept.	E		815	408	611	204	(2038)
Service Dept.	D		41	61	82	(204)	20
Service Dept.	E		8	4	6	2	(20)
Service Dept.	D		—	1	1	(2)	(—)
Total (X)			**9,339**	**9,061**	**12,200**		
			A Rs.	B Rs.	C Rs.		
Working hours **(as per problem) (Y)**			6,226	4,028	4,066		
Rate per hour $\left(\frac{X}{Y}\right)$			1.50	2.25	3.00		

Statement of Total Cost :

	Rs.
Direct Materials	50.00
Direct Labour (wages)	30.00
Prime Cost	80.00
Overhead	26.25
Total Cost	106.25

☐ "Sir, how has the figures for overhead, Rs. 26.25, been arrived at?"

- Please note the workings :

	Rs.
Department A 4 hours @ 1.50 =	6.00
Department B 5 hours @ 2.25 =	11.25
Department C 3 hours @ 3.00 =	9.00
	26.25

I think you have followed the above computation. Now let me work out a few more problems. Take down the following problems:

Problem

In a light engineering factory, the following particulars have been collected for the 3 monthly period ended 31st Dec. 2005.

Compute the departmental overhead rates for each of the production departments assuming that overheads are recovered as a percentage of direct wage.

Particulars	Production Departments			Service Departments	
	A	B	C	D	E
Direct Wages (Rs.)	2,000	3,000	4,000	1,000	2,000
Direct Materials (Rs.)	1,000	2,000	2,000	1,500	1,500
Staff Nos.	100	150	150	50	50
Electricity Kwh	4,000	3,000	2,000	1,000	1,000
Light Point Nos.	10	16	4	6	4
Assets Value Rs.	60,000	40,000	30,000	10,000	10,000
Area Occupied (Sq. Yds)	150	250	50	50	50

The expenses for the period were :

	Rs.
Motive Power	550
Lighting Power	100
Stores Overheads	400
Amenities to Staff	1,500
Depreciation	15,000
Repairs and Maintenance	3,000
General Overheads	6,000
Rent and Taxes	275

Apportion the expenses of Service Department E proportionate to Direct Wages and that of Service Department D in the ratio 5 : 3 : 2 to Departments A, B and C, respectively.

[I.C.W.A.I., Adapted]

Solution

Computation of Overhead Rates for the last quarter ended 31.12. 2005

Overhead Expense Items	Basis of Recovery	Total	Production Depts. A	B	C	Service Depts. D	E
		Rs.	Rs.	Rs.	Rs.	Rs.	Rs.
Direct Wages	Actual	3,000	—	—	—	1,000	2,000
Direct Materials	Actual	3,000	—	—	—	1,500	1,500
Motive Power	Elect. Kwh.	550	200	150	100	50	50
Light Power	Light Points	100	25	40	10	15	10
Stores Overheads	Direct Material	400	50	100	100	75	75
Amenities	Staff nos.	1,500	300	450	450	150	150
Depreciation	Assets Value	15,000	6,000	4,000	3,000	1,000	1,000
Repairs etc.	Assets Value	3,000	1,200	800	600	200	200
General Overhead	Direct Wages	6,000	1,000	1,500	2,000	500	1,000
Rent and Taxes	Area Occupied	275	75	125	25	25	25
Total		**32,825**	**8,850**	**7,165**	**6,285**	**4,515**	**6,010**
Apportionment E			1,202	1,803	2,404	601	(6,010)
			10,052	8,968	8,689	5,116	Nil
Apportionment D			2,558	1,534.8	1,023.2	(5,116)	—
Total			12,610	10,502.8	9,712.2	—	—
Direct Wages			2,000	3,000	4,000		
Overhead Rate (Per Rupee of Direct Wages)			6.305	3.5	2.428		

Problem

X Y Z and Co. Ltd. manufactures a number of sizes of product P. They have grouped various sizes into 4 main groups called A, B, C & D groups. If the company manufactures only one group in the factory, the monthly production can be either Nos. 5,000 of A group, or Nos. 10,000 of B group, or Nos. 15,000 of C group, or Nos. 30,000 of D group.

From the following information you are required to find out the profit/loss made on each group of product showing Prime cost, Works Cost and Total Cost :

Production Group	A	B	C	D
Actual Production during March 2006 :	675	1,800	4,050	9,450
Direct Labour Cost Rs.	3,000	5,500	7,500	21,000
Direct Material Cost Rs.	3,500	6,500	9,000	27,500
Sales Price Per Unit Rs.	30	20	15	12

Overhead expenses for the month of March 2006, is Rs. 81,000. Selling and Distribution Cost is to be calculated @ 10% on Works Cost.

Overhead Expenses are to be allocated to each product on the basis of number of units produced. **[I.C.W.A.I., Adapted]**

Solution

Please note that, first of all, overhead for each unit A, B, C and D is to be calculated. Production of A, B, C and D are to be made in the following ratios:

I Unit of A = 2 Units of B

= 3 Units of C

= 6 Units of D

Here overhead charges would be in the inverse ratio. This means, ratio of capacity used. Hence Overhead Ratios are :

For every Re. 1 for A, Re. $\frac{1}{2}$ for B

For every Re. 1 for A, Re. $\frac{1}{3}$ for C

For every Re. 1 for A, Re. $\frac{1}{6}$ for D

As the total overhead for the month of March 2006 is Rs. 81,000

Overhead for Unit of A = Rs. 18.00

Overhead for Unit of B = Rs. 9.00

Overhead for Unit of C = Rs. 6.00

Overhead for Unit of D = Rs. 3.00

☐ "Sir, how figure for A, Rs. 18.00, calculated?"

● Well, please note below the workings :

$$\frac{\text{Rs. } 81{,}000}{675 + (1{,}800 \times 1/2) + (4{,}050 \times 1/3) + (9{,}450 \times 1/6)}$$

$$\frac{\text{Rs. } 81{,}000}{\text{Rs. } 4{,}500} = \text{Rs. } 18.00$$

WORKINGS OF PROFIT/LOSS

Group of Products	A	B	C	D
	Rs.	Rs.	Rs.	Rs.
Direct Material	3,500	6,500	9,000	27,500
Direct Labour Wages	3,000	5,500	7,500	21,000
Prime Cost	6,500	12,000	16,500	48,500
Overheads (as per unit rate computed earlier)	12,150	16,200	24,300	28,350
Works Cost	18,650	28,200	40,800	76,850
Selling and Distribution Expenses or Cost @ 10% on Work Cost.	1,865	2,820	4,080	7,685
	20,515	31,020	44,880	84,535
Profit (Loss)	(265)	4,980	15,870	28,865
Sales	20,250	36,000	60,750	1,13,400

Problem

A company makes a product in a standard model whose ratio of direct materials cost to direct wage was 7 to 3. In 2005, total prime costs were Rs. 1,00,000 and no direct expense was incurred. The company uses a direct wages percentage rate of overhead absorption; for 2005 this was 230% but there was an under–absorption of overhead of Rs. 6,000 even though total direct wages were as budgeted. The profit margin on total costs incurred was 20%.

For 2006, the company proposes to take up a contract for a different model which will require more processing per unit than the standard model, and will have a direct material cost to direct wages ratio of 3 to 7.

For 2006, the company expects the total prime cost to remain the same as in 2005, though 20% of the total will relate to the new contract model. It also expects to incur an additional Rs. 8,600 of overhead above the 2005 actual total overhead incurred. It cannot,however, alter the selling price of the standard model.

The contract customer is prepared to accept a price which covers prime cost, overhead at the prime cost percentage rate, that would have applied for 2005, and a 20% profit margin on total costs.

You are required to :

(a) Calculate the total price that would be payable for the contract models for 2006 if the company were to accept the contract :

(i) On the customer, term;

(ii) On its present method of overhead absorption calculated on the basis of the 2006 budgeted figures, plus a 20% margin on total costs.

(b) Show Budgeted Trading and Profit and Loss Statements for the company for 2006 for each of the situations in (a) (i) and (a) (ii) above.

[Adapted from I.C.W.A. Final, London]

Solution

For 2005 :		
Direct Mateials	Rs. 70,000	
Direct Wages	Rs. 30,000	Rs. 1,00,000
Overhead absorbed on the basis of 230% Direct Wages		69,000
		1,69,000
Overhead Absorbed		6,000
Total		1,75,000
Profit 20% of total costs (16.67% of sales)		35,000
Sales Value		Rs. 2,10,000

a.

(i) Customer's Term for 2006

Particulars	Standard Model	Contract Model	Total
	Rs.	Rs.	Rs.
Prime Cost	80,000	20,000	1,00,000
Overhead			
(Contract model 75% of prime cost)	68,600	15,000	83,600
	1,48,600	35,000	1,83,600
Profit Margin	19,400	7,000	26,400
Sales Value	1,68,000	42,000	2,10,000
% Profit to Sales	11.5%	16.7%	12.6%

The price to be paid for the contract model would be Rs. 42,000.

(ii) On the present method

Direct Material	56,000	6,000	62,000
Direct Wages	24,000	14,000	38,000
Prime Cost	80,000	20,000	1,00,000
Overhead absorption to recover Rs. 83,600, 220% of Direct Wages	52,800	30,800	83,600
	1,32,800	50,800	1,83,600
Profit Margin (Contract model)	35,200	10,160	45,360
20% on Total Costs	1,68,000	60,960	2,28,960
% Profit to Sales	21%	16.4%	19.8%

b. Budgeted Profit and Loss Statement for the year 2006

Particulars	Situation (a)	Situation (b)
Sales of Standard Model	1,68,000	1,68,000
Sales of Contract Model	42,000	60,960
	2,10,000	2,28,960
Prime Costs	1,00,000	1,00,000
Budgeted Overhead	83,600	83,600
	1,83,600	1,83,600
Profit	26,400	45,360
% Profit to Sales	12.6%	19.8%

Problem

A B C and Co. Ltd. is distributing their estimated yearly overhead expenses to departments and recover each department overhead expenses on various jobs on the basis of the direct labour hour method. Figures are estimated on the basis of the normal capacity of the factory.

Following are the estimates for the year 2005 :

Department X :

Estimated overhead expenses.	Rs. 48,000
Estimated direct labour hour	Hrs. 12,000

At the end of June 2005, they found the actual position as :

Actual overhead expenses	Rs. 28,000
Actual direct labour hours	Hrs. 8,400

The department was required to work at its full capacity and overtime due to pressure of work in the factory. The actual overhead expenses and direct labour hours for the excess working hours over the normal capacity are Rs. 4,000 and Hrs. 2,000, respectively.

Calculate actual over-absorbed overhead expenses for the normal capacity working and the actual working from January 2005 to June 2005. Explain how you will treat the over-absorbed overhead expenses.

For the remaining 6 months the estimates are :

	For Normal Capacity Working	For Actual Working
Estimated overhead expenses	Rs. 25,350	Rs. 31,500
Estimated direct labour hrs.	Hrs. 6,500	Hrs. 9,000

What overhead rate do you recommend for the remaining 6 months? Give reasons.

[I.C.W.A.I., Adapted]

Solution

A. (i) Estimated Overhead Rate Per Hour = Rs. 4.00

(ii) Amount Recovered from January to June on actual workings (Rs. 4.00 × 8, 400) = Rs. 33,600.00

(iii) Amount Over-recovered (Rs. 33,600 – Rs. 28,000) = Rs. 5,600.00

(iv) Normal working hours January/June (8,400 – 2,000) = 6,400.00

(v) Recovery of Overhead on normal hours (Rs. 4.00 × 6, 400) = Rs. 25,600.00

(vi) Actual overhead for normal hours (Rs. 28,000 – Rs. 4,000) = Rs. 24,000.00

(vii) Over-recovered on normal hours (Rs. 25,600 – Rs. 24,000) = Rs. 1,600.00

B. It should be noted in this context that amount for over-recovered overhead should not be reduced from the overhead expenses of the next period. Adjustments to the extent of over-recovered overhead should be made on work-in-progress and the cost of finished goods.

C. **For the remaining 6 months :**

(i) Overhead Rate for Normal Workings $= \text{Rs. } \frac{25,350}{6,500}$

$= \text{Rs. } 3.90$

(ii) Overhead Rate for Excess Working Hours $= \frac{\text{Rs. } 31,500 - \text{Rs. } 25,350}{9,000 - 6,500}$

$= \text{Rs. } \frac{6,150}{2,500} = \text{Rs. } 2.46$

(iii) Overhead for Actual Hours $= \text{Rs. } \frac{31,500}{9,000} = \text{Rs. } 3.50$

To have two different rates for the same period should be avoided and it is recommended that average rate should be accepted. Here average rate is Rs. 3.50.

Problem

You have been engaged to instal a cost system for Martin Co. Your investigation of the manufacturing opertions of the business discloses these facts :

(1) The company makes a line of lighting fixtures and lamps. The material cost of any particular item ranges from 15% to 60% of total factory cost, depending on the kind of metal and fabric used in making it.

(2) The business is subject to wide cyclical fluctuations, since the sales volume follows new housing construction.

(3) About 60% of the manufacturing is normally done in the first quarter of the year.

(4) For the whole plant, the wage rates range from Rs. 1.25 to Rs. 3.75 an hour. However, within each of the eight individual dept.'s, the spread between the high and low wage rates is less than 5%.

(5) Each of the products uses all eight of the manufacturing departments but not proportionately.

(6) Within the individual manufacturing departments, factory overhead ranges from 30% to 80% of conversion cost.

Based on the above information, you are to prepare a statement or letter for the President of the company explaining whether, in its cost system, Martin Company should use :

a. A normal overhead rate or an expected actual capacity annual overhead rate;

b. An overall overhead rate or a departmental overhead rate.

c. A method of factory overhead application based on direct labour hours; direct labour costs; or prime costs.

Include the reasons supporting each of your three recommendations.

Prepare your answer on scratch paper before glancing at the answer.

[Adapted from C. P. A. (U.S.A.) Examination]

Solution

To
The President
Martin Company
Kolkata

Sir,

With reference to the above information, I have the pleasure to give you my considered views :

1. On review of the manufacturing process I find that your company, on its application of manufacturing overhead, uses normal departmental overhead rates which is applied as percentages of direct labour cost.

2. In view of the wide cyclical seasonal fluctuations in business, the company should use normal overhead rates instead of expected actual overhead rates. During low production period, expected actual overhead rates would result per-unit overhead cost high. This is due to large fixed overhead expenses. Conversely, during the period of high production, the per unit overhead cost would be lower. The application of normal rates would result in the same per-unit overhead costs, regardless of wide fluctuation—may be in month-to-month and year-to-year. The use of per-unit cost for both inventories and quoting pricing is welcome, but it should neither be inflated nor deflated by unused factory facilities and by the gain of 'better than normal use' of factory facilities.

3. It is recommended that the company should use departmental overhead rates. Since this rate varies obviously from department to department, the use of blanket rate as an average rate is not recommended. Because, a large part of the factory cost is represented by overhead cost resulting from the use of blanket rate may be substantial.

If all the products made used all the departments proportionately, a blanket rate would result in substantially accurate total (but not departmental) unit overhead costs. But in your company the use of the products are not made proportionately in all the departments.

4. The labour costs are proportionate to labour time in each and every department because of substantial uniformity in wage rates in all the different departments. Because of non-requirement of accumulation of direct labour hour number applicable to each, the clerical expense of per-paisa of direct labour cost method would be low.

5. For the wide differences in cost of materials the application of per-paisa-of-prime cost method of overhead cannot be recommended. Here factory overhead is mainly the cost of using factory facilities. The factory facilities applied to make up a lamp made of silver is almost similar to a lamp made of copper. As prime cost includes materials cost, it would result in an excessive charge to lighting lamps which use material of higher cost.

If you would need any other further classifications and answers to other pertinent queries, please feel free to contact us.

Thanking you,

Yours faithfully,
X, Y, Z

Problem

From the following particulars prepare a Machine Utilisation Statement for bringing to the notice of the top management the true cost of idle time :

(i) Machine standing charges Rs. 2,400 per annum

(ii) Maximum capability of possible machine hours = 2,300 hrs.

(iii) Standard Machine hour capacity expected = 1,840 hrs.

(iv) Actual Machine Hours recorded = 1,750 hrs.

(v) Operator's total idle time = 70 hours.

The details of idle time are :

460 hours spoiled for idle facilities (unavoidable)

40 hours spoiled for the arrival of supervisor.

30 hours spoiled for load shading.

20 hours spoiled for idle facilities (avoidable)

(vi) The operator's remuneration = Re. 0.30 per hour.

(vii) Fixed Administrative Overhead Cost = Rs. 10,000.

(viii) Standard Machine Hour capacity of whole factory = 14,000 hrs.

Solution

1. **Capacity Usage Ratio** $= \dfrac{\text{Standard Capacity Expected.}}{\text{Maximum Possible Machine Hrs.}}$

$= \dfrac{1,840}{2,300} = 80\%$

2. Capacity Utilisation Ratio $= \dfrac{\text{Actual Machine Hours Recorded}}{\text{Standard Machine Hour Expected}}$

$= \dfrac{1,750}{1,840} = 95\%$

3. Details of Idle time

(a) Unavoidable : (2,300–1,840)	460	hrs.
(b) Avoidable :		
Idle Facilities	20	hrs.
Supervisor's Arrival	40	hrs.
Load Shading	30	hrs
	550	Hours

4. Cost of Avoidable Idle Facilities	Rs.
In Terms of Operator's Remuneration	21
@ Re. 0.30 per hour (70 hrs. × Rs. 0.30)	
Apportionment of lost total machine hour in relation to proportionate fixed Overhead and Administrative Charges.	888
	909

Do you follow the above workings? Is there any question please!

□ "Sir, why have you not taken ideal facilities into account in the above calculation the appropriate amount for 20 hrs. which have been spolied due to?"

● Thank you for your question. You can take into account that I have assumed that during that period the operators might have been engaged with available machinery. That's why it has been omitted. I think you have followed.

□ "Sir, how has the above figure of Rs. 888.00 been arrived at? Please give us the working."

● Well, note below the workings :

You know the figure for standing charges for machine is Rs. 2,400. To it should be added the proportion of administrative cost applicable to the machine. This can be done in the following manner :

$$\frac{\text{Standing Capacity of Machine}}{\text{Standard Capacity of Whole Factory}} \times \text{Administrative Cost}$$

$$= \frac{1{,}840 \times 10{,}000}{14{,}000} = \text{Rs. } 1{,}314$$

So the total of fixed overhead charge — i.e., machine standing charges and proportionate administration charges — should be apportioned with the relationship between hours lost and maximum hours.

The total figure here is (Rs. 2,400 + Rs. 1,314) Rs. 3,714

The figure Rs. 888 has been computed in the following way :

$$\frac{\text{Total Hours Lost} \times 3{,}714}{\text{Maximum Hours}} = \frac{550 \times 3{,}714}{2{,}300} = \text{Rs. } 888$$

I hope that this time you have followed.

□ "Thank you Sir."

- Now I would like to compute the "Break Down" Analysis of Cost :

5. **Break Down of Cost :**

Avoidable Causes :		Rs.
Idle Facilities $\frac{20}{550} \times 888$	=	32
Supervisor's Arrival $\frac{40}{550} \times 888$	=	65
Load Shading $\frac{30}{550} \times 888$	=	48
Labour Cost of Idle Time Unavoidable	=	21
Idle Facilities $\frac{460}{550} \times 888$	=	743
		909

Problem

A machine shop of a light engineering factory has three cost centres having distinct sets of machines. The following are the details available to your for the year 2005 :

Particulars	Figures in lakhs			
	Total for the factory	**Centre A**	**Centre B**	**Centre C**
	Rs.	Rs.	Rs.	Rs.
Value of Assets		4.00	5.00	6.00
Direct Wages		0.50	0.40	0.50
Repairs and Maintenance	0.60			
Indirect Labour	0.28			
Insurance on Assets	0.15			
Supervision	0.70			
Power	0.15			
Labour Welfare	0.42			
Other Expenses	1.40			
Estimated Working Hours		16,000	13,000	15,000

Work out a comprehensive machine hour rate in detail for the three centres after providing for depreciation at 6¼%. The ratio of the horse power : hours is 6 : 4 : 5.

[I.C.W.A.I., Adapted]

Solution

Figures in lakh of Rupees

Items of Expenses	Basis of Apportionment	Total	Centre A	Centre B	Centre C
Direct Wages	Direct	1.40	0.50	0.40	0.50
Repair and Maintenance	Asset Value	0.60	0.16	0.20	0.24
Indirect Labour	Direct Wages	0.28	0.10	0.08	0.10
Insurance on Assets	Asset Value	0.15	0.04	0.05	0.06
Supervisors	Direct Wages	0.70	0.25	0.20	0.25
Power	Horse Power	0.15	0.06	0.04	0.05
Labour Welfare	Direct Wages	0.42	0.15	0.12	0.15
Other Expenses	Direct Wages	1.40	0.50	0.40	0.50
Depreciation	Asset Value	0.94	0.25	0.31	0.38
	Total	6.04	2.01	1.80	2.23
Estimated Working Hours		44,000	16,000	13,000	15,000
Machine Hour Rate Rs.			12.56	13.86	14.83

Problem

The following figures have been extracted from the book of Agantuk Bros. Manufacturing Company. All jobs pass through the company's two departments :

	Working Department (X)	Finishing Department (Y)
	Rs.	Rs.
Material Used	6,000	500
Direct Labour	3,000	1,500
Factory Overhead	1,800	1,200
Direct Labour Hours	12,000	5,000
Machine Hours	10,000	2,000

The following information relates to Job A 100

	Working Department (X)	Finishing Department (Y)
Material Used	Rs. 120	Rs. 10
Direct Labour	65	25
Direct Labour Hours	265	70
Machine Hours	255	25

You are required :

(a) To enumerate four methods of absorbing factory overheads by jobs, showing the rates for each department under the methods quoted.

(b) To prepare a statement showing the different cost result for **Job A 100** under any two of the methods referred to. **[Adapted from I.C.W.A. London]**

Solution

Part (a)

Method I. Machine Hour Rate :

$$\text{Machine Hour Rate for Dept. X} = \frac{1{,}800}{10{,}000} = \text{Re. } 0.18 \text{ per hour}$$

$$\text{Machine Hour Rate for Dept. Y} = \frac{1{,}200}{2{,}000} = \text{Re. } 0.60 \text{ per hour}$$

Method II. Direct Labour Hour Rate :

$$\text{For Department X} = \frac{1{,}800}{12{,}000} = \text{Re. } 0.15 \text{ per hour}$$

$$\text{For Department Y} = \frac{1{,}200}{5{,}000} = \text{Re. } 0.24 \text{ per hour}$$

Method III. Direct Wages :

$$\text{For Department X} = \frac{1{,}800 \times 100}{3{,}000} = 60\%$$

$$\text{For Department Y} = \frac{1{,}200 \times 100}{1{,}500} = 80\%$$

Method IV. Prime Cost :

$$\text{For Department X} = \frac{1{,}800 \times 100}{9{,}000} = 20\%$$

$$\text{For Department Y} = \frac{1{,}200 \times 100}{2{,}000} = 60\%$$

PART (b)

JOB NO. : A100

Statement Showing Different Cost Results Under Method Of Charging Overhead,under Direct Labour Hour Rate & Machine Hour Rate

Details	LABOUR HOUR RATE							MACHINE HOUR RATE						
	Department (X)			Department (Y)				Department (X)			Department (Y)			
	Hrs	Rate	Cost	Hrs	Rate	Cost	Total	Hrs.	Rate	Cost	Hrs	Rate	Cost	Total
		Rs.	Rs.		Rs.	Rs.	Rs.		Rs.	Rs.		Rs	Rs.	Rs.
Direct Materials	—	—	120.00	—	—	10.00	130.00	—	—	120.00	—	—	10.00	130.00
Direct Labour	—	—	65.00	—	—	25.00	90.00	—	—	65.00	—	—	25.00	90.00
Overhead (application)	265	0.15	39.75	70	0.24	16.80	56.55	225	0.18	40.50	25	0.60	15.00	55.50
							276.55							275.50

Problem

As Management Accountant you are requested by the Chairman of a progressing company to advice on the best method of absorbing overheads and to compute rate or rates to be applied. No cost account has been kept, but estimates have been prepared for jobs undertaken on the following basis :

Estimated materials and direct wages, plus 150% on direct wages for factory overheads, plus 15% on factory cost for all other overheads. To this figure a further 15% is added for profit.

The accounts for the year show the following figures :

	Rs.
Direct Material	21,000
Factory Overheads	27,500
Selling Overheads	3,000
Sales	75,000
Direct Wages	18,500
Administration Overheads	5,000
Distribution Overheads	1,500
Net Loss	1,500

There are two production departments, and the overhead rates for the departments vary considerably.

(A) Summarise your computation and observations.

(B) State what advice you would give to the Chairman.

(C) Suggest lines on which further investigation should proceed.

[Adapted from I.C.W.A. London]

Solution

(A) % of Factory Overheads in Relation to Actual Direct Wages

$$= \frac{\text{Actual Factory Overheads}}{\text{Actual Direct Wages}} \times 100$$

$$= \frac{27,500 \times 100}{18,500} = 149\%$$

As per problem given above, overheads have been applied at 150% of Direct Wages.

% of Actual Administrative and Selling and Distribution Overheads in relation to Factory Cost is 14%. This can be computed as :

Factory Cost :	Rs.
Direct Material	21,000
Direct Wages	18,500
Factory Overheads	27,500
	67,000

$$\frac{\text{Actual Administrative and Selling and Distribution Overheads}}{\text{Factory Cost}}$$

$$= \frac{\text{Rs. } (5{,}000 + 3{,}000 + 1{,}500)}{\text{Rs. } 67{,}000} = \frac{\text{Rs. } 9{,}500 \times 100}{\text{Rs. } 67{,}000} = 14\%$$

As per information supplied in the problem it is clear that Administrative, Selling and Distribution Overheads have been applied at 15% of Factory Cost.

So the overall rates used in the problem are satisfactory. Further, the figure for cost of goods sold as per information supplied in the problem is Rs. 76,500. And the sales figure is estimated at Rs. 75,000.

Thus the expected profit on cost of goods sold is not realised; moreover, a loss for Rs. 1,500 is there.

Did you follow?

□ "No Sir, how is the figure of cost of goods sold for Rs. 76,500 computed? Moreover, what is the figure for expected profit?"

● Well, please note below the workings :

Cost of Goods Sold = (Opening Stock + Purchase) – Closing Stock

Again, Sales = Cost of Goods Sold + Profit

So, 75,000 = Cost of Goods Sold – 1,500 (since loss here)

Cost of Goods Sold = 75,000 + 1,500 = Rs. 76,500

$$\text{Expected Profit} = \frac{\text{Rs. } 15 \times 76{,}500}{100} = \text{Rs. } 11{,}475$$

So, it is clear that the sales of the company should be boost up to the extent (Rs. 11,475 + 1,500) Rs. 12,975 to avoid the above situation.

I think you have followed now. Let me show the remaining two parts of the answer :

(B) As a Management Accountant I should give the following advice to the Chairman of the company :

(i) Two different overhead rates for two production departments should be applied. Overall overhead rate should not be applied. Similarly, instead of an overall rate, separate rates for Administrative, Selling and Distribution should be applied.

(ii) The cost of production of the company under review are not correct because of the fact that overheads were not properly charged to different products of the company. Moreover, the selling prices as a percentage of cost of production is not justifiable.

Other defects of the company's financial management are :

(a) High selling price of a few products which are beyond the normal reach of customers.

(b) Sale of a few products at a loss.

(c) Adoption of unprofitable lines.

(iii) It is recommended to establish two overhead rates—one for fixed overhead and the other for absorbing variable overheads.

(C) For maintaining high integrity or cost and financial management of the company, investigations are to be made on the following lines of approach :

(a) Production and distribution cost should be compared with prevailing market price.

(b) Company's product should be sold at the prevailing market price and the selling price should not be based on as a percentage of the costs.

(c) Market research should be conducted for profitable line of sale and adequate measures should be adopted to bring down the overhead cost of the company in order to sell the products at or either below the market price.

I think the above discussions and different worked-out typical problems will help you to gain an insight into the concept of overhead cost control and its recovery.

In my next lecture I shall be discussing the concept of Cost Control Accounts.

Now I am showing a few worked out problem for your study.

Problem

Atlas Engineering Ltd. accepts a variety of jobs which require both manual and machine operations. The budgeted Profit and Loss A/c for the period 2005-06 is as follows :

		(in lakhs of rupees)
Sales		75
Cost :		
Direct Materials	10	
Direct Labour	5	
Prime Cost	15	
Production Overhead	30	
Production Cost	45	
Administration, Selling and Distribution Overhead	15	60
Profit		15
Other budgeted data :		
Labour hours for the period		2,500
Machine hours for the period		1,500
No. of jobs for the period		300

An enquiry has been received recently from a customer and the production department has prepared the following estimate of the prime cost required for the job:

	Rs.
Direct Material	2,500
Direct Labour	2,000
Prime Cost	4,500

Labour hours required 80

Machine hours required 50

You are required to :

(a) Calculate, by different methods, six overhead absorption rates for absorption of production overhead and comment on the suitability of each.

(b) Calculate the production overhead cost of the order based on each of the above rates.

(c) Give your recommendations to the company. **[I.C.W.A.I. Inter]**

Solution

(a) Computation of overhead absorption rate by using six methods :

Method I :

$$\text{Direct material cost rate} = \frac{\text{Production overhead}}{\text{Direct material cost}}$$

$$= \frac{\text{Rs. } 30,00,000}{\text{Rs. } 10,00,000} \times 100$$

$$= 300\%$$

Method II :

$$\text{Direct labour cost rate} = \frac{\text{Production overhead}}{\text{Direct labour cost}}$$

$$= \frac{\text{Rs. } 30,00,000}{\text{Rs. } 5,00,000} \times 100$$

$$= 600\%$$

Method III :

$$\text{Prime cost rate} = \frac{\text{Production overhead}}{\text{Prime cost}}$$

$$= \frac{\text{Rs. } 30,00,000}{\text{Rs. } 15,00,000} \times 100$$

$$= 200\%$$

Method IV :

$$\text{Labour hour rate} = \frac{\text{Production overhead}}{\text{Labour hour}}$$

$$= \frac{\text{Rs. } 30,00,000}{2,500}$$

$$= \text{Rs. } 1,200$$

Method V :

$$\text{Machine hour rate} = \frac{\text{Production overhead}}{\text{Machine hours}}$$

$$= \frac{\text{Rs. } 30,00,000}{1,500}$$

$$= \text{Rs. } 2,000$$

Method VI :

$$\text{Cost unit rate} = \frac{\text{Production overhead}}{\text{No. of jobs}}$$

$$= \frac{\text{Rs. } 30,00,000}{300}$$

$$= \text{Rs. } 10,000$$

(b) Absorption Rates	Overhead Absorption
(i) Direct material cost rate	300% of Rs. 2,500 = Rs. 7,500
(ii) Direct labour cost rate	600% of Rs. 2,000 = Rs. 12,000
(iii) Prime cost rate	200% of Rs. 4,500 = Rs. 9,000
(iv) Labour hour rate	Rs. 1,200 × 80 = Rs. 96,000
(v) Machine hour rate	Rs. 2,000 × 50 = Rs. 1,00,000
(vi) No. of jobs	Rs. 10,000 × 1 = Rs. 10,000

Problem

A manufacturing unit has added a new machine to its fleet of five existing machines. The total cost of purchase and installation of the machine is Rs. 7,50,000. The machine has an estimated life of 15 years and is expected to realise Rs. 30,000 as scrap at the end of its working life.

Other relevant data are :

(i) Budgeted working hours is 2,400 based on 8 hours per day for 300 days. This includes 400 hours for plant maintenance.

(ii) Electricity used by the machine is 15 units per hour at a cost of Rs. 2.00 per unit. No current is drawn during maintenance.

(iii) The machine requires special oil for heating which is replaced once every month at a cost of Rs. 2,500 on each occasion.

(iv) Estimated cost of maintenance of the machine is Rs. 500 per week of 6 working days.

(v) 3 operators control the operations of the entire battery of six machines and the average wages per person amounts to Rs. 450 per week plus 40% fringe benefits.

(vi) Departmental and general works overheads allocated to the operations during the last year was Rs. 60,000. During the current year it is estimated that there will be an increase of 12.5% of this amount. No incremental overhead is envisaged for the installation of the new machine.

You are required to compute the machine hour rate for recovery of the running cost of the machine. **[I.C.W.A.I. (Inter)]**

Solution

Computation of Machine Hour Rate

Effective Machine Hours : 2,000

Particulars	Amount	Rate per hour
	Rs.	Rs.
Standing Changes :		
Operator wages $\frac{\text{Rs. } 450 \times 3 \times 50}{6}$	11,250	
Add: Fringe benefits (40%)	4,500	
	15,750	
Departmental and General Works Overhead :		
$\frac{(60{,}000 + 60{,}000 \times 12.5\%)}{6}$	11,250	
	27,000	13.50
Machine Expenses :		
Electricity $\frac{(15 \times 2{,}000 \times \text{Rs. } 2.00)}{2{,}000}$		30.00
Depreciation $\frac{(7{,}50{,}000 - 30{,}000)}{15 \times 2{,}000}$		24.00
Special oil $\frac{(2{,}500 \times 12)}{2{,}000}$		15.00
Maintenance $\frac{(500 \times 300)}{6 \times 2{,}000}$		12.50
Machine Hour Rate		95.00

Working : Effective Working Hours :

Budgeted working hours	=	2,400
Less : Maintenance hours	=	400
Effective hours		2,000

Problem

The following expenses were incurred in respect of a shop having 5 identical machines :

	Per month (Rs.)
1. Rent and Rates	21,600
2. Repair and Maintenance	10,000
3. Power (at 54 paise per unit)	32,400
4. Lighting	9,700
5. Supervisor's Salary (He devotes his time equally on all the 5 machines)	3,120
6. Oil, grease and cotton waste	560
7. Hire-purchase instalment including interest (Rs. 6,000)	46,600
8. Each machine consumes 8 units of power per hour	
9 The purchase price of each machine is	92,000

The life of each machine is estimated at 10 years, at the end of which it would have a residual value of Rs. 12,000. Calculate machine hour rate. **[B.Com., Mangalore]**

Solution

Power expenses per month for 5 machines = Rs. 32,400

Power charge is Re. 0.54 per unit.

Each machine consumes 8 units of power per hour.

∴ Power expense per hour for 5 machines = $8 \times 5 \times 0.54$ = Rs. 21.60

∴ Machine hours per machine = $\frac{32,400}{21.60}$ = 1,500 hours

Computation of Machine Hour Rate

Particulars	Per month	Per hour
	Rs.	Rs.
Standing Changes :		
Rent and Rates	21,600	
Lighting	9,700	
Supervisor's Salary	3,120	
Oil, grease and cotton waste	560	
Total for 5 machines	34,980	
For 1 machine 1 hour $\left(\frac{34,980}{5 \times 1,500}\right)$		4.664
Machine Expenses :		
Depreciation $\left(\frac{92,000 - 12,000}{10 \times 12}\right)$	666.67	0.444
Repairs and Maintenance for 1 machine $\left(\frac{10,000}{5}\right)$	2000	1.333
Power 8 units per hrs. @ 54 paise		4.320
Machine hour rate		10.761

Note : Interest on hire-purchase is ignored as it is of financial nature.

Problem

Three machines P, Q and R which are of different nature are used in a department of a factory. From the following information compute machine hour rate of machine R :

(i) Total cost of machines P, Q and R is Rs. 50,000 out of which cost of machine R is Rs. 10,000. Its estimated scrap value and working life are Rs. 1,000 and 18,000 hours, respectively.

(ii)	Rent (Total area 1,000 sq.ft and machine R occupies 250 sq.ft.)	Rs. 780 p.a.
(iii)	Lighting (Total light points 12, out of which 2 points used for machine R)	Rs. 288 p.a.
(iv)	Insurance for all machines	Rs. 45 per quarter
(v)	Consumable stores for machine R	Rs. 60 p.m.
(vi)	Salary of supervisor (Supervisor devotes ¼th of his time for machine R)	Rs. 6,000 p.m.
(vii)	Repairs and maintenance for the entire life of machine R	Rs. 1,800
(viii)	Machine R consumes 5 units of power per hour at a cost of Rs. 16 per 100 units	

(ix) Machine R will work 2,000 hours p.a. out of which normal idle time estimated at 8% of total working hours and time for routine maintenance estimated at 40 hours p.a.

[C.U. B.Com. (Hons.)]

Solution

Computation of Machine Hour Rate of Machine R

Particulars	Amount per annum	Rate per hour
	Rs.	Rs.
Fixed Charges :		
Rent $\left(\text{Rs. } 780 \times \frac{250}{1,000}\right)$	195	
Lighting $\left(\text{Rs. } 288 \times \frac{2}{12}\right)$	48	
Insurance $\left(\text{Rs. } 45 \times 4 \times \frac{10,000}{50,000}\right)$	36	
Consumable Stores (Rs. 60 × 12)	720	
Salary of supervisor $\left(\text{Rs. } 6,000 \times \frac{1}{4}\right)$	1,500	
	2,499	1.388

Particulars	Amount per annum	Rate per hour
	Rs.	Rs.
Machine Expenses :		
Depreciation $\left\{(10,000 - 1,000) \times \frac{1,800}{18,000} \times \frac{1}{1,800}\right\}$		0.50
Repair & Maintenance $\left(1,800 \times \frac{1,800}{18,000} \times \frac{1}{1,800}\right)$		0.10
Power $\left(\frac{16}{100} \times \frac{1,800 \times 5}{1,800}\right)$		0.8
Machine Hour Rate		2.788

Working note :

	Hrs.
Total working hours p.a. of machine R	= 2,000
Less : Idle Time (8%)	= 160
	1,840
Less : Maintenance Hours	40
Effective Machine Hours	1,800

Problem

A machine shop has 6 identical machines manned by 5 operators. A machine cannot be worked without any operator wholly engaged on it. The original cost of all these 6 machines works out at Rs. 6 lakhs.

The following estimates are available for the year 2005 :

(a)	Normal working hours per month	220 hours
(b)	Absenteeism (without pay) per month	20 hours
(c)	Leave, with pay, per month	20 hours
(d)	Normal idle time (unavoidable)	20 hours
(e)	Average rate of wages per day of 8 hours	Rs. 40
(f)	Production bonus	15% of wages
(g)	Cost of power for the period	Rs. 20,700
(h)	Supervision and indirect labour cost for the year	Rs. 8,100
(i)	Lighting and electricity per annum	Rs. 3,070
(j)	Repairs and maintenance of machines	2% of the value of the machines p.a.
(k)	Insurance charges	Rs. 30,000 p.a.
(l)	General management expenses as allocated for the year	Rs. 84,000
(m)	Depreciation under Straight Line Method	15% on orginal cost of machines

You are required to work out a comprehensive Machine Hour Rate for the machine shop. **[C.U. B.Com. (Hons.)]**

Solution

Computation of Comprehensive Machine Hour Rate

Particulars	Amount per month	Rate per hour
	Rs.	Rs.
Fixed Charges :		
Supervisor and Indirect Labour Cost $\left(\frac{8,100}{12}\right)$	675	
Wages of Operators $\left(\frac{\text{Rs. } 40}{8} \times 200 \times 5 \times \frac{115}{100}\right)$	5,750	
Lighting and Electricity $\left(\frac{\text{Rs. } 3070}{12}\right)$	255.8	
Insurance Charges $\left(\frac{\text{Rs. } 30000}{12}\right)$	2,500	
General Management Expenses $\left(\frac{84000}{12}\right)$	7,000	
	16,180.8	101.13
Machine Expenses :		
Power $\left\{\left(\text{Rs. } 20,700 \times \frac{1}{12}\right) \times \frac{1}{160}\right\}$		10.78
Repairs and Maintenance $\left[6,00,000 \times 2\% \times \frac{1}{12} \times \frac{1}{160}\right]$		6.25
Depreciation $\left[6,00,000 \times 15\% \times \frac{1}{12} \times \frac{1}{160}\right]$		46.875
Comprehensive Machine Hour Rate		165.035

Working note :

	Hrs.
Normal working hours	220
Less : Absenteeism without pay	20
	200
Less : Leave with pay	20
	180
Less : Idle time (unavoidable)	20
Effective working hours	160

Problem

A company has three production departments and two service departments.

Production Departments	Overhead Expenses
A	Rs. 13,600
B	Rs. 14,700
C	Rs. 12,800
Service Departments	
X	Rs. 9,000
Y	Rs. 3,000

The expenses of service departments are charged on a percentage basis which is as follows :

	A	B	C	X	Y
X Deptt.	40%	30%	20%	—	10%
Y Deptt.	30%	30%	20%	20%	—

Apportion the cost of Service Departments by using the Repeated Distribution Method.

[C.A. Inter]

Solution

Distribution of Overhead
(Repeated Distribution Method)

Particulars	Production Departments			Service Departments	
	A	B	C	X	Y
	Rs.	Rs.	Rs.	Rs.	Rs.
Total Overhead as per Distribution Summary	13,600	14,700	12,800	9,000	3,000
Overhead Distribution of Service Department X (4 : 3 : 2 : — : 1)	3,600	2,700	1,800	– 9,000	900
	17,200	17,400	14,600	—	3,900
Overhead Distribution of Service Department Y (3 : 3 : 2 : 2 : —)	1,170	1,170	780	780	– 3,900
	18,370	18,570	15,380	780	—
Overhead Distribution of Department X (4 : 3 : 2 : — : 1)	312	234	156	– 780	78
	18,682	18,804	15,536	—	78

Particulars	Production Departments			Service Departments	
	A	B	C	X	Y
	Rs.	Rs.	Rs.	Rs.	Rs.
Overhead Distribution of Department Y (3 : 3 : 2 : 2 : —)	23.4	23.4	15.6	15.6	– 78
	18,705.4	18,827.4	15,551.6	15.6	—
Overhead Distribution of Department X (4 : 3 : 2 : — : 1)	6.24	4.68	3.12	– 15.6	1.56
	18,711.64	18,832.08	15,554.72	—	1.56
Overhead Distribution of Department Y (3 : 3 : 2 : 2 : —)	.47	.47	.62	—	–1.56
	18,712.11	18,832.55	15,555.34	—	—

Problem

A factory is having three production departments, A, B and C, and two service departments— Boiler-House and Pump-Room. The boiler-house has to depend upon the pump-room for supply of water and the pump-room, in its turn, is dependent on the boiler house for supply of power for driving the pump. The expenses incurred by the production departments during a period are : A Rs. 8,00,000; B Rs. 7,00,000; and C Rs. 5,00,000. The expenses for boiler-house are Rs. 2,34,000 and the pump-room Rs. 3,00,000.

The expenses of the boiler-house and pump-room are apportioned to the production departments on the following basis :

	A	B	C	B.H.	P.R.
Expenses of boiler-house	20%	40%	30%	—	10%
Expenses of pump-room	40%	20%	20%	20%	—

Show clearly as to how the expenses of boiler-house and pump-room would be apportioned to A, B and C departments. Use algebrical equations. **[CS Final]**

Solution

Let X be the total overhead of boiler-house, Y be the total overhead of pump-room.

$$X = \text{Rs. } 2{,}34{,}000 + 20\% \text{ of } Y.$$

$$Y = \text{Rs. } 3{,}00{,}000 + 10\% \text{ of } X.$$

$X = 2{,}34{,}000 + .2Y$

or, $10X - 2Y = 23{,}40{,}000$ .... (i)

$Y = 3{,}00{,}000 + .1Y$

or, $10Y = 30{,}00{,}000 + 1X$

or, $-X + 10Y = 30{,}00{,}000$ .... (ii)

Multiplying equation (i) by 5 and adding it to (ii) we get

$$50X - 10Y = 1,17,00,000$$
$$-X + 10Y = 30,00,000$$
$$49X = 1,47,00,000$$

$$\text{or, } X = \frac{147,00,000}{49}$$

$$= \text{Rs. } 3,00,000$$

Putting value of X in equation (ii) we get

$$-3,00,000 + 10Y = 30,00,000$$

$$\text{or, } 10Y = 30,00,000 + 3,00,000$$

$$\text{or, } 10Y = 33,00,000$$

$$\text{or, } Y = 3,30,000$$

Distribution of Overhead

Particulars	Total	Production Depts.			Service Depts.	
		A	B	C	B.H.	P.R.
	Rs.	Rs.	Rs.	Rs.	Rs.	Rs.
Expenses Incurred	25,34,000	8,00,000	7,00,000	5,00,000	2,34,000	3,00,000
Actual overhead of boiler house apportioned on the given ratio		60,000	1,20,000	90,000	(3,00,000)	30,000
Actual overhead of power-room apportioned on the given ratio		1,32,000	66,000	66,000	66,000	(3,30,000)
	25,34,000	9,92,000	8,86,000	6,56,000	—	—

Problem

A Ltd. has three production departments P_1, P_2 & P_3 and two service departments S_1 and S_2. The following data are extracted from the records of the company for a particular given period :

	Rs.		Rs.
Rent and rates	25,000	Power	7,500
General lighting	3,000	Depreciation on machinery	50,000
Indirect wages	7,500	Sundries	50,000

OTHER INFORMATION :

	P_1	P_2	P_3	S_1	S_2
Direct Wages (Rs.)	15,000	10,000	15,000	7,500	2,500
H.P. of machines used	60	30	50	10	—
Cost of machinery (Rs.)	3,00,000	4,00,000	5,00,000	25,000	25,000
Floor Space (sq. ft.)	2,000	2,500	3,000	2,000	500
No. of light-points	10	15	20	10	5
Production hour worked	6,226	4,028	4,066	—	—

Expenses of the service departments S_1 and S_2 are apportioned as :

	P_1	P_2	P_3	S_1	S_2
S_1	20%	30%	40%	—	10%
S_2	40%	20%	30%	10%	—

You are required to :

(a) Compute overhead rate per production hour of each production department.

(b) Determine the total cost of product X which is processed for manufacture in departments P_1, P_2 and P_3 for 4 hours, 5 hours and 3 hours, respectively, given that its direct material cost is Rs. 250 and indirect labour cost is Rs. 150.

[C.U. B.Com. (Hons.)]

Solution

(a)

Distribution of Overhead

Overhead Expenses	Bases of Apportionment	Total	Production Depts. P_1	P_2	P_3	Ser. Deps. S_1	S_2
		Rs.	Rs.	Rs.	Rs.	Rs.	Rs.
Direct wages	Actual	10,000	—	—	—	7,500	2,500
Rent and rates	Floor space (4 : 5 : 6 : 4 : 1)	25,000	5,000	6,250	7,500	5,000	1,250
General Lighting	No. of light-points (2 : 3 : 4 : 2 : 1)	3,000	500	750	1,000	500	250
Indirect wages	Direct wages (6 : 4 : 6 : 3 : 1)	7,500	2,250	1,500	2,250	1,125	375
Power	H.P. of machine (6 : 3 : 5 : 1 : —)	7,500	3,000	1,500	2,500	500	—
Depreciation on Machinery	Cost of machinery (12 : 16 : 20 : 1 : 1)	50,000	12,000	16,000	20,000	1,000	1,000
Sundries	Direct wages (6 : 4 : 6 : 3 :1)	50,000	15,000	10,000	15,000	7,500	2,500
		1,53,000	37,750	36,000	48,250	23,125	7,875

Overhead Expenses	Bases of Apportionment	Total	Production Depts.			Ser. Depts.	
			P_1	P_2	P_3	S_1	S_2
		Rs.	Rs.	Rs.	Rs.	Rs.	Rs.
Secondary Distribution							
Actual overhead of S_1 apportioned on the basis of given ratio	(2 : 3 :4 : — : 1)		4,831	7,246	9,662	(24,154)	2,415
Actual overhead of S_2 apportioned on the basis of given ratio	(4:2:3:1:—)		4,116	2,058	3,087	1,029	(10,290)
			46,697	45,304	60,999	—	—
Production hours worked			6,226	4,028	4066		
Overhead rate per hour (Rs.)			7.50	11.25	15.00		

Workings :

Let x be the total overhead of service department S_1 and y be the total overhead of service department S_2.

Then, x = 23,125 + 10% of y

y = 7,875 + 10% of x.

x = 23,125 + .1 y

or, 10x = 2,31,250 + y

or, 10x – y = 2,31, 250 .... (i)

y = 7,875 + 10% of x

or, 10y = 78,750 + x

or, 10y – x = 78,750 .... (ii)

On multiplying equation (i) by 10 and adding it to equation (ii) we get

$$\begin{aligned} 100x - \cancel{10y} &= 23{,}12{,}500 \\ -x + \cancel{10y} &= 78{,}750 \\ \hline 99x &= 23{,}91{,}250 \end{aligned}$$

$$\text{or, } x = \frac{23{,}91{,}250}{99} = \text{Rs. } 24{,}154$$

Putting the value of x in equation (ii) we get

10y – 24,154 = 78,750

or, 10y = 78,750 + 24,154

or, $10y = 1,02,904$

or, $y = \frac{1,02,904}{10}$

$= 10,290$

(b) **Determination of total cost of production of Product X**

		Rs.
Direct material		250
Direct labour		150
Prime Cost		400
Overhead		
P_1 — Rs. 7.50 × 4 =	30	
P_2 — Rs. 11.25 × 5 =	56.25	
P_3 — Rs. 15.00 × 3 =	45.00	131.25
Total Cost		531.25

● I hope you have followed the above discussion. Now I would like to go for next chapter. Is there any question from your side?

☐ "Excuse me Sir, I could not attend your classes on Fixed Cost and Overhead Cost. Kindly enlighten me the concept in brief."

● You see, it is not possible to discuss it again. Here I would like to give my experience while delivering my lecture to engineers of different organisations.

I hope this experience will help you to distinguish between overhead cost and fixed Cost.

An engineer, who attended my lecture, asked me to give an example from day to day life which may help to distinguish between the two. I asked the engineer.

Are you married?

His answer was "yes Sir, I am married. I have my wife, my two sons, one daughter and also I have father-in-law, mother-in-law and sister-in-law." Then I told him maintenance for your sons, daughter and wife is Fixed Cost and maintenance for your father-in-law, mother-in-law and sister-in-law is a Overhead Cost i.e., to say indirect cost. Then the engineer told me, Sir! it is a beautiful example. Now I need not go through the chapters on Fixed Cost and Overhead Cost. The example will help me to distinguish between the two by application of mind, experience, knowledge and education.

QUESTIONS

1. A company is about to produce two articles whose prime cost is composed of as follows :

Cost per dozen : X	Rs.	Cost per dozen : Y	Rs.
Direct Material	10.00	Direct Material	15.00
Direct Wages (8 hours at Rs. 3.00 including 5 machine hours)	24.00	Direct Wages (4 hrs. at Rs. 4.50 including 2 machine hours)	18.00
	34.00		33.00

For the three months ending 31st March 2005, the budget shows the following information :

Budgeted output of A 1,000 dozen

Budgeted output of B 2,000 dozen

Overhead Rs. 6,000

You are requested :

(a) to name three cost rates by which overhead to be absorbed by each product could be calculated.

(b) to calculate the overhead to be absorbed by each product under each of the cost rates that you name. Show your workings.

[Adapted from I.C.W.A. London]

2. Calculate from the following data the machine hour rate for Machine B :

Cost of the machine	Rs. 1,050
Estimated scrap value	Rs. 50
Effective working life	20,000 hours
Running time per 4-weekly period	150 hours
Weekly amount payable under a maintenance agreement covering all repairs	Rs. 2.50
Standing charges allocated to machine per 4-weekly period	Rs. 5.00
Power used by machine	5 units per hour at Re. 0.20 per unit

[Adapted from I.C.W.A. London]

3. "Proper Overhead Cost control helps to enter comparative market." —Explain.

9

COST CONTROL ACCOUNTS

☐ "Good evening Sir."

• Good evening my dear students.

Well in my last lecture I discussed in detail about Elements of Cost Control such as Material Cost Control, Labour Cost Control and Overhead Cost Control. Now I would like to take up for discussion different Cost Control Accounts.

You see, accounts which are used in controlling expenditures chargeable to cost and which form a means and medium of reconciliation of cost and financial accounts, may be termed as cost control accounts. What is reconciliation and how it is reconciled will be discussed in the subsequent chapter. I had already given you a basic and constructive idea of financial accounting. In my earlier chapters 'Accounting Mechanism' and 'Highlights of Basic Accounting Concept' I explained in detail the concept of Debit and Credit. I would request you to recapitulate the earlier discussions.

Concept of Debit and Credit in Control Accounting

This would help us to understand better the concept of Cost Control Accounts.

However, we had seen earlier that accounts in general are of two types — Personal, and Impersonal. Again, Impersonal Accounts may be divided under two heads — (i) Real, and (ii) Nominal. Please note one fundamental difference between Cost Department and Accounting Department — the former is interested in Impersonal Accounts, i.e. Real and Nominal, and the latter is interested in both Personal and Impersonal Accounts, i.e. Personal, Real and Nominal. Thus, in general, cost department is mainly concerned with income and expenditure of any enterprise or business.

The ways in which cost control is generally accomplished are of two natures :

(i) Control of Expenditure in Detail

Ways of Cost Control

This process accommodates the cost of individual order, article and analysis according to total cost of production, i.e., expenses, selling, distribution and administration cost.

(ii) Control of Expenditure in Total

This process provides for integration and reconciliation of the detailed cost as shown earlier with the total expenditure as shown in General Accounting Records, i.e. the General Ledger.

From the above discussions it is clear that Financial Ledger includes :

(i) General Ledger,
(ii) Debtors Ledger, and
(iii) Creditors Ledger.

Again, Cost Ledger can generally be classified under the following heads :

Classification of Cost Ledger

(i) Cost Ledger : It is the main ledger account maintained by the Cost Department. As stated earlier it is mainly concerned with impersonal accounts, i.e. Income and Expenditure.

(ii) Stores Ledger : Stores accounts are maintained in the ledger. It is concerned with 'In' and 'Out' of material received from the suppliers and distribution of the same to all departments on receipt of Stores Requisition.

(iii) Work-in-Progress Ledger : It records the details of cost incurred during production process; as well as the production during a particular period.

(iv) Finished Goods Ledger : It records the details of completely finished products as well as the total cost incurred.

Different Types of Cost Control Accounts

Well, in order to facilitate effective control over cost accounts, following important control accounts are to be opened in the Cost Ledger :

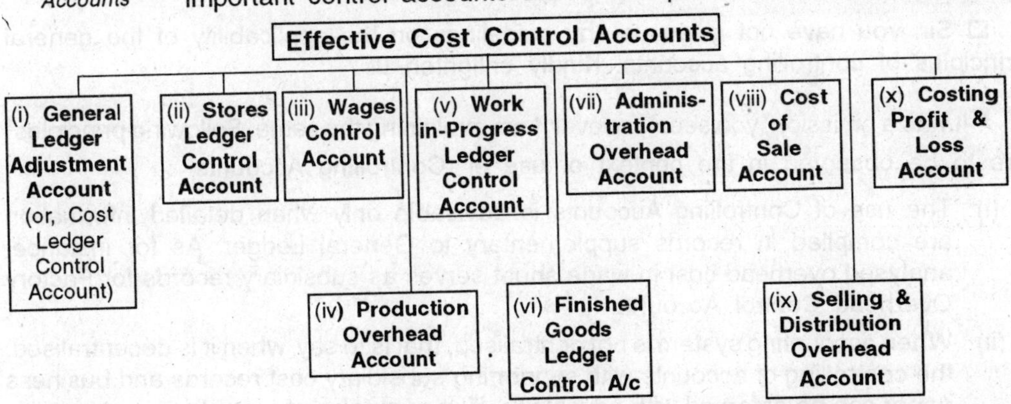

You see, the nature and purpose of the above control accounts would be self-explanatory when I shall be working out a few practical problems dealing with the above control accounts. Now I would like to show you how a transaction appears in Financial Books. That is to say, recording of a transaction both in Financial Book and Cost Book. Before that I want to hear from you any point which is not clear to you.

Yes, yes .... what do you want to say?

☐ "Sir, can Cost Ledger Accounts be opened in Financial Book?"

● Why not? It can. Here all items of Income and Expenditure 'which affect cost accounts' are recorded.

Any other questions please!

☐ "Sir, you have not given us any light on the **advantages of Cost Control Accounts**".

● You see, you can easily realise the importance of the Control Accounts from the discussions made earlier. Well, when requested by you I would like to refer your attention to the work of Blocker and Weltmer. In their work, '***Cost Accounting***', Blocker and Weltmer listed five advantages of using control accounts :

1. "Controlling Accounts are invaluable to Management in policy formulation because they summarise masses of detailed information contained in subsidiary records.
2. Controlling accounts make possible a division of labour among clerks and accountants and a greater degree of specialisation in work performed.
3. A system of internal check exists through the use of controlling accounts because the work of one individual is checked against the work of others. This is an important factor in assuring accuracy, maintaining honesty and detecting errors.
4. The use of controlling accounts permits the prompt preparation of financial statements at the end of each accounting period without waiting for all work to be done in balancing individual subsidiary ledgers.
5. Controlling accounts permit the general ledger to remain under executive control, and since the accounting system is decentralised through the use of subsidiary records, costs and the financial position of the concern may be treated confidentially."

I think you all have followed the above discussions.

☐ "Sir, you have not given us any guidelines on the applicability of the general principles of controlling accounts. Kindly enlighten us."

● It was a omission, you see. However, I am explaining the same. Following principles[1] are to be observed in the context of use of 'Controlling Accounts' :

(i) The use of Controlling Accounts is advisable only when detailed information are compiled in records supplementary to General Ledger. As for instance, analysed overhead cost in wage sheet serves as subsidiary records for Factory Overhead Control Account.

(ii) When accounting system is not centralised, that is to say, when it is decentralised, the controlling of accounts with supporting subsidiary cost records and business paper can be enforced with advantage. The examples of subsidiary cost records are bound or loose-leaf ledger accounts, card files, columnar analysis sheets and examples of business papers are Time Ticket, Payroll Sheets, Production Orders and Expense Voucher.

(iii) The plan of operation is to be accounted in General Ledger which is designated as Control Account for an individual or group of accounts. The forms of subsidiary records are schemed and analysis of day-to-day transactions are to be made. Posting of all transactions are to be made from journal or from business papers to the subsidiary records. However, posting to controlling accounts in General Ledger is to be made from either journal or summarised statement of transactions. Controlling account balances are to be proved frequently against the sum of the balances of subsidiary records 'which it controls'. That is to say, the total of the balances of Stores Ledger Control Account, Work-in-Progress Ledger Control Account, Finished Goods Ledger Control Account should agree with the balance of General Ledger Adjustment Account.

I think you have followed the above principles of Control Accounts. Now I would like to show you the proforma of different important control accounts and also other accounts which are opened in this connection. Please note :

[1] Blocker and Weltmer, ***Cost Accounting.***

Dr. **General Ledger Adjustment A/c** **Cr.**

Particulars	Amount	Particulars	Amount
	Rs.		Rs.
To Stores Ledger Control A/c : Returns		By Balance b/d	
To Capital Order		By Stores Ledger Control A/c	
To Profit & Loss A/c Sales		By Material Purchased	
To Special Job		By Work-in-Progress Ledger Control A/c	
To Balance c/d		By Materials for Special Orders	
		By Production Overhead A/c : Carriage Inwards	
		By Wage Control A/c	
		By Work-in-Progress	
		By Ledger Control A/c Direct Expenses	
		By Production Overhead A/c	
		By Administration Overhead A/c	
		By Selling & Distribution Overhead A/c	
		By Costing Profit & Loss A/c	
		By Profit during the year	

Dr. **Stores Ledger Control A/c** **Cr.**

Particulars	Amount	Particulars	Amount
	Rs.		Rs.
To Balance b/d		By Work-in-Progress A/c Materials Issued to Production	
To General Ledger Adjustment A/c		By Production Overhead A/c Materials Used for Repairs	
To Purchase		By General Ledger Adjustment A/c Materials Returned	
		By Abnormal Loss A/c Materials Lost by Pilferage	
		By Production Overhead A/c Normal Material Loss	
		By Balance c/d	
To Balance b/d			

Wages Control A/c

Dr. Particulars	Amount	Particulars	Cr. Amount
	Rs.		Rs.
To General Ledger Adjustment A/c Wages		By Work-in-Progress Control A/c Direct Wages	
		By Production Overhead Indirect Wages	
		By Abnormal Loss A/c Idle Time	
		By Production Overhead A/c Normal Idle Time	

Production Overhead A/c

Dr. Particulars	Amount	Particulars	Cr. Amount
	Rs.		Rs.
To Stores Ledger Control A/c Material for Repairs		By Work-in-Progress Control A/c	
To General Ledger Adjustment A/c Carriage Inward		By Overhead Recovered	
To Wages Control A/c Indirect Wages Normal Idle Time		By Overhead Adjustment A/c Under-recovered	
To General Ledger Adjustment A/c			
To Stores Ledger Adjustment A/c Normal Loss			
To Special Repairs and Maintenance			

Administration Overhead A/c

Dr. Particulars	Amount	Particulars	Cr. Amount
	Rs.		Rs.
To General Ledger Adjustment A/c		By Finished Goods Ledger Control A/c Overhead Recovered	
To Special Repair & Maintenance		By Overhead Adjustment A/c Under-recovered	

Dr. **Selling and Distribution Overhead A/c** *Cr.*

Particulars	Amount	Particulars	Amount
	Rs.		Rs.
To General Ledger Adjustment A/c		By Cost of Sales A/c Overhead Recovered	
To Special Repairs & Maintenance			
To Overhead Adjustment A/c Overhead Recovered			

Dr. **Works-In-Progress Ledger Control A/c** *Cr.*

Particulars	Amount	Particulars	Amount
	Rs.		Rs.
To Balance b/d		By Special Repairs and Maintenance Order No.	
To General Ledger Adjustment A/c Purchases		Material	
To Stores Ledger Control A/c Materials Issued		Labour	
To Wage Control A/c Direct Wages		Production Overhead	
To General Ledger Adjustment A/c Direct Expenses		By Capital Order Materials	
To Production Overhead A/c		Labour	
		By Special Job No. Materials	
		Labour	
		Overhead	
		Special Purchase	
		By Finished Goods Ledger Control A/c	
		By Balance c/d	

Dr. **Finished Goods Ledger Control A/c** *Cr.*

Particulars	Amount	Particulars	Amount
	Rs.		Rs.
To Balance b/d		By Cost of Sale A/c Sale of Finished Goods	
To Work-in-Progress		By Balance c/d	
To Ledger Control A/c			
To Administration Overhead A/c			
To Balance b/d			

Special Repair and Maintenance Order A/c

Dr. Particulars	Amount	Cr. Particulars	Amount
	Rs.		Rs.
To Work-In-Progress		By Production Overhead A/c	
To Ledger Control A/c		By Administration Overhead A/c	
Materials		By Selling Overhead A/c	
Labour			
Production Overhead			

Capital Order No.

Dr. Particulars	Amount	Cr. Particulars	Amount
	Rs.		Rs.
To Work-in-Progress		By General Ledger Adjustment A/c	
To Ledger Control A/c		By Cost of Capital Work	
Materials			
Labour			

Special Job No.

Dr. Particulars	Amount	Cr. Particulars	Amount
	Rs.		Rs.
To Work-in-Progress		By General Ledger Adjustment A/c	
To Ledger Control A/c		By Sales	
Materials			
Labour			
Overhead			
Special Purchases			
To Profit and Loss A/c			
Profit			

Abnormal Material Loss A/c

Dr. Particulars	Amount	Cr. Particulars	Amount
	Rs.		Rs.
To Stores Ledger Control A/c		By Costing Profit & Loss A/c	

Abnormal Idle Time A/c

Dr. Particulars	Amount	Cr. Particulars	Amount
	Rs.		Rs.
To Wages Control A/c		By Costing Profit and Loss A/c	

Dr. Overhead Adjustment A/c Cr.

Particulars	Amount	Particulars	Amount
	Rs.		Rs.
To Production Overhead A/c		By Selling Overhead A/c	
To Administration Overhead A/c		By Costing Profit & Loss A/c	

Dr. Cost of Sales A/c Cr.

Particulars	Amount	Particulars	Amount
	Rs.		Rs.
To Finished Goods Ledger A/c		By Costing Profit & Loss A/c	
To Selling & Distribution Overhead A/c			

Costing Profit & Loss A/c

Dr. for the year ended 31st December .... Cr.

Particulars	Amount	Particulars	Amount
	Rs.		Rs.
To Cost of Sales		By Sales	
To Abnormal Loss :		By Profit on Special Job (No.)	
Materials			
Labour			
To Overhead Adjustment A/c			
Overhead Under-recovered			
To General Ledger Adjustment A/c			
To Profit during the year			

Trial Balance as at 31st December 20...........

Particulars	Debit	Credit
	Rs.	Rs.
Finished Goods Ledger Control A/c	X	
General Ledger Adjustment A/c	—	XX
Stores Ledger Control A/c	X	
Work-in-Progress Ledger Control A/c	X	
	XX	XX

I hope that the above explained proformas would help you to work out any practical problems on Cost Control Accounts. I think you have followed. Is there any question?

☐ "Sir, give us a few specimen Book-Keeping entries for Material, Labour, Direct Expenses and Overhead as would appear in Financial Books and Cost Book".

● You see, I was just thinking of giving the same. I would like to give the entries as :

Nature of Transactions	Financial Book	Cost Book
(A) MATERIAL		
1. Purchase of Material on credit	**Dr.** Purchase A/c or, Cost Ledger Control A/c (Memorandum) **Cr.** Creditors A/c	**Dr.** Stores Ledger Control A/c **Cr.** General Ledger Adjustment A/c
2. Purchase of Material on credit for special job	**Dr.** Purchase A/c or, Cost Ledger Control A/c (Memorandum) **Cr.** Creditors A/c	**Dr.** Work-in-Progress Ledger Control A/c **Cr.** General Ledger Adjustment A/c
3. Purchase of Materials on cash	**Dr.** Purchase A/c or, Cost Ledger Control A/c (Memorandum) **Cr.** Cash	**Dr.** Stores Ledger Control A/c **Cr.** General Ledger Adjustment A/c
4. Return of Material to Suppliers	**Dr.** Creditors A/c **Cr.** Purchase Return or, Cost Ledger Control A/c (Memorandum)	**Dr.** General Ledger Adjustment A/c **Cr.** Stores Ledger Control A/c
5. Issue of Direct Material to Production	No effects as such no entries	**Dr.** Work-in-Progress Ledger Control A/c **Cr.** Stores Ledger Control A/c
6. Issue of Indirect Material to Production	Do	**Dr.** Production Overhead A/c **Cr.** Stores Ledger Control A/c
7. Return of Material from Production to Stores	Do	**Dr.** Stores Ledger Control A/c **Cr.** Work-in-Progress Ledger Control A/c
8. Transfer of Materials from Job No. (a) to Job No. (b)	Do	**Dr.** Job No. (b) **Cr.** Job No. (a)
(B) LABOUR		
1. Wages are paid to the employees or workers after following deduction, say, Provident Fund and Income Tax etc.	**Dr.** Wages A/c. or, Cost Ledger Control A/c (Memorandum) **Cr.** Employees Provident Fund A/c **Cr.** Income Tax A/c **Cr.** Cash A/c	**Dr.** Wages Control A/c **Cr.** General Ledger Adjustment A/c
2. Wages paid to Direct Labour	No Entry	**Dr.** Work-in-Progress Ledger Control A/c **Cr.** Wage Control A/c
3. Wages paid to Indirect Labour (for example, Production Staff, Administration Staff and Selling and Distribution Staff)	No Entry	**Dr.** Production, Administration & Selling & Distribution Overhead A/c **Cr.** Wages Control A/c

Note : General Ledger Adjustment A/c. sometimes referred to as Cost Ledger Control Account

Nature of Transactions	Financial Book	Cost Book
(C) DIRECT EXPENSES		
1. Total Direct Expenses incurred during a year or job No. (assuming paid in cash)	**Dr.** Expenses A/c or Cost Ledger Control A/c (Memorandum) **Cr.** Cash A/c	**Dr.** Work-in-Progress Ledger Control A/c **Cr.** General Ledger Adjustment A/c
(D) OVERHEAD 1. Supply of service by the creditors in the nature of Production Overhead, Administration, Selling & Distributing Overhead	**Dr.** Expenses A/c or Cost Ledger Control A/c (Memorandum) **Cr.** Creditors	**Dr.** Production, Administration, Selling & Distributing Overhead A/c **Cr.** General Ledger Adjustment A/c
2. Miscellaneous Petty Cash expenditure incurred during a period in connection with Production, Selling & Distributing Overhead	**Dr.** Expenses A/c or Cost Ledger Control A/c (Memorandum) **Cr.** Cash	**Dr.** Production, Administration, Selling & Distributing Overhead A/c **Cr.** General Ledger Adjustment A/c
3. Production Overhead Absorbed	No Entry	**Dr.** Work in Progress Ledger A/c **Cr.** Production Overhead A/c
4. Difference between actual overhead incurred and Overhead absorbed. (Causes for difference are-increased or decreased production, above or below estimation of actual expenditure. The balance of this account represents either over or under-recovered overhead and this may be transferred either to Overhead Adjustment A/c or Costing Profit & Loss A/c directly	No Entry	**Dr.** Overhead Adjustment A/c **Cr.** Production Overhead A/c
5. Administration Overhead Absorbtion	No Entry	**Dr.** Finished Goods Ledger Control A/c **Cr.** Administration Overhead A/c
6. Transfer of balance of Overhead Absorption Account	—Do—	**Dr.** Administration Overhead A/c **Cr.** Overhead Adjustment A/c
7. Recovery of Selling & Distribution Overhead on Goods sold	—Do—	**Dr.** Cost of Sales A/c **Cr.** Selling & Distribution Overhead A/c
8. Transfer of the balance of the above Account	—Do—	**Dr.** Overhead Adjustment A/c **Cr.** Selling & Distribution Overhead A/c

□ "Sir, please work out a few practical problems".

• Well, now I would like to work out a few practical problems on Cost Control Accounts.

Problem

Following balances appeared in the book of Light and Shade Engineering Co. Ltd. at the beginning of 1st January 2005 :

Particulars	Dr. Rs.	Cr. Rs.
Stores Ledger Adjustment A/c	17,502	
Work-in-Progress Ledger Control A/c	8,574	
Finished Goods Ledger Control A/c	4,398	
General Ledger Adjustment A/c		30,474
	30,474	30,474

Following information was collected at the end of the year 2005 :

Purchase for Stores	1,15,280
Purchase for Special Job No. 78	3,500
Direct Wages	77,254
Factory Wages (Indirect)	19,086
Salaries (Administrative)	13,462
Salaries (Selling and Distribution)	8,504
Expenses for Production	24,864
" " Administration	17,092
" " Selling and Distribution	10,874
Materials Returned to Supplier	414
Issue of Material from Stores to Production	1,09,402
Stores Issued to Maintenance Account	4,952
Absorption of Production Overhead by Production	49,000
Absorption of Administration Overhead by Finished Goods	30,500
Recovery of Selling Overhead on Sales	19,200
Production of Finished Products during 2005	2,35,434
Finished Goods Sold at Cost	2,64,584
Sales	3,00,000

Show all the Control Accounts including Costing Profit and Loss Account and a Trial Balance as at 31.12.05.

Solution

General Ledger Adjustment A/c

Dr. Date	Particulars	Amount	Date	Particulars	Cr. Amount
		Rs.			Rs.
2005			2005		
Dec.31	To Stores Ledger Control A/c	414	Jan. 1	By Balance b/d	30,474
"	" Profit & Loss A/c —Sales	3,00,000	Dec. 31	" Stores Ledger Control A/c —Purchase	1,15,280
"	" Balance c/d	36,058		" Work in-Progress A/c —Sp. Purchase	3,500
				" Wages A/c— Direct Wages	77,254
				Indirect Factory Wages	19,086
				" Admn.–Salaries	13,462
				" Selling & Distributing Salaries	8,504
				" Production Overhead A/c	24,864
				,, Adm. Overhead A/c	17,092
				" Selling and Distribution Overhead.	10,874
				" Costing Profit and Loss A/c	16,082
		3,36,472			3,36,472
			2006		
			Jan. 1	By Balance b/d	36,058

Stores Ledger Control A/c

Dr. Date	Particulars	Amount	Date	Particulars	Cr. Amount
		Rs.			Rs.
2005			2005		
Jan. 1	To Balance b/d	17,502	Dec. 31	By Work-in-Progress Ledger Control A/c (Store issued to Production)	1,09,402
Dec. 31	To General Ledger Adjustment A/c (Purchase)	1,15,280		" Production Overhead A/c (Stores issued to Maintenance)	4,952
				By General Ledger Adjustment A/c (Return to Supplier)	414
				" Balance c/d	18,014
		1,32,782			1,32,782
2006					
Jan. 1	To Balance b/d	18,014			

Wages Control A/c

Date	Particulars	Amount	Date	Particulars	Amount
Dr.					Cr.
		Rs.			Rs.
2005			2005		
Dec. 31	" General Ledger Adjustment A/c	1,18,306	Dec. 31	By Work-in-Progress Ledger Control A/c (Direct Wages)	77,254
				" Production Overhead A/c (Indirect Factory Wages)	19,086
				" Administrative Overhead A/c (Admn. Salaries)	13,462
				" Selling & Distribution Overhead A/c (Selling and Distribution Salaries)	8,504
		1,18,306			1,18,306

Production Overhead A/c

Date	Particulars	Amount	Date	Particulars	Amount
Dr.					Cr.
		Rs.			Rs.
2005			2005		
Dec.31	To General Ledger Adjustment A/c (Production Exp.)	24,864	Dec. 31	By Work-in-Progress Ledger Control A/c	49,000
"	" Stores Ledger Control A/c (Stores issued to Maintenance A/c)	4,952			
"	" Wages A/c (Indirect Factory Wages)	19,086			
"	" Overhead Adjustment A/c (Balancing figure)	98			
		49,000			49,000

Administration Overhead A/c

Date	Particulars	Amount	Date	Particulars	Amount
Dr.					Cr.
		Rs.			Rs.
2005			2005		
Dec.31	To General Ledger Adjustment A/c (Administration Expenses)	17,092	Dec. 31	By Finished Goods Ledger Control A/c (Admn. Overhead absorbed by finished goods)	30,500
"	" Wages A/c (Admn. Salaries)	13,462	"	Overhead Adjustment A/c (Balancing figure)	54
		30,554			30,554

Dr. Selling & Distribution Overhead A/c Cr.

Date	Particulars	Amount	Date	Particulars	Amount
		Rs.			Rs.
2005			2005		
Dec. 31	To General Ledger Adjustment A/c (Selling and Distributing Expenses)	10,874	Dec. 31	By Cost of Sales A/c (Selling Overhead Recovered)	19,200
"	" Wages A/c (Selling and Distribution Salaries)	8,504	"	" Overhead Adjustment A/c (Balancing figure)	178
		19,378			19,378

Dr. Work-in-Progress Ledger Control A/c Cr.

Date	Particulars	Amount	Date	Particulars	Amount
		Rs.			Rs.
2005			2005		
Jan. 1	To Balance b/d.	8,574	Dec. 31	By Finished Goods Ledger Control A/c (Products finished during the year)	2,35,434
Dec. 31	" Gen. Ledger Adjustment A/c (Purchase for Special Job. 78)	3,500		By Balance c/d	12,296
"	" Stores Ledger Control A/c (Stores Issued to Production)	1,09,402			
"	" Wages A/c (Direct Wages)	77,254			
"	" To Production Overhead A/c (Absorption of Production Overhead by Production)	49,000			
		2,47,730			2,47,730
2006					
Jan 1	To Balance b/d	12,296			

Dr. Finished Goods Ledger Control A/c Cr.

Date	Particulars	Amount	Date	Particulars	Amount
		Rs.			Rs.
2005			2005		
Jan. 1	To Balance b/d	4,398	Dec 31	By Cost of Sales A/c (Sales of Finished Goods at Cost)	2,64,584
Dec. 31	" Admn. Overhead A/c	30,500			
"	To Work-in-Progress Ledger Control A/c	2,35,434	Dec 31	By Balance c/d	5,748
		2,70,332			2,70,332
2006					
Jan. 1	To Balance b/d	5,748			

Dr. **Cost of Sales A/c** Cr.

Date	Particulars	Amount	Date	Particulars	Amount
		Rs.			Rs.
2005			2005		
Dec. 31	To Selling & Distribution Overhead A/c	19,200	Dec. 31	By Costing Profit & Loss A/c	2,83,784
	" Finished Goods Ledger Control A/c	2,64,584			
		2,83,784			2,83,784

Dr. **Overhead Adjustment A/c** Cr.

Date	Particulars	Amount	Date	Particulars	Amount
		Rs.			Rs.
2005			2005		
Dec. 31	To Administration Overhead A/c	54	Dec.31	By Production Overhead A/c	98
"	" Selling and Distribution Overhead A/c	178	"	By Costing Profit and Loss A/c	134
		232			232

Dr. **Costing Profit and Loss A/c for the year ended 31st December 2005** Cr.

Particulars	Amount	Particulars	Amount
	Rs.		Rs.
To Cost of Sale A/c	2,83,784	By Sales	3,00,000
Overhead Adjustment A/c	134		
Gen. Ledger Adjustment A/c. – Profit	16,082		
	3,00,000		3,00,000

Trial Balance as at 31st December 2005

Particulars	Dr.	Cr.
	Rs.	Rs.
Stores Ledger Control A/c	18,014	
Work-in-Progress Ledger Control A/c	12,296	
Finished Goods Ledger Control A/c	5,748	
General Ledger Adjustment A/c		36,058
	36,058	36,058

Problem

From the following figures, ascertained from the Costing Records and Financial Books of a factory, you are required to pass the necessary entries in the Cost Journal (assume that a system of maintaining Control Accounts prevails in the organisation):

	Rs.
Purchases	3,90,000
Carriage Inwards	5,850
Stores Issued	3,58,800
Productive Wages	3,46,320
Unproductive Labour	1,21,680
Works-on-Cost	3,48,400
Material used in repairs	3,120
Cost of completed jobs	12,80,630

[C.A. India, Final]

Solution

Entries in the Cost Journal

		Particulars	Rs.	Rs.
(1)	Dr :	Stores Ledger Control A/c	3,90,000	
	Cr :	Cost Ledger Control A/c Or, General Ledger Adjustment A/c (Being the total amount of purchase of the period ascertained from finished book)		3,90,000
(2)	Dr :	Stores Ledger Control A/c	5,850	
	Cr :	Cost Ledger Control A/c Or, General Ledger Adjustment A/c (Being the amount for carriage inwards)		5,850
(3)	Dr :	Work-in-Progress A/c	3,58,800	
	Cr :	Stores Ledger Control A/c (Being the amount of stores issued as per Material Abstract)		3,58,800
(4)	Dr :	Wages A/c. Direct 3,46,320 Indirect 1,21,680	4,68,000	
	Cr :	Cost Ledger Control A/c (Being expenditure incurred for wages)		4,68,000
(5)	Dr :	Work-in-Progress A/c	3,46,320	
	Cr :	Wages A/c (Being the allocation of direct wages to job)		3,46,320
(6)	Dr :	Works Overhead A/c	1,21,680	
	Cr :	Wages A/c. (Being the allocation of indirect labour to works overhead)		1,21,680
(7)	Dr :	Works Overhead A/c	3,48,400	
	Cr :	Cost Ledger Control A/c (Being the amount for works on Cost accounted for)		3,48,400
(8)	Dr :	Works Overhead A/c	3,120	
	Cr :	Stores Ledger Control A/c (Being the amount for materials used in repairs)		3,120
(9)	Dr :	Stores Ledger Control A/c	12,80,630	
	Cr :	Work-in-Progress A/c (Being the amount for completed job)		12,80,630

Problem

From the following figures (standard, except where otherwise stated) relating to a month's activities, draw, up the various Control Accounts required, showing the total variances from standard. Please note that here total variance is only required, and no attempt should be made to analyse by causes :

Particulars			Amount Rs.	Amount Rs.
Stock Brought Forward				
Steel bars		....	7,000	
Pressings		....	5,000	
Tools		....	1,000	
Consumable Stores		....	2,000	15,000
Work-in-Progress brought forward				11,000
Direct Wages				
Machine Shop		....	3,000	
Assembly Shop		....	7,000	
Tool room		....	2,000	12,000
Overheads				
Machine Shop		....	6,000	
Assembly		....	3,500	
Tool room		....	2,000	11,500
Sales (actual)				42,000
			Actual Rs.	**Standard Rs.**
Purchase				
Steel bars			6,140	6,000
Pressings			6,090	6,000
Tools			1,050	1,000
Consumable stores			1,020	1,000
			14,300	14,000
Issues from stores				
Steel bar to Machine Shop			6,500	
Pressings to Assembly Shop			5,500	
Tools			500	
Consumable Stores				
Machine Shop	750			
Tool room	250		1,000	13,500
Production				
Machine Shop			20,000	
Assembly Shop			16,750	
Scrapped Work-in-progress				
Machine Shop	750			
Assembly Shop	250		1,000	
Work-in-progress carried forward			12,000	
Cost of Sales			35,250	
Allocation of Tool room cost				
Machine Shop	5,000			
Assembly Shop	750		5,750	

[Adapted from I.C.W.A. London, Final]

Solution

General Ledger Adjustment Account

Dr. Particulars	Amount	Particulars	Cr. Amount
	Rs.		Rs.
To Profit & Loss A/c			
Sales....	42,000	By Balance b/d	26,000
" Balance c/d	28,547	" Wage Control	12,000
		" Manufacturing Expenses :	
		Machine Shop	6,000
		Assembly Shop	3,500
		Tool room	3,000
		" Material control	13,000
		" Tools–Purchases	1,000
		" Material Price Suspense	300
		" Profit & Loss A/c –Profit	5,747
	70,547		70,547
		By Balance b/d	28,547

Materials Control Account

Dr. Particulars	Amount	Particulars	Cr. Amount
	Rs.		Rs.
To Balance b/d	14,000	By Machine Shop	6,500
" General Ledger Adjustment A/c	13,000	" Assembly Shop	5,500
		" Manufacturing Overhead	
		—Machine shop	750
		Tool room	250
		" Balance c/d	14,000
	27,000		27,000
To Balance b/d	14,000		

Tools Account

Dr. Particulars	Amount	Particulars	Cr. Amount
	Rs.		Rs.
To Balance b/d	1,000	By Overhead — Tool room	500
" General Ledger Adjustment A/c	1,000	" Balance c/d	1,500
	2,000		2,000
To Balance b/d	1,500		

Wages Control Account

Dr. Particulars	Amount	Particulars	Cr. Amount
	Rs.		Rs.
To General Ledger		By Machine Shop	3,000
Adjustment A/c	12,000	" Assembly Shop	7,000
		" Tool room	2,000
	12,000		12,000

Manufacturing Overhead (Machine Shop)

Dr. Particulars	Amount	Particulars	Cr. Amount
	Rs.		Rs.
To General Ledger Adj. A/c	6,000	By Machine Shop	12,500
" Material Control A/c	750		
" Machine Shops Cost	750		
" Overhead – Tool Room	5,000		
	12,500		12,500

Dr. **Manufacturing Overhead A/c (Assembly Shop)** Cr.

Particulars	Amount	Particulars	Amount
	Rs.		Rs.
To General Ledger Adj. A/c	3,500	By Assembly Shop	4,500
" Assembly Shop Cost	250		
" Overhead — Tool room	750		
	4,500		4,500

Dr. **Overhead Tool Room** Cr.

Particulars	Amount	Particulars	Amount
	Rs.		Rs.
To Wages Control A/c	2,000	By Manufacturing Overhead	
		Assembly Shop	750
		Machine Shop	5,000
" Material Control A/c	250		
" Tool room A/c	500		
" General Ledger Adjustment A/c	3,000		
	5,750		5,750

Dr. **Machine Shop Cost** Cr.

Particulars	Amount	Particulars	Amount
	Rs.		Rs.
To Control A/c		By Variance A/c	750
Material	6,500	" Work-in-progress	20,500
Wages	3,000	" Manufacturing Overhead	
" Manufacturing Overhead		Machine Shop	750
— Machine Shop	12,500		
	22,000		22,000

Dr. **Assembly Shop Cost** Cr.

Particulars	Amount	Particulars	Amount
	Rs.		Rs.
To Wage Control A/c	7,000	By Work-in-Progress	16,750
" Material Control A/c	5,500	" Manufacturing	
" Manufacturing Overhead		Overhead—Assembly Shop	250
Assembly Shop	4,500		
	17,000		17,000

Dr. **Work-in-Progress A/c** Cr.

Particulars	Amount	Particulars	Amount
	Rs.		Rs.
To Balance b/d	11,000	By Finished Goods Control A/c	36,250
" Assembly Shop cost	16,750		
" Machine Shop cost	20,500	" Balance c/d	12,000
	48,250		48,250
To Balance b/d	12,000		

Dr. Finished Goods Control A/c Cr.

Particulars	Amount	Particulars	Amount
	Rs.		Rs.
To Work-in-Progress A/c	36,250	By Cost of Sales	35,250
		" Balance c/d	1,000
	36,250		36,250
To Balance b/d	1,000		

Dr. Material Price Suspense A/c Cr.

Particulars	Amount	Particulars	Amount
	Rs.		Rs.
To General Ledger Adjustment A/c	300	By Variance A/c	253
		" Balance c/d	47
	300		300
To Balance b/d	47		

Dr. Variance A/c Cr.

Particulars	Amount	Particulars	Amount
	Rs.		Rs.
To Machine Shop Cost	750	By Profit and Loss A/c	1,003
" Material Price Suspense	253		
	1,003		1,003

Dr. Cost of Sales A/c Cr.

Particulars	Amount	Particulars	Amount
	Rs.		Rs.
To Finished Goods Control A/c	35,250	By Profit & Loss A/c	35,250
	35,250		35,250

Trial Balance

Particulars	Dr.	Cr.
General Ledger Adjustment A/c		28,547
Material Control A/c	14,000	
Tool A/c	1,500	
Work-in-Progress A/c	12,000	
Finished Goods A/c	1,000	
Material Suspensse A/c	47	
	28,547	28,547

Dr. Costing Profit and Loss A/c Cr.

Particulars	Amount	Particulars	Amount
	Rs.		Rs.
To Variance	1,003	By General Ledger Adjustment A/c – Sales	42,000
" Cost of Sales	35,250		
" Profit transferred to General Ledger Adjustment A/c	5,747		
	42,000		42,000

I think you have followed the above worked-out problems.

Now I would like to give few problems for your working :

Problem

Aene Manufacturing Co. Ltd. opens the costing records, with the balances as on 1st July 2006 as follows :

Particulars	Amount	Amount
	Rs.	Rs.
Material Control Account	1,24,000	—
Work-in-progress Account	62,500	—
Finished Goods Account	1,24,000	—
Production Overhead Account	8,400	—
Administration Overhead Account	—	12,000
Selling and Distribution Overhead Account	6,250	—
General Ledger Control Account	—	3,13,150
	3,25,150	3,25,150

The following are the transactions for the quarter ended 30th September 2006:

	Rs.		Rs.
Materials Purchased	4,80,100	Absorbed Overheads Production	3,59,100
Materials Issued to jobs	4,77,400	Administration Overheads	74,000
Materials Issued to works maintenance	41,200	Administration Allocation to Production	52,900
Materials Issued to administration office	3,400	Administration Allocation to Sales	14,800
Materials Issued to selling department	7,200	Sales Overheads	64,200
Wages Direct	1,49,300	Sales Overheads absorbed	82,000
Wages Indirect	65,000	Finished Goods produced	9,58,400
Transportation for incoming materials	8,400	Finished Goods sold	9,77,300
Production Overheads	2,42,250	Sales Realisation	14,43,000

Make up the various accounts as you envisage in the Cost Ledger and prepare the Trial Balance as at 30th September 2006. **[CA (Final) Adapted]**

Solution

Dr. **COST LEDGER OF AENE MANUFACTURING CO. LTD.** *Cr.*

General Ledger Control A/c

Particulars	Amount	Particulars	Amount
	Rs.		Rs.
To Costing P/L A/c	14,43,000	By Balance b/d	3,13,150
" Balance c/d	3,22,300	" Material Control A/c	4,80,100
		" Productions Overhead A/c (8400 + 2,42,250)	2,50,650
		" Wages Control A/c	2,14,300
		" Administration Overhead A/c	74,000
		" Selling & Distribution Overhead A/c	64,200
		" Costing P/L A/c	3,68,900
	17,65,300		17,65,300
		By Balance b/d	3,22,300

Material Control A/c

Dr. Particulars	Amount	Cr. Particulars	Amount
	Rs.		Rs.
To Balance B/d	1,24,000	By Work-in-progress A/c	4,77,400
" General Ledger Control A/c	4,80,100	" Production Overhead A/c	41,200
		" Admn. Overhead A/c	3,400
		" Selling and Distribution Overhead A/c	7,200
		" Balance c/d	74,900
	6,04,100		6,04,100
To Balance B/d	74,900		

Wages Control A/c

Dr. Particulars	Amount	Cr. Particulars	Amount
	Rs.		Rs.
To General Ledger Control A/c (Rs. 1,49,300 + Rs. 65,000)	2,14,300	By Work-in-progress A/c	1,49,300
		" Production Overhead A/c	65,000
	2,14,300		2,14,300

Production Overhead A/c

Dr. Particulars	Amount	Cr. Particulars	Amount
	Rs.		Rs.
To Balance b/d	8,400	By Work-in-progress A/c	3,59,100
" Material Control A/c	41,200	" Balance c/d	6,150
" Wages Control A/c	65,000		
" General Ledger Control A/c (Transportation)	8,400		
" General Ledger Control A/c	2,42,250		
	3,65,250		3,65,250
To Balance b/d	6,150		

Administration Overhead A/c

Dr. Particulars	Amount	Cr. Particulars	Amount
	Rs.		Rs.
To Material Control A/c	3,400	By Balance b/d	12,000
" General Ledger Control A/c	74,000	" Work-in-progress A/c	52,900
" Balance c/d	2,300	" Cost of Sales A/c	14,800
	79,700		79,700
		By Balance b/d	2,300

Selling and Distribution Overhead A/c

Dr. Particulars	Amount	Cr. Particulars	Amount
	Rs.		Rs.
To Balance b/d	6,250	By Cost of Sales A/c	82,000
" Material Control A/c	7,200		
" General Ledger Control A/c	64,200		
" Balance c/d	4,350		
	82,000		82,000
		By Balance b/d	4,350

Dr. Work-in-Progress A/c Cr.

Particulars	Amount	Particulars	Amount
	Rs.		Rs.
To Balance b/d	62,500	By Finished Goods A/c	9,58,400
" Material Control A/c	4,77,400	By Balance c/d	1,42,800
" Wages Control A/c	1,49,300		
" Administration Overhead A/c	52,900		
" Production Overhead A/c	3,59,100		
	11,01,200		11,01,200
To Balance b/d	1,42,800		

Dr. Finished Goods A/c Cr.

Particulars	Amount	Particulars	Amount
	Rs.		Rs.
To Balance b/d	1,24,000	By Cost of Sales A/c	9,77,300
" Work-in-Progress A/c	9,58,400	By Balance c/d	1,05,100
	10,82,400		10,82,400
To Balance B/d	1,05,100		

Dr. Cost of Sales A/c Cr.

Particulars	Amount	Particulars	Amount
	Rs.		Rs.
To Administration Overhead A/c	14,800	By Costing P/L A/c	10,74,100
" Selling and Distribution Overhead A/c	82,000		
" Finished Goods A/c	9,77,300		
	10,74,100		10,74,100

Dr. Costing P/L A/c Cr.

Particulars	Amount	Particulars	Amount
	Rs.		Rs.
To Cost of Sales A/c	10,74,100	By General Ledger Control A/c (Sales)	14,43,000
" General Ledger Control A/c (Profit)	3,68,900		
	14,43,000		14,43,000

Trial Balance
as at 30th September 2006

Particulars	Dr. Amount Rs.	Cr. Amount Rs.
Material Control A/c	74,900	—
Production Overhead A/c	6,150	—
Administration Overhead A/c	—	2,300
Selling and Distribution Overhead A/c	—	4,350
Work-in-Progress A/c	1,42,800	—
Finished Goods A/c	1,05,100	—
General Ledger Control A/c	—	3,22,300
	3,28,950	3,28,950

Problem

The following balances were extracted from a company's ledger as on December 31, 2005 :

Particulars	Dr. Amount	Cr. Amount
	Rs.	Rs.
Raw Materials Control A/c	48,836	—
Work-in-Progress Control A/c	14,745	—
Finished Stock Control A/c	21,980	—
Nominal Ledger Control A/c	—	85,561
	85,561	85,561

Further transactions took place during the following quarter as follows :

Particulars	Amount
	Rs.
Factory overhead — allocated to work-in-progress	11,786
Goods finished — at cost	36,834
Raw materials purchased	22,422
Direct wages — allocated to work-in-progress	18,370
Cost of goods sold	42,000
Raw materials — issued to production	17,000
Raw materials — credited by suppliers	1,000
Inventory audit — raw materials losses	1,300
Work-in-Progress rejected (with no scrap value)	1,800
Customers' return (at cost) of finished goods	3,000

Prepare all the ledger accounts in the cost ledger. **[C.A. Inter]**

Solution

Dr. **Nominal Ledger Control A/c*** Cr.

Particulars	Amount	Particulars	Amount
	Rs.		Rs.
To Raw Material Control A/c	1,000	By Balance b/d	85,561
To Balance c/d	95,039	" Raw Material Control A/c	22,422
		" Wages Control A/c	18,370
		" Factory Overhead Control A/c	8,686
		" Finished Goods Control A/c	3,000

Dr. **Raw Material Control A/c** Cr.

Particulars	Amount	Particulars	Amount
	Rs.		Rs.
To Balance b/d	48,836	By Work-in-Progress Control A/c	17,000
" Nominal Ledger Control A/c	22,422	" Nominal Ledger Control A/c	1,000
		" Factory Overhead Control A/c	1,300
		" Balance c/d	51,958
	71,258		71,258
To Balance B/d	51,958		

Dr. **Work-in-Progress Control A/c** Cr.

Particulars	Amount	Particulars	Amount
	Rs.		Rs.
To Balance b/d	14,745	By Finished Stock Control A/c	36,834
" Factory Overhead	11,786	" Factory Overhead Control A/c	1,800
" Wage Control A/c	18,370	" Balance c/d	23,267
" Raw Material Control A/c	17,000		
	61,901		61,901
To Balance B/d	23,267		

* This A/c can not be closed due to unavailability of actual sales figure.

Dr. **Finished Stock Control A/c** Cr.

Particulars	Amount	Particulars	Amount
	Rs.		Rs.
To Balance b/d	21,980	By Cost of Goods Sold A/c	42,000
" Work-in-progress Control A/c	36,834	" Balance c/d	19,814
" Nominal Ledger Control A/c	3,000		
	61,814		61,814
To Balance b/d	19,814		

Dr. **Wages Control A/c** Cr.

Particulars	Amount	Particulars	Amount
	Rs.		Rs.
To Nominal Ledger Control A/c	18,370	By Work-in-progress Control A/c	18,370
	18,370		18,370

Dr. **Factory Overhead Control A/c** Cr.

Particulars	Amount	Particulars	Amount
	Rs.		Rs.
To Raw Material Control A/c	1,300	By Work-in-progress Control A/c	11,786
" Work-in-progress Control A/c	1,800		
" Nominal Ledger Control A/c	8,686		
	11,786		11,786

Dr. **COST OF GOODS SOLD A/C** Cr.

Particulars	Amount	Particulars	Amount
	Rs.		Rs.
To Finished Goods Control A/c	42,000	By Costing P/L A/c	42,000
	42,000		42,000

QUESTIONS

1. Using suitable figures, journalise the transactions regarding Material in Cost and Financial Account.
2. What principles are to be followed before introducing the Cost Control Accounts System?
3. What are the advantages of maintaining Cost Control Accounts ?
4. Following balances appeared in the book of ABC's Cost Ledger at the beginning of the year 2006 :

Particulars	Dr.	Cr.
	Rs.	Rs.
Raw Material Control A/c	60,287	
Factory Overhead Control A/c		2,105
Work-in-Progress Control A/c	24,473	
Finished Stock Control A/c	50,389	
Cost Ledger Control A/c		1,33,044
	1,35,149	1,35,149
During the year 2006, following items arose :		
Finished Output (at cost)		42,167
Factory overhead incurred		18,302

Particulars		Dr.	Cr.
		Rs.	Rs.
Raw materials purchased			24,600
Payment made for :			
Direct Labour	Rs.10,106		
Factory Salaries	Rs. 4,333		14,439
Cost of Sales			37,178
Material issued to production			25,463
Sales return (at cost)			1,076
Materials returned to and credited by Suppliers			580
Factory Overhead allocated to production			15,440

You are requested to open Control Accounts and also prepare the Costing Profit and Loss Account. **[Adapted from I.C.W.A. (London)]**

5. Following balances were found in the Cost Ledger of an Engineering Company in the beginning of the year 2006 :

Particulars	Cr.	Dr.
	Rs.	Rs.
Stores Ledger Control A/c	7,000	
Work-in-Progress A/c	12,800	
Finished Stock A/c	2,000	
Cost Ledger Control A/c		21,800
	21,800	21,800

Following information was collected during the year 2006 :		Rs.
Purchase of materials	.....	40,000
Factory Wages (direct)	.....	60,000
Manufacturing Expenses	.....	34,600
Selling and Distribution Expenses	.....	5,400
Issue of Materials to Production	.....	37,200
Manufacturing Expenses Recovered	.....	34,440
Selling & Distribution Expenses Recovered	.....	5,320
Sales	.....	1,50,000
Stock of Material (31.12.06)	.....	9,800
Stock of Finished Goods (31.12.06)	.....	4,700
Work-in-Progress (31.12.06)	.....	14,700

You are requested to show all the Control Accounts, to prepare Costing Profit and Loss A/c and extract a Trial Balance. **[Adapted from C.I.S. Final, London]**

10

RECONCILIATION AND INTEGRATED ACCOUNTS

• Good morning to you all.

□ "Good morning Sir."

You see, in my last lecture I discussed in details about different cost control accounts. Now I would like to discuss with you about the concept of Reconciliation of Cost and Financial Accounting.

Importance of Reconciliation

It is a fact that the profit or loss as shown in General Profit and Loss Account and Costing Profit or Loss Account generally differ. So reconciliation between the two is very much important, both for management purpose and for effective control. The fundamental cause for the differences between the two is due to the fact that cost accounting system takes into account expenses or gains relating to cost of production, whereas financial accounts take into account all actual expenses and gains—whether it is related to production or not. However, the reconciliation between the two systems is possible through checking of results and verification of items of expenditures or gains as shown in the two systems of accounting —Cost and Financial. This process of reconciliation will bring to light any omission or wrong addition in either books of accounts.

The advantages of reconciliation are summed up as :

Advantages :

i. Cross Verification of entries can be made possible.
ii. Policies regarding charging of overheads, fixation of standard and reliability of cost data can be made effective.
iii. It is a basis of control device.
iv. Coordination between the cost and financial accounting departments can be made effective.

There is no denying the fact that whenever causes are identified, the processes of reconciliation become an easy job. So first let us find out the causes of differences or discrepancies between the Cost and Financial Accounts :

CAUSES OF DISCREPANCY

- (A) Items included in Financial Accounts, but not in Cost Accounts
- (B) Items included in Cost Accounts but not in Financial Accounts
- (C) Different Methods of Depreciation
- (D) Difference due to varying bases of stock valuation

I think, you have followed the above discussions.

☐ "No Sir, please explain to us in details".

• Well, please note below the causes of discrepancies :

(A) Items that are included in only financial ledgers but not included in cost account ledger. For example, items like loss of capital assets, stamp duty or expenses in connection with issue and transfer of capital stock, loss on investment, Discount on issue of shares or Debenture, penalties and fines, Interest on bank loan or mortgage, capital gains, rent received, interest and dividend received and amounts for appropriation of profits are of purely financial nature and not connected with cost of production. Accordingly, these are not included in cost accounts, rather, these are included in financial accounts.

(B) Certain items that are included in cost accounts but are not included in financial accounts. For example, items like interest on capital, charge in lieu of rent and over- and under-recovery of overheads etc. are taken as notional expenses in cost accounts. As these are not actually paid, these do not appear in financial accounts.

(C) The methods of charging depreciation in financial and cost accounting system differ. Since, in case of financial accounts, Straight Line Method, Diminishing Balance Method etc. are taken into account, whereas, in cost accounting system, generally Production Hour Method is adopted.

(D) In cost accounts, stock frequently appears in one figure and in the financial accounts it appears in different figures. That is to say, valuation of Closing stock and Work-in-Progress in financial accounting may be done on different bases.

I hope that you have now followed the above discussions.

Is there any question, please?

☐ "Sir, please work out a few problems on Reconciliation Account".

• Yes, I will .... but before that I would like to explain to you about the mechanism of reconciliation between Cost and Financial Accounts.

Mechanism of Reconciliation

You see, in reconciling between the two, the accountants can start either with Costing Profit and Loss Account in arriving at financial figure, or with General or Financial Profit and Loss Account to arrive at cost figure, by adding and subtracting different items.

☐ "How is it possible Sir? Please sir, start with Costing Profit and Loss Account figure".

• Well, look here. If it is started from Costing-Profit and Loss Account the procedures would be as :

Statement Reconciling the Profit as disclosed by the Cost and Financial Accounts

	Rs.	Rs.
Profit as disclosed by the Costing Profit & Loss Account :		***
Add :		
(i) Dividend Received and Credited to the Financial P & L A/c	**	
(ii) Over-absorbed Factory Expenses	**	
(iii) Over-absorbed Selling & Distribution Exp.	**	***
		***

	Rs.	Rs.
Less (or deduct) :		
(i) Preliminery or other expenses written-off in the Financial Profit and Loss A/c	**	
(ii) Goodwill or other fictitious assets written-off in the Financial Profit and Loss A/c	**	
Net Profit as per Financial Profit and Loss A/c		***
		***

Now if you analyse the above example, that is, if you arrive at financial profit from cost profit you would see that charges that are taken only in the cost accounts and not in financial accounts should be added to Costing Profit and Loss Account.

Again, incomes that are taken in financial accounts and not in cost accounts should be added to Costing Profit and Loss Account.

On the other hand, charges that are taken in the financial accounts but not in the cost accounts should be deducted.

Now, I think, you have followed. Is there any question?

□ "Sir, what would be the case if it is started from Financial Profit and Loss Account? Just show us the proforma".

● Well, note below the procedure if it is started from Financial Profit and Loss Account :

Profit and Loss Reconciliation Statement

	Rs.	Rs.
Profit as per Financial Account		***
Add : Charges made in the Financial Account, but not in Cost Account :		
(a) Discount on Issue of Debentures	**	
(b) Loss on Sale of Assets	**	
(c) Fines etc.	**	***
		***
Less : Income taken in the Financial Accounts but not in the Cost Accounts :		
(a) Dividend Received ...	**	
(b) Interest on Bank Deposit etc.	**	***
Profit as per Cost Account		***

May I think that the concept of reconciliation is clear to you. Did you follow?

□ "Very interesting Sir, for your very simple approach to the concept. You have explained the concept as lucidly as possible. For that, we thank you Sir".

● Many thanks to you also for your patient hearing and understanding.

"However, I am working out a few typical problems on this topic. After that I would like to discuss the integrated accounting system."

Problem

The following is a summary of the Trading and Profit and Loss Account of M/s Alpha Manufacturing Co. Ltd. for the year ended 31st December, 2005 :

Dr. **Trading and Profit and Loss Account** *Cr.*

	Particulars	Amount		Particulars		Amount
		Rs.				Rs.
To	Material Consumed	27,40,000	By	Sales (1,20,000 Units)		60,00,000
"	Wages	15,10,000	"	Finished Stock (4,000 Units)		1,60,000
"	Factory Expenses	8,30,000	"	Work-in-progress :		
"	Administration Exp.	3,82,400		Material	64,000	
"	Selling & Distribution Exp.	4,50,000		Wages	36,000	
"	Preliminery Expenses (written-off)	40,000		Factory Expenses	20,000	1,20,000
"	Goodwill (written-off)	20,000	"	Dividend Received		18,000
"	Net Profit	3,25,600				
		62,98,000				62,98,000

The company manufactures a standard unit. In the Cost Account :

(i) Factory expenses have been allocated to the production at 20 per cent on Prime Cost;

(ii) Administration Expenses at Rs. 3 per unit on units produced;

(iii) Selling and Distribution Expenses at Rs. 4 per unit on units sold.

You are required to prepare a Costing Profit and Loss Account of the company and to reconcile the profit disclosed with that shown in the Financial Accounts. **[I.C.W.A. India]**

Solution

M/S ALPHA MANUFACTURING CO. LTD.
Costing Profit and Loss Account for the year ended 31.12.2005

Dr. *Cr.*

	Particulars	Amount		Particulars	Amount
		Rs.			Rs.
To	Material Consumed	26,76,000	By	Sales (1,20,000 Units)	60,00,000
"	Wages	14,74,000	"	Finished Stock (4,000 Units)	1,60,000
"	Factory Expenses	8,30,000			
"	Administration Expenses (Rs. 3 per unit on units produced)	3,72,000			
"	Selling & Distribution Exp. (Rs. 4 per unit sold)	4,80,000			
"	Net Profit	3,28,000			
		61,60,000			61,60,000

Statement Showing Reconciliation between Costing Profit and Loss Account and Financial Profit and Loss A/c

		Rs.	Rs.
Profit as per Costing Profit and Loss A/c			3,28,000
Add:	(i) Over-recovery of Selling & Distribution Overheads i.e., selling expenses over-charged	30,000	
	(ii) Dividend Received, being the financial transaction not included in Cost Book	18,000	
	(iii) Factory Exp. in Work-in-progress	20,000	68,000
			3,96,000
Deduct:	(i) Under-recovery of Administrative Overhead	10,400	
	(ii) Preliminary Expenses written-off	40,000	
	(iii) Goodwill written-off	20,000	70,400
	Profit as per Financial Book		3,25,600

I think you have followed the above problem and its solution.

☐ "Sir, how are the figures for Material Consumed, Wages and Factory Expenses arrived at? Please enlighten us".

● Well, note below the workings :

	Rs.
Material consumed	27,40,000
Less : Work-in-Progress	64,000
	26,76,000
Wages Paid	15,10,000
Less : Work-in-Progress	36,000
	14,74,000

Prime Cost of Production (Rs. 26,76,000 + Rs. 14,74,000) = 41,50,000

Factory Expenses @ 20% on Prime Cost = Rs. 8,30,000

I hope you have followed.

☐ "Thank you, Sir".

Problem

You are required, as a Management Accountant of a manufacturing organisation, to prepare a statement reconciling the financial records with the cost records.

You are also required to write briefly on the possible causes of such differences between the two sets of records as disclosed by the comparison.

The following information relating to the operations for a given month has been supplied to you :

(a) Extract from Profit and Loss Statement prepared from financial books

	Rs.	Rs.	Rs.
Sales			36,128
Less : Cost of Goods Sold :			
Stock at the beginning of the period :			
Raw Material	3,984		
W.I.P.	2,216		
Finished Goods	7,842	14,042	
Raw Materials		10,224	
Direct Wages		7,163	
Manufacturing Wages		5,289	
		36,718	
Less : Stock at the end of the period :			
Raw Materials	4,285		
W.I.P.	3,072		
Finished Goods	8,177	15,534	21,184
Gross Profit			14,944

(b) Data obtained from costing records

Work-in-Progress at the beginning of the period :	Rs.	Rs.
Materials	956	
Wages	700	
Expenses, 80% of wages	560	2,216
Work-in-Progress at the end of the period		
Materials	1,398	
Wages	930	
Expenses, 80% of Wages	744	3,072
Materials and Wages charged to W.I.P. during the period :		
Materials		9,528
Wages		6,634

[Adapted from I.C.W.A. London, Final]

Solution

COST LEDGERS

General Ledger Adjustment Account

Dr. | | | Cr.

Particulars	Amount	Particulars	Amount
	Rs.		Rs.
To Cost of Goods Sold	36,128	By Balance b/d	14,042
" Balance c/d	16,440	" Materials Control	10,224
		" Wages Control	7,163
		" Manufacturing Exp.	5,289
		" Costing Profit & Loss A/c	15,850
	52,568		52,568
		" Balance b/d	16,440

Materials Control Account

Dr. | | | Cr.

Particulars	Amount	Particulars	Amount
	Rs.		Rs.
To Balance b/d	3,984	By Material in Process	9,528
" General Ledger Adjustment A/c	10,224	" Balance c/d	4,680
	14,208		14,208
To Balance b/d	4,680		

Wages Control Account

Dr. | | | Cr.

Particulars	Amount	Particulars	Amount
	Rs.		Rs.
To General Ledger Adjustment A/c	7,163	By W.I.P.	6,634
		" Balance c/d	529
	7,163		7,163
To Balance b/d	529		

Manufacturing Expenses Control Account

Dr. | | | Cr.

Particulars	Amount	Particulars	Amount
	Rs.		Rs.
To General Ledger Adjustment A/c	5,289	By Overhead in Process	5,307
" Balance c/d	18		
	5,307		5,307
		By Balance b/d	18

Material Process Account

Dr. | | | Cr.

Particulars	Amount	Particulars	Amount
	Rs.		Rs.
To Balance b/d	956	By Finished Goods Control A/c	9,086
" Material Control	9,528	" Balance c/d	1,398
	10,484		10,484
To Balance b/d	1,398		

Dr. **Labour in Process Account** Cr.

Particulars	Amount	Particulars	Amount
	Rs.		Rs.
To Balance b/d	700	By Finished Goods Control A/c	6,404
" Wages Control A/c	6,634	" Balance c/d	930
	7,334		7,334
To Balance b/d	930		

Dr. **Overhead in Process Account** Cr.

Particulars	Amount	Particulars	Amount
	Rs.		Rs.
To Balance b/d	560	By Finished Goods Control A/c	5,123
" Manufacturing Exp.	5,307	" Balance c/d	744
	5,867		5,867
To Balance b/d	744		

Dr. **Finished Goods Control Account** Cr.

Particulars	Amount	Particulars	Amount
	Rs.		Rs.
To Balance b/d	7,842	By Cost of Goods Sold A/c	20,278
" Material in Process	9,086	" Balance c/d	8,177
" Labour in Process	6,404		
" Overhead in Process	5,123		
	28,455		28,455
To Balance b/d	8,177		

Dr. **Cost of Goods Sold Account** Cr.

Particulars	Amount	Particulars	Amount
	Rs.		Rs.
To Finished Goods Control A/c	20,278	By Costing Profit and Loss A/c	20,278
	20,278		20,278

Dr. **Costing Profit and Loss Account** Cr.

Particulars	Amount	Particulars	Amount
	Rs.		Rs.
To Cost of Goods Sold	20,278	By General Ledger Adjustment A/c — Sale	36,128
" Profit transferred to General Ledger Adjustment A/c	15,850		
	36,128		36,128

Statement of Reconciliation of Profit as per Cost & Financial Accounts

	Rs.	Rs.
Profit as per Cost Accounts		15,850
Add: Over-absorbed Manufacturing Overhead		18
		15,868

	Rs.	Rs.
***Deduct*:**		
(i) Differences between the value of Raw Materials, Inventory as per cost, and Financial Books	395	
(ii) Wages incurred but not charged to WIP	529	924
Profit as per Financial A/c		14,944

Problem

The financial Profit and Loss Account of a Manufacturing Company, for the year ended 31st March 2006, is given :

Profit and Loss Account

for the year ended 31.3.06

Dr. *Cr.*

Particulars	Amount Rs.	Amount Rs.	Particulars	Amount Rs.	Amount Rs.
To Opening Stock :			By Sales		4,60,000
Raw Material	25,000		" Closing Stock :		
Finished Stock	40,000		Raw Materials	30,000	
Work-in-Progress	12,500	77,500	Finished Stock	15,000	
To Purchases		1,20,000	Work-in-Progress	20,700	65,700
" Wages (Factory)		30,000			
" Electric Power (Factory)		65,000			
" Factory Overheads		45,000			
" Gross Profit c/d		1,88,200			
		5,25,700			5,25,700
To Administration Exp.		20,500	By Gross Profit b/d		1,88,200
" Selling & Distribution Exp.		46,500	" Miscellaneous		
" Bad Debts		15,600	Revenue		26,800
" Net Profit		1,32,400			
		2,15,000			2,15,000

The cost accounts of the concern showed a net profit of Rs. 1,32,200.

It is seen that the Costing Profit and Loss Account is arrived at on the basis of figures furnished below :

Opening Stock of Raw Materials, Finished Good & WIP	Rs. 90,800
Closing Stock of Raw Materials, Finished Goods	Rs. 69,500

You are required to prepare Memorandum Reconciliation Account and reconcile the difference in the Profit and Loss Account. **[C.A. India, Final]**

Solution

Dr. **Memorandum Reconciliation Account** *Cr.*

	Particulars	Amount Rs.		Particulars	Amount Rs.
To	Under-valuation of Opening Stock	13,300	By	Net Profit as per General Profit and Loss A/c	1,32,400
"	Miscellaneous Revenues	26,800	"	Bad Debts	15,600
"	Net Profit as per Cost A/c	1,32,200	"	Administration Exp.	20,500
			"	Under-valuation of Closing Stock	3,800
		1,72,300			1,72,300

I think you have followed the working of the above problems. You see, I would like to work out a few more problems on Reconciliation. Is there any question?

☐ "Sir, the problems you worked out are quite sufficient. Please Sir, enlighten us on the concept of Integrated Accounting".

• Thank you very much. Of course, I would definitely give you some light about 'Intergrated Accounting'. Well, before that I place before you the views expressed by the Cost Accounting Sub-Committee of the Institute of Chartered Accountants in England and Wales. The Committee, in their report entitled '***Development in Cost Accounting***', says that 'we consider it fundamental that there should be complete integration between the cost and financial records not only for the purpose of cost control but also for the purpose of cost ascertainment. In order to achieve such an integration it is necessary that an all-embracing accounting scheme should be planned in relation to which accounting records can be developed for all purposes; both financial and costing.

Need for Integrated Accounts

The financial accounts and cost accounts of an organisation should be regarded as but two parts of one whole; both utilise the same basic information although in different ways. In our opinion, the chief accounting executive of any organisation should be responsible for seeing that all the sections of the accounting organisation contribute to the common end; that redundancies and unnecessary operations are eliminated; that information is brought forward promptly and reflected accurately; and that, in short, financial accounting and costing are so keyed together that they contribute, each in its proper sphere, towards the common objective.

So, in integrated accounting system, recordings of both cost and financial transactions are combined in the ledger.

☐ "Sir, what is 'Integrated' Accounting"?

Meaning of Integrated Accounts

• You see, the method of keeping cost and financial accounts in a single set of books is called Integrated Accounting. I think you have followed. Is there any question?

☐ "Sir, why should Integrated Accounting system be introduced?"

• You see, in many large firms, Integrated or Integral Accounting system has been introduced for the following advantages :

i. Under this method excessive cost for keeping two sets of accounts – Financial and Cost — may be minimised.

Advantages of Integrated Accounts

ii. Under this method there is no necessity for making reconciliation of cost profit and financial profit.

iii. This method provides data in a single ledger in respect of both Financial and Cost.

iv. This method satisfies the needs of both Proprietor and Management by providing pertinent cost and financial information.

However, I am explaining below the 'Method of Keeping Accounting' under 'Integrated' or 'Integral' accounts :

Nature of items	Under Financial Book	Under Cost Book	Under Integrated Method
1. Purchase of Material	Purchase A/c Dr. Creditors A/c Cr.	Stores Ledger Control A/c Dr. General Ledger Adjustment A/c Cr.	Stores A/c Dr. Creditors A/c Cr.
2. Payment for Wages	Wages A/c Dr. Cash A/c Cr.	Wages Control A/c Dr. General Ledger Adjustment A/c Cr.	Wages Control A/c Dr. Cash A/c Cr.
3. Overhead	Expenses A/c Dr. Cash A/c Cr.	Overhead Control A/c Dr. General Ledger Adjustment A/c Cr.	Overhead Control A/c Dr. Cash A/c Cr.

I hope you have followed the underlying philosophy of the integrated accounting system. On analysis of the above, it is clear that one entry has been taken from the Financial Book and the other from the Cost Book. However, it is clear from the above chart that Integrated Accounting system consists of two items – Debit item from Cost Book, and Credit item from the Financial Book.

Now, is there any question?

☐ "Sir, what are the main requirements of 'Integrated Accounting' system? Please enlighten us".

● Please note below the main requirements :

Main Requirements of Integrated or Integral Accounting System

(1) Capital & Other Financial Accounts
(2) Fixed Asset Accounts
(3) Stores Accounts
(4) Work-in-Progress Accounts
(5) Finished Goods Stock Accounts
(6) Control Accounts
(7) Expenses Accounts
(8) Variance Accounts

You see, I do not like to explain the above accounts since all these are self-explanatory.

☐ "Sir, please work out a few problems on 'Integrated' or Integral Accounts."

• Yes, I am planning to work out the same. Please note:

Problem

Give Journal entries (narrations are not required) to give effect to the double entry principles of Integral Accounting in respect of the following :

		Rs.
(a)	Payment of Net wages by cheque	800
	National Insurance by cheque	100
	Deduction from wages of Income Tax	100
(b)	Allocation of gross wages and National Insurance—	
	Direct wages (In Progress)	600
	Departmental Indirect wages	150
	(Wages are paid a week in arrear)	
(c)	Credit Purchases of Raw Materials	2,000
	and returnable packages	120
(d)	Charging into departmental costs of a proportion of annually paid insurances	70
(e)	Credit charging by outside engineers for departmental plant repair	240
(f)	Payment of supplier's accounts (after Rs. 60 taken for cash discounts)	1,130
(g)	Factory cost of production of finished stocks (Ratios : Direct materials 12, Direct wages 2, Factory overhead 6)	
(h)	Factory cost of finished stocks sold	8,000
(i)	Sale of finished stocks on Credit (after showing Rs. 370 sales rebate)	10,370
(j)	Payment by customers of credit sales (after taking Rs. 120 in cash discounts)	13,380

[Adapted from I.C.W.A. London]

Solution

No	Particulars	Dr. Rs.	Cr. Rs.
(a)	Wage Control A/c	900	
	National Insurance Withholding A/c	100	
	To Bank A/c		900
	" Withholding for Income Tax		100
(b)	Labour in Process A/c	600	
	Departmental Manufacturing Overhead Control A/c	150	
	To Wage Control A/c		750

No	Particulars	Dr.	Cr.
(c)	Material Control A/c	2,000	
	Returnable Packages A/c	120	
	To Sundry Creditors A/c		2,120
(d)	Departmental Manufacturing Overhead Control A/c	70	
	To Accrued Insurance A/c		70
(e)	Departmental Mfg. Overhead Control A/c	240	
	To Sundry Creditors A/c		240
(f)	Sundry Creditors A/c	1,190	
	To Bank A/c		1,130
	" Cash Discount Received A/c		60
(g)	Finished Goods Control A/c	10,000	
	To Material In Process A/c		6,000
	" Labour in Process A/c		1,000
	" Overhead in Process A/c		3,000
(h)	Cost of Sales A/c	8,000	
	To Finished Goods Control A/c		8,000
(i)	Sundry Debtors A/c	10,000	
	Selling Overheads A/c	370	
	To Sales A/c		10,370
(j)	Bank A/c	13,260	
	Cash Discount (allowed) A/c	120	
	To Sundry Debtors A/c		13,380

□ "Excuse me Sir, you have not given Narration for each journal".

● Yes, yes, I know. I have done it intentionally to see whether you are alert or not. I think you are now expert in the subject; so why don't you prepare the same".

□ Thank you, sir.

Problem

Following are the balances existed in Charming Company Ltd.'s Integrated Accounts as on 31st December 2004 :

Trading Accounts	Rs.	
Sales (Budgeted)	11,70,000	
Sales Variances	24,000	Debit
Direct Wages Variances	14,000	Debit
Factory Overhead Variances	4,000	Debit
Material Variances	10,000	Credit
Selling and Administration Expenses	28,000	
Factory Cost of Sales (standard)	9,86,000	

Balance Sheet items	Rs.
Share Capital	4,00,000
General Reserve	2,00,000
Sundry Creditors and Accruals	1,76,000
Fixed Assets	2,80,000
Raw Material in process and in Stores (at Standard)	1,60,000
Direct Wages in process (at Standard)	40,000
Factory Overhead (at Standard)	20,000
Finished Stock (at Standard)	1,80,000
Debtors	2,00,000
Cash at Bank	20,000
During the year 2005, following transactions took place	
Sales (Budgeted)	2,10,000
Sales (Actual)	1,96,000
Factory expenses incurred	34,000
Selling and Administration	6,000
Purchase of raw materials (at actual cost)	80,000
Issue of excess materials (at standard cost)	2,000
Cash payment to creditors	1,26,000
Paid for wage (Direct)	46,000
Receipt of cash from Debtors	1,90,000
Cost of Materials purchased (at Standard Cost)	84,000
Output Finished	
Material (at standard cost)	1,00,000
Direct Wages (at standard cost)	52,000
Factory Overhead (at standard cost)	26,000
Factory Cost of actual sales (standard)	1,64,000
Closing valuation of Work-in-Progress A/c are	
—Standard Direct Wages	30,000
—Standard Factory Overhead	26,000

Note : Work-in-Progress Account is debited at actual cost and Credited at standard cost.

From the above information you are requested

(i) to write-up and close-off the Accounts

(ii) to prepare a Trial Balance, and

(iii) a Profit and Loss Account and Balance Sheet as at 31st December 2005.

I hope, you would be able to work out the problem. Now I like to conclude my lecture.

□ "Sir, this is a complicated problem. Please work out the problem".

● Well, note below the workings of this problem :

Solution

Capital A/c

Dr. Particulars	Amount Rs.	Particulars	Cr. Amount Rs.
To Balance c/d	4,00,000	By Balance b/d	4,00,000
	4,00,000		4,00,000
		By Balance b/d	4,00,000

General Reserve A/c

Dr. Particulars	Amount Rs.	Particulars	Cr. Amount Rs.
To Balance c/d	2,00,000	By Balance b/d	2,00,000
	2,00,000		2,00,000

Creditors and Accruals A/c

Dr. Particulars	Amount Rs.	Particulars	Cr. Amount Rs.
To Bank	1,26,000	By Balance b/d	1,76,000
" Balance c/d	1,70,000	" Purchase	80,000
		" Factory Expenses	34,000
		" Administration Expenses	6,000
	2,96,000		2,96,000
		By Balance b/d	1,70,000

Fixed Assets A/c

Dr. Particulars	Amount Rs.	Particulars	Cr. Amount Rs.
To Balance b/d	2,80,000	By Balance c/d	2,80,000
	2,80,000		2,80,000
To Balance b/d	2,80,000		

Raw Materials in Stores and in Process A/c

Dr. Particulars	Amount Rs.	Particulars	Cr. Amount Rs.
To Balance b/d	1,60,000	By Finished Goods (Material Variance Rs. 2,000 and Finished Stock A/c 1,00,000)	1,02,000
" Creditors	84,000	By Balance c/d	1,42,000
	2,44,000		2,44,000
To Balance b/d	1,42,000		

Direct Wages in Process A/c

Dr. Particulars	Amount Rs.	Particulars	Cr. Amount Rs.
To Balance b/d	40,000	By Finished Goods	52,000
" Bank	46,000	" Direct Wages Variance A/c	4,000
		" Balance c/d	30,000
	86,000		86,000
To Balance b/d	30,000		

Finished Stock A/c

Dr. Particulars	Amount	Particulars	Cr. Amount
	Rs.		Rs.
To Balance b/d	1,80,000	By Cost of Sales	1,64,000
" Raw Material in Process	1,00,000	" Balance c/d	1,94,000
" Wages in Process	52,000		
" Factory Overhead in Process	26,000		
	3,58,000		3,58,000
To Balance b/d	1,94,000		

Factory Overhead in Process A/c

Dr. Particulars	Amount	Particulars	Cr. Amount
	Rs.		Rs.
To Balance b/d	20,000	By Finished Goods	26,000
" Sundry Creditors	34,000	" Factory Overhead Variance	2,000
		" Balance c/d	26,000
	54,000		54,000
To Balance b/d	26,000		

Debtors A/c

Dr. Particulars	Amount	Particulars	Cr. Amount
	Rs.		Rs.
To Balance b/d	2,00,000	By Bank	1,90,000
" Actual Sales	1,96,000	" Balance c/d	2,06,000
	3,96,000		3,96,000
To Balance b/d	2,06,000		

Cash at Bank A/c

Dr. Particulars	Amount	Particulars	Cr. Amount
	Rs.		Rs.
To Balance b/d	20,000	By Wages	46,000
" Debtors	1,90,000	" Creditors	1,26,000
		" Balance c/d	38,000
	2,10,000		2,10,000
To Balance b/d	38,000		

Budgeted Sales A/c

Dr. Particulars	Amount	Particulars	Cr. Amount
	Rs.		Rs.
To Balance b/d	13,80,000	By Balance b/d	11,70,000
		" Debtors (actual sales)	1,96,000
		" Sales Variance	14,000
	13,80,000		13,80,000
		By Balance b/d	13,80,000

Dr. **Sales Variance A/c** Cr.

Particulars	Amount	Particulars	Amount
	Rs.		Rs.
To Balance b/d	24,000	By Balance c/d	38,000
" Debtors (Budgeted Sales)	14,000		
	38,000		38,000
To Balance b/d	38,000		

Dr. **Standard Factory Cost of Sales A/c** Cr.

Particulars	Amount	Particulars	Amount
	Rs.		Rs.
To Balance b/d	9,86,000	By Balance c/d	11,50,000
" Finished Goods	1,64,000		
	11,50,000		11,50,000
To Balance b/d	11,50,000		

Dr. **Material Variance A/c** Cr.

Particulars	Amount	Particulars	Amount
	Rs.		Rs.
To Raw Material (Excess)	2,000	By Balance b/d	10,000
" Balance c/d	12,000	" Material Purchase	4,000
	14,000		14,000
		By Balance b/d	12,000

Dr. **Direct Wage Variance A/c** Cr.

Particulars	Amount	Particulars	Amount
	Rs.		Rs.
To Balance b/d	14,000	By Balance c/d	18,000
" Direct Wages	4,000		
	18,000		18,000
To Balance b/d	18,000		

Dr. **Factory Overhead Variance A/c** Cr.

Particulars	Amount	Particulars	Amount
	Rs.		Rs.
To Balance b/d	4,000	By Balance c/d	6,000
Factory Overhead	2,000		
	6,000		6,000
To Balance b/d	6,000		

Dr. **Selling and Administration Expenses A/c** Cr.

Particulars	Amount	Particulars	Amount
	Rs.		Rs.
To Balance b/d	28,000	By Balance c/d	34,000
" Sundry Creditors	6,000		
	34,000		34,000
To Balance b/d	34,000		

Trial Balance as on 31st December 2005

Particulars	Dr. Rs.	Cr. Rs.
Selling and Administration Expenses	34,000	
Factory Overhead Variance	6,000	
Direct Wages Variance	18,000	
Material Variance	—	12,000
Capital	—	4,00,000
General Reserve	—	2,00,000
Standard Factory Cost of Sales	11,50,000	
Budgeted Sales	—	13,80,000
Sales Variance	38,000	
Cash at Bank	38,000	
Debtors	2,06,000	
Factory Overhead In Process	26,000	
Finished Stock	1,94,000	
Direct Wages in Process	30,000	
Raw Materials in Stores and In Process	1,42,000	
Fixed Assets	2,80,000	
Creditors and Accruals	—	1,70,000
	21,62,000	21,62,000

Profit and Loss Account for the year 2005

Dr. Particulars	Amount Rs.	Cr. Particulars	Amount Rs.
To Cost of Sales	11,50,000	By Budgeted Sales	13,80,000
" Sales Variance	38,000	" Material Variance	12,000
" Wage Variance	18,000		
" Factory Overhead Variance	6,000		
" Selling and Administration Overhead	34,000		
" Net Profit	1,46,000		
	13,92,000		13,92,000

Charming Co. Ltd.

Balance Sheet as at 31st December 2005

Liabilities	Amount Rs.	Assets	Amount Rs.
Share Capital	4,00,000	Fixed Assets	2,80,000
General Reserve	2,00,000	Finished Stock	1,94,000
Profit for the year	1,46,000	Raw Material in Stores & Process	1,42,000
Creditors and Accruals	1,70,000	Labour	30,000
		Factory Overhead in Process	26,000
		Debtors	2,06,000
		Bank	38,000
	9,16,000		9,16,000

Problem

Organic Products Co. Ltd. keeps its financial accounts separate from its cost accounts. In the cost ledger on 1st January 2004 the balances were as follows:

Particulars		Rs.
Stores Ledger Control		15,000
Work-in-progress Control		23,250
Finished Stock Control		5,250
Cost Ledger Control		43,500
Transactions for the year ended 31st December 2004 were :		
Purchases of Raw Materials		82,500
Wages : Direct	1,18,500	
Indirect	31,500	
		1,50,000
Factory Overhead Expenses :		
Incurred		54,000
Absorbed		82,500
Administration Overhead Expenses :		
Incurred		18,750
Absorbed		18,600
Selling Overhead Expenses :		
Incurred		11,250
Absorbed		11,400
Materials Issued to Production		86,250
Sales		3,97,500
Work-in-progress : Value at 31.12.2004		20,250
Finished Stock : Value at 31.12.2004		6,000
The value of stocks and work-in-progress in the company's balance sheet were :		
As at 31st December 2003		46,500
2004		36,750
The following items have been recorded in the financial accounts only :		
Debenture interest paid		12,000
Loss on sale of investments		3,750
Dividends received		4,500

You are required to :

(a) Show the accounts in the cost ledger for the year ended 31st December 2004.

(b) Prepare statement reconciling the profit disclosed by the Cost Accounts with the Profit shown in the Financial Accounts. **[C.A. (Final), Adapted]**

Solution

Dr. **Cost Ledger Control A/c** *Cr.*

Date	Particulars	Amount	Date	Particulars	Amount
2004		Rs.	2004		Rs.
Dec. 31	To Costing Profit & Loss A/c	3,97,500	Jan. 1	By Balance b/d	43,500
	" Balance c/d	37,500		" Stores Ledger Control A/c	82,500
				" Wages Control A/c	1,50,000
				" Factory Overhead control A/c	54,000
				" Administration Overhead Control A/c	18,750
				" Selling Overhead Control A/c	11,250
				" Costing Profit & loss A/c	75,000
		4,35,000			4,35,000

Dr. **Finished Stock Control A/c** *Cr.*

Date	Particulars	Amount	Date	Particulars	Amount
2004		Rs.	2004		Rs.
Jan. 1	To Balance b/d	5,250		By Cost of Sales A/c	2,89,500
	To Work-in-progress Control A/c	2,90,250		By Balance c/d	6,000
		2,95,500			2,95,500

Dr. **Stores Ledger Control A/c** *Cr.*

Date	Particulars	Amount	Date	Particulars	Amount
2004		Rs.	2004		Rs.
Jan. 1	To Balance b/d	15,000		By Work-in-progress Control A/c	86,250
	To Cost Ledger Control A/c	82,500	Dec 31	By Balance c/d	11,250
		97,500			97,500

Dr. **Work-in-Progress Control A/c** *Cr.*

Date	Particulars	Amount	Date	Particulars	Amount
2004		Rs.	2004		Rs.
Jan. 1	To Balance b/d	23,250		By Finished Stocks Control A/c	2,90,250
	To Wages Control A/c	1,18,500		By Balance c/d	20,250
	To Stores Ledger Control A/c	86,250			
	To Factory Overhead Control A/c	82,500			
		3,10,500			3,10,500

Dr. Factory Overhead Control A/c Cr.

Date	Particulars	Amount	Date	Particulars	Amount
2004		Rs.	2004		Rs.
	To Wages Control A/c	31,500		By Works-in-progress Control A/c	82,500
	To Cost Ledger Control A/c	54,000		By Overhead Adj. A/c	3,000
		85,500			85,500

Dr. Wages Control A/c Cr.

Date	Particulars	Amount	Date	Particulars	Amount
2004		Rs.	2004		Rs.
	To Cost Ledger Control A/c	1,50,000		By Factory Overhead Control A/c	31,500
				By Work-in-Progress Control A/c	1,18,500
		1,50,000			1,50,000

Dr. Cost of Sales A/c Cr.

Date	Particulars	Amount	Date	Particulars	Amount
2004		Rs.	2004		Rs.
	To Finished Stocks Control A/c	2,89,500		By Costing Profit & Loss A/c	3,19,500
	To Administration Overhead Control A/c	18,600			
	To Selling Overhead Control A/c	11,400			
		3,19,500			3,19,500

Dr. Administration Overhead Control A/c Cr.

Date	Particulars	Amount	Date	Particulars	Amount
2004		Rs.	2004		Rs.
	To Cost Ledger Control A/c	18,750		By Cost of Sales A/c	18,600
				By Overhead Adj. A/c	150
		18,750			18,750

Dr. Selling Overhead Control A/c Cr.

Date	Particulars	Amount	Date	Particulars	Amount
2004		Rs.	2004		Rs.
	To Cost Ledger Con. A/c	11,250		By Cost of Sales A/c	11,400
	To Overhead Adj. A/c	150			
		11,400			11,400

Dr. **Overhead Adjustment A/c** *Cr.*

Date	Particulars	Amount	Date	Particulars	Amount
2004		Rs.	2004		Rs.
	To Factory Overhead Control A/c	3,000		By Selling Overhead Control A/c	150
	To Administration Overhead Control A/c	150		By Costing Profit & Loss A/c	3,000
		3,150			3,150

Dr. **Costing Profit & Loss A/c** *Cr.*

Date	Particulars	Amount	Date	Particulars	Amount
2004		Rs.	2004		Rs.
	To Cost of Sales A/c	3,19,500		By Costing Ledger Control A/c	3,97,500
	To Overhead Adjustment A/c	3,000			
	To Cost Ledger Control A/c	75,000			
		3,97,500			3,97,500

Reconciliation of Profit
(as shown by Cost Accounts and Financial Accounts)

	Amount	Amount
	Rs.	Rs.
Profit as per Cost Accounts	—	75,000
Add : **Income not recorded in Cost Accounts :**		
Dividend Received	4,500	
		4,500
		79,500
Less : **Expenditure not recorded in Cost Accounts :**		
Debenture Interest paid	12,000	
Loss on Sale of Investment	3,750	
		15,750
		63,750
Add : Opening Stock as per Cost Accounts		43,500
		1,07,250
Less : Opening Stock as per Financial Accounts		46,500
		60,750
Add : Closing Stock as per Financial Accounts		36,750
		97,500
Less : Closing Stock as per Cost Accounts		37,500
Profit as per Financial Accounts		60,000

Problem

BB Ltd. keeps its Financial Accounts separate from its Cost Accounts. The Cost Control Accounts show the following balances as on 1.1.2004 :

Cost Ledger Control		Rs. 70,960
Stores Ledger Control		Rs. 21,600
Work-in-progress Control		Rs. 34,850
Finished Stock Control		Rs. 14,510
The transactions during the year 2004 were :		
Raw Material Purchased		Rs. 1,34,420
Material Issued to Production		1,42,600
Wages : Direct	1,67,900	
Indirect	4,550	1,72,450

Overhead Expenses:	**Incurred**	**Absorbed**
	Rs.	Rs.
Factory Overhead	62,600	57,000
Administration Overhead	36,560	38,600
Selling Overhead	22,420	21,500
Sales	5,16,500	
Balances as at 31.12.2004 :		
Work-in-progress	31,600	
Finished Stock	16,200	
The value of stocks in the Balance sheet of BB Ltd were :		
As at 31.12.2003	Rs. 68,500	
31.12.2004	Rs. 51,600	

The following items have been recorded in the Financial Account only :

Loss on Sale of Investments	Rs. 4,400
Debenture Interest paid	Rs. 12,600
Dividends Received	Rs. 6,300

You are required to :

(a) Prepare Control Accounts and Costing Profit and Loss Account in the Cost Ledger for the year ended 31st December 2004.

(b) Prepare a Statement reconciling the profit disclosed by the Cost Accounts with the profit shown by the Financial Accounts. **[C.U. M.Com. Adapted]**

Solution

Dr. **Cost Ledger Control A/c** *Cr.*

Date	Particulars	Amount	Date	Particulars	Amount
2004		Rs.	2004		Rs.
	To Costing Profit and Loss A/c	5,16,500	Jan. 1	By Balance b/d	70,960
Dec. 31	To Balance c/d	61,220		By Stores Ledger Control A/c	1,34,420
				" Wages Control A/c	1,72,450
				" Production Overhead A/c	62,600
				" Administration Overhead A/c	36,560
				" Selling Overhead A/c	22,420
				" Costing Profit & Loss A/c	78,310
		5,77,720			5,77,720

Dr. **Work-in-Progress Control A/c** **Cr.**

Date	Particulars	Amount	Date	Particulars	Amount
2004		Rs.	2004		Rs.
Jan. 1	To Balance b/d	34,850		By Finished Stock Control A/c	3,70,750
	„ Stores Ledger Control A/c	1,42,600		By Balance c/d	31,600
	„ Wages Control A/c	1,67,900			
	„ Production Overhead A/c	57,000			
		4,02,350			4,02,350

Dr. **Finished Stock Control A/c** **Cr.**

Date	Particulars	Amount	Date	Particulars	Amount
2004		Rs.	2004		Rs.
Jan 1	To Balance b/d	14,510		By Cost of Sales A/c	4,07,660
	„ W-I-P Control A/c	3,70,750			
	„ Administration Overhead A/c	38,600	Dec 31	By Balance c/d	16,200
		4,23,860			4,23,860

Dr. **Production Overhead A/c** **Cr.**

Date	Particulars	Amount	Date	Particulars	Amount
2004		Rs.	2004		Rs.
Jan 1	To Wages Control A/c	4,550		By W-I-P Control A/c	57,000
	„ Cost Ledger Control A/c	62,600		„ Overhead Adj. A/c	10,150
		67,150			67,150

Dr. **Wages Control A/c** **Cr.**

Date	Particulars	Amount	Date	Particulars	Amount
2004		Rs.	2004		Rs.
Jan 1	To Cost Ledger Control A/c [1,67,900 + 4,550]	1,72,450		By W-I-P control A/c	1,67,900
				By Production Overhead A/c	4,550
		1,72,450			1,72,450

Dr. **Administration Overhead A/c** **Cr.**

Date	Particulars	Amount	Date	Particulars	Amount
2004		Rs.	2004		Rs.
Jan 1	To Cost Ledger Control A/c	36,560		By Finished Stock Control A/c	38,600
	To Overhead Adj. A/c	2,040			
		38,600			38,600

Dr. **Selling Overhead A/c** Cr.

Date	Particulars	Amount	Date	Particulars	Amount
2004		Rs.	2004		Rs.
Jan 1	To Cost Ledger Control A/c	22,420		By Cost of Sales A/c	21,500
			Dec 31	By Overhead Adj. A/c	920
		22,420			22,420

Dr. **Cost of Sales A/c** Cr.

Date	Particulars	Amount	Date	Particulars	Amount
2004		Rs.	2004		Rs.
	To Finished Stock Control A/c	4,07,660		By Costing Profit & Loss A/c	4,29,160
	To Selling Overhead A/c	21,500			
		4,29,160			4,29,160

Dr. **Overhead Adjustment A/c** Cr.

Date	Particulars	Amount	Date	Particulars	Amount
2004		Rs.	2004		Rs.
Jan 1	To Production Overhead A/c	10,150		By Administration Overhead A/c	2,040
	To Selling Overhead A/c	920		By Costing Profit and Loss A/c	9,030
		11,070			11,070

Dr. **Costing Profit & Loss A/c** Cr.

Date	Particulars	Amount	Date	Particulars	Amount
2004		Rs.	2004		Rs.
Jan 1	To Cost of Sales A/c	4,29,160		By Cost Ledger Control A/c	5,16,500
	To Overhead Adj. A/c	9,030			
	To Cost Ledger Control A/c	78,310			
		5,16,500			5,16,500

Dr. **Stores Ledger Control A/c** Cr.

Date	Particulars	Amount	Date	Particulars	Amount
2004		Rs.	2004		Rs.
Jan 1	To Balance b/d	21,600		By W-I-P Control A/c	1,42,600
	To Cost Ledger Control A/c	1,34,420			
			Dec 31	By Balance c/d	13,420
		1,56,020			1,56,020

Statement showing Reconciliation of Profit as shown by Cost Accounts and Financial Accounts

Particular	Amount Rs.	Amount Rs.	Amount Rs.
Profit as per Cost Accounts	—	—	78,310
Add : Dividend received	—	6,300	
Add : Op. Stock as per Cost Accounts	70,960		
Less: Op. Stock as per Financial Accounts	68,500		
		2,460	
			8,760
			87,070
Less : Loss on Sale of Investment		4,400	
Debenture Interest paid		12,600	
Closing Stock as per Cost Accounts	61,220		
Less : Closing Stock as per Financial Accounts	51,600		
		9,620	
			26,620
Profit as per Financial Accounts			60,450

Problem

Journalise the following transactions in the integrated books of accounts :

Particulars	Amount Rs.
(a) Credit purchase	12,50,000
(b) Production wages paid	5,00,000
(c) Stocks issued to production order	7,00,000
(d) Works expenses charged to production	3,10,000
(e) Finished goods transferred from production order	13,50,000
(f) Administration expenses charged to production	2,00,000
(g) Work expenses outstanding	1,00,000
(h) Work expenses paid	3,50,000

[I.C.W.A. Inter, Adapted]

Solution

Journal Entries under Integrated System of Accounting

Particulars		Dr. Rs.	Cr. Rs.
(a) Stores Ledger Control A/c	Dr.	12,50,000	—
To Sundry Creditors A/c		—	12,50,000
(Being purchase of goods on credit)			
(b) Wages Control A/c..............	Dr.	5,00,000	
To Bank A/c		—	5,00,000
(Being wages paid)			
(c) Work-in-Progress Control A/c........	Dr.	7,00,000	
To Stores Ledger Control A/c		—	7,00,000
(Being stores issued against production order)			
(d) Work-in-progress Control A/c.........	Dr.	3,10,000	
To Production Overhead Control A/c			3,10,000
(Being works expenses charged to production)			

Particulars		Dr. Rs.	Cr. Rs.
(e) Finished Goods Control A/c.........	Dr.	13,50,000	
To Work-in-progress Control A/c			13,50,000
(Being finished goods transferred)			
(f) Work-in-progress Control A/c..........	Dr.	2,00,000	
To Administration Overhead Control A/c			2,00,000
(Being administration overhead charged to production).			
(g) Production Overhead Control A/c........	Dr.	1,00,000	
To Outstanding Works Overhead Expenses A/c			1,00,000
(Being work expenses outstanding)			
(h) Production Overhead Control A/c.......	Dr.	3,50,000	
To Bank A/c			3,50,000
(Being work expenses paid)			

Problem

Dutta Enterprises operates an integral system of accounting. You are required to pass the Journal Entries for the following transactions that took place for the year ended 30.6.05. Narrations are not required.

	Rs.		Rs.
Raw materials purchased (50% on credit)	6,30,000	Selling and Distribution overheads incurred	40,000
Materials issued to production	4,50,000	Finished Goods at cost	5,00,000
Wages paid (50% direct)	2,00,000	Sales (50% credit)	7,50,000
Wages charged to production	1,00,000	Closing stock	Nil
Factory overheads incurred	80,000	Receipts from Debtors	2,00,000
Factory overhead charged to production	1,00,000	Payments to creditors	2,00,000

[B.Com. (Hons.), Delhi University, Adapted]

Solution

Journal Entries under Integral System of Accounting

Particulars		Dr. Rs.	Cr. Rs.
Stores Ledger Control A/c	Dr.	6,30,000	—
To Sundry Creditors A/c			3,15,000
To Bank A/c			3,15,000
Work-in-progress Control A/c	Dr.	4,50,000	
To Stores Ledger Control A/c			4,50,000
Wages Control A/c	Dr.	2,00,000	
To Bank A/c			2,00,000
Work-in-Progress Control A/c	Dr.	1,00,000	
To Wages Control A/c			1,00,000
Factory Overhead Control A/c	Dr.	80,000	
To Bank A/c			80,000

Particulars		Dr.	Cr.
		Rs.	Rs.
Work-in-progress Control A/c..............	Dr.	1,00,000	
To Factory Overhead Control A/c			1,00,000
Selling and Distribution Overhead Control A/c	Dr.	40,000	
To Bank A/c			40,000
Finished Goods Control A/c	Dr.	5,00,000	
To Work-in-progress Control A/c			5,00,000
Cost of Sales A/c	Dr.	5,40,000	
To Finished Goods Control A/c			5,00,000
To Selling and Distribution Overhead Control A/c			40,000
Sundry Debtors A/c	Dr.	3,75,000	
Bank A/c	Dr.	3,75,000	
To Sales A/c			7,50,000
Sales A/c	Dr.	7,50,000	
To Cost of Sales A/c			7,50,000
Bank A/c	Dr.	3,75,000	
To Sundry Debtors A/c			3,75,000
Sundry Creditors A/c	Dr.	2,00,000	
To Bank A/c			2,00,000

QUESTIONS

1. Discuss for and against Reconciliation of Cost and Financial Accounts.
2. What are the causes of discrepancy in Financial and Cost Accounts?
3. Explain the mechanism of Reconciliation of Financial and Cost Accounts.
4. What is 'Integrated' or 'Integral' Accounts? Do you justify the introduction of 'integral' accounts in medium type business? If so, why?
5. Is 'Integral Accounting' system quite separate from Financial and Cost Accounting?
6. Following balances were extracted from the Cost Ledger of Illusion Co. Ltd. as on 1st January 2005 :

	Rs.
Work-in-Progress	5,000
Finished goods	2,000
Stores	3,600
Transactions during the year :	
Stores purchases	21,000
Productive wages	60,000
Unproductive wages	18,000
Stores issued	22,000

Works Expenses	12,000
Selling & Administrative Expenses	8,000
Works expenses recovered	19,500
Selling & Administrative Expenses recovered	15,200
Sales	1,30,000

On 31st December 2005, stocks were valued as :

	Rs.
Work-in-Progress	7,350
Finished Goods	4,200
Stores	2,900

Unproductive wages are allocated equally between Works and Selling and Administrative Expenses.

You are requested to write-up the appropriate accounts in the Cost Ledger of the Co. and to prepare a Trial Balance as on 31.12.2005.

[Adapted from I.C.W.A. London]

7. The "Paints and Chemicals" company maintains its Cost Accounts on double entry system. The Cost Control Accounts show the following balances :

	As on 1.4.04	As on 31.3.05
	Rs.	Rs.
Material Control Account	20,000	10,000
Work-in-Progress Account	30,000	28,000
Finished Goods Account	50,000	80,000
Total	1,00,000	1,18,000

The transactions during the year 2004-05 were :

	Rs.	Rs.
Total Materials Purchased		1,60,000
Total Wages Paid — Direct	80,000	
Indirect	20,000	1,00,000
Indirect Expenses Incurred :		
Depreciation	30,000	
Power and Fuel	50,000	
Sundry Expenses	80,000	1,60,000
Loss on Sale of Capital Assets		2,000
Abnormal Loss		8,000

	Rs.	Rs.
Interest		10,000
Direct Materials Consumed on Jobs		1,20,000
Indirect Materials Consumed		50,000
Overhead Expenses Recovered from Jobs		2,20,000
Sales		5,00,000

Show :

(a) All the Control Accounts including Works-in-Progress, Finished Goods, and Cost of Sales Account.

(b) Profit and Loss Account; and

(c) Cost and Financial Profit and Loss Reconciliation. [C.A. India, Final]

11

OPERATING COSTING/ SERVICE COSTING

● Good afternoon to you all.

□ "Good afternoon Sir."

● Now I would like to take up for discussion the aspect which is very important in the study of Cost Accounting. Previously we were concerned with Cost of Production—Material, Labour, Overhead Cost etc. The study of Cost Accounting will not be fulfilled unless the costs of rendering services are taken into account. This chapter relates to the study of 'Cost of Rendering Services'. So operating costs are costs of rendering a particular or a group of services. That is to say, costs and expenditures incurred for operating and providing a service is called Operating Costs. According to the Terminology of Cost Accountancy, Operating Cost may be defined as 'the cost of providing a service'. Here costs are determined in terms of units of services rendered, that is to say, cost per tonne mile/km or per passenger mile/km in case of transport services. This method of costing is applicable to those undertakings that render service viz. Transport, Catering, Hospital and other services etc.

Meaning of Operating Cost

APPLICABILITY OF OPERATING COSTS IN UNDERTAKINGS

- **(A) Transport Services** (Motor Transport, Railways etc.)
- **(B) Catering** (Canteens, Hotels etc.)
- **(C) Hospital**
- **(D) Other Services** (Electricity, Water, Gas, Telephone etc.)

In this chapter I would like to take up for discussion :

(a) Transport Services, (b) Canteen, and (c) Electricity Undertakings.

Well, let me take up the matter for discussion one by one –.

Transport Services :

Advantages of Operating Costing

The advantages which can be derived from Operating Costing are :

i. Comparison can be made between different types of transport facilities; whether it is advantageous to transport by train or by lorry.
ii. Comparison about the cost of maintaining different types of vehicles can be made.
iii. Comparison can be made between the hired vehicle and owned vehicle.

iv. Comparison as to determination of the basis for fixing rate and for charging the same to department can be drawn.

I hope you have followed the above discussion. Well, now I would like to discuss about the different heads of Motor Transport Expenditure :

EXPENDITURE OF MOTOR TRANSPORT

- **Operating Cost or Charges**
- **Maintenance Cost or Charges**
- **Fixed Cost or Charges**

DETAILS OF OPERATING CHARGES

Petrol . . .
Grease . . .
Oil . . .
Driver . . .
Mechanics . . .
Assistants . . .

DETAILS OF MAINTENANCE CHARGES

Tyres . . .
Overhead . . .
Repairs . . .
Garage Charges . . .

DETAILS OF FIXED CHARGES

Insurance . . .
Depreciation . . .
Interest . . .
Tax . . .
Licence . . .

So the Total Expenses relating to Motor Transport consists of :

a. Operating Charges,

b. Maintenance Charges, and

c. Fixed Charges.

Please note that the following information are to be collected or computed before working out any problems on Motor Transport :

i. No. of days operated . . .

ii. No. of days the vehicle remained idle . . .

iii. Days Maintained . . .

iv. Hours Operated . . .

v. Trips Made . . .

vi. Miles Covered . . .

vii. Average miles/kms per day maintained $\left[\frac{\text{item vi}}{\text{item iii}}\right]$ . . .

viii. Average miles/kms per trip $\left[\frac{\text{item vi}}{\text{item v}}\right]$ . . .

ix. Average miles/kms per day operated $\left[\frac{\text{item vi}}{\text{item i}}\right]$ . . .

x. Cost per hour $\left[\frac{\text{Total Expenses}}{\text{Hours Operated}}\right]$ . . .

xi. Cost per day maintained $\left[\frac{\text{Total Expenses}}{\text{Days Maintained}}\right]$ . . .

xii. Cost per mile/km operated $\left[\frac{\text{Total Expenses}}{\text{Miles / kms Covered}}\right]$ . . .

xiii. Cost per day operated $\left[\frac{\text{Total Expenses}}{\text{No. of Days Operated}}\right]$ . . .

I hope that you have followed the above discussion. Is there any questions, please?

□ "Sir, how does a Transport Manager exercise control" ?

● Well, the Transport Manager maintains control through Log Sheet.

□ "Sir, what is Log Sheet"?

● You see, the ordinary meaning of log sheet is that it is a statement which maintains the information of (a) Trip record, (b) Details of workers and time, (c) Supplies, and (d) Causes of delay.

Well, you may get details of the same in Wheldon's book ***Cost Accounting and Cost Method***. So I would suggest you to go through the book.

□ "Sir, please show us a specimen of Log Sheet".

● Well, Please note :

LOG SHEET

Driver's Name . . .	Date . . .
Vehicle No. . . .	Time Left . . .
Route No. . . .	Time Returned . . .

TRIP RECORD

Trip No.	Distance From – To	Miles/kms. Covered Total Miles/kms.	Time Out – In	Tonne or Packages Carried
. . .	. . .	. . .		. . .
. . .	. . .	. . .	. . .	
	. . .			

Exceptional Delays	Workers' Time	Supplies
Traffic . . . Loading . . . Accidents . . .	Driver . . . Assistants . . . Mechanics . . . Cleaners . . .	Petrol Grease . . .

I hope you have followed the above discussion.

☐ "Yes Sir".

● Is there any question?

☐ "Sir, would you kindly enlighten us about the concept of Fuel Consumption and Tyre Performance" ?

● Yes, yes, I should. Please note :

Here fuel includes – Petrol, Oil, Diesel etc.

Assessment of Fuel Consumption = (OQ + NQ) – CQ.

OQ = Opening quantity in tank

NQ = Newly poured in quantity in tank

CQ = Closing quantity in tank

Please note here in this context that it is necessary to maintain a record in case of new and after every retreading the contribution of per ml/km tyre cost.

In case of new tyres :

$$\text{Cost per mile/km run} = \frac{\begin{pmatrix}\text{Purchase value}\\ \text{of Tyres}\end{pmatrix} - \begin{pmatrix}\text{Estimated values}\\ \text{when removed for 1st retreading}\end{pmatrix}}{\text{Miles / Kms Covered in 1st Run}}$$

In case of first retreading :

Cost per mile/km run =

$$\frac{\left(\begin{array}{l}\text{Estimated value when}\\\text{removed for 1st retreading}\end{array}\right)+\left(\begin{array}{l}\text{Cost of}\\\text{retreading}\end{array}\right)-\left(\begin{array}{l}\text{Estimated value when}\\\text{removed for 2nd retreading}\end{array}\right)}{\text{Miles / Kms Covered in 2nd Run}}$$

Now, I think, you have followed the concept of assessment of fuel consumption and tyre performance.

Are there any questions? You can ask me any question without any hesitation.

☐ "Sir, what is Absolute Ton Mile and Commercial Ton Mile. Kindly enlighten us.

● Well, please note

Absolute Ton Mile/Km = Load × Distance to and fro.

Commercial Ton Mile/Km = Average Load × Total distance

$$\text{Average Load} = \left(\frac{\text{Maximum Load} + \text{Minimum Load}}{2}\right)$$

Now I would like to discuss about Railway Transport. You see, the costs of railways can be classified under four broad heads :

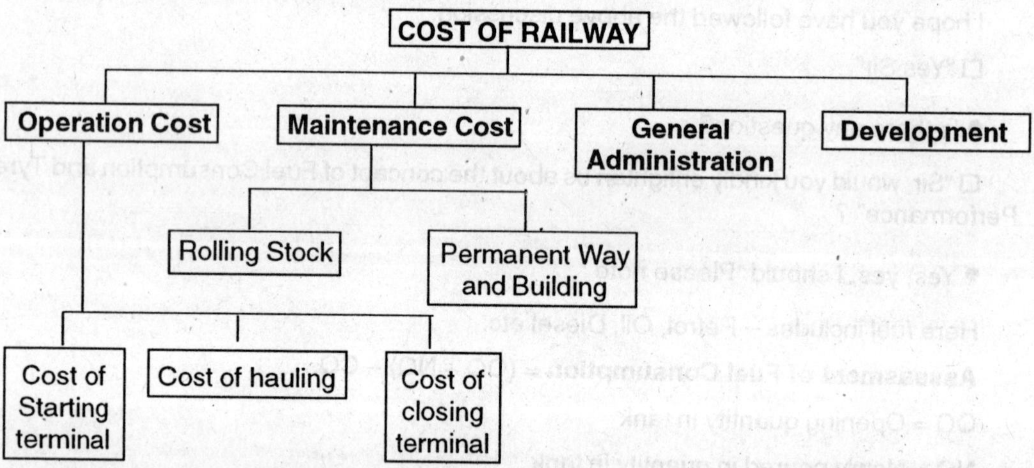

So long I was discussing with you Transport Costing. I hope you have followed the above discussion. Is there any question?

☐ "Sir, would you please enlighten us on the concept of Canteen Costing."

● Yes I will . . .

Please note the details about Canteen Costing —

Heads of Canteen Expenses can be classified as :

CANTEEN EXPENSES

- **Provisions** (Meat, fish, soft drinks tea, etc.)
- **Labour** (**Cooks,** Kitchen etc.)
- **Services** (Elect. Power light etc.)
- **Consumable Stores** (Cleaning materials, cutlery etc.)
- **Misc. Overhead** (Rent, Rates, Depreciation etc.)
- **Credit** (Charges for meal, tea etc.)

The above items of expenses are taken into account in operating cost of Canteen.

Well, regarding electricity undertaking, I am to say that electricity undertakings are of two types :

CLASSIFICATION OF ELECTRICITY UNDERTAKINGS

- **Generation of Electricity**
  - Hydroelectric Power
  - Thermal Power
- **Distribution of Electricity**

So, the cost and nature of expenses of electricity undertakings are dependent on the above classification. Now I do hope that you have followed my earlier discussion.

□ "Yes Sir."

● Is there any question?

□ "Sir what is the Load Factor?"

● You see, Load Factor can be studied from two points of view :

$$\textbf{Load Factor} = \frac{\text{Units Generated}}{\text{Per hour Maximum Capacity} \times \text{No. of Hrs.}} \times 100$$

(With reference to Generator)

$$\textbf{Load Factor} = \frac{\text{Units Consumed}}{\text{Per hour Maximum Demand} \times \text{No. of Hrs.}} \times 100$$

(with reference to transmission and distribution)

Now I would like to work out a few practical problems on Operating Costing. Please note them very carefully.

Problem

A factory which uses a large amount of coal is situated between two collieries "Ashman" and "Bhainkar", the former being 5 miles and latter 10 miles distant from the factory. A fleet of lorries of 5-ton carrying capacity is used for the collection of coal from the pit-heads. Records reveal that the lorries average a speed of 20 miles an hour when running and regularly take 10 minutes in the factory yard to unload. At colliery "Ashman", loading time averages 30 minutes per load; at colliery "Bhainkar" 20 minutes per load.

Drivers' licenses, depreciation, garage and similar charges are found to cost Rs.6.00 per hour operated. Fuel, oil, tyres, repairs, and similar charges are found to cost Re.0.50 per mile run.

Draw up a statement showing the cost per ton-mile of carrying coal from each colliery. If the coal is of equal quality and priced at pit-head, from which colliery should the purchase be made? **[Adapted from I.C.W.A. (London) Final]**

Solution

COMPARATIVE COST-PER-TON-MILE STATEMENT OF COLLIERIES 'ASHMAN' AND 'BHAINKAR'

	'Ashman'	'Bhainkar'
Time taken from Commencement to Unloading WN-1	70 Minutes	90 Minutes
Mileage covered from Commencement till Unloading	10 Miles	20 Miles
Ton-Miles WN-2	25	50
Drivers' wages, licenses, depreciation, garage and similar charges for carrying 5 ton coal @ Rs.6.00 per hour	Rs. 7.00	Rs. 9.00
Fuel, oil, tyres, repairs for carrying Coal Re.0.50 per mile run	Rs. 5.00	Rs.10.00
	Rs.12.00	Rs.19.00
Cost per ton of coal	Rs. 2.4	Rs. 3.8
Cost per ton-mile WN-2	Re. 0.48	Re. 0.38

Working Note 1 (WN 1)

	Ashman	**Bhainkar**
Time taken per trip		
Loading time	30 min	20 min
Unloading time	10 min	10 min
To-and-fro travelling time		
(i) Ashman $\frac{60}{20} \times 10$	30 min	60 min
(ii) Bhainkar $\frac{60}{20} \times 20$		
	70 min	90 min

Working Note 2 (WN 2)

Ton mile	$5 \times 5 = 25$	$5 \times 10 = 50$
Cost per ton of coal	2.4	3.8
Cost per ton mile	$\frac{12}{25}$ = 0.48	$\frac{19}{50}$ = 0.38

Purchases should certainly be made from colliery "Ashman" the reason being that five tons of coal can be transported for Rs. 12 in 70 min whereas in the case of colliery "Bhainkar" the same tonnage would cost Rs. 19 and take 90 min.

I hope, you have followed the above problem.

□ "Yes Sir".

• Well, now I would like to conclude my lecture on Operating Costing. Is there any question?

□ "Sir, please work out a few more problems".

• Please note the following problems :

Problem

The following cost data pertaining to the year 2004-2005 are collected from the books of A.B.C. Power Co. Ltd.

Prepare a Cost Sheet showing the cost of power per unit of Kwh :

Total Units Generated	...	15,00,000 Units
Operation		Rs.
Labour	...	16,500
Plant Supervision	...	5,250
Lubricant and Supplies	...	10,500
Repairs and Maintenance	...	21,000
Administrative Overhead	...	9,000
Capital Cost	...	1,50,000

Coal consumed per Kwh for the year is 1.5 lbs. and cost of coal delivered to the power station is Rs.33.06 per metric tonne.

Depreciation rate chargeable is 4% per annum and interest on capital is to be taken at 1% higher than the Reserve Bank rate of 6% per annum. **[Adapted from C.A. Final]**

Solution

Cost Sheet of A.B.C. Power Co. for the year 2004-2005

Total Units Generated	...	15,00,000 Units
Operation Cost :	...	Rs.
Labour	...	16,500
Consumption of Coal	...	33,741
Supervision of Plant	...	5,250
Depreciation	...	6,000
Lubricant and Supplies	...	10,500
Repairs and Maintenance	...	21,000
		92,991

Administrative and Other Costs :

Administrative Overhead	...	9,000
Interest on Capital @ 7%	...	10,500
Total Costs		Rs.1,12,491

Cost per unit $= \frac{\text{Total Costs}}{\text{Units Generated}} = \frac{\text{Rs.1,12,491}}{\text{15,00,000 units}}$ = 7.5 paise per unit (app).

☐ "Sir, please show us how the figure for Coal Consumed is calculated".

● Well, please note the working :

1 lb = 0.4536 kg.

Coal Consumed per Kwh for the year is 1.5 lbs.

Total Units Generated = 15,00,000 Units.

Quantity of Coal Consumed during the year is 1.5 lbs × 15,00,000 Units = 22,50,000 lbs = 22,50,000 × 0.4536 = 1,020.6 metric tonnes.

1,020.6 metric tonnes × Rs.33.06 = Rs.33,741

I hope you have followed the workings.

☐ "Yes Sir",

● Well, take another problem.

Problem

From the following data, calculate the cost per mile of a vehicle :

		Rs.
Value of vehicle	...	25,000
Garage rent per year	...	1,200
Insurance charge per year	...	400
Road tax per year	...	500
Driver's wage per month	...	400
Cost of petrol per litre	...	1.40
Miscellaneous—including tyres and maintenance per mile	...	Re. 0.20
Estimated life	...	1,50,000 miles
Miles per litre of petrol	...	5
Estimated annual mileage	...	10,000 miles
Ignore interest on capital		**[I.C.W.A.I.]**

Solution

Estimated Annual Mileage	...	10,000 miles
		Rs.
Garage rent	...	1,200
Insurance charge	...	400

Road Tax	...	500
Driver's wages (Annual)	...	4,800
Cost of petrol $\left(\frac{10,000}{5} = 2,000 \times \text{Rs.}1.40\right)$	...	2,800
Miscellaneous Expenses (Re 0.20 × 10,000 miles)	...	2,000
Depreciation	...	1,667
Total Annual Cost		Rs.13,367

$$\text{Cost per Mile} = \frac{\text{Total Annual Cost}}{\text{Total Annual Mileage}} = \frac{\text{Rs.}13,367}{10,000 \text{ miles}} = \text{Rs.}1.34 \text{ (app.)}$$

I hope you have followed the workings of the problem. Did you follow?

□ "Sir, I could not follow how the figure for depreciation is arrived at. Please explain.

• You see, depreciation is to be calculated on the basis of the total mileage during the life of the vehicle. So depreciation is calculated on the following basis :

$$\left(\frac{\text{Estimated Annual Mileage}}{\text{Estimated life of the vehicle}} \times \text{Value of the vehicle}\right)$$

$$\left(\frac{10,000}{1,50,000} \times \text{Rs.}25,000\right) = \text{Rs.}1,667 \text{ (app.)}$$

I think you have understood the problems.

Is there any question(s) ?

□ "Sir, if I am excused, I want to say something."

• Yes, Please feel free.

□ "Sir, now a days is it possible to have a vehicle for Rs. 25,000, cost of Petrol per litre Rs.1.40 etc."

Well, you are right. But I am here to make you understand the principle and mechanism of the calculations.

You can prepare a problem taking into present market value of vehicle and petrol cost and other aspect.

Do you follow me?

□ Yes, Sir. Thank you, Sir.

• Please take down the following problems for your workings :

Problem

Mr. X owns a bus which runs according to the following schedule :

(i) Delhi to Chandigarh and back the same day.
Distance Covered : 150 kms one way
Number of days run each month : 8
Seating capacity occupied 90%.

(ii) Delhi to Agra and back the same day.
Distance Covered : 120 kms one way.
Number of days run each month : 10
Seating capacity occupied 85%.

(iii) Delhi to Jaipur and back the same day.
Distance covered : 270 kms one way.
Number of days run each month : 6
Seating capacity occupied 100%.

(iv) Following are the other details :

	Rs.	
Cost of the bus	6,00,000	
Salary of the drivers	2,800	p.m.
Salary of the conductors	2,200	p.m.
Salary of the Part-time Accountant	200	p.m.
Insurance of the bus	4,800	p.a.
Diesel Consumption 4 kms per litre, at	6	per litre
Road Tax	1,500	p.a.
Lubricant Oil	10	per 100 kms
Permit Fee	315	p.m.
Repairs and Maintenance	1,000	p.m.
Depreciation of the bus	@ 20% p.a.	
Seating Capacity of the bus	50 persons	

Passenger tax is 20% of the total takings.

Calculate the bus fare to be charged from each passenger to earn a profit of 30% on total takings.

The fares are to be indicated per passenger for the journeys :
(i) Delhi to Chandigarh
(ii) Delhi to Agra
(iii) Delhi to Jaipur. **[C.A. Inter]**

Solution

Statement of Operating Cost (per month)

Particulars	Amount Rs.	Amount Rs.
Fixed Costs :		
Salary of Drivers	2,800	
Salary of Conductors	2,200	
Salary of Part-time Accountant	200	
Insurance (Rs.4,800/12)	400	
Road tax (Rs.1,500/12)	125	
Permit Fee	315	
Depreciation of Bus (Rs.6,00,000 × 20% × 1/12)	10,000	
		16,040

Particulars	Amount	Amount
	Rs.	Rs.
Running Costs :		
Diesel $\left(\frac{8,040}{4} \times Rs.6.00\right)$(W.N.1)		12,060
Lubricant oil $\left(\frac{8,040}{100} \times Rs.10\right)$		804
Repair and Maintenance		1,000
Total Cost per month		29,904
Passenger tax (W.N.3.)		11,961 .60
Profit (W.N. 3)		17,942 .40
Total taking		59,808 .00

$\therefore$ Rate per passenger Km = $\frac{59,808}{3,72,000} = 0.1608$

$\therefore$ **Rate to be charged per passenger :** Rs.

(i) Delhi to Chandigarh (Re. 0·1608 × 150) = 24.12
(ii) Delhi to Agra (Re. 0·1608 × 120) = 19.30
(iii) Delhi to Jaipur (Re. 0·1608 × 270) = 43.42

Working Notes :

(1) Total running kms. per month :

(i) Delhi to Chandigarh (150 × 2 × 8) = 2,400
(ii) Delhi to Agra (120 × 2 × 10) = 2,400
(iii) Delhi to Jaipur (270 × 2 × 6) = 3,240

8,040

(2) Total Passenger kms. per month :

(i) Delhi to Chandigarh (50 × 2 × 8) × 90% × 150 = 1,08,000
(ii) Delhi to Agra (50 × 2 × 10) × 85% × 120 = 1,02,000
(iii) Delhi to Jaipur (50 × 2 × 6) × 100% × 270 = 1,62,000

3,72,000

(3) Let the total taking be X

$\therefore$ Passenger tax 20% of x = .2x

Profit 30% of x = .3x

$\therefore$ 29,904 + .2x + .3x = x

or, x – .2x – .3x = 29,904

or, .5x = 29,904

or, $x = \frac{Rs.29,904}{.5}$ = Rs.59,808

$\therefore$ Passenger tax Rs.59,808 × 20% = Rs.11,961.60

Profit = Rs. 59,808 × 30% = Rs.17,942.40

Problem

A company presently brings coal to its factory from a nearby yard and the rate paid for transportation of coal from the yard, located 6 km away, to factory is Rs. 50 per tonne. The total coal to be handled in a month is 24,000 tonnes.

The company is considering proposal to buy its own truck and has the option of buying either a 10-tonne capacity or a 8-tonne capacity truck.

The following information are available :

Particulars	10-tonne Truck	8-tonne Truck
Purchase price	Rs.10,00,000	Rs.8,50,000
Life (years)	5	5
Scrap value at the end of 5th year	Nil	Nil
Km. per litre of diesel	3	4
Repair/maintenance p.a. per truck	60,000	48,000
Other fixed expenses p.a.	60,000	36,000
Lubricants & Sundries per 100 km	Rs. 20	Rs. 20

Each truck will daily make 5 trips (to and fro) on an average for 24 days in a month.

Cost of Diesel Rs.15 per litre.

Salary of Drivers Rs.3,000 per month – Two Drivers will be required for a truck.

Other staff expenses Rs.1,08,000 p.a.

Present a comparative Cost Sheet on the basis of the above data showing transport cost per tonne of operating 10-tonne and 8-tonne trucks at full capacity utilisation.

[C.A. Final]

Solution

Comparative Cost Sheet (per month)

Particulars		Truck Capacity 10-tonne Rs.		8-tonne Rs.
Fixed Expenses :				
Staff Expenses		9,000		9,000
Driver's Salary	(Rs. 3,000 × 40)(WN–1)	1,20,000	(Rs. 3,000 × 50)	1,50,000
Other Fixed Expenses	$\left(\text{Rs. } 60{,}000 \times \frac{1}{12}\right)$	5,000	$\left(\text{Rs. } 36{,}000 \times \frac{1}{12}\right)$	3,000
Repairs & Maintenance	$\left(\frac{\text{Rs. } 60{,}000 \times 20}{12}\right)$	1,00,000	$\left(\frac{\text{Rs. } 48{,}000 \times 25}{12}\right)$	1,00,000
Running Expenses :				
Depreciation	$\left(\frac{\text{Rs. } 10{,}00{,}000 \times 20}{5 \times 12}\right)$	3,33,333	$\left(\frac{\text{Rs. } 8{,}50{,}000 \times 25}{5 \times 12}\right)$	3,54,167
Diesel (W.N. 2)		1,44,000		1,35,000
Lubricant & Sundries	$\left(\frac{28{,}800 \times \text{Rs. } 20}{100}\right)$	5,760	$\left(\frac{36{,}000 \times \text{Rs. } 20}{100}\right)$	7,200
		7,17,093		7,58,367

Total tonnes	24,000	24,000
Cost per tonne	Rs.29.88	Rs.31.60

Working Notes

1. Computation of no. of trucks and drivers required :

	10-tonne	8-tonne
Effective trips per day	5	5
No. of days per month	24	24
Effective trips per month	5 × 24 = 120	5 × 24 = 120
Coal carried per month per truck	1,200 (120 × 10)	960 (120 × 8)
No. of trucks required	24,000 / 1,200 = 20	24,000 / 960 = 25
No. of drivers required	20 × 2 = 40	25 × 2 = 50

2. Cost of diesel :

	10-tonne	8-tonne
Kms. covered per day per truck (5 × 2 × 6)	60	60
Kms covered per day by the trucks	1,200 (60 × 20)	1,500 (60 × 25)
Total kms covered by all the trucks per month	28,800 (1,200 × 24)	36,000 (1,500 × 24)
Kms per litre of diesel	3	4
Diesel required	9,600 (28,800/3)	9,000 (36,000/4)
Cost of diesel	1,44,000 (9,600 × 15)	1,35,000 (9,000 × 15)

Problem

A manufacturing firm facing shortage of electric power supply from the State Electricity Board has set up its own power generation plant for efficient running of its production units in the factory.

The following information has been taken from the records in connection with the generations of power for a month :

(1) Number of units generated was 10,00,000 for the month, of which 10% was utilised by the generator department.

(2) Consumption data of materials, etc. for the month :

(a) Coal consumption	300 MTs @ Rs.3,600 per MT
(b) Oil Consumption	4.5 MTs @ Rs.40,000 per MT
(c) Cost of water extraction and treatment	for 6 lakh litres @ Rs.1.25 per litre

(3) Steam boiler cost Rs. 20 lakhs with a residual value of Rs. 2 lakhs after a life of 10 years.

(4) Salaries and wages per month :

(a) For staff of generating plant :

(i) 100 skilled workers @ Rs. 3,000 p.m.

(ii) 150 helpers @ Rs.1,500 p.m.

(b) For staff of boiler house :

(i) 60 Category A workers @ Rs.1,500 p.m.

(ii) 100 Category B workers @ Rs.1,000 p.m.

(5) Cost of generating plant : Rs.36 lakhs with no residual value. Depreciation @ 10% on straight line basis is to be charged.

(6) Repairs and maintenance of generating plant and boiler Rs. 50,000 p.m.

(7) Share of administrative charges Rs. 40,000 p.m.

(8) Sales value of ash disposed of Rs.15,000 p.m.

Calculate the per unit cost of electricity generated using a cost sheet format.

[I.C.W.A.I. Inter]

Solution

COST SHEET
for the month of . . . . **Units 9,00,000**

Particulars	**Total Cost Rs.**	**Cost per Unit Rs.**
Coal consumed 300 MTs @ Rs. 3,600 per MTs	10,80,000	1.20
Oil consumption 4.5 MTs @ Rs. 40,000 per MTs	1,80,000	.20
Water extraction and treatment 6 lakh litre @ Rs.1.25 per litre	7,50,000	.833
	20,10,000	2.233
Depreciation $\left[\frac{20,00,000 - 2,00,000}{10 \times 12}\right]$	15,000	.017
	20,25,000	2.250
Less: Sale of ash	15,000	.017
	20,10,000	2.233
Salaries and Wages :		
Generating Plant	5,25,000	.583
Boiler House	1,90,000	.211
Depreciation of generating plant $\left(\frac{\text{Rs. } 36,00,000 \times 10\%}{12}\right)$	30,000	.033
Repairs and maintenance of generating plant and boiler	50,000	.056
Administrative Expenses	40,000	.044
	28,45,000	3.160
Add: Electricity consumed by generation department (1 ̓0,000 × Rs. 3.160)	3,16,000	.351
Total Cost	31,61,000	3.511

Here, total cost is cost of 9,00,000 units and not 10,00,000 units, because 1,00,000 units of electricity generated are used by generation department.

Problem

A lodging home is being run in a small hill-station with 50 single rooms. The home offers concessional rates during six off-season months in a year. During this period, half of the full-room rent is charged. The management's profit margin is targeted at 20% of the room rent.

The following are the cost estimates and other details for the year ending 31st March 2005 (assume a month to be of 30 days) :

(a) Occupancy during the season is 80%, while in the off-season is 40% only.

(b) Expenses :

	Rs.
(i) Staff salary (excluding room attendants)	2,75,000
(ii) Repairs to Buildings	1,30,500
(iii) Laundry and Cleaner	40,000
(iv) Interior and Tapestry	87,500
(v) Sundry Expenses	95,400

(c) Annual depreciation is to be provided for building at 5% and on furniture and equipments at 15% on straight line basis;

(d) Room attendants are paid Rs.5 per room-day on the basis of occupancy of the rooms in a month;

(e) Monthly light charges are Rs.120 per room except in four months of winter when it is Rs. 30 per room, and this cost is on the basis of full occupancy for a month; and

(f) Total investments in the home is Rs.100 lakhs of which Rs.80 lakhs relate to buildings and balance for furniture and equipments.

You are required to work out the room rent chargeable per day both during the season and the off-season month, on the basis of the foregoing information.

[I.C.W.A. Inter, Adapted]

Solution

(i) Calculation of number of room-days in a year :

During 6 months' season ($50 \times 80\% \times 6 \times 30$)	=	7,200 room-days
During 6 months' off-season ($50 \times 40\% \times 6 \times 30$)	=	3,600 room-days
Total Room-days	=	10,800 room-days

(ii) Attendants' salary = $10,800 \times$ Rs.5.00 = Rs.54,000

(iii) Light charges per room-day during season of 8 months = Rs.120/30 = Rs.4.00

Light charges per room-day during off-season of 4 months = Rs.30/30 = Re.1.00

Total light charges

for 8 months :

	Rs.
6 months : 7,200 × Rs. 4	= 28,800
2 months : 3,600 × $\frac{2}{6}$ × Rs. 4	= 4,800
Off season 4 months : 3,600 x $\frac{4}{6}$ × Re.1.00	= 2,400
	36,000

Statement of Total Estimated Cost

	Rs.	Rs.
Staff Salary		2,75,000
Repairs to Buildings		1,30,500
Laundry and Cleaner		40,000
Interior and Tapestry		87,500
Sundry Expenses		95,400
Depreciation :		
Building (80,00,000 × 5%)	4,00,000	
Furniture and Equipment (20,00,000 × 15%)	3,00,000	7,00,000
Attendants' Salary		54,000
Light Charges		36,000
		14,18,400

Computation of total full room - day

(i.e., on the basis of 80% occupancy)

During season	= 7,200
During off-season (50% of 3,600)	= 1,800
	9,000

$$\therefore \text{Cost per room-day} = \frac{\text{Rs.}14{,}18{,}400}{9{,}000} = \text{Rs. } 157.60$$

Computation of Room-rent

During season

		Rs.
Cost per room-day	=	157.60
Add: Profit 157.60 × 25%	=	39.40
		197.00

During off-season = 197.00 × 50% = Rs. 98.50

Problem

Public Health Centre runs an Intensive Care Unit. For this purpose, it has hired a building at a rent of Rs. 5,000 per month with the understanding that it would bear the repairs and maintenance charges also.

The unit consists of 25 beds and 5 more beds can be comfortably accommodated when the occasion demands. The permanent staff attached to the unit are :

2 Supervisors, each at a salary of Rs. 500 per month.

4 Nurses, each at a salary of Rs. 300 per month.

2 Ward-boys, each at a salary of Rs. 150 per month.

Though the unit was open for the patients all the 365 days in a year, scrutiny of accounts in 2004 revealed that only for 130 days in the year the unit had the full capacity of 25 patients per day and, for another 70 days, it had on an average 20 beds only occupied per day. But there were occasions when the beds were full, extra beds were hired at a charge of Rs. 5 per bed per day and this did not come to more than 5 beds extra above the normal capacity on any one day. The total hire charges for extra beds incurred for the whole year amount to Rs. 2,000.

The unit engaged expert doctors from outside to attend on the patients and the fees were paid on the basis of the number of patients attended and time spent by them and on an average worked out to Rs. 10,000 per month in 2004.

The other expenses for the year were :

	Rs.
Repairs and Maintenance	3,600
Food supplied to patients	44,000
Janitor and other services for them	12,500
Sundry charges for their bed linen	28,000
Medicines supplied	35,000
Cost of oxygen, X-ray etc. other than directly borne for treatment of patients	54,000
General Administration charges allocated to the unit	49,550

(i) If the unit recovered an overall amount of Rs. 100 per day an average from each patient what is the profit per patient day made by the unit in 2004 ?

(ii) The unit wants to work on a budget for 2005 but the number of patients requiring intensive medical care is a very uncertain factor. Assuming that same revenue and expenses prevail in 2005, in the first instance, work out the number of patient-days required by the unit to break-even. **[I.C.W.A.I. Final, Adapted]**

Solution

(i) Calculation of number of Patient-days in 2004 :

25 beds × 130 days	3,250
20 beds × 70 days	1,400
Extra $\left(\frac{\text{Rs. } 2{,}000}{5}\right)$	400
	5,050

Statement of Profit

			Rs.	Rs.
	Gross Income received from patients [5,050 × 100]			5,05,000
Less:	Variable Cost :			
	Food		44,000	
	Janitor and other Services		12,500	
	Sundry Charges for their bed linen		28,000	
	Medicines		35,000	
	Doctors' Fees (Rs. 10,000 × 12)		1,20,000	
	Hire Charges for extra beds		2,000	2,41,500
	Contribution			2,63,500
Less:	Fixed Cost :			
	Salary —	Supervisors (500 × 2) × 12	12,000	
		Nurses (300 × 4) × 12	14,400	
		Ward-boys (150 × 2) × 12	3,600	
		Rent (5,000 × 12)	60,000	
	Repair and Maintenance		3,600	
	General Administration		49,550	
	Cost of Oxygen, X-ray etc.		54,000	
				1,97,150
		Profit		66,350

$$\therefore \text{ Profit per Patient-day} = \frac{\text{Rs. } 66{,}350}{5{,}050} = \text{Rs. } 13.139$$

(ii) Break-even point $= \dfrac{\text{Fixed Cost}}{\text{P/v ratio}}$

$$= \frac{\text{Fixed Cost}}{\dfrac{\text{Contribution}}{\text{Gross Income}}}$$

$$= \text{Fixed Cost} \times \frac{\text{Gross Income}}{\text{Contribution}}$$

$$= 1{,}97{,}150 \times \frac{5{,}05{,}000}{2{,}63{,}500}$$

$$= \text{Rs. } 3{,}77{,}839.63$$

$$= \text{Rs. } 3{,}77{,}839.$$

or, 3,77,839/100 = 3,778 Patient-days.

Note : It is assumed that the cost of janitor and other charges as variable cost and the cost of oxygen and X-ray as fixed cost.

QUESTIONS

1. What is Operating Costing? What are its advantages ? To what industries the Operating Cost Method is applicable?
2. Write short notes on : (a) Commercial Ton-Mile. (b) Absolute Ton-Mile. (c) Load Factor.
3. Is Operating Costing an independent method of costing?
4. A Transport Service Company is running 4 buses between two towns which are 50 miles apart. Seating capacity of each bus is 40 passengers.

   The following particulars were obtained from their books for April 2004 :

	Rs.
Wages of drivers, conductors and cleaners	2,400
Salaries of office and supervisory staff	1,000
Diesel oil and other oils	4,000
Repairs and maintenance	800
Taxation, Insurance etc.	1,600
Depreciation	2,600
Interest and other charges	2,000
	14,400

   Actual passengers carried were 75 per cent of the seating capacity. All the four buses ran on all the days of the month. Each bus made one round trip per day.

   Find out cost per passenger-mile. **[Adapted from C.A. Inter]**

5. From the following data relating to two different vehicles A and B, compute the cost per running mile :

	A	B
Mileage run (annual)	15,000	6,000
Cost of vehicle	Rs. 25,000	Rs. 15,000
	Rs.	Rs.
Road licence (annual)	750	750
Insurance (annual)	700	700
Garage rent (annual)	600	500
Supervision and Salaries (annual)	1,200	1,200
Drivers' wages per hour	3	3
Cost of petrol per gallon	3	3
Miles run per gallon	20 miles	15 miles
Repairs and Maintenance per mile	1.65	2
Tyre allocation per mile	Re. 0.80	Re. 0.60
Estimated life of the vehicles	1,00,000 miles	75,000 miles

   You are to charge interest on cost of vehicles at 5 per cent per annum. The vehicles run 20 miles per hour, on an average. **[Adapted I.C.W.A.I.]**

12

STANDARD COSTING

● Good morning to you all.

□ "Good morning Sir."

● Well, I would like to take up for discussion 'Standard Costing'. Because, a basic concept about Standard Costing would help us to understand the inherent idea of Budgetary Control. Both Budgetary Control and Standard Costing methods are comparable systems of cost accounting since "they are both predetermined or forward-looking". They are concerned with comparing actual results of manufacturing a product or service with predetermined target. There is no doubt that both Standard Costing and Budgetary Control are quite helpful to management in the context of cost control and right management decisions. Standard Cost may be defined as a 'predetermined cost of material, labour and overhead chargeable' to product or service—which is the yardstick of comparing with actual cost. The difference between actual and standard is called Variance.

Standard Costing & Budgetary Control

Now let us see how Standard Costing has been defined by others :

Definitions :

'The preparation and use of standard costs, their comparison with actual costs and the analysis of variance to their causes and points of incidence' – ***Terminology of the Institute of Cost and Works Accountants of London***.

'A system of cost accounting which makes use of predetermined standard costs relating to each element of cost — labour, material and overhead – for each line of product manufactured or service supplied. Actual costs incurred are compared with the standard costs as the work proceeds, the differences between the two being known as 'variance'; these are analysed by 'reason' so that inefficiencies may be quickly brought to the notice of the persons responsible for them, and appropriate action may be taken. – Dr. J. Batty

'Standard Costs are predetermined, or budgeted estimates of costs to manufacture a single unit, or a number of units of a product, during a specified immediate future period. They are used as a measure with which the actual cost, as ascertained, may be compared.

– Wheldon

'Standard Costing may be defined basically as a technique of cost accounting which compares the "Standard Cost" of each product or service with the actual cost, to determine the efficiency of the operation, so that any remedial action may be taken immediately. The "Standard Cost" is a predetermined cost which determines what each product or service should cost under given circumstance". Brown & Howard

So it is clear from the above discussion that the management accountant is concerned with finding out the causes and nature of variation. I have already said that the difference between Standard Cost and Actual Cost represents '*Variance*'; depending on the nature and circumstances of respective and individual cases. However, before I would like to take up for discussion the different aspects of 'Variance Analysis', I think it proper to discuss about the process of setting standard cost, types of standard, points of similarity and difference between Standard Costing and Budget, and advantages of Standard Costing. I think you have followed the above discussion. Now let me discuss the above aspects one by one.

Variance

Process of Standard Costing

Process of Setting Standard : It has been stated earlier that standard cost is a predetermined cost which is, in most of the cases, a basis of controlling expenses and cost. It is not an easy task on the part of management to set up a standard which is really a difficult process. However, the process should include the following :

a. Right and careful selection of materials.

b. Time and Motion Study of manufacturing operation.

c. Careful study of industrial equipment and manufacturing facilities.

d. Careful review of all elements of cost as a whole.

Different Types of Standard

Types of Standard : Standard may be defined as a 'base' or 'level of attainment' established by authority and accepted by management for measuring and comparing the actual performance. So the term 'Standard Costing' or 'Standard Cost' is dependent on the concept of standard. However, in the context of the predominance of the term 'Standard' in Standard Costing, 'Standard' can be classified in the following broad types :

TYPES OF STANDARD

Ideal Standard	**Normal Standard**	**Basic Standard**	**Expected Standard**	**Current Standard**
(It would result if ideal conditions prevailed, such as, satisfactory rate for labour, overhead cost, best output, best possible price for material. It is not generally changed when ideal standard is set)	(It represents the average figure and is expected to 'characterise the entire business cycle'. Any fluctuations arising from cyclical and seasonal fluctuations can be overcome through the normal standard)	(Basic standard is seldom revised. It is a level of standard which is fixed in relation to a particular base year. Thus 'they represent a fixed base analogous to the base' upon which a price index no. is computed)	(Expected standard is one which is based on the current or present business condition which is subject to adjustment and revision)	(It reflects 'what performance should be in the period for which the Standard is to be used)

I think you have followed my lectures. Now I would like to discuss about the advantages of Standard Costing.

☐ "Sir, before that, please explain to us the points of similarity and difference between Budgets and Standard Costing".

• For that I refer to you the book – '***Principles of Management Accountancy***' by Brown and Howard.

Points of Similarity

Relationship between Budget & Standard Costing

Regarding the points of similarity between budgets and budgetary control and Standard Cost, Professor Brown and Howard explained that 'both are comparable systems of cost accounting in that they are both predetermined or "forward-looking". However, there is one big difference in that budgetary control is concerned with comparison of the estimated and actual results of a department, company or even country while standard costing is concerned with comparison of estimated and actual results of manufacturing a product or providing a service'.

☐ Please Sir, give us more points of difference between Budgets and Standard Costing."

• **Points of Difference**

Thank you for your interest in the subject. Well, for details of the same I like to refer you to the works of Prof Henrici. Prof. Henrici in his book '***Standard Cost for Manufacturing***' explained that both 'consider departmental expenses according to accounts. Both assumes that costs are controllable along with fixed lines of supervision and responsibility. Both require the issuance of periodic comparative cost reports. Both require the measurement of cost as related to some other variable, such as prices, standard hours etc.' However, differences between Standard Cost and Budget, according to Henrici, can be explained as :

BUDGET	STANDARD COST
1. It is a statement of expected cost.	1. It shows what cost should be if desirable performance is attained.
2. It emphasises the level of cost which should not be allowed to exceed.	2. It emphasises the level to which cost should be reduced.
3. It is set for all departments of the company, as for example from sales to manufacturing.	3. It is set only for manufacturing cost.
4. Any saving in budgets are not investigated.	4. Any adverse or marked variance from the standards are investigated.

I think the above discussions – the difference between budget and standard cost— are clear to you. Now I would like to discuss about the advantages of Standard Costing. You see the advantages of the same can be classified under two broad heads :

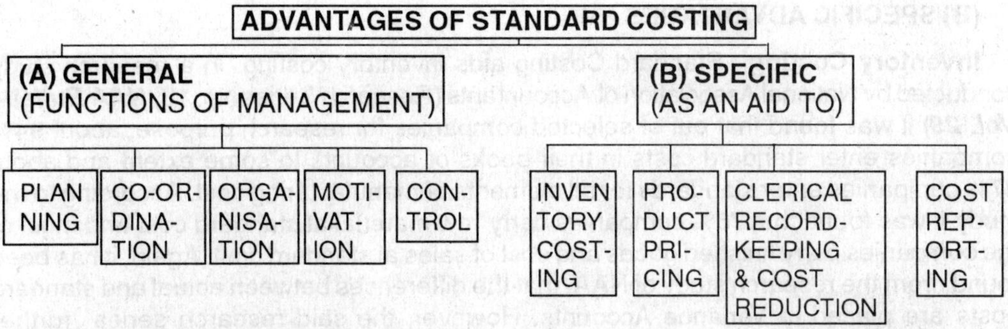

(A) GENERAL ADVANTAGES

Standard Costing renders assistance to five functions of management. These are, as already stated—Planning, Coordination, Organisation, Motivation and Control.

Planning : Heckert and Wilson in their book "***Business Budgeting and Control***" defined management planning as a means 'basing action upon thorough investigation, study and research. All these are needed in setting standard cost and expenses as well as product lines and manufacturing method.' In this context I have the pleasure to draw your attention to the work of Mr. Vance. He, in his book "***Theory and Technique of Cost Accounting***", rightly observed that preparation of standard involves a scrutiny of the operations that often discloses inefficiencies even though no further use of the standard cost is made.

Coordination : Coordination means a process of striving for both principal and subordinate business aims and all the elements of business organisation towards the common aim. So standard costs are an integral part of accounting, management and engineering thinking. Bennett, in his book '***Standard Cost : How they serve Modern Management***', explained that 'Management must determine the volume level to be adopted and the set of circumstances to be assumed. The engineer's job is to set the standard within the framework of management's prescription. The accountant's job is to show how these standards are then compared with the actual results and why there were differences'.

Organisation : It is a fact, as has been rightly observed by Prof. Keller, that standard should be established or set up depending on clearly defined lines of authority and responsibility, as for example, for cost centre as per the cost responsibility concept.

Motivation : There is no denying the fact that employees or workers may be inclined to do a job if the nature of the job is clearly clarified. So setting a standard is a right step to motivational aid. Mr. Roe notes, in the ***National Association of Accountants Bulletin No. 36***, that 'Men are more willing to be judged against such standard ... a man is less likely to 'pass-the-buck' for his own deficiencies'.

Control : The term control is a function which regulates all the four functions of management – Planning, Coordination, Organisation, Motivation. Sometimes it acts as control of Control—which is an item of five functions of management. Here standard cost method plays an important role in controlling all elements of cost. As, a control device, standard is compared with actual, and the adverse variances are investigated—either for regulating and controlling future cost or for reviving the concept 'standard' in light of the cause of adverse variance.

(B) SPECIFIC ADVANTAGES

Inventory Costing : Standard Costing aids inventory costing. In a research study conducted by National Association of Accountants (Research Series No. 13, ***NAA Bulletin Vol. 29***) it was found that out of selected companies for research purpose, about 94% companies enter standard costs in their books of accounts to some extent and about 87% companies enter standards for all elements of manufacturing cost. According to the study it was found that 75% companies carry raw material at standard cost and most of the companies carry finished goods and cost of sales at standard cost. Again, it has been found, from the research study of NAA, that the differences between actual and standard costs are placed in Variance Accounts. However, the said research series further expressed the view that 'this reasoning seems to require standards which are current and attainable. Changes in external factors such as prices or changes in methods and performance efficiency which are made or accepted by management require revision of standards using in costing'.

Product Costing : In actual practice it has been found that very few companies have little control over the prices of their products and services. However, companies are found to obtain prices in excess of the cost of product. National Association of Accountants in their Research Series No. 14 (***Bulletin Vol. 30***) found that 62 companies out of 67 companies make use of standard costs in their product pricing. Professor Dickey, while editing '***Accountant's Hand Book***' states that "for companies having products produced for stock and listed in catalogue, the NAA reports distinguishes four groups in respect to cost figure supplied to pricing executive" :

"1. 'Companies which supply pricing executives with standard costs without application of any adjustments to the standards. These companies use current standard brought up to date each time a catalogue appears.

2. Companies in which costs supplied to the pricing executives are standard costs adjusted by the ratio of actual cost to the standard cost as shown by the variance accounts. These companies use current standards revised annually.

3. Companies which use current market prices for materials, and in a few cases for labour, together with standard costs for other elements of product cost when preparing pricing costs. These companies have materials standards, but use current prices because materials cost is such a large element of their total costs, and their materials costs fluctuate frequently.

4. Companies which adjust their standard costs to reflect actual costs which are anticipated during the period for which prices are to be in effect."

Clerical Record Keeping and Cost Reduction : The installation of standard cost tends to minimise or reduce the clerical expenses and it acts as an instrument of cost control. This will be clear if we take into account the view expressed by Prof. Neuner. Professor Neuner, in his book '***Cost Accounting***' states that 'materials requisitions, labour time tickets, cost sheets, and operating instructions can be prepared on standard printed forms for use in costing any such production order, since all production orders for a given product will be identical'.

Cost Reporting : If management is to take time to time, hour to hour and even minute to minute management decision, they will have to depend on time to time and hour to hour report regarding the various courses of business activities. Here standard costing plays an important role in comparing the actual report and expected report. So the adverse variance can be taken into account for alternative course of action.

I think you have followed the above advantages of Standard Costing. Please tell me frankly any point which is not clear to you.

□ "Sir, we are very glad for your detailed discussions on the concept. Would you kindly enlighten us about the concept of variance and its different aspects".

● Surely, I will.

You see, I have already given you a general idea about variance. However, I am explaining the same now in detail :

VARIANCE

I find, in actual practice, that students are confused by the term 'Variance' or 'Variation' — firstly, whether it will be 'Variation' or 'Variance'. Fundamentally, there lies no difference between the two. Both terms are used in Cost literature. Schlatter and Schlatter in their book "***Cost Accounting***" said that 'variation is the better word for our purpose unless variance can be said to be the correct word because of the sanction of special usage by cost accountants'. However, it is a fact that the concept 'variance', which is the valuable contribution of standard costing to cost accounting literature, is the pillar or basis of the principle — 'Management by Exception'. Please note that, of the different methods of management, the most common methods of management in the area of Financial Management are (a) Management by Exception, and (b) Management by Objective. So if you can study fully the different aspects of variance analysis, then, I think, you will be expert in 'Management by Exception'. Regading the concept 'Management by Objective', I would like to discuss the same in my subsequent discussions. However, there is no deying the fact that variance analysis aids management in the following ways:

Basis of the Management by Exception Theory

Contribution of Variance in Management Decision

(a) Where variance occurred?

(b) Why it has occurred?

(c) Who is responsible?

Here we can see that the concept Variance Analysis is the direct contribution to the idea of Responsibility Accounting. You see, now I like to refer to the work of Prof. Bennett. Professor Bennett, in his book "***Standard Costs : How They Serve Modern Management***", explained the significance of variance analysis. He is of opinion that 'it is probably a fair and accurate statement to say that the analysis of cost variances is usually the most important job to be done in operating a standard cost system. Without proper analysis and intelligent, factual interpretation, the cost variances are just so many figures. Only through the medium of this analytical device can the figures tell the story of what is happening and point the way to improvement procedures. Here is where the standard cost system leaves the realm of technical accounting and dull debits and credits and enters the rarefied atmosphere of interpretive and creative analysis for management guidance. At this point, also, the accountant who is blessed with the gift of vision and imagination steps out from the maze of debits and credits and becomes the valued interpreter of the business facts of life'.

Significance of Variances

I hope you have followed the above discussions. By the by, I would like to make clear one point that nature of Variance is of two types:

(a) General Variance, and
(b) Mix Variance.

I have already given you some idea about General Variance. I have not yet discussed Mix Variance.

□ "Sir, what is Mix Variance?"

● Suppose product 'X' is to be produced and for that different quantities of 'E' and 'Y' were used in production. This is known as Product Mix.

Again, suppose, standard material for product 'O' is

6 kg of "IYE" at Rs. 5 per kg = Rs. 30, and

10 kg of "YUE" at Rs. 6 per kg. = Rs. 60.

So the above situation may be termed as 'Standard Mix' of the product. So the difference between Actual Quantity (AQ) and Revised Standard Quantity (RSQ) represents Mix Variance.

Now I think you have understood the term 'Mix Variance'.

□ "Sir, can Mix Variance arise in case of labour variance?"

● I mean, you want to know about Labour Mix Variance.

□ "Yes Sir".

● You see, during any manufacturing period, when different grades of labours are employed from those budgeted, the variance will arise.

So the formula of Labour Mix Variance is :

$$\textbf{Labour Mix Variance} = \begin{pmatrix}\text{Standard Cost of} \\ \text{Standard Mix}\end{pmatrix} - \begin{pmatrix}\text{Standard Cost of} \\ \text{Actual Mix}\end{pmatrix}$$

So the concept 'Variance' discussed earlier is not only confined to material and labour, it can also be extended to the area of Variable Overhead, Fixed Overhead and Sales. However, basically, there are two types of variance — (a) Price Variance, and (b) Volume Variance. These two types of variance — Price and Volume—can be studied in the context of elements of Cost and Sales of the manufacturing concern.

So 'Variance' can be studied in respect of :

a. Direct Material.
b. Direct Labour.
c. Variable Overhead.
d. Fixed Overhead based on units.
e. Sales based on Turnover and Profits.

Please note one point again that—variance in case of Sales is known as Value Variance. Similarly, for each elements of cost (Material, Labour, Overhead) there is a total variance known as Cost Variance.

□ "Sir, what are the components of *Cost Variance* in case of each element of cost and *Value Variance* in case of sale? Please enlighten us as to those concept".

Please note :

Cost Variance = Cost/Price Variance + Volume Variance
Value Variance = Sales/Price Variance + Volume Variance

Now I would like to discuss all the elements of cost and sales in light of the basic two types of variance – Price and Volume :

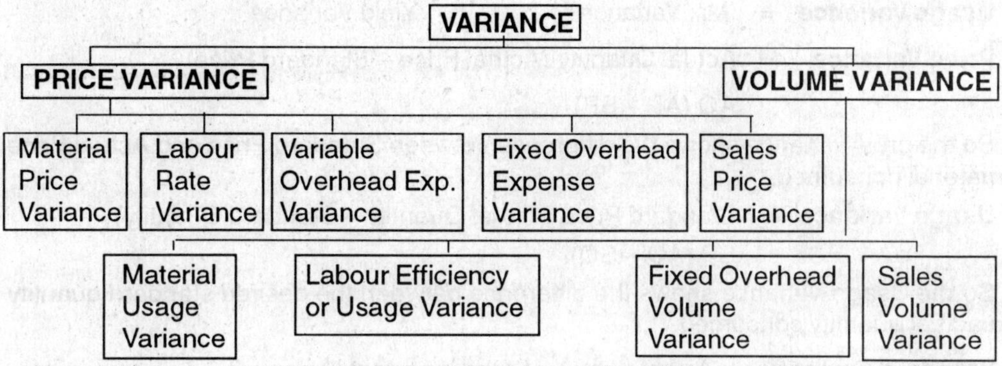

Now I think that you have followed the above classification. Is there any question, please?

☐ "Sir, variable overhead cost is represented only by one variance, that is, from the point of Price Variance, or, in other words, Expenditure Variance. Why, sir, is it not classified from the point of Volume Variance? Please explain it."

● You see, per unit overhead rate, it is assumed, is constant, irrespective of any amount of quantity or qualities produced. So it is desirable to find out only a Standard cost per hour or per unit. So any variance in variable overhead should be attributed to expenditure variance. According to the Institute of Cost and Works Accountants of London, variable cost is a cost which tends to vary directly with volume of output. As it varies directly with production, a change in expenditure can affect cost.

Well, besides all these variances there are many other types of variances : Mix Variance, Yield Variance, Idle Time Variance, Capacity Variance, Calendar Variance, and Quantity Variance.

Now let me represent all those variances under each element of cost as well as sale:

MATERIAL COST VARIANCE :

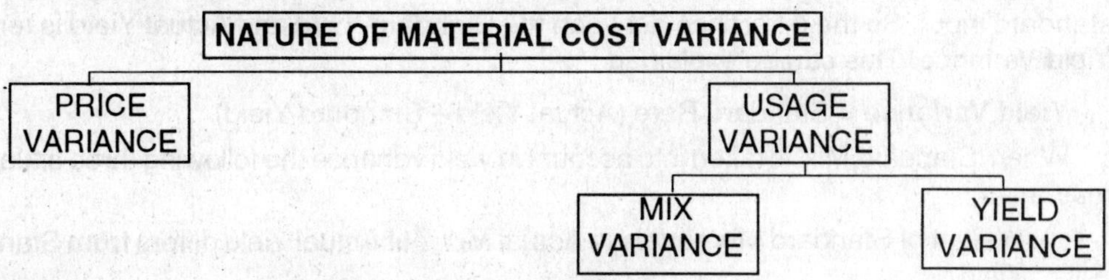

Material Cost Variance = Standard Cost – Actual Cost
SC – AC

Standard Cost = Actual Production x Standard Rate
AP × SR

Standard Rate $= \dfrac{\text{Standard Cost per ton or metric ton}}{\text{Standard output per ton or metric ton}}$

Check of Material Cost Variance = Price Variance + Usage Variance

Usage Variance = Mix Variance + Yield Variance

Price Variance = Actual Quantity (Actual Price – Standard Price)

AQ (AP – SP)

So the price variance shows the difference between Standard Price and Actual Price of material consumed.

Usage Variance = Standard Price (Actual Quantity – Standard Quantity)

SP (AQ – SQ).

So the Usage Variance shows the difference between the desired standard quantity and actual quantity consumed.

Standard Quantity = Actual output × Standard quantity per unit

Again, usage variance can also be calculated in case of 'Standard Mix'. Then the formula will be :

Standard Price (Revised Standard Quantity for Actual input – Actual Quantity)

SP (RSQ – AQ)

The Revised Standard Quantity (RSQ) can be found out in the following manner:

$$\left(\frac{\textbf{Standard Quantity for Each Material}}{\textbf{Total of Standard Quantity}} \times \textbf{Actual Total Quantity}\right)$$

Mix Variance = Standard Price (Revised Standard Quantity for Actual Input – Actual Quantity)

SP (RSQ – AQ)

So the above situation shows the difference between 'the actual proportions of the actual quantity used and the standard proportion of the actual quantity used'.

Yield Variance : It is a fact that in manufacturing process normal losses in processes are expected, so it is desirable as well as possible to set a standard for expected normal yield. Hence, Standard Yield may be conceived of as that output which is expected from standard input. So the difference between the Standard Yield and Actual Yield is termed Yield Variance. This can be explained :

Yield Variance = Standard Rate (Actual Yield – Standard Yield)

When 'Standard Mix' is taken into account in yield variance the following three situations may arise :

i. Weight of Standard Mix equals to Actual Mix, but Actual Yield differs from Standard Yield.

ii. Weight of Standard Mix differs from Actual Mix and Actual Yield differs from Standard Yield.

iii. Weight of Standard Mix differs from Actual Mix but Actual Yield equals to Standard Yield.

The formula to find out yield variance in all the above three situations is

$$\text{Yield Variance} = \text{Standard Cost}\left[\begin{array}{l}\text{Standard Loss}\\ \text{on Actual Mix}\end{array} - \begin{array}{l}\text{Actual Loss}\\ \text{on Actual Mix}\end{array}\right]$$

LABOUR COST VARIANCE

NATURE OF LABOUR COST VARIANCE

- RATE VARIANCE
- EFFICIENCY VARIANCE
- IDLE TIME VARIANCE
- MIX VARIANCE

Labour Cost Variance = Standard Cost – Actual Cost

= SC – AC

Standard Cost = Actual Output × Standard Rate

$$\textbf{Standard Rate per Unit} = \frac{\text{Standard Rate per hour}}{\text{Standard Output per hour}}$$

Check of Labour Cost Variance. = Rate Variance + Efficiency Variance + Idle time Variance + Mix Variance

Now let us see details about the different natures of Labour Cost Variance :

Rate Variance = Actual Hours(Actual Rate – Standard Rate)

AH (AR – SR)

So, it shows the difference between Standard Rate and Actual Rate of pay.

Efficiency Variance = Standard Rate (Actual Hrs. – Standard Hrs.)

SR (AH – SH)

It shows the difference between the standard time and the actual time taken in completing a job.

☐ "Sir, how is Standard Hour calculated?"

● Please note :

$$\textbf{Standard Hour} = \frac{\text{Quantity Produced or Actual Output}}{\text{Standard Output per Hour}} \times \text{No. of Men}$$

Idle Time Variance : It shows that the standard cost of actual hours of workers are idle due to certain reasons.

Idle Time = Standard Rate × Hour Idle

= SR × HI

Mix Variance : When actual grades of labour differ from the Standard, the variance is said to be Mix Variance.

Mix Variance = (Standard Cost of Standard Mix) – (Standard Cost of Actual Mix)

= SC of SM – SC of AM

Variable Overhead Cost Variance : The delails of it I have discussed already.

Please note, the variance is calculated as :

SC – AC

FIXED OVERHEAD COST VARIANCE

NATURE OF FIXED OVERHEAD COST VARIANCE

- Expenditure Variance
- Volume Variance
- Efficiency Variance
- Capacity Variance
- Calendar Variance

Please note that the different aspects of Fixed Overhead Cost Variance can be studied in light of the below-mentioned situations. However, the principles involved in finding out the different variance formulae will, more or less, be same in the two situations:

(a) Variance based on Units of Output, and
(b) Variance based on Standard Hour.

Expenditure Variance : It is the difference between the Budgeted Expenditure and Actual Expenditure.

Volume Variance : It is that part of fixed overhead cost variance which arises due to difference in Actual Volume of Production and Budgeted Quantity of Products.

Efficiency Variance : This arises due to the difference between Standard Quantity and Actual Quantity. This is related to the Labour Efficiency Variance.

Capacity Variance : It is that part of Profit Variance which arises due to the difference in planned capacity and actual capacity. It arises owing to over-utilisation or under-utilisation of plant or machinery and other equipment.

Calendar Variance : It arises due to the under- or over-recovery of fixed overhead that results from the difference between the standard allowed working hours and actual possible working hours in the specified year, month or a week.

I hope you have followed the above discussion.

Now I would like to take up for discussion the said variances in the context of

(a) Variances Based on Units of Output, and
(b) Variances Based on Standard Hours.

(a) **Variances Based On Units of Output**

Fixed Overhead Cost Variance = Standard Cost – Actual Cost
SC – AC

Standard Cost = Actual Output × Standard Rate
AO × SR

Standard Rate = $\dfrac{\text{Budgeted Fixed Overhead}}{\text{Budgeted Output}}$

Expenditure Variance = Budgeted Cost – Actual Cost
BC – AC

Budgeted Cost $= \dfrac{\text{Budgeted Fixed Overhead}}{\text{Budgeted Number of Weeks}}$

Volume Variance = Standard Rate (Actual Quantity – Budgeted Quantity)
SR (AQ –BQ)

Budgeted Quantity $= \dfrac{\text{Budgeted Output per Annum}}{\text{Budgeted Number of Weeks}}$

Efficiency Variance = Standard Rate (Actual Quantity – Standard Quantity)
SR (AQ – SQ)

Standard Quantity = Actual Hours × Standard Quantity Per Hour
Or
Average Hours Worked × Standard Quantity Per Hour

Capacity Variance = (i) Standard Rate (Standard Quantity – Budgeted Quantity)
SR (SQ – BQ)
= (ii) Standard Rate (Standard Quantity – Revised Budgeted Quantity)
= SR (SQ – RBQ)

Revised Budgeted Quantity = Budgeted Output For Period $\times \dfrac{\text{Actual Days}}{\text{Budgeted Days}}$

Calendar Variance : Standard Rate (Revised Budgeted Quantity – Budgeted Quantity)
= SR (RBQ – BQ).

I hope you have followed the above discussions.

Now please note the following interpretations:

Fixed Overhead Cost Variance = Expenditure Variance + Volume Variance

Volume Variance = Efficiency Variance + Capacity Variance + Calendar Variance + Yield Variance

Yield Variance = Standard Cost (Standard Loss on Actual Mix – Actual Loss on Actual Mix)

Check of Fixed Overhead Cost Variance = Expenditure Variance + Volume Variance
or
= Exp. Variance + Efficiency Variance + Capacity Variance + Calendar Variance + Yield Variance

Now let us see all these formulae based on standard hour:

(b) Variances Based On Standard Hours

Fixed Overhead Cost Variance = SC – AC

Standard Cost = Standard Hour × Standard Rate Per Hour

Standard Hour $= \dfrac{\text{Actual Units Produced}}{\text{Standard Output per Hour}}$

Standard Rate = $\frac{\text{Budgeted Overhead In Period}}{\text{Budgeted Hours In Period}}$

Expenditure Variance = Budgeted Cost – Actual Cost
BC – AC

Volume Variance = Standard Rate (Standard Hour – Budgeted Hour)
SR (SH – BH)

Efficiency Variance = Standard Rate (Standard Hour – Actual Hour)
SR (SH – AH)

Capacity Variance = Standard Rate (Actual Hour – Budgeted Hour)
SR (AH – BH)
or
SR (AH – RBH)

Revised Budgeted Hours

RBH = Budgeted Hours per Period × $\frac{\text{Actual days}}{\text{Budgeted days}}$

Calendar Variance = SR (RBH – BH).
or SR (BH – AH)

I think you have followed the above formula. I hope you would be able to work out any type of practical problem with the help of the discussed formulae.

☐ "Sir, You have not discussed about Sales".

☐ "Sir, Please work out a few practical problems".

● You see, I would like to work out a few typical problems on Standard Costing after explaining different aspects of Sales Variance.

Sales Variance

(a) From the point of Turnover Method

It indicates the effect of change in sale, and it can be computed as:

Value Variance = Budgeted Sales – Actual Sales
BS – AS

Price Variance = Standard Sales – Actual Sales
SS – AS
or
Actual Sales Qty. (Budgeted Price – Actual Price)

Volume Variance = Budgeted Sales – Standard Sales
BS – SS

Quantity Variance = Budgeted Sales – Revised Standard Sales
Or, this can be presented as

Budgeted Price (Budgeted Qty. – Qty. in Revised Mix)
Mix Variance = Revised Standard Sales – Standard Sales
RSS – SS

Check : (1)

Value Variance = Price Variance + Volume Variance
VV = PV + VV

Check : (2)

Volume Variance = Mix Variance + Quantity Variance
VV = MV + QV

So, VV = PV + MV + QV

(b) From the point of view of Profit Method

Standard Profit = Budgeted Sales Price – Standard Cost
BS – SC

Value Variance = Budgeted Profit – Actual Profit
BP – AP

Price Variance = Standard Profit – Actual Profit
SP – AP

Volume Variance = Budgeted Profit – Standard Profit
BP – SP

Quantity Variance = Budgeted Profit – Revised Standard Profit
BP – RSP

Sales Quantity Variance and its effect on Sale Value
= Budgeted Price (Budgeted Qty. – Qty. in Revised Mix)

Mix Variance = Revised Standard Profit – Standard Profit
RSP – SP

Please note that the principles of check would be similar to (a) as explained earlier.

Now I have the pleasure to work out a few standard problems on 'Standard Costing'.

Problem

The Standard mix of a compound of four materials is :

Material :	A	B	C	D
Percentage by weight	30	40	20	10
Price per lb	Rs. 1.33	1.50	3.50	3.00

This compound should be used at the rate of 4 lb of compound cubic foot of production. During a period in which 1,000 cubic foot of finished product was made, actual usage was :

Material :	A	B	C	D
Lbs used	1,180	1,580	830	440
Price per lb	Rs. 1.25	1.66	3.33	3.00

Present these figures to the management of an undertaking where standard costing is used. **[Adapted from I.C.W.A. (London) Final]**

Solution

Please note here, Standard Quantity of the Compound 4,000 lbs. And other information relating to quantities, actual Standard Rates are given in the below-mentioned statements :

Material Cost Variance Analysis Statement

Material	Material Price Variance (6 – 7)	Material Mix Variance (7 – 8)	Material Yield Variance (8 – 9)	Material Cost Variance (6–9)
	Rs.	Rs.	Rs.	Rs.
A	(–) 98.33	(–) 38.67	(+) 12.00	(–) 125.00
B	(+) 260.66	(–) 48.00	(+) 18.00	(+) 230.66
C	(–) 141.00	(+) 84.00	(+) 21.00	(–) 36.00
D	Nil	(+) 111.00	(+) 9.00	(+) 120.00
Total :	(+) 21.33	(+) 108.33	(+) 60.00	(+) 189.66

Standard Cost of Production and Variance Statement

Material	Standard Cost	Material Price Variance	Material Mix Variance	Material Yield Variance	Actual Cost of Production
	Rs.	Rs.	Rs.	Rs.	Rs.
A	1,600	(–) 98.33	(–) 38.66	(+) 12.00	1,475.00
B	2,400	(+) 260.66	(–) 48.00	(+) 18.00	2,630.66
C	2.800	(–) 141.00	(+) 84.00	(+) 21.00	2,764.00
D	1,200	(Nil)	(–) 111.00	(+) 9.00	1,320.00
Total :	8,000	(+) 21.33	(+) 108.33	(+) 60.00	8,189.66

Material Cost Variance Analysis Statement

Material	Actual Qty.	Actual Price	Standard Qty.	Standard Price	Standard Mix in Actual Qty.	Actual Cost 1 × 2	Actual Qty. × Standard Price 1 × 4	5 × 4	3 × 4
	1	2	3	4	5	6	7	8	9
	Lbs	Rs.	Lbs.	Rs.	Lbs.	Rs.	Rs.	Rs.	Rs.
A	1,180	1.25	1,200	1.33	1,209	1,475.00	1,573.33	1,612.00	1,600.00
B	1,580	1.66	1,600	1.50	1,612	2,630.66	2,370.00	2,418.00	2,400.00
C	830	3.33	800	3.50	806	2,764.00	2,905.00	2,821.00	2,800.00
D	440	3.00	400	3.00	403	1,320.00	1,320.00	1,209.00	1,200.00
Total :	4,030				4,030	8,189.66			

Problem

From the following records of the Apollo Bolt-Nut Manufacturing Company you are required to compute the Material and Labour Variances :

Input 100 kg of material yield a
Standard output of .... 10,000 units
Standard price per kg of material .... Rs. 20

Actual quantity of material issued and used by production department	.... 10,000 kg
Actual price per kg of material	.... Rs. 21
Actual output	.... 9,00,000 units
No. of employees	 200
Standard wage rate per employee per day	..... Rs. 4
Standard daily output per employee	..... 100 units
Total number of days worked	..... 50 days
Idle time paid for and included in above	..... Half-day
Actual wage rate per day	..... Rs. 4.50

[I.C.W.A.]

Solution

Material Variances

Actual output	.... 9,00,000 units
Standard Material Cost :	
Standard quantity	100 kg per 10,000 units
Standard quantity for 9,00,000 units	..... 9,000 kg
Standard cost of 9,000 kg	..... Rs. 20 per kg
(Rs. 20 × 9,000)	Rs. 1,80,000
Actual material cost :	
Actual quantity issued	..... 10,000 kg
Actual price	..... Rs. 21 per kg
Actual cost of 10,000 kg	..... Rs. 2,10,000
(Rs. 21 × 10,000)	

Material Cost Variance = Standard material cost – Actual material cost
= Rs. 1,80,000 – Rs. 2,10,000
= Rs. 30,000 (Adverse)

(i) Price Variance = Actual quantity (Standard Price – Actual Price)
= 10,000 kg. (Rs. 20 – Rs. 21)
= Rs. 10,000 (Adverse)

(ii) Usage Variance = Standard Price (Standard Quantity – Actual Quantity)
= Rs. 20 (9,000 kg – 10,000 kg)
= Rs. 20,000 (Adverse)

(iii) Yield Variance = Standard Cost (Standard Yield – Actual Yield)

Actual Input = 10,000 kg
Standard Output = 10,000 units per kg
Standard Yield for 10,000 kg = 10,00,000 Units

$$\left[\frac{(10{,}000 \times 10{,}000)}{100}\right]$$

Actual Yield 9,00,000 units

Standard cost per unit is Re. 0.20

☐ "Sir, how is this calculated?"

- Well, please note the workings : $\frac{\text{Rs. } 20 \times 100 \text{ kg}}{10{,}000 \text{ Units}} = \text{Re. } 0.20$

Yield Variance = Re. 0.20 × (10,00,000 units – 9,00,000 units)
= Re. 0.20 × 1,00,000 units = Rs. 20,000 (Adverse)

Check :

Material Cost Variance = Price Variance + Usage Variance
Rs. 30,000 (Adverse) = Rs. 10,000 (Adverse) + Rs. 20,000 (Adverse)

Labour Cost Variance

Actual Labour .... Rs. 45,000
(200 workers × 50 days × Rs. 4.50)

Standard Labour Cost :

Actual output ..... 9,00,000 Units
Standard daily output per employee 100 Units
Number of employees 200
Output per day ..... 20,000 Units
(No. of employees 200 × daily output per employee 100)

Number of days required for, 9,00,000 units = 45 days

$$\left\{\frac{9{,}00{,}000}{20{,}000}\right\} = 45 \text{ days}$$

Standard Labour Cost Rs. 36,000

(200 workers × 45 days × Rs. 4 per day)

Standard Cost – Actual Cost = Labour Cost Variance

Rs. 36,000 – Rs. 45,000 = Rs. 9,000 (adverse)

(i) No. of Worker day (Standard Rate – Actual Rate) = Labour Rate Variance

200 × 50 (Rs. 4.00 – Rs. 4.50) = 5,000 (Adv)

(ii) Standard Labour Cost per day = 200 × Rs. 4.00 = Rs. 800

Idle Time $\frac{1}{2}$ day

Idle time variance = $\frac{1}{2}$ × Rs. 800 = 400.00 (Adv)

(iii) Labour Efficiency Variance

= Standard Rate (Standard man days – Actual man days)

Or, in other words, it can be stated as

Standard Rate (Standard man-hour days – Actual man-hour days)

= Labour Efficiency Variance

Rs. 4.00 (9,000 – 9,900) = Rs. 3,600 (Adv)

● Do you follow the computation?

☐ "No Sir, Please work it out".

● Well, note below

Actual No. of man days	
(200 × 50)	10,000
Less : Idle time = $\frac{1}{2}$ day × 200 workers	100
Actual man days utilised	9,900

Regarding the calculation of Standard man-days, it is to be found out by multiplying the number of days required for 9,00,000 units by number of workers. Here the figure is 200 workers. So the Standard man days = 45 days × 200 workers = 9,000.

Check :

Labour Cost Variance = Rate Variance + Idle Variance + Efficiency Variance

Rs. 9,000 (Adv) = Rs. 5,000 (Adv) + Rs. 400 (Adv) + Rs. 3600 (Adv)

Problem

The Pioneer Manufacturing Co. Ltd. lost its works accounting records in the plant due to an accidental fire in May 2006. But following information was collected from Head Office :

(a) All payments were made by Head Office on behalf of the Plant.

(b) A copy of the Variance report for April 2006 showed the following information:

		Unfavourable	Favourable
		Rs.	Rs.
Raw Material	Price Variance		4,000
	Usage	8,000	
Direct Labour	Rate	6,000	
	Usage		7,400
Production			2,000
Overhead :	Budget		
	Capacity	6,000	
	Efficiency		4,400
	Total :	20,000	17,800

(c) Production in April 2006 was 20,000 units.

(d) Standard costs are revised annually at the beginning of each financial year (April)

(e) Direct labour payments for April 2006 were Rs. 80,000 (Actual)

(f) During April 2006, 40,000 units of raw materials were purchased for Rs. 76,000. The standard rate of consumption is 2 units of raw material for each unit of production.

(g) Price Variance is accounted for at the time of purchase and inventory is carried at standard rate.

(h) Overhead is applied to production on a direct labour hour basis. Budgeted overhead expenses = Rs. 50,000 per month.

(i) No incomplete work either at beginning or end of the month.

You are required to reconstruct average monthly product standard cost (ignoring calendar variance) and actual cost in April 2006. **[I.C.W.A.I. Final]**

Solution

Standard and Actual Costs of Production for April 2006

1. Raw Materials

	Rs.
Cost of Purchase (Actual)	... 76,000
Add: Favourable Price Variance	 4,000
Standard Cost of Purchase	.... Rs. 80,000
Quantity Purchased	..... 40,000 units
Standard Rate $\left\{\frac{\text{Rs } 80,000}{40,000}\right\}$ per unit	.... Rs. 2

As per information supplied, the standard rate of consumption is 2 units of raw material for each unit of production.

∴ Per unit product standard material cost (Rs. 2×2) = Rs. 4.00

Here 40,000 units of raw material are the standard consumption for 20,000 units of production.

Unfavourable Variance = Rs. 8,000

Per Unit Standard Rate = Rs. 2

Actual Consumption of Raw Material = 40,000 + 4,000 = 44,000 units

Here 4,000 units of raw material were used in excess of standard quantity.

Actual cost of 44,000 units Consumed :-

Standard cost (44,000 × Rs. 2.00)	....	Rs. 88,000
Less: Price Variance	....	Rs. 4,000
Actual Material Cost	....	Rs. 84,000
Per Unit Actual Material Cost	....	Rs. 4.20

2. Labour Cost

Actual Labour Cost	.....	Rs. 80,000
Production (units)	....	20,000
Per Unit Actual Labour Cost	....	Rs 4.00
Actual Labour Cost	....	Rs. 80,000
Less: Unfavourable Rate Variance	....	Rs. 6,000
		Rs. 74,000
Add: Usage Variance (Favourable)	....	7,400
Standard Labour Cost	....	81,400

Per Unit Standard Labour Cost $= \dfrac{\text{Standard Labour Cost}}{\text{Units of Production}}$

$= \dfrac{\text{Rs. } 81{,}400}{20{,}000} = \text{Rs. } 4.07$

3. Overhead

Budgeted as shown in the information	...	Rs. 50,000
Less : Expenditure variance	...	
(Budget Variance)	...	Rs. 2,000
Actual Overhead	...	Rs 48,000
Per Unit Actual Overhead $\left[\dfrac{\text{Rs. } 48{,}000}{20{,}000 \text{ units}}\right]$ =		Rs. 2.40
Budgeted Overhead	...	Rs. 50,000
Deduct : Capacity Variance	...	6,000
Overhead Capacity Utilised	...	44,000
Add : Favourable Efficiency Variance		4,400
Standard Overhead		48,400
Per Unit Standard Overhead Variance	....	Rs 2.42

Cost Sheet for the month of April 2006

	Standard Per unit Rate	Total	Actual Per unit Rate	Total
	Rs.	Rs.	Rs.	Rs.
Raw Materials	4.00	80,000	4.20	84,000
Direct Labour	4.07	81,400	4.00	80,000
Overhead	2.42	48,400	2.40	48,000
	10.49	2,09,800	10.60	212,000

Problem

From the following details reconcile the Budgeted Sales with Actual Sales and Standard Profit with Actual Profit in terms of variances :

Product	Budget Qty.	Budget Selling Price	Budget Standard Cost	Actual Qty.	Actual Selling Price	Actual Cost
A	8,000	Rs. 12	Rs. 7	9,000	Rs. 11	Rs. 7.50
B	12,000	Rs. 9	Rs. 6	6,000	Rs. 10	Rs. 5.50

[C.A. Final]

Solution

1. Sales Price Variance (SPV)

SPV = Actual Sales Quantity (Actual Price – Budgeted Price)

Product A

Price Variance = 9,000 (Rs. 11 – Rs. 12)
= Rs. 9,000 (Adverse)

Product B

6,000 (Rs. 10 – Rs. 9)
Rs. 6,000 (Favourable)

Total Price Variance of Products A & B is Rs. 3,000 (Adverse)

This can be calculated as :

Product A = Rs. 9,000 (Adverse)
Product B = Rs. 6,000 (Favourable)
Rs. 3,000 (Adverse)

2. Sales Mix Variance

(a) Effect on Sale Value

Budgeted Mix of Product A & B
A : B = 8,000 : 12,000 = 2 : 3
Actual Total Sales : 15,000 units
Revised Sales Mix :

Product A = 2/5 × 15,000 = Rs. 6,000
B = 3/5 × 15,000 = Rs. 9,000

Actual Sales at Budgeted Price :
A = 9,000 @ Rs. 12 = 1,08,000
B = 6,000 @ Rs. 9 = 54,000
Total : = 1,62,000

Revised Sales Mix at Budgeted Prices : (RSBP)
A = 6,000 @ Rs. 12 72,000
B = 9,000 @ Rs. 9 81,000
Total : 1,53,000

Mix Variance = (ASBP – RSBP)
= (Rs. 1,62,000 – 1,53,000)
= Rs. 9,000

(b) Effect on Profit

Standard Profit
= Budgeted Sales — Standard Cost
Product A = Rs. 12 – Rs. 7 = Rs. 5
Product B = Rs. 9 – Rs. 6 = Rs. 3

Budgeted Profit on Actual Sales Mix (BPASM)

	Rs.
Product A = 9,000 × Rs. 5 =	45,000
Product B = 6,000 × Rs. 3 =	18,000
Total :	63,000

Budgeted Profit on Revised Sales Mix (BPRSM)

	Rs.
Product A = 6,000 × 5 =	30,000
Product B = 9,000 × 3 =	27,000
Total :	57,000

Mix Variance = BPASM – BPRSM
(Rs. 63,000 – 57,000)
= Rs. 6,000 (Favourable)

3. Sales Quantity Variance (SQV)

(a) Effect on Sales value

SQV = Budgeted Price (Budgeted Quantity – Quantity in Revised Mix)

Product A

12 (8,000 – 6000) = Rs. 24,000 (A)

Product B

9 (12,000 – 9,000) = Rs. 27,000 (A)

Total : Rs. 51,000 (A)

(b) Effect on Profit

Sales Quantity Variance depending on the effect on profit
= Budgeted Price (Budgeted Quantity – Quantity in Revised Mix)

Product A

5 (8,000 – 6,000) = Rs. 10,000 (A)

Product B

3(12,000 – 9000) = 9,000 (A)

Total : Rs. 19,000 (A)

4. Cost Variance : (CV)

	Rs.	
AQ (BC – AC) = CV		
Product A = 9,000 (7 – 7.50) =	4,500	(Adverse)
Product B = 6,000 (6 – 5.50) =	3,000	(Favourable)
	1,500	(Adverse)

5. Budgeted and Actual Sales and Profit of Products A and B

Product	Budgeted Sales	Budgeted Profit	Actual Sale	Actual Profit
A	8,000 × 12 = 96,000	8,000 × 5 = 40,000	9,000 × 11 = 99,000	9,000 × 3.50 = 31,500
B	12,000 × 9 = 108,000	12,000 × 3 = 36,000	6,000 × 10 = 60,000	6,000 × 4.50 = 27,000
Total	2,04,000	76,000	1,59,000	58,500

Check (1)

Budgeted Sales + Total Variance = Actual Sale
Rs. 204,000 + Rs. 45,000 (Adv) = Rs. 1,59,000

Check (2)

Budgeted Profit + Total Variance = Actual Profit
Rs. 76,000 + (– Rs. 17,500) = Rs. 58,500
Rs. 76,000 – Rs. 17,500 = Rs. 58,500

DETAILS OF VARIANCES

Particulars	Profit	Sales
	Rs.	Rs.
Price	(–) 3,000	(–) 3,000
Mixture	(+) 6,000	(+) 9,000
Quantity	(–) 19,000	(–) 51,000
Cost Variance	(–) 1,500	Nil
	(–) 17,500	(–) 45,000

Note (–) indicates Adverse Variance and (+) indicates Favourable Variance.

Problem

The standard mix to produce one unit of product is :

	Units		Rs.
Material A	60	@ Rs. 15 per unit	900
Material B	80	@ Rs. 20 per unit	1,600
Material C	100	@ Rs. 25 per unit	2,500
	240		5,000

During the month of April, 10 units were actually produced and consumption was as follows :

	Units		Rs.
Material A	640	@ Rs. 17.50 per unit	11,200
Material B	950	@ Rs. 18 per unit	17,100
Material C	870	@ Rs. 27.50 per unit	23,925
	2,460		52,225

Calculate :

(i) Material Price Variance.
(ii) Material Usage Variance.
(iii) Material Cost Variance.
(iv) Material Yield Variance.
(v) Material Mix Variance.
(vi) Material sub-usage Variance. **[B.B.M. Bangalore]**

Solution

Standard quantity of material for 10 units of actual output :

Material A	: 60	×	10	=	600 units
Material B	: 80	×	10	=	800 units
Material C	: 100	×	10	=	1000 units
					2,400 units

(i) Material Price Variance :

(Standard Price – Actual Price) × Actual Quantity

Material A	:	(Rs. 15 – Rs. 17.50)	×	640	=	Rs. 1,600 (A)
Material B	:	(Rs. 20 – Rs. 18)	×	950	=	Rs. 1,900 (F)
Material C	:	(Rs. 25 – Rs. 27.50)	×	870	=	Rs. 2,175 (A)
						Rs. 1,875 (A)

(ii) Material Usage Variance :

Standard Price × (Standard Quantity for actual production – Actual Quantity used)

Material A	:	Rs. 15	×	(600 – 640)	= Rs. 600 (A)
Material B	:	Rs. 20	×	(800 – 950)	= Rs. 3,000 (A)
Material C	:	Rs. 25	×	(1,000 – 870)	= Rs. 3,250 (F)
					Rs. 350 (A)

(iii) Material Cost Variance :

(Standard Cost for actual porduction – Actual Cost)

Material A	:	(600 × Rs. 15)	–	(Rs. 11,200)	=	Rs. 2,200 (A)
Material B	:	(800 × Rs. 20)	–	(Rs. 17,100)	=	Rs. 1,100 (A)
Material C	:	(1,000 × Rs. 25)	–	(Rs. 23,925)		Rs. 1,075 (F)
						Rs. 2,225 (A)

(iv) Material Mix Variance :

(Revised Standard Quantity for actual output – Actual Quantity) × Standard Price

Material A : $600 \times \frac{2,460}{2,400} = 615$ units

Material B : $800 \times \frac{2,460}{2,400} = 820$ units

Material C : $1,000 \times \frac{2,460}{2,400} = 1,025$ units

2,460 units

Material A	:	(615 – 640) × Rs. 15 =	Rs. 375	(A)
Material B	:	(820 – 950) × Rs. 20 =	Rs. 2,600	(A)
Material C	:	(1,025 – 870) × Rs. 25 =	Rs. 3,875	(F)
			Rs. 900	(F)

(v) Material Yield Variance :

(Standard Yield – Actual Yield) × Standard Cost per unit

$$= \left(10 \times \frac{2,460}{2,400} - 10\right) \times \text{Rs. } 5,000$$

= (10.25 – 10) × Rs. 5,000 = Rs. 1,250 (A)

(vi) Material Sub-usage Variance/Revised Usage Variance
= (Standard Quantity – Revised Standard Quantity) × Standard Price

A	:	(600 – 615)	× Rs. 15 =	Rs. 225	(A)
B	:	(800 – 820)	× Rs. 20 =	Rs. 400	(A)
C	:	(1,000 – 1,025)	× Rs. 25 =	Rs. 625	(A)
				Rs. 1,250	(A)

Problem

The Standard specification for a batch of 500 kg of output of a factory is :

Material	Input (kg)	Std. Price per kg (Rs.)
A	250	4.00
B	200	3.00
C	100	2.00
D	50	1.00

In October 2006 the factory obtained a production of 9,750 kgs output for which 20 batches consisting of standard input to materials were issued to the shop floor in the following ratio at the actual prices indicated against each :

Material	Ratio of Material Issued %	Actual Price per kg Rs.
A	60	5.00
B	20	2.50
C	10	2.25
D	10	0.75

Calculate the Material Yield, Mix, Usage, Price and Total Material Cost Variances.

[C.A. Final, Adapted]

Solution

Standard output for a batch		500 kg
Standard input for 500 kg of standard output		600 kg
Actual output for 20 batches of production		9,750 kg
Standard output for 20 batches of production	500 × 20 =	10,000 kg
Actual input of material used	600 × 20 =	12,000 kg
Standard input of material used	$9,750 \times \frac{600}{500} =$	11,700 kg

Actual Material used :

Material A : 12,000 × 60% = 7,200 kg
Material B : 12,000 × 20% = 2,400 kg
Material C : 12,000 × 10% = 1,200 kg
Material D : 12,000 × 10% = 1,200 kg

Calculation of Variances :

Material Cost Variance = Standard Cost for actual output – Actual Cost of material

$$A: \left(11{,}700 \times \frac{250}{600} \times \text{Rs. } 4\right) - (7{,}200 \times \text{Rs. } 5.00) = \text{Rs. } 16{,}500 \ (A)$$

$$B: \left(11{,}700 \times \frac{200}{600} \times \text{Rs. } 3\right) - (2{,}400 \times \text{Rs. } 2.50) = \text{Rs. } 5{,}700 \ (F)$$

$$C: \left(11{,}700 \times \frac{100}{600} \times \text{Rs. } 2\right) - (1200 \times \text{Rs. } 2.25) = \text{Rs. } 1{,}200 \ (F)$$

$$D: \left(11{,}700 \times \frac{50}{600} \times \text{Re. } 1\right) - (1200 \times \text{Rs. } 0.75) = \text{Rs. } 75 \ (F)$$

Rs. 9,525 (A)

Material Price Variance :

(Standard Price – Actual Price) × Actual quantity

A	:	(Rs. 4.00 – Rs. 5.00)	× 7,200	=	Rs.	7,200	(A)
B	:	(Rs. 3.00 – Rs. 2.50)	× 2,400	=	Rs.	1,200	(F)
C	:	(Rs. 2.00 – Rs. 2.25)	× 1,200	=	Rs.	300	(A)
D	:	(Rs. 1.00 – Rs. 0.75)	× 1,200	=	Rs.	300	(F)
					Rs.	6,000	(A)

Material Usage Variance :

Standard Price × (Standard Quantity – Actual Quantity).

A	:	Rs. 4.00	× (4,875 – 7,200)	=	Rs.	9,300	(A)
B	:	Rs. 3.00	× (3,900 – 2,400)	=	Rs.	4,500	(F)
C	:	Rs. 2.00	× (1,950 – 1,200)	=	Rs.	1,500	(F)
D	:	Re. 1.00	× (975 – 1,200)	=	Rs.	225	(A)
					Rs.	3,525	(A)

Direct Material Mix Variance :

Standard Rate × (Revised Standard Qty. – Actual Qty.)

$$A: \text{Rs. } 4.00 \times \left(12{,}000 \times \frac{250}{600} - 7{,}200\right) = \text{Rs. } 8{,}800 \ (A)$$

$$B: \text{Rs. } 3.00 \times \left(12{,}000 \times \frac{200}{600} - 2{,}400\right) = \text{Rs. } 4{,}800 \ (F)$$

$$C: \text{Rs. } 2.00 \times \left(12{,}000 \times \frac{100}{600} - 1{,}200\right) = \text{Rs. } 1{,}600 \ (F)$$

$$D: \text{Re. } 1.00 \times \left(12{,}000 \times \frac{50}{600} - 1200\right) = \text{Rs. } 200 \ (A)$$

Rs. 2,600 (A)

Direct Material Yield Variance =
Standard Cost per unit × (Standard Output – Actual Output)
= Rs. 3.70 × (10,000 – 9750)
= Rs. 925 (F)

Workings

Standard Cost of output of 500 kgs

				Rs.
250	×	Rs. 4.00	=	1,000
200	×	Rs. 3.00	=	600
100	×	Rs. 2.00	=	200
50	×	Re. 1.00	=	50
				1,850

$\therefore$ Standard Cost per unit = $\frac{\text{Rs. } 1{,}850}{500}$ = Rs. 3.70

Problem

Vinak Ltd. produces an article by blending two basic raw materials. It operates a Standard Costing system and the following standards have been set for raw materials :

Material	Standard Mix	Standard Price per kg
A	40%	Rs. 4.00
B	60%	Rs. 3.00

The standard loss in processing is 15%.

During April 2006, the company produced 1,700 kg of finished output.

The position of stock and purchases for the month of April 2006 is :

Material	Stock on 1.4.06	Stock on 30.4.06	Purchased during April 2006	
	kg	kg	kg	Cost (Rs.)
A	35	5	800	3,400
B	40	50	1,200	3,000

Calculate the following variances :

(i) Material Price Variance.

(ii) Material Usage Variance.

(iii) Material Yield Variance.

(iv) Material Mix Variance.

(v) Total Material Cost Variance. **[C.A. Inter, Adapted]**

Solution

Type of Material	Standard Qty. (kg)	Standard Rate (Rs.)	Standard Amount (Rs.)	Actual Qty. (kg)	Actual Rate (Rs.)	Actual Amount (Rs.)
A	800	4.00	3,200	35	4.00	140.00
				795	4.25	3,378.75
B	1,200	3.00	3,600	40	3.00	120.00
				1,150	2.50	2,875.00
	2,000		6,800	2,020		6,513.75

(i) Material Price Variance :

(Standard Price – Actual Price) × Actual Qty.

A	:	(Rs. 4.00 – Rs. 4.25) × 795 =	Rs. 198.75 (A)
B	:	(Rs. 3.00 – Rs. 2.50) × 1,150 =	Rs. 575.00 (F)
			Rs. 376.25 (F)

(ii) Material Usage Variance :

Standard Rate × (Standard Qty. – Actual Qty.)

A	:	4.00 × (800 – 830) =	Rs. 120 (A)
B	:	3.00 × (1,200 – 1,190) =	Rs. 30 (F)
			Rs. 90 (A)

(iii) Material Yield Variance :

Standard Cost per unit × (Standard Output – Actual Output)

$$\frac{\text{Rs. } 6{,}800}{1{,}700} \times (2{,}020 \times 85\% - 1{,}700)$$

= Rs. 4.00 × (1,717 – 1,700)

= Rs. 68 (F)

(iv) Material Mix Variance = Standard Rate × (Revised Standard Quantity – Actual Quantity)

A : Rs. 4.00 × $\left(800 \times \frac{2{,}020}{2{,}000} - 830\right)$ = Rs. 88 (A)

B : Rs. 3.00 × $\left(1{,}200 \times \frac{2{,}020}{2{,}000} - 1{,}190\right)$ = Rs. 66 (F)

Rs. 22 (A)

(v) Total Material Cost Variance = Standard Cost of Actual Output – Actual Cost

(Rs. 6,800 – Rs. 6,513.75)

= Rs. 286.25 (F)

Problem

The standard output of product 'EXE' is 25 units per hour in manufacturing department of a company employing 100 workers. The standard wage rate per labour hour is Rs. 6.

In a 42-hour week, the department produced 1,040 units of 'EXE' despite 5% of the time paid was lost due to an abnormal reason. The hourly wage rate actually paid was Rs. 6.20, Rs. 6 and Rs. 5.70, respectively, to 10, 30 and 60 of the workers.

Compute relevant variances. **[C.A. Inter, Adapted]**

Solution

Labour Cost Variance

Standard Cost of labour for actual output – Actual Cost of labour

Standard hour for actual output = $\frac{1,040}{25}$ = 41.6 hours

Standard wage rate per hour of 100 workers = 100 × Rs. 6

= Rs. 600

∴ Standard Cost of labour for actual output = 41.6 × Rs. 600 = Rs. 24,960

Actual Cost of Labour :

						Rs.
42	×	10	×	Rs. 6.20	=	2,604
42	×	30	×	Rs. 6.00	=	7,560
42	×	60	×	Rs. 5.70	=	14,364
						24,528

∴ Labour Cost Variance = Rs. 24,960 – Rs. 24,528

= Rs. 432 (F)

Labour Rate Variance

(Standard Rate – Actual Rate) × Actual Hours

						Rs.	
10	×	(Rs. 6 – Rs. 6.20)	×	42	=	84	(A)
30	×	(Rs. 6 – Rs. 6.00)	×	42	=	Nil	
60	×	(Rs. 6 – Rs. 5.70)	×	42	=	756	(F)
						672	(F)

Labour Efficiency Variance

(Standard hours for actual output – Actual effective hours) × Standard Rate

= (41.6 × 100 – 42 × 100 × 95%) × Rs. 6.00

= (4,160 – 3,990) × Rs. 6.00

= Rs. 1,020 (F)

Idle Time Variance :

Idle Time × Standard Rate

4,200 × 5% × Rs. 6.00

= 1,260 (A)

Problem

The Standard Labour Complement and the Actual Labour Complement engaged during month are :

	Skilled	Semi-skilled	Unskilled
(a) Standard no. of workers in a group	30	10	10
(b) Standard wage rate (Rs.)	5	3	2
(c) Actual no. of workers employed during the month in the group	24	15	12
(d) Actual wage rate per hour (Rs.)	6	2.5	2

During the month of 200 working hours the group produced 9,600 standard hours of work.

Required :

Calculation showing wage rate variance, labour efficiency variance, labour mix variance and total labour cost variance. **[I.C.W.A.I. Inter]**

Solution

Calculation of standard labour hour rate from standard group :

	No. of workers	Hours per month	Total Hours	Standard rate Rs.	Standard total cost Rs.
Skilled	30	200	6,000	5	30,000
Semi-skilled	10	200	2,000	3	6,000
Unskilled	10	200	2,000	2	4,000
			10,000		40,000

$\therefore$ Standard rate = Rs. $\frac{40,000}{10,000}$ = Rs. 4.00

Calculation of standard labour hour rate from actual group :

	No. of workers	Hours per month	Total Hours	Standard rate Rs.	Standard total cost Rs.
Skilled	24	200	4,800	5	24,000
Semi-skilled	15	200	3,000	3	9,000
Unskilled	12	200	2,400	2	4,800
			10,200		37,800

Standard labour hour rate of actual mix = $\frac{37,800}{10,200}$ = Rs. 3.71

Calculation of actual labour hour rate of actual group :

	No. of workers	Hours per month	Total Hours	Actual rate Rs.	Actual total cost Rs.
Skilled	24	200	4,800	6	28,800
Semi-skilled	15	200	3,000	2.5	7,500
Unskilled	12	200	2,400	2	4,800
			10,200		41,100

$\therefore$ Actual labour hour rate = $\frac{41,100}{10,200}$ = 4.03

Wage rate variance = Standard labour cost of actual group – actual labour cost of actual group

= (Rs. 37,800 – Rs. 41,100) = Rs. 3,300 (A)

Efficiency Variance

= Standard rate × (Standard hours equivalent to production – Actual hours worked)

= Rs. 4.00 × (9,600 – 10,200)

= Rs. 2,400 (A)

Mix Variance = (10,200 × Rs. 4) – Rs. 37,800

= Rs. 40,800 – Rs. 37,800

= Rs. 3,000 (F)

Labour Cost Variance = Standard Cost – Actual Cost

= (9,600 × Rs. 4.00) – Rs. 41,100

= Rs. 38,400 – Rs. 41,100

= Rs. 2,700 (A)

Problem

In Department X, the following data are submitted for the week ending 8th January :

Standard Output for 40 hours per week	1400 units
Standard fixed overhead	Rs. 1400
Actual output	1200 units.
Actual hours worked	32
Actual fixed overhead	Rs. 1500

Calculate (a) Overhead Cost variance (b) Overhead expenditure variance and (c) Overhead volume variance. **[I.C.W.A.I. Inter]**

Solution

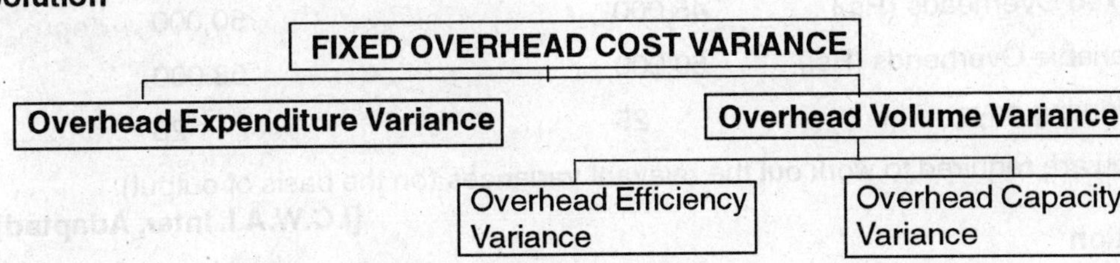

(a) Fixed Overhead Cost Variance = (Overheads recovered – Actual Overheads Incurred)

$$\left(\frac{\text{Rs. } 1,400}{1,400} \times 1,200 - \text{Rs. } 1,500\right)$$

= (Rs. 1,200 – Rs. 1,500) = Rs. 300 (A)

(b) Overhead Expenditure Variance
= (Budgeted Fixed Overhead – Actual Fixed Overhead)
= (Rs. 1,400 – Rs. 1,500) = Rs. 100 (A).

(c) Overhead Volume Variance
= (Budgeted Production – Actual Production) × Standard Overhead rate per unit

$$= (1,400 - 1,200) \times \text{Rs. } \frac{1,400}{1,400}$$

= 200 × Re. 1.00
= Rs. 200 (A)
(i) Overhead Efficiency Variance = (Standard production in actual hours – Actual produc-

tions) × Standard overhead rate per unit

$$= \left(\frac{1,400}{40} \times 32 - 1,200\right) \times \text{Re. } 1.00$$

= (1,120 – 1,200) × Re. 1.00

= 80 × Re. 1.00

= Rs. 80.00 (F)

(ii) Overhead Capacity Variance = (Standard production in actual hours – Budgeted Production) × Standard overhead rate per unit

= (1,120 – 1,400) × Re. 1.00

= 280 × Re. 1.00

= Rs. 280 (A)

Problem

AB Company Limited is having standard costing system in operation for quite some time. The following data relating to the month of April 2007 is available from the Cost records :

	Budgeted	Actual
Output (in units)	30,000	32,500
Operating Hours	30,000	33,000
Fixed Overheads (Rs.)	45,000	50,000
Variable Overheads (Rs.)	60,000	68,000
Working days	25	26

You are required to work out the relevant variances (on the basis of output).

[I.C.W.A.I. Inter, Adapted]

Solution

$$\text{Variable Overhead Recovery Rate.} = \frac{\text{Budgeted Variable Overhead}}{\text{Budgeted Output}}$$

$$= \frac{\text{Rs. } 60,000}{30,000}$$

= Rs. 2.00

Variable Overhead Variances

Variable Overhead Cost Variance

= (Variable Overhead Recovered – Actual Overhead Incurred)

= (32,500 × Rs. 2.00) – Rs. 68,000

= Rs. 65,000 – Rs. 68,000

= Rs. 3,000 (A)

(i) Variable Overhead Expenditure Variance
= (Standard Variable Overhead Rate – Actual Variable Overhead Rate) × Actual Time

$$= \left(\frac{\text{Rs. } 60{,}000}{30{,}000} - \frac{\text{Rs. } 68{,}000}{33{,}000}\right) \times 33{,}000$$

= (Rs. 2.00 – Rs. 2.0606) × 33,000

= Rs. 2,000 (A) (App.)

(ii) Variable Overhead Efficiency Variance
= (Standard Time for Actual Output – Actual Time Taken) × Standard Rate

$$= \left(\frac{30{,}000}{30{,}000} \times 32{,}500 - 33{,}000\right) \times \text{Rs. } 2.00$$

= (32,500 – 33,000) × Rs. 2.00

= Rs. 1,000 (A)

Fixed Overhead Variance :

Fixed Overhead Cost Variance
= (Fixed Overhead Recovered – Actual Overhead Incurred)

$$= \left(\frac{\text{Rs. } 45{,}000}{30{,}000} \times 32{,}500 - \text{Rs. } 50{,}000\right)$$

= (Rs. 1.50 × 32,500 – Rs. 50,000)

= (Rs. 48,750 – Rs. 50,000)

= Rs. 1,250 (A).

(i) Fixed Overhead Expenditure Variance =
(Budgeted Fixed Overhead – Actual Fixed Overhead)

= Rs. 45,000 – Rs. 50,000

= Rs. 5,000 (A).

(ii) Fixed Overhead Volume Variance
= (Actual Production – Budgeted Production) × Standard Overhead Rate per unit

$$= (32{,}500 - 30{,}000) \times \frac{\text{Rs. } 45{,}000}{30{,}000}$$

= 2,500 × Rs. 1.50

= Rs. 3,750 (F).

(a) Fixed Overhead Efficiency Variance
= (Standard Time for Actual Output – Actual Time Taken) × Std. Rate per hour

$$= \left(\frac{30{,}000}{30{,}000} \times 32{,}500 - 33000\right) \times \frac{\text{Rs. } 45{,}000}{30{,}000}$$

= (32,500 – 33,000) × Rs. 1.50

= Rs. 750 (A)

(b) Fixed Overhead Capacity Variance =

(Standard Production in Actual Hours – Budgeted Production) × Standard Rate per unit

$$= \left(\frac{30{,}000}{30{,}000} \times 33{,}000 - 30{,}000\right) \times \frac{\text{Rs. } 45{,}000}{30{,}000}$$

= (33,000 – 30,000) × Rs. 1.50

= Rs. 4,500 (F)

(i) Fixed Overhead Calendar Variance

= Extra hours worked × Standard rate per hour

$$= \frac{30{,}000}{25} \times 1 \times \text{Rs. } 1.5 = \text{Rs. } 1{,}800 \text{ (F)}$$

(ii) Fixed Overhead Revised Capacity Variance

= (Actual hours worked – Revised budgeted hours) × Standard overhead rate

$$= \left(33{,}000 - \frac{30{,}000}{25} \times 26\right) \times \text{Rs. } 1.50$$

= Rs. 2,700 (F).

Problem

PH Ltd. furnishes the following information relating to budgeted sales and actual sales for April 2006 :

	Product	Sales Quantity units	Selling Price per unit Rs.
Budgeted Sales :	A	1,200	15
	B	800	20
	C	2,000	40
Actual Sales :	A	880	18
	B	880	20
	C	2,640	38

Calculate the following variances :

(i) Sales Quantity Variance.

(ii) Sales Mix Variance.

(iii) Sales Price Variance.

(iv) Total Sales Variance. **[C.A. Inter, Adapted]**

Solution

Statement showing Budgeted Sales and Actual Sales

Product	Budgeted Qty.	Budgeted Rate Rs.	Budgeted Amount Rs.	Actual Qty.	Actual Rate Rs.	Actual Amount Rs.
A	1200	15	18,000	880	18	15,840
B	800	20	16,000	880	20	17,600
C	2,000	40	80,000	2,640	38	1,00,320
	4,000		114,000	4,400		1,33,760

(i) Sales Quantity Variance = (Budgeted Quantity – Actual Quantity) × Standard Rate

A : (1,200 – 880) × Rs. 15 = Rs. 4,800 (A)
B : (800 – 880) × Rs. 20 = Rs. 1,600 (F)
C : (2,000 – 2,640) × Rs. 40 = Rs. 25,600 (F)
Rs. 22,400 (F)

(ii) Sales Mix Variance = (Revised Budgeted Quantity – Actual Quantity) × Standard rate.

$$A: \left(1{,}200 \times \frac{4{,}400}{4{,}000} - 880\right) \times \text{Rs. } 15 = \text{Rs. } 6{,}600 \text{ (A)}$$

$$B: \left(800 \times \frac{4{,}400}{4{,}000} - 880\right) \times \text{Rs. } 20 = \text{Nil}$$

$$C: \left(2{,}000 \times \frac{4{,}400}{4{,}000} - 2{,}640\right) \times \text{Rs. } 40 = \text{Rs. } 17{,}600 \text{ (F)}$$

Rs. 11,000 (F).

(iii) Sales Price Variance = (Standard Price – Actual Price) × Actual Quantity

A : (Rs. 15 – Rs. 18) × 880 = Rs. 2,640 (F)
B : (Rs. 20 – Rs. 20) × 880 = Nil
C : (Rs. 40 – Rs. 38) × 2,640 = Rs. 5,280 (A)
Rs. 2,640 (A)

(iv) Total Sales Variance = Budgeted Sales – Actual Sales
= Rs. 1,14,000 – Rs. 1,33,760
= Rs. 19,760 (F)

Problem

The budgeted sales for one month and the actual results achieved are :

Product	Budget Qty.	Budget Rate	Budget Amount	Actual Qty.	Actual Rate	Actual Amount
		Rs.	Rs.		Rs.	Rs.
A	1,000	100	1,00,000	1,200	125	1,50,000
B	700	200	1,40,000	800	150	1,20,000
C	500	300	1,50,000	600	300	1,80,000
D	300	500	1,50,000	400	600	2,40,000
	2,500		5,40,000	3,000		6,90,000

Calculate in respect of each product the sales variances. **[I.C.W.A.I. Final, Adapted]**

Solution

Sales Value Variance = Budgeted Sales – Actual Sales
= Rs. 5,40,000 – Rs. 6,90,000
= Rs. 1,50,000 (F)

Sales Quantity Variance = (Budgeted Quantity – Actual Quantity) × Standard Rate

A :	(1000 – 1,200)	×	Rs. 100	=	Rs.	20,000 (F)
B :	(700 – 800)	×	Rs. 200	=	Rs.	20,000 (F)
C :	(500 – 600)	×	Rs. 300	=	Rs.	30,000 (F)
D :	(300 – 400)	×	Rs. 500	=	Rs.	50,000 (F)
					Rs.	1,20,000 (F)

Sales Price Variance = (Standard Rate – Actual Rate) × Actual Quantity

A	:(Rs. 100 – Rs. 125)	×	1,200	=	Rs.	30,000 (F)
B	:(Rs. 200 – Rs. 150)	×	800	=	Rs.	40,000 (A)
C	:(Rs. 300 – Rs. 300)	×	600	=		Nil
D	:(Rs. 500 – Rs. 600)	×	400	=	Rs.	40,000 (F)
					Rs.	30,000 (F)

Verification :

Sales Value Variance = Sales Quantity Variance + Sales Price Variance
= Rs. 1,20,000 (F) + Rs. 30,000 (F)
= Rs. 1,50,000 (F)

Sales Quantity Variance can be classified into the following two classes of variance :

(i) Sales Mix Variance

= (Revised Budgeted Quantity – Actual Quantity) × Standard Rate

$$A: \left(1{,}000 \times \frac{3{,}000}{2{,}500} - 1{,}200\right) \times \text{Rs. } 100 = \text{Nil}$$

$$B: \left(700 \times \frac{3{,}000}{2{,}500} - 800\right) \times \text{Rs. } 200 = \text{Rs. } 8{,}000 \text{ (A)}$$

$$C: \left(500 \times \frac{3{,}000}{2{,}500} - 600\right) \times \text{Rs. } 300 = \text{Nil}$$

$$D: \left(300 \times \frac{3{,}000}{2{,}500} - 400\right) \times \text{Rs. } 500 = \text{Rs. } 20{,}000 \text{ (F)}$$

Rs. 12,000 (F)

(ii) Revised Quantity Variance = Budgeted Sales – Revised Standard Sales
Or, (Budgeted Qty. – Revised Standard Qty.) × Standard Rate

A :	(1,000 – 1,200)	× Rs. 100	=	Rs. 20,000 (F)
B :	(700 – 840)	× Rs. 200	=	Rs. 28,000 (F)
C :	(500 – 600)	× Rs. 300	=	Rs. 30,000 (F)
D :	(300 – 360)	× Rs. 500	=	Rs. 30,000 (F)
				Rs. 1,08,000 (F)

Verification : Sales Volume Variance = Sales Mix Variance + Revised Quantity Variance.
= Rs. 12,000 (F) + Rs. 1,08,000 (F).
= Rs. 1,20,000 (F)

QUESTIONS

1. What is Standard Costing? Discuss its advantages from management point of view.
2. (a) Define :
   (i) Material Cost Variance.
   (ii) Material Usage Variance.
   (iii) Material Price Variance.
   (b) From the following particulars find out the three variances mentioned in (a) above :

Quantity of material purchased	3,000 units
Value of material purchased	Rs. 9,000
Standard quantity of material required per ton of finished product	25 units
Standard rate of material	Rs. 2 per unit
Opening stock of material	Nil
Closing stock of material	500 units
Finished product during the period	80 ton

[I.C.W.A.I.]

3. From the following data, calculate overhead variances which have arisen and present them in a form suitable for management appraisal :

Item	Budget	Actual
Number of working days in period	20	21
Man-hours in period	40,000	43,000
Output per-man-hour in units	3.2	3.0
Total output in units	1,28,000	1,29,000
Overheads : Variable	5,120	5,720
Fixed	1,280	1,250

[I.C.W.A., London]

4. A factory specialises in the production of a single component for an improved equipment. The accounts for February 2006, showed :

	Rs.
Material used 1,000 units @ Rs. 5.250	5,250
Labour 1,000 hrs @ Rs. 3.00	3,000
Overhead for 1000 hrs @ Rs. 2.00 per hr	2,000
	10,250

The output at the close of the month was 900 units of the components (completed) and 100 units for which materials were drawn fully but only 50% completed with reference to labour and overheads.

Find out the average cost of completed units under each element of cost, and in total.

Standard cost of the product was	Rs. 10
Material single item	Rs. 5
Labour 1 hr @ Rs. 3/- per hour	Rs. 3
Overhead for 1 hr @ Rs. 2/- per hr	Rs. 2
	Rs. 10

Calculate the (i) Material Price Variance, and (ii) Labour Efficiency Variance.

[C.A. Final, Adapted]

13

ACTIVITY-BASED COSTING

● Good morning to my dear students.

☐ "Good morning, Sir."

● What will be discussed this morning ?

☐ "Sir, you said in your last class that you will be discussing Activity-Based Costing."

● Well, before I am to discuss about this, let us discuss the genesis of Activity-Based Costing (ABC). Activity Based Costing is concerned with the allocation of overhead costs to products and/or services on the basis of several activities being performed. It originates to overcome the drawbacks of traditional overhead cost accounting which allocates cost to product as the principle of single overhead allocation rate.

Following are the reasons which demand for the introduction of refined costing system, termed as Activity-Based Costing (ABC) —

Traditional costing system allocates overhead costs to products, services or jobs by using single or multiple volume related allocation base, such as labour hours, machine hours, etc. This method is useful when different products or services consume overhead costs uniformly. But this may not always happen and result in inaccurate product or service costing. This, in turn, affects the decision-making process of managers.

Reasons for Activity-Based Costing

Traditional costing system is useful for companies producing or providing few products or services. But nowadays cut-throat competition compels companies to produce or provide different types of products or services in order to survive in a competitive environment. In other words, companies have diversified their operations. Naturally, these products or services may not consume overhead resources uniformly based on volume. Traditional costing system fails to identify the actual amount of resources consumed by these products or services and allocates overhead costs based on volume only.

Nowadays most of the companies have implemented computer-assisted production technology. In this new production environment, direct labour costs have decreased significantly and, at the same time, indirect costs of automation have increased. This necessitates the change in the method of overhead allocation. For traditional costing system fails to recognise the cause-effect relationship between cost allocation bases (e.g. labour hour, machine hour etc.) and overhead costs.

☐ "Sir, I could not follow you, first of all please define what is activity-based costing."

● Well, I am giving you a glimpse of Activity Based Costing. Though the example given here is not exhaustive; however, it will give you an insight about activity-based costing.

Suppose, total overhead cost of one agricultural firm for three crops– Rice, Wheat and Sugarcane are Rs. 3,00,000, Rs.1,00,000 and Rs. 50,000, respectively, and total labour hour used for production of all crops on an average is 10,000 each.

Items	Overhead cost (Rs.)	Agricultural labour hour
Rice	3,00,000	10,000
Wheat	1,00,000	10,000
Sugarcane	50,000	10,000
Total	4,50,000	30,000

Under traditional costing system, average overhead cost for all these products is

$$\text{Average} = \frac{\text{Rs. } 4{,}50{,}000}{30{,}000 \text{ hours}} = \text{Rs. } 15/\text{hour}$$

As per Activity-Based Costing (ABC)

$$\text{Rice} = \frac{\text{Rs. } 3{,}00{,}000}{10{,}000 \text{ hours}} = \text{Rs. } 30/\text{hour}$$

$$\text{Wheat} = \frac{\text{Rs. } 1{,}00{,}000}{10{,}000 \text{ hours}} = \text{Rs. } 10/\text{hour}$$

$$\text{Sugarcane} = \frac{\text{Rs. } 50{,}000}{10{,}000 \text{ hours}} = \text{Rs. } 5/\text{hour}$$

If the farmer wants to produce extra sugarcane for which 40 agricultural labour hour is required then

As per traditional system, overhead cost would be –

40 hours × Rs. 15 = Rs. 600

as per ABC

40 hours × Rs. 5 = Rs. 200

Here, the moot point is, which one is correct ?

This example will lead you to follow my following lecture.

Is it clear to you ?

☐ "Thank you, Sir ! Now you can proceed."

● Thus, to have a true and fair view of actual cost consumed, a refined costing system should be followed. Activity-Based Costing System is one of the best tools for refining a costing system.

☐ "Sir, what exactly is Activity-Based Costing ?"

Meaning of Activity-Based Costing

- The pioneers of Activity-Based Costing (ABC) are Robin Cooper and Robert S. Kaplan.[1] According to them, ABC systems give better measure of Product or Service Cost. These systems focus on activities as fundamental cost objects and costs of these activities are assigned to products or services on the basis of activities consumed by these products or services. Thus, ABC systems not only help to understand Cost Behaviour but also to identify the causes of overhead cost.

Now I am giving you some definitions of renowned authors :

According to C.T. Horngren, S.M. Datar and G. Foster[2] "one of the best tools for refining a costing system is activity based costing. Activity-Based Costing (ABC) refines a costing system by focusing on individual activities as the fundamental cost objects. An activity is an event, task or unit of work with a specified purpose; for example, designing products, setting up machines, operating machines and distributing products. ABC systems calculate the costs of individual activities and assign costs to cost objects, such as, products and services on the basis of the activities needed to produce each product or service."

According to Barfield, Raiborn and Kinney[3] "ABC is a cost accounting system that focuses on the various activities performed in an organisation and collects costs on the basis of the underlying nature and extent of these activities. This costing method focuses on attaching Costs to products and services based on the activities conducted to produce, perform, distribute or support those products and services."

Thus, Activity-Based Costing (ABC) may be defined as a system of overhead cost accounting under which activities are first identified and the cost of these activities are assigned to products or services on the basis of extent of activities consumed by these products or services :

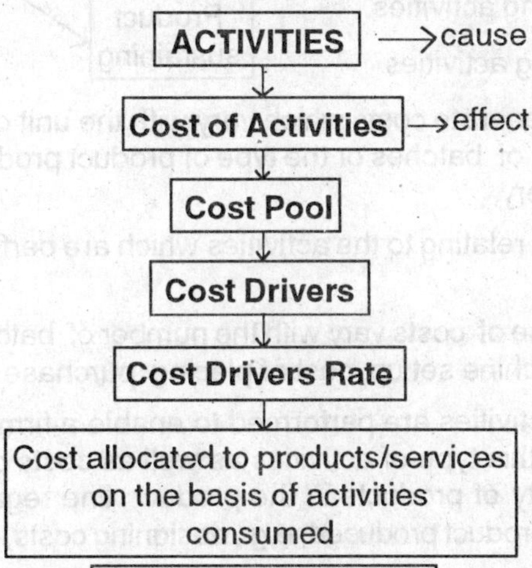

Activity Based Costing

---

[1] R. Cooper and R.S. Kaplan, ***The Design of Cost Management Systems***, Prentice Hall, 1999

[2] C.T. Horngren, S.M. Datar & G. Foster, ***Cost Accounting : A Managerial Emphasis***, Prentice Hall of India Pvt. Ltd, New Delhi, 2003

[3] Barfield, Raiborn and Kinney, ***Cost Accounting — Tradition and Innovation***, Third Edition, South-Western College Publication.

☐ "Sir, what is cost driver?"

Meaning of Cost Driver

● Cost driver is transaction or activity of support department, which drives or, better to say, accelerates overhead cost, that is to say, indirect cost. Thus, cost driver dictates cost behaviour. The example of cost drivers are number of production run, number of parts inserted by machine, number of parts inserted by man, quality testing time, number of set up, number of hours spent in supervision etc.

Kaplan and Cooper—for the purpose of designing this system—have classified costs into short-term variable costs, long-term variable costs and fixed costs. In other words, fixed costs as classified under traditional costing system is again classified in ABC, as long-term variable cost and fixed costs.

☐ "Sir, give us some light on short term, long term variable cost as well as fixed cost."

● You see, short term variable costs vary proportionately with the volume of production and are identical with the variable costs of traditional costing systems. Long term variable costs do not vary with the volume of production but vary with the extent of activities, such as, number of set up, number of orders. In ABC, fixed costs are those costs which do not vary for a given period of time with the extent of activities.

In ABC approach, all activities within the organisation are classified into four categories —

i. Unit level activities

ii. Batch level activities

iii. Product sustaining activities

iv. Facility sustaining activities

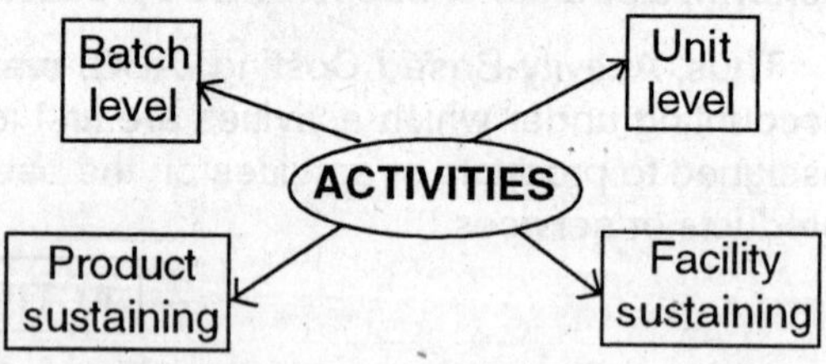

Unit level activities generate costs which vary with the unit of output produced but do not vary with the number of batches or the type of product produced, e.g., cost of repair, depreciation of machinery.

There are some costs relating to the activities which are performed each time a group of product is produced.

In other words, this type of costs vary with the number of batches of product produced, e.g., costs relating to machine set up, cost of placing purchase orders, inspection costs.

Product-sustaining activities are performed to enable a firm to produce each type of product. In other words, this type of activities as well as costs of activities increase with the increase in the variety of products in the product line regardless of the number of units or batches of each product produced, e.g., designing costs, engineering cost, product specification cost.

Facility sustaining activities[4] support the organisation as a whole instead of supporting any product or services. For example, administration cost arising from administration activities. These costs are either deducted from operating income or allocated to products or services on some basis.

---

[4] C.T. Horngren, S.M. Datar & G. Foster, ***Cost Accounting — A Managerial Emphasis***, Prentice Hall of India, Pvt. Ltd, New Delhi, 2003

Now, I shall discuss the steps for implementing ABC system :

Steps of Activity-Based Costing

(i) Identify all major activities performed in an organisation to support the process of production and distribution of products or services.

(ii) Assign overhead resources to the above activities by using the most appropriate cost drivers.

(iii) Identify the cost allocation bases or cost drivers and create activities cost pool. A cost pool is a combination of costs of activities which can be allocated to products by using a single cost driver. In other words, costs of activities having the same cause and effect relationship with a single cost driver are combined to create a cost pool.

(iv) Determine the cost driver rate by dividing the cost pool by the units of cost driver which has cause and effect relationship with that cost pool.

(v) Identify the benefit derived by each product from each activity pool.

(vi) Allocate the cost of each activity pool to products on the basis of benefit derived. In other words, cost driver rate, here, is multiplied by the quantity of activities consumed by each product.

(vii) Complete the total cost of each product by adding direct cost with the indirect cost so allocated to the product.

It can be shown diagramatically as :

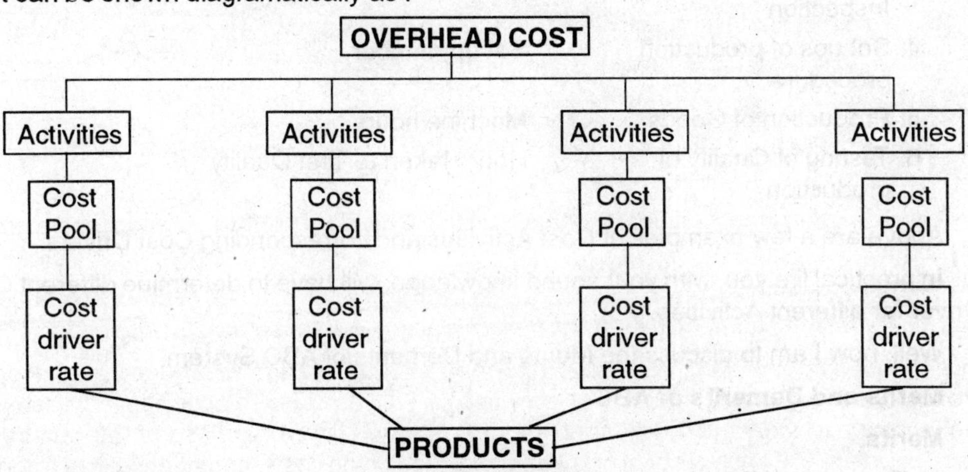

Activity Based Costing

Your attention please ! Why you are talking to each other?

Silence please !

Now I would like to discuss the Merits and Demerits of the ABC system.

Before that, I want to know whether you have any question(s).

☐ "Sir, the concept of Cost Driver is not yet clear to me."

● Well, I am discussing the same in brief. I have already mentioned at the outset of this part of Cost Accounting that core meaning of the term cost is '*Sacrifice*' which is used to achieve some specific object. Objects of Cost are activities[5]. Activities justify cost driver.

☐ "Excuse me Sir. Still now I do not understand how activities justify cost driver(s)".

● Well, have a look here. Perhaps you have a personal car, say Maruti 800 or any other model. If so who drives the car.?

☐ "Yes Sir I have Santro .... I drive it locally or some short distance."

● Can you drive a big lorry from your residence to a long long distance, say, from Kolkata to Patna ?

☐ "No Sir, for this I have to select a driver having efficiency for driving heavy vehicle."

● Now you can realise that your object(s) or activities justify your selection of appropriate person. This selection of appropriate person is Driver. So in case of some cost activities it is called Cost Driver(s).

Now, you Jot down different Cost Driver for different Activities.

Activities	Cost Driver
1. Material Purchase	Number of purchase orders placed or processed
2. Handling of Materials and Parts	Number of Materials and Parts
3. Material and parts Inspection	Number of Materials and parts inspected
4. Set ups of production procedure	Set up number
5. Production of Goods	Machine hours
6. Testing of Quality of production	Hours taken to Test Quality

Above are a few examples of Cost Activities and corresponding Cost Drivers.

In practical life you, with your sound knowledge, will have to determine different Cost Driver for different Activities.

Well, now I am to discuss the Merits and Demerits of ABC System.

Merits and Demerits of ABC

Merits

(i) The use of ABC results in accurate product or service costing. For, ABC allocates overhead costs to products or services based on activities consumed by these products or services.

(ii) The identification of non-value added activities is possible by the use of ABC. The non-value added activities are those activities which are not adding value or utility to the products or services.

5 "... activity or item for which a separate measurement of cost is desired"—C.T. Horngren and others. ***Cost Accounting—A Managerial Emphasis***. Prentice Hall (1994) p. 2.

(iii) ABC is useful in advanced manufacturing technology (AMT) environment where significant portion of total manufacturing cost is overhead cost.

Advantages

(iv) ABC results in better management of activities. It recognises that product or services consume activities which, in turn, consume resources. Thus, resources management is possible only if activities are properly managed.

(v) ABC helps management in many important decision making processes, such as, selection of most profitable product mix, product design, rejection of non-value added activities.

Demerits of ABC

Disadvantages

(i) ABC is suitable only when products and services consume resources disproportionately. It has no use so far as product costing is concerned when products and services consume indirect resources uniformly.

(ii) ABC is a costly method and therefore can only be used in large organisation.

(iii) There are some activities for which it is really difficult to identify cost allocation bases. For example, "advertising to build corporate rather than brand image".

(iv) ABC has no use in those organisations where a significant portion of total cost is represented by direct cost. That is why a small percentage of total cost is represented by indirect cost.

□ "Sir, I have a question".

● Yes, yes speak up.

□ "Sir, I have heard about Activity Based Management. What is it, Sir ? Please explain".

Concept of Activity-Based Management

● We know that the aim of modern business is to improve profitability and, at the same time, satisfy customers. Activity Based Management (ABM) refers to the use of Activity Based Costing information in the management of the organisation's activities to improve profitability and satisfy customers. You know, the decision-making is one of the important functions of management and appropriate decision-making requires timely and accurate information in the decision areas. Activity based management involves the use of activities based costing information in the process of decision-making. The decision includes-product pricing , product mix, product design, process improvements etc.

□ "Sir, give us some practical problems on ABC".

● Your attention please, Here are a few worked out problems. Have a look here.

Problems

Problem on Product Complexity :

You are given the following information about two products X and Y produced by a company.

	Product X	Product Y
Production (Units)	1,000	1,000
Number of production run	8	16
Direct labour hours per unit	1.5	1.5

Budgeted machine set up cost Rs. 36,000.

Compute :

(i) Machine set up cost per unit of the products using traditional costing, and also ABC.

(ii) Explain the reason for the difference, if any.

Solution

(i) Total direct labour required to produce X and Y.

$= (1{,}000 \times 1.5 + 1{,}000 \times 1.5) \quad = 3{,}000 \text{ hours}$

$$\text{Machine set up cost per labour hour} = \frac{\text{Rs. } 36{,}000}{3{,}000}$$

$= \text{Rs. } 12.00$

Machine set up cost per unit (Using Labour hour rate) :

	Product X	Product Y
Direct labour hour per unit	1.5 hrs	1.5 hrs
Machine set up cost per hour	Rs.12.00	Rs.12.00
Machine set up cost to per unit (12.00 × 1.5)	Rs.18.00	Rs.18.00

$$\text{Machine set up cost per production run} = \frac{\text{Rs. } 36{,}000}{(8+16)} = \frac{\text{Rs. } 36{,}000}{24} = \text{Rs.}1{,}500$$

Machine set up cost per unit (Using Activity-based Costing) :

	Product X	Product Y
Number of production runs	8	16
Machine set up cost per production run	Rs. 1,500	Rs. 1,500
Total machine set up cost	Rs.12,000	Rs. 24,000
Production (Units)	1,000	1,000
Machine set up cost per unit (Rs.)	12.00	24.00

(ii) Under traditional costing, machine set up cost per unit of both X and Y is Rs.18.00. It ignores the fact that product Y is more complex and requires production runs double than product X. But, ABC takes product complexity into consideration and allocates machine set up cost according to the production runs (which drives machine set up costs) consumed by the products. Based on ABC, machine set up cost per unit of X is Rs. 12, while, per unit of Y is Rs. 24.00.

Problem on Volume Diversity :

A company produces two products M and N. The following information are available about these two products —

	Products	
	M	N
Production (Units)	10,000	5,000
Labour hour per unit	2.5	2.5
Number of orders placed	10	10

Purchasing material cost Rs. 15,000.

Compute purchasing material cost per unit of M and N under

(i) Traditional Costing

(ii) Activity-Based Costing; and compare the difference, if any.

Solution

$$\text{Labour hour rate} = \frac{\text{Rs. } 15{,}000}{10{,}000 \times 2.5 + 5{,}000 \times 2.5}$$

$$= \frac{\text{Rs. } 15{,}000}{37{,}500} = \text{Re. } 0.40$$

(i) Purchasing material cost per unit under Traditional Costing :

	Products	
	M	N
Labour hour per unit	2.5	2.5
Labour hour rate	Re.0.40	Re.0.40
Purchasing material cost per unit	(0.40 × 2.5) = Re.1.00	(0.40 × 2.5) = Re.1.00

$$\text{Purchasing material cost per order} = \frac{\text{Rs. } 15{,}000}{10 + 10} = \text{Rs. } 750$$

(ii) Purchasing material cost per unit under Activity-Based Costing :

	Products	
	M	N
Production Units	10,000	5,000
Number of Orders	10	10
Purchasing material cost per order (Rs.)	750	750
Purchasing material cost per unit (Re./Rs.)	$\frac{\text{Rs.}750 \times 10}{10{,}000}$ = 0.75	$\frac{\text{Rs.}750 \times 10}{5{,}000}$ = 1.5

It is clear that traditional costing does not consider the cost driver for Overhead Cost— overcost product M and undercost product N. But, ABC allocates overhead cost based on Cost allocation require for each product. As a result, overhead cost per unit of M is lower because of high volume of production, than product N.

Problem

Executive Power (EP) manufactures and sells computers and computer peripherals to several nationwide retail chains. Mr. Bose is the manager of the printer division. Its two largest selling printers are P41 and P63.

The manufacturing cost of each printer is calculated using EPs activity-based costing system. EP has one direct manufacturing cost category (direct materials) and the following indirect manufacturing cost pools :

Indirect manufacturing cost pool	**Allocation Rate Rs.**
Material handling	1.20
Assembling management	40.00
Machine insertion of parts	0.70
Manual insertion of parts	2.10
Quality testing	25.00

(a) What are the allocation bases ?

Product characteristics of P41 and P63 are :

	P41	**P63**
Direct material costs	Rs. 407.50	Rs. 292.10
No. of parts	85 parts	46 parts
Hours of assembling time	3.2 hrs	1.9 hrs
No. of machine-inserted parts	49 parts	31 parts
Hours of quality testing	1.4 hrs	1.1 hrs
No. of manually-inserted parts	36 parts	15 parts

(b) What is the manufacturing cost of P41 and P63 ?

Mr. Bose has just received some bad news, A foreign competitor has introduced products very similar to P41 and P63. Given their announced selling price, Mr. Bose estimates the P41 alone to have a manufacturing cost of approximately Rs. 680 and the P63 alone to have a manufacturing cost of approximately Rs. 390.

The following revised designs of P41 and P63 (termed P41 REV and P63 REV respectively) are arrived at :

	P41 REV	**P63 REV**
Direct material costs	Rs. 381.20	Rs. 263.10
No. of parts	71	39
Hours of assembly time	2.1	1.6
No. of machine inserted parts	59	29
No. of manually inserted parts	12	10
Hours of quality testing	1.2	0.9

(c) What is the target cost per unit ?

(d) Explain the differences between P41 and P41 REV and between P63 and P63 REV. **[M.Com. C.U.]**

Solution

(a) The cost allocation bases are the activities which are consumed by the two products P41 and P63. They are number of material handled, hours spent for assembling, management, number of parts inserted by machine, number of parts inserted manually and quality testing time.

(b) Calculation of manufacturing cost of P41 and P63

	P41 (Rs.)	P63 (Rs.)
Direct Material Cost	407.5	292.10
Material Handling Cost		
(85 × 1.20)	102	—
(46 × 1.20)	—	55.20
Assembling Cost		
(Rs. 40 × 3.20)	128	—
(Rs. 40 × 1.90)		76.00
Machine Insertion of Parts		
(49 × Re. 0.70)	34.30	—
(31 × Re. 0.70)	—	21.70
Manual Insertion of Parts		
(36 × 2.10)	75.60	—
(15 × 2.10)	—	31.5
Quality Testing		
(25 × 1.4)	35.00	—
(25 × 1.1)	—	27.5
	782.40	504.00

Thus, manufacturing cost of P41 is Rs. 782.40 and that of P63 is Rs.504.

(c) Calculation of target cost per unit

	P41 REV Rs.	P63 REV Rs.
Direct Material Costs	381.20	263.10
Material Handling Cost		
(71 × 1.20)	85.20	—
(39 × 1.20)	—	46.80
Assembling Cost		
(40 × 2.10)	84.00	—
(40 × 1.60)	—	64.00

Machine Insertion Cost		
(59 × 0.70)	41.30	—
(29 × 0.70)	—	20.30
Manual Insertion Cost		
(12 × 2.10)	25.20	—
(10 × 2.10)	—	21.00
Quality Testing		
(25 × 1.20)	30.00	—
(25 × 0.90)	—	22.50
	646.90	437.70

(d) The cost per unit of P41 is higher than the cost per unit of P41 REV. All items of costs, except cost of parts inserted by machine, in case of P41 are higher than the items costs of P41 REV.

The cost per unit of P63 is higher than the cost of P63 REV. All items of costs of P63 are higher than the cost of items of P63 REV.

Problem

The following information provides details of the cost volume and transaction cost driver for a particular period of a hypothetical company :

Particulars	**Products**			**Total**
	X	**Y**	**Z**	
Production and Sales (Units)	35,000	25,000	10,000	
Raw material (Units)	6	6	12	
Direct material cost per unit (Rs.)	30	24	12	Rs.17,70,000
Direct labour hour per unit	1¼	2	1	1,03,750 hrs.
Machine hours per unitt	1¼	1	2	88,750 hrs.
Direct Labour Cost (Rs.)	10	12	8	—
Number of Production run	3	7	20	30
Number of deliveries	10	4	20	34
Number of receipt	15	35	220	270
Number of production order	15	10	25	50

Overhead Costs :	Rs.
Set up	36,000
Machining	7,10,000
Receiving	4,33,350
Packing	2,65,200
Engineering Cost	3,72,500
	18,17,050

Find out and compare product cost under traditional approach, multiple volume base allocation method and activity-based costing and analyse the situation when it is known that the target profit margin of the company is 40% on selling price.

Product Y has achieved the plan margin but product X is achieving a margin of only 30% because of increase in foreign competition while product Z achieved a margin of 50% (when overheads are allocated on the basis of direct labour hours).

Solution

Traditional Method (using direct labour hours as basis of allocation)

Total overhead = Rs. 18,17,500

Total labour hour = 1,03,750 hrs.

Labour hour rate $= \frac{\text{Rs.}18,17,500}{1,03,750}$

= Rs. 17.518

Statement of Product Cost

Particulars	X	Y	Z
Raw material cost	30	24	12
Direct labour cost	10	12	8
	40	36	20
Add : Overhead			
X : (17.514 × 1¼)	21.89	—	—
Y : (17.514 × 2)	—	35	—
Z : (17.514 × 1)	—	—	17.51
	61.89	71	37.51
Market Price : $X = \left(61.89 \times \frac{100}{70}\right)$	88.41	—	—
$Y = \left(71 \times \frac{100}{60}\right)$	—	118.33	—
$Z = \left(37.51 \times \frac{100}{50}\right)$	—	—	75

Multiple volume based costing method :

Machine cost = Rs. 7,10,000

Machine hours = 88,750 hrs.

Machine hour rate $= \frac{\text{Rs. } 7,10,000}{88,750}$ = Rs. 8.00

Other overhead cost as a percentage of material cost $= \frac{11,07,050}{17,70,000} \times 100 = 62.545\%$

Statement of Product Cost

Particulars	X (Rs.)	Y (Rs.)	Z (Rs.)
Direct Material Cost	30	24	12
Direct Labour Cost	10	12	8
Prime Cost	40	36	20
Overhead : Machine			
X : (8 × 1¼)	10	—	—
Y : (8 × 1)	—	8	—
Z : (8 × 2)	—	—	16
Other Overheads :			
X : (30× 62.545%)	18 .76	—	—
Y : (24 ×62.545%)	—	15	—
Z : (12×62.545%)	—	—	7.51
	68 .76	59	43.51

It is clear from the above that Product Y is earning return more than target return. Whereas, Products X and Z are earning return lower than the target return.

Activity-Based Costing Method:

We have to indentify activities, cost drivers and to calculate cost driver rates first :

Statment showing Calculation of Cost Driver Rate

Activities	Cost Driver	Cost (Rs.)	No. of transactions			Total	Cost driver rate (Rs.)
			X	Y	Z		
set up	No.of Production run	36,000	3	7	20	30	1,200
Machining	Machine hours	7,10,000	43,750	25,000	20,000	88,750	8
Receiving	No.of receipts	4,33,350	15	35	220	270	1,605
Packing	No. of deliveries	2,65,200	10	4	20	34	7,800
Engineering	No. of Production order	3,72,500	15	10	25	50	7,450
		18,17,050					

Calculation of Overhead Cost per unit of X, Y & Z

	X	Y	Z
Set up:	$\frac{1,200 \times 3}{35,000}$ = 0.103	$\frac{1,200 \times 7}{25,000}$ = 0.336	$\frac{1,200 \times 20}{10,000}$ = 2.40
Machining	$\frac{8 \times 43,750}{35,000}$ = 10	$\frac{8 \times 25,000}{25,000}$ = 8	$\frac{8 \times 20,000}{10,000}$ = 16

Receiving	$\frac{1605 \times 15}{35,000}$	$\frac{1605 \times 35}{25,000}$	$\frac{1605 \times 220}{10,000}$
	= 0.69	= 2.247	= 35.31
Packing	$\frac{7800 \times 10}{35,000}$	$\frac{7800 \times 4}{25,000}$	$\frac{7800 \times 20}{10,000}$
	= 2.23	= 1.248	= 15.6
Engineering	$\frac{7450 \times 15}{35,000}$	$\frac{7450 \times 10}{25,000}$	$\frac{7450 \times 25}{10,000}$
	= 3.19	= 2.98	= 18.625

Statement of Product Cost :

	X	Y	Z
Direct Material (Rs.)	30	24	15
Direct Labour Cost (Rs.)	10	12	8
	40.00	36.00	23.00
Overhead :			
Set up	.103	.336	2.40
Machining	10.00	8.00	16.00
Receiving	.69	2.247	35.31
Packing	2.23	1.248	15.6
Engineering	3.19	2.98	18.625
	56.213	50.811	110.935

Statement showing Product Cost under different methods :

	X	Y	Z
	Rs.	Rs.	Rs.
Traditional method	61.89	71	37.51
Multiple volume method	68.76	59	43.51
Activity-based costing	56.21	50.81	110.935

It is clear from the above that, under traditional costing method, Product Z is under costed whereas, Product X and Y are over costed. But ABC results in accurate product costing because overhead costs are allocated based on activities consumed by the products. Thus, actually Products X and Y are earning profit more than the target profit of 40% whereas, Product Z is incurring loss [Cost of Rs. 110.935 is more than the setting price of Rs.75].

Problem

You are given the following information in respect of a manufacturing company producing three products .

(i) **Budgeted Overhead Expenses :**

	Rs.
Machine depreciation & maintenance	1,68,000
Receiving	83,720
Engineering	72,000
Machine set up	7,480
Inspection	38,400
	3,69,600

(ii) **Other particulars :**

	Product A	Product B	Product C	Total
Units of produced and sold	28,000	18,000	6,000	
Direct material cost per unit (Rs.)	40	30	26	
Direct labour cost per unit (Rs.)	24	28	20	
Machine hour per unit	1.5	2	1	84,000
Number per product line :				
Receiving orders	16	40	200	256
Production orders	14	12	19	45
Production runs	4	8	22	34
Inspections	8	4	20	32

Required :

(a) Statement showing total cost per unit for each product using machine hour rate;

(b) Statement showing total cost per unit of each product using relevant activities for recovery of overhead expenses;

(c) Explain the reasons for differences, if any, in costs between (a) and (b).

[M.B.M., C.U.]

Solution

Total Overhead Expenses = Rs.3,69,600

Total Machine Hours = 84,000

$$\text{Machine Hour Rate} = \frac{\text{Rs. } 3,69,600}{84,000} = \text{Rs. } 4.40$$

(a) Statement showing total cost per unit for each product using machine hour rate :

	Product A	Product B	Product C
	Rs.	Rs.	Rs.
Direct Material Cost	40.00	30.00	26.00
Direct Labour Cost	24.00	28.00	20.00
Prime Cost	64.00	58.00	46.00
Overhead Expenses			
A : (Rs. 4.40 × 1.5)	6.60	—	—
B : (Rs. 4.40 ×2)	—	8.80	—
C : (Rs. 4.40 ×1)	—	—	4.40
	70.60	66.80	50.40

Statement Showing Calculation of Cost Driver Rates

Activities	Cost Drivers	Total Overhead Cost	Product A	Product B	Product C	Total	Cost Driver Rate (Rs.)
Depreciation & Maintenance	Machine hours	1,68,000	42,000	36,000	6,000	84,000	2.00
Receiving	No. of order received	83,720	16	40	200	256	327.03125
Engineering	No.of production orders	72,000	14	12	19	45	1,600
Machine set up	No.of production run	7,480	4	8	22	34	220
Inspection	No. of Inspection	38,400	8	4	20	32	1200

Calculation of Overhead Cost per unit of A, B and C

	A	B	C
Depreciation and Maintenance	$\frac{42,000 \times 2}{28000}$ = 3	$\frac{36,000 \times 2}{18000}$ = 4	$\frac{60,00 \times 2}{6000}$ = 2
Receiving	$\frac{16 \times 327.03125}{28,000}$ = 0.187	$\frac{40 \times 327.03125}{18,000}$ = 0.727	$\frac{200 \times 327.03125}{6,000}$ = 10.9
Engineering	$\frac{14 \times 1,600}{28,000}$ = 0.80	$\frac{12 \times 1,600}{18,000}$ = 1.067	$\frac{19 \times 1,600}{6,000}$ = 5.067

Machine set up	$\frac{4 \times 220}{28,000}$ = 0.0314	$\frac{8 \times 220}{18,000}$ = 0.098	$\frac{22 \times 220}{6,000}$ = 0.807
Inspection	$\frac{8 \times 1200}{28,000}$ = 0.343	$\frac{4 \times 1200}{18,000}$ = 0.267	$\frac{20 \times 1200}{6,000}$ = 4

(b) Statement showing total cost per unit of each product using relevant activities for recovery of overhead expenses

	Product A		Product B		Product C	
Direct material		40.00		30.00		26.00
Direct labour		24.00		28.00		20.00
Prime cost		64.00		58.00		46.00
Overhead Cost						
Depreciation & Maintenance	3.00		4.00		2.00	
Receiving	0.187		.727		10.9	
Engineering	0.80		1.067		5.067	
Machine set up	.0314		.098		.807	
Inspection	.343	4.361	.267	6.159	4.00	22.774
Total Cost per unit		68.361		64.159		68.774

	Products A Rs.	Products B Rs.	Products C Rs.
Product cost per unit as per traditional costing	70.60	66.80	50.40
Cost per unit as per Activity-based costing	68.361	64.159	68.774

(c) Reasons for differences

It is clear from the above that traditional costing over-costs Products A and B and under-costs Product C. The reasons are that traditional costing allocates overhead costs based on machine hour without considering activities consumed by the products. But an analysis of supporting activities will reveal that Product C requires much of the receiving, engineering, machine set up and inspection activities compared with Products A and B.

Activity based costing considers the activities consumed by the products and allocates overhead costs accordingly. Thus, ABC results in accurate product cost.

Problem

PQR Ltd. produces two products A and B. The product A has sales units of 1,00,000 p.a. and B 40,000 units p.a. Both products require 4 labour hour for completion and the company works 1,00,000 direct labour hour each year.

Details of costs for material and labour for each product are given below :

	Product A	Product B
	Rs.	Rs.
Direct Materials	12.50	7.5
Direct Labour/hour	5	5

Total Manufacturing Overhead Cost Rs. 17,50,000

The company has analysed its operation and determined 5 activities as cost drivers in the occurrence of overhead cost. Data relating to these 5 activities are as under :

Sl. No.	Activities	Traceable Costs (Rs.)	No. of events or transaction	
			Product A	Product B
1.	Machines Set ups	4,60,000	6,000	4,000
2.	Quality Inspections	3,20,000	1,000	6,000
3.	Production Orders	1,62,000	400	800
4.	Machine Hour Works	6,28,000	24,000	56,000
5.	Material receipts	1,80,000	300	1,200

Your are require to compute per unit cost for each unit of each product using.

(i) Direct labour hour rate method for absorption of overhead.

(ii) Activity-Based costing technique for absorption of overhead cost.

Solution

(i) **Under Direct Labour Rate Method**

$$\frac{\text{Total Overhead}}{\text{Total Labour Hour}} = \frac{\text{Rs.}17{,}50{,}000}{1{,}00{,}000} = \text{Rs.}17.50/\text{hr}$$

Calculation of Cost Per Unit :

Elements of Costs	Product A	Product B
Material Cost	12.50	7.50
Labour Cost (4 Hrs @ Rs.5)	20.00	20.00
Overhead Cost (4 Hrs @ Rs. 17.50)	70.00	70.00
Total Cost	102.50	97.50

(ii) **Activity-Based Costing Technique**

Calculation of Overhead rate per activity

Sl. No.	Activities	Traceable Cost (Rs.)	No. of Events or Transaction	Rate Per Event/Transaction (Rs.)
(1)	(2)	(3)	(4)	(5) = (3) ÷ (4)
1.	Machine set up	4,60,000	10,000	46.00/setup
2.	Quality Inspection	3,20,000	16,000	20.00/Inspection
3.	Production Order	1,62,000	1,200	135.00/Production Order
4.	Machine Hour worked	6,28,000	80,000	7.85/Machine Hour
5.	Material Receipts	1,80,000	1,500	120.00/Receipts

Calculation of Overhead Cost Per Unit

Sl. No.	Activities	Rate Per Event (Rs.)	Product A		Product B	
			No. of Events	Amount (Rs.)	No. of Events	Amount (Rs.)
1.	Machine set up	46.00	6,000	2,76,000	4,000	1,84,000
2.	Quality Inspection	20.00	10,000	2,00,000	6,000	1,20,000
3.	Production order	135.00	400	54,000	800	1,08,000
4.	Machine hour worked	7.85	24,000	1,88,400	56,000	4,39,600
5.	Material Receipts	120.00	300	36,000	1,200	1,44,000
	Total	—	—	7,54,400	—	9,95,600
	Overhead Cost Per Unit			$\frac{7,54,400}{1,00,000}$ = 7.544		$\frac{9,95,600}{40,000}$ 24.89

Calculation of cost per unit

Elements of Cost	Product A	Product B
	Rs.	Rs.
Material Cost	12.50	7.50
Labour Cost	20.00	20.00
Overhead Cost	7.544	24.89
Total Cost	40.044	52.39

QUESTIONS

1. What is Activity-Based Costing? Why is it used ?
2. In spite of having traditional overhead cost system what prompts you for the introduction of Activity-Based Costing ? Justify your argument.
3. What is Cost Driver? How Cost Driver is selected ?
4. Give, with an imaginary example, different cost drivers for different cost activities.
5. What measures do you suggest to guard against the possibilities of smooth application of Activity-Based Costing ?
6. What do you mean by the term Activity-Based Management ? Explain how Activity-Based Costing helps the management to arrive at correct management decisions.
7. Having attended a CIMA course on Activity Based Costing (ABC) you decide to experiment by applying the principles of ABC to the four products currently made and sold by your company. Details of the four products and relevant information are given below for one period :

Product	**A**	**B**	**C**	**D**
Output in units	120	100	80	120
Costs per unit :	Rs.	Rs.	Rs.	Rs.
Direct material	40	50	30	60
Direct labour	28	21	14	21
Machine hours (per unit)	4	3	2	3

The four products are similar and are usually produced in production runs of 20 units and sold in batches of 10 units. The production overhead is currently absorbed by using a machine hour rate, and the total of the production overhead for the period has been analysed as follows :

	Rs.
Machine department costs	10,430
(rent, business, rates, depreciation and supervision)	
Set-up costs	5,250
Stores receiving	3,600
Inspection/Quality control	2,100
Materials handling and despatch	4,620

You have ascertained that the "cost drivers" to be used are as listed below for the overhead costs shown;

Cost	**Cost Driver**
Set-up costs	Number of production runs
Stores receiving	requisitions raised
Inspection/Quality control	Number of production runs
Materials handling and dispatch	Orders executed

The number of requisitions raised on the stores was 20 for each product and the number of orders executed was 42, each order being for a batch of 10 a product.

You are **required** :

a. to calculate the total costs for each product if all overhead costs are absorbed on a machine hour basis;
b. to calculate the total costs for each product, using activity based costing;
c. to calculate and list the unit product costs from your figures in (a) and (b) above, to show the differences and to comment briefly on any conclusions which may be drawn which could have pricing and profit implications.

[C.I.M.A. London, Adapted]

8. ABCD & co. manufactures four products viz. A,B.C and D using the same plant and process. The following information relates to a production period :

Product	Volume	Material Cost Per unit (Rs.)	Direct labour per unit	Machine time per unit	Labour Cost per unit
A	500	5	1/2 hour	1/4 hour	3
B	5,000	5	1/2 hour	1/4 hour	3
C	600	16	2 hours	1 hour	12
D	7,000	17	1-1/2 hours	1-1/2 hours	9

Total production overhead recovered by the cost accounting system is analysed under the following headings :

	Rs.
Factory overhead applicable to machine-oriented activity	37,424
Set-up costs are	4,355
Cost of ordering materials	1,920
Handling materials	7,580
Administration for spare parts	8,600

These overhead costs are absorbed by products on a machine hour rate of Rs. 4.80 per hour giving an overhead cost per product of

A = Rs. 1.20, B = Rs. 1.20, C = Rs. 4.80, D = Rs. 7.20

However, investigation into the production overhead activities for the period reveals the following totals :

Product	Number of set-ups	Number of material Orders	Number of times material was handled	Number of spare parts
A	1	1	2	2
B	6	4	10	5
C	2	1	3	1
D	8	4	12	4

You are required :

i. to compute an overhead cost per product using Activity Based Costing, tracing overheads to production units by means of cost drivers.
ii. to comment briefly on the differences disclosed between overheads traced by the present system and those traced by Activity Based Costing.

[C.I.M.A. London, Adapted]

PART IV

FINANCIAL MANAGEMENT

"One of the gravest problems in the sphere of modern politics is that of making democracy work, evolving a system which will give suitable expression to democratic aspirations while at the same time ensuring a satisfactory level of efficiency in the social and economic life of the community. It is not only in the political life, however, that democracy is on trial. A similar, in a less obvious but equally important form, is taking place in the field of joint stock finance".

14

MANAGEMENT FOR FINANCE AND WORKING CAPITAL

● Good morning to you all my dear students.

□ "Good morning Sir."

● Well from the discussions made earlier, we can come to the conclusion that Management Accountancy embraces :[1]

Anatomy of Management Accountancy

1. Financial Accounting
2. Cost Accounting
3. Financial Management
4. Decision Accounting, and finally,
5. Control Accounting.

Components of Management Accounting

Of the five components, I had already discussed in detail about Financial Accounting and Cost Accounting. I shall be discussing with you in my subsequent lectures about the concept of Decision and Control Accounting. Well, before that I would like to discuss about Financial Management. Here I would like to give you a diagram which is vital in the context of discussion on Financial Management.

□ "Excuse me Sir, before discussion on the chart, please enlighten us what is Financial Management."

Definition of Financial Management

● Well, you see, Financial Management may be defined as efficient handling of financial resources of any organisation—inflow and outflow of finance. Judicious financial planning and efficient control of finance are the key factors of Financial Management. I feel you have understood what is Financial Management. Are there any questions? Please do not feel shy. Yes, tell me.

□ "Sir, I have two questions to ask — What is finance ? What are the functions of Financial Management ?"

● Well you will get all answers to your questions in subsequent lectures. However, as you are very eager to know, I am discussing the same in brief.

---

[1] *Lecture delivered by Dr. B.K. Basu as Chairman at the National Seminar on Auditing held at Garhwal University, Srinagar in 1982.*

Functions of Financial Management

Regarding what is finance, I am to say that it is the life blood of business or any organisation. Please note below the functions of Financial Management :

1. Raising of fund
2. Utilisation of fund in an effective and efficient manner.
3. Maintaining necessary liquidity
4. Protecting capital from erosion
5. Monitoring flow of finance
6. Allocation and distribution of profit

Now I am presenting the diagram.

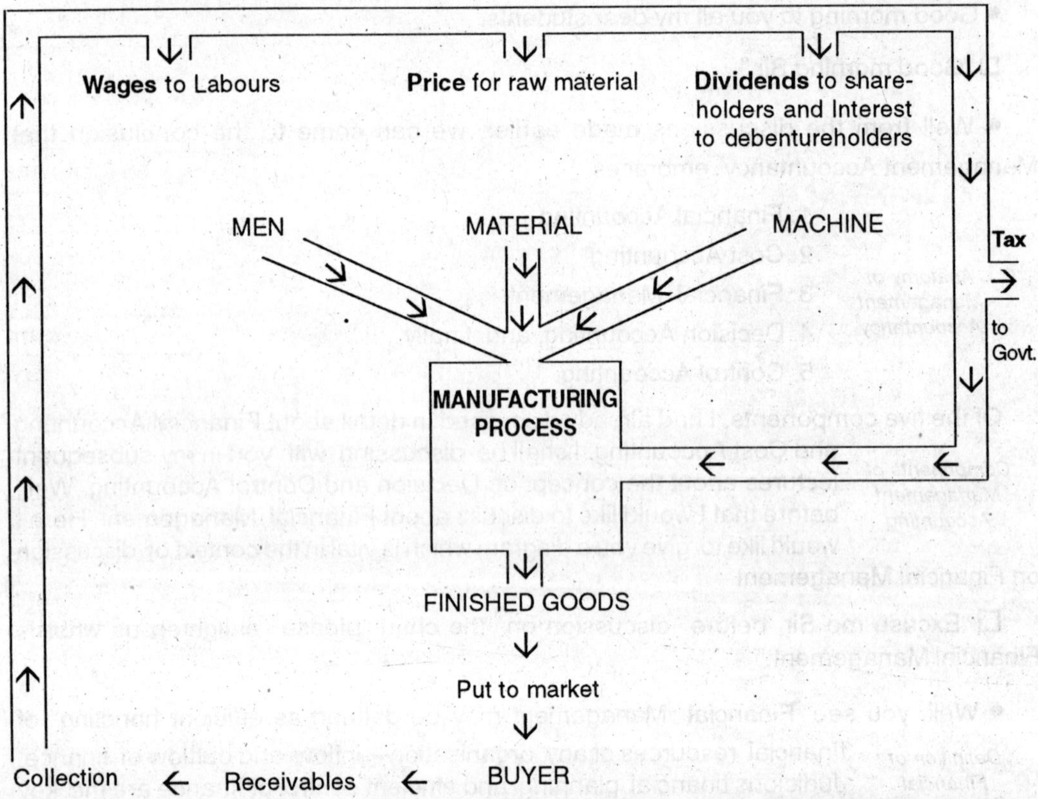

I am sure that you have understood the chart. However, I would like to explain the same. Three 'M's i.e. Men, Materials and Machines are needed for the manufacturing process. The ultimate aim of the manufacturing process is to manufacture goods which would be sold either against cash or on credit. In case of cash sale, no problem arises,

Management Efficiency

as it has its direct flow into the business. Problem arises in respect of credit sale. This is because in respect of collection of the same. Reported profit in majority of the cases includes a portion of the debtors. Now the debtors are to play an important role in regulating the forces in working capital of the business. Problems arise in a situation where proper adjustment between the date of receipt and date of payment is not possible. Suppose, date of receipt is within 30 days and the date of payment is within 28 days. In such a situation the company will have to suffer 2 days for its working capital. To overcome the situation the management can adopt a number of alternatives; such as loan from banks, issue of debenture etc. Now, which one would be more profitable depends upon the judgement on the part of the top management. That is to say, how the management is able to draw up the scheme for the capital structure of the business. If the company concentrates more on loan capital, instead of equity capital, dividend per share will be higher. If the company depends too much on equity capital instead of loan capital, dividend per share, other things being equal, will be lower. This aspect of financial management can be explained with the help of two examples, assuming that the two companies are doing same type of business under similar circumstances.

Exhibit 1

Assumed Balance Sheet of X. Co. Ltd. as at.......

Liabilities	Amount	Assets	Amount
	Rs.		Rs.
Equity Share Capital	50,000	Fixed Assets	40,000
		Current Assets	10,000
	50,000		50,000

Exhibit 2

Assumed Balance Sheet of Y. Co. Ltd. as at ......

Liabilities	Amount	Assets	Amount
	Rs.		Rs.
Equity Share Capital	10,000	Fixed Assets	40,000
6% Preference Share Capital	30,000	Current Assets	10,000
5% Debenture	10,000		
	50,000		50,000

Now, you see that the two types of company have equal amount of capital employed in the business. One concentrates wholly on Equity Capital and other partly in Equity and partly on Loan Capital. Suppose Rs. 10,000 is return on Capital Employed in both the cases. Now rate of return on Ordinary or Equity Share Capital will vary accordingly.

In case of X Co. Ltd.

$$\frac{\text{Return i.e., Profit}}{\text{Ordinary Share Capital}} = \frac{\text{Rs. } 10{,}000}{\text{Rs. } 50{,}000} \times 100 = 20\%$$

In case of Y Co. Ltd.

Profit—Amount necessary to pay fixed Interest bearing securities.

Profit Rs. 10,000 – (Pref. dividend Rs. 1,800 + Debenture interest Rs. 500)

= Rs. 10,000 – Rs. 2,300

= Rs. 7,700

The rate of return on Ordinary Share Capital.

$$\frac{\text{Rs. } 7{,}700}{\text{Rs.} 10{,}000} \times 100 = 77\%.$$

Though the two companies invest similar amount of capital in the business, rate of return per share differs largely. This is because one depends more on loan capital and other depends more on equity capital. This is an aspect of capital gearing. I shall be discussing the same afterwards. You see, upon the construction of the capital structure depends the efficiency and performance of the company. However, if you are interested to have a thorough idea on the said concept, please consult my research publication ***"Accounting for Goodwill".*** I think the discusssions made there will be sufficient to cater to the needs of the advanced students of this subject.

Types of Business

By Financial Management I mean here Planning for Profit, Sources and Disposition of Funds etc. Before I go into details of all these points under review, I would like to give you some idea about the different types of business found in the present society — (i) Proprietorship, (ii) Partnership, and (iii) Corporate form of business. Now corporate form of business have been developed out of the experience from Proprietorship and Partnership business. However, the owners of the corporate form of business are the shareholders who contribute capital to the business against promise from the management as to its payment of dividend and the protection of real capital. Use of funds is not less difficult as are found in case of sources of the same. Collection of funds and its proper use—or both—are problems to management. Now, no financial plan is said to be sound unless it is well-integrated with some financial policies.

Financial Policies

However, the financial policies of any enterpirse are comprise of :

(i) Capital Sources

(ii) Capital Use

(iii) Capital Protection

(iv) Capital Cost and finally, .

(v) Planning for Profit.

Need for Capital

Before discussing all these points in detail, I would like to give you some ideas about the need for capital. You know that capital is one of the factors of production. Decision, Action, Control and Follow-up, which are the four processes of management evolution, cannot function properly unless capital flows into the business. Any decision for the expansion programme as to present and future will not be put into action if the management is not assured for its funds. Now you can very well realise the importance of capital or finance in the business. 'Like blood in human system, finance flows through every artery and capillary of the business system. And like circulation of blood, circulation of finance too is an essential requirement to keep the business alive. It must be a continuous process. If the supply of finance fails to feed the system at any stage, the process would come to standstill. Business would shrink, or it may even die.'

However, the need for capital of any business can be ascertained depending upon the circumstances of the same. Following are the situations which may occur in the business – you need no further capital in the business, yet actually capital is needed in the business, and further if you need capital in the business : yet actually no capital is needed. To overcome the situation should be the ultimate motto of the financial management. Accordingly you are to study the situation and action should follow after proper diagnosis of the same. Whether the business has been suffering from over capitalisation or under-capitalisation should be studied properly before recommending for the introduction of further capital into the process of business, or viceversa.

Management Decision vs Capital Sources

Business has two types of capital— Fixed and Working. The very classification of the two types of capital seeks different types of sources. It is not source which is a predominating factor but it is the purpose of the sources. Take for an example : There are many medicines found in Drug House; having so many medicines is not an important factor unless they are used for different purposes. Whether a particular medicine will be used or not depends upon the types of diseases. Similarly nature of capital indicates the source for the same. However, decisions as to the source of capital depend upon the type of capital or upon the use of the same. Similar, type of treatment cannot be made to the individual owner of a sewing machine and the owner of sewing machine factory.

What is a fixed asset to me may be current asset to other. Accordingly, the nature of sources and the use of capital may be confined to the nature of the business and the circumstances of respective cases.

Equity of Newly Started Business and Continuing Business

However, the sources of capital or funds to be used differ from company to company. That is to say, I mean by 'company'—newly started business or continuing business. Now, you see, both types of business— continuing and newly started, have to purchase assets — fixed and other. So it is not always possible, unlike the Proprietorship or Partnership business who trade within the range of the funds available to them, to start a new business with proprietors' fund itself. He is to take loan from outsider. That is, from bank and other sources. The sources of fund of newly started business and continuing business are indicated below. However, it may be said, in other words,that the equities of the two types of business are as follows :

Newly Started Business	**Continuing Business**
Issue of Shares	Issue of Share
+	+
Issue of Debentures	Issue of Debentures
+	+
Other Sources	Reserve and Surplus
	+
	Other Sources

Now the continuing business can use their Reserve and Surplus which is absent in case of newly started business. 'Equities are claims against the assets owned by a business'. Equities or claim against the assets indicate the source from which the assets of a business were obtained. While the owner usually provides most of the assets, assets are too frequently provided by outsiders— people with no ownership rights in the business. For example, merchandise which is bought on credit, that is on the promise to pay in the future, is an asset provided by an outsider. There are, therefore, two kinds of equities or claims against the assets of a business— Liabilities and Net-Worth.

Liabilities

'Claims of outsiders against the business, such as notes or accounts owned by the business are called liabilities. Notes owed, called notes payable, are written promises to pay, upon a specified date, outsiders who provides merchandise, equipment, supplies, or service to the business. Accounts payable are verbal promises to pay, made for the same reasons. People to whom the business owes money are called creditors.

Net-Worth

The terms Net-Worth, proprietorship, owner's investment, or capital have the same meaning in book- keeping, namely, the owner's equity or interest in the assets of the business. Net-Worth is the difference between what the business owns and what it owes. The owner's investment in a business is usually called capital'.

Net-Worth = OWN – OWE.

Net-Worth = Assets – Liabilities.

Assets = NetWorth + Liabilities

However, the influences of Net Worth and Liabilities on the Balance Sheet are indicated below. Besides, this influence indicates their use.

Proforma of Balance Sheet

Liabilities			Assets
Share Capital	✓	→	**Fixed Assets**
Plus : Reserve and Surplus	✓	↑	Land and Building
Retained Profit	✓	↑	Plant and Machinery
Net-Worth	✓✓	→→	Furniture and Fixture
Loan Capital		↑→	**Current Assets**
Current Liabilities		→→	Stock
			Work-in-Progress
			Cash and Bank

From the pro-forma Balance Sheet and the arrowmarks indicated above, it is clear about the source of capital or fund and their respective uses. The idea fixed capital for fixed assets, loan capital for current assets, cannot be accepted for a 'dynamic nature of financial management'. Sometimes it is found in actual practice that a part of the loan capital is blocked in the fixed assets of the business. The whole situation regarding sources and uses of fund can be explained with the help of the above chart.

From the discussions made earlier, I think you have understood that there are two types of assets—fixed assets and current assets. The fixed assets of the business are never sold, not to speak of replacement. Replacement and selling are not the same thing. You know that the business is a continuous process. In order of keep the process of business alive, old and obsolete machines are to be replaced. That is to say, you are purchasing a new machine as a replacement for the old. Please note this difference. The fixed tangible assets are to be replaced. Now, from the proforma it is clear that the fixed tangible assets consists of Land and Building, Plant and Machinery, Furniture and Fittings etc.—assets retained in the business to carry on its production. So it is 'synonymous with the fixed capital of business.' Current Assets such as cash, accounts receivables, stock etc. arise as a result of day-to-day operation of the business. It is 'synonymous with working capital of business.'

Here I would like to mention one interesting point for your understanding : (i) to Businessmen working capital comprises the current assets of the business. (ii) to Economists also the term means all current assets. (iii) to Investor, Credit-man, Accountant and Investment Analysts the term denotes as excess of current assets over current liabilities. However, in this connection I would like to mention that, generally, the working capital of the business indicates Current Assets—Current Liabilities. If the working capital of the current year is greater than working capital of last year, it indicates increase in working capital. Now from the proforma given earlier you can easily grasp the idea of the different types of assets—fixed and current.

Your attention please. Well... it is you, yes you. What do you want to say ?

☐ "Sir, What is Negative and Positive Working Capital?"

Negative and Positive Working Capital

● You see, Positive Working Capital refers to a situation where current assets is greater than current liabilities, that is to say current assets exceed current liabilities. Besides other reasons, it may happen when a part of the current assets is financed from fixed sources; i.e. using long term finance (Capital).

On the other hand, Negative Working Capital denotes a situation where current liabilities exceed current assets. This situation arises when a part of the current liabilities is used to finance fixed assets.

☐ "Sir, we have understood the discussions made earlier—types of Capital; but Sir, we shall be obliged if you please give us some idea about the Financial Capital and its relationship with Capital Stock."

Financial Capital vs Capital Stock

● I am really very happy that you want to understand Financial Management in detail. Here I would like to give you a reference where you can get some light in the concept. Dr. A. K. Sur M.A. D.Sc. (Econ.) in his book ***"Principles of Corporate Finance"*** explains: 'Financial capital implies monetary counterpart of real capital, that is to say the money which has been employed for acquisition of the real capital of the business. Now financial capital can be supplied either by the owners of the business or by others who constitute its creditors. That part of financial capital which is supplied by the owner is known as capital stock. Capital stock implies long-term finance.'

Now I would like to give you some idea about the nature of fixed and working capital of the business.

☐ "Sir, you have already given us some concept about the nature of fixed assets and fixed capital and as well as working capital and current assets."

● However, you please note the chart, given below, which will help you to recapitulate the whole discussions made earlier.

NATURE AND SOURCES OF BUSINESS CAPITAL

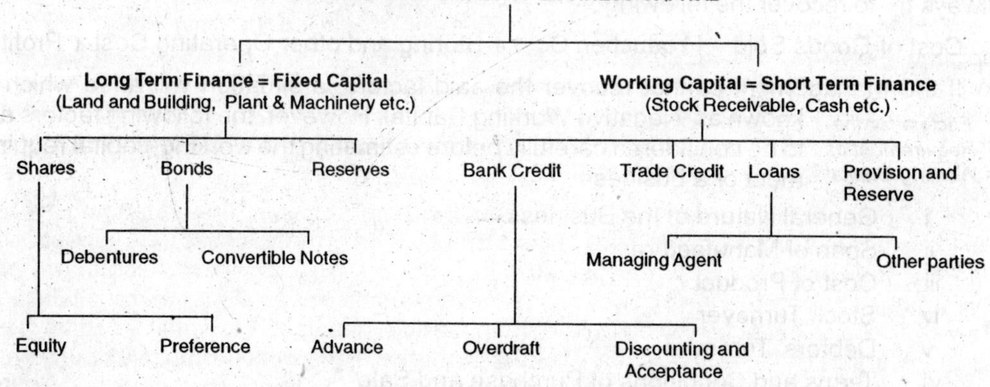

(Source : Dr. Sur. *Principles of Corporate Finance.*)

Now I want to discuss in detail about the working capital and the factors to be considered for its requirement. You know that cash, inventory, finished goods, receivable etc. are the components of working capital of the business. Cash is needed to buy raw materials and raw materials are put into production process; after the goods are produced, the goods would be sold against either cash or credit; upon the collection of the receivables, cash is again needed for buying and manufacturing process. During the period of manufacture, raw materials are to be purchased, wages are to be paid to the workers. Here we can realise the need for working capital. By working capital some people understand 'Idle Working Capital'! Take for an example old stock which cannot be sold in the market at a figure shown in the books of accounts. So I should better to say it as 'Sentimental Stock'. Well, by working capital I only mean the effective working capital of the business. However, Dr. Sidney M. Robbins of Columbia University explained the nature of working capital with the help of cycle and also suggested a number of factors to be considered before estimating the working capital requirement of a business. The above figure would help you to understand the nature of working capital of a business.

Flow of Working Capital

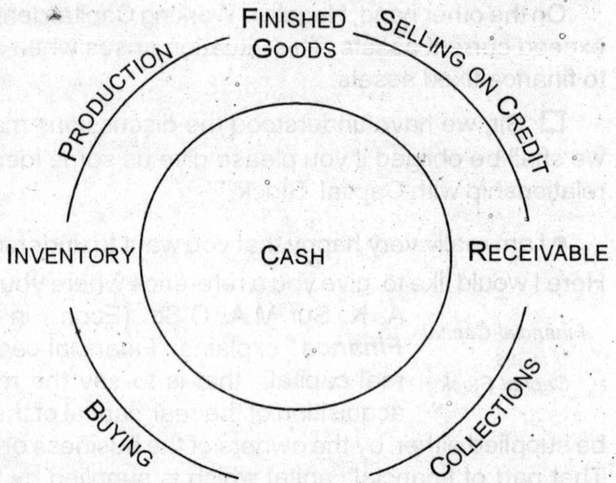

Here one point which I would like to make clear is that there is area in between finished goods and cash, as shown in the cycle is the 'crucial area' of the business. The 'crucial area' can be managed or tackled for the benefit of management needs if cash is properly managed and controlled. I mean that there should be a proper system of Cash Management in the organisation. The circulation of different parts of the 'cycle' mentioned earlier depends entirely on the proper flow of cash. If cash remains standstill and get obstackle in its flow, the entire cycle will remain standstill. However, the management will always try to recover the following :

Cost of Goods Sold + Production Cost + Storing and other Operating Cost + Profit

If the management cannot recover the said factors, a situation will arise which is known as Negative Working Capital. However, the following factors are to be considered carefully before estimating the working capital requirement of a business :

Factors for the Requirement of Working Capital

i. General Nature of the Business
ii. Span of Manufacture
iii. Cost of Product
iv. Stock Turnover
v. Debtors' Turnover
vi. Terms and Conditions of Purchase and Sale
vii. Business Expansion
viii. Seasonal Variation
ix. Hazard and Contingencies

I do not like to discuss all these points in detail. You can ordinarily understand its nature and meaning. Regarding debtors turnover and stock turnover I would like to bring to your attention that I shall be discussing all these points— Debtors and Stock Turnover, under the discussion of 'Accounting Ratios and Interpretation of Accounts.'

☐ "Sir, would you please give us some idea about the variation in Working Capital statement ?"

Variation in Working Capital

● I think you know the different components of working capital. Variation in the working capital components is natural. If you can study the earlier discussions that the working capital of the business is changing its form regularly, you can get some idea about the variation in working capital. So, it is a method of analysing the change in working capital—of a business. This portion—the change in working capital would be more clear to you if you can follow my subsequent lecture on 'Fund Flow' and 'Cash Flow' Statement. However, for the time being, for your understanding I am giving you two illustrations.

Condensed Balance Sheet of Mithu Trading Co.

Figures for the Previous Year	Liabilities and Capital	Figures for the Current Year	Figures for the Previous Year	Assets	Figures for the Current Year
Rs.		Rs.	Rs.		Rs.
2,00,000	Share Capital	2,40,000	60,000	Plant and Machinery	50,000
20,000	Reserve and Surplus	40,000	1,00,000	Inventories	1,60,000
30,000	Accounts Payable	90,000	70,000	Accounts Receivable	1,00,000
			20,000	Bank	60,000
2,50,000		3,70,000	2,50,000		3,70,000

Now from the data supplied, I would like to make you clear the 'Statement Showing Variation of Working Capital.' That is to say, this will indicate how the funds, used for the increase in working capital, are coming from the different sources.

From the illustration it is clear that the working capital of the business has increased to the extent of Rs.1,30,000. This Rs.1,30,000 is supplied from the different sources.

Statement showing the Variation of Working Capital of Mithu Trading Company

Sources

	Rs.
Depreciation/Sale of Fixed Assets	10,000
Increase in Reserve and Surplus	20,000
Loan from Creditors	60,000
Increase in Share Capital	40,000
	1,30,000

Application of Fund

	Rs.
Accounts Receivable	30,000
Bank	40,000
Inventories	60,000
	1,30,000

Now I think, you have understood the different sources of working capital for its use. Is there any question ?

☐ "Sir, you have told earlier that 'Cash' is the pivot of Working Capital. For that you suggested proper Cash Management".

• Yes it is.

☐ "Would you, kindly Sir, enlighten us about the concept of Cash Management ?"

Cash Management

• You see, cash management is a 'Universal Business Activity'. The main aim of any company is to manage day-to-day cash transactions. It is sometime found in actual practice that in spite of high reported profit in the books of accounts the company cannot pay dividend to the shareholders of the company. This is because the said reported profit is blocked in receivable which constitute the item of 'Dormant Capital'. To overcome the said adverse effect—shortage of liquid cash, management should concentrate their attention how cash should be made available for the smooth running of the business. That requires the knowledge of 'Cash Management'.

One important point that should be borne in mind is that though excessive cash holding may increase liquidity position of any firm or organisation, but, in actual practice, it may affect profitability. On the other hand, holding of lesser amount of cash reflects lack of liquidity. Thus it appears that excess amount of cash holding and less amount of cash holding—both are problems to management. Under the circumstances to overcome the problem, the necessity of Cash Management is felt.

Do you follow ?

☐ "Yes Sir, Please enlighten us what is Cash Management. What are the motives of Cash holding?

Definition of Cash Management

• You see, your attention please ....

Cash Management is a trade-off between two objectives—maximising liquidity and minimising cost associated with liquidity.

Well, you wanted me to let you know the motives for holding cash.

Note down, the motives for cash holding are :

Motives for Cash Holding

1. Transaction Motives
2. Speculative Motives
3. Precautionary Motives.

Now, have a detail of these motives :

1. Transaction Motives

For day to day operation of the business such as payment for purchase, wages and salaries and other expenses—holding of cash is a 'must'.

It is important to note that receipt of cash and payment of cash may not be always equal. Sometime payment of cash may be greater than receipt of cash which results in deficit of cash. So management should aim at surplus of cash for meeting necessary expenses by applying judicious management decisions.

2. Speculative Motives

Sometimes cash holding stems from speculative motives. That is to say investing cash for purchase of securities or other items when prices are low with the expectation to sale the same when prices are high. This may be termed 'Profitable Investment Opportunity.'

3. Precautionary Motive

To guard against unforseen future events and to meet future contingencies holding of cash as precaution is necessary. For this, prediction or forecasting of in flow and out-flow of cash deserve special attention of management. Therefore, firms or businesses should maintain some amount of cash to meet future unexpected happenings.

Now let me explain about the tools or techniques of Cash Management :

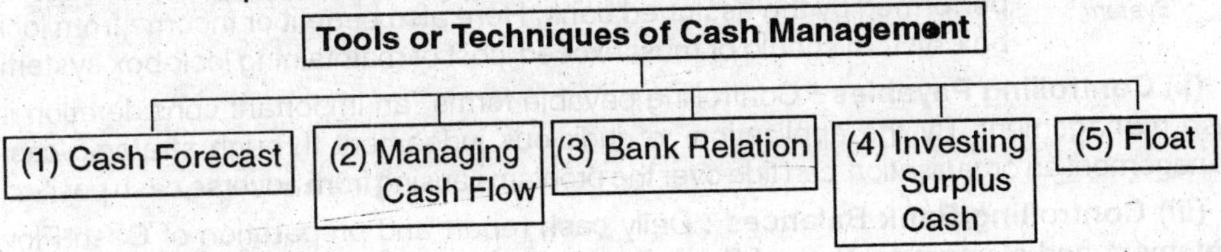

1. Cash Forecast

Regarding Cash forecast I am to say that the main aspect of Cash Forecast is to estimate cash requirements in advance. That is to say, take for an example, in the month of January you are to forecast about the requirement of cash for the month of June. Here we see that the forecast is made before six months. It may be for 2 yrs, 1 yr, 6 months, 3 months, 1 month, 15 days and even for a week. This process estimates the expected receipts and payments of cash. However, the details of cash forecast will be discussed in the subsequent part of this book. This would be discussed under the caption 'Business Budget'.

2. Managing Cash Flows

It has been stated earlier that the main aim of any type of business is to keep adequate flow of cash. That is to say, managing cash flow. The concept of Cash Flow Management embraces the following points :

(i) Speeding up Collections

(ii) Controlling Payables

(iii) Controlling Bank Balances

Are you following my lecture ?

□ "Yes Sir, kindly enlighten us on speeding up collection, Controlling payable, controlling Bank Balances etc."

• Well, jot down the following :

(i) Speeding up Collection

There is no denying the fact that speeding up collection strengthens the cash position of any firm or organisation.

You see, following are the two methods usually used to speed up cash collections :

(a) Concentration Banking : It is a system to collect dues from by opening collection centre at different parts of the country. Collection of money from each and every centre are deposited in the respective local banks. It is a decentralised collection system. As opening of different collection centres involves cost, it is the volume of billing which determines to take decision whether opening of collection is justifiable or not. The collection from all local banks are then transferred to the main bank account of the concerned organisation. This system reduces mail float as well as bank float. It is important to note that maintaining a large number of Current Accounts involves cost. So, it is desirable that benefits arising from the centres should exceed the costs

Necessity of Concentration Banking

(b) Lock Box System : Under the system special post office boxes are rented at different regions; customers are advised to mail their payment in post box, cheques are collected by the assigned bank and deposited to the local bank account. This system reduces cheque processing time as the same are being performed by the assigned bank. Here also benefit or income from lock box system should or must exceed cost of maintaining lock-box system.

Necessity of Lock Box System

(ii) Controlling Payables : Controlling payable forms an important consideration in cash management. By the application of judicious judgement through strategic cash management an organisation can tide over the problems arising from adverse cash position.

(iii) Controlling Bank Balances : Daily cash report and preparation of Cash Flow Statement and also preparation of Bank Reconciliation Statement—all form a basis of Cash Management.

3. Bank Relation

There should be proper understanding between Company Management and the Bank. Sometimes it may be necessary to have overdraft facilities at the time of acute working capital crisis. Besides, amicable bank relation will speed up the 'clearing and collection facilities.'

4. Investing Surplus Cash

If the total receipts during a year or a period is higher than the total payments during that year or period, the situation represents cash surplus. So it would be wise to invest the surplus either in the money market or within the same business. For that a comparison should be made whether investment in outside business would be profitable or not. However, if it is decided to invest in money market, the management should weigh the following four factors :

i. Price stability
ii. Marketability
iii. Maturity
iv. Yield.

5. Float

Float is one of the important tools or techniques of Cash Management.

You all know that cheques are received from traders or customers and the same are issued to suppliers. All these cheques are sent or deposited to Bank for clearance. There is always a time gap between date of issue of cheque or deposit the cheque to bank and the date of clearance. This time gap is known or referred as *Float.* A few examples of Float are Billing Float, Mail Float, Bank Processing Float, Processing Float etc.

Meaning of Float

There are two types of Float
(i) Payment Float and
(ii) Receipt Float.

☐ "Sir, Please explain the said two types of Floats."

• Please note :

(i) Payment Float

It refers to a situation where issued cheques are not presented to bank for payment.

☐ "Excuse me Sir, I cannot follow it."

Positive Float

• Well, take an example. Suppose on 1st August 2006 I issued a cheque to you for Rs.1,000/- to celebrate our Independence day 15th August; the said cheque you presented to the Bank for payment on 14th August 2006. So, in between 1st August and 14th August Bank Pass Book balance will be Rs.1,000/- more than the Ledger balance provided there are no other transactions. It reflects Positive Float.

Do you follow ?

☐ "Yes, Sir. Thank you Sir, Please enlighten us on receipt float."

• Well, please note.

(ii) Receipt Float

Cheque deposited to the Bank but not cleared by the Bank; that is to say, not credited in the Bank's Account.

Do you follow ?

☐ "But Sir...... Please explain it giving a suitable example."

Negative Float

• Well,take a look here. Suppose on 2.1.2006 Avator Co. Ltd. received a cheque for Rs. 1 lakh and deposited the same in the Bank on 3.1.2006; but not cleared till 31.1.2006. It was cleared on 1.2.2006. It shows from the above example that Bank Pass Book balance would show Rs. 1 lakh less than the Bank balance if no other transactions took place in between the date of depositing the cheque and the date the Bank cleared the cheque.

Therefore, Receipt Float during the said period is Rs. 1 lakh, which is negative.

☐ "Sir, What is Net Float ?"

Net Float

• You see, it is the difference between Receipt Float and Payment Float. It may be Negative or Positive. The Net Float, on a particular date, is the difference between **Book Balance** and **Bank Balance** — it may be positive or Negative. In case of Positive Net Float, available Bank Balance is greater than Book Balance (i.e. Payment Float is greater than Receipt Float). In case of Negative Net Float, Book Balance is greater than available Bank Balance (i.e Receipt Float is greater than the Payment Float).

Playing the Float

You see, through efficient Management of Float a firm or organisation can control payment and reduce its collection time. Float Management is known as Playing the Float.

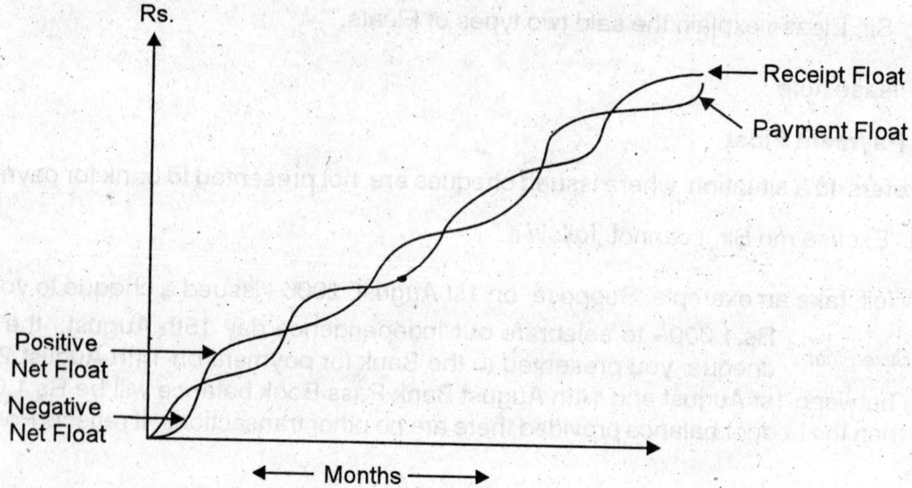

Net Float Diagram

However, the ranking of the Company's investment criteria, as stated earlier, depends on the following two important considerations :

a. The general investment philosophy of the business.

b. How the Company "foresees" its cash requirements.

I think you have followed my lecture. Is there any question?

□ "Sir, I have one question."

● What is that?

□ "Sir, Is or are there any formula or model(s) to determine optimum Cash Balance(s)."

● Well, yes, there are two models to determine it. One is BAUMOL MODEL and another one is MILLER-ORR MODEL. I am explaining the same one by one.

A. BAUMOL MODEL

William J. Baumol suggested a model which is applicable to the concept of Economic Order Quantity (EOQ) in determining optimum Cash Balance. Here optimum cash balance is a level at which total opportunity cost and transaction cost is minimum. If a firm wants to maintain high level of cash, then the firm will have to forgo opportunity cost and it will increase with the increase in the level of cash balance. On the other hand if a firm holds too little cash balance(s)—in that case transaction cost will increase and other costs resulting from shortage of cash; such as cost of forgoing trade and quantity discount etc. So, optimum cash balance is one at which both opportunity costs and transaction costs are minimum.

The formula, under this model, to determine optimum cash balance is :

$OC = \sqrt{\frac{2AO}{C}}$ where OC = Optimum Cash Balance

A = Total Amount of Cash Required

O = Per order conversion cost or Transaction cost

C = Carrying Cost/Interest earned on marketable Securities

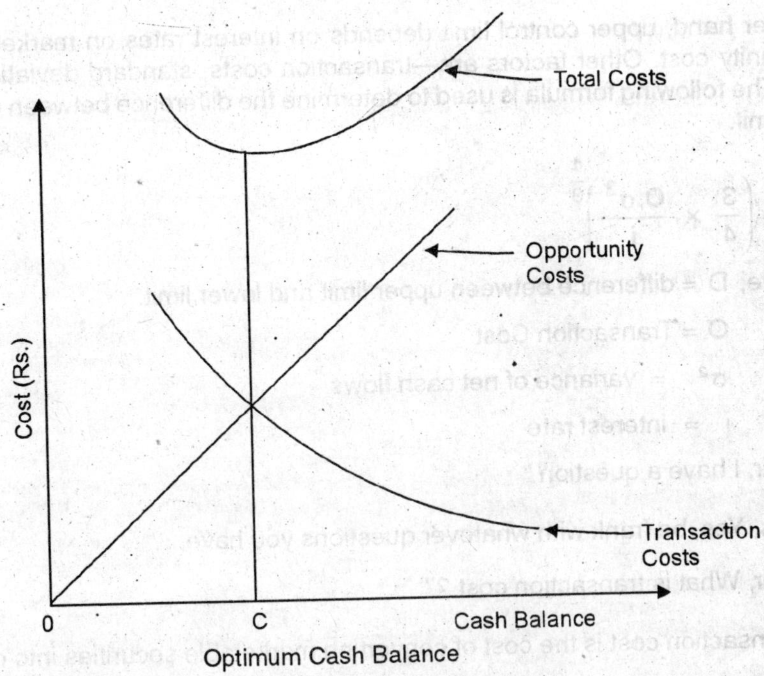

B. MILLER-ORR MODEL

Before discussing about Miller-Orr Model I am to say something about Baumol model which I had discussed earlier.

You see, Baumol's model is good no doubt but it raises some problems to determine optimum cash balance when cash balance over the period is not uniform. That is to say, Baumol's model is suitable in a situation where cash balance over the period is uniform. But in actual practice cash balance fluctuates owing to continuous inflows and outflows of cash. It is a fact that inflow and outflow of cash cannot be predicted with precision. Under the circumstances the use of Control Theory, which is used in Miller-Orr Model, gives better result.

Two control limits are there under this model. One is uppper limit, another is lower control limit; The results of the two control limits are average which is taken as a middle point or return point. When cash balance touches the upper limit, the firm buy marketable securities to reach the return point. Similarly, when cash balance touches the lower limit, in that case marketable securities are sold by the firm to come back to the middle point i.e. return point.

I think you are following my lecture. Any problem to follow my lecture ?

☐ "No Sir. No problem.Sir, please give us a diagram or a formula in this respect."

● Well, I would discuss all this aspect in due course of time. I have not completed my earlier lecture.

● What was I discussing ?

Yes, I remember, return point. Now, coming back to our earlier discussion!; I am to say that the lower control limit is set after considering liquidity requirements of the firm. On the other hand, upper control limit depends on interest rates on market securities i.e. opportunity cost. Other factors are—transaction costs, standard deviation of net cash flows. The following formula is used to determine the difference between upper limit and lower limit.

$$D = \left(\frac{3}{4} \times \frac{O.\sigma^2}{i}\right)^{\frac{1}{3}}$$

where, D = difference between upper limit and lower limit

O = Transaction Cost

σ^2 = variance of net cash flows.

i = interest rate

□ "Sir, I have a question."

● Yes, Yes, be frank with whatever questions you have.

□ "Sir, What is transaction cost ?"

● Transaction cost is the cost of converting marketable securities into cash.

Now I would like to show the model through a figure :

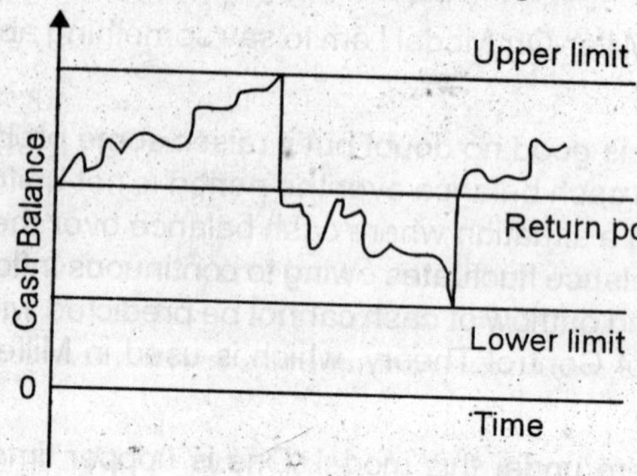

□ "Sir we are very glad in having all these points and discussions. If you please don't mind, Sir, work out at least one practical problem."

● I think you would not face any difficulty which may stand on your way to work out practical problems if you have really followed my last lectures. Besides, you may get a few typical worked out problems in Brown and Howard's book ***"Principles of Management Accountancy"*** which, I think, will be very helpful to you.

□ "Sir, I have Batty's book. Is it not sufficient ? Besides, what book is by far the best in the market Sir ?"

● You see, many books are good no doubt, but one particular book is best for a particular topic which may not be the case for other books too. That's why I would suggest you to do your library work and follow the lecture. But you see, my request to you is not to underestimate any author in the subject, please !

Now I would like to discuss with you about 'Capital Gearing'. You see, Capital Gearing is the...

☐ "Sir, would you not please work out a few practical problems on the discussions of 'Requirement of Working Capital'?"

● Yes yes, I have totally forgotten. Here are your problems :

Problem

On 1st January 19... the Board of Directors of Nilmani Co., Ltd. wish to know the amount of working capital that will be required to meet the programme they have planned for the year.

From the following information, prepare a Working Capital Requirement Forecast and a Forecast Profit and Loss Account as well as Balance Sheet :

Issued Capital	Rs. 2,00,000
5% Debentures (Secured)	Rs. 50,000
Fixed Assets Value on 1st January	Rs. 1,25,000

Production during the previous year was 60,000 Units and it is planned that this level of activity should be maintained during the present year (current year). The expected ratios of cost to selling price are : raw materials 60%, direct wages 10%, overheads 20%.

Raw materials are expected to remain in stores for an average of two months before issue of production.

Each unit of production is expected to be in process for one month.

Finished goods will stay in the warehouse awaiting despatch to customers for approximately three months.

Credit allowed by creditors is two months from the date of delivery of raw materials.

Credit given to debtors is three months from the date of despatch.

Selling price is Rs. 5 per unit.

There is a regular production and sales cycle.

Before going to work out this sum I would like to discuss some important points which will be more helpful to you in the matter. Now you remember my last lecture where I explained a figure showing the changes in the components of working capital. You see, during the manufacturing process as well as during the period of sale and collection, working capital is needed. Because, during these two periods — (i) in between sales and collection and (ii) in between the manufacturing process and date of sale, wages are to be paid and other expenditure are to be incurred.

In this problem we can clarify the whole thing under the following heads :

(1) Materials, (2) Wages, (3) Overheads, (4) Profit.

However, the total period required apparently for the maintenance of working capital is 9 (nine) months and the period of credit allowed by the Creditors is 2 (two) months. So the problem as to working capital is solved by 2 (two) months. Now net requirements for working capital in connection with Material is 7 months (9 months – 2 months). Now as per our Forecast Revenue Accounts which is worked out below, we can get the figure for raw materials consumed for Rs. 1,80,000 (60,000 units $\times$ Rs. 5 = Rs. 3,00,000 $\times \frac{60}{100}$ = Rs.1,80,000). This figure is the for one year. Now if you want to get the figure for 1 (one) month, divide it by 12 months. Now figure for each month is Rs.15,000. Now, total requirement of working capital in connection with materials is Rs. 15,000 $\times$ 7 = Rs. 1,05,000.

Similarly, requirement of working capital in connection with wages can be found out :

60,000 units $\times$ Rs. 5 = 3,00,000 $\times \frac{10}{100}$ = Rs. 30,000; Rs. 30,000 $\times \frac{7}{12}$ = Rs.17,500.

Now you are to assume that no wages are to be paid to the workers for the stocks which are in store. The total period for the requirement of working capital in connection with wages is 7 (seven) months. Similar is the period of overhead which is 7 (seven) months, 60,000 units $\times$ Rs. 5 $\times \frac{20}{100} \times \frac{7}{12}$ = Rs. 35,000.

Now what is more complicated is that the profit of the business includes a part of the figure arising from credit sale. This will be more clear if you can understand the below—mentioned relationship :

$$\frac{\text{Profit}}{\text{Cash Sales}} \text{ or } \frac{\text{Profit}}{\text{Credit Sales}} \text{ or } \frac{\text{Profit}}{\text{Cash and Credit Sales}} \text{ or } \frac{\text{Profit}}{\text{Sales}}$$

You know that cash is one of the items of working capital, after collection, the credit sale will be converted into cash. Now we have to find out the period in which the actual profit of the business depends upon the collection of receivables. Though profit is there in the business, the company cannot enjoy a part of it which will be converted in reality after the collection of the receivables, as a source of working capital for a certain period of time. During this period, in order to keep the process of business running, the company will have to think for its working capital. It reveals from the Forecast Revenue Account that the profit of the business for the year is Rs. 30,000. Now the average profit is Rs. $\frac{30,000}{12}$ = Rs. 2,500. This Rs. 2,500 for 3 months—i.e., 2,500 $\times$ 3 = Rs.7,500—will be collected after three months. Now to overcome the present situation the company will have to think for Rs. 7,500 which I explained to you earlier. Now total working capital requirement is (Rs. 1,05,000 + Rs.17,500 + Rs.35,000 + Rs.7,500) Rs.1,65,000. From it will be deducted any balance for Bank Overdraft which is one of the components of working capital. We have to see now after working out the Forecast Balance Sheet if there be any figure traced for Bank Overdraft.

Now I am working out the problem :

Dr. **Forecast Revenue Account** *Cr.*

	Particulars	Amount Rs.		Particulars	Amount Rs.
To	Material Consumed	1,80,000	By	Cost of Manufacture Account c/d	2,70,000
,,	Direct Wages	30,000			
,,	Overhead	60,000			
		2,70,000			2,70,000
To	Cost of Manufacture Account b/d	2,70,000	By	Sales	3,00,000
,,	Gross Profit c/d	30,000			
		3,00,000			3,00,000
To	Debenture Interest	2,500	By	Gross Profit b/d	30,000
,,	Net Profit	27,500			
		30,000			30,000

Forecast Balance sheet as at............

Capital and Liabilities	Amount	Assets and Properties		Amount
	Rs.			Rs.
Share Capital	2,00,000	Fixed Assets		1,25,000
Net Profit	27,500	Current Assets :		
5% Debenture	50,000	Raw Materials	30,000	
Current Liabilities :		Work-in-Progress	22,500	
Creditors	30,000	Finished Goods	67,500	
Bank Overdraft	12,500			1,20,000
		Debtors		75,000
	3,20,000			3,20,000

You may put me question "Sir how have you found out Bank overdraft".

Now you see, it is a balancing figure of the two sides (Assets and Liabilites) of the Balance Sheet. Regarding the figures appearing in the columns of the Current Assets and Current Liabilities, you, please, consult below-mentioned statement— "Statement of Working Capital Requirement Forecast".

Now you see that the total Working Capital will be required as follows :

	Rs.
Working Capital Requirement (as per the Working Capital Requirement Forecast)	1,65, 000
Less : Bank Overdraft (as per Forecast Balance Sheet)	12, 500
Total Working Capital Required is	1,52, 500

Well, regarding the figures for Rs.1,65,000, please consult the contents of the following table.

Working Capital Requirement Forecast

Items	Period (Month)	Total	Raw Materials	Work-in-Progress	Finished Goods	Debtors	Creditors
		Rs.	Rs.	Rs.	Rs.	Rs.	Rs.
1. Materials :							
(i) In Stock	2		30,000				
(ii) In Work-in-Progress	1			15,000			
(iii) In Finished Goods	3				45,000		
(iv) Credit to Debtors	3					45,000	
	9						
Less: (v) Credit from Creditors	2						30,000
Total	7	1,05,000					

Items	Period (Month)	Total	Raw Materials	Work-in-Progress	Finished Goods	Debtors	Creditors
		Rs.	Rs.	Rs.	Rs.	Rs.	Rs.
2. Wages :							
(i) In Work-in-Progress	1			2,500			
(ii) Finished Goods	3				7,500		
(iii) Credit to Debtors	3					7,500	
Total	7	17,500					
3. Overheads :							
(i) In Work-in-Progress	1			5,000			
(ii) In Finished Goods	3				15,000		
(iii) Credit to Debtors	3					15,000	
Total	7	35,000					
4. Profit :							
Credit to Debtors	3					7,500	
Total	3	7,500					
Grand Total :		1,65,000	30,000	22,500	67,500	75,000	30,000

Now I think, you have understood the problem. Try to go into the details of the problem. If you can grasp the idea contained in the problem, you will be in a position to work out other problems of similar type.

☐ "Sir, one more problem please !"

● Oh, yes. Now I would like to give you another problem. This is for your home task. Here is the problem.

Problem

You are required to prepare for the Board of Directors of Hind Ltd., a statement showing the working capital needed to finance a level of activity of 5,200 units for 1970.

You are given the following information :

Elements of cost :	Amount per unit
	Rs.
Raw Material	8
Wages	2
Overheads	6
Total Cost	16
Profit	4
Selling Price	20

Raw materials are in stock on average one month. Materials are in process on average, half a month.

Finished goods are in stock on average Six weeks.

Credit allowed by Creditors is One Month.

Credit allowed to Debtors is Two Months.

Lag payment of wages is 1½ weeks.

Cash on hand and at Bank is expected to be Rs.7,300.

You are informed that production is carried on evenly during the year and the wages and overheads accrue similarly. **[M.Com. (C.U.)]**

Now I think, you have understood the problem. Try to go into the details of the problem. If you can grasp the idea contained in the problem, you will be in a position to work out other problems of similar type.

☐ "Sir, one more problem please !"

● Oh, yes. Now I would like to give you another problem. This is for your home task. Here is the problem."Sir, Please work out the problem".

● You see, it is not possible to work out each and every problem. You are to try yourself. If not, you will not be in a position to work out a complete problem. However, as per your request I am working out the problem.

Solution

	Rs.
Total Required Working Capital will be like this :	
Required Working Capital (as per Working Capital Requirement Forecast	27,700
Cash on hand and at Bank expected (as per information supplied)	7,300
	35,000

Working Capital Requirement Forecast

Items	Period Week	Total Rs.	Raw Materials Rs.	Work-in-Progress Rs.	Finished Goods Rs.	Debtors Rs.	Creditors Rs.
1. Materials :							
(i) In Stock	4		3,200				
(ii) In Work-in-Progress	2			1,600			
(iii) In Finished Goods	6				4,800		
(iv) Credit to Debtors	8					6,400	
	20						
(v) Credit from Creditors	4						3,200
Total	16	12,800					
2. Wages :							
(i) In Work-in-Progress	1			200			
(ii) Finished Goods	6				1,200		
(iii) Credit to Debtors	8					1,600	
	15						
(iv) Credit from Employees	1½						300
Total	13½	2,700					
3. Overheads :							
(i) In Work-in-Progress	1			600			
(ii) In Finished Goods	6				3,600		
(iii) Credit to Debtors	8					4,800	
Total	15	9,000					
4. Profit :							
Credit to Debtors	8					3,200	
Total	8	3, 200					
Grand Total		27,700	3,200	2,400	9,600	16,000	3,500

I think you all have understood the two problems worked out here. So I do not like to discuss anything more regarding your working capital.

☐ "Sir, are all these discussions sufficient ?"

● Oh yes; but you see, all these are the guidelines. Now you can apply your experience and knowledge, and you can bring all these discussions under suitable footings with the aid of your developed knowledge and experience.

Now I shall be glad much to hear from you any question, of course within our discussions.

☐ "Sir, we have nothing to say about the discussions made ealier. We are very glad to have your able guidance in the matter. Will you please, sir, discuss at present about Capital Gearing ?"

● I am really very glad to see that you have followed my lectures successfully. At present I do not like to discuss anything about Capital Gearing which I like to take up for discussion in my next lecture. For the time being please try to recapitulate the whole discussions. For that I suggest you to work out a few more advanced problems on Working Capital Requirement. Please observe the following :

Problem

X & Co. is desirous to purchase a business and has consulted you, and one point on which you are asked to advise them is the average amount of working capital which will be required in the first year's working.

You are given the following estimates and are instructed to add 10% to your computed figure to allow for contingencies :

		Figures for year Rs.
(i)	Average amount locked up for stocks :	
	Stock finished product	5,000
	Stock of Stores, Materials, etc.	8,000
(ii)	Average credit given :	
	Inland Sales — 6 weeks credit	3,12,000
	Export Sales — $1\frac{1}{2}$ weeks credit	78,000
(iii)	Lag in payment of wages and other outgoings :	
	Wages — $1\frac{1}{2}$ weeks	2,60,000
	Stores materials etc — $1\frac{1}{2}$ weeks	48,000
	Rent, Royalties, etc.,— 6 months	10,000
	Clerical Staff — $\frac{1}{2}$ month	62,000
	Manager — $\frac{1}{2}$ month	4,800
	Miscellaneous expenses — $1\frac{1}{2}$ months	48,000

(iv) Payment in advance :
(Sundry expenses paid quarterly in advance) 8,000

(v) Undrawn profits on the average throughout the year 11,000

Set up your calculations for the average amount of working capital required.

[C.A. Final]

Solution

STATEMENT SHOWING AVERAGE WORKING CAPITAL REQUIREMENTS

Particulars	Amount	Amount
	Rs.	Rs.
Inventories :		
Stock of Finished Products	5,000	
Stock of Stores, Materials, etc.	8,000	13,000
Book Debt :		
Inland Sales — 6 weeks' of Rs. 3,12,000 p. a. $\left[\frac{3,12,000 \times 6}{52}\right]$	36,000	
Export Sales — $1\frac{1}{2}$ weeks' of Rs. 78,000 p.a. $\left[\frac{7,8000 \times 3}{52 \times 2}\right]$	2,250	38,250
Advance payment of Expenses $\left[8000 \times \frac{1}{4}\right]$		2,000
Investment in Current Assets		53,250
Less : Lags in Payment :		
Wages $\left(\text{Rs. } 2,60,000 \times 1\frac{1}{2} / 52\right)$	7,500	
Stores, Materials etc. $\left(\text{Rs. } 48,000 \times 1\frac{1}{2} / 12\right)$	6,000	
Rent, Royalties etc.	5,000	
Clerical Staff	2,600	
Manager	200	
Miscellaneous Expenses	6,000	
		27,300
Net Working Capital		25,950
Add : 10% for Contingencies		2,595
Average Working Capital Required		28,545

Note : Undrawn profit has not been taken into account. Because, it is a source of Fund. This may or may not be used as working capital. This does not affect the requirement of working capital.

Besides, figures given in the question show loss, not profit.

Problem

The following is the Balance Sheet of A.B. Co. Ltd. on 31st March 2006 :

Liabilities	Amount	Assets	Amount
	Rs.		Rs.
Capital	10,00,000	Fixed Assets (Land, Furniture etc.)	4,00,000
Creditors (Trade)	1,40,000	Stock	3,00,000
Profit and Loss A/c	60,000	Debtors	1,50,000
		Cash and Bank	3,50,000
	12,00,000		12,00,000

The management estimates the purchases and sales for the year ended 31st March, 2006 as under :

28.2.06	Up to 2006	March
	Rs.	Rs.
Purchases	14,10,000	1,10,000
Sales	19,20,000	2,00,000

It was decided to invest Rs.1,00,000 in purchases of fixed assets which are depreciated 10% on cost.

The time lag for payment to trade creditors for purchase and receipts from sales is one month. The business earns a gross profit of 30% on turnover. The expenses against profit amount to 10% of the turnover. The amount of depreciation is not included in these expenses.

Draft a Balance Sheet as at 31st March, assuming that creditors are all trade creditors for purchases and debtors for sales and there is no other item of current assets and liabilities apart from stock and cash and bank balances. **[Adapted from C.A. Final]**

Solution

Projected Trading & Profit and Loss Account
for the year ending 31st March 2006

Dr. Cr.

Particulars	Amount	Particulars	Amount
	Rs.		Rs.
To Opening Stock	3,00,000	By Sales	21,20,000
,, Purchase	15,20,000	,, Closing Stock	
,, Gross Profit c/d (30% on sales)	6,36,000	(balancing figure)	3,36,000
	24,56,000		24,56,000
To Sundry Expenses (10% on sales)	2,12,000	By Gross Profit b/d	6,36,000
,, Depreciation	50,000		
,, Net Profit	3,74,000		
	6,36,000		6,36,000

Projected Balance Sheet of A.B.Co. Ltd.
as on 31st March 2006

Liabilities		Amount	Assets		Amount
		Rs.			Rs.
Capital		10,00,000	Fixed Assets		
Profit & Loss A/c :			Land, Furniture etc.	4,00,000	
Balance on 1.4.05	60,000		Additions	1,00,000	
Profit for the year	3,74,000	4,34,000		5,00,000	
Sundry Creditors		1,10,000	*Less* : Depreciation	50,000	4,50,000
			Stock-in-trade		3,36,000
			Sundry Debtors		2,00,000
			Cash & Bank		5,58,000
		15,44,000			15,44,000

Calculation of Cash and Bank Account :

Dr. **Cash and Bank Account** *Cr.*

Particulars	Amount	Particulars	Amount
	Rs.		Rs.
To Balance b/d	3,50,000	By Sundry Creditors (Rs. 1,40,000 + Rs. 14,10,000)	15,50,000
,, Sundry Debtors (Rs. 1,50,000 + Rs.19,20,000)	20,70,000	,, Expenses	2,12,000
		,, Fixed Assets	1,00,000
		,, Balance c/d	5,58,000
	24,20,000		24,20,000

Problem

A Proforma cost sheet of a company provide the following particulars :

Elements of Cost	Amount Per Unit
	Rs.
Raw Material	80
Direct Labour	30.
Overheads	60
Total Cost	170
Profit	30
Selling Price	200

The following further particulars are available :

Raw materials are in stock on average one month. Materials are in process, on average, half a month. Finished goods are in stock, on average, one month.

Credit allowed by suppliers is one month. Credit allowed to debtors is two months. Lag in payment of wages is $1\frac{1}{2}$ weeks. Lag in payment of overhead expenses is one month.

One-fourth of the output is sold against cash. Cash on hand and at bank is expected to be Rs.25,000.

You are required to prepare a statement showing the working capital needed to finance a level of activity of 1,04,000 units of production.

You may assume that production is carried on evenly throughout the year, wages and overheads accrue similarly and a time period of 4 weeks is equivalent to a month.

[C.A. Final]

Solution

Statement Showing the Requirement of Working Capital

Particulars		Amount Rs.	Amount Rs.
Current Assets :			
Finished Goods : (for 1 month 8,000 Units @ Rs.170)			13,60,000
Stock of Materials (for 1 month 8,000 Units @ Rs.80 $Rs.80 \times 1,04,000 \times \frac{4}{52}$)			6,40,000
Work-in-Progress: (for $\frac{1}{2}$ month)	Materials Cost for 4,000 units @ Rs.80 per unit	3,20,000	
	Labour and Overheads Cost 2,000 units @ Rs.90	1,80,000	5,00,000
Debtors : (for 2 months)	Material Cost $\frac{Rs.\ 80 \times 1,04,000 \times 3 \times 8}{4 \times 52}$	9,60,000	
	Labour Cost $\frac{Rs.\ 30 \times 1,04,000 \times 3 \times 8}{4 \times 52}$	3,60,000	
	Overheads $\frac{Rs.\ 60 \times 1,04,000 \times 8 \times 3}{4 \times 52}$	7,20,000	20,40,000

Particulars	Amount	Amount
	Rs.	Rs.
Cash Balances :		25,000
		45,65,000
Less : **Current Liabilities :**		
Credit allowed by Creditors (8,000 @ Rs. 80 Materials for 1 month)	6,40,000	
Lag in payment of Overheads (1 month 80,000 @ Rs. 60)	4,80,000	
Lag in payment of wages ($1\frac{1}{2}$ weeks 3,000 @ Rs. 60) $\left(\frac{\text{Rs. } 30 \times 1,04,000 \times 3}{52 \times 2}\right)$	90,000	12,10,000
Estimated Requirement of Working Capital		33,55,000

One thing please note here that, in the absence of adequate information, depreciation—included in the overhead, cannot be excluded.

Problem

While preparing a project report on behalf of a client you have collected the following facts. Estimate the net working capital required for that project. Add 10% to your computed figure to allow contingencies :

Estimated cost per unit of production	Amount per unit (Rs.)
Raw Materials	80
Direct Labour	30
Overheads (exclusive of depreciation Rs.10 per unit)	60
Total Cash Cost	170

Additional information :

Selling price Rs. 200 per unit.

Level of activity 1,04,000 units of production per annum.

Raw Materials in stock, average 4 weeks. Work-in-progress (assume 50% completion stage in respect of conversion costs and 100% completion in respect of materials), average 2 weeks.

Finished Goods in stock, average 4 weeks. Credit allowed by suppliers, average 4 weeks. Credit allowed to debtors average 8 weeks. Lag in payment of wages, average 1.5 weeks. Cash at Bank is expected to be Rs.25,000.

You may assume that production is carried on evenly throughout the year (52 weeks) and wages and overhead accrue similarly.

All sales are on Credit basis only. **[C.S. Final—Adapted]**

Solution

Working Notes :

(i) Average weekly production = $\frac{1,04,000 \text{ units}}{52}$ = 2,000 units

(ii) Average cost and profit per week :

	Rs.
Raw materials (2,000 × Rs. 80)	1,60,000
Direct Labour (2,000 × Rs. 30)	60,000
Overheads (2,000 × Rs. 60)	1,20,000
Overheads — depreciation (2,000 × Rs.10)	20,000
Total Cost	3,60,000
Profit (Balancing Figure)	40,000
Sales (2,000 × Rs. 200)	4,00,000

Statement Showing the Working Capital Requirement

Particulars	Average Cost per Week	Net Block (in week)	Amount	
A. Current Assets:	Rs.		Rs.	Rs.
1. Stock :				
(i) Raw Materials	1,60,000	4		6,40,000
(ii) Work-in-Progress:				
Raw Materials	1,60,000	2	3,20,000	
Labour	60,000	1	60,000	
Overhead	1,20,000	1	1,20,000	5,00,000
(iii) Finished Goods :				
Raw Materials	1,60,000	4	6,40,000	
Labour	60,000	4	2,40,000	
Overhead	1,20,000	4	4,80,000	13,60,000
2. Debtors : (Equivalent to Cost only) :				
Raw Materials	1,60,000	8	12,80,000	
Labour	60,000	8	4,80,000	
Overheads	1,20,000	8	9,60,000	27,20,000
3. Expected Bank Balance				25,000
Total Current Assets (A)				52,45,000
B. Current Liabilities:				
1. Creditors for Materials	1,60,000	4		6,40,000
2. Outstanding Wages	60,000	1.5		90,000
Total Current Liabilities B				7,30,000
Net Working Capital (A – B)				45,15,000
Add: Contingencies (10% of Rs.45,15,000)				4,51,500
Final Working Capital Requirement				49,66,500

Alternatively :

Statement Showing the Working Capital Requirement

Particulars	Weekly average Cost	Time Lag (Weeks)	Raw Materials	Work-in-Progress	Finished Goods	Debtors	Creditors	Total
	Rs.		Rs.	Rs.	Rs.	Rs.	Rs.	Rs.
1. Material :	1,60,000							
(i) in Store		4	6,40,000					
(ii) in WIP		2		3,20,000				
(iii) in finished goods		4			6,40,000			
(iv) in debtors		8				12,80,000		
gross block		18						
Less Creditors		4					(6,40,000)	
Net Block		14						22,40,000
2. Labour :	60,000							
(i) in WIP		1		60,000				
(ii) in finished goods		4			2,40,000			
(iii) in debtors		8				4,80,000		
gross block		13						
Less : Outstanding Wages		1.5					(90,000)	
Net Block		11.5						6,90,000
3. Overhead :	1,20,000							
(i) in WIP		1		1,20,000				
(ii) in finished goods		4			4,80,000			
(iii) in debtors		8				9,60,000		
Net Block		13						15,60,000
			6,40,000	5,00,000	13,60,000	27,20,000	(7,30,000)	44,90,000
Add : Expected Cash and Bank Balance								25,000
								45,15,000
Add : Contingencies (10% of 45,15,000)								4,51,500
Requirement Working Capital								49,66,500

Problem

With the following information, prepare a statement showing the working capital required to finance level of activity of 10,400 units per annum :

(i) Selling price is Rs. 5 per unit.

(ii) The expected ratios of cost of selling price are :

(a) Raw material 40% (b) Direct Wages 10% (c) Overhead 30% (d) Profit 20%.

(iii) Raw Materials are expected to remain in store for an average period of two months before being used for production and materials are in process on an average period of six weeks.

(iv) Finished goods will stay in store approximately for six weeks before despatch to customers.

(v) Credit allowed to debtors is for a period of two months.

(vi) Credit allowed by Creditors is for a period of two months.

(vii) Lag in Payment of wages and overheads is for a period of two weeks.

(viii) Cash in hand and bank expected to be Rs.10,000.

It may be noted that production is carried on evenly during the year and wages and overheads accrue similarly. Assume 4 weeks a month. **[C.U., B.Com. (H)]**

Solution

Working Notes :

(1) Calculation of Cost per unit (elementwise)

		Rs.
Raw Material	(40% of Rs. 5)	2.00
Direct Wages	(10% of Rs.5)	0.50
Overheads	(30% of Rs.5)	1.50
Total Cost per Unit		4.00
Profit (20% of Rs.5)		1.00
Selling Price Per Unit		5.00

(2) Average Weekly production= $\frac{10,400 \text{ units}}{52}$ = 200 units

(3) Calculation of Average Cost per Week and Average Weekly Profit

	Rs.
Raw Materials (Rs. 2.00×200)	400
Direct Wages (Re. 0.50×200)	100
Overheads (Rs. 1.50×200)	300
Total Cost	800
Profit (Re. 1.00×200)	200
Selling Price Per Week	1,000

(4) Since the production is carried on evenly during the year and wages and overhead accrue similarly, time lag for wages and overhead in processing has been taken as half of the given period.

(5) Profit is included in debtors considering normal profit is an element of cost.

Statement Showing the Working Capital Requirement

Particulars	Weekly Average Cost	Time Lag (Weeks)	Raw Materials	Work-in-Progress	Finished Goods	Debtors	Creditors	Total
	Rs.		Rs.	Rs.	Rs.	Rs.	Rs.	Rs.
1. Raw Materials :	400							
(i) in Store		8	3,200					
(ii) in WIP		6		2,400				
(iii) in Finished goods		6			2,400			
(iv) in Debtors		8				3,200		
Gross Block		28						
Less : Credit from Suppliers		8					(3,200)	
Net Block		20						8,000
2. Direct Wages :	100							
(i) in WIP		3		300				
(ii) in Finished goods		6			600			
(iii) in Debtors		8				800		
Gross Block		17						
Less : Lag in payment of wages (Credit from employees)		2					(200)	
Net Block		15						1,500
3. Overhead :	300							
(i) in WIP		3		900				
(ii) in Finished goods		6			1,800			
(iv) in Debtors		8				2,400		
Gross Block		17						
Less : Lag in payment of overhead		2					(600)	
Net Block		15						4,500
4. Profit :	200							
in Debtors		8				1,600		1,600
			3,200	3,600	4,800	8,000	(4,000)	15,600
Add : Expected Cash and Bank Balance								10,000
Working Capital Requirement								25,600

Problem

From the following information, prepare a statement showing the estimated working capital requirements :

(i) Projected annual Sale – 26,000 units
(ii) Selling Price per unit – Rs. 60.00
(iii) Analysis of Selling price :
Material 40%, Labour 30%, Overhead 20%, Profit 10%.
(iv) Time Lag (on average)
Raw materials in stock 3 week
Production process 4 weeks.
Credit to Debtors 5 weeks
Credit from Suppliers 5 weeks
Lag in payment of wages and overheads 2 weeks
Finished goods are in warehouses 2 weeks
(v) Cash in hand is expected to be 10% of net working capital. **[C.U., B.Com.(H)]**

Solution

Working Notes

(1) **Calculation of elementwise cost per unit :**

	Rs.
Material (40% of Rs. 60.00)	24.00
Labour (30% of Rs.60.00)	18.00
Overhead (20% of Rs. 60.00)	12.00
Total Cost per unit	54.00
Profit (10% of Rs. 60.00)	6.00
Selling Price Per Unit	60.00

(2) **Average weekly production** $= \frac{26,000}{52}$

$= 500$ units

Here, it has been assumed that annual production is equal to the projected annual sale.

(3) **Calculation of Average Cost per week and Average weekly Profit :**

	Rs.
Raw Material (500 × Rs. 24)	12,000
Labour (500 × Rs.18)	9,000
Overhead (500 × Rs.12)	6,000
Total Cost	27,000
Profit (500 × Rs. 6)	3,000
Total Selling Price	30,000

(4) It has been assumed that production is carried on evenly during the year and wages and overheads accrue similarly.

(5) Profit is included in debtors.

Statement Showing the Estimated Working Capital Requirement

Particulars	Average Cost per week	Time Lag (Weeks)	Raw Materials	Work-in Progress	Finished Goods	Debtors	Creditors	Total
	Rs.		Rs.	Rs.	Rs.	Rs.	Rs.	Rs.
1. Raw Materials :	12,000							
(i) in Stock		3	36,000					
(ii) in WIP		4		48,000				
(iii) In Debtors		5				60,000		
(iv) in Finished goods		2			24,000			
Gross Block		14						
Less : Credit from Suppliers		3					(36,000)	
Net Block		11						1,32,000
2. Labour :	9,000							
(i) in WIP		2		18,000				
(ii) in Finished goods		2			18,000			
(iii) in Debtors		5				45,000		
Gross Block		9						
Less : Lag in wage payment (Credit from employees)		2					(18,000)	
Net Block		7						63,000
3. Overhead :	6,000							
(i) in WIP		2		12,000				
(ii) in Finished goods		2			12,000			
(iii) in Debtors		5				30,000		
Gross Block		9						
Less : Lag in payment		2					(12,000)	
Net Block		7						42,000
4. Profit :	3,000							
In Debtors		5				15,000		15,000
Add : Expected Cash and Bank Balance			36,000	78,000	54,000	1,50,000	(66,000)	2,52,000
Net working capital before adding expected cash in hand								2,52,000
Add : Expected Cash in Hand 10% of net working capital or 1/9th of net working capital before adding cash i.e., 1/9th of Rs.2,52,000								28,000
Estimated Working Capital								2,80,000

Problem

20th Century Fox Ltd. plans to sell 30,000 units next year. The expected cost of goods sold is as follows :

	Rs. (Per unit)
Raw materials	100
Manufacturing Expenses	30
Selling Expenses	20
Selling price	200

The duration at various stages of the operation is expected to be :

Raw materials stage	2 months
Work-in-Progress stage	1 month
Finished goods stage	½ month
Debtors stage	1 month

Assuming the monthly sales level of 2,500 units :

(i) Calculate the investment in various Current Assets; and

(ii) Estimate the Gross Working Capital requirement if the desired cash balance is 5% of Gross Working Capital requirements.

[C.S. (F) (Adapted)]

Solution

(i) Calculation of Investment in Current Assets :

		Rs.
(a) Raw materials	$= \text{Rs.}30{,}00{,}000 \times \frac{2}{12} =$	5,00,000
(b) Work-in-Progress	$= \text{Rs. } 39{,}00{,}000 \times \frac{1}{12} =$	3,25,000
(c) Finished Goods	$= \text{Rs. } 39{,}00{,}000 \times \frac{1}{24} =$	1,62,500
Total for Inventory		9,87,500
(d) Debtors	$= \text{Rs.}60{,}00{,}000 \times \frac{1}{12} =$	5,00,000
		14,87,500

(ii) Gross Working Capital Requirement :

	Rs.
Inventory	9,87,500
Debtors	5,00,000
	14,87,500
Cash: 5% of Gross Working Capital	78,290
	15,65,790

Working Notes

Statement of Cost and Profit

	Per Unit (Rs.)	30,000 units Amount (Rs. in lakhs)
Raw materials	100	30
Manufacturing Expenses	30	9
Cost of Production	130	39
Add : Selling, Admin. & Financial Exp.	20	6
Total Cost of Sales	150	45
Sales	200	60
Profit	50	15

Problem

Warner Brothers Ltd. has obtained the following data concerning the average working capital cycle for other companies in the same industry :

Raw Material stock turnover	20 days
Debtors velocity	60 days
Creditors velocity	40 days
Work-in-Progress turnover	15 days
Finished goods stock turnover	40 days

Using the following data, calculate the current working capital cycle for Warner Brothers Ltd :

	(Rs. in thousands)
Sales	3,000
Cost of Production	2,100
Purchases	600
Average Stock of Materials	80
Average Work-in-Progress	85
Average Stock of Finished Goods	180
Creditors on an Average	100
Debtors on an Average	400

[C.A. Final Adapted]

Solution

Calculations of operating cycle of Warner Bros. Ltd. :

1. **Raw Material**

$$\frac{\text{Average stock of Raw Material}}{\text{Total Raw Materials Purchased}} \times \text{Length of the Accounting Period}$$

$$= \frac{80}{600} \times 365 = 49 \text{ days}$$

2. **Work in Progress**

$$\frac{\text{Average Work in Progress}}{\text{Cost of Production}} \times \text{Length of the accounting period}$$

$$= \frac{85}{2,100} \times 365 = 15 \text{ days}$$

3. **Finished Goods**

$$\frac{\text{Average stock of finished goods}}{\text{Cost of Production}} \times \text{Length of the accounting period}$$

$$= \frac{180}{2,100} \times 365 = 31 \text{ days}$$

4. **Debtors**

$$\frac{\text{Average Debtors}}{\text{Credit Sales}} \times \text{Length of Accounting Period}$$

$$= \frac{400}{3,000} \times 365 = 49 \text{ days}$$

5. **Creditors**

$$\frac{\text{Average Creditors}}{\text{Credit Purchase}} \times \text{Length of the Accounting Period}$$

$$= \frac{100}{600} \times 365 = 61 \text{ days}$$

∴ Operating Cycle

= 49 days + 15 days + 31 days + 49 days – 61 days

= 83 days

Problem

Columbia Ltd. sells its product on a gross margin of 20% Profit on Sales. Following information is extracted from its annual accounts for the year ending 31st Dec. 2005 :

	Rs.
Sales (at 3 months' credit)	45,00,000
Raw Material	15,00,000
Wages (15 days in arrears)	9,60,000
Manufacturing & General Expenses (one month arrears)	15,00,000
Administration overheads ($1\frac{1}{2}$ months' lag)	5,00,000
Sales Promotion expenses (Payable half-yearly in advance)	2,00,000

The company enjoys one months' credit from its suppliers of materials and maintains $1\frac{1}{2}$ months' stock of Raw Material and 1 months' finished goods. Cash Balance is maintained at Rs.1,25,000 as a precaution.

Assuming 10% margin, Calculate the working capital requirement of Columbia Ltd.

[C.A. Final Adapted]

Solution

Statement of Working Capital Requirement

Particulars	Amount Rs.
1. **CURRENT ASSETS**	
Debtors $\left(4,500,000 \times \frac{3}{12} \times 80\%\right)$	9,00,000
Stock of Raw Materials $\left(15,00,000 \times \frac{1.5}{12}\right)$	1,87,500
Finished goods' stock (Sales × 80%) × $\frac{1}{12}$	3,00,000
Prepaid Sales Promotion Expenses (half)	1,00,000
Cash	1,25,000
Total Current Assets (A)	16,12,500
2. **CURRENT LIABILITIES**	
Creditors $\left(15,00,000 \times \frac{1}{12}\right)$	1,25,000
Wages $\left(9,60,000 \times \frac{1}{24}\right)$	40,000
Manufacturing Expenses $\left(15,00,000 \times \frac{1}{12}\right)$	1,25,000
Administrative Expenses $\left(5,00,000 \times \frac{1.5}{1.2}\right)$	62,500
Total Current Liabilities (B)	3,52,500
Working Capital (A – B)	12,60,000
Add : 10% Margin	1,26,000
Net Working Capital Required	13,86,000

Problem

Following are the particulars of X Ltd. :

Annual cash requirement is Rs.10,00,000, Marketable securities in lot sizes of Rs.50,000, Rs.1,00,000, Rs. 2,00,000, Rs.2,50,000 and Rs. 5,00,000. Cost of conversion per lot is Rs.1000. Annual yield 5%.

Prepare a table showing the required lot size to be sold by X Ltd.

Also, show that the Economic lot size as per Baumol's Model.

[C.A. Final, Adapted]

Solution

Table showing lot size of Securities

Particulars	(1)	(2)	(3)	(4)	(5)
A) Annual Cash requirement (Rs.)	10,00,00	10,00,000	10,00,000	10,00,000	10,00,000
B) Lot Sizes (Rs.)	50,000	1,00,000	2,00,000	2,50,000	5,00,000
C) No. of Lots (A/B)	20	10	5	4	2
D) Cost of Conversion per lot (Rs.)	1,000	1,000	1,000	1,000	1,000
E) Total cost of Conversion (C) × (D)	20,000	10,000	5,000	4,000	2,000
F) Interest = B/2 × 5/100	1,250	2,500	5,000	6,250	12,500
G) Total Cost	21,250	12,500	10,000	10,250	14,500

Therefore, the required lot of securities is Rs.2,00,000 (total cost of holding cash is minimum i.e. Rs. 10,000).

Solution as per Baumol's model

$$OC = \sqrt{\frac{2AO}{C}}$$

where OC = Optimum Cash Balance

A = Total Amount of annual cash requirement i.e. Rs. 1000000

O = Cost of Conversion/Transaction i.e. Rs. 1000

C = Interest rate on Securities i.e. 5% p.a. or 0.05

$$\therefore \quad OC = \sqrt{\frac{2 \times 10,00,000 \times 1000}{0.05}}$$

= Rs. 2,00,000

QUESTIONS

1. Explain the idea that Business Finance is a part and parcel of Financial Management.
2. What are the different sources of finance? Write about the respective advantages and disadvantages.
3. What is Working Capital ? What are the different factors that are to be taken into account in estimating working capital of a business?
4. What is 'Cash Management'? Is there any relationship between 'Cash Management' and 'Working Capital Management'.
5. Explain the idea that 'Working Capital is the Pivot of Financial Management'.

6. Bring out clearly the essential nature of the Projected Balance Sheet Method of forecasting fund requirements. What major steps are involved in preparing the Projected Balance Sheet? **[M.Com., Delhi University]**

7. Explain clearly what is meant by 'working capital'. As a management consultant, you are required to state the consideration involved in estimating the amount of the required working capital. Suggest ways and means to meet need for working capital in the case of a newly started business. **[C.A. Final]**

8. From the following information prepare a statement in columnar form showing the estimated working capital requirements as regards each constituents part of working capital :

Budgeted Sales Rs, 2,60,000 per annum, Analysis of cost of each unit :

	Rs.
Raw material	3
Labour	4
Overheads	2
Profit	1
	10

It is estimated that :

(a) Pending use, raw materials are carried in Stock for three weeks and finished goods for two weeks.

(b) Factory processing will take three weeks,

(c) Suppliers will give five weeks' credit and customers require eight weeks credit,

It may be assumed that production and overheads accrue evenly throughout the year. **[M.Com., C.U.]**

9. (a) As a Management Accountant you are required to state the considerations involved in estimating the amount of working capital required for a business engaged in manufacturing cum-marketing.

(b) EXE Ltd. are engaged in large-scale consumer retailing. From the following information, you are required to forecast their working capital requirement :

Projected Annual Sales — Rs. 65 lakhs.

Percentage of Net profit on cost of Sales — 25%

Average credit period allowed to Debtors — 10 weeks

Average credit period allowed by creditors — 4 weeks

Average stock carrying (in terms of sales requirement) — 8 weeks.

Add 10% to computed figures to allow for contingencies. **[M.Com., C.U.]**

10. What do you understand by the term 'Working Capital' ? What is the significance of an increase in Working Capital ?

You are preparing a project report for an investment project. From the following data calculate the working capital requirement at the end of the first month of full operations of the project :

Investment in fixed assets :	Rs. 96 lakhs (raised by mortgage—bearing interest @ 10% per annum payable at the end of each month).
Sales (which take place uniformly over the year) :	Rs. 3 crores (annual) 20% of sales are for cash. 80% are on credit receivable 31 days after date of sale.
Cost of production of the quantity sold :	Rs. 2 crores 4 lakhs (annual). Materials (30% : of cost of production) bought on credit payable 30 days after date of purchase. Wages (15% of cost of production) payable on the first of every month.
	Fixed overheads (55% of cost of production) include depreciation @10% of fixed assets per annum. The rest of overheads are payable uniformly over the month.
Selling and distribution cost :	Rs. 36 lakhs (annual) payable uniformly over the month.
Stock holdings :	Finished goods : 45 days' sale. Materials : 15 days' consumption.
Bank :	An overdraft arrangement up to Rs. 7.50 lakhs exists with the bankers.

Ignore taxation.

Assume each month to be of 30 days' duration.

[M.Com., C.U.]

11. From the following particulars of Sun Ltd., determine the working capital requirement :

(a) Monthly Sales (expected) - 16,000 units of Rs. 10 each.

(b) Analysis of Sales : Material 40%, Labour 30%, Overhead Rs.8,000 per week.

(c) Stock will include raw-material for Rs.48,000 and 8,000 units of finished goods.

(d) Processing Periods 2 weeks

(e) Credit to Debtors 5 weeks

(f) Credit from Creditors 1 month

(g) Lag in payment of overhead -2 weeks

(h) Production is carried out evenly during the year and expenses accrue similarly.

[C.U., B.Com. (H)]

12. From the following information of Bright Ltd, you are required to determine the Working Capital requirement :

(a) Annual (expected) Sales
Rs. 12,00,000

(b) Analysis of Sales :
Material - 60%, Expenses - 15%, Profit - 25%

(c) Credit allowed to debtors	2.5 months
Credit allowed by Creditors	1.5 months
Raw Material in store	1 month
Processing period	2 months
Finished goods in store	3 months
(d) Bank Overdraft	Rs. 80,000
(e) Cash in hand for contingencies	Rs. 20,000

(f) Production is carried on evenly during the year and expenses accrue similarly.

[C.U., B.Com. (H)]

13. Your company is operating on 60% capacity, producing 24,000 units per annum at the following cost-price structure :

	Rs.
Raw Material	5 per unit
Wages	3 per unit
Overheads—variable	2 per unit
Overheads—fixed	1 per unit
Profit	2 per unit
	13 per unit

On 31st December 1984, the current assets and liabilities were :

	Rs.
Raw Material 4,000 units, at cost	20,000
Work-in-Progress 1,000 units, at cost	8,000
Finished Goods 3,000 units, at cost	33,000
Sundry Debtors	78,000
Creditors for Goods	30,000
Liability for Wages	3,000
Liability for expenses	6,000

In view of increased demand for the product, it has been decided that from 1st January 1985, the unit should operate at 90% capacity.

You are required to ascertain the additional working capital as would be necessary in view of additional production. The prices of materials, rates of wages and the expenses and the selling prices per unit will not change. The period of credit allowed to customers, credit allowed by suppliers and also time lag in payment of wages and expenses shall remain the same as before. **[C.U., B.Com. (H)]**

14. The components of current assets of a new trading concern are Stock, Debtors, and Cash. The only component of its current liabilities is Creditors.

Ascertain the concern's Working Capital requirement for the first year from the following information:

(a) Expected Sales at a profit of 20% on Cost — Rs. 9,00,000 (20% Cash)

(b) Expected Stock Turnover — 6 times

(c) Expected Credit period to Debtors — 2 months

(d) Expected Credit period from Creditors — 1½ months

(e) The concern intends to maintain a Cash Balance equal to 1 month's cash Sales. **[C.U., B.Com. (H)]**

15. On 1st January 2004, the management of PQ Ltd. desires to forecast Working Capital to be needed to meet the programme they have Planned for the year.

From the particulars of the Company, forecast (a) its Working Capital requirement (b) its Profit and Loss Account for the year ending 31st December, 2004 and (c) its Balance Sheet as on that date :

Issued Capital :

8,000 equity shares of Rs. 10 each, fully paid — Rs. 8,00,000

12% Debentures — Rs. 5,00,000

Fixed Assets o 1st January 2004 — Rs. 12,00,000

Estimated annual production 90,000 units

Expected ratio of cost of selling price are :

Material 60%, Wages 15%, Variable Overheads 10%

Fixed Overhead (including depreciation) at 90,000 units Rs.3,60,000 per annum.

Fixed Assets are depreciated at 10% p.a. Raw Materials are expected to remain in stock for 1½ months on average before issued to production.

Processing time 1 month.

Finished goods are in stock on average 2 months.

Credit to Debtors 1½ months.

Credit from Creditors 2 months.

Time lag in payment of wages ½ month.

Lag in payment of overhead 1 month.

Selling price is Rs. 40 per unit

Production is carried evenly throughout the year. **[C.U., M.Com.—Adapted]**

16. Prepare a statement to determine the working capital requirement from the following information :

(i) Expected Sales 36,000 units per annum.

(ii) Analysis of Selling price :

	Rs.
Raw Material	6 per unit
Labour	4 per unit
Overhead	3 per unit
Profit	2 per unit
Selling Price	15 per unit

(iii) Additional information :

(a) Raw materials remain in stores on an average 1 month.

(b) Processing time 2 months.

(c) Finished goods are kept in stores 3 months.

(d) Credit allowed to debtors 4 months.

(e) Credit allowed by suppliers 2 months.

(f) Wages and overhead are paid twice a month—on the 1st and on the 16th.

(g) Production is carried on evenly during the year and wages and expenses accrue in the same way. **[C.U., B.Com. (H)]**

17. You are the responsible officer in the finance department of Wholesom Co. Ltd. The data given below are estimates relating to the year ending 31st December 2004 :

		Rs./Lakhs
(i)	Opening Balances	
	Raw Materials	410
	Work in Progress	100
	Finished Goods	450
	Receivables	600
	Payables	450
(ii)	Estimated Closing Balances	
	Raw Materials	450
	Work in Progress	120
	Finished Goods	500
	Receivables	740
	Payables	420
(iii)	Raw Materials purchased	1,600
(iv)	Manufacturing Expenses	1,100
(v)	Selling, Administration and Financing costs	480
(vi)	Sales	4,000

You are required to compute the operating cycle period and prepare a statement showing the Cash Working Capital of the company. Assume 360 days in the year. **[C.U., M.Com.]**

18. From the following information you are asked to forecast the Working Capial requirement of X Ltd :

Projected Annual Sales	Rs. 130 lakhs
Percentage of net profit on cost of Sales	25%
Average Credit period allowed to Debtors	10 weeks
Average Credit period allowed by Creditors	4 weeks
Average Stock Carrying (in terms of Sales requirement)	8 weeks

Add 10% to computed figures to allow for contingencies. **[C.U., M.Com.]**

19. From the following information of Moon Ltd. prepare a cash budget for the three months commencing from 1st June 2005, when the bank balance was Rs.10,000:

Month	Sales Rs.	Purchases Rs.	Wages Rs.	Selling Expenses Rs.	Overhead Rs.
April	1,00,000	70,000	8,500	3,500	4,000
May	1,20,000	80,000	9,500	3,500	4,500
June	1,40,000	90,000	9,500	3,500	6,000
July	1,60,000	1,00,000	12,000	3,500	6,500
August	1,80,000	1,10,000	14,000	3,500	7,000

A commission 5% on Sales, due 2 months after Sales—is payable in addition to the above selling expenses. Credit terms of Sale are—Payment by the end of the month following the month of supply. On average one half sale is paid on the due date, while the other half is paid during the next month. Creditors are paid during the month following the month of supply. Plant purchased in June Rs. 78,000 out of which Rs.48,000 is payable on delivery and balance in two equal monthly instalments in July and in August. A dividend of Rs.30,000 will be paid in September. Wages are paid ¾th on due date while ¼th during the next month. Lag in payment of selling expenses and overheads is one month. **[C.U., B.Com. (H)]**

15

CAPITAL STRUCTURE —GEARING, LEVERAGE

● Good morning to you all my dear students.

☐ "Good morning Sir".

● Now I discuss on Capital Structure.

You see, capital structure is the mix of several securities such as equity and debt securities (fixed interest bearing securities i.e. preference share, debenture etc.) of a firm or company. It is to note in this context that fixed interest bearing securities, now a days, are termed as fixed charge bearing securities.

Meaning of Capital Structure, Capital Gearing

Capital Gearing what is called Capital Leverage is one of the important aspects of financial planning. It is the base of capital structure. By capital gearing is meant a relationship between the Ordinary or Equity Share Capital and the Preference Share Capital, Debenture etc. However, the very relationship indicates whether capital structure is high-geared or low-geared. The relationship can be drawn from two points of view —(a) Structural and (b) Profit Distribution.

CAPITAL GEARING

- (a) Structural Relationship
- (b) Profit Distribution Relationship

☐ "Sir, what is Structural Relationship and Profit Distribution Relationship ? Besides, what is high-gearing and what is low-gearing?"

● Now I like to explain the Structural Relationship in the following way with the help of a few exhibits:

(a) Relationship drawn from the point of view of equity capital and loan capital i.e. relationship drawn from the Structural point of View is :

$$\frac{\text{Equity Share Capital}}{\text{Fixed Charge Bearing Securities (Preference Share Capital + Debenture and other long term loan)}} \quad \text{... (i)}$$

(b) Relationship drawn from Profit Distribution Point of View is :

$$\frac{\text{Amount Payable on the Fixed Charge Bearing Securities i.e., Loan Capital}}{\text{Total Distributable Profit}} \quad \text{... (ii)}$$

However, capital gearing can be measured having due regard to the relationship (b) drawn earlier—profit distribution. Gear ratio is the measurable relation or proportion of the annual amount payable on the fixed charge or prior charge capital to the distributable profit.

Now I would like to explain Capital Gearing — High/Low with the help of a few Exhibits.

High/Low Geared Capital under the structural relationship—Capital.

Exhibit 1

Balance Sheet of X Y Z Co. Ltd.

Liabilities	Amount	Assets	Amount
	Rs.		Rs.
Share Capital :		Sundry Assets	1,05,000
Equity Shares of Rs. 100 each	50,000		
6% Preference Shares of Rs. 10 each	10,000		
Reserve and Surplus (Retained Earning)	30,000		
5% Debentures	10,000		
Current Liabilities	5,000		
	1,05,000		1,05,000

Exhibit 2

Balance Sheet of A B C Company Ltd.

Liabilities	Amount	Assets	Amount
	Rs.		Rs.
Share Capital :		Sundry Assets	1,00,000
Equity Shares of Rs. 100 each	30,000		
6% Preference Shares of Rs. 10 each	10,000		
Reserve and Surplus	10,000		
5% Debentures	50,000		
	1,00,000		1,00,000

Exhibit 3

Balance Sheet of ABXY Co. Ltd.

Liabilities	Amount	Assets	Amount
	Rs.		Rs.
Share Capital :		Sundry Assets	1,00,000
Equity Shares of Rs. 100 each	50,000		
6% Preference Shares of Rs. 10 each	40,000		
5% Debentures	10,000		
	1,00,000		1,00,000

Please note the whole situation in the following manner :

Exhibit No.	Equity Share Capital or Net Worth	Loan Capital (Preference Shares and Debentures)	Relationship	Result
	Rs.	Rs.		
1.	80,000	20,000	80,000 / 20,000	Low Geared Capital (Over Capitalised)
2.	40,000	60,000	40,000 / 60,000	High Geared Capital (Under Capitalised)
3.	50,000	50,000	50,000 / 50,000	Fair Capitalisation

High Gear and Low Gear

I think you have understood all these points. In Exhibit No. 1, it is revealed that the proportion of the Loan Capital is much lower than the Equity Share Capital. So is the case of Low-Geared Capital i.e., Low Gearing. Now Exhibit No. 2 is an example of High Geared Capital, since the proportion of Loan Capital is much higher than the Equity Share Capital. Exhibit 3 is a stage which reveals a proportionate balance between the two equities—own capital and loan capital. 'The analysis of financial statements sometimes reveals a disproportionate balance between these interests, and the resulting conditions may be referred to as under-capitalisation or over-capitalisation.'

Capitalisation

☐ "Sir, what is Under-Capitalisation and Over-Capitalisation and what are the causes and effects of Over-and Under-Capitalisation? Please explain us all these things in detail".

● Let me discuss the whole thing i.e., Capital Gearing, first. Do not get worried. I would like to discuss these in my following lectures after discussing the Capital Gearing in all its aspects. However, the discussions so far made relate to the discussion of Capital Gearing—high/low, under the structural/capital point of view.

Now I would like to discuss the other portion of our present task—the profit distribution point of view.

Where the gearing is high, the percentage rate of possible dividend on the ordinary share capital rises or falls disproportionately to the percentage rate of increase or decrease in the profits. We can explain the same with the help of an example.

Example : A company having capital of Rs. 10,000 in 6% Preference Shares and Rs. 1,000 in Ordinary Shares, making a profit of, say, Rs. 2,000 would be able, after payment of the preference dividend, to pay a dividend of 140 percent on the Ordinary share capital; if the profits were reduced to, say, Rs. 650, it would only be possible to pay a dividend of 5 percent on Ordinary shares. High geared shares must be regarded as the most speculative, and subject to greater price fluctuation. "... high gearing, that is greater use of borrowed capital, makes profits high in case of boom and losses high in case of slump." Now for the practical case study regarding high/low gearing, you may consult my research publication ***"Accounting for Goodwill and its Effects on Enterprise and Social Economy."***

Now I think I am clear to you. If you do not understand any point please tell me, so that I can make clear the points again.

☐ "Sir, we shall be glad much if you give us some light about the terms 'Over-Capitalisation' and 'Under-Capitalisation'?"

● You see, this portion of capitalisation I will take up for discussion afterwards. Moreover, I will discuss the same in the chapter on 'Accounting Ratios'.

☐ "Why Sir ?"

● You see, it is related to the concept of Proprietary Ratio.

☐ "Sir, what is Proprietary Ratio ?"

● I have told you earlier that I will discuss the same under the head of "Accounting Ratios." However, you please note that Proprietary Ratio brings a relationship between proprietor's fund and total assets of the business. It gives an indication to what degree owner (proprietary capital) contributes to the total assets of the business. This situation calls for to what degree the outsiders (loan capital) contribute in the total assets of the business. That is to say, the degree of reliance between the two equities, own capital and loan capital has to be found out.

This 'Degree of Reliance' indicates whether the capital structure is said to be high-geared or low-geared. If we consider the dimension of the whole capital structure as 360° degree it would be very helpful for our analysis. If the own resources i.e., proprietor's fund are 200° and the outsider's i.e., Loan Capital is 160° the dimension of the capital structure is said to be low geared, and vice-versa. "A rise in the proprietary ratio denotes a tendency for Over-Capitalisation and a fall in the same that for Under-Capitalisation .... Under-Capitalisation speaks of a situation under which the proportion of borrowed or loan capital becomes usually high."

Loan Capital > Equity Capital = Under-Capitalisation.

Loan Capital< Equity Capital = Over-Capitalisation.

Relationship between Capital Gearing and Capitalisation

Equity Capital > Loan Capital = Over-Capitalisation = Low Gearing.

Equity Capital < Loan Capital = Under-Capitalisation = High Gearing.

From this it is clear that from the result of the Gear Ratio we can find out or we can diagnose the stage of Under-Capitalisation or Over-Capitalisation as the case may be.

I think, you all have followed my lectures. I shall be glad much to hear from you any points which come in your mind. Please, do not feel shy. Yes, tell, ...

☐ "Sir, what are the causes of Under-Capitalisation?"

● You see, Under-Capitalisation is the result of Over Trading.

☐ "What is Over-Trading Sir?"

● You see Over-Trading is an expansion of sales without adequate capital support. Over trading is indicated by inadequate working capital, low proprietary ratio, low current ratio. In this respect I like to place before you the views of Mr. T. G. Rose as expressed in his book, ***"The Internal Finance of Industrial Undertaking"***. Mr. Rose is of opinion that 'the danger that lies in over-trading—in other words in attempting the expansion of a business without an adequate background of liquid capital—is that the management, dazzled by the opportunity offered by the market and the profits undoubtedly being made, do not appreciate that the cash return during the expansion period inevitably lags behind the expenditure. Many individuals spend their lives in industry without realising that as many companies go into liquidation through doing too much business as through doing too little. The whole affair appears to be a complete anomaly. A concern has a good product, ample markets, excellent opportunities for doing well, and is actually making good profits—yet the machine seems to be clogging itself, and eventually breaks down. It is, in fact, the inevitable result of commercial expansion when working with a profit margin which in itself is sufficient to supply the cash necessary to cover that expansion, and where no additional source of temporary funds is available to take its place.'

Over-Trading

☐ "Sir, what is Trading on Equity?"

I find no reason why you could not catch the point which I explained you in the last lectures. You may not have the same thing exactly, but you can get the idea of the same contained in the lectures. However, by 'trading on the equity' is meant the situation where the amounts paid to the fixed interest-bearing securities are proportionately less than the earning on the capital contributed from these sources— Preference Shares and Debentures.

Trading on Equity

Did you follow what I discussed so far?

☐ "Yes Sir".

• If so, please tell me what are the symptoms of Under-Capitalisation and Over-Capitalisation.

☐ "I cannot answer Sir."

☐ "I cannot follow your lecture Sir, if possible please explain, in a nutshell."

• If you go on like this, the rate of progress will be hampered. However, note here the following :

Over-Capitalisation denotes a stage where the capital of the business is found far in excess of the requirement of the business. Besides, in this stage the reasonable rate of return on investment is not found. Existence of intangibles such as Goodwill, Patents, Trade marks etc., in some cases, has evolved the idea of Over-Capitalisation. Because it denotes a condition where major part of the capital or fund invested in is represented by inflated value owing to the existence of intangibles such as Goodwill etc. Now from this we can come to the conclusion that recording of goodwill follows overstatement of the nominal value of share capital. For this I request you or suggest you to go through my research publication, ***"Accounting for Goodwill and its Effects on Social and Enterprise Economy."***

Over-Capitalisation of the business is indicated by :

i. Unnecessary investment of fund in the fixed assets which are in excess of its actual needs.

ii. Low earning capacity of the business.

iii. High proprietary ratio.

iv. Inadequate earning per share.

Now I hope that you all have understood the causes and effects of Capitalisation i.e. I mean here Over-Capitalisation. I shall be glad to hear from you if you really face any difficulties in the last lectures.

☐ "Sir, please explain in detail the meaning of Earning Per Share."

• You know that there are two types of Equities— Owner and Outsider, or, in other words, Proprietary Capital and Loan Capital. A situation is said to be under-capitalisation when the proportion of Loan Capital is comparatively higher than Equity or Proprietary capital. It means that the business has no sufficient fund or, better to say, cash, to meet its requirement. Sometimes it happens that a business has to borrow in order to keep the cycle of working capital running. So, some writer is of opinion that over-trading is the cause of under- capitalisation. What is over-trading, I explained you earlier.

Earning Per Share (EPS) can be calculated, dividing the amount arising from profit after payment to fixed charge bearing securities by total number of equity or ordinary shares.

You see, followings are the symptoms of Under-Capitalisation :

i. Unlike low earning per share in case of over-capitalisation, the earning per share is higher.

ii. Shortage of Working Capital.

iii. Low Proprietary Ratio.

☐ "Sir, will you not give us some idea about 'Capital Protection', 'Cost of Capital' and 'Planning for Profit'?"

• Now, do you remember my first lecture where I explained that the business is a continuous process. During this process we have to keep a constant watch on the process of the capital flow. It is sometimes found that the capital of the business wear away slowly, that is to say, 'erosion of capital' is found in the process of business. So this aspect of capital protection, I would like to take up for discussion in my subsequent lectures under the head of "Accounting for Inflation." Regarding Cost of Capital and Planning for Profit, I would like to bring to your attention that all these will be discussed under suitable heads in my subsequent lectures. However, in my next lecture I will take up Fund Flow and Cash Flow for discussion separately. Before that let me know whether you have followed my earlier discussions or not.

Silence please! yes, yes you, why have you raised your hand?

☐ "Sir, would you kindly discuss different concepts such as Capitalisation, Capital Structure and Financial Capital?"

• You see, I have discussed the theme of the concepts earlier. Is it so that you could not follow my lectures?

☐ "Sir! I could not attend your classes; because my mother was in death bed; ultimately she expired. That's why I was absent."

• Don't worry. I feel sad that you have lost your mother. I am explaining all these again.

You see, I have already told you at the outset of the discussions that Capital Structure is the mix of several securities such as equity shares, debt securities i.e., preference shares and debentures etc. It is the ***'Qualitative Aspect'*** of financial planning. The proportionate amount of different types of securities such as equity shares, preference shares and debentures make the capital structure of a firm or company. Total amount of securities viz, equity or ordinary shares, preference shares and debentures issued by a firm or company is termed as capitalisation. Capitalisation may be considered '***Quantitative Aspect***' of financial planning. Total of liabilities side of a Balance Sheet is considered as Financial Structure of a firm or company. It depicts all sources of finance viz. equity or ordinary share capital plus all sorts of long term and short term debts.

Meaning of Capitalisation, Capital Structure and Financial Structure

I feel that you have followed my lecture. You please stand up. I think, you want to say something yes, yes... tell me if you have any problem. Please frank with me.

You see, I feel that teacher is the machine and students are raw materials. Unless there is a close understanding between teachers and the students like machine and raw materials, the products (students) will not be of high standard.

You see, if you obtain your degree from University or from and Institute(s) without adequate knowledge of the subject(s), you will be selling in the **Job Market** not at a **premium** but at a **discount** like issue of shares by companies.

Well, I have lost so many times by giving you advice. Now tell me what is your question.

☐ "Sir, I could not follow the term proportionate balance and the proportionate amount. as well as, capitalisation-Capital Structure and Financial Structure. Please explain these with an example."

• Well, have a look at the board where I have shown three Exhibits—Exhibit 1, Exhibit 2 and Exhibit 3. Direct your attention to Exhibit 1. Where compositions of Liabilities side of the Balance Sheet are as follows :

	Rs.
Equity Share Capital	50,000
% Preference Share Capital	10,000
Reserve and Surplus (Retained Earning and Capital Reserve)	30.000
% Debentures	10,000
Current Liabilities	5,000
	1,05,000

Here **Capitalisation** is Rs. 70,000. I have already told you that total amount of securities issued by the company is called capitalisation. Total amount of securities are Equity Share Capital Rs. 50,000. Preference Share Capital Rs. 10,000 and Debentures Rs. 10,000. You add all these, you will get Rs. 70,000.

It is to note is this context that most of the students understand Capitalisation as Capitalisation of Reserve Fund, that is to say, company converts reserve fund to Equity Capital through issue of **Bonus Share**. In that case it forms a part of Securities. The said understanding relates to process of Capitalisation, that is good no doubt.

Regarding **Capital Structure** I have told you earlier that **mix** of Securities is capital Structure; or it may be stated as **proportional** amount of the securities that constitute capitalisation. Here Capital Structure is Rs. 70,000. Please have a look on the Board.

	Rs.	Proportion or Mix of Securities %
Equity share Capital	50,000	71.42
% Preference Share Capital	10,000	14.29
% Debenture	10,000	14.29
	70,000	100.00

Here it is seen that out of total Capital Structure (100%) 71.42% is owned by the Equity or Ordinary shareholder. So, it reflects Low Levered (Low Geared) capital Structure.

☐ "Excuse me Sir! I have one question. Is capitalisation and capital structure same which we see from the figures where both show Rs. 70,000?"

● You see, though both appear similar but it differs from conceptual point of view, you recapitulate my previous lecture where I told you that capital structure is the **'Qualitative Aspect'** of financial planning where as capitalisation is **'Quantitative Aspect'** of financial planning.

Is it clear to you?

☐ "Yes Sir, but I have one more question to ask. That is Sir! when I was doing library work I saw that a few writers included Reserve and Surplus in the list of capital structure. Would you, please kindly enlighten us on this issue?"

● Well, you have put a nice question.

You see, after a few years of start of the business, companies are found to create Reserve Fund; that Reserve Fund is a part of Net-worth.

You see, you all know that when Reserve and Surplus is added to Equity or Ordinary Share Capital it is called Net-worth. When there is a scope for capitalisation of Reserve and Surplus which I mentioned earlier through issue of Bonus Share, it results increase in the amount of Equity or Ordinary Share capital which may be termed as internal security. On the other hand Reserve and Surplus play an important role to regulate gearing (levering) the capital structure i.e., High Geared or High Levered and Low Geared or Low Levered.

For example, Capital Structure consists of

	Rs.
Equity or Ordinary Share Capital	10,000
6% Preference Share Capital	20,000
7% Debentures	10,000

The example exhibits a situation of High Levered or High Geared Capital Structure. Because, out of total capital structure for Rs. 40,000 the contribution of external securities, i.e., Preference Share Capital and Debentures is Rs. 30,000 which is 75% of the total capital structure, whereas 25% is represented by Equity or Ordinary Share Capital (Internal Securities). Suppose, subsequently over the years if Reserve and Surplus amounts to say Rs. 60,000, the situation is bound to change, i.e., High Geared (High Levered) changed to Low Levered (Low Geared) Capital Structure.

Have a look here

	Rs.
Equity Share Capital	10,000
% Preference Share Capital	20,000
Reserve and Surplus	60,000
% Debentures	10,000
	1,00,000

Our of total Capital Structure Rs. 1,00,000, Rs. 70,000 (Equity Share Capital Rs. 10,000 Plus (+) Reserve and Surplus Rs. 60,000) is represented as Proprietor's Fund i.e., shareholders fund. Here 70% is represented by Internal source and 30% is represented by external source. So, from the said logic, if any author includes Reserve and Surplus in the list of capital structure it is acceptable.

● Have you followed?

☐ "Yes Sir, please give us an example of Financial Capital Structure".

● Well, look here—Exhibit I

All sources of finance which appear in the Liability side of a Balance Sheet for the acquisition of Assets which appear in the Assets side of a Balance Sheet are called Financial Capital Structure.

It includes :

Equity Share Capital
% Preference Share Capital
Reserve and Surplus
% Debentures
Current Liabilities

● Do you follow what I discussed?

☐ "Yes Sir. Please enlighten us about different Theories of Capital Structure".

● Well, before discussing the different theories of capital structure I am to say some important points on this aspect.

Whether, by changing capital mix or financial mix[1] that is to say, changing capital gearing, from high gearing to low gearing and low gearing to high gearing (high leverage to low leverage and low leverage to high leverage) it is possible or not for a firm or

[1] James C. Van Horne. *"Financial Management and Policy"*

company to affect its cost of capital and total valuation of the firm, is a subject matter of analytical study taking cognition of other factors in the arena of ***mood of the capital market***. Professor James C. Van Horne had righty observed that "attention is directed to the question of what happens to the total valuation of the firm and to its cost of capital when the ratio of debt to equity, or degree of leverage, is varied."[2]

Capital or Financing Mix

Is there any problem(s) that stands on the way to follow my lecture?

☐ "No Sir, we have followed your lecture. You can proceed for further discussions. We are enjoying the discussions Sir!"

● Well, please note that following assumptions are considered pre-requisite to the discussions of several rate of returns of capital structure as well as different theories of capital structure.

Your attention please, have your look on the board where I have shown different assumptions.

Assumptions :

Assumptions Pre-requisite to the Discussions of Capital Structure Theories

(i) Tax aspects i.e., income tax or corporate tax is ignored; subsequently this tax aspect is taken care of.

(ii) Capital Structure ratio i.e., Debt Equity ratio is subject to change through different mechanisms such as issue of equity or ordinary shares, redemption of loan or debt capital; similarly issue of loan capital (Preference shares and Debentures), as a device to re-purchase of equity share (stock). Here transaction cost is ignored.

(iii) Entire earnings i.e., profit of the business is to be paid as dividend which implies that no profits or earnings are to be retained for the firm.

(iv) Future operating profits or operating earnings for each and every similar types of firms or companies as well as distribution of operating earnings or operating profits are expected to be similar.

(v) Present operating earnings or operating profits are expected to be guiding factor for all future operating earnings or operating profits of the firm, that is to say, increase in operating earnings or operating profits in the future should not be taken into cognigence.

I think you have followed the above assumptions. Now I am showing you here 3 (three) rates of capital structures, based on said assumptions-K_i (i.e., yied on company's debt) K_e (i.e., cost of equity capital) and K_o (i.e., overall capitalisation rate) Please note that It was Ezra Solomon[3] who had shown the said 3 (three) rates which I am presenting before you for your study.

---

[2] *Ibid.*

[3] *The Theory of Financial Management* Columbia University Press New York 1963, chapters 7-9 as reproduced in James c. Van Horne *Financial Management and Policy*. 5th Edition.

$$K_i = \frac{F}{B} = \frac{\text{Annual Interest Charges}}{\text{Market Value of debt outstanding}}$$

In this equation, K_i is the yield on the company's debt to be perpetual

$$K_e = \frac{E}{S} = \frac{\text{Earning available to Common Stockholders}}{\text{Market Value of stock outstanding}}$$

The required rate of return for investors in a firm whose earnings are not expected to grow and that has a 100 percent dividend-payout ratio, is the earning/price ratio. Given our restrictive assumptions, then, the earnings/price ratio represents the market rate of discount that equates the present value of the stream of expected future dividends with the current market price of the stock........ The final rate we consider is

$$K_o = \frac{O}{V} = \frac{\text{Net operating earnings}}{\text{Total market value of the firm}}$$

where V = B + S. Here K_o is an overall capitalisation rate for the firm. It is defined as the weighted-average cost of capital and may be expressed as

$$K_o = K_i\left(\frac{B}{B+S}\right) + K_e\left(\frac{S}{B+S}\right)$$

our concern will be with what happens to K_i, K_e and K_o when degree of leverage, as denoted by the ratio B/S, increases.

By the by, I am to bring to your attention that here cost of debt is shown as K_i. Many authors has shown it as K_d. So, don't get confused.

I hope, you have understood the said discussions. Is there any question from your side, please don't feel shy. Yes, yes, what do you want to say?

☐ "Excuse me Sir! I have one question to ask."

● What is your question?

☐ "Sir, Can K_e be calculated other than methods you described earlier"

● Yes, Prof James C. Van Horne in his book *Financial Management and Policy* had shown it, which is as follows :

$$K_e = K_o + (K_o - K_i)\frac{B}{S}$$

☐ Please explain how to find out

(i) Market value of debt outstanding. (B)

(ii) Market value of stock, i.e., equity shares outstanding. (S)

(iii) Total market value of the firm. (V)

● Well, please refer to *situation No. 1*, discussed earlier.

$$K_i = \frac{F}{B}$$

or, $k_i B = F$ — K_i = Debt Capitalisation Rate

or $B = \frac{F}{K_i}$ — F = Annual Interest charge

B = Market Value of Debt outstanding

Situation No. 2

$$K_e = \frac{E}{S}$$ — K_e = Equity Capitalisation Rate

or $K_e S = E$ — E = Earning available to Common Stockholder

$S = \frac{E}{K_e}$ — S = Market Value of Stock outstanding (Equity)

Situation No. 3

$$K_o = \frac{O}{V}$$ — K_o = Overall Capitalisation Rate

or $K_o V = O$ — O = Net Operating Earning

or, $V = \frac{O}{K_o}$ — V = Total Market Value of the Firm

Now, as stated earlier value of the firm (V) = B + S

So, it can be expressed as follows :

$$V = \frac{F}{K_i} + \frac{E}{K_e}$$

☐ Sir, can O, as you mentioned earlier, be taken as EBIT (Earning Before Interests and Taxes)?

● It is perfectly alright, I am very happy to note that you have gone into the deep of the concept.

Your attention please!

The Weighted-Average Cost of Capital (K_o) which was stated earlier as

$$K_o = K_i\left(\frac{B}{B+S}\right) + K_e\left(\frac{S}{B+S}\right)$$

can be expressed as

$$K_o = K_i\left(\frac{B}{V}\right) + K_e\left(\frac{S}{V}\right)$$

Have a look here, should I continue my lecture; or if you feel tired It may be deferred for the next day, please tell me frankly.

☐ Sir! it is very interesting; please continue Sir! If possible give us a break for ten minutes.

● Ok

● Well, I feel that now you are happy after break. Now I am discussing different important Theories of Capital Structures proposed by different authors, in the context of cost of capital and value of the firm.

Theories of Capital Structure

Different Theories of Capital Structure

1. Net Income Approach (NIA)
2. Net Operating Income Approach (NOIA)
3. Traditional Approach (TA)
4. Modigliani-Miller Approach (M-MA)

Now I am explaining the said approaches one by one.

1. Net Income Approach (NIA)

David Durand[4] propounded two extreme theories of capital structure—the Net Income Approach Theory (NIA) and the Net Operating Income Approach Theory (NOIA) to determine the valuation of earnings of a firm. These two approaches symbolize, as different as possible, to measure the worthiness of a firm or a company with regard to 'the degree of leverage'. However, the effectiveness of NI Approach (Theory) is that the use of debt financing i.e., loan capital can invite the following situations to a firm or company

(a) Decrease in Weighted Average Cost of Capital

(b) Increase in Total Valuation of the Firm

(c) Increase in Market Price of Equity Share.

Thus, it appears that increase and decrease in the leverage (capital gearing) influence the capital structure of a firm.

However, this theory of capital structure (NIA) is established on the following assumptions :

(i) Cost of debt is less than cost of equity ($K_i<K_e$)

(ii) Increase in degree of leverage bears no effects on cost of equity as well as cost of debt; that is to say, cost of equity (capital) and cost of debt (loan capital) remain unchanged (constant).

(iii) Corporate taxes are ignored.

(iv) The perception of risk is not changed by the use of increased degree of debt

---

[4] "The Cost of Debt and Equity Funds for Business" ***in the Management of Corporate Capital.*** Edited by Ezra Soloman. Free Press NY 1959, Pp. 91-116.

financing. It has been nicely expressed by Prof. Van Horne that "the firm does not become increasingly more risky in the minds of investors and creditors as the degree of leverage is increased"[5]

I think that you have followed the above discussions. Is there any question?

☐ "Sir, give us an illustration showing total value of a firm as well as overall capitalisation rate of a firm or company".

☐ "Sir, please graphically illustrate it".

• You see, I am showing you the nature of the graph of NIA just to give you an instant impression. It is not supported by any figure or information which it is based on. I would request you to prepare a diagram with supporting information on a graph paper. This is your home-task.

Please have your look on the board.

☐ "Excuse me Sir! I cannot follow your lecture. Please explain if cost of debt (K_i) and cost of equity (K_e) remain unchanged, the question arises where the effect can be reflected or traced".

• Thank you very much for your question.

You see, I have already explained the same in my previous lecture(s).

Have a look here. Three aspects are involved in this theory of capital structure.

There are as follows.

K_i = Cost of Debt, i.e., yield on firm's or company's debt.

K_e = Cost of Equity.

K_o = Overall Capitalisation rate which is known as Weighted-Average Cost of Capital.

Perhaps you remember my advice to you which is "*Make Common sense your Best Friend*". So, if you apply your common sense you will find your answer. When K_i and K_e remain unchanged, effect is reflected on K_o. Professor Van Horne had rightly observed that "As the proportion of cheaper debt funds in the capital structure is increased, the weighted-average cost of capital, K_o, decreases and approaches the cost of debt, K_i. The optimal capital structure would be the one at which the total value of the firm is greatest and the cost of capital is the lowest. At that structure, the market price per share of stock is maximized".

Please note that it may be the case that K_o may meet the line of K_i.

You please stand up. Have you followed my lecture now. Is there any question?

☐ "Thank you Sir, Now I have followed it. It appears to me so simple like a glass of drinking water".

• Now I am constructing the diagram. Please direct your attention on the Board.

[5] Van Horne opcit. p. 265

Ox-axis shows leverage or gearing.

Oy-axis shows % Cost of Capital.

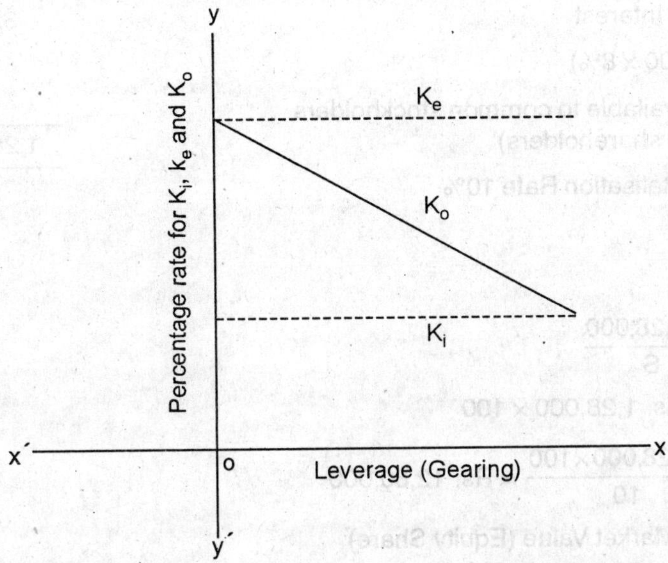

Do you follow the said diagram? I suggest that you should prepare the diagram in a graph paper for better presentation.

☐ "Sir, give us an example for understanding the said diagram."

● Well, please note the following illustration.

Illustration

From the following information find out.

(a) Market Value of Equity

(b) Value of Firm or Company

(c) Overall Capitalisation Rate (i.e., overall cost of capital) and

(d) Situation arising from increase in Market Value of Debt.

Information

Net Income Rs. 1,60,000

Market Value of Debt Rs. 4,00,000

Interest Rate of Debt 8%

Equity Capitalisation Rate 10%

Increase in Market Value of Debt Rs. 6,00,000, interest rate remaining the same.

Solution

Computation of Market Value of Equity (Stock), Value of the Firm (Company) and Overall Capitalisation Rate (Overall Cost of Capital)

	Rs.
Net Income	1,60,000
Less : Debt Interest	32,000
(Rs. 4,00,000 × 8%)	
Earnings available to common stockholders (1.e., equity shareholders)	1,28,000

Equity Capitalisation Rate 10%

$$K_e = \frac{E}{S}$$

$$\frac{10}{100} = \frac{\text{Rs.} 1{,}28{,}000}{S}$$

or, 10 S = Rs. 1,28,000 × 100

$$\therefore S = \frac{\text{Rs.} 1{,}28{,}000 \times 100}{10} = \text{Rs. } 12{,}80{,}000$$

Therefore, Market Value (Equity Share)

Rs. 12,80,000

Market Value of Debt Rs. 4,00,000

Value of the Firm or Company

V = B + S

= Rs. 4,00,000 + Rs. 12,80,000

= Rs. 16,80,000

Overall Capitalisation Rate (% overall capitalisation)

$$K_o = \frac{O}{V}$$

$$= \frac{\text{Rs.} 1{,}60{,}000}{\text{Rs.} 16{,}80{,}000}$$

= 0.95238 × 100

= 9.52380%

Computation of Market Value of Equity (Stock), Value of the Firm (Company) and Overall Capitalisation Rate (Overall Cost of Capital) **arising** from **increase in Market Value of Debt.**

	Rs.
Net Income	1,60,000
Less : Debt Interest	48,000
(Rs. 6,00,000 × 8%)	
Earnings available to common stock holders (1.e., equity shareholders)	1,12,000

Equity Capitalisation Rate 10%

$$K_e = \frac{E}{S}$$

$$\frac{10}{100} = \frac{\text{Rs.}1{,}12{,}000}{S}$$

or, 10 S = Rs. 1,12,000 × 100

$$\therefore S = \frac{\text{Rs.}1{,}12{,}000 \times 100}{10} = \text{Rs. } 11{,}20{,}000$$

Therefore, Market Value (Equity Share)

Rs. 11,20,000

Market Value of Debt Rs. 6,00,000

Value of the Firm or Company

V = B + S

= Rs. 6,00,000 + Rs. 11,20,000

= Rs. 17,20,000

Overall Capitalisation Rate (% Overall Capitalisation)

$$K_o = \frac{O}{V}$$

$$= \frac{\text{Rs.}1{,}60{,}000}{\text{Rs.}17{,}20{,}000}$$

= 0.0930232 × 100

= 9.30232%

You see, I have already brought to your notice that the application of increased debt financing increases value of the firm in the one hand and decreases overall cost of capital on the other. Now, it is clear to you, from the said illustration, that the use of increased debt financing has decreased overall capitalisation rate to the extent of 0.22148% (9.52380% – 9.30233%).

I think that you have followed my lecture.

Is there any question?

☐ "Sir, can overall capitalisation rate be termed as overall cost of capital; that is to say, are both terms same?"

● You are perfectly right. I am happy to note that you have understood the concept(s).

Now I would like to discuss other theory of capital structure.

☐ "Sir, Is it Net Operating Income Approach?"

• Yes, yes.

Your attention please! Have a look on the Board.

2. Net Operting Income Approach (NOIA)

David Durand, as has been stated earlier, is the exponent of this theory of capital structure. It is completely different, better to say opposite, from his another theory of capital structure — Net Income Approach (NIA). The Net Operating Income Approach (NOIA) depicts extreme effects of leverage on firm's value. The market value of any firm, according to NOIA, is not affected by the change in capital structure, arising from debt-equity mix. Another important point to note in this context is that overall cost of capital of any firm or company does not change, i.e., remains constant, at any level of mix of debt-equity which is considered as methods of financing capital structure. Under this approach, what is peculiar to note in this context, both cost of equity and debt are equal. Under the said state of affair it appears that there is no as such optimal capital structure; every capital structure is said to be optimal capital structure.

In this context Van Horne has rightly said that "Cost of debt has two parts : the explicit cost represented by the rate of interest, and the implicit cost, or "hidden" cost, which is represented by the increase in the equity capitalisation rate that accompanies an increase in the proportion of debt to equity. Because the cost of capital of the firm cannot be altered through leverage; this approach implies that there is no one optimal capital structure.

All capital structures are optimal, for market price per share does not change with leverage... Thus capital structure would be a matter of indifference to the investor."[6]

It is very important to note in this context that the financial risk, under this approach, of the stockholders (Equity shareholders) appears to be high thanks to the use of increased debt financing, resulting increase in cost of equity capital. Here financial risk of debt financier is not affected.

To find out market value of a firm, under this method, operating income or net operating income of a firm is capitalised at the rate of overall cost of capital, i.e., overall capitalisation rate.

• I think, you are following my lecture.

Is there any question?

☐ "Sir, are not there any assumptions to this theory like previous one?"

• Don't worry. I will explain every thing and every aspects of the theory.

Well, I was talking about market value of a firm.

Is it so?

☐ "Yes, you can proceed Sir!"

• Now to find out the market value of equity (stock), market value of debt is to be deducted from market value of a firm or company; after that if you are asked to calculate equity capitalisation rate, i.e., cost of equity, you can calculate the same from the formula given below which I discussed earlier.

---

[6] Van Horne op. cit., p. 287

Formula of equity capitalisation rate (Cost of equity)

$$K_e = \frac{E}{S}$$

E = Earning available to equity shareholders, i.e., common stockholder after deduction of debt capital

S = Market value of equity i.e., stock.

Now I am discussing a few assumptions which the Net Operating Income Approach is based on.

Assumptions

Assumptions of Net Operating Income Approach

(i) Overall capitalisation rate of a firm or company does not fluctuate at any level of mix of debt-equity.

(ii) Increased debt financing is offset by increased cost of equity. This aspect has nicely been explained by Van Horne which runs as follows :

> "An increase in the use of supposedly 'cheaper' debt funds is offset exactly by the increase in the equity-capitalisation rate, K_e. Thus the weighted average of K_e and K_i remains unchanged for all degrees of leverage."[7]

(iii) Market takes the advantage to value the firm or company as a whole.

Now I am showing you the nature of a diagram as per NOIA.

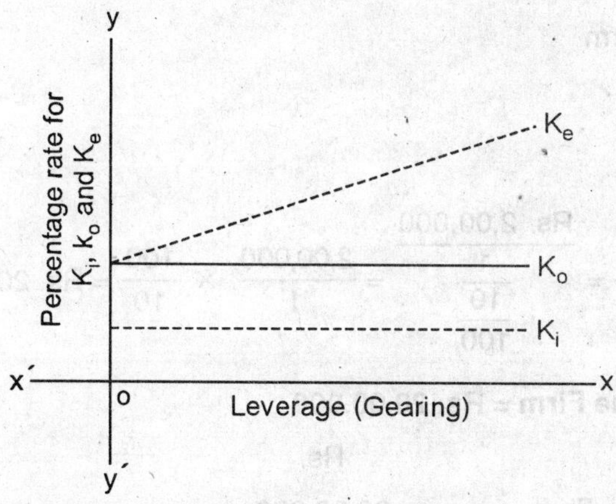

OX-axis shows leverage or Gearing, where as OY-axis shows percentage rate for K_i, K_o and K_e.

I think, you have followed the discussions made earlier. Now I am showing you an illustration. Please note it very carefully.

---

[7] Van Horne op. cit., p. 267

Illustration

From the following information find out.

(A) Market Value of the Firm

(B) Market Value of Equity

(C) Equity Capitalisation Rate

(D) Situation arising from increase in debt financing.

Information

Net Operating Income Rs. 2,00,000

Market Value of Debt Rs. 10,00,000

Interest Rate of Debt 6%

Overall Capitalisation Rate 10%

Increase in Market Value of Debt Rs. 15,00,000

Interest Rate remaining the same

Solution

Computation of Market Value of the Firm (Company), Market Value of Equity and Equity Capitalisation Rate

Net operating Income Rs. 2,00,000

Overall Capitalisation Rate 10%

Market Value of Firm

$$V = \frac{O}{K_o}$$

$$= \frac{\text{Rs. } 2{,}00{,}000}{\frac{10}{100}} = \frac{\frac{\text{Rs. } 2{,}00{,}000}{1}}{\frac{10}{100}} = \frac{2{,}00{,}000}{1} \times \frac{100}{10} = \text{Rs. } 20{,}00{,}000$$

A. Market Value of the Firm = Rs. 20,00,000

		Rs.
Market Value of the Firm	=	20,00,000
Less : Market Value of Debt	=	10,00,000
Market Value of Equity		10,00,000

B. Market Value of Equity = Rs. 10,00,000

Equity Capitalisation Rate

$K_e = \frac{E}{S}$ E = Earning available to common Stockholders

S = Market Value of Stock (Equity)

Earning available to Common Stockholders :

Net Operating Income – Debt Interest

Rs. 2,00,000 – Rs. 60,000

= Rs. 1,40,000

Equity Capitalisation Rate (K_e) is

$$K_e = \frac{E}{S} = \frac{\text{Rs. } 1,40,000}{\text{Rs. } 10,00,000} \times 100 = 14\%$$

C. Equity Capitalisation Rate = 14%

Computation of Equity Capitalisation Rate (K_e) in a situation where Debt financing increased to Rs. 15,00,000.

● Your attention please! why are you talking with each other?

☐ "Sir, I am not talking. I am just trying to find out K_e with help of my friend".

● Please note that I am here for your help; your attention please.

You see, the value of a firm or company does not change with the change in debt financing.

	Rs.
Here value of the firm stands at	20,00,000
Increased debt financing (Market Value of Debt)	15,00,000
Market Value of Equity	5,00,000
Net operating income	2,00,000
Less : Debt interest	90,000
Earning available to Equity Shareholders (Common Stockholders)	1,10,000

$$\text{So, } K_e = \frac{\text{Rs. } 1,10,000}{5,00,000} \times 100 = 22\%$$

D. Situation arising from increase in debt financing = 22%

☐ "Excuse me Sir, I have one question i.e., can the said sum be worked out taking the working of previous result?"

● Well, come to the Board and show it.

☐ "Sir, you have told that value of the firm or company remains unchanged."

So, the market value of the firm comes at Rs. 20,00,000 after capitalising net operating income of Rs. 2,00,000 at overall capitalising rate 10%.

Market value of Equity as per previous

calculation comes at Rs. 10,00,000 after deducting Market value of Debt Rs. 10,00,000

So, increased market value is Rs. 5,00,000

So, if I deduct Rs. 5,00,000 from previous calculated market value Rs. 10,00,000 it comes at Rs. 5,00,000.

Earning available to common stock holders, i.e., equity shareholders as per previous calculation is Rs. 1,40,000.

So, from Rs. 1,40,000 I am deducting increased interest on increased figure for debt financing which is Rs. 5,00,000. So, interest on Rs. 5,00,000 @6% comes at Rs. 30,000.

Therefore, earning available to equity shareholders is as follows :

Rs. 1,40,000 – Rs. 30,000 = Rs. 1,10,000

$$\text{So, } K_e = \frac{\text{Earning available to equity shareholders}}{\text{Market value of equity}}$$

$$= \frac{\text{Rs. } 1,10,000}{\text{Rs. } 5,00,000} \times 100 = 22\%$$

Sir, is it correct?"

● Thank you very much. I am happy to see that I am able to make you understand the concept.

Now you see that the cost of equity increases with the increase in debt financing.

Now I am discussing other theory of capital structure which is the Traditional Approach.

3. Traditional Approach (TA)

The Traditional Approach (T.A.) which is one of the theories of capital structure may be termed as 'Composite Approach'[8], because it contains all the properties that lie between the two extremes of Net Income Approach (NIA) and Net Operating Income Approach (NOIA). Many authors coined this approach as '**Intermediate Approach**'.

[8] Lecture delivered by Prof. B. K. Basu before MBA Students at different Management Institutes at Bareilly. U.P. Nov. 2006.

This theory portrays the following aspects :

(i) By use of more cheaper debt financing, a firm can, initially, increase its value resulting decrease in the cost of equity i.e., capitalisation rate of equity.

(ii) By judicious mix of debt-equity financing a firm can attain optimum capital structure which, according to Ezra Solomon, 'is the point at which overall cost of capital is the minimum ... value of the firm maximum.'

Features of Traditional Approach

(iii) By virtue of inherent risk of the stock holders, i.e., equity shareholders, involved in increased debt financing of a firm, the capitalisation rate of equity (K_e) increases beyond at a particular point. The beneficial feature of cheaper debt financing at that point of capital structure is offset by increase in capitalisation rate of common stockholders (Equity Shareholders)

(iv) By application of cheaper debt financing (Low cost of debt), it is not always possible for a firm to reap the advantage of the same. Because after that "there comes a stage, when increased cost of equity cannot be offset by the advantage of low-cost debt".

I think you have followed my lecture.

Are there any questions?

☐ "Sir, I could not follow optimum structure of capital."

☐ "Sir, show us the nature of diagram of Traditional Approach."

• Well I will answer to your all questions .... Silence please.

☐ "Excuse me Sir, please give us an illustration covering every aspects that are embodied in this Traditional Approach (TA)".

• Thank you my dear students for your queries. I will explain every aspects raised by you. Before that I am to bring to your knowledge how nicely Van Horne explained the Traditional Approach.

According to Van Horne

"... the traditional position implies that the cost of capital is not independent of the capital structure of the firm and that there is an optimal capital structure. At that optimal structure, the marginal real cost of debt (explicit and implicit) is the same as the marginal real cost of equity in equilibrium. For degrees of leverage before that point, the marginal real cost of debt is less than that of equity; beyond that point, the marginal real cost of debt exceeds that of equity"[9].

Do you follow the above statement?

☐ "Yes Sir, We have no problems you can proceed Sir!"

• You see, I have seen in my practical life that to have no problem is really a great problem; and to solve a greater problem I had to create a small problem as a token of measure.

---

[9] Van Horne op. cit., pp. 269-270

Are you feeling bore, as I am sharing my experience?

☐ "Not at all Sir. It is more interesting to me, not to speak of other, than any thing else".

• You see, I had seen in my school days a family with severe poverty. When poverty was there in the family all members of the family were disciplined—love, regards, co-feeling etc. every things were found; but when poverty vanished, thanks to inflow of finance from the earnings like service, business etc, the members of the family appeared to be indisciplined. Please note that the example and the experience cited above should not be taken as representative model applicable in all cases. It may be treated as an exceptional case.

All these I am saying is that shortage of finance for a firm or company is a problem to the firm no doubt; the same can be solved by inducting loan capital. Induction of loan capital is risky after a certain stage or stages. So, judicious application of mind as to debt-equity financing may avoid many problems. Too much under-capitalisation and too much over-capitalisation both are problems to an organisation. So, close understanding of the concepts and integration of K_i, K_e and K_o may help for long and efficient survival of a firm or company or organisation. What to stop, when to stop and how to stop, where to stop; that is say, what to finance, when to finance, how to finance where to stop financing—all these are to be properly assessed for long term benefits of a firm. You should always observe that your body shadow should not be much less than the length of your body and the same should not be much more than the length of your body. This should be, according to me, the real philosophy of judicious application of mind with regard to debt-equity financing.

Are you feeling tired? should I stop my discussion?

☐ "No Sir, it is really exciting. We are hearing your lecture for two hours (two classes), but sir, your different examples give us stimulant energy which guard against bore and tiredness. You can proceed now."

• Well, I need, hope you too need, a break for thirty minutes. When we will meet this venue after 30 minutes I will show you the Diagram of Traditional Approach. Thank you all.

Are you all present in the class?

☐ "Sir, please wait for five minutes more; four or five classmates yet to come."

• Now I think you all are present. Please have your look on the board for the Diagram.

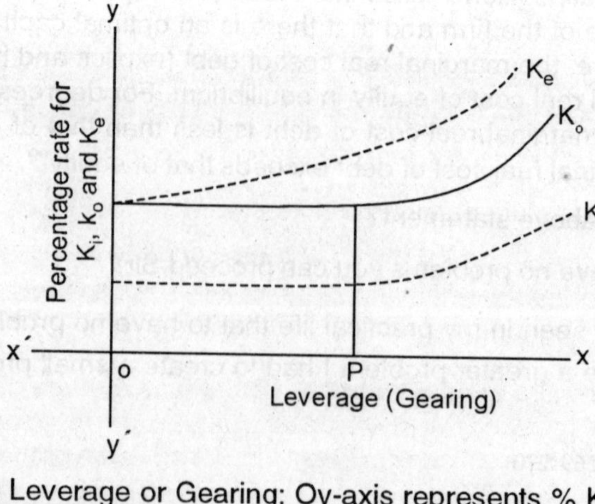

Ox-axis represents Leverage or Gearing; Oy-axis represents % K_i, K_o and K_e. Optimal Capital Structure point is P.

I think, you have understood the diagram.

You see, overall cost of capital of a firm is found to change or behave differently with the change in capital structure. That is to say, increased debt financing (leverage) must have strong effect on the total market value of a firm. This behavioural aspect of reaction has been nicely observed by Ezra Solomon. Accordingly he classified this effect into Three (3) Stages — Stage I, Stage II and stage III

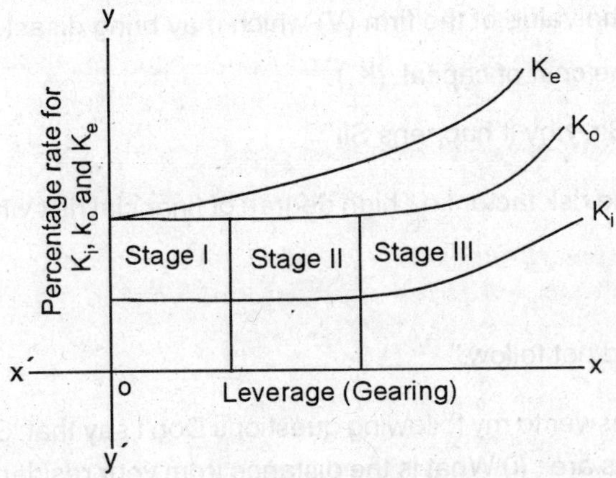

Stage I

In this stage both K_e and K_i remain unchanged. Though K_e remains unchanged, but in actual practice it is found to increase of little value with the increase in debt financing. It is also observed in this stage that the said increase is so slow that cannot reap the benefit of 'cheaper' debt financing. It is to note again that rise in the value of debt financing (K_i) is observed no doubt, but that rise appears to be so unimportant which is not worth considering. The reason for assuming 'not worth considering' is that it is persuaded by logical argument that use of debt financing is a matter of common general financial policy of a firm or company.

In brief, this situation depicts increasing market value (V_o) of business or firm and declining trend of average cost of capital (K_o).

I think you are following my lecture.

Are there any problems? Should I explain it again.

☐ "Sir, we have followed; because your delivering of lecture is so lucid and beautiful that even non-accountant that is to say, man of any discipline can understand. Please Sir proceed for remaining stages."

● Thank you my dear students that you interpreted my lecture beautiful. I feel that as you are beautiful and well behaved my deliberation of lecture appears to be good. I am grateful to you for your patient hearing. Well, I am discussing Stages II and III.

Stage II

There is no denying the fact that when a firm attains a stage of relative amount or intensity of leverage (gearing) any increase in leverage or gearing appears to be insignificant. Therefore, it bears no significant impact on value of the firm as well as cost of capital. So, it may be interpreted that this stage II 'is a range of capital structure' which depicts minimum overall capitalisation rate (K_o) and maximum value of the firm (V_o).

Stage III

After saturated stage of capital leverage, two things are observed due to inflow of debt financing into the capital structure of a firm.

(i) Decrease in the value of the firm (V) which may bring disaster to the firm.

(ii) Increase in the cost of capital. (K_o).

☐ "Excuse me Sir, why it happens Sir".

• You see, it is the risk factor i.e., high degree of financial risk which is responsible for the situations.

Do you follow?

☐ "No Sir, I could not follow."

• Well, please answer to my following questions Don't say that 'Sir I was absent in the last class'. Questions are : (i) What is the distance from your residence to the University? (ii) How do you come to the University, whether by your own car or any cheaper hired car of your friend's? (iii) What time is taken if you drive your own car and what time is taken if you drive a car which is hired at a cheaper rate or your friend's car? Do you find any difference between the two, with regard to **time** and **speed**? Is there any risk factor with regard to the two types of driving? Before answering these questions consider you V (Value to your family and society) K_o may be assumed as **speed** and **time**.

☐ "Thank you Sir! I have got my answer. Because Sir, hired car or car of my friend is considered loan capital which is high levered or high geared capital structure. In case of high levered (high geared) capital structure rate of return on equity capital is high (after payment of fixed interest bearing securities); but risk to the value of the firm increases."

☐ "Excuse me Sir! I have a question."

• What is that?

☐ "Sir, the example you have given is quite enough to understand the concept no doubt, from where it is clear that from behaviour of person(s) one can understand whether a man is following the theme of leverage (gearing)—high lever (high gearing) and low lever (low gearing). Give us some examples, if possible."

• You see, time to time, a few years back, I was requested to deliver lectures to the Officers, Executives, Management Trainees of different industrial organisations. All were non-accountants, i.e., engineers. I explained them the concept of leverage or gearing citing two examples. These examples I gave them to make the concept clear, instant. I told them these examples should not be taken as a representative model applicable in all cases. I told them that if you keep your eye open and observe the behaviour of person(s) you will realize that from the study of financial management you can read the attitude of person(s) like *How to Read the Balance Sheet*.

Examples :

1. I saw two cars (Maruti) were plying on a rough road. One with low speed and other at a speed more than the other. On enquiry it is revealed that low speed car is **personal car** and high speed car is a **hired car** (other factors of comparison being the same). So, low speed car may be treated as low leverage and high speed car may be treated as high leverage.
2. Once I attended a dinner party of a marriage ceremony where I found four persons (Men and Women), sitting on a dining table, were eating Rosgollas, (juicy sweets made of posset and sugar). On observation it was revealed that one man and one woman—two were eating the juicy sweets sitting straight at an angle of 90° carelessly resulting a situation (Situation A) where juicy drops of sweets were falling on their respective dresses—suit in case of man and silken sari in case of woman. The other two persons (one man and one woman) were eating the said juicy sweets carefully, just bending at an angle of 45° (Situation B) to see that the juicy drops of sweets do not fall on their respectives dresses—suit and silken sari.

As soon as they completed their dinner I went to make friendship with them and praised their respective dresses and wanted to know the name of the shop(s) from where they purchased the same. Man and woman under Situation A reported that those dresses belong to others; they collected these only to attend the marriage ceremony. This situation appeared to me like debt financing (K_i).

Man and woman under Situation B reported that those dresses are of their own and they purchased it from a big shop of Kolkata. This situation appears to me as equity financing (K_e).

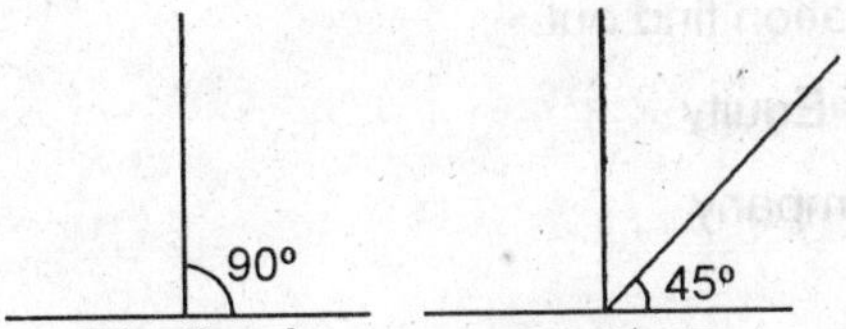

Situation A (Depicting K_i) Situation B (Depicting K_e)

From the above examples you can get an idea of the effects of K_i and K_e please note that many authors used K_i as K_d. So, do not get confused for the same.

Do you follow what I explained.

☐ "Yes Sir, Thank you for giving beautiful and exciting examples".

● Thank you, let me come to the original discussion.

I was talking about two situations, —decrease in the value of the firm and increase in cost of capital. Under the situation cost of equity (K_e) and cost of debt (K_i) are found to increase exceptionally (not usual) thanks to high involvement of financial risk of the firm or company.

You have seen the graphical presentations of different stages of Traditional Approach where K_o (Cost of Capital Curve) appears as 'Saucer shape' which indicates the range where cost of capital (K_o) is minimised. It depicts a situation of optimum range which crosses the boundary of normal range of leverage. An insight into the matter would reveal that here changes in leverage does not bring any worth considering effect on the value (V) and cost of equity (K_e) of a firm or company.

I think, you have followed what I was discussing. Now I would like to give an illustration on this aspect.

Illustration

Information

		Rs.
(i)	Total capital employed (investment)	20,00,000
(ii)	Net operating Income	4,00,000
(iii)	Split of debt financing :	
	5% Debentures	8,00,000
	6% Debentures	12,00,000

(iv) Equity Capitalisation Rate under different contexts :

(a) 10% in case the company does not use debt i.e., the situation of unlevered firm

(b) 11% in case the company uses 5% Debentures as mentioned earlier i.e., the situation of levered firm.

(c) 13% in case the company uses 6% Debentures as mentioned earlier i.e., the situation of levered firm.

From the above information find out.

(A) Market Value of Equity

(B) Value of the Company

(C) Cost of Capital.

Solution

Computation of Value of Equity (S) Value of the Company (V) and Cost of Capital (K_o)

Details	No Debt	5% Debentures Rs. 8,00,000	6% Debentures Rs. 12,00,000
	Rs.	Rs.	Rs.
Net Income	4,00,000	4,00,000	4,00,000
Less : Cost of Debt.	—	40,000	72,000
Earning available to			
Equity Shareholders	4,00,000	3,60,000	3,28,000
Equity Capitalisation Rate	10%	11%	13%
$K_e = \frac{E}{S}$			

Details	No Debt	5% Debentures Rs. 8,00,000	6% Debentures Rs. 12,00,000
	Rs.	Rs.	Rs.
Market Value of Equity	$4,00,000 \times \frac{100}{10}$	$3,60,000 \times \frac{100}{11}$	$3,28,000 \times \frac{100}{13}$
$S = \frac{E}{K_e}$	= 40,00,000	= 32,72,727	= 25,23,077
Market value of debt			
Debentures	—	8,00,000	12,00,000
Market value of company	40,00,000	40,72,727	37,23,077
Cost of capital	$\frac{4,00,000}{40,00,000} \times 100$	$\frac{4,00,000}{40,72,727} \times 100$	$\frac{4,00,000}{37,23,077} \times 100$
$K_o = \frac{O}{V}$	= 10%	= 9.82%	= 10.74%

Comments :

From the above it reveals that when Debentures for Rs. 8,00,000 are inducted to the capital structure the value of the company increases no doubt; but cost of capital decreases. It also indicates the use of more debt (in this case for Rs. 12,00,000) decreases the value of the company but it also increases the cost of capital.

- Is the illustration clear to you?

☐ "Yes Sir, Give us some light on Modigliani-Miller Approach."

- Do you know who was Modigliani.

☐ "No Sir".

- Now I am discussing the Modigliani-Miller Approach (M-M Approach)

4. The Modigliani-Miller Approach

Franco Modigliani was a Nobel laureate and Professor at the Massachusetts Institute of Technology U.S.A. He got Nobel Prize in the year 1985 for economics.

This approach is exactly same with Net Operating Income Approach, if concept of income tax is not taken into consideration. Here income tax is also taken care of at the latter stage.

According to this approach debt-equity mix does not play any significant role to determine total value of the firm. The argument put forward in this regard is that debt financing is cheaper than equity financing; so, as a result of excessive debt financing in the capital structure, capital structure appears to be high gearing. I have said earlier that in case of high geared capital structure the rate of return to equity capital is high and thereby the cost of equity is increased. This increase in cost of equity balances (offset) the benefit of cheaper or low cost of debt financing. Under this situation the overall cost of capital remains unchanged. There is no denying the fact, as emphasised in this theory, that the operating income is a determinant factor of total value of a firm. The theory put forward the view that due to increased financial risk, the cost of debt financing, after certain limit of debt will be higher than cost of equity. That is to say, cost of debt increases "but cost of equity falls thereby again balancing the two costs". It is to note in this context that two firms exactly same in all respect other than their structure of capital, in the opinion of Modigliani and Miller, should have the same market value and cost of capital, thanks to **"Arbitrage Process";** that is to say, there cannot be different market value or cost of capital. If under the said situation, reverse results are found to exist that is to say, appearance of different market value and cost of capital; in that case **"arbitrage"** would lead the situation resulting an entry of 'personal leverage' of the investors in place of corporate leverage; that is to say, substitution of 'personal leverage for corporate leverage'[10] on the part of the investors.

It is important to note in this context that this switch over of investor's decision from corporate leverage to personal leverage will melt the situation down, to bring value of the two firms on a same footing.

I think you are following my lecture. Is there any question?

☐ "Sir, I have one question?"

● What is that?

☐ "Sir, what is Personal Leverage? Please give us some light on it".

● You see, the term 'lever' is engineering or mechanical concept. It indicates a force with mechanical advantage. It is a mechanical device to pull or move a heavy object or weight without putting much physical strength.

In the context of discussion on theory of capital structure it may be considered as influence or strategic advantage. Therefore, 'Personal Leverage' may be defined as personal influence of the investors to choose or buy the equity of those company or companies other than company or companies having lesser value.

I think, it is clear to you. Now I am explaining a few assumptions of The Modigliani-Miller Approach.

Assumptions :

(i) Existence of perfect capital markets.

(ii) Availability of readily cost less information to all investors.

(iii) Non-existence of transaction cost.

(iv) Expectation of reasonable or sensible conduct from investors.

(v) All securities of a firm are divisible without any limit.

(vi) No discrimination or no distinction among the investors with regard to distribution of desired probable monetary worth.

---

[10] Modigliani and Miller, *'Cost of Capital, Corporation Finance and Theory of Investment'*. American Economic Review June, 1958. pp. 270-72.

(vii) Exactly same uniformity of expectation among present and future investors as to estimate of average income of a firm.

(viii) Categorisation of all firms into uniform risk class.

(ix) Distribution of entire profit (100% pay-out) of a firm to the shareholders in a form of dividend.

(x) Non-existence of corporate income tax (subsequently this assumption was removed).

Illustration

X Co. has earning before interest and taxes of Rs. 4,00,000. It expects a return on its investment at a rate of 12.5% you are required to find out the total value of the firm according to the Modigliani Miller theory.

Solution

As per Modigliani Miller theory, the total value of the firm remains constant. It does not change with the change in Capital Structure.

$$\text{Total Value of Firm (V)} = \frac{\text{Earning Before Interest and Taxes (EBIT)}}{\text{Overall Cost of Capital } (K_o)}$$

$$= \frac{\text{Rs. } 4{,}00{,}000}{12.5\%}$$

$$= \text{Rs. } 4{,}00{,}000 \times \frac{100}{12.5}$$

$$= \text{Rs. } 32{,}00{,}000$$

Is there any question please?

☐ "Sir, what is 'Leverage in Capital'?"

● You see, 'lever' is a mechanical device which enables one to raise a heavy weight easily. In business finance the term "leverage' refers to denote the use of loan or borrowed capital. You see, leverage is sometimes termed as 'trading-on equity'. I have explained to you earlier about the meaning of 'trading on equity'. The use of loan capital (borrowed fund + preferred stock) for financing the company is termed as trading on equity. This aspect I discussed earlier. However, both 'leverage' and 'trading on equity' refer to the relationship between the amount of Loan Capital (borrowed capital) and Equity Capital (amount contributed by the owner).

Leverage in Capital

☐ "Sir what is the use of Leverage in Business Finance?"

You see, Leverage is used to measure risk of business operation. There are two types of leverages—

(1) **Operating Leverage** measuring operating risk

(2) **Financial Leverage** measuring financial risk of business firms.

Now I would like to discuss in brief about these two types of leverage and risk.

(1) **Operating Leverage**

Operating leverage refers to the incurring of fixed operating cost in order to intensify the Earning Before Interest and Tax (EBIT). Higher the fixed operating cost, greater will be the operating risk. As we know, we cannot imagine a situation where there is no fixed operating cost, it is not possible to reduce operating leverage, which is a measure of operating risk, to zero.

☐ "Sir, what is operating risk ?"

● We know risk can be defined as the possibility of unfavourable happening. By operating risk we mean the fluctuation of operating income (i.e. EBIT).

The Degree of Operating Leverage (DOL) can be measured by the equation :

$$\text{DOL} = \frac{\text{Contribution}}{\text{Contribution} - \text{Fixed Cost}}$$

$$= \frac{\text{Contribution}}{\text{Operating Profit (EBIT)}}$$

or, alternatively

$$\text{DOL} = \frac{\text{\% Change in Operating Profit}}{\text{\% Change in Sales}}$$

The value of DOL is always greater than 1, because we cannot assume a situation where there is no fixed operating cost.

(2) **Financial Leverage**

Financial leverage refers to the use of borrowed funds or fixed cost funds in the Capital Structure so that a given change in operating income will have an intensifying effect on the Earning Per Share (EPS). Financial Leverage is used to measure financial risk. It is also termed Trading On Equity.

Degree of Financial Leverage (DFL) can be measured by using the following equation :

$$\text{DFL} = \frac{\text{Operating Profit Before Interest \& Tax (EBIT)}}{\text{Operating Profit Before Interest \& Tax (EBIT)} - \text{Interest}}$$

$$\text{DFL} = \frac{\text{EBIT}}{\text{EBIT} - \text{I}}$$

Alternatively,

$$\text{DFL} = \frac{\text{\% change in EPS}}{\text{\% change in EBIT}}$$

Here, also, the value of DFL must be greater than '1'.

☐ "Sir, what is **Combined Leverage** ?"

● Please note that Combined Leverage provides the total risk measure of the firm. It is the 'mix' of Operating Leverage and Financial Leverage. In other words, Combined Leverage is the product of Operating Leverage and Financial Leverage.

Combined Leverage

It will be clear from the following :

Degree of Combined Leverage (DCL) = DOL × DFL

$$= \frac{\text{Contribution}}{\text{EBIT}} \times \frac{\text{EBIT}}{\text{EBIT} - \text{I}}$$

$$= \frac{\text{Contribution}}{\text{EBIT} - \text{I}}$$

$$= \frac{\text{Contribution}}{\text{EBT}}$$

Alternatively, we can calculate DCL as follows :

$$\text{DCL} = \frac{\text{\% change in EBIT}}{\text{\% change in Sales}} \times \frac{\text{\% change in EPS}}{\text{\% change in EBIT}}$$

$$= \frac{\text{\% change in EPS}}{\text{\% change in Sales}}$$

DCL gives the risk profile of the firm. Therefore, if the operating risk is high then financial risk should be kept low and vice versa.

Problem

Calculate the operating leverage, financial leverage and combined leverage from the following data under situation I and II and Financial Plan A & B :

Installed capacity	5,000 units
Actual capacity utilised	75%
(Production & Sales)	
Selling Price	Rs. 50 per unit
Variable Cost	Rs. 25 per unit
Fixed cost :	
under situation I	Rs. 25,000
under situation II	Rs. 30,000

Capital Structure	**Financial Plan**	
	A	B
	Rs.	Rs.
Equity	15,000	20,000
Debt (at 20% interest)	15,000	10,000
	30,000	30,000

[C.A. (F), Adapted]

Solution

Situation 1

	Financial Plan A Rs.	Financial Plan B Rs.
Sales [3,750 × Rs.50]	1,87,500	1,87,500
Less : Variable Cost [3,750 × Rs.25]	93,750	93,750
Contribution	93,750	93,750
Less : Fixed Cost	25,000	25,000
EBIT	68,750	68,750
Less : Interest (20%)	3,000	2,000
EBT	65,750	66,750
Operating Leverage $\left[\frac{\text{Contribution}}{\text{EBIT}}\right]$	$\frac{93,750}{68,750}$ = 1.36	$\frac{93,750}{68,750}$ = 1.36
Financial Leverage $\left[\frac{\text{EBIT}}{\text{EBT}}\right]$	$\frac{68,750}{65,750}$ = 1.045	$\frac{68,750}{66,750}$ = 1.03
Combined Leverage	= 1.36 × 1.045 = 1.42	= 1.36 × 1.03 = 1.40

Situation 2

	Financial Plan A Rs.	Financial Plan B Rs.
Sales [3,750 × Rs. 50]	1,87,500	1,87,500
Less : Variable Cost [3,750 × Rs.25]	93,750	93,750
Contribution	93,750	93,750
Less : Fixed Cost	30,000	30,000
EBIT	63,750	63,750
Less : Interest (20%)	3,000	2,000
EBT	60,750	61,750
Operating Leverage	$\frac{93,750}{63,750}$ = 1.47	$\frac{93,750}{63,750}$ = 1.47
Financial Leverage	$\frac{63,750}{60,750}$ = 1.05	$\frac{63,750}{61,750}$ = 1.032
Combined Leverage	= 1.47 × 1.05 = 1.5435	= 1.47 × 1.032 = 1.517

Problem

Calculate degree of operating leverage and degree of financial leverage under situation A,B and C and financial plans 1, 2 and 3, respectively, from the following information of ABC Ltd.

What are the combinations of operating and financial leverage which give the highest and the least value?

How are these information useful to the financial manager of ABC Ltd. ?

Production and Sales	800 units
Selling Price per unit	Rs. 15
Variable Cost per unit	Rs. 10
Fixed Costs (operating):	
Situation A	Rs. 2,000
Situation B	Rs. 1,000
Situation C	Rs. 3,000

Capital Structure :

	Plan 1	Plan 2	Plan 3
Equity	7,500	5,000	2,500
Debt (12%)	2,500	5,000	7,500
	10,000	10,000	10,000

[C.U., M.Com.]

Solution

Operating Leverage under alternative situation

	Situation A Rs.	Situation B Rs.	Situation C Rs.
Sales [800 × Rs.15]	12,000	12,000	12,000
Less : Variable Cost [800 × Rs.10]	8,000	8,000	8,000
Contribution	4,000	4,000	4,000
Less : Fixed Cost	2,000	1,000	3,000
EBIT	2,000	3,000	1,000
Degree of Operating Leverage $\left(\frac{\text{Contribution}}{\text{EBIT}}\right)$	$\frac{4,000}{2,000}$ = 2	$\frac{4,000}{3,000}$ = 1.33	$\frac{4,000}{1,000}$ = 4

Financial Leverage under alternative financial plan

Situation A	Plan 1 Rs.	Plan 2 Rs.	Plan 3 Rs.
EBIT	2,000	2,000	2,000
Less : Interest	300	600	900
EBT	1,700	1,400	1,100

Degree of Financial Leverage $\left(\frac{EBIT}{EBT}\right)$	$\frac{2,000}{1,700}$ = 1.18	$\frac{2,000}{1,400}$ = 1.43	$\frac{2,000}{1,100}$ = 1.82

Situation B

	Plan 1	2	3
	Rs.	Rs.	Rs.
Contribution	4,000	4,000	4,000
Less : Fixed Cost	1,000	1,000	1,000
EBIT	3,000	3,000	3,000
Less : Interest	300	600	900
EBT	2,700	2,400	2,100
Degree of Financial Leverage $\left(\frac{EBIT}{EBT}\right)$	$\frac{3,000}{2,700}$ = 1.11	$\frac{3,000}{2,400}$ = 1.25	$\frac{3,000}{2,100}$ =1.43

Situation C

	Plan 1	2	3
	Rs.	Rs.	Rs.
EBIT	1,000	1,000	1,000
Less : Interest	300	600	900
EBT	700	400	100
Degree of Financial Leverage $\left(\frac{EBIT}{EBT}\right)$	$\frac{1,000}{700}$ = 1.43	$\frac{1,000}{400}$ = 2.5	$\frac{1,000}{100}$ = 10

Degree of Combined Leverage = Operating Leverage × Financial Leverage

Situations :	Financial Plan 1	2	3
A	2 × 1.18 = 2.36	2 × 1.43 = 2.86	2 × 1.82 = 3.64
B	1.33 × 1.11 = 1.48	1.33 × 1.25 = 1.66	1.33 × 1.43 = 1.9
C	4 × 1.43 = 5.72	4 × 2.5 = 10	4 × 10 = 40

Low operating leverage and high financial leverage is an ideal situation for maximising return to the equity shareholders and hence gives the highest value for the firm. Whereas, the situation where both the leverages are high or low will give least value for the firm.

The information about different combination of situations and financial plans are very useful to the Finance Manager of ABC Ltd. Because he/she can select the combination which is best suited for the firm.

● I hope, you have followed the above discussions. Is there any question please !

☐ "Sir, you have explained in detail about over-capitalisation. But you have not explained anything about the **Management of Fair, Over and Under-Capitalisation**. Sir, please explain these from practical point of view."

● I am really very glad to see that you have taken so much interest in this aspect. I appreciate your curiosity.

Well, before explaining these I would like to give you some introductory ideas about Par Value, Book Value, Real Value and Market Value of shares.

Par Value : It is the face value of the share.

Book Value : It is the proprietary value of share. It is calculated as.

$$\frac{\text{Share Capital} + \text{Reserve and Surplus}}{\text{Number of Equity Shares}}$$

Real Value : It is the capitalised earning value of share. It is found out like below.

$$\frac{\text{Capitalised Value of Earning}}{\text{Number of Equity Shares}}$$

Market Value : It the market value of share. It is found out like below.

$$\frac{\text{High Market Value of Share} + \text{Low Market Value of Shares}}{2}$$

Now please note the test of Fair-Over and Under-Capitalisation in light of the discussions made earlier :

Book Value = Real Value = Fair-Capitalisation.

Book Value > Real Value = Over-Capitalisation.

Book Value < Real Value = Under-Capitalisation.

Or, in other words, above matter can be represented :

Real Value = Book Value = Fair-Capitalisation.

Real Value < Book Value = Over-Capitalisation.

Real Value > Book Value = Under-Capitalisation.

I hope you have followed. Is there any question ?

☐ "Sir, please explain the above concepts with the help of a practical example or problem".

● Yes, I will explain. Please note very carefully.

Problem

From the following information test Fair-Capitalisation, Over-Capitalisation and Under-Capitalisation :

Balance Sheet of Taste Company Limited
as at 31st March 2007

Liabilities and Capital	Amount	Assets and Properties	Amount
	Rs.		Rs.
Share Capital		**Fixed Assets**	
2,000 Equity Shares of		Land and Building	50,000
Rs. 100 each, fully paid	2,00,000	Plant and Machinery	1,00,000
Reserve and Surplus		Furniture & Fittings	50,000
General Reserve	8,000	**Current Assets**	
Profit and Loss A/c	42,000	Stock	10,000
Current Liabilities		Sundry Debtors	1,25,000
Loans and Advances		Cash	15,000
Sundry Liabilities	1,00,000		
	3,50,000		3,50,000

Other Information :

i. During the year market value of share fluctuated in between Rs. 80 to Rs. 130.

ii. The average rate of returns or capitalisation rate is 6%;and the average earning over first four months was Rs. 15,000, second four months was Rs. 9,000 and third four months was Rs. 18,000.

Solution

In this problem it is clear that the average earning of the company fluctuates during the year which has got some far-reaching effect on the different types of capitalisation.

☐ "Sir, how can the capitalised earning value of different periods of the year be calculated"?

● Well, note below the workings :

1st Four Months :

When Capitalisation is Rs. 6 then, Capital Invested Rs. 100

" " " 1 $\frac{100}{6}$

" " " Rs. 15,000 $\frac{100\times \text{Rs. } 15{,}000}{6}$

= Rs. 2,50,000

So the Real Value of Share = $\frac{2{,}50{,}000}{2{,}000}$ = Rs. 125

Similarly we can find out the figure for Real value of Share for the remaining two four months periods :

2nd Four Months = $\frac{100 \times 9,000}{6}$ = Rs. 1,50,000 = Real value $\left[\frac{1,50,000}{2,000}\right]$ = Rs. 75

3rd Four Months = $\frac{100 \times 18,000}{6}$ = Rs. 3,00,000 = Real Value $\left[\frac{3,00,000}{2,000}\right]$ = Rs. 150

Next, let us see the workings of Book Value and Market Value :

Book Value = $\left[\frac{\text{Share Capital Rs. 2,00,000 + Reserve and Surplus Rs. 50,000}}{\text{Number of shares 2,000}}\right]$

= Rs. 125

Average Market Value = $\left[\frac{\text{High Market Price Rs. 130 + Low Market Price Rs. 80}}{2}\right]$

= Rs. 105

☐ "Sir, what is the Par Value of Share?"

● It is the face value of share which, in this problem, is Rs. 100 each.

Now we will have to compare the Book Value of Shares with Real Value of Shares in different periods of the year. This is to find out fair, over, and under-capitalisation. Please note that each four months represents a period. So, here there are three periods.

Periods	Analysis for Test	Indication
I	Book value of shares = Real value of shares Rs. 125 = Rs. 125	Fair-Capitalisation
II	Book value of shares > Real value of shares Rs. 125 > Rs. 75	Over-Capitalisation
III	Book value of shares < Real value of shares Rs. 125 < Rs. 150	Under-Capitalisation

● I think, you have followed the above discussions.

☐ "Yes Sir. Please Sir, workout a few more problems."

● Well, have a book on the board.

Problem

X Co. has net operating income of Rs. 3,60,000 when its investment in assets is Rs. 20,00,000. It can raise debt at 12% rate of interest.

(i) Using the NI Approach and an equity capitalisation rate of 18%, compute the total value of firm and the weighted average cost of capital if the firm has :

(a) No debt, and

(b) Rs. 6,00,000 debt.

(ii) Using the NOI Approach and an overall capitalisation rate of 15%, compute the total value of firm, value of shares and the cost of equity if the firm has :

(a) No debt, and

(b) Rs. 6,00,000 debt.

Assume that taxes do not exist. **[C.U., M.Com.]**

Solution

(i) Computation of Total Value Of The Firm (V) and the Weighted Average Cost of Capital (K_o) under Net Income (NI) Approach.

Particulars	(a) No Debt	(b) Rs. 6,00,000 Debt
	Rs.	Rs.
Net Operating Income/EBIT	3,60,000	3,60,000
Less : Interest on Debt (I)	—	72,000
Earning available to Equity Shareholders/ Equity Earnings (E_e)	3,60,000	2,88,000
Equity Capitalisation Rate (K_e)	18%	18%
Market Value of Equity (S) = $\left[\frac{E_e}{K_e}\right]$	20,00,000	16,00,000
Market Value of Debt (K_i) = $\left[\frac{I}{K_i}\right]$	—	6,00,000
Total Market Value of the firm (V) = [B + S]	20,00,000	22,00,000
Weighted Average Cost of Capital (K_o) $\left[\frac{EBIT}{V}\right]$	18%	16.36%

(ii) Computation of the total value of the Firm (V), Value of Shares (S) and the Cost of Equity (K_e) under Net Operating Income (NOI) Approach.

Particulars	(a) No Debt	(b) Rs. 60,000 Debt
	Rs.	Rs.
EBIT	3,60,000	3,60,000
Overall Capitalisation Rate (K_o)	15%	15%
Total Value of the Firm (V) = $\left[\frac{EBIT}{K_o}\right]$	24,00,000	24,00,000
Less : Market Value of Debt Capital (B)	—	6,00,000
Market Value of Equity Share Capital (S) $\because$ V = B + S	24,00,000	18,00,000
Cost of Equity Capital (K_e) = $\left[\frac{(EBIT - I)}{S}\right]$		
(a) $\frac{(\text{Rs. } 3,60,000 - \text{Nil})}{\text{Rs. } 24,00,000} \times 100$	15%	—
(b) $\frac{(\text{Rs. } 3,60,000 - \text{Rs. } 72,000)}{\text{Rs. } 18,00,000} \times 100$	—	16%

Problem

From the following information relating to a company determine the optimum capital structure :

Debt as % total Capital employed	Before tax Cost of Debt (%)	Cost of Equity (%)
0	12	15
10	12	15
20	12	16
30	13	17
40	15	18
50	16	19
60	18	22
70	21	24

Corporate tax may be taken at 50% **[C.U., M.Com.]**

Solution

The optimum capital structure for the company would be that point where the overall cost of capital (WACC) would be minimum. Therefore, we have to calculate WACC (K_o) for each alternative mix by using the following formula :

$K_o = W_1K_i + W_2K_e$

Where k_o = Overall Cost of Capital or WACC

K_i = Cost of Debt after tax [i.e., cost before tax (1–t)]

K_e = Cost of Equity after tax

W_1 = Proportion of Debt to Capital Employed

W_2 = Proportion of Equity to total Capital Employed

Computation of Weighted Average Cost of Capital (WACC)

K_i (%)	K_e (%)	W_1	$W_2 = (1-W_1)$	W_1K_i (%)	W_2K_e (%)	$W_1K_i + W_2K_e = K_o$(%)
6.0	15.0	0.0	1.0	0.00	15.00	15.00
6.0	15.0	0.1	0.9	0.60	13.50	14.10
6.0	16.0	0.2	0.8	1.20	12.80	14.00
6.5	17.0	0.3	0.7	1.95	11.90	13.85
7.5	18.0	0.4	0.6	3.00	10.80	13.80
8.0	19.0	0.5	0.5	4.00	9.50	13.50
9.0	22.0	0.6	0.4	5.40	8.80	14.20
10.5	24.0	0.7	0.3	7.35	7.20	14.55

It is ascertained from the above computation that the minimum cost of capital 13.50. Thus, the capital structure will be optimum when the debt equity ratio is 1:1.

I hope you have followed the workings of the problem. I shall be happy to hear from you any point which is not clear to you.

☐ "Thank you, Sir, for the trouble you have taken in explaining the above concepts in detail."

• Well, in my next lecture I shall be discussing the concept of Fund Flow.

QUESTIONS

1. What do you understand by 'Over-trading'and 'Under-trading'? What are the symptoms of these? **[C.A. Final]**
2. For a medium-sized manufacturing unit what Capital Structure would you suggest (a) When profit is anticipated to be widely fluctuating? (b) when profit is estimated to be reasonably steady? **[MBA C.U.]**
3. What do you mean by the term 'Over-Capitalisation' and 'Under-Capitalisation'? Expalin their impacts on Business Finance.
4. What do you understand by "Capital Gearing"? Which points you consider in deciding upon Capital Gearing? **[I.C.W.A.]**
5. The Share Capital of KPR Manufacturing Company is as follows :

		Authorised Rs.	Issued and Fully Paid Rs.
6% Preference Shares	(Rs. 20 each)	1,00,000	1,00,000
Ordinary Shares	(Rs. 20 each)	4,50,000	2,50,000

The profits of the Company have been steadily increasing and for the year to 31st December 2006 amounted to Rs. 80,000 before taxation.

For that year, in addition to the dividend on the Preference Shares, a dividend was paid on the ordinary shares of 12 ½%, less tax.

Further expansion of the company's manufacturing activities involves capital expenditure of Rs. 2,50,000, which cannot be financed from existing resources. Consequently, it has been suggested that this amount should be provided in one of two ways:

(i) A Debenture Issue of Rs. 2,50,000 at a rate of 6% per annum, associated with an increase to 7% per annum in the rate of dividend on the Preference Shares to compensate for the prior ranking of the Debenture issue; or

(ii) A "right" issue to the existing ordinary shareholders of four ordinary shares of Rs. 20 each for every five ordinary shares held, at an issue price at Rs. 25 a share.

Your are required :

(a) To prepare statements showing the amount which would have been retained, if any, for ordinary shareholders under each scheme, starting with a profit of

Rs. 80,000 before charging debenture interest and taxation at current rates; and, thereafter, make provision for dividends, including a dividend less tax of 12½% on the ordinary shares.

(b) To calculate the increase in profits required under each scheme to allow the ordinary dividend of 12% to be twice covered, and

(c) To comment on which of the suggested financing would be more attractive to the ordinary shareholders, assuming the trend of profits continues.

[Adapted from C.A. (London) Examination]

6. From the following information relating to a company determine the optimum capital structure :

Debt as percentage of total Capital employed	Before tax Cost of Debt (%)	Cost of Equity (%)
0	10	15
10	10	15
20	10	16
30	11	17
40	12	18
50	14	19
60	15	21
70	18	24

Corporate tax may be taken at 50% **[C.U., M.Com.]**

7. Joy Engineering Company and Pleasure Engineering Company are in the same risk class and are identical in all respects except that Joy Engineering uses debt while Pleasure Engineering does not resort to debt financing.

Joy Engineering has Rs. 18,00,000 debentures carrying coupon rate 10%. Both the firms earns 20% before interest and taxes [EBIT] on their total assets of Rs. 30,00,000. Assume perfect capital markets, rational investors and so on. Corporate Tax rate is 50% and capitalisation rate is 15% for on all equity capital.

You are required to compute the value of both the companies using the NI and NOI Approach. **[C.A. Final, Adapted]**

8. A firm has sales of Rs. 5,00,000, variable cost of Rs. 3,50,000 and fixed cost of Rs. 1,00,000 and debt of Rs. 2,50,000 at 10% rate of interest. What is Combined Leverage? If the firm wants to double its EBIT, how much of a rise in sales would be needed on a percentage basis? **[C.U., B.Com.]**

16

FUNDS FLOW STATEMENT

• Good morning to you all.

□ "Good morning Sir."

• Well, in my last lectures I explained you in detail about the different aspects of financial management, such as sources of capital, components of capital structure, under-capitalisation, over-capitalisation and, finally, capital gearing. Now I would like to explain before you in detail about fund flow statement. I assume that you all know the meaning of fund. So I do not like to discuss anything about the term 'fund'.

□ "Sir, please work out a few practical problems on Fund Flow."

• You see if you do not get any idea about the theoretical aspects of the subject it would be very difficult on your part to work out any practical problem. Now I will explain the whole thing under the following heads — (i) Meaning, (ii) Impact of Fund Flow on Business Finance, (iii) Components of Fund Flow, (iv) A Proforma of Fund Flow and, finally, (v) A few practical problems in the subject. Now I would like to explain the whole thing systematically. You please note carefully.

Meaning

Fund Flow Statement or Flow of Funds is a statement of source and application of funds. Or, in other words, it is a statement of sources and uses of funds. Some writer had described it as 'where got, where gone' statement. It may be stated that Fund Flow Statement records the events of the periods—increase in working capital and decrease or release in working capital.

□ "Sir, who is the writer who explained it by way of 'where got where gone statement?' Besides, what is the meaning of where got, where gone?"

• Professor Anthony in his book ***"Management Accounting—Text and Cases"*** has explained the fund flow by way of 'where got where gone statement.'

Where Got = Sources of Fund.

Where Gone = Applications of Fund.

I think you have understood the concept of 'Got and Gone' Statement.

□ "Sir, what is the impact of fund flow on Business Finance?"

• Do not worry, I will explain everything step by step. The effects of fund flow are

Impact of Funds Flow

indicated by increase and decrease in assets and liabilities or equities. That is to say, increase in equities and decrease in assets will always be represented by increase in assets and decrease in equities or liabilities. Sources of fund, according to some, should always be represented by increase in assets and decrease in equities or liabilities; sources of fund should always be represented by the application of funds. But no such guarantee is there. The difference in the statement indicates either increase or decrease/release in working capital. This can be explained in the following way :

Sources > Application = Increase in Working Capital.

Sources < Application = Decrease/Release in Working Capital.

So, the increase and release/decrease in working capital may be revealed from a statement— 'Statement of Change in Working Capital' which is prepared by comparing the Balance Sheets of different periods. The result can be arrived at by deducting the working capital of the current year from the working capital of the previous year. By working capital I mean current assets minus current liabilities. If the current year's working capital is greater than the previous year's working capital, it indicates increase in working capital. If the current year's working capital is less than the previous year's working capital, it indicates decrease/release in working capital of the business.

Current year's W. C. > Previous year's W. C. = Increase in Working Capital.

Current year's W. C. < Previous year's W. C. = Decrease/Release in Working Capital.

However, increase and decrease or release in working capital can be found out by the effect (+/–) of each transaction on its working capital. To revise again, increase in assets and decrease in liabilities have favourable effect (+) on the working capital. On the other hand, decrease in assets and increase in liabilities have unfavourable or adverse effect (–) on the working capital of the business. So, the balance of the "Statement of Change in Working Capital" should always be equal to the balance of "Funds Flow Statement" or the "Statement of Sources and Uses of Funds".

Now I would like to explain the whole thing as follows :

Source	>	Application	= Increase in Working Capital
Current Year's W. C.	>	Previous Year's W. C.	= Increase in Working Capital
Source	<	Application	= Decrease in Working Capital
Current Year's W. C.	<	Previous Year's W. C.	= Decrease in Working Capital

I think you have understood all these points. If you find any difficulties, please ask. Now I would like to explain about the components of Fund Flow which are :

Sources Sources = Increase in profit; Increase in share capital or Issue of shares, share premium, Issue of Debenture, Sale of assets, Bank loan, Depreciation, Sale of investments etc.

Application = Payment of Dividend, Purchase/Addition of assets. Redemption of *Application* Debentures, Purchase of Investment.

Do you follow what I have discussed so far?

☐ "Sir, why is Depreciation a source of Fund?"

● I am really very glad that you want to go into details of the subject. Definitely I will try to make it clear why depreciation is a source of fund of the business.

It is 'retention' of profit. That is to say, out of the profit of the business you are setting aside a portion of profit for the replacement of the said machine in the year of replacement.

Depreciation as a Source of Fund

Sometimes depreciation expense is added back to net income to determine the fund flow from operation. So, instead of showing two items, such as (i) Profit of the business, and (ii) Depreciation, you can use one term which is known as 'Income from Operations'.

However, you note below the proforma of the "Statement of Change in Working Capital" or "Statement Showing Change in Working Capital" and the "Statement Showing Sources and Application of Funds" or "Statement of Flow of Funds."

Statement showing change in Working Capital for the year ended 20XX

	Previous year Rs.	Current year Rs.	Effects (+) Rs.	Effects (–) Rs.
Current Assets				
Cash in hand				
Debtors				
Inventory				
Bills Receivable				
Total Current Assets				
Current Liabilities				
Trade Creditors				
Bills Payable				
Total Current Liabilities				
Working Capital or Net Current Assets				
Increase/Decrease in W.C.				

Statement of Funds Flow for the year ended ...

Sources	Amount Rs.	Uses/Application	Amount Rs.
Increase in Share Capital		Purchase of Assets	
Sale of Assets		Purchase of Investment	
Depreciation		Payment of Dividend	
Loan from Bank		Other Payments	
Sale of Investments		Increase in Working Capital	
Increase in Profit			
Other Receipts			
Buy-back of Shares			

Statement of Flow of Funds
for the year ended ...

Sources	Amount	Uses/Application	Amount
	Rs.		Rs.
Increase in Share Capital		Purchase of Assets	
Sale of Assets		Purchase of Investment	
Depreciation		Payment of Dividend	
Profit		Other Payments	
Other Receipts etc.			
Decrease in Working Capital			

Now I would explain the fund flow with the help of a exhibit given to the next page which, I think, will be very helpful to understand this concept.

Well, I shall be glad to hear from you any questions which come in your mind.

☐ "Sir, please tell us what are the Advantages of the Funds Flow Statement."

Advantages of Funds Flow Statement

● You see, from the Fund Flow analysis we can find out or make out the basis of the relationship of the funds provided by profitable operation to the requirement of the working capital of the business and to the different policies of the business such as debt retirement, financial and investment policy. By the by, I have forgotten to tell you that the Fund Flow Statement is a top management report, and from this report the management can recommend the ways and means by which the position of the working capital can be improved. That's why Perry Mason in his book ***"Cash Flow Analysis and the Funds Statement***, Accounting Research Study No. 2", published by the American Institute of Certified Public Accountants, had expressed his views that the funds statement shall be treated as a major financial statement and it should be presented in all Annual Reports of the company.

Besides, the funds statements can assist the management in implementing plan and policy as to financing various types of investment. H. G. Guthmann and H. E. Dougall, in their book ***"Corporate Financial Policy"*** (4th edn. Prentice-Hall, 1962), have described the utility of the statement of fund as : '...comparison of these sources and applications of working 'funds' may reveal that current funds have been diverted to permanent uses, or that working capital has been drained out by operating losses or dividends; or the statement may show that inappropriate means of financing have been used. Another purpose of this exhibit is to reveal why funds (working capital) may have increased or decreased while accounting profits moved in an opposite direction. This statement does not, however, reveal shifts among the items making up current assets or current liabilities nor tell whether any loss of working capital has unduly weakened financial position. Only an examination of the balance sheet at the end of the period will show the end effects of these changes and permit ratio analysis to check solvency.'

Now I hope that you have understood the advantages of the fund flow statement. That is to say, how the management is benefitted from this statement. I have already told you the views of Perry Mason in this respect. Do you remember? He suggests that the fund flow statement should be treated as a major financial statement and it should be presented in all annual reports of business. Apprehending the possible misunderstanding arising from, considering the sources of funds as being owner's equity, the Accounting Principles Board of the AICPA, in their Opinion No. 3 (The Statement of Sources and Application of Funds) have expressed the following opinion. This is only to alarm at the misunderstandings

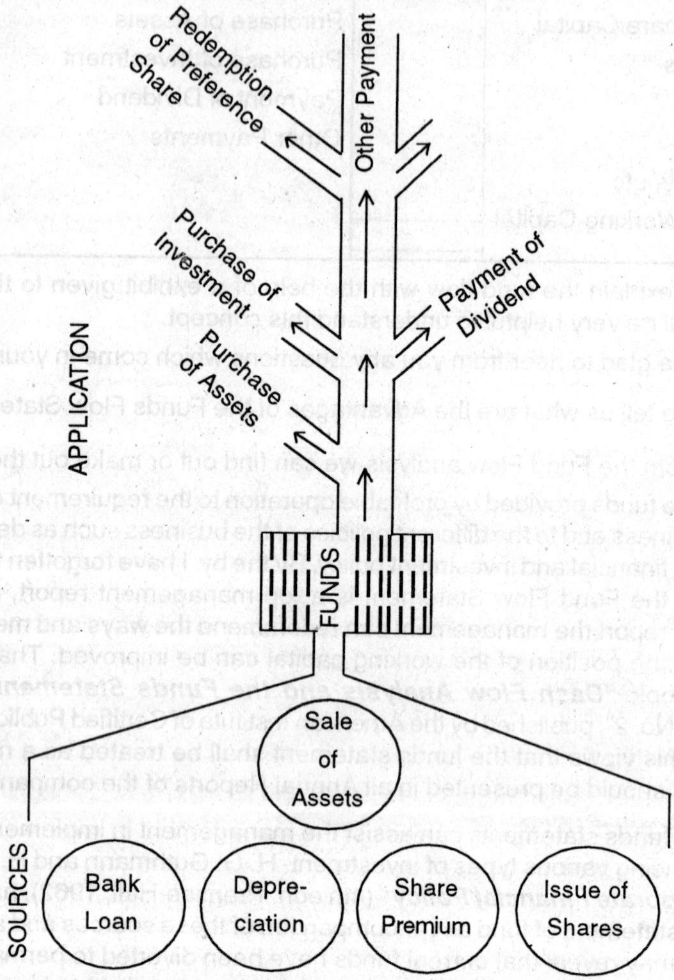

expressed earlier. Accountants have long prepared statements of sources and application of funds for management, which are in fact reports on the flow of funds in individual company. These statements have often been presented in annual reports. The concept of "funds" used in these statements has varied somewhat in practice, and variations in the concept have resulted in variations in the nature of the statements. For example, "funds" has sometimes been interpreted to mean cash or its equivalent; in such cases the resulting statement of source and application of funds is a statement of cash receipts and disbursements. The most common concept of "funds" has, however, been that of working capital, i.e., current assets less current liabilities. If the definition is applied literally, the resulting statement includes only those transactions which affect the current assets or the current liabilities. A broader interpretation identifies "funds" as all financial resources arising from transactions with parties external to the business enterprise.

In recent years a new concept (or more correctly, an old concept with a new name) has become increasingly important in the analysis of the flow of funds. The term "cash flow" has been used to refer to a variety of concepts, but its most common meaning in financial literature—and to a lesser extent in accounting literature—is the same as 'funds derived from operations' in a statement of sources and application of funds. It is often defined as "net income plus depreciation", or "net income before deducting depreciation, depletion, amortisation etc." Synonyms which are sometimes used include "cash earnings", "cash income," and "cash throw-off."

Many of the comments made in connection with "cash flow" analysis leave the reader with the erroneous impression that "cash flow" or "cash earnings" is superior to net income as a measure of a company's real earning power. Calculations of the price/cash flow ratio are sometimes made and presented as a substitute for or supplement to Price/Earnings ratio in evaluating a company's stock. The amount of "cash flow" or the "cash flow per share" has often been presented in the president's letter, the financial review or the statistical section of the annual report of a corporation apart from or in the absence of a complete statement of source and application of funds in the report. In other words, there has been a growing tendency on the part of some people to single out one of the items on the statement of source and application of funds, thereby implying that this figure is more important than other information regarding the flow of funds and often carrying the implication that "net income plus depreciation" is the best measure of the company's profitability. There is a strong implication running through the comment in the literature, including those in the annual reports of some corporations, that the total "cash flow" can be considered available for the payment of dividends.

☐ "Sir, what is Cash Flow Statement? Please give a proforma of the same."

☐ "Sir, you have told us that 'depreciation' is a source of fund. But I have seen in other book that it is not included in the list of the sources of fund. Please give us some reference in the matter."

• You want to know what is Cash Flow Statement. I am really very glad to see your keen interest in the matter. I will take up that matter in my next chapter in detail.

Oh yes, you are speaking about depreciation. I have already pointed it out at the outset of this lecture. You can show it separately or you may include it in the profit of the company. Now you take down a few references where you may get detailed discussions on the issue of depreciation.

(i) W. J. Vatter, ***"Operating Confusion in Accounting"***— Journal of Business, July 1963, University of Chicago.

(ii) Charles J. Gaa, ***"Depreciation—the Good provider?"***—Business Topics, Michigan State University, Winter, 1962.

Now I like to work out a few practical problem. This, I think, will be very helpful to understand all the theoretical discussions make earlier.

☐ 'Please Sir, at first start with an easy problem'.

Problem

From the following Condensed Balance Sheet as at 31st December 2004 and 2005 prepare a Fund Statement :

Assets	**2005**	**2004**
	Rs.	Rs.
Cash in hand	25,000	15,000
Cash at Bank	22,000	15,000
Debtors	1,00,000	1,00,000
Stock	45,000	50,000
Bills Receivable	15,000	20,000
Work-in-Progress	45,000	30,000
Land and Building	30,000	25,000
Plant and Machinery	36,000	25,000
	3,18,000	2,80,000
Liabilities		
Share Capital	2,50,000	2,00,000
Creditors	20,000	35,000
Bills Payable	25,000	35,000
Profit and Loss Account	23,000	10,000
	3,18,000	2,80,000

Now, you see that this is a very easy problem. In this problem and also for the following problems, you will have to prepare two statements—(i) Statement Showing Change in Working Capital, and (ii) Statement Showing Sources and Application of Funds. I think I discussed all these things earlier, in my last lectures. Before preparing all these statements, first of all select the items for current assets and current liabilities. Confusion arises as to a particular item, whether it will be included in the lists of the current liabilities or not. Take for an example, whether provision for taxation will be shown in the lists of the current liabilities or it will be adjusted against the Profit and Loss Account. However, note below the workings.

☐ "Sir, can we show the 'effect of each transaction on its 'working capital' in the Statement showing Change in Working Capital?"

● Oh yes; why not, you can show it along with the 'Statement Showing Change in Working Capital' or you can show it separately under the head of 'Statement Showing the effect of each transaction on the Working Capital.'

Statement Showing Change in Working Capital

Particulars	2004	2005	Effect of each transaction (Favourable) +	Effect of each transaction (Unfavourable) –
Current Assets	Rs.	Rs.		
Cash	15,000	25,000	10,000	
Bank	15,000	22,000	7,000	
Debtors	1,00,000	1,00,000		
Bills Receivables	20,000	15,000		5,000
Stock	50,000	45,000		5,000
Work-in-Progress	30,000	45,000	15,000	
Total Current Assets	2,30,000	2,52,000		

Particulars	2004	2005	Effect of each transaction (Favourable) +	(Unfavourable) –
Current Liabilities	Rs.	Rs.		
Creditors	35,000	20,000	15,000	
Bills Payable	35,000	25,000	10,000	
Total Current Liabilities	70,000	45,000		
Working Capital/Net Current Assets (Total C.A. – Total C.L.)	1,60,000	2,07,000		
Increase in Working Capital or, Increase in Net Current Assets	47,000			47,000
	2,07,000	2,07,000	57,000	57,000

Now you see that the balance of the 'Statement of Effect of Each Transaction' will be equal to the balance of the 'Statement Showing the Change in Working Capital.' The increase in working capital as per the statement of the change in Working Capital is Rs. 47,000.

The increase in working capital as per the Effect of working capital is :

+ 57,000 = (total of plus column)

– 10,000 = (total of minus column)

47,000 = (increase in working capital)

Now I hope that you all have understood all these points. Now, I would like to prepare the "Statement of Sources and Application of Funds." I shall be glad to hear from you any point which you cannot follow. Do you follow what I say?

☐ "Yes Sir."

Statement Showing Sources and Applications of Funds
for the year ended December 2005

Sources	Amount	Application	Amount
	Rs.		Rs.
Issue of shares	50,000	Purchase/Addition of Land	5,000
Increase in profit	13,000	Purchase/Addition of Plant and Machinery	11,000
		Increase in Working Capital	47,000
	63,000		63,000

Do you remember my last lecture where I tried to bring a relationship between sources and application of fund. If the sources are greater than application, it denotes increase in working capital. In this case Source is Rs. 63,000 and Application is Rs. 16,000, so the increase in working capital is Rs. 47,000 which is indicated in the statement.

I shall be glad to hear any problem you face.

☐ "Sir, we have understood the problem and its underlying principles. Please work out a few practical problems."

Problem

Given the following figures :

Assets	**31.12.05** Rs.	**31.12.04** Rs.
Cash	40,000	1,30,000
Debtors	1,60,000	1,00,000
Stock and work-in-progress	2,55,000	2,35,000
Land & Building	10,20,000	5,40,000
Plant and Machinery	35,44,000	28,04,000
Furniture and Fittings	2,10,000	2,10,000
	52,29,000	40,19,000
Liabilities		
Creditors	3,65,000	3,19,000
Provision for Dividend	2,00,000	—
Long term Loan	5,35,000	—
Net Worth		
Equity Capital	40,00,000	36,00,000
Surplus	1,29,000	1,00,000
	52,29,000	40,19,000

Prepare Statement of Sources and Application of Fund during the year. **[I.C.W.A.]**

If you go through this sum you will see that this is a very easy problem. First of all you select figures for current assets and current liabilities. From the assets side you can easily find out items for current assets. Difficulties arise from the liabilities side, particulary from the item of Provision for Dividend, whether you can include it in the list of the current liabilities or you can show it as an item of source of fund. You can apply your judgement on the matter for your convenience. I like to prepare in this sum three statements—Statement Showing the Change in Working Capital; Statement Showing the effect of each transaction on its Working Capital; Statement Showing Sources and Application of Funds.

(A) Statement Showing Change in Working Capital

Current Assets	**2005** Rs.	**2004** Rs.
Cash	40,000	1,30,000
Debtors	1,60,000	1,00,000
Stock and Work-in-Progress	2,55,000	2,35,000
Total Current Assets	4,55,000	4,65,000
Current Liabilities		
Creditors	3,65,000	3,19,000
Total Current Liabilities	3,65,000	3,19,000
Working Capital	90,000	1,46,000
Decrease/Release in Working Capital	56,000	
	1,46,000	1,46,000

(B) Statement showing the effect of each transaction on its Working Capital

	Effect	
	Favourable (+) (Increase in assets and Decrease in liability) Rs.	Unfavourable (–) (Decrease in assets and Increase in liability) Rs.
Cash (From 1,30,000 to 40,000)		90,000
Debtors (From 1,00,000 to 1,60,000)	60,000	
Stock and work-in-progress (From 2,35,000 to 2,55,000)	20,000	
Creditors (From 3,19,000 to 3,65,000)		46000
	+ 80,000	– 1,36,000

Now the net unfavourable effect on the working capital of the business is Rs. 80,000 – Rs. 1,36,000) Rs. 56,000. This unfavourable effect on the working capital indicated decrease or release in working capital of the business.

Now I would like to explain to you the Statement of Funds.

Statement of Sources and Applications of Fund

Sources	Amount Rs.	Application	Amount Rs.
Issue of shares	4,00,000	Purchase of Land and Building	4,80,000
Increase in Surplus	29,000	Purchase/addition of	
Long term Loan	5,35,000	Plant and Machinery	7,40,000
Provision for dividend	2,00,000		
Decrease/Release in Working Capital	56,000		
	12,20,000		12,20,000

Problem

From the following Balance Sheet as at 1.1.05 and the Budgeted Balance Sheet as at 31.12.05 prepare a Funds Flow Statement as estimated.

	1.1.05 Rs.	31.12.05 Rs.
Equity Share Capital	20,00,000	25,00,000
Share Premium	—	1,00,000
Profit on Sale of Leasehold Property	—	25,000
Profit on Redemption of Debenture	—	4,000

	1.1.05 Rs.	31.12.05 Rs.
Profit and Loss A/c—balance b/f	4,50,000	4,50,000
Profit for the year before taxation	—	4,85,000
4% Debentures	5,00,000	4,00,000
Creditors	6,40,000	5,90,000
Reserve for Income-tax	3,10,000	31,200
Proposed Dividend	1,00,000	—
	40,00,000	45,85,200

		1.1.05 Rs.		31.12.05 Rs.
Freehold Property at Cost		14,50,000		18,50,000
Leasehold Property at Cost		50,000		—
Plant and Machinery at cost	18,00,000		21,00,000	
Less: Depreciation	7,20,000	10,80,000	9,30,000	11,70,000
Investments		1,60,000		2,24,000
Work-in-Progress		1,70,000		1,50,000
Stock-in-trade		2,70,000		3,60,000
Debtors		6,20,000		6,47,200
Bank Balance		2,00,000		1,84,000
		40,00,000		45,85,200

During 2005, it is estimated, Plant Costing Rs. 1,30,000 (Depreciation Rs. 90,000) will be sold for Rs. 30,000. This transaction has been allowed for in preparing the estimated Balance Sheet as at 31.12.2005, the loss on sale having been charged against profit for the year. **[Adapted from C.A. Final]**

First of all read the problem several times. Try to go into the depth of the problem. Your first step will be to select items for Current Assets and Current Liabilities which are :

Work-in-Progress, Stock-in-trade, Debtors, Bank Balance, Creditors, Provision for Income tax.

After selection you plot them under suitable heading. Then you find out the result—either increase or decrease/release in Working Capital. I think you remember the items for sources of fund and the items for application of fund.

In this problem sources of funds are :

(i) Profit during the year (ii) Issue of share (increase in share capital) (iii) Premium on issue of share (iv) Sale of Leasehold Property (v) Sale of Plant and Machinery.

Now application of funds in this problem includes :

(i) Payment of Dividend (ii) Purchase of Freehold Property (iii) Redemption of Debenture (iv) Purchase of Plant and Machinery (v) Purchase of Investment etc.

Now you will get some items without any difficulties and some items with difficulties. That is to say, you will have to compute the same with the help of scattered information given in the problem. Now I like to work out the problem. You note below each step of workings. If you cannot understand you can tell me without any hesitation.

Statement Showing Change in Working Capital

	1.1.05	31.12.05
Current Assets	Rs.	Rs.
Work-in-Progress	1,70,000	1,50,000
Stock-in-Trade	2,70,000	3,60,000
Debtors	6,20,000	6,47,200
Bank Balance	2,00,000	1,84,000
	12,60,000	13,41,200
Current Liabilities		
Creditors	6,40,000	5,90,000
Provision for Income Tax	3,10,000	31,200
	9,50,000	6,21,200
Working Capital	3,10,000	7,20,000
Increase in Working Capital	4,10,000	—
	7,20,000	7,20,000

Statement Showing Sources and Applications of Funds

Sources	Amount	Application	Amount
	Rs.		Rs.
Profit during the year	7,95,000	Payment of Dividend	1,00,000
Issue of Share Capital	5,00,000	Purchase of Freehold Property	4,00,000
Premium on Issue of Shares	1,00,000	Redemption of Debenture	96,000
Sale of Leasehold Property	75,000	Purchase of Plant and Machinery	4,30,000
Sale of Plant and Machinery	30,000	Purchase of Investment	64,000
		Increase in Working Capital	4,10,000
	15,00,000		15,00,000

"Sir, why haven't you worked out the effect of (+/–) each transaction on its Working Capital?"

Thank you, I am really very glad that you are observing every step of its working. You can prepare the statement. You can easily work out the same with the help of previous sum. However, note below the detail workings of the figures appearing in the statement of Sources and Application of Funds :

Dr. **Plant and Machinery A/c** *Cr.*

Particulars	Amount	Particulars	Amount
	Rs.		Rs.
To Balance b/d	18,00,000	By Bank—Sales	30,000
" Bank—Purchase	4,30,000	" Depreciation on Machine sold	90,000
		" Profit and Loss A/c—(Loss on Sale of Plant & Machinery (A)	10,000
		" Balance c/d	21,00,000
	22,30,000		22,30,000

Workings of (A) Profit and Loss A/c

(Rs. 18,000 + Rs. 4,30,000) – (Rs. 30,000 + Rs. 90,000 + Rs. 21,000)

= Rs. 10,000. Figure being Loss on Sale of Plant and Machinery.

Dr. **Depreciation on Plant and Machinery A/c** *Cr.*

	Particulars	Amount		Particulars	Amount
		Rs.			Rs.
To	Plant and Machinery	90,000	By	Balance b/d	7,20,000
"	Balance c/d	9,30,000	"	Profit and Loss A/c (B) (Depreciation provided)	3,00,000
		10,20,000			10,20,000

Workings of (B) Profit and Loss A/c

(Rs. 90,000 + Rs. 9,30,000) – Rs. 7,20,000 = Rs. 3,00,000. Figures being the depreciation provided.

Now the figure appearing in (A) and (B), that is to say Loss on Sale of Plant and Machinery and Depreciation provided will come in the Debit side of Profit and Loss A/c which will be prepared to find out the profit during the year.

Dr. **Profit and Loss A/c** *Cr.*

	Particulars	Amount		Particulars	Amount
		Rs.			Rs.
To	Depreciation (B)	3,00,000	By	Balance b/d	4,50,000
"	Loss on Sale of Plant & Machinery (A)	10,000	"	Profit during the year (the balancing figure)	7,95,000
"	Balance c/d (4,50,000 + 4,85,000)	9,35,000			
		12,45,000			12,45,000

Dr. **Leasehold Property A/c** *Cr.*

	Particulars	Amount		Particulars	Amount
		Rs.			Rs.
To	Balance b/d	50,000	By	Bank—Sales	75,000
"	Profit on Sale of Leasehold Property	25,000			
		75,000			75,000

Dr. **Investment A/c** *Cr.*

	Particulars	Amount		Particulars	Amount
		Rs.			Rs.
To	Balance b/d	1,60,000	By	Balance c/d	2,24,000
"	Bank—Purchase	64,000			
		2,24,000			2,24,000

Dr. **Equity Share Capital A/c** Cr.

Particulars	Amount	Particulars	Amount
	Rs.		Rs.
To Balance c/d	25,00,000	By Balance b/d	20,00,000
		" Bank—Issue of Shares	5,00,000
	25,00,000		25,00,000

Dr. **Share Premium A/c** Cr.

Particulars	Amount	Particulars	Amount
	Rs.		Rs.
To Balance c/d	1,00,000	By Bank	1,00,000
	1,00,000		1,00,000

Dr. **Proposed Dividend A/c** Cr.

Particulars	Amount	Particulars	Amount
	Rs.		Rs.
To Bank	1,00,000	By Balance b/d	1,00,000
	1,00,000		1,00,000

Dr. **Freehold Property A/c** Cr.

Particulars	Amount	Particulars	Amount
	Rs.		Rs.
To Balance b/d	14,50,000	By Balance c/d	18,50,000
" Bank—Purchase	4,00,000		
	18,50,000		18,50,000

Dr. **4% Debenture A/c** Cr.

Particulars	Amount	Particulars	Amount
	Rs.		Rs.
To Profit on Redemption of Debenture	4,000	By Balance b/d	5,00,000
" Bank—Redeemed	96,000		
" Balance c/d	4,00,000		
	5,00,000		5,00,000

Dr. **Profit on Sales of Leasehold Property A/c** Cr.

Particulars	Amount	Particulars	Amount
	Rs.		Rs.
To Balance c/d	25,000	By Leasehold Property	25,000
	25,000		25,000

Dr. **Profit on Redemption of Debenture A/c** Cr.

Particulars	Amount	Particulars	Amount
	Rs.		Rs.
To Balance c/d	4,000	By 4% Debenture A/c	4,000
	4,000		4,000

Now I would like to discuss another problem. Before that let me know whether you have followed the previous problem. If not, please tell me if I may be helpful to you in the matter.

☐ "Sir, can I show Depreciation in the list of the sources of the fund?"

● Yes, you can. I have not shown it separately. It does not mean that I have omitted it. I have included it in the figure appearing for the 'profit during the year.' If you want to show it separately the workings will be :

Dr. **Profit and Loss A/c** *Cr.*

	Particulars	Amount		Particulars	Amount
		Rs.			Rs.
To	Loss on Sale of Machinery	10,000	By	Balance b/d	4,50,000
"	Balance c/d (4,50,000 + 4,85,000)	9,35,000	"	Profit during the year	4,95,000
		9,45,000			9,45,000

Profit during the year	Rs. 4,95,000
Depreciation	Rs. 3,00,000
	Rs. 7,95,000

Now you see that the result is same. So you can follow any one of the methods of working.

Any point please?

☐ "Sir, can we prepare horizontal 'Statement Showing the Sources and Application of Funds?"

● I mean, you want to know the following :

Statement Showing the Sources and Application of Funds

	Rs.
Sources	
Profit during the year	***
Issue of Shares	***
Sale of Assets etc.	***
	***
Application	Rs.
Payment of Dividend	***
Purchase of Property	***
Increase in Working Capital	***
	***

Statement of Sources and Applications of Funds

Sources	Amount	Uses Application	Amount
	Rs.		Rs.
Profit during the year	***	Payment of Dividend	***
Issue of Shares	***	Purchase of Property	***
Sale of Assets etc.	***	Increase in Working Capital	***
	***		***

Now you can follow any one of the two methods. Now I will take up another problem.

Here is your problem.

Problem

Following are the summaries of the Balance Sheets of Time and Talent Limited as at 31st December 2004 and 31st December 2005 :

	2004	2005
	Rs.	Rs.
Sundry Creditors	39,500	41,135
Bills Payable	33,780	11,525
Bank Overdraft	59,510	—
Provision for Taxation	40,000	50,000
Reserves	50,000	50,000
Profit and Loss A/c	39,690	41,220
Share Capital	2,00,000	2,60,000
	4,62,480	4,53,880
Cash at Bank	2,500	2,700
Sundry Debtors	85,175	72,625
Sundry Advances	2,315	735
Stock	1,11,040	97,370
Land and Building	1,48,500	1,44,250
Plant and Machinery	1,12,950	1,16,200
Goodwill	—	20,000
	4,62,480	4,53,880

The following additional information is obtained from the General Ledger :

(i) During the year ended 31st December 2005, an interim dividend of Rs. 26,000 was paid.

(ii) The assets of another company were purchased for Rs. 60,000, payable in fully paid shares of the company. The assets consisted of Stock Rs. 21,640, Machinery Rs. 18,360 and Goodwill Rs. 20,000. In addition, sundry purchase of plant were made totalling Rs. 5,650.

(iii) Income-tax paid during the year amounted to Rs. 25,000.

(iv) The net profit for the year before tax was Rs. 62,530.

You are required to prepare a statement showing source and application of funds for the year 2005 and a schedule setting out changes in working capital.

[Adapted from C.A. Final]

Statement/Schedule of Changes in Working Capital

Particulars	2004	2005	(+)	(–)
	Rs.	Rs.	Rs.	Rs.
Current Assets				
Cash	2,500	2,700	200	
Debtors	85,175	72,625		12,550
Advances	2,315	735		1,580
Stock	1,11,040	97,370		13,670
Total Current Assets	2,01,030	1,73,430		
Current Liabilities				
Sundry Creditors	39,500	41,135		1,635
Bills Payable	33,780	11,525	22,255	
Bank Overdraft	59,510	—	59,510	
Total Current Liabilities	1,32,790	52,660		
Working Capital	68,240	1,20,770	81,965	29,435
Increase in Working Capital	52,530	—		52,530
	1,20,770	1,20,770	81,965	81,965

Now you will have to prepare a Statement of Sources and Application of Funds. Before that I would like to clear certain points which will be very helpful to prepare the statement. The Plant and Machinery (Rs. 1,16,200) for the current year (2005) includes new purchase of Plant and Machinery which are Rs. 18,360 for Machinery and Rs. 5,650 for Plant. Now you will have to find out the original amount of Plant and Machinery for the year 2005. The working will be :

Plant and Machinery for 2005 is		Rs. 1,16,200
New purchase during the year :		
Machinery	Rs. 18,360	
Plant	Rs. 5,650	24,010
Original amount of Plant and Machinery for year 2005		= 92,190

From this calculation you can easily find out the sources of fund. Now, Plant and Machinery for 2004 was Rs. 1,12,950 which became, as per our new calculation, Rs. 92,190 in the year 2005.

From Rs. 1,12,950 to Rs. 92,190

Rs. 1,12,950

Rs. 92,190

Rs. 20,760 can be treated either as sale of assets or depreciation. Whatever the case may be, it is a source of fund. However, in this sum I have assumed it as Depreciation which is an item for source of fund.

☐ "Sir, what is the effect of the purchase of stock to the extent of Rs. 21,640?"

• You see, it is included in the stock for the current year which constitutes a part of the working capital of the business.

Now some problems may arise as to finding out the figure for profit for the year which is a source of fund. The profit for the year is Rs. 62,530.

	Rs.
Profit for the Current Year	41,220
Payment of Income-tax	25,000
Interim Dividend	26,000
Increase in Provision for Tax	10,000
	1,02,220
Less : Profit for the last year	39,690
Profit for the year	62,530

☐ "Sir, Please show it in the form of Profit and Loss Appropriation Account."

● Well, Please, note below :

Dr. **Profit and Loss Appropriation A/c** Cr.

Particulars	Amount	Particulars	Amount
	Rs.		Rs.
To Payment of Income-tax	25,000	By Profit for the last year	39,690
" Dividend	26,000	" Profit for the year	62,530
" Provision for Taxation	10,000		
" Net profit	41,220		
	1,02,220		1,02,220

Now I would like to prepare a statement of Source and Application of Funds. Here is the statement.

Statement Showing Sources and Applications of Funds
for the year ended 31st December 2005

Sources		Amount	Application	Amount
	Rs.	Rs.		Rs.
Increase in Share Capital		60,000	Purchase of Machinery (Rs. 18,360 + Rs. 5,650)	24,010
Profit for the year before taxation		62,530	Purchase of Goodwill	20,000
Depreciation :			Payment of Dividend	26,000
Land and Building	4,250		Payment of Income-tax	25,000
Plant and Machinery	20,760	25,010	Increase in Working Capital	52,530
		1,47,540		1,47,540

Problem

The provisional Balance Sheet of C. Ltd. as on 31st December 2005 and the final Balance Sheet of the said Co. as on 31st December 2004 were as follows :

	2005 Rs.	2004 Rs.
Plant and Machinery at cost	25,000	20,000
Deduct : Depreciation	12,000	8,000
	13,000	12,000
Freehold property at cost	1,00,000	—
Trade Investment at cost	—	15,000
Stock and Work-in-Progress	44,000	30,000
Trade Debtors	30,000	20,000
Cash in Hand and at Bank	1,000	15,000
	1,88,000	92,000
Share Capital : Authorised, Issued and fully Paid up 5,000 Ordinary Shares of Rs. 10 each	50,000	50,000
General Reserve—Profit on Sale of Trade Investment	3,000	—
Profit and Loss Account	35,000	15,000
6% Debenture (Secured)	50,000	—
Bank Loan	20,000	—
Trade Creditors	22,000	18,000
Proposed Dividend	—	3,000
Provision for Taxation	8,000	6,000
	1,88,000	92,000

The Directors of the company decide the following adjustments to be made in connection with 1974 accounts.

(i) General Reserve provision of Rs. 2,000 for doubtful debts.

(ii) Reduction in book value of work-in-progress by Rs. 6,000 to conform with a new basis of valuation.

(iii) Transfer of Rs. 5,000 to General Reserve.

(iv) Recommendation of a dividend at the rate of 8% per annum.

You are required to prepare a statement showing the Sources and Application of funds for the calendar year 2005. **[Adapted from C.A. (Eng.) Final]**

This is to some extent a critical problem. In this problem a few additional points are to be incorporated. These are :

(a) Reduction in the book value of work-in-progress by Rs. 6,000. This figure is to be deducted from the figure for stock of 2005. The computation is given below.

(b) General provision for doubtful debts by Rs. 2,000. That means, this figure will be deducted from the figure for Debtors of 2005. The working of it is given below.

(c) Proposed Dividend @ 8% is Rs. 4,000 ($\frac{8}{100} \times 50{,}000$). This figure may be shown in the list of the current liabilities for 2005.

(d) Transfer General Reserve for Rs. 5,000. So, this will be adjusted out of the profit of the current year (2005). That is why you are to find out the figure for profit for the current year.

☐ "Sir, are there any effect of these facts to the profit of the business? If so, please show the effects of these facts on the Profit and Loss Account of the Company."

• Yes, there are effects. I explain them by way of working out the problem.

	Rs.
Now, profit for the year 2005 is (as per information given)	35,000
Profit for the year 2004 is	15,000
Apparent increase in Profit is	20,000

☐ "Sir, is this figure Rs. 20,000 a source of fund?"

Do not worry, first of all try to go deep into the problem. I have already told you that reduction in work in progress, provision for doubtful debts, proposed dividend and transfer of fund to general reserve—all have their effects on the Profit and Loss Account of the company. That is to say, the 'Apparent Increased Profit' for the year (2005) Rs. 20,000 will come down to Rs. 3,000, after deducting Rs. 17,000 which is the total of the adjusting items indicated earlier.

I think you have followed the points. Is there any question which you would like to ask?

☐ "Sir, frankly speaking, I could not follow your lecture in this respect."

• I find no reason why you could not follow. Do you admit that there is an apparent increase in profit for Rs. 20,000?

☐ "Yes Sir".

• If you can really understand this point, I think the following workings will help you to understand the basic principle :

		Rs.
Apparent Increase in Profit, as per our previous conclusion		20,000
Deduct :	Rs.	
Reduction in Work in Progress	6,000	
Provision for Doubtful Debts	2,000	
Proposed Dividend	4,000	
Transfer of General Reserve	5,000	17,000
Actual Profit for the year is		3,000

Now, this actual profit Rs. 3,000 plus General Reserve Rs. 5,000 will be shown separately in the list of the source column or it may be shown in the condensed form, as being 'the Profit of the Year' which is Rs. 8,000.

☐ "Sir, from the information given in the Balance Sheet it is clear that there is a General Reserve for Rs. 3,000 which, I think, is a source of fund. You have said nothing yet about the same. What type of fate are you going to prescribe for it? Please give us some light."

• Your question is very interesting. Please note that this fund is created out of the profit on the sale of investment. Now from the information given in the Balance Sheet, it is clear that there is a sale of investment to the extent of Rs. 15,000 which, I think, as well as you should think, is a source of fund. Now you can show Rs. 15,000 as a source of fund; in that case Rs. 3,000 will be shown separately in the list of the source of fund or it can be merged with the profit of the company, as being non-trading profit. Then the figure for profit will be Rs. 11,000. Or, you can show it as follows :

Sale of Investment is Rs. 18,000 (Rs. 15,000 being actual sale and Rs. 3,000 being profit on sale of investment). In this sum I have taken this idea.

Now I like to work out the problem. If you really face any difficulties, please be frank.

☐ "Sir, we are really very glad and satisfied, having these thorough discussions on the subject. Please Sir, work out the problem."

● You better know that two types of statements are to be prepared :

(i) Statement showing change in Working Capital.

(ii) Statement of Sources and Applications of funds.

Statement Showing Change in Working Capital

	2005 Rs.	2004 Rs.
Current Assets		
Stock and Work-in-Progress (44,000 – 6,000)	38,000	30,000
Sundry Debtors (30,000 – 2,000)	28,000	20,000
Cash and Bank	1,000	15,000
	67,000	65,000
Current Liabilities		
Creditors	22,000	18,000
Provision for Taxation	8,000	6,000
Proposed Dividend	4,000	3,000
	34,000	27,000
Working Capital	33,000	38,000
Release/Decrease in Working Capital	5,000	
	38,000	38,000

Statement Showing Sources and Applications of Funds
for the year ended 31st December 2005

Sources	Amount Rs.	Application	Amount Rs.
Profit for the year including general reserve	8,000	Purchase of Freehold premises	1,00,000
Sale of Investment	18,000	Addition to/Purchase of Plant and Machinery	5,000
Depreciation on Plant & Machinery	4,000		
Issue of Debenture	50,000		
Bank loan	20,000		
Release in Working Capital	5,000		
	1,05,000		1,05,000

Problem

You have been given the following financial statement of Adariji Estates Limited as at 31st December 2004 and 31st December 2005 :

	2005	2004
Assets	Rs.	Rs.
Cash at Bank	45,000	1,30,000
Sundry Debtors	1,40,000	90,700
Stock-in-Trade	1,96,000	1,42,500
Fixed Assets less depreciation	6,00,000	3,60,000
Investments	10,000	11,250
Prepaid Expenses	21,000	14,000
	10,12,000	7,48,450
Liabilities		
Sundry Creditors	2,98,000	2,51,450
Provision for Taxation	1,72,000	65,000
Secured Loan from Bank		87,000
Reserve and Surplus	3,12,000	1,48,000
Share Capital—Ordinary Shares of Rs. 100 each	2,30,000	1,97,000
	10,12,000	7,48,450

The following further information is available from the records :

(i) The position in respect of Reserve and Surplus is as under :

Balance as on 1st January 2005	1,48,000
Net Profit for the year	1,98,500
	3,46,500
Less : Dividend	34,500
	3,12,000

(ii) On 31st December 2005 the accumulated depreciation on fixed assets was Rs. 1,80,000 and on 31st December 2004 Rs. 1,60,000, Machinery costing Rs. 20,000 was one-half depreciated and discarded and written off in 2005. Depreciation for the year 2005 amounted to Rs. 30,000.

(iii) Investment costing Rs. 5,000 were sold during the year 2005 for Rs. 4,800 and Govt. Securities of the face value of Rs. 4,000 were purchased during the year for Rs. 3,750.

You are required to prepare the following :

(a) Statement of Sources and Application of Funds.

(b) Statement showing in detail the item-wise increase or decrease in Net Working Capital. **[C.A. Final]**

Solution

Statement Showing Change in Working Capital

Particulars	2004	2005	Effect (change) +	Effect (change) –
Current Assets	Rs.	Rs.	Rs.	Rs.
Cash at Bank	1,30,000	45,000		85,000
Sundry Debtors	90,700	1,40,000	49,300	
Stock-in-Trade	1,42,500	1,96,000	53,500	
Prepaid Expenses	14,000	21,000	7,000	
	3,77,200	4,02,000		
Current Liabilities				
Sundry Creditors	2,51,450	2,98,000		46,550
Provision for Taxation	65,000	1,72,000		1,07,000
	3,16,450	4,70,000		
Working Capital	60,750	– 68,000		
Decrease in Working Capital			1,28,750	
			2,38,550	2,38,550

☐ "Sir, why the Working Capital for the year 2005 has shown a negative balance for Rs. 68,000?"

● You see, current assets for the year 2005 is less than current liabilities of the said year, that's why it is a negative balance. Decrease in the working capital in this case is Rs. 1,28,750 (Rs. 60,750 + 68,000). If the working capital of the year 2005 were not a negative balance, then the working capital would have been increased by Rs. 7,250. However, this is a tendency which is spoken of here. Now I will prepare the statement of Sources and Applications of Funds for the year 1963.

Statement of Sources and Applications of Funds
for the year ended 2005

Sources	Amount Rs.	Application	Amount Rs.
Profit for the year (A)	2,38,700	Purchase of Fixed Assets (B)	2,80,000
Increase in Share Capital	33,000	Repayment of Loan	87,000
Sale of Investment	4,800	Payment of Dividend	34,500
Decrease/Release in Working Capital	1,28,750	Purchase of Government Securities	3,750
	4,05,250		4,05,250

Workings

	Rs.	Rs.
(A) Net Profit (given)		1,98,500
Add: Depreciation	30,000	
Writing-off discarded Machinery	10,000	
Loss on Sale of Investment	200	40,200
		2,38,700

(B) Value of the fixed assets (2005) before charging depreciation is (Rs. 6,00,000 + Rs. 1,80,000) Rs. 7,80,000 and the value of the fixed assets (2004) before charging depreciation is (Rs. 3,60,000 + Rs. 1,60,000) Rs. 5,20,000.

Now you see, Value of Fixed Assets before charging depreciation as on 31.12.05	Rs. 7,80,000
Value of Fixed Assets before charging depreciation and writing off discarded machine Rs. (7,80,000 + 20,000)	Rs. 8,00,000
Value of Fixed Assets as on 31.12.04 before charging depreciation	Rs. 5,20,000
	Rs. 2,80,000

Now I think, you have followed the workings of this sum. Is there any question?

☐ "Sir, what will be the position if we do not show 'Provision for Taxation' under the head of Current Liabilities?"

• Your question, indeed, is very interesting. Please note below the working of the same :

Statement Showing Change in Working Capital

	2004 Rs.	2005 Rs.
Current Assets		
Cash	1,30,000	45,000
Debtors	90,700	1,40,000
Stock	1,42,500	1,96,000
Prepaid Expenses	14,000	21,000
	3,77,200	4,02,000
Current Liabilities		
Creditors	2,51,450	2,98,000
	2,51,450	2,98,000
Working Capital	1,25,750	1,04,000
Decrease in Working Capital		21,750
	1,25,750	1,25,750

Statement of Sources and Applications of Funds

Sources	Amount	Applications	Amount
	Rs.		Rs.
Share Capital	33,000	Bank Loan	87,000
Profit for the year (A)	4,75,700	Purchase of Fixed Assets, Machinery (C)	4,10,000
Sale of Investment (B)	4,800	Purchase of Investment	3,750
Decrease in Working Capital	21,750	Payment of Dividend	34,500
	5,35,250		5,35,250

Workings

	Rs.
Machinery discarded and written-off in 2005 (Rs. 1,80,000 + Rs. 20,000)	2,00,000
Less: Depreciation	30,000
Actual amount of obsolete machinery	1,70,000

Dr. **(A) Profit and Loss A/c** *Cr.*

	Particulars	Amount		Particulars	Amount
		Rs.			Rs.
To	Taxation	1,07,000	By	Balance b/d	1,48,000
"	Dividend	34,500	"	Profit for the year	4,75,700
"	Loss on Sale of Investment	200			
"	Depreciation (obsolete)	1,70,000			
"	Balance c/d	3,12,000			
		6,23,700			6,23,700

Dr. **(B) Investment A/c** *Cr.*

	Particulars	Amount		Particulars	Amount
		Rs.			Rs.
To	Balance b/d	11,250	By	Bank (Sale)	4,800
"	Purchase	3,750	"	Profit & Loss A/c (Loss)	200
			"	Balance c/d	10,000
		15,000			15,000

Dr. **(C) Fixed Asset A/c** *Cr.*

	Particulars	Amount		Particulars	Amount
		Rs.			Rs.
To	Balance b/d	3,60,000	By	P/L A/c (obsolete)	1,70,000
"	Purchase	4,10,000	"	Balance c/d	6,00,000
		7,70,000			7,70,000

Problem

The following are the summarised Trial Balances of C. Ltd. as on 31st December 2005 and 2006 :

Particulars	2005		2006	
	Dr.	Cr.	Dr.	Cr.
	Rs.	Rs.	Rs.	Rs.
Issued Share Capital		2,00,000		2,00,000
Capital Reserve				47,600
5½% Debentures				50,000
Debenture Discount			1,000	
Freehold at cost	1,12,500			
at Valuation			1,51,000	
Plant and Machinery at cost	2,48,000		2,96,000	
Provision for depreciation of Plant and Machinery		1,14,200		1,25,350
Current Assets	1,86,150		1,78,950	
Current Liabilities		1,09,250		82,550
Balance on Profit and Loss Account from previous years		92,200		1,22,000
Net Profit for the year		29,800		36,850
Dividend paid for the year 2005			20,000	
Provision for doubtful debts		1,200		1,350
Trade Investment at cost			18,750	
	5,46,650	5,46,650	6,65,700	6,65,700

(1) The Capital Reserve on 31st December 2006 represented

(a) the profit on the sale, for cash, of one freehold property, and

(b) the surplus arising on the revaluation of the remaining freeholds.

(2) During the year 2006, machinery costing Rs. 24,000 (accumulated depreciation Rs. 15,500) was sold for Rs. 10,300.

(3) On 1st July 2006, Rs. 50,000 Debentures were issued for cash, at a discount of Rs. 1,500.

(4) the net profit for the year 2006 is arrived at after crediting profit on sale of machinery and after charging debenture interest and writing-off debenture discount Rs. 500.

You are required to prepare Statements showing :

(a) the net increase in Working Capital during the year 2006, and

(b) the Sources and Application of working capital during the year.

Taxation has been and is to be ignored. **[Adapted from C.A. (Eng.) Final]**

Solution

Statement Showing Change in Working Capital

	2005 Rs.	2006 Rs.
Current Assets	1,86,150	1,78,950
	1,86,150	1,78,950
Current Liabilities	1,09,250	82,550
	1,09,250	82,550
Working Capital	76,900	96,400
Increase in Working Capital	19,500	—
	96,400	96,400

Statement of Sources and Applications of Funds

Sources	Rs.	Amount Rs.	Application	Amount Rs.
Profit for the year (A)		35,700	Purchase of Plant and Machinery	72,000
Depreciation (B)		26,650	Purchase of Trade Investment	18,750
Issue of Debenture	50,000		Payment of Dividend	20,000
Less : Discount	1,500	48,500	Increase in Working Capital	19,500
Sale of Freehold Property (C)		9,100		
Sale of Plant and Machinery (D)		10,300		
		1,30,250		1,30,250

Workings

(A) Profit for the year :

	Rs.
Balance as at 31.12.2006	36,850
Add : Provision for doubtful debts	150
Discount on Debenture written-off	500
	37,500
Less : Profit on Sale of Machinery	1,800
	35,700

(B) Depreciation for the year :

Dr. **Provision for Depreciation (Plant and Machinery) A/c** *Cr.*

Particulars	Amount Rs.	Particulars	Amount Rs.
To Transfer of Plant and Machinery	15,500	By Balance b/d	1,14,200
" Balance c/d	1,25,350	" Depreciation	26,650
	1,40,850		1,40,850

(C) Sale of Freehold Property :

Dr.	Freehold Property A/c		Cr.
Particulars	**Amount**	**Particulars**	**Amount**
	Rs.		Rs.
To Balance b/d	1,12,500	By Bank—sale	9,100
" Capitalization	47,600	" Balance c/d	1,51,000
	1,60,100		1,60,100

(D) Sale of Plant and Machinery

Dr.	Plant and Machinery A/c		Cr.
Particulars	**Amount**	**Particulars**	**Amount**
	Rs.		Rs.
To Balance b/d	2,48,000	By Bank—sale	10,300
" Profit on Sale	1,800	" Depreciation	15,500
" Bank (Purchase)	72,000	" Balance c/d	2,96,000
	3,21,800		3,21,800

Problem

The following are the summarised Balance Sheets of NVN Ltd. as on 31st December 2005 and 31st December 2006 :

Balance Sheet

Particulars	2005	2006	Particulars	2005	2006
	Rs.	Rs.		Rs.	Rs.
Issued Share Capital	60,000	75,000	Freehold Plant at cost	33,000	24,000
Share Premium A/c	—	5,000	Plant and Machinery at		
Capital Reserve	—	17,000	cost, Less depreciation	20,800	60,300
(Profit on Sale of			Preliminery Expenses	1,200	600
freehold premises)			Stock	30,350	32,850
Profit and Loss A/c	21,500	21,200	Debtors	20,100	24,750
Trade Creditors	27,200	32,600	Bank	9,250	16,800
Proposed Dividends	6,000	8,500			
	1,14,700	1,59,300		1,14,700	1,59,300

The following is a summary of the Profit and Loss Account for 2006 :

	Rs.		Rs.
Proposed Dividends	8,500	Net Profit for year	8,200
Balance c/f	21,200	Balance from 2005	21,500
	29,700		29,700

No Plant and Machinery was sold during 2006. The net profit Rs. 8,200 is the amount after charging Rs. 7,500 for depreciation of plant and machinery and after writing-off preliminary expenses Rs. 600.

You are required to prepare a statement showing :

(a) The net increase in working capital during 2006.

(b) The sources and applications of funds during that year.

Ignore taxation. **[Adapted from C.I.S., London]**

Well, would you work out the problem?

☐ "Sir, let me see whether I can work out the problem or not. Please give us some guidance".

● You see, no guidance is required. Because you have previously worked out many advanced problems on Funds Flow Statement.

☐ "Sir, I have worked out the problem. Here it is !"

● Thank you, let me see your problem.

Statement Showing Sources and Applications of Funds

Particulars	Sources	Application
	Rs.	Rs.
Profit	8,200	
Add: Depreciation	7,500	
" Preliminary Expenses	600	
	16,300	
Share Capital and Premium	20,000	
Sale of Assets	26,000	
Purchase of Assets	—	47,000
Payment of Dividend	—	8,500
Increase in Working Capital	—	6,800
	62,300	62,300

Statement Showing Movement of Working Capital

		2005		2006
Current Assets		Rs.		Rs.
Stock		30,350		32,850
Debtors		20,100		24,750
Bank		9,250		16,800
		59,700		74,400
Less : **Current Liabilities**				
Creditors	27,200		32,600	
Proposed Dividend	6,000		8,500	
		33,200		41,100
		26,500		33,300
Increase in Working Capital		6,800		
		33,300		33,300

Workings

Freehold Premises A/c

Dr. Particulars	Amount	Particulars	*Cr.* Amount
	Rs.		Rs.
To Balance b/d	33,000	By Cash A/c	26,000
" Capital Reserve	17,000	" Balance c/d	24,000
	50,000		50,000

Plant and Machinery A/c

Dr. Particulars	Amount	Particulars	*Cr.* Amount
	Rs.		Rs.
To Balance b/d	20,800	By Provision for Depreciation	7,500
" Cash	47,000	" Balance c/d	60,300
	67,800		67,800

Proposed Dividend A/c

Dr. Particulars	Amount	Particulars	*Cr.* Amount
	Rs.		Rs.
To Cash A/c	6,000	By Balance b/d	6,000
" Balance c/d	8,500	" P/L Appropriation A/c	8,500
	14,500		14,500

I am really very glad to see that you have completely grasped the subject. Now I would like to work out a few problems; for that I think no prior discussion is required.

☐ "Yes Sir, you just work out the problem. No discussion is required."

Problem

Balance Sheet of A Co. Ltd.
as at 31st December 2006

	2005			2006
Rs.	Rs.		Rs.	Rs.
		Fixed Assets		
	25,000	Goodwill		25,000
1,00,000		Building	1,00,000	
30,000		*Less* : Depreciation	40,000	
	70,000			60,000
2,60,000		Machinery	2,60,000	
		Addition	40,000	
2,60,000			3,00,000	
1,40,000		*Less* : Depreciation	1,92,000	
	1,20,000			1,08,000
	20,000	Investment (Trade) at cost		25,000

2005 Rs.	2005 Rs.		2006 Rs.	2006 Rs.
		Current Assets		
50,000		Stock	70,000	
60,000		Debtors	90,000	
46,000		Cash	60,000	
1,56,000			2,20,000	
		Less : Current Liabilities		
1,00,000		Creditors	1,10,000	
20,000		Current Taxation	24,000	
	36,000	Working Capital		86,000
	2,71,000	Total Resources		3,04,000
		Represented by		
1,00,000		Issued Share Capital	1,00,000	
60,000		Revenue Reserve	70,000	
37,000		Profit & Loss Appropriation :	56,000	
	1,97,000			2,26,000
	24,000	Future Taxation		28,000
	50,000	10% Debenture		50,000
	2,71,000	**Capital Employed**		3,04,000

Revenue Account
for the year 2006

	Rs.	Rs.
Profit & Loss A/c		
Operation profit		1,40,000
Less : Reserve for Bad Debts	8,000	
Depreciation	62,000	
Debenture Interest	5,000	75,000
		65,000
Less : Loss on Sale of Investment (Cost Rs. 10,000)		2,000
		63,000
Adjustment for taxation		29,000
		34,000
Add : Profit & Loss A/c 2005		37,000
		71,000
Less : Revenue Reserve	10,000	
Dividend	5,000	15,000
Balance on 2006		56,000

Required : A Statement of Sources and Applications of Funds.

[Adapted from C.C.S. London]

Solution

Increase in Working Capital :

	Rs.
Working Capital in the year 2006	86,000
Working Capital in the year 2005	36,000
	50,000

Sources :

Profit during the period (Reserve + Profit & Loss A/c)	29,000
* Depreciation	62,000
Future Taxation ‡	4,000
	95,000

Applications :

Addition to Plant & Machinery	40,000
Debenture interest (Appropriation)	5,000
Increase in Working Capital	50,000
	95,000

* Taking depreciation amount as an inflow in funds.

‡ In England such provision is allowed in Income Tax Act. As it has been stated in P/L Appropriation A/c so I have not taken the provision amount in calculating working capital.

Problem

Given the following Statements :

Statement No. 1

Flow of Funds Statement of A.B.C. Co. Ltd.

for the year ended 30 September 2006

Sources	Amount	Application	Amount
	Rs.		Rs.
Profit during the year	8,00,000	Payment of Dividend	
Discount on issue of Debenture	20,000	(Pref. and Ordinary)	6,00,000
Depreciation	1,80,000	Machinery	14,00,000
Loan from Bank	1,00,000	Redemption of Debentures	2,12,000
Sale of Investment	4,00,000	Redemption of Preference	
Release in Working Capital	13,24,000	Shares	6,12,000
	28,24,000		28,24,000

Statement No. 2

Statement Showing Changes in Working Capital

Particulars	30.9.05	30.9.06	(+)	(–)
	Rs.	Rs.	Rs.	Rs.
Current Assets				
Sundry Debtors	10,20,000	11,00,000	80,000	
Stocks	26,00,000	16,00,000		10,00,000
Cash and Bank	2,60,000	1,60,000		1,00,000
	38,80,000	28,60,000		
Current Liabilities				
Sundry Creditors	18,00,000	21,04,000		3,04,000
	18,00,000	21,04,000		
			(+) 80,000	(–) 14,04,000
Working Capital	20,80,000	7,56,000		
Release in Working Capital		13,24,000		(–) 13,24,000
	20,80,000	20,80,000		

Further information

The trend of sales of the company remained more or less constant during the past three years.

From the above information you are requested to report the Managing Director of the company about the weakness as well as financial trend of the company.

Solution

To
The Managing Director
ABC Company Limited
Kolkata

Dear Sir

With reference to the financial information supplied to me, I have the pleasure to give you my opinion regarding the financial trend and weakness of your business :

1. On review the sources and application side of the fund flow statement it is quite apparent that the use of Capital Account (Rs. 14,00,000 for the purpose of plant and machinery, Rs. 2,12,000 for Redemption of Debenture and Rs. 6,12,000 for Redemption of Preference Shares) totalling Rs. 22,24,000 is more than capital receipt Rs. 4,00,000 which represents sale proceeds of investment. This results in release of fund to the extent of Rs. 18,24,000 for use of Capital Account. If preference and equity dividend Rs. 6,00,000 is added to the list, the total release of fund appears to be Rs. 24,24,000. This total release of fund has been compensated to the extent of Rs. 11,00,000 (Rs. 8,00,000 arising from Profit for the year and Rs. 2,00,000 arising from Non-Cash changes viz. Depreciation and Discount on issue of Debentures, and Rs. 1,00,000 from short term Bank Loan). Thus, net release of fund stands at Rs. 13,24,000 which may be considered as a serious reduction in working capital.

2. Purchase of Plant and Machinery for Rs. 14,00,000 seems to me unwise. Because, as there is no proper guarantee that the output from new machinery will find ready market, no such remarkable record for increase of sales figures was found in the last year, it will result in idle investment in capital assets which, instead of showing good result, has accelerated the cause for release of working capital.

3. Apparently the fall in the stock figure to the extent of Rs. 10,00,000 seems large stock turnover which is considered one of the signs of sound financial health. But in actual practice this soundness in financial health was not reflected in Cash and Bank Balances as well as Debtors of the business. So this seems to me that the value of stock were either inflated previously without appropritae market price backing or of uncomfortable condition which results loss on sale.

4. Regarding slight increase in the value of creditors indicated that the purchases of the business remains more or less uniform. Regarding increase in the value of the debtors to the extent of 8% indicates less remarkable improvement in Sales frontier. This increase in the figure may also indicate 'laxity' in credit collection.

5. Regarding fall in the Cash Balance to the extent of Rs. 1,00,000 indicates that total payments during the year is more than, say, to the extent of Rs. 1 lakh than receipts of cash. The flow of cash receipt is checked to the extent of Rs. 80,000, being increase in the value of Debtors. Similarly, increase in. Sundry Creditors results in a check in the payment of cash to the extent of Rs. 3,04,000.

6. However, under the situation, it was not wise to purchase the new Plant and Machinery and the payment of ordinary dividend may be deferred and an arrangement should have been made either to issue new shares or to issue Debentures in the market to avoid the serious reduction in Working Capital Balance.

Thanking you.

Yours faithfully

Mr. Pleasure

20 Sept. 2006 Management Accountant

Kolkata ABC. Co. Ltd.

Problem

The following are the summarised Balance Sheets of A Ltd. as on 31st December :

Liabilities	2005	2006	Assets	2005	2006
	Rs.	Rs.		Rs.	Rs.
Share Capital :					
6% Preference Shares	1,00,000	80,000	Fixed Assets at Cost	2,40,070	2,53,730
Redeemable 2002/07			Depreciation provided	90,020	98,480
at Rs. 22 Ordinary	75,000	1,20,000		1,50,050	1,55,250
Revenue Reserve :			Subsidiary Company		
Plant Replacement	15,000	10,000	Shares at Cost	61,000	76,000
Profit and Loss A/c	1,00,350	1,02,700	Current Assets :		
6½% Debenture	—	40,000	Stock	98,000	1,04,000
Current Liabilities :			Debtors	88,000	85,000
Bank Loan	22,000	—	Cash	11,750	32,000
Creditors and Accruals	84,450	75,550			
Proposed Ordinary					
Dividends	12,000	24,000			
	4,08,800	4,52,250		4,08,800	4,52,250

You ascertain that during 2006 :

(a) Rs. 25,000, part of the unappropriated balance on Profit and Loss Account, was capitalised and applied in paying up on the issued ordinary shares making them fully paid-up.

(b) On 31st December 2006, 20,000 Preference shares were redeemed at the specified premium 10% out of the proceeds of a rights issue of 20,000 new ordinary shares issued for cash at Re. 1.00 per share. The premium was written-off to Profit and Loss Account.

(c) The movement on plant replacement reserve represents a transfer to Profit and Loss Account.

(d) The ordinary dividend proposed for 2005 was paid and in addition an interim dividend on the ordinary shares absorbing Rs. 4,000 was paid. The preference dividend was paid on 31st December in each year.

(e) In regard to fixed assets (i) Rs. 3,000 was added to the book value of a property, following a revaluation, and credited to Profit and Loss Account (ii) Expenditure totalling Rs. 1,700 which, at 31st December 2005, has been carried forward in Suspense (included in "debtors") was transferred to fixed assets (iii) Depreciation of fixed assets of Rs. 13,260 was charged to Profit and Loss Account, and (iv) Plant (Cost Rs. 6,000, depreciation provided Rs. 4,800) was sold for Rs. 250 and the loss written-off to Profit and Loss Account.

(f) The increase in the investment in the subsidiary company represents the cost of additional shares purchased during the year.

You are required to prepare a statement showing the sources and application of funds during the year.

Ignore taxation. **[Adapted from C.A. (Eng.) Final]**

Solution

A Ltd.

Statement Showing Change in Working Capital

	2005	2006
Current Assets	Rs.	Rs.
Stock	98,000	1,04,000
Debtors (88,000 – 1,700)	86,300	85,000
Cash	11,750	32,000
	1,96,050	2,21,000
Current Liabilities		
Creditors and Accruals	84,450	75,550
	1,11,600	1,45,450
Increase in Working Capital	33,850	
	1,45,450	1,45,450

Statement at Sources and Applications of Funds

Sources	Amount	Application	Amount
	Rs.		Rs.
Issue of Shares	20,000	Payment for Redeemable	
Profit for the year (A)	56,300	Preference Shares	22,000
Issue of Debenture	40,000	(20,000 + 10% Premium)	
Depreciation (C)	13,260	Payment for Bank loan	22,000
Sale of Machinery	250	Payment for Dividend (2005)	
		Ordinary	12,000
		Interim	4,000
		Preference	6,000
		Purchase of Fixed Assets (B)	14,960
		Purchase of Investment	15,000
		Increase in Working Capital	33,850
	1,29,810		1,29,810

Workings :

Dr. **(A) Profit and Loss A/c** *Cr.*

Particulars	Amount	Particulars	Amount
	Rs.		Rs.
To Share Capital	25,000	By Balance b/d	1,00,350
" Share Premium on Redeemable Preference Shares (10% on Rs. 20,000)	2,000	" Plant Replacement Reserve	5,000
" Interim Dividend	4,000	" Profit on revaluation of Fixed Assets	3,000
" Proposed Dividend	24,000	" Profit for the year (balancing figure)	56,300
" Preference Dividend (6% on Rs. 1,00,000)	6,000		
" Loss on Sale of Plant	950		
" Balance c/d	1,02,700		
	1,64,650		1,64,650

Dr. **(B) Fixed Assets** *Cr.*

Particulars	Amount	Particulars	Amount
	Rs.		Rs.
To Balance b/d	2,40,070	By Depreciation	4,800
" Debtors	1,700	" Cash (Sale)	250
" Addition	3,000	" Loss on Sale	950
" Bank (Purchase)	14,960	" Balance c/d	2,53,730
	2,59,730		2,59,730

(C)		
Depreciation as per last A/c	90,020	
Less : Depreciation	4,800	
	85,220	
Add : Depreciation provided	13,260	(balancing figure)
Depreciation as per Balance Sheet	98,480	

QUESTIONS

1. What is Funds Flow Statement? Explain its advantages.
2. How is Financial Management benefitted from the underlying philosophy of Funds Flow Analysis?
3. Is Depreciation a Source of Fund? If so, explain it with arguments.
4. The following are the Balance Sheets of Bharat Industries Limited as at 31.12.2005 and as at 31.12.2006.

	2005 Rs.	2006 Rs.
Building and Machinery	1,72,778	2,07,782
Investments	1,17,500	90,000
Stock-in-Trade	83,164	95,438
Sundry Debtors	67,186	65,638
Advances	9,025	9,816
Cash and Bank Balances	40,409	30,337
Unamortised Debenture Account	4,305	2,867
	4,94,367	5,01,878
Share Capital (Face value of Rs. 100 per share)	1,00,000	92,500
Reserve for Contingencies	34,500	63,600
Reserve and Surplus	80,231	80,753
Allowance for Inventory Loss	2,000	8,500
Accumulated Depreciation	99,618	81,633
Allowance for loss on Sundry Debtors Accounts	4,630	3,815
4% Mortgage Debentures	82,000	68,500
Accrued Interest, Taxes etc.	12,307	21,263
Sundry Creditors	79,081	81,314
	4,94,367	5,01,878

The following information concerning the transaction is available :

(1) Net profit for 2006 was shown by the Profit and Loss Statement as Rs. 48,097.

(2) The share capital account as at 31.12.2005 includes 75 Redeemable Preference shares. These were redeemed during the year at Rs. 111 per share. Subsequent to the redemption a 10 percent cash dividend was paid.

(3) Machinery was purchased for Rs. 31, 365 and machinery costing Rs. 32,625 was scrapped. The scrapped machinery had accumulated depreciation of Rs. 29,105 at the date of scrapping. The scrap was sold for Rs. 1,000 which was credited against the profit and loss on scrapping of the asset. The remaining increase in fixed assets resulted from construction of a building.

(4) The debentures mature at the rate of Rs. 5,000 per year. In addition to the redemption of Rs. 5,000 debenture due in 2006, the company purchased and redeemed Rs. 8,500 of the debentures at Rs. 103. Both the premium on redemption and the applicable discounts were charged as expense.

(5) The allowance for inventory loss was created by a charge to expense in each year. It was set up to reduce the inventory value of obsolete items to estimated market value.

(6) A sum of Rs. 11,400 was debited to Reserve for Contingencies Account during the year. It represented the amount of Income-tax liability of an earlier year in dispute.

You are required to prepare a statement showing the sources and application of funds for the year 2006. **[C.A. Final]**

5. From the following Balance Sheets of Alpha Ltd. make out (1) Statement of Change in the Working Capital (2) Funds Flow Statement :

Liabilities	2005	2006	Assets	2005	2006
	Rs.	Rs.		Rs.	Rs.
Equity Share Capital	3,00,000	4,00,000	Goodwill	1,00,000	80,000
8% Redeemable Preference Share	1,50,000	1,00,000	Land & Buildings	2,00,000	1,70,000
			Plant	80,000	2,00,000
Capital Reserve	—	20,000	Investment	20,000	30,000
General Reserve	40,000	50,000	Sundry Debtors	1,40,000	1,70,000
Profit and Loss A/c	30,000	48,000	Stock	77,000	1,09,000
Proposed Dividend	42,000	50,000	Bills Receivable	20,000	30,000
Sundry Creditors	25,000	47,000	Cash in hand	15,000	10,000
Bills Payable	20,000	16,000	Cash at Bank	10,000	8,000
Liability for Expenses	30,000	36,000	Preliminary Expenses	15,000	10,000
Provision for taxation	40,000	50,000			
	6,77,000	8,17,000		6,77,000	8,17,000

Note : (1) A piece of land had been sold out in 2006 and the profit on Sale has been credited to Capital Reserve.

(2) A machine has been sold for Rs. 10,000. The written-down value of the machine was Rs. 12,000. Depreciation of Rs. 10,000 is charged on Plant Account in 2006.

(3) The Investments are trade investments, Rs. 3,000 by way of dividend is received including Rs. 1,000 from pre-acquisition profit which has been credited to Investment Account.

(4) An interim dividend of Rs. 20,000 has been paid in 2006. **[C.A. Final]**

6. The following are the summarised Trial Balances of a Limited Company as at 31st March 2005 and 2006 :

Particulars	2005		2006	
	Dr.	Cr.	Dr.	Cr.
	Rs.	Rs.	Rs.	Rs.
Fixed Assets	23,36,960		24,60,500	
Current Assets	9,60,540		7,91,800	
Debenture Discount	30,000		25,000	
Issued Capital—Equity		15,00,000		15,00,000
Preference		3,00,000		4,00,000
Share Premium Account		30,000		40,000
Debentures		5,00,000		5,00,000
Current Liabilities		6,20,000		4,40,000
Provision for Depreciation		1,80,000		1,95,000
Provision for Doubtful Debts		6,000		5,000
Dividend for 2004-05			1,50,000	
Balance of P/L A/c from Previous year		24,400		1,91,500
Net Profit for the year		1,67,100		1,55,800
	33,27,500	33,27,500	34,27,300	34,27,300

(a) During the year ended 31st March 2006, Machinery costing Rs. 2,00,000 (accumulated provision for depreciation Rs. 60,000) was sold for Rs. 1,50,000.

(b) Rs. 1,00,000 preference share capital was issued during 2005-06 at a premium of Rs. 10,000.

(c) The net profit for 2005-06 has been arrived at after taking credit for the profit on sale of machinery, reduction in the provision for doubtful debts and writing-off the discount on issue of debentures.

You are required to prepare :

(a) A statement showing the net increase in working capital during the year 2005-06, and,

(b) A statement showing the sources of the increase in the working capital and application thereof during the year. **[C.A. Final]**

7. From the following comparative summary and information, prepare a statement of sources and application of funds :

Adams Product Limited
Balance Sheet
as at 31st December

Particulars	2005 Rs.	2006 Rs.
Assets		
Cash and Bank	2,87,800	1,70,650
Sundry Debtors	1,53,030	1,38,760
Inventories	2,87,640	2,35,800
Prepaid Expenses	4,600	3,200
Current Assets	7,33,070	5,48,410
Investments	25,000	1,05,000
Debenture Discount	5,000	6,875
Patents	24,000	30,000
Goodwill	5,000	85,000
Property, Plant and Equipment, less depreciation	4,13,000	4,26,000
	12,05,070	12,01,285
Liabilities		
Sundry Creditors	1,43,000	1,12,000
Dividend Payable	25,000	—
Provision for Taxation	48,000	8,000
(In between dividend payable and Accrued Interest)		
Accrued Interest on Debenture	3,000	3,750
	2,19,000	1,23,750
6% Debentures	1,00,000	1,25,000
Share Capital	5,75,000	5,25,000
Reserves	2,52,000	2,52,000
Surplus	59,070	1,75,535
	12,05,070	12,01,285

Supplemetary Information

(1) Depreciation on Property, Plant and Equipment amounts to Rs, 4,24,000 to 31st December 2005 and to Rs. 4,11,000 to 31st December 2006. Depreciation for the year amounts to Rs. 66,000.

(2) A machine was sold for Rs. 20,000. At the time of sale, the net book value of the machine was Rs. 30,000 (cost Rs. 70,000 and accumulated depreciation Rs. 40,000).

(3) Investments, book cost of which was Rs. 80,000, were sold for Rs. 1,00,000.

(4) During the year 2006, debentures of the face value of Rs. 25,000 were redeemed at a premium of 5 percent.

(5) The surplus as at 31st December, 2006 has been arrived at as under :

	Rs.
Balance as on 31st December 2006	1,75,535
Less : Net Loss for the year after providing for all write-offs	66,465
	1,09,070
Less : Dividend declared	50,000
	59,070

[Adapted from C.A. Final]

17

CASH FLOW STATEMENT

● Good afternoon my dear students.

☐ "Good afternoon Sir."

● Well, I already discussed about the fund flow statement in my last lecture. Now I would like to discuss about the Cash Flow Statement.

☐ "Sir what is Cash Flow Statement ? What is the difference between the Cash Flow Statement and the Fund Flow Statement ?"

● If you can really understand the concept of fund flow, it would not be difficult to understand the concept of cash flow.

You perhaps know that planning may be of two types—(a) Long range planning and (b) Short-range planning. The success of the long range planning depends on how far the short range plannings are tackled. In this respect Funds Flow analysis are needed in a long range planning and 'for more detailed planning over relatively short period of times, a cash flow statement will probably prove to be more valuable. A plan of cash flow will show whether or not a company can expect a sufficient flow of cash from operations to enable it to meet debt payment schedules promptly with enough remaining for additional investment'. If you think a little, you will see that from fund flow analysis we cannot find out how cash, accounts receivable, or inventories are affected. The changes in cash position—increase and decrease—can be found out from a detailed analysis of financial statement.

Funds Flow and Cash Flow Analysis in Profit Planning

The proforma of Cash Flow Statement is given:

Case No. I
B and Co. Limited
Cash Flow Statement for the year ended 31st December

	Rs.	Rs.	Rs.
Bank Overdraft as at 31st Dec. 2003			XXX
Payment during the year			
	XX		
	XX		
	XX	XXX	
Less : Received during the year :			
	XX		
	XX		
	XX	XXX	XXX
Bank Overdraft (increase)			XXX

Case No. II

	Rs.	Rs.	Rs.
Bank Balance as on 1st January 2004			XXX
Received during the year			
Share Capital and Premium	XXX		
Sale of Plant	XXX		
Depreciation Fund	XXX		
Profit for the year	XXX		
	XXX		
Less : Increase in Debtors	XX	XXX	
Paid during the year			
Loan to Subsidiary Company	XXX		
Increase/Purchase in Stock	XXX		
Payment to Creditors	XXX		
Purchase of Property	XXX		
Purchase of Plant	XXX		
Payment of Tax	XXX		
Proposed Dividend	XXX		
Redemption of Debenture	XXX	XXX	XXX
Bank Balance as at 31st December 2004			XXXX

Now with the help of the information given, you are to find out what are the items to be included under the head of Receipts and Payments. Now if Receipt > Payment, then the favourable (surplus) balance will be added with the opening balance of the cash of the year under review. If Receipts < Payment; then the unfavourable (deficit) balance will be deducted from the opening cash balance of the year under review.

I think you have understood the real significance of the cash flow statement. If you want to know anything, please tell me.

☐ "Sir, what is the distinction between the Funds Flow Statement and Cash Flow Statement?"

Difference between Funds Flow and Cash Flow Statement

● I think, you have followed my last lecture where I explained that Fund Flow Statement is appropriate in long range planning and Cash Flow Statement is appropriate for a short range planning. However, ' the primary difference in analysis lies in the relationship drawn between the income statement and current assets and current liabilities on the balance sheet. In cash flow analysis, each item of the revenue and expense is placed on a cash basis by relating it to a particular current assets or current liability classification. This refinement of analysis is not necessary if only the change in the net working capital is to be explained'.

Now I think you have really understood the difference between the two.

☐ "Sir, Please work out a few practical problems in the matter."

● Oh, yes, take down a few problems on the discussion of cash flow statement. This will definitely help you to understand its basic principles.

Problems

From the following condensed Balance sheet of XYZ Co. Ltd. for the years 2005 and 2006, prepare a Cash Flow Statement :

Liabilities		**31-12-05** Rs.		**31-12-06** Rs:
Equity Share Capital				
Share of Rs. 10 each		30,00,000		40,00,000
Share Premium				1,00,000
Profit and Loss A/c				
Balance b/f		10,00,000		10,00,000
Profit for the year				20,00,000
6% Debentures		15,00,000		10,00,000
Profit on Redemption of Debenture				20,000
Sundry Creditors		14,00,000		11,00,000
Provision for Taxation		5,00,000		10,00,000
Proposed Dividend		1,50,000		2,00,000
		75,50,000		1,04,20,000
Assets		**31-12-05** Rs.		**31-12-06** Rs.
Property		20,00,000		25,00,000
Plant and Machinery	40,00,000		45,00,000	
Less: Depreciation	14,00,000	26,00,000	15,00,000	30,00,000
Loan to Subsidiary Co.				1,50,000
Shares in Subsidiary Co.		2,00,000		2,00,000
Stock		14,00,000		15,00,000
Debtors		10,00,000		15,00,000
Bank		3,50,000		15,70,000
		75,50,000		1,04,20,000

Following further information was supplied :

During the year, Plant and Machinery costing Rs. 5,00,000 accumulated depreciation thereon being Rs. 3,00,000 was sold for Rs. 1,00,000. The Loss on Sale being charged to Profit and Loss Account; Taxation for Rs. 6,00,000 for the last year was paid.

Process of Cash Flow

Please go through the problem carefully. Try to understand what is expected from you. In our previous analysis (Funds Flow Analysis) we were concerned with the increase and decrease in working capital. Here we shall be concerned with the increase and decrease in the cash and Bank balance.

☐ "Sir, I cannot follow your lecture."

• I do not find any reason why you cannot follow this particular point. Please note below :

	Rs.
Bank Balance as at 31.12.05	3,50,000
... ...	
... PROCESS	
... ...	
Bank Balance as at 31.12.06	15,70,000

Now how much is to be added to Rs. 3,50,000 to make it Rs. 15,70,000 ? You please tell me.

☐ "Sir, Rs. 12,20,000 is to be added".

• Now you can realise that this Rs.12,20,000 is obtained after thorough examination of the 'PROCESS' indicated earlier.

☐ "How it is possible Sir ?"

Receipts will be higher than your payment. The process so indicated earlier reveals what you have received and what you have paid. If the receipt is higher than the payment, it indicates surplus. If the receipt is less than payment, it indicates deficit. Now this can be explained in the following ways :

Cash Flow and Management Decision

Situation	Result	Decision
Receipt > Payment	Surplus	Add to the Cash-Bank balance of the last year or add to the opening balance.
Receipt < Payment	Deficit	Deduct from the Cash-Bank Balance of the last year.

The working of the sum under review will be :

	Rs.		Rs.
Bank Balance as at 31.12.05			3,50,000
Receipt during the year			
Items	XXX		
	XXX		
	XXX		
	XXX		
Less : Increase			
In Debtors	XXX	45,00,000	
Paid during the year			
Items	XXX		
	XXX		
	XXX		
	XXX	32,80,000	12,20,000
Less : Increase			
In Creditors	XXX		
			15,70,000

Now you will have to find out the items for the receipt or payment from the information supplied to you. Now you can try to follow the workings of the problem given earlier.

Statement Showing the Movement of Funds (Cash/Bank)
for the year ended 31-12-06

		Rs.
Bank Balance as at 31.12.05		3,50,000
Received during the year	Rs.	
Share Capital	10,00,000	
Share Premium	1,00,000	
Sale of Plant and Machinery	1,00,000	
Depreciation	4,00,000 (A)	
Profit for the year	34,00,000 (B)	
	50,00,000	
Less : Increase in Debtors	5,00,000	45,00,000
Paid during the year		
Loan to Subsidiary Company	1,50,000	
Increase in Stock	1,00,000	
Payment to Creditors	3,00,000	
Purchase of Property	5,00,000	
Purchase of Plant and Machinery	10,00,000 (C)	
Payment of Dividend	1,50,000	
Redemption of Debenture	4,80,000 (D)	
Payment for Tax	6,00,000	32,80,000
		12,20,000
Bank Balance as on 31st Dec., 2006		15,70,000

(A) Depreciation Rs. 4,00,000

Dr. **Provision for Depreciation Account** *Cr.*

Particulars	Amount	Particulars	Amount
	Rs.		Rs.
To Plant and Machinery Account	3,00,000	By Balance b/d	14,00,000
Balance c/d	15,00,000	By Plant and Machinery Account (Depreciation for the year)	4,00,000
	18,00,000		18,00,000

(B) Profit for the year Rs. 34,00,000

Profit and Loss Account

Dr. Cr.

Particulars	Amount	Particulars	Amount
	Rs.		Rs.
To Provision for Taxation (X)	11,00,000	By Profit for the year	34,00,000
Plant and Machinery (Provision for the Placement of loss of sale of assets)	1,00,000		
Proposed Dividend	2,00,000		
Balance c/d	20,00,000		
	34,00,000		34,00,000

(C) Purchase of Plant and Machinery Rs. 10,00,000

Plant and Machinery Account

Dr. Cr.

Particulars	Amount	Particulars	Amount
	Rs.		Rs.
To Balance	40,00,000	By Cash (Sales)	1,00,000
" Cash Purchase	10,00,000	,, Provision for Depreciation	3,00,000
		,, Profit and Loss A/c (Loss on Sale of Assets)	1,00,000
		,, Balance	45,00,000
	50,00,000		50,00,000

(X) Provision for Taxation Account

Dr. Cr.

Particulars	Amount	Particulars	Amount
	Rs.		Rs.
To Cash (Payment for Tax)	6,00,000	By Balance	5,00,000
,, Balance	10,00,000	,, Provision for Taxation for the current year (P/L A/c) (X)	11,00,000
	16,00,000		16,00,000

(D) Redemption of Debenture at a profit for Rs. 20,000

Rs. 5,00,000 – Rs. 20,000 = Rs. 4,80,000

Problem

The abridged Profit and Loss Account for the year ended 31st December 2005 and 31st December 2006 and the Balance Sheet as on those dates of B. Ltd. were :

Profit and Loss Account

		2005		2006
	Rs.	Rs.	Rs.	Rs.
Trading Profit		45,000		70,000
Profit on Sale of Investment		—		2,000
		45,000		72,000
Taxation of Profit of the year :				
Income Tax	21,000		33,000	
Profit Tax	6,700		12,000	
		27,700		45,000
		17,300		27,000
Brought Forward				
from the previous year	15,000		17,300	
Income tax over-provided	—		4,000	
in Previous year		15,000		21,300
		32,300		48,300
Proposed Dividend	15,000		15,000	
Transfer to General Reserve	—		10,000	
		15,000		25,000
Balance of Undistributed Profit		17,300		23,300
Fixed Assests				
Land	50,000		60,000	
Addition during the year	10,000	60,000	8,000	68,000
Depreciation		20,000		32,000
		40,000		36,000
Current Assets				
Investments	12,000		—	
Stock at cost	1,78,000		2,00,000	
Debtors	1,30,000		2,18,500	
	3,20,000		4,18,500	
Current Liabilities				
Bank Overdraft	1,15,000		1,40,000	
Trade Creditors	70,000		90,000	
Expenses Creditors	8,000		9,200	
Current Taxation :				
Income Tax	13,000		18,000	
Profit Tax	6,700		12,000	
Proposed Dividend	15,000		15,000	
	2,27,700		2,84,200	
Net Current Assets		92,300		1,34,300
		1,32,300		1,70,300

	Rs.	2005 Rs.	Rs.	2006 Rs.
Ordinary Share Capital		70,000		80,000
General Reserve		25,000		35,000
Profit and Loss Account		17,300		23,300
Future Taxation		20,000		32,000
		1,32,300		1,70,300

For the year ended 31st December 2006, trading purchases totalled Rs. 6,50,000 and Sales Rs. 8,00,000; the trading profit was arrived at after charging depreciation Rs.12,000 and director's remuneration Rs.10,000.

You are required to prepare a summarised Cash Flow Statement of B. Ltd. for the year ended 31.12.06. **[Adapted from C.A. (Eng.) Final]**

Solution

B. Ltd.
Cash Flow Statement
for the year ended 31.12.06

		Rs.		Rs.
Bank Overdraft as at 31.12.05				1,15,000
Paid during the year		Rs.		
Creditor				
	Trade	6,30,000 (A)		
	Expenses	78,800 (B)		
			7,08,800	
Income Tax		12,000 (C)		
Profit Tax		6,700	18,700	
Dividend			15,000	
Director's Remuneration			10,000	
Purchase of Fixed Assets (Rs.68,000 – Rs. 60,000)			8,000	
			7,60,500	
Less : **Received during the year**				
Debtors		7,11,500 (D)		
Sale of Investments (Rs.12,000 + Rs. 2,000 profit)		14,000		
Issue of Share Capital		10,000	7,35,500	
Bank Overdraft (Increase) (Deficit in Cash Position)				25,000
Bank Overdraft as at 31.12.2006				1,40,000

Notes :

	(A) Trade Creditors		Rs.
	Balance 31.12.12005		70,000
Add :	Purchases during the year		6,50,000
			7,20,000
Less :	Balance, 31st December 2006		90,000
	Cash Paid		6,30,000
	(B) Opening Stock (31.12.2005)		1,78,000
Add :	Purchases		6,50,000
			8,28,000
Less :	Closing Stock (31.12.2006)		2,00,000
	Cost of Goods Sold		6,28,000
Add :	Depreciation	12,000	
"	Director's Remuneration	10,000	22,000
	Total Cost of Goods Sold		6,50,000
Add :	Trading Profit (as per question)		70,000
			7,20,000
	Sales		8,00,000
	Expenses		80,000 *

Or, in other words,

Revenue = Cost of Goods Sold + Profit + Expenses

Let Expenses = x

8,00,000 = 6,50,000 + 70,000 + x

8,00,000 = 7,20,000 + x

Or, x = 80,000

Creditors Expenses

	Rs.	
Opening Expenses (2005)	8,000	
Add : Expenses incurred during the year	80,000 *	
	88,000	
Less : Closing Expenses—Creditors (2006)	9,200	
	78,800	PAID

(C) Computation of Income Tax paid

Balance : 1st January 2006 —Current	13,000	
Future	20,000	33,000
Profit and Loss Account —		
Profit for the year (given)	33,000	
Less : Over-provision	4,000	29,000
		62,000

	Rs.	Rs.
Balance: 31st December 2006 —Current	18,000	
Future	32,000	50,000
Income-Tax paid		12,000

(D) Received from Debtors

	Rs.
Opening Debtors (2005)	1,30,000
Add : Sales during the year	8,00,000
	9,30,000
Less : Closing Debtors (2006)	2,18,500
Received from Debtors	7,11,500

I think, you all have followed the problem and its workings. Let me know first of all 'hether you have followed the last lectures or not.

☐ "Yes, Sir."

• I shall be glad to hear from you anything relating to the discussions on cash flow statement.

☐ "Sir, give us another problem so that we can prepare the same without your help."

• I am really very glad to see your confidence in the matter. So, please take down another problem. I would like to take up for discussion a few more problems.

Problem

The summarised Balance Sheets of a company for two successive years are :

	Year 1 Rs.000s	Year 2 Rs.000s
Sources of Funds :		
Ordinary Share Capital	1,760	1,760
Share Premium Account	207	207
Other Capital Reserves	440	440
Revenue Reserves	2,192	2,434
	4,599	4,841
Taxation Equalisation Account	618	622
	5,217	5,463
Employment of Funds :		
Land and Buildings	1,388	1,354
Plant, Equipment and Vehicles	1,243	1,161
	2,631	2,515
Goodwill and Patents	314	341
	2,945	2,856

	Year 1 Rs.000s	Year 2 Rs.000s
Net Current Assets :		
Stocks	2,294	2,287
Debtors	1,879	1,974
Cash and Bank Balances	46	186
	4,219	4,447
Less :		
Creditors	1,069	1,118
Current Taxation	394	358
Bank Overdraft	282	109
Proposed Dividend (gross)	202	255
	1,947	1,840
	2,272	2,607
	5,217	5,463

Notes on the accounts show that :

(1) Depreciation has been charged for Year 2 as follows :

	Rs.
Land and Buildings	35,000
Plant, Machinery and Vehicles	2,40,000
Goodwill and Patents	9,000

(2) Plant sold during year 2 realised Rs. 16,000. It was included at cost in the balance sheet for Year 1 at Rs. 61,000 with depreciation accumulated of Rs. 53,000. The difference between realisation and written-down value was credited to Profit and Loss Account.

(3) The Balance of profit for Year 2 after taxation charge and dividend appropriation has been transferred to Revenue Reserve.

Further enquiries reveal that during Year 2 the company made cash payments for total dividends, including tax thereon amounting to Rs. 3,71,000 and other taxation amounting to Rs. 4,52,000.

You are required to prepare a statement which explains the improvement in the net Cash and Book Balances during Year 2. **[Adapted from C.A. (Eng.) Final]**

Solution

				Rs.
Cash balance on 1st Year				46,000
Receipt during the year		Rs.		
Increase in Reserve		2,42,000		
Taxation Equalisation Reserve		4,000		
Depreciation		2,84,000		
Sale of Plant		8,000		
Sale of Stock		7,000		
		5,45,000		
Less : Increase in Debtors		95,000		
			4,50,000	
Payment during the year				
Purchase of Land and Building		9,000		
Purchase of Plant and Vehicle		1,58,000		
Purchase of Goodwill and Patents		36,000		
Payment of Tax		36,000		
Payment of Overdraft		1,73,000		
		4,12,000		
Less :				
Increase in Creditors	49,000			
Increase in Proposed Dividend	53,000	1,02,000	3,10,000	(+) 1,40,000
Cash Balance on 2nd Year				1,86,000

Problem

A company finds on 1st January, 2006, that it is short of funds with which to implement its programme of expansion. On 1st January 2005 it had a credit balance of Rs. 1,80,000. From the following information prepare a statement for the Board of Directors to show how the overdraft of Rs. 68,750 as at 31st December 2005 has arisen :

Figures as per Balance Sheet as at 31st December

	2004 Rs.	2005 Rs.
Fixed Assets	7,50,000	11,20,000
Stock and Stores	1,90,000	3,30,000
Debtors	3,80,000	3,35,000
Bank Balance	1,80,000 (Cr.)	68,750 (O/D)
Trade Creditors	2,70,000	3,50,000
Share Capital in shares of Rs.10 each	2,50,000	3,00,000
Bills Receivable	87,500	95,000

The profit for the year ended 31st December 2005 before charging depreciation and taxation amounted to Rs. 2,40,000.

The 5,000 shares were issued on 1st January 2005 at a premium of Rs.5 per share. Rs.1,37,500 was paid in March 2005 by way of inoome tax. Dividend was paid as follows :

2004 (final) on the Capital on 31-12-2004 at 10 per cent less tax at 25 per cent.

2005 (interim) 5 per cent free of tax. **[Adapted from C.A. Final]**

Solution

	Rs.	Rs.	Rs.
Cash Balance as on 31st December 2004			1,80,000
Received during the year	Rs.	Rs.	
Profit before Depreciation and Taxation	2,40,000		
Issue of Shares (at a premium of Rs. 5 per share)	75,000		
Received from Debtors	45,000		
	3,60,000		
Less : Increase in Bills receivable	7,500	3,52,500	
Payments during the year			
Purchase of Fixed Assets	3,70,000		
Addition in Stock and Stores	1,40,000		
Payment of Tax	1,37,500		
Payment of Dividends			
Final (2004)	18,750		
Interim	15,000		
	6,81,250		
Less : Increases in Creditors	80,000	6,01,250	
			(–)2,48,750
Bank Overdraft as on 31st December 2005			68,750

☐ "Sir, Please give us proforma of Cash Flow Statement (Both Direct and Indirect Method) as per **Accounting Standard (AS)-3** and please work out a few problems on it."

● Well, note here.

CASH FLOW STATEMENT AS-3

Cash Flow Statement (Direct Method)

1. Cash flows from operating activities			
Collection from customers		***	
Less : Cash paid to suppliers	***		
Cash paid to employees	***		
Payment for other operating expenses		***	
	***		
Cash generated from operation		***	
Less : Income taxes paid		***	
Cash flow before extraordinary item		***	
Add : Extraordinary receipts e.g. earthquake disaster settlement		***	
Net cash from operation activities			***
2. Cash flows from investing activities			
Sale of fixed assets	***		
Sale of securities that are not cash equivalents	***		
Interest Collected		***	
Dividend Collected		***	
Less : Purchase of fixed assets	***	***.	
Purchase of securities that are not cash equivalents		***	
Giving loan	***		
	***		
Net Cash form investing activities			***
3. Cash flows from financing activities			
Proceeds from issuance of share capital		***	
Proceeds from long-term borrowing		***	
		***	
Less : Repayment of amount borrowed	***		
Redemption of preference shares	***		
Buy-back of equity shares	***		
Payment of interest	***		
Payment of dividend	***		
		***	
			***
Net increase/Decrease in cash and cash equivalents			***
Add: Cash and cash equivalents to beginning of period			***
Cash and cash equivalent at end of the period			***

CASH FLOW STATEMENT AS-3

Cash Flow Statement (Indirect Method)

1. Cash flows from operating activities			
Operating Profit		***	
(To be found out by opening Adjusted P/L A/c)			
Add : Decrease in Current Assets	***		
(Other than cash & cash equivalents)			
Increase in Current Liabilities	***		
	***		
	***		
Less : Increase in Current Assets	***		
(Other than cash & cash equivalents)			
Decrease in Current Liabilities	***		
Cash generated from operations		***	
Income taxes paid		***	
Cash Flow before extraordinary item		***	
Add : Extraordinary receipts e.g., earthquake disaster settlement		***	
Net Cash from operating activities			***
		***	
2. Cash flows from investing activities			
(Same as discussed under direct method)			***
3. Cash flows from financing activities			***
(Same as discussed under direct method)			
Net increase/(decrease) in cash and cash equivalents			***
Add : Cash and cash equivalents at beginning of period			***
Cash and cash equivalents at end period			

Problem

From the following Balance Sheet and information prepare Cash Flow Statement of Ryan Ltd. for the year ended 31st March 2003 :

Liabilities	31.03.2004 Rs.	31.03.2003 Rs.
Equity Share Capital	6,00,000	5,00,000
10% Redeemable Preference Capital	—	2,00,000
Capital Redemption Reserve	1,00,000	—
Capital Reserve	1,00,000	—
General Reserve	1,00,000	2,50,000
Profit and Loss Account	70,000	50,000
9% Debentures	2,00,000	—
Sundry Creditors	95,000	80,000
Bills Payable	20,000	30,000
Liabilities for Expenses	30,000	20,000
Provision for Taxation	95,000	60,000
Proposed Dividend	90,000	60,000
	15,00,000	12,50,000

Assets	31.03.2004	31.03.2003
	Rs.	Rs.
Land and Building	1,50,000	2,00,000
Plant and Machinery	7,65,000	5,00,000
Investments	50,000	80,000
Inventory	95,000	90,000
Bills Receivable	65,000	70,000
Sundry Debtors	1,75,000	1,30,000
Cash and Bank	65,000	90,000
Preliminary Expenses	10,000	25,000
Voluntary Separation Payments	1,25,000	65,000
	15,00,000	12,50,000

Additional Information :

i. A piece of land has been sold out for Rs.1,50,000 (Cost Rs.1,20,000) and the balance land was revalued. Capital Reserve consisted of profit or sale and profit on revaluation.

ii. On 1st April 2003 a plant was sold for Rs.90,000 (original cost Rs.70,000 and WDV. Rs.50,000) and debentures worth Rs. 1 lakh was issued at par, as part consideration for plant worth Rs. 4.5 lakhs acquired.

iii. Part of the investments (Cost Rs. 50,000) was sold for Rs. 70,000.

iv. Pre-acquisition dividend received Rs. 5,000 was adjusted against cost of investment.

v. Directors have proposed 15% dividend for the current year.

vi. Voluntary separation cost of Rs. 50,000 was adjusted against General Reserve.

vii. Income-Tax liability for the current year was estimated at Rs. 1,35,000.

viii. Depreciation @15% has been written-off from plant account but no depreciation has been charged on Land and Building. **[C.A.P.E. II]**

Solution

Cash Flow Statement of Ryan Ltd.
for the year ended 31.03.2004

Cash flows from operating activities:	**Rs.**	**Rs.**	**Rs.**
Profit before taxation		2,45,000	
Add : **Non-cash, non-operating items debited to P/L A/c :**			
Depreciation	1,35,000		
Interest on Debenture (2,00,000 × 9% × ½)	9,000		
Preliminary Expenses	15,000		
		1,59,000	
		4,04,000	

Less : **Non-operating items Credited to P/L A/c :**			
Profit on Sale of Plant	40,000		
Profit on Sale of Investment	20,000	60,000	
Operating Profit before Working Capital Adjustment :		3,44,000	
Add : **Decrease in Current Assets or Increase in Current Liabilities**			
Decrease in Bills Receivable	5,000		
Increase in Sundry Creditors	15,000		
Increase in Liabilities for Expenses	10,000	30,000	
		3,74,000	
Less : **Increase in Current Assets or Decrease in Current Liabilities**			
Inventory	5,000		
Sundry Debtors	45,000		
Bills Payable	10,000	60,000	
Operating Cash Inflow before Income Tax Paid		3,14,000	
Income Tax Paid		1,00,000	
Operating Cash Flow before extraordinary items :		2,14,000	
Less : Voluntary Separation payments		1,10,000	
Cash from Operating Activities :			1,04,000
Cash Flows from Investing Activities			
Inflows: Sale of Land	1,50,000		
Sale of Plant	90,000		
Sale of Investment	70,000		
Dividend received	5,000	3,15,000	
Outflows :			
Purchase of Plant	3,50,000		
Purchase of Investment	25,000	3,75,000	
Net Cash used in Investing Activities			(–) 60,000
Cash Flows from Financing Activities			
Inflows: Issue of Equity Shares	1,00,000		
Issue of Debentures	1,00,000	2,00,000	
Outflows: Redemption of Preference Share	2,00,000		
Dividend paid	60,000		
Interest paid on Debenture	9,000	2,69,000	
Net Cash used in Financing Activities			(–) 69,000
Changes in Cash and Cash equivalent during the period			(–) 25,000
Opening Cash and Cash equivalent			90,000
Closing Cash and Cash equivalent			65,000

Working Notes

(1)

Dr. **Adjusted P/L A/c** *Cr.*

	Particulars	Amount		Particulars	Amount
		Rs.			Rs.
To	Provision for Taxation A/c	1,35,000	By	Balance b/d	50,000
"	Proposed Dividend A/c	90,000	"	Profit before Taxation (balancing figure)	2,45,000
"	Balance c/d	70,000			
		2,95,000			2,95,000

(2)

Dr. **Provision for Taxation Account** *Cr.*

	Particulars	Amount		Particulars	Amount
		Rs.			Rs.
To	Bank A/c (balancing figure)	1,00,000	By	Balance b/d	60,000
"	Balance c/d	95,000	"	Adjusted P/L A/c	1,35,000
		1,95,000			1,95,000

(3)

Dr. **Proposed Dividend A/c** *Cr.*

	Particulars	Amount		Particulars	Amount
		Rs.			Rs.
To	Bank A/c	60,000	By	Balance b/d	60,000
"	Balance c/d	90,000	"	Adjusted P/L A/c (balancing figure)	90,000
		1,50,000			1,50,000

(4)

Dr. **Land and Building A/c** *Cr.*

	Particulars	Amount		Particulars	Amount
		Rs.			Rs.
To	Balance b/d	2,00,000	By	Cash A/c	1,50,000
"	Capital Reserve A/c (Profit on Sale)	30,000			
"	Capital Reserve A/c (Profit on revaluation)	70,000	"	Balance c/d	1,50,000
		3,00,000			3,00,000

(5)

Dr. **Plant and Machinery A/c** *Cr.*

	Particulars	Amount		Particulars	Amount
		Rs.			Rs.
To	Balance b/d	5,00,000	By	Bank A/c	90,000
"	Profit and Loss A/c	40,000	"	Depreciation A/c	1,35,000
"	Debenture A/c	1,00,000			
"	Bank A/c	3,50,000	"	Balance c/d	7,65,000
		9,90,000			9,90,000

(6)

Dr. **Investment A/c** *Cr.*

	Particulars	Amount		Particulars	Amount
		Rs.			Rs.
To	Balance b/d	80,000	By	Bank A/c	70,000
"	Profit and Loss A/c	20,000	"	Dividend A/c	5,000
"	Bank A/c	25,000		(Pre-acquisition dividend	
	(balancing figure)			adjusted)	
			"	Balance c/d	50,000
		1,25,000			1,25,000

(7)

Dr. **Capital Reserve A/c** *Cr.*

	Particulars	Amount		Particulars	Amount
		Rs.			Rs.
			By	Balance b/d	000
			"	Profit on Sale of Land	30,000
			"	Profit on Revaluation of Land and Building	70,000
To	Balance c/d	1,00,000			
		1,00,000			1,00,000

(8)

Dr. **General Reserve A/c** *Cr.*

	Particulars	Amount		Particulars	Amount
		Rs.			Rs.
To	Capital Redemption Reserve	1,00,000	By	Balance b/d	2,50,000
"	Voluntary Separation Cost	50,000			
"	Balance c/d	1,00,000			
		2,50,000			2,50,000

(9)

Dr. Voluntary Separation Payments A/c Cr.

	Particulars	Amount		Particulars	Amount
		Rs.			Rs.
To	Balance b/d	65,000	By	General Reserve A/c	50,000
"	Bank A/c (balancing figure)	1,10,000	"	Balance c/d	1,25,000
		1,75,000			1,75,000

Cash Flow Statement [As per AS3 (R)]

Problem

You are presented with the Balance Sheet of X Ltd and following further information :

Balance Sheet

as on 31.3.2003 and 31.3.2004

Assets	2004 (Rs.)	2003 (Rs.)
Cash and Bank Balance	4,00,000	6,00,000
Debtors	8,00,000	6,50,000
Inventory	14,00,000	15,50,000
Prepaid Expenses	65,000	80,000
Land	15,00,000	18,00,000
Equipment	20,00,000	16,00,000
Building	25,00,000	25,00,000
	86,65,000	87,80,000
Liabilities		
Provision for Taxation	1,25,000	1,00,000
Provision for Depreciation		
on Equipment	3,00,000	2,00,000
on Building	6,00,000	5,00,000
Trade Creditors	6,50,000	8,00,000
10% Debentures	20,50,000	22,00,000
Profit & Loss A/c	6,40,000	9,80,000
Equity Shares of Rs.10 each, fully paid	43,00,000	40,00,000
	86,65,000	87,80,000

Additional information

(i) Land was sold for cash at a profit of Rs. 50,000.

(ii) Dividends paid during the year Rs. 4,50,000.

(iii) Equipment costing Rs.6,00,000 was purchased. In addition, equipment costing Rs.2,00,000 (W.D.V. Rs.40,000) was sold for Rs.30,000.

(iv) Debentures were converted into Equity Shares of similar amount on 1.4.2003.

(v) Amount transferred to provision for taxation during the year Rs. 1,60,000.

You are required to prepare a cash flow statement for the year ended 31.3.2004 as per AS3. **[C.U., M.Com.]**

Solution

Cash Flow Statement
for the year ended 31.03.2004

			Rs.
	Opening Cash and Bank Balance		6,00,000
Add :	**Receipt during the year**		
	Cash from Operating Activities (W.N. 12)		5,25,000
			11,25,000
Less :	**Payment during the year :**		
	Cash Outflow from Investing Activities (W.N.13)	2,20,000	
	Cash Outflow from Financing Activities (W.N.14)	5,05,000	
			7,25,000
	Closing Cash and Bank Balance		4,00,000
	Non-Cash Investing and Financing Activities		
	Conversion of Debenture into Equity Share		1,50,000

Working Notes

(1)

Dr. **Profit and Loss Adjustment A/c** *Cr.*

	Particulars	Amount		Particulars	Amount
		Rs.			Rs.
To	Dividend A/c	4,50,000	By	Balance b/d	9,80,000
"	Sale of Equipment A/c (Loss on Sale)	10,000	"	Land A/c (Profit on Sale)	50,000
"	Provision for Taxation A/c	1,60,000	"	Net Operating Profit (balancing figure)	4,35,000
"	Interest on Debenture	2,05,000			
"	Balance c/d	6,40,000			
		14,65,000			14,65,000

(2)

Dr. **Land A/c** *Cr.*

	Particulars	Amount		Particulars	Amount
		Rs.			Rs.
To	Balance b/d	18,00,000	By	Bank A/c (balancing figure)	3,50,000
"	Profit and Loss Adjustment A/c (Profit on Sale)	50,000	"	Balance c/d	15,00,000
		18,50,000			18,50,000

(3)

Equipment A/c

Dr. Particulars	Amount	Cr. Particulars	Amount
	Rs.		Rs.
To Balance b/d	16,00,000	By Sale of Equipment A/c	2,00,000
" Bank A/c	6,00,000	" Balance c/d	20,00,000
	22,00,000		22,00,000

(4)

Sale of Equipment A/c

Dr. Particulars	Amount	Cr. Particulars	Amount
	Rs.		Rs.
To Equipment A/c	2,00,000	By Provision for depreciation on Equipment A/c	1,60,000
		" Bank A/c	30,000
		" Profit and Loss Adj. A/c (Loss on Sale)	10,000
	2,00,000		2,00,000

(5)

Provision for Depreciation on Equipment A/c

Dr. Particulars	Amount	Cr. Particulars	Amount
	Rs.		Rs.
To Sale of Equipment A/c	1,60,000	By Balance b/d	2,00,000
" Balance c/d	3,00,000	" Depreciation A/c	2,60,000
	4,60,000		4,60,000

(6)

Provision for Taxation A/c

Dr. Particulars	Amount	Cr. Particulars	Amount
	Rs.		Rs.
To Bank A/c	1,35,000	By Balance B/d	1,00,000
" Balance c/d	1,25,000	" Profit & Loss Adjustment A/c	1,60,000
	2,60,000		2,60,000

(7)

10% Debenture A/c

Dr. Particulars	Amount	Cr. Particulars	Amount
	Rs.		Rs.
To Equity Shares (balancing figure)	1,50,000	By Balance b/d	22,00,000
" Balance c/d	20,50,000		
	22,00,000		22,00,000

(8)

Dr. **Building A/c** *Cr.*

Particulars	Amount	Particulars	Amount
	Rs.		Rs.
To Balance b/d	25,00,000		
		By Balance c/d	25,00,000
	25,00,000		25,00,000

(9)

Dr. **Provision for Depreciation on Building A/c** *Cr.*

Particulars	Amount	Particulars	Amount
	Rs.		Rs.
		By Balance b/d	5,00,000
		" Depreciation A/c	1,00,000
To Balance c/d	6,00,000		
	6,00,000		6,00,000

(10)

Dr. **Equity Shares A/c** *Cr.*

Particulars	Amount	Particulars	Amount
	Rs.		Rs.
		By Balance b/d	40,00,000
		" 10% Debenture	1,50,000
		" Bank A/c	
To Balance c/d	43,00,000	(balancing figure)	1,50,000
	43,00,000		43,00,000

(11)

Dr. **Interest on Debenture A/c** *Cr.*

Particulars	Amount	Particulars	Amount
	Rs.		Rs.
To Bank A/c	2,05,000	By Profit & Loss	
(20,50,000 × 10%)		Adjustment A/c	2,05,000
	2,05,000		2,05,000

(12) Calculation of Cash Flow from Operation

		Rs.	Rs.
	Net Operating Profit		4,35,000
Add :	**Non-Cash expenses**		
	Depreciation on Equipment	2,60,000	
	Depreciation on Building	1,00,000	3,60,000
			7,95,000
Add :	**Decrease in Current Assets**		
	Inventory	1,50,000	
	Prepaid expenses	15,000	1,65,000
			9,60,000
Less :	**Increase in Current Assets**		
	Debtors	1,50,000	
Less :	**Decrease in Current Liabilities**		
	Trade Creditors	1,50,000	3,00,000
			6,60,000
Less :	Payment of Tax		1,35,000
	Cash Flow from Operation		5,25,000

(13) Calculation of Cash Flow from Investment Activities

		Rs.	Rs.
Inflow :	Sale of Land	3,50,000	
	Sale of Equipment	30,000	3,80,000
Outflow :	Purchase of Equipment		6,00,000
Cash Outflow from Investing Activities			2,20,000

(14) Cash Flow from Financing Activities

		Rs.	Rs.
Inflow :	Issue of Equity Shares		1,50,000
Outflow :	Payment of Dividend	4,50,000	
	Interest on Debenture	2,05,000	6,55,000
Cash Outflow from Financing Activities			5,05,000

Problem

From the information given below relating to XYZ Ltd. prepare a cash-flow statement for the year ended March 31, 2002 clearly classifying the cash flow into operating cash-flow, financing cash-flow and investing cash flows as per the provisions of AS3.

Balance Sheet

Liabilities	31.03.01	31.03.02	Assets	31.03.01	31.03.02
	Rs.	Rs.		Rs.	Rs.
Equity Share Capital	3,00,000	4,00,000	Fixed Assets at cost	8,00,000	9,50,000
Capital Reserve	—	10,000	*Less* : Depreciation	2,30,000	2,90,000
P/L Account	2,30,000	2,75,000		5,70,000	6,60,000
10% Debentures	2,00,000	1,40,000	Investment	1,00,000	80,000
Sundry Creditors	1,20,000	1,30,000	Current Assets	2,80,000	3,30,000
Provision for			Preliminary Expenses	20,000	10,000
Income Tax	90,000	85,000			
Proposed Dividend	30,000	36,000			
Unclaimed Dividend	—	4,000			
	9,70,000	10,80,000		9,70,000	10,80,000

You have also been given the following additional information :

(i) One machine was sold for Rs.25,000, the cost of which was Rs. 50,000 and depreciation provided on it was Rs. 21,000.

(ii) Depreciation on fixed assets provided during the year was Rs. 95,000.

(iii) 30% of the debentures were redeemed at a premium of 3%.

(iv) Some investments were sold at a profit which had been credited to capital reserve account.

(v) Fixed assets costing Rs.14,000 had been written-off. These assets had been depreciated fully.

(vi) Current assets include a cash balance of Rs.80,000 and Rs.1,00,000 as on 31.03.01 and 31.03.02, respectively. **[C.U. M.Com, Adapted]**

Solution

Cash Flow Statement

for the year ended 31.03.02

		Rs.
	Opening Cash Balance	80,000
Add:	Cash Inflow from Operating Activities [W.N.(12)]	1,83,800
		2,63,800
Less :	Cash Outflow from Financing Activities [W.N.(13)]	4,800
		2,59,000
Less :	Cash Outflow from Investing Activities [W.N.(11)]	1,59,000
	Closing Cash Balance	1,00,000

Working Notes

(1)

Dr. **P/L Adjustment A/c** *Cr.*

Particulars	Amount	Particulars	Amount
	Rs.		Rs.
To Dividend	36,000	By Balance b/d	2,30,000
" Provision for Income Tax	85,000	" Net Profit (balancing figure)	1,66,000
" Balance c/d	2,75,000		
	3,96,000		3,96,000

(2)

Dividend A/c

Dr. Particulars	Amount	Particulars	Cr. Amount
	Rs.		Rs.
To Unclaimed Dividend A/c	4,000	By Balance b/d	30,000
" Bank A/c	26,000	" P/L Adjustment A/c	36,000
" Balance c/d	36,000		
	66,000		66,000

(3)

Provision for Income Tax A/c

Dr. Particulars	Amount	Particulars	Cr. Amount
	Rs.		Rs.
To Bank A/c	90,000	By Balance b/d	90,000
" Balance c/d	85,000	" P/L Adjustment A/c (balancing figure)	85,000
	1,75,000		1,75,000

(4)

Fixed Assets A/c

Dr. Particulars	Amount	Particulars	Cr. Amount
	Rs.		Rs.
To Balance b/d	8,00,000	By Sale of Machine A/c	50,000
" Bank A/c	2,14,000	" Provision for Dep. A/c	14,000
		" Balance c/d	9,50,000
	10,14,000		10,14,000

(5)

Provision for Depreciation A/c

Dr. Particulars	Amount	Particulars	Cr. Amount
	Rs.		Rs.
To Sale of Machine A/c	21,000	By Balance b/d	2,30,000
" Fixed Assets A/c	14,000	" P/L A/c (Depreciation)	95,000
" Balance c/d	2,90,000		
	3,25,000		3,25,000

(6)

Sale of Machine A/c

Dr. Particulars	Amount	Particulars	Cr. Amount
	Rs.		Rs.
To Fixed Assets A/c	50,000	By Provision for Dep. A/c	21,000
		" Bank A/c	25,000
		" P/L A/c (Loss on Sale)	4,000
	50,000		50,000

(7)

Dr. **Investment A/c** *Cr.*

Particulars	Amount	Particulars	Amount
	Rs.		Rs.
To Balance b/d	1,00,000	By Sale of Investment A/c	20,000
		" Balance c/d	80,000
	1,00,000		1,00,000

(8)

Dr. **Sale of Investment A/c** *Cr.*

Particulars	Amount	Particulars	Amount
	Rs.		Rs.
To Investment A/c	20,000	By Bank A/c	30,000
" Capital Reserve A/c	10,000	(balancing figure)	
	30,000		30,000

(9)

Dr. **10% Debenture A/c** *Cr.*

Particulars	Amount	Particulars	Amount
	Rs.		Rs.
To Redemption of Debenture A/c	60,000	By Balance b/d	2,00,000
" Balance c/d	1,40,000		
	2,00,000		2,00,000

(10)

Dr. **Redemption of Debenture A/c** *Cr.*

Particulars	Amount	Particulars	Amount
	Rs.		Rs.
To Bank A/c	61,800	By 10% Debenture A/c	60,000
		" P/L A/c (Premium on redemption of debenture)	1,800
	61,800		61,800

(11) Calculation of Cash Flow Investing Activities

	Rs.	Rs.
Inflow : Sale of Machine	25,000	
Sale of Investment	30,000	
		55,000
Outflow : Purchase of Fixed Assets		2,14,000
Net Cash Outflow from Investing Activities		1,59,000

(12) Calculation of Cash from Operation

		Rs.	Rs.
	Net Profit		1,66,000
Add :	**Non-operating items debited to P/L A/c**		
	Loss on Sale of Machine	4,000	
	Premium on redemption of debenture	1,800	
	Interest on Debenture	17,000	
Add :	**Non-Cash items debited to P/L A/c**		
	Depreciation	95,000	
	Preliminary Expenses	10,000	1,27,800
			2,93,800
Less :	Increase in Current Assets : [(3,30,000 – 1,00,000) – (2,80,000 – 80,000)]		30,000
			2,63,800
Add :	Increase in Current Liabilities Sundry Creditors (1,30,000 – 1,20,000)		10,000
			2,73,800
Less :	Tax Paid		90,000
Cash Inflow from Operating Activities			1,83,800

(13) Calculation of Cash from Financing Activities

		Rs.	Rs.
	Issue of Equity Shares		1,00,000
Less :	Redemption of debenture including premium	61,800	
	Interest on Debenture	17,000	
	Dividend paid	26,000	1,04,800
Cash outflow from Financing Activities			4,800

(14) Interest on Debenture

$$\text{Rs. } 2{,}00{,}000 \times 10\% \times \frac{6}{12} + 1{,}40{,}000 \times 10\% \times \frac{6}{12}$$

$$= \text{Rs. } 10{,}000 + \text{Rs. } 7{,}000$$

$$= \text{Rs. } 17{,}000$$

Assumptions

(1) Provision for Income Tax of the last year had been paid in full in the current year.

(2) Debentures were redeemed at the middle of the year.

Problem

From the information given below relating to ABC Ltd. prepare a cash flow statement for the year ended March 31, 2001, clearly classifying the Cash-flows into Operating Cashflows, Financing Cash-flows and Investing Cash-flows as per the provisions of AS 3 :

Balance Sheet

Liabilities	31.03.2000	31.03.2001	Assets	31.03.2000	31.03.2001
	Rs.	Rs.		Rs.	Rs.
Equity Share Capital	3,00,000	3,50,000	Fixed Assets (Net)	5,10,000	6,20,000
General Reserve	1,00,000	2,70,000	Investments	30,000	80,000
10% Debentures	3,00,000	3,00,000	Current Assets	2,40,000	3,75,000
Current Liabilities	70,000	1,45,000	Discount on Debentures	—	5,000
Provision for Doubtful Debts	10,000	15,000			
	7,80,000	10,80,000		7,80,000	10,80,000

You have also been given the following additional information :

(i) A machine costing Rs. 70,000 (W.D.V. Rs.40,000) was disposed off for Rs. 25,000.

(ii) The provision for depreciation stood at the beginning of the current year at Rs.1,50,000 and Rs. 1,90,000 at the end of the year.

(iii) A dividend at the rate of 15% was paid on equity shares on the 1st April 2000.

(iv) Fresh equity shares were issued on the 1st April 2000.

(v) Rs.1,00,000 debentures were redeemed on 1st April 2000 at a premium of 5%. On the same date, debentures of the same amount were issued at a discount of 5%.

(vi) Current Assets include a cash balance of Rs. 40,000 and Rs. 75,000 as on 31.03.2000 and 31.03.2001, respectively. Ignore Income Tax.

[C.U., M.Com.]

Solution

Cash Flow Statement
for the year ended 31.03.2001

		Rs.	Rs.
	Opening Cash Balance	40,000	
Add :	Cash-Inflow from Operation [W.N.8]	3,15,000	3,55,000
Less :	Cash Outflow from Investing Activities [W.N.9]		2,45,000
			1,10,000
Less :	Cash Outflow from Financing Activities [W.N.10]		35,000
	Closing Cash Balance		75,000

Working Notes (W.N.)

(1)

Dr. **Fixed Assets** *Cr.*

	Particulars	Amount Rs.		Particulars	Amount Rs.
To	Balance b/d (5,10,000 + 1,50,000)	6,60,000	By	Sale of Machine A/c	70,000
"	Bank A/c (balancing figure)	2,20,000	"	Balance c/d	8,10,000
		8,80,000			8,80,000

(2)

Dr. **Provision for Depreciatoin A/c** Cr.

Particulars	Amount	Particulars	Amount
	Rs.		Rs.
To Sale of Machine A/c	30,000	By Balance b/d	1,50,000
" Balance c/d	1,90,000	" P/L A/c	
		(Depreciation charged)	70,000
	2,20,000		2,20,000

(3)

Dr. **Investment A/c** Cr.

Particulars	Amount	Particulars	Amount
	Rs.		Rs.
To Balance b/d	30,000	By Balance c/d	80,000
" Bank A/c (balancing figure)	50,000		
	80,000		80,000

(4)

Dr. **10% Debenture A/c** Cr.

Particulars	Amount	Particulars	Amount
	Rs.		Rs.
To Redemption of Debenture A/c	1,00,000	By Balance b/d	3,00,000
		" Bank A/c	95,000
" Balance b/d	3,00,000	" Discount on Debenture A/c	5,000
	4,00,000		4,00,000

(5)

Dr. **Redemption of Debenture A/c** Cr.

Particulars	Amount	Particulars	Amount
	Rs.		Rs.
To Bank A/c	1,05,000	By 10% Debentures A/c	1,00,000
		" P/L A/c (Premium on redemption)	5,000
	1,05,000		1,05,000

(6)

Dr. **P/L Adjustment A/c** Cr.

Particulars	Amount	Particulars	Amount
	Rs.		Rs.
To General Reserve	1,70,000	By Net Profit	2,15,000
" Dividend	45,000	(balancing figure)	
	2,15,000		2,15,000

(7)

Dr. **Sale of Machine A/c** *Cr.*

	Particulars	Amount		Particulars	Amount
		Rs.			Rs.
To	Fixed Assets A/c	70,000	By	Provision for Depreciation A/c	30,000
			"	Bank A/c	25,000
			"	P/L A/c (Loss on Sale)	15,000
		70,000			70,000

(8) Calculation of Operating Cash Flow

		Rs.	Rs.
	Net Profit		2,15,000
Add :	**Non-operating items debited to P/L A/c**		
	Loss on Sale of Fixed Assets	15,000	
	Interest on Debenture	30,000	
	Premium on redemption of debenture	5,000	
Add :	Non-Cash operating items :		
	Depreciation	70,000	1,20,000
			3,35,000
Less :	Increase in Current Assets		95,000
			2,40,000
Add :	Increase in Current Liabilities		75,000
Cash Inflow from Operating Activities			3,15,000

(9) Calculation of Cash from Investing Activities

		Rs.	Rs.
Inflow :	Sale of Machine		25,000
Outflow :	Purchase of Fixed Assets	2,20,000	
	Purchase of Investment	50,000	2,70,000
Cash Outflow from Investing Activities			2,45,000

(10) Calculation of Cash from Financing Activities

		Rs.	Rs.
Inflow :	Issue of Shares		50,000
	Issue of Debenture		95,000
			1,45,000
Outflow :	Redemption of Debenture	1,05,000	
	Dividend paid	45,000	
	Interest on Debenture	30,000	1,80,000
Cash Outflow from Financing Activities			35,000

Problem

From the following information you are required to prepare a Cash-flow Statement as per AS3 :

The summarised Balance Sheet of X Ltd as on 31.3.06 and 31.3.07 are as follows :

Balance Sheet

Liabilities	31.03.06	31.03.07	Assets	31.03.06	31.03.07
	Rs.	Rs.		Rs.	Rs.
Equity Shares of Rs.10 each fully paid	3,00,000	3,50,000	Fixed Assets (Net)	4,00,000	4,75,000
General Reserve	1,50,000	2,25,000	Long-term Investment (at cost)	90,000	90,000
Capital Reserve (Profit on Sale of Investment)	—	5,000	Current Assets :		
			Stock (at cost)	1,00,000	1,35,000
			Debtors	1,12,500	1,22,500
15% Debentures	1,50,000	1,00,000	Cash	32,500	43,500
Accrued Expenses	5,000	6,000			
Creditors	80,000	1,25,000			
Proposed Dividend	15,000	17,000			
Provision for tax	35,000	38,000			
	7,35,000	8,66,000		7,35,000	8,66,000

Additional Information

(i) The balance of accumulated depreciation stood at Rs. 1,00,000 on 31.3.06 and Rs. 1,25,000 on 31.3.07.

(ii) During the year ended 31.3.07 fixed asset with a net book value of Rs. 5,000 (accumulated depreciation Rs. 15,000) was sold for Rs. 4,000.

(iii) During the year ended 31.3.07 investment costing Rs. 40,000 were sold.

(iv) Debentures were redeemed at a premium of 10%.

(v) Tax of Rs.27,500 was paid.

(vi) The proposed dividend for the year ended 31.3.06 was paid in 2007.

[C.U. M.Com., Adapted]

Solution

Cash Flow Statement
for the year ended 31.03.2007

		Rs.	Rs.
	Opening Cash Balance	32,500	
Add :	Cash-Inflow from Operating Activities [W.N.10]	1,60,750	
			1,93,250
Less :	Cash Outflow from Investing Activities [W.N.11]	1,11,000	
	Cash Outflow from Financing Activities [W.N.12]	38,750	
			1,49,750
	Closing Cash Balance		43,500

Working Notes

(1)

Dr. **Fixed Assets A/c** *Cr.*

	Particulars	Amount		Particulars	Amount
		Rs.			Rs.
To	Balance b/d (4,00,000 + 1,00,000)	5,00,000	By	Sale of Fixed Assets A/c	20,000
”	Bank A/c (balancing figure)	1,20,000	”	Balance c/d (4,75,000 + 1,25,000)	6,00,000
		6,20,000			6,20,000

(2)

Dr. **Provision for Depreciation A/c** *Cr.*

	Particulars	Amount		Particulars	Amount
		Rs.			Rs.
To	Sale of Fixed Assets A/c	15,000	By	Balance b/d	1,00,000
”	Balance c/d	1,25,000	”	P/L A/c (balancing figure)	40,000
		1,40,000			1,40,000

(3)

Dr. **Sale of Fixed Assets A/c** *Cr.*

	Particulars	Amount		Particulars	Amount
		Rs.			Rs.
To	Fixed Assets A/c	20,000	By	Bank A/c	4,000
			”	P/L A/c (Loss on Sale)	1,000
			”	Provision for Depreciation A/c	15,000
		20,000			20,000

(4)

Dr. **Long-term Investment A/c** *Cr.*

	Particulars	Amount		Particulars	Amount
		Rs.			Rs.
To	Balance b/d	90,000	By	Bank A/c	45,000
”	Capital Reserve A/c	5,000	”	Balance c/d	90,000
”	Bank A/c (balancing figure)	40,000			
		1,35,000			1,35,000

(5)

Dr.	**15% Debentures A/c**		*Cr.*
Particulars	**Amount** Rs.	**Particulars**	**Amount** Rs.
To Bank A/c	55,000	By Balance b/d	1,50,000
" Balance c/d	1,00,000	" P/L A/c (Premium on redemption of Debenture)	5,000
	1,55,000		1,55,000

(6)

Dr.	**Proposed Dividend A/c**		*Cr.*
Particulars	**Amount** Rs.	**Particulars**	**Amount** Rs.
To Bank A/c	15,000	By Balance b/d	15,000
" Balance c/d	17,000	" P/L Appropriation A/c	17,000
	32,000		32,000

(7)

Dr.	**Provision for Tax A/c**		*Cr.*
Particulars	**Amount** Rs.	**Particulars**	**Amount** Rs.
To Bank A/c	27,500	By Balance b/d	35,000
" Balance c/d	38,000	" P/L Appropriation A/c (balancing figure)	30,500
	65,500		65,500

(8)

Dr.	**General Reserve A/c**		*Cr.*
Particulars	**Amount** Rs.	**Particulars**	**Amount** Rs.
To Balance c/d	2,25,000	By Balance b/d	1,50,000
		" P/L Appropriation A/c (balancing figure)	75,000
	2,25,000		2,25,000

(9)

Dr.	**P/L Appropriation A/c**		*Cr.*
Particulars	**Amount** Rs.	**Particulars**	**Amount** Rs.
To General Reserve	75,000	By Net Profit (balancing figure)	1,22,500
" Proposed Dividend	17,000		
" Provision for Tax A/c	30,500		
	1,22,500		1,22,500

(10) Calculation of Cash from Operating Activities

		Rs.	Rs.
	Net Profit		1,22,500
Add :	**Non-operating items debited to P/L A/c**		
	Loss on Sale of Fixed Assets	1,000	
	Premium on redemption of debenture	5,000	
	Interest on Debenture	18,750	24,750
	(1,50,000 × 15% × ½ + 1,00,000 × 15% × ½)		1,47,250
Add :	**Non-Cash operating items debited to P/L A/c**		
	Depreciation		40,000
			1,87,250
Less :	**Increase in Current Assets :**		
		Rs.	
	Stock	35,000	
	Debtors	10,000	45,000
			1,42,250
Add :	**Increase in Current Liabilities**		
	Accrued Expenses	1,000	
	Creditors	45,000	46,000
			1,88,250
Less :	Tax paid		27,500
Cash from Operation			1,60,750

(11) Cash from Investing Activities

		Rs.	Rs.
Inflows :	Sale of Fixed Assets	4,000	—
	Sale of Long-term Investment	45,000	
			49,000
Outflows :	Purchase of Fixed Assets	1,20,000	
	Purchase of Investment	40,000	1,60,000
Cash Outflow from Investing Activities			1,11,000

(12) Cash from Financing Activities

		Rs.	Rs.
Inflows :	Issue of Shares		50,000
Outflows :	Redemption of debenture with premium	55,000	
	Payment of interest on debenture	18,750	
	Payment of dividend	15,000	
			88,750
Cash outflow from Financing Activities			38,750

(13) It is assumed that debenture were redeemed during middle of the accounting year.

Problem

From the following condensed Balance Sheets of M/s Chanda Enterprises Ltd prepare a Cash Flow statement as at 31.12.2006 in accordance with AS 3 :

Account Heads	31.12.2005	31.12.06
	Rs.	Rs.
Capital and Liabilities		
Share Capital	1,40,000	1,48,000
Debentures	24,000	12,000
Reserve for Bad Debts	1,400	1,600
Creditors	20,720	23,680
Profit and Loss Account	20,080	21,120
	2,06,200	2,06,400
Assets		
Goodwill	20,000	10,000
Land	40,000	60,000
Stock	98,400	85,400
Cash	18,000	15,600
Debtors	29,800	35,400
	2,06,200	2,06,400

Other Information

(1) Dividend paid for the year ending 31.12.2006 Rs. 7000.

(2) Land was acquired for Rs. 20,000.

(3) Amount provided for the amortisation of Goodwill is Rs. 10,000.

(4) Debentures paid-off Rs. 12,000.

Solution

Cash Flow Statement of Chanda Enterprises Ltd. for the year ended 31.12.2006

Particulars	Amount	Amount
	Rs.	Rs.
1. Cash Flow from Operating Activities		
Operating Profit	18,240	
Decrease in Stock	13,000	
Increase in Debtors	(5,600)	
Increase in Creditors	2,960	
Cash generated from operations	28,600	
Less : Income Tax paid	Nil	
	28,600	
Add : Extraordinary Receipts/Payments	Nil	
Net Cash from Operating Activities		28,600
2. Cash Flows from Investing Activities		
Purchase of Land	(20,000)	
Net Cash from Investing Activities		(20,000)

Particulars	Amount	Amount
	Rs.	Rs.
3. Cash Flows from Financing Activities		
Issue of Share Capital	8,000	
Debentures Paid-off	(12,000)	
Payment of dividend	(7,000)	
Net Cash from Financing Activities		(11,000)
Net decrease in Cash and Cash Equivalents		(2,400)
Add: Cash and Cash Equivalents at the beginning of the year		18,000
Cash and Cash Equivalents at the end of the year		15,600

Working Notes

(i)

Dr. **Adjusted Profit and Loss Account** *Cr.*

Particulars	Amount	Particulars	Amount
	Rs.		Rs.
To Reserve for Bad Debts	200	By Balance b/d	20,080
" Goodwill written-off	10,000	" Operating Profit	
" Dividend	7,000	(balancing figure)	18,240
" Balance c/d	21,120		
	38,320		38,320

Problem

Balance Sheets of M/s Black and White as on 31.3.04 and 31.03.2005 were :

Liabilities	31.03.2004	31.03.2005	Assets	31.03.04	31.03.05
	Rs.	Rs.		Rs.	Rs.
Creditors	16,000	17,600	Cash	4,000	2,800
Jayram's Loan	10,000	—	Debtors	12,000	20,000
Loan from Yes			Stock	14,000	10,000
Bank Ltd.	16,000	20,000	Plant & Machinery	32,000	22,000
Capital	54,000	65,200	Land	16,000	20,000
			Building	18,000	28,000
	96,000	1,02,800		96,000	1,02,800

Additional Information

(a) During the year a machine costing Rs. 4,000 (accumulated depreciation Rs. 1,200) was sold for Rs. 2,000. The provision for depreciation against Plant and Machinery as on 31.03.04 was Rs. 10,000 and on 31.3.05 it was Rs. 16,000.

(b) Net Profit for the year ending 31.3.05 amounted to Rs.18,000.

Prepare a Cash Flow Statement as per Accounting Standard 3.

Solution

Cash Flow Statement of M/s Black and White for the year ended 31.3.2005

Particulars	Amount Rs.	Amount Rs.
1. Cash Flow from Operating Activities		
Net profit during the year	18,000	
Add: Depreciation	7,200	
Loss on Sale of Machine	800	
Operating Profit	26,000	
Increase in Creditors	1,600	
Increase in Debtors	(8,000)	
Decrease in Stock	4,000	
Net Cash from Operating Activities		23,600
2. Cash Flow from Investing Activities		
Sale of Machinery	2,000	
Acquisition of land	(4,000)	
Acquisition of Building	(10,000)	
Net Cash from Investing Activities		(12,000)
3. Cash Flow from Financing Activities		
Jayram's loan repayment drawings	(10,000)	
Drawings (54,000+18,000–65,200)	(6,800)	
Loan from Yes Bank Ltd.	4,000	
Net Cash from Financing Activities		(12,800)
Net Cash and Cash Equivalents during the year		(1,200)
Add: Cash and Cash Equivalents at the beginning of the year	2,000	4,000
Cash and Cash Equivalents at the end of the year		2,800

Working Notes

(1)

Dr. **Plant and Machinery Account** Cr.

Particulars	Amount Rs.	Particulars	Amount Rs.
To Balance b/d	42,000	By Machine Disposal A/c	4,000
		" Balance c/d	38,000
	42,000		42,000

Dr. **Provision for Depreciation Account** Cr.

Particulars	Amount Rs.	Particulars	Amount Rs.
To Machine Disposal A/c	1,200	By Balance b/d	10,000
		" Depreciation A/c (balancing figure)	7,200
" Balance c/d	16,000		
	17,200		17,200

Dr. Machine Disposal Account Cr.

Particulars	Amount	Particulars	Amount
	Rs.		Rs.
To Plant and Machinery A/c	4,000	By Provision for Depreciation A/c	1,200
		" Bank A/c	2,000
		" Profit & Loss A/c (loss on sale)	800
	4,000		4,000

QUESTIONS

1. What is Cash Flow Statement ? What are its advantages?
2. How does preparation of Cash Flow Statement help management in taking decision regarding flow of funds?
3. Does Cash Flow Statement differ from Fund Flow Statement ? If so, explain.
4. Does the preparation of Cash Flow Statement bear any significance in the context of 'Cash Management'?
5. You are introduced to a new client company by a friend who sends you the latest accounts for your consideration prior to introducing you to the managing director of the company. The accounts include :

Summarised Balance Sheet — 31st December 2006

2005	Share Capital	Authorised	Issued and fully paid
Rs.		Rs.	Rs.
44,257	50,000, 5½ preference shares of Re. 1 each	50,000	44,257
29,585	Ordinary shares of Rs. 5 each	50,000	29,585
73,842		1,00,000	73,842
	Reserve		
Rs.		Rs.	Rs.
5,694	Capital	5,694	
11,128	Revenue Surplus	12,831	18,525
—	Future taxation		565
	Current Liabilities		
31,981	Bank Overdraft (secured)	32,726	
62,676	Creditors and accrued expenses	54,732	
1,488	Dividend Payable	2,422	89,880
1,86,809			1,82,812

Rs.	Fixed Assets	Rs.
67,314	Freehold and Leasehold premises	66,935
40,466	Plant, equipment, motor vehicle	41,098
1,07,780		1,08,033
1	Goodwill and Copyrights	1
	Investment	
2,328	at cost leasehold redemption policies	2,421
	Current Assets	
33,553	Stock and Work-in-progress	37,718
43,027	Debtors Less Provisions for Doubtful Debts	34,372
120	Balance at Bank and Cash in hand	267
1,86,809		1,82,812

Profit and Loss Account

Year ended 31st December 2005 Rs.				Year ended 31st December 2006 Rs.
15,282		Balance on Trading		18,360
		Deduct :		
	2,728	Depreciation on Plant, Equipment and Motor Vehicles	2,760	
	286	Depreciation of Freehold Property	287	
	92	Lease hold property redemption	92	
	450	Auditor's redemption	450	
11,596	8,040	Director's remuneration	8,357	11,946
3,686		Profit for the year before charging Taxation		6,414
		Deduct :		
		Taxation based on the Profit for the year —		
	—	Corporate Tax	798	
(10)	(10)	Income Tax	—	798
3,696		Profit after charging Taxation		5,616
		Deduct dividend for the year :		
	2,434	Preference Shares	2,434	
3,174	740	Ordinary Shares at 5%	1,479	3,913
522		Surplus for the year carried to Balance Sheet		1,703

Notes to the Accounts

	Cost	Depreciation	Net
	Rs.	Rs.	Rs.
(1) Freehold and leasehold premises	75,200	8,265	66,935
2005	75,200	7,886	67,314
Plant, equipment and motor vehicles	85,639	44,541	41,098
2006	82,247	41,781	40,466

Since 31st December 2006, a freehold property costing Rs. 40,000 has been sold for Rs. 1,60,000.

You are required to prepare a statement for the year ended 31st December 2006, showing the sources and application of funds and cash flow.

[Adapted from C.A. (Eng.) Final]

6. From the Profit & Loss A/c for the year ended 31st December 2006 of a firm and the Balance Sheets as on 31.12.05 and 31.12.06, respectively, prepare a Cash Flow Statement.

Profit & Loss A/c for the year ended 31.12.06

Particulars	Amount	Particulars	Amount
	Rs.		Rs.
To Cost of materials consumed	1,90,000	By Sales	2,50,000
,, Wages	20,000	,, Profit on Sale of Plant	10,000
,, Gross Profit	65,000	,, Misc. Income	15,000
	2,75,000		2,75,000
To Salaries	10,000	By Gross Profit	65,000
,, Office Expenses	15,000		
,, Depreciation	10,000		
,, Deferrred expenses	2,000		
,, Interest paid	2,000		
,, Net Profit	26,000		
	65,000		65,000
To Dividend	10,000	By Net Profit	26,000
To Balance c/d	16,000		
	26,000		26,000

Balance Sheet

Liabilities	2005	2006	Assets	2005	2006
	Rs.	Rs.		Rs.	Rs.
Share Capital	90,000	1,00,000	Fixed Assets	50,000	70,000
Profit & Loss A/c	15,000	31,000	Inventories	30,000	25,000
Secured Loan	10,000	20,000	Debtors	50,000	75,000
Trade Creditors	25,000	30,000	Cash & Bank Balance	5,000	15,000
Liabilities for Expenses	4,000	6,000	Prepaid Expenses	8,000	5,000
Outstanding Wages & Salaries	2,000	4,000	Deferred Expenses	3,000	1,000
	1,46,000	1,91,000		1,46,000	1,91,000

An old plant was sold for Rs. 15,000.

7. From the following particulars prepare a cash flow statement of Sundry Ltd. for the year ended 31st December 2006:

Profit and Loss A/c for the year ended 31.12.06

Particulars	Amount	Particulars	Amount
	Rs.		Rs.
To Opening Stock	5,500	By Sales	2,16,000
,, Purchase	80,500	,, Closing Stock	20,000
,, Wages	16,000	,, Loss on Stock	5,000
,, Gross Profit c/d	1,39,000		
	2,41,000		2,41,000
To Expenses	10,000	By Gross Profit b/d	1,39,000
,, Loss on Stock	1,000	,, Other Income	6,000
,, Loss on Sale of Plant	5,000		
,, Deferred Expenses	5,000		
,, Depreciation	12,000		
,, Bad Debt	1,000		
,, Income Tax	10,000		
,, Net Profit c/d	1,01,000		
	1,45,000		1,45,000
To Dividend	8,000	By Balance b/d	30,000
,, Reserve	23,000	,, Net Profit b/d	1,01,000
,, Balance c/d	1,00,000		
	1,31,000		1,31,000

Balance Sheet

Liabilities	2005	2006	Assets	2005	2006
	Rs.	Rs.		Rs.	Rs.
Share Capital	80,000	90,000	Fixed Assets	60,000	1,80,000
Profit & Loss A/c	30,000	1,00,000	Investments	68,500	30,000
Reserve	50,000	73,000	Stock-in-Trade	5,500	20,000
Creditors	30,000	20,000	Debtors	50,000	55,000
Liabilities for Expenses	8,000	10,000	Cash & Bank	3,500	1,500
Advance Income	5,000	3,000	Deferred Expenses	10,500	5,500
			Prepaid Expenses	5,000	4,000
	2,03,000	2,96,000		2,03,000	2,96,000

A machine was sold for Rs. 10,000.

8. The following are the summarised balance sheets of Brad Pitt Ltd. as on 31st December 2005 and 31st December 2006 :

Balance Sheet

Liabilities	2005 Rs.	2006 Rs.	Assets	2005 Rs.	2006 Rs.
Share Capital	12,00,000	16,00,000	Plant & Machinery (at cost)	8,00,000	12,90,000
Debentures	4,00,000	6,00,000	Land & Building (at cost)	6,00,000	8,00,000
Profit & Loss A/c	2,50,000	5,00,000	Stock	6,00,000	7,00,000
Creditors	2,30,000	1,80,000	Bank	40,000	80,000
Provision for :			Preliminary Expenses	14,000	12,000
Bad & Doubtful Debts	12,000	6,000	Debtors	1,38,000	1,22,000
Depreciation on Land & Buidling	40,000	48,000			
Depreciatoin on Plant & Machinery	60,000	70,000			
	21,92,000	30,04,000		21,92,000	30,04,000

Additional Information :

i. During the year a part of machinery costing Rs. 1,40,000 (accumulated depreciation thereon Rs. 4,000) was sold for Rs. 12,000.

ii. Dividend for Rs. 1,00,000 was paid during the year.

9. From the following information, prepare a cash flow statement for the year ending 31st March 2006 :

Balance Sheet (Figures in Lac)

As on 31.3.05	Liabilities	As on 31.3.06	As on 31.3.05	Assets	As on 31.3.06
10.00	Equity Shares of Rs.100 each	15.00	15.00	Plant at W.D.V.	18.00
5.00	Redeemable Preference Shares of Rs. 100 each Rs.50 paid	Nil	6.00	Stock	3.00
0.25	Share Premium	Nil	15.00	Debtors	10.00
Nil	Capital Redemption Reserve	5.00	2.00	Cash Balance	5.00
10.00	General Reserve	7.00			
2.75	P/L A/c	3.00			
10.00	Current Liabilities	6.00			
38.00		36.00	38.00		36.00

Additional Information

(a) During the year the company paid Rs. 2,00,000 as equity dividend and Rs. 56,250 as preference dividend.

(b) The company redeemed the preference shares at a premium of 5% after making a call of Rs.50 per share to make the shares fully paid.

(c) During the year one plant, whose book value was Rs. 1,00,000, was sold at a loss of Rs.25,000 and the company purchased a plant for Rs. 6,00,000.

10. The comparative Balance Sheets of Crook Bond Ltd. are indicated in a condensed form as under :

Balance Sheets as at 31.3.05 & 31.3.06

Liabilities	As on 31.3.05	As on 31.3.06	Assets	As on 31.3.05	As on 31.3.06
	Rs.	Rs.		Rs.	Rs.
Share Capital			Fixed Assets	4,80,000	5,20,000
Equity Shares of Rs.100 each			*Less* : Dep. to date	(1,08,000)	(1,40,000)
Issued for cash	3,60,000	4,00,000		3,72,000	3,80,000
General Reserve	1,10,000	60,000	Investment at Cost	1,00,000	50,000
Profit & Loss A/c	20,450	53,450	Stocks	55,600	90,500
Sundry Creditors	1,83,650	1,75,350	Sundry Debtors	1,18,300	1,67,800
Proposed Dividend	28,800	15,000	Cash & Bank	49,800	47,500
Provision for Taxation	—	32,000	Preliminary Expenses	7,200	—
	7,02,900	7,35,800		7,02,900	7,35,800

1. The net profit for the year 2005-06 (after providing for depreciation Rs.40,000; writing-off preliminary expenses Rs. 7,200 and making provision for taxation Rs. 32,000) amounted to Rs. 58,000.
2. The company sold during the year 2005-06 old machinery costing Rs. 9,000 for Rs. 3,000. The accumulated depreciation on the said machinery was Rs. 8,000.
3. A portion of the company's investments become worthless and was written off to General Reserve during 2005-06. The cost of such investment was Rs. 50,000.

   During the year 2005-06, the company paid an interim dividend of Rs. 10,000 and the directors have recommended a final dividend Rs. 15,000 for the year 2005-06.

11. The following are the summarised Balance Sheets of Roma Sanyasin Limited as on March 2005 and 2006 :

Liabilities	31.3.05	31.3.06	Assets	31.3.05	31.3.06
	Rs.	Rs.		Rs.	Rs.
Share Capital	4,60,000	4,60,000	Land & Building	3,00,000	3,00,000
Profit & Loss A/c	32,000	46,000	Machinery	1,04,000	1,40,000
Reserve	1,20,000	1,20,000	Investments	2,20,000	1,48,000
8% Debenture	1,80,000	1,40,000	Stock	1,64,000	2,12,000
Depreciation Fund	80,000	88,000	Debtors	1,34,000	86,000
Creditors	2,06,000	1,92,000	Cash	1,80,000	1,80,000
Outstanding Expenses	26,000	24,000	Prepaid Expenses	2,000	4,000
	11,04,000	10,70,000		11,04,000	10,70,000

Additional Information

1. 10% dividend was paid during 2005-06.
2. Machinery for Rs. 6,000 was purchased and old Machinery costing Rs. 24,000 (accumulated depreciation Rs. 12,000), was sold for Rs. 8,000.

3. 40,000, 8% debentures were redeemed by purchase from open market at Rs. 96 for a debenture of Rs.100.
4. Investments worth Rs.72,000 were sold at book value.
5. Bad Debt written-off during the year Rs. 10,000.

Prepare a Statement of Cash Flow for the year ended 31.3.06

12. The Balance Sheets of Jhawar Ltd. as on 31st December 2005 and 2006 are as under :

Liabilities	2005	2006	Assets	2005	2006
	Rs.	Rs.		Rs.	Rs.
Share Capital :			Goodwill	60,000	47,000
Equity	1,50,000	2,50,000	Land & Building	1,00,000	75,000
8% Preference	1,50,000	1,00,000	Plant & Machinery	90,000	1,91,000
Reserve & Surplus :			Trade Investment	10,000	35,000
General Reserve	20,000	30,000	Current Assets		
Capital Reserve		25,000	Loans & Advances :		
Profit & Loss A/c	18,000	27,000	Stock	85,000	78,000
Current Liabilities			Sundry Debtors	60,000	90,000
& Provisions :			Bills Receivable	15,000	18,000
Sundry Creditors	26,000	53,000	Cash at Bank	10,000	22,000
Bills Payable	18,000	12,000	Cash in hand	7,000	6,000
Provision for Taxation	28,000	32,000			
Proposed Dividend	27,000	33,000			
	4,37,000	5,62,000		4,37,000	5,62,000

The following further particulars are given :

1. In 2006, Rs. 18,000 depreciation has been written-off Plant & Machinery and no depreciation has been charged on Land & Building.
2. A piece of land has been sold out and the balance has been revalued, profit on such sale and revaluation being transferred to capital reserve. There is no other entry in Capital Reserve Account.
3. A plant was sold for Rs. 12,000 (WDV Rs. 15,000).
4. Dividend received amounted to Rs. 2,100, which included pre-acquisition dividend of Rs. 600.
5. An interim dividend of Rs. 10,000 has been paid 2006.

You are required to prepare a cash flow statement for the year 2006.

13. From the following information, prepare a statement of Cash Flow Statement :

Balance Sheets

Liabilities	2005	2006	Assets	2005	2006
	Rs.	Rs.		Rs.	Rs.
Share Capital (Rs.100)	5,00,000	6,00,000	Building & Machinery	6,20,000	6,90,000
Reserve & Surplus	1,32,500	60,000	Advances	40,000	60,000
8% Debentures	1,50,000	2,00,000	Inventories	1,80,000	1,95,900
Accrued Debenture Int.	3,000	4,000	Debtors	1,50,000	1,80,000
Proposed Dividend	50,000	60,000	Goodwill	20,000	30,000
Unclaimed Fund	6,000	4,000	Debenture Discount	4,000	5,000
Depreciation Fund	1,25,000	1,75,800	(unamortised)		
Inventory Provision	8,000	9,500			
Provision for Taxation	19,500	17,600			
Sundry Creditors	20,000	30,000			
	10,14,000	11,60,900		10,14,000	11,60,900

Other Information

- Net loss amounts to Rs. 1,25,000.
- Debentures were issued at 5% Discount.
- Machine costing Rs. 20,500 (accumulated depreciation Rs.16,000) has been written-off and discarded. At the end of the year, however, the scrap was sold for Rs. 300.
- A running business was purchased in the year by issue of Rs. 1,00,000 shares at par. The business had machinery Rs. 30,000, Stock Rs. 40,000, Sundry Debtors Rs. 40,000 and Sundry Creditors Rs. 35,000.
- No shares were issued for cash.

14. From the following Balance Sheets and other information, prepare a cash flow statement for the year 2006 : (Figures in thousand)

Particulars	2005	2006	Particulars	2005	2006
	Rs.	Rs.		Rs.	Rs.
Equity Share Capital	300	350	Goodwill	100	89
8% Preference Shares	150	100	Land & Building at cost	200	170
Share Premium	20	25	Plant & Machinery (Net)	80	200
Capital Reserve	—	20	Investment	20	35
General Reserve	40	75	Debtors	140	170
Profit & Loss Appro. A/c	30	73	Stock	77	100
Creditors	55	83	Bills Receivable	20	30
Bills Payable	20	16	Cash & Bank	25	18
Proposed Dividend	42	50	Preliminary Expenses	35	30
Provision for Tax	40	50			
	697	842		697	842

Additional Information

- One piece of land was sold at a profit and the profit was transferred to capital reserve.
- One machine was sold for Rs. 15,000 (written-down value on the date of sale was Rs.18,000).
- Depreciation charged on Plant and Machinery amounted Rs. 16,000.
- Dividend of Rs. 4,000 was received from investment of which Rs. 2,000 was credited to investment account—being dividend declared from pre-acquisition profit.
- Actual amount of dividend and taxes paid were Rs. 35,000 and Rs. 38,000, respectively.

You are also required to make comments on the financial position of the company on the basis of cash flow information.

18

ACCOUNTING RATIOS ANALYSIS AND INTERPRETATION OF FINANCIAL STATEMENTS

● Good morning to you all my dear students.

☐ "Good morning Sir."

● Are you all present in the class?

☐ "Yes Sir."

● Now I would like to give you some idea about the Accounting and Financial ratios which aid management to take its decision. In day to day business operation every person is interested to know about the workings of the company or companies. This is possible at the end of the year with the help of analysis and interpretation of financial statement.

☐ "Sir, what is financial statement and what are its purposes?"

☐ "Sir, is management interested in the financial statements which are published at the end of the year when they take time to time day to day and hour to hour, even minute to minute management decision."

● Have patience, please I will satisfy you all, one by one.

You see, management does not depend on the statement which are published at the end of the year. Because, they are to tackle the changing conditions of the business. However, this, I will discuss when I shall be discussing with you the chapter on 'Management Report'.

☐ "Sir, is Fund Flow Statement a Management Report?"

● Yes, a top management report. You can even prepare Fund Flow Statement on quarterly basis if you want to pinpoint managment decision.

Purpose of Financial Statement

However, I was discussing with you financial statement. You see, Profit and Loss Account and Balance Sheets are the main financial statements of any Company or Organisation. The purpose of the Profit and Loss Account and Balance Sheet are :

(a) To indicate the result— Profit/Loss of the Company; and

(b) To show the position of Assets and Liabilities at the end of the year.

☐ "Sir, please enlighten us about the meaning and use of Financial Statements."

Real Meaning and Use of Financial Statements

• I have told you earlier that from the financial statements we can understand the result of operations of the business as well as position of assets and liabilities of the company at the end of the period. However, the real meaning and use of financial statements is something different from the apparent ones. Financial Statements are those statements from which one can understand the past condition, present position and the future trend of the financial position as well as the 'integrity' of the future capital structure of the business.

Now you may put me the question.

☐ "Sir, who are the **parties interested in the financial statements** and what are their aims?"

• You see, the following parties are interested in the financial statements of any enterprise :

1. Management : i) Formulation of policy
   ii) Arriving at management decision
   iii) Understanding the trend of the business.
2. Shareholders : i) Understanding the working of the business
   ii) The effect of the operating result on the shares in the Stock Exchange.
3. Creditors : To understand the solvency and liquidity position of the business.
4. Investors : i) Understanding the operational efficiency and 'financial health' of the business.
   ii) To understand the long term solvency of the business.
5. Government : i) To see whether the shareholders' interests are protected or not
   ii) Tax collection.
6. Auditors : i) In case of internal auditor, to report to the management after analysing and interpreting the financial statements
   ii) In case of external auditor, to report to the shareholders about the correctness of the information contained in the financial statements.

☐ "Sir, what is Internal Audit?"

• Look here, Audit can be classified under two heads— (a) Internal Audit, and (b) External or Statutory Audit. I think you know in detail about the purpose of statutory audit. I will discuss the concept of internal audit when I shall be discussing the chapter 'Internal and Management Audit' later on.

☐ "Sir, what is the difference between 'Analysis' and 'Interpretation'?"

Difference between Analysis and Interpretation

• You see, 'Analysis' means breaking down a complete set of figures into simple elements or segments. 'Interpretation,' on the other hand, explains the real significance of those scattered elements.

Now, it becomes very difficult to arrive at any concrete decision from a large number of figures—whether a business is progressing or not. This will be clear from the following situation.

Situation	Capital Employed	Profit Earned
	Rs.	Rs.
1.	50,000	10,000
2.	40,000	10,000
3.	60,000	12,000

From the situation indicated earlier it is very difficult to recommend any situation as being the best of the above. One without a, b, c knowledge of accountancy and ordinary arithmetical knowledge will perhaps recommend situation 3 which indicates the highest profit figure. Or, they will be at a dilemma which one of the above three situations is by far the best. To overcome this dilemma the only solution will be if they try to establish a relationship between the two figures appearing therein and express them in terms of percentage :

Situation	Relationship	Result
1.	$\frac{10,000}{50,000} \times 100$	20%
2.	$\frac{10,000}{40,000} \times 100$	25%
3.	$\frac{12,000}{60,000} \times 100$	20%

Now from the relationship drawn above it is clear that situation 2 is by far the best of all the situations. So 'ratio analysis is the process of determining and interpreting meaningful numerical relationships based on financial statements. Presentation of these ratios enables the user to better understand financial statements than by looking at the absolute quantities alone'. However, the relationship between the two figures can be drawn from the Balance Sheet, Profit and Loss Account and even both from Balance Sheet and Profit and Loss Account.

Meaning and Use of Ratio

I think, you have followed what I discussed so far. If you have not understood, please tell me frankly.

☐ "Sir, we have followed your lecture. Please give us some light about its advantages and disadvantages, if any."

● I was just thinking to discuss about its merits and demerits. You see, the advantages can outweigh its disadvantages if the shortcomings of the same are properly adjusted in light of the changing conditions of the business. However, I would like to mention a few of its advantages :

Advantages of Ratio Analysis

1) Accounting ratios are most commonly used for management control purpose, by comparing its own performance with the performance of similar types of business.

2) Accounting and financial ratios can play a significant and important role in cost accounting, financial accounting, budgetary control and auditing.

3) It is one of the medias to 'link between the past and the future'.

4) Besides its aids to management, it helps the general public to understand the financial trend and the financial health of the business. From ratio analysis it is possible, without any difficulty, to have a general impression of the past performance of the business and is possible to have a forecast about the uncertain future.

5) Identification of financial responsibility is possible from thorough and critical ratio analysis.

6) It is one of the factors which accelerate the development of the art of intuition in the field of financial management.

All these are some of the important advantages. However, it should be noted in this context that whether accounting and financial ratios will render valuable services to all concerned depends on the persons who handle it. That is to say, the current ratio will lose its purpose if the practice of 'window-dressing' is followed.

☐ "Sir what is Current ratio and Window-Dressing?"

• Wait please. I wil discuss all these points in due course of time.

Limitations of Ratio Analysis

Now I would like to discuss a few drawbacks of accounting and financial ratios. The limitations of ratio analysis are :

1) The ratios so drawn are based on the historical figures appearing in the balance sheet. So the performance of one enterprise based on only historical data gives a wrong direction to the approach.

2) In preparing different ratios, assets and liabilities are not grouped under money-value and real-value items. This could have given a realistic approach to the concept.

3) Financial and Accounting ratio will tend to interpret in wrong direction if based on unauthehtic data.

4) One particular ratio is not sufficient to review the whole operation of the business. It should be considered along with other ratios.

5) In practice, ratio analysis is useful only to understand the trend of the particular business, not the particular type of business as a whole. This can be done by comparing the past result with that of the present. Management and financial policies differ from concern to concern. For this, in practice, it is difficult to compare the performance of one company with another. However, this study will give us some guidelines. Though 'a ratio which is satisfactory for one particular enterprise, may be the reverse in the case of another.'

6) From the points discussed earlier, it can be stated that ratio analysis can be regarded 'only as an aid to making judgement and not a substitute to judgement'.

I think you have followed what I wanted to make clear. Now I would like to discuss......

☐ "Sir, what is Money Value Assets and Liabilities and Real Value Assets and Liabilities"?

• Wait please, you will have all these ideas when I shall be discussing the topic on 'Accounting for inflation.'

Oh yes, now I would like to discuss the different types of accounting ratios. The whole aspects of Accounting Ratios can be studied from two points of view :

Structural and Functional Ratios Analysis

(a) Structural point of view; and

(b) Functional point of view.

Now I discuss the accounting ratios under structural point of view :

Ratio Analysis

- Balance Sheet Ratios
- Profit and Loss Account Ratios or Revenue Statement Ratios
- Composite Ratios or Balance Sheet and Profit and Loss Account Ratios

☐ "Sir, what are Balance Sheet Ratios, Profit and Loss Account Ratios and, the Composite Ratios?"

● I will definitely discuss all these points in detail. First of all I discuss the Balance Sheet Ratios.

Balance Sheet Ratios

A. Balance Sheet Ratios— These show the meaningful relationship between the two figures appearing in a Balance sheet. The Balance Sheet ratios consist of :

1. Current Ratio or Working Capital Ratio

Current Ratio

It brings a relationship between the total current assets and total current liabilities. Now we may get the total current assets and total current liabilities from balance sheet items. Please note that Current Ratio can be found out in the following manner :

$$\text{Current Ratio} = \frac{\text{Total Current Assets}}{\text{Total Current Liabilities}}$$

However, from this ratio you can study the current financial position of the business.

Standard Ratio is 2 : 1. But in actual practice 1 : 1 ratio is found suitable than 2 : 1. High ratio (more than 2 : 1, say 3 : 1, 4 : 1; 5 : 1 and so on) indicates Under-Trading and the same also indicates one of the sign of Over-Capitalisation. Conversely, low ratio, say less than 1 : 1. i.e. 0·5 : 1, indicates over trading and as well as give an indication of Under Capitalisation of business.

2. Liquid Ratio

Liquid Ratio

This is also known as Quick Asset Ratio, or Acid Test Ratio. It establishes a relationship between quick assets and quick liabilities.

$$\text{Liquid Ratio} = \frac{\text{Liquid Assets}}{\text{Liquid Liabilities}}$$

The standard ratio is 1 : 1

☐ "Sir what are Quick Assets and Quick Liabilities"?

● Quick Assets are those assets which can be immediately converted into cash. Similarly quick liabilities include those liabilities which may have to be paid immediately.

Now, you note :

Quick Assets = Current Assets – Stock

Quick Liabilities = Current Liabilities – Bank Overdraft.

Now I would like to mention one point in this connection—some writers do not prefer to exclude Bank Overdraft. However, you can give a note in this respect whether you have excluded it or not. This quick assets ratio or acid test ratio can help one to study the ability of an enterprise to meet its quick debt obligation out of its quick assets.

☐ "Sir, you told us that you would discuss about the concept of window-dressing."

● Oh yes, I have totally forgotten about the same. I shall discuss it now, because it relates to the concept of current or working capital ratio. Do you remember that at the outset of this chapter I explained you that different parties are interested in the different aspects, of the business? Take for an example, creditors will allow credit only when fully aware of the current financial condition of the business. That is to say, he will always see that the current assets of the business should be higher, better to say twice, than the current liabilities. You see, window-dressing is an artificial practice to show current ratio position favourable. That is to say, current ratio, after the process of window-dressing, does not show the real current financial position.

Window-Dressing

☐ "Sir, how can window-dressing be effected ? For this, do not think that I will adopt the process of window-dressing".

● Well, Window-dressing may be done in the following ways :

i) Deferring purchases.
ii) Extensive drive is made for the collection of debts in order to keep the bank balances in a favourable footing.
iii) Manipulating the value of inventory.
iv) Recording in advance in the current year the cash receipt of the next year.
v) Treating borrowed capital as being long term loan capital, etc.

Well let me show you the mechanism. I am explaining the mechanism of window-dressing taking into account (2) item. Please note very minutely.

Example :

Balance Sheet

Liabilities	Amount Rs.	Assets	Amount Rs.
Capital	15,000	Land and Building	5,000
Sundry Creditors	4,000	Machinery	3,000
Bills Payable	1,000	Furniture	2,000
		Debtors	5,000
		Cash	5,000
	20,000		20,000

Here total Current Assets = Rs.10,000

Total Current Liabilities = Rs. 5,000

$$\text{Current Ratio} = \frac{10{,}000}{5{,}000} = 2:1$$

If the needed credit purchase of stocks for Rs. 6,000 was not possible to defer, the position of Current Ratio would have been :

$$\frac{16{,}000}{11{,}000} = 1{\cdot}45:1$$

So, if the said purchase of stock for Rs.6,000 was deferred then the current ratio would have been 2 : 1—which is said to be an ideal ratio. So, deferring purhcase is one of the techniques of window-dressing, Clear ?

☐ "Yes Sir".

3. Proprietary Ratio

Proprietary Ratio

It brings a relationship between the proprietor's fund (equity share capital, retained earnings) and total assets. From this relationship you can find out the proportion of owners' equity in assets. Or, it expresses the proportion of Net-Worth to Total Assets.

$$\text{Proprietary Ratio} = \frac{\text{Proprietary Fund}}{\text{Total Assets}}$$

Express this ratio in terms of percentage (%). This ratio indicates long term financial stability of the business. This ratio tests the capitalisation of business. That is to say, from the study of this ratio it can be ascertained whether a business or a Company is Over-Capitalised or Under-Capitalised. Higher the ratio, i.e. closer to 100%, stronger the future financial position of the business. On the other hand, the ratio indicates insufficient use of external equities (Loan Capital) to finance the business. This high proprietary ratio indicates over-capitalisation and low ratio indicates under-capitalisation.

High ratio indicates low earning per share.

Low ratio indicates high earning per share.

Do you follow what I have discussed so far.?

☐ "Sir, please explain the concept that low ratio indicates high earning per share and high ratio a low earning per share with the help of practical example."

● Well, please note the following examples to explain the said concept :

Suppose expected return on Investment of Rs.50,000 is Rs. 10,000. Now from this example we can construct two Balance Sheets, one showing high proprietary ratio and the other low proprietary ratio. From this example you will be able to grasp the idea.

Balance Sheet 1

Liabilities	Amount	Assets	Amount
	Rs.		Rs.
Equity Share Capital	50,000	Total Fixed Assets	30,000
		Total Current Assets	20,000
	50,000		50,000

Balance Sheet 2

Liabilities	Amount	Assets	Amount
	Rs.		Rs.
Equity Share Capital	10,000	Total Fixed Assets	30,000
6% Pref. Shares	30,000	Total Current Assets	20,000
5% Debentures	10,000		
	50,000		50,000

Well Expected Return in both cases is same—Rs.10,000.

Balance Sheet 1

$$\text{Proprietary Ratio} = \frac{\text{Proprietor's Fund}}{\text{Total Assets}} = 50,000 \times \frac{100}{50,000} = 100\%$$

$$\text{Rate of Return} = \frac{\text{Profit}}{\text{Equity Share Capital}} = \frac{10,000}{50,000} \times 100 = 20\%$$

Here high ratio (100%) indicates low earning (20%) per share.

Balance Sheet 2

$$\text{Proprietary Ratio} = \frac{\text{Proprietor's Fund}}{\text{Total Assets}} = \frac{10,000}{50,000} \times 100 = 20\%$$

$$\text{Rate of Return} = \frac{\text{Profit*}}{\text{Equity Share Capital}} = \frac{7,700}{10,000} \times 100 = 77\%$$

*Profit Rs.10,000 – (Pref. Div. Rs. 1,800 + Debenture interest Rs.500) = Rs.7,700.

4. Debt-Equity Ratio

Debt-Equity Ratio It brings a relationship between the external equities and internal equities. This is known as liabilities-proprietorship ratio.

Debt-Equity Ratio

(i) Total Debt to Equity (ii) Long term Debt to Equity

So, the computation of Debt-Equity Ratio under the two above situations will be :

(i) Total Debt to Equity =

$$\frac{\text{Long term Loan + Short term Credit + Current Liability and Provision}}{\text{Shareholders' Equity}}$$

$$\text{(ii) Long term Debt to Equity} = \frac{\text{Long term Debt}}{\text{Equity Share Capital + Reserve and Surplus}}$$

Express this ratio in terms of percentage (%). 'Margin of Safety' of the Creditors is lost as a result of too heavy debt burden.

Do you follow ? Is there any question ?

☐ "Sir, what is 'Debt Ratio' and what is 'Equity Ratio'?"

● Well, please note.

$$\text{Debt Ratio} = \frac{\text{Debt}}{\text{Total Assets}}$$

$$\text{Equity Ratio} = \frac{\text{Equity}}{\text{Total Assets}}$$

So, the analysis of Debt-Equity Ratio will be :

$$\frac{\text{Debt}}{\text{Equity}} = \frac{\dfrac{\text{Debt}}{\text{Total Assets}}}{\dfrac{\text{Equity}}{\text{Total Assets}}}$$

$$= \frac{\text{Debt}}{\text{Total Assets}} \times \frac{\text{Total Assets}}{\text{Equity}}$$

$$= \frac{\text{Debt}}{\text{Equity}}$$

5. Capital Gearing Ratio

Capital Gearing Ratios

It brings a relationship between the Equity Share Capital and Fixed Interest bearing long term securities (Preference Share Capital + Debentures).

So, Capital Gearing Ratio can be expressed as :

$$\text{Capital Gearing Ratio} = \frac{\text{Equity Share Capital}}{\text{Fixed Interest bearing Securities*}}$$

(*Debentures and Preference Share Capital. This is known as Loan Capital).

This ratio indicates High or Low Gearing.

If Loan Capital > Equity Captial = High Gearing

If Equity Capital > Loan Capital = Low Gearing

The Capital Gearing Ratio may be termed as Leverage Ratio.

Now I would like to discuss Profit and Loss Account ratio or Revenue Statement ratios.

Revenue Statement Ratio

B. Revenue Statement Ratio— It brings a meaningful relationship between the two figures appearing in Profit and Loss Account or Revenue Statement. Revenue Statement ratios consist of :

1. Gross Profit Ratio

Gross Profit Ratio

It brings a relationship between Gross Profit and Net Sales. This ratio indicates the operational efficiency of the business.

The ratio can be expressed as :

$$\text{Gross Profit Ratio} = \frac{\text{Gross Profit}}{\text{Net Sales}} \times 100 = \%$$

Always express this ratio in percentage.(%)

Causes for increase of this ratio are :

(i) If the figures for closing stock are inflated.

(ii) If the sale price of goods or products are increased while the Cost of Production or cost price remains constant.

(iii) If the sales figures are inflated.

(iv) If the opening stock figures are undervalued.

Now if you can apply your common sense you will see that the causes for decrease of this ratio is opposite to the causes for increase.

2. Net Profit Ratio

It brings a relationship between net profit and net sales. This ratio also measures the *Net Profit Ratio* operational efficiency of the business. This is sometimes known as profit margin ratio.

3. Expense Ratio

Expense Ratio It brings a relationship between each item of expenses and net sales. It measures the operating efficiency of the business.

Express the ratio in percentage.
The ratio can be expressed as :

$$\frac{\text{Each item of Expenses}}{\text{Net Sales}} \times 100$$

4. Operating Ratio

It brings a relationship between the cost of goods sold plus operating expenses and net sales. Please note that some experts prefer not to include operating expenses to find *Operating Ratio* out operating ratio. In that case, operating ratio brings a relationship between Cost of Goods Sold and Net Sales. You can follow any one of the systems adding a note stating whether you have taken operating expenses to find out the ratio. Please note that Cost of Goods Sold = Opening Stock + Purchase – Closing Stock.

However, the ratio can be expressed as :

$$\text{Operating Ratio} = \frac{\text{Cost of Goods Sold} + \text{Operating Expenses}}{\text{Net Sales}} \times 100 \quad \text{(i)}$$

$$= \frac{\text{Cost of Goods Sold}}{\text{Net Sales}} \times 100 \quad \text{(ii)}$$

Express this ratio in percentage.

This ratio measures the operational as well as financial management efficiency—specially during inflationary period.

Higher ratio indicates lower profit margin. The high ratio ensures managements to protect erosion of real capital which results from inflation of profit. Since, dividend declared or paid out of inflated profit amounts to payment of dividend out of capital. On the other hand, Low ratio indicates High profit margin and less 'ploughing-back' or 'retention of profit' which permits replacing the goods which was sold. This can be explained with the help of two examples :

CASE I

Trading A/c

Dr. Cr.

	Particular	Amount		Particular	Amount
		Rs.			Rs.
To	Opening Stock	10,000	By	Sales	30,000
"	Purchase	10,000	"	Closing Stock	15,000
"	Gross Profit	25,000			
		45,000			45,000

Here, Cost of Goods Sold = Opening Stock (Rs.10,000) + Purchase (Rs.10,000) – Closing Stock (Rs. 15,000) = Rs. 5,000

CASE II

Trading A/c

Dr. Cr.

	Particular	Amount		Particular	Amount
		Rs.			Rs.
To	Opening Stock	10,000	By	Sales	30,000
"	Purchase	10,000	,,	Closing Stock	10,000
"	Gross Profit	20,000			
		40,000			40,000

Here, Cost of Goods Sold = Opening Stock (Rs.10,000) + Purchase (Rs.10,000) – Closing Stock (Rs.10,000) = Rs. 10,000.

Sales = Cost of Goods Sold + Profit.

Case I

Rs. 30,000 = Rs. 5,000 + Rs. 25,000.

$$\text{Operating Ratio} = \frac{\text{Cost of Goods Sold}}{\text{Net Sales}} = \frac{\text{Rs. } 5{,}000}{\text{Rs. } 30{,}000} \times 100 = 16\%$$

Please remember my earlier lecture where I told you that Low Ratio (here 16%) indicates high profit margin. The situation will be more clear if its result is compared with Case II :

Sales = Cost of Goods Sold + Profit.

Rs. 30,000 = Rs. 10,000 + Rs. 20,000.

$$\text{Operating Ratio} = \frac{\text{Cost of Goods Sold}}{\text{Net Sales}} = \frac{\text{Rs. } 10{,}000}{\text{Rs. } 30{,}000} \times 100 = 33\tfrac{1}{3}\%$$

So it is clear that high ratio indicates low profit margin.

5. Stock Turnover Ratio

Stock Turnover Ratio

It brings a relationship between the Cost of Goods Sold and Average Stock Carried. It is also known as Turnover Ratio. The Stock Turnover Ratio can be expressed as :

$$\text{Stock Turnover} = \frac{\text{Cost of Goods Sold}}{\text{Average Stock}}$$

Express the ratio in terms of TIMES. It is stated by an expert that 'greater the merchandise turnover, the larger the amount of profit, the smaller the amount of capital is tied up in inventory'. It measures the merchandise efficiency. High Stock Turnover indicates Over-Trading and Low Stock Turnover indicates Under-Trading in general.

☐ "Sir, what is Average Stock ?"

• Note the following as to average stock :

$$\frac{\text{Opening Stock} + \text{Closing Stock}}{2} = \text{Average Stock Carried}$$

Now I would like to give you some idea about the composite or Inter-Statement or Profit and Loss Account and Balance Sheet Ratio.

C. Composite Ratio — It brings a relationship between the two figures, one appearing in Balance Sheet and the other in Profit and Loss Account. Composite ratios consist of the following.

Composite Ratio

1. (a) Return on Proprietor's Fund

Return on Proprietor's Fund

It brings a relationship between the Proprietor's Fund and Net Profit or Net Operating profit, as the case may be.

Proprietor's Fund =	Equity Share Capital	XXXX
	Reserve and Surplus	XXX
	Retained Profit	XXX
	Proprietor's Fund	Rs. XXXXX

The ratio can be expressed as :

$$\frac{\text{Profit}}{\text{Proprietor's Fund}} \times 100$$

Express the ratio in percentage. This ratio measures profitability of the business.

(b) Return on Proprietor's Equity

Return on Proprietor's Equity

It brings a relationship between the proprietor's equity (Net Worth + Pref. Share Capital) and net profit or net operating profit as the case may be.

The ratio can be expressed as :

$$\frac{\text{Profit}}{\text{Proprietor's Equity}} \times 100$$

Express this ratio in terms of percentage. This ratio also indicates the profitability of the business.

(c) Return on Ordinary Share Capital

Return on Ordinary Share Capital

It brings a relationship between the Ordinary Share Capital and Net Profit after satisfying the dividend to the preference shareholders.

This ratio can be expressed as :

$$\frac{\text{Profit}}{\text{Ordinary Share Capital}} \times 100$$

Express the ratio in percentage. This ratio measures the profitability of any business.

(d) Return on Capital Employed

Return on Capital Employed

It brings a relationship between the Total Capital Employed (Proprietor's Fund + Loan Capital) and Net Profit or Net Operating Profit as the case may be.

This ratio can be expressed as :

$$\frac{\text{Profit}}{\text{Capital Employed}} \times 100$$

Express the ratio in percentage. This ratio measures the total profitability of business.

(e) Return on Total Resources

Return on Total Resources

The other name of Return on Capital Employed is Return on Total Resources. It brings a relationship between the Net Total Assets (Net Current Assets + Fixed Assets) and Net Profit or Net Operating Profit.

This ratio can be expressed as :

$$\frac{\text{Profit}}{\text{Total Resources}} \times 100$$

Always express this ratio in percentage.

☐ "Sir, please explain how **Capital Employed** in the business represents the **Net Total Assets** or **Total Resources** of the business."

• Your question is indeed very interesting. I would like to explain your point after explaining the different aspects of Composite Ratio.

2. Turnover of Fixed Assets

Turnover of Fixed Assets

It brings a relationship between the Cost of Goods Sold (Sale of goods at cost) and the amount invested in fixed assets.

The ratio can be expressed as :

$$\frac{\text{Cost of Goods Sold}}{\text{Fixed Assets}}$$

Express the ratio in terms of proportion, say 1·5 to 1 or 2 to 1 and so on.

For example : Cost of Goods Sold Rs. 30,000 and Fixed Assets Rs.21,000.

$$\frac{\text{Rs. } 30{,}000}{\text{Rs. } 21{,}000} = 1{\cdot}43 \text{ to } 1$$

This indicates that for every investment of Re. 1·00 in Fixed Assets of the business, Rs. 1·43 worth of Goods are sold. This ratio indicates operational efficiency.

3. Turnover of Total Assets

Turnover of Total Assets

It brings a relationship between the Cost of Goods Sold and the amount invested in Total Assets (Fixed and Current).

This ratio can be expressed as :

$$\frac{\text{Cost of Goods Sold}}{\text{Total Assets}}$$

4. Turnover of Debtors

Turnover of Debtors

It brings a relationship between the Net Sales and Receivables (Bills Receivable and Debtors) during the year. This relationship indicates the credit and collection policy of the enterprise. That is to say, this relationship indicates 'the number of days' credit outstanding at the date'.

This ratio can be expressed as :

$$\frac{\text{Debtors or Receivable}}{\text{Net Sales}} \times 365 \text{ days}$$

Always express this ratio in Days.

☐ "Excuse me Sir, you have forgotten to give us Turnover of Creditors".

• Well, I have done it intentionally to see that you are attentive or not.

Take a look here.

$$\text{Turnover of Creditor} = \frac{\text{Creditors or Payable}}{\text{Credit Purchase}} \times 365 \text{ days}$$

5. Turnover of Capital Employed

Capital Turnover Efficiency

This ratio indicates how many times Capital turned over during a particular period. High turnover reflects higher profitability of business. This ratio gives an indication of managerial efficiency. This can be expressed as :

$$\frac{\text{Sales}}{\text{Capital Employed}}$$

Express this ratio in terms of TIMES.

However, I like to explain the whole ratios (Balance Sheet, Profit and Loss Account and Composite) in a tabular form.

Accounting and Financial Ratios

Balance Sheet Ratios	Indication	Components	1st year	2nd year	3rd year	4th year	5th year
1. Current Ratio	Current Financial Position and short-term solvency	$\frac{\text{Current Assets}}{\text{Current Liabilities}}$	X	X	X	X	X
2. Liquid Ratio	Immediate cash position	$\frac{\text{Quick Assets}}{\text{Quick / Current Liabilities}}$	X	X	X	X	X
3. Proprietary Ratio	Future financial position	$\frac{\text{Proprietor's Fund}}{\text{Total Assets}}$	X	X	X	X	X
4. Assets Proprietorship Ratio	Contribution of proprietor's fund to assets	$\frac{\text{Current or Fixed Assets}}{\text{Proprietor's Fund}}$	X	X	X	X	X
5. Debt-Equity Ratio	Source of Capital	$\frac{\text{External Equities}}{\text{Internal Equities}}$	X	X	X	X	X
6. Capital Gearing Ratio	High and Low Gearing of the business	$\frac{\text{Equity Share Capital}}{\text{Fixed Charge Bearing Long term Securities (Pref. Sh. Capital + Debentures)}}$	X	X	X	X	X

Accounting and Financial Ratios

Operating Ratios or Profit and Loss Account Ratios	Indication	Components	1st year	2nd year	3rd year	4th year	5th year
1. Gross Profit Ratio	Profitability	$\frac{\text{Gross Profit}}{\text{Net Sales}}$	X	X	X	X	X
2. Net Profit Ratio	do	$\frac{\text{Net Profit}}{\text{Net Sales}}$	X	X	X	X	X
3. Expense Ratio	Operational Efficiency	$\frac{\text{Each item of Expenses}}{\text{Net Sales}}$	X	X	X	X	X
4. Operating Ratio	do	$\frac{\text{Cost of Goods Sold + Operating Expenses}}{\text{Net Sales}}$	X	X	X	X	X
5. Stock Turn Over Ratio	do	$\frac{\text{Cost of Goods Sold}}{\text{Average Stock Carried}}$	X	X	X	X	X

Accounting and Financial Ratios

Composite Ratios	Indication	Components	1st year	2nd year	3rd year	4th year	5th year
1. Return on Proprietor's Fund	Profitability	Net/Operating Profit / Proprietor's Fund	X	X	X	X	X
2. Return on Proprietor's Equity	do	Net/Operating Profit / Proprietor's Equity	X	X	X	X	X
3. Return on Ordinary Share Capital	Operational Efficiency and Profitability	Net Profit – Pref. Div. / Ordinary Share Capital	X	X	X	X	X
4. Return on Capital Employed or Return on Total Resources	Profitability	Profit / Capital Employed	X	X	X	X	X
5. Turnover of Fixed Assets	Operational Efficiency	Cost of Goods Sold / Fixed Assets	X	X	X	X	X
6. Turnover of Total Assets	do	Cost of Goods Sold / Total Assets	X	X	X	X	X
7. Creditors' Velocity	Borrowing and Payment Policy	Total Creditor or Payables / Credit Purchase	X	X	X	X	X
8. Turnover of Debtors	Credit and Collection Policy	Debtors or Receivables / Net Sales	X	X	X	X	X
9. Turnover of Capital Ratio	Operational Efficiency	Sales / Capital Employed	X	X	X	X	X

Now I would like to explain how Ratio Analysis can be studied from Functional or Working point of View.

Ratio Analysis

- **Solvency**
  - **Short Term**
    - (1) Current Ratio or Working Capital Ratio
  - **Immediate**
    - (1) Quick Ratio or Acid Test Ratio
  - **Long Term**
    - (1) Proprietary Ratio
- **Profitability**
  - (1) Gross Profit Ratio
  - (2) Net Profit Ratio
  - (3) Dividend Per Share Ratio
  - (4) Return on Capital Employed
  - (5) Return on Total Resources
  - (6) Return on Equity etc.
- **Efficiency and Performance**
  - (1) Solvency Ratio
  - (2) Profitability Ratio
  - (3) Capital Gearing Ratio
  - (4) Stock Turnover Ratio
  - (5) Operating Ratio
  - (6) Turnover of Total Assets etc.
  - (7) Turnover of Capital
  - (8) Expense Ratio

☐ "Sir, Please work out a few practical problems which will be helpful to understand the whole discussions".

• Yes, yes, I will definitely work out a few practical problems. Before that, I would like to discuss a few points. When you try to interpret any Balance Sheet and Profit and Loss Account, I think you should study the financial

Approach to Financial Study

statement beforehand. Your interpretation will remain confirmed within the information supplied to you. Take for example, if no information as to the profit of the business is supplied to you, how can you find out the result of operation of the business? Besides, whenever you go to interpret the working of the business, you are to study the ratio analysis from the Functional Point of View as indicated earlier. However, you can interpret the financial statement with the help of certain Exhibits or Tables :

Exhibit I

Showing the Solvency of the Business

	Years				
	1st	2nd	3rd	4th	5th
Current Ratio	...	...	...	...	...
Liquid Ratio	...	...	...	...	...
Proprietary Ratio	...	...	...	...	...

Exhibit II

Showing the Profitability of the Business

	Years				
	1st	2nd	3rd	4th	5th
Net Profit Ratio	...	...	...	...	...
Return on Capital Employed	...	...	...	...	...
Earning Per Share Ratio	...	...	...	...	...

Exhibit III

Showing the Efficiency of the Business

	Years				
	1st	2nd	3rd	4th	5th
Turnover of Capital	...	...	...	...	...
Capital Gearing Ratio	...	...	...	...	...
Turnover of Debtors	...	...	...	...	...
Turnover of Creditors	...	...	...	...	...
Operating Ratio	...	...	...	...	...
Stock Turnover	...	...	...	...	...

After this you can interpret about the working of the business.

Before you go to interpret the Statement you should tabulate them in a suitable form if possible. The proforma of tabulation of accounting information for different years are given :

I **hope**, you have understood my lectures. Is there any question?

☐ "Sir, can you interpret the financial statement without tabulating accounting information?"

• Yes, you can. If you are asked to tabulate it at that time, it should be given :

Comparative Revenue Statement/Profit and Loss Account

Particulars	**2005**	**2005**	**2006**	**2006**
	Rs.	Rs.	Rs.	Rs.
Sales	XXXXX		XXXXX	
Less : Cost of Goods Sold :				
(Opening Stock + Purchase +				
Manufacturing Expenses– Closing Stock)	XXXX		XXXXX	
Gross Profit		XXXX		XXXXX
Less : Expenses—Operating :				
Salaries	XX		XX	
Insurance	XX		XX	
Stationeries	XX		XX	
Postage and Telegram	XX		XX	
Depreciation	XX		XX	
Provision for Taxation	XX		XX	
Bad Debt	XX		XX	
Provisoin for Bad and Doubtful Debts	XX		XX	
Discount Allowed	XX		XX	
Advertising and Travelling Expenses	XX		XX	
Directors' Fees	XX		XX	
Other Debit Items of Profit and Loss Account	XX	XXXX	XX	XXXX
Operating Profit		XXXX		XXXX
Non-Operating Income:				
Interest	XX		XX	
Profit on Sale of Investment	XX		XX	
	XXX		XXX	
Non-Operating Expenses :				
Loss on Sale of Assets	XX		XX	
Net Non-Operating Income or				
Net Non-Operating Loss				
Net Profit		XXX		XXX
		XXX		XXX

Comparative Balance Sheet

Particulars	2005 Rs.	2005 Rs.	2006 Rs.	2006 Rs.
Share Capital :				
Ordinary or, Equity Share Capital	XXXX		XXXX	
Reserve and Surplus	XXX		XXX	
Proprietor's Fund or Net Worth	XXXX		XXXX	
Less :				
Goodwill	XX		XX	
Patent	XX		XX	
'Know-how'	XX		XX	
Preliminary and Development Expenses	XX		XX	
Profit and Loss A/c. (Dr)	XX		XX	
Tangible Net Worth	XXX		XXX	
Add : Loan Capital		XX		XX
(Pref. share capital, Debenture and other long-term loan)		XXXX		XXXX
Capital Employed in the Business (Total Fund Employed)		XXXX		XXXX
Represented by Total Resources				
Tangible Fixed Assets :				
Land and Building	XX		XX	
Furniture and Fittings	XX		XX	
Plant and Machinery	XX		XX	
Investment	XX		XX	
Current Assets :		XXX		XXX
Stock in Trade	XX		XX	
Finished Goods	XX		XX	
Debtors	XX		XX	
Bills Receivable	XX		XX	
Payment in Advance	XX		XX	
Total Current Assets (T.C.A.)	XXX		XXX	
Less : Current Liabilities :				
Sundry Creditors	XX		XX	
Bills Payable	XX		XX	
Bank Overdraft	XX		XX	
Accrued Expenses	XX		XX	
Dividend	XX		XX	
Total Current Liabilities (T.C.L.)	XX		XX	
Working Capital or Net Current Assets (T.C.A. – T.C.L.)		XXX		XXX
Total Net Assets (Total Resources)		XXXX		XXXX

Is there any question please?

☐ "Sir, what is Weighted Current Ratio? Give us some light about the concept".

● Thank you for your question. You know that the other names of Current Ratio are Working Capital Ratio and Liquidity Ratio. This ratio is found out by drawing a relationship between Current Assets and Current Liabilities. You see, all types of current assets are not equally liquid and, similarly, all types of current liabilities are not payable with same speed. So to make the current assets more dependable 'weights' may be imposed on the respective current assets and current liabilities, depending on the actual degree of liquidity and payment urgency.

Weighted Current Ratio

Now you may put me question, sir how actual selection of weights would be made? I am to say that it depends upon the nature and circumstances of individual case. Take for an example, cash may be treated as hundred percent liquid, similarly Sundry Debtors may be treated at 75% liquid, similarly, work-in-progress and Stock-in-trade may be treated as 60% and 50% liquid, respectively. Regarding items of current liabilities, the urgency of payment may be treated as follows : Provision for Taxation 60%, Provision for Dividend 100%, Sundry Creditors 75%, Bank overdraft 100%.

The specification of above weights is not final and rigid, it may vary. So to test the real solvency or liquidity of a business, the idea of Weighted Current Ratio should be implemented. The whole thing may be discussed with the help of an example :

Balance Sheet

Capital and Liabilities	I year	II year	Assets and Properties	I year	II year
	Rs.	Rs.		Rs.	Rs.
Share Capital	1,00,000	1,00,000	Total Tangible Fixed		
Reserve and Surplus	30,000	50,000	Assets, *Less* depreciation	1,50,000	1,60,000
5% Debentures	50,000	50,000	Sundry Debtors	50,000	60,000
Bank Overdraft	10,000	15,000	Stock	50,000	70,000
Sundry Creditors	40,000	50,000	Cash in hand	5,000	10,000
Proposed Dividend	15,000	20,000			
Provision for Taxation	10,000	15,000			
	2,55,000	3,00,000		2,55,000	3,00,000

Now I show the position of current assets and liabilities by applying weight :

Particulars	Weight %	1st year figure	2nd year figure	Weight 1st year figure	Weight 2nd year figure
Current Assets	y	a	b	a × y	b × y
Sundry Debtors	75	50,000	60,000	37,500	45,000
Stock	50	50,000	70,000	25,000	35,000
Cash	100	5,000	10,000	5,000	10,000
		1,05,000	1,40,000	67,500	90,000
Current Liabilities					
Bank Overdraft	100	10,000	15,000	10,000	15,000
Sundry Creditors	80	40,000	50,000	32,000	40,000
Proposed Dividend	80	15,000	20,000	12,000	16,000
Provision for Taxation	50	10,000	15,000	5,000	7,500
		75,000	1,00,000	59,000	78,500

Now let us compare the normal Current Ratios of respective years with that of weighted Current Ratio :

Ratios / Year	General or Normal Current Ratio (Total Current Assets / Total Current Liabilities) X	Weighted Current Ratio (Weighted Current Assets / Weighted Current Liabilities) Y	Extent to which Normal Current Ratio has been inflated (X – Y)
1.	$\frac{\text{Rs. } 1,05,000}{\text{Rs. } 75,000} = 1.4$	$\frac{\text{Rs. } 67,500}{\text{Rs. } 59,000} = 1.144$	0.256
2.	$\frac{\text{Rs. } 1,40,000}{\text{Rs. } 1,00,000} = 1.4$	$\frac{\text{Rs. } 90,000}{\text{Rs. } 78,500} = 1.146$	0.254

I think the discussions made earlier is clear to you. Please be frank if there are any questions you like to put me.

☐ "Sir, how we can interpret Financial Statements?"

• I have already discussed how to interpret Financial Statements. Do you remember? I told you that the main aim of interpretation is to assess Solvency, Profitability and Efficiency. And I explained about different types of accounting ratios which may be applied to test Solvency, Profitability and Efficiency. Do you follow?

☐ "Sir, do the concepts of Over-trading, Under-trading, Over-capitalisation and Under-capitalisation bear any significance in the context of interpertation of Financial Statement?"

• Yes they have. Besides commenting on Solvency, Profitability and Efficiency, you should comment on whether a particular business is over-capitalised or under-capitalised and overtraded or undertraded.

You see, I had given you the basic and overall conception about Over-trading, Under-trading, Under-Capitalisation and Over-Capitalisation in the chapter on 'Capital gearing'. I think you remember.

☐ "Yes Sir, but give us the name of ratios which can be used to test Over-Capitalisation, Under-Capitalisation, Over-Trading and Under-Trading".

• Well, please note :

Diagnosis	Symptoms	Tools Used
Over-Trading	Inadequate working capital, Declining normal and future solvency, Excessive creditors' figure, High Debtor turnover, High Stock turnover etc.	Current Ratio—Low Proprietary Ratio—Low Stock turnover Ratio—High Debtors Turnover—High Creditors Velocity—High
Under-Trading	Adequate working capital. Increasing normal and future solvency.	Current Ratio—Very High Proprietary Ratio—High
Over Capitalisation	Low earning per share, Increasing future solvency	Earning per share Ratio—Low Proprietary Ratio—High

Diagnosis	Symptoms	Tools Used
Under-Capitalisation	Insufficient working capital, Declining future and long term solvency. High earning per share, High Capital Gearing—Dependence (too much) on Loan Capital	Current Ratio—Low Proprietary Ratio—Low Earning per share—High Capital Gearing Ratio—High

☐ "Sir, what is Earning Per Share Ratio"?

● I think, it is very easy. I find no reason why you cannot conceive of the idea of Earning Per Share Ratio, Dividend Per Share Ratio, Payout Ratio.

☐ "Sir, please explain".

● Earning Per Share Ratio (EPS) = $\frac{\text{Net Profit after Pref. Dividend}}{\text{No. of Shares}}$ = Rs. ... per share

Dividend Per Share Ratio (DPS) = $\frac{\text{Dividend for Ordinary Shares}}{\text{No. of Shares}}$ = Rs. ... per share

Payout Ratio = $\frac{\text{DPS}}{\text{EPS}}$ = ...%.

☐ "Excuse me Sir, I have one more question. Sir, suppose return on capital employed of a company for four consecutive years are 40%, 30%, 25% and 20% respectevely. Here we see a decline or fall in earnings. Now, if I am asked by the company to analyse the causes for decline, then how am I to proceed? Please enlighten me".

● You see, you have put a very apt question. You know that the return on capital employed is judged by drawing a relationship between capital employed and profit. And this return is the result of multiplied result of Turnover of Capital and Margin on sale. So your first and foremost work should be to scrutinise the two aspects—percentage margin on sale and capital turnover :

$$\text{Return on Capital Employed} = \frac{\text{Profit}}{\text{Capital Employed}}$$

$$\text{Return on Capital Employed} = \text{\% Margin on Sale} \times \text{Capital Turnover}$$

$$= \frac{\text{Profit}}{\text{Sales}} \times \frac{\text{Sales}}{\text{Capital Employed}}$$

Profit = Sales – (Cost of Goods Sold + Operating Expenses)

Capital Employed = Tangible Fixed Assets + Working Capital

I think you have followed the above discussions. Now I wish to work out a few practical problems on Accounting Ratios and Interpretation of Financial Statements.

☐ "Sir, so long you were discussing about the different types of accounting and ratios, statements needed for management for management decision. Before working out a few problems on accounting ratios, would you kindly enlighten us about the types of **Accounting Statements for Management of a Manufacturing Business**?"

• Your question really is very interesting. You want to know the types of accounting statements for management of manufacturing concern.

Isn't it so? For that would like to refer you to an address delivered by Mr. W. W. Fea to the members of the Summer Course of the Institute of Chartered Accountants of England and Wales on 16th July 1949. In his lecture on "Presentation of Accounting Statements for Management" Mr. Fea circulated to all the participants at the Summer Course a table containing information about types of Accounting Statements for management of a manufacturing business. This I present before you for your knowledge. Here is the table. Please note it very minutely.

No.	Name of statement	To whom addressed	Additional copies to	Information conveyed	Purpose	Frequency
1.	Balance sheet	Managing director	—	Sources of capital, Employment of capital, Liquidity of capital	Aids control of finance. Shows employment of capital in different assets. Aids credit control, shows surplus funds available for investment	Monthly
2.	Fixed Assets	Managing director	Plant engineer	Analysis of expenditure between replacements and additions. Comparison of expenditure with budget authorisations and depreciation	Controls maintenance of productive capacity. Controls planned expansion of capacity	Monthly
3.	Profit & Loss Account Summary	Managing director	—	Sales, cost of sales and profit. Actual compared with budget/standard to disclose variances	Shows actual against expected. Shows actual costs against allowed cost for volume attained. Shows gain/deficiency of actual profit from standard profit analysed by causes	Monthly
3.a.	Departments	Managing director	—	Ditto by departments	Ditto by departments	Monthly
4.	Expenses Analysis Administrative	Managing director	—	Analysis of expenses for administrative departments. Actual compared with budget allowances for volume or activity achieved	Provides a basis of control of administrative expenses	Monthly

No.	Name of statement	To whom addressed	Additional copies to	Information conveyed	Purpose	Frequency
	Sales	Sales Manager	Managing director	Analysis of expenses for sales division. Actual compared with budget allowances for volume achieved	Ditto for sales expenses	Monthly
	Works	Works Manager	Managing director	Analysis of expenses for works. Actual compared with budget allowance for volume achieved	Ditto for works expenses	Monthly
5.	Sales Analysis Markets	Sales Manager	Managing director	Suitable analysis of qualities, values, profit and loss	Provides check on sales force	Monthly
	Customers	Sales Manager	Managing director	Ditto by customers	Shows where follow up by representatives is necessary	
	Products	Sales Manager	Managing director	Ditto by products	Shows slow moving-lines Aids consideration of price policy and production policy	
6.	Orders Received and on Hand Markets	Sales Manager	Managing director	Suitable analysis of quantities, values and production load	Aids market research	Weekly
	Customers	Sales Manager	Managing director	Ditto by customers	Provides data for advertising and sales drives	Ditto
	Products	Sales Manager	Managing director Planning Manager	Ditto by products	Provides check on production programme	Ditto
7.	Stocks Finished	Sales manager	Managing director Planning Manager	Suitable analysis of quantities and values	Provides check on production programme and flexibility of factory processes	Monthly
	Work in Progress	Works Manager	Managing director Planning Manager	Ditto by departments	Ditto by departments	Ditto

No.	Name of statement	To whom addressed	Additional copies to	Information conveyed	Purpose	Frequency
8.	Activity & Efficiency Summary	Works manager	Managing director	Actual activity, utilisation and efficiency compared with standard	Provides check on the use of plant capacity, and of direct labour	Weekly/ Monthly
	Departments	Departmental Supervisor	Works manager Planning manager	Ditto by departments	Ditto by departments	Ditto
9.	Stopped Time analysis Summary	Works manager	Plant engineer	Causes of stopped time in hours and value	Aids consideration of replacement of old plant, and adequacy of maintenance. Provides check on availability of materials and on tool service	Weekly
	Department	Departmental Supervisor	Works manager Planning manager	Ditto by department	Ditto by departments	Ditto
10.	Operating Statements Summary	Works manager	Managing director	Comparison of actual expenses with standard for materials, labour and variable expenses controlled by works	Provides information concerning the elements of cost for which direct responsibility is accepted so as to permit effective control of them by appropriate means that will lead to maximum economy	Monthly
	Department	Departmental supervisor	Works manager	Ditto by departments	Ditto by departments	Ditto
11.	Production Analysis	Works manager	Managing director Planning manager	Volume of output, compared with budget	Provides check on production programme including balance between departments	Weekly
12.	Labour Performance	Works manager	Labour manager	Operator efficiency, direct and indirect labour.	Aids consideration of transfer or elimination of sub-standard and operation Aids consideration of	Weekly
	Accidents and	Works manager	Labour manager	Frequency and severity rates, number of acci-		

No.	Name of statement	To whom addressed	Additional copies to	Information conveyed	Purpose	Frequency
	safety		Works medical offcer	dents hours lost, causes	accident prevention	Weekly
	Lateness and Absenteeism	Works manager	Labour manager Works medical officer	Numbers, amount of lost time, reasons	Shows quality of labour and influence of outside factors, e.g. public transport. Shows incidence and influence of sickness.	Ditto
	Turnover	Works manager	Labour manager	Number starting and leaving, sexes and grades, reasons for leaving	Aids consideration of policy as to transfer of labour, and welfare organisation	Quarterly
13.	Materials Stocks outstanding Orders and receipts.	Works manager	Planning manager	Availability to meet production plan	Shows whether stocks and expected deliveries are sufficient to meet production plan	Weekly
	Consumption	Works manager	Planning manager	Usage of material	Shows redundant or slow moving stock. Shows efficiency of usage	Ditto
14.	Scrap report	Chief inspector	Works manager	Causes of scrap, rejects and spoilt work in quantity and values, compared with standard allowances	Aids economy in use of materials Shows where improvement of methods and of labour training is demanded	Weekly
15.	Power Consumption	Works manager	Engineer	Power factor, load factor, maximum demand, consumption in relation to output	Aids economy in use of power	Weekly
16.	Activity and Efficiency (Sectional)	Foreman	Works manager	Actual activity, utilisation and efficiency compared with standard	Provides check on the use of plant capacity and of direct labour	Weekly
17.	Stopped Time Analysis (Sectional)	Foreman	Works manager	Causes of stopped time in hours and value	Aids consideration of adequacy of maintenance; provides check on availability of materials and on tool service	Weekly
18.	Operating Statement (Sectional)	Foreman	Works manager	Comparison of actual expense with standard for materials, labour and variable expenses in cost centres controlled	Provides information concerning the elements of cost for which direct responsibility is accepted,	Weekly/ Monthly

No.	Name of statement	To whom addressed	Additional copies to	Information conveyed	Purpose	Frequency
				by foreman	so as to permit effective control of them by appropriate means that will lead to maximum economy	
19.	Scrap Report (Sectional)	Foreman	Works manager	Causes of scrap, rejects and spoilt work in quantity and value compared with standard allowances	Aids economy in use of materials Shows where improvement of methods and of labour training is demanded	Weekly

Problem

Rearrange the following statements in a form suitable for analysis and calculate five ratios which are significant in analysing the finanacial trend of the business :

Condensed Balance Sheet

	Year I Rs.	Year II Rs.
Assets :		
Cash at Bank	15,380	26,020
Trade Debtors	11,260	11,710
Stock on hand	56,160	49,460
Fixed Assets (Less Depreciation)	2,17,200	2,19,810
Total Assets	3,00,000	3,07,000
Liabilities and Capital :		
Creditors	20,000	16,000
Bills Payable	12,750	6,500
Debentures	1,00,000	1,00,000
Reserves and Appropriation Account Balance	67,250	84,500
Paid-up Capital	1,00,000	1,00,000
	3,00,000	3,07,000
Sales	1,80,000	1,95,000

Note : Calculate ratios to nearest second decimal place. **[C.A. Final]**

Try to understand the problem, you are to note here one important point. That is to say, no figure for the profit is given.

Now you may put me the question "Sir, how can we find out the profitability ratio?" For this I told you already that your answer should remain confined within the information supplied. So in this case you cannot speak anything about the profitability of the company. Before discussing all these ratios, let me first of all show how statement can be tabulated in a form suitable for analysis.

Solution

Comparative Balance Sheets of ... Co. Ltd. as at 31st December

		Year I Rs.		Year II Rs.
Share Capital :				
Paid-up Capital		1,00,000		1,00,000
Reserves and Surplus		67,250		84,500
Proprietor's Fund or Net Worth		1,67,250		1,84,500
Add : Loan Capital		1,00,000		1,00,000
Total Capital Employed		2,67,250		2,84,500
Represented by :				
Fixed Assets		2,17,200		2,19,810
Total Current Assets	82,800		87,190	
Less : Total Current Liabilities	32,750		22,500	
Net Working Capital or Net Current Assets		50,050		64,690
Net Total Assets or Total Resources		2,67,250		2,84,500

I have already given you a proforma chart as to how the financial statement can be re-arranged in a form suitable for analysis.

☐ "Sir, please work out the different ratios."

• From the information given above, you can find out the following ratios :

1. Current Ratio.
2. Acid Test Ratio.
3. Proprietary Ratio.
4. Turnover of Debtors Ratio.
5. Turnover of Capital Ratio.
6. Fixed Assets to Net worth Ratio.

However, you are to point out five ratios. For this, Acid Test Ratio can be avoided for the time being :

Ratios	Components	Years I	Years II
Ratio Indicating Solvency :			
1. Current Ratio or Working Capital Ratio	$\frac{\text{Current Assets}}{\text{Current Liability}}$	$\frac{82,800}{32,750} = 2.53$	$\frac{87,190}{22,500} = 3.87$
2. Proprietary Ratio	$\frac{\text{Proprietor's Fund}}{\text{Total Assets}}$	$\frac{1,67,250}{3,00,000} = 56\%$	$\frac{1,84,500}{3,07,000} = 60\%$

Ratios	Components	Years I	Years II
Ratios Indicating the Efficiency of the Business			
1. Turnover of Debtors Ratio or, Debtors' Velocity	$\frac{\text{Debtors}}{\text{Net Sales}} \times \text{Days}$	$\frac{11,260}{1,80,000} \times 365$ days =23 days (app.)	$\frac{11,710}{1,95,000} \times 365$ days = 22 days (app.)
2. Turnover of Capital Ratio	$\frac{\text{Sales}}{\text{Capital Employed}}$	$\frac{1,80,000}{2,67,250}$ = 0.67 times	$\frac{1,95,000}{2,84,500}$ = 0.69 times
3. Fixed Assets to Net Worth	$\frac{\text{Fixed Assets}}{\text{Net Worth}}$	$\frac{2,17,200}{1,67,250}$ = 1.30	$\frac{2,19,810}{1,84,500}$ = 1.19

Problem

From the following information, for the accounting year 2005 you are requested

(a) to arrange them in a form suitable for analysis, and

(b) to find out the following ratios — (i) Gross Profit Ratio, (ii) Operating Ratio, and (iii) Stock Turnover Ratio.

	Rs.
Sales	5,20,000
Purchases	3,22,250
Opening Stock	76,250
Closing Stock	98,500
Sales Return	20,000
Selling and Distribution Expenses :	
Salaries	15,300
Advertising	4,700
Travelling	2,000
Administrative Expenses :	
Salaries	27,000
Rent	2,700
Stationery, Postage etc.	2,500
Depreciation	9,300
Other charges	16,500
Provision for Taxation	40,000
Non-operating Income :	
Dividend on Shares	9,000
Profit on Sale of Shares	3,000
Non-operating Expenses :	
Loss on Sale of Assets	4,000

[Adapted from C.A. Final]

Solution

(a)

Revenue Statement

		Rs.	Rs.
Net Sales		5,00,000	
Less : Cost of Goods Sold		3,00,000	
Gross Profit			2,00,000
Operating Expenses :			
Total of Selling and Distribution Expenses		22,000	
Administrative Expenses		98,000	1,20,000
Operating Profit			80,000
Non-Operating Income	12,000		
Non-Operating Expenses	4,000		
Net Non-Operating Income			8,000
Net Profit			88,000

(b)

(i) Gross Profit Ratio $= \frac{\text{Gross Profit}}{\text{Net Sales}} \times 100$

$= \frac{\text{Rs. } 2,00,000}{\text{Rs. } 5,00,000} \times 100$

$= 40\%$

(ii) Operating Ratio $= \frac{\text{Cost of Goods Sold + Operating Expenses}}{\text{Net Sales}} \times 100$

$= \frac{\text{Rs. } 3,00,000 + \text{Rs. } 1,20,000}{\text{Rs. } 5,00,000} \times 100$

$= 84\%$

(iii) Stock Turnover Ratio $= \frac{\text{Cost of Goods Sold}}{\text{Average Stock carried}}$

$= \frac{\text{Rs. } 3,00,000}{\text{Rs. } 87,375}$

$= 3.43$ (app.) times a year.

Problem

The following are the summarised Profit and Loss Account of Hind Products Limited for the year ending 31st December, 2005 and the Balance sheet as on that date :

Dr. **Profit and Loss A/c** *Cr.*

Particular	Amount	Particular	Amount
	Rs.		Rs.
To Opening Stock	99,500	By Sales	8,50,000
" Purchases	5,45,250	" Closing stock	1,49,000
" Incidental Expenses	14,250		
" Gross Profit c/d	3,40,000		
	9,99,000		9,99,000

Particular		Amount	Particular		Amount
		Rs.			Rs.
To Operating Expenses :			By Gross Profit b/d		3,40,000
Selling and Distribution Expenses	30,000		" Non-Operating Income		
Administration Expenses	1,50,000		Interest	3,000	
Finance Expenses	15,000	1,95,000	Profit on Sale of Shares	6,000	9,000
To Non-Operating Expenses :					
Loss on Sale of Assets		4,000			
To Net Profit		1,50,000			
		3,49,000			3,49,000

Balance Sheet

Liabilities	Amount	Assets	Amount
	Rs.		Rs.
Issued Capital :		Land and Building	1,50,000
2,000 ordinary shares of		Plant & Machinery etc.	80,000
Rs. 100 each	2,00,000	Stock-in-Trade	1,49,000
Reserve	90,000	Sundry Debtors	71,000
Current Liabilities	1,30,000	Cash & Bank Balance	30,000
Profit and Loss Account	60,000		
	4,80,000		4,80,000

From the above statements, you are required to calculate the following ratios and state the purposes they serve :

(i) Current Ratio.

(ii) Operating Ratio.

(iii) Stock Turnover Ratio.

(iv) Turnover of Fixed Assets.

(v) Return on Total Resources. **[C.A. Final]**

Solution

$$1. \text{ Current Ratio} = \frac{\text{Current Assets}}{\text{Current Liabilities}} = \frac{\text{Rs. } 2,50,000}{\text{Rs. } 1,30,000} = 1.92$$

Purposes of Current Ratio :

(i) To understand the financial planning.

(ii) To test the normal solvency of the business.

(iii) To scrutinise whether the business is over-trading. As for example, a fall in the Current Ratio is a sign of over-trading.

(iv) To aid management in taking decision, since low Current Ratio indicates inadequacy of the working capital, and high ratio sometimes indicates the existence of the Idle Capital (fund).

2. **Operating Ratio** $= \dfrac{\text{Cost of Goods Sold* + Operating Expenses}}{\text{Net Sales}}$

$$= \frac{\text{Rs. } 7{,}05{,}000}{\text{Rs. } 8{,}50{,}000} = 83\% \text{ (app.)}$$

*Cost of Goods Sold = (Op. Stock + Purchase + Incidental Expenses) – Closing Stock.

Purposes of the Operating Ratio :

(i) To ascertain the operational efficiency of the management.

(ii) To help the management in ploughing back sufficient profit during the period of inflation.

(iii) It helps management in arriving at its decision.

3. **Stock Turnover Ratio** $= \dfrac{\text{Cost of Goods Sold}}{\text{Average Stock Carried*}}$

$$= \frac{\text{Rs. } 5{,}10{,}000}{\text{Rs. } 1{,}24{,}250} = 4 \text{ (app.) times per year}$$

$$\text{*Average Stock Carried} = \left[\frac{\text{Opening Stock + Closing Stock}}{2}\right]$$

Stock turnover is 4 times per year. That is to say, once in every $\left(\dfrac{52}{4}\right)$ 13 weeks.

Purposes of Stock Turnover Ratio :

(i) To indicate the operational and marketing efficiency of the business.

(ii) It aids management in arriving at the management decision.

(iii) It is one of the instruments by which operational efficiency of the sales frontier of the business can be measured.

A low ratio indicates a bad sign. Low stock turnover ratio arises out of the followings :

(a) Unwise buying policy of the company.

(b) Unnecessary existence of stock.

(c) Existence of obsolete stock.

4. **Turnover of Fixed Assets**

$$= \frac{\text{Cost of Goods Sold}}{\text{Fixed Assets}} = \frac{\text{Rs. } 5{,}10{,}000}{\text{Rs. } 2{,}30{,}000} = 2.21 \text{ to } 1$$

Purposes of Turnover of Fixed Assets Ratio :

(i) To measure the productivity of Fixed Assets.

(ii) To indicate the proportion of goods sold in relation to investment in fixed assets.

5. **Turnover of Total Resources :**

$$\frac{\text{Net Operating Profit}}{\text{Capital Employed or, Total Resources}} = \frac{\text{Rs. 1,45,000}}{\text{Rs. 3,50,000}} \times 100 = 41.4\%$$

Statement of Capital Employed/Total Resources

	Rs.	Rs.
Share Capital		2,00,000
Reserve		90,000
Profit and Loss Account		60,000
Capital Employed		3,50,000
Represented by Fixed Assets :		
Land and Building		1,50,000
Plant and Machinery etc.		80,000
		2,30,000
Current Assets (A) :		
Stock in Trade	1,49,000	
Sundry Debtors	71,000	
Cash and Bank Balances	30,000	
	2,50,000	
Current Liabilities (B) :		
Total Current Liabilities	1,30,000	
	1,30,000	
Net Current Assets or Working Capital (A – B)		1,20,000
Total Resources or Net Total Assets		3,50,000

Statement of Operating Profit :

Net Profit of Business		1,50,000
Less : Net Non-Operating Income :		
(i) Non-operating Income (as per Cr. side of P.L. A/c)	9,000	
(ii) *Less* : Non-operating Expenses (as per Dr. side of P.L. A/c)	4,000	5,000
		1,45,000

Purposes of Return on Total Resources :

(i) To test the profitability of the business.

(ii) To assess the efficiency of the operation of the business.

(iii) To act as a yardstick of industrial performance.

(iv) To guide management in achieving its goal.

Problem

The following are the Final Accounts of Alpha Trading Company Limited relating to the year ended 31st December 2005 :

Trading and Profit and Loss Account

Dr *for the year ended 31.12.05* *Cr.*

	Particular	Amount		Particular	Amount
		Rs.			Rs.
To	Opening Stock	5,000	By	Sales	2,00,000
"	Purchase	1,20,000	"	Closing Stock	7,000
"	Wages c/d	50,000			
"	Gross Profit c/d	32,000			
		2,07,000			2,07,000
To	Salaries	8,000	By	Gross Profit b/d	32,000
"	Depreciation	1,500			
"	Rent	4,000			
"	Advertisement	1,200			
"	Interest on Loan	800			
"	General Expenses	1,400			
"	Net Profit	15,100			
		32,000			32,000

Balance Sheet

as at 31st December 2005

Liabilities		Amount	Assets		Amount
		Rs.			Rs.
Share Capital :			Goodwill		5,000
5,000 shares of Rs. 10 each		50,000	Land and Building		55,000
Reserve Fund		10,000	Plant and Machinery	20,500	
Profit and Loss Account :			*Less* : Dep.	1,500	19,000
Balance	5,000		Stock		7,000
Add : Profit of this year	15,100		Sundry Debtors		8,000
	20,100		Bills Receivable		2,000
Less : Dividend paid	10,000	10,100	Cash in hand		100
Loan		16,000			
Sundry Creditors		4,000			
Bills Payable		2,000			
Bank Overdraft		4,000			
		96,100			96,100

Calculate the following Accounting Ratios from the above Revenue Account and Balance Sheet :

(a) Current Ratio (b) Acid Test Ratio (c) Proprietary Ratio (d) Turnover of Debtors.

[C.U., M.Com.]

Solution

1. **Current Ratio**

$$= \frac{\text{Total C.A.}}{\text{Total C.L.}} = \frac{\text{Rs. } 17{,}100}{\text{Rs. } 26{,}000} = 0.66$$

Current Assets
= Stock + Dr. + B.R. + Cash

This ratio indicates the normal solvency position of the business

Current Liabilities
= Loan + Cr. + B.P. + B.O.

2. **Acid Test Ratio**

$$= \frac{\text{Liquid Assets}}{\text{Liquid */ Current Liabilities}} = \frac{\text{Rs. } 10{,}100}{\text{Rs. } 26{,}000} = 0.39$$

Liquid Assets
= Dr. + B.R. + Cash

This ratio indicates the immediate solvency position of the business

Liquid Liabilities
= Loan + Cr. + B.P. + B.O.*

3. **Proprietary Ratio**

$$\frac{\text{Proprietor's Fund}}{\text{Total Assets **}} = \frac{\text{Rs. } 70{,}100}{\text{Rs. } 91{,}100} = 0.77$$

			Rs.
Proprietors' Fund	=	Equity Share Capital	50,000
		Reserve Fund	10,000
		Retained Profit	10,100
			70,100

This ratio indicates the future solvency position of the business. This ratio indicates how much of the total assets is owned by the proprietor

4. **Turnover of Debtors**

$$\frac{\text{Debtors}}{\text{Net Sales}} \times 365 \text{ days}$$

$$= \frac{\text{Rs. } 8{,}000}{\text{Rs. } 2{,}00{,}000} \times 365 = 15 \text{ days (app.) Collection Period.}$$

This ratio indicates credit and collection policy of the business.

* Bank overdraft may be included in or excluded from the list of total Liquid Liabilities.

** Goodwill has been excluded from the total of Assets. For details, See, ***Accounting for Goodwill*** by Dr. B. K. Basu (Ghosh Dastidar Publishing Concern, 9/1A Tamer Lane, Kolkata 9)

Problem

The condensed annual accounts of Sivalingam and Venkatesh Trading Company Ltd. for 2004 and 2005 were :

		2004		2005
	Rs.	Rs.	Rs.	Rs.
Sales :				
Cash	30,000		32,000	
Credit	2,70,000	3,00,000	3,42,000	3,74,000
Cost of Sales		2,36,000		2,98,000
Gross Margin		64,000		76,000
Expenses :				
Warehousing		13,000		14,000
Transport		6,000		10,000
Administration		19,000		19,000
Selling		11,000		14,000
Debenture interest				2,000
		49,000		59,000
Net Profit		15,000		17,000
Fixed Assets (*Less* : Depreciation)		30,000		40,000
Current Assets :				
Stock	60,000		94,000	
Debtors	50,000		82,000	
Cash	10,000	1,20,000	7,000	1,83,000
Less : Current Liabilities :				
Trade Creditors		50,000		76,000
Net Current Assets		70,000		1,07,000
Net Total Assets		1,00,000		1,47,000
Share Capital		75,000		75,000
Reserve and Undistributed Profit		25,000		42,000
Debenture Loan		—		30,000
		1,00,000		1,47,000

You are informed that :

(1) All sales were from stocks in the company's warehouse.

(2) The range of merchandise was not changed and buying remained steady throughout the two years.

(3) Budgeted total sales for 2006 were Rs. 3,90,000.

(4) The Debenture loan was received on 1st January 2005 and additional fixed assets were purchased on that date.

You are required to state the internal accounting ratios that you would use in this type of business to assist the management of the company in measuring the efficiency of its operation, including its use of capital.

Your answer should name the ratios and give the figures (calculated to one decimal place) for 2004 and 2005, together with possible reasons for changes in the ratios for the two years. Ratio relating to capital employed should be based on the capital at the year end. Ignore taxation. **[Adapted from C.A. (Eng.) Final]**

I think you have understood the problem. In this problem they ask you to name a few internal ratios which are important to assist the management in measuring the efficiency of the company. I think you remember my last lectures where I explained the whole ratio from the point of view of (a) Structure, and (b) Function. The success of any enterprise is tested by its solvency, profitability and efficiency. To have adequate solvency and profitability is the sign of efficiency. Moreover, to have adequate use of capital is a sign of efficiency. You remember that chart which I gave you previously. Now this sum can be studied applying a few Exhibits or Charts; such as Exhibit I showing the Solvency of the company, and Exhibit II, showing the Profitability of the company; and the Exhibit III, Showing the Efficiency of the company.

☐ "Sir, how this can be done"?

● I think you could not follow my last lecture. Please go through those lectures again. Then I will try to make you clear this point.

☐ "Yes Sir, I have followed. Excuse me Sir, Please".

● Well, you please note here the solution of the problem, under review.

Exhibit 1
Showing the Solvency of the Business

Ratios	Components	2004	2005	Comments
1. Current Ratio	$\frac{\text{Current Assets}}{\text{Current Liabilities}}$	$\frac{\text{Rs. } 1,20,000}{\text{Rs. } 50,000} = 2.4$	$\frac{\text{Rs. } 1,83,000}{\text{Rs. } 76,000} = 2.4$	No change in the Current Ratio. The normal solvency position of the business can be considered satisfactory.
2. Liquid Ratio	$\frac{\text{Liquid Assets}}{\text{Current Liabilities}}$	$\frac{\text{Rs. } 60,000}{\text{Rs. } 50,000} = 1.2$	$\frac{\text{Rs. } 89,000}{\text{Rs. } 76,000} = 1.2$	No change in the immediate solvency position of the business. The immediate solvency position is said to be satisfactory.
3. Proprietary Ratio	$\frac{\text{Proprietor's Fund}}{\text{Total Assets}}$	$\frac{\text{Rs. } 1,00,000}{\text{Rs. } 1,50,000} = 67\%$ (app.)	$\frac{\text{Rs. } 1,17,000}{\text{Rs. } 2,23,000} = 52\%$	Though the future solvency position of the business has decreased by 15%, yet this position cannot be said to be unsatisfactory. This indicates the maximum utilisation of loan capital. On the other hand, this ratio indicates good financial planning on the part of the management. However, the decrease in the ratio indicates switch over from over-capitalisation to normal capitalisation.

Exhibit 2
Showing the Profitability of the Business

Ratios	Components	2004	2005	Comments
1. Return on Capital Employed	$\frac{\text{Net Profit *}}{\text{Capital Employed}}$	$\frac{\text{Rs. } 15,000}{\text{Rs. } 1,00,000} \times 100$ = 15%	$\frac{\text{Rs. } 19,000}{\text{Rs. } 1,47,000} \times 100$ = 12.9 or 13% (app.)	Extra Capital employed in the business had not been properly utilised in a profitable manner. The same has been possibly blocked in Stock and Debtors. This (increase in Stock and Debtors) indicates that the activities of the business has increased but the profit of the business has not increased considerably.
2. Gross Profit Ratio	$\frac{\text{Gross Profit}}{\text{Sales}}$	$\frac{\text{Rs. } 64,000}{\text{Rs. } 3,00,000} \times 100$ = 21.3%	$\frac{\text{Rs. } 76,000}{\text{Rs. } 3,74,000} \times 100$ = 20.3%	The reasons for change in the ratio are : i) Reduction in the selling price for the increased demand. ii) Increase in operating cost.
3. Net Profit Ratio	$\frac{\text{Net Profit *}}{\text{Sales}}$	$\frac{\text{Rs. } 15,000}{\text{Rs. } 3,00,000} \times 100$ = 5%	$\frac{\text{Rs. } 19,000}{\text{Rs. } 3,74,000} \times 100$ = 5.1%	The slight change in the ratio is due to the increased sale or Profit.

*Profit before Debenture Interest.

Exhibit 3
Showing the Efficiency of the Business

Ratios	Components	2004	2005	Comments
1. Turnover of Capital	$\frac{\text{Sales}}{\text{Capital Employed}}$	$\frac{\text{Rs. } 3,00,000}{\text{Rs. } 1,00,000}$ = 3 Times.	$\frac{\text{Rs. } 3,74,000}{\text{Rs. } 1,47,000}$ = 2.5 Times	The velocity or turnover of capital has decreased due to the following possible reasons : (a) Unscientific adoption of loan capital without proper diagnosis in the sales frontier. (b) The operational side of the business is said to be unsatisfactory. It should be noted that more times capital is turned over, the better it is.
2. Debt-Equity Ratio	$\frac{\text{External Equities}}{\text{Internal Equities}}$	$\frac{\text{Rs. } 50,000}{\text{Rs. } 1,00,000}$ = 50%	$\frac{\text{Rs. } 1,06,000}{\text{Rs. } 1,17,000}$ = 90.6%	The reasons for the change in the ratio are possibly : (a) The issue of long term debenture. (b) A change in the financial policy of the business.
3. Velocity of Debtors	$\frac{\text{Debtors}}{\text{Credit Sales}} \times 365$	$\frac{\text{Rs. } 50,000}{\text{Rs. } 2,70,000} \times 365$ = 68 days	$\frac{\text{Rs. } 82,000}{\text{Rs. } 3,42,000} \times 365$ = 88 days	The reasons for change in the collection days are possibly as follows : (a) Necessity for granting long term credit with a view to achieving increased turnover. (b) Inefficient follow-up in the 'financial follow-up'.
4. Operating Ratio	$\frac{\text{Cost of Goods Sold}}{\text{Net Sales}}$	$\frac{\text{Rs. } 2,36,000}{\text{Rs. } 3,00,000} \times 100$ = 78.67%	$\frac{\text{Rs. } 2,98,000}{\text{Rs. } 3,74,000} \times 100$ = 79.68%	The ploughing back of profit of the business tends to be higher. This is possibly to meet the challenging threat of rising in price level.

Check : Return on Capital Employed = % Margin on Sales × Turnover of Capital

For 2004 = 5% × 3 times = 15%

For 2005 = 5.1% × 2.5 Times = 13% (app.)

You see, Proprietary Ratio is used to indicate the future solvency of the business Again, the profitability of the business is indicated by Gross Profit Ratio or Gross Margin Ratio, Net Profit Ratio, Dividend Per Share Ratio and Return on Capital Employed. The efficiency of any business is indicated by the Solvency and Profitability of the business. Besides the Profitability and Solvency, Capital Gearing Ratio, Stock Turnover Ratio. Operating Ratio, Turnover of Total Assets Ratio, Turnover of Capital and Expenses Ratio contribute much in analysing the efficiency of the business.

☐ "Sir, are all these ratios to be followed strictly?"

• You see, whether you apply all of these ratios or part of it, depends on as circumstances dictate.

Now I think, you have understood the whole discussions. I would like to say a few words about the respective ratios indicated earlier. That is to say about the Current Ratio, Liquid Ratio and Proprietary Ratio. The Standard of Current Ratio is 2 : 1 and that of Liquid Ratio is 1 : 1. Now in practice and day to day business operations 1 : 1 current ratio is found more successful than that of the 2 : 1 ratio. If the business turnover is satisfactory then the business can carry out its operation more efficiently with the minimum amount of working capital. As to proprietary ratio, it can be said that if most of the assets are covered by the proprietor's fund, it indicates a weak financial policy of the management. So a better equilibrium between the proprietor's fund and the loan capital is sought for.

Do you like further discussions in the matter? Besides, I shall be glad to hear from you any new points which arise in your mind.

☐ "Sir, we shall be obliged if you, please give us some light as to how Balance Sheet and Profit and Loss Account can be prepared with the help of different types of Ratios?"

Definitely, I will discuss the point with the help of a few practical examples. One thing you may note—for the preparation of Profit and Loss Account and Balance Sheet you will be given at least a few figures, such as total current assets and issued capital. However, you note below a few problems on the concept.

Problem

The financial statements of Efficient Limited, for the year 2005, contain the following information :

Ratio of Current Assets to Current Liabilities	1.75 to 1
Liquidity Ratio—total of debtors and bank balances to current liabilities	1.25 to 1
Net Current Assets	Rs. 37,500
Issued Capital in ordinary shares	Rs. 50,000
Fixed Assets—percentage of shareholder's equity	60%
Average age of outstanding debtors for the year 2005 (based on a year of 52 weeks)	7 weeks
Net Profit—percentage of issued share capital	15%
Annual rate of turnover of stock (based on cost on 31.12.2005)	4.16 times
Gross Profit—percentage of turnover	20%

On 31st December 2005, there were (a) current assets other than stock, debtors and bank balances (b) liabilities other than share capital and current liabilities, and (c) assets or debit balances other than fixed and current assets.

You are required to reconstruct in as much detail as possible

(1) the Balance sheet as on 31st December 2005, and

(2) the Trading and Profit and Loss Accounts for the year 2005.

Ignore Taxation. **[Adapted from C.A. (Eng.) Final]**

Solution

(1) Summarised Balance Sheet of Efficient Limited
as at 31st December 2005

		Rs.
Share Capital :		
Ordinary shares of Rs. 10 each		50,000
Profit for the current year		7,500 (F)
Reserve and surplus		36,250 (L)
Proprietor's Fund		93,750
		Rs.
Represented by :		
Fixed Assets		56,250 (I)
Current Assets :		
Stock	25,000 (C)	
Debtors	17,500 (G)	
Bank balances	45,000 (H)	
	87,500 (B)	
Deduct :		
Current Liabilities	50,000 (A)	37,500
		93,750

(2) Summarised Profit and Loss Account
for the year ended 31st December 2005

	Rs.
Sales	1,30,000 (E)
Cost of Goods Sold	1,04,000 (D)
Gross Profit	26,000
Overheads	18,500 (K)
Net Profit	7,500 (J)

Now you note below the workings of the figures marked against the letters (A to L) :

Calculation of A

As per information supplied, the current assets are 175 to 100. So the net current assets is 75.

When net current assets is Rs. 75 then current liabilities is Rs. 100

" " " " Rs. 37,500 " " $\frac{100}{75} \times 37{,}500$ = Rs. 50,000

Calculation of B

The net current assets figure Rs. 37,500 given in the problem is arrived at after deducting the current liabilities Rs. 50,000.

So the total Current Assets is Rs. 87,500 (Rs. 50,000 + Rs. 37,500).

Calculation of C

From the Liquidity Ratio 1.25 to 1 (given in the problem) which is total of debtors and bank balance to current liabilities, it is clear that total of Debtors and Bank are 125% of current liabilities which is Rs. 50,000 (see calculation A). Now the figure $\left(\frac{125}{100} \times 50{,}000\right)$ Rs. 62,500 is the total of debtors and bank balance. Current Assets Rs. 87,500 consist of figure of stock, debtors and bank balance. Total of Debtors and Bank balances, calculated just now, is Rs. 62,500.

Debtors and Bank balances and Stock	Rs. 87,500
Debtors and Bank balances	Rs. 62,500
Stock	Rs. 25,000

Calculation of D and E

As per information supplied, annual rate of stock turnover is 4·16 times. Now stock calculated, as per calculation C, is Rs. 25,000. Total stock which rounded during a year is (4·16 × Rs. 25,000) = Rs. 1,04,000.

Now, as per infomation supplied gross profit — percentage of turnover, is 20%. So it is 25% on cost. Now the whole thing can be summarised as :

The turnover at cost	Rs. 1,04,000
Gross Profit 25%	Rs. 26,000
Sales	Rs. 1,30,000

Calculation of F, J and K

Net Profit 15% of share capital (Rs. 50,000) = 7,500

Gross Profit as per above calculation	26,000	Difference
Overheads	18,500	
Net Profit	Rs. 7,500	

Calculation of G and H

Average time of outstanding debt 7 weeks

(as per information supplied)

Sales Rs. 1,30,000 as per calculation of D and E.

The formula of Turnover of Debtors :

$$\frac{\text{Debtors}}{\text{Sales}} \times 365 \text{ days, or } 52 \text{ weeks.}$$

Let Debtors be X

$$\therefore \frac{X}{1{,}30{,}000} \times 52 = 7$$

$$\text{Or, } \frac{52X}{1{,}30{,}000} = \frac{7}{1}$$

Or $52X = 7 \times 1{,}30{,}000$

$$\text{Or } X = \frac{7 \times 1{,}30{,}000}{52}$$

$X = 17{,}500$

So the figure for Debtors is Rs. 17,500.

The total of Debtors and Bank balance, as per Calculation C, is Rs. 62,500

Debtors as per above calculation is Rs. 17,500

So Bank balances (Rs. 62,500 – Rs. 17,500) = Rs. 45,000.

Calculation of I

As per information, fixed assets is 60% of the shareholders' Equity. Now as per my last lecture I told you that Capital Employed= Total Net Assets.

Total Net Assets = Fixed Assets + Net Current Assets

As per information supplied, Net Current Assets = Rs. 37,500 which is 40% (100% – 60%) of the total net assets.

When contribution of Net Current Assets is 40 then contribution of Fixed Assets is 60

" " " " " 1 " " $\frac{60}{40}$

" " " " " 37,500 " " $\frac{60}{40} \times 37{,}500$

= Rs. 56,250

Calculation of L

The difference between the Assets side and Liabilities side of the Balance Sheet—assumed that it represents the balance of the profit of the last year.

Problem

From the following given ratios and figures prepare a summarised Balance Sheet of XYZ Co. Ltd for the year ended 31st December 2005 :

(a) Working Capital	Rs. 60,000
(b) Reserve and Surplus	Rs. 40,000
(c) Bank Overdraft	Rs. 10,000
(d) Asset (Fixed)-Proprietorship Ratio	0.75
(e) Current Ratio	2.5
(f) Liquid Ratio	1.5

[Adapted from C.A. Final]

Solution

Summarised Balance Sheet of XYZ Co. Ltd.
as at 31st December 2005

	Rs.		Rs.	
Share Capital :				
Equity Shares of Rs. 10 each			2,00,000	(D)
Reserve and Surplus			40,000	
Proprietor's Fund			2,40,000	(C)
Represented by			Rs.	
Fixed Assets			1,80,000	(G)
Current Assets :	Rs.			
Stock	55,000	(F)		
Liquid Assets	45,000			
	1,00,000	(E)		
Current Liabilities :			Rs.	
Bank Overdraft	10,000			
Creditors	30,000	(B)		
	40,000	(A)		
Net Current Assets			60,000	
Net Total Assets			2,40,000	

I hope you have followed the workings.

☐ "No, Sir, I cannot follow, please show us the workings of the problem."

• I am working out the calculation. This will help you to understand the significance of the figures appearing in the summarised Balance Sheet.

Calculation of A, B, E

As per information, Current Ratio is 2.5 : 1
C.A. — C.L. = W.C. (Working Capital)

Given :
C.A. = 2.5
W.C. = 60,000
C.L. = 1

2.5 – 1 = 60,000

1.5 = 60,000

$$1 = \frac{60,000 \times 10}{15} = \text{Rs. } 40,000$$

Current Liabilities = Rs. 40,000

C.A – C.L. = W. C.

Let Current Assets = X

Or, X – 40,000 = 60,000

Or, X = 60,000 + 40,000

$\therefore$ X = 1,00,000

So the Current Assets = Rs. 1,00,000

Bank Overdraft = Rs. 10,000 (given); Current Liabilities as per calculation = Rs. 40,000

So other creditors (Rs. 40, 000 – Rs. 10,000) = Rs. 30,000

Calculation of C,D, and G

From our comparative Balance sheet, the following situation can be observed :

Proprietor's Fund = Fixed Assets + (Current Assets – Current Liabilities)

or, Proprietor's Fund = Fixed Assets + Working Capital

or, Proprietor's Fund – Fixed Assets = Working Capital.

Let Proprietor's Fund = X or, X – F.A = W.C.

$$\text{or, } X - \tfrac{3}{4}X = \text{Rs. } 60,000 \therefore \left[\frac{F.A}{X} = \frac{3}{4},\ F.A = \frac{3}{4}X\right]$$

$$\text{or, } \frac{X}{4} = \text{Rs. } 60,000$$

or, X = Rs. 2,40,000

So the Proprietor's Fund, which is the total of Share Capital and Reserve and Surplus, is Rs. 2,40,000.

The Reserve and Surplus as per information = Rs. 40,000.

So, Share Capital = (Rs. 2,40,000 – Rs. 40,000) = Rs. 2,00,000.

Now the formula of assets Proprietor's Ratio is like thus :

$$\frac{\text{Fixed Assets}}{\text{Proprietor's Fund}}$$

This is equal to 0.75 i.e., $\frac{3}{4}$

Now, Let the fixed assets be x,

The formula can be written :

$$\frac{x}{\text{Rs. } 2,40,000} = \frac{3}{4}$$

or, $4x = 3 \times \text{Rs. } 2,40,000$

or, $x = \frac{3 \times \text{Rs. } 2,40,000}{4}$

$x = \text{Rs. } 1,80,000$

So, the Fixed Assets = Rs. 1,80,000.

Calculation of F

The formula of Liquid Ratio is :

$$\frac{\text{Liquid Assets}}{\text{Quick Liabilities}}$$

$\frac{\text{L. A.}}{\text{Q. L.}} = 1.5$ Let Liquid Assets be = x

$\frac{x}{\text{Q. L.}} = 1.5$

or, $\frac{x}{\text{Rs. } 30,000} = 15$

or, $x = 1.5 \times \text{Rs. } 30,000$

$\therefore$ $x = \text{Rs. } 45,000.$

Liquid Assets = Rs. 45,000.

Total Current Assets	=	Rs. 1,00,000
Total Liquid Assets	=	Rs. 45,000
Stock	=	Rs. 55,000

Now I hope that you have followed all these points. I shall be glad to hear any points in the matter.

☐ Sir, it is really very exciting to see the method of solving problems in this chapter. Please do some more problems.

• Well, I am solving some more problems for the purpose of your practice.

Problem

Current Ratio	2.5
Liquidity Ratio	1.5
Working Capital	Rs. 3,00,000
Stock Turnover Ratio	6

Gross Profit Ratio	0.20
Ratio of Turnover to Fixed Assets	2
Debtors' velocity	2 months
Fixed Assets to Net Worth	0.80
Reserves and Surplus to Capital	0.50

Draw up the Balance Sheet from the above figures.

[Delhi University, B.Com. (Adapted)]

Solution

Balance Sheet as at ...

Liabilities	Amount	Assets	Amounts
	Rs.		Rs.
Share Capital	5,00,000	Net Block of Fixed Assets	7,50,000
Reserve & Surplus	2,50,000	Current Assets :	
Long-term Loans	3,00,000	Stock	2,00,000
Balance figure		Debtors	2,50,000
Current Liabilities	2,00,000	Cash	50,000
	12,50,000		12,50,000

Working Notes

(i) Current Ratio = 2.5

or, $\frac{\text{Current Assets}}{\text{Current Liabilities}} = 2.5$

or, Current Assets = 2.5 (Current Liabilities)

or, Current Assets – Current Liabilities = 1.5 Current Liabilities

or, Working Capital = 1.5 Current Liabilities

or, 1.5 Current Liabilities = 3,00,000

or, Current Liabilities = $\frac{\text{Rs. } 3,00,000}{1.5}$

or, Current Liabilities = Rs. 2,00,000

$\therefore$ Current Assets = 2.5 × Rs. 2,00,000 = Rs. 5,00,000

(ii) Liquidity Ratio = 1.5

or, $\frac{\text{Current Assets} - \text{Stock}}{\text{Current Liabilities} - \text{Bank O/D}} = 1.5$

or, $\frac{5,00,000 - \text{Stock}}{2,00,000 - 0} = 1.5$

or, Stock = (– 1.5 × Rs. 2,00,000) + Rs. 5,00,000

or, Stock = Rs. 2,00,000

(iii) Stock Turnover = 6

$$\text{or, } \frac{\text{Cost of Goods Sold}}{\text{Stock}} = 6$$

or, Cost of Goods Sold = 6 × Rs. 2,00,000 = Rs. 12,00,000

(iv) G.P. Ratio = 20%

$$\text{or, } \frac{\text{Gross Profit}}{\text{Sales}} \times 100 = 20$$

i.e., Sales – Gross Profit = Rs. 12,00,000

or, Sales – Sales × 0.20 = Rs. 12,00,000

or, 0.80 sales = Rs. 12,00,000

$$\text{or, Sales} = \frac{\text{Rs. } 12,00,000}{0.80} = \text{Rs. } 15,00,000$$

(v) Fixed Assets Turnover Ratio = 2

$$\text{or, } \frac{\text{Sales}}{\text{Net Block}} = 2$$

or, Rs. 15,00,000 = 2 × Net Block

or, Net Block = Rs. 7,50,000

$$\text{(vi) Debtor's Velocity} = \frac{\text{Receivables}}{\text{Credit Sales}} \times 12 \text{ months}$$

$$\text{or, } 2 = \frac{\text{Receivables}}{\text{Rs. } 15,00,000} \times 12$$

or, Receivables = Rs. 2,50,000

(vii) Cash = Current Assets – Stock – Receivables

= Rs. 5,00,000 – Rs. 2,00,000 – Rs. 2,50,000 = Rs. 50,000

(viii) Fixed Assets to Net Worth = 0.80

$$\therefore \text{Net worth} = \frac{\text{Rs. } 6,00,000}{0.80} = \text{Rs. } 7,50,000$$

(ix) Reserves and Surplus to capital is 0.5, hence Reserves and Surplus is one-third of Net Worth ie. (Share Capital + Reserves & Surplus)

$$\therefore \text{Reserves \& Surplus} = \frac{\text{Rs. } 7,50,000}{3} = \text{Rs. } 2,50,000$$

(x) ∴ Share Capital = Rs. 7,50,000 – Rs. 2,50,000 = Rs. 5,00,000

Problem

From the following information M/s Paramount Ltd. requests you to prepare a projected Trading and Profit and Loss Account and the Balance Sheet for the Next Financial year ending 31st March 2007 :

Gross Profit Ratio	25%
Stock Turnover Ratio	5 times
Average Debt collection period	3 months
Creditiors' Velocity	3 months
Current Ratio	2
Proprietary Ratio	80%
Capital Gearing Ratio	30%
Net Profit to Equity Share Capital	10%
General Reserve and Profit & Loss A/c to issued equity capital	25%
Preference Share Capital to Debentures	2

Cost of sales consists of 50% for materials. Gross Profit Rs. 12,50,000.

[C.A. (Final) Adapted]

Solution

Projected Trading and Profit & Loss Account of Paramount Ltd.

for the year ending 31st March 2007

Dr. *Cr.*

Particulars	Amount Rs.	Particulars	Amount Rs.
To Materials Used	18,75,000	By Sales	50,00,000
To Expenses (direct)	18,75,000		
To Gross Profit c/d	12,50,000		
	50,00,000		50,00,000
		By Gross Profit b/d	12,50,000
To Sundry Expenses Bal. fig.	9,70,000		
To Net Profit	2,80,000		
	12,50,000		12,50,000

Projected Balance Sheet of Paramount Ltd.

as at 31st March 2007

Liabilities	Amount Rs.	Assets	Amount Rs.
Equity Share Capital	28,00,000	Fixed Assets	40,00,000
Preference Share Capital	10,00,000	Stock	7,50,000
General Reserves	4,20,000	Debtors	12,50,000
Profit & Loss A/c	2,80,000		
Debentures	5,00,000		
Creditors	4,68,750		
Bank Overdraft	5,31,250		
	60,00,000		60,00,000

Working Notes

(i) Gross Profit Ratio = 25%

$\therefore$ Sales = Rs. 12,50,000 $\times \frac{100}{25}$ = Rs. 50,00,000

(ii) Cost of Sales = Sales – Gross Profit

= Rs. 50,00,000 – Rs. 12,50,000

= Rs. 37,50,000

(iii) Materials = 50% of Cost of Sales

= Rs. 37,50,000 $\times \frac{50}{100}$ = Rs. 18,75,000

(iv) Other Expenses = Rs. 37,50,000 – Rs. 18,75,000

= Rs. 18,75,000

(v) Current Assets :

(a) Stock = $\frac{\text{Cost of Sales}}{\text{Stock Turnover Ratio}}$ = Rs. $\frac{37,50,000}{5}$ = Rs. 18,75,000

(b) Debtors = Sales for 3 months

= Rs. 50,00,000 $\times \frac{3}{12}$ = Rs. 12,50,000

$\therefore$ Total Current Assets = Rs. 7,50,000 + Rs. 12,50,000 = Rs. 20,00,000

(vi) Current Liabilities = 50% of Current Assets

= $\frac{\text{Rs.}20,00,000}{2}$ = Rs. 10,00,000

(vii) Trade Creditors = Materials Consumption in 3 months

= Rs. 18,75,000 $\times \frac{3}{12}$ = Rs. 4,68,750

(viii) Bank Overdraft = Current Liabilities – Creditors

.= Rs. 10,00,000 – Rs. 4,68,750

= Rs. 5,31,250

(ix) Fixed Assets to Capital Employed = 80%

$\therefore$ Working Capital = 20% of Capital Employed

or Working Capital = Current Assets – Current Liabilities

= Rs. 20,00,000 – Rs. 10,00,000

= Rs. 10,00,000

So, Fixed Assets = $\frac{10,00,000}{20} \times 80$ = Rs. 40,00,000

(x) Long Term Funds = Fixed Assets + Working Capital

= Rs. 40,00,000 + Rs. 10,00,000

= Rs. 50,00,000

Now, Capital Gearing Ratio = 30%

∴ Preference Share Capital + Debentures

= Rs. 50,00,000 × $\frac{30}{100}$ = Rs. 15,00,000

Preference Share Capital = Rs. 15,00,000 × $\frac{2}{3}$ = Rs. 10,00,000

Debentures = Rs. 15,00,000 × $\frac{1}{3}$ = Rs. 5,00,000

(xi) Equity Shareholders' Funds = Rs. 50,00,000 – Rs. 15,00,000

= Rs. 35,00,000

Now, (General Reserve + Profit & Loss A/c) = 25% of Equity Share Capital

⇒ 20% of (Equity Shareholders' Funds)

⇒ 20% of Rs. 35,00,000

⇒ Rs. 7,00,000

(xii) ∴ Equity Share Capital = Rs. 35,00,000 – Rs. 7,00,000

= Rs. 28,00,000

(xiii) Profit & Loss A/c = 10% of Equity Share Capital

= Rs. 28,00,000 × 10%

= Rs. 2,80,000

and, General Reserve = Rs. 7,00,000 – Rs. 2,80,000

= Rs. 4,20,000

Problem

From the Following details, prepare Final Accounts and Balance Sheet of Clooney Ltd. :

a) Gross Profit ratio = 25%
b) Net Profit Ratio = 20%
c) Inventory Turnover Ratio = 10
d) Fixed Assets : Current Assets = 5 : 8
e) Current Ratio = 1
f) Fixed Assets to Share Capital = $\frac{5}{4}$
g) Fixed Assets = Rs. 8,00,000
h) Closing Stock = Rs. 80,000, there was no opening stock.

[C.U. B.Com. (H) Adapted]

Solution

Books of Clooney Ltd.

Trading and Profit & Loss Account
for the year ended...

Dr. *Cr.*

Particulars	Amount	Particulars	Amount
	Rs.		Rs.
To Purchases	6,80,000	By Sales	8,00,000
To Gross Profit c/d	2,00,000	By Closing Stock	80,000
	8,80,000		8,80,000
		By Gross Profit b/d	2,00,000
To Expenses	40,000		
To Net Profit	1,60,000		
	2,00,000		2,00,000

Balance Sheet as at .....

Liabilities	Amount	Assets	Amount
	Rs.		Rs.
Share Capital	6,40,000	Fixed Assets	8,00,000
Profit & Loss A/c	1,60,000	Stock	80,000
Current Liabilities	12,80,000	Other Assets & Cash	12,00,000
	20,80 000		20,80,000

Working Notes

(i) $\dfrac{\text{Fixed Assets}}{\text{Share Capital}} = \dfrac{5}{4}$

or, $\dfrac{\text{Rs. } 8,00,000}{\text{Share Capital}} = \dfrac{5}{4}$

or, Share Capital = Rs. 8,00,000 $\times \dfrac{4}{5}$ $\Rightarrow$ Rs. 6.40,000

(ii) $\dfrac{\text{Fixed Assets}}{\text{Current Assets}} = \dfrac{5}{8}$

or, Current Assets = $\dfrac{8}{5} \times$ Rs. 8,00,000 $\Rightarrow$ Rs. 12,80,000

(iii) Current Ratio = 1

$\Rightarrow$ Current Assets = Current Liabilities $\Rightarrow$ Rs. 12,80,000

$\therefore$ Closing Stock = Rs. 80,000 $\therefore$ Other Assets = Rs. 12,00,000

(iv) Inventory Turnover Ratio = 10

or, $\frac{\text{Sales}}{\text{Closing Stock}} = 10$

or, Sales = 10 × Rs. 80,000 ⇒ Rs. 8,00,000

(v) Gross Profit Ratio = 25%

or, $\frac{\text{GP}}{\text{Sales}} \times 100 = 25$

or, Gross Profit = $\cancel{25} \times \frac{\text{Rs. } 8,00,000}{\cancel{100}\ 4}$ ⇒ Rs. 2,00,000

☐ "Sir, Please give us a standard problem so that from same information we can prepare Fund flow statement, Cash flow statement, and Accounting Ratio".

● Well, I am giving you but I had already discussed the same in the part of Financial Accounting. However, I am giving you a Balance sheet of an Old Indian Company Ltd. from which we can work out Accounting Ratio, Fund flow statement and Cash flow statement. Do you follow ?

☐ "Excuse me Sir, give us some worked out problems."

● Well, here is a problem.

Problem

Old Indian Company Limited

Profit and Loss Account

for the year ended 30th September of 2nd Year

	2nd year	1st year
	Rs.	Rs.
Income		
Sales	17,37,28,112	15,86,02,932
Other Sources	12,42,623	12,21,514
	17,49,70,735	15,98,24,446
Expenditure		
Materials Consumed	6,38,39,969	5,95,48,626
Expenses	8,16,53,961	7,29,77,260
Depreciation	83,98,000	97,71,000
Interest Paid	20,57,774	23,44,612
	15,59,49,704	14,46,41,498

	2nd year Rs.	1st year Rs.
Profit before Taxation :	1,90,21,031	1,51,82,948
Provision for Tax	1,14,00,000	92,00,000
Profit after Taxation :	76,21,031	59,82,948
Excess provision of tax in earlier years	36,00,000	—
	1,12,21,031	59,82,948
Transfer to Development Rebate Reserve (inclusive of Rs. 2,00,000 transferred as per Board Resolution dated 19th September of 2nd year)	3,50,000	7,00,000
	1,08,71,031	52,82 948
Transfer from Development Rebate Reserve	13,00,000	12,00,000
Balance Available For Appropriation		
Transferred to General Reserve (inclusive of Rs. 93,00,000 transferred as per Board Resolution dated 19th September of 2nd year)	1,21,71,031	64,82,948

Schedules :

	2nd year Rs.	1st year Rs.
Income From Other Sources		
Rent	2,10,268	1,48,680
Commission	1,39,708	3,05,280
Interest (Net) —On Investments	1,736	1,736
— Others	29,814	31,783
Profit on Disposal of Capital Assets	3,78,351	3,55,605
Miscellaneous	4,82,746	3,78,430
	12,42,623	12,21,514
Materials Consumerd		
Commencing Stock :		
Raw Materials and Components	1,56,71,299	1,23,11,477
Finished Goods	1,66,86,646	1,76,73,126
Work-in-Progress	13,71,040	14,01,408
	3,37,28,985	3,13,86,011
Purchases During the year	6,93,86,411	6,18,91,600
	10,31,15,396	9,32,77,611

	2nd year	1st year
	Rs.	Rs.
Less:		
Closing Stock :		
Raw Materials and Components	1,68,94,640	1,56,71,299
Finished Goods	2,01,18,056	1,66,86,646
Work-in-Progress	22,62,731	13,71,040
	3,92,75,427	3,37,28,985
Materials Consumed during the year	6,38,39,969	5,95,48,626
Expenses :		
Stores and Spare Parts Consumed	65,81,668	58,15,557
Salaries, Wages and Bonus	3,49,34,556	3,01,84,129
Contributions to Provident and Pension Funds	34,64,878	32,91,132
Workmen and Staff Welfare Expenses	26,53,383	22,06,324
Power and Fuel	92,06,998	83,92,110
Repairs to Plant and Machinery	30,60,259	27,76,422
Repairs to Buildings	7,91,999	8,22,797
Insurance	13,59,996	14,43,016
Freight and Transport	92,12,626	84,50,547
Rent	9,79,710	9,24,195
Rates and Taxes	4,99,558	4,88,753
Miscellaneous	89,32,143	82,61,653
	8,16,77,774	7,30,56,635
Less :		
Transferred to Fixed Assets	23,813	79,375
	8,16,53,961	7,29,77,260

Balance Sheet as at 30th September 2nd year

Liabilities	2nd year		1st year
Share Capital :	Rs.	Rs.	Rs.
Authorised :			
80,00,000 Ordinary Shares of Rs. 10/- each		8,00,00,000	8,00,00,000
Issued and Subscribed			
25,00,000 for Cash	2,50,00,000		2,50,00,000
2,22,666 for other considerations pursuant to Contracts	22,26,660		22,26,660
18,97,334 as Bonus Shares by Capitalisation of Reserves and Share Premium Account	1,89,73,340		1,89,73,340
46,20,000 Ordinary Shares of Rs. 10/- each fully paid		4,62,00,000	4,62,00,000
Of these, 30,52,000 Ordinary Shares are held by the holding company			
Reserves and Surplus :			
Capital Reserve	1,20,93,399		1,20,93,399
Share Premium Account	39,20,000		39,20,000
Development Rebate Reserve	96,00,000		1,05,50,000
General Reserve	3,08,13,768		2,41,86,737
		5,64,27,167	
Total Capital and Reserves :		10,26,27,167	9,69,50,136
Loans:			
Secured	1,29,91,344		2,01,60,499
Unsecured	40,54,189		45,04,655
		1,70,45,533	2,46,65,154
Current Liabilities and Provisions :			
Current Liabilities :			
Trade and other Creditors	2,87,92,469		2,60,30,909
Current Account with The British Oxygen Co. Ltd.	13,29,126		28,75,478
Unclaimed Dividend	1,38,822		1,24,338

Provisions :			
Taxation less Advance Payments	57,61,131		66,76,532
		3,60,21,548	3,57,07,257
		15,56,94,248	15,73,22,547
Assets	**2nd year**		**1st year**
Fixed Assets	Rs.	Rs.	Rs.
At Cost or Valuation less			
Depreciation	6,26,79,037		6,85,23,519
Capital Projects in Progress	40,54,776		32,32,871
		6,67,33,813	7,17,56,390
Investment :			
At Cost		3,99,500	5,99,500
Current Assets, Loans and Advances :			
Current Assets :			
Stocks — at lower of cost or market value			
Stores and Spare Parts	1,18,00,046		1,13,68,565
Raw Materials and Components	1,68,94,640		1,56,71,299
Finished Goods	2,01,18,056		1,66,86,646
Work-in Progress	22,62,731		13,71,040
	5,10,75,473		4,50,97,550
Trade Debtors	2,83,44,208		2,93,37,078
Cash and Bank Balances :			
Bank Balances			
With Scheduled Banks in			
Current Accounts	26,61,295		43,12,051
With The Chartered Bank in Current Accounts			
Karachi	1,40,541		1,40,541
London	—		23,326
Cash Balances			
In Transit	6,76,338		5,73,208
In Hand	2,59,977		2,24,950
Loans and Advances	54,03,103		54,57,953
		8,85,60,935	8,51,66,657
		15,56,94,248	15,73,22,547

Well, from the above published Balance Sheet and Revenue Statement I am showing you Fund Flow Statement, Cash Flow Statement and different Accounting Ratios Please note :

An Old INDIAN COMPANY LTD.
Statement Showing Change in Working Capital

	II year Rs.	I year Rs.
Total C.A.	8,85,60,935	8,51,66,657
Total C.L.	3,60,21,548	3,57,07,257
Working Capital	5,25,39,387	4,94,59,400
Increase in W.C.		30,79,987
	5,25,39,387	5,25,39,387

Statement Showing Sources and Application of Fund or Fund Flow Statement

Sources	Amount Rs.	Application	Amount Rs.
Sales of Assets	50,22,577	Payment of Loan	76,19,621
Increase in Profit	56,77,031	Increase in W.C	30,79,987
	1,06,99,608		1,06,99,608

Old INDIAN COMPANY LTD.
Cash Flow Statement
(as per old method)

			Rs.
Cash Balance as at 30th September of I year			52,74,076
Received during the year :			
Sale of Fixed Assets	50,22,577		
Increase in Profit (Reserve Fund)	56,77,031		
Received from Loans and Advances	54,850		
Received from Debtors	9,92,870		
		1,17,47,328	
Payment during the year :			
Payment of Loan	76,19,621		
Addition to Stock	59,77,923		
Payment of Current A/c (with British Oxygen Co. Ltd.)	15,46,352		
Payment of Taxes	9,15,401		
	1,60,59,297		
Less : Increase in Creditors*	27,76,044	1,32,83,253	
			(−) 15,35,925
***Increase in Creditor**			
Sundry Creditor	27,61,560		
Increase in Unclaimed Dividend	14,484		
Balance on 30th September II year			37,38,151

Now I would request you to prepare the same as per As 3.

Can you prepare ?

☐ Yes, Sir.

- Now I am showing Comparative Revenue Statement.

Comparative Revenue Statement of Old Indian Company Ltd.

Particulars	II yr.	II yr.	I yr.	I yr.
	Rs.	Rs.	Rs.	Rs.
Sales		17,37,28,112		15,86,02,932
Less : Cost of Goods Sold or Material Consumed		6,38,39,969		5,95,48,626
(Opening Stock	3,37,28,985		3,13,86,011	
Purchase	6,93,86,411		6,18,91,600	
	10,31,15,396		9,32,77,611	
Closing Stock	3,92,75,427		3,37,28,985	
Gross Profit		10,98,88,143		9,90,54,306
Less : Expenses				
Expenses	8,16,53,961		7,29,77,260	
Depreciation	83,98,000		97,71,000	
Interest Paid	20,57,774	9,21,09,735	23,44,612	8,50,92,872
Operating Profit		1,77,78,408		1,39,61,434
Non Operating Income :				
Income from other Sources		12,42,623		12,21,514
Profit before Tax		1,90,21,031		1,51,82,948

Old Indian Company Limited

Comparative Balance Sheet

Particulars	II yr.	II yr.	I yr.	I yr.
	Rs.	Rs.	Rs.	Rs.
Share Capital :				
Ordinary Shares	4,62,00,000		4,62,00,000	
Reserve and Surplus	5,64,27,167		5,07,50,136	
Proprietor's Fund or Net Worth		10,26,27,167		9,69,50,136
Add : Loan Capital		1,70,45,533		2,46,65,154
Capital Employed		11,96,72,700		12,16,15,290
Reperesented by				
Total Resources				
Aggregate of Fixed Assets		6,67,33,813		7,17,56,390
Investment		3,99,500		3,99,500
		6,71,33,313		7,21,55,890

Particulars	II yr.	II yr.	I yr.	I yr.
	Rs.	Rs.	Rs.	Rs.
Current Assets				
Stock	5,10,75,473		4,50,97,550	
Debtors	2,83,44,208		2,93,37,078	
Cash and Bank	37,38,151		52,74,076	
Loans and Advances	54,03,103		54,57,953	
Total C.A.	8,85,60,935		8,51,66,657	
Current Liabilities				
Trade and other Creditors	2,87,92,469		2,60,30,909	
Current Account with British Oxygen Ltd.	13,29,126		28,75,478	
Dividend	1,38,822		1,24,338	
Provision for Taxation	57,61,131		66,76,532	
	3,60,21,548		3,57,07,257	
Net Current Asssets or Working Capital		5,25,39,387		4,94,59,400
Total Resources		11,96,72,700		12,16,15,290

Old Indian Company Limited

Different Types of Accounting Ratios

Accounting Ratios		II yr.	I yr.
Current Ratio		2.46 : 1	1.38 : 1
Liquid Ratio		1.05 : 1	1.12 :1
Proprietary Ratio		0.659 to 1 or 65%	0.616 to 1 or 61%
Debt Equity Ratio		17%	25%
Gross Profit Ratio		63%	64%
Net Profit Ratio		10% (app)	9% (app)
Operating Ratio		36%	37%
Stock turnover Ratio	1.8 times (app.) (Once for every 28.8 weeks)	1.8 times (app.) (Once for every 28.8 weeks)	

Turnover of Capital	1.5 times		1.3 times
Return on Capital Employed (RCE)	15%		11.7%
Check of RCE :	= % Margin of Sale	×	Turnover of Capital
	= 10%	×	1.5 times
	= 9%	×	1.3 "

I think you all have understood the working of the problem.

☐ "Sir, really speaking, the problem you worked out (i.e, from one information the chain or mechanism of working out different aspects of Cash flow, Fund flow and Accounting Ratios) is really meaningful in the context of day-to-day financial management requirement."

● You attention please. Now I am concluding discussions on Accounting Ratios and Interpretation of Financial Statements. If you want to put me any question(s) you can. Why you are talking with each other. You please stand up. What do you want to say?

☐ "Sir! I have one question relating to Accounting Ratio."

● What is that? Please don't feel shy. I am here to help you, you can put me any question. Tell me the question(s). Yes...yes, tell....

☐ "Sir, Is it possible from the study of Accounting Ratios to predict the alarming conditions say bankruptcy, sickness of any firm or company?"

● Well, all these aspects I have already mentioned in course of my lectures on Solvency (Liquidity) Ratio, Profitability Ratio and Efficiency Ratio.

However, on these respect I am refering the work of Professor E.I. Altman who in his work "**Financial Ratios, Discriminate Analysis and Prediction of Corporate Bankruptcy**[1] mentioned a set of Accounting Ratios with their respective results (Weights). The summation of respective results (Weights) of ratios gives an indication of alarming condition relating to bankruptcy. In this respect the name of Professor L.C. Gupta may be made who in his study to predict sickness of Indian firms mentioned **Five Ratios** which according to him have high degree of forewarning indications of sickness.

● Are you feeling any bore?

☐ "No Sir, we are much delighted from your lecture Sir. Please give us the Five Ratios given by Professor Altman and Professor Gupta."

● Well, have a look here.

Five Ratios given by Altman to predict bankruptcy of firm(s) or Companies.

or Enterprise(s)

[1] *Journal of Finance*. (September 1968)

Components of Ratios	Weights
1. $\frac{\text{Working Capital}}{\text{Total Assets}}$	0.012
2. $\frac{\text{Retained Earning}}{\text{Total Assets}}$	0.014
3. $\frac{\text{EBIT}}{\text{Total Assets}}$	0.033
4. $\frac{\text{MVE}}{\text{Total Assets}}$	0.016
5. $\frac{\text{Sales}}{\text{Total Assets}}$	0.999

☐ "Excuse Sir, what are MVE, BVD and EBIT. Please explain Sir."

• Well, Please note.

EBIT stands for Earning Before Interest and Tax

MVE stands for Market Value of Equity

BVD stands for Book Value of Debts.

• Do you follow?

☐ "Yes, Sir".

• Coming to our discussion on Professor Altman I am to say that if summation of weights (ΣW) which Prof Altman described Z (Combined value of weights) in 1.81 there shows the signal of danger of bankruptcy.

You see, if the combined value, according Professor Altman Comes to 2.999, it depicts no danger zone (Ż); if the situation lies in between 1.81 and 2.99, it indicates the zone of insolvency.

It is to note in this context that out of Five Ratios, Prof Altman gave much emphasis on Ratio No 1, 3 and 5. Ratio No. 1 which gives indication of solvency i.e., Liquidity, Ratio 3 is Profitability and Efficiency (Activity) are the important areas where all time attention should be given by the Management to avoid unpleasant situation.

• Do you follow my lecture?

☐ "Yes Sir, we are feeling it to be very interesting."

• Well, coming to the discussion of sickness prediction ratios as emphasised by Prof. L.C. Gupta, following ratios should be to constant vouching to avoid sickness.

1. $\frac{\text{EBDIT *}}{\text{Sales}}$

2. $\frac{\text{Profit after Tax plus (+) Depreciation}}{\text{Sales}}$

3. $\frac{\text{EBDIT *}}{\text{Total Assets plus (+) Accumulated Depreciation}}$

4. $\frac{\text{Profit after tax plus (+) Depreciation}}{\text{Total Assets plus (+) Accumulated Depreciation}}$

5. $\frac{\text{EBDIT *}}{\text{Interest + 0.25 Debt}}$

*Earning Before Depreciation, Interest and Tax

- Is it clear to you?

☐ "Yes Sir, Thank you Sir."

- Thank you all.

☐ "Same to you Sir."

QUESTIONS

1. Discuss the role of ratio analysis as a tool and technique in financial management.
2. How can financial statement be interpreted ? And what are the areas of study?
3. What is Accounting Ratio ? What are its Advantages and Disadvantages?
4. Explain in details about Balance Sheet Ratios, Revenue Statement Ratios and Composite Ratios.
5. From the following two years' Balance Sheet and Profit and Loss Account of Basu Company Limited, you are to examine the Profitability, Solvency and Efficiency of the business :

Balance Sheet at the end of the year

	1st year	2nd year
	Rs.	Rs.
Equity Shares of Rs. 100 each	2,00,000	2,00,000
Reserve and Surplus	20,000	40,000
Profit and Loss Account	28,000	4,000
Loan on Mortgage	2,20,000	1,60,000
Bank Overdraft	—	40,000
Creditors	60,000	1,80,000
Provision for Taxation	68,000	26,000
Proposed Dividend	20,000	30,000
	6,16,000	6,80,000

	1st year	2nd year
	Rs.	Rs.
Fixed Assets, less depreciation	4,16,000	3,96,000
Stock-in-trade	60,000	1,20,000
Debtors	80,000	1,60,000
Cash and Bank Balances	60,000	4,000
	6,16,000	6,80,000

Profit and Loss Account for the two years

Particulars	1st year	2nd year	Particulars	1st year	2nd year
	Rs.	Rs.		Rs.	Rs.
To Interest on Mortgage Loan	4,800	9,600	By Balance b/f	—	28,000
" Directors' remuneration	20,000	60,000	" Profit for the year after normal running cost and depreciation	1,60,800	1,21,600
" Provision for Taxation	68,000	26,000			
" Dividend	20,000	30,000			
" Transfer to Reserve	20,000	20,000			
Balance c/d	28,000	4,000			
	1,60,800	1,49,600		1,60,800	1,49,600

[Adapted from C.A. Final]

6. **From the following information you are to (a) arrange them suitabily for analysis and (b) to find out the following ratios :**

   (1) Return on Capital Employed.
   (2) Stock : Fixed Assets.
   (3) Current Assets : Current Liabilities.
   (4) Sales : Debtors and Receivables.

Information :

	Rs.
Cash	89,200
Land and Buildings at Cost	16,00,000
Deposits and Payments in advance	1,24,000
Stock	7,45,600
Trade Creditors	8,11,500
General Reserve	2,00,000
Debtors	10,46,000
Bills Receivable	45,200

	Rs.
Plant and Machinery at Cost, less depreciation	10,88,000
Secured Debenture	5,00,000
Bank Overdraft	1,04,000
Equity Shares of Rs. 10 each	20,00,000
Balance of Profit and Loss Account	4,34,000
Proposed Dividend for the current year	1,72,500
Trade Investment	40,000
Provision for Taxation	2,48,000
Dividend Reserve	2,80,000
Bills Payable	36,000
Net Sales	43,64,800
Net Profit for the current year before Taxation and Dividend	6,55,660

[Adapted from C.A. Final]

7. From the following Profit and Loss Appropriation Account and Balance Sheet of a company, work out ratios that you know, and comment on the changes of such ratios during the year :

Profit and Loss Appropriation Account

31.12.04		31.12.05
Rs.		Rs.
6,000	To Income Tax	6,600
10,000	" Dividend	10,000
7,970	" Balance c/f	2,110
23,970		18,710
31.12.04		**31.12.05**
Rs.		Rs.
23,970	By Balance b/d	18,710
23,970		18,710

Balance Sheet as at 31st December 2005

31-12-04		31-12-05
Rs.		Rs.
2,00,000	Equity Shares	2,00,000
1,00,000	Pref. Shares	1,00,000
28,670	Reserves (including balance of profits)	30,710

31-12-04		31-12-05
Rs		Rs.
22,970	Creditors	27,600
21,210	Bank Overdraft	67,290
5,320	Current Taxation	5,960
740	Accrued Charges	690
4,600	Deferred Repairs	4,600
3,83,510		4,36,850

31-12-04		31-12-05
Rs.		Rs.
5,10,550	Fixed Assets	5,29,140
3,09,120	*Less* : Depreciation	3,11,120
2,01,430		2,18,020
90,000	Goodwill	90,000
37,840	Stock of Raw-materials	60,700
22,700	Stock of Finished goods	7,400
21,620	Debtors	37,820
9,600	Cash	22,730
320	Prepaid Expenses	180
3,83,510		4,36,850

[Adapted form C.U., M.Com. Examination]

8. M/s PQR and Co. presents the following Balance Sheet to you :

Balance Sheet as at 31st December 2005

Liabilities	Amount	Assets	Amount
	Rs.		Rs.
Partners' Capital	6,80,000	Cash and Bank	2,80,000
Creditors	35,60,000	Machinery	22,50,000
Reserves for Development Rebate	3,36,000	Stocks	33,26,000
Profit and Loss Account for the year	5,90,000	Debtors	25,08,000
		Land and Buildings	9,52,000
Deposits from			
Family Members	14,50,000		
Others	23,64,000		
Depreciation	3,36,000		
	93,16,000		93,16,000

The Turnover of the firm is Rs. 1 Crore.

The firm approaches you for a cash credit arrangement of Rs. 50 lacs so as to repay the Deposits and certain Creditors.

Present a note of your recommendations containing the Balance Sheet in a rearranged form suitable for interpretation.

[Indian Institute of Bankers' Examination]

9. PQR Private Ltd. was formed on 1st April 2001 for taking over the business of a partnership firm. The Partners were paid the purchases consideration partly in cash and partly by issue of capital.

The Balance Sheet as at 31st March 2002 shows the following position :

Liabilities	Amount	Assets	Amount
	Rs.		Rs.
Equity Capital	10,00,000	Goodwill	10,00,000
Debentures	2,50,000	Fixed Assets	5,00,000
Deposits from Directors' friends	1,50,000	Stock	50,00,000
		Debtors	25,00,000
Sundry Creditors	80,00,000	Cash	25,000
		Profit and Loss Account	3,75,000
	94,00,000		94,00,000

The sales for the year 2001-2002 were Rs. 75,00,000.

The Company approaches you for borrowing facilities.

Prepare a note setting out your recommendations and the reasoning for the same.

[Indian Institute of Bankers' Examination]

10. State what is meant by :

(i) Gross Profit Ratio.

(ii) Operating Ratio.

(iii) Stock Turnover Ratio.

State briefly how these are determined and what are the purpose of each.

[Indian Institute of Bankers' Examination]

11. (a) Discuss the utility of Ratio Analysis to Management Accounts.

(b) From the following figures make out a statement of Proprietors' Fund :

Current Ratio 2.5 ; Liquid Ratio 1.75; Proprietary Ratio (Fixed Assets to Proprietary Fund) 0.80 and Capital Gearing Ratio (Equity share capital to Preference share Capital) 6.

Working Capital Rs. 75,000; Reserve and Surplus Rs. 25,000 and Bank Overdraft Rs. 20,000.

There is no long term loan, investment or fictitious asset.

[M.Com. C.U. Management Accounting]

12. From the following different information you are requested to comment on the financial trend of Light and Shade manufacturing Company :

Ratios	Years				
	2000	2001	2002	2003	2004
Current Ratio	1.5	3.1	3.5	4.1	4.5
Acid Test Ratio	0.70	0.60	0.90	0.50	0.80
Stock Turnover Ratio (Times)	4	3	3	2	2.1
Margin on Sale	5%	4%	3%	2%	5%
Return on Capital	15%	16%	12%	12%	15%
Proprietary Ratio	40%	50%	65%	70%	70%
E.P.S. Ratio (Earning per share of Rs. 20).	.6	.5	.4	.3	.3

19

COST OF CAPITAL ANALYSIS

• Good morning my dear students.

☐ "Good morning Sir."

• Now I would like to give you some idea about the 'Cost of Capital'.

Introduction

You know, finance is one of the most important aspects of business management. Like circulation of blood in the human body, finance flows through every process of business. But it is not an easy task to keep the flow of finance steady in this process. It requires efficiency on the part of the management and continued patronage of the investors. Declaration of dividend at a higher rate, selling the shares in the share market at a higher value, possessing business solvency—all are the attractions of continued investors' patronage. However, all these depend upon sound and efficient financial management.

Financial Planning

Out of the two sources of tapping finance—internal and external—which one would be more profitable? Whether it would be possible to maintain the bare cost of capital and to reject the capital expenditure project on the ground of high cost of capital? All these are questions of financial management. Some author has described this financial management as a 'forward looking appraisal of the financial aspect of the business programme, leading to decisions regarding the most effective course of action to be taken over a future period.'

Planning for profit, besides coordinating and controlling the same, is one of the important aspects of financial management. The success of financial managers will be justified when they are able to maximise the present value of the owners' future income. This requires a close study of the internal rate of return and the cost of capital.

However, the financial management is concerned with :

Revenue = Cost of Goods Sold + Profit before Interest and Tax (PBIT) + Other Expenses

Profit before Interest and Tax = Tax + Cost of Capital + Retained Surplus

or, in other words,

Revenue = Cost of Goods Sold + Other Expenses + Tax + Cost of Capital + Retained Surplus.

Cost of Capital = Revenue – (Cost of Goods Sold + Other Expenses + Tax + Retained Surplus)

The whole can be explained as :

$R = C + E + T + K_o + S.$

or, $K_o = R - (C + E + T + S)$

where, K_o = Cost of Capital
R = Revenue
C = Cost of Goods Sold
T = Tax
E = Expenses
S = Retained Surplus

Finding out and estimating the cost of capital is not an easy task. Evaluating the Cost of Capital is a dynamic process since computing the cost of capital in a given situation 'involves such variables as capital structure...floating cost, dividend policies and the level of the security prices.' In spite of this, attempts had already been made in U.S.A. to find out the cost of capital for nearly 300 companies in the year 1963.

Do you follow my lecture?

☐ "Yes Sir".

☐ "Sir, what is the definition of Cost of Capital?"

Definition of Cost of Capital

• Cost of capital may be defined as a minimum acceptable rate of return on capital employed in the business. Some author has described the minimum rate as being the cost of capital input. The minimum rate of return may be equal to the cost of input, when the company's output is not enough to plough back profit for future expansion which could have been invested in the business as an internal source of finance. So, a close study of the cost of input and output can be made in case of Indian concerns. However, the National Association of Accountants has defined the cost of capital as :

1. 'The rate that a company must pay for capital whether obtained by borrowing or by issue of capital stock. This is commonly termed 'the borrowing rate'.'

2. 'The rate that can be earned on alternative investments having a like degree of risk. This is often called the 'lending rate'.'

By cost of capital one author has assumed the weighted cost of capital because of its advantages in actual practice, that weights are based upon present market value which helps the management to take concrete management decision. Even there are authors who consider the cost of capital of a firm as being weighted average cost of capital which in practice, indicates minimum acceptable rate of return for accepting or rejecting any capital investment proposal.

However, in my view, it should be understood as the weighted average of the costs of various sources of finance, namely, equity, preference or debt.

I hope you have understood the meaning and definition of cost of capital. Is there any question you would like to put me?

☐ "Sir, who are the exponents of the Theory?"

Exponents of the Theory

• Well, you see, though various financial experts have worked out various formulae to find out the cost of capital, yet the credit goes to

Myron J. Gordon and Shapiro for original formulation of the growth model. As an expert of this theory and model Prof. Solomon explained the same in a modified way. However, different formulae have been originated—thanks to different problems of the situation. This problem relates to the structure and components of the capital structure of the business. It has already been pointed out at the outset that the difficulties in selecting a number of alternative sources of capital or finance are obvious. The capital structure consists of Equity capital, Loan capital and Borrowed capital. The company can secure finance from all of these quarters against the promise to distribute a portion of output for the input contributed by them. No problem arises as to the cost of Preference Shares and Debentures. Difficulties arise to find out the cost of Equity Share Capital and Retained Earnings. Declaration of dividends depends upon the management policy which varies as circumstance dictates. 'Another fundamental problem in determining the cost of common stock capital is that the stockholders participate in Company Profits. There is no fixed ceiling as to what he is to be paid, as in the case of a lender. If management's objective is to maximise growth through reinvestment of earnings, the dividend can be considered as interest cost.' Similar difficulties are found to be more acute in case of retained earnings which constitute a part of the Net Worth of the business. Capital from this source has no cost; since it is generated within. But retained earnings definitely has opportunity cost. Determination of the cost of capital from static point of view is not less complicated as is found more in case of dynamic approach to the problem. Since it is affected by :

Problems in Computing Cost of Capital

(i) Current Capital Structure, (ii) Changes in the Rate of Earnings, (iii) Financial Plan for the future and, finally, (iv) the Industrial Climate of a country. But it is not possible always at a time to take all these variables as constant while computing the cost of capital of any enterprise.

Well, I think you have followed my lecture as well as different problems which arise while computing the cost of capital.

Now I am explaining the different formulae given by different experts in the line :

☐ "But before that Sir, would you explain why it is essential to calculate cost of capital?"

• It is absolutely essential to calculate the cost of capital. The cost of capital is an important concept in financial management. It is used as a decision criterion in a number of decision areas of financial management. Such as, in investment decision, cost of capital is used as a minimum acceptable rate of return. In financing decision, while setting capital structure the financial manager tries to keep cost of capital at minimum level. The cost of capital is also used for evaluating performance of divisional managers in the area of working capital management, lease proposal assessment etc.

Now, we discuss the methods to calculate each component of cost of capital :

(1) Cost of Equity Capital (K_e) : Cost of Equity Capital means the cost of the sale of new equity for the present stakeholders of the company. Also, the rate of return that an investor expects to earn when investing in ordinary shares of a company is known as cost of equity share capital.

For Example : If an investor expects a 5% return from A Ltd. stock and he buys a share at Rs. 50, his expectation is to receive Rs. 2.50 during the year in the form of dividend. This rate of 5% is known as cost of equity.

The formulae to calculate cost of equity are discussed here :

(a) Realised Return Method : Under this method, cost of equity is the aggregate of two historical returns to the equity shareholders. The two returns are average dividend yield and average capital gain. That is

$$K_e = \frac{D + G}{P_0} \times 100$$

K_e = Cost of equity

D = Average dividend per share

G = Average capital gain per share $(P_1 - P_0)$

P_0 = Face value per share

P_1 = Expected market price per share

Thus, the formula can be expressed as

$$K_e = \frac{D}{P_0} + \frac{P_1 - P_0}{P_0}$$

(b) Earnings Price Ratio Method : Under this method cost of equity capital :

$$K_e = \frac{\text{Earning per share (EPS)}}{\text{Market price per share } (P_1)} \times 100$$

(c) Dividend Valuation Model : If flotation costs are ignored the cost of equity for new shares and its retained earnings could be estimated by dividend valuation approach. Here it is assumed that share prices in the market is related to expected future dividend.

I. Dividend Growth Approach (Model) :

$$P_0 = \frac{D_1}{1 + K_e} + \frac{D_1(1 + g)}{(1 + K_e)^2} + \frac{D_1(1 + g)^2}{(1 + K_e)^3} + \ldots\ldots\ldots \infty$$

$$\text{or, } P_0 = \frac{\dfrac{D_1}{1 + K_e}}{1 - \dfrac{1 + g}{(1 + K_e)}}$$

$$\text{or, } P_0 = \frac{\dfrac{D_1}{1 + K_e}}{\dfrac{1 + K_e - 1 - g}{1 + K_e}}$$

$$\text{or, } P_0 = \frac{D_1(1 + K_e)}{(1 + K_e)(K_e - g)}$$

$$\text{or, } P_0 = \frac{D_1}{K_e - g}$$

$$\text{Also, } K_e = \frac{D_1}{P_0} + g$$

The above formula is also known as 'Gordon's Model'.

Here K_e = Cost of equity capital

g = growth rate

P_0 = Current market price of a share

D_1 = Dividend after a year

Now, the formula to calculate growth is given as :

g = br

where g = growth rate

b = retention ratio

r = rate of return

The above method is based on the following assumptions :

(a) Dividend pay out ratio is constant.

(b) Dividend will grow at a constant rate.

(c) Market price of a share depends upon expected dividend.

II. Constant Dividend Approach : Under this approach, it is presumed that dividend will remain constant throughout a number of years. The cost of Equity is derived as

$$P_0 = \frac{D_1}{1 + K_e} + \frac{D_1}{(1 + K_e)^2} + \frac{D_1}{(1 + K_e)^3} + \frac{D_1}{(1 + K_e)^4} + \ldots\ldots\ldots \infty$$

$$\text{or, } P_0 = \frac{\dfrac{D_1}{1 + K_e}}{1 - \dfrac{1}{1 + K_e}}$$

$$\text{or, } P_0 = \frac{\dfrac{D_1}{(1 + K_e)}}{\dfrac{1 + K_e - 1}{(1 + K_e)}}$$

$$\text{or, } P_0 = \frac{D_1 (1 + K_e)}{(1 + K_e) K_e}$$

$$\text{or, } P_0 = \frac{D_1}{K_e}$$

This model is based on the principle of perpetuity.

(d) Bond Yield Plus Risk Premium Method : Under this method, cost of equity is calculated by adding premium for risk to the required return on the long term bond.

Thus, $K_e = B_Y + r$

K_e = Cost of equity

B_Y = Yield on long term bond

r = Premium for risk

(e) Capital Asset Pricing Model (CAPM) Method : According to this method, the cost of equity is calculated by using the following formula :

$$K_e = R_f + (R_m - R_f)\,\beta$$

where K_e = Cost of equity

R_f = risk-free rate of long term bond

R_m = average market rate of return

β = systematic risk.

CAPM method is the most objective method of determining cost of equity. Under this method, risk premium for the systematic risk is added to the rate of return on long-term government bond in order to determine cost of equity. Here the risk premium is $(R_m - R_f)\,\beta$, which is a compensation for bearing systematic risk.

Now I am discussing on cost of debt and preference share capital.

(2) Cost of Preference Share Capital : We know that the preference shareholders are paid a fixed rate of dividend and are redeemed at maturity.

The following formula is used to calculate cost of preference :

$$K_p = \frac{D + \dfrac{F - F_M}{n}}{\dfrac{F + F_M}{2}}$$

where, K_p = Cost of preference

F = Face value

F_M = Market price (present)

n = maturity period

D = Dividend per year.

(3) Cost of Debt Capital : The cost of debt capital is, what the firm must pay to the purchasers of its debentures, or, bonds. This is stated as a percentage which is also known as rate of interest.

In case of perpetual debt

K_d = rate of Interest × (1 – tax rate).

This method is used to calculate cost of term loan (K_t).

In case of debt having fixed maturity

$$K_d = \frac{I(1 - t) + \frac{(F - F_m)}{n}}{\frac{F + F_m}{2}}$$

where, K_d = Cost of debt capital
I = Interest on debt per annum
F = Face value
F_m = Current market value
n = Maturity period
t = rate of tax.

Also, if a clever investor is ready to purchase a bond or debenture, he has to consider future cash flows i.e., interest and the redemption value of debenture.

The current market price

$$P_0 = \frac{I}{(1 + r)} + \frac{I}{(1 + r)^2} + \frac{I}{(1 + r)^3} + \ldots\ldots\ldots + \frac{R_v + I}{(1 + r)^n}$$

By method of Interpolation and Extrapolation, the value of 'r' can be calculated.

This 'r' is also the cost of debt (redeemable) capital

P_0 = Current price of debentures
I = Interest per year
r = discounting rate i.e., cost of debt
R_v = redeemable value.

It is important to note in this context that the value of I is assumed to be same, as debenture is a fixed interest-bearing security. R_v may be at par, premium or discount. Also, if the debenture is convertible into equity share, the issue price should be taken here.

☐ "Sir, is retained earning cost-free"? "What is weighted cost of capital Sir"?

• You have asked interesting questions. Although companies do not have to incur any actual cost for retained earnings, it is not cost-free. The opportunity cost is considered as cost of retained earnings, the opportunity cost is the dividend foregone by the equity shareholders. Thus, the cost of retained earnings can be taken as equal to the cost of equity share capital. The cost of retained earnings can be calculated with the help of formulae used for calculating cost of equity.

Weighted Average Cost of Capital (WACC) : It is also known as implicit or composite cost of capital. WACC is the weighted average cost of specific sources of capital. The weights are the proportion of individual component of various sources of funds. Financial decisions are made on the basis of after tax cost of capital.

The formula of Weighted Average Cost of Capital

$$K_c = K_d W_d + K_t W_t + K_p W_p + K_e W_e + K_r W_r$$

where K_c = Overall cost of capital

W_d = weight of debt

W_t = weight of term loans

W_p = weight of preferred capital

W_e = weight of equity capital

W_r = weight of retained earnings

K_d = cost of debt, K_t = Cost of term loans, K_p = Cost of Preference Capital, K_e = Cost of equity capital, K_r = Cost of retained earnings.

Now I am discussing on determination of weights. You know that the weighted average cost of capital calculation requires two types of information. One information is about specific cost of individual sources and second, their respective weights in the total capital structure. Weights may be, again, weights in the current capital structure or in target capital structure. The current capital structure or target capital structure may be taken either in book value term or in market value term. Now, what is acceptable,—current capital structure at book value or market value or, target capital structure at book value or market value?

Financial experts believe that target capital structure at market value is appropriate.

Again, unlike book value, market value information is very difficult to obtain. Book value remains unchanged, but market value changes with the change in market conditions. There is no doubt about the fact which I gave you in inflation accounting where I explained that, on the date of purchase, cost and value remains the same but with the passage of time, cost remains the same, value changes.

Do you remember this?

□ "Yes Sir".

• If so, similarly, on the date of issue, book value and market value of share remains the same but, with the passage of time, they fail to coincide. That is to say, book value of share remains the same and market value fluctuates. We know, one of the use of cost of capital is its use as cut-off rate and, in order to remain in competition, a firm must earn required rate of return on capital at market value—not book value. Thus, market value gives more appropriate measure of cost of capital.

Marginal Cost of Capital : It is the cost of raising an additional capital. In raising new funds, this approach is normally applied. It may be calculated as the weighted average cost of fresh capital using marginal weights.

However, various models cited above to find out the cost of capital is nothing but an attempt made by different leaders of the financial front. Because it is very difficult to determine or compute 'the cost of capital of any enterprise with precision.' Besides, opinion varies from expert to expert as to the supremacy of these models. Because, while much of this debate over the cost of capital is theoretical and of interest mainly to economists, there are some aspects of the controversy of practical interest to accounting and financial manager. The practical question in the cost of capital controversy is what kind of rate should be used for cut-off purposes in the Project Selections.

I think, you have understood my lecture.

☐ "Sir, really speaking, I cannot understand the concept of Cut-off Rate and Opportunity Cost".

● Well, I am explaining the same. Please note carefully the following discussions.

Management is to take decision in order to keep the process of business running. Management decision is not confined to the field of business management alone, rather it can be extended in the financial side of the business too, which is known as financial management decision. Selling the share in the share market at a higher value depends on sound and efficient dividend policy and the future stability of the company. 'Companies which fail to pay dividends will experience difficulty in raising finance on the stock exchange and also will find the value of their share depressed in the market'. The success of the financial management depends on how they are successful to earn more than the cost of capital. Because no investment proposal will be accepted unless the rate of earnings does not exceed the cost of capital. Earning over and above dividends means excess of return on investment over the cost of capital.

Success of Financial Management

Please note the management decision in the context of Cost of Capital :

Situation	Decision
(a) Return on Investment <	Cost of Capital = Reject
(b) Return on Investment >	Cost of Capital = Accept
(c) Return on Investment =	Cost of Capital = Observation

Above are the situations which the management can face and take its decision accordingly. Conflict of judgement arises when the management is to tackle the third (c) situation when cut off point return on investment is equal to the cost of capital. This is known as the cut-off rate. That is to say, the cost of capital is looked upon as a cut-off point; that is, point of equilibrium of 'Satisfaction' and 'Tolerance'. Constructing this line depends upon how the management are efficient in the financial side. Management will derive considerable benefits if decision is taken from this equilibrium point. Side shown figure indicates the point of equilibrium—the stage of 'wait and see'.

Cut-off Point

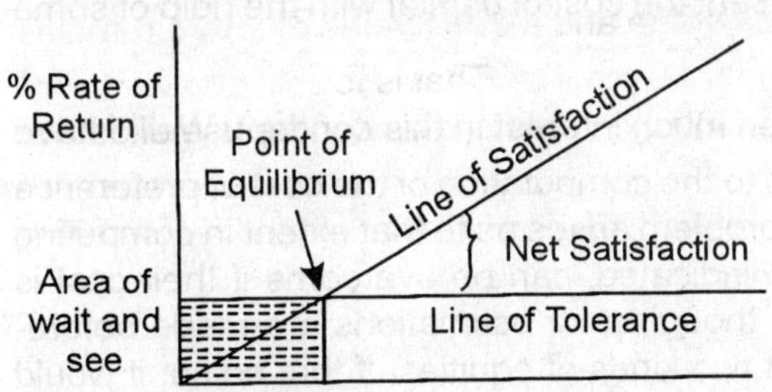

It is very difficult to bring all businesses under a set policy which varies from firm to firm, industry to industry and unit to unit. The practical question, accordingly, in the cost of capital controversy is what kind of rate should be used for cut-off purposes in project selection.

However, the third situation (c), as indicated earlier, can be accepted for a minimum period of time. If this situation continues in the business, two alternatives are open to management—either (i) to close down the project, or (ii) to construct the capital structure which helps the company to pay higher dividend, besides adequate provision for the same, which enhances the prices in the share market. It should be noted in this connection that the market value of the share depends on various factors of which one is even 'psychological'—creating what is known as the 'mood of the market'. However, this cut-off rate can be regarded, other factors being standardised, as a minimum cut off rate of other similar types of company. The controversy as to what kind of rate should be taken for cut-off purpose can be overcome if the minimum rate of return of other similar types of company or companies are taken into account for guiding purposes. This cut-off rate is regarded as the 'opportunity cost' of capital when there is a scarcity of investment opportunity. This opportunity cost is the best return which 'can be obtained, with comparable risks, by investing the firm's available funds either internally or externally. The opportunity cost of capital, when there is a paucity of profitable investment opportunities, approaches the cost of capital but not otherwise.'

Opportunity Cost

However, a diagram is shown below bringing all the factors together, discussed earlier. The diagram shown here only indicates the behaviour which varies from concern to concern or even industry to industry.

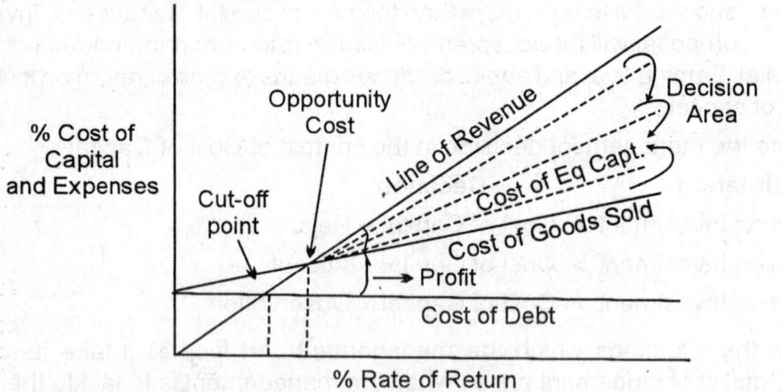

I hope you have followed the diagram given above. Do you follow?

☐ "Yes Sir."

"We shall be glad Sir, if you please represent the cost of capital with the help of some case study".

• I am really very glad that you have taken much interest in this concept. Well, I have already discussed that no problem arises as to the computation of the cost of preference share and fixed interest bearing securities; problem arises as to that extent in computing the cost of equity capital. This problem, as indicated, can be overcome if their cost is estimated beforehand. It would be unwise, though prior estimations are made beforehand in the either cases, to treat the cost of two kinds of equities. If that be so, it would lead to a situation where the company would be compelled to pay dividend out of capital.

The scheme to overcome existing difficulties by inviting a new problem cannot be welcome. If the capital structure of the company is low geared, the equity shareholder will be deprived of getting higher dividend in case of boom. If the cost of equity share capital is fixed beforehand, the basic philosophy of gearing of capital will not be realised then, rather, it would bring a new problem in a period of slump when the return or output will not be commensurate with the cost of input.

However, following are the names of companies with more or less similar amount of capital, selected from different industries to indicate the cost of equity capital. This study of cost of capital relates to the 'compensation to be paid' for the use of capital, or it is the price paid for the use of capital.

Exhibit 1

% Cost of Capital of Different Companies for a certain period—year

Name of Companies	I	II	III	IV	V
1. A	7.5	10	10	10	12
2. B	7.2	10	10	10	10
3. C	45	20	15	15	20
4. D	10	5	—	40	35
5. E	22	15	10	15	6
6. F	17.5	12.5	17.5	10	12.5

Exhibit 2

Average Market Value of Shares for a certain period

Name of Companies	Face value of share	Years I	II	III	IV	V
1. A	10	—	—	19	20	15
2. B	5	6.5	8	8.5	7	6
3. C	10	36.5	29	41.5	31	25
4. D	100	133.5	125	121	142	145
5. E	10	19	25	23	23	23
6. F	100	200	164	152	151	151

Cost of Capital and Market Value of Shares

From the above figures, it is clear that the cost of Equity Capital of industry C, E and F is higher. One peculiarity to be noted is that the market value of share does not fluctuate with the rise or fall of the cost of equity share capital. It has been stated earlier that this depends on the 'mood of the market'.

However, Now I like to work out a few problems on Cost of Capital. Here are the problems. Note these very minutely.

☐ "Sir, how can the relationship between corporate earning and share price be established?"

• You see, the relationship between share price and corporate earnings can be expressed as under :

$P = m\overline{n}$ P = Co's share price (market)

$\frac{1}{m}$ or $\frac{\overline{n}}{P}$ is the cost of capital $\overline{n}$ = Earning per share

m = The multiple that shareholders use to relate current earnings

Problem

A manufacturing company has assets Rs. 1,600 which are financed with Rs. 520 of Debt and Rs. 1,080 of equity share capital. The total profit of the company after tax is Rs. 135. It pays 8% interest on debt (borrowed fund or capital). It has 90 shares of stock outstanding, selling at a market price of Rs. 12 per share. Tax 50%.

(a) What is the company's share valuation multiplier?

(b) What is the weighted average cost of capital?

Solution

(a) $P = m\bar{n}$ $\qquad$ Earning per share $= \dfrac{\text{Rs. } 135}{90} = \text{Rs. } 1.50$

or $P = m\,(1.50)$

or $12 = m\,(1.50)$

or $= \dfrac{1}{m} = \dfrac{1.5}{12}$

or $1.5\,m = 12$, or $m = 8$

(b) Since m is 8, then $\dfrac{1}{m} = 12.5\%$ and cost of equity before tax = 25%.

The Debt and Equity ratios are :

$$\text{Debt Ratio} = \frac{\text{Debt}}{\text{Total Assets}} = \frac{\text{Rs. } 520}{\text{Rs. } 1{,}600} = .325$$

$$\text{Equity Ratio} = \frac{\text{Equity}}{\text{Total Assets}} = \frac{\text{Rs. } 1{,}080}{\text{Rs. } 1{,}600} = .675$$

And since the proportions of Debt and Equity are .325 and .675, respectively, then the weighted cost of capital is = .325 (.08) + .675 (.25) = .195 or 19.5%.

☐ "Sir, how is the figure (.08) calculated"?

● It is very easy, it has been calculated as :

$$\frac{8}{100} = .08$$

Do you follow ?

☐ "Yes Sir".

Problem

At present X, Y, Z Co. has Rs. 5,000 Loan Capital and Rs. 15,000 in Equity Share Capital. The Company pays 8% interest on loan capital. The Company has 1,000 shares of common stock outstanding at the current price Rs. 24 per share. The Co. pays 50% income tax. The Profit for the year after taxes is Rs. 2,400.

The Company has chosen to finance a new Rs. 1,800 project entirely through sale of additional shares with no underwriting cost involved. The aim of the Company is to maintain earning per share Rs. 2.40. What is the project's required rate of return?

Solution

	Original Situation	Situation arising from the floating of New Shares
	Rs.	Rs.
Earning Before Interest and Taxes (EBIT)	5,200	5,560 (C)
Interest	400	400
Profit Before Tax (PBT)	4,800	5,160
Tax (50%)	2,400	2,580 (B)
Profit After Tax (PAT)	2,400	2,580
No of Shares	1,000	1,075 (A)
Earning Per Share (EPS)	2.40	2.40
Change in EBIT	—	360
Required Return on Rs. 1,800		20% (D)

Calculations : (A) No. of extra shares $= \dfrac{\text{Value of Shares}}{\text{Market Value}} = \dfrac{1,800}{24} = 75$ Shares

Old Share 1,000 + New Share 75 = 1,075 Shares

(B) Expected earning per share Rs. 2.40.

So expected earnings on 1,075 share is (1,075 × Rs. 2.40) Rs. 2,580.

(C) (Rs. 2,580 × 2) + Rs. 400 = Rs. 5,560

(D) $\dfrac{360}{1,800} \times 100 = 20\%$

Problem

The current capital structure of a firm is :

	Amount (Rs./lakh)
Equity Share Capital (Rs. 100 each)	400
Retained Earnings	200
12% Debentures (Rs. 100 each)	400
	1,000

You are given the following further information :

(i) Current market value per share : Rs. 300
    Dividend paid per share in the last year Rs. 45
    Growth rate in dividend 10%

(ii) The market value of Debenture is Rs. 110 per Debenture

(iii) Corporate tax rate : 40%

Using market values as weights, find out the average cost of capital of the firm.

[C.U., M.Com.]

Solution

Working notes

(i) **Cost of Equity Capital (K_e)** $= \frac{D_1}{P_0} + g$

$$= \frac{D_0(1+g)}{P_0} + g$$

$$= \frac{45\ (1 + 0.10)}{300} + 0.10$$

$$= \frac{49.50}{300} + 0.10$$

$= 0.265$

i.e. 26.5%

(ii) **Cost of Debt Capital (K_r)** $= R\ (1 - t)$

$= 12\%\ (1 - 0.40)$

$= 7.2\%$

(iii) **Cost of Retained Earnings (K_s)** = 26.5%, i.e., same as equity capital.

(iv) **Ascertainment of weights of Components of Cost of Capital :**

	Market value (Rs. in lakhs)
Equity Share Capital (Rs. 300)	1,200.00
Retained Earnings	200.00
12% Debentures (Rs. 110)	440.00
	1,840.00

∴ Weight of Equity Share Capital (W_e) = 65.22%

Weight of Retained Earnings (W_r) = 10.87%

Weight of Debentures (W_D) = 23.91%

∴ Weighted Average Cost of Capital

$= K_e W_e + K_D W_D + K_r W_r$

$= 26.5\ (0.6522) + 7.2\ (0.2391) + 26.5\ (0.1087) = 17.28 + 1.72 + 2.88$

$= 21.88\%$

Problem

Wisconson Company has assets of Rs. 32,00,000 that have been financed by Rs. 18,00,000 of Equity (Shares of Rs. 100 each), General Reserve of Rs. 3,60,000 and Debt of Rs. 10,40,000. For the year ended 31.03.02 the company's total profit before interest and taxes were Rs. 6,23,200. Wisconson pays 8% interest on borrowed capital and is in a 40% tax bracket. The market value of Equity as on 31.03.02 was Rs. 150 per share.

What was the Weighted average cost of capital? Use market values as weights.

[C.U. M.Com., Adapted]

Solution

(i) **Calculation of Cost of Equity**

	Rs.
Profit before interest and tax	6,23,200
Less : Interest [Rs. 10,40,000 × 8%]	83,200
Profit before tax	5,40,000
Less : Tax (40%)	2,16,000
Profit after tax	3,24,000
No. of Equity Shares	18,000
Earning Per Share (Rs.)	18.00
Market Value Per Share (Rs.)	150
Cost of Equity	$18/150 \times 100$
	=12%

(ii) Cost of Borrowed Capital = 8% (1 – .40)

= 4.8%

Calculation of Weighted Average Cost of Capital :

Source	Capital (Rs.)	Cost (%)	Market Value (Rs.)	Proportion	Weighted Average Cost of Capital (%)
Equity share	18,00,000	12	27,00,000	.72	8.640
Retained Earnings	3,60,000	12	—		
Debt	10,40,000	4.8	10,40,000	.28	1.344
			37,40,000	1.00	9.984

∴ Weighted average cost of capital = 9.984%

Problem

Calculate weighted average cost of capital from the following particulars of a company :

(i) Rs. 10,00,000 Equity shares of Rs. 100 each. Present dividend per share is Rs. 25 with a market price of Rs. 250 per share. Estimated growth rate in dividend 5%.

(ii) Rs. 5,00,000 8% Preference shares of Rs. 100 each issued at Rs. 95.

(iii) 10% Term Loan Rs. 5,00,000. The company received the entire proceeds of the loan.

(iv) 11% 5 year Debentures of Rs. 5,00,000 (Rs. 100 each). The company received Rs. 105 per debenture.

Assume that the optimum mix of capital of the company is represented in the amounts as mentioned above and that the company is in a 40% tax bracket.

[C.U., M.Com.]

Solution

Calculation of Specific Cost of Capital

(i) **Cost of Equity**

$$K_e = \frac{D}{P} + g$$

where K_e = Cost of equity

D = Dividend per share

P = Market price per share

g = Growth rate in dividend

$$\therefore K_e = \frac{25}{250} + .05$$

$$= 0.1 + .05$$

$$= 0.15 \text{ or } 15\%$$

(ii) **Cost of Preference Share Capital**

$$K_P = \frac{D}{I}$$

where K_P = Cost of preference share

D = Dividend per preference share

I = Issue price per share

$$\therefore K_P = \frac{8}{95} \times 100$$

$$= 8.42\%$$

(iii) **Cost of Term Loan**

$$K_T = 10\% \, (1 - .4)$$

$$= 6\%$$

(iv) **Cost of Debenture**

$$K_D = \frac{I(1-t) + \frac{F-P}{n}}{\frac{F+P}{2}}$$

where K_D = Cost of debenture

I = Rate of interest

t = Rate of tax

F = Face value

P = Proceeds from issue

n = Maturity period

$$K_D = \frac{11\,(1 - 0.4) + \dfrac{100 - 105}{5}}{\dfrac{100 + 105}{2}}$$

$$= \frac{6.6 + (-1)}{102.5}$$

$$= \frac{5.6}{102.5}$$

$= 0.0546$ or, 5.46%

Calculation of Weighted Average Cost of Capital

Source	Amount Rs.	Cost (%)	Book value weight	Weighted average (%) cost of capital
Equity	10,00,000	15	.4	6.000
8% Preference	5,00,000	8.42	.2	1.684
10% Term loan	5,00,000	6	.2	1.200
11% 5 year Debenture	5,00,000	5.46	.2	1.092
	25,00,000		1.00	9.976

∴ Weighted Average Cost of Capital is 9.976%.

Problem

Calculate weighted average cost of capital from the following information :

	(Rs. '000)
(i) Capital Structure of H Ltd. :	
Equity share capital (shares of Rs. 10 each fully paid)	200
Reserves & Surplus	100
14% Bond (before tax)	600
Total	900

(ii) Market price per share of H. Ltd. is Rs. 90 and dividend per share is Rs. 13.50. Expected growth rate in dividend is 5% p.a.

(iii) Corporate tax rate : 40%.

What is the weighted average cost of Capital of H. Ltd.?

Use market value as weights and show your workings. **[C.U. M.Com., Adapted]**

Solution

Cost of equity by using Dividend Growth Model :

$K_e = \frac{D}{P} + g$ where K_e = Cost of equity

D = Dividend per share

P = Market price per share

g = Expected growth rate

$$\therefore K_e = \frac{13.50}{90} + .05$$

$$= 0.15 + 0.05$$

$$= .2 \text{ or } 20\%$$

Cost of bond where, K_d = Cost of bond

$K_d = r(1 - t)$ r = Rate of interest

t = Tax rate

$$\therefore K_d = 14\% (1 - 0.4)$$

$$= 8.4\%$$

Calculation of Weighted Average Cost of Capital

Source	Book value (Rs.)	Cost (%)	Market value (Rs.)	Proportion	Weighted Average Cost of Capital (%)
Equity share	2,00,000	20	18,00,000	0.75	15.0
Reserve & Surplus	1,00,000	20	—		
14% Bond	6,00,000	8.4	6,00,000	0.25	2.1
	9,00,000		24,00,000	1.00	17.1

∴ Weighted Average Cost of Capital = 17.1%

Problem

From the following information relating to a company calculate the cost of institutional loan (after tax and before tax) after making assumption where necessary :

(i) Weighted average cost of capital (K_0) 13.91%

(ii) Capital structure and cost of capital :

Source	Amount Rs./Lakhs	After tax cost of capital (%)
Equity share capital	800	15
Reserve & Surplus	400	?
Institutional loan	200	?
	1,400	

(iii) Corporate tax : 40% **[C.U., M.Com.]**

Solution

Cost of Reserve & Surplus

Reserve & Surplus do not have any explicit cost; no cash outflow occurs for reserve & surplus. But it definitely has opportunity cost. If we think reserve & surplus as investment by equity shareholders, the opportunity cost would be the cost of equity.

Thus, the cost of reserve and surplus, here, will be 15%.

Cost of Institutional Loan :

We know that

$K_o = K_eW_1 + K_rW_2 + K_LW_3$

where, K_o = cost of capital (weighted average)

K_e = cost of equity

K_r = cost of retained earnings

K_L = cost of institutional loan

W_1, W_2, W_3 = respective weights

$$\therefore 13.91\% = 15\% \times \frac{800}{1{,}400} + 15 \times \frac{400}{1{,}400} + K_L \times \frac{200}{1{,}400}$$

$$\text{or, } 13.91\% = 8.57\% + 4.29\% + K_L \frac{200}{1{,}400}$$

$$\text{or, } 13.91\% - 8.57\% - 4.29\% = K_L \frac{200}{1{,}400}$$

$$\text{or, } 1.05\% = K_L \frac{200}{1{,}400}$$

$$\text{or, } K_L = \frac{1.05 \times 1{,}400}{200} = 7.35\%$$

$$\therefore \text{Before tax Cost of Institutional Loan} = 7.35 \times \frac{1}{.6} = 12.25\%$$

QUESTIONS

1. What is Cost of Capital? How is it concerned with Financial Management?
2. Find out the relationship between Share Price and Corporate Earnings.
3. What is 'Cut-off Point'? Explain its significance.
4. The average cost of capital of a firm is 15.36%. The following particulars are ascertained from its books of accounts :

   (i) Equity share capital : 40,000 shares of Rs. 10 each. Cost of equity is 20%.

   (ii) Retained earnings : Rs. 2,00,000.

   (iii) Debentures : 4,000 at Rs. 100 each issued at par.

   Calculate cost of retained earnings (K_r) and cost of debentures (K_d) (after-tax and before-tax) if the corporate tax rate is 40%. Make assumptions where necessary. **[C.U., M.Com.]**
5. The directors of X Ltd. are considering the feasibility of issuing 12% debentures at par to raise Rs. 10,00,000 for financing a new project. The project is expected to

produce a return of Rs. 2,50,000 per year indefinitely before tax and interest.

At present the company has the following capital structure :

	Rs.
Equity shares of Rs. 10 each	30,00,000
8% Preference shares of Rs. 10 each	60,00,000
Reserves and surplus	60,00,000
	1,50,00,000

The current market value of the equity and preference shares are Rs. 40 and Rs. 8, respectively, and the company's current maintainable profit before meeting taxes at an effective rate of 40% is Rs. 40,00,000.

You are required to :

(i) Compute the market value of the equity shares immediately after the issue of debentures; and

(ii) Calculate the weighted average cost of the capital before and after the issue of debentures.

It may be assumed that the cost of preference and equity capital will not be affected as a result of introduction of debt into the capital structure of the company.

[C.U., M.Com.]

6. BHX Ltd. has the following structure :

	Rs.
14% Preference Shares of Rs. 10 each	20,00,000
Equity Shares of Rs. 10 each	50,00,000
General Reserve	25,00,000
Profit and Loss Account	15,00,000
12% Debentures of Rs. 1,000 each	90,00,000
	2,00,00,000

You are given the following additional information about the company :

Equity Shares	:	Current market price per share Rs. 40, expected dividend per share one year from now Rs. 6 and this amount is expected to grow @ 5% per year thereafter to infinity.
Preference Shares	:	Current market price Rs. 9.40 per share, the shares have perpetual life.
Debentures	:	Current market price Rs. 925 per debenture; the debentures will mature 10 years from now, interest is payable annually.
Tax rate	:	45%

You are required to compute the weighted average cost of capital for BHX Ltd. Use market values as weights.

[C.U., M.Com.]

7. Your company proposes to undertake an investment project at a cost of Rs. 200 lakhs. The various sources from which the same can be financed and their relative specific costs are :

	Amount (Rs./Lakhs)	Cost of Capital (%)
Equity	100	18
Retained Earnings	50	?
Debentures	50	See note below
	200	

Note : 13.5% Debentures of Rs. 1,000 each to be issued at a premium of 10%, redeemable after 5 years.

What minimum rate of return (after-tax) do you recommend for the project? Assume corporate tax at 40%. **[C.U., M.Com.]**

8. You are given the following particulars with respect to a firm for the year just ended :

Source	Amount (Rs./Lakhs)	After-tax Cost of capital
Equity Share Capital	200	15
Retained Earnings	100	?
Long-term Debt	200	?
	500	

The corporate tax rate is 40% and the average cost of capital of the firm is 11.88%. Determine cost of retained earnings (K_r) and cost of debt (K_d) (after-tax and before-tax). Make assumptions where necessary. **[C.U., M.Com.]**

9. Calculate weighted average cost of capital (K_o) from the following information and comment on the results :

(i) Capital structure :

	Rs./Lakh
Equity share Capital (Shares of Rs. 100 each)	200
Reserves and Surplus	100
9% Debentures	200
	500

(ii) Current market value per share : Rs. 300

Last year's dividend per share : Rs. 45

Growth rate in dividend : 10%

(iii) Corporate tax : 40%

Use book values and market values as weights.

[MBA in Finance, Calcutta University]

20

EFFECT OF TAX ON MANAGEMENT FOR FINANCE

• Good morning to you all my dear students.

☐ "Good morning Sir."

• Now I would like to discuss the effects of corporate tax on financial management.

You see, like human beings, every business has some philosophy of its own. The philosophy of business may be summed up as :

Introduction

(i) Maximising profits, (ii) Reduction of cost, (iii) Increase of turnover, (iv) Production of quality goods at a reduced price for general welfare, (v) Efficient purchases and sales, (vi) Elimination of unnecessary expenditures, (vii) Increase in business efficiency, (viii) Proper utilisation of resources, and, finally (ix) Preserving the integrity of capital investment in the business.

Planning

For the proper striving towards profitability or for achieving the proper business philosophy,[1] finance plays an important part in regulating all the activities mentioned above. Because, finance is needed for generating further finance into the business. For accelerating finance in every sector of the business the following are needed :

1. Planning for Profit.
2. Planning for future investment decision; and
3. Planning for finance.

But of all the plannings mentioned above the most important one should be to study the environment in which a business operates, and an important part of the environment is the 'Tax structure' of the country[2], which has 'decisive effects'[3] on the development of the modern accounting world. It is to be noted in this context that well-developed and well-diversified tax-structure of a country contribute to its business environment. In many developed and developing countries there are many efficient authorities to levy taxes of different types. For example, in India there are two categories of taxes levied by the local, state or central governments : (i) Direct taxes; and (ii) Indirect taxes. Direct taxes are

---

[1] *Dr. Basu : "How Business Budget can help in taking Management Decision". Capital, 29.4.71, p. 757. But Mr. R. N. Bhaduri in his paper 'Management Accounting—its contribution to Productivity', Chartered Accountant, Sept. 1971, p. 245, has explained most of the business philosophy as objectives.*

[2] *Wright : "Discounted Cash Flow", Mc Graw Hill, p. 38.*

[3] *Ross : "The Elusive Art of Accounting", Ronald Press Company, p. 104.*

collected by the tax collecting authority directly from the tax payers e.g. income tax, wealth tax etc. Again, indirect taxes are collected by the tax collecting authority indirectly from the tax payers through the suppliers of the goods or service provider e.g. sales tax, customs duty, excise duty, value added tax (VAT), octroi, entry tax, service tax, expenditure tax.

I think you are following my lecture.

☐ "Sir, I have one question to ask."

• What is your question?

☐ "Sir, would you please highlight some aspects of tax planning, tax avoidance and tax evasion?"

• Why are you putting such a question?

☐ "Sir, I feel it has much impact on inflow of finance to the Government exchequer. Because, these aspects are very important to management consultants for further knowledge of the subject."

• You are perfectly right. It has much impact on corporate tax planning also.

Well have a look here ...... your attention please. Well, under a particular statute when an assessee carries out an exercise to meet his tax obligation in a systematic and orderly manner to avail maximum possible exemptions, reliefs and deductions it is called tax planning. It reduces the tax liability as well as avoid controversies. Proper tax planning includes—(i) Filing of various returns in time, (ii) Compliance of different provisions of law, (iii) Avoiding the levy of interest, (iv) Avoiding the imposition of penalty.

An efficient "Tax Management" system deals with all above exercises, and it can avoid the penalty up to Rs. 1 lakh due to delay in furnishing tax audit report u/s 44AB, by proper tax planning.

All assessees are expected to make faithful disclosure truly about his income and pay taxes abiding by the law. Sometime it is found that the tax payer deliberately hides the material particulars or furnishes false return or attempts to defraud the state by violating the mandatory provisions of law, which is termed as **tax evasion**, eg. suppressing income, recording fictitious transactions, knowingly claiming wrong deductions etc.

You see, two things are observed in day to day life—one is legitimate and another is illegitimate. In between the two i.e. legitimate and illegitimate there remains an aspect which may be considered neither legitimate nor illegitimate. This middle ground between legitimacy and illegitimacy may be considered as *taking the advantage of legitimacy*. Similarly there are two aspects in tax study —

(i) Payment of tax and

(ii) Evasion of tax.

In between these, two there remains a gap which is called tax avoidance. To make this aspect clear I am to give you an example of fasting of persons for religious matter, which I observed in my school days in my family. In Hindu mythology day starts from the time of rising the sun. Before that it is considered previous day.

My mother was very religious and orthodox lady as well as very weak in health. For performing Laxmi (Godess of Wealth) Puja she started fasting from the time of sunrise of the day. My maternal aunty was also religious minded and weak in health, started fasting from the start of the sunrise. Needless to mention my maternal aunty was very clever and she had some flavour of management education. While both were fasting, in the evening my mother had fallen ill for lack of food as reported by doctor. But curiously enough my maternal aunty was found very sound in her health, no trace of fasting from her face reading. After a while at a time of performing worship of Laxmi (Godess of Wealth) the priest reported that he is happy that both ladies (my mother and maternal aunty) have completed their fasting as per accepted principle of Hindu mythology which in the word of auditing may be termed as *true and fair*.

The said situation lead me to think that when both are of ill health only my mother get fainted why not my maternal aunty? On enquiry from management audit point of view it was revealed that my maternal aunty taken her 'lunch' just before sunrise (suppose sunrise at 5.00 am; she had taken the food, assuming lunch for the next day at 4.30 am) In Hindu mythology 4.30 a.m. goes to previous day.

An analysis of the two situation reveals that my maternal unty has taken the advantage of Hindu mythology which may be treated in the case of tax study as avoidance of tax. An insight into the matter would reveal that her fasting though in the eye of law (here in Hindu mythology) appears to be fair; but from ethical point of view, what appears to me, it is illegitimate.

Apparantly **tax planning** and **avoidance of tax** appear to be similar; but a hair splitting logic to differentiate the same is difficult. Here, in this regard I am quoting a report of Wanchoo Committee, which will speaks for itself. The distinction between 'evasion' and 'avoidance' therefore, is largely dependent on the difference in methods of escape resorted to. Some are instances of merely availing, strictly in accordance with law, the tax exemptions or tax privileges offered by the government. Others are manoeuvres involving an element of deceit, misrepresentation of facts, falsification of accounts, including down right fraud. The first represents what is truly *tax planning*, the latter tax evasion. However, between these two extremes, there lies a vast domain for selecting a variety of methods which constitute "*tax avoidance*".

By the by I am to bring your attention to court's decision with regard to avoidance of Tax and evasion of Tax, in the case *Aruna Group of Estates Vs State of Madras [1965] 55 IRT 642 [Mad]* which runs as follows.

"Avoidance of tax in not tax evasion and it carries no ignominy with it, for, it is sound law and certainly not bad morality for any body so to arrange his affairs as to reduce the brunt of taxation to the minimum."

It is a fact that 'Taxes are accepted fact—a cost—a tangible cash expenditure—an expense beyond management control'[4]. Though taxes are governmental levies which are based on the economic requirement of the environment in which business operates and, hence, beyond management control, yet the efficiency of the financial management will be justified by how they are able to stop the capital erosion resulting from taxation[5], by adopting the concept that 'pattern of operating activity may have tax effects'[6]. But this in

[4] *"Return on capital as a Guide to Managerial decisions", N. A. A. Research Report 35 p.21.*

[5] *Jaedicke and Sprouse : "Accounting flows : Income, Funds and Cash". Prentice-Hall, p.52.*

[6] *Paton and Dixon; "Essentials of Accounting" Macmillan Co., p 118.*

no way restores the confidence of the shareholders and investors that already exists following the conflict[7] between tax rules and ordinary accounting principles. And 'the divergence of taxable income from reported net income has set the accounting profession one of its toughest problems'[8]. Because most accountants will be at a dilemma before introducing any modification in the procedure of accounting following the threat of risk that two sets of figures are to be computed for reporting purposes—one for annual report and the other for the tax purposes. This follows that the accounting principles, which are acceptable or suitable for corporate law purposes, may not be accepted or found unsuitable for Revenue Court'[9]. As for example, in the case of Patrick and Broadstone Mills Ltd. (1954) I All E R 163 (C. A.) and the Minister of National Revenue vs. Anaconda American Brass Ltd., (1956) A. C. 85 (P.C.), the Base Stock and Life Method of Stock valuations were either rejected or found unsuitable for the computation of Income tax. And this divergence in the procedure stands on the way of development of accounting principles.

Though theoretically it is advocated that 'Accounting must not be subservient to tax law'[10], but in actual practice accountants wink the same by adopting 'two sets of books'[11]—one for tax purposes and other for shareholders. In view of the above and in view of tax effects on the modern business thinking, this chapter aims at finding out some effects of corporate tax on the different aspects of business. Because 'management must always plan ahead and must constantly take decisions effecting the future of the company. The majority of these decisions will affect the profitability of the company, and management is constantly seeking to know the effect of any action will have on profits and on the structure of the company'[12].

Did you follow what I have discussed so far?

☐ "Yes Sir".

• Well, it should be noted in this connection that the system of accounting has been developed or has been originated out of the necessity of social demand. So it is clear that the system of accounting is for the society and not the society for accounting[13]. Though theoretically it is advocated, as mentioned earlier, that accounting must not be subservient to tax law, yet from social point of view there cannot be any bar why it should not be subservient to tax when there is much scope for the improvement of existing accounting system or orientation of new accounting principles. 'Accounting is a practical common sense discipline. However, this does not mean that clear thinking is not required. We do indeed require the coolest, most clear headed survey of our dogma'[14]. If accounting principles and tax principles are correlated,

Structural Adjustment

[7] *Ibid, p. 494.*

[8] *Ross : op. cit., p. 107.*

[9] *Edey; "Accounting Principles and Business Reality" 'Accountancy', Vol. 74 (1963), pp. 998-1002 and pp. 1083-1088.*

[10] *Accountant's Encyclopaedia, Vol. 1.*
(A paper by Joseph A Mauriell entitled "Depreciation, Depletion, and Fixed Asset valuation")

[11] *Jaedicke and Sprouse, op. cit., p.14.*

[12] *Morrow; "Standard System of Accounting Control Embracing Financial and Cost Accounts", 'The Accountant' 18.6.1949.*

[13] *Dr. Basu : "Impact of conversion of Loans into Equity on Company Finances". 'Capital'; 17.12.70, p. 1043.*

[14] *Ross : Op. cit., p. 20.*

the shortcomings arising from keeping two sets of books, as mentioned earlier, may be removed. One of the shortcomings is that shareholders and investors are deprived of getting the real and transparent picture of the 'state of affairs' of the business. On this ground one may argue that oil and water cannot be mixed. But in actual practice mixtures have been made possible which, other things remaining the same, consists of water and oil.

One of the greatest effects of corporate tax lies on its distributable profit, because taxation on corporate profit in most of the countries of the world is becoming higher and higher. This impairs the company to finance expansion out of its retained profit which is one of the sources of finance. It involves no cost. Since it is generated within. If the rate of corporate tax is higher, the management will be at a loss what to do with the distribution of dividend. Good company will always try to distribute good dividends having due regard to the integrity of the capital structure of the business. Sometimes, in actual practice, companies are found to declare higher dividend inspite of the fact that their reserve position is at a stake. This practice is definitely one of the ways of back biting the shareholders of the business. It is not always possible to declare higher dividends when the major portion of the corporate profit is taxed at an excessive dose with the result that it may kill the market for equity capital[15]. However, it should be noted in this connection that profit tax and income tax and its level may influence the volume of production in the following ways :

Business Finance

(1) 'By affecting, generally adversely, the willingness of an individual to put forward his maximum effort and by discouraging risk taking.

(2) By preventing industry from setting aside out of profits a sufficiently large sum to ensure adequate working capital and replacement of capital equipment.

(3) By preventing the private individual from saving sufficiently to provide industry with fresh capital as and when required'.

Not only the volume of production may be affected by the level of taxation, the planning for constructing the capital structure, on the other hand, may need further planning for choice of preference. As we stated earlier, the level of taxation may kill the market for equity capital—this will lead financial management to think whether they should prefer high geared capital to low geared capital or not. 'The most obvious reason for raising debt finance is the fact that debt interest payments are deductible against earning before Corporation tax is charged, whereas equity dividend payments are not. A company with debt in its capital structure will pay less Corporation tax than all-equity company with the same gross earnings'[16]. However, the high level of corporate tax may, on the other hand, stand : on the way of inviting future investment in the society. This may put inconvenience to medium and small type of businesses who are always struggling for their existence 'The heavy tax burden on corporate sector will also affect the climate for new investment, thereby reducing the tempo of industrial growth'[17]. The tempo of industrial growth may be disturbed if the profit of the business cannot be reinvested properly. Since, major part of the profit of the business is being taxed. This leads to erosion of real capital of the business. Do you find any difficulty?

---

[15] *Hume : "The use of published accounts—the viewpoint of an investor". The Accountant, December 16, 1950, p.613.*

[16] *Stapleton : "The Theory of Corporate Finance", George G. Harrap and Co. Ltd. (1970), p. 196*

[17] *"Threat of New Taxes Depresses Equities" 'The Statesman', The Calcutta, 12.6.1971, p. 11.*

☐ "No Sir".

- Can I proceed?

☐ "Yes Sir".

- You see, It is a fact that inflation coupled with over-taxation of corporate profits have torn a gap in the physical resources of industry of alarming dimension. During the period of inflation income and capital sometimes get confused and the business tends to live on its capital, previously the business managed to keep its physical resources intact by ploughing back corporate profit at an excessive dose. During the period of inflation and high level of corporate tax as mentioned earlier, it has made it difficult to keep the real capital of the business intact. This leads to erosion[18] of real capital of the business.

Capital Erosion

Owing to inadequate provision for depreciation and improper valuation of closing stock, the profit of the business is inflated. Any dividend declared and any tax paid out of the inflated profit is nothing but dividend declared out of capital and tax paid dragging the real capital of the business. Overdrawing the revenue resources by the owner of the business and payment of corporate profit tax, following the inflation of profits, may put the business with the resources indicating high money values in terms of less commodities. The real capital of the business may be consumed unnoticed if the revenue is not matched with proper cost.

That capital erosion results through taxation will be clear if the published annual report of the company is envisaged. 'So long as depreciation that is deductible for tax purposes is measured by the relatively smaller number of dollars of greater buying power expended in an earlier period, it will be inadequate to recover the original purchasing power invested in the facilities consumed in production. Real wear and exhaustion costs are thus understated, real profits are overstated, and their results are erosion of capital through taxation'[19]. To stop the adverse effects of taxes on corporate finance; proposals have been suggested by the accountants[20] to include tax 'as an element of manufacturing cost' on the ground that taxes on income are a cost'. But it would not be surprised if any accountant does not agree to accept the proposal from the point of view that 'most companies account in the profit and loss statement for income taxes as a deduction from net profit'. This treatment recognises income taxes as a distribution of net income rather than as a manufacturing cost or an expense[21]. Now it is clear that none of the proposals are proper and fit to relieve the financial management from headache and anxiety arising from taxes.

Tax-Shield

It is a fact that erosion of capital through taxes can be safeguarded if the reported profit of the business stands at a standard level—a level which permits the financial management to protect the real value of capital. Erosion of capital is found to be more explicit if the retention and ploughing back of profit is not adequate. Charging depreciation on the historical cost method and valuing closing

Tax Shield

---

[18] *For details of capital erosion, see chapter on Accounting for Inflation.*

[19] *United States Steel Corporation, Annual Report, 1952, p. 4-5.*

[20] *"Some writers in the N.A.A. Bulletin and in a study made by National Industrial Conference Board have recommended its inclusion as an element of cost"—Neuner, Cost Accounting—Principles and Practice, 5th Ed.*

[21] *Lang-Mc. Farland-Schiff, "Cost Accounting". The Ronald Press Co., New York (1953)*

stock at an inadequate rate are the main causes of erosion of capital. Depreciation is a regular business expense—an expense which has a far-reaching effect in the determination of net cash inflow. Moreover, different methods of amortisation of assets, viz Declining (Diminishing) Balance Method, Straight Line Method and Sum of the Years' Digits Method etc. may alter the net cash flow into the business.

This can be explained following some imaginary figures—Investment Rs. 30,000; Annual cash flow expected to receive Rs. 22,000 over the next 50 years of the actual investment.

EXHIBIT I

Showing the pattern of cash inflow after taxes under sum of years' Digits Method of Depreciation

Year	Cash inflow before taxes	Depreciation	Incremental Income subject to tax	Tax (Assuming 50%)	Netcash inflow
	Rs.	Rs.	Rs.	Rs.	Rs.
1	22,000	10,000	12,000	6,000	16,000
2	22,000	8,000	14,000	7,000	15,000
3	22,000	6,000	16,000	8,000	14,000
4	22,000	4,000	18,000	9,000	13,000
5	22,000	2,000	20,000	10,000	12,000
Total Net Cash Inflow after Taxes					70,000

EXHIBIT II

Showing the pattern of cash inflow after taxes under Straight Line Method of Depreciation

Year	Cash inflow before taxes	Depreciation	Incremental Income subject to tax	Tax (Assuming 50%)	Netcash inflow
	Rs.	Rs.	Rs.	Rs.	Rs.
1	22,000	6,000	16,000	8,000	14,000
2	22,000	6,000	16,000	8,000	14,000
3	22,000	6,000	16,000	8,000	14,000
4	22,000	6,000	16,000	8,000	14,000
5	22,000	6,000	16,000	8,000	14,000
Total Net Cash Inflow after Taxes					70,000

So, it is clear from the exhibits indicated earlier that none of the methods of charging depreciation is found suitable to stop erosion of capital general reserve arising through taxation; though it is a fact that depreciation on asset is a tax deduction, thereby reducing the tax payment.[22] So, only Current Replacement Method (depending on Depreciation Base Method) will be the wise step to retain profit to check capital erosion in general. This will be clear if Exhibit 3 mentioned next is reviewed properly :

EXHIBIT III

Showing the pattern of cash inflow after taxes (under Current Replacement Method of Depreciation)

Year	% index	Cash Inflow Before Tax	Depreciation	Incremental Income Subject to tax	Tax (Assuming 50%)	Net-cash Inflow
		Rs.	Rs.	Rs.	Rs.	Rs.
1	101	22,000	6,060	15,940	7,970	14,030
2	103	22,000	6,300	15,700	7,850	14,150
3	106	22,000	6,720	15,280	7,640	14,360
4	107	22,000	6,600	15,400	7,700	14,300
5	109	22,000	6,930	15,070	7,535	14,465
Total Net Cash Inflow after Taxes						71,305

On review of the exhibits it is crystal clear that the payments of taxes under SYD (Sum year's—Digit) and Straight Line Method of Depreciation is Rs. 40,000 and the net cash inflow under both the methods is Rs. 70,000, whereas under Current Replacement methods the payment of taxes stood at Rs. 38,695 which falls short of Rs. 1,305 to arrive at Rs. 40,000 as payment of taxes. This additional amount is saved and enters into net cash flow (Rs. 70,000 + Rs. 1,305) which is Rs. 71,305. This method of depreciation may help the financial management to stop erosion of capital and general reserve to the extent of Rs. 1,305—particularly under this illustration. So, it is advocated that Income Tax Act and Companies Act should recognise Current Replacement Method of Depreciation in case of tangible fixed assets and current cost of replacement in computing 'cost of goods sold'.

QUESTIONS

1. Explain the effects of Corporate Tax on Financial Management.
2. "There results........erosion of Real Capital through taxation"—Explain.
3. What is "Tax-Shield"? Explain its significance in the context of Financial Management.

[22] *Lynch, "Accounting for Management"*, p. 402

21

DIVIDEND POLICY

● Good morning to you all.

☐ "Good morning Sir."

● You see in my last chapter I discussed in details about the effect of corporate tax on management for finance. It is a fact, and has been discussed earlier, that tax is paid on the net corporate profit. So, payment of tax is one of the two aspects of accomplishment of business liabilities or obligation. You know that a business has two liabilities—(i) Enterprise; and (ii) Social. The discussions made earlier, i.e. in the last chapter, relate to the effect arising from the accomplishment of social obligation of the business. Now I would like to explain the determinant factors for the accomplishment of enterprise liabilities.

Business Obligation

BUSINESS LIABILITIES OR OBLIGATION

- **Enterprise Obligation**
  - Investor (Payment of Interest)
  - Creditors (Payment of Interest)
  - Directors' Remuneration (Payment of Commission)
  - Self-Protection or Integration (Retaining sufficient Profit)
  - Shareholder (Payment of Dividend)
- **Social Obligation** (Payment of Tax)

From the above-mentioned chart it is very clear that discharge of the above liabilities is not an easy thing, and it is done through disposition of profit. Here we see that shareholders—who are the owners of the business—are paid off at the last.

This chapter concentrates on the different aspects of payment of dividend. However, a slice of profit which goes to the credit of the shareholder after meeting different obligations as explained in the above is termed Dividend. Profit which is legally distributed to the shareholders in the form of dividend is generally called Divisible Profit. Here I like to point out before you one important point—computation and basis of computation of profit is the prerequisite to the concept of Divisible Profit. Because sometimes, as has been found out in actual practice, profits of the business are inflated with certain motives of self-interest. And any dividend declared and paid out of the inflated profit amounts to payment of dividend out of capital.

Divisible Profit and Dividends

Payment of dividend out of capital is legally prohibited. It results in erosion of real capital of the business. You see, there exists no difference between the payment of dividend out of capital and out of inflated profit. Since payment of dividend out of inflated profits results unnoticed erosion of real capital of business. However, one important characteristic of corporate form of business you might have already observed, — the 'ownership' and 'control' of the business are separated. You know what I mean about ownership. Well, regarding 'Control,' aspect of the business I am to say that the business is conducted by a group of people who is termed as 'Board of Directors.' So, because of the existing separation of ownership and control of the business, there should be certain payout and retention policy of the business.

It should be noted in this context that while framing out 'determinant factors of dividend policies', the following important aspects should be taken into account :

Key to Dividend Policy

* To keep high the 'integrity' of the capital structure of the business.
* To keep active the stability and continuity and future growth of the business.
* To keep alive the 'mood' of the shareholders and morale of investors.
* To keep high the image of the shares in the Share Market so that the shares of the company may be sold like hot cake.

However, the different aspects of the dividend policy can be studied under two broad heads :

* Declaration of Dividend.
* Payment of Dividend.

Of the above two broad aspects, as mentioned earlier, the declaration of dividend is most important. Because, how much is to be distributed without injuring the integrity of the company's capital structure is really a difficult determination on the part of the management. However, let me discuss the above two broad heads of study of dividend policy :

Declaration of Dividend : Under this head following aspects could be studied properly :

* Factors affecting dividend policy, i.e. determinants of dividend policy.
* Types of dividend that can be declared for payment.

Payment of Dividend : Under this head following aspects could be considered properly :

(i) Nature of payment.

(ii) Basis of payment practices.

Now I would like to discuss the whole one by one (a) Factors affecting dividend policy i.e. determinant of dividend policy, (b) Types of dividend, (c) Nature and types of payment, (d) Basis of payment.

I hope you have followed the basis of my lecture. Is there any question please?

☐ "Sir, please go on speaking. It's really very interesting. We feel no boreing."

● I am really very glad to see that you have taken much interest in this respect. However, I am explaining below the above aspect of discussions. Please note it carefully.

(a) Factors Affecting Dividend Policy i.e. Determinants of Dividend Policy

Considerations that should be taken into account in formulating dividend policy are :

Legal Right

Legal Right : It is significant in the context of dividend policy, since management will have to formulate its policy within the framework provided by law. The essence of legal restriction is to protect the creditors and investors as well as, self-protection, i.e., preserving business integrity. Thus it provides that :

(i) No dividend can be paid out of capital.

(ii) No dividend can be declared or paid without providing for adequate depreciation for the replacement of fixed assets.

(iii) No dividend can be declared or paid except either from current year's earnings or earnings of the last year, i.e., retained earnings.

Earning Capacity

Earning Capacity : Generally, no dividend can be declared except in certain exceptional cases if a company incurs loss. There is no hard and fast rule that a company would earn fixed rate of earnings; it may fluctuate—high and low. It is a fact that a company cannot declare or pay dividend in excess of its earnings. However, an ideal dividend policy is the one which takes into account the behaviour of earnings of the business.

Tax Aspect

Tax Consequences : The dividend which goes to the individual shareholder is treated as personal income and added to his total individual income. That is to say, shareholders who are in high income tax bracket desire that a company should not declare or pay high dividend in form of cash, rather, they influence to capitalise a part of the profit, through issue of Bonus Share, which could have been distributed in the form of cash. This is insisted because of the following reasons :

(i) Evasion of personal income tax.

(ii) More shareholding motive.

(iii) Selling the shares at a higher price in the share market.

Bonus Share and Tax Consideration

Whether dividend can be paid in cash or the benefits of which can be paid by way of declaring bonus share is fully dependent on the choice and judgement of the Board of Directors. Besides, to fulfil the interest of a few shareholders who are in high income tax bracket, the interest of the poor shareholders cannot be denied. However, in the interest of society the declaration and payment of Bonus Share should be treated as declaration and payment of cash dividend which should be added to the total income of individual influential interested shareholders. If it is done, fluctuations of the share price—arising from the declaration of the bonus share—in the share market can be controlled. Besides, it would help in implementing 'Garibi Hatao Policy' of the government in the sphere of corporate finance. For that it is suggested on the ground of the social needs to take Bonus Share in the computation of total income of the shareholders and should be subject to tax.

Reinvestment of Earnings

Reinvestment of Earnings : Whether entire earnings of the business or a part of it should be retained in the business is a matter of consideration on the part of the management. Since earning is a source of fund which is generated within and which involves no general cost for its procurement, a part of it may be reinvested for future expansion, growth and future stability of the business. It should be wise on the part of the management to measure and compare the expected rate of return arising from the investment of retained earnings which should have been distributed to the shareholder with the rate of return if invested outside the business. However, the payment of dividend may influence Over-Capitalisation and Under-Capitalisation of business.

Working Capital Position : You know that cash dividend reduces the current solvency position of business. The dividend policy may influence the short term and long term solvency of the business. Here we can feel the importance of projection of long term 'inflow' and 'outfolw' of cash. This projection will definitely help in the formulation of sound dividend policy. It would be unwise to "impair" the working capital position for dividend payment purpose. It does not mean that declared dividend should not be paid, it should be at the suitable moment which can be determined from the projection of cash inflow and cash outflow. Professor Walter G. Kell of Michigan State University in his "Corporate Surplus, Reserves and Dividends" had rightly observed that 'since cash dividends reduce current assets of the corporation, the effects of dividend distribution upon the Working Capital position of the enterprise must be carefully weighed. It is obviously short-sighted and unsound to impair working capital for dividend purposes; particularly if there is any question about the adequacy of current assets to meet current liabilities and operating expenses. Therefore a projection of cash requirements should be made to ensure that fund to be used for dividend distributions can be spared. The fact that current cash holding are adequate does not alone justify a dividend declaration. If a corporation must borrow some years hence to replenish working capital that has been impaired by dividend distributions, in effect it borrows to pay the dividend. For this reason a projection of cash income and outgo for a period of 2 years or longer ahead should be weighed in formulating dividend policy where capital resources are scant'.

Declaration of Dividend Vs Working Capital Position

Control Aspect : You know that sources of finance are Issue of Share, Loan from Outside, and Retention of Profit. If a running company raises its capital through Issue of share for the expansion and growth of the business, one of the shortcomings arising from the situation is that the issue of additional share may dilute the control of the dominating group of the firm or the company. The situation can be avoided—that is to say, the right of the dominating group can remain unaffected—if internal earning can be used for investment purposes. And this object of maintaining control may motivate management to reduce dividend payment.

Control Aspect of Dividend Policy

Besides the points mentioned earlier, following factors may be acted in some cases as a basis of dividend policy :

i. Past dividend policy of the company.
ii. Rate of expansion of the business which requires extra fund.
iii. Capital market consideration.
iv. Influence of powerful stockholders or shareholders.
v. The effects of debt, contract on the imposition of dividend policy.
vi. The influence of dividend policy as persuaded by other similar type of competitive concern.

(b) Types of Dividend

Different types of dividends that are declared for payment are :

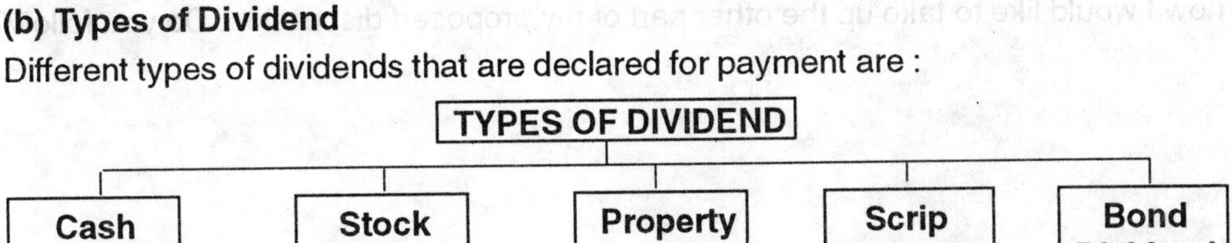

Cash dividend

Cash Dividend : Cash dividends require no introduction for its explanation. Dividends paid or payable in cash are known as cash dividends.

Stock Dividend : Stock dividends rank next to cash dividends. In the interest of overall business position, it may be sometime necessary to keep working capital position at a favourable position. For that it becomes unwise on the part of the management to declare cash dividend. In these situations a firm may be required to issue and distribute to the stockholders extra or additional shares of the same firm or stock of other company 'that is in the possession of the firm declaring dividend'. From accounting point of view the transaction may be defined as reclassifying a portion of the earned surplus as capital stock'. Such stocks may be cashed and stockholders may cash it by disposing their new shares at the prevailing market price. Well, we see here a process of converting the earned surplus to its capital stock. This process of declaration and payment of dividend is termed stock dividends.

Stock Dividend

Property Dividend : Dividends that are payable in non-cash assets are known as property dividends. Most common form of property dividend is the distribution of securities to the shareholders. That is to say, declaration and payment of dividends by distributing securities held as investments by the declaring company. That's why property dividends are sometimes referred as "Security Dividends". However, the payment of property dividends results from anti-trust policies of management. For this reason a company may be forced to 'divest' itself of the securities.

Property Dividend

Scrip Dividends : A company may seek to maintain or keep regular records of dividend payment without paying it by liquid cash.

☐ "Sir, how is it done?"

• Please wait. I will explain everything. You see in these cases it is done by distributing notes Payable or better to say, by distributing Written Evidences of the liability. The written certificates that are paid, instead of immediate cash payment, to the shareholder are known as 'Scrip'. So, dividends that are payable or paid by the 'issuance' of 'scrip' certificates are known as Scrip Dividends. Scrip dividends, until obligations are mitigated by instalments over a period of years, may be classified as an item of current liabilities.

Scrip Dividend

Bond Dividend : These are similar to Scrip Dividend with the exception that the 'obligation has a longer maturity'. The mechanism of bond dividend is the transformation of the amount of declared dividend into long term debt. That is to say, instead of selling bonds to the outside investor, these are distributed to the stockholders. So other major point of distinction between scrip dividend and bond dividend is that Scrip Dividend is current liability and Bond Dividend is loan capital.

Bond Dividend

I hope you have followed the above discussions. Is there any question please? Well, now I would like to take up the other part of my proposed discussion. Do you follow?

(c) Nature of Payment

NATURE AND TYPES OF DIVIDEND PAYMENT

- **Regular Dividend** (Normal cash dividend)
- **Extra Dividend** (In addition to regular dividend)
- **Special Dividend** (In the nature of 'windfall' to shareholder)
- **Interim Dividend** (Partial distribution of earning in the middle of a year)
- **Final Dividend** (Declaration made at the end of the year)
- **Liquidating or Capital Dividend** (Arises in mining co. investment, Trust Distribution—some part of contributory Capital)

(d) Basis of Payment Practices

BASIS OF DIVIDEND PAYMENT PRACTICES

- **Fixed Rupee Amount**
- **Minimum Rupee Amount**
- **Fixed Percentage on Net Profit**
- **Fixed Percentage of Market Value**

☐ "Sir, please explain the above concept in brief."

- Yes, I will.

Fixed Rupee Amount

You see, distribution of fixed rupee amount of dividends means that ordinary shareholders are paid off at a fixed rate—whether profit is earned or not. Under this policy, ordinary shareholders are treated as Preference Shareholders. The main defect of this policy is that, in the event of losses, the company will have to pay dividend at the cost of working capital.

Minimum Rupee Amount

Minimum Rupee Amount of dividend may be treated as a 'step up feature' of dividend policy. Since, this dividend policy ensures the payment of regular dividend to the shareholder—however small it may be. Unlike fixed rupee amount of dividend, determination of dividend here is dependent on the earnings of the company. Chances of 'ever missing' of regular dividend are eliminated under the basis of this payment practice. This dividend payment policy may stimulate the Board of Directors to concentrate its ideas for the growth, expansion and strengthening the 'integrity' of business capital and status.

Fixed Percentage on Net Profit

Regarding payment of dividend on the basis of fixed percentage on net profit, I am to say that here dividends are a fixed percentage of net profits of a business. This fixed percentage of profit is called payout ratio. In this basis of determination, internal financing of the business is an automatic process. Take an example—If 40% is payout, is 60% pay-in ratio? However, this payout ratio is subject to fluctuation with the change in the rate of profit. That is to say, percentage of profit should be increased with the decline in the net profit and percentage of profit should be decreased with the increase in the rate of profit.

The last part of this head of discusson is the fixed percentage of market value. This method relates to the determination of dividend as a fixed percentage on market value of shares rather than the net profit of the company.

Fixed Percentage of Market value

The shareholders, in most of the cases, try to draw the relationship between dividend income as a percentage return of market value of shares, not dividend income as a percentage return of net profit. To fulfil the desire of the shareholders the management should 'tie' dividends to the value of the market price of the company's share. So to have this tie in actual practice, as a target rate there should be setting up a representative rate of dividend return which may either be average dividend rate for the industry as a whole or the rate of similar type of competitive business. Under the basis of payment practices, the importance of internal financing for future prospect and expansion of business is ignored.

I hope you have followed the discussions made earlier. Please be frank if you cannot follow my lecture. Yes, please.

☐ "Sir, what is 'Cum-Dividend and Ex-Dividend' and what is 'Cum-right and Ex-right'? Please explain."

● You see, Cum-Dividend means inclusive of the forthcoming dividend and Ex-dividend means exclusive of the forthcoming dividend. Do you follow?

☐ "No Sir, I cannot follow. Please excuse me Sir".

● You see, for detailed discussions I would suggest you to go through the book of Dr. A. K. Sur's 'Principles of Business Finance'. I hope that is sufficient for your understanding.

☐ "Sir, give us some note from the said source."

Ex-dividend and Cum-dividend

● Well, Dr. A. K. Sur in his book, as mentioned earlier, while writing about 'Marketing of Securities' states that near about the dividend rate, transactions in the shares of a company are done either on c.d. or x. d. basis—c d. means inclusive of the forthcoming dividend, and x. d. exclusive of it. If a transaction done on c. d, basis is delivered on or after the date fixed by the Stock Exchange Committee for x. d. transactions, then the buyer would pay the price of the shares less the value of the dividend. Professor Sur, while explaining the ideas of 'Cum-right' and 'Ex-right', states that one of the convenient methods of raising new capital is by the issue of 'right shares'. A shareholder who does not wish to exercise his right may, of course, (a) sell the right, or, (b) simply allow them to expire.

When, however, the right is sold off the theoretical value of the right is calculated on the basis of the following formulas :

1. Before the Ex-right date : $\dfrac{MP - SP}{N+1} = VR$

2. After the Ex-right date : $\dfrac{MP - SP}{N} = VR$

MP, in the first formula, stands for 'market price of old stock per share', and, in the second formula, 'the ex-right price'; SP stands for subscription price of new stock per share; N for 'number of shares required to purchase one new share', and VR for 'theoretical value of right.'

A buyer is entitled to obtain the rights if the transaction is done on cum-right basis. The seller will have to give the right to the buyer, if a cum-right delivery is effected on or after the date fixed for ex-right transaction.

☐ "Excuse me Sir, I have one question. You have not discussed about different **models of dividend policy.**"

• Oh, yes, thank you for remembering the same. I had decided to discuss it earlier but it has escaped my attention.

Well, take a look here on the board. You see there are three models on dividend policy which are based on the concept of relationship between dividend policy and the value of the firm.

One theory views that dividends are relevant because they affect positively to the value of the firm. There is another theory which views that dividends are irrelevant, because they do not affect the value of the firm. However, they are discussed :

Walter's Model : According to Professor James E. Walter, dividend policy always affects the value of the firm. He showed that the choice of dividend policy depends on the relationships between the firm's internal rate of return and the cost of capital. His theory is based on the following assumptions—

1. **No external financing :** There is no external financing, only retained earnings are used to finance investment.

2. **Constant rate of return and cost of capital :** Firm's cost of capital and rate of return always remain constant.

3. **There is either 100% dividend or retention :** There is either 100% reinvestment of earnings or 100% dividend payout.

4. **Earnings per Share** (E) and **Dividend per Share** (D) remain constant.

5. **Perpetual life** : The firm has perpetual life.

Professor Walter gave the following formula to determine the market value per share—

$$P = \frac{D}{K} + \frac{(E - D)\frac{r}{k}}{K}$$

where, P = market value per share
D = dividend per share
E = earnings per share
K = cost of capital
r = rate of return

According to him, market value per share is obtained by adding the present value of two sources of income — dividend income [i.e. $D/_K$] and Capital gain $\left[\text{i.e. } \frac{(E-D)\frac{r}{k}}{K}\right]$

James E. Walter, "Dividend Policy : Its influence on the value of the Firm", Journal of Finance. (May, 1963).

Prof. Walter classified all firms into three classes based on the relationship between firm's internal rate of return and cost of capital. Optimum Dividend policy varies with the types of firms. The optimum dividend policy, based on types of firms, are :

1. **Growth Firms :** Growth firms have internal rate of return greater than cost of capital (r > k). These firms have ample profitable investment opportunities. Thus, the optimum dividend policy would be to retain entire earnings for investments in profitable opportunities. In other words, optimum dividend policy of growth firms would be 100% retention and 0% dividend.

2. **Normal firms :** Normal firms have rate of return equal to the cost of capital (r = k). These firms have exhausted all profitable investment opportunities and earn rate of return equal to the cost of capital. Dividend policy of this type cannot affect the value of the firm. Thus, there is no one optimum dividend policy—when r = k.

3. **Declining Firms :** Declining Firms have internal rate of return less than the cost of capital (r < k). Here the optimum dividend policy to maximise market value of shares would be to distribute all earnings as dividend and there would be no retention.

Walter's theory would be more clear when you go through the following illustration—

Suppose a firm has EPS = Rs. 20.00. We can determine the value per share by using Walter's model for the growth firm, normal firm and declining firm under different assumptions of payout ratio. Again, assume the following data :

	Growth Firm	Normal Firm	Declining Firm
Firms rate of return (r)	25%	20%	15%
Cost of Capital (K)	20%	20%	20%

When the payout ratio is 0% [i.e. D = 0]

The value per share for the

Growth Firm

$$P = \frac{0}{.20} + \frac{(20 - 0)\frac{.25}{.20}}{.20}$$

$$= 0 + \frac{20 \times \frac{.25}{.20}}{.20}$$

= Rs. 125

Normal Firm

$$P = \frac{0}{.20} + \frac{(20-0)\frac{.20}{.20}}{.20}$$

$$= 0 + \frac{20}{.20}$$

= Rs. 100

Declining Firm

$$P = \frac{0}{.20} + \frac{(20-0)\frac{.15}{.20}}{.20}$$

$$= 0 + \frac{20\frac{.15}{.20}}{.20}$$

= Rs. 75.

When the payout ratio is 30% [i.e., D = Rs. 6.00]

The value per share for the

Growth Firm

$$P = \frac{6}{.20} + \frac{(20-6)\frac{.25}{.20}}{.20}$$

= 30 + 87.5

= Rs. 117.50

Normal Firm

$$P = \frac{6}{.20} + \frac{(20-6)\frac{.20}{.20}}{.20}$$

= 30 + 70

= Rs. 100

Declining Firm

$$P = \frac{6}{.20} + \frac{(20-6)\frac{.15}{.20}}{.20}$$

= 30 + 52.50

= Rs. 82.50

When the payout ratio is 75% [i.e., D = Rs. 15]

The value per Share for the

Growth Firm	Normal Firm	Declining Firm
$P = \frac{15}{.20} + \frac{(20-15)\frac{.25}{.20}}{.20}$	$P = \frac{15}{.20} + \frac{(20-15)\frac{.20}{.20}}{.20}$	$P = \frac{15}{.20} + \frac{(20-15)\frac{.15}{.20}}{.20}$
= 75 + 31.25	= 75 + 25	= 75 + 18.75
= Rs. 106.25	= Rs. 100	= Rs. 93.75

When the payout ratio is 100% [i..e. D = Rs. 20]

The value per share for the

Growth Firm	Normal Firm	Declining Firm
$P = \frac{20}{.20} + \frac{(20-20)\frac{.25}{.20}}{.20}$	$P = \frac{20}{.20} + \frac{(20-20)\frac{.20}{.20}}{.20}$	$P = \frac{20}{.20} + \frac{(20-20)\frac{.15}{.20}}{.20}$
= 100 + 0	= 100 + 0	= 100 + 0
= Rs. 100	= Rs. 100	= Rs. 100

From the above it is clear that the value per share of growth is maximum (i.e. Rs. 125) when the payout ratio is 0%. For the declining firm the optimum dividend payout ratio is 100%. For the normal firm, dividend policy has no effect on the value per share.

Walter's model suffers from the following limitations :

(i) In Walter's model, it is assumed that firm finances from retained earnings only for investment and no external finance is used. But in actual practice firm raises external fund to finance profitable investment. Walter's model fails to reach optimum level of investment.

(ii) It is also assumed that rate of return and cost of capital are constant. This is not true in actual practice. In actual practice, rate of returns decreases with the increase in the level of investment. And cost of capital increases with the increase in risk of the firm.

(iii) The model is applicable to all equity firms. This model does not recognise the importance of using cheap debt capital in the Capital structure.

Gordon's Model : Another theory, developed by Myron Gordon, also views that dividend decision is relevant decision, that is, it affects the value of the firm. His theory is based on the following assumptions :

1. The firm is an all-equity firm. In other words, only retained earnings are used to finance new investment and no debt capital is used.

2. The internal rate of return and cost of capital is constant.

3. The growth rate is the product of internal rate of return (r) and retention ratio (b) and is constant. This is because of the constant retention ratio.

4. The growth rate is lower than the cost of capital.

5. Firm's life is perpetual.

6. There is no corporate tax.

Gordon's model has given the following formula to determine the market value per share—

$$P_0 = \frac{E(1-b)}{K-br}$$

where
P_0 = market value per share
E = earning per share
b = retention ratio
K = cost of capital
r = internal rate of return

Thus, according to Myron Gordon, market value of a share is affected by earning per share, retention ratio, cost of capital, and internal rate of return. He shows the dividend policies under different conditions of relationship between internal rate of return and cost of capital as :

Dividend policy in case of growth firm (r > k)

In case of growth firm, market value per share increases with the increase in retention ratio (b). But it should be increased in such a way that the growth rate (br) does not exceed the cost of Capital (K). Because, if growth rate exceeds the cost of capital we would get meaningless result.

Thus, to have meaningful result of P, the value of b should be less than $^k/_r$. [$g < k$, or $br < k$ or $b < {^k/_r}$].

Dividend policy in case of declining firm (r < k)

In case of declining firm, the market value per share increases with the decrease in retention ratio. Under this condition, market value per share will be maximum when the retention ratio is zero.

Dividend policy in case of normal firm (r = k)

When the rate of return is equal to the cost of capital, the market value per share is not affected by the dividend policy. Thus, dividend policy is irrelevant for normal firm. These would be more clear from the following example :

	Growth Firm	**Normal Firm**	**Declining Firm**
	(r>k)	(r=k)	(r<k)
r	20%	15%	10%
k	15%	15%	15%
E (Rs.)	20	20	20

Show the effect of dividend policy for the growth firm, normal firm and declining firm.

Retention ratio, b = 70%, Pay-out ratio (1 – b) = 30%

Growth Firm	Normal Firm	Declining Firm
$P_0 = \frac{20(1-0.7)}{0.15-(0.7\times.2)}$	$P_0 = \frac{20(1-0.7)}{0.15-(0.7\times0.15)}$	$P_0 = \frac{20(1-0.7)}{0.15-(0.7\times0.10)}$
$= \frac{6}{0.01}$	$= \frac{6}{.15-0.105}$	$= \frac{6}{.15-0.07}$
= Rs. 600	= Rs. 133.33	= Rs. 75.00

Retention ratio, b = 40%, Pay-out ratio (1 – b) = 60%

Growth Firm	Normal Firm	Declining Firm
$P_0 = \frac{20(1-0.4)}{0.15-(0.4\times.2)}$	$P_0 = \frac{20(1-0.4)}{0.15-(0.4\times0.15)}$	$P_0 = \frac{20(1-0.4)}{0.15-(0.4\times0.10)}$
$= \frac{12}{0.07}$	$= \frac{12}{0.09}$	$= \frac{12}{0.11}$
= Rs. 171.43	= Rs. 133.33	= Rs. 109.09

Retention ratio, b = 10%, payout ratio (1 – b) = 90%

Growth Firm	Normal Firm	Declining Firm
$P_0 = \frac{20(1-0.10)}{0.15-(0.10\times.20)}$	$P_0 = \frac{20(1-0.10)}{0.15-(0.10\times.15)}$	$P_0 = \frac{20(1-0.10)}{0.15-(0.10\times.10)}$
$= \frac{18}{0.13}$	$= \frac{18}{0.135}$	$= \frac{18}{0.14}$
= Rs. 138.46	= Rs. 133.33	= Rs. 128.57

The above model also suffers from the same limitations as Walter's model.

Dividend and Uncertainty

Under condition of uncertainty, dividend policy affects the value of the firm even when r = k. If we assume that the investors are risk-averse and uncertainty increases with futurity, the value of the firm cannot remain unaffected even when r = k. Because, risk, averse inverstors will discount distant capital gain at a higher rate than current dividends. In other words, investors prefer current dividends over future dividends. Thus, investors will pay higher price for shares of companies with higher current dividends and, as a result, increase the value of shares. This view is called 'bird in the hand' argument.

Gordon modified his conclusion and argued that under condition of uncertainty, dividend decision affects the value of the firm even when r = k.

Dividend Irrelevance Theory

According to **Modigliani and Miller (M - M)**, when capital market is perfect dividend policy cannot affect the value of the firm. His theory is based on the following assumptions:

(i) The Capital markets are perfect. In other words, there is no transaction cost and all shares are fairly priced in the market.

(ii) There is no tax or both dividends and capital gains are equally taxed. In other words, investors equally prefer dividends and capital gains so far as tax is concerned.

(iii) Investors can expect dividends and capital gain, with certainty.

(iv) The rate of return, (r) is equal to the cost of capital (K) for all firms and all times.

The rate of return which is equal for all firms, is composed of dividends and capital gains, symbolically

$$r = \frac{Div_1 + (P_1 - P_0)}{P_0} \quad \text{.................(1)}$$

where Div_1 = Dividend per share after one year

r = rate of return

P_0 = Price per share at time 0

P_1 = Price per share after one year

or, $rP_0 = Div_1 + P_1 - P_0$

or, $rP_0 + P_0 = Div_1 + P_1$

or, $P_0 = \dfrac{Div_1 + P_1}{(1+r)}$

Since r = K we can write

$$P_0 = \frac{Div_1 + P_1}{(1+K)} \quad \text{..............(2)}$$

Now if the total number of outstanding shares are n, the value of the firm is

$$nP_0 = \frac{n(Div_1 + P_1)}{(1+K)} \quad \text{...............(3)}$$

If m number of shares are issued at times, the value of the firm at time 0 is

$$nP_0 = \frac{n(Div_1 + P_1) + mP_1 - mP_1}{(1+K)}$$

$$= \frac{nDiv_1 + nP_1 + mP_1 - mP_1}{(1+K)}$$

$$= \frac{nDiv_1 + P_1(n+m) - mP_1}{(1+K)} \quad \text{..............(4)}$$

Thus, unlike Walter and Gordon's model, firms in MM model can issue new shares to finance new investments. The amount of fund to be raised by issuing new shares is the excess of funds required for investment over retained earnings. Symbolically

$mP_1 = I_1 - (E_1 - n\,Div_1)$ ....(5)

Now, substituting equation (5) into equation (4) we get

$$np_0 = \frac{nDiv_1 + p_0(n+m) - [I_1 - (E - nDiv_1)]}{(1+K)}$$

$$= \frac{nDiv_1 + (n+m)P_1 - I_1 + E - nDiv_1}{(1+K)}$$

$$= \frac{(n+m)P - I_1 + E}{(1+K)} \quad ....(6)$$

There is no dividend in equation (6). Thus, value of the firm is not affected by the dividend policy.

The following illustration will make the model more clear to you :

Suppose, a firm has 60,000 outstanding shares with face value of Rs. 10 each. It wants to make a new Capital investment of Rs. 2,00,000 during the period. The firm's current dividend is Rs. 2.00 per share. It has earned net profits of Rs. 2,20,000. The cost of capital is 10%.

Determine according to the above model the Wealth of shareholders before and after the payment of dividend and also the number of shares to be issued to finance new investments.

The price per share (P_1) at the end of the year

$$P_0 = \frac{Div_1 + P_1}{(1+K)}$$

or, $P_1 = P_0\,(1+K) - Div_1$

= Rs. 10 (1 + 0.10) – Rs. 2.00 = Rs. 11 – Rs. 2 = Rs. 9.00

If no dividends are paid

$P_1 = 10\,(1 + 0.10) - 0$

= Rs. 11.00

The wealth of shareholders if dividends are paid = Rs. 9.00 + Rs. 2.00 = Rs. 11.

The wealth of shareholders when no dividends are paid = Rs. 11.

Thus the wealth is not affected by the payment of dividends.

The funds to be raised to finance new investments—

= Rs. 2,00,000 – [2,20,000 – (60,000×Rs. 2.00)]

= Rs. 2,00,000 – Rs. 100,000.

= Rs. 1,00,000

Number of shares to be issued

$$= \frac{\text{Rs.}1{,}00{,}000}{\text{Rs. }9} = 11{,}111 \text{ shares}$$

Criticism of MM Model : MM model of dividend irrelevance is based on certain assumptions which are not realistic. Thus the assumptions can be easily challenged. Such as—

1. **Uncertainty :** Under condition of uncertainty, MM model cannot remain valid. Rational investors would prefer current dividend to future dividend and, in turn, affect the value of the firm with changes in dividend policy.

2. **Flotation costs :** MM assumes that there is no flotation cost. But in actual practice flotation cost such as underwriting fee, brokerage etc. do exist for issuing new shares. Thus, internal financing and external financing cannot be considered equal.

3. **Tax differential :** MM assumes that there is no tax advantages associated with dividend or capital gain. But in many countries dividend and capital gains are taxed differently. Thus investors' preference for dividend or capital gain is influenced by the tax differential and value of the firm is affected.

4. **Information content of dividend :** Dividends convey information about the future prospects of the company. A high and regular dividend pay-out ratio suggests that in the judgement of management the future prospects of the company is good. This information content of dividends reduces the agency cost on the part of the investors.

I think you have followed the discussions made earlier.

☐ "Yes Sir, thank you Sir for your detailed discussions on the concept".

• Well,now I am working some more problems of different examinations for your better understanding.

Problem

The following data are available for P.P. Ltd.

Earnings per share	Rs. 3.00
Internal Rate of Return	15%
Cost of capital	12%

If Walter's valuation formula holds, what will be the price per share when the dividend pay-out ratio is 50%, 75% and 100%? **[C.U., M.Com.]**

Solution

Here, Earning per share, E = Rs. 3.00

Internal rate of return, $r = 15\%$ or 0.15

and Cost of capital $k = 12\%$ or 0.12

Now, the price per share (P) according to the Walter's model.

$$P = \frac{D}{K} + \frac{(E - D)\frac{r}{k}}{k}$$ where D = Dividend per share

Calculation of Price per share

Situation 1

D/P Ratio = 50%
(Dividend per share
= 50% of Rs. 3.00
= Rs. 1.50)

$$P = \frac{\text{Rs. } 1.50}{0.12} + \frac{(\text{Rs. } 3.00 - \text{Rs. } 1.50)\frac{0.15}{0.12}}{0.12}$$

= 12.5 + 15.625
= Rs. 28.13

Situation 2

D/P Ratio = 75%
(Dividend per share
= 75% of Rs. 3.00
= Rs. 2.25)

$$P = \frac{\text{Rs. } 2.25}{0.12} + \frac{(\text{Rs. } 3.00 - \text{Rs. } 2.25)\frac{0.15}{0.12}}{0.12}$$

= 18.75 + 7.8125
= Rs. 26.56

Situation 3

D/P Ratio = 100%
(Dividend per share
= 100% of Rs. 3.00
= Rs. 3)

$$P = \frac{\text{Rs. } 3.00}{0.12} + \frac{(\text{Rs. } 3.00 - \text{Rs. } 3.00)\frac{0.15}{0.12}}{0.12}$$

= 25 + 0
= Rs. 25.00

Problem

You are given the following information in respect of ABC Ltd.

Earning	Rs. 1,00,000
Equity Capital	5,000 shares of Rs. 10 each
Cost of capital	10%

Expected rates of return (i) 9% (ii) 10% and (iii) 12% Assuming that dividend pay-out ratios are 0%, 50% and 100% respectively determine the effect of the different dividend policies on the share price of ABC Ltd. for the above mentioned three alternative levels of rate of return using Gordon's model. **[C.U., M.Com.]**

Solution

The share price (p) of ABC Ltd., according to Gordon's Model, is given as

$$P_0 = \frac{E(1-b)}{k-br}$$

where, Earning per share $= \frac{\text{Total Earning}}{\text{Total number of Equity Share}}$

$$= \frac{\text{Rs. } 1,00,000}{5,000}$$

= Rs. 20

b = Retention Ratio,

(1 – b) = D/P Ratio

k = Cost of Capital = 10% or 0.10

and r = internal rate of return.

Now, the following share price of ABC Ltd. at different dividend pay-out ratio (D/P ratio) and at different expected rate of return (r) may be calculated as under :

D/P Ratio = (1 – b)%	Situation 1 r = 9% or 0.09	Situation 2 r = 10% or 0.10	Situation 3 r = 12% or 0.12
0%	$P = \frac{\text{Rs. } 20 \times 0}{0.10 - (1 \times 0.09)}$ = 0	$P = \frac{\text{Rs. } 20 \times 0}{0.10 - (1 \times 0.10)}$ = 0	$P = \frac{\text{Rs. } 20 \times 0}{0.10 - (1 \times 0.12)}$ = 0
50%	$P = \frac{\text{Rs. } 20 \times 0.50}{0.10 - (0.50 \times 0.09)}$ = Rs. 181.81 = Rs. 182 (App.)	$P = \frac{\text{Rs. } 20 \times 0.50}{0.10 - (0.50 \times 0.10)}$ = Rs. 200	$P = \frac{\text{Rs. } 20 \times 0.50}{0.10 - (0.50 \times 0.12)}$ = Rs. 250
100%	$P = \frac{\text{Rs. } 20 \times 1}{0.10 - (0 \times 0.09)}$ = Rs. 200	$P = \frac{\text{Rs. } 20 \times 1}{0.10 - (0 \times 0.10)}$ = Rs. 200	$P = \frac{\text{Rs. } 20 \times 1}{0.10 - (0 \times 0.12)}$ = Rs. 200

Here retention ratio (b) was calculated with different D/P ratio.

when D/P ratio (1 – b) = 0%, retention ratio (b) = 100% or 1

D/P ratio (1 – b) = 50%, retention ratio (b) = 50% or 0.50

D/P ratio (1 – b) = 100%, retention ratio (b) = 0% or 0

Problem

A company has a book value per share of Rs. 137.80. Its return on equity is 15% and it follows a policy of retaining 60% of its earnings. If the opportunity cost of capital is 18%, what is the price of the share today?

[C.A. Final]

Solution

Book value per share = Rs. 137.80

Return on Equity, r = 15% or 0.15

Earning per share, E = 15% of Rs. 137.80 = Rs. 20.67

Retention Ratio, b = 60% = 0.60

∴ D/P Ratio (1 – b) = 40% = 0.40

Now, Dividend per share D = 40% of EPS

= 40% of Rs. 20.67

= Rs. 8.27

Opportunity cost of capital, k = 18% or 0.18

I. Share Price (P) using Walter's Model is

$$P = \frac{D}{K} + \frac{(E - D)\frac{r}{k}}{k}$$

Substituting the values, we get,

$$P = \frac{\text{Rs. } 8.27}{0.18} + \frac{(\text{Rs. } 20.67 - \text{Rs. } 8.27)\frac{0.15}{0.18}}{0.18}$$

$$= \text{Rs. } 45.944 + \text{Rs. } 57.407$$

$$= \text{Rs. } 103.35$$

II. Share price (P) using Gordon's Model is

$$P = \frac{E(1-b)}{k - br}$$, Substituting the values, we get,

$$P = \frac{\text{Rs. } 20.67 \times 0.40}{0.18 - (0.60 \times 0.15)} = \text{Rs. } 91.87$$

Problem

A company currently has 1,00,000 shares. The company needs Rs. 10,00,000 to finance its new investments. The total earnings of the firm during the current year would be Rs. 10,00,000 and Rs. 5,00,000 would be paid by way of dividends. The market price per share at the end of the current year is expected to Rs. 110. If the cost of capital is 15%, ascertain the present value of a share under the Modigliani-Miller model.

[C.U., M.Com.]

Solution

Under the Modigliani-Miller model, the present value of a share P can be ascertained as—

$$P_0 = \frac{Div_1 + P_1}{1 + k}$$

where P_0 = current value of a share

Div_1 = Dividend per share at the year end

$$= \frac{\text{Total Dividends}}{\text{Number of share}} = \frac{\text{Rs. } 5,00,000}{1,00,000} = \text{Rs. } 5$$

P_1 = Market price per share at the year end

= Rs. 110

and k = cost of capital = 15% or 0.15

$$\text{Thus } P_0 = \frac{\text{Rs. } 5 + \text{Rs. } 110}{1 + 0.15}$$

= Rs. 100

Hence the present value of a share is Rs. 100.

☐ Thank you Sir for detail working which helped to understand the problems.

● Well, Good-bye.

QUESTIONS

1. What is Dividend Policy? How it is related to the aspect of Financial Management?
2. What are the different factors that should be taken into account before declaration of Dividends?
3. What are the different types of dividends that can be declared for payment? Explain the basic philosophy which motivates behind the declaration of respective types of Dividends.
4. Write short notes on—(a) Scrip dividend, (b) Interim and Final Dividend, (c) Ex-Dividend and Cum-Dividend, (d) Divisible Profit, (e) Regular Dividend.
5. Explain the idea that 'payment of dividend out of Inflated Profits amounts to payment of Dividend out of Capital'.
6. A company has a present 1,00,000 shares. The company requires Rs. 10,00,000 to finance a new project of which Rs. 4,00,000 would be available out of profits after paying Rs. 10,00,000 as dividends. The balance amont can be raised either by issuing new shares or new debentures. The company decides to procure finance through the issue of new shares. The market price per share at the end of the current year is expected to be Rs. 120. If the cost of capital is 18%, determine the present value of a share using the M-M model. **[C.U. M.Com.]**
7. Zee company has 1,00,000 equity shares of Rs. 10 each fully paid. The company expects its earning at Rs. 12,00,000 and cost of capital at 10% for the next financial year. Using the Walter's model, what dividend policy would you recommend when the rate of return on investment of the company is estimated at 8% and 12% respectively? What will be the price of equity share if your recommendations are accepted? **[C.U. M.Com.]**
8. A company has total investment of Rs. 10,00,000 in assets and 10,000 outstanding shares of Rs. 100 each. It's rate of return is 24% and it has a policy of retaining 50% of the earnings. If the cost of capital is 18%, determine the market price of the share using Gordon's model. How would the market price change if the pay-out ratio is 90% or 10%? What should be the optimum dividend policy and why? **[C.U. M.Com.]**
9. The following data are available for KPI Ltd :

   Earnings per share — Rs. 8.00

   Rate of Return on Investment — 16%

   Rate of Return required by shareholders — 12%

   If Gordon's basic valuation formula hold, what will be price per share when the dividend pay out ratio is 25% and 60%. **[C.U. M.Com.]**
10. (a) What is the substance of Modigliani Miller and "dividend irrelevence theorem"? Prove the 'dividend irrelevance' theorem.

    (b) The appropriate capitalization rate for a company which belongs to a risk class is 10%. Presently the company has 1,00,000 shares selling at Rs. 100 each. the company is contemplating the declaration of Rs. 5 as dividend at the end of the current financial year, which has just begun. What will be the price of the share at the end of the year, if a dividend is not declared? What will be if dividend is declared? Answer these on the basis of Modigliani and Miller model and assume no taxes.

22

ACCOUNTING FOR INFLATION

● Good afternoon to you all.

□ "Good afternoon Sir."

● I think you followed my earlier lectures. Now I like to discuss with you about the Accounting for Inflation. This is known as 'Revaluation Accounting,' 'the Replacement Value Theory', 'Stabilised Accounting', and 'Accounting for price level changes'.

□ "Sir, what is Accounting for Inflation ?"

● I will definitely discuss in detail what is Accounting for Inflation. Before that I like to draw your attention to the fact that the Rupee of yesterday is not equal to the Rupee of today and it will not be equal to Rupee of tomorrow. Do you admit this point ?

□ "Yes Sir."

● Well the method of accounting which takes into account the recorded book value to be adjusted owing to change in prices, is known as accounting for inflation. That is to say, the system of accounting which pays due regard to the money value and real value assets and liabilities, is known as accounting for inflation.

Meaning of Inflationary Accounting

□ "Sir, what is Money Value Assets and Liabilities and Real Value Assets and Liabilities?"

● Wait please, I will discuss all these classification in due course of time.

Now I like to discuss a few problems arising during the period of inflation.

□ "Excuse me, Sir, please explain, what is the effect of a change in price level, specially inflationary effects on accounting results".

● Thank you very much for your special interest in the topic. However, here I have the pleasure to refer you to a paper of my respected teacher Professor Sitala charan Sengupta M.A., G.D.A, F.C.A., A.I.C.W.A. Professor Sengupta in his paper "Accounting for Inflation" which he read at the 10th All India Commerce Conference held at Ranchi in 1956, explained the effect of change by way of, as if, a story which he quoted from "Financial Times" (dated July 17, 1951). I am quoting from the said source.

Once upon a time there was a Chinese merchant named Tu Bad, who lived in Singapore. He was a poor man and in 1941 he locked up all his capital in the purchase of sack of rice which cost him $7. A few weeks later, the Japanese unfortunately invaded the country and Tu Bad, seeing hard times ahead hid his sack of rice in the loft and earned his living by tapping rubber trees.

All went well for the next three years, but then, as his sack of rice was going mouldy, he sold it. And as the country's currency having depreciated rapidly during the Japanese occupation, he received for his sack of rice no less than $20,000.

Famine was fairly wide spread, however, and seeing even worse time ahead Tu Bad reinvested his money a month later in more rice which, not being mouldy, cost him $25,000 for a mere half-sack to raise which he had to borrow the odd $5000 from his cousin. Un Sam.

Being an honest man, Tu Bad then asked his friend, the accountant, See Ay to draw up his accounts. His stock at cost, being unsold, had no effect on his profit and loss account but the sale of the first sack of rice showed a profit of $19,993. This put him well into top bracket for sur-tax, and in due course he received a demand from the tax-gatherer for $19,498.

"Alas" said Tu Bad "a twelve months ago I had one sack of rice and no debts. Now I have a half sack of rice only and I owe my cousin $5,000. How can you say I have made a vast profit and ask me for $19,498 ?"

"Ask See Ay", said the tax-gatherer roughly leading Tu Bad off to the dungeons. "He drew up your accounts, not I, and who am I to question the established accounting principles of one so learned ?"

However, after explaining the story Prof. Sengupta rightly said that 'during inflation huge profits may be shown on the basis of monetary units while in reality there may not be any accretion of net assets.'

Well, please note below the problems arising from Inflationary Accounting.

Problems of Inflationary Accounting

1. **The Problem of Replacement of Fixed Assets :** As depreciation is charged on historical cost method, it accounts more for cost than for values. Cost means sacrifice in the acquisition of an item and value implies benefits accruing on its acquisition of an item and value implies benefits accruing on its acquisition. Only on the date of acquisition, the cost and value of an item would be the same. Subsequently, cost remains the same but the value changes. If depreciation is charged on the historical cost method, the ploughing back of profit due to charging of depreciation would be less than what it would have been if it was charged on current values. So, there is less retention of profit. So the total fund arising out of the depreciation does not permit the company to replace the assets, say machines at current values. So the problem of replacement becomes more and more acute during the period of inflation. So, the alternative in this case is to bring or introduce further capital into the business. This will be clear from the examples given below :

Difference between Cost and Value

Suppose a Machine was purchased in 1994

Cost price of the machine	Rs. 12,000
Estimated life	say 10 years
Scrap value of the machine say,	Rs. 2,000

Now from the example given, it is clear that the year of replacement of the existing machine is 2004 when the market price of similar type of machine was 20,000.

	Rs.
Cost of Machine	12,000
Less : Scrap value of the Machine	2,000
	10,000

This Rs. 10,000 will be spread-out over 10 years, because the life of the machine was estimated at 10 years. Now each year $\left[\frac{\text{Rs.}10{,}000}{10\text{years}}\right]$ Rs. 1,000 will be charged for depreciation. This provision for depreciation for the replacement of machine is known as 'ploughing back of profit.'

Dr. **Profit and Loss Account** *Cr.*

Particulars	**Amount**	**Particulars**	**Amount**
	Rs.		Rs.
To		By Gross Profit	12,000
To Depreciation on Machine	1,000		
Net Profit	11,000		

Now at the end of 10th year Rs. 10,000 will be ploughed back out of the revenue of the years :

$$x_1 + x_2 + \ldots\ldots x_{10} = \Sigma x$$

This Rs. 10,000 plus Rs. 2,000 being the amount for scrap value, will be the total amount to be used for replacement purpose. Now most important point is that this Rs. 12,000 will not be sufficient to replace similar type of machine, when the price of the said machine had gone up, say, Rs. 20,000. From all these facts it is clear that the replacement of assets is one of the most important problems during the period of inflation.

2. **Problem of Inventory Valuation :** Conventional method of valuation of stock is either at cost or at market price whichever is less. But trading profit usually takes the valuation at latest purchase which is higher than the previous purchase. So profit is inflated. This will be clear from the two examples given below, assuming the market price to replace the 'cost of goods sold' is Rs. 9,000.

Exhibit 1

Assuming stock valuation at latest purchase

Dr. **Trading Account** *Cr.*

Particulars	**Amount**	**Particulars**	**Amount**
	Rs.		Rs.
To Opening Stock	10,000	By Sales	30,000
" Purchase	10,000	" Closing Stock	15,000
" Operating Expenses	1,000		
" Gross Profit	24,000		
	45,000		45,000

Exhibit 2

Assuming stock valuation either at cost or at market price, whichever is less :

Dr. **Trading Account** Cr.

Particulars	Amount	Particulars	Amount
	Rs.		Rs.
To Opening Stock	10,000	By Sales	30,000
" Purchase	10,000	" Closing Stock	10,000
" Operating Expenses	1,000		
" Gross Profit	19,000		
	40,000		40,000

Analysis of Exhibit 1 and 2

Cost of Goods Sold = (Opening Stock + Purchase) – Closing Stock.

Sales = Cost of Goods Sold + Operating Expenses + Profit.

Exhibit 1

	Rs.
Opening Stock	10,000
Purchase	10,000
	20,000
Closing Stock	15,000
Cost of Goods Sold	5,000

Sales = Cost of Goods Sold + Operating Expenses + Profit.

Rs. 30,000 = Rs. 5,000 + Rs. 1,000 + Rs. 25,000.

Exhibit 2

	Rs.
Opening Stock	10,000
Purchase	10,000
	20,000
Closing Stock	10,000
Cost of Goods Sold	10,000

Sales = Cost of Goods Sold + Operating Expenses + Profit

Rs. 30,000 = Rs. 10,000 + Rs. 1,000 + Rs. 19,000.

From the analysis of Exhibits 1 and 2 it is clear that retention of profit is higher in the case where closing stock takes the valuation either at cost price or market price, whichever is less. Conversely, retention of profit is lower in the case where closing stock takes the valuation of latest purchase. Now the market price of the 'cost of goods sold' as indicated earlier is say Rs. 9,000. Retention of profit in case of Exhibit 1. will not help the management to replace similar type of goods sold. Retention of profit in case of Exhibit 2 is sufficient to meet the situation arising from inflation. Here also replacement of stock is another problem to be observed during the period of inflation.

3. **Erosion of Real Capital :** From the discussions made earlier, it has now become clear that erosion of real capital is the greatest curse of inflation. Owing to inadequate provision for depreciation and improper valuation of closing stock, the profit of the business is inflated. This gives rise to some industrial problem, as to distribution of dividend, payment of bonus, etc. The owner of the business 'overdraws revenue resources and what is left indicates high money value in terms of less commodity.' It is a fact that as revenue is not matched with proper cost, a part of the real capital of the business is consumed.

Erosion of Real Capital

4. **Problem of Proper Interpretation of Financial Statement :** Changes in the purchasing power of money will definitely affect accounting for real value. Value may be of two types – (a) Real Value, and (b) Money Value. The assets and liabilities which are reassessed owing to rise in price level are known as real value items; and which do not permit reassessment under similar circumstance are termed money value items. Examples of real value assets and liabilities are Land, Machinery, Building, Capital Reserve etc. This indicates the items of tangible assets and net worth of the business. The examples of money value assets and liabilities are Cash, Debtors, Bills Receivable, Bills Payable etc. It is a fact that appropriate technique for the new method of accounting for inflation has not been arrived at by any uniformity. However, the presentation of corporate accounts, in view of the situation depicted earlier, is the subject matter of research of the Institute of Chartered Accountants of India.

The gist of the analysis made earlier can be summed up as :

(a) The Balance sheet does not show a 'true and fair' view of the state of affairs of the business.

(b) Trading and Profit and Loss Account shows a 'distorted' picture of the business operation. If the depreciation is charged at current value, the reported profit will come down. Such statement of the operation of the business 'understate assets and overstates profit.'

This will be clear from the examples given :

(A)

Dr.	**Profit & Loss A/c**	*Cr.*
To Depreciation	1,000	
" Net Profit	9,000	

(B)

Dr.	**Profit & Loss A/c**	*Cr.*
To Depreciation	2,000	
" Net profit	8,000	

Now, you see that in case of A, the reported profit is higher because depreciation was charged at historical cost method. In case of B, the reported profit is lower to the extent of Rs. 1,000, if the same is compared with A. This indicates greater retention of profit. This is possible because the depreciation was charged at current replacement value.

5. **Problem of Distribution of Dividend and Payment of Taxation for Profit :** It was explained to you earlier that the under-statement of assets and over-statement of profits invites many problems in accounting literature. This results in payment for higher dividend and taxation.

6. **Disparity of the Rate of Dividend** : Preference shareholders and other fixed interest bearing securities, that is to say, providers of long term loan, suffer during the period of inflation. Because their 'capital and income both depreciate' in terms of purchasing power of money.

7. Problem of Proper Managerial Decision : I think you know that management needs accurate meaningful report on a day-to-day, week-to week, month to month and even hourly basis, for taking its decision in right perspective. So the financial ratio computed from unadjusted balance sheet would provide misleading information. Only the adjusted rate of return ratio would be very helpful to take correct management decision. Management policies can be formulated following the experience of the past condition of the present and intuition about the future. The efficiency of the management will be tested from the ratio mentioned below :

$$\text{Earning Ratio} = \frac{\text{Net Profit}}{\text{Equity Capital / Capital Employed}}$$

X	Y	Z
Earning Ratio (depending on past experience)	Earning Ratio (depending on present experience)	Earning Ratio (depending on intuition about the future)

The function of top management is to make reconciliation among the past, present, and uncertain future. According to Mr. Parkinson, 'it is a fact that 'management efficiency is a relationship between a ratio fact and ratio ideal.'

● Now I hope that you all have understood all the basic problems arising from accounting for inflation. I shall be glad to hear from you any point which is not clear to you.

☐ "Sir, we are really very glad to have all these discussions in details, but, Sir, you did not say anything about Goodwill. Please explain : whether Goodwill can be considered as real value assets or not ?"

● You have put a smart question. I will definitely explain. Before that I like to appreciate your keen interest in the subject. However, I told you earlier that assets are sometimes classified as real value and money value items. Value of real assets such as machinery, equipment, buildings, land etc rises with the rise in price level, whereas that of money value assets, such as cash, debtors etc. remains constant. At the time of rise in price level, stated book values of real value assets are only subject to revision. It is, of course, difficult to suggest what category, real value or money value, goodwill as an asset will belong to. If goodwill is treated simply as an annuity of some periodical receipts of money in future, it has reasonably to be considered a money value asset. As such its value will not rise with the rise in prices. On the other hand, if the future periodical money receipts stated to represent income of the business which are also likely to rise with the rise of price level, then goodwill is evidently a real value asset. But even if goodwill is considered a real value asset in this way, a rise in its value owing to rise in price level will not possibly be recorded because the said rise will not be represented by any cost.

Money Value and Real Value Assets and Liabilities

Goodwill as Money Value and Real Value Asset

Any question, please. Tell me frankly, so that I may be helpful to you. Now it is clear that you have understood the different aspects of inflationary accounting.

Problem

The following is the Trial Balance of a company at the end of a certain year (where accounting was done on orthodox principles) :

Particulars	Dr. Amount	Cr. Amount
	Rs.	Rs.
Opening Stock	4,000	
Purchases	20,000	
Sales		27,000
Expenses	4,000	
Depreciation	800	
Fixed Asset (at cost)	8,000	
Provision for Depreciation		3,200
Sundry Debtors	6,000	
Bank	3,400	
Capital		12,000
Reserve		1,000
Sundry Creditors		3,000
	46,200	46,200

The following information are supplied :

(a) Closing stock which was purchased at the beginning of the fourth quarter is valued at cost price at Rs. 4,600.

(b) The accounts relate to the first year of inflation after a period of stable price. During this year, the general "index of inflation" rose steadily from 100 to 140. The price of the commodity in which the company dealt also increased steadily, but only by 20 per cent, while the prices of its fixed assets increased by 40 per cent.

Prepare the final account in such a way, which according to you will be best under such inflationary conditions. (Ignore Income-Tax)

[Adapted from M.Com.; C.U.]

Solution

Trial Balanced

Accounts	Orthodox System		Converted to Present day Currency (Revaluation System)			
			Rate			
	Dr.	*Cr.*	From	To	*Dr.*	*Cr.*
Profit and Loss Items :	Rs.	Rs.			Rs.	Rs.
Opening Stock	4,000		100	120	4,800	
Purchases	20,000		120	120	20,000	
Sales		27,000	120	120		27,000
Closing Stock		4,600	130	120		4,246
Expenses	4,000		120	120	4,000	
Depreciation	800		100	120	960	
Balance Sheet Items :						
Fixed Assets (at cost)	8,000		100	140	11,200	
Provision for Depreciation		3,200	100	140		4,480
Closing Stock	4,600		130	140	4,954	
Sundry Debtors	6,000		140	140	6,000	
Bank	3,400		140	140	3,400	
Capital		12,000 }	100	140		12,000 }
Reserve		1,000 }				6,200 }
Sundry Creditors		3,000	140	140		3,000
Total	50,800	50,800			55,314	56,926
Loss on Inflation					1,612	
					56,926	56,926

Dr. **Trading Account** *Cr.*

Particulars	Amount	Particulars	Amount
	Rs.		Rs.
To Opening Stock	4,800	By Sales	27,000
" Purchases	20,000		
	24,800		
Less : Closing Stock	4,246		
Cost of Goods Sold	20,554		
To Gross Profit c/d	6,446		
	27,000		27,000

Dr. **Profit and Loss Account** Cr.

Particulars	Amount	Particulars	Amount
	Rs.		Rs.
To Expenses	4,000	By Gross Profit b/d	6,446
" Depreciation	960		
" Net Trading Profit	1,486		
	6,446		6,446

Dr. **Profit and Loss Appropriation Account** Cr.

Particulars	Amount	Particulars	Amount
	Rs.		Rs.
To Loss on Inflation	1,612	By Net Trading Profit	1,486
		" Net Loss transferred to Balance Sheet	126
	1,612		1,612

Balance Sheet

Liabilities		Amount	Assets		Amount
		Rs.			Rs.
Capital	12,000		Fixed Assets at Cost	11,200	
Reserve	6,200		*Less* : Provision for		
	18,200		Depreciation	4,480	6,720
Less : Loss on			Closing Stock		4,954
Appropriation	126	18,074	Sundry Debtors		6,000
Sundry Creditors		3,000	Bank		3,400
		21,074			21,074

Problem

The following is the Trial Balance of A. Co. Ltd. as on 30th June 2005 you are required to prepare the Trading and Profit and Loss Account for the year ended and the Balance sheet as at that date both on Orthodox and the Replacement system of accounting assuming that —

(a) the year in question is the first year of inflation;

(b) during this year the general index number of prices rose by 40 per cent, the prices of the commodity in which the company dealt rose by 20 per cent, and the prices of its fixed assets by 50 per cent.

(c) The quality and quantity of the Closing Stock is the same as those of the Opening Stock.

Trial Balance

Dr. Particulars	Amount	Particulars	Cr. Amount
	Rs.		Rs.
Opening Stock	37,000	Share Capital	75,000
Plant and Machinery (at cost)	50,000	Provision for Depreciation	20,000
Sundry Debtors	48,000	Sundry Creditors	15,650
Purchases	1,14,000	Sales	1,72,000
Closing Stock	42,550	Provision for Taxation	8,000
Cash in Hand	2,250	Closing Stock	42,550
Cash at Bank	14,600	General Reserve	10,000
Postage and Stationery	3,000		
Salary	8,000		
Wages	6,000		
General Expenses	4,200		
Bad Debt	600		
Taxation	8,000		
Depreciation	5,000		
	3,43,200		3,43,200

[Adapted from M.Com. (C.U.) Examination]

Solution

Trading and Profit and Loss Account
for the year ending June 2005

Dr. Particulars	Orthodox	Replacement	Particulars	Orthodox	Cr. Replacement
	Rs.	Rs.		Rs.	Rs.
To Opening Stock	37,000	37,000	By Sales	1,72,000	1,72,000
" Purchases	1,14,000	1,14,000			
	1,51,000	1,51,000			
Less : Closing Stock	42,550	37,000 (A)			
	1,08,450	1,14,000			
To Wages	6,000	6,000			
" Gross Profit c/d	57,550	52,000			
	1,72,000	1,72,000		1,72,000	1,72,000
To Postage and Stationery	3,000	3,000	By Gross Profit	57,550	52,000
" Salary	8,000	8,000			
" General Expenses	4,200	4,200			
" Bad Debts	600	600			
" Depreciation	5,000	7,500 (B)			
" Net Trading Profit	36,750	28,700			
	57,550	52,000		57,550	52,000

Profit and Loss Appropriation Account

Dr. Particulars	Orthodox	Replacement	Particulars	Orthodox	Replacement Cr.
	Rs.	Rs.		Rs.	Rs.
To Taxation	8,000	8,000	By Net Trading Profit b/d	36,750	28,700
" Arrears Depreciation	—	7,500(C)			
" Net Profit transferred to Reserve	28,750	13,200			
	36,750	28,700		36,750	28,700

Balance Sheet as at 30.6.2005

Particulars	Orthodox	Replacement	Particulars	Orthodox	Replacement
	Rs.	Rs.		Rs.	Rs.
Share Capital	75,000	75,000	Plant and		
General Reserve	10,000	10,000	Machinery (at cost)	50,000	50,000
Appropriation A/c	28,750	13,200	*Less:* Depreciation	20,000	30,000(B)
Sundry Creditiors	15,650	15,650		30,000	20,000
Provision for Taxation	8,000	8,000	Sundry Debtors	48,000	48,000
			Closing Stock	42,550	37,000
			Cash in hand	2,250	2,250
			Cash at Bank	14,600	14,600
	1,37,400	1,21,850		1,37,400	121,850

Working

(A) Closing Stock

As per information supplied, closing stock is the same as opening stock.

(B) Depreciation

$$5,000 \times \frac{150}{100} = \text{Rs. } 7,500$$

$$20,000 \times \frac{150}{100} = \text{Rs. } 30,000$$

(C) Arrears Depreciation

In this problem under Orthobox system, depreciation provided up to 30th June amounted to Rs. 15,000.

So arrears depreciation will be :

Rs. 30,000 – (Rs. 15,000 + Rs. 7,500, being current year's dep.)

= Rs. 30,000 – Rs. 22,500

= Rs. 7,500.

Problem

Information :

(i) Machine purchased on the 30th December 2000.

(ii) Value/Cost of the Machine as on that date is Rs. 5,000.

(iii) Estimated life of the Machine, 5 years.

(iv) Machine to be replaced on 30th December 2005; when the cost of the machine is expected to be Rs. 5,500.

(v) Following Forecast Index Nos. are supplied :

Year	% Forecast Index Nos.
1	101
2	103
3	106
4	107
5	109

From the information given above you are requested to calculate the amount to be provided for each year in order to avoid the threat arising from inflation (rise in prices).

Your calculation should be based on the following methods :—

(a) Depreciation Base Method.

(b) Asset Valuation Method.

Solution

(a) Amount to be provided in each year under Depreciation Base Method

a.	Years	1	2	3	4	5
b.	% Index No. (Current Replacement)	101 (1 × 101)	103 (2 × 103)	106 (3 × 106)	107 (4 × 107)	109 (5 × 109)
c.	Current Replacement years i.e. (a × b)	101	206	318	428	545
d.	Cumulative Replacement Index No.	101	(101 + 103) 204	(204 + 106) 310	(310 + 107) 417	(417 + 109) 526
e.	Cumulative deficiency index per cent (c – d)	—	2	8	11	19
f.	Current deficiency index per cent	—	2	6	3	8
g.	Depreciation Charges Rs.	1,000	1,000	1,000	1,000	1,000

h.	Current Replacement Cost Charge Rs. $\left(\frac{g \times b}{100}\right)$	1,010	1,030	1,060	1,070	1,090
i.	Deficiency in appropriation $\left(\frac{g \times f}{100}\right)$	—	20	60	30	80
	Total current provision Rs. (h + i)	1,010	1,050 (1,010+1,050)	1,120 (2,060+1,120)	1,100 (3,180+1,100)	1,170 (4,280+1,170)
	Total Provision to Date	1,010	= 2,060	= 3,180	= 4,280	= 5,450

(b) Amount to be provided in each year under Asset Valuation Method

a.	Years	1	2	3	4	5
b.	Current Replacement Index per cent	101	103	106	107	109
c.	Cumulative Replacement Index per cent	101	204	310	417	526
d.	Depreciation charge up to date (Rs.)	1,000	2,000	3,000	4,000	5,000
d_1	Depreciation charges	1,000	1,000	1,000	1,000	1,000
e.	Depreciation charge up to date converted into Current Repalcement (Rs.) $\frac{d \times b}{100}$	1,010	2,060	3,180	4,280	5,450
f.	Reserve to be provided for current depreciation (Based on Cumulative Index) $\left(\frac{di \times c}{100}\right)$ (Rs.)	1,010	2,040	3,100	4,170	5,260
g.	Deficiency, (e – f)	—	20	80	110	190
h.	Appropriation of Deficiency (Rs.)	—	20	60	30	80
i.	Current Replacement Cost Charge $\left(\frac{di \times b}{100}\right)$ = (Rs.)	1,010	1,030	1,060	1,070	1,090
	Current Provision (h + i) = (Rs.)	1,010	1,050 (1,010+1,050)	1,120 (2,060+1,120)	1,100 (3,180+1,100)	1,170 (4,280+1,170)
	Total Current Provision up to date (Rs.)	1,010	2,060	3,180	4,280	5,450

Now you see, the result is same as per the calculation of the two methods. I hope you have followed the workings of this problem. Is there any question you like to put to me?

☐ "Sir, what are the definitions of the Depreciation Base Method and Assets Valuatior Method ?"

• The Institute of Cost and Works Accountants of London, defines the two methods as under :

Depreciation Base Method :

'Where this method is used, the amounts required are calculated by applying the index to the depreciation charge .....'

Assets Valuation method :

'Where this method is employed, the amounts required are calculated by applying the index to the cost of the assets ....'

Problem

	Units	Unit Cost	Total Cost
		Rs.	Rs.
Inventory –January 1	1,600	10.00	16,000
Purchase –January 5	800	11.00	8,800
Purchase –January 20	500	13.00	6,500
Purchase –January 31	1,400	12.00	16,800

Above Units were sold at the following intervals :

January 3	900
January 10	800
January 23	700

What were the January *cost of goods sold* and the 31st inventory valuation :

(a) Assuming cost to be determined on a 'first-in first-out basis'?

(b) Assuming application of the "cost or market" rule in connection with (a) above?

(c) Assuming cost to be determind on an average cost basis?

Solution

		Rs.
(a) Opening Stocks (inventories) (1,600 X Rs. 10)		16,000
Plus : Purchases :		
5th Janauary	8,800	
20th January	6,500	
31st January	16,800	32,100
		48,100
Less : Closing Stocks (ending inventories) **1,900 Units**		
1,400 @ Rs. 12.00	16,800	
500 @ Rs. 13.00	6,500	23,300
Cost of Good Sold	→	24,800
(b) Closing Stock 1,900 @ 12.00 (Market price)		22,800
Cost of goods Sold : (Rs. 48,100 – Rs. 22,800)		25,300

(c) Moving Weighted Average Method

Date	Receipts		Issues		Balances	
		Rs.		Rs.		Rs.
Jan.1					1,600 @10.00	16,000
" 3			900 @ 10.00	9,000	700 @10.00	7,000
" 5	800 @ 11.00	8,800			1,500 @10.53	15,800
" 10			800 @ 10.53	8,427	700 @ 10.53	7,373
" 20	500 @ 13.00	6,500			1,200 @ 11.56	13,873
" 23			700 @ 11.56	8,093	500 @ 11.56	5,780
" 31	1,400 @12.00	16,800			1,900 @ 11.88	22,580
Total Cost of Goods Sold				25,520		

Working

$$\text{Moving Weighted Average Method} = \frac{\text{Total cost of Materials}}{\text{Total number of units}}$$

(1) $\frac{7,000 + 8,800}{1,500} = \text{Rs. } 10.53$ (2) $\frac{7,373 + 6,500}{1,200} = \text{Rs. } 11.56$

(3) $\frac{5,780 + 16,800}{1,900} = \text{Rs. } 11.88$

Problem

Rahu, Ketu and Sani Company, a dealer of varieties of articles, adopted a LIFO Method of inventory valuation as on January 2003 at which time FIFO inventory balances amounted to Rs. 2,00,000. No atempt was made to keep separate inventory balances for each of the company's merchandise items a rupee value method was adopted.

You are given the following information for the years 2003-2006 :

(1) The company's inventory had the following LIFO Valuation on December 31,2005 :

	Rs.
LIFO base (1.1.03 prices)	2,00,000
2004 layer	35,000
2005 layer	19,500
Total	2,54,500

(2) All increments to the LIFO inventory are priced at beginning of year prices. (For this purpose, it is assumed that at the beginning of the year prices are the same as the prices prevailing at the end of the previous year).

(3) Year ending inventories were :

	End-of-year Prices Rs.	Beginning-of-year Prices Rs.
December 31, 2005	3,33,000	3,02,727
December 31, 2006	3,12,000	3,00,000

(4) Merchandise purchases during 2006 amounted to Rs. 25,00,000.

(5) The ratios of end-of-year prices to beginning-of-year prices were*

2003	1.10
2004	1.05
2005	1.10
2006	1.04

(*Note that these index number have not been "chained")

(a) Compute the cost of goods sold for 2006 and the December 31, 2006 inventory valuation.

(b) What was the price level gain or loss reflected in the 2006 income statement? (Assume that adequate supplies of merchandise could have been bought at year-end to keep inventories constant.

(c) What was the price level gain or loss eliminated from reported income for the years 2003 through 2006 by the adoption of the LIFO method? **[Adapted from C.P.A.]**

Solution

(a) Cost of Goods Sold : Rs. 25,29,500*

LIFO Inventory	**Rs.**
Base	2,00,000
2004 layer	25,000
	2,25,000

* Rs. 25,00,000 + Rs. 29,500

Computation : 2006 decrement.

Decrement = Rs. 3,33,000 – Rs. 3,00,000
= Rs. 33,000 @ 1.1.2006 prices.
= 33,000/Rs.1.1 = Rs. 30,000 @ 1.1.2005 prices.

But only Rs. 19,500 in 2005 layer (@ 1.1.2005 prices) leaving Rs. 10,500. This is equivalent to Rs. 10,500/Rs. 1.05 = Rs.10,000 @ 1.1.2004 prices.

Therefore, the decrement is Rs 19,500 + Rs.10,000 = Rs.29,500.

(b) Price level gain = Rs. 33,000 × 1.04 – Rs. 29,500 = Rs. 4,820

The 1.04 factor is necessary to get decrement in end-of-year prices to calculate the effect of not re-building inventory at year end.

(c) Cumulative gain eliminated from income by use of LIFO = Rs. 3,12,000 – Rs. 2,25,000 = Rs. 87,000.

QUESTIONS

1. The following is a summary of the accounts of a company for a period of over 20 years :

Balance Sheets at year-end

	1984 Rs. '000	1991 Rs. '000	1998 Rs. '000	2005 Rs. '000	2006 Rs. '000
Fixed Assets at cost	200	200	317	504	519
Less : Depreciation	25	132	148	235	243
Trading assets	175	68	169	269	276
Net current assets	200	300	460	560	580
Equity capital and retained Profit	375	368	629	829	856

Profit and Loss Accounts for the respective years :

	1984 Rs. '000	1991 Rs. '000	1998 Rs. '000	2005 Rs. '000	2006 Rs. '000
Trading Profit	80	120	184	224	232
Depreciation	25	10	24	39	40
Profit before taxation	55	110	160	185	192
Index Numbers (base 1984)	100	150	230	280	290

A financial commentator has observed that because of the changing value of money, the company has, in effect, been paying dividend out of capital. You are asked to comment on this statement giving detailed workings on which you base your findings. **[Adapted from M.Com., C.U.]**

2. What is Accounting for Inflation? Explain different types of problems arising from inflationary accounting.
3. What are money value assets and liabilities ? What are real value assets and liabilities ? Explain the above concepts in detail.
4. Explain the character of goodwill from the point of view of 'money value and real value asset concept'.
5. "Erosion of real capital is the greatest curse of inflation" — Explain.
6. (a) In a period of continuous rise in price level it is difficult to maintian real capital in the business under conventional accounting. Explain how this happens.

(b) A company has a number of plant and machinery, the details in respect of which are :

Date of purchase	Cost Rs.	Estimated life (years)	Hypothetical price index at date of purchase
1.1.1990	30,000	20	100
1.1.1998	20,000	10	200
31.10.2003	12,000	5	300

Depreciation has been charged under straight-line method up to 31st December 2003. Determine the amount of replacement reserve up to 31.12.03 and explain its treatment in the books of accounts.

[Adapted from M.Com. (C.U.) Management Accountancy]

7. The operating results of Lotus Ltd. for the last three years were as under :

	2002-03 Rs./lakhs	2003-04 Rs./lakhs	2004-05 Rs./lakhs
Sales	50.00	63.00	69.30
Material Consumed	20.00	26.40	30.36
Wages	20.00	24.00	28.80
Factory Expenses	6.00	7.00	7.50
Administrative Expenses	2.50	3.20	3.50
Selling Expenses	0.50	2.00	2.50
Interest	—	0.60	1.00
	49.00	63.20	73.66
Profit/(Loss)	1.00	(0.20)	(4.36)

The following index numbers have been worked out and are applicable to the whole of the year concerned :

	2002-03	2003-04	2004-05
Sales Price	100	105	105
Price of Raw Material	100	110	120
Wages	100	120	144

You are required to analyse the figures and work out the efficiency at constant prices. Offer your comments. **[I.C.W.A. Final, C.A. Final, Adapted]**

8. The Balance Sheet of XYZ Ltd. as on 31st December 2005 and the Profit and Loss Account during the year 2006 are as under :

Balance Sheet as at 31.12.2005

Liabilities	Rs.	Assets	Rs.
Share Capital	40,000	Plant and Machinery	60,000
13.5% Debentures	24,000	Stocks	9,600
Sundry Creditors	14,400	Debtors	4,800
		Cash	4,000
	78,400		78,400

Profit & Loss A/c for the year ended 31.12.2006

	Rs.		Rs.
To Opening Stock	9,600	By Sales	40,000
" Purchases	18,400	" Closing Stock	8,000
" Gross Profit	20,000		
	48,000		48,000
To Expenses	3,200	By Gross Profit	20,000
" Interest on Debenture	3,240		
" Depreciation	6,000		
" Net Profit	7,560		
	20,000		20,000

The following information is relevant :

(i) There is no change in Debtors and Creditors during the year.

(ii) Following indices are to be taken :

On 1st January 2006	200
Average of 2006	240
On 31st December 2006	300

(iii) First-In-First-Out method is used

You are required to prepare the final accounts for the 2006 after adjusting for price level changes under CPP Method. **[I.C.W.A. Final, Adapted]**

9. The summarised profit and loss account of Alfa Ltd. for 2006 prepared under the historical cost convention, was as follows :

Profit and Loss Account for 2006

	(Rs. '000)	(Rs. '000)
Turnover		3,60,000
Less : Opening Stock	35,000	
Purchase	2,00,000	
Closing Stock	(50,000)	
Cost of goods sold		1,85,000
Gross Profit		1,75,000

	(Rs. '000)	(Rs. '000)
Gross Profit b/f		1,75,000
Less : Depreciation	20,000	
Other running costs	1,26,000	1,46,000
Operating profit		29,000
Less : Interest payable		5,000
Profit before taxation		24,000
Taxation		10,000
Profit after tax		14,000
Less : Dividends		7,000
Retained profit for the year		7,000

The following additional information is provided :

(i) Relevant indices for stocks are as follows :

Average for October/December 2005	120
At 31st December 2005	124
Average for 2005	135
Average for October/December 2006	142
At 31st December 2006	145

On an average the company holds stock for three months.

(ii) All the company's fixed assets were purchased when the company was incorporated in January 2000. Their original cost was Rs. 20,00,00,000 and they are being depreciated over a ten-year period assuming a nil residual value. The original estimate of these assets' lives is still considered appropriate. The following current cost valuations are provided :

	Rs.'000
At 1st January 2006	3,10,000
Average for 2006	3,30,000
At 31st December 2006	3,55,000

Required

A summarised profit and loss account for 2006 prepared on the current basis so far as the information permits.

Note : All calculations are to be made to the nearest Rs. '000.

[Adapted, I.C.W.A. Final]

10. The following information has been extracted from the accounts of Sigma Ltd. prepared under the historical cost convention for 2006.

Profit and Loss Accounts Extracts 2006

	(Rs. in millions)
Turnover	200
Operating profit	15
Less : Interest payable	3
Net Profit	12

Summarised Balance Sheet at 31st December 2006

	(Rs. in millions)	(Rs. in millions)
Fixed assets at cost less depreciation		60
Current assets : Stock	20	
Debtors	30	
Bank	2	
	52	
Less : Current Liabilities	30	
Net current assets		22
Total assets less current liabilities		82
Less : 15% debentures		20
		62
Capital and reserves		62

The company's accountant has prepared the following current cost data :

	(Rs. in millions)
Current cost adjustment for 2006 :	
Depreciation adjustment	3
Cost of sales adjustment	5
Replacement cost at 31st December 2006 :	
Fixed assets, net of depreciation	85
Stocks	21

Required :

(a) A calculation of the current cost operating profit of N Ltd. for 2006 and summaries current cost balance sheet of the company at 31st December 2006, so far as the information permits.

(b) Calculations of the following ratios from both the historical cost accounts and current cost accounts :

(i) interest cover;

(ii) rate of return on shareholder's equity;

(iii) debt/equity ratio.

(c) A discussion of the significance of the ratios calculated under (b) and of the reason for differences between them.

Note : Ignore taxation. **[I.C.W.A. Final, Adapted]**

23

PORTFOLIO MANAGEMENT

● Good evening to you all.

□ "Good evening, Sir".

● Well, what would be discussed this evening?

□ "Sir, you promised us that you would give us some basic idea on **Portfolio Theory** and its Management."

● Well, do you know what is meant by the term **Portfolio**?

□ "No, Sir, give us the meaning of the term Portfolio and its theory and how it is managed."

● You see, the term Portfolio means list of investments held by investor or it may be stated as bundle of savings. I had already given in my earlier lectures, what is the term security means. Yes, yes, you stand up. What do you want to say?

□ "Sir! it is Share(s) or Debenture(s)".

Meaning of Portfolio Management

● Yes, you have rightly answered. You see, Portfolio management is the technique to get advantage out of the processes of purchase and sales of securities.

You see, **expected return** and **risk** are the two important aspects or factors which invite the attention of the investors to take decision—whether it is worthy to invest money in individual security or single project. Have a look here—the formula to determine the rate of return from a secruity.

$$\text{Rate of Return (R)} = \frac{D + (P_1 - P_0)}{P_0} \times 100$$

Here D stands for dividend per share, P_0 and P_1 stand for market price per share today, and one year hence, respectively. It is clear from the above that the return is the aggregate of dividend yield and capital gain.

□ "Sir, what is capital gain, here?"

Definition of Capital Gain

You see $(P_1 - P_0)$ is the capital gain. That is to say, it is the difference between the expected market price per share after one year and today's market price.

Let us illustrate the rate of return of a share with an example.

Suppose market price of ACC on 2nd September 2003 is Rs. 212, dividend paid during the year Rs. 3.50 per share and the market price per share on 2nd September, 2004 is Rs. 262. The rate of return would be

$$R = \frac{\{\text{Rs. } 3.50 + \text{Rs. } (262 - 212)\}}{212} \times 100$$

$$= \frac{\{\text{Rs. } 3.50 + \text{Rs. } 50\}}{212} \times 100 = 25.24\%$$

- I think you are following my lecture.

☐ "Sir, we are feeling much satisfied. No problem Sir!"

Factors Affecting Rate

- You see, the number of factors, such as dividend policy of the firm(s), different economic conditions, market price of shares at different points of time, etc., that affect the rate of return, cause the **Variability of rate of return**. Actually, this variability of rate of returns is the **risk**.

Have you followed what I want to say?

☐ "Yes Sir. Sir! give us the formula to measure the risk of a share".

- Is there any question(s) besides this from your side for clarification?

☐ "No Sir! for the present. Please give the formula".

- Thank you, my dear students. I am very happy to see that you have taken so much interest in the subject.

You see, Standard Deviation(σ) or Variance(σ^2) is used to calculate the **risk**.

The **risk** of a **share** is measured by using the following formula of **Variance** or **Standard Deviation**:

$$\text{Variance } (\sigma^2) = \frac{(R_1 - \bar{R})^2 + (R_2 - \bar{R})^2 + (R_3 - \bar{R})^2 + \ldots + (R_n - \bar{R})^2}{n}$$

$$= \frac{1}{n}\sum_{i=1}^{n}(R_i - \bar{R})^2$$

$$\text{or, Standard deviation } (\sigma) = \sqrt{\frac{1}{n}\sum_{i=1}^{n}(R_i - \bar{R})^2}$$

where, R_i = Rate of return at time 'i'

$\overline{R}$ = Average rate of return

n = number of year

Let us now see how to calculate expected rate of return. The expected rate of return of a share is the weighted average of returns under different possible economic conditions—the weights being the probability of occurrence of each of the economic conditions.

The following example will illustrate the calculation of weighted average rate of return :

Economic Conditions	Rate of Return	Probability	Expected Return	
A	–8	0.2	$-8 \times 0.2 =$	$-$ 1.60
B	10	0.3	$10 \times 0.3 =$	3.00
C	18	0.3	$18 \times 0.3 =$	5.40
D	15	0.2	$15 \times 0.2 =$	3.00
				9.8

Therefore, we can use the following equation to calculate the expected rate of return :

$$E(R) = R_1P_1 + R_2P_2 + R_3P_3 + \ldots + R_nP_n.$$

$$\text{or,}\quad E(R) = \sum_{i=1}^{n} R_iP_i$$

where, E(R) = Expected rate of return

R_i = Rate of return at time i

P_i = Probability of occurrence of return at time i

It is to be noted from the above example that the rates of return range between –8% to 18%. Thus, it involves risk which can be calculated in the following way :

$$\sigma^2 = (-8-9.8)^2 \times 0.2 + (10-9.8)^2 \times 0.3 + (18-9.8)^2 \times 0.3 + (15-9.8)^2 \times 0.2$$

$$= 63.368 + 0.012 + 20.172 + 5.408.$$

$$= 88.96$$

$$\sigma = \sqrt{88.96} = 9.43$$

Therefore, we can use the following formula to calculate the risk :

$$\sigma^2 = [R_1 - E(R)]^2 P_1 + [R_2 - E(R)]^2 P_2 + [R_3 - E(R)]^2 P_3 + \ldots + [R_n - E(R)]^2 P_n$$

$$\sigma^2 = \sum_{i=1}^{n} [R_i - E(R)]^2 P_i$$

The meaning of R_i, P_i and E(R) are the same as above.

I think you have followed the said example.

☐ "Yes Sir. Thank you Sir for creating interest in the subject".

• Can I proceed for further discussion?

☐ "If I am excused Sir, please give us a break for fifteen minutes."

• Well, your request is gladly accepted.

Now fifteen minutes is over. I feel, all of you are present in the class.

You see, I had already brought to your notice at the outset, i.e., at the begining of this chapter, that expected **rate of returns** and **risks** are the two important aspects that influence the investors to take decision to invest money in the share market. That is to say, **risks** and **expected returns** are associated with investment decision.

It is an accepted fact, you know better than me, that rational investors do not like to take **risk** which means 'risk averse'. Investors always choose those types of investments which are either risk-free or of minimum risk having moderate or maximum returns.

Again I am to say that, when there exists more than one investment opportunities having equal rates of return, investors may choose those types of investments that bear minimum **risk**.

Intuitive Art and Mood of the Market

It is important to note that, selection of a particular type of investment and of so many, in actual practice which I had seen while conducting a survey long years back on trends of share prices at the Calcutta Stock Exchange, not only geared by academic exercises but, championed by the **Intuitive Art** of Investor(s) also. It is also seen, in actual practice, that valuation of shares depends upon the **'Mood of the Market**.'[1]

I think that you are feeling bore. Can I stop the discussions for the moment?

☐ "No Sir! We are not feeling bore. You can proceed further."

Human Behaviour and Portfolio

☐ "Sir! if I am excused, please give us an example as you did with the help of human behaviour. Sir! different examples given by you earlier such as convertible Debenture, difference between Equity Share and Preference Shares by drawing an analogy of father and father-in-law—all are really exciting and thought-provoking. Similary, please Sir! give us an example of human behaviour associated with investment and risk. We have seen Sir, you can prepare story instantly relating to a particular situation. Please Sir...."

• Well, I am telling you two practical case studies side by side. I do not like to mention the names of persons because they are very close friends of mine. So, they are represented as Friend X and Friend Y. My friend X had two daughters. He is very rich person. He wanted to give marriage of his younger daughter with a brilliant son(B) of his friend Z who was very poor so far as his wealth is concerned. Daughter of X was equally brilliant who passed class Twelve Examination with high percentage of mark. The boy B (son of Z) was very ambitious and wanted to study MBA in Sydney University, Australia. The father of B could not afford money to get his son educated in Australia which costs minimum

---

[1] Dr. A.K. Sur. "*New Issue Market and Stock Exchange.*"

Rs. 15 Lakhs. There was a deal between X and Z that X will provide the said amount provided, after return from foreign country crowned with MBA degree, son of Z that is B, will marry the daughter of X. The deal was made out of sentiment; not backed by portfolio analysis which concerned with **risk** and **return on investment factor**.

After returning from Australia, the boy B (son of Z) refused to marry the daughter of X on the ground that he (B) had already married a foreign girl at Australia. His answer was "I am sorry".

The situation of my another friend Y was quite different. He had his only daughter studying at college for Commerce degree. Similar deal was made between Y and his another poor friend (O). Y was very expert in portfolio management. His deal was based upon the **risk free** and profitable investment model which in this case refers to the theory that "I am willing to afford all educational expenses to be incurred in foreign country **provided** your son (L) will marry my daughter before going to foreign country".

This approach is, perhaps, a process of risk-free investment analysis. This may be treated as portfolio investment decision. My friend Y was benefitted, thanks to his expertise in Portfolio Management. How do you like this example, my dear students? Do you like to say anything? How do you enjoyed the example?

☐ "Very exciting, Sir! we are satisfied. It is really wonderful example".

• I hope that you are not feeling tired. Now I am proceeding for the next discussion on Portfolio Theory.

Portfolio Theory

I have given you earlier a general or first-hand impression of portfolio. However, a portfolio may be defined as a 'bundle or combination of securities or other assets' which are held in such a fashion that the total risk of holding securities can be reduced to minimum through the process of **Diversification.** Under the circumstances, the **Portfolio Theory** is based on the concept or assumption that "investors are risk-averse".

Portfolio Theory

You see, I have already explained the concept of **risk averse**. Guidelines for constructing portfolio have been provided in **Portfolio Theory**. It should be noted in this connection that two important aspects or criteria—**risk** and **return**—play a dominating factor for constructing portfolio. These aspects should be considered as a whole and should not be considered separately for each security in the portfolio.

Risk Averse

For constructing portfolio of securities following considerations deserve special attentions —

Consideration for Constructing Portfolio

(i) Decision of the investor as to selection of securities.

(ii) Decision of the investor regarding distribution of total amount in different securities with the object to minimise **risk**.

The following is an example of hypothetical portfolio :

An investor has made investment of his/her fund in the following shares :

Shares of	Proportion
Ashok Leyland	20%
Raymond	30%
Tata Steel	10%
Satyam Computer	30%
HPCL	10%
	100%

● I think, you have followed my lecture. Is there any question(s)?

☐ "Sir, I have one question to ask".

● What is that?

☐ "What is Diversification?"

● Well, you see, the dictionary meaning of the term 'diversification' is quality of being different or varied. But, when the said term is used in the context of portfolio, it means spreading securities, i.e., investments over several companies or enterprises.

Meaning of Diversification

Let me come to my original discussion—factors to be taken into consideration by the investors while constructing portfolio. That is to say, proper weightage to the factors for constructing portfolio. You please stand up and say what are those factors.

☐ "Sir, two factors are (i) types of securities, and (ii) the proportion of fund invested in each security."

● Thank you. You are absolutely correct.

☐ "Excuse me Sir! Please enlighten us as to how portfolio **return** and **risk** is calculated in case of two securities portfolio."

● Well, let us now see how portfolio return and risk is calculated in case of two securities portfolio.

The following steps are involved in calculating portfolio return —

Steps to Calculate Portfolio Return

Step 1 : Calculate expected return of each security in the portfolio.

Step 2 : Multiply expected rate of return of each security with proportion of fund invested in that security.

Step 3 : Add all the outcomes obtained in step 2 to get expected rate of return on portfolio.

● Did you follow my lecture? Is there any question?

☐ "Sir, kindly explain this with an example".

• Well take a look at the following example.

Example

Possible rates of return of two securities along with probability of occurrence under different economic conditions are given below :

State of economy	Probability	Rate of return (%)	
		A	B
P	0.10	– 5	10
Q	0.40	15	– 2
R	0.30	10	18
S	0.20	8	15

Ascertain the expected rate of return of security A and B. Find also the expected rate of return from portfolio assuming that funds are distributed equally in both the securities.

Solution

Expected rate of return of —

Security A = (–5% × 0.10) + (15% × 0.40) + (10% × 0.30) + (8% × 0.20)

= 10.1%

Security B = (10% × 0.10) + (–2% × 0.40) + (18% × 0.30) + (15% × 0.20)

= 8.6%

∴ Expected rate of return of portfolio assuming that total available funds are equally distributed —

(10.1% × 0.5) + (8.6% × 0.5)

= 5.05% + 4.3%

= 9.35%

I think you have followed the above calculation. Now I would like to discuss on Portfolio Risk.

Portfolio Risk

Portfolio risk is not simply the weighted average of variance or standard deviation of individual securities. Because, portfolio variance is affected by the co-movement of securities. Thus, the following formula is used to measure portfolio risk of two securities portfolio :

Formula to Calculate Portfolio Risk

$$\sigma_P^2 = W_A^2\sigma_A^2 + W_B^2\sigma_B^2 + 2.W_A.W_B.Cov(A,B)$$

where, σ^2_P = Portfolio Variance

W_A = Weight of security 'A'

W_B = Weight of security 'B'

σ_A = Standard deviation of security 'A'

σ_B = Standard deviation of security 'B'

Cov (A,B) = Covariance of security A and B.

Covariance measures the co-movement of return of security A and B. Again,

$$\text{Cov (A,B)} = \sigma_A . \sigma_B .\text{Cr (A,B)}.$$

$$\text{or, Cr (A,B)} = \frac{\text{Cov (A,B)}}{\sigma_A . \sigma_B}.$$

Let us now calculate portfolio risk from the above Example :

$W_A = 0.5$

$W_B = 0.5$

$$\sigma^2_A = (-5 - 10.1)^2 \times 0.10 + (15 - 10.1)^2 \times 0.40 + (10 - 10.1)^2 \times 0.3 + (8 - 10.1)^2 \times 0.2$$

$$= 22.8 + 9.6 + .003 + .882$$

$$= 33.285\%$$

$$\sigma^2_B = (10 - 8.6)^2 \times 0.1 + (-2 - 8.6)^2 \times 0.4 + (18 - 8.6)^2 \times 0.3 + (15 - 8.6)^2 \times 0.2$$

$$= 0.196 + 44.94 + 26.508 + 8.192$$

$$= 79.836\%$$

Cov (A, B)

The following formula is used to calculate the coefficient of variance of two securities :

$$\text{Cov (A, B)} = \sum_{i=1}^{n}[R(A_i) - E(R_A)][R(B_i) - E(R_B)]P_i$$

where, $R(A_i)$ = Returns of security 'A'

$R(B_i)$ = Returns of security 'B'

$E(R_A)$ = Expected rate of return of security 'A'

$E(R_B)$ = Expected rate of return of security 'B'

P_i = Probability of occurrence of the state of economy

$$\text{Cov (A, B)} = (-5 - 10.1)(10 - 8.6) \times 0.1 + (15 - 10.1)(-2 - 8.6) \times 0.4 + (10 - 10.1)(18 - 8.6) \times 0.3 + (8 - 10.1)(15 - 8.6) \times 0.2$$

$$= -2.114 - 20.776 - 0.282 - 2.688$$

$$= -25.86$$

Portfolio risk :

$$\sigma^2_p = W_A^2\sigma_A^2 + W_B^2\sigma_B^2 + 2\,W_A W_B \text{Cov (A,B)}$$

$$\sigma^2_p = (0.5)^2 (33.285) + (0.5)^2 (79.836) + 2(.5)(.5)(-25.86)$$

$$= 8.32 + 19.96 - 12.93$$

$$= 15.35\%$$

Let us now calculate correlation coefficient of securities A and B. We know

$$Cr\ (A, B) = \frac{Cov\ (A,B)}{\sigma_A . \sigma_B}$$

$$\sigma_A = \sqrt{33.285} = 5.769\%$$

$$\sigma_B = \sqrt{79.836} = 8.935\%$$

$$Cov\ (A, B) = \frac{-25.86}{5.769 \times 8.935} = -0.5017$$

Here correlation between securities is – 0.5017. Portfolio should be constructed among securities having negative correlation in order to have favourable impact on risk of portfolio. This aspect will be discussed later on.

I feel you are following my lecture. Is there any problem?

☐ "Sir, would you please enlighten us how risk is minimised by changing weight."

• Well, here is your answer.

Minimising Risk by Changing Weights

I have mentioned earlier that portfolio risk can be reduced by changing weights. Theoritically, we can reduce risk to zero by changing weights. Let us now see how it is possible.

Let us assume that we have two securities portfolio and α is the weight attributed to security 1 and $(1 - \alpha)$ is the weight attributed to security 2.

∴ The risk of two securities portfolio $= \sigma^2_p = \alpha^2\sigma_1^{\ 2} + (1 - \alpha)^2\sigma_2^{\ 2} + 2.\alpha.(1 - \alpha)\ r\ (1,2)\ \sigma_1\sigma_2$.

where, σ_1 = Standard deviation of security 1.

σ_2 = Standard deviation of security 2.

r(1,2) = Correlation of returns between two securities.

For minimising risk to zero, derivative of portfolio risk with respect to weight should be equal to zero. That is

$$\frac{\delta\sigma_p^2}{\delta_\alpha} = 0$$

$$\sigma^2_p = \alpha^2\sigma^2_1 + (1 - 2\alpha + \alpha^2)\ \sigma^2_2 + 2\ \alpha\ r\ (1,2)\ \sigma_1\sigma_2 - 2\alpha^2\ r(1,2)\ \sigma_1\sigma_2$$

$$= \alpha^2\sigma^2_1 + \sigma^2_2 - 2\alpha\sigma^2_2 + \alpha^2\sigma^2_2 + 2\ \alpha\ r\ (1,2)\ \sigma_1\sigma_2 - 2\alpha^2\ r(1,2)\ \sigma_1\sigma_2$$

$$\frac{\delta\sigma_p^2}{\delta_\alpha} = 2\alpha\sigma^2_1 + 0 - 2\sigma^2_2 + 2\alpha\sigma^2_2 + 2\ r(1,2)\ \sigma_1\sigma_2 - 2\ r(1,2)\ \sigma_1\sigma_2 .\ 2\alpha$$

Since, $2\alpha\sigma^2_1 + 2\alpha\sigma^2_2 - 2\ r(1,2)\ \sigma_1\sigma_2 .\ 2\alpha - 2\sigma^2_2 + 2\ r(1,2)\ \sigma_1\sigma_2 = 0$

∴ $2\alpha\sigma^2_1 + 2\alpha\sigma^2_2 + 2\ r(1,2)\ \sigma_1\sigma_2 = 2\sigma^2_2 + 2\ r(1,2)\ \sigma_1\sigma_2 .2\alpha$

or, $\not{2}(\alpha\sigma^2_1 + \alpha\sigma^2_2 + r(1,2)\ \sigma_1\sigma_2 = \not{2}(\sigma^2_2 + r(1,2)\ \sigma_1\sigma_2 .2\alpha)$

or, $\alpha(\sigma^2_1 + \sigma^2_2 - 2\, r(1,2)\, \sigma_1\sigma_2) = \sigma^2_2 - r(1,2)\, \sigma_1\sigma_2$

or, $$\alpha = \frac{\sigma_2^2 - r(1,2)\sigma_1\sigma_2}{\sigma_1^2 + \sigma_2^2 - 2r(1,2)\sigma_1\sigma_2}$$

☐ "Sir, what is Derivative?"

• You know, variables can be classified as dependent and independent. Derivative is a technique of calculas used for investigating the rate of change of a dependent variable for a given change in independent variable.

Definition of Derivative

In our discussion, the weight of security i.e. α, is independent variable and portfolio risk, i.e. σ^2_p, is dependent variable. A detailed discussion on derivative is irrelevant here. You may consult any well-known calculas book for detail study.

So, risk-minimising weight of

Security 1 $$= \frac{\sigma_2^2 - r(1,2)\sigma_1\sigma_2}{\sigma_1^2 + \sigma_2^2 - 2.r(1,2)\sigma_1\sigma_2}$$

Security 2 $$= 1 - \frac{\sigma_2^2 - r(1,2)\sigma_1\sigma_2}{\sigma_1^2 + \sigma_2^2 - 2.r(1,2)\sigma_1\sigma_2}$$

Now I am to discuss on

Correlation and Portfolio Risk Reduction

Portfolio risk is affected by relationship of returns between two securities constituting portfolio. This relationship is measured by calculating coefficient of correlation. There exist three types of relations between returns of securities constituting portfolio — positive correlation, negative correlation and no correlation.

Different types of Correlation

(i) **Positive Correlation**

Positive Correlation is said to exist between two securities when an increase in return of one security is always accompanied by a similar increase in return of another security.

(ii) **Negative Correlation**

In the case of negative correlation an increase in return of one security is always accompanied by decrease in return of another security.

(iii) **No Correlation**

Two securities are uncorrelated when return of one security is independent of returns of another security.

Diversification of portfolio risk involves holding of securities which have negative correlation. The value of correlation lies between –1 and +1. According to portfolio theory, maximum risk reduction is possible when securities are perfectly negatively correlated (i.e., value of correlation is –1). But in actual practice such a perfectly negative correlation rarely exist and its value generally lies between – 1 and +1. Therefore, next preference after negative correlation should be no significant correlation between returns of securities.

Diversification of Portfolio Risk

☐ **"Sir, please give an example which will be more suitable for our understanding."**

• **Well, take the following example.**

Example

The following particulars are available regarding equity shares of two companies X Ltd and Y Ltd :

Particulars	X Ltd.	Y Ltd.
Expected Return	30%	35%
Weight	0.5	0.5
Risk (σ)	20%	20%

Calculate portfolio variance (σ^2_P) if correlation coefficient between securities return is—

(i) +1

(ii) –1

(iii) + 0.2

(iv) – 0.2

Solution

(i) When correlation Coefficient (Cr.) is + 1.

$$\sigma^2_P = (.5)^2(.2)^2 + (.5)^2(.2)^2 + 2.(.5)(.5)(+1)(.2)(.2)$$
$$= 0.01 + 0.01 + 0.02$$
$$= 0.04.$$

(ii) When Cr. is – 1.

$$\sigma^2_P = (.5)^2(.2)^2 + (.5)^2(.2)^2 + 2.(.5)(.5)(-1)(.2)(.2)$$
$$= 0.01 + 0.01 - 0.02$$
$$= 0.02 - 0.02$$
$$= 0$$

(iii) When Cr. is + 0.2

$$\sigma^2_P = (.5)^2(.2)^2 + (.5)^2(.2)^2 + 2.(.5)(.5)(0.2)(.2)(.2)$$
$$= 0.01 + 0.01 + 0.004$$
$$= 0.024.$$

(iv) When Cr. is – 0.2

$$\sigma^2_P = (.5)^2(.2)^2 + (.5)^2(.2)^2 + 2.(.5)(.5)(-0.2)(.2)(.2)$$
$$= 0.01 + 0.01 - 0.004$$
$$= 0.016.$$

It is clear from the above that portfolio risk is reduced when correlation coefficient is perfectly negatively correlated (–1) or at least weakly negatively correlated (Say – 0.55, – 0.25, – 0.75, etc.).

From the study of your face, it is clear to me that you have taken much interest in the subject. Now I am to discuss on—

Portfolio Return and Risk of More than Two Securities Portfolio

The following formula is used for calculating expected return of portfolio consisting of more than two securities :

$$E(R_P) = W_1 E(R_1) + W_2 E(R_2) + W_3 E(R_3) + ... + W_n E(R_n)$$

$$= \sum_{i=1}^{n} W_i E(R_i)$$

where, $E(R_P)$ = expected portfolio return

$W_1, W_2, ... W_n$ = Weights of securities (1, 2,...n)

$E(R_1), E(R_2), E(R_3) ... E(R_n)$ = Expected rate of returns of securities (1, 2, 3,...,n).

The risk of portfolio consisting of more than two securities can be calculated by using the following formula

$$\sigma^2_P = \sum_{i=1}^{n} W_i^2 \sigma_i^2 + \sum_{i=1}^{n}\sum_{j=1}^{n} W_i W_j \, Cov(i, j)$$

Thus, in case of, say, three securities portfolio, risk is calculated by using the following formula :

$$\sigma^2_P = W_1^2\sigma_1^2 + W_2^2\sigma_2^2 + W_3^2\sigma_3^2 + 2\, W_1W_2\, Cov(1, 2) + 2.W_1W_3\, Cov(1, 3) + 2W_2W_3\, Cov(2, 3)$$

Let us illustrate with an example :

Example

	Three securities Portfolio		
	X Ltd.	Y Ltd.	Z Ltd.
E(r)	20%	25%	30%
σ	10%	20%	25%

Correlation Coefficient

(X, Y) = 0.5

(X, Z) = –0.5

(Z, Y) = 0.2

An investor has decided to invest in these securities in the following proportions :

X = 40%

Y = 30%

Z = 30%

Calculate portfolio return and risk of the investor.

Solution

Portfolio Return

$E(r_p) = 20\% \times 0.4 + 25\% \times 0.3 + 30\% \times 0.3$

$= 8\% + 7.5\% + 9\%$

$= 24.5\%$

Portfolio Risk

$$\sigma^2_P = W_x^2\sigma_x^2 + W_y^2\sigma_y^2 + W_z^2\sigma_z^2 + 2\,W_xW_y\,Cov(x,\,y) + 2.W_xW_z\,Cov(x,\,z) + 2.W_yW_z\,Cov(y,\,z)$$

Let us first find out covariances

$Cov(x, y) = Cr(x, y)\,\sigma_x\,\sigma_y$

$= (0.5)\,(10)\,(20)$

$= 100$

$Cov(x, z) = Cr(x, z)\,\sigma_x\,\sigma_z$

$= (-0.5)\,(10)\,(25)$

$= -125$

$Cov(y, z) = Cr(y, z)\,\sigma_y\,\sigma_z$

$= (0.2)\,(20)\,(25)$

$= 100$

$$\sigma^2_P = (.4)^2(10)^2 + (.3)^2(20)^2 + (.3)^2(25)^2 + 2\,(.4)\,(.3)\,(100) + 2\,(.4)\,(.3)\,(-125) + 2\,(.3)\,(.3)\,(100)$$

$= 16 + 36 + 56.25 + 24 - 30 + 18$

$= 120.25\%$

$\sigma_P = 10.966\%$

- Are the above discussions clear to you?

☐ "Yes Sir, would you please give us an idea about Portfolio opportunity set?"

- I have decided to explain it afterwards.

☐ "Please Sir, discuss it now".

- To satisfy your thirst for knowledge I am explaining it now.

Silence please! Take a look at the board.

Portfolio Opportunity Set

Portfolio Opportunity set

You see, Portfolio opportunity set represents all possible portfolios which can be constructed between/among securities. In case of two securities portfolio, the portfolio opportunity set is looked like a triangle as illustrated in the following figure—

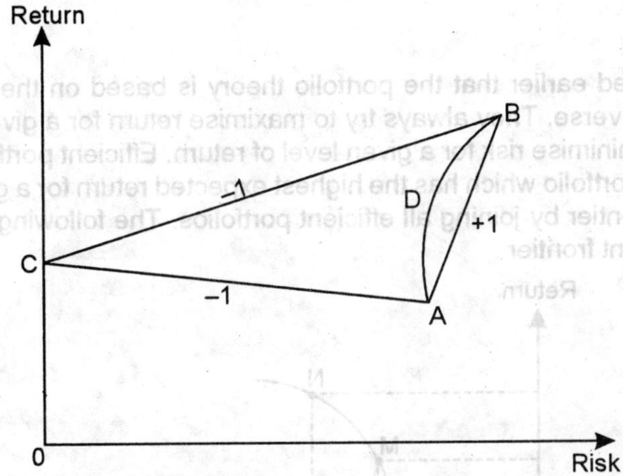

Diversification of Risk in case of Two Securities Portfolio

The above figure illustrates the risk-return relationship of all possible portfolio which can be constructed by changing weights between two securities. Line AB shows all possible portfolios when correlation coefficient between securities is perfectly positive (+1). Similarly, ACB is the locus of all possbile portfolios when correlation coefficient between securities is perfectly negative (–1). But in actual practice securities are positively or negatively correlated; perfect correlation rarely happens. In such a case risk-return relationship is depicted by the curve ADB. Thus, it is clear that all possible portfolios fall within the zone ABC and it specifies the limit of diversification in case of two securities portfolio.

● I assume that you have followed the above discussion.

□ "Yes Sir. But Sir! I have one question to ask—what is the impact of combining more than two securities?"

● Well, let us now see the impact of combining more than two securities on portfolio opportunity set. The following figure illustrates the portfolio opportunity set in case of more than two securities portfolio.

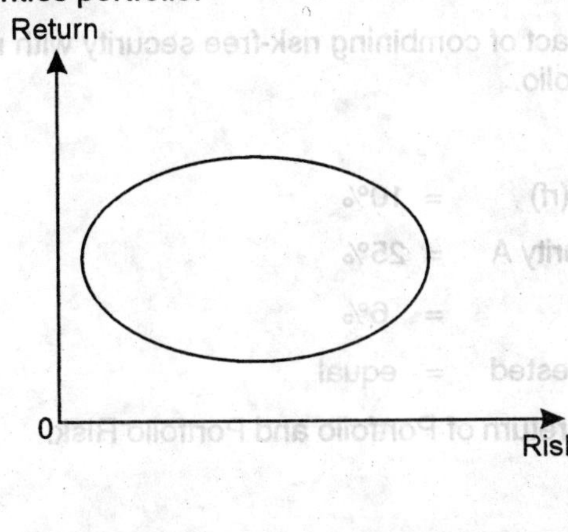

The above figure shows that, here portfolio opportunity set is egg-shaped. All possible portfolios lie within this zone.

☐ "Sir, would you kindly enlighten us on Efficient Portfolio."

- Well, have a look on the board.

Efficient Portfolio

I have mentioned earlier that the portfolio theory is based on the assumption that investors are risk averse. They always try to maximise return for a given level of risk or minimise risk for a given level of return. Efficient portfolio refers to that portfolio which has the highest expected return for a given level of risk. We get efficient frontier by joining all efficient portfolios. The following figure illustrates the shape of efficient frontier :

Efficient Frontier

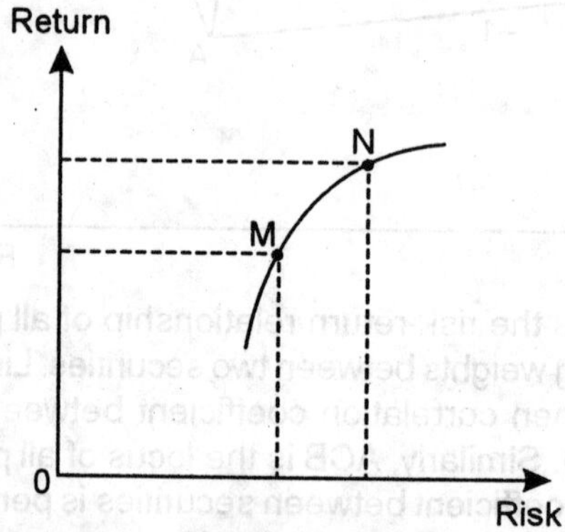

Efficient Frontier

In the above figure, M and N are all efficient portfolios because, they have the highest expected returns for a given level of risk. Thus, we can say, efficient frontier is a *locus of all efficient* portfolios.

Introduction of Risk-free Security

A risk-free security is one whose return can be expected with certainty. In other words, return of a risk-free security remains fixed under all possible economic situations. Thus, a risk-free security has zero variance or standard deviation. Govt. bonds, treasury bills, etc. are examples of these types of securities.

Example of Risk-free Securities

Let us now see the impact of combining risk-free security with risky security on risk-return relationship for portfolio.

Illustration

Risk-free rate of return (rf)	=	10%
Expected return of security A	=	25%
risk (σ_A)	=	6%
Proportion of wealth invested	=	equal

Ascertain the expected return of Portfolio and Portfolio Risk.

Solution

Expected return of portfolio = $E(r_P)$ = $0.50 \times 10\% + 0.50 \times 25\%$
= $5\% + 12.5\%$
= 17.5%

$$\text{Portfolio risk} = \sigma_P = \sqrt{(0.5)^2(0)^2 + (0.5)^2(0.06)^2 + 2.\,(.5)\,(.5)\,Cr(rf.A)\,\sigma_{rf} \cdot \sigma_A}$$

σ_{rf} = risk of security rf = 0

σ_A = standard deviation of security A = 6%

$$\sigma_P = \sqrt{0 + (.5)^2(.06)^2 + 0}$$

$$= \sqrt{(.5)^2(.06)^2}$$

$= (.5)\,(.06)$

$= .03$ i.e. 3%

Combining Risky and Risk-free Security

It is clear, from the above illustration that portfolio risk in this type of portfolio, is the product of standard deviation of risky security and its weight. It is also clear that, by combining risky security with risk-free security an investor is able to increase his/her return from 10% to 17.5% and at the same time he/she is able to reduce risk from 6% to 3%. This is illustrated in the following figure—

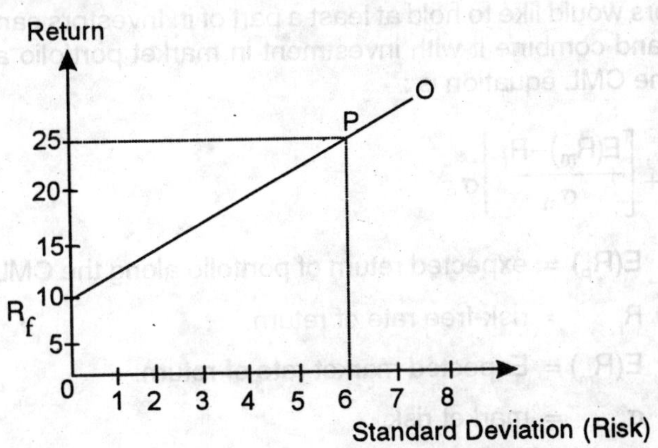

The above straight line ($R_f$po) is a locus of all possible portfolios which can be constructed by changing weights between securities. An investor can invest his/her entire wealth either in risk-free security or risky security. If entire wealth is invested in risk-free security, his/her return will be 10%. But if entire wealth is invested in risky security, the return will increase to 25%, but he will have to assume 6% risk. Thus, the straight line R_fo illustrates the portfolio opportunity set for portfolios consisting of a risk-free security and a risky security.

I feel that you have followed my lecture. Now I am to give you some basic ideas on Capital Market line.

Capital Market Line (CML)

You see, we can construct a portfolio consisting of a risk-free security and a portfolio of all risky securities. The following figure illustrates the Capital Market Line (CML) :

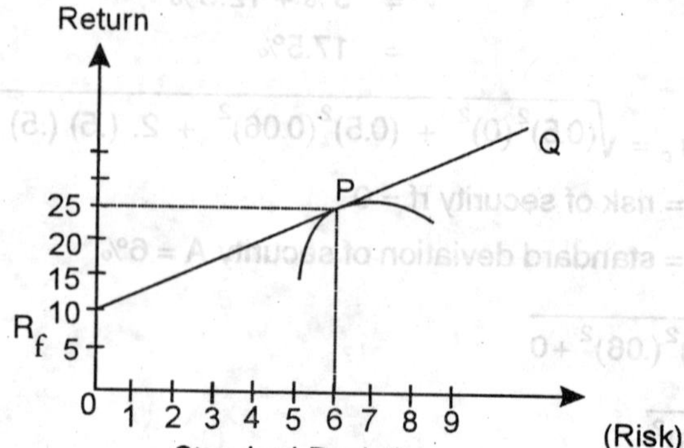

When we combine risk-free security with portfolio of risky securities, we get a new portfolio opportunity set, which will discuss the risk-return relationship of all efficient portfolios. All investors now would choose portfolios along the line R_fPQ, for these portfolios offer highest return for a given level of risk. The line R_fPQ is called Capital Market Line (CML), because it shows the risk-return relationship of various combinations of risk-free security with market portfolio (P).

Importance of Capital Market Line

A market portfolio is a portfolio of all risky securities which a rational investor wants to hold in proportion of their market values. Market portfolio dominates all other portfolios and all investors would like to hold at least a part of it. Investors can borrow or lend at the risk-free rate and combine it with investment in market portfolio according to their risk preference. The CML equation is :

$$E(R_p) = R_f + \left[\frac{E(R_m)-R_f}{\sigma_m}\right]\sigma_P$$

where, $E(R_p)$ = expected return of portfolio along the CML.

R_f = risk-free rate of return.

$E(R_m)$ = Expected market rate of return.

σ_m = market risk.

σ_P = risk of portfolio along the CML.

$\left[\frac{E(R_m)-rf}{\sigma_m}\right]$ measures the slope of Capital Market Line.

Illustration

Let, the risk-free rate of return $(R_f) = 10\%$

Market rate of return $E(R_m) = 30\%$

risk (S.D.) of market portfolio $(\sigma_P) = 8\%$

In what proportion should an investor hold risk-free security and market portfolio to earn —

(i) 25% rate of return?

(ii) 30% rate of return?

(iii) 35% rate of return?

Solution

Let 'α' be the weight of market portfolio and (1 – α) the weight of risk-free security.

$\therefore E(R_p) = \alpha \,.\, E(R_m) + (1 - \alpha).R_f$

Now,

(i) $25\% = \alpha \,.\, 30\% + (1 - \alpha)10\%$

or, $25\% = \alpha 30\% + 10\% - \alpha 10\%$.

or, $25\% - 10\% = \alpha 30\% - \alpha 10\%$.

or, $15\% = \alpha 20\%$.

or, $\alpha = \frac{15}{20} = 0.75$ or, 75%.

$(1 - \alpha) = (1 - 0.75) = 0.25$ or, 25%.

∴ Proportion of funds to be invested in market portfolio is 75% and in risk-free security is 25% in order to earn 25% rate of return.

(ii) $30\% = \alpha E(R_m) + (1 - \alpha)R_f$

or, $30\% = \alpha 30\% + (1 - \alpha)\ 10\%$

or, $30\% = \alpha 30\% + 10\% - \alpha 10\%$.

or, $30\% = 10\% + \alpha 20\%$

or, $30\% - 10\% = \alpha 20\%$

or, $\alpha = \frac{20}{20} = 1$.

∴ Entire funds should be invested in market portfolio to earn 30% rate of retrun.

(iii) $35\% = \alpha 30\% + (1 - \alpha)\ 10\%$

or, $35\% = \alpha 30\% + 10\% - 10\% \alpha$.

or, $35\% - 10\% = \alpha 30\% - \alpha 10\%$

or, $25\% = \alpha 20\%$

or, $\alpha = \frac{25}{20} = 1.25$ or, 125%.

∴ 125% of funds should be invested in market portfolio and (–)25% of funds in risk-free security. In other words, instead of lending, one would borrow 25% of its funds at the risk-free rate of interest and invest 125% in market portfolio in order to earn 35% rate of return.

☐ "Excuse me Sir, I have one question — Are there any classification of risk in Portfolio management?"

• Well, please note the following :

Systematic Risk and Unsystematic Risk

Classification of Risks

We know that risk can be reduced by holding a large number of securities. In other words, a well-diversified portfolio can reduce risk. But a question arises, can diversification reduce risk completely? The answer is no. Then why? In order to understand the underlying causes we have to know the sources of risk, that is to say, the causes of variation in return. Risk can be classified according to underlying causes into two parts—Systematic risk and Unsystematic risk.

Systematic Risk

Systematic risks are caused by overall market related factors that affect all securities in the same direction. These factors include changes in government policies, change in corporate tax rate, credit policy of RBI, etc. This part of risk cannot be diversified away by holding a well-diversified portfolio.

Unsystematic Risk

The other part of risk, that is, unsystematic risk, is caused by industry or firm related factors. Such as, non-availability of raw materials, strike declared by workers, inefficiency of management, increase in competition etc. This part of risk can totally be eliminated by holding a well-diversified portfolio. Thus, total risk which is measured by using standard deviation has two parts—

Total risk = Systematic risk + Unsystematic risk.

The following figure illustrate that with the increase in the number of securities in the portfolio, the unsystematic risk is reduced but systematic risk remains unchanged :

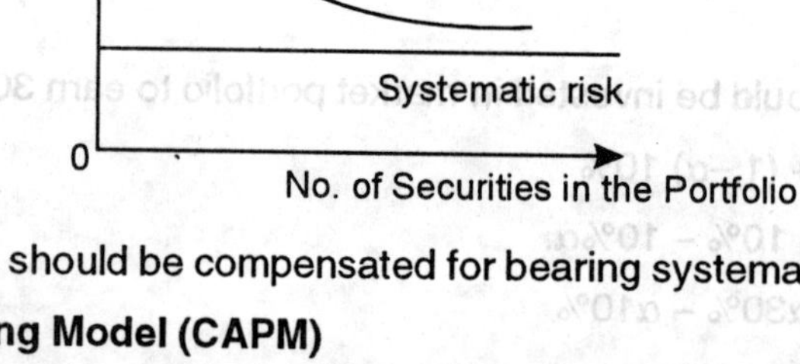

Therefore, investors should be compensated for bearing systematic risk.

Capital Asset Pricing Model (CAPM)

Importance of Capital Asset Pricing Model

We have seen that risk has two parts—systematic risk and unsystematic risk. Diversification of unsystematic risk is possible by holding a well-diversified portfolio. But diversification cannot reduce systematic risk. Therefore, systematic risk has influence on the expected return of individual security. In other words, investors should be compensated by risk premium for assuming systematic risk.

Capital Asset Pricing Model (CAPM) is used to measure the systematic risk, risk premium and the resulting expected return of individual security.

The CAPM equation is :

$E(R_i) = R_f + [E(R_m) - R_f]b$

$E(R_i)$ = expected rate of return of security 'i'.

R_f = risk-free rate of return

$E(R_m)$ = expected market rate of return.

b = beta-coefficient which measures the systematic risk.

The CAPM is based on certain *assumptions* :

(i) The capital market is efficient which means that share prices reflect all relevant information.

(ii) Investors are risk-averse which means that they will take additional risk if they are compensated by additional return.

Assumptions of Capital Asset Pricing Model

(iii) Investors' decisions are based on single time period.

(iv) Risk-free rate of interest is used to lend or borrow by investors.

(v) All investors have homogeneous expectation about the expected risk and return of securities.

It is clear from the above equation that the expected rate of return of a security is equal to the risk-free rate of return plus the risk premium which is measured by $[E(R_m) - R_f]b$. The risk premium depends on the relative value of beta (b). Beta (b) measures the responsiveness of return of a security relating to any variation in return of market portfolio. It measures the systematic risk.

The following formula is used to measure the value of beta :

$$b_i = \frac{Cov(R_i, R_m)}{\sigma_m^2} = \frac{Cr(i,m).\sigma_m.\sigma_i}{\sigma_m.\sigma_m} = \frac{Cr(i,m).\sigma_i}{\sigma_m}$$

Thus, beta of a security is the product of that security's standard deviation and its correlation with the market portfolio divided by the standard deviation of market portfolio.

The beta value of each security can be used to calculate beta value of well diversified portfolio. The beta value of a portfolio is the weighted average of beta values of securities constituting portfolio. Thus,

$$b_P = W_1b_1 + W_2b_2 + W_3b_3 + ... + W_nb_n.$$

where, b_P is the beta of a portfolio of 'n' securities and $W_1, W_2, ..., W_n$ and $b_1, b_2, b_3, ..., b_n$ are weights and betas of securities constituting portfolio.

Security Market Line (SML)

We have seen that investors are compensated by risk premium for taking systematic risk. The CAPM is used to measure risk-adjusted rate of return of any security or portfolio. In other words, CAPM expresses systematic risk-

Importance of SML

return relationship of portfolio or individual security. The Security Market Line (SML) is the graphical presentation of CAPM. The following figure shows the SML which depicts the systematic risk-return relationship. The beta (b) value is plotted along the x axis and return along the y axis. When value of b is zero, return is equal to risk-free rate of return (R_f). With the increase in the value of 'b', return increases and when value of 'b' becomes '1', return becomes equal to market rate of return (R_m). The value of 'b' determines the premium to be added to the risk free rate of return to determine the overall rate of return.

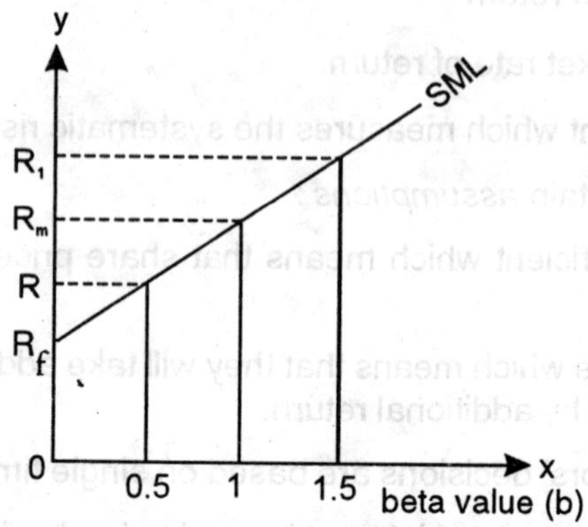

Problem

As an investment manager you are given the following information :

Investment in equity shares of	Initial price	Dividends	Market Price at the end of the year	Beta risk factor
	Rs.	Rs.	Rs.	
A. Infar India Ltd.	28	4	60	0.7
Godrej India Ltd.	42	4	75	0.6
Exxon Ltd.	62	4	145	0.5
B. Government Bonds	600	96	610	0.99

Risk-free return may be considered at 16%.

You are required to calculate :

(i) Expected rate of return of each security in the portfolio using Capital Asset Pricing Model.

(ii) Average expected return of the portfolio. **[C.U., M.Com.]**

Solution

(a) We know that rate of return of each security can be calculated by using Capital Asset Pricing Model (CAPM) in the following way :

$$R_P = R_f + (R_m - R_f)b$$

where, R_P = return of individual security

R_f = risk-free rate of return

b = beta of individual security

Calculation of market rate of return :

Type of Investment	Initial Price (P_0) Rs.	Dividend Rs.	Market Price at the end of one year (P_1) Rs.	Capital Gain ($P_1 - P_0$)
Infar India Ltd.	28	4	60	32
Godrej India Ltd.	42	4	75	33
Exxon Ltd.	62	4	145	83
Govt. Bond	600	96	610	10
	732	108		158

$$\therefore \text{Market rate of return} = \frac{\text{Total Dividend} + \text{Total Capital Gain}}{\text{Total initial price of shares}} \times 100$$

$$= \frac{108 + 158}{732} \times 100$$

$= 36.34\%$

(i) Expected rate of return using CAPM :

Infar India Ltd. : $16\% + (36.34\% - 16\%) \times 0.7 = 30.24\%$

Godrej India Ltd. : $16\% + (36.34\% - 16\%) \times 0.6 = 28.20\%$

Exxon Ltd. : $16\% + (36.34\% - 16\%) \times 0.5 = 26.17\%$

Govt. Bond : $16\% + (36.34\% - 16\%) \times 0.99 = 36.14\%$

$$\text{(ii) Portfolio beta} = \frac{(0.7 + 0.6 + 0.5 + 0.99)}{4}$$

$= 0.6975$

Portfolio return $= 16\% + (36.34\% - 16\%) \times 0.6975 = 30.187\%$

Problem

(a) You, as a portfolio manager of SUN F & Co. Mutual Fund, are considering purchasing the equity shares of LML Co. Ltd. The current price per share is Rs. 30. You expect the dividend per share one year hence to be Rs. 3.00. You expect the price per share of the LML Co. Ltd. for a year hence to have the following probability distribution :

Price for a year hence	Probabilities
Rs. 30	0.4
Rs. 33	0.4
Rs. 36	0.2

What is the expected return if Rs. 3,000 is invested in shares of the company?

(b) The risk-free return is 8% and the return on market portfolio is 12%.

If the required return on a share is 15%, what is its beta? **[C.U., M.Com.]**

Solution

(a) Current market price (P_0) = Rs. 30.00

Dividend per share after one year (D) = Rs. 3.00

Average market price after one year (P_1) = Rs. 30 × 0.4 + Rs. 33 × 0.4 + Rs. 36 × 0.2

= Rs. 32.4

$$\text{Expected rate of return on 3,000 shares} = \frac{\text{Rs. } 3.00 + (\text{Rs. } 32.4 - \text{Rs. } 30)}{30} \times 3{,}000$$

= Rs. 540

(b) We know that, according to CAPM, required rate of return (R) = $R_f + (R_m - R_f)b$

where, R_f = risk-free rate of return

R_m = market rate of return

b = measure of systematic risk

here, R_f = 8%

R_m = 12%

R = 15%

b = ?

15% = 8% + (12% – 8%) × b

or, 15% = 8% + 4% × b

or, 15% – 8% = 4%b

or, 7% = 4%b

or, $b = \frac{7\%}{4\%} = 1.75$

∴ b = 1.75

Problem

Mr. X invests 60% of his fund in stock A and 40% in stock B. Standard deviation of expected return on A is 10 and that on B is 20. Estimate the variance of the portfolio return when returns from the two stocks are perfectly negatively correlated.

What should be the proportions of fund to be invested by him in A and B, so that the portfolio risk is completely eliminated? **[C.U., M.Com.]**

Solution

	Security	
	A	B
Standard deviation (σ)	10	20
Proportion of funds invested	60%	40%

Correlation coefficient (r) = –1

Portfolio variance (σ^2_P) = $W_A^2\sigma_A^2 + W_B^2\sigma_B^2 + 2\,W_A.W_B\,.\,r(A,B).\sigma_A\sigma_B$

where, W_A = proportion of fund invested in stock A = .60

W_B = proportion of fund invested in stock B = .40

r(A,B) = correlation between returns from stock A and stock B = –1

σ_A = S.D. of expected return on A = 10

σ_B = S.D. of expected return on B = 20

$$\therefore \sigma^2_P = (.6)^2(10)^2 + (.4)^2(20)^2 + 2\,(.6)(.4)(-1)(10)(20)$$

$$= (.36)(100) + (.16)\,(400) + (-96)$$

$$= 36 + 64 - 96$$

$$= 4$$

Let, α be the proportion of fund invested in security A. Therefore, $(1-\alpha)$ is the proportion of fund invested in security B, which will reduce risk to zero.

$$\therefore \sigma^2_P = \alpha^2\sigma^2_A + (1-\alpha)^2\sigma^2_B + 2\,(\alpha)\,(1-\alpha).\,r(A,B).\,\sigma_A.\sigma_B$$

$$= \alpha^2\sigma^2_A + (1-2\alpha+\alpha^2)\sigma^2_B + 2\,(\alpha-\alpha^2).\,r(A,B).\,\sigma_A.\sigma_B$$

$$= \alpha^2\sigma^2_A + \sigma^2_B - 2\alpha\sigma^2_B + \alpha^2\sigma^2_B + 2\,\alpha\,r(A,B).\,\sigma_A.\sigma_B - 2\,\alpha^2\,r(A,B).\,\sigma_A.\sigma_B$$

differentiating with respect to weight.

$$\frac{\delta\sigma_P^2}{\delta\alpha} = 2\alpha\sigma^2_A + 0 - 2\sigma^2_B + 2\alpha\sigma^2_B + 2r(A,B)\,\sigma_A.\sigma_B - 2.2\alpha\,r(A,B).\,\sigma_A.\sigma_B$$

In order to reduce risk to zero

$$2\alpha\sigma^2_A - 2\sigma^2_B + 2\alpha\sigma^2_B + 2r(A,B)\,\sigma_A.\sigma_B - 4\alpha\,r(A,B).\,\sigma_A.\sigma_B = 0$$

or, $\alpha\,(2\sigma^2_A + 2\sigma^2_B - 4r(A,B).\,\sigma_A.\sigma_B) = 2\sigma^2_B - 2r(A,B)\,\sigma_A.\sigma_B$

or, $\alpha\,(\sigma^2_A + \sigma^2_B - 2r(A,B)\,\sigma_A.\sigma_B) = (\sigma^2_B - r(A,B).\,\sigma_A.\sigma_B)$

$$\text{or, } \alpha = \frac{\sigma_B^2 - r(A,B)\sigma_A\,\sigma_B}{\sigma_A^2 + \sigma_B^2 - 2r(A,B)\sigma_A\,\sigma_B}$$

$$\text{or, } \alpha = \frac{\sigma_B^2 - \text{Cov}(A,B)}{\sigma_A^2 + \sigma_B^2 - 2\,\text{Cov}(A,B)}$$

In this problem

σ_A = 10

σ_B = 20

Cov(A, B) = r (A, B) $\sigma_A.\sigma_B$

= (–1)(10)(20)

= –200

$$\therefore \alpha = \frac{(20)^2 - (-200)}{(10)^2 + (20)^2 - 2(-200)}$$

$$= \frac{400 + 200}{100 + 400 + 400}$$

$$= \frac{600}{900} = 0.67$$

$\therefore$ Proportion of funds to be invested in security B = $(1 - \alpha) = (1 - 0.67) = .33$

Investment of funds in this proportion will reduce risk to zero.

Problem

The Vice President (Finance) of a company is planning to invest surplus fund of Rs. 1,00,000 in the shares of A Ltd. and B Ltd. Shares of A Ltd. and B Ltd. are currently selling at Rs. 100 and Rs. 50 per share, respectively. Rupee return (dividend plus share price) of these two shares under possible business situation are :

Situation	Probability	Return	
		Shares of A Ltd. (Rs.)	Share of B Ltd. (Rs.)
High growth	0.3	110	75
Low growth	0.3	100	65
Stagnation	0.2	120	50
Recession	0.2	140	40

Calculate the expected return in (%) and standard deviation when :

(i) full amount is invested in shares of A Ltd.

(ii) full amount is invested in shares of B Ltd.

Also calculate expected return of the portfolio both in (%) and rupee term if 70% of the fund is invested in shares of A Ltd. and the rest is invested in shares of B Ltd.

[C.U., M.Com.]

Solution

Calculation of expected return in (%) and standard deviation when —

(i) **Full amount is invested in shares of A Ltd. :**

Calculation of return under different situation

	(%) return (A Ltd.)
High growth	$\left(\frac{110 - 100}{100}\right) \times 100 = 10\%$
Low growth	$\left(\frac{100 - 100}{100}\right) \times 100 = 0\%$

Stagnation $\left(\dfrac{120 - 100}{100}\right) \times 100 = 20\%$

Recession $\left(\dfrac{140 - 100}{100}\right) \times 100 = 40\%$

$\therefore$ Expected rate of return $[E(R)_A] = 10\% \times 0.3 + 20\% \times 0.2 + 40\% \times 0.2 = 15\%$

Standard deviation (σ)

$$= \sqrt{0.3 \times (10\% - 15\%)^2 + 0.3 \times (0\% - 15\%)^2 + 0.2 \times (20\% - 15\%)^2 + 0.2 \times (40\% - 15\%)^2}$$

$$= \sqrt{7.5\% + 67.5\% + 5\% + 125\%}$$

$$= \sqrt{205\%} = 14.318\%$$

(ii) **Full amount is invested in shares of B Ltd. :**

Calculation of return under different situation :

(%) Return (B Ltd.)

High growth $\left(\dfrac{75 - 50}{50}\right) \times 100 = 50\%$

Low growth $\left(\dfrac{65 - 50}{50}\right) \times 100 = 30\%$

Stagnation $\left(\dfrac{50 - 50}{50}\right) \times 100 = 0\%$

Recession $\left(\dfrac{40 - 50}{50}\right) \times 100 = [-]\ 20\%$

$\therefore$ Expected rate of return $[E(R_B)] = 0.3 \times 50\% + 0.3 \times 30\% + 0.2 \times 0\% + 0.2 \times (-20\%)$

$= 20\%$

Standard deviation (σ_B)

$$= \sqrt{0.3 \times (50\% - 20\%)^2 + 0.3 \times (30\% - 20\%)^2 + 0.2 \times (0\% - 20\%)^2 + 0.2 \times (-20\% - 20\%)^2}$$

$$= \sqrt{270\% + 30\% + 80\% + 320\%}$$

$$= \sqrt{700} = 26.458\%$$

If 70% invested in shares of A Ltd. and 30% invested in shares of B Ltd., the

Portfolio Return $(P_r) = 0.7 \times 15\% + 0.3 \times 20\% = 16.5\%$

Problem

A portfolio consists of five securities whose particulars are :

Name of the Company	Amount invested (Rs. in Crore)	Beta factor of security
Hindusthan Lever	100	1.30
ITC	50	1.20
Ranbaxy Labs	50	.90
TELCO	100	1.15
Hindusthan Petroleum	200	1.25
	500	

If the risk-free rate of return is 10% and the average market return is 15%, what is the expected return of the portfolio? **[C.U., M.Com.]**

Solution

Let us first calculate the rate of return of individual security.

Risk-free rate of return (R_f) = 10%

Average market rate of return (R_m) = 15%

Rate of return of security of

(1) Hindusthan lever = R_{HL} = $R_f + (R_m - R_f)b$

= 10% + (15% – 10%) × 1.3

= 10% + 6.5%

= 16.5%

(2) ITC = R_{ITC} = 10% + (15% – 10%) × 1.20

= 16%

(3) Ranbaxy Labs = R_{RL} = 10% + (15% – 10%) × 0.90

= 14.5%

(4) TELCO = R_{TC} = 10% + (15% – 10%) × 1.15

= 15.75%

(5) Hindusthan Petroleum = R_{HP} = 10% + (15% – 10%) × 1.25 = 16.25%

Calculation of expected return of Portfolio :

Company	Rate of Return	Proportions	Overall Return
Hindusthan lever	16.5%	.20	3 .30%
ITC	16%	.10	1 .60%
Ranbaxy Labs	14.5%	.10	1 .45%
TELCO	15.75%	.20	3 .15%
Hindusthan Petroleum	16.25%	.40	6 .5%
			16 .00%

∴ Expected Portfolio return = 16%

Problem

Return on market portfolio has a standard deviation of 20% and covariance between the returns on the market portfolio and that of security A is 800.

What is the beta of security A? **[C.U., M.Com.]**

Solution

Let, market rate of return = R_M

Return on security A = R_A

$Cov(R_M, R_A) = 800$

Standard deviation of return on market portfolio (σ_M) = 20%

$\therefore$ Variance $\sigma^2_M = 400$

We know that

$$\beta_A = \frac{Cov(R_M.R_A)}{Var(R_M)} = \frac{800}{400} = 2$$

$\therefore$ beta of security A = 2.

Problem

An investor has chosen a risky portfolio, P_3, with an expected return of 10% and standard deviation of 12%. The risk-free rate on security RF, is 6%. The investor invests 25% in security RF and 75% in P_3.

(i) What is the RF – P_3 portfolio's expected return?

(ii) What is the portfolio standard deviation?

(iii) Draw the Capital Market Line (CML) for portfolio P_3.

Solution

(i) Expected portfolio return = $W_{RF} \times R_{RF} + W_{P_3} \times E(R_{P_3})$.

where, W_{RF} = Weight of risk-free security

R_{RF} = risk-free rate of return

W_{P_3} = weight of risky portfolio P_3

$E(R_{P_3})$ = Expected rate of return of risky portfolio P_3

$\therefore$ Expected portfolio return $= 0.25 \times 6\% + 0.75 \times 10\%$

$= 1.5\% + 7.5\% = 9\%$

(ii) Capital Market Line (CML) equation

$$E(R_P) = R_{RF} + \left[\frac{E(R_{P3}) - R_{RF}}{\sigma_{P3}}\right]\sigma_P$$

$$\text{or, } 9\% = 6\% + \left[\frac{10\% - 6\%}{12\%}\right]\sigma_P$$

$$\text{or, } 3\% = 0.333\ \sigma_P$$

$$\text{or, } \sigma_P = \frac{3}{.333} = 9\%$$

(iii)

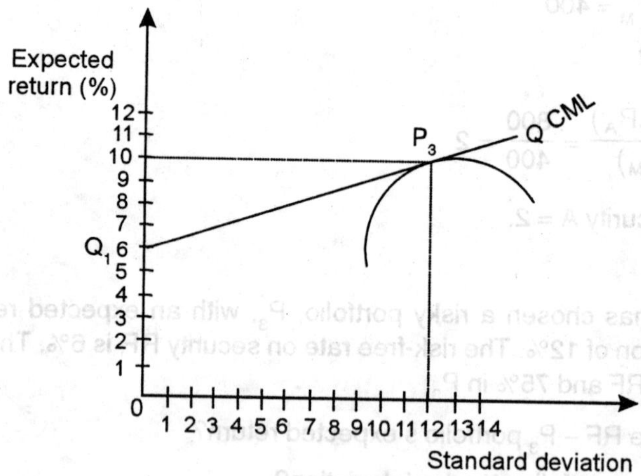

QUESTIONS

1. What do you mean by Portfolio Management? What is the importance of Portfolio Management?
2. What do you mean by the term 'risk' in the context of an investment?
3. Can diversification reduce the risk of investment? Explain.
4. Explain the nature of the Capital Market Line (CML).
   How does the CML differ from the Security Market Line (SML)?
5. Distinguish between systematic risk and unsystematic risk.
6. Explain the concept of an "efficient portfolio".
7. What is a market portfolio? How would you measure its expected return?
8. Explain in details the underlying philosophy of efficient frontier.
9. An investor has Rs. 1,000 to invest. The following information is available :

Return on market portfolio 15%

Risk of market portfolio 10%

Risk-free return 6%

You are required to plot the Capital Market Line and show that :

(i) a lending portfolio of Rs. 500 invested at the risk-free rate and Rs. 500 invested in market portfolio, and

(ii) a borrowing portfolio of Rs. 500 borrowed at risk-free rate and Rs. 1,500 invested in market portfolio lies on this line. **[C.U., M.Com.]**

10. Two securities, x and y, have the following mean returns and standard deviations :

Securities	Mean returns	Standard deviations
x	15%	8%
y	25%	14%

The correlation between the shares is –0.50.

(i) Estimate the proportions of x and y that make up the minimum variance portfolio.

(ii) What are the expected return and risk of the minimum variance portfolio?

(iii) If one invests 40% in x and 60% in y, what are the portfolio expected return and standard deviation? **[C.U., M.Com.]**

11. Securities x and y have the following characteristics :

Probabilities	Possible Return Outcomes (%) Security x	Security Y
0.1	30	30
0.2	20	20
0.4	(–) 10	(–) 20
0.2	50	40
0.1	10	70

A risk-averse investor realises that it is not possible to form a portfolio of the above two securities. Which security would then the investor select for investment and why? **[C.U., M.Com.]**

12. Given the following information about two stocks Alpha and Beta :

	Stocks Alpha	Beta
Expected Return (%)	20	15
Expected Standard Deviation (%)	5	4
Co-variance between the stocks	16	

(i) Is there any advantage for an investor to hold a combination of the above two stocks according to Markowitz Principle of Diversification?

(ii) Will your answer change if the co-variance between the two stocks Alpha and Beta is 12 in the above problem?

If you recommend the information of a portfolio in any of the above situations, then also determine the minimum variance portfolio for such situation(s) and portfolio risk and return for the minimum variance portfolio. **[C.U., M.Com.]**

13. A financial analyst is analysing two investment alternatives of y and z. The estimated rates of return and their chances of occurrence for the next year are given in the table below :

Probability of occurrence	Rates of Return	
	Y	Z
0.20	22%	5%
0.60	14%	15%
0.20	– 04%	25%

(i) Determine the expected rate of return, variance and standard deviation of each alternative.

(ii) Is Y comparatively riskless?

(iii) If the financial analyst wishes to invest half in y and another half in z, would it reduce risk? Explain with reasons. **[MBA (IGNOU)]**

14. Given expected return from security A to be 35% and that from security B to be 15% and standard deviation of such returns to be 40 and 20, respectively.

Determine the portfolio risk when coefficient of correlation, r_{AB}, is equal to –1 and 75% of the fund stands invested in security A and 25% in B.

Also determine the proportion of fund to be invested in A and B so as to reduce the portfolio risk to zero, other things remaining the same. **[C.U., M.Com.]**

PART V

DECISION ACCOUNTING

> "Be not a traitor in your thought. Be sincere; act according to your thought and you shall surely succeed."

24

COST-VOLUME-PROFIT ANALYSIS

● Good afternoon my dear students.

☐ "Good afternoon, Sir."

● Now I would like to discuss about the cost-volume-profit analysis. Cost-volume-profit analysis is a technique by which the relationship between cost-volume-profit is ascertained. It attempts to find out the impact or effect of change in price, cost, and volume on the profitability of the business. However, the following chart attempts to show the behaviour of the influence of change of price, volume and cost on the profit of the enterprise.

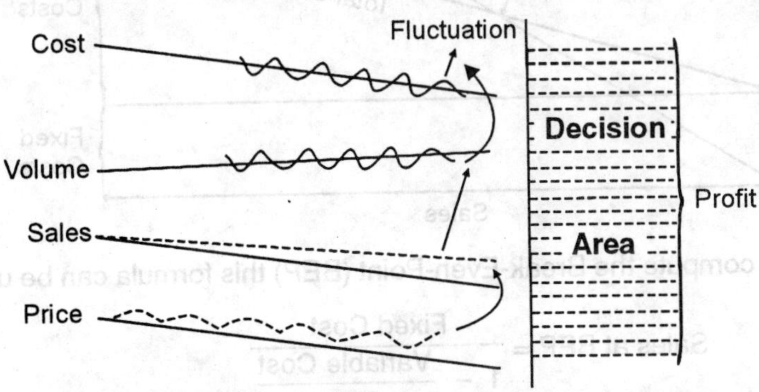

However, cost-volume-profit analysis helps management in arriving at its final decision. It should be noted in this connection and context that management decision itself can control overall activities of the cost-volume-profit area. 'Since costs are not inherently fixed or variable but acquire these characteristics principally as a result of managerial decisions, any method for determining how costs should vary with volume must look to the decisions and policies which control cost variations. For this reason it seems important to focus attention upon the need for planning and control of costs as an important factor underlying behaviour of cost with fluctuations in volume. Many companies already have standards and flexible budgets which provide the basic data from which to construct reliable measure of cost-volume relationships, where these are lacking it appears desirable to begin by establishing such standards in order that management may have the means to control cost with volume when it is desired to do so.'

Cost-Volume-Profit Analysis and Management Decision

I hope you have understood my lecture on cost-volume-profit analysis which aids management to take its decision on planning and control.

☐ "Sir, what is Break-Even-Analysis? Are there any fundamental differences between the Break-Even Analysis and Cost-Volume-Profit Analysis?"

● Well, you see, there is no fundamental difference between the two. The Cost-Volume Profit analysis is also termed Break-Even Analysis.

Break-Even Analysis is a technique which determines the equilibrium point of cost and revenue. Variations in the respective degree of cost and revenue have some impact on the area of the profit and loss of the business. The equilibrium point so indicated reveals 'no profit no loss' stage. The National Association of Accountants in their research report series 16-17-18 explains the break-even-point as : 'The break-even-point indicates the volume of sales which the company must obtain in order to cover its costs without profit.' However, it should be noted in this connection that it is one of the important devices that transmit management the relationship that exists among volume of output, cost and profit.

Definition of Break Even Analysis

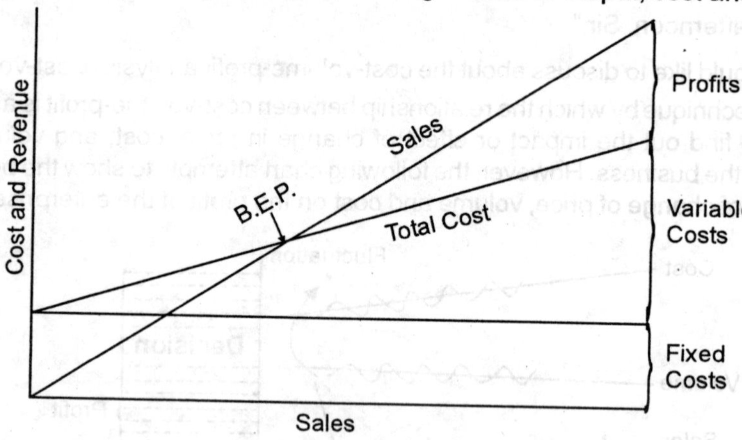

However, to compute the Break-Even-Point (BEP) this formula can be used :

Formulae of BEP

$$\text{Sales at BEP} = \frac{\text{Fixed Cost}}{1 - \dfrac{\text{Variable Cost}}{\text{Sales}}}$$

Illustratration

Fixed Costs Rs. 6,00,000, Variable Costs Rs. 10,00,000, Sales Rs. 20,00,000.

$$\text{BEP} = \frac{\text{Rs. } 6,00,000}{1 - \dfrac{\text{Rs. } 10,00,000}{\text{Rs. } 20,00,000}} = \frac{6,00,000}{1} \times \frac{2}{1} = \text{Rs. } 12,00,000$$

Check

	Rs.
Fixed Cost	6,00,000
Variable Cost (50% of Rs. 12,00,000)	6,00,000
	12,00,000

The above formula can be expressed in the following ways :

$$\text{Units Sales at BEP} = \frac{\text{Fixed Cost}}{\text{Sales price per unit} - \text{Variable Cost per unit}}$$

$$\text{Break Even Point of Sales} = \text{Fixed Overhead} \div \frac{\text{Contribution}}{\text{Sales}}$$

Well, it should be noted in this context that BEP concept can further be extended to find out sales at desired profit level. The formula will be :

$$\text{Sales at desired profit level} = \frac{\text{Fixed Costs} + \text{Desired Profit}^{*}}{\text{Marginal Contribution Rate}}$$

*(treating it an additional fixed cost)

Illustration

Fixed Cost for the coming year estimated at Rs. 7,50,000; Desired Profit Rs. 2,50,000; Variable Costs 80% of Sales. Marginal Contribution Rate 20%.

$$\text{Sales at desired profit level} = \frac{\text{Rs. } 7{,}50{,}000 + \text{Rs. } 2{,}50{,}000}{20\%} = \text{Rs. } 50{,}00{,}000$$

So, it is clear that sales revenue should be estimated at Rs. 50,00,000 in order to realise the desired profit for Rs. 2,50,000.

By the by, I have forgotten to tell you the other formula by which the level of sales at BEP can be calculated. Take down the formula :

$$\frac{\text{Fixed Costs} \times \text{Sales Value}}{\text{Sales Value} - \text{Variable Costs}}$$

Illustration

Fixed Cost estimated to produce 3,300 units, sales price at the rate of Rs. 20 per unit, is Rs. 11,055. Variable costs estimated at Rs. 45,150.

$$\text{BEP at Sales} = \frac{Fc \times Sv}{Sv - Vc} = \frac{\text{Rs. } 11{,}055 \times \text{Rs. } 66{,}000}{\text{Rs. } 66{,}000 - \text{Rs. } 45{,}150} = \text{Rs. } 35{,}000 \text{ (app.)}$$

Now I shall be glad to hear from you any point which is not clear to you.

☐ "I understand the different formulas to compute the BEP. But, Sir, the chart which you have given earlier is not clear to me. Please explain the same in detail."

● Well, now I will construct a diagram considering all of its aspects. Before that I would like to inform you about certain assumptions which are essential for constructing break-even diagram. Please note carefully :

1. Total cost can easily be divided into two categories : (a) Fixed Cost, and (b) Variable cost. If there is semi-variable cost, it can also be segregated into fixed cost and variable cost.
2. Both revenue and cost functions are linear.
3. The price of input and output should remain the same.
4. Productivity or operating efficiency of the factors of production must not be changed.
5. The product specification, state of technology, the process of production and methods of selling will remain the same.

6. There will be no change in the level of opening and closing inventory. Total number of units produced must be sold out, i.e., No. of units sold = No. of units produced.
7. The firm manufactures a single product. In case of a multi-product, the sales mix or proportion remains the same.
8. The pricing policy will not be changed in response to changes in volume, competition, market condition etc.

With these assumptions you can draw the BE chart on a graph paper. Output or volume or activity level can be plotted on X-axis, and costs and revenues (sales) are plotted on Y-axis.

First, draw the fixed cost (FC) line parallel to X-axis and variable cost (VC) line over FC line for the different levels of output. Then join the VC line with FC line at zero level of output, it will be the total cost (TC) line. Thereafter sales (revenue) line can be drawn by ascertaining the sales value for the different levels of output. The sales (revenue) line will make a 45º angle with the X-axis. Here it is important to observe that the point, where TC line intersects the sales line, is the BEP. You can easily ascertain the amount of output and sales by drawing two perpendicular lines to the X-axis and Y-axis, respectively.

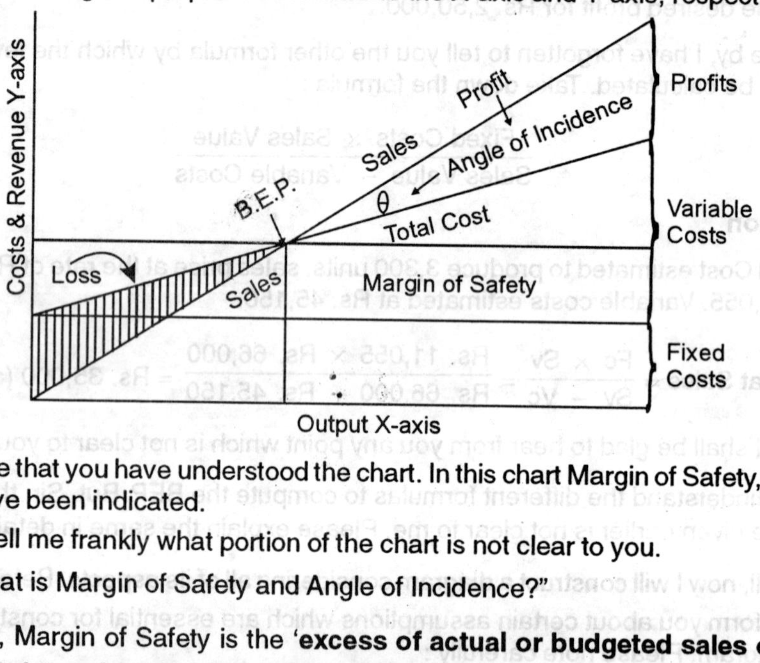

Now I hope that you have understood the chart. In this chart Margin of Safety, Angle of Incidence have been indicated.

Yes, you tell me frankly what portion of the chart is not clear to you.

☐ "Sir, what is Margin of Safety and Angle of Incidence?"

• You see, Margin of Safety is the '**excess of actual or budgeted sales over the break-even Sales volume**'. Owler and Brown described the margin of safety with the analogy of cushion. They are of opinion that margin of safety 'measures the "cushion" which exists against "a bad fall" in the sales.' It should be noted in this connection that finding out the proportion* of safety factor in a rupee will help, or, better to say, assist, the management to chalk out a plan and programme for its future course of action. Because 'the Margin of Safety indicates' the

Margin of Safety

*Suppose Sales figure is Rs. 4,00,000. Margin of Safety is Rs. 2,40,000.

The Proportion of safety factor $\left[\frac{\text{Rs.}\,2,40,000}{\text{Rs.}\,4,00,000}\right]$ is Re. 0.60 per Re. sales.

drop in sales volume which can take place before profits disappear. The trend in the ratio between sales value and break-even point also furnishes an indication of fundamental changes affecting the ability of the company to make a profit. However, it is important for management to know what the conditions are which have caused the change in this ratio before drawing conclusions or planning action. For example, the break-even-point varies up and down directly with the amount of the fixed costs and inversely with the margin per unit of selling price over variable cost.

Margin of Safety (MOS) can be computed with the help of the following formula :

$$P \div \frac{\text{Contribution}}{\text{Sales}}$$

P = Profit

Contribution = Sales – Variable Costs

= Fixed Cost + Profit = Sales × P/V Ratio

$$\text{or, MOS} = \frac{\text{Profit}}{\text{P / V Ratio}}$$

$$\text{Margin of Safety Ratio} = \frac{\text{Total Sales} - \text{B / E Sales}}{\text{Total Sales}} \times 100$$

I think, you have understood the concept of Margin of Safety.

☐ "Yes Sir."

☐ "But Sir, what is the Angle of Incidence?"

● You see, it is an angle arising from the intersection of the sales line and total cost lines (See the diagram) :

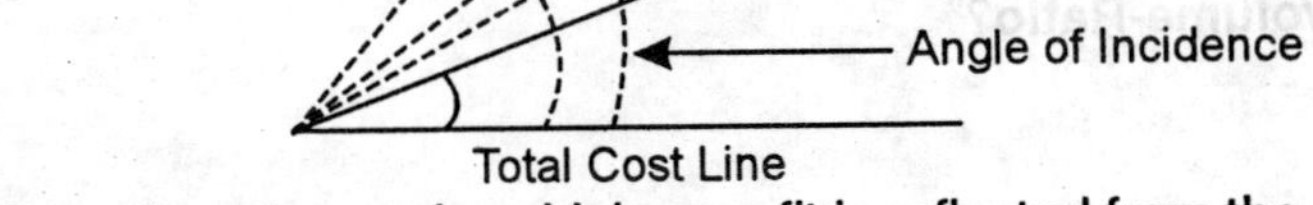

That a Company enjoys higher profit is reflected from the angle of incidence.

☐ "How is it Sir"?

● Large angle indicates higher profit and the small angle indicates lower profit.

I think you have understood all the aspects of Break-Even-Analysis.

☐ "Yes Sir."

☐ "Sir, we shall be obliged if you, please, give us some light on the various uses of break-even analysis in planning for profit."

● Your question is very interesting indeed. Well, I have discussed all the various uses in course of my lecture given earlier. However, I am referring your attention to the Journal of Finance, Vol XII, where Robbins and Foster summed up the different uses of Break-even analysis in profit-planning. You note the following which are collected from the said source :

'As an aid in budgeting they (financial analysts) show the pre-tax profits generated at various volume levels above the break-even point output base; management may then determine at a glance the expected profits relative to the break-even point at the budgeted volume and the effect of variations from this figure. A Safety Factor measure may be constructed by determining the relationship between actual production and the volume at break-even. Relative efficiency may be checked by comparing the dates during each year when break-even production is reached.

Use of Break-Even Analysis in Profit Planning

More importantly, however, when the ties that link break-even investigations with the chart form are cut and the traditional emphasis on determining the profit of no-return is lifted, the technique is broadened to cover a variety of volume-cost relationship. By directing attention to cost differentials rather than totals, it throws light on the **profitability of product lines**. Decisions to abandon items that show losses on the basis of total costs may be waived so long as they provide income balances over variable costs that contributed towards the recovery of fixed costs.

The variable-fixed cost break-down facilitates translating pricing problems affecting individual products into policy action. In appraising the advisability of introducting price cuts recommened by the sales department, for example, the availability of such data makes it easy to determine the increase in sales volume necessary to compensate for the reduction. With respect to the long-range view-point, this information is employed to gauge the influence of physical expansion on costs and profits. In these cases, the changes in plant facilities lead to shift in the levels of fixed costs which must be taken into account in the analysis. The technique also provides an **administrative tool** to control costs and to establish benchmarks in developing operating policies.'

I think the above discussions are sufficient for you to have a general understanding of the concept of Break-Even Analysis. I shall be happy to hear from you any points which have not been discussed so far. Yes?

☐ "Sir, what is **Profit-Volume-Ratio?**"

● Please note :

$$\text{Profit Volume Ratio} = \frac{\text{Contribution}}{\text{Sales}}$$

The above ratio can be re-stated as :

$$\frac{\text{Sales} - \text{Variable Costs}}{\text{Sales}}$$

$$\%\ \text{Profit Volume Ratio} = \frac{\text{Contribution}}{\text{Sales}} \times 100$$

$$\text{P/V Ratio} = 1 - \frac{\text{Variable Cost}}{\text{Sales}}$$

$$\text{or, } \frac{\text{Change in Contribution}}{\text{Change in Sales}}$$

$$\text{or, } \frac{\text{Change in Profit}}{\text{Change in Sales}}$$

Profit Volume Ratio

So, it is clear from the above that the P/V Ratio indicates a relationship between Contribution and Sales. It should be noted in this context that this profit/volume ratio aids management to take its vital decision as to planning for profit. If the ratio is high, it is definitely a sign of sound financial health of the business. The profitability of the business is reflected by this ratio.

☐ "Sir, how can the ratio be increased?"

• Well, it can be done in the following ways :

(1) By reducing the variable cost.

(2) By increasing prices.

However, a profit-volume chart is given below for your general understanding.

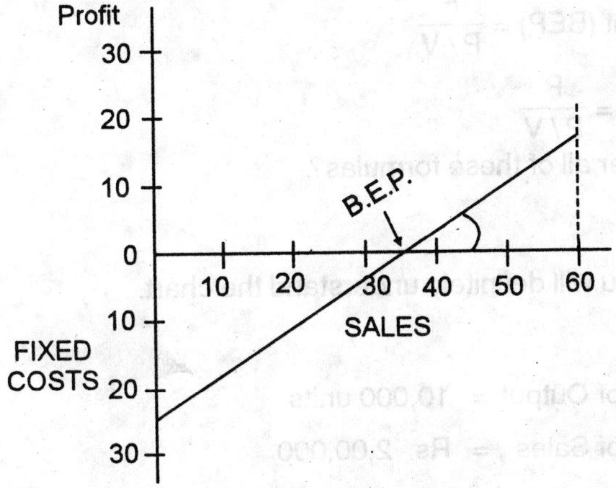

☐ "Sir, please explain the Profit/Volume ratio with the help of a few practical examples."

• Well, take down a problem which will help you to understand how variable cost for any volume of sales is determined.

Illustration

From the given information find out variable Costs of the Joy Bangla Product Limited :

Turnover Rs. 60,000

Profit/Volume Ratio 20%

Solution

$$\text{Profit/Volume Ratio} = \frac{S - V}{S}$$

$$\text{or, } \frac{20}{100} = \frac{60{,}000 - V}{60{,}000}$$

or, 100 V = 60,00,000 – 12,00,000

∴ V = 48,000

So the Variable Cost is Rs. 48,000.

Now I think that you have followed the Profit-Volume Chart.

Well, did you follow?

☐ "Really speaking, Sir, I could not follow the profit-volume chart. Please sir, construct a profit-volume chart with the help of some appropriate data".

● Well, before I go to explain the profit-volume chart let me recapitulate in a nutshell the whole discussion made earlier :

$$\text{Profit-Volume Ratio} = \frac{S - V}{S}$$

$$\text{Break-Even Point (BEP)} = \frac{F}{P/V}$$

$$\text{Margin of Safety} = \frac{P}{P/V}$$

Do you remember all of these formulas?

☐ "Yes, Sir."

● Then I hope you will definitely understand the chart.

Illustration

Present Volume of Output	=	10,000 units
Present Volume of Sales	=	Rs. 2,00,000
Fixed Costs	=	Rs. 50,000
Variable Costs	=	Rs. 1,20,000

From the figure given above, you are requested to construct a profit volume chart.

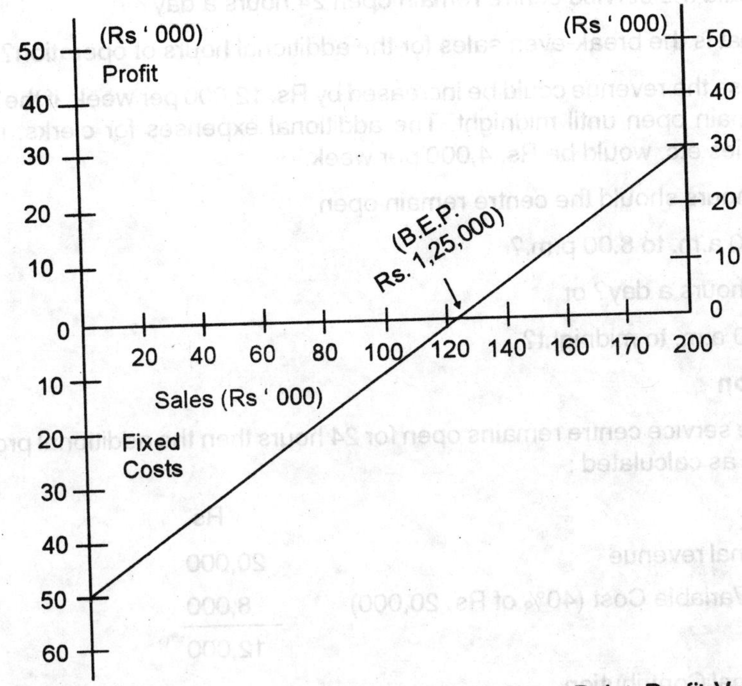

So, from the above information you can find out Break-Even-Point, Profit-Volume Ratio and Margin of Safety.

Profit-Volume Ratio $= \dfrac{S - V}{S} = \dfrac{\text{Rs. } 2{,}00{,}000 - \text{Rs. } 1{,}20{,}000}{\text{Rs. } 2{,}00{,}000} \times 100 = 40\%$

Margin of Safety $= P \div \dfrac{\text{Contribution}}{\text{Sales}}$ or $\dfrac{P}{P/V}$

$= 30{,}000 \div \dfrac{80{,}000}{2{,}00{,}000}$

$= \text{Rs. } 75{,}000$

Sales at BEP $= \dfrac{\text{F.C.}}{1 - \dfrac{VC}{S}} = \dfrac{50{,}000}{1 - \dfrac{1{,}20{,}000}{2{,}00{,}000}} = \text{Rs. } 1{,}25{,}000$

I hope now you have understood the profit volume chart.

☐ "Yes Sir".

- Now I am working out some more problems for your practice as well as better understanding; observe them carefully.

Problem

A service centre remains open from 8.00 a.m. to 8.00 p.m. for 7 days a week. The manager wants to keep it open for 24 hours a day. He estimates that additional revenue would be Rs. 20,000 per week. Additional expenses for clerks, insurance and other utilities will be Rs. 9,000 per week. Variable Cost is 40% of sales.

(i) Should the service centre remain open 24 hours a day?

(ii) What is the break-even sales for the additional hours of operation?

Suppose the revenue could be increased by Rs. 12,000 per week, if the service centre would remain open until midnight. The additional expenses for clerks, insurance and other utilities etc. would be Rs. 4,000 per week.

What hours should the centre remain open

(a) 8.00 a.m. to 8.00 p.m.?

(b) 24 hours a day? or

(c) 8.00 a.m. to midnight?

Solution

(i) If the service centre remains open for 24 hours then the additional profit/loss would be earned as calculated :

	Rs.
Additional revenue	20,000
Less : Variable Cost (40% of Rs. 20,000)	8,000
	12,000
Additional Contribution	
Less : Additional fixed cost	
(Expenses for clerks, insurance and other utilities etc.)	9,000
Additional Profit	3,000

Thus, the service centre should remain open 24 hours a day.

(ii) P/V Ratio $= \dfrac{\text{Additional Contribution}}{\text{Additional Sales}}$

$= \dfrac{12,000}{20,000} = \dfrac{3}{5}$

BEP Sales $= \text{Fixed cost} \times \dfrac{1}{\text{P/V Ratio}}$

$= \text{Rs } 9,000 \times \dfrac{1}{3/5}$

$= \text{Rs. } 9,000 \times \dfrac{5}{3}$

$= \text{Rs. } 15,000$

If the service centre remains open till midnight then the additional profit would be :

	Rs.
Additional Sales/revenue	12,000
Less : Variable Cost (40% of Rs. 12,000)	4,800
Additional Contribution	7,200
Less : Additional Fixed cost (Expenses for clerks, insurance and other utilities etc.)	4,000
Additional Profit	3,200

Thus, the manager may decide to keep open the service centre till midnight which will give Rs. 200 more profit.

Problem

If margin of safety is 40% of sales, find fixed cost when profit is Rs. 30,000.

Solution

$$\text{Margin of safety} = \frac{\text{Profit}}{\text{P / V Ratio}} = \frac{2}{5} \text{ i.e. } 40\%$$

$$\text{Break-Even Sales} = \frac{\text{Fixed Cost}}{\text{P/V Ratio}} = \frac{3}{5} \text{ (i.e. } 1 - 40\%)$$

$$\text{Now, } \frac{\text{Margin of Safety}}{\text{Break - Even Sales}} = \frac{\text{Profit}}{\text{P/V Ratio}} \times \frac{\text{P/V Ratio}}{\text{Fixed Cost}} = \frac{2}{5} \times \frac{5}{3}$$

By given condition we have

$$\frac{\text{Profit}}{\text{Fixed Cost}} = \frac{2}{3}$$

$$\text{or, } \frac{\text{Rs. } 30{,}000}{\text{Fixed Cost}} = \frac{2}{3}$$

or, Fixed Cost = Rs. 45,000

Now I am giving you a few typical problems on this topic.

Problem

M. Manufacturing Company, operating in a single region, contemplates expanding its activities by stages to cover the whole Bangla Desh. Market research and extensive cost investigation indicate that the following figures will be applicable to the first stage of expansion :

	Rs.
Additional Buildings required	5,00,000
Additional Equipment	8,45,000
Additional Annual Sales	6,00,000

Depreciations of Buildings and Equipment are to be made @5% and 10% per annum, respectively, by the Straight-Line Method. Fixed Overhead, other than depreciation, is estimated to increase by Rs. 10,500.

Present figures, before the expansion, are summarised as :

	Rs.
Annual Fixed Overheads	2,00,000
Annual Materials	2,00,000
Annual Wages and Variable Overheads	4,00,000
Annual Sales	9,00,000

The proposed scale of operations is expected to yield some minor economies in material purchase price for all of the output so that the proposed sales total will be reached if a further Rs. 1,20,000 annually is spent on materials. Similarly, other economies will result in a less than proportional increase in the wages and variable overheads, upon which annual outlay will be increased by Rs. 90,000.

Present the information represented by the above figures, graphically on a single Break-Even Chart. Extract from the chart summarised details of interest to the management.

[I.C.W.A., London, Adapted]

Solution

In this problem we can assume present capacity 60% increased to 100%. In this problem no figures as to the present and proposed capital employed have been supplied. So it is not possible to have a full analysis of Turnover and Return on capital employed ratio. However, Break-even chart to illustrate proposed and present trading position of M. Manufacturing Co. Ltd. is given below :

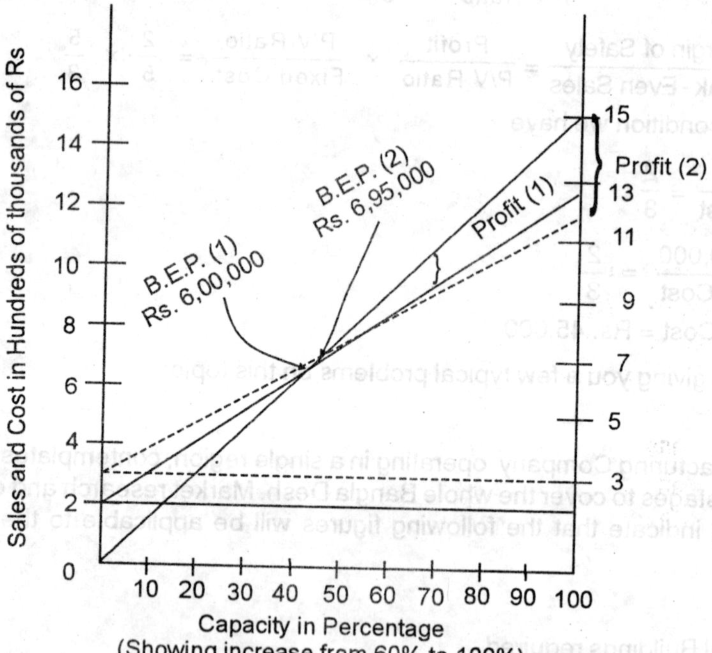

	Present	Proposed
Break-Event Point	Rs. 6,00,000	Rs. 6,95,000
Margin of Safety	Rs. 3,00,000	Rs. 8,05,000

	Present	Proposed
Margin of Safety per Re. of Sales	$33\frac{1}{3}$%	53.5%
Profit	Rs. 1,00,000	Rs. 3,70,000
Contribution Ratio	$33\frac{1}{3}$%	46%
(S – V) ÷ S		
Profit ÷ Sales %	$33\frac{1}{3}\% \times 33\frac{1}{3}$	53.5×46
	$= 11\frac{1}{9}\%$	= 24.6%

Problem

LBK Company manufactures a machine which is sold at Rs. 100. In the year 2006, monthly accounts showed the following figures :

Months	Unit made and Sold	Total Costs Rs.	Profits (Loss) Rs.
January	1,500	1,20,000	30,000
February	1,375	1,05,000	32,500
March	1,200	1,00,000	20,000
April	1,700	1,27,500	42,500
May	1,300	1,07,500	22,500
June	1,825	1,30,000	52,500
July	1,100	1,00,000	10,000
August	825	85,000	(2,500)
September	2,175	1,45,000	72,500
October	1,900	1,40,000	50,000
November	1,575	1,15,000	42,500
December	975	85,000	12,500

Present these figures graphically to show :

(a) the effect of volume on Profit;

(b) the fixed expenses of the company per month;

(c) the profit-volume ratio.

(d) the profits which it would be expected to earn in future months, assuming that the structure of the business is unaltered, if sales were :

(i) 1,000 Units

(ii) 1,400 Units

(iii) 2,000 Units.

[Adapted from the Advanced Cost and Management Accountancy Examination of London I.C.W.A.]

Solution

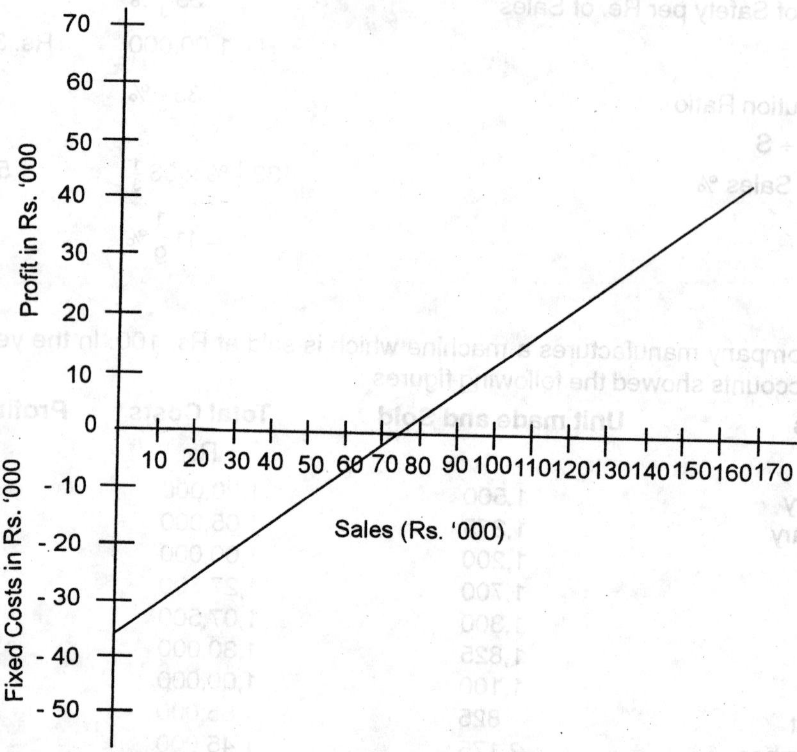

It appears that the 'August' result is exceptional. It should be discarded when considering the shape of contribution line. However, note below the workings :

	Units	Total costs.
		Rs.
High	2,175	1,45,000
Low	975	85,000
Difference	1,200	60,000

The difference is attributed to Variable Costs so that,

$$\frac{\text{Rs. } 60{,}000}{1{,}200 \text{ Units}} = \text{Rs. } 50 \text{ per Unit.}$$

Total Costs – Variable Costs = Fixed Costs.

2,175 × Rs. 50 = 1,08,750; Rs. 1,45,000 – Rs. 1,08,750 = Rs. 36,250.

975 × Rs. 50 = Rs. 48,750; Rs. 85,000 – Rs. 48,750 = Rs. 36,250

∴ Fixed Costs are Rs. 36,250

Now, since, at BEP, P = O

We have BEP of Sales = S – V = F.

Substituting and making n = number sold

$$100n - 50n = \text{Rs. } 36,250$$

$$50n = \text{Rs. } 36,250$$

$$n = 725$$

∴ BEP of Sales is Rs. 72,500.

Therefore, contribution line has been drawn from Rs. 36,250 on the 'y'-axis through the point Rs. 72,500 on the sales line.

(a) The effect of volume on profit can be seen in the general slope of the contribution line. As for example, when sales are at Rs. 2,00,000; Fixed Cost is Rs. 36,250 and the Profit is Rs. 62,750.

That is to say Rs. 36,250 + Rs. 62,750 = 99,000

But P + F = S – V

So that $S - V/S = \frac{99,000}{2,00,000} = .495$ which is equal to Tan 26º (app). $\text{Tan} = \frac{\text{Perpendicular}}{\text{Base}}$

(b) The fixed expenses of the Company are Rs. 36,250 or Rs. 3,000 per month.

(c) The Profit/Volume Ratio is 49.5%

(d) The profits would be :

In 1,000 Units = Rs. 14,000
In 1,400 Units = Rs. 34,000
In 2,000 Units = Rs. 62,750

Problem

The following figures relate to the Beta Bagh Manufacturing Co. :

	Rs.	Rs.
Annual Sales		7,00,000
Direct Materials	1,00,000	
Direct Wages	1,50,000	
Semi-Variable Overheads	1,20,000	
Fixed Overheads	80,000	
Fixed Administrative and Selling Costs	42,000	
Variable Selling and Distribution Costs	1,00,000	

Apart from the cost described as fixed overhead there is included in the semi-variable overhead a figure for fixed element amounting to Rs. 50,000.

On a single graph, display the Cost-Volume Relationship from each category of cost, and also for the total costs.

Plot the sales line on the graph. What is the Break-Even Point?

[Adapted from Advanced Cost and Management Accountancy Examination of London I.C.W.A.]

Solution

Chart to Display Cost-Volume Relationship

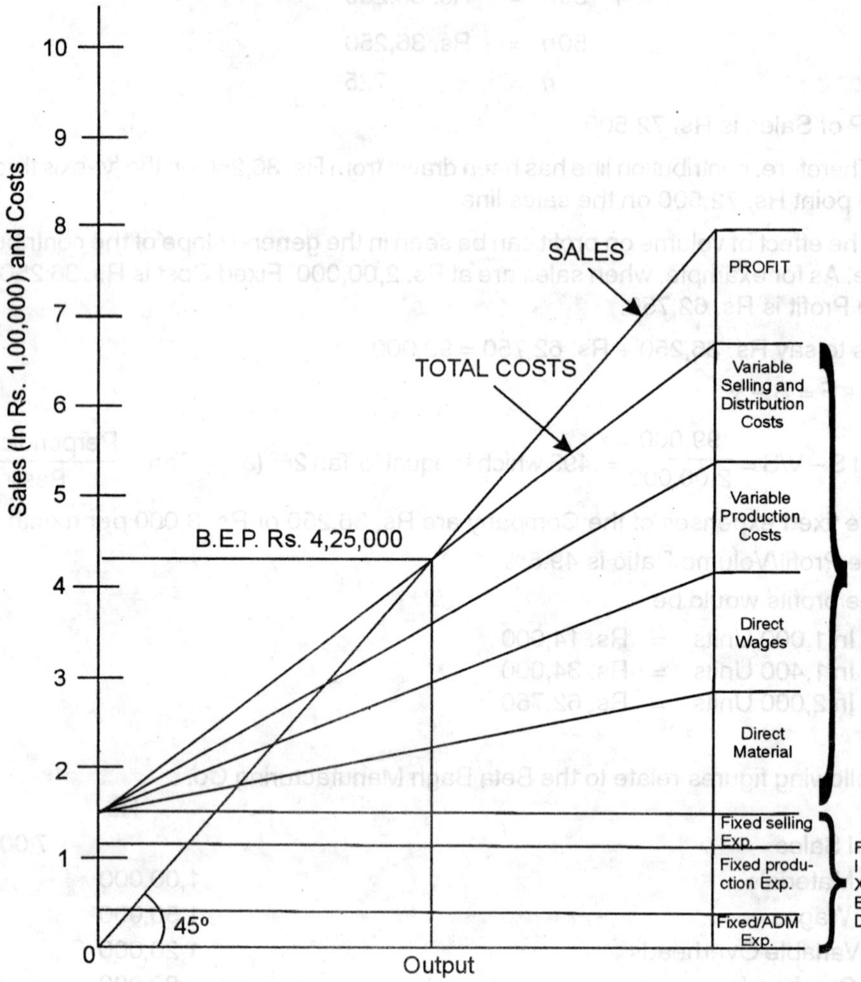

The Break Even Point at sales is Rs. 4,25,000

Check

BEP = Fixed Cost ÷ Contribution/Sales

= 1,70,000 ÷ 2,80,000/7,00,000

= 1,70,000 ÷ 28/70

= Rs. 4,25,000

Well, I hope you have followed the lecture on Cost-Volume-Profit Analysis.

☐ "Yes Sir, but Sir, we shall be obliged if you please explain to us cost-volume profit analysis with the help of a practical example considering the following points :

(i) The influence of Price changes on the Profit.

(ii) The influence of Volume changes on the Profit.

(iii) The influence of changes in Price and Volume on the Profit.

(iv) The influence of an increase or decrease in Variable Costs on the Proift.

(v) the influence of an increase or decrease in Fixed Costs on the Profit, and

(vi) The influence of all four factors, i.e.
Price, Volume, Variable and Fixed Cost on the Profit?"

• Well, you take down a problem which, I think, will be very helpful to understand all the said points mentioned by you. Here is your problem.

Problem

Normal Volume of Surprise Industries are given :

	Normal Volume
Units	2,00,000
	Rs.
Sales	4,00,000
Variable Costs	2,00,000
Marginal Income	2,00,000
Fixed Costs	1,60,000
Net Profit	40,000
Net Profit per Unit	0.20
Return on Investment	20%
Break-Even Point	3,20,000

In view of the above you are requested to report to the top management about the situation arising from :

(a) the proposal to increase or decrease 10% or 20% in the prices with the same volume.

(b) the proposal to increase or decrease 10% or 20% in the volume with the same price.

(c) the proposal of a 10% increase in price and 10% decrease in volume; a 20% increase in price and a 20% decrease in volume; a 10% increase in volume and a 10% reduction in price; a 20% increase in volume and a price reduction of 20%.

(d) the proposal of 10% and 20% increase or decrease in variable cost without changing sales price, volume, and fixed expenses.

(e) the proposal of keeping constant sales price, sales volume and variable expenses but increasing or decreasing 10% or 20% in fixed expenses.

(f) the proposal of the following composite change :

(i) 10% decrease or increase in price.

(ii) 10% decrease or increase in volume.

(iii) 4% decrease or increase in variable costs.

(iv) 5% decrease or increase in fixed costs.

Solution

(a) The Effect of Changes in Prices on Profit (Net)

	% Increase		% Decrease	
	10%	20%	10%	20%
Units	2,00,000	2,00,000	2,00,000	2,00,000
	Rs.	Rs.	Rs.	Rs.
Sales	4,40,000	4,80,000	3,60,000	3,20,000
Variable Cost	2,00,000	2,00,000	2,00,000	2,00,000
Marginal Income	2,40,000	2,80,000	1,60,000	1,20,000
Fixed Cost	1,60,000	1,60,000	1,60,000	1,60,000
Net Proift/Loss	80,000	1,20,000	—	(40,000)
Net Profit/Loss Per Unit	0.40	0.60	—	(0.20)
%Change in Profit	+ 100%	200%	– 100%	– 200%
Return on Investment	40%	60%	0%	– 20%
Break-Even Point	2,93,333	2,74,286	3,60,000	4,26,667

(b) The Effect of Changes in Volume on Profit (Net)

	% Increase		% Decrease	
	10%	20%	10%	20%
Units	2,20,000	2,40,000	1,80,000	1,60,000
	Rs.	Rs.	Rs.	Rs.
Sales	4,40,000	4,80,000	3,60,000	3,20,000
Variable Cost	2,20,000	2,40,000	1,80,000	1,60,000
Marginal Income	2,20,000	2,40,000	1,80,000	1,60,000
Fixed Cost	1,60,000	1,60,000	1,60,000	1,60,000
Net Proift/Loss	60,000	80,000	20,000	—
Net Profit/Loss Per Unit	0.273	0.33	0.11	—
%Change in Profit	+ 50%	100%	– 50%	– 100%
Return on Investment	30%	40%	10%	—
Break-Even Point	3,20,000	3,20,000	3,20,000	3,20,000

(c) The Effect of Price and Volume Changes on Profit (Net).

	% Increase in Volume		% Decrease in Volume	
	20%	10%	20%	10%
	Decrease in Price		Increase in Price	
	20%	10%	20%	10%
Units	2,40,000	2,20,000	1,60,000	1,80,000
	Rs.	Rs.	Rs.	Rs.
Sales	3,84,000	3,96,000	3,84,000	3,96,000
Variable Cost	2,40,000	2,20,000	1,60,000	1,80,000
Marginal Income	1,44,000	1,76,000	2,24,000	2,16,000
Fixed Cost	1,60,000	1,60,000	1,60,000	1,60,000
Net Proift/Loss	(16,000)	16,000	64,000	56,000
Net Profit/Loss Per Unit	(0.066)	0.0727	0.40	0.31
%Change in Profit/Loss	– 140%	– 60%	+ 60%	+ 40%
Return on Investment	8% (Loss)	8%	32%	28%
Break-Even Point	4,26,667	3,60,000	2,74,286	2,93,333

(d) The Effect of Increase of Decrease in Variable Costs on Profit (Net)

	% Increase		% Decrease	
	10%	20%	10%	20%
Units	2,00,000	2,00,000	2,00,000	2,00,000
	Rs.	Rs.	Rs.	Rs.
Sales	4,00,000	4,00,000	4,00,000	4,00,000
Variable Cost	2,20,000	2,40,000	1,80,000	1,60,000
Marginal Income	1,80,000	1,60,000	2,20,000	2,40,000
Fixed Cost	1,60,000	1,60,000	1,60,000	1,60,000
Net Proift/Loss	20,000	—	60,000	80,000
Net Profit/Loss Per Unit	0.10	—	0.30	0.40
%Change in Profit	– 50%	– 100%	+ 50%	+ 100%
Return on Investment	10%	—	30%	40%
Break-Even Point	3,55,555	4,00,000	2,90,909	2,66,666

(e) The Effect of Increase or Decrease in Fixed Costs on Profit (Net)

	% Increase		% Decrease	
	10%	20%	10%	20%
Units	2,00,000	2,00,000	2,00,000	2,00,000
	Rs.	Rs.	Rs.	Rs.
Sales	4,00,000	4,00,000	4,00,000	4,00,000
Variable Cost	2,00,000	2,00,000	2,00,000	2,00,000
Marginal Income	2,00,000	2,00,000	2,00,000	2,00,000
Fixed Cost	1,76,000	1,92,000	1,44,000	1,28,000
Net Proift/Loss	24,000	8,000	56,000	72,000
Net Profit/Loss Per Unit	0.12	0.04	0.28	0.36
%Change in Profit	– 40%	– 80%	+ 40%	+ 80%
Return on Investment	12%	4%	28%	36%
Break-Even Point	3,52,000	3,84,000	2,88,000	2,56,000

I hope, you have followed the above discussions. Is there any question please?

☐ "Sir, we employ Break-Even Analysis to indicate the likely profits and losses at different levels of sales activities. Isn't it so?"

● Yes, yes, then what?

☐ "Sir, what are the several factors which can invalidate the findings and how these factors can suitably be allowed for in the use of B.E.A."?

● You see, if you go through the discussions made earlier, you may get the answer to the question put by you. However, I explain here specifically the factors which can invalidate the findings indicated by the employment of B.E.A. Just notice the following factors :

Factors that Invalidate the BEA (Limitations)

a. A change in one item may influence change in another item. Take for an example, increase in the volume of sale may necessitate a decrease in sales price of a commodity.

b. In the case of a concern manufacturing a variety of products, the study of Break-Even-Analysis which is related to the total costs and sales of a concern, may not be explanatory of position in regard to one product.

c. The B.E.A. does not pay due regard to the aspect of 'employment of capital'.

d. With the introduction of additional plant and machinery, the fixed costs may change at varying levels of activity.

However, to overcome the above factors allowances should be made as to the following :

a. The introduction of Budgetary Control system will help to understand the estimated future trend in production. Besides, the mechanism of market research system will help to ascertain market condition and demands of a product. Thus a decrease in the sales price of a product, which results in decrease in revenue, can be reflected in the B.E.A. chart.

Solution to Overcome the Problems

b. In case of concerns making variety of products, the B.E.A., by the use of profit graph, can be applied to various product mixes.

The situation can be illustrated as follows :

Fixed Costs Rs. 39,600

Case No.	P/V Ratio	Product Mix	P/V Ratio Weighted by Product Mix	Average P/V
Case 1 A	60%	1	60%	
B	20%	1	20%	$\frac{80\%}{2} = 40\%$
		2	80%	
Case 2 A	60%	3	180%	
B	20%	2	40%	$\frac{220\%}{5} = 44\%$
		5	220%	
Case 3 A	60%	2	120%	
B	20%	3	60%	$\frac{180\%}{5} = 36\%$
		5	180%	

The Break-Even Point in each case is ascertained as below :

Case Nos. / Formula	1	2	3	Comments
$\frac{\text{Fixed Cost}}{\text{P/V Ratio}}$	$\frac{\text{Rs. } 39,600}{40\%}$ = Rs. 99,000	$\frac{\text{Rs. } 39,600}{44\%}$ = Rs. 90,000	$\frac{\text{Rs. } 39,600}{36\%}$ = Rs. 1,10,000	It appears that the mix in case of Nos. 2,3, : 2 gives the lowest B.E.P.

c. Although generally the aspects of capital employed are not taken into account in the B.E.A. but the study of this aspect will help to understand the interaction of different ratios. This can be stated as :

$$\text{P/V} \times \frac{\text{Margin of Safety}}{\text{Sales}} = \frac{\text{Profit}}{\text{Sales}}$$

$$\text{and } \frac{\text{Profit}}{\text{Sales}} \times \frac{\text{Sales}}{\text{Capital Employed}} = \frac{\text{Profit}}{\text{Capital Employed}}$$

d. It may be possible to draw a fixed cost line on a B.E. Chart which is "stepped". It shows 'any increased fixed costs incurred at changing levels of activity'. So, it is, possible to get on the chart more than one break-even point and it is possible to justify at what point the gap between the sales and total cost lines is "at its maximum".

I hope, you have followed my lecture.

☐ "Yes, Sir, please work out a few practical problems."

● Well, please note below.

Problem

The following figures apply to a manufacturing co. :

	Rs.
Annual Sales at 100% effective capacity	12,00,000
Fixed Overhead	4,00,000
Total Variable Costs	6,00,000

It is proposed to increase capacity by the acquisition of 30% additional space and plant. One result will be to increase Fixed Overhead by Rs. 1,00,000 per annum.

Plot the foregoing on a single Break-Even Chart, and determine from the Chart at what capacity utilisation the same profits as before will be produced after the extensions have been made. **[Adapted from I.C.W.A. (Lond.) Final]**

Solution

Here at 100% capacity profit is Rs. 2,00,000

Contribution per percentage of capacity utilisation = Rs. 6,00,000 ÷ 100 = Rs. 6,000

Contribution (total) required to earn profit Rs. 2,00,000 after extension and after covering the Fixed Overhead Rs. 5,00,000 is Rs. 7,00,000.

$$\text{So the Capacity to be utilised} = \frac{\text{Rs. } 7{,}00{,}000}{6{,}000} = 116\frac{2}{3}\%$$

☐ "Sir, how figures for Rs. 7,00,000 and Rs. 5,000 are calculated?

● Well, note below :

Rs. 5,00,000 = Rs. 4,00,000 + Rs. 1,00,000 (as per information)

Rs. 7,00,000 = Rs. 5,00,000 + Rs. 2,00,000

Problem

Two businesses AB Ltd. and CD Ltd. sell same type of product in the same type of market. Their budgeted profit and loss account for the year ending 2006 are :

	AB Ltd.		CD Ltd.	
	Rs.	Rs.	Rs.	Rs.
Sales		1,50,000		1,50,000
Less : Variable Costs	1,20,000		1,00,000	
Fixed Costs	15,000	1,35,000	35,000	1,35,000
Net Profit Budgeted		15,000		15,000

You are required to :

(a) Calculate the Break-Even Point of each business, and

(b) State which business is likely to earn greater profit in condition of

(i) Heavy demand for the product.

(ii) Low demand for the product.

Give your reasons. **[Adapted from I.C.W.A. Lond., Inter]**

Solution

(a)

	AB Ltd.	CD Ltd.
P/V Ratio = $\frac{\text{Contribution}}{\text{Sales}} \times 100\%$ =	$\frac{1{,}50{,}000 - 1{,}20{,}000}{1{,}50{,}000} \times 100$	= $\frac{1{,}50{,}000 - 1{,}00{,}000}{1{,}50{,}000} \times 100$
	= 20%	= $33\frac{1}{3}\%$
Break-Even Sales (BS) × P/V Ratio Fixed Overhead (FO)	BS × 20% = 15,000	BS × $33\frac{1}{3}\%$ = 35,000
(BS) × P/V Ratio = (FO)	BS × $\frac{1}{5}$ = 15,000	BS × $\frac{1}{3}$ = 35,000
BS	$\frac{BS}{5}$ = 15,000	$\frac{BS}{3}$ = 35,000
	BS = 75,000	BS = 1,05,000

(b) (i) It appears from the above that the P/V Ratio in the case of CD Ltd. is higher than AB Ltd. and, hence, in the conditions of heavy demand for the product it will earn higher profit.

(ii) It appears that in the conditions of low demand for the product the profits of AB Ltd. will be higher than DC Ltd.

- I think you have followed all worked out problems.

I hope that you can solve any problem(s) on Cost-Volume-Profit Analysis, if you really understand all these worked out problem.

If you don't understand, please be frank with me; I will discuss again.

☐ "Sir! We have understood all those problems. We feel that we would be able to solve any problem."

● You please stand up what you want to say.

☐ "Sir, we have 20 minutes time left to this period of the class; give us a problem for class test which we can complete within 20 minutes."

● Thank you for your interest in the subject. Are you all agreed to work out a problem?

☐ "Yes Sir."

● Well take a problem. Please don't discuss with each other; and also don't copy from others.

Problem

From the following information find out—

1. Break-Even (Sales Value)
2. Break-Even (Units)
3. Calculation of Profit for Different Turnover.
4. Calculation of Turnover for Desired Profit.

Information

(a) Fixed Costs (F.C.) Rs. 8,00,000.

(b) Variable Cost (V.C.) Rs. 40 per unit.

(c) Selling Price (S.C.) Rs. 200 per unit.

(d) Sales turnover (St) Rs. 16,00,000.

(e) Budgeted Profit target, i.e., Desired Profit (DP) Rs. 6,00,000.

☐ "Thank you Sir. We are working out the problem."

Solution

1. **Break-Even (Sales Value)**

$$\frac{\text{F.C}}{1-\dfrac{\text{V.C.}}{\text{S.P}}} = \frac{\text{Rs. } 8,00,000}{1-\dfrac{\text{Rs. } 40}{\text{Rs. } 200}} = \frac{\text{Rs. } 8,00,000}{\dfrac{4}{5}} = \text{Rs. } 10,00,000$$

2. **Break-Even (Units)**

$$\frac{\text{F.C}}{\text{S.P} - \text{V.C.}} \text{ or, } \frac{\text{F.C.}}{\text{Contribution}} = \frac{\text{Rs. } 8,00,000}{\text{Rs. } 200 - \text{Rs. } 40} = \frac{\text{Rs. } 8,00,000}{\text{Rs. } 160} = 5,000 \text{ units}$$

3. Calculation of Profit for Different Turnover

$$\text{Contribution} = \text{St}\left(1 - \frac{\text{V.C.}}{\text{S.P.}}\right)$$

$$= \text{Rs. } 16{,}00{,}000\left(1 - \frac{\text{Rs. } 40}{\text{Rs. } 200}\right) = \text{Rs. } 16{,}00{,}000 \times \frac{4}{5} = \text{Rs. } 12{,}80{,}000$$

Profit = Contribution – F.C.

= Rs. 12,80,000 – Rs. 8,00,000

= Rs. 4,80,000

4. Calculation of Turnover for Desired Profit

$$\frac{\text{F.C.} + \text{D.P.}}{1 - \frac{\text{V.C.}}{\text{S.P.}}} = \frac{\text{Rs. } 8{,}00{,}000 + \text{Rs. } 6{,}00{,}000}{1 - \frac{\text{Rs. } 40}{\text{Rs. } 200}}$$

$$= \text{Rs. } 14{,}00{,}000 \times \frac{5}{4}$$

= 17,50,000 Turnover.

☐ "Sir, Are the answer correct?"

• Yes, Thank you all.

I will meet you tomorrow morning class.

Bye.

QUESTIONS

1. What is Cost-Volume Profit relationship? How it aids management in taking decision.
2. Explain the effects of Price Changes on the Break-Even Point.
3. What are the uses of Break-Even Analysis in Profit Planning?
4. Explain the following terms :
   (a) Profit-Volume Ratio (b) Angle of Incidence (c) Margin of Safety.
5. You wish to employ Break-Even Analysis to indicate likely profits and losses at different levels of sales activity, but you are aware of several factors which could invalidate your findings.
   What might these factors be and how could they be suitably allowed for in the use of B.E.A?
   [Advanced Cost and Management Accountancy, I.C.W.A., London]
6. (a) Explain P/V Ratio.
   (b) The Sales Turnover and Profit during two periods were :
   Period 1 Sales Rs. 20 lakhs—Profit Rs. 2 lakhs
   Period 2 Sales Rs. 30 lakhs—Profit Rs. 5 lakhs

Calculate :

(i) P/V Ratio.

(ii) The Sales required to earn a profit of Rs. 5 lakhs. **[I.C.W.A. (India) Inter]**

7. (a) Describe what do you understand by :

(i) Break-Even Chart

(ii) Break-Even Point.

(b) From the following particulars draw a Break-Even Chart and find out the Break-Even Point :

Variable Cost per Unit	Rs. 15
Fixed Expenses	Rs. 54,000
Selling price per unit	Rs. 20

(c) What should be the selling price per unit, if the Break-Even Point should be brought down to 6,000 units? **[I.C.W.A. India]**

8. Assuming that the Cost structure and Selling prices remain the same in periods I and II find out :

(a) Profit/Volume Ratio; (b) Break-Even Point for sales; (c) Profit when sales are Rs. 1,00,000; (d) Sales required to earn a profit of Rs. 20,000, and (e) Safety Margin in period II :

Period	Sales	Profit
	Rs.	Rs.
I	1,20,000	9,000
II	1,40,000	13,000

[C.A. Final, Management Accounting]

9. Explain the term 'Break-Event Point'. Give an example illustrating your answer. **[C.A. Final]**

10. What do you understand by the term 'Break-Even Point'? Mention the types of problems which an accountant expect to solve with the help of such analysis.

You are required to calculate the break-even point in the following case :

The Fixed Costs for the year are Rs. 80,000, Variable Cost per unit for the single product being made is Rs. 4.

Estimated sales for the period are value at Rs. 2,00,000. The number of units involved coincides with the expected volume of output. Each units sells at Rs. 20. **[C.A. Final]**

11. From the following data, work out :

(i) The Marginal (Differential) Cost

(ii) The Marginal Unit Cost.

(iii) Average costs at two levels of production :

	Production	
	10,000 Units	15,000 Units
	Rs.	Rs.
Fixed Expenses	20,000	20,000
Variable Expenses	30,000	45,000
Total Expenses	50,000	65,000

[C.A. Final]

12. Assuming that the cost structure and selling prices remain the same in periods I and II, find out :
    (a) Profit Volume Ratio;
    (b) Break-Even Point for sales;
    (c) Profit when sales are Rs. 1,00,000;
    (d) Sales required to earn a profit of Rs. 20,000; and
    (e) Safety Margin in period II.

Periods	Sales Rs.	Profit Rs.
I	1,20,000	9,000
II	1,40,000	13,000

[C.A. Final]

13. The budgeted results for A. Co. Ltd. include the following :

	Rs. in Lakhs	Variable Cost as % of Sale Value
Sales		
Product A	50.00	60%
Product B	40.00	50%
Product C	80.00	65%
Product D	30.00	80%
Product E	44.00	75%
Total	244.00	65.17%

Fixed overheads for the period Rs. 90.00 lakhs.

You are asked to (a) produce a statement showing the amount of loss expected, and (b) recommend a change in the sales volume of each product which will eliminate the expected loss, assuming that the sale of only one product can be increased at a time. **[Adapted from C.A. Final]**

14. The profits for 2006 are given together with expenses :

	2005	2006
	Rs.	Rs.
Materials Consumed	1,00,000	1,40,000
Wages	80,000	1,20,000
Overheads : Fixed	30,000	32,000
Variable	24,000	34,000
Net Profit	10,000	20,500

The wages rate was increased by 20% in 2006 than 2005. Similarly, materials price were higher by 10%. Sales prices were increased by 10% in 2006.

Analyse the causes of increase in profits in 2006. **[Adapted from C.A. Final]**

15. (a) What do you understand by Break-Even Analysis?

(b) From the following, find out :

(i) Profit Volume Ratio,

(ii) Break-Even Point,

(iii) Net Profit from the sales of Rs. 3,00,000, and;

(iv) Required sales for the Net Profit of Rs. 70,000.

Position of A Ltd. for the year	2006
	Rs.
Sales	2,00,000
Variable Overheads	1,50,000
Gross Profit	50,000
Fixed Overheads	15,000
Net Profit	8,000

[Adapted from M.Com., Agra]

16. (a) "The effect of a price reduction is always to reduce the P/V Ratio, to raise the break-even point and to shorten the margin of safety".

—Explain and illustrate by a numerical example.

(b) Mr. X manufactures and sells four products P_1, P_2, P_3 and P_4. He sells P_1 worth Rs. 20,000, P_2 worth Rs. 25,000, P_3 worth Rs. 10,000, and P_4 worth Rs. 5,000 every month. His total fixed cost per month is Rs. 14,700. The variable costs are : on P_1— 60%, on P_2 — 68%, P_3— 80% and P_4— 40%.

Mr. X, being basically a non-commerce graduate, wonders at what combined sales volume does he really start earning profit.

You are asked to help him in arriving at such a sales volume.

(c) If margin of safety is 40% of sales find out the amount of fixed costs where profit is Rs. 25,000. **[C.U., M.Com.]**

17. (a) A manufacturing firm sells its product at Rs. 200 per unit. Variable costs per unit is Rs. 75 and total fixed cost is Rs. 20,00,000 per annum. Based on the above the budgeted profit for the next year is fixed at Rs. 10,00,000. However, market survey suggests that sales may be increased by reducing the selling price and recommends the following three alternatives.

Suggest the most profitable alternative clearly showing the profits of all the alternatives :

	Reduction in Selling Price	Increase in Sales
Alternative I	5%	10%
Alternative II	10%	20%
Alternative III	15%	25%

(b) A company incurs a loss of Rs. 10 per unit when it sells 10,000 units @ Rs. 25 per unit. However, it can earn a profit of Rs. 8 per unit if it sells 25,000 units at the same selling price.

Calculate the break-even sales. **[C.U., M.Com.]**

25

CAPITAL EXPENDITURE DECISION
(INVESTMENT DECISION)

• Good afternoon to my dear students.

☐ "Good afternoon Sir."

• How are you enjoying my lecture? Do you like any further clarification for your better understanding?

☐ No Sir, not at all, it is quite understandable. Please proceed to the next topic.

• Well now I am to discuss different aspects of Capital Expenditure Decision. i.e., Investment decision.

It is one of the crucial decisions a firm has to take. The other name of capital expenditure decision is capital budgeting decision. The financial managers have to decide how the funds they have raised could be invested in assets from which benefits are expected to derive in future. The growth and survival of a business require expansion and replacement of assets at periodical intervals—capital expenditure decision deals with this crucial aspect.

The capital expenditure can be defined as an expenditure to be incurred in capital assets or any other areas from which benefits are expected to be derived in future. For example, investment in plant and equipment, research and development, major advertising campaign etc.

Following are the essential features of capital expenditure :

Features of Capital Expenditure

1. Capital expenditure requires huge amount of funds as against revenue expenditure.
2. The benefits from capital expenditure are expected to derive in the years to come.
3. It involves greater amount of risk, as future is uncertain.
4. Capital expenditure decision is to be taken with prudence and judicious application of mind on the part of the management to avoid possible reversal of that expenditure which may entail heavy cost burden to the firm.

The different types of capital expenditure are shown in the following diagram :

Types of Capital Expenditure Projects :

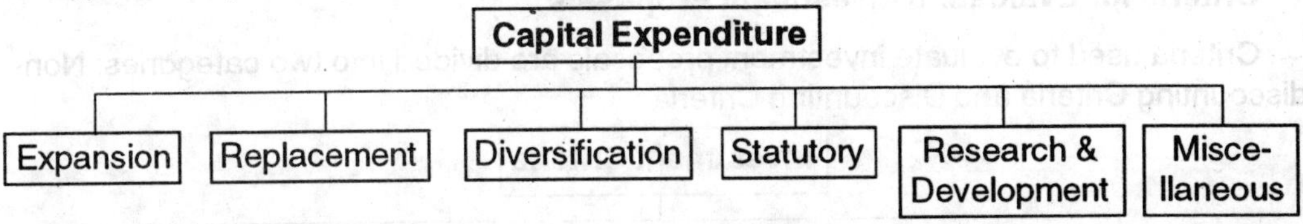

Expansion Project

Expansion projects are taken up by the growing firms for the purpose of expansion of fixed assets base so that its capacity is increased.

Replacement Project

Replacement of fixed assets after the expiry of useful lives or any other reasons is required for the purpose of continuing the firm's normal operation. The objective is to improve quality and quantity at reduced cost.

Diversification Project

Diversification projects are taken up for the purpose of diversifying operation. This involves investment in a completely new area of business for producing new products or providing services. Diversification is required in the competitive market for survival.

Statutory Project

Statutory Investment Projects are taken up to comply with any statutory requirement. For example, investment in pollution control equipment, fire fightings equipment etc.

Research and Development Project

Research and development activities also require huge investment, particularly in knowledge-intensive industries. Thus, research and development projects should be carefully analysed.

Miscellaneous Projects

Interior decoration, education and training etc.

There are two types of investment decision :

Types of Investment Decision

(i) Accept/Reject decision.

(ii) Mutually exclusive decision.

(i) Accept/Reject Decision

When investment proposals are independent of each other, the selection of one proposal will not lead to the rejection of the other. Each proposal is evaluated separately by using a particular investment criterion and thereafter either accepted or rejected. For example, if Net Present Value Method is used to evaluate independent proposal, it will be accepted if NPV ≥ O and will be rejected if NPV < O. Again, if Interal Rate of Return (IRR) Method is used, a project will be accepted if IRR > cost of capital (K_0) and will be rejected if IRR < K_0.

(ii) Mutually Exclusive Decision

When investment proposals are such that the selection of one proposal leads to the rejection of others, the investment decision is called mutually exclusive decision. When projects are mutually exclusive, they should be ranked by using any investment criterion to select the best one.

Criteria for Evaluating Investment Proposals

Criteria used to evaluate investment proposals are divided into two categories. Non-discounting Criteria and Discounting Criteria :

Investment Criteria

Non-discounting Criteria	Discounting Criteria
(A) Accounting Rate of Return (ARR)/ Profitability	(C) Net Present Value (NPV)
	(D) Profitability Index (PI)
(B) Pay-back Period	(E) Internal Rate of Return (IRR)

Before I go on to explain profitability, I would like to put you one question. You, please tell me, who is by far the best among Mr. A, Mr. B and Mr. C?

☐ "Mr. A, Sir".

☐ "Mr. C, Sir".

● You see, it is not possible to tell who is the best, until and unless different data as to their different activities are supplied to you. Take for an example, they all are students. They have secured 20 marks, 25 marks and 30 marks, respectively. In this stage also you cannot tell who has secured the highest marks; whether they have secured all these marks out of 50 or 100 or 150. If you express the relationship between the marks obtained and the total marks of the subject, then you can pass your judgement, only after comparing all these relationships so drawn—who is by far the best?

Origin of the Concept of Profitability

Similarly, in business too, you cannot comment on the performance of any company if you do not prepare a Profitability Statement. You are to prepare the profitability statement after expressing the relationship between profit earned and capital employed in the business in terms of percentage. However, the term 'profitability' bears an important meaning in Financial Cost and Management Accountancy. It may be described as a yardstick of Industrial or Business performance. It is a relative term and is concerned with the 'key factor' of the business, besides change in the capital structure of the business as well as design and volume of production, adoption of new product line, selling price, replacement and management policy of the business; as indicated earlier; a relative concept which regulates and controls management policy and decision. However, profitability can be expressed in the following ways :

Profitability and Management Decision

☐ "Sir, what are the Key Factors"?

● I would like to discuss this point after discussing the different aspects of profitability :

Aspects of Profitability

$$\% \text{ Profitability} = \frac{\text{Profit}}{\text{Capital Employed}} \times 100$$

$$\% \text{ Profitability} = \frac{\text{Sales Revenue} - \text{Cost}}{\text{Capital Employed}} \times 100$$

Profitability $\left[\frac{\text{Profit}}{\text{Capital Employed}}\right]$ is the product of two aspects of the activities of the business — (i) Margin on Sales, and (ii) Turnover of Capital Rate.

Profitability = Margin on Sale × Rate of Capital Turnover.

$$\text{Margin on Sale} = \frac{\text{Profit}}{\text{Sales}}$$

$$\text{Rate of Capital Turnover} = \frac{\text{Sales}}{\text{Capital Employed}}$$

$$\text{Profitability} = \frac{\text{Profit}}{\text{Sales}} \times \frac{\text{Sales}}{\text{Capital Employed}}$$

The whole point can be re-written in the following ways :

$$\% \text{ Profitability} = \frac{\text{Profit}}{\text{Capital Employed}} \times 100 \qquad \text{(i)}$$

$$\% \text{ Profitability} = \left[\frac{\text{Profit}}{\text{Sales}} \times \frac{\text{Sales}}{\text{Capital Employed}}\right] \times 100 \qquad \text{(ii)}$$

Profitability = Margin on Sales × Turnover of Capital Rate (iii)

No I think that the whole thing will be clear if you consider the followings data (Capital Employed Rs. 5,000. Net Sales Rs. 10,000 Profit Rs. 1,000).

$$\% \text{ Profitability} = \frac{1{,}000}{5{,}000} \times 100 = 20\% \qquad \text{(i)}$$

$$\% \text{ Profitability} = \left[\frac{1{,}000}{10{,}000} \times \frac{10{,}000}{5{,}000}\right] \times 100\% = 20\% \qquad \text{(ii)}$$

% Profitability = % Margin on Sales × Turnover Rate of Capital

$$= 10\% \times 2 = 20\% \qquad \text{(iii)}$$

I hope you have followed all the points discussed. If you find any difficulty, please tell me frankly.

☐ "No Sir, I cannot follow, please work out a Comparative Profitability Statement."

Example

X, Y and Z companies are doing same type of business. The respective figures for these three companies—as to their sales, cost of production and capital employed—are given below :

Companies	Sales	Cost	Capital Employed
	Rs.	Rs.	Rs.
X and Co.	10,000	9,000	5,000
Y and Co.	5,000	4,500	50,000
Z and Co.	1,00,000	99,500	50,000

From the information given above, prepare a Profitability Statement of the above three companies.

Solution

	Company X	Company Y	Company Z
	Rs.	Rs.	Rs.
Sales	10,000	5,000	1,00,000
Cost	9,000	4,500	99,500
Profits	1,000	500	500
Capital Employed	5,000	50,000	50,000
Profitability	20%	1%	1%
Margin on Sales	10%	10%	0.5%
Turnover of Capital Rate	2 times	0.1 times	2 times

From the situation it is clear that the profitability of X Company is higher than Y and Z Companies. Though the margin on sales in both the companies X and Y are equal, yet the turnover rate of Y Company is lower than all other companies. In view of the situations indicated above company X is preferred.

By the by, I have forgotten to tell you about the Key Factor. You better know the term 'Key', which indicates the most important and vital to anything. The production, sales and purchase budgets fail to achieve its target if it is disturbed by the Key Factor. That's why the Key Factor has been termed as 'Limiting or Principal Budget Factor.' Key Factors do not concentrate in one area of the business, say, sales, rather, it may exist in material, labour plant and management activities too. While preparing different types of budgets management should try to understand with the help of forecast and following the art of intuition whether the supply of labour may be affected by the introduction of computer and the possible industrial dispute and whether policy of installation or expansion of plant may be affected by the invention of automatic up to date economy plant as well as shortage of capital, whether the supply of material may be disturbed due to imposition of new licence or rules and regulations. Similarly, the management will change its decision following the market research on sales—whether a particular product should be produced or sold at a lower price or stop the production or plant for the introduction of new product line.

Key Factor

☐ "Sir, what is Planning for Profitability"?

● It should be noted in this connection that the management attempts to increase the profitability of the business. If it fails to achieve its target it must plan for the better and desired profitability. This is possible if the management check out the plan on the basis of the existing information and fact. The management is to keep its all eyes to the day-to-day and current performance and check it up with the desired performance or target. The variances should be scrutinised and the ways and means to overcome the adverse variance should be sought for. This is possible through the four phases of management science—Directing, Coordinating controlling,and Motivating.

Planning for Profitability

However, I was discussing with you about the key factor. Now, I hope, you have followed what key factors are.

☐ "Sir, what is the formula which measures the Profitability in terms of Key Factor?"

● You see, I explained you the formula of profitability at the outset of this chapter. Now I would like to explain you profitability in terms of the key-factor :

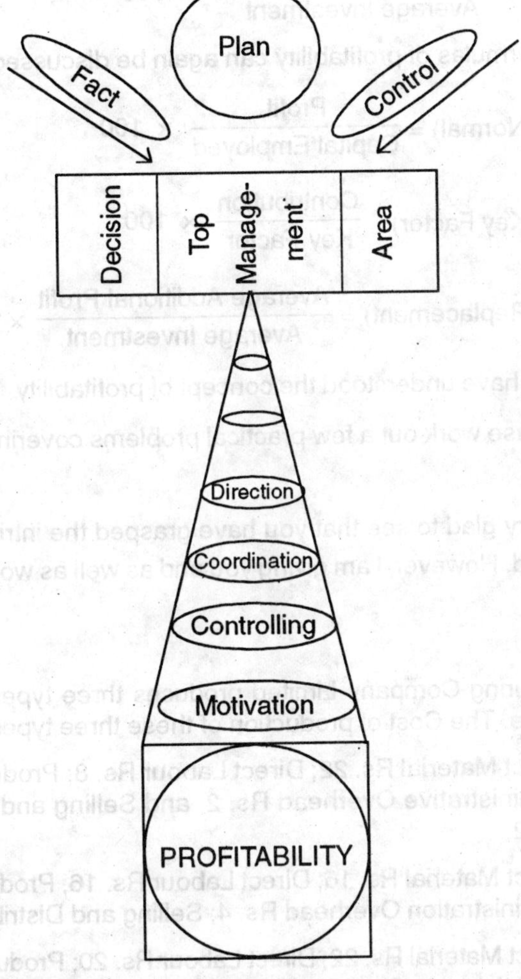

$$\text{Profitability} = \frac{\text{Contribution}}{\text{Key Factor}}, \text{ Total Contribution} = \text{Fixed Overhead} + \text{Profit.}$$

$$\%\ \text{Profitability} = \frac{\text{Contribution}}{\text{Key Factor}} \times 100$$

Different Formulae of Profitability

Besides expressing profitability in general and in terms of key factor, as indicated earlier, profitability can be expressed when the existing assets are to be replaced with a view to increasing output and reduction of cost. Then the formula will be :

$$\text{Profitability} = \frac{\text{Average Additional Profit}}{\text{Average Investment}^{*}}$$

*Average Investment

$$= \frac{\text{Cost of New Machine} - \text{Sale Value of Old Machine}}{2}$$

$$\% \text{ Profitability} = \frac{\text{Average Additional Profit}}{\text{Average Investment}} \times 100$$

Now different formulas of profitability can again be discussed :

$$\% \text{ Profitability (Normal)} = \frac{\text{Profit}}{\text{Capital Employed}} \times 100 \qquad (1)$$

$$\% \text{ Profitability (Key Factor)} = \frac{\text{Contribution}}{\text{Key Factor}} \times 100 \qquad (2)$$

$$\% \text{ Profitability (Replacement)} = \frac{\text{Average Additional Profit}}{\text{Average Investment}} \times 100 \qquad (3)$$

Now I think you have understood the concept of profitability.

☐ "Yes Sir. Please work out a few practical problems covering all the formulas given in this chapter."

• I am really very glad to see that you have grasped the intricate idea of profitability within a short period. However, I am giving you and as well as working out a few practical problems :

Problem

Hallo Manufacturing Company Limited produces three types of Cigarettes—Taste, Sweet and Pleasure. The Cost of production of these three types of cigarettes are :

Taste : Direct Material Rs. 22; Direct Labour Rs. 8; Production Overhead Rs. 4; Administrative Overhead Rs. 2, and Selling and Distribution Overhead Rs. 2.

Sweet : Direct Material Rs. 16; Direct Labour Rs. 16; Production Overhead Rs. 8; Administration Overhead Rs. 4; Selling and Distribution Overhead Rs. 2.

Pleasure : Direct Material Rs. 22; Direct Labour Rs. 20; Production Overhead Rs. 10; Administrative Overhead Rs. 6; Selling and Distribution Overhead Rs. 4.

Budgeted Output = Taste 140; Sweet 100, and Pleasure 50.

Selling Price = Taste Rs. 42; Sweet Rs. 52; Pleasure Rs. 72.

Note : Machines are in full capacity.

From the information given above, prepare a Profitability Statement.

Now you see, in this problem first of all you are to find out the total cost of each Brand and then you are to find out the margin on sale. I hope that you know what is margin on sale :

$$\text{Margin on Sale} = \frac{\text{Profit}}{\text{Sales}}$$

After that you are to find out the net profit per product and the net profit per day. After preparing all these indicated above, you will have to prepare a profitability statement, and you can comment which one of these three is more profitable.

However, I am working out the problem now.

Solution

Profitability Statement of Taste, Sweet and Pleasure

Explanation	**Budgeted Sales**	**140**	**100**	**50**
	Products	**Taste**	**Sweet**	**Pleasure**
Elements of Cost :		Rs.	Rs.	Rs.
Direct Material		22	16	22
Direct Labour		8	16	20
Prime Cost		30	32	42
Production Overhead		4	8	10
Production Cost		34	40	52
Administrative Overhead		2	4	6
Selling and Distribution Overhead		2	2	4
Total Cost		38	46	62
Selling Price		42	52	72
Net Profit per product		4	6	10
% Margin on Sale		9.5%	11.5%	13.9%
Daily Net Profit		560	600	500

From the situation indicated above, it is clear that the product 'Sweet' is found to be more profitable. But a little thinking over the matter will reflect that, if the management concentrates its attention to the product 'Pleasure' and plan for their large sale, it will be more profitable than the product Sweet. However, in this situation, product 'Sweet' is preferred. If in anticipation for a large sale on product 'Sweet', the management decides to bring down its selling price at Rs. 50, then the position of product 'Sweet' will be thus :

	Rs.
Selling Price	50
Total Cost as per Statement	46
Net Profit	4
% Margin on Sale	8%
Daily Net Profit	400

In this stage product 'Taste' will be preferred. However, for the steady progress of the organisation, the management should stick to the product 'Sweet' at Rs. 52.

Problem

A decision is to be taken relating to the possible introduction of a new product. There are three basic design versions of this product, aimed at different sections of the consumer market. The relevant figures are :

Variable Cost (per unit) :	Model I	Model II	Model III
	Rs.	Rs.	Rs.
Materials	1.54	1.22	0.86
Labour	1.06	0.95	0.58
Variable Overheads	0.40	0.33	0.31
	3.00	2.50	1.75
Selling Price (per unit)	4.25	3.50	2.50
Expected Sales Volume per month (units)	800	200	4,000
Capital Expenditure before Production can commence (financed by bank overdraft at 5% per annum)	800	3,000	4,000
Fixed Overheads per month attributable to new models, including depreciation on Capital Expenditure, but excluding interest	280	850	1,100

You are required to prepare a Schedule of Relative Profitablility, showing for each model the figures making up expected total cost per unit, the expected net profit per unit, and the percentage of net profit to selling price at the expected sales volume.

[Adapted from C.A. (Eng.) Final]

First of all, read this problem again and again. Next you see what is asked for. In this problem they ask you to prepare a profitability statement for Models I, II and III. Find out what is the 'contribution to fixed overhead'; then deduct total of fixed overhead from the contribution to fixed overhead to find out net profit.

Next, find out the percentage of Margin on Sale $\left[\frac{\text{Net Profit}}{\text{Sales}} \times 100\right]$

This principle will be applied to find out the profitability of all three models.

Solution

Profitability Statement

	Model I		Model II		Model III	
Expected Monthly Sales Volume	800 Units		2,000 Units		4,000 Units	
Expenses	Total	Cost per unit	Total	Cost per unit	Total	Cost per unit
Variable Costs :	Rs.	Rs.	Rs.	Rs.	Rs.	Rs.
Materials	1,232	1.54	2,440	1.22	3,440	0.86
Labour	848	1.06	1,900	0.95	2,320	0.58
Variable Overheads	320	0.40	660	0.33	1,240	0.31
Total Variable Cost	2,400	3.00	5,000	1.50	7,000	1.75
Sales	3,400	4.25	7,000	3.50	10,000	2.50
Contribution to Fixed Overheads	1,000	1.25	2,000	2.00	3,000	.075
Interest on Bank Overdraft	280	0.35	850	0.42	1,100	2.27
	40	0.05	150	0.07	200	0.05
Total Fixed Overhead	320	0.40	1,000	0.49	1,300	2.32
Net Profit	680	0.85	1,000	1.51	1,700	0.43
Percentage of net profit to selling price (% Margin on Sale)	20%		14.3%		17%	

In this Profitability Statement, Model I apparently is found to be more profitable. It appears that the management should concentrate its all attention to Model I. But the total net profit in case of Model III is higher. The margin on sale in Model III is lower in comparison to Model I. In spite of that, for the betterment and all-round progress of the company, Model III is preferred.

I think you have understood this problem.

☐ "Sir, please work out a few practical problems."

● Oh yes, I am working out a few more practical problems.

Problem

The Directors of the Basu Industries have sought your help on costing and the type of information reporting system which they should have in the following circumstances :

(1) The company comprises a Head Office at Kolkata and two Production Centres—one in Western India and the other in Southern India. The Head Office expenses for the year ended 31st December 2006 are :

	Rs.
Marketing Expenses (including Advertising)	1,00,000
General Administration and Finance Expenses	75,000
Production Expenses (certain Technical Services)	10,000
	1,85,000

(2) The Western Production Centre makes two products—A, which is made only at the Centre, and D, which is made also in Southern India.

Its result for the year ended 31st December 2006 are :

	Product A	Product D	Total
	Rs.	Rs.	Rs.
Sales	3,20,000	1,80,000	5,00,000
Standard Cost of Sales	1,50,000	1,20,000	2,70,000
Production Variances (Loss)	2,000	10,000	30,000
Production Overhead	—	—	60,000

(3) The Southern India production centre makes three products—B and C, which are made only at the centre, and D, which is made also in Western India.

Its results for the same period are :

	Product B	Product C	Product D	Total
	Rs.	Rs.	Rs.	Rs.
Sales	2,10,000	3,50,000	75,000	6,35,000
Standard Cost of Sales	1,80,000	2,50,000	55,000	4,85,000
Production Variances (Gain)	(10,000)	(15,000)	(5,000)	(30,000)
Production Overhead (Fixed)	—	—	—	1,00,000

You are required to prepare a Statement of Operations showing profitability by product for Basu Industries for the year ended 31st December 2006, in the form which you consider most informative for the Directors to enhance control (not for pricing purposes) and on the lines of which, for example, you recommend that monthly reports should be prepared.

[Adapted from C.A. (Eng.) Final]

Solution

Basu Industries

Operating Statement for the year ended 31st December 2006

Particulars	Total		Southern India								Western India					
	All Products		All Products		Product B		Product C		Product D		All Products		Product A		Product D	
	Rs. '000	%	Rs '000	%	Rs. '000	%	Rs. '000	%	Rs. '000	%	Rs. '000	%	Rs. '000	%	Rs. '000	%
Sales	1,135	100.0	635	100.0	210	100.0	350	100.0	75	100.0	500	100.0	320	100.0	180	100.0
Standard Cost of Sales	755	66.5	485	76.4	180	85.7	250	71.4	55	73.3	270	54.0	150	46.9	120	66.7
Standard Contribution	380	33.5	150	23.6	30	14.3	100	28.6	20	26.7	230	46.0	170	53.1	60	33.3
Production Variances Profit/ (Loss)	—	—	30	4.7	10	4.7	15	4.3	5	6.6	(30)	(6.0)	(20)	(6.2)	(10)	(5.3)
Actual Contribution	380	33.5	180	28.3	40	19.0	115	32.9	25	33.3	200	40.0	150	46.9	50	27.8
Production Overheads	160	14.1	100	15.7							60	12.0				
Net Contribution (a)	220	19.4	80	12.6							140	28.0				
Head Office Expenses :																
Marketing	100	8.8														
General Administration and Finance	75	6.6														
Technical Service	10	0.9														
Total Head Office Expenses (b)	185	16.3														
Net Profit before Taxation (a – b)	35	3.1														

Problem

Following information are supplied to you for your opinion—whether the replacement of an existing machine, which has been in operation for six (6) years, will be profitable :

Details	Existing Machine	Proposed Machine
	Rs.	Rs.
Cost	60,000	1,20,000
Per Annum Expenditures :		
Power	7,000	8,000
Stores	4,000	5,000
Repairs	5,000	4,000
Labour Cost (per running hour)	2	2.25
Unit per hour	40 unit	60 unit
Per annum running hour machine	2,000 hours	2,000 hours
Per unit material cost	Re. 0.40	Re. 0.40
Per unit output selling price	Re. 1.00	Re. 1.00
Estimated life of the machine	10 years	10 years

Ignore Taxation.

[Adapted from I.C.W.A., Final, London]

Solution

Profitability Statement of New Machine

		Existing Machine	Proposed Machine	Remarks
	p.a. output	80,000	1,20,000	The proposed machine will yield additional profit of 27.5%. So it will be profitable to replace the existing machine
	Output Per hour	40	60	
	Cost of Machine	60,000	1,20,000	
	Machine running p.a.	2,000 hrs.	2,000 hrs.	
	Life of Machine	10 years	10 years	
Cost of Production :		Rs.	Rs.	
Materials		32,000	48,000	
Labour		4,000	4,500	
Power		7,000	8,000	
Consumable Stores		4,000	5,000	
Repairs		5,000	4,000	
Marginal Cost		52,000	69,500	
Depreciation		6,000	12,000	
Total Cost		58,000	81,500	
Selling Price		80,000	1,00,000	
Profit		22,000	18,500	
Profitability of Proposed Machine			5.83% (additional profit)	

Calculation

Output per annum

Limit of output per hour × Machine running hour p.a.

Existing Machine = 40 × 2,000 = 80,000 Units

Selling Price 80,000 × Re. 1.00 = Rs. 80,000

Proposed Machine = 60 × 2,000 = 1,20,000

Selling Price = 1,20,000 × Re. 1.00 = Rs. 1,20,000

$$\% \text{ Profitability} = \frac{\text{Average Additional Profit}}{\text{Average Investment}} \times 100$$

Average Additional Profit = Rs. 22,000 – Rs. 18,500 = Rs. 3,500

$$\text{Average Investment} = \frac{\text{Cost of New Machine} - \text{Sale Value of Old Machine}}{2}$$

$$= \frac{\text{Rs. } 1{,}20{,}000 - 0}{2} = \text{Rs. } 60{,}000$$

$$\text{Profitability} = \frac{\text{Rs. } 3{,}500}{\text{Rs. } 60{,}000} \times 100 = 5.83\%$$

I think you have understood the problem. If you do not understand any point, please feel free to tell me.

☐ "Sir, what are the different factors which should be considered in assessing the profitability of the proposed project"?

● You see, the following **points are to be considered before assessing the profitability of the proposed project**.

(1) To prepare a profitability statement of the existing machine and compare it with the similar type of profitability statement of the proposed project, and to find out the maximum life of the existing machine.

(2) To predict within a reasonable range of accuracy of the expected additional expenditure of the proposed plant and its relationship with the margin of the possible sale.

(3) To estimate before-hand the expected income of the proposed plant and the periods of its flow of fund.

(4) To assess before-hand the anticipated life of the new plant.

(5) To plan the cost of capital of the proposed factory and its equipment and the timing of the capital expenditure.

I hope you have understood all these points.

☐ "Sir, we have understood. Please work out a few more practical problems. We are much interested in it."

• I have told you at the outset of the lecture that it is not possible to work out each and every problem. However, as the chapter on Investment Decision is bound to be complicated, I am working out a few more problems :

Problem

A warehousing concern proposes to purchase Electric High-lift Trucks and Auxiliary Equipment to replace hand trucks used now. The new trucks would necessitate additional capital expenditure being made on Buildings and Fittings.

The following information appeared in last year's Profit and Loss Account :

	Rs.		Rs.
Management and Clerical Cost	32,000	Space rentals	2,50,000
Warehouse Wages Cost	1,04,000		
Rates and Licence Cost	18,000		
Power, Light, and Water cost	15,000		
Insurance Cost	7,000		
Maintenance Cost	3,000		
Depreciation :			
Buildings	10,000		
Hand-Trucks (final)	2,000		
	1,91,000		2,50,000

Proposed new expenditures :

Trucks etc. Rs. 60,000, life 10 years, residual value Rs. 10,000. Building and Fittings Rs. 50,000 to be written off over 20 years.

Estimated increased operating cost :

Management and Clerical : estimated increase 10%

Warehouse Wages : estimated increase 25%

Power etc.	Rs. 3,000
Insurance	Rs. 2,000
Maintenance	Rs. 500

Rental income : increase of space available for renting : 50%

It is estimated that an overall reduction of charges of 50% will be possible.

From the above information, present a forecast comparing the present Profit and Loss Account with the Projected Profit and Loss Account when the scheme is in full working.

[Adapted from I.C.W.A., London]

Solution

Comparative Profit and Loss Account

Dr. Details	Present Rs.	Projected Rs.	Details	Present Rs.	Projected Rs. Cr.
Management and clerical cost	32,000	35,200	Space rental	2,50,000	3,75,000 (A)
Warehouse cost	1,04,000	1,30,000			
Rates and Licence cost	18,000	18,000			
Power, Light and Water cost	15,000	18,000			
Insurance cost	7,000	9,000			
Maintenance cost	3,000	3,500			
Depreciation :					
Buildings	10,000	12,500 (B)			
Hand Truck (final)	2,000				
Electric high lift Truck		5,000 (C)			
Profit	59,000	1,43,800			
	2,50,000	3,75,000		2,50,000	3,75,000

Workings (A) : $2,50,000 \times \frac{50}{100} + 2,50,000$

$= 1,25,000 + 2,50,000 = \text{Rs. } 3,75,000$

(B) $\frac{50,000}{20} = 2,500;\ 10,000 + 2,500 = 12,500$

(C) 60,000

$\frac{60,000 - 10,000}{10} = 5,000$

Problem

Sundry Company Limited has a machine which has been in operation for 5 years. The management is considering the purchase of a new machine to replace the old machine. Following information is supplied to you for your opinion.

You are to find out whether it would be profitable to replace the old machine.

	Old Machine	New Machine
	Rs.	Rs.
Cost of machine	6,000	10,000
Life of the machine	10 years	10 years
Per annum running hour	2,000	2,000
Miscellaneous expenses (Rs.)	600	800
Power per annum (Rs.)	300	850
Consumable stores (Rs.)	500	700
Output per hour	20	20
Disposal value (Re.)	2,000	
Sale price per unit (Re.)	0.23	0.20
Material cost per unit (Re.)	0.10	0.10
Wage cost (Re.)	0.40	0.60
Ignore taxation		

[Adapted from I.C.W.A., London]

Solution

Sundry Company Limited
Profitability Statement

	Old Machine	New Machine
Cost of Machine	Rs. 6,000	Rs. 10,000
Output units	40,000 units	80,000 units
Life of the Machine	10 yrs.	10 yrs.
Cost of Production	Rs.	Rs.
Direct Material	4,000	8,000
Direct Labour	800	1,200
Power	300	850
Consumable Stores	500	700
Miscellaneous Expenses	600	800
Marginal cost	6,200	11,550
Depreciation	600	1,000
Total Cost	6,800	12,550
Selling Price	9,200	16,000
Profit before Tax	2,400	3,450

$$\% \text{ Profitability} = \frac{\text{Average Additional Profit}}{\text{Average Investment}} \times 100$$

$$= \frac{1{,}250}{4{,}000} \times 100 = 31\%$$

Profit as per new machine	=	Rs.	3,450
Reduced Depreciation	=	Rs.	200
		Rs.	3,650

Average Additional Profit (Rs. 3,650 – Rs. 2,400) = Rs. 1,250

$$\text{Average Investment} = \frac{\text{Cost of New Machine} - \text{Sale Value of Old Machine}}{2}$$

$$= \frac{\text{Rs. } 10{,}000 - \text{Rs. } 2{,}000}{2} = \frac{\text{Rs. } 8{,}000}{2} = \text{Rs. } 4{,}000$$

Problem

XYZ Limited is a manufacturer of certain goods viz. A, B and C. The following information given as to their Production Budget :

Product A :	Output 5,560 Units	
	Machine hour per unit	2
	Direct Materials	Rs. 20
	Direct Labour	Rs. 15
	Direct Expenses	Rs. 3
	Variable Overhead	Rs. 7
Product B :	Output 2,000 Units	
	Machine hour per unit	2
	Direct Materials	Rs. 30
	Direct Labour	Rs. 17
	Direct Expenses	Rs. 3
	Variable Overhead	Rs. 9
Product C :	Output 4,000 Units	
	Machine hour per unit	1
	Direct Material	Rs. 15
	Direct Labour	Rs. 12
	Direct Expenses	Re. 1
	Variable Overhead	Rs. 3

Selling Prices; A—Rs. 60; B—Rs. 80; C—Rs. 40.

The year's Fixed Overhead Budget—Rs. 1,05,600

Fixed overheads are to be allocated to total production of Product A, Product B and Product C on the machine hour rate basis.

Key factor : Shortage of raw materials.

This is a very important problem. This problem should be considered from the point of view of Key factor. I think you remember the formula of profitability from the point of view of Key factor.

☐ "Yes, Sir".

● However, I am writing this formula again and for this you, please, consult my last lectures :

$$\% \text{ Profitability} = \frac{\text{Contribution}}{\text{Key Factor}} \times 100$$

Contribution = Fixed Overhead + Profit.

$$\text{So, } \% \text{ Profitability} = \frac{\text{Fixed Overhead} + \text{Profit}}{\text{Key Factor}} \times 100$$

One point you please note in this problem is that the Budgeted Fixed Overhead are to be allocated to total production of Product A, Product B, and Product C on the machine hour per unit rate of each product at 2, 3 and 1, respectively.

The workings are given :

Budgeted Machine Hour =	A; 5,560 × 2 =	11,120
	B; 2,000 × 3 =	6,000
	C; 4,000 × 1 =	4,000
		21,120

$$\text{Now the Machine Hour Rate} = \frac{\text{Budgeted Fixed Overhead}}{\text{Total Budgeted Machine Hour}}$$

$$= \frac{\text{Rs. } 1{,}05{,}600}{21{,}120} = \text{Rs. } 5.00$$

Now the Budgeted Fixed Overhead are to be allocated at the rate of Rs. 5. Then the position will be :

A =	11,120 × Rs. 5 = Rs.	55,600
B =	6,000 × Rs. 5 = Rs.	30,000
C =	4,000 × Rs. 5 = Rs.	20,000
		1,05,600

Bearing all these points in mind, I work out the problem :

Solution

Profitability Statement

Particulars	Products		
	A	B	C
	5,560 output	2,000 output	4,000 output
	2 hours per unit	3 hours per unit	1 hour per unit
	Rs.	Rs.	Rs.
Direct Materials	1,11,200	60,000	60,000
Direct Labour	83,400	34,000	48,000
Direct Expenses	16,680	6,000	4,000
Variable Overhead	38,920	18,000	12,000
Marginal Cost	2,50,200	1,18,000	1,24,000
Fixed Overhead	55,600	30,000	20,000
Total Cost	3,05,800	1,48,000	1,44,000
Profit	27,800	12,000	16,000
Selling Price	3,33,600	1,60,000	1,60,000
% Margin on Sale	8.3%	7.5%	10%
Profit per article	5	6	4
% Profitability	75%	70%	60%

Profitability calculated in the statement given earlier on the basis of the formula given :

$$\frac{\text{Fixed Overhead + Profit}}{\text{Key Factor}} \times 100$$

Profitability of Product A

$$\frac{\text{Rs. } 55,600 + \text{Rs. } 27,800}{\text{Rs. } 1,11,200} \times 100 = 75\%$$

Profitability of Product B

$$\frac{\text{Rs. } 30,000 + \text{Rs. } 12,000}{\text{Rs. } 60,000} \times 100 = 70\%$$

Profitability of Product C

$$\frac{\text{Rs. } 20,000 + \text{Rs. } 16,000}{\text{Rs. } 60,000} \times 100 = 60\%$$

From the statement given earlier it is clear that the Product A seems to be more profitable; and Product A shall be considered the best.

☐ "Sir, what is the **utility of preparing the profitability statement**? Can we concentrate our attention for greater production of a product which shows greater profitability?"

● I am really very glad to see that you have realised the real philosophy of the concept of profitability. The main aim of preparing the comparative profitability statement is to indicate which product is more profitable; whether it would be wise to concentrate on the product which seems apparently more profitable. This is possible if you follow the line of 'trial and error approach' procedure.

☐ "How is this possible, Sir?"

● As Product A seems apparently more profitable, let concentration be given for the production on Product A. For this you will have to calculate the total contribution of all the products the company produce. In this case the total contribution of Product A, B, C will be needed to be found out. Then the total material costs for Products A, B and C will have to find out. And this total Direct Material is to be converted to the profitability rate of Products A, B and C which are 75%, 70% and 60%, respectively. The result of Product A (Profitability of Direct Materials) will be compared with the present total contribution. This will indicate the greater contribution than expectation. The workings are :

Budgeted Contribution Statement

	Product A	**Product B**	**Product C**	
	Rs.	Rs.	Rs.	Rs.
Fixed Overheads	55,600	30,000	20,000	1,05,600
Contribution	27,800	12,000	16,000	55,800
Total Contribution	83,400	42,000	36,000	1,61,400

☐ "Sir, what do you mean by Contribution and Total Contribution? Can we write Profit instead of Contribution?"

● Yes, Instead of writing Contribution you can write Profit.

Now, Total Contribution = Fixed Overhead + Profit.

I think you have understood now all these points. Now let me complete the problem first of all.

Total cost of materials to be purchased as to the following products :

Product A =	Rs.	1,11,200
Product B =	Rs.	60,000
Product C =	Rs.	60,000
		2,31,200

Now the following position will be revealed if the management concentrates attention on one product only :

Particulars	Product	A	B	C
	Profitability	75%	70%	60%
		Rs.	Rs.	Rs.
Direct Material		2,31,200	2,31,200	2,31,200
Contribution		1,73,400	1,61,840	1,38720

The position if Product A is produced

Total Contribution if the Product A is produced	1,73,400
Present Total Contribution	1,61,400
Additional Contribution	12,000

From the situation indicated above it is clear that if the management concentrates its attention on the manufacture of Product A, it will give them additional profit to the extent of Rs. 12,000.

The above situation can be verified from the following observations.

	Rs.
Total Purchase of Raw Materials for the production of Product A only	2,31,200
Cost of Direct Material of Product A	20

$$\text{Units Produced} = \frac{\text{Rs. } 2{,}31{,}200}{\text{Rs. } 20} = 11{,}560 \text{ Units}$$

Sale of 11,560 units @ Rs. 60	6,93,600
Marginal Cost of 11,560 units @ Rs. 45	5,20,200
Contribution	1,73,400

Budgeted Contribution = Rs. 1,61,400

So the additional/increased contribution = Rs. 1,73,400 – Rs. 1,61,400 = Rs. 12,000

I hope, you have followed my lecture and the problems worked out earlier.

☐ "Yes Sir, we have followed."

• Good bye.

• Now I will discuss in detail about the Pay-Back Period which is one of the important aspects of investment decision. Before I take up for discussion this chapter, you please assure me whether you have followed my last lecture or not. That is to say, let me know whether you have understood the discussion on 'Profitability'.

☐ "No Sir."

☐ "Sir, you have not discussed how profitability of a proposed business can be improved?"

☐ "Sir, you have not discussed about the Return on Investment. I shall be obliged if you, please sir, discuss it in detail."

☐ "Sir, really speaking I cannot understand the head or tail of Investment Decision."

Motives of Business

• From the different questions put by you it is clear that most of you could not understand the concept of Investment Decision and how it is related with profitability and pay-back period. However, do you admit that business has two motives — (1) Profit motive, and (2) Service motive. Production of quality and quantity goods at a reduced price should be the Service motive of any enterprise. Any drive for the increase in profit, having due regard to the service motive of the business, is said to be the constructive motive of the business. All the drive is nothing but the technique for improving the profitability. Now the point is how profitability can be improved?

Following are the **ways by which profitability can be improved** :

1. Implementing sound Financial Planning.
2. Proper utilisation of Man and Machine Power.
3. Increasing Productivity.
4. Reducing cost of production by introducing the system of Budgetary Control and Standard Costing etc.
5. Increase in Turnover.
6. Production of uptodate goods following the outcome of Market Research. This is only to avoid unnecessary blockage of capital blocked in stock.
7. Increase in selling price for the products which have low turnover; conversely, reduction in selling price in order to boost up the market for a commodity which has high turnover.
8. Elimination of unnecessary expenses, etc.

INVESTMENT DECISION

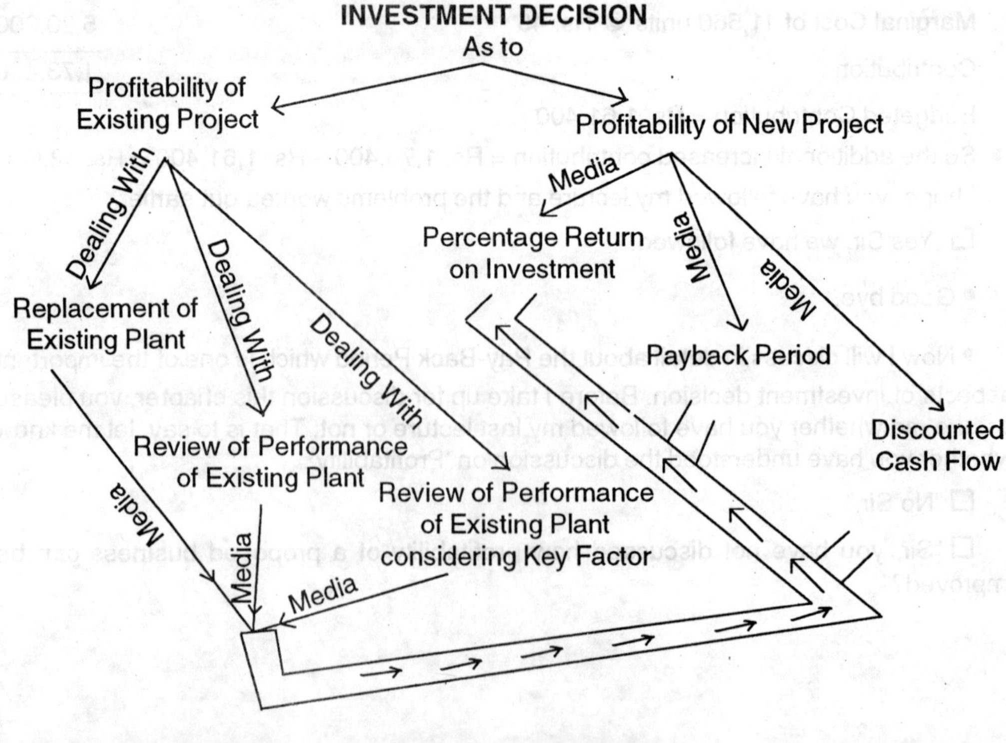

I think it is clear to you—how profitability of the old business and newly set up business can be improved. You please note below the different aspects of investment decision which will help you to understand its basis.

Now, from the chart given earlier it is clear that percentage Return on Investment is expressing the profitability of the enterprise in terms of percentage. However, Investment Decision deals with the concept of Return on Investment, Pay-back period and Discounted Cash Flow. So the percentage of return on investment methods embracing all its aspects such as key factor for replacement of existing plant have already been discussed in detail under the head of Profitability. So I hope that you have understood the concept of Percentage Return on Investment. Now I like to discuss about the Pay-Back Period.

□ "Excuse me Sir, I cannot understand till now the concept of Percentage Return on Investment Method."

● So, I am discussing the concept of Percentage Return on Investment Method in a nutshell having due regard to the discussions made earlier in the chapter on Profitability.

Now you tell me, do you follow this concept?

$$\% \text{ Profitability} = \frac{\text{Profit}}{\text{Capital Employed}}$$

$$= \frac{\text{Profit}}{\text{Sales}} \times \frac{\text{Sales}}{\text{Capital Employed}}$$

□ "Yes Sir. I can follow the concept explained earlier."

● If that be so, I would like to discuss a few more words from different angles and approach to make clear the concept of Return on Capital Employed. If you can really follow the point of return on capital employed which had been discussed in your Ratio Analysis chapter then it would be very easy to understand the other part of the discussion.

The Return on Investment is a method which is used to express the profitability of an enterprise. The Return on Capital Employed, on the other hand, discloses the efficiency of the management. The efficiency of the management is tested in general by the ratio of the Net Profit to Capital Employed. The other term of the Return on Capital Employed is a percentage 'Yield on Capital'. On this basis comparison as to the efficiency of different companies and different departments of the same company or different companies and even of different plants of the existing company or different plant of other companies can be made. However, it has already been mentioned that Return on Investment is aimed to measure or express the profitability of any enterprise. The formulas of Percentage Return on Capital Employed, Percentage Return on Investment, Average Gross Annual Rate of Return per Re. 1.00 Capital Outlay are given :

$$\% \text{ Return on Capital Employed} = \frac{\text{Profit}}{\text{Capital Employed}} \times 100$$

This attempts to find out the overall efficiency or inefficiency of the management.

$$\% \text{ Return on Investment} = \frac{\text{Average Additional Profit}}{\text{Average Investment}} \times 100$$

This attempts to find out the expected profitability arising from the replacement of the old machine.

Average Gross Annual Rate of Return per Re. 1.00 Capital Outlay :

$$= \frac{\text{Total Gross Anticipated Income}}{\text{Expected life} \times \text{Capital outlay}}$$

Now, I hope, you have followed all these points. If you do not understand, please tell me frankly.

☐ "Sir, now I understand the concept of Return on Capital Employed and Return on Investment under the head of Profitability".

☐ "Sir, please explain the concept of Average Gross Annual Rate of Return per Re. 1.00 Capital Outlay with the help of an example."

- You take down an example in this regard.

Capital Outlay (Expended now)	Rs. 25,000
Expected/Anticipated Life	10 years
Total Anticipated Profit excluding Depreciation	Rs. 50,000

The Percentage Average Gross Annual Rate of Return per Re 1.00 Capital Outlay

$$= \frac{\text{Total Anticipated Profit or Total Gross Income}}{\text{Expected Life or Anticipated Life} \times \text{Capital Outlay}}$$

$$= \text{Rs. } \frac{50,000}{10 \times 25,000} \times 100 = 20\%$$

Now, I hope, you have understood the different aspects of Return on Investment Method which had been discussed in detail when I discussed before you the chapter on 'Profitability.' Now I like to discuss about the concept of Pay-Back Period.

Pay-Back Period—It is a method of evaluating the profitability of the proposed capital expenditure project. It attempts to find out the period of time required to recover the original cost of the project from the additional profit from the operation of the machine before charging depreciation. Professors Brown and Howard, in their book "Principles of Management Accountancy," has described the 'pay-back' period as a method which 'attempts to measure the period of time it takes for the original cost of a project to be recovered from the additional earnings of the project itself'. But the most comprehensive definition was given by Mr. Wheldon. He is of opinion that 'this is the period required for saving in marginal cost to recover the investment. The real profitability of an investment depends on the number of years it will continue to operate after the pay-off period'.

Meaning of Pay-Back

Formula of Pay-Back The formula of Pay-Back = $\frac{I}{S}$

That is to say

$P = \frac{I}{S}$ P = Pay-Back Period

I = Cost of Assets/Original Investment

S = Saving Per Year/Annual Cash in Flow.

☐ "Sir I cannot follow all these."

• You will definitely follow the concept of Pay-Back Period if we can work out a few practical problems;

Example

Cost of Machine	Rs. 20,000
Estimated life	10 years
Estimated Saving Per Annum	Rs. 20,000
Estimated Expenditure	Rs. 15,000

Now, you are required to find out the Pay-Back Period.

You know the formula of Pay-Back Period :

$$\text{Pay-Back Period} = \frac{\text{Cost of Assets or Original Investment}}{\text{Net Saving Per Year or Annual Cash in Flow}}$$

Now with the help of this formula you will have to find out the Pay-Back Period—the number of years within which the cash outlay will be recovered. It should be noted in this context that the life of the assets should be higher than the Pay-Back Period. Otherwise, the project will not be worth mentioning.

	Situations		**Decision**
	Life-span of the Machine or Estimated life of the Machine	Pay-Back Period	
	4	5	Reject
Pay-Back and	5	4	Accept
Management	10	5	Accept
Decision	4	4	Observation

The table given above will be clear to understand the inner philosophy of the Pay-Back Period. As already been pointed out at the outset of this discussion—'the real profitability of an investment depends on the number of years it will continue to operate after the pay-off period'. However, I like to work out the example given earlier.

Profitability Statement

	Rs.
Cost of the Machine	20,000
Estimated life	10 years
Per Annum Estimated Saving	20,000
Per Annum Estimated Expenditure	15,000
Profit (before tax)	5,000
50% tax	2,500
Profit (after tax)	2,500

$$\text{Pay-Back Period before Tax} = \frac{\text{Cost of Machine}}{\text{Saving per year}} = \text{Rs. } \frac{20,000}{5,000} = 4 \text{ yrs}$$

$$\text{Pay-Back Period after Tax} = \frac{\text{Cost of Machine}}{\text{Saving per year after tax}} = \text{Rs. } \frac{20,000}{2,500} = 8 \text{ yrs}$$

The project seems to be more profitable, because the assets will continue to operate for 6 years more, after the pay-back period. So the project indicates extra profitability to the extent of (10 yrs. – 4 yrs. = 6 yrs. × Rs. 5,000) = Rs. 30,000.

☐ "Sir what are the Advantages and Disadvantages of Pay-Back Period?"

● You see, I will work out first of all a few practical problems on Pay-Back Period, then I would like to discuss the relative Advantages and Disadvantages of the Pay-Back Period.

Problem

Basu Industries in their Annual General Meeting passed a resolution wishing to expand production. For this they decide to purchase a machine from the market. Sales of the Industries are limited by the market which is estimated at Rs. 15,000 per annum.

Information	**Machine X**	**Machine Y**
	Rs.	**Rs.**
Cost of Machine	21,000	7,500
Estimated Life	6 Years	7 Years
Cost per annum :		
Labour	1,000	5,000
Materials	6,000	6,000
Variable Overheads	2,000	1,500

From the information supplied to you, advise the management which machine should be purchased.

Now the point is, if you go deep into the problem you will see that management would be interested with the minimum period of time within which the cash outlay is recovered.

Solution

Profitability Statement 1

	X	Y
	Rs.	Rs.
Cost of the Machine	21,000	7,500
Expected Life of the Machine	6 years	7 years
Estimated Sales	15,000	15,000
Marginal Cost	9,000	12,500
Marginal Profit	6,000	2,500
Pay-Back Period	3½ years	3 year
Profitability	15,000	10,000

	Machine X	Machine Y
Pay-Back Period	$\left(\frac{\text{Rs. } 21,000}{\text{Rs. } 6,000}\right)$ = 3½ years	$\left(\frac{\text{Rs. } 7,500}{\text{Rs. } 2,500}\right)$ = 3 years

Profitability Statement 2

Machine	Estimated Life a	Pay-Back Period b	Difference (a – b) = d	Marginal Profit c	Profitability c × d	Comments
X	6 yrs	3½ yrs.	(6 – 3½) = 2½	6,000	15,000	On review of the Pay-Back and Profitability, Machine X may be purchased
Y	7 yrs.	3 yrs.	(7 – 3) = 4	2,500	10,000	

Problem

Joy Bangla Trading Co. Ltd. proposed to increase the production of their company. For this they are willing to purchase a new machine. There are four types of Machine found in the market. As a Management Accountant of the company, you are requested to advise the management which type of machine should be purchased.

	Type A	Type B	Type C	Type D
	Rs.	Rs.	Rs.	Rs.
Cost of Machine	25,000	18,000	15,000	35,000
Estimated Saving in Scrap	1,500	500	1,000	800
Wages per Employee	600	500	600	500
Cost of Indirect Material	800	—	600	—
Expected Saving in Indirect Materials	—	500	—	200
Additional Cost of Maintenance	1,100	1,000	700	1,500
Additional Cost of Supervision	1,600	—	1,200	—
Operative not required	20	9	15	11
Estimated life of Machine	6 years	5 years	5 years	10 years

Taxation 50% of Profit

I think you can work out the problem. It is a very easy problem.

☐ "No Sir, it is a difficult problem, please solve it."

Solution

Profitability Statement No. 1

	Machine A	Machine B	Machine C	Machine D
	Rs.	Rs.	Rs.	Rs.
Cost of Machine	25,000	18,000	15,000	35,000
Life of the Machine	6 years	5 years	5 years	10 years
Saving per year :	13,500 (X)	5,500 (Y)	10,000 (Z)	6,500 (L)
Extra cost per year :	3,500 (M)	1,000 (N)	2,500 (Q)	1,500(R)
Profit	10,000	4,500	7,500	5,000
50% tax	5,000	2,250	3,750	2,500
Profit after tax	5,000	2,250	3,750	2,500
Pay-Back Period :				
(i) After tax	5 years	8 years	4 years	14 years
(ii) Before tax	2½ years	4 years	2 years	7 years

Calculation : Savings Arising from	Machine A (X) Rs.	Machine B (Y) Rs.	Machine C (Z) Rs.	Machine D (L) Rs.	Note :
Wages	12,000	4,500	9,000	5,500	Wages per Employee X
Scrap	1,500	500	1,000	800	operative not
Indirect Materials	—	500	—	200	required
	13,500	5,500	10,000	6,500	

Extra Cost :	M Rs.	N Rs.	Q Rs.	R Rs.
Indirect Material	800	—	600	—
Maintenance	1,100	1,000	700	1,500
Supervision	1,600	—	1,200	—
	3,500	1,000	2,500	1,500

One important point, please note that before arriving at the final decision which one of the above four machines is to be purchased, you will have to prepare another profitability statement, indicating the overall profitability of the above machines.

☐ "How is it possible Sir?"

● You note the following workings and Profitability Statement 2.

Profitability Statement 2

Machine	Estimated Life a (yrs.)	Pay-Back Period b (yrs.)	Difference (a – b) = d	Marginal Profit c Rs.	Profitability d × c Rs.	Comments
A	6	2½ yrs.	(6 – 2½) = 3½	10,000	35,000	Type A Machine is
B	5	4 yrs.	(5 – 4) = 1	4,500	4,500	the more
C	5	2 yrs.	(5 – 2) = 3	7,500	22,500	profitable
D	10	7 yrs.	(10 – 7) = 3	5,000	15,000	investment

I think, you have understood all the problems discussed earlier.

☐ "Sir, what are the advantages and disadvantages of Pay-Back Period?"

● **Advantages**

(i) The pay-back period is very indispensible to the concerns where liquidity is the main objective of the business.

(ii) It is easy to calculate. Because, it estimates before-hand the economic desirability of cash outlay.

(iii) It is one of the ways of assessing the managerial performance of any organisation.

(iv) It guarantees and warns the management before-hand against the possible threat arising from the fear of obsolescence.

Disadvantages

(i) 'The pay-back period does not take into account the number of years beyond that earning will continue, nor does it consider the rate at which these inflows occur'.

(ii) The pay-back period is quite under the direct control and supervision of the management.

(iii) Possible manipulations in the real profitability are possibly evident when the estimated life of the machine is twisted by the management in their own way.

I hope you have understood my discussion.

Yes, ... Do you like to put me any question?

☐ Sir, kindly enlighten us about the concept of Discounted pay back period.

• Well, take a look at the concept of Discounted pay back period.

Discounted Payback Period

Discounted Pay-Back Period is the modification of payback period method to consider the time value of money. We know that one of the shortcomings of payback period is that it does not consider the time value of money. In order to avoid this shortcoming, discounted payback period method is suggested. In this method, cash inflows are discounted to their present values and then pay-back period is calculated.

☐ "Excuse me Sir, please, clarify with an example."

• O.K., see the following example.

Let, a project require initial investment of Rs. 10,000. The life of the project is 5 years. The cash inflows generated by the project are :

1	2	3	4	5
Rs. 3,000	Rs. 4,000	Rs. 4,000	Rs. 3,500	Rs. 3,500

Calculate discounted payback period assuming discounting factor at 10%.

Solution

Year	Cash flow (Rs.)	Discounting factor at 10%*	Present value (Rs.)	Cumulative Present value
0	(10,000)	1.000	(10,000)	(10,000)
1	3,000	0.909	2,727	(7273)
2	4,000	0.826	3,304	(3969)
3	4,000	0.751	3,004	(965) }
4	3,500	0.683	2,391	1426 }
5	3,500	0.621	2,174	3,600

Discounting factors

1st year = $\frac{1}{(1+0.1)^1}$, 2 year = $\frac{1}{(1+0.1)^2}$, 3rd year = $\frac{1}{(1+0.1)^3}$

It is clear from the above calculation that the discounted payback period is between 3 and 4 years.

Now I would like to discuss about the Discounted Cash Flow which is known as Net Present Value Return on Investment Method. However, it attempts to evaluate a proposal in the form of 'rate of return that is applied to the unrecovered capital of each period instead of to the initial investment.' I have told you earlier that one of the main defects of the Pay-Back Period is that 'it does not take into account the number of years beyond that earnings will continue nor does it consider the rate at which these inflows occur'. It would be more helpful to the top management to locate the amount, being the recovery of original cash outlay and profit therefrom.

Scientific Approach to Investment Decision

Annual Cash Flow = Recovery of Investment + Profit.

The Discounted Cash Flow Technique attempts to find out the 'net Cash Flow as representing the recovery of original investment plus a return on capital invested'. Besides the point indicated earlier, the D.C.F. technique attempts to find out the inner meaning of the idea that Re. 1 received today is worth more than the right to receive Re. 1 at the end of, say, 5 years. For example, the right to receive Re. 1 five years after today is worth about say Re. 0.75 (following suitable interest rate) on today. 'Thus the present value of a sum to be received at some future time is such an amount as will be based upon time factor. For this D.C.F. Method; which aims to find out the return on cash outlay, considers over the life of the assets, the timing factor both as to capital expenditure and the profit arising from the projected investment. Similar type of idea has been expressed by Broad and Carmichael when they opined, 'the method of expressing the return on a projected investment takes into account the timing both of the capital expenditure and the accrual of profits over the asset life. Distant profits are worthless today than more immediate profit.' The National Association of Accountants, New York, in their Research Monograph 1, states that 'the rate of return is the discount rate which equates present worth of cash inflows to present worth of cash outflows. This method is commonly called the Discounted Cash Flow Method.'

Meaning of Discounted Cash Flow

The whole point will be clear if the following Exhibits are deeply observed :

Exhibit No. 1

Showing Recovery of Capital Outlay

Years	Unrecovered capital outlay at the beginning of the year	Cash inflow	Rate of interest	Proportion of recovery of cash outlay
1st year	XX	XX	XX	XX
2nd year	XX	XX	XX	XX
3rd year	XX	XX	XX	XX
4th year	XX	XX	XX	XX
5th year	XX	XX	XX	XX

Internal Rate of Return (IRR)

Internal Rate of Return is the discount rate at which the present value of net cash inflows exactly equal the initial amount of investment. In other words, it is the discount rate at which the net present value of investment proposal is zero. Graphically, we can show the internal rate of return (r) by drawing a NPV profile :

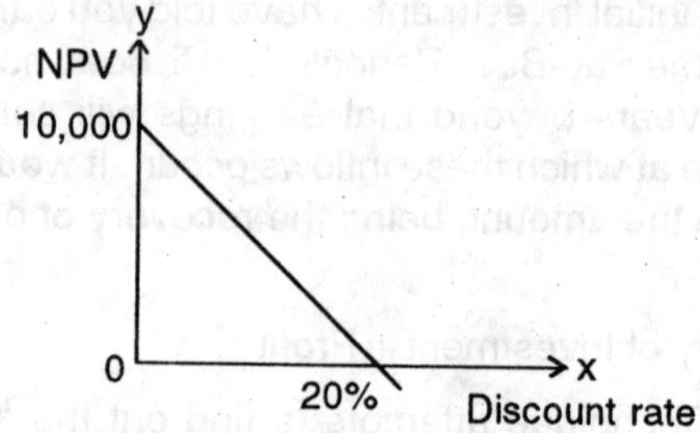

The above NPV profile shows that on the Y-axis NPV is plotted and on the X-axis discount rate is plotted. When discount rate is zero, NPV is equal to the difference between all cash inflows and outflow. NPV is zero at 20% rate of discount. This 20% discount rate is the internal rate of return for the project.

Now, we can use this internal rate for evaluating investment proposals. Under the criterion, internal rate is compared with the cost of capital. So long as the internal rate is greater than the cost of capital, the project is accepted.

Let us now see how the internal rate of return is determined. For determining internal rate we have to find out two discount rates by applying trial and errors between which the internal rate of return falls. Then we have to apply linear interpolation to find out the internal rate which makes the net present value zero. The following illustration will make you clear on the point :

A project requires initial investment of Rs. 20,000 and expected cash inflows from the project are Rs. 10,000 in the first year, Rs. 8,000 in the second year, Rs. 6,000 in the third year and Rs. 4,000 in the fourth and final year.

Determine the internal rate of return of the project.

Solution

First we have to find out the two rates between which the internal rate of return lies.

Let, the IRR or r = 20%

NPV at 20% is calculated :

Year	Cash flow	Discounting factor at @ 20%	Discounted cash flows	Cumulative cash flows
0	(20,000)	1	(20,000)	(20,000)
1	10,000	0.833	8,330	(11,670)
2	8,000	0.694	5,552	(6118)
3	6,000	0.579	3,474	(2644)
4	4000	0.482	1928	(716)

∴ NPV = – 716. So, IRR is below 20%.

Let, IRR be 16%

Year	Cash flow	Discounting factor at @ 16%	Discounted cash flows	Cumulative cash flows
0	(20,000)	1	(20,000)	(20,000)
1	10,000	0.862	8,620	(11,380)
2	8,000	0.743	5,944	(5436)
3	6,000	0.641	3,846	(1590)
4	4,000	0.552	2,208	618

∴ NPV = Rs. 618

So, it is clear that IRR is between 16% and 20%.

Now, by linear interpolation :

$$r = 16\% + \frac{618}{618 + 716} \times [20\% - 16\%]$$

$$= 16\% + \frac{618}{1334} \times 4\%$$

$$= 16\% + 1.85\%$$

$$= 17.85\%$$

So, IRR = 17.85%

☐ "Sir, please explain it with the help of one more numerical problem."

- Well, I would like to explain it with the help of the following example :

Problem

Investment	Rs. 5,982
Annual cash inflow	Rs. 2,000
Life of the machine	5 years
Discount factors (Rate of Return)	20%

From the information given above you are requested to find out the recovery of original investment and return on capital invested.

Solution

Year	Investment Unrecovered at beginning of the Year Rs.	Cash inflow (Annual) Rs.	Discount Factor at 20% Rs.	Recovery of Investment Rs.
1	5,982	2,000	1,196	804
2	5,178	2,000	1,036	964
3	4,214	2,000	842	1,158
4	3,056	2,000	612	1,388
5	1,668	2,000	334	1,666 *

*Error of Rs. 2.00 is due to round-off.

Now I hope, you have followed my lecture.

Now I would like to explain the other Exhibit, showing the 'Trial and Error Approach'.

Exhibit 2

Showing the possible amount to be invested for achieving the maximum and reasonable Return on Investment.

(Trial and Error Approach) Investment Rs. 50,000

Years	Present Value of Re. 1.00 at Discount Factor			Cash Inflow	Present value of Cash Inflow		
	16%	17%	18%		(16%) Rs. (x)	(17%) Rs. (y)	(18%) Rs. (z)
1st	0.8621	0.8547	0.8475	10,000	8,621	8,547	8,475
2nd	0.7432	0.7305	0.7182	15,000	11,148	10,957	10,773
3rd	0.6047	0.6244	0.6086	20,000	12,814	12,488	12,172
4th	0.5523	0.5337	0.5158	20,000	11,046	10,674	10,316
5th	0.4761	0.4561	0.4371	15,000	7,141	6,841	6,556
				80,000	50,770	49,507	48,292
					ΣX	ΣY	ΣZ

Suitable Rate of Retrun

$$\frac{\Sigma X - I}{\Sigma X - I + I - \Sigma Y} \times (17\% - 16\%)$$

$$= \frac{50{,}770 - 50{,}000}{50{,}770 - 49{,}507} \times 1\%$$

$= 0.6\%$

The Rate of Return = 16% + 0.6% = 16.6%

Now I hope that you have followed the discussion made earlier. I shall be glad to hear from you any point which come in to your mind.

☐ "Sir, what are the Advantages and Disadvantages of Discounted Cash Flow Method?"

☐ "Sir, what is the formula of Present value Method"?

- Oh! Yes, I will discuss all these points in detail. First of all take down the formula of Present Value Method :

$$V = \frac{A}{r}\left[1 - (1 + r)^{-n}\right]$$

Now : V = Present Value
A = Earnings
r = Rate of Interest; Discount Factor.
n = No. of years

☐ "Sir, I cannot follow all these points".

● Wait please, it would be clear to you if a few practical problems are taken into account on this concept. Before that I would like to discuss the merits and demerits of the Discounted Cash Flow Method.

Advantages

(i) It has been told earlier that the pay-back period considers only a limited period. But that defects of the pay-back period have been eliminated by the introduction of the D.C.F. technique. Since, this technique considers the full period of the project.

(ii) This method recognises the inner philosophy of the business finance—'money due in the near future is not worth face value in the present.'

(iii) The evaluation of this method helps the management to arrive at some correct decision.

Disadvantages

(i) Application of this method requires more computation which is not, in many cases, welcome by business-men.

(ii) Difficulties arise in selecting appropriate discount factors (rate of interest).

I hope that you all have understood my lecture. Now I work out a few practical problems on the concept of D.C.F. Technique which, I think, will be very helpful to understand the whole lectures. Here are a few problems.

☐ "Excuse me Sir, I could not follow your lecture. Please explain it as simply as possible. Besides, Sir, I cannot make out the inner relationship of Trial and Errors, Present Value and Net Gain Method."

● I find no reason why you could not follow my lectures. I do not like to discuss the same again.

☐ "Please Sir, discuss it in a nutshell. This is our earnest request."

You see, I have explained earlier that the D.C.F. Method takes into consideration the fact that nominal value of money received today is more valuable than the same to be received after one year. This is because money of today can be invested to earn certain amount of interest which can be collected after specified periods or years. Thus I told you earlier that the right or claim to receive Re. 1.00 after a year or so on is not equivalent to Re. 1.00 of today. It is, as explained earlier, Re 0.75. From this we can come to an inference that the present value of Rs. 100 to be received after 'one year hence' is approximately Rs. 94.3, if the discounting rate is 6%. I think you are following my lecture.

Basic Idea of DCF

☐ "One point Sir."

● Yes, what do you want me to tell?

☐ "Sir, how Rs. is 94.3 calculated"?

● This is done by discounting Rs. 100 at 6% discounting rate. 6% discounting rate is 0.943. So Rs. 100 × 0.943 = Rs. 94.3.

☐ "Sir, where can we get the discounting rate?"

Well, after the discussion I would like to give you for your reference two tables : (1) Present Value of Re. 1, (2) Present Value of Re. 1 received annually for N years. Well, you will get these two tables in due course of time.

Now I hope that you have followed.

☐ "Yes Sir, you can put to me any types of question on Discounted Cash Flow."

● Now you please tell me what ideas you have grasped from the discussions made earlier.

☐ "Sir, I have understood that the process of adjusting the face value of future cash flows to their present value by means of imputed interest rate is called disounting. This imputed rate is the rate of return. The rate of return calculation that takes into account the time value of money is called discounted cash flow method. The discounted rate of return is that rate which, when applied to a series of future cash flows, brings the sum of their present value to the same level of original investment. It has been developed from the simple defects of the pay-back period. D.C.F. calculation reveals not only the pay-back period but also profit accruing therefrom. This method takes into account the entire life of the project together with profit. Thus D.C.F. method considers the net cash flow as representing the recovery of original investment plus return on capital employed."

● Thank you very much. I am really very glad to note that you have really grasped the concept of D.C.F. Is there any question please?

☐ "Sir, please explain us the reasons how D.C.F. (Discounted Cash Flow) method offers us a much better measure of a Project's Profitability."

● You have put me a very interesting question. Thank you for your curiosity. However, for that I would like to refer you Dr. George B. Baldwin. He in his writing "Discounted Cash Flow", which appeared in 'Finance and Development', explained three main reasons which offer better measure of a firm's or project's profitability. I am explaining the three reasons from the said source :

Reasons why D.C.F. offer better Measure of Projects Profitability

* D.C.F. washes out year-to-year variations in profit and gives us a single valid figure for the whole life of the project.

* D.C.F. automatically takes into account the timing of cash payments and receipts, so that no one can neglect the importance of this factor.

* D.C.F. gets around the difficulty of interpreting what accountants mean by "profit" and gives us a simple, unambiguous definition based on project earnings over the entire life of a project.

Now I think that you have followed the above discussions. Well, regarding the interrelationship of DCF, I am to say that the Discounted Cash Flow Method can be studied under the following heads :

Discounted Cash Flow

(a) Present Value System	**(b) Trial and Error System**	**(c) Net Gain System**
(what sum of money to be invested in order to arrive such and such future streams of income at some discounting rate, i.e., dates for annual cash flow, discounting rate and estimated life of the machine to be given)	(Here, no discounting rate is given. This is to be found out through trial and error method. Given information : Annual cash flow, Estimated life of the machine or asset and capital cost. In this approach care should be taken to select such discounting rate which equates the sum of the discounted future cash flow to capital cost)	(This is to be found out by *deducting* the total present value of future cash flow, or, computed at a predetermined discounting rate from capital cost (payment for the acquisition of assets) Given information : Capital cost, Predetermined Discounting Rate, and Annual Cash Flow)

Now I would like to take up a few problems for discussion under the above three heads—(a) Present Value System, (b) Trial and Error System (c) Net Gain System.

Please note the following examples.

Profitability Index (PI) or Benefit-Cost Ratio

One of the investment criteria used for evaluating investment projects is Profitability Index (PI) or Benefit-Cost Ratio. It is the ratio of present value of net cash flows arising from the project and the initial cost of investment. Symbolically

$PI = \frac{PNCF}{I}$ where, PNCF = Present value of Net cost flows expected to generate from project

1 = Cost of investment

The basic conditions according to this criterion for accepting an investment project is, PI ≥ 1 and when projects are mutually exclusive, the one with the higher Profitability Index is selected.

Net Present Value vs Profitability Index

You have seen that both net present value method and profitability index method consider the time value of money. While NPV method considers the acceptability of a project in absolute term, profitability index method measures the profitability in relative term. But both method gives the same result regarding the acceptability of a project where projects are independent and firms have unlimited source of funds for investment. In other words, firms with unlimited source of funds for investment in independent project can use any of the two methods of evaluating investment projects. But, in case of mutually exclusive projects, profitability index method gives the better result under condition of capital rationing. Because, PI method measures the profitability per unit of capital invested which is a limiting factor here. The following example will clarify further—

A firm is considering two alternative projects—Project A and Project B. The detail information regarding these two projects are :

	Project A (Rs.)	Project B (Rs.)
Initial Investment	40,000	47,500
Net Cash inflow p.a.	12,000	10,000
Expected life	5 years	8 years

Calculate Net Present Value (NPV) and Profitability Index (PI) of these two projects assuming discounting rate at 10% and comment on acceptability of project under conditions of limited supply of capital and unlimited supply of capital.

Solution

Net Present Value of

Project A =

$$\frac{\text{Rs. } 12{,}000}{(1+0.1)^1} + \frac{\text{Rs. } 12{,}000}{(1+0.1)^2} + \frac{\text{Rs. } 12{,}000}{(1+0.1)^3} + \frac{\text{Rs. } 12{,}000}{(1+0.1)^4} + \frac{\text{Rs. } 12{,}000}{(1+0.1)^5} - \text{Rs. } 40{,}000$$

= Rs. (10,909 + 9,917 + 9,016 + 8,196 + 7,451) – Rs. 40,000

= Rs. 45,489 – Rs. 40,000

= Rs. 5,489

Project B =

$$\frac{\text{Rs. } 10{,}000}{(1+0.1)^1} + \frac{\text{Rs. } 10{,}000}{(1+0.1)^2} + \frac{\text{Rs. } 10{,}000}{(1+0.1)^3} + \frac{\text{Rs. } 10{,}000}{(1+0.1)^4} + \frac{\text{Rs. } 10{,}000}{(1+0.1)^5}$$

$$+ \frac{\text{Rs. } 10{,}000}{(1+0.1)^6} + \frac{\text{Rs. } 10{,}000}{(1+0.1)^7} + \frac{\text{Rs. } 10{,}000}{(1+0.1)^8} - \text{Rs. } 47{,}500$$

= Rs. (9,091 + 8,264 + 7,513 + 6,830 + 6,209 + 5,645 + 5,132 + 4,665) – Rs. 47,500

= Rs. 53,349 – Rs. 47,500

= Rs. 5,849

Profitability Index (PI) of

$$\text{Project A} = \frac{\text{Present value of net cash inflows}}{\text{Cost of investment}}$$

$$= \frac{\text{Rs. } 45{,}489}{\text{Rs. } 40{,}000} = 1.14$$

$$\text{Project B} = \frac{\text{Rs. } 53{,}349}{\text{Rs. } 47{,}500} = 1.12$$

Net Present Value (NPV) and Profitability Index (PI) is :

	Project A	Project B
Net Present value	Rs. 5,489	Rs. 5,849
Profitability Index	1.14	1.12

When supply of capital is unlimited, NPV method should be used and Project B is accepted because NPV of Project B is better than Project A. But under condition of limited supply of capital Profitability Index method should be used and Project A is more profitable because Project A has higher Net Cash inflows per unit of capital.

(a) Problem or Example on Present Value Method

Problem

A. Co. Limited is considering to purchase one automatic machine. The life of the machine is estimated at 5 years. The machine is expected to earn Rs. 10,000 per annum before deduction of tax. The company considers a yield of 20% necessary before investment is made in a project.

How much would be spend for the machine?

Assume tax 50%. Given log 1.2 = .0792; Antilog 0.604 = 4.018.

Solution

$$V = \frac{A}{r}\left\{1 - (1 + r)^{-n}\right\} = \frac{5{,}000}{.2}\left\{1 - (1.2)^{-5}\right\}$$

$$= \frac{5{,}000}{.2}[1 - .4018] = \frac{5{,}000}{.2} \times .5982$$

$$= \frac{5{,}000 \times 10 \times 5{,}982}{2 \times 10{,}000} = 14{,}955$$

Now, I hope that you have understood its workings. I shall be glad if you tell me frankly any point which is not clear to you.

☐ "Sir, can we prepare this sum without applying the formula?"

• Yes, you can.

Please note the workings :

Exhibit 1

Year	Cash Inflow	Present Value of Re. 1.00 at Discount Factor 20%	Present Value of Cash Inflow
	Rs.	Rs.	Rs.
1	5,000	0.833	4,165
2	5,000	0.694	3,470
3	5,000	0.579	2,895
4	5,000	0.482	2,410
5	5,000	0.402	2,010
	25,000		14,950 *

*Error of Rs. 5 is due to rounding.

This can be checked with the help of Exhibit 2.

Exhibit 2

Year	Capital unrecovered at the beginning of each year	Discount Factor (20%)	Inflow of Cash	Recovery of Capital
	Rs.	Rs.	Rs.	Rs.
1	14,950	2,990	5,000	2,010
2	12,940	2,588	5,000	2,412
3	10,528	2,106	5,000	2,894
4	7,634	1,527	5,000	3,473
5	4,161	832	5,000	4,168
			25,000	14,957 *

*Error of Rs. 7 is due to rounding in calculation.

However, on review of the above it is clear that the company can afford Rs. 15,000 (app) on the automatic machine.

(b) Problem on Trial and Error Method

Taking into account all the information contained in Exhibit 2, I want to make you clear the concept of Trial and Error Method.

☐ "Sir please dictate it, I have forgotten to bring the exercise book on which I had written all the information."

• That's not good. You should have. However, Please note :

Problem

Information

Investment Rs. 50,000

Year	Cash Flow (annual)
1	10,000
2	15,000
3	20,000
4	20,000
5	15,000

Calculate the suitable Rate of Return.

Year	Present Value of Re. 1.00 at discounting factor			Cash in-flow	Present Value of cash flow		
	16%	17%	18%	Rs.	16%	17%	18%
					X	Y	Z
1	0.8621	0.8547	0.8475	10,000	8,621	8,547	8,475
2	0.7432	0.7305	0.7182	15,000	11,148	10,957	10,773
3	0.6407	0.6244	0.6086	20,000	12,814	12,488	12,172
4	0.5523	0.5337	0.5168	20,000	11,046	10,674	10,316
5	0.4761	0.4561	0.4371	15,000	7,141	6,841	6,556
				80,000	50,770	49,507	48,292
					ΣX	ΣY	ΣZ

Suitable Rate of Return $= \dfrac{\Sigma X - I}{\Sigma x - I + I - \Sigma y} \times$ (Maximum rate – Minimum rate)

$$= \frac{50,770 - 50,000}{50,770 - 49,507} \times (17\% - 16\%)$$

$$= 0.6\%$$

The rate of return = 16% + 0.6% = 16.6%

(c) Problem on Net Gain Method

Problem

Particulars	**Machine Y**	**Machine X**
	Rs.	Rs.
Capital Cost	3,000	3,000
Cash Inflow (before tax)		
1st year	1,000	2,000
2nd year	2,000	3,000
3rd year	3,000	2,000
4th year	2,000	1,000
5th year	2,000	1,000

From the information given above you are requested by the top management to advise which one of the two machines is productive under the net present value method if the rate of interest is assumed to be : Machine X—5%; Machine Y—15%

Assume Income Tax 50%.

Solution

Year	Discount Factor		Present Value of Future Receipts			
			Under (5%) Discount Factor, machines		Under (15%) Discount Factor, Machines	
	5%	15%	Y	X	Y	X
	Rs.	Rs.	Rs.	Rs.	Rs.	Rs.
1st	0.952	0.869	476.0	952.0	434.5	869.0
2nd	0.907	0.756	907.0	1,360.5	756.0	1,134.0
3rd	0.864	0.657	1,296.0	864.0	985.5	657.0
4th	0.823	0.571	823.0	411.5	571.0	285.5
5th	0.784	0.497	784.0	392.0	497.0	248.5
Total Present Value			4,286.0	3,980.0	3,244.0	3,194.0
Cost of the Machine			3,000.0	3,000.0	3,000.0	3,000.0
Net Present Value			1,286.0	980.0	244.0	194.0

On review of the above it is clear that Machine Y seems to be more profitable with either rate.

Net, Present Value (NPV) vs Internal Rate of Return (IRR)

Both net present value (NPV) and internal rate of return (IRR) method consider the time value of money. Under NPV method the initial capital investment is deducted from the present value of expected future cash inflows from the proposed project. The project under evaluation is accepted if the NPV is positive and rejected otherwise. Under IRR method, project is accepted if the IRR is greater than the cost of capital. Again, NPV is positive only when the IRR is greater than the cost of capital. Thus, both NPV and IRR gives the same accept/reject decision provided that all cash inflows from the project under evaluation are positive and the projects are independent. But when projects are mutually exclusive, NPV and IRR methods may not always give the identical results. This can be illustrated with the following example :

Example :

A firm is considering two mutually exclusive proposals Proposal A and Proposal B. The investment required, cash inflows generated and other related information are :

	Proposal A	Proposal B
	Rs.	Rs.
Investment Required	18,160	18,160
Cash inflows :		
1st year	15,000	1,500
2nd year	7,500	9,000
3rd year	1,500	16,500
IRR	22%	17%
Ner Present value at 8% discount rate	3,350	4,043

[Calculations are not shown]

In the above situation conflict between NPV and IRR exists. If IRR is used Proposal A is preferred but under NPV method Proposal B is more profitable. Now what to do in such a situation?

In order to explain the situation let us construct a NPV profile of these two projects in the following table.

☐ "Excuse me Sir." What is NPV profile?

• NPV profile is a profile of NPVs at different discount rates. Now see the profile table :

Discount rate (%)	Proposal A Rs.	Proposal B Rs.
0%	5,840	8,840
5%	4,225	5,685
8%	3,350	4,043
11.1%	2,511	2,513
15%	1,540	798
20%	416	(1111)
25%	(592)	(2752)

The above table can be presented graphically as :

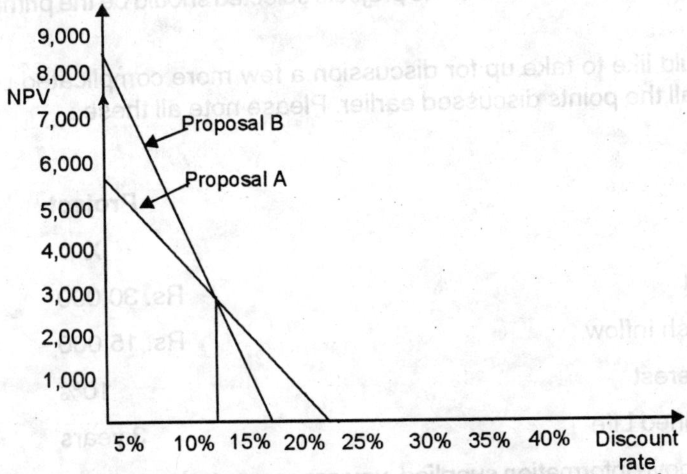

It is clear from the above table and graph that when the discount rate is approximately 11.1%, the NPV of two projects are almost equal. It is also clear that the NPV and IRR will contradict when the discount rate is below 11%. For example, at 8% discount rate NPV of Proposal B is greater than the Proposal A while IRR of Proposal B is lower than the Proposal A. However, No conflict will arise when the discount rate is above 11%. For example, at 15% discount rate, both NPV and IRR of Proposal A are greater than the Proposal B. So there is no conflict.

The reason for the conflict between IRR and NPV method is the assumption about the reinvestment rate of return. The IRR method assumes internal rate as the reinvestment rate; while NPV method assumes the minimum required rate of return as the reinvestment rate. Now, which one is the best? If IRR is used, we shall have more than one reinvestment rate. Since, different proposals have different IRR. But if NPV method is used we shall have only one reinvestment rate—which is the minimum required rate of return. Thus, assumption under NPV method about reinvestment rate is more realistic than IRR method and NPV method is therefore, preferred. Again, since the objective of business is to maximise the value of the firm one should prefer NPV method for selecting investment proposal when conflict exists between NPV and IRR method.

- I think, you have followed my lecture. Is there any question?

☐ "Sir what is **Capital Rationing**?

In actual practice, firms do not have unlimited supply of funds for making capital investment. Firms usually have capital expenditure budget for a particular period and have to incur capital expenditure within the limit specified in the budget. This situation refers to the capital rationing situation. This situation arises due to both external such as, various consequences of market imperfections as well as internal or self-imposed reasons such as management policy of financing from internally generated funds having maximum amount that can be invested by each department, specifying minimum rate of return of each project etc.

Capital Rationing

Under capital rationing situation projects should be evaluated by applying profitability index criterion and ranked in descending order of profitability. This selection of alternative will continue till the funds available for the project is exhausted. Maximisation of total net present value of the combination of the projects selected should be the prima facie objective of the firm.

Now I would like to take up for discussion a few more complicated problems taking into account all the points discussed earlier. Please note all these :

Problem :

Details	**Project X**	**Project Y**
Investment	Rs. 30,000	Rs. 35,000
Annual Cash Inflow	Rs. 15,000	Rs. 10,000
Rate of Interest	10%	10%
Predetermined Life	3 years	6 years

From the above information supplied, you are requested to report the Top Management which one of the two investments would be more profitable under the (a) Pay-Back Period Method, and (b) Net Gain Method (Discounted Cash Flow).

Other Special Information :

Ignore Taxation.

Log 1.10 = 0.0414 and antilog .8758 = .7513
.7516 = .5644

Solution

The formula of Pay-back Period

$P = \frac{1}{S}$

P = Pay-Back Period

I = Cost of Assets/Original Investment

S = Annual Cash Inflow

(a) Pay-Back

	Project X	Project Y
Cost	Rs. 30,000	Rs. 35,000
Cash Inflow	Rs. 15,000	Rs. 10,000
Pay-Back Period	2 years	3½ years
Profitability		
X = (3 yrs. – 2 yrs.)	1 × 15,000 = 15,000	
Y = (6 yrs. – 3½ yrs.)		2½ × 10,000 = 25,000

On overall review of the situation, it is clear that Project Y seems to be more profitable under the Pay-back Period.

(b) Discounted Cash Flow

Project X

$$V = \frac{A}{r}\left\{1 - (1 + r)^{-n}\right\}$$

$$= \frac{15,000}{0.1}\left\{1 - (1.1)^{-3}\right\}$$

$$= \frac{15,000}{0.1}(1 - .7513)$$

$$= \frac{15,000}{0.1} \times .2487$$

$$= \frac{15,000 \times 10 \times 2487}{1 \times 10,000} = 37,305$$

Project Y

$$V = \frac{A}{r}\left\{1 - (1 + r)^{-n}\right\}$$

$$= \frac{10,000}{0.1}\left\{1 - (1.1)^{-6}\right\}$$

$$= \frac{10{,}000}{0.1}(1 - .5644)$$

$$= \frac{10{,}000}{0.1} \times .4356$$

$$= \frac{10{,}000 \times 10 \times 4356}{1 \times 10{,}000} = 43{,}560$$

	Project X	Project Y
	Rs.	Rs.
Present value of Cash Flow	37,305	43,560
Less : Cost of Investment	30,000	35,000
Net Present Value	7,305	8,560

Investment in Project Y seems to be more profitable.

Problem

ABC Company Limited is willing to purchase a machine for the expansion of their existing factory. With this end in view they seek your advice as to which one of the following machines would be more profitable. For this you are supplied with the following data :

Cost of each type of machine	Rs. 1,00,000
Discount rate for all types of Investment	10%

Cash Flow

Years	Machine A	Machine B	Machine C	Machine D
	Rs.	Rs.	Rs.	Rs.
1	30,000	10,000	20,000	20,000
2	40,000	30,000	40,000	30,000
3	50,000	40,000	50,000	35,000
4	30,000	60,000	35,000	40,000
5	20,000	40,000	30,000	40,000

You see, this is a very easy problem.

☐ "No Sir, It is a very difficult problem. Please, Sir, work out the problem."

• Well, I will work out the problem. Before that I would like to discuss a few points. First of all, you are to see and observe the total cash inflow for each type of machine :

Machine A Rs. 1,70,000; B Rs. 1,80,000; C Rs. 1,75,000; D Rs. 1,65,000.

It is clear from the figures shown earlier that cash inflow in case of Machine B is higher. But this does not mean that Machine B would be more profitable. This will be tested from the Profitability Statement :

Solution

Profitability Statement

Years	Machine A		Machine B		Machine C		Machine D		Discount factor (10%)
	Cash in-flow	Present value	Cash in-flow	Present value	Cash in-flow	Present value	Cash in-flow	Present value	
	Rs.	Rs.	Rs.	Rs.	Rs.	Rs.	Rs.	Rs.	Rs.
1	30,000	27,270	10,000	9,090	20,000	18,180	20,000	18,180	0.909
2	40,000	33,040	30,000	24,780	40,000	33,040	30,000	24,780	0.826
3	50,000	37,550	40,000	30,040	50,000	37,550	35,000	26,285	0.751
4	30,000	20,490	60,000	40,980	35,000	23,905	40,000	27,320	0.683
5	20,000	12,420	40,000	24,840	30,000	18,630	40,000	24,840	0.621
	1,70,000	1,30,770	1,80,000	1,29,730	1,75,000	1,31,305	1,65,000	1,21,405	

This statement indicates that Machine C would be the more profitable investment, though cash inflow in this machine is less than Machine B; Machine C has more or less standard cash inflow early in its working life. For this, present value in case of C is relatively higher.

Problem

		(figures in thousand) Rs.
1st year	Initial Investment	40
2nd year	Investment in Fixed Assets	40
	Working Capital	15
3rd year	Investment in Working Capital	5
		100
1st year	Return in initial year	Nil
2nd year	Return in initial year	Rs. 6,000
3rd year	Return in initial year	Rs. 14,000
4th year	Return in initial year	Rs. 32,000
5th year	Return in initial year	Rs. 33,000
6th year	Return in initial year	Rs. 30,000

Return before charging depreciation allowance @ 20% of the W.D.V. of fixed assets. Development rebate 20% of the original cost of fixed assets. Rate of tax @ 50%. After the expiry of 6th year the working capital is drawn in full. A scrap value of Rs. 6,000 will be realised. The present value of Re. 1 in amount @ 8% will be as under :

1st year	Rs. .92
2nd year	Rs. .86
3rd year	Rs. .79
4th year	Rs. .74
5th year	Rs. .68
6th year	Rs. .63

From the above information comment on whether investment will be profitable or not.

[Adapted from I.C.W.A.]

Solution

Profitability Statement

Years	Cost	Cost of Machine	Capital Allowance	Cash Flow	Taxable Income	Tax	Years of Payment
1	Value of Machine	40,000					
	Development Rebate		8,000				
	Depreciation Allowance	8,000	8,000				
	W.D.V.	32,000	16,000	Nil	(–) 16,000	(–) 8,000	2nd
2	Addition	40,000					
		72,000					
	Development Rebate		8,000				
	Depreciation Allowance	14,400	14,400				
	W.D.V.	57,600	22,400	6,000	(–) 16,400	(–) 8,200	3rd
3	Depreciation Allowance	11,520	11,520	14,000	+ 2,480	1,240	4th
	W.D.V.	46,080					
4	Depreciation Allowance	9,216	9,216	32,000	+ 22,784	11,392	5th
	W.D.V.	36,864					
5	Depreciation Allowance	7,372	7,372	33,000	+ 25,628	12,814	6th
	W.D.V.	29,492					
6	Scrap	6,000					
		23,492	23,492	30,000	(+) 6,508	3,254	7th

Cash Outflow

Years	Capital Exp.	Working Capital	Discount Factor	Present Value
1	40,000	—	.92	36,800
2	40,000	15,000	.86	47,300
3	—	5,000	.79	3,950
6	(–) 6,000	(–) 20,000	(–) 26,000 × .63	(–) 16,380
				71,670

Net Cash Outflow

Years	Cash in-Flow	Tax	Net Cash Flow	Discount Factor	Present Value
1	—	(–) 8,000	8,000	.94	7,360
2	6,000	(–) 8,200	14,200	.86	12,212
3	14,000	1,240	12,760	.79	10,080
4	32,000	11,392	20,608	.74	15,249
5	33,000	12,814	20,186	.68	13,726
6	30,000	3,254	26,746	.63	16,849
					75,476

From the above calculation it is found that cash outflow is less than cash inflow; so the project may be accepted.

Problem

A company has the choice of continuing making a product on its existing machine or obtaining one of two alternative machines in lieu.

The following details are available in respect to these machines :

	Machines		
	Present	**E**	**F**
Book value (Rs.)	50,000		
Re-sale value now (Rs.)	55,000		
Purchase price (Rs.)		90,000	1,00,000
Fixed costs p.a. (including dep.) (Rs.)	46,000	54,000	66,000
Variable running costs per unit (including labour) (Rs.)	1.50	0.75	1.25
Units produced per hour	8	8	12

Additional data :

Selling Price per unit	Rs. 10
Materials cost per unit	Rs. 5
Annual operating hours	2,000
Life of each machine (as from now)	5 years
Residual value of machines	Nil

Depreciation was calculated by straight-line method using book value or purchase price, as the case may be. The Sales Manager believes that the production from the present machine or machine *E* can all be sold without further expenditure, but that an extra Rs. 4,000 p.a. will need to be spent on advertising to sell the extra production given by machine *F*.

Assuming that the rate of tax is 50% and that the cost of finance is 9%, evaluate the projects using Net Present Value Method.

The P.V. of Re. 1 (to be received at the end of each year) at 9% is given :

Year	1	2	3	4	5
P.V.	.92	.84	.77	.71	.65

[M.Com., (C.U.) Management Accountancy]

Solution

Profitability Statement

	Machines					
		Present		E		F
		Rs.		Rs.		Rs.
Sales Value		1,60,000		1,60,000		2,40,000
Less :						
Variable Cost	24,000		12,000		30,000	
Material Cost	80,000		80,000		1,20,000	
Fixed Cost (excluding Depreciation)	36,000		36,000		46,000	
Advt. Cost	—		—		4,000	
		1,40,000		1,28,000		2,00,000
		20,000		32,000		40,000
Less : Depreciation		10,000		18,000		20,000
		10,000		14,000		20,000
Less : Tax@ 50%		5,000		7,000		10,000
		5,000		7,000		10,000
Add : Depreciation		10,000		18,000		20,000
Net Cash Flow		15,000		25,000		30,000

Profitability of Machines

Years	Present	Pv	E	Pv	F	Pv
1	.92 × 15,000 =	13,800	× 25,000 =	23,000	× 30,000 =	27,600
2	.84 × 15,000 =	12,600	× 25,000 =	21,000	× 30,000 =	25,200
3	.77 × 15,000 =	11,550	× 25,000 =	19,250	× 30,000 =	23,100
4	.71 × 15,000 =	10,650	× 25,000 =	17,750	× 30,000 =	21,300
5	.65 × 15,000 =	9,750	× 25,000 =	16,250	× 30,000 =	19,500
		58,350		97,250		1,16,700
Less : Original Value		55,000		90,000		1,00,000
		3,350		7,250		16,700

Hence the present machine should be replaced and Machine F, which yields highest net present value, should be installed.

Note

Sales Value : Present = 2000 × 8 = 16,000 units × Rs. 10 = 1,60,000

E = 2000 × 8 = 16,000 units × Rs. 10 = 1,60,000

F = 2000 × 12 = 24,000 units × Rs. 10 = 2,40,000

Depreciation : Present $= \frac{\text{Rs. } 50,000}{5}$ Rs. 10,000 p.a.

$E = \frac{\text{Rs. } 90,000}{5} = \text{Rs. } 18,000 \text{ p.a. } F = \frac{\text{Rs. } 1,00,000}{5} = \text{Rs. } 20,000 \text{ p.a.}$

● I hope that you have followed my workings. Is there any question?

☐ "Sir, I would like to put to you one question."

● Yes.

☐ "Sir, wherefrom we can get the figure for, say .92, .84, when only Discounting factors, say 6%, 8%, are given?"

● Well, you see you will be supplied with the source from where you may get all these. Please note that in the Appendix I have given details of the same. However, I am giving you two Tables here for your calculation :

Table I

Present Value of Re. 1

Years	5%	6%	8%	10%	12%	14%	15%	16%	18%	20%	22%	24%	25%
1	0.952	0.943	0.926	0.909	0.893	0.877	0.870	0.862	0.847	0.833	0.820	0.806	0.800
2	0.907	0.890	0.857	0.826	0.797	0.769	0.756	0.743	0.718	0.694	0.672	0.650	0.640
3	0.864	0.840	0.794	0.751	0.712	0.675	0.658	0.641	0.609	0.579	0.551	0.524	0.512
4	0.823	0.792	0.735	0.683	0.636	0.592	0.572	0.552	0.516	0.482	0.451	0.423	0.410
5	0.784	0.747	0.681	0.621	0.567	0.519	0.497	0.476	0.437	0.402	0.370	0.341	0.328
6	0.746	0.705	0.630	0.564	0.507	0.456	0.432	0.410	0.370	0.335	0.303	0.275	0.262
7	0.711	0.665	0.583	0.513	0.452	0.400	0.376	0.354	0.314	0.279	0.249	0.222	0.210
8	0.677	0.627	0.540	0.467	0.404	0.351	0.327	0.305	0.266	0.233	0.204	0.179	0.168
9	0.645	0.592	0.500	0.424	0.361	0.308	0.284	0.263	0.225	0.194	0.167	0.144	0.134
10	0.614	0.558	0.463	0.386	0.322	0.270	0.247	0.227	0.191	0.162	0.137	0.116	0.107
11	0.585	0.527	0.429	0.350	0.287	0.237	0.215	0.195	0.162	0.135	0.112	0.094	0.086
12	0.557	0.497	0.397	0.319	0.257	0.208	0.187	0.168	0.137	0.112	0.092	0.076	0.069
13	0.530	0.469	0.368	0.290	0.229	0.182	0.163	0.145	0.116	0.093	0.075	0.061	0.055
14	0.505	0.442	0.340	0.263	0.205	0.160	0.141	0.125	0.099	0.078	0.062	0.049	0.044
15	0.481	0.417	0.315	0.239	0.183	0.140	0.123	0.108	0.084	0.065	0.051	0.040	0.035
16	0.458	0.394	0.292	0.218	0.163	0.123	0.107	0.093	0.071	0.054	0.042	0.032	0.028
17	0.436	0.371	0.270	0.198	0.146	0.108	0.093	0.080	0.060	0.045	0.034	0.026	0.023
18	0.416	0.350	0.250	0.180	0.130	0.095	0.081	0.069	0.051	0.038	0.028	0.021	0.018
19	0.396	0.331	0.232	0.164	0.116	0.083	0.070	0.060	0.043	0.031	0.023	0.017	0.014
20	0.377	0.312	0.215	0.149	0.104	0.073	0.061	0.051	0.037	0.026	0.019	0.014	0.012

Table II

Present Value Received Annually for N Years

Years	5%	6%	8%	10%	12%	14%	15%	16%	18%	20%	22%	24%	25%
1	0.952	0.943	0.926	0.909	0.893	0.877	0.870	0.862	0.847	0.833	0.820	0.806	0.800
2	1.859	1.833	1.783	1.736	1.690	1.647	1.626	1.605	1.566	1.528	1.492	1.457	1.440
3	2.723	2.673	2.577	2.487	2.402	2.322	2.283	2.246	2.174	2.106	2.042	1.981	1.952
4	3.546	3.465	3.312	3.169	3.037	2.194	2.855	2.798	2.690	2.589	2.494	2.404	2.362
5	4.330	4.212	3.993	3.791	3.605	3.433	3.352	3.274	3.127	2.991	2.864	2.745	2.689
6	5.076	4.917	4.623	4.355	4.111	3.889	3.784	3.685	3.498	3.326	3.167	3.020	2.951
7	5.786	5.582	5.206	4.868	4.564	4.288	4.160	4.039	3.812	3.605	3.416	3.242	3.161
8	6.463	6.210	5.747	5.335	4.968	4.639	4.487	4.334	3.078	3.837	3.619	3.421	3.329
9	7.108	6.802	6.247	5.759	5.328	4.946	4.772	4.607	4.303	4.031	3.786	3.566	3.463
10	7.722	7.360	6.710	6.145	5.650	5.216	5.019	4.833	4.494	4.192	3.923	3.682	3.571
11	8.306	7.887	7.139	6.495	5.937	5.453	5.234	5.029	4.656	4.327	4.035	3.776	3.656
12	8.863	8.384	7.536	6.814	6.194	5.660	5.421	5.197	4.793	4.439	4.127	3.851	3.725
13	9.394	8.853	7.904	7.103	6.424	5.842	5.583	5.342	4.910	4.533	4.203	3.912	3.780
14	9.899	9.295	8.244	7.367	6.628	6.002	5.724	5.468	5.008	4.611	4.265	3.962	8.824
15	10.380	9.712	8.559	7.606	6.811	6.142	5.847	5.575	5.092	4.675	4.375	4.315	3.859
16	10.838	10.106	8.851	7.824	6.974	6.265	5.954	5.669	5.162	4.730	4.357	4.033	3.887
17	11.274	10.447	9.122	8.022	7.120	6.373	6.047	5.749	5.222	4.775	4.391	4.059	3.910
18	11.690	10.828	9.372	8.201	7.250	6.467	6.128	5.818	5.273	4.812	4.419	4.080	3.928
19	12.085	11.158	9.604	8.365	7.366	6.550	6.198	5.877	5.316	4.844	4.442	4.097	3.942
20	12.462	11.470	9.818	8.514	7.469	6.623	6.259	5.929	5.353	4.870	4.460	4.110	3.954

Problem

Which of the following competing projects would you recommend using (a) Pay-Back Period, (b) Pay-Back Profitability, and (c) Net Present Value Methods?

		Project I	Project II
Initial Outlay (Rs.)		20,000	25,000
Estimated Life (years)		5	7
Estimated Net Cash Flow (Rs.)			
End of year	1	5,000	5,000
	2	6,000	5,000
	3	4,000	5,000
	4	4,000	5,000
	5	6,000	5,000
	6	—	5,000
	7	—	5,000
Estimated Scrap Value		Nil	Nil

Discount rate may be taken at 10% p.a. and the P.V. of Re. 1 to be received at the end of each year at 10% is given :

Year	1	2	3	4	5	6	7
P.V. (Re.)	0.91	0.83	0.75	0.68	0.62	0.57	0.51

[C.U., M.Com. Adapted]

Solution

(a) Pay-Back Period

Project I

Year	Cash Flows (Rs.)	Cumulative Cash Flows (Rs.)
0	(20,000)	(20,000)
1	5,000	(15,000)
2	6,000	(9,000)
3	4,000	(5000)
4	4,000	(1,000)
5	6,000	5,000

$$\therefore \text{Pay-Back Period} = 4 \text{ year} + 12 \times \frac{1{,}000}{6{,}000}$$

$$= 4 \text{ years } 2 \text{ months}$$

Project II

$$\text{Pay-Back Period} = \frac{\text{Initial Outlay}}{\text{Estimated net cash inflow per year}}$$

$$= \frac{\text{Rs. } 25{,}000}{\text{Rs. } 5{,}000} = 5 \text{ years}$$

Project I has shorter pay-back period. Thus Project I is recommended under this method.

(b) Pay-Back Profitability

Project I : Total cash inflows – Initial outlay

= Rs. 25,000 – Rs. 20,000

= Rs. 5,000

Project II = Rs. 35,000 – Rs. 25,000

= Rs. 10,000

Thus, when Pay-Back Profitability is used Project II is recommended for selection.

(c) Net Present Value

Project I :

Year	Cash Flows Rs.	Discounting Factors @ 10% p.a.	Discounted Cash Flows (Rs.)	Cumulative Discounted Cash Flows (Rs.)
0	(20,000)	1.00	(20,000)	(20,000)
1	5,000	0.91	4,550	(15,450)
2	6,000	0.83	4,980	(10,470)
3	4,000	0.75	3,000	(7,470)
4	4,000	0.68	2,720	(4,750)
5	6,000	0.62	3,720	(1,030)

∴ NPV = Rs. (–) 1,030

Project II :

Year	Cash Flows Rs.	Discounting Factors @ 10% p.a.	Discounted Cash Flows (Rs.)	Cumulative Discounted Cash Flows (Rs.)
0	(25,000)	1.00	(25,000)	(25,000)
1	5,000	0.91	4,550	(20,450)
2	5,000	0.83	4,150	(16,300)
3	5,000	0.75	3,750	(12,550)
4	5,000	0.68	3,400	(9,150)
5	5,000	0.62	3,100	(6,050)
6	5,000	0.57	2,850	(3,200)
7	5,000	0.51	2,550	(650)

$\therefore$ NPV = Rs. – 650

Since, both projects have negative NPV at 10% discount rate, none of them are acceptable.

Problem

A company is considering two mutually exclusive proposals. Each proposal requires an investment of Rs. 50,000 and has a life-time of five years. The depreciation is charged on Straight Line Method. The applicable tax rate is 50%.

The estimated cash flows (before depreciation and tax) are :

Years	Proposal X (Rs.)	Proposal Y (Rs.)
1	20,000	30,000
2	22,000	27,000
3	28,000	22,000
4	25,000	25,000
5	30,000	20,000

Advice the company which proposal is acceptable under Internal Rate of Return Method. The present value of Re. 1 to be received at the end of each year, at different cost of capital, is given :

Year	18%	22%	25%
1	0.847	0.820	0.800
2	0.718	0.672	0.640
3	0.609	0.551	0.512
4	0.516	0.451	0.410
5	0.437	0.370	0.328

[C.U., M.Com, Adapted]

Solution

$$\text{Depreciation per year} = \frac{\text{Rs. } 50{,}000}{5} = \text{Rs. } 10{,}000$$

Calculation of net cash inflows from the projects after tax but before depreciation :

Proposal X

Year	Cash Flows Rs.	Depreciation Rs.	Tax @ 50% Rs.	Net Cash flow after tax (Rs.)
	a	b	c = (a – b) × 50%	(a – c)
0	20,000	10,000	5,000	15,000
1	22,000	10,000	6,000	16,000
3	28,000	10,000	9,000	19,000
4	25,000	10,000	7,500	17,500
5	30,000	10,000	10,000	20,000

Proposal Y

Year	Cash Inflow before depreciation and tax	Depreciation	Tax	Net Cash Inflow after tax
	a	b	$c = \frac{(a-b)}{100} \times 50$	(a – c)
	Rs.	Rs.	Rs.	Rs.
1	30,000	10,000	10,000	20,000
2	27,000	10,000	8,500	18,500
3	22,000	10,000	6,000	16,000
4	25,000	10,000	7,500	17,500
5	20,000	10,000	5,000	15,000

Calculation of Internal Rate of Return :

Proposal X

NPV at 22% discount rate and 18% discount rate.

Year	Net cash inflows (Rs.)	Discount rate 18%	Discount Factor @22%	Discounted Cash Flow at 18% Discount rate (Rs.)	Discount Cash Flow at 22% Discount rate (Rs.)
0	(50,000)	1.00	1.000	(50,000)	(50,000)
1	15,000	.847	.820	12,705	12,300
2	16,000	.718	.672	11,488	10,752
3	19,000	.609	.551	11,571	10,469
4	17,500	.516	.451	9,030	7,893
5	20,000	.437	.370	8,740	7,400
Net Present Value				3,534	– 1,186

By Interpolation

$$\text{IRR} = 18\% + \frac{3534}{3534 + 1186} \times (22\% - 18\%)$$

$$= 18\% + \frac{3534}{4720} \times 4\%$$

$$= 18\% + 2.99\%$$

$$= 20.99\%$$

or near 21% (approx).

Proposal Y

NPV at 22% discount rate and 18% discount rate.

Year	Net cash inflows after tax (Rs.)	Discount Factor at 22%	Discount Factor at 25%	Discounted Cash Flow at 22% Discount rate (Rs.)	Discount Cash Flow at 25% Discount rate (Rs.)
0	(50,000)	1.000	1.000	(50,000)	(50,000)
1	20,000	0.820	0.800	16,400	16,000
2	18,500	0.672	0.640	12,432	11,840
3	16,000	0.551	0.512	8,816	8,192
4	17,500	0.451	0.410	7,893	7,175
5	15,000	0.370	0.328	5,550	4,920
Net Present Value				1,091	–1,873

By Interpolation

$$\text{IRR} = 22\% + \frac{\text{Rs. } 1{,}091}{(\text{Rs. } 1{,}091 + \text{Rs. } 1{,}873)} \times (25\% - 22\%)$$

$$= 22\% + 1.10\%$$

$$= 23.1\%$$

$\therefore$ near 23%

Since, IRR of Proposal Y, i.e., 23% is greater than the IRR of Proposal X, i.e., 21%, Proposal Y is acceptable.

Problem

The SRL Hospital has its own laundry. It is considering replacement of existing laundry equipments. Currently two options are available—the purchase of Machine A or the rental of Machine B. Information on both options are given :

Machine A (Purchase)		Machine B (Rental)
Material Cost per kg.	Rs. 2	Rs. 1.80
Labour Cost per kg.	Rs. 3	Rs. 3.40
Fixed Cost p.a.	Rs. 20,000	Rs. 18,000
Life of Machine	3 Years	Rental Agreement 3 Years
Rental per annum	—	Rs. 20,000
Depreciation p.a.	Rs. 20,000	Nil
Capital Cost	Rs. 60,000	

Other information :

(i) Machine A will have no residual value at any time. (ii) The existing laundry equipment could be sold for Rs. 10,000, (iii) The hospital's discount rate for projects of this nature is 15%, (iv) The fixed cost are direct cost of operating the laundry (v) Last year the laundry processed 1,20,000 kgs of washing and this year the total is forecast to grow to 1,32,000 kgs. The growth in laundry processed is forecast to continue at the same percentage rate for the next 7 years.

Evaluate the options for operating the laundry using discounted cash flow techniques and give your recommendations.

Note : Inflation and income tax can be ignored.

Solution

Growth in laundry processing

$$= \frac{1{,}32{,}000 \text{ kgs.} - 1{,}20{,}000 \text{ kgs.}}{1{,}20{,}000 \text{ kgs.}} \times 100$$

$$= \frac{12{,}000 \text{ kgs.}}{1{,}20{,}000 \text{ kgs.}} \times 100 = 10\%$$

∴ Laundry Processing in 2nd year = 1,32,000 × 110%

= 1,45,200 kgs.

and in 3rd year = 1,45,200 kgs × 110%

= 1,59,720 kgs

Let us first consider Proposal 1, that is purchase of Machine A.

Initial cash outflow :

Capital Cost	Rs. 60,000
Less : Expected sale proceeds of laundry equipment	Rs. 10,000
	Rs. 50,000

Cash outflows of subsequent three years :

	Years		
	1	2	3
Units expected to be processed	1,32,000 kgs	1,45,200 kgs	1,59,720 kgs
	Rs.	Rs.	Rs.
Material (Rs. 2.00 each)	2,64,000	2,90,400	3,19,440
Labour (Rs. 3.00 each)	3,96,000	4,35,600	4,79,160
	6,60,000	7,26,000	7,98,600
Add : Fixed Cost	20,000	20,000	20,000
	6,80,000	7,46,000	8,18,600

Calculation of Present value of cash outflows if Proposal 1 is selected :

Year	Cash outflows Rs.	Present value Factor at 15% Discount rate	Present value Rs.
0	50,000	1.00	50,000
1	6,80,000	0.87	5,91,600
2	7,46,000	0.756	5,63,976
3	8,18,600	0.658	5,38,639
			17,44,215

Now if Proposal 2 is considered :

Net cash outflow if Machine B is rented :

	Years		
	1	2	3
Units expected to be processed	1,32,000 kgs	1,45,200 kgs	1,59,720 kgs
	Rs.	Rs.	Rs.
Material (Rs. 1.80 each)	2,37,600	2,61,360	2,87,496
Labour (Rs. 3.40 each)	4,48,800	4,93,680	5,43,048
	6,86,400	7,55,040	8,30,544
Fixed cost	18,000	18,000	18,000
	7,04,400	7,73,040	8,48,544
Rental p.a.	20,000	20,000	20,000
	7,24,400	7,93,040	8,68,544

∴ Present Value of Net Cash Outflow

= Rs. (7,24,400 × 0.87 + 7,93,040 × 0.756 + 8,68,544 × 0.658) – Initial cash inflow

= Rs (6,30,228 + 5,99,538 + 5,71,502) – Rs. 10,000

= Rs. 18,01,268 – Rs. 10,000

= Rs. 17,91,268

	Machine A (Purchase)	Machine B (Rental)
Present value of cash outflows	Rs. 17,44,215	17,91,268

Present value of net cash outflows of Proposal 1 is lower than the Proposal 2, hence, Proposal 1 is preferred for acceptance.

Problem

An investor facing two multually exclusive investment proposals, having life span of four years each, furnishes the following information :

		Proposal A	Proposal B
Initial Investment needed (Rs.)		80,000	24,000
Net after tax inflows expected at the			
end of year	1	28,000	9,800
	2	28,000	9,800
	3	28,000	9,800
	4	28,000	9,800

You are asked to rank the two proposals by the IRR method and the P.V. Method, assuming cost of capital to be 10%.

Explain the reasons for contradiction in ranking, if any, and state with reasons which of the two methods the investor should rely upon in making his final choice.

[C.U., M.Com.]

Solution

Let us first calculate IRR of Proposal A and Proposal B :

Proposal A

Let, IRR = 13%

We know that IRR is that rate which equates the present value of future cash inflows with the initial investment.

∴ at 13% discount rate, present value of future cash inflows :

$$\frac{\text{Rs. } 28{,}000}{(1.13)} + \frac{\text{Rs. } 28{,}000}{(1.13)^2} + \frac{\text{Rs. } 28{,}000}{(1.13)^3} + \frac{\text{Rs. } 28{,}000}{(1.13)^4}$$

= Rs. 24,779 + Rs. 21,928 + Rs. 19,405 + Rs. 17,173

= Rs. 83,285 > Rs. 80,000

∴ NPV = Rs. 83,285 – Rs. 80,000

= Rs. 3,285

Let, IRR = 16%

∴ Present value of cash inflows =

$$\frac{\text{Rs. } 28{,}000}{(1.16)} + \frac{\text{Rs. } 28{,}000}{(1.16)^2} + \frac{\text{Rs. } 28{,}000}{(1.16)^3} + \frac{\text{Rs. } 28{,}000}{(1.16)^4}$$

= Rs. 24,138 + Rs. 20,809 + Rs. 17,938 + Rs. 15,464

= Rs. 78,349 < Rs. 80,000

∴ NPV = Rs. – 1651

Now, by interpolation we get

$$\text{IRR} = 13\% + \frac{3{,}285}{3{,}285 + 1{,}651} \times (16\% - 13\%)$$

= 13% + 1.99%

= 14.99%

∴ IRR of proposal A is 14.99%.

Proposal B

Let, IRR = 22%

∴ NPV at 22%

$$= \frac{\text{Rs. } 9{,}800}{(1.22)} + \frac{\text{Rs. } 9{,}800}{(1.22)^2} + \frac{\text{Rs. } 9{,}800}{(1.22)^3} + \frac{\text{Rs. } 9{,}800}{(1.22)^4} - \text{Rs. } 24{,}000$$

= Rs. 8,033 + Rs. 6,584 + Rs. 5,397 + Rs. 4,424 – Rs. 24,000

= Rs. 24,438 – Rs. 24,000

= Rs. 438

Let, IRR = 25%

∴ NPV at 25%

$$= \frac{\text{Rs. } 9{,}800}{(1.25)} + \frac{\text{Rs. } 9{,}800}{(1.25)^2} + \frac{\text{Rs. } 9{,}800}{(1.25)^3} + \frac{\text{Rs. } 9{,}800}{(1.25)^4} - \text{Rs. } 24{,}000$$

= Rs. 7,840 + Rs. 6,272 + Rs. 5,018 + Rs. 4,014 – Rs. 24,000

= Rs. 23,144 – Rs. 24,000

= Rs. – 856

∴ By interpolation we get

$$\text{IRR} = 22\% + \frac{438}{438 + 856} \times (25\% - 22\%)$$

$= 22\% + 1.01\%$

$= 23\%$ (Approx).

∴ IRR of proposal B is 23%.

Let us now calculate Net Present Value (NPV) at 10% cost of capital.

Proposal A

$$\text{NPV} = \frac{\text{Rs. } 28{,}000}{(1.1)} + \frac{\text{Rs. } 28{,}000}{(1.1)^2} + \frac{\text{Rs. } 28{,}000}{(1.1)^3} + \frac{\text{Rs. } 28{,}000}{(1.1)^4} - \text{Rs. } 80{,}000$$

= Rs. 25,455 + Rs. 23,140 + Rs. 21,037 + Rs. 19,124 – Rs. 80,000

= Rs. 88,756 – Rs. 80,000

= Rs. 8,756

Proposal B

$$\text{NPV} = \frac{\text{Rs. } 9{,}800}{(1.1)} + \frac{\text{Rs. } 9{,}800}{(1.1)^2} + \frac{\text{Rs. } 9{,}800}{(1.1)^3} + \frac{\text{Rs. } 9{,}800}{(1.1)^4} - \text{Rs. } 24{,}000$$

= Rs. 8,909 + Rs. 8,099 + Rs. 7,363 + Rs. 6,694 – Rs. 24,000

= Rs. 31,065 – Rs. 24,000

= Rs. 7,065

Let us now present the above results of calculation in the following table :

	Proposal A	Proposal B
IRR	14.99%	23%
NPV (Rs.)	8,756	7,065

Ranking of Proposals :

Under IRR method

I — Proposal B

II — Proposal A

Under NPV method

I — Proposal A

II — Proposal B

In case of mutually exclusive proposals, contradiction arises after ranking under two methods of project evaluation—Internal Rate of Return (IRR) and Net Present Value (NPV). Where the NPV profiles of the two projects intersect with one another, contradiction in ranking arises for all discount rate below the intersection rate. Thus, no contradiction arises if the discount rate is above the intersection rate.

When contradiction arises it is better to select a proposal with higher NPV. The reason for giving preference to NPV method is that the objective of business is to maximise value of the firm and selection of proposal by using NPV leads to the achievement of that objective. Another reason is that NPV method assumes minimum required rate of return, that is, cost of capital or the discount rate as reinvestment rate for intermediate cash inflows as against IRR method which assumes IRR as the reinvestment rate. The cost of capital remains constant for all projects but all projects do not have the same IRR. Thus, using IRR means shifting reinvestment rate from one project to another.

Problem

W Ltd. is faced with a decision to purchase or acquire on lease a car. The price of the car is Rs. 2,52,000. The car can be obtained on lease by paying 5 advance equal lease rentals of Rs. 60,500 annually. W Ltd. can also obtain car loan at a rate of 15% p.a. and the loan will be paid in five annual equal instalments exclusive of interest. Interest is payable annually on reducing balance of loan. The effective tax rate is 40%. As per Income Tax Act, depreciation allowable on Motor Car is 20% on W.D.V. basis. Cost of Capital is 9%.

Which of the two alternatives do you recommend?

Use the following discount factors.

Discount rate	Year				
	1	2	3	4	5
9%	0.92	0.84	0.77	0.71	0.65

[C.U., M.Com]

Solution

Alternative 1 : Purchase of car by taking loan at a rate of 15% p.a.

Calculation of Present value of net cash outflows if loan is taken :

Year	Repayment of Principal (Rs.) 1	Interest (Rs.) 2	Depreciation (Rs.) 3	Net outflow at Interest due to tax shield 4 = 2 s [1 – 40%] (Rs.)
1	50,400	37,800	50,400	22,680
2	50,400	30,240	40,320	18,144
3	50,400	22,680	32,256	13,608
4	50,400	15,120	25,805	9,072
5	50,400	7,560	20,644	4,536

Depreciation tax savings (Rs.) 5 = 3 × 40%	Net cash outflow (Rs.) 6 = [1 + 4 – 5]	P/V factor at 9% discount rate 7	Present value
20,160	52,920	0.92	48,686.40
16,128	52,416	0.84	44,029.40
12,902	51,106	0.77	39,351.62
10,322	49,150	0.71	34,896.50
8,258	46,678	0.65	30,340.70
			1,97,304.62

If the car is taken on lease the present value of net cash outflows would be :

Year	Lease Rental 1 (Rs.)	Lease Rental net of tax shield 2 = 1 × [1 – 40%]	P/V factor at 9% discount rate 3	Present value 2 × 3 (Rs.)
0	60,500	36,300	1	36,300
1	60,500	36,300	0.92	33,396
2	60,500	36,300	0.84	30,492
3	60,500	36,300	0.77	27,951
4	60,500	36,300	0.71	25,773
				1,53,912

Since present value of cash outflows in case of car is taken on lease is lower than the purchase by taking loan, leasing is less costly and, hence, recommended.

Problem

A firm proposes to market a cheaper variety of its existing brand to be sold for Rs. 20 per unit, estimated product life being five years. The sales volume for the five years has been estimated to be 30,000 units for the first year, 40,000 units for each of the next two years, and 20,000 units for each of the last two years. Production of the cheaper brand will entail an initial expenditure of Rs. 4,50,000 in purchasing and installing a new plant with estimated economic life of five years and scrap value of Rs. 50,000 at the end. Variable cost of Rs. 10 per unit and fixed cost of Rs. 2,00,000 per annum including depreciation on the plant on straight line basis will be needed for producing and marketing the cheaper brand. Introduction of this cheaper variety is also likely to have an adverse impact on the demand of the existing year resulting in loss of contribution estimated at Rs. 20,000 per annum.

Assuming cost of capital to be 10% and marginal tax rate to be 40%, you are required to evaluate the proposal and give your reasoned recommendation as to its acceptance or rejection. The PV factors at 10% for five years are 0.909, 0.826, 0.751, 0.683 and 0.62.

[C.U., M.Com.]

Solution

Calculation of future net cash flows arising from the project for the next five years :

	Year 1	2	3	4	5
Sales volume (units)	30,000	40,000	40,000	20,000	20,000
(a) Selling Price (Rs.)	20.00	20.00	20.00	20.00	20.00
(b) Variable cost (Rs.)	10.00	10.00	10.00	10.00	10.00
Contribution per unit (Rs.) (a – b)	10.00	10.00	10.00	10.00	10.00

	Rs.	Rs.	Rs.	Rs.	Rs.
Total Contribution (Sales volume x per unit contribution) (Rs.)	3,00,000	4,00,000	4,00,000	2,00,000	2,00,000
Less : Loss of Contribution estimated	20,000	20,000	20,000	20,000	20,000
	2,80,000	3,80,000	3,80,000	1,80,000	1,80,000
Less : Fixed cost	2,00,000	2,00,000	2,00,000	2,00,000	2,00,000
Profit before tax	80,000	1,80,000	1,80,000	(–) 20,000	(–) 20,000
Tax (40%)	32,000	72,000	72,000	—	—
Profit after tax	48,000	1,08,000	1,08,000	(–) 20,000	(–) 20,000
Add : Depreciation being non-cash expenses $\left[\frac{4{,}50{,}00 - 50{,}000}{5}\right]$	80,000	80,000	80,000	80,000	80,000
Add : Scrap value	—	—	—	—	50,000
	1,28,000	1,88,000	1,88,000	60,000	1,10,000

Initial Investment Rs. 4,50,000.

∴ Net Present value at 10% discount.

Rate = Rs (1,28,000 × 0.909 + 1,88,000 × 0.826 + 1,88,000 × 0.751 + 60,000 × 0.683 + 1,10,000 × 0.62) – Rs. 4,50,000

= Rs. 5,22,008 – Rs. 4,50,000

= Rs. 72,008

Here NPV is positive, hence the project is acceptable.

I think you have followed my previous lecture.

Is there any question?

☐ "No Sir, we have followed your lecture. It is really worth grasping. But, Sir, kindly enlighten us about Risk and Uncertainty."

• I mean you want discussions on 'Investment Decisions under risk and uncertainty.' Is it so?

Well, have a look on the Board.

Investment (Capital Budgeting) under Risk and Uncertainty

You see, there is no denying the fact that investment decisions (capital budgeting decisions) are, more or less, associated with risk and uncertainty. Management has to take decision under different situations (i) ***Persuasive Situation*** which has many meanings such as certainty, best, optimum etc. In this situation, future occurrence of a particular or different results such as inflow and outflow of cash as well as rate of discount are expected to be sure, thanks to past record and series of trend analysis (ii) ***Risk Situation*** which implies more or most likely situation. Here probabiliity distribution of a particular or different results i.e., outcome, could be known in advance objectively with possible danger of loss. (iii) ***Uncertain Situation***. This situation is also known as worst or pessimistic situation — here probability distribution of income in a particular or different situation(s) cannot be known in advance, it is guessed, not based by objective consideration. In a sense, it is based on subjective consideration.

I think, you have followed my lecture.

Are there any questions from your side?

☐ "Sir, we have followed your lecture. But Sir, I have two questions."

● Well, what are those questions?

☐ "Sir, my questions are

(1) What are the other objective causes that may stand on the way of the decision-maker to invest under uncertainty besides inherent character of uncertainty?

(2) What are the possible ways the decision-maker may adopt to tackle or manage uncertainty?"

● Well, the questions you have thrown are really praise-worthy. This indicates that you have concentrated on the deep concept.

Please, have a look here.

The answer to your first question is :

The Objective causes are :

Causes Adding to Degree of Uncertainty

(i) Sudden loss of demand for the product for which you intend to invest money.

(ii) Obsolescence of manufacturing process as well as product.

(iii) Change in the policy of the Government.

(iv) Fluctuations i.e., rise and fall in prices.

(v) Impact of inflation.

(vi) Impact of globalisation.

(vii) Consideration of the effect of share market.

(viii) Restrictions on foreign exchange.

(ix) Inflow of foreign capital.

The answer to your other question is :

Remedial Measures

(i) Application of Forecast Audit[1] regarding the estimates of various variables depending upon the nature of industry where proposal of investing money is aimed at.

[1] Dr. B.K. Basu, *"An Insight into Auditing—a Multidimensional Appr᾽ach"* —chapter on Forecast Audit

(ii) Application of judicious and strategic mind to deal with unforeseen events while forming decision at initial level of investment through different market research, operation research, system analysis etc.

(iii) Review of performance of industry at each level of organisational behaviour.

(iv) Application of modern methods like Sensitivity Analysis, Probability Analysis, Expected Value Analysis and Decision Tree Analysis.

By the by, I am to bring to your attention that before application of modern method to deal with uncertainty in capital budgeting or investment decision a few moderate methods, which were based on subjective or intuitive consideration, were applied. These are Lesser Pay Back Period, Moderate Forecast Method backed by certainty Intuitive Equivalent Co-efficient and Risk Premium Method which may be termed 'Risk Adjusted Discount Rate'.

Now I am explaining all these, in brief, one by one. This will give you some insight of the concept. Are you feeling bored? Should I stop my lecture for the day?

☐ "No Sir, we are enjoying your lecture. Please Sir, continue your lecture."

- Your attention please! Note below.

Lesser Pay-Back Period

Suppose a Firm has three projects say X_1, X_2 and X_3, with their respective economic lives 10, 11 and 6 years and their respective payback periods are 5, 6 and 4 years. In this situation project X_3 will be preferred. Because it has shorter payback period. So, it denotes that to avoid future risk this method gives much emphasis on the '**tolerance level**' of the firm. This tolerance level is considered as '**Cut-off-period**'.

Moderate Forecast Method

This method implies that to avoid the risk of inflow of cash the investment decision-maker tries to eliminate the degree of risk perceived by intuition which is called Certainty Equivalent Coefficient. This Certainty Equivalent Coefficient (CEC) level enhances the confidence of the decision-maker of investment.

$$CEC = \frac{\text{Expected cash inflow}}{\text{Estimated cash inflow}}$$

Greater the ratio i.e., nearer to 1, i.e., 0.60, 0.70, 0.80 and so on, greater is the satisfaction on the part of the investor.

Risk Premium Method

This method is known as Risk Adjusted Discounted Rate. Here, the firm's cost of capital is treated as cut-off rate which is increased by adding risk premium. Risk premium implies protection to investors to guard against possible losses. Premium is found to increase with the increase in Risk in the project. Suppose cost of capital for a project which most of the authors consider risk free discount rate, is 15%, it appears a risky project so the decision maker may add another 2.5% to the above risk free discount rate. Here risk adjusted discount rate is 17.5%. Need less to mention this discount rate may be used under net present value as well as internal rate of return method.

Sensitivity Analysis

The meaning of the term sensitivity implies acutely affected by external impressions or recording changes of conditions affected by susceptible to any situation or conditions. That is to say, key variables like cost, market price, life of the project, share market. Consideration are subject to change with the change in varied situation and its result is reflected in rate of return. Here, selection of variables are made from significant errors or any element of uncertainty. And these errors are to be taken into account for examination for avoiding adverse situation for the purpose of present value rate of the project.

Probability Analysis

Probability implies likelihood of any event, occurrence of any certainty or uncertainty. It ranges from 1 to 0. In a probability distribution, situations are graded as optimistic (when probability of occurrence of any favourable outcome is 1), pessimistic (when the probability of occurrence of any favourable outcome is 0) and most likely (when value of probability ranges in between 1 to 0). Obtaining probability distribution is difficult but not impossible. However, in a situation of uncertainty, decision-makers are found to use two types of probability—objective and subjective. Objective probabilities are based on large number of observations of identical nature.

But investment decisions which are not coming under identical situations are found to switch over to subjective consideration whose bases are wisdom and strong belief and intuitive art of the decision maker.

Expected Value

The Expected value (EV) of any project implies potential value of the project. It is a summation of products of estimated values (X_i) of the project and their respective probabilities (P_i).

$EV = \sum_{i=1}^{n} X_i P_i$, where X_i = estimated value of the project.

P_i = Probability distribution of estimated value.

Take for an example the estimated present value of a project under three different situations :

Situations	Estimated Present Value (Rs.) (Xi)	Probability Factors (Pi)	Expected value (Rs.) (P_iX_i)
S_1	8,00,000	0.25	2,00,000
S_2	12,00,000	0.60	7,20,000
S_3	16,00,000	0.15	2,40,000
		ΣP_iX_i =	11,60,000

It is to be noted in this context that if project cost is lesser than the estimated expected value of the project, the project should not be discarded, that is to say, the project should be accepted.

Decision-Tree Analysis

It implies a bunch of various decisions which are subject to assessment of alternative decisions and are correlated with individual decisions — this is called decisions tree.

I hope you have followed my lecture. Is there any question from your side?

☐ "Sir, please enlighten us about the steps in decision-free process."

• Well, please note :

1. There should be a well-defined and clear investment decision.
2. Proper identification of decision alternatives should be clearly indicated.
3. Best alternatives of investment should be chosen through analysing the result.

QUESTIONS

1. What do you understand by the term Profitability? Explain the different aspects of Profitability.
2. A factory producing pressed metal components has a four-year-old production line which costs Rs. 40,000 and which was estimated to have a total life of ten years and a residual value of approximately Rs. 5,000. Its output averages 12 units per minute and it runs for 3,000 hours per annum.

   A proposal is submitted to replace this line with a new and much improved line which will cost Rs. 1,00,000. It is estimated that this new plant will have a life of no more than six years and a residual value of approximately Rs. 10,000. If the new plant is purchased the existing plant can be disposed off for Rs. 15,000. The new plant would give an output of 24 units per minute and would run for 3,000 hours per annum.

	Present Plant	New Plant
Operator's Wages	3,000	4,000
Power Cost	6,000	9,000
Repairs and Maintenance	3,000	5,000
Tools and Consumables	9,000	12,000
Apportionment of general Factory Fixed Costs	4,000	6,000

   From the above information prepare a Comparative Cost Statement to show marginal costs and total costs per dozen unit for each plant.

   [Adapted from I.C.W.A. (London, Final)]

3. A cigarette manufacturer proposes to replace his existing cigarette machine by the latest type of high speed machine, to operate at the rate of 2,000 cigarettes per minute.

   The existing machines cost Rs. 6,000 each, ten years ago. New and old machines have an estimated total useful life of 20 years; the depreciation provision is by the "straight line" method, the residual value for each machine being Rs. 1,000. The price of the new machine is Rs. 10,000. The present part exchange value of the existing machines is Rs. 1,500 each.

The new machine will occupy only 80% of the effective floor space of an old machine, the cost of which is Rs. 50 per year.

The following details also apply :

	Old Machine Rs.	New Machine Rs.
Annual operating hours	1,500	1,500
Operator's annual wages	550	550
Annual repairs and maintenance cost	150	190
Annual power cost	50	110

Any probable capital loss on the old machines is to be included in the estimated cost of the new machine.

(a) Tabulate a comparative cost estimate for one year for an old and a new machine.

(b) Calculate how many cigarettes must be produced by the new machine to yield savings equal to the extra capital outlay it involves. (Ignore tax).

[Adapted from I.C.W.A. (London) Final]

4. A business manufactures two products A and B and during the past year the following figures in respect of these products were obtained :

	A Rs.	B Rs.
Sales units	500	500
Selling price per unit	350	31.50
Standard cost per unit :		
Direct materials	100	18
Direct labour	200 hrs	10 hrs

Standard direct labour hour rate is Re. 0.30 per hour, and standard overhead rate Re. 0.45 per hour in respect of variable overheads.

Fixed overheads for the business amount to Rs. 60,000 and it has been the practice to absorb these as a percentage on direct labour.

The business has ample finance and facilities available to increase production, and it is envisaged that total direct labour hours can be increased by 10%.

The market for both products at current selling prices is considerably in excess of current production and material and labour may be used on either product, as desired. It is not considered good policy, however, to reduce production of Product A below 300 units per year, or Product B below 5,000 units per year.

It is anticipated that the increase of 10% in labour activity will not cause any increase in fixed expenses of the business.

Present information to management regarding the profitability of the products for the past year and a separate statement indicating the best course of action for the coming year.

[Adapted from I.C.W.A. (London) Final]

5. Three different product lines are sold by Mohan Mills. Product A contributes 20% of its revenue to fixed costs and profit Product B contributes 10% and Product C contributes 60%. The products sell for the following prices :

	Rs.
Product A	8.00
Product B	2.00
Product C	3.00

The company earned a net profit of Rs. 50,000 before income taxes last year by selling 50,000 units of Product A, 1,50,000 units of Product B and 60,000 units of Product C. Rajendra, the Sales Manager, believes that the profit picture can be improved by eliminating Product B and concentrating the sales effort on Products A and C. He sees an opportunity to increase the sales of Product A to 70,000 units but admits that Product C will probably sell at the same amount next year.

Prepare a Projected Income Statement using Rajendra's assumptions. Do you agree with him? Explain what would cause the profit to increase or decrease as the case might be. **[M.Com., University of Delhi]**

6. What is Pay-Back Period? Discuss its relative Advantages and Disadvantages.

7. Discuss, in detail, at least two methods employed for the appraisal of long term investment projects. **[M.Com., C.U.]**

8. Explain briefly the following methods of ascertaining the profitability of Capital Expenditure Projects, bringing out the Merits and Limitations of each :

   (a) Pay-Back Method

   (b) Return on Investment Method.

9. To increase the production capacity of a Department it is proposed to introduce a new machine. Type X and Type Y machines are available in the market.

Detailed Information

	Type X	**Type Y**
Cost of Machine	Rs. 36,000	Rs. 70,000
Expected life of machine	10 yrs.	20 yrs.
Number of operatives not required if project introduced	9	11
Average earning of operatives per year	Rs. 1,000	Rs. 1,000
Additional Cost of maintenance, men, supervisors etc. required if project is introduced	Rs. 2,000	Rs. 3,000
Expected saving in direct material	Rs. 1,000	Rs. 400
Expected savings in scrap losses due to better efficiency.	Rs. 500	Rs. 800

From the above information state which one of the two types of machine can be purchased.

10. (a) Explain with suitable illustrations the limitation of Pay-Back Method of evaluating capital projects?

(b) A plant is offered for Rs. 1,00,000. Its estimated life is 20 years. During that period it is estimated that the net cash flow of the plant will be at the rate of Rs. 10,000 p.a. and the rate of interest to be taken is 8% p.a. Is it worth while to accept the offer? Given log 1.08 = 0.0334 anti log 1.332 = 0.2148.

[M.Com., (C.U.) Management Accounting]

11. Examine the proposition that the Discounted cash flow method for the appraisal of long term investments provides to the investment analysts what the pay-back method or the return on capital employed method, individually, cannot.

[M.Com., (C.U.) Management Accounting]

12. What is Discounted Cash Flow Method? Explain its advantages and disadvantages.

13. Your factory's product range includes 'Product A' which sales at a loss, as detailed :

	Rs.	Rs.
Sales Price per unit		4,000
Costs—variable	3,000	
Fixed—specific to Product 'A'	1,200	
Fixed—general	800	5,000
Loss per unit		1,000

The fixed costs specific to the Product 'A' wil be annually Rs. 3,00,000 for the next three years after which they will be discontinued with the termination of the product. The sales forecast for the next three years are :

2001	Rs.12,00,000
2002	8,00,000
2003	2,50,000 —thereafter nil

Existing finished stocks at book value (variable cost) amounts to Rs. 8,00,000. There is also a stock of service Spares amounting to Rs. 18,00,000 (at variable cost, i.e., sales less 50%). Forecast sales appear at Rs. 4,20,000 for each of the next three years and Rs. 1,80,000 for each of the following three years. After this, the business will fade away.

Your competitor has offered to take over the manufacture and sale of Product 'A' including that of the service spares. The terms offered are :

(a) Rs. 2,00,000 to be paid for the manufacturing rights.

(b) A royalty @ 5% on total sales, including spare sales for the next three years—payable at the end of each year.

(c) Finished stock to be taken over at book values and paid for immediately, and Rs. 10,00,000 to be paid for spares on take over.

The cost of finance to your company is @ 8% per annum. You have been asked by your directors to suggest, with reasons, if this offer should be accepted.

Present value of Re. 1 assuming that the Re. 1 is received in a single payment on the last day of each year, regard being given to interest @ 8%, is :

After 1 year	.93
After 2 years	.86
After 3 years	.79
After 4 years	.74
After 5 years	.68
After 6 years	.63

[M.Com., (C.U.) Adapted Management Accounting]

14. A construction firm in need of an automatic digger at a construction site for a period of five years can either buy it outright or hire it on payment of rent. If hired, rent of Rs. 35,000 per annum has to be paid. In addition, a security deposit of Rs. 20,000 payable at the beginning has to be made which, however, will be refunded with 15% compound interest per annum at the end of the fifth year. Cost of repair and maintenance will be borne by the owner.

    If purchased, the initial cost will be Rs. 1,00,000, estimated scrap value being Rs. 10,000 at the end of its five-year life. Repair and maintenance costs are expected to be Rs. 5,000 at the end of the second year and Rs. 6,000 at the end of the 4th year. The machine will be entitled to accelerated depreciation at 40% in each of the first two years and 20% in the third year.

    If marginal tax rate is 40% and cost of capital is 15%, which of the two alternatives should the firm go for?

    The relevant P.V. factors at 15% for the five years are 0.870, 0.756, 0.658, 0.572 and 0.497. **[M.Com., (C.U.)]**

15. Following data pertain to the proposed project to manufacture and sell computer parts of existing profit making company, M/s Pentium (I) Ltd. :

    (i) Project cost Rs. 1,00,000, (ii) Installation cost Rs. 5,000, (iii) Initial working capital required Rs. 1,000, (iv) Selling price per unit Rs. 20.00, (v) Variable cost ratio 60%, (vi) Annual capacity 4,000 units (vii) Annual fixed cost Rs. 2,000 (excluding depreciation), (viii) Promotional expenses at the beginning of the project Rs. 2,000, (ix) Depreciation allowed @ 25% on WDV, (x) Working capital required each year 25% of sales, (xi) Estimated life 4 years, (xii) Terminal value of the project 20% of the original cost, (xiii) Annual capacity utilisation :

Year	1	2	3	4
%	75%	80%	100%	100%

    (xiv) Discount rate 16%.

    The relevant P.V. factors at 16% for four years are 0.862, 0.743, 0.641 and 0.552.

    Should the project be accepted? **[M.Com., (C.U.)]**

16. MNC (I) Ltd. is considering a proposal to acquire a plant costing Rs. 12 lakhs which has an economic life of five years with no residual value.

Management has following three alternative options :

(a) Purchase the plant outright by taking term loan at 16% p.a. payable in five equal instalments (Principal) along with interest on balance outstanding.

(b) Taking the plant on lease at yearly lease rental of Rs. 3,24,000 payable in advance.

(c) Taking the plant on hire-purchase basis with annual instalment of Rs. 3,84,000 payable at the end of the year. Further, a security deposit of Rs. 5 lakhs to be kept with the vendor which will be refunded at the end of the contract.

The company adopts straight line method of depreciation.

If marginal tax rate is 40% and cost of capital is 16%, which of the above alternatives do you recommend? Give reasons for your recommendation.

The relevant P.V. factors at 16% for five years are 0.862, 0.743, 0.641, 0.552 and 0.476. **[M.Com., (C.U.)]**

17. NC Ltd. is considering a number of capital investment projects for which Rs. 2,00,000 have been allocated. The following projects are under consideration :

Project	Investment (Rs.)	NPV (Rs.)
A	1,20,000	25,000
B	1,00,000	20,000
C	80,000	20,000
D	60,000	20,000
E	40,000	15,000
F	10,000	5,000

Projects A and B are mutually exclusive; if Project A is undertaken, the initial cost is reduced by Rs. 10,000 (without affecting its benefits). If Project B is undertaken, the initial cost of D is reduced by Rs. 10,000 (without affecting its benefits). The benefit cost ratio of unutilised funds is 0.90.

Which projects should be chosen? **[M.Com., (C.U.)]**

26

TRANSFER PRICING

- Good Evening, my dear students.

☐ "Good evening, Sir."

- What would you want me to discuss today?

☐ "Sir, Give us some idea on Transfer Pricing (TP)."

- Well before discussing the same, I present before you my views regarding the transfer of academic product of an institution. This will help you to understand the concept of TP.

There is no denying the fact that the output of a system or department is the input of another system or department.

You, please stand up. Why are you talking? Any problem there?

☐ "No Sir. No problem; but I have one question to ask."

- What is your question?

☐ "Sir! What do you mean by the term ***academic product***? Please enlighten us".

Example of Transfer Pricing of Academic Product

Well, ***academic product*** of a university is what one becomes after successful complection of Master Degree. You see, you are not attending your ***Post Graduate Classes*** suddenly, you have come here step-by-step i.e. through different stages or processes, with some value addition of knowledge of your respectives stages or processes of initial cost (knowledge).

That is to say, some knowledge is imputed to existing stock of knowledge in respective stages. Note below the different stages of ***academic product***

Primary Level → Secondary Level → Higher Secondary Level → Graduation Level → Postgraduation Level

To explain it you may consider initial knowledge as initial cost, at the end of each stages, the situation appears :

Starting point →	**At the end of Primary Level** →	**Secondary Level** →
(Initial cost means initial education) This level is treated as Primary Level	Initial cost (initial knowledge) + Imputed cost i.e., addition to existing knowledge ↓ This whole aspect is treated as ***Output*** of Primary Education. This ***Output*** is the ***Input*** of next Level i.e., Secondary Level.	Input cost i.e., knowledge from Primary Level + Imputed cost i.e., addition to Secondary Level of Education ↓ This whole aspect is treated as ***Output*** of Secondary Education. This ***Output*** is the ***Input*** of next level i.e., Higher Secondary Level

University Level ←	**Graduation Level** ←	**Higher Secondary Level**
Input cost i.e., knowledge from Graduation Level + Imputed cost i.e., addition to knowledge at Post-graduation Level ↓ This whole aspect is the ***Output*** of Postgraduation Level	Input cost i.e., knowledge from Higher Secondary Level + Imputed cost i.e., addition to knowledge at Graduation Level ↓ This whole aspect is the ***Output*** of Graduation Level which is the ***Input*** of University Level	Input cost i.e., knowledge from Secondary Level + Imputed cost i.e., addition to knowledge at Higher Secondary Level ↓ This whole aspect is the ***Output*** of Higher Secondary Level. This ***Output*** is the ***Input*** of Graduation Level

The said example of academic product will be more appropriate in an institution where graduation and postgraduation levels exist; as if Graduation Level is one Division and Postgraduate Level is another division. These divisions may be treated as cost of knowledge centres or added value of knowledge centres. Moreover, these centres may be treated as Responsibility centres. Now the moot point is what should be the quantum of knowledge used to record the transfer of academic product from Graduation Level to Postgraduation Level, i.e., from one division to another?

The transfer of this quantum of knowledge—initial knowledge plus added knowledge—of academic product from one division (stage, level) to another division(s) is called transferred knowledge.

I hope you have followed the intention of the said example to make clear a first-hand impression of transfer pricing.

☐ "Yes Sir, It is quite clear to me that for transferring goods and services from one division to another division of the same organisation, the price charged to record to goods and services is Transfer Price (TP)."

• I am hapy to note that you have understood the concept from the example of transfer of academic product. Now I explain the concept in details—well-designed transfer price, advantages (benefits), methods of transfer pricing, objectives etc.

☐ "Excuse me Sir; first give us the definition of Transfer Pricing (TP)".

• Well, before giving you the definition of TP, I find it essential to narrate organisational structure of a company in a nutshell.

Organisational structure may be centralised or decentralised. To facilitate effective management control, big companies are found to prefer decentralisation where divisional managers enjoy much freedom to take decision independently. They are responsible for the performance of their respective divisions. Because, each division is considered as ***responsibility centre***. The performances of managers or in-charges of respective departments are required to evaluate; since each division is considered as cost centre or profit centre. There is no denying the fact that performance of different departments have direct impact on the overall performance of a company or organisation. So, the performances of different departments as well as price charged to transfer of goods and services from one division to another division of the same firm should aim at goal congruence of the organisation or firm.

Market Force

Regarding transfer of goods and services from one division of a firm to an external firm there arises no problem; because prevailing ***market force*** of the time will determine the price at which goods and services will be sold to external firm. But problem arises to determine at which price goods and services will be transferred from one division to another division of the same firm.

Example of Transfer Price

Take for an example, a computer company, which manufactures and sells computers, has two Divisions—Division A, concerned with manufacturing memory devices and other parts of computer; Division B, engaged with assembling of desktop computer. Here price charged or labelled by Division A for transfer of memory devices and other parts of computer to Assembly Department B is transfer price.

I hope you have followed my lecture.

☐ "Yes Sir! Please give your own definition of Transfer Price (TP)".

Definition of Transfer Pricing

• Well, please note it— Price labelled to goods and services, while transferring the same from one division or department to another division or department of the same firm, is called Transfer Price."

Sometimes TP is viewed as "Charge Back" or "Internal" Price. It is to be noted in this context that as divisional performance is evaluated on the basis of profit criteria, a tendency may arise among the different divisional managers to enhance the TP in the garb of profit which is more than rational transfer price. This type of motivation of department manager(s) —which jeopardises the spirit of TP—should be curbed if overall objective of an organisation is to be achieved, i.e., to stand in competitive market with adequate profitability.

So, in order to avoid the said problem and to achieve the overall objectives of an organisation, i.e, goal congruence, the Management Accountant can play an important role through constant vouching of the activities of different divisions or departments. This aspect can be made effective with the help of Management Auditors. The technique to be used, it is recommended, is Propriety Audit.

You see, the meanings of the word 'propriety' are manifold—justness, fitness, rightness, correctness of behaviour or morals etc. On the other hand, the term 'audit', in a broad sense, means to make an enquiry[1]. Therefore, the term Propriety Audit, in the context of TP, means to make an inquiry into the rightness of the price charged by the respective divisions or departments for transfer of goods and services keeping in view the goal congruence of the organisation or firm. Needless to mention, the introduction of Propriety Audit in TP will stop the tendency of extending benefit to a department or division at the cost of other department or division of a same firm.

I think you have followed my lecture. Is there any problem?

☐ "Sir, we are facing no problem. We have understood your lecture. Please explain the different methods of transfer pricing."

● Well, take a look at the board.

You see, there are three (3) methods of Transfer Pricing :

Methods of Transfer Pricing

- Cost-Based Transfer Price
- Market-Based Transfer Price
- Negotiated Transfer Price

1. Cost Based Transfer Price

You see, I have already discussed in Part III of this book that general meaning of the term 'Cost', which is applicable in all cases, is ***sacrifice***. But if the term ***sacrifice*** means mere cost, i.e., Cost of production, without taking into account the concept of profit, the basic philosophy of the test of transaction—Change in the financial condition—may be lost. So, from seller's and transferer point of view, ***sacrifice*** includes cost of production or cost of procurement plus 'something'. This 'something' may be termed from seller's and transferer point of view *profit*.

However, several costs are involved there in the context of TP—Variable Cost, Full cost, Absorption Cost, Full cost plus margin, Standard Cost and Modified Cost (cost plus some added amount). Section of cost out of so many, as stated above, for inclusion in price for transfer of goods and services by the transferer department or division to transferee departement or division depends upon the decision of the management as well as nature of the form or business.

2. Market-Based Transfer Price

When transfer of goods and services from one division or department to another division or department is made at a prevailing market price of similar good and services,

[1] Dr. B.K. Basu *"An Insight into Auditing—a Multi Dimensional Approach"*

it is called Market-based Transfer Price. This method is suitable in perfect by competitive market.

3. Negotiated Transfer Price

Negotiated transfer price implies an agreement, based on bargaining, between transferer division or department and transferee division or department at what price goods or services are to be transferred from one division or department to another division or department. Note in this context that existing cost and market price may form an important consideration in arriving at a decision to fix up negotiated price, but this negotiated price should have no impact on the existing market price or cost.

I hope you have followed my lecture. Now I would like to give you some idea on the factors that bear some impact on TP.

Is there any questions from your side? Can I proceed for discussion?

☐ "No Sir, we have nothing to say. All aspects are discussed; you can proceed Sir!"

• Please note

Factors Affecting Transfer Price (TP)

These are —

Factors Affecting Transfer Pricing

(i) Prevailing market condition.

(ii) Mood of the market.

(iii) Object of TP.

(iv) Compatible goal of the firm or organisation.

(v) Accomplished management.

(vi) Effective decentralisation with responsibility and accountability.

(vii) Judicious evaluation of the performance of different divisions or departments or sub-units.

Now a formula can be developed on the basis of the rule as suggested by Horngren, Datar and Foster.[2] This can be used as ***first step general rule*** in fixing minimum TP :

$$\text{Minimum Transfer Price} = \left(\begin{array}{l}\text{Incremental Cost}\\ \text{of transferring one}\\ \text{unit of intermediate}\\ \text{component}\end{array}\right) + \left(\begin{array}{l}\text{Opportunity cost}\\ \text{per unit to the}\\ \text{transferring division}\\ \text{arising from transfer}\end{array}\right)$$

Incremental cost = All additional costs incurred by selling division while transferring intermediate goods and services.

Opportunity Cost = Contribution margin per unit foregone by the selling department or division while transferring goods and services to other department or division instead of selling in the external market. It is the difference between the market price and the variable cost of intermediate goods and services.

---

[2] "*Cost Accounting : A Managerial Emphasis*", Prentice Hall of India Ltd., 11th edition

I think you have followed my lecture. Are there any questions which you want me to discuss?

☐ "Sir! we have understood your lecture. We shall be grateful to you if you please discuss (i) Well-Designed Transfer Pricing and (ii) Benefits or Advantages of Transfer Pricing".

• Thank you all for your interest in the subject. Let me first discuss Well-Designed Transfer Pricing; after that I will discuss the advantages of TP.

Please note.

Well-Designed Transfer Pricing

Harmonious Relation in Transfer Pricing

Well Designed Transfer Pricing

You see, a Well-Designed Transfer Pricing depicts a situation in a firm or organisation where harmonious relationship among different sub-units or divisions or departments exist; and transfer prices from one division or department or unit to another division or department or unit should be consistent with the overall objective of the organisation. Besides these, scope for application of managerial skill, effective decentralisation (freedom of department or division or sub-unit to take decision), proper appraisal of managerial performance etc.—all are found to exist in an organisation.

All these aspects have been explained by Horngren and others in their work ***Cost Accounting : A Managerial Emphasis***—under 4 (four) criteria :

1. Goal Congruence
2. Management Effort
3. Sub-unit Performance Evaluation
4. Sub-Unit Autonomy.

1. Goal Congruence

Transfer of goods and services from one division or unit to another division or unit should aim at goal congruence of the firm or organisation; that is to say, it must be consistent with the overall objectives of the firm or organisation. In other words, respective divisional managers are expected to make the best of their performance to achieve their respective departmental or divisional or unit goal which, in turn, automatically will reach goal congruence.

2. Management Effort

It implies determined attempt on the part of managers of respective departments or divisions or sub-units to attain high level of managerial performance.

3. Sub-unit Performance Evaluation

Concept of TP invites manifold activities of any firm or organisation. For example, in the 1st stage the manager of respective sub-unit tries to exert high level of performance to reach the desired objective; in the second stage their performances are assessed or evaluated by the top management, the third stage envisages judicious application of mind of the top management to confirm whether activities of all managers are in tune with the overall objectives of a firm.

4. Sub-unit Autonomy

TP method calls for elevations of different sub-units, as decision-making processes, by the top management. It implies that managers of different sub-units are given freedom either to transact with other sub-unit of the same firm or with external parties.

It is to be noted in this context that to transact with external parties should not, in principle, be considered as transfer pricing. Because it may be treated as ***Sale*** to external parties.

Now I discuss the benefits (advantages) of transfer pricing (TP).

Benefits of TP

Advantages of TP

(i) It offers scope for coordination among different departments or divisions — the end-goal can be visualised.

(ii) Evaluation of the performance of different divisions or departments can be made possible through assessment of TP.

(iii) Managerial efficiency can be promoted.

(iv) Exercise of managerial control over the departments or divisions or sub-units will help productivity and profitability of an organisation.

I hope you have followed my lecture.

Is there any question from your side?

☐ "Excuse me sir, what are the disadvantages of TP."

• You see, benefits or advantages of TP outweigh its disadvantages. If any shortcoming or disadvantage is to be traced, these can be stated :

Disadvantages of TP

1. Inter-conflicts among different departments or divisions may mar (spoil) the spirit of TP.
2. Fixing TP by one department or division at the cost of other department or division may stand on the way of coordination among various departments or divisions.
3. Lack of work culture may stand on the way of objective of TP.

I think you have followed the discussion.

Is there any question?

☐ "Sir, we have understood your lecture. But Sir, please work out a few problems on TP."

• Well, I am giving you a few worked-out problems.

Problem

A company has two divisions, Division X and Division Y. The component produced by X has both external market as well as internal market. Division Y receives internal transfer from Div. X and sells in the external market after further processing. The detailed costs and other information of these two divisions are :

	Div. X	Div. Y
Direct Material [Rs. per unit]	9.00	—
Direct Labour [Rs. per unit]	5.00	—
Variable Overhead per unit (Rs.)	3.00	3.00
Transfer Price	—	20.00
	17.00	23.00
Fixed Overhead (Rs.)	75,000	45,000
Market Price (Rs.)	25.00	30.00
Internal Transfer	25,000 units	
External Sales	15,000 units	25,000 units

Division X has capacity to produce 40,000 units but it could not sell beyond 15,000 units in external market.

Now if in the next period Div. Y finds an external supplier of its input at Rs. 18.00 per unit, what course of action should Div. X follow?

Should Div. X revise its Transfer Price or retain as it is? Offer your suggestions.

Solution

Profitability Statement when the Transfer Price is Rs. 20.00 :

	Div. X	Div. Y	Co. as a Whole
	Rs.	Rs.	Rs.
Sales			
External [X : 15,000 units × Rs. 25]	3,75,000	—	
[Y : 25,000 units × Rs. 30]	—	7,50,000	
Internal [25,000 units × Rs. 20]	5,00,000	—	
	8,75,000	7,50,000	16,25,000
Less : Variable Cost (40,000 × Rs. 17.00)	6,80,000		
(25,000 × Rs. 23.00)		5,75,000	12,55,000
Contribution	1,95,000	1,75,000	3,70,000
Fixed Overhead	75,000	45,000	1,20,000
	1,20,000	1,30,000	2,50,000

Now, let us take the situation of the next period when the external market price of intermediate product would reduce to Rs. 18.00 and thereby Div. Y would purchase from external market and Div. X would sell only 15,000 units in the external market.

The division as well as company profit as a whole can be shown as :

Profitability Statement

	Div. X	Div. Y	Co. as a Whole
	Rs.	Rs.	Rs.
Sales (External)	3,75,000	7,50,000	11,25,000
Less : Variable Cost			
X : [15,000 × Rs. 17.00]	2,55,000		
Y : [25,000 × (3 + 18)]	—	5,25,000	7,80,000
Contribution	1,20,000	2,25,000	3,45,000
Less : Fixed Cost	75,000	45,000	1,20,000
	45,000	1,80,000	2,25,000

It is clear from the above that profit of Div. X and the company as a whole have come down to Rs. 45,000 and Rs. 2,25,000 respectively.

Now, if Div. X starts transferring to Div. Y at Rs. 18.00 per unit the profits of the divisions and the company as a whole can be shown as :

Profitability Statement

	Div. X	Div. Y	Co. as a Whole
	Rs.	Rs.	Rs.
Sales			
External	3,75,000	7,50,000	
Internal [25,000 × Rs. 18]	4,50,000	—	
	8,25,000	7,50,000	15,75,000
Less : Variable Cost	6,80,000	5,25,000	12,05,000
Contribution	1,45,000	2,25,000	3,70,000
Less : Fixed Cost	75,000	45,000	1,20,000
	70,000	1,80,000	2,50,000

Thus, the company profit has again increased to Rs. 2,50,000 and the company has come to an equilibrium situation. Therefore, Div. X should fix its transfer price at Rs. 18.00 per unit and it should be revised with changes in the external market condition.

Problem

A company has two divisions A and B. Div. A produces 4,00,000 units of product P_1 and entirely transfers it to Div. B where it is further processed and product P is produced. The external market price of P is Rs. 80 per unit. Unlimited quantities of P_1 can be purchased and sold in the external market at Rs. 45 per unit.

The following table gives details of manufacturing cost per unit of the two divisions :

	Division A	Division B
	Rs.	Rs.
Direct Material	6.00	3.00
Direct Labour	8.00	10.00
Variable Overhead	12.00	5.00
	26.00	18.00
Fixed Overhead	4.00	7.50
	30.00	25.50

You are required to calculate :

(1) Operating income of both divisions using — (a) market-based transfer pricing (b) 120% of full cost.

(2) Which transfer pricing method will Div. A prefer and why?

Solution

1. (a) Profitability Statement when the transfer Price is market based i.e., Rs. 45.00 per unit.

	Div. A	Div. B	Co. as a Whole
	Rs.	Rs.	Rs.
Sales (Rs. 45 × 4,00,000)	1,80,00,000	3,20,00,000	5,00,00,000
Less : Variable Cost :			
(4,00,000 × Rs. 26.00)	1,04,00,000		
(4,00,000 × Rs. 63 i.e. Rs. 45 + Rs. 18)	—	2,52,00,000	3,56,00,000
Contribution	76,00,000	68,00,000	1,44,00,000
Fixed Overhead	16,00,000	30,00,000	46,00,000
	60,00,000	38,00,000	98,00,000

(b) TP based on 120% of full cost :

∴ Transfer Price = Rs. 30 × 120% = Rs. 36.00

Statement of Operating Income

	Div. A	Div. B	Co. as a Whole
	Rs.	Rs.	Rs.
Sales	1,44,00,000	3,20,00,000	4,64,00,000
[4,00,000 × Rs. 36.00]			
Less : Variable Cost :			
[4,00,000 × Rs. 26.00]	1,04,00,000	2,16,00,000	3,20,00,000
[4,00,000 × Rs. 54.00]			
Contribution	40,00,000	1,04,00,000	1,44,00,000
Less : Fixed Overhead	16,00,000	30,00,000	46,00,000
	24,00,000	74,00,000	98,00,000

2. Div. A will prefer market-based transfer pricing, because market-based transfer pricing increases its operating profit and if the transfer price is fixed at Rs. 36.00 [i.e., 120% of full cost], Div. A would sell its products in the external market at Rs. 45.00 per unit instead of transferring to Div. B at Rs. 36.00; and Div. B would have to purchase component P_1 from external market at Rs. 45 per unit. Therefore, for the overall interest of the company, transfer price should be fixed at Rs. 45.00 per unit. This also ensures standard good quality of the intermediate product.

Problem

X Ltd. has capacity to produce 10,000 units of product P. This product is processed through three divisions A, B & C. Division C ultimately sells the product in the external market. At present, external market demand for the product P is 8,000 units.

The other information related to X Ltd. is given :

	A	B	C	Co. as a whole
TP/Selling Price (Rs.)	3.00	6.00	12.00	12.00
Less : Variable Cost (Rs.)	1.50 (3+1.50)	4.50 (6+2)	8.00	5.00
	1.50	1.50	4.00	7.00

Now suppose that X Ltd. has received an order from Y Ltd. to supply 2,000 untis of P at a price of Rs. 7.00 per unit. Y Ltd. will further process 'P' to produce new product. Should X Ltd. accept the proposal or reject it? Offer your suggestions.

Solution

If X Ltd. accepts the order, the additional contribution of division C will be

	Rs.
Sales [2,000 × Rs. 7.00]	14,000
Less : Variable Cost [2,000 × Rs. 8.00]	16,000
	– 2,000

Therefore, Division C will not accept the proposal because it would lead to loss of contribution of Rs. 2,000. But if we consider the proposal from overall point of view, the additional contribution will be

	Rs.
Sales [2,000 × Rs. 7.00]	14,000
Less : Variable Cost [2,000 × Rs. 5.00]	10,000
Additional Contribution	4,000

Since X Ltd. has idle capacity, additional contribution to X Ltd. leads to additional profit. Therefore, from overall company point of view, it is worthwhile to accept the order.

Thus, when a company has idle capacity, transfer price based on market price often leads to suboptimal decision.

Problem

Division A of a company, with capacity to produce 40,000 units of a component can sell 30,000 units in the external market and can transfer the balance to Division B of the same company. External selling prices is determined as to get a return of 25% on assets employed. The following particulars of Division A are known :

Fixed Overhed	Rs. 10,00,000
Variable Overhead	Rs. 20.00 per unit
Asset Employed	Rs. 20,00,000

Division A wants to supply the components to Division B at Rs. 50 per unit but Division B is willing to accept it at Rs. 40.00 only.

If Division A produces only 30,000 units it can reduce its fixed overhead by Rs. 2,00,000 and asset holding by Rs. 4,00,000.

Offer your suggestions as to what course of action the Division A should take.

[C.U., M.Com.]

Solution

Determination of External Selling Price of 30,000 units

Variable Cost [30,000 × Rs. 20.00]	6,00,000
Add: Fixed Overheads	8,00,000
Full cost	14,00,000
Add: Return [25% on assets employed] [16,00,000 × 25%]	4,00,000
Sales	18,00,000

$$\therefore \text{ Selling Price} = \frac{\text{Rs. } 18,00,000}{30,000} = \text{Rs. } 60.00.$$

Now, if Division A starts to produce additional 10,000 units, it would have to incur additional fixed overhead of Rs. 2,00,000 and have to employ additional assets worth Rs. 4,00,000.

Incremental Cost per unit

Variable Cost	Rs. 20.00
Fixed Overhead $\left(\frac{2,00,000}{10,000}\right)$	Rs. 20.00
	40.00

Now, it is clear from the above that if transfer price is fixed at Rs. 40.00, Division A could recover only the incremental cost without any contribution to additional assets employed. Thus, overall return on assets employed would reduce to 20% $\left[\text{i.e., } \frac{4,00,000}{20,00,000} \times 100\right]$.

Therefore, Division A will never accept transfer price of Rs. 40.00 per unit.

However, if transfer price is fixed at Rs. 50.00, Division A would get additional profit of Rs. 10.00 per unit or in total Rs. 1,00,000. Thus, overall return will increase to 25% $\left[\text{i.e., } \frac{4,00,000 + 1,00,000}{20,00,000} \times 100\right]$ as before.

Any transfer price below Rs. 50.00 will reduce overall rate of return of Division A.

Thus, if divisional performance is measured on the basis of rate of return on assets employed, Division A should not accept transfer price below Rs. 50.00 per unit.

Problem

Division M is a profit centre which produces three products—O, P and Q. Each has an external market :

	O Rs.	P Rs.	Q Rs.
External market price per unit	44	42	36
Variable Cost of product in Division M (per unit)	29	20	24
Labour hour required per unit in Division M	3	4	2

Product P can be transferred to Division N, but the maximum quantity that might be required for transfer is 900 units of P.

The maximum External Sales :

O	2,400 units
P	1,500 units
Q	900 units

Instead of receiving transfers of product from Division M, Division N could buy similar product in the open market at a slightly cheaper price of Rs. 41.00 per unit.

What should be the transfer price for each unit of 900 units of P, if the total labour hours available in Division M are :

(a) 11,400 hours?

(b) 16,800 hours? **[C.U., M.Com.]**

Solution

Total labour hour required to meet external demand and internal transfer :

Labour hour required to meet external demand :

O	2,400 × 3	7,200 hours
P	1,500 × 4	6,000 hours
Q	900 × 2	1,800 hours
		15,000 hours

Internal transfer :

P	900 × 4	3,600 hours
		18,600 hours

Calculation of contribution per labour hour for the three products :

	O	P	Q
	Rs.	**Rs.**	**Rs.**
Market Price	44	42	36
Less : Variable Cost	29	20	24
Contribution/unit	15	22	12
Labour hour required per unit	3	4	2
Contribution per labour hour (Rs.)	5	5.50	6.00

Therefore, when labour hour is the limiting factor, Division M should produce three products in the following order :

1. Q
2. P
3. O

(a) Labour hours available — 11,400 hours

Determination of number of units of Q, P and O can be produced with the available labour hours :

Available labour hours		11,400 hrs
Labour hours required to produce :		
Q : 900 × 2	1,800 hrs	
P : 1,500 × 4	6,000 hrs	
		7,800 hrs
		3,600 hrs

∴ Number of units of O that can be produced = $\frac{3,600}{3}$ = 1,200 units

Thus, total labour hour is exhausted by producing 900 units of Q, 1,500 units of P and 1,200 units of O to meet external demand.

Division M can produce additional 900 units of P to meet internal demand only if production of O is foregone [Production of 900 units of P also require 3,600 labour hours].

Therefore, transfer price of P would be—Variable Cost per unit of P + Contribution from O to produce per unit of P.

∴ TP = Rs. 20 + Rs. 5.00 × 4 = Rs. 20 + Rs. 20 = Rs. 40.

(b) Labour hours available—16,800 hrs.

∴ No. of units of Q, P and O that can be produced with the available labour hours :

Available labour hours		16,800 hrs
Q : 900 × 2	1,800 hrs	
P : 1,500 × 4	6,000 hrs	
O : 2,400 × 3	7,200 hrs	
		15,000 hrs
Idle labour hour		1,800 hrs

No. of units of P that can be produced with available labour hours = $\frac{1,800}{4}$ = 450 units.

Therefore, transfer price of 450 units of P will be only the variable cost of producing per unit of P, i.e., Rs. 20.00 per unit.

The transfer price of remaining 450 units will be as before, that is Rs. 40 per unit, because, for this 450 unit Division M will have to forego 600 units $\left[\text{i.e., } \frac{1,800}{3}\right]$ of O.

Therefore, on an average Division M can charge Rs. 30.00 $\left[\text{i.e., } \frac{20 + 40}{2}\right]$ per unit for the internal transfer of 900 units of P.

QUESTIONS

1. (a) What is Transfer Pricing?

   (b) What are its advantages and disadvantages?
2. Explain in brief the different methods of Transfer Pricing.
3. Explain the term "Well Designed Transfer Pricing".
4. Work out the cost-plus desired return based transfer price from the following data :

Investment : Fixed Assets (average)	Rs. 10 lakhs
Investment : Average working capital	Rs. 10 lakhs
Budgeted volume	50,000 units
Fixed costs	Rs. 8 lakhs
Desired return	25 per cent per annum

   Variable cost per unit is Rs. 20

   All the above figures are for the budget year ending 31st March 2006.

   [Adapted from I.C.W.A. Inter]
5. A company fixes the inter-divisional transfer prices for its products on the basis of cost *plus* and estimated return on investment in its divisions. The relevant portion of the budget for the Division A for the year 2006-07 is given below :

Fixed assets	Rs. 5,00,000
Current assets (other than debtors)	3,00,000
Debtors	2,00,000
Annual fixed cost of the division	8,00,000

Variable cost per unit of product	10
Budgeted volume of production per year (units)	4,00,000
Desired return on investment	28%

You are required to determine the transfer price for the Division A.

[Adapted from I.C.W.A. Inter]

6. A company has two divisions, Division 'A' and Division 'B'. Division 'A' has a Budget of selling 2,00,000 no. of a particular component 'x' to fetch a return of 20% on the average assets employed.

The following particulars of Division 'A' are also known :

Fixed Overhead	Rs. 5 lakhs
Variable Cost	Re. 1 per unit
Average Assets	
Sundry Debtors	Rs. 2 lakhs
Inventories	Rs. 5 lakhs
Plant and Equipments	Rs. 5 lakhs

However, there is constraint in marketing and only 1,50,000 units of the component 'x' can be directly sold to the market at the proposed price.

It has been gathered that the balance 50,000 units of component 'x' can be taken up by Division 'B'. Division 'A' wants a price of Rs. 4 per unit of 'x' but Division 'B' is prepared to pay Rs. 2 per unit of 'x'.

Division 'A' has another option on hand, which is to produce only 1,50,000 units of component 'x'. This will reduce the holding of assets by Rs. 2 lakhs and fixed overhead by Rs. 25,000.

You are required to advise the most profitable course of action for Division 'A'.

[Adapted from C.A. Final]

7. X Ltd.—which has a system of assessment of divisional performance on the basis of Residual Income—has two divisions—A and B. A has annual capacity to manufacture 15 lakhs of a special component which it sells to outside customers; but has idle capacity.

The budgeted residual income of B is Rs. 120 lakhs while that of A is Rs. 100 lakhs. Other relevant details extracted from the Budget of A for the year are :

Sale (to outside customers)	12 lakh units @ Rs. 1.80 per unit
Variable Cost per unit	Rs. 160
Divisional Fixed Cost	Rs. 80 lakhs
Capital Employed	Rs. 750 lakhs
Cost of Capital	12%

B has just received a special order for which it requires components similar to the ones made by A. Fully aware of A's unutilised capacity, B has asked A to quote for manufacture and supply of 3,00,000 numbers of the components with a slight modification during final processing. A and B agree that this will involve an extra variable cost of Rs. 5 per unit.

(i) Calculate the transfer price which A should quote to B to achieve its budgeted residual income.

(ii) Indicate the circumstances in which the proposed transfer price may result in a sub-optimal decision for the X group as a whole. **[Adapted from I.C.W.A. Final]**

PART VI

CONTROL ACCOUNTING

> "Planning is the basis for Control, Information is the guide for Control and Action is the essence of Control."

27

CAPITAL EXPENDITURE CONTROL

• Good morning to you all my dear students.

□ "Good morning, Sir."

• So long we were considering about the Capital Expenditure Decision. Now I would like to discuss about Capital Expenditure Control. I would request you to go through the works of Dr. Batty as well as NAA Accounting Practice Report 7. However, I am delivering this lecture from the said sources.

Importance of Controlling Capital Expenditure

Controlling the capital expenditure means financial control over capital expenditure. This financial control over capital expenditure is the basic to the proper administration of a business.

The effects of decision regarding capital expenditure are permanent, far-reaching and determining factor for the success and failure of an enterprise.

Importance of Capital Expenditure Control

Once acquired, capital assets cannot be disposed of except at a substantial loss. If purchased on a long term credit basis, a substantial down payment is usually required, and a continuing liability is incurred for the balance—payable over a long period of time.

The issuance of long term bonds to finance the acquisition of capital assets mortgages the future earning of the company. If the purchase of the additional capital assets does not guarantee the increased earnings, the ability of the company to discharge its financial obligations may be impaired with disastrous results.

Expansion of capital assets is by means of the sale of stocks for the ownership of the company, and, if not carefully planned and controlled, it may result in loss of voting control by management or the inability of the company to earn an adequate return on its invested capital.

The basic principles involved in managing and controlling fixed assets will be the same for all business, regardless of size or nature.

In a **small business**, investment in fixed capital is usually made by the owner who personally supervises all activities of the business. He can control the affairs of investment in both fixed and current assets.

In a large organisation no man can personally oversee the activities of the entire business. Management must rely carefully on the devised procedures, standards, and recommendations of individuals and committees to whom authority has been delegated.

As a business increases in size, procedure for the control of capital expenditure must be tightened.

Classification of Outlays for the Proper Integration of Capital Expenditure Control

Control over capital expenditure is facilitated by classification of the following outlays such as :

Steps towards Proper Integration of Capital Expenditure Control

1. Major Project
2. Routine Expenditure
3. Replacements

Well, the line of demarcation between the Major Project and Routine Project depends upon the following :

a. The size of the company, and

b. The consequent degree of control of capital expenditure exercised by the top management.

Sound control over major project involves :

a. Careful analysis of initial cost of each purchase as installation

b. Maintenance Cost—Maintenance Cost necessitated by major capital expenditures include repairs, depreciation (property taxes), insurance, additional labour cost etc.

The effects of proposed capital expenditure on fixed charges, cash requirement and proposed earning should be weighed.

Prior to the approval request for capital appropriation, careful comparison should be made with the cost of production of existing and that of proposed equipment.

Routine expenditure requires control so that multiples of small authorisation, in aggregate, should not exceed a major single project.

Principles of Capital Expenditure Procedure

Any form of capital expenditure procedure should incorporate following principles :

Principles of Capital Expenditure Control

1. **Justification :** It is vital to see that each project should be justified by a statement of reason for expenditure and forecast profitability—Pay Back, Return on Average Investment, Discounted Cash Flow.

2. **Authorisation :** Before any capital expenditure is incurred, or any commitment entered into, it should be authorised within the over all Capital Budget which incorporates all projects in progress or to be commenced during the budget period.

3. **Authentication :** As a project is carried out, all expenditure should be authenticated as being within the previously authorised budget for the proejct of the Company.

Steps in Capital Expenditure Control

1. Capital Expenditure Budget
2. Appropriation Request

3. Measuring Expenditures against Appropriation
4. Post-Completion Audit or follow up of realisation from expenditure.

1. **Capital Expenditure Budget** — Budget of an organisation incorporates all the ideas for the future expansion programme. The Capital Expenditure Budget takes into account expenditure required both to replace worn out or depleted assets and requirement of additional assets needed for enterprise growth. Budget is the only means to see projects side by side and to evaluate the contribution of each the aspect for the future period.

The proposal made by various departments and layers of management are incorporated in the budget.

Capital Expenditure Budget is also of prime importance in developing the Company's Cash Budget.

Before submitting the budget to management for approval, the major project must be summarised as to size and classified or grouped. Classification is important because it permits the higher management to see the relationship among the various proposals of the company being made.

Capital Expenditure Budget

For, the most part of capital expenditure budgeting begins at the lowest level of responsibility and works through management level to the Managing Director and Board of Directors. The consolidated budget, representing the thought-process of the management, is then presented to a Budget Committee.

2. **Request for Appropriation of Fund**

Do not start anything if you cannot finish. Failure may result from (1) Lack of Planning (2) Lack of Finance. Individual appropriation requests are required for each item of Capital Expenditure Budget. The individual appropriation requests are approved after review by authorised official or committee of the company.

The appropriation request may specify or originate the reasons for the expenditure. The reasons are :

Appropriation of Fund

(i) New business.
(ii) Increased needs of present business
(iii) Normal replacement
(iv) Change in manufacturing method

It is important to note that the appropriation requests are to be approved in light of the company's resources and the economy of the company as a whole.

3. **Measuring Expenditure Against Appropriation**

The next step in the capital expenditure control plan consist of issuance of report during the period in which the project is being performed. The report may be quarterly and monthly. The control emphasis at this level is aimed at observing that, overall, programme remains within limits set by the policy of the company.

Measurement of Capital Expenditure

4. **Post-Completion Audit**

This is an overall review of the entire project. This approach analyses critically the three steps of capital expenditure control — Budget, Appropriation Request, and Project Reporting.

This Post-Completion Audit is considered as ***after-the-fact approach.***

Post-Completion Audit

The purposes of Post-Completion Audit are :

(i) To detect those areas where action can be taken to improve future results

(ii) The information gained from the evaluation will be helpful in improving forecast techniques for new projects.

(iii) It tends to serve the integrity of future capital expenditure request and justification.

QUESTIONS

1. What is Capital Expenditure Control? How can Capital Expenditure Control be made effective?
2. Explain the importance of Capital Expenditure Control in the context of Management Decision.
3. Explain the steps in Capital Expenditure Control.
4. Explain the principles of Capital Expenditure Procedure.

28

BUSINESS BUDGETS AND BUDGETARY CONTROL

• Good morning my dear students.

☐ "Good morning Sir, what will you discuss today, Sir?"

• Today I would like to discuss about the Business Budgets and Budgetary Control.

☐ "Sir, what is Budget and Budgetary Control"?

• Well, I will discuss it after discussing its relevant aspects. Do you remember my previous lectures where I discussed the business philosophy in detail. Do you remember?

☐ "Yes Sir."

☐ "Please Sir, discuss it from the beginning."

• Do not worry, I will explain all the points so that you may understand.

Like human beings, every business has some philosophy of its own. The philosophy of business can be summed up as :

Business Philosophy

Business Philosophy

(1) Maximisation of profit
(2) Increase in turnover
(3) Reduction in cost
(4) Production of quality goods at a reduced price for the general welfare
(5) Efficient purchase and sale
(6) Elimination of unnecessary expenditures
(7) Preserving the integrity of the capital investment of the business
(8) Proper utilisation of resources, and finally
(9) Increase in business efficiency

But in actual practice very few businesses are found successful in achieving the aforesaid objectives of business which have been termed here as business philosophy. It is also found in actual case that a business with sufficient fund at its disposal cannot compete with the firm running with small amount of capital. There are many causes for it. One of the causes is the lack of planning. So planning is the key of success of any organisation. 'Some people do their planning entirely in their heads, others make notes and rough estimates on the backs of old envelopes, and still others express their plans in quantitative terms and commit these to

Planning vs Budgeting

papers in some orderly, systematic fashion. The process engaged in by the latter group is called "budgetings," for a budget is merely a plan expressed in quantitative terms. So it can be assumed that a budget is a plan and 'can be regarded as the statement of what an account is expected to look like after the events that have been planned for a given period have taken place.'

So the successful achievement of the basic business philosophy — earning profit, depends upon the successful planning to be framed by management. To make the plan successful, budgets should be allowed to enter in the process of business. The importance of budgeting in business organisation cannot be rejected when it was found to be 'part of plan'; rather it can be extended irrespective of the size of the business. Without planning there can be no budgeting. 'For, good planning and good budgeting go hand in hand.' Budgets and Plannings are correlated. It should be noted in this connection that budgets cannot guarantee success towards the desired objective. The success of the same depends upon a number of factors of which most vital is the performance factor. To make the business budget successful and more fruitful, Performance Budget and Responsibility Accounting should be developed and even encouraged. Otherwise, budgets will not be useful for control device. The budget which is most appropriate for planning purposes is not best suited for control.' Besides, if business budget are to be used for the purposes of control device then Flexible Budget should be allowed to enter in.

Functions of Budgeting

1. It encourages and forces the top management to make a coordinated plan for the accomplishment of objective.

2. It serves as a yardstick to measure individual performance.

3. It acts as a control device by comparing the budgeted figure with the actual figure.

4. It will help to reduce control cost. "They will save you many costly arguments and painful ulcers, because they will more exactly fix accountability for results."

5. It is very useful for keeping control on all the departments; accordingly it keeps the departments together harmoniously.

Effectiveness of Budgeting

1. Experience of the past and the condition of the present should be taken into account.

2. Better human performance; — effort should be executed from all levels of management.

3. Application of intuition and better hypotheses are necessary for its effectiveness. 'Nevertheless, business conditions, though fluid, are sufficiently stable for some condition, conclusions to be drawn from the past and these can form the basis for plans about the future. Each day amended hypotheses will probably be needed, yet the conditions of yesterday are in some degree useful in setting up-to-day's hypothesis'.

4. Constantly changing condition of the society—such as labour policy, product, taste and economic condition—should be taken into account in order to make a business budget more effective. Besides, changing prices should be taken into account in the prepartion of budgets because problem arises in making correct estimate in respect of real value assets.

5. Effectiveness of business budget will be more fluid and lucid if it is based upon market research. For example, for the preparation of Sales Budget, the future and existing selling trend is first to be justified and verified.

6. The preparation of budget would be more effective if it is based on 'trial and error approach'.

7. The ideal budget control record should be self-explanatory and reveal at a glance just what was going on in the business and why certain changes were called for.

Business Budgeting : For the accomplishment of each and every aspect of business philosophy, there should be a separate planning. Accordingly, there should be budget for purchase, sales, production, debtors, creditors, expenses, selling and distribution cost, raw materials, labour production overhead, administration cost, and, finally, cash budget. The development and introduction of cash budget depends upon the success of other budgets, that is to say, sales budget, production budget etc. and in some cases it is found that modification of sales budget, production budgets etc. will be made in light of cash budget.

Different Types of Budgets

Coordination : it is a potent fact that coordination is necessary among all other budgets. It would be sound business policy to consider the budget as a whole and not as separate. This is because whenever any change in the production budget is likely to be made, some repercussion is likely to follow on the purchase and sales budget. If the management wishes to cut down the production budget, some alteration is likely to be made on the purchase and selling policy of the business in order to keep the business on right footing. This is the policy of adjustment which is needed for efficient running of business. This policy of adjustment necessitates the origin and development of Flexible Budget which is very helpful for controlling the cost. So it is very helpful for control device, 'the sales budget is likely to have repercussions on the production, material and finance and other budgets. But as our mental faculties are limited, we have to be content with a step by step approach considering one departmental budget at a time.'

Co-ordination in Budgeting

For the increase in production, or purchase or sale, there will be proportionate increase or decrease in the expenditure too. All these wil be taken into account for the preparation of budgets. The performance of purchase, production and sales budget depends upon the proper success of debtors and creditors budgets. 'The sales, production and materials budgets must be related to budgets of changes in amounts owing to the business by debtors and from the business to creditors ......'

I have already pointed out in course of general discussions that the sources of profit are—increase in turnover and reduction of cost or expenditure. Whenever a business is found efficient in sales it does not necessarily mean that the company is making higher profit thereby. Expenses may be of various types—manufacturing expenses, buying expenses, selling expenses, general office expenses etc.

If, $S = E$ = No Profit/no Loss

$S > E$ = Profit   S = Total Sales

$S < E$ = Loss   E = Total Expenses.

So it is clear that, other things remaining the same, Profit/Loss is the result of favourable/ unfavourable movement of Sales and Expenditures as indicated above. With the increase in turnover, expenses have a tendency to rise constantly and, as they increase, the profit of the business tends to decrease. So a clear understanding should be there among the sales budget, the production budget and the expense budget. 'When examining actual expenditure, allowance must be made for the effect of any rise or fall in production upon those expenses, such as direct labour, which vary directly with production.' So without proper coordination of sales and expenditure the control of the latter will definitely be a difficult task.

Besides, the preparation of cash budget will be more effective if the ideas of accumulated sales and the collection of the same can be drawn. Because, sales may be of two types—cash sales and credit sales. No problem arises as to cash sale, because cash is collected on the day of transaction. Problem is there in respect of credit sales and respective collection periods. So the preparation or formulation of cash budget will be more effective if a clear understanding between the sales and collection can be developed.

Cash Budget

Though cash results from the movement in other assets and liabilities, yet cash itself is needed for lubricating the said movement. If there be sufficient fund after payment, i.e., purchase, expenses etc. the said fund is treated as one of the items of cash receipts. Cash itself has two functions of its own—receipt and payment. Accordingly, there are cash receiving budget and cash disbursement budget. The cash receiving budget and cash disbursement budget, in general, may be termed as Cash Budget. So Cash Budget is a statement of the expected position of the business which begins with cash balance at the beginning of the month or period and to which is added the expected receipt during the month and from which is deducted the expected payments to be made during the month or period. At the end of the month or period there is a balance,—favourable or unfavourable—which indicates whether overdraft facilities need to be provided or not. So a diagram can be drawn in respect of the receipt and payment of cash budget. It should be noted in this context that American Technical Society (A.T.C. 1942) had given a diagram showing the estimate of accumulated cash receipts and disbursements. However, the diagram given below is an advanced thinking of the concept :

Meaning of Cash Budget

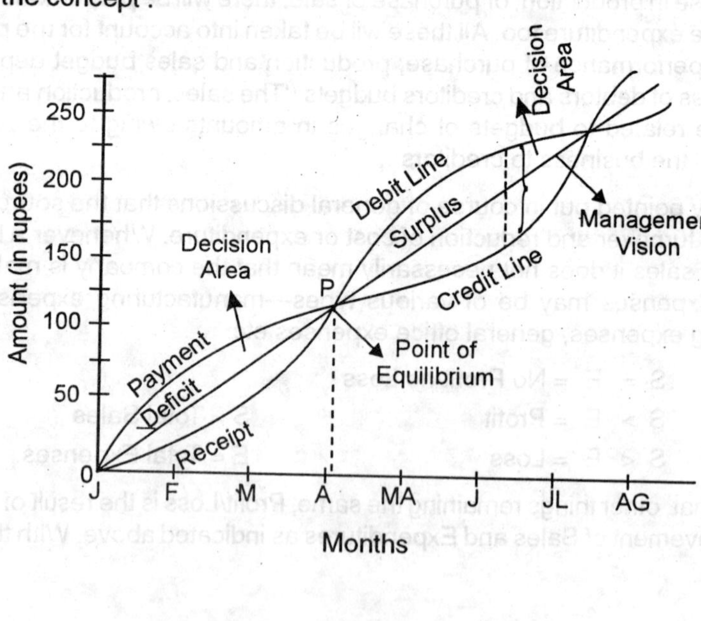

Cash Budget and Management Decision

Cash budget or financial budget as shown in the diagram indicates that after certain point or stage (Point 'P' shown in the diagram) the surplus areas starts. This area may be termed as the 'Problem Area'. This is the area which the management is concerned with. To overcome this is the ultimate desire of the management. What management can do to solve this problem is a matter of headache. The management can :

Cash Budget as an Aid to Management Decision

1) Make arrangement with the bank for overdraft facilities.

2) Issue shares or debentures in the period of deficit. This can be done only when there is such scope for the same.

3) Make arrangement with the creditors so that the payment can be deferred for a considerable period.

4) Stop purchase if it does not affect the continuity of the business.

5) Provide some attraction to the debtors for early payment.

6) Modify the different policies of the business in light with above policy. 'Sales, production, pricing, financing and other policies should be critically re-examined in the light of the cash budget, and modified where the latter indicates this to be desirable.'

It is not always advisable that the management should follow all of the methods indicated above, the application of any one of the said methods depends upon the suitability of individual case.

Control

Decision is the ultimate result of all causes and effects. Decision-taking would be more effective if the relevant data, as far as possible, are communicated to top management. These data are communicated through reports which are very useful for making decision. Budgets are the top management report which is required for making management decision and used as control device. Besides, the budgetary process consists of control at three points—the budget itself, the appropriation and the expenditure. Whatever may be the points of control it is a fact that control is essential for better implementation of coordination. This co-ordination is possible only when the management compares the budgeted figures with actual figures. The resultant figures, if in adverse variance, may alert the management to institute investigation and decision to avoid cause and effect of this adverse variance in light with the past and present experience should be taken while preparing the budgets for the next month; if that be so, the performance appraisal would be more effective. The variance, say in the Sales Budget, may be due to inefficiency on the part of the management, lack of proper coordination among other budgets and finally lack of proper estimation of market research. But it cannot be denied that the deviation may be due to the errors contained in the budget itself. These errors are unforeseen errors which come after the sales and purchase budgets or forecasts are prepared. This is due to the fact that the budgets, say the purchase and sales, are based on the objective forecast based on the analysis of past. A subjective approach in the matter is welcome and the forecast or the budget should be based on the subjective forecast based on the analysis of the past, the judgement of the present and the intuition of the future. As for example, the budget will give us an adverse result in

Control in Budgeting

Responsibility Accounting and Budgeting

actual practice if it does not take into account the aspect of change in price level in the budget preparation. The Re of yesterday is not equal to the Re of today and it will not even be equal to the Re of tomorrow. In many cases, the budgets for tomorrow are prepared in terms of today's Re. If the preparation of sales budget and the purchase budget etc. does not pay due regards to the accounting for stewardship in a period of inflation, it would misguide the management in the preparation of financial budgets.

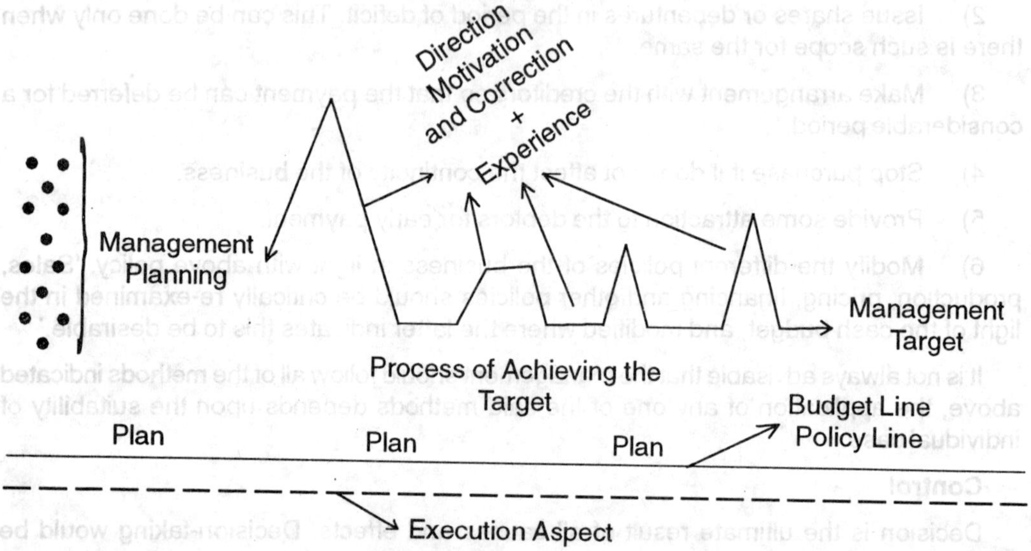

So, it is suggested, if the performance appraisal is to be made more effective, budgets should be prepared at three months' intervals having due regard to the discussion made earlier in this chapter, though it is normally prepared for one year. Besides, responsibility accounting and, if possible, performance audit, should be welcome in the process of management in order to make the performance appraisal more effective.

Now I hope you have understood the different aspects of budget and budgetary control. Please tell me if you really face any difficulties.

☐ "Sir, really speaking I cannot understand."

• Well, which portion do you find difficult? Should I discuss the whole thing in a nutshell?

☐ "No Sir, please clear the portion."

• What? Please clarify what do you want to say?

☐ "Sir, what is the difference between the Budget and Budgetary Control and what are the objects of Budgetary Control?"

• You see, I have already discussed all these points in course of my lectures. You could have grasped all these if you could follow my last lectures very carefully.

From the Exhibit given earlier it is clear that budgetary control is the counterpart of the business budget. Had there been no control aspect, the plan and policy of the business from the practical point of view would have been static. However, the Institute of Cost and Works Accountants of London, in their book "An Introduction to Budgetary Control, Standard Costing, Material Control and Production Control," has given the definition of Budgets and Budgetary Control and the objects of Budgetary Control in separate which I am giving you from the same source.

Difference between Budget and Budgetary Control

A Budget can be defined as 'a financial or quantitative interpretation, prior to a defined period of time, of a policy to be pursued for that period to attain a given objective'.

Definition of Budget

Budgetary Control can be defined as 'the establishment of Departmental Budgets relating the responsibilities of executives to the requirement of a policy, and the continuous comparison of actual with budgeted results, either to secure by individual action the objective of that policy or to provide a basis for its revision.'

Definition of Budgetary Control

Now if you go through the definition given above you will find that every point have been incorporated in my last lectures. However, the **Objects of Budgetary Control**, as given by the Institute of Cost and Works Accountants of London, are :

(a) To plan and control the income and expenditure of manufacturing and trading operations so that the most practicable profit is obtained;

(b) To plan and control the capital expenditure of a business.

(c) To plan and control expenditure on Development and Research in so far as such expenditure is not applicable to normal manufacturing and trading operations or is not covered by a Capital Expenditure Budget.

(d) To plan and control the financing of a business so that adequate working capital, including liquid resources, is available for carrying the policy of the business.

(e) To act as an instrument of management policy whereby the extension of the scheme to lower level of management enables top management to decentralise responsibility and centralise control.

Now I hope that all these discussions are sufficient for your level of thinking. By the by, you can ask me about points which are not clear to you.

☐ "Sir, please work out a few practical problems on Budgeting".

● Well, I am also thinking the same. Here are the different types of practical problems which will definitely help you to understand the whole process of business budgets.

Problem

From the following information prepare a Cash Budget for the months of January to April :

Expected Sales :

January	—	Rs	60,000
February	—	Rs	40,000
March	—	Rs	45,000
April	—	Rs	40,000

Expected Purchase :

January	—	Rs.	48,000
February	—	Rs.	80,000
March	—	Rs.	81,000
April	—	Rs.	90,000

Wages to be paid to workers Rs. 5,000 each month

Balance at bank on 1st January Rs. 8,000

Solution

Cash Budget for the months of January to April

Receipts :	January Rs.	February Rs.	March Rs.	April Rs.
Balance	8,000	15,000	—	—
Sales	60,000	40,000	45,000	40,000
Deficit	—	30,000	71,000	1,26,000
	68,000	85,000	1,16,000	1,66,000
Payments :				
Deficit b/f	—	—	30,000	71,000
Creditors	48,000	80,000	81,000	90,000
Wages	5,000	5,000	5,000	5,000
Balance c/d	15,000			
	68,000	85,000	1,16,000	1,66,000

Problem

Assuming the same information as contained in the previous problem, it has been decided by the management as to the following :

(i) In case of deficit of fund within the limit of Rs. 10,000 arrangement can be made with the Bank.

(ii) In case of deficit of fund exceeding Rs. 10,000 but within the limit of Rs. 42,000 issue of Debenture is preferred.

(iii) In case of deficit of fund exceeding Rs. 42,000 issue of shares is preferred (considering the fact that it is within the limit of Authorised Capital).

Solution

Cash Budget for the months of January to April

	January Rs.	February Rs.	March Rs.	April Rs.
Receipts :				
Balance b/f	8,000	15,000	—	—
Sales	60,000	40,000	45,000	40,000
Issue of Debenture	—	30,000	41,000	—
Issue of Shares	—	—	—	55,000
	68,000	85,000	86,000	95,000
Payments :				
Creditors	48,000	80,000	81,000	90,000
Wages	5,000	5,000	5,000	5,000
Balance c/d	15,000	—	—	—
	68,000	85,000	86,000	95,000

Now I hope that you have understood these two problems. I shall be glad to hear from you any points which you want to know or any new questions you can put me.

☐ "Sir, give us a Proforma of long-term Cash forecast."

• Well, it is a nice question. Here is your Proforma of Cash Forecast.

Pro-forma of Long-term Cash Forecast

	1st quarter Rs.	2nd quarter Rs.	3rd quarter Rs.	4th quarter Rs.
Receipts :				
Balance b/f	xx	xx	xx	xx
Issue of shares	xxx	xxx	xxx	xxx
Sales	xxx	xxx	xxx	xxx
Receipts from Debtors	xx	xx	xx	xx
Any Other Receipts	xx	xx	xx	xx
Deficit for the Quarter	xx	xx	xx	xx
	xxxx	xxxx	xxxx	xxxx
Payments :				
Deficits b/f	xx	xx	xx	xx
Purchase of Assets	xxx	xxx	xxx	xxx
Creditors	xxx	xxx	xxx	xxx
Expenses	xx	xx	xx	xx
Payment of Taxation	xx	xx	xx	xx
Payment of Dividend	xx	xx	xx	xx
Balance c/d	xx	xx	xx	xx
	xxxx	xxxx	xxxx	xxxx

Now I hope you have understood what I wanted to clarify.

☐ "Yes Sir, But Sir, Please work out at least one complicated problem in this respect."

- Well, take down the problem.

Problem

From the following information prepare a Cash Forecast for the first quarter of 2007 :

(1) Cost

Prime cost is estimated at Rs. 20 per unit, being Rs. 10 direct labour and Rs. 10 direct material. Factory and administrative overhead cost is estimated for each month to be Rs. 10,000. A publicity campaign is to be lanuched from February. It is to cost Rs. 10,000 for the first month and then Rs. 2,000 for the subsequent months. Selling expenses are expected Rs. 15,000 per month, commencing from 1st February.

Initial contingencies have been estimated at Rs. 25,000

(2) Sales

They have been estimated as :

January	2,000 Units
February	3,000 Units
March	4,000 Units

The selling price has been fixed at Rs. 50 per unit.

(3) Stocks

- Raw materials costing Rs. 60,000 are to be purchased for the initial stock and this is to be maintained at this level. A stock of finished goods is also to be maintained at 500 units.

(4) Terms of Purchases and Sales

Materials purchased are to be paid for within one month, 20% of sales will be for cash and the balance on credit receivable within one month. On an average the credit sales will be allowed a cash discount of 5%.

All overheads are payable within the month in which they are incurred.

[Adapted from C.A. Final]

You see, this is a most typical problem on Cash Forecast. Read this problem again and again. You see, in this problem there is no opening cash balance. You are to think out yourself the details of the Receipts side and the Payment side of Cash Forecast. Now, following are the possible items of Receipts and Payments of this Problem.

Receipts : Cash Sales, Receivable from Debtors

Payments : Direct Material, Direct Labour, Factory and Administrative Cost, Publicity Expenses, Selling Expenses, Initial Contingencies

From the problem it is clear that 20% of the sales are to be made at cash and the balance on credit, receivable within one month. that is to say, January's money will be received in of February and similarly February's money in March. However, 5% cash discount will be allowed on the credit sales. The calculation will be :

Sales figure for January is 2,000 unit. Per unit selling price is Rs. 50

Sales (2,000 x 50) = Rs. 1,00,000

Cash Sales .... 20% of Rs. 1,00,000 = Rs. 20,000. This amount will be collected within the current month and the balance (Rs. 1,00,000 — Rs. 20,000) Rs. 80,000 will be collected in the following month after deducting 5% discount. The figure will be :

$$\frac{5}{100} \times 80{,}000 = \text{Rs. } 4{,}000.$$

The amount to be received from Debtors in the month of February will be :

Rs.	80,000
Rs.	4,000
Rs.	76,000

☐ "Sir, how figures for February and March will be calculated?"

• Oh yes, similar type of principles will be followed in the future, particularly in this problem."

I hope that you have followed my lecture. If you find any point complicated, you can ask me.

☐ "Sir, how the figures for Direct Material and Direct Labour will be calculated?"

• From the information supplied, it is clear that materials purchased are to be paid within one month. In this sum it is assumed that materials were purchased in the middle of January. Naturally payment would be made in February. You know that business is a continuous process. In this process we see three stages — Purchase, Production and Sales. What is sold is to be replaced. Thus the calculation runs :

Direct Materials

		Rs.
Payment for January to be made in February	Purchase of raw materials	60,000
	Stock of Finished goods (500 units x Rs. 10)	5,000
	Sales (2,000 units X Rs. 10)	20,000
		85,000

Calculation for February :

Sales figures (3,000 units X Rs. 10)	Rs. 30,000
	Rs. 30,000

Payment for Rs. 30,000 would be made in the month of March.

Calculation of Direct Labour :

January,	Sales figures (2,000 units X Rs. 10)	Rs.	20,000
	Finished goods	Rs.	5,000
		Rs.	25,000

From the information supplied it is clear that all overheads are payable within the months in which they are incurred. So, this Rs. 25,000, being figure for January, will appear on the Payment side of the Cash Forecast. Thus Rs. 30,000 and Rs. 40,000, being the figures for the month of February and March, respectively, will appear on the payment side of the Cash Forecast.

Regarding Publicity Expenses it can be said that it starts from February in which month it is estimated at Rs. 10,000. After that Rs. 2,000 will be charged for respective subsequent months.

Selling expenses start from February. Now I hope that you have understood all the complicated points of this sum.

☐ "Sir, Please work out the problem."

• Well note below the workings of this problem :

Solution

Cash Forecast of .... Co. Ltd.
for the first quarter of 2007

	Jan. Rs.	Feb. Rs.	March Rs.
Receipts :			
Balance b/f	—	—	—
Cash Sales	20,000	30,000	40,000
Debtors (to be received)	—	76,000	1,14,000
Deficit	40,000	84,000	27,000
	60,000	1,90,000	1,81,000
Payments :			
Deficit b/f	—	40,000	84,000
Direct Materials	—	85,000	30,000
Direct Labour	25,000	30,000	40,000
Factory Administrative Cost	10,000	10,000	10,000
Advertisement Expenses	—	10,000	2,000
Selling Expenses	—	15,000	15,000
Initial Contingency	25,000	—	—
	60,000	1,90,000	1,81,000

Problem

From the following budgeted figures prepare a Cash Budget in respect of three months to June 30 :

Months	Sales Rs.	Materials Rs.	Wages Rs.	Overheads Rs.
January	60,000	40,000	11,000	6,200
February	56,000	48,000	11,600	6,600
March	64,000	50,000	12,000	6,800
April	80,000	56,000	12,400	7,200
May	84,000	62,000	13,000	8,600
June	76,000	50,000	14,000	8,000

Expected Cash Balance on 1st April Rs. 20,000

Other Information :

(a) Materials and Overheads are to be paid during the month following the month of supply

(b) Wages are to be paid during the month in which they are incurred

(c) Terms of Sales—

The terms of Credit Sales are payment by the end of the month following the month of sales; 1/2 of the Sales are paid when due, the other half to be paid during the next month.

5% Sales commission is to be paid within the month following actual sales

(d) Preference dividend for Rs. 30,000 is to be paid on 1st May

(e) Share call money for Rs. 25,000 is due on 1st April and 1st June

(f) Plant and Machinery worth Rs. 10,000 is to be installed in January and the payment is to be made in the month of June.

Solution

Cash Budget

Receipts :	April Rs.	May Rs.	June Rs.
Balance b/f	20,000	32,600	—
Sales	60,000 (A)	72,000 (B)	82,000 (C)
Share Capital	25,000	—	25,000
Deficit	—	5,600	—
	1,05,000	1,10,200	1,07,000

Payments :	Rs.	Rs.	Rs.
Deficit b/f	—	—	5,600
Materials	50,000	56,000	62,000
Wages	12,400	13,000	14,000
Overheads	6,800	7,200	8,600
Sales Commission	3,200 (D)	4,000 (E)	4,200 (F)
Preference Dividend	—	30,000	—
Installation of Plant and Machinery	—	—	10,000
Balance c/d	32,600	—	2,600
	1,05,000	1,10,200	1,07,000

Calculations :

		Rs.			Rs.
(A)	1/2 March	32,000	(B)	1/2 April	40,000
	1/2 February	28,000		1/2 March	32,000
		60,000			72,000
(C)	1/2 May	42,000	(D)	$\frac{5}{100} \times 64,000$	= Rs. 3,200
	1/2 April	40,000			
		82,000			
(E)	$\frac{5}{100} \times 80,000$	= Rs. 4,000	(F)	$\frac{5}{100} \times 84,000$	= Rs. 4,200

Problem

From the following information prepare a Cash Budget for the three months commencing 1st June, when the bank balance was Rs. 1,10,000 :

Months	Sales	Selling Over-heads	Pur-chases	Wages	Factory Over-heads	Adminis-tration Overheads	Research Expendi-tures
	Rs.	Rs.	Rs.	Rs.	Rs.	Rs.	Rs.
April	88,500	3,250	37,000	8,000	5,680	2,500	2,400
May	84,000	4,100	40,000	8,400	5,920	2,760	2,400
June	93,000	3,710	39,060	8,800	5,440	2,480	2,400
July	72,000	3,210	39,900	6,000	5,880	2,600	2,400
August	82,500	3,600	35,000	9,600	6,000	2,520	2,600

A Sales Commission of 5% on Sales are due 2 months after sales, and is payable in addition to the above selling overheads. Capital Expenditure : Plant purchased, June, Rs. 38,000, payable on delivery; building purchased, June, Rs. 80,000, payable in two half yearly instalments, the 1st in July.

A dividend of Rs. 20,000 will be paid in October.

Period of Credit allowed by suppliers and to customers—8 weeks. Lag in payment as to the following are to be taken into account :

Wages	1/8th month
Factory Overheads	4 weeks
Administration Overheads	4 weeks
Research Expenditure	4 weeks
Selling Overheads	4 weeks

[Adapted from C.A. (India) Final]

Solution

Cash Budget
for the Period ended 31st August 20.........

	June Rs.	July Rs.	August Rs.
Receipts :			
Balance b/f	1,10,000	95,145	74,565
Cash Received from Debtors	88,500	84,000	93,000
	1,98,500	1,79,145	1,67,565
Payments :	Rs.	Rs.	Rs.
Purchases	37,000	40,000	39,060
Wages	8,750	6,350	9,150
Factory Overheads	5,920	5,440	5,880
Administration Overheads	2,760	2,480	2,600
Research Expenditure	2,400	2,400	2,400
Selling Overheads	4,100	3,710	3,210
Selling Commission	4,425	4,200	4,650
Capital Expenditure	38,000	40,000	—
Balance c/d	95,145	74,565	1,00,615
	1,98,500	1,79,145	1,67,565

Now I hope that you have understood the details of Cash Forecast and Cash Budget. Is there any question?

☐ "Sir, what is Master Budget? Give us some ideas about Master Budget."

• I am really very glad to see that you try to go deep into the subject matter. Now I am explaining Master Budget in general.

You see, Master Budget is the summary budget of the different Functional or Departmental Budgets. That is to say, the management accountant prepares the master budget as soon as all individual and departmental budgets are prepared. Here I like to bring to your attention the fact that there exist differences of opinion about the concept of Master Budget. Some consider it as a summary of all other principal budgets which I explained to you earlier. And others consider Master Budget as the Budgeted Balance Sheet and Profit and Loss Account. However, whatever the approach it might be, it cannot be denied that Master Budget portraits the overall financial planning of the business.

Master Budget

I think you have understood what are Budgeted Profit and Loss Account and Balance Sheet.

☐ "Yes, Sir, I shall be obliged if you please give us the format of Budgeted Profit and Loss Account and the Master Budget."

• Oh yes. You note below specimen of the two :

Budgeted Profit and Loss Account

				Current Year Products			**Previous Year Products**		
				X	**Y**	**Z**	**X**	**Y**	**Z**
				Rs.	Rs.	Rs.	Rs.	Rs.	Rs.
Sales at Budgeted Price				X	X	X			
Deduct :									
Budgeted Cost of Production :									
	X	**Y**	**Z**						
Materials	X	X	X						
Wages	X	X	X						
Factory	X	X	X						
				X	X	X			
Gross Profit Margin				X	X	X			
Less :									
Adm. Exp.	X	X	X						
Selling Exp.	X	X	X						
				X	X	X			
Anticipated Profit				X	X	X			

Master Budget
for the year ended 31st December 20.............

				Products		
				X	Y	Z
				Rs.	Rs.	Rs.
Sales at Budgeted Price				XX	XX	XX
Less : Cost of Goods Sold				XX	XX	XX
Gross Margin				XX	XX	XX
Deduct :						
	X	Y	Z			
Adm. Exp.	XX	XX	XX			
Selling Exp.	XX	XX	XX			
				XX	XX	XX
Anticipated Profit				XX	XX	XX
Anticipated Appropriation of Profit						
	X	Y	Z			
General Reserve	XX	XX	XX			
Dividend	XX	XX	XX			
				XX	XX	XX
Profit and Loss Balance				XX	XX	XX
Fixed Assets				XX	XX	XX
Net Current Assets				XX	XX	XX
Capital Employed				XX	XX	XX
Profitability				%	%	%
Margin on Sale				%	%	%
Capital Turnover				%	%	%
Solvency Ratio				%	%	%

I think you have understood what is Master Budget. Is there any question?

□ "Sir Please work out at least one practical problem on Master Budget.".

• Well, take down the problem.

Problem

From the following information, prepare Profit and Loss Account for September 20........

Budget output :	Product X	... ...	20,000 Units
	Product Y	... ...	10,000 Units

Selling price per unit of Product X is Re 1.00

Selling price per unit of Product Y is Re 0.50

Other information relating to cost applicable to each unit are :

	X	Y
	Rs.	Rs.
Direct Material	0.40	0.15
Direct Labour	0.25	0.13
Factory Overheads	0.12	0.05
Administration Expenses	0.03	0.03
Selling Expenses	0.08	0.05

Solution

Budgeted Profit and Loss Account for September 20.....

	Product X		Product Y	
	Rs.	Rs.	Rs.	Rs.
Budget Sales Process		20,000		5,000
Deduct : Budgeted Cost of Production				
Direct Material	8,000		1,500	
Direct Labour	5,000		1,300	
Factory Overheads	2,400	15,400	500	3,300
Gross Profit Margin		4,600		1,700
Deduct :				
Administration Exp.	600		300	
Selling Expenses	1,600	2,200	500	800
Anticipated Profit		2,400		900

Problem

The following is a summary of the Balance Sheet of A.B. Ltd. as at 30th September 2005 :

Liabilities	Amount	Assets	Amount
	Rs.		Rs.
Issued Share Capital	10,00,000	Fixed Assets	2,80,000
Reserves & Surplus	2,40,000	Stock	7,20,000
Bank Overdraft	3,60,000	Debtors	10,00,000
Sundry Creditors	4,00,000		
	20,00,000		20,00,000

The creditors represent September 2005 purchases : Debtors represent August and September 2005 sales which were Rs. 5,00,000 each. The sales for the half year ended 30th September 2005 amounted to Rs. 31,50,000 and the Gross Profit was at a uniform rate of 20% on the selling price.

On 1st October 2006 the company's suppliers increased the prices of all goods by 25% and A.B. Ltd. raised its selling prices by 20% immediately. The following estimates were made for the half year ended 31st March 2006 :

(a) Sales, in quantities, would be 10% more than in the preceding half-year. Sales in November will be Rs. 8,58,000, the remaining sales being evenly spread over the other five months.

(b) The stock at the end of each month would be the same, in quantity, as on 30th September 2005 except that on 31st March 2006 it will be 10% above that level.

(c) The credit policy as regards suppliers and customers will not change.

(d) Wages and expenses will aggregate Rs. 40,000 each month.

(e) Fixed assets are to depreciate at the rate of 10% per annum and a dividend at the rate of 20% on issued capital will be paid in January 2006.

You are required to prepare statements in the form of a National Balance Sheet as at 31st March 2006 and a Profit and Loss Account for the year ended on that date.

[C.U., M.Com. Management Accounting Exam. (Adapted)]

Solution

Sales on the basis of the last half year :

	Rs.
Sales of last half year	31,50,000
Add : 10% increase	3,15,000
Projected Sales at old prices	34,65,000
Add : 20% increase in prices	6,93,000
Projected Sales	41,58,000
Expected Sales in November	8,58,000
Sales in other 5 months	33,00,000
Sales in each month other than November	6,60,000

	Sales Price	Cost	G.P.
Old	100	80	20
			100
Add : Increase	20 (20%)	20 (25%)	20
	120	100	120

However, in respect of the opening stock the cost was	Rs. 80
while the revised price is 120, margin being	Rs. 40
	Rs. 120

The old stock thus may be sold at 50% above cost

Sales realisation will be out of the same

	(a)	Rs. 10,80,000	In Oct.	6,60,000
			In Nov.	4,20,000
Sales out of purchase new prices	(b)	Rs. 30,78,000		
Gross Margin on (b)		Rs. 5,13,000		
Cost of Sales out of new purchase		Rs. 25,65,000		

Stock at Close on 31.3.2006		
At Sept. 30 level	Rs. 7,20,000	
Add: 10% Rise in quantity	Rs. 72,000	
	Rs. 7,92,000	
Add: 25% price rise	Rs. 1,98,000	9,90,000
Purchases during the period		Rs. 35,55,000

	Oct.	Nov.		Dec.	Jan.	Feb.	March
Sales	6,60,000	8,58,000		6,60,000	6,60,000	6,60,000	6,60,000
		1,40,000	Old				
	*2,20,000	73,000	New	1,10,000	1,10,000	1,10,000	1,10,000
Cost of Sales	4,40,000	6,45,000		5,50,000	5,50,000	5,50,000	5,50,000
Cl. Stock							
Old	2,80,000						
New	5,50,000	9,00,000		9,00,000	9,00,000	9,00,000	9,00,000
	12,70,000	15,45,000		14,50,000	14,50,000	14,50,000	15,40,000
Less Op. Stock	7,20,000	8,30,000		9,00,000	9,00,000	9,00,000	9,00,000
Purchases	5,50,000	7,15,000		5,50,000	5,50,000	5,50,000	6,40,000

*Sale out of old stock

Creditors on 30.9.2005	Rs. 4,00,000	Debtors on 30.9.2005	Rs. 10,00,000
Add: Purchases	Rs. 35,55,000	*Add*: Sales	Rs. 41,58,000
	Rs. 39,55,000		Rs. 51,58,000
Less: Creditors on 31.3.2006	Rs. 6,40,000	*Less*: on 31.3.2006	Rs. 13,20,000
Payment to Creditors	Rs. 33,15,000	Collection	Rs. 38,38,000

Cash Forecast

	Rs.
Overdraft on 30.9.2005	3,60,000
Add : Payment to Creditors	33,15,000
Add : Payment for Expenses	2,40,000
Add : Payment for Dividend	2,00,000
	41,15,000
Less : Collection from Customers	38,38,000
Overdraft on 31.3.2006	2,77,000

Dr. **Budgeted Profit & Loss A/c** *Cr.*

Particulars	Amount	Particulars	Amount
	Rs.		Rs.
To Stock on 30.9.2005	7,20,000	By Sales	41,58,000
" Purchases	35,55,000	" Stock on 31.3.2006	9,90,000
" Wages & Expenses	2,40,000		
" Depreciation	14,000		
" Net Profit for the half year	6,19,000		
	51,48,000		51,48,000

Notional Balance Sheet as at 31.03.2006

Liabilities		Amount	Assets	Amount
		Rs.		Rs.
Share Capital		10,00,000	Fixed Assets	2,66,000
Reserve and Surplus			Stock	9,90,000
Balance on 30.9.2005	2,40,000		Debtors	13,20,000
Add : Profit to 31.3.2006	6,19,000			
	8,59,000			
Less : Dividend	2,00,000	6,59,000		
Bank Overdraft		2,77,000		
Creditors		6,40,000		
		25,76,000		25,76,000

Now I hope you have understood the problem. Is there any question?

☐ "Sir, we are very glad to have all these information. We shall be obliged, Sir, if you please work out a few problems on Cash Budget."

☐ "Sir, before that please work out a few problems on Budgeted Profit and Loss A/c and Budgeted Balance Sheet. Besides, Sir, you have not explained anything about Flexible Budget."

• I will explain everything. Before that I would like to work out one problem on Budgeted Profit and Loss Account and Balance Sheet.

Problem

From the particulars of Arab Ltd. given below, prepare a Forecast Profit and Loss Account for the year ended 31st December 2007 and a Cash Forecast for that year :

(a) Extracts from Profit & Loss Account for the year ended 31st December 2006

Material consumed	Rs.	24,000
Wages	Rs.	20,000
Overheads (50% variable)	Rs.	40,000
Sales (all production)—1,000 units @ Rs. 100	Rs.	1,00,000

(b) Balance Sheet as at 31.12.2006

Liabilities	Amount	Assets	Amount
	Rs.		Rs.
Share Capital	70,000	Fixed Assets	60,000
Reserve & Surplus	24,000	(Cost less dep.)	
Sundry Creditors	4,000	Stock (materials)	8,000
Proposed Dividend	7,000	Debtors	25,000
		Cash & Bank	12,000
	1,05,000		1,05,000

(c) Other relevant information :

(i) Arab Ltd. contemplates an increase in the sales volume by 20%. This would necessitate a 5% reduction in the selling price.

(ii) Estimated increase in costs : Materials 2%; Wages 3%; Variable Overheads 2% and Fixed Overheads 1%.

(iii) Terms of payments : Debtors 3 months; Creditors 2 months; Wages and Expenses—within the month in which they are due.

(iv) Stock (materials) carrying policy—4 months' production requirements. Materials are issued on FIFO basis.

(v) Income-tax at 30% should be paid in advance. A dividend at 10% may be proposed to be paid in the subsequent year.

(vi) Fixed costs include depreciation which is a fixed instalment of Rs. 10,000 p.a. charged in full to Overheads.

Assume that there will not be any closing work-in-progress and production and sales will coincide.

[M.Com. (C.U.) Management Accounting (Adapted)]

Solution

1. Sales Budget :

(a) Estimated units = 1,200 Units
Unit Selling price = 100 – 5 = 95
Estimated Sales = 1200 Units X Rs. 90 = 1,14,000 (P/L A/c)

(b) Closing Debtors :
3/12 X 1,14,000 = Rs. 28,500

(c) Receipts from Debtors (i.e. Collection)

		Rs.
Opening Balance		25,000
Add : Sales		1,14,000
		1,39,000
Less : Closing Debtors		28,500
		1,10,500

2. Purchase Budget :

		Rs.
(a) Material Consumed (as per last Profit and Loss A/c)		24,000
Add : (+) 20% increase in Volume		4,800
		28,800
Add : (+) Closing Stock (4/12 X 28,800)		9,600
Total Requirements		38,400
Less : (–) Opening Stock		8,000
Net Requirement at Old Price		30,400
Add : (+) 2% increase in Price		608
		31,008
(b) Closing Creditors = 2/12 X 31,008 =		5,168

(c) Payment to Creditors :

Opening Balance of Sundry Creditors (as per last Balance Sheet)		4,000
Add : (+) Purchases to be made		31,008
		35,008
Less : Closing Creditors		5,168
		29,840

3. Wages (assuming variables) as per last P/L A/c		20,000
20% increase in value		4,000
		24,000
3% Increase in Price		720
		24,720

4. Raw Materials Consumed		8,000
Add : (+) Raw Materials Purchased		31,008
		39,008
Less : (–) Closing Stock at old Price	9,600	
Plus : (+) 2% Increase in Price	192	9,792
		29,216

5. Overhead : Rs. 40,000

Fixed Rs. 20,000			Variable	Rs. 20,000
For Depreciation (Rs. 10,000)	For Others (Rs. 10,000)		*Plus* : (+) 20% Increase in Volume	4,000
	Plus : 1% Increase in Price = Rs. 100			24,000
			(+) *Plus* : 2% increase in Price	480
So Fixed Overhead	= Depreciation	Rs. 10,000		Rs. 24,480
	= Others	Rs. 10,100		
		20,100		

So Total Overhead Cost = Rs. 20,100 + Rs. 24,480 = Rs. 44,580

I hope that your have followed the above workings.

Now I would like to work out the Budgeted Trading and Profit and Loss Account and Budgeted Balance Sheet

Please note that after that a Cash Budget should be prepared to find out the expected surplus of cash at the end of the year under review.

However, I am now working out the Budgeted Trading and Profit and Loss Account and Balance Sheet.

Budgeted Trading and Profit and Loss A/c
for the year ended .....

Dr. *Cr.*

Particulars		Amount	Particulars	Amount
		Rs.		Rs.
To Raw Material Consumed		29,216	By Sales	1,14,000
" Wages		24,720		
" Overhead :				
Fixed	20,100			
Variable	24,480	44,580		
Net Profit c/d		15,484		
		1,14,000		1,14,000
To Proposed Dividends (10% on Capital Rs. 70,000)		7,000	By Net Profit b/d	15,484
" Income Tax (30% of 15,484)		4,625	" Reserve and Surplus as per given Balance Sheet	24,000
" Surplus		27,859		
		39,484		39,484

Budgeted Balance Sheet as at ....

Liabilities	Amount	Assets		Amount
	Rs.			Rs.
Share Capital	70,000	Fixed Assets	60,000	
Reserve and Surplus	27,859	Less Depreciation	10,000	50,000
Sundry Creditors	5,168	Stock		9,792
Proposed Dividend	7,000	Debtors		28,600
		Cash and Bank		21,735 *
	110,027			110,027

Cash Budget

		Rs.
Receipts :		
Opening Cash Balance		12,000
Receipts from the Debtors		110,500
		122,500
Payments :		
Payment to Creditors		29,840
Payment for Wages		24,720
Payment for Overhead	44,580	
Less : Depreciation	10,000	
		34,580
Payment for Proposed Dividend		7,000
Payment for Income Tax		4,625
		100,765

Cash Balances = Rs. 122,500 – 100,765 = Rs. 21,735*

Problem

The accounts of a company for the year ended 31.3.2006 were :

	Rs.
Direct Material	96,000
Wages	48,000
Variable Overheads	24,000
Fixed Overheads	48,000
Profit	24,000
Sales	2,40,000

The Balance Sheet as at 31st March 2006 appeared as :

Liabilities	Amount	Assets	Amount
	Rs.		Rs.
Share Capital	50,000	Freehold Land and Buildings	20,000
Capital Reserve	20,000	Plant and Machinery	40,000
Profit and Loss A/c	20,000	Stock	40,000
Taxation Reserve	10,000	Debtors	40,000
Trade Creditors	16,000		
Bank Overdraft	24,000		
	1,40,000		1,40,000

Experience shows that Creditors can be maintained at the equivalent of two months' purchases of direct materials, while stock and debtors should each continue to be kept at the value of two months' sales.

The budget for the year commencing 1st April 2006 gives quarterly sales as follows :

		Rs.
Quarters	1	60,000
	2	66,000
	3	72,000
	4	78,000

It is expected that all variable costs will be incurred at the same relative prices and efficiences as in the year to 31st March 2006. Fixed overheads will remain at Rs. 48,000 paid evenly over the year.

Taxation (Rs. 10,000) will be paid in January 2007. Plant and Machinery costing Rs. 10,000 will be purchased and paid for in March 2007, but will not be subject to depreciation during the budgeted year. Other plant and machinery will be depreciated at 10% per annum.

Prepare a forecast of the accounts, with balance sheets as at the end of each quarter of the budget year.

[Adapted from I.C.W.A. Final, London. Advanced Cost and Management Accountancy]

Solution

		Quarters						
Details		**1**		**2**		**3**		**4**
		Rs.		Rs.		Rs.		Rs.
D.M.		24,000		26,400		28,800		31,200
D.L.		12,000		13,200		14,400		15,600
V. Overheads		6,000		6,600		7,200		7,800
		42,000		46,200		50,400		54,600
Changes in Stock:								
Op. Stock	40,000		40,000		44,000		48,000	
Cl. Stock	40,000		44,000	4,000	48,000	4,000	52,000	4,000
		42,000		42,200		46,400		50,600
Depreciation		1,000		1,000		1,000		1,000
Fixed Overheads		12,000		12,000		12,000		12,000
		55,000		55,200		59,400		63,600
Profit		5,000		10,800		12,600		14,400
Sales		60,000		66,000		72,000		78,000

Forecast Balance Sheet

	Quarters 1	2	3	4
	Rs.	Rs.	Rs.	Rs.
Share Capt.	50,000	50,000	50,000	50,000
Capital Res.	20,000	20,000	20,000	20,000
P/L A/c	25,000	35,800	48,400	62,800
Taxation Resv.	10,000	10,000	10,000	—
Trade Crs.	16,000	17,600	19,200	20,800
Bank Overdrafts	18,000	12,600	5,400	16,400
Total	139,000	146,000	153,000	170,000
Freehold				
Building	20,000	20,000	20,000	20,000
Plant and Machinery	39,000	38,000	37,000	46,000
Stock	40,000	44,000	48,000	52,000
Debtors	40,000	44,000	48,000	52,000
Total	139,000	146,000	153,000	170,000

Notes :

$$\text{D.M.} = \frac{96,000}{240,000} \times 100 = 40\%$$

$$\text{D.L.} = \frac{48,000}{240,000} \times 100 = 20\%$$

$$\text{V.O.} = \frac{24,000}{240,000} \times 100 = 10\%$$

Bank Overdraft

Details	Quarters 1	2	3	4
	Rs.	Rs.	Rs.	Rs.
B/debts	(24,000)	(18,000)	(12,600)	(5,400)
Dr.	60,000	62,000	68,000	74,000
Total	36,000	44,000	55,400	68,600
Cr.	24,000	24,800	27,200	29,600
Wages	12,000	13,200	14,400	15,600
V.O.	6,000	6,600	7,200	7,800
Fixed Overhead	12,000	12,000	12,000	12,000
	54,000	56,000	60,800	65,000
Plant				10,000
Tax				10,000
Total	54,000	56,000	60,800	85,000
c/d	(18,000)	(12,600)	(5,400)	(16,400)

Problem

XYZ Engineering Ltd. proposes to increase its output by reorganising the factory layout, installing some additional plant and increasing the labour force.

The plan is intended to be put into operation during the four months to 31st December 2006, and has the following financial implications :

(1) The Forecast Balance Sheet as on 31st August 2006 is :

Liabilities	Amount	Assets	Amount
	Rs.		Rs.
Issued Share Capital	7,00,000	Plant and Machinery at cost	6,00,000
Reserves	1,00,000	*Less* : Depreciation	2,64,000
			3,36,000
Profit and Loss Account	1,40,000	Raw Material stocks	1,15,000
	9,40,000	Work-in-progress and finished stocks	1,25,000
Trade Creditors	85,000	Debtors	3,00,000
Accrued charges :		Cash	1,63,000
Rent 8,000			
Other 6,000			
	14,000		
	10,39,000		10,39,000

Note : Trade creditors represent the purchases of raw materials during August 2006. Debtors represent sales in July and August 2006 at the rate of Rs. 1,50,000 per month.

(2) The additional plant, costing Rs. 2,00,000 will be delivered and paid for in September.

(3) Raw materials to be consumed per month :

	September	October to December
	Rs.	Rs.
	70,000	100,000

(4) Stocks of raw materials are to be increased to Rs. 130,000 at the end of September and maintained at that level.

(5) Monthly figures of other costs of production :

	September	October to December per month
	Rs.	Rs.
Direct wages	16,000	24,000
Indirect wages	5,000	7,000
Other factory expense	3,000	5,000

One quarter of each of each of the above costs would be outstanding at the end of the respective month and would be paid in the following month.

Rent of the factory at Rs. 4,000 per month is paid quarterly in arrears on 30th September and 31st December, etc.

Depreciation on plant and machinery is to be provided throughout at the rate of Rs. 7,000 per month.

(6) Administration and selling expenses monthly :

	September	October to December per month
	Rs.	Rs.
Salaries	20,000	22,000
Other office expenses	2,000	3,000

Advertising and publicity will continue at Rs. 10,000 monthly, but will be increased to Rs. 30,000 in October and November.

Each of the above expenses is to be considered as paid in the month in which they arise.

(7) Forecast Sales are :

	Rs.	
September and October	150,000	per month
November	160,000	
December	250,000	

(8) To meet the higher level of sales planned, work-in-progress and finished stocks are to be increased to Rs. 1,60,000 at the end of October and to Rs. 1,95,000 at the end of November.

A fall to Rs. 175,000 is expected at 31st December.

(9) It is expected that existing credit terms will continue to be observed.

(10) The parent company has agreed to advance on a loan account monthly such sums as may be necessary to limit to Rs. 100,000 the bank overdraft of XYZ Engineering Ltd. (Interest on overdraft and loan is to be ignored).

As Chief Accountant you are required to prepare the following for discussion with your Managing Director :

(a) A Forecast Trading and Profit and Loss Account for each of the four months September to December 2006 and a supporting forecast Balance Sheet as on 31st December 2006.

(b) A cash forecast, month by month, for the four months to 31st December 2006, showing when any advance on the Parent Company Loan Account will be required.

Ignore taxation and investment grants.

[Adapted from C.A. (Eng.) Final]

Solution

(a) XYZ Engineering Ltd.

Forecast Monthly Trading and Profit and Loss Accounts
September to December 2006

Particulars	September Rs. '000s	October Rs. '000s	November Rs. '000s	December Rs. '000s
1. Sales	Rs. 150	Rs. 150	Rs. 160	Rs. 250
2. Raw materials consumed	70	100	100	100
3. Direct wages	16	24	24	24
4. Indirect wages	5	7	7	7
5. Depreciation	7	7	7	7
6. Factory rent	4	4	4	4
7. Other factory expenses	3	5	5	5
8. (Increase)/Decrease in work in progress and finished stocks		(35)	(35)	(20)
9. Factory Cost of Sales	105	112	112	167
10. Gross Profit	45	38	48	83
11. Salaries	20	22	22	22
12. Advertising and publicity	10	30	30	10
13. Other Office Expenses	2	3	3	3
14. Administration and Selling Expenses	32	55	55	35
15. Net Profit/(Loss)	13	(17)	(7)	48

Balance Sheet as at 31st December 2006

Liabilities	Amount Rs. '000	Assets	Amount Rs. '000
Issued Share Capital	700	Plant and Machinery at cost	800
Reserves	100	*Less* : Depreciation	292
Profit and Loss Account	177		
			508
	977	Raw material stocks	130
Trade Creditors	100	Work in progress and Finished Stocks	175
Bank Overdraft	100	Debtors	410
Loan from parent company	37		
Accrued Charges	9		
	1,223		1,223

(b)

Cash Forecast
for four months to December 31st 2006

Particulars	September	October	November	December
	Rs. '000	Rs. '000	Rs. '000	Rs. '000
Payments :				
Additional plant	200			
Trade creditors	85	85	100	100
Rent	12	—	—	12
Direct wages	16	22	24	24
Indirect wages and other factory expenses	8	11	12	12
Administration and selling — salaries and other office expenses	22	25	25	25
Advertising and publicity	10	30	30	10
	353	173	191	183
Receipts :				
Debtors	150	150	150	150
Excess of Payments over Receipts	203	23	41	33
Less : Cash balance at end of previous month	163	—		—
Add : Overdraft at end of previous month	—	40	63	100
Add : Advance on parent company loan account in previous month	—		—	4
Total Overdraft and Loan Facilities required	40	63	104	137
Advance on Parent Company Loan Account	—	—	4	37
Overdraft at end of month (Rs.)	40	63	100	100

Please note the following working notes :

(i) Balance Sheet as on December 31st

		Rs. '000
(a)	Profit and Loss Account, August 31st	140
	Add : Net profit, September to December	37
	Profit and Loss Account, December 31st	Rs. 177
(b)	Trade creditors at December 31st represent purchases of raw materials during November	
(c)	Accrued charges are 1/4th of the December costs (Rs. 36,000) given in item (5) of the question	
		Rs. '000
(d)	Plant and machinery at cost, August 31st	600
	Add : Purchased in September	200
	Plant and machinery at cost, December 31st	800

		Rs. '000
(e)	Depreciation provision at August 31st	264
	Add: Provided, September to December	28
	Depreciation provision at December 31st	292

(f) Debtors represent sales in November and December

(g) The bank overdraft and loan from the parent company are the balancing figures and this is confirmed when the cash forecast required in the second part of the question has been prepared.

(ii) Cash Forecast for September to December

(a) Payments to trade creditors each month represent the purchase in the preceding month.

September purchases (paid October) are Rs. 85,000 as follows :

	Rs. '000
Raw material stocks required at end of September	130
September consumption	70
	200
Less : Raw material stocks at August 31st	115
September purchases	85

In October and November purchases (paid in November and December, respectively) are equal to consumption since stocks are to be maintained at the end of September level.

(b) Payments in respect of direct wages and indirect wages and other factory expenses equal 3/4ths of the monthly cost plus 1/4th of the preceding month's cost. The total cost of these items in September is Rs. 24,000 of which 1/4th is Rs. 6,000 and this is equivalent to the amount outstanding shown in the Balance Sheet at the end of August. It may be assumed that the make-up of the charges outstanding in August will be identical to that in September.

(c) Receipts from debtors in September represent sales in July.
Receipts from debtors in October represent sales in August.
Receipts from debtors in November represent sales in September.
Receipts from debtors in December represent sales in October.

I hope, you have followed the above workings. Is there any question please?

☐ "Sir, would you kindly enlighten us about the concept of Flexible Budget?"

• Yes, I will ....

Definition of Flexible Budgeting

You see, The Institute of Cost and Works Accountants of London defined Flexible Budget as 'budget which by recognising the difference between fixed, semi-fixed and variable costs, is designed to change in relation to the level of activity attained'. The essence of flexible budget lies in the fact that original budget should be revised as necessitated by demand of the situation, viz., changes in the volume and the revised budget should be compared with actual figure. And the process of adjusting the original budget with the changed conditions is called flexible budgeting.

☐ "Sir, why are Flexible Budgets desirable?"

• Your question indeed is very interesting. Your question embraces many aspects. Take for example, that are the prerequisite to the introduction of flexible budget. For that I would like to refer you to the work of Mr. Broad and Carmichael. Mr. Broad and Carmichael in their book "A Guide to Management Accounting" explained the circumstances for the introduction of flexible budgets. The circumstances are :

Pre-requisition to the introduction of Flexible Budget

(a) 'When sales are unpredictable because of the nature of business; for example, in the case of jobbing builder or engineer or in those luxury and semi-luxury trades where demand is largely affected by politico-economic conditions.

(b) In case of new ventures, where it is impossible to forecast public demand, e.g., Novelties in fashion or domestic hardware industries.

(c) Where the business is subject to the vagaries of weather, e.g., in soft drinks, i.e. cream and rainwear industries.

(d) Where process depends upon on adequate labour supply as in an area of over full employment.'

I think you have followed the above discussion. Now I like to work out a few practical problems on the concept of Flexible Budget.

Problem

Prepare a Flexible Budget from the following data made available in respect of half yearly period and forecast the working results at 70%, 85% and 100% of capacity when the respective sales are Rupees 50 lakhs, Rupees 60 lakhs and Rupees 85 lakhs.

Where Fixed Expenses remain constant, semivariable expenses are constant, between 55% and 75% of capacity, increasing by 10% between 75% and 90% of capacity and by 20% between 90% and 100% of capacity. The expenses at 60% capacity are :

	Rupees in Lakhs
Semi-Variable	
Maintenance and Repairs	1.25
Indirect Labour	5.00
Sales Department Expenses	1.50
Sundry other Overheads	1.25
Variable	
Materials	12.00
Labour	13.00
Other Expenses	2.00
Fixed	
Wages and Salaries	4.20
Rent, Rates and Taxes	2.80
Depreciation	3.50
Sundry Overheads	4.50
	51.00

[I.C.W.A. (India) Final]

Solution

Flexible Budget

Cost	Cost at 60% capacity Rs. (lakhs)	Cost at 70% capacity Rs. (lakhs)	Cost at 85% capacity Rs. (lakhs)	Cost at 100% capacity Rs. (lakhs)
Maintenance and Repairs	1.25	1.25	1.38	1.50
Indirect Labour	5.00	5.00	5.50	6.00
Sales Department Exp.	1.50	1.50	1.65	1.80
Sundry Other Overheads	1.25	1.25	1.38	1.50
Materials	12.00	14.00	17.00	20.00
Labour	13.00	15.17	18.42	21.67
Other Expenses	2.00	2.33	2.83	3.33
Wages and Salaries	4.20	4.20	4.20	4.20
Rent, Rates and Taxes	2.80	2.80	2.80	2.80
Depreciations	3.50	3.50	3.50	3.50
Sundry Overheads	4.50	4.50	4.50	4.50
	51.00	55.50	63.16	70.80
Sales		50.00	60.00	85.00
Profit (Loss)		(5.50)	(3.16)	14.20

Problem

Demand for the output of a certain company is very elastic and modern plant recently installed is capable of greatly increased production. Output at present is 80,000 units per year, and half a million units annually are estimated to be within the capacity of the new plant.

The present selling price per unit is Rs. 15.

The need for flexible budgeting is recognised and six alternative levels of output in addition to the present level are contemplated. Six equal increments in annual output level, up to a maximum of 5,00,000 units, would involve corresponding reductions of Re 1 each in unit price to Rs. 9 per unit at the maximum output.

The present variable costs amount to Rs. 4,00,000. Fixed Costs which at present amount to Rs. 2,00,000 are not expected to increase for any of the six alternative output levels contemplated. Semi-fixed costs are expected to vary from the present annual figure of Rs. 2,30,000 to Rs. 3,20,000, the upward steps being to Rs. 2,60,000 at 2,20,000 units, Rs. 2,80,000 at 3,60,000 units, and Rs. 3,20,000 at 5,00,000 units. The cost classified as variable at six projected levels of output are calculated to be as :

Rs. 7,50,000	Rs. 11,00,000	Rs. 15,00,000
Rs. 17,50,000	Rs. 20,50,000	Rs. 25,00,000

(a) Tabulate the above data and show total costs, incremental costs, total and incremental sales income at the various output levels.

(b) Which volume should be set for budgeted output?

(c) What is the selling price at what volume?

[Adapted from I.C.W.A. (London), Advanced Cost and Management Accountancy]

Solution

Flexible Budget

(a) **Levels of Output** ('000 units)

	80	150	220	290	360	430	500
	Rs.	Rs.	Rs.	Rs.	Rs.	Rs.	Rs.
Sales ('000)	1,200	2,100	2,860	3,480	3,960	4,300	4,500
Variable Cost	400	750	1,100	1,500	1,750	2,050	2,500
Semifixed Costs	230	230	260	260	280	280	320
Fixed Costs	200	200	200	200	200	200	200
Total Costs	830	1,180	1,560	1,960	2,230	2,530	3,020
Profit ('000)	370	920	1,300	1,520	1,730	1,770	1,480

(b) Increase of profit from level to level are :

	Rs.
80 — 150	5,50,000
150 — 220	3,80,000
220 — 290	2,20,000
290 — 360	2,10,000
360 — 430	40,000
430 — 500	Loss

From the above it is clear that profit increases up to the level of 4,30,000 units, and it appears from the above that this increase in profit is at a diminishing rate and as soon as the level of output reached at 3,60,000 units the drop is noticeable. However, the aimed volume should be 3,60,000 units as minimum and 4,20,000 as a maximum.

(c) The selling price should be Rs. 11 per unit for 3,60,000 units and for the remainder the selling price should be Rs. 10 and Rs. 11 per unit.

Problem

The Pleasure Shoe Company Ltd. prepared the following forecasts

2006-07 Month	Sales	Raw Material	Wages	Production Overhead	Office Overheads	Selling Overhead	Research Overhead	Capital Expenditure
	Rs.	Rs.	Rs.	Rs.	Rs.	Rs.	Rs.	Rs.
Oct 2006	1,35,000	53,000	12,500	8,100	3,450	9,000	1600	1,000
Nov 2006	1,20,000	42,000	11,506	7,600	3,400	8,000	1600	2,000
Dec 2006	1,08,000	45,000	9,080	6,000	3,800	7,500	1600	61,000
Jan 2007	90,000	48,000	9,790	6,500	3,600	6,400	1,800	4,000
Feb 2007	82,000	46,000	9,400	6,100	500	6,200	1800	6,000
Mar 2007	96,000	48,000	10,212	6,700	3,350	6,500	1800	3,000
Apr 2007	94,000	49,000	9,300	6,100	3,400	6,400	1,800	—
May 2007	1,08,000	47,000	10,304	6,900	3,250	7,300	1,900	8,000
June 2007	1,05,000	40,000	10,032	6,600	3,500	7,400	1,750	63,000

From the above information prepare the Cash Budget for the 1st half of the 2007. The following further details are given :

(a) The Cash Balance on 1st Jan 2007 Rs. 87,500

(b) Debtors are allowed two (2) months' credit, 90% payable within the period, the rest pay in three months with the exception of Bad Debts which is equal to 1% of sales.

(c) Creditors for goods and services allow one month credit.

(d) 40% of the creditors for Raw Materials allow 2½% Discount to payment in the same month and advantages is taken.

(e) The budget figure for wages is for those earned in each month.

A 5 day working week is followed and wages are paid one week in arrears in Friday. Assume 1st Jan 2007 as a Sunday.

(f) Interest on Rs. 30,000 @ 5% debenture is due in February and August.

(g) Ordinary shares dividend of Rs. 31,000 for half-year is due in March and in September.

(h) Capital Expenditure is payable in the month indicated in the table.

[Adpated from C.I.A.]

Solution

Cash Budget

Particulars	January	February	March	April	May	June
	Rs.	Rs.	Rs.	Rs.	Rs.	Rs.
Receipts :						
1. Balance b/d	87,500	1,30,085	1,57,070	1,69,668	1,45,513	1,56,818
2. Collection from Customers ...	1,20,000	1,08,000	90,720	81,900	93,780	93,240
3. Income from Investment ...	—	—	80	—	—	—
Rs.	2,07,550	2,38,085	2,47,870	2,51,568	2,39,293	2,50,058
Payments :						
1. Raw Materials	45,720	46,740	46,320	47,610	47,730	43,800
2. Wages	8,945	9,225	11,282	9,195	9,045	11,336
3. Factory Overheads	6,000	6,500	6,100	6,700	6,100	6,900
4. Office	3,800	3,600	3,500	3,350	3,400	3,250
5. Selling Overheads	7,500	6,400	6,200	6,500	6,400	7,300
6. Research Overheads	1,600	1,800	1,800	1,800	1,800	1,900
7. Capital Expenditure	4,000	6,000	3,000	—	8,000	63,000
8. Interest on Debenture ...	—	750	—	—	—	—
9. Ord Sh. Dividend	—	—	—	31,000	—	—
Balance C/d.	1,30,085	1,57,070	1,69,668	1,45,513	1,56,818	1,12,572
Rs.	2,07,650	2,38,086	2,47,870	2,51,568	2,39,293	2,50,059

Wages Calculation

January 1st Jan. Sunday :

1 2 3 4 5 6 7 8 9 10 11 12 13 14 15 16 17 18 19 20 21 22 23 24 25 26 27 28 29 30 31 (Tues)

(1) 7–8 (2) 14–15 (3) 20–21 (4) 28–29

No. of working days in the month of Jan = 22 days $\left[\frac{9{,}790 \times 15}{22}\right]$ = 6,675 Payment in Jan.

But Wages will be paid for 15 days 3,115 Arrear of Jan.

Now Arrear of December

9,080 for 4 weeks : For 1 week = $\frac{9{,}080}{4}$ = Rs. 2,270

Total Wages Payment of January = Rs. 6,675 + Rs. 2,270 = **Rs. 8,945**

Febaruary

W

1 2 3 4 5 6 7 8 9 10 11 12 13 14 15 16 17 18 19 20 21 22 23 24 25 26 27 28 (Tues)

(1) 4–5 (2) 11–12 (3) 18–19 (4) 25–26

	Rs.	Arrear of February	Rs.
No. of Working days : 20 days. But payment will be made for 13 days on	9,400		
$\frac{9{,}400 \times 13}{20}$	6,110		9,400
Add : Arrear of January	3,115		6,110
Total Wages Payment in February	**9,225**		3,290

Wages Calculation

March

1 2 3 4 5 6 7 8 9 10 11 12 13 14 15 16 17 18 19 20 21 22 23 24 25 26 27 28 29 30 31 (Tues)

(1) 4–5 (2) 11–12 (3) 18–19 (4) 25–26 (5) 31

∴ No. of working days = 23 days

But Wages will be paid for 18 days on Rs. 10,212

$= \frac{10,212 \times 18}{23} =$ Rs. 7,992 (Arrear of March = Rs. 10,212 – Rs. 7,992) = Rs. 2,220

Add: Arrear of February	Rs. 3,290
Total for March	**11,282**

April

W

1 2 3 4 5 6 7 8 9 10 11 12 13 14 15 16 17 18 19 20 21 22 23 24 25 26 27 28 29 30 (Tues)

(1) 8–9 (2) 15–16 (3) 21–23 (4) 29–30

∴ No. of working days = 20 days

But Wages will be paid for 15 days

$= \frac{9,300 \times 15}{20}$	Rs. 6,975	Arrear of April	= Rs. 9,300
Add: Arrear of March	Rs. 2,220		= Rs. 6,975
Payment for April	Rs. **9,195**		Rs. 2,325

Wages Calculation

May

1 2 3 4 5 6 7 8 9 10 11 12 13 14 15 16 17 18 19 20 21 22 23 24 25 26 27 28 29 30 31

(1) 6–7   (2) 13–14   (3) 20–21   (4) 27–28   (5) 31

∴ No. of Working days = 23 days

But Wages will be paid for 15 days on Rs. 10,304

$\frac{10,304 \times 15}{23} =$ Rs. 6,720   Arrear of May 10,304 – 6,720 = Rs. 3,584

Add: Arrear of April Rs. 2,325

Payment of May **Rs. 9,045**

June

1 2 3 4 5 6 7 8 9 10 11 12 13 14 15 16 17 18 19 20 21 22 23 24 25 26 27 28 29 30

(1) 3–4   (2) 10–11   (3) 17–18   (4) 24–25

∴ No. of Working days = 22 days

But Wages will be paid for 17 days on Rs. 10,032

$\frac{10,032 \times 17}{22} =$ Rs. 7,752

Add: Arrear of May Rs. 3,584

Payment in June **Rs. 11,336**

Problem

The month by month forecast of profitability of a company for the five months May to September is :

(Rs. '000)

	May	**June**	**July**	**Aug.**	**Sept.**
Materials Consumed	60	70	80	102	90
Wages	32	32	32	40	32
Depreciation	7	7	7	7	7
Factory Expenses	5	5	5	5	5
Rent	3	3	3	3	3
Salaries and Office Expenses	32	32	32	32	32
Advertising and Publicity	12	14	10	16	20
Sales Commission	8	9	10	13	11
	159	172	179	218	200
Sales	160	180	200	260	220
Profit	1	8	21	42	20
Raw Material Stock (end month)	70	80	90	70	60

The following additional information is given :

(1) On average payment is made to suppliers one month after delivery

(2) The lag in payment of wages is 1/8th month

(3) Factory Expenses are paid during the month incurred

(4) Rent is paid quarterly on the last day of March, June, September and December

(5) Salaries and Office Expenses are paid in the month in which they arise

(6) Advertising and Publicity Expenditure is paid monthly but 2 months' credit is taken

(7) Sales Commission is paid one month in arrear

(8) On average Debtros take two months' credit

(9) Cash Balance at 1st July is Rs. 52,000

(10) In September Rs. 30,000 will be paid for machinery. A dividend and tax thereon amounting to Rs. 6,000 will be paid in August. Investment grants of Rs. 20,000 will be received in September.

You are required to prepare a Cash Budget for each of the three months to 30th September. (Give figures to the nearest Rs. 1,000). **[Adapted from C.A. (Eng.) Final]**

Solution

Cash Budget
for three months to 30th September

(Rs. '000)

	July	August	September
Receipts :			
Sales	160	180	200
Investment Grants	—	—	20
Total Inflow	160	180	220
Payment :			
Materials	80	90	82
Wages	32	39	33
Factory Expenses	5	5	5
Rent	—	—	9
Salaries	32	32	32
Advertising and Publicity	12	14	10
Sales Commission	9	10	13
	170	190	184
Capital Expenditure	—	—	30
Dividend and Tax	—	6	—
Total Outflow	170	196	214
Net Movement	– 10	– 16	6
Opening Balance	52	42	26
Closing Balance	42	26	32

I hope you have understood the problem.

☐ "Sir how the figures for purchase of material Rs. 80,000, Rs. 90,000 and Rs. 82,000 for the respective months of July, August and September are arrived at?"

• Well, if you go through the problem very carefully you will find that the figures for payment of raw material have been obtained from the figures for consumption and stock which are :

(Rs. '000)

	June	July	August	September
Closing Stock	80	90	70	60
Add : Consumption	70	80	102	90
	150	170	172	150
Less : Opening Stock	70	80	90	70
Purchases	80	90	82	80

I think, this time you have followed my lecture and the problem.

☐ "Yes Sir, please work out another complicated problem."

• I hope the problems so far discussed are sufficient.

☐ "Please Sir, ..."

• You see, it is not possible to work out each and every problem, you please collect the same from different examination question papers.

I shall be glad to hear from you any points which have not been discussed so far.

☐ "We shall be glad Sir, if you please, Sir, work out a few problems on Budgeted Statement of Operation."

• Well, please take down a problem on Budgeted Statement of Operation.

Problem

A manufacturer provides you with the following Cash Budget covering the 6 months ending 31st October 2006 :

	May Rs.	**June** Rs.	**July** Rs.	**August** Rs.	**Sept.** Rs.	**Oct.** Rs.
Overdraft at the Beginning of the Month	540,340	536,565	573,160	563,755	553,450	549,095
Add : Expenditures Direct						
Variable Costs						
Material	3,500	3,770	4,000	3,730	3,500	4,000
Labour	8,000	8,000	8,000	8,000	—	8,000
Power etc.	7,000	6,800	7,000	6,700	—	7,500
	18,500	18,570	19,000	18,430	3,500	19,500
Fixed Overhead Exp—						
Work Management etc.	4,470	4,470	4,470	4,470	16,470	4,470
Rates (for six months' periods)	—	3,250	—	—	—	—
Office Exp. etc.	5,755	5,955	5,825	6,195	10,875	5,125
Insurance (for the year to 30 April 2007)	—	1,000	—	—	—	—
Legal etc. (for the six month period)	—	2,650	1,200	500	500	500
	10,225	17,325	11,495	11,165	27,845	10,095

	May Rs.	June Rs.	July Rs.	August Rs.	Sept. Rs.	Oct. Rs.
Financial and other—						
Interest on debenture and overdraft	—	8,750	—	—	4,700	—
Capital Expenditure	2,500	31,450	1,600	1,600	1,100	600
	2,500	40,200	1,600	1,600	1,100	600
Sub-Total	5,71,565	6,12,660	6,05,255	5,94,950	5,90,595	5,79,290
Less : Receipt from sales— equivalent to production in the month of sales	35,000	36,000	38,000	38,000	38,000	—
Representing a reduction in finished stock	—	3,500	3,500	3,500	3,500	40,000
	35,000	39,500	41,500	41,500	41,500	40,000
Overdraft at the end of the month	5,36,565	5,73,160	5,63,755	5,53,450	5,49,095	5,39,290

You are given :

(1) all direct variable cost expenditures relate to production in the month in which paid with the exception of Rs. 3,500 spent on materials in September which represents an accretion to raw material stocks. There will be no production in September because the factory shut down for the month for holdiays; certain extra expenditure for the month account for the additional Rs. 12,000 paid for works management etc. in September;

(2) office etc. expenses are up Rs. 5,000 in September because of a payment for advertising charges attributable to the 6 months' period;

(3) fixed overhead expenses and sales collections have been budgeted to be paid and received one month in arrear. The Cash Budget for November 2006 shows :

	Rs.
Fixed Overhead Expenses	
Works Management etc.	4,470
Office expenses etc.	5,965
	10,435
Receipt from sales—equivalent to production in the month of sale	38,000

(4) opening and closing finished stocks are valued at standard cost prices ascertained with refernce only to the direct variable costs of production. The relationship between these cost and selling prices remains unchanged throughout;

(5) fixed overhead expenses are incurred on a time basis and there are 20 working days in each calendar month worked.

You are required to :

(a) prepare a budgeted statement of operations for the half-year to 31st October 2006, showing Sales, Cost of Sales in terms of direct variable expenses, fixed overheads and the result before charging interest.

(b) prepare a budgeted statement of production costs in relation to production sold for May, 2006 showing the value of production at selling prices, the direct costs and the fixed overheads atributable thereto and the costed result before charging interest.

[Adapted from C.A. (Eng.) Final]

☐ "Sir, please work out the problem."

● Well, you try yourself, for that I am giving you some instructions and I hope that it will be helpful to work out the problem.

Instruction :

(1) $\frac{1}{6}$th of Advertising charges for Rs. 5,000 are to be apportioned to each calendar month.

(2) $\frac{1}{6}$th of the Rates for the six month period (the figure appearing in the Cash Budget) are to be apportioned to each calender month.

(3) $\frac{1}{12}$th of the Insurances for the year to 30.4.2007 (the figure appearing in the Cash Budget) are to be apportioned to each calendar month.

(4) The Legal Expenses for the 6 month period are to be apportioned equally over the said period.

(5) $\frac{1}{12}$th of the certain extra expenditure in September for Rs. 12,000 are to be apportioned to each calendar month.

Well, regarding the decrease of stock I would like to give the idea that the standard cost of finished stock are to be taken 50% of sales value. The calculation runs :

Months	Direct Variable Cost of Production Rs.	Sales Value of Production Rs.
May	18,500	36,000
June	18,570	38,000
July	19,000	38,000
August	18,430	38,000
September	—	—
October	19,500	38,000
	94,000	1,88,000

So the Direct Varaible Cost of Production is 50% of Sales Value of Production.

Well, now I am working out the problem.

☐ "Thank you Sir."

Solution

(a) Budgeted Statement of Operation for the half-year to October 31st 2006

Particulars	May	June	July	August	September	October	Total	Percentage
	Rs.	Rs.	Rs.	Rs.	Rs.	Rs.	Rs.	
Sales	39,500	41,500	41,500	41,500	40,000	38,000	242,000	100%
Cost of Production	18,500	18,570	19,000	18,430	—	19,500	94,000	
Stock Decrease	1,750	1,750	1,750	1,750	20,000	—	27,000	
Cost of Sales	20,250	20,320	20,750	20,180	20,000	19,500	1,21,000	50%
Gross Margin	19,250	21,180	20,750	21,320	20,000	18,500	1,21,000	
Works Management etc.	4,470	4,470	4,470	4,470	4,470	4,470	26,820	
Shut-down Expenses	1,000	1,000	1,000	1,000	1,000	1,000	6,000	
Rates and Insurance	625	625	625	625	625	625	3,750	
Office Expenses	5,955	5,825	6,195	5,875	5,125	5,965	34.940	
Legal and Advertising Exp.	1,725	1,725	1,725	1,725	1,725	1,725	10,250	
Total Fixed Overheads	13,775	13,645	14,015	13,695	12,945	13,785	81,860	34%
Margin before charging interest, depreciation and tax	5,475	7,535	6,735	7,625	7,055	4,715	39,140	16%

(b) Budgeted Statement of Production Cost in relation to production sold for the month of May 2006 :

	Rs.
Sales Value of Production	36,000
Materials	3,500
Labour	8,000
Power etc.	7,000
Direct Cost	18,500
Fixed Overhead Cost	14,884
Total Cost	33,384
Margin before charging Interest, Depreciation and Tax	Rs. 2,616

I think all these discussions are sufficient to understand what is Budget and Budgetary Control. In my next lecture I would like to discuss about 'Management by Objective.' Before that I shall be glad to hear any point which is not clear to you.

☐ "Sir, you have not discussed anything about Selling Expenses Budget."

● You see, I discussed in general the basic principles of all the budgets as well as Selling Expenses Budget.

Well, if you want a practical problem on the concept, I will give you a problem.

☐ "Please Sir, work out a practical problem."

● Here is your problem.

Problem

Details of Expenditures	Areas		
	Eastern	Southern	Western
	Rs.	Rs.	Rs.
Advertising Contracts	700	1,000	1,300
Salaries	400	1,000	400
Rent, Rates, Light and Heat	150	450	100
Miscellaneous Exp.	30	100	20
Representatives' Salaries and Commission	800	1,400	800
Representatives' Expenses	500	800	400
Carriage Outwards	250	200	350
Warehouse Wages	800	1,600	600
Warehouse General Expenses	300	500	100
Total	3,930	7,050	4,070

Following changes are likely to be made during the ensuing budget period :

(a) The Commission on the Representatives employed in areas Eastern, Southern and Western is to be enhanced by Rs. 60. This is because of increased turnover.

(b) The expenses of Representatives in the Northern area will be Rs. 1,000.

(c) As a result of good market in the new Northern area, it has been necessitated the transfer of representatives from the Southern area. It will cost Rs. 360 (both for Salary and Commission). Further, to meet a large number of demand, besides the transfer of representatives from Southern area, a few representatives are to be employed. This will cost Rs. 1,440.

(d) Salaries at the Sales Office in the Eastern, Western and Southern areas will be increased by 10%, while Rs. 320 is to be charged in the Northern area.

(e) Carriage Outward Expenses (depending the sales variation) as to the different areas are :

Eastern Area Rs.	Western Area Rs.	Southern Area Rs.	Northern Area Rs.
20% (Rise)	20% (Rise)	40% (Fall)	500 (Anticipated)

(f) An increase of Rs. 10 in Miscellaneous Expenses will be charged in all the areas—Eastern, Southern, and Western.

(g) Rs. 400 additional advertising contracts will be charged in the Southern area.

(h) Advertising contracts for Rs. 1,500; Warehouse General Expenses for Rs. 500; Miscellaneous Expenses for Rs. 20 and Warehouse Wages for Rs. 1,000 are to be charged to the new North area.

(i) Rs. 50 in respect of Rent, Rates, Light and Heat of the Sales Office is to be transferred from the Southern area to the Northern area.

From the information supplied you are requested by the Top Management to set out the Selling Expenses Budget.

I think you will be able to work out the problem. If you find any point difficult, you can ask me.

☐ "Sir, please work out the problem."

Solution

Selling Expenses Budget for the period ended ....

Submitted to ....

Prepared by ....

Details of Expenditures	**Total**	**North**	**East**	**South**	**West**
	Rs.	Rs.	Rs.	Rs.	Rs.
Distribution Expenses :					
Carriage Outward	1,300	500	270	160	370
Warehouse Wages	4,000	1,000	800	1,600	600
Warehouse General Expenses	1,400	500	300	500	100
Direct Selling Expenses :					
Representatives' Salaries and Commission	4,620	1,800	860	1,100	860
Representatives' Expenses	2,700	1,000	500	800	400
Publicity :					
Advertising Contracts	4,900	1,500	700	1,400	1,300
Sales Office :					
Salaries	2,300	320	440	1,100	440
Rent, Rates, Light etc.	700	50	150	400	100
Miscellaneous Expenses	200	20	40	110	30
Total	22,120	6,690	4,060	7,170	4,200

QUESTIONS

1. Define Budgetary Control and name a few types of Functional Budgets. **[I.C.W.A. India]**

2. The Management process of forecasting, planning, selecting plans for operation and then controlling them should be a continuous one and not merely an annual exercise. Discuss and mention the essential steps in the formulation of business policies, basd on forecasting methods. **[I.C.W.A. India]**

3. (a) Sales forecasting is an essential element in budgetary control. Set out in short notes the points you would make to a sales manager to enlist the effective co-operation in a budgetary scheme.

   (b) Prepare a ruling of sales forecast form, providing for certain details to be entered by the cost accountant and others to be entered by the sales manager, for use in connection with budgeting. **[I.C.W.A. London]**

4. A manufacturing business has drawn up a budget for the current year, the proportion of the expected costs, etc. being :

	% (Percentage)
Direct Material	34.0
Direct Labour	22.0
Variable Factory Overheads	16.5
Fixed Factory Overheads	12.0
Other Variable Costs	5.5
Other Fixed Costs	4.0
Profit	6.0
	100.0

After six months' working it becomes apparent that the volume of business anticipated will not be obtained, and management considers that a figure of approximately 75% of budgeted sales will be obtained, i.e., Rs. 3,30,000 for the full year.

As Management Accountant of the business, present information to the management at this stage which will enable decisions to be made on matters of policy. **[Adapted from I.C.W.A. London]**

5. As an accountant of a company making, selling and distributing a wide range of products you are preparing to instal system of Budgetary Control.

   In a report to your managing director :

   (a) state the factors to be taken into consideration in establishing the length of the proposed budget periods;

   (b) describe the operation of a budgeting system for a given period; and

   (c) state your recommendations on the level of attainment that should be adopted. **[M.Com. C.U.]**

6. Discuss the importance of cash budget in an organisation.

   A company making for stock in the first quarter of the year is assisted by its bankers with overdraft accommodation. The following are the relevant budget figures :

	Sales (Credit) Rs.	Purchases (Credit) Rs.	Wages and Expenses Rs.
November	1,20,000	83,000	10,000
December	1,28,000	96,000	10,000
January	72,000	1,62,000	11,000
February	1,16,000	1,64,000	10,000
March	84,000	40,000	12,000

Given the following further information, you are required to prepare a cash budget for the quarter January to March, showing the budgeted amount of bank facilities required, if any, at each month-end :

(a) Budgeted cash at bank on 1st January : Rs. 20,000

(b) Credit terms of sale are payment by the end of the month following the month of supply. On average, one-half of sales are paid on the due date, whilst the other half are paid during the next month. Creditors are paid during the month following the month of supply.

(c) Wages and expenses are paid twice in a month on the 1st and 16th, respectively.

[M.Com. (C.U.) Management Accounting]

7. Make out a Cash Budget for April-June 2007 from the following information :

(1) **Actual and Budgeted Sales :**

	Actual Rs.		**Budgeted** Rs.
January	80,000	April	90,000
February	80,000	May	85,000
March	75,000	June	80,000

(2) **Actual and Budgeted Purchases :**

	Actual Rs.		**Budgeted** Rs.
January	45,000	April	50,000
February	40,000	May	45,000
March	42,000	June	35,000

(3) **Actual and Budgeted Wages and Expenses :**

	Actual			**Budgeted**	
	Wages Rs.	**Expenses** Rs.		**Wages** Rs.	**Expenses** Rs.
January	20,000	5,000	April	24,000	7,000
February	18,000	6,000	May	20,000	6,000
March	22,000	6,000	June	18,000	5,000

(4) **Special :**

Advance Income tax in May Rs. 4,000

Plant in April Rs. 10,000

(5) Rent Rs. 300/- payable each month, not included in expenses.

(6) 10% of purchases and sales are on cash terms.

(7) Credit purchases are after 1 month and credit sales are collected after 2 months. Time lag in wages and expenses : ½ month.

(8) Cash and Bank balances on April 1 Rs. 13,000. **[C.A. Final]**

29

MANAGEMENT BY OBJECTIVES

● Good morning students.

☐ "Good morning Sir. Sir! you have promised us to discuss 'Management by Objectives' today."

● Oh, yes as requested by you I have the pleasure to discuss about Management by Objectives. You see, in the context of implementing control devices in the process of Business, Management by Objectives is abbreviated to MBO. Now I would like to discuss MBO under the following heads :

An Approach to Management by Objectives

(a) Historical Growth

(b) Definition

(c) Advantages

(d) Possible Disadvantages; and, finally

(e) Conclusion.

(a) **Historical Growth :** The idea that has been expressed by many authors that MBO is of recent origin is not an appropriate one, since the term appears to have originated in Personnel Management. It is very difficult to say that who has originated the idea. Is it Dr. Peter Drucker or Mr. John W. Humble? Both were American Management Consultants. It has been suggested that Dr. Drucker "coined" the expression. Similarly 'the development has been attributed to other management consultants, notably Mr. John W. Humble.'

Early History of MBO

However, the two main areas of development of MBO are :

i. Management Accounting

ii. Personnel Management.

That is to say, one associated with Management Accounting, particularly Standard Costing and Budgetary Control, and the other associated with Personnel Management, particularly Management Development. However, that the two branches—(a) Management Accounting, and (b) Personnel Management, are merged into MBO will be evident if the following chart is carefully considered :

Components of MBO

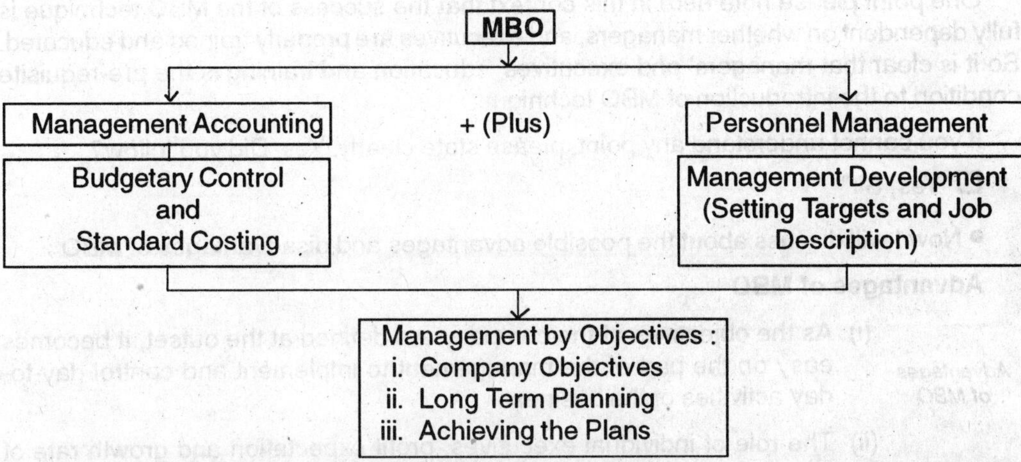

I hope you have followed the chart. Now you see, as a tool and technique in planning and control, budgetary control originated in 1920s. Since then the concepts of Budgetary Control and Standard Costing were greatly recognised. So it is clear that since then the two branches—Budgetary Control and Standard Costing and Personnel Management—merge into MBO, and had wide spread application of their respective principles. So it cannot be stated that MBO is of recent origin. But the manner in which it has been widely used is definitely a new introduction.

I hope you have followed the above discussions. Is there any question please?

☐ "Sir, How can MBO be defined?"

● I think you want to know the exact definition of MBO. Isn't it so?

☐ "Yes, Sir."

● Please note below the definition of MBO.

Definition of MBO

You see, MBO is a management technique 'which purports to be all-embracing as a system of planning and control'. Here 'correct attitude of mind' is the predominating factor in the evolution of the technique. However, defining business objectives, regular tangible meetings, manager's participation in establishing and revising the target in light with the changing environments-are the key to introducing MBO successfully. Harmonising the individual goals with those of the goal of the company as a whole can be made possible if MBO is introduced. You see, one of the features of MBO is that here a real attempt is made to write out fully the responsibilities of each manager and foreman. Once a job description or specification has been prepared this becomes the basis for the targets. A job analysis is made and major areas of a specific job are defined, for example :

1. A Stated Output
2. Labour Efficiency
3. Material Utilisation
4. Work in Progress Control
5. Acceptable Standard of Quality.

These guides should be described in detail so that each manager would know precisely what is expected of him.

One point please note here in this context that the success of the MBO technique is fully dependent on whether managers, and executives are properly trained and educated. So it is clear that managers' and executives' education and training is the pre-requisite condition to the introduction of MBO technique.

If you cannot understand any point, please state clearly. Yes, Did you follow?

☐ "Yes, Sir"

● Now I will discuss about the possible advantages and disadvantages of MBO :

Advantages of MBO

Advantages of MBO

(i) As the objectives of the company are defined at the outset, it becomes easy on the part of the management to implement and control day-to-day activities of the business.

(ii) The role of individual executives, profit expectation and growth rate of the company can be defined.

(iii) Active manager's participation in day-to-day activities in the business and regular meetings to review the said activities in light of the company's objectives and goal would lead to 'better planning and control.'

(iv) Clearly defined responsibilities of each executive will give proper guidance and everyone's endeavour 'to give of his best'.

(v) The appraisal of the business conditions relating to solvency, profitability and efficiency will help the person concerned to tackle the adverse situations.

(vi) 'Decision-making prerogatives,' individual responsibilities, areas of work and other different and vital aspects of management can be well-guided by clearly defined 'job description'.

Please note below the possible disadvantages of MBO technique :

Disadvantages of MBO

Disadvantages of MBO

(i) It has been regarded by many consultants as a 'gimmick'.

(ii) The supporters of MBO put much emphasis on the aspect of 'ideas and plans' which are the basis for control, but less emphasis has been given to 'how the detailed control is to be achieved'.

(iii) Less emphasis has been given by the supporters of MBO to the operation of Budgetary Control which is one of the keys to control.

So from the above it appears that an efficient system of Budgetary Control will give the same results as MBO.

☐ "Sir, what is the utility of wide application of MBO when Budgetary Control system are in force in the operation of business"?

● You see, if only Budgetary Control is introduced, the other part of Personnel Management is denied to. So the MBO system embraces—(1) Personnel Management (2) Management Accounting. Please note that if the principles of MBO is applied within the framework of Budgetary Control system, a higher degree of success is likely to be achieved.

☐ "Sir, what are points of comparison between Budgetary Control System and MBO"?

● Well, please note below the points of difference :

Management by Objectives	Budgetary Control
1. It is concerned with the setting target within an organisation or part of it, as a basis for achieving greater efficiency and providing motivation and an incentive to managers. Factors impeding the attainment of objectives are identified and action is taken to overcome them. Results are periodically appraised and new targets set where necessary.*	1. It is concerned with the establishment of budgets relating to the responsibilities of executives to the requirements of a policy, and the continuous comparison of actual with budgeted results, either to secure by individual action the objective of that policy or to provide a basis for its revision.**
2. Company objectives are reflected in the form of general statement which, subsequently, converted into forecasts and budgets.	2. Company objectives are reflected initially in long term forecasts and budgets.
3. After assaying and considering profitable course of action, 'strategic' plans are developed. Here participation is an essential requirement.	3. After comparing a few of the alternative forecastings, the basis of budgetary control is decided. Here participation is not essentially stressed.
4. Coordination in the process of management is made effective through individual objectives, detailed target and team's action.	4. Coordination is made effective through flexible budgets.
5. As a control device actions are taken only when deviation from target occurs.	5. As a control device actions are taken by management so that deviations are corrected. The basis for correction is decided through review and analysis of variance.
6. It is not generally accepted as a management tool.	6. It is generally accepted as a management tool. This principles can be applied to all types of business.

I think, you have fully understood the concept.

☐ "Thank you Sir for your new and simple discussion."

☐ "Excuse me Sir."

● Yes, Yes, what do you want to know?

☐ "Sir, we have understood the concept of MBO. But, Sir, what is MBE"?

* Management Glossary, Longman's
** Terminology of I.C.W.A., London

● You have put a nice question. You see, the mechanism of MBO will be successful if it is assisted by the principles of MBE. Do you follow?

☐ "Sir, please explain the idea of MBE."

● You see, M Stands for Management

B Stands for By

E Stands for Exception.

Now you see the basic philosophy of MBE is to collect information by comparing the actual performance with the predetermined standard or target at different stages of operation. Please note that managerial attention is a 'must' as to the areas of deviation. Mr. Bittel defined it (MBE) as a 'system of identification and communication that signals the manager when his attention is needed; conversely, it remains silent when his attention is not required.'

Definition of MBE

However, the Elements of MBE are :

Elements of MBE

(i) Measuring the performance

(ii) Projecting business objectives

(iii) Selecting the criteria to check target

(iv) Observing the current performance

(v) Comparing the actual performance with the expected

(vi) Making decision as to deviation.

QUESTIONS

1. What do you understand by the term MBO? Discuss its advantages and disadvantages.
2. What are the points of difference between MBO and Budgetary Control?
3. Can MBO be applied universally? If so, give arguments to support your view.

30

INTERFIRM COMPARISON

• Good morning dear students.

□ "Good morning, Sir."

• How often has a Managing Director reviewed his firm's progress and wondered

Are we doing as well as we could?

Are we following the right policies and practices?

Are other firms doing better than us?

If so, how?

How often has he wondered whether there was some way of comparing his performance in detail with that of other similar firms, so as to get answers to these questions?

There is a means of doing exactly this—It is called Interfirm Comparison.

The above is the **definition of Interfirm Comparison**, as defined by ***The Centre for Interfirm Comparison.***

However, now I like to discuss Interfirm Comparison in detail which means that the performances of own firm or firms will be compared with the performance of other similar firms. You see, the need for comparing own performance with that of the other arises out of the following situations :

(1) The development of trade and industry;

(2) The increasing complexities in the business; and

(3) The growing competition in industrial circle.

Now you see, I have told you just earlier that comparison will be made between two similar types of industry. Take for an example, comparison with one Engineering Industry will be made with that type of Engineering Industry, not with Clothing or Chemical Industry.

□ "Sir, Is the technique of Interfirm Comparison a new origin?"

• You see, I think the idea of Interfirm Comparison was felt in 1889 when the National Association of Stove Manufacturers, USA, introduced first the scheme of Uniform Costing.

□ "Sir, what is Uniform Costing?"

• You see, it is a system which attempts to 'standardise' the method of accounting and cost in order to assist the management in fixing its prices. The Institute of Cost and Works Accountants of England defines **Uniform Costing** as :

The use by several undertakings of the same costing principles and/or practices.

I think you have understood the concept of Uniform Costing. Is there any question?

□ "Sir, does it mean that under Uniform Costing System cost in different businesses will be the same?"

• Your question, indeed, is very interesting—you have put really a nice question. Here I would like to refer to the "Target" (A bulletin of the British Productivity Council) where one article under the title "Costing in Printing" was published in December 1956, where it was found that "the use of Uniform Costing methods does not mean that cost in different businesses will be the same. It does mean, however, that a comparison of the costs of different firms will be logical if they have been computed on similar lines. Uniform Costing makes possible the exchange or comparison of cost figures prepared on a similar basis in each business and this provides a means of improving efficiency throughout the industry. By profiting from the experience of the most efficient firms, others are able to reduce costs. It facilitates investigations into specific cost problems on the industry."

Now I hope that you have understood the idea given above.

□ "Yes Sir."

□ "Sir, give us some ideas about the growth and origin of the Interfirm Comparison".

• Well, please note below.

Need for Interfirm Comparison

You see, in day to day business operation every trader wants to know whether he is making sufficient profit or not, whether he is efficient in purchase sales and production. These can be known if he compares his own peformances with the performances of other similar concerns.

Origin of Interfirm Comparison

With this end in view, The British Institute of Management **(B.I.M.)**, in collaboration with the British Productivity Council, set up in 1959 a body known as Interfirm Comparison. It is a non-profit motive organisation which carried out its investigation not only in its own country but also it carried on an extensive investigation in USA and some other countries of Europe in the field of chemical, clothing, food, light, medium and heavy engineering industries. This body analyses and scrutinises the different aspects of the business operation of the participant concerns which pay their fees for the services rendered by the body of Interfirm Comparison.

Interfirm Comparison Ratios

$$\text{Primary Ratio} = \frac{\text{Operating Profit}}{\text{Assets Employed}}$$

$$\text{Supporting Ratio} = \text{(A)}\ \frac{\text{Operating Profit}}{\text{Sales}} : \text{(B)}\ \frac{\text{Sales}}{\text{Assets Employed}}$$

General Explanatory Ratios = (A) $\frac{\text{Factory Cost of Goods Sold}}{\text{Sales}}$

$\frac{\text{Marketing and Distribution Cost}}{\text{Sales}}$

$\frac{\text{Administration Cost}}{\text{Sales}}$

(B) $\frac{\text{Sales}}{\text{Fixed Assets}}$: $\frac{\text{Sales}}{\text{Current Assets}}$

Specific Explanatory Ratio

(A) $\frac{\text{Production Cost}}{\text{Sales Value of Production}}$ $\frac{\text{Direct Material Cost}}{\text{Sales Value of Production}}$

$\frac{\text{Direct Labour Cost}}{\text{Sales Value of Production}}$

$\frac{\text{Production Overhead}}{\text{Sales Value of Production}}$

(B) $\frac{\text{Sales at Cost}}{\text{Material Stock}}$; $\frac{\text{Sales at Cost}}{\text{Work - in - Progress}}$

$\frac{\text{Sales at Cost}}{\text{Finished Goods Stock at Cost}}$; $\frac{\text{Sales}}{\text{Debtors}}$

I think you have understood the ratios of Interfirm Comparison. Is there any question?

☐ "Sir, what are the purposes of Interfirm Comparison?"

Importance of Interfirm Comparison

• (1) One of the purposes of this system is to render competition less destructive, by ensuring that all the members know what is included in cost and how to arrive at it.

(2) Another purpose is to standardise a method of collecting figures in order to fix selling prices on a basis acceptable to those engaged in the industry.

Well, now I would like to discuss about the advantages and disadvantages of Interfirm Comparison.

☐ "Excuse me Sir. Please give the chart of Pyramid Ratio."

• You see, I have already explained the same. However, please note the chart :

PYRAMID OF RATIOS

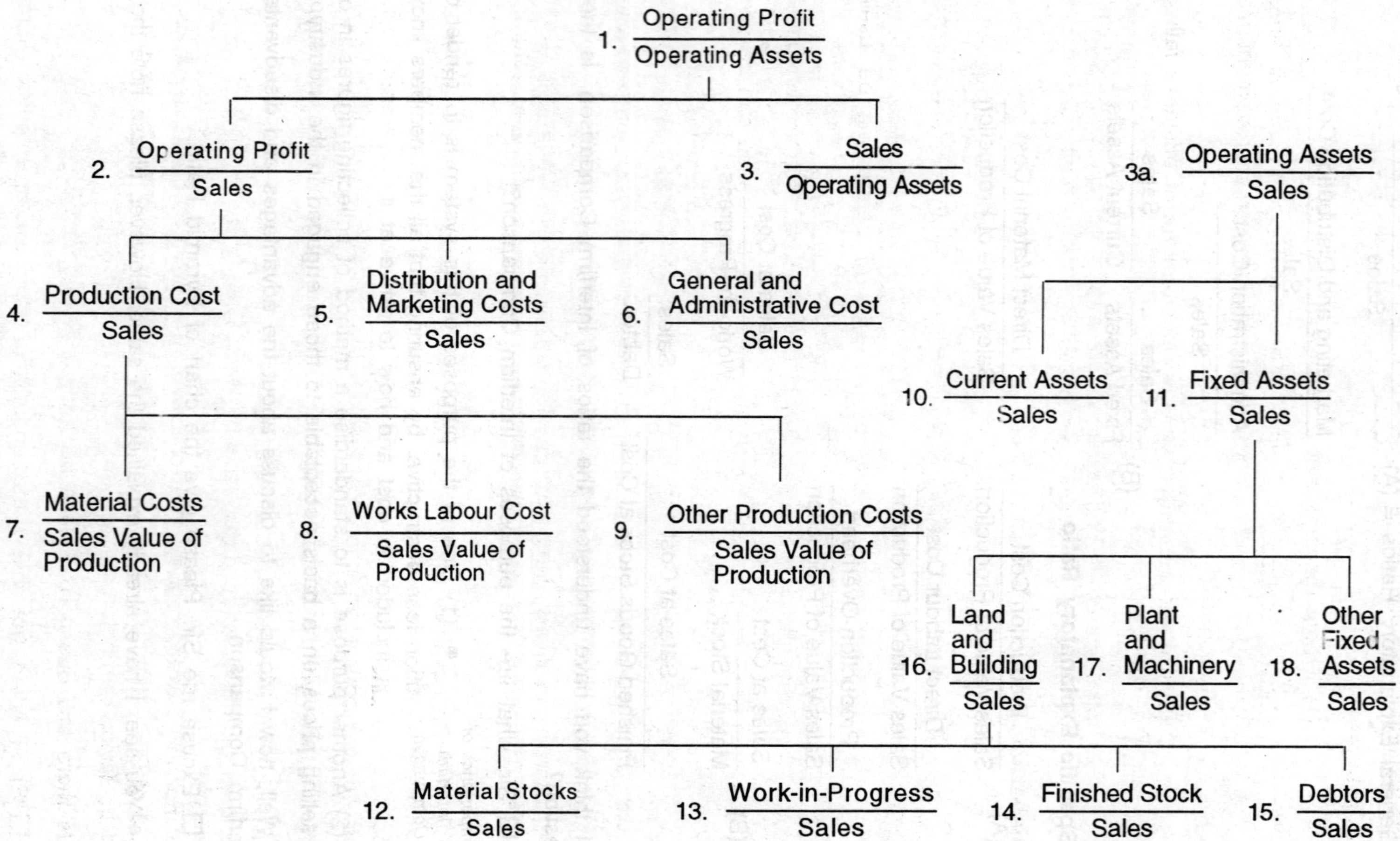

(Source : H. Ingham, Interfirm Comparison for Management)

I hope you have followed the above chart. Well, please note below the advantages and disadvantages of IFC.

Advantages

Advantages of IFC

(1) It aids management in taking its decision.

(2) The drawbacks and possible weakness of different firms are revealed and, accordingly, techniques for improvement may be suggested.

(3) It is an instrument by which postmortem of business failure can be performed.

(4) Secrecy is the greatest advantage of this body which is a process in achieving success in management science.

Disadvantages

Disadvantages of IFC

(1) Shyness of the members to disclose confidential matter.

(2) As it is a voluntary organisation, it cannot enforce every firm to enjoy its benefit.

(3) The main purpose of this type of centre will be useless if secrecy is not maintained.

Now I think that the whole discussion is clear to you. Is there any question?

☐ "Sir, you have not discussed how the Interfirm Comparison can be operated. If possible, throw some light on it."

• You see, I had already given you some light on the concept. Please go through my earlier lectures on Interfirm Comparison. However, I am explaining the same again. Well, **Interfirm Comparison operates** in two ways :

(1) Each and every firm which register their names under the Centre for Interfirm Comparison are sent different questionnaires which they return to the Centre after duly filled up.

(2) The Centre then analyses the activities of different firms under different circumstances. After proper scrutiny, the Centre recommends the weaker firms—whose performances are not stated to be satisfactory if compared with other firms—for the course of action to be taken by the latter.

Now, I think, you have understood how Centre for Interfirm Comparison operates.

☐ "Sir, you have told about questionnaires. Would you please give us some specimen of the questionnaires used by the Centre."

• For this I would request you to consult the **Management Economics Series No. 3** of BIM—"Interfirm Comparison for Management" prepared by Herbert Ingham and L. Taylor Harrington.

Is there any question? Please be frank with me.

☐ "Sir, I could not follow the underlying principles of Interfirm Comparison Ratio."

I find no reason why you could not follow. It is based on the financial and other records of the business. From these financial statements and other records are computed different ratios which are tabulated on the Comparative Statement to assist the top management in making its decision. Well, I think you have studied properly the chapter on 'Accounting Ratio Analysis and Interpretation of Financial Statement.'

☐ "Yes Sir."

• If you can understand that chapter, I think it would not be difficult to have a general understanding of the concept of Interfirm Comparison Ratio. Well, you note below the underlying principles of the ratios discussed earlier in this chapter.

You see, the success of management is tested by the Primary Ratio which is :

$$\frac{\text{Profit}}{\text{Capital Employed or Total Assets Employed}}$$

In actual practice it has been found that this ratio varies from firm to firm. The causes of variances and the differences between the participants of the Interfirm Comparison Centre as to the above ratio can be found out, following a 'close observation and study' of the components of the Profitability which are : (i) Margin on Sale $\left(\frac{\text{Profit}}{\text{Sales}}\right)$, and (ii) Turnover rate of Capital $\left(\frac{\text{Sales}}{\text{Total Assets or Capital Employed}}\right)$

I think you have understood this point, that is to say, the differences in the Primary Ratio $\left(\frac{\text{Profit}}{\text{Total Assets or Capital Employed}}\right)$ of the participants concerned might be either due to the differences in the ratio of $\frac{\text{Profit}}{\text{Sales}}$ (Margin on Sale) or to the differences in the ratio of $\frac{\text{Sales}}{\text{Capital Employed}}$ (Turnover of Capital).

Again, interfirm differences in the Margin on Sale are either due to the differences in the Gross Profit Ratio $\left(\frac{\text{Gross Profit}}{\text{Sales}}\right)$ or the Expenses Ratio $\left(\frac{\text{Different Departmental Cost}}{\text{Sales}}\right)$.

Do you follow what I have discussed so far?

☐ "Yes Sir."

• It is really very nice that you have understood. Well, it should be noted in this context that business or firms can raise their Profit 'either by earning higher gross profits on those items in their range which represent a high proportion of total sales or by achieving a higher volume in those items of their range which earn high gross profits'.

Further, interfirm differences in the turnover rate of capital are either due to the differences in the relationship between Sales and Fixed Assets $\left(\frac{\text{Sales}}{\text{Fixed Assets}}\right)$ or in the relationship between Sales and Current Assets $\left(\frac{\text{Sales}}{\text{Current Assets}}\right)$. Again, the differences between the participants in the relationship as indicated later is due to the differences either in the Turnover of Debtors :

$\left(\frac{\text{Debtors}}{\text{Net Sales}} \times 365 \text{ days}\right)$ Ratio or Stock Turnover

$\left(\frac{\text{Cost of Goods Sold}}{\text{Average Stock Carried}}\right)$ Ratio.

I hope you have followed what I discussed so far. Is there any question please?

☐ "Sir, we shall be obliged if you please give us a few specimen tables showing Comparison of Financial and Operating Ratio, Comparison of Cost of Production and finally Productivity Comparison."

• Well, I am giving you a few tables of Interfirm Comparison from the **Management Economic Series No. 3** as published by The British Institute of Management.

☐ "Sir, please work out at least one problem on Interfirm Comparison."

• You see, first of all I would like to give you a few tables, after that I will give you a problem on Interfirm Comparison.

COMPARISON OF FINANCIAL AND OPERATING RATIOS

Ratios	Measurement		Figures of 10 Firms of Similar size and making Similar Products		Figures of our firm	
			Figures for last year	Figures for current year	Figures for the last year	Figures for current year
$\frac{\text{Profit}}{\text{Capital/Total Assets Employed}}$	%	First Quartile Average Third Quartile				
$\frac{\text{Profit}}{\text{Sales}}$	%	"				
$\frac{\text{Sales}}{\text{Capital Employed}}$	Times	"				
$\frac{\text{Cost of Production}}{\text{Sales}}$	%	"				
$\frac{\text{Different Costs}}{\text{Sales}}$	%	"				
$\frac{\text{Marketing and Distribution Cost}}{\text{Sales}}$	%	"				
$\frac{\text{Fixed Assets}}{\text{Total Assets}}$	%	"				
$\frac{\text{Cost of Administration}}{\text{Sales}}$	%	"				
$\frac{\text{Sales}}{\text{Average Stocks}}$	Times	"				
$\frac{\text{Average of Outstanding Debts}}{\text{Average Sales per day}}$	Days	"				

COMPARISON OF COST OF PRODUCTION

per...Kilogram of Molten Iron (... Foundries)

Type of Cost	Firms							Average
	1	2	3	4	5	6	7	
Wages								
Salaries								
Compulsory Social Security								
Voluntary Social Security								
Fuel								
Maintenance								
Auxiliary materials								
Incoming transport								
Depreciation								
Actual or imputed rent								
Power								
Welfare								
General Production overheads								
Main factory profit								
Other Costs								
Cost of Smelting								
Cost of Smelting								
Cost of Iron ore, scrap etc.								
Cost of iron								
Liquid Iron (tons)								

PRODUCTIVITY COMPARISON

Direct Man hour Expended per 100 units for the Production of Electrically Operated Automatic Irons, by Major Operations :

Items	Firms			
	A	B	C	D
Total Direct Man hours				
Machining				
Metal Forming				
Plating and Polishing				
Painting				
Sub and Final Assembly				
Number of Direct Workers				
Number of Indirect Workers				
Direct Labour as % of Cost of Production				
Direct Materials as % of Cost of Production				
Other Factory Costs (including Indirect Labour) as % of Cost of Production				
Production of Iron as % of Total Production				
Minimum order accepted				
Retail price				
Volume—Daily				

Problem

From the information given below you are requested to comment on the performance strategy of Firm D. The last year's performances of all the firms are given below for your perusal :

Ratios	Measurement	Firm A		Firm B		Firm C		Firm D	
		This year	Last year	This year	Last year	This year	Last year	This year	Last year
Operating Profit / Operating Assets	%	14.3	14.3	18	21	7.9	7	10	8.24
Operating Profit / Sales	%	13.1	13.2	15	14	8.1	7	6.1	5.5
Sales / Operating Assets	Times	1.09	1.08	1.2	1.5	0.98	1	1.65	1.5
Operating Assets / Average Daily Sales	Days	335	340	304	320	372	380	222	249
Production Cost of Sales / Sales	%	69.4	68.5	73	80	72.5	70.5	70.4	71
Distribution and Marketing Expenses / Sales	%	13.1	12.5	8	7	13.7	12.7	17.7	17.7
General and Administrative Expenses / Sales	%	4.4	4	4	3	5.7	6	5.8	5.8
Current Assets / Average Daily Sales	Days	219	230	213	210	288	290	188	21.5
Finished Stock / Average Daily Sales	Days	59	50	71	66	93	92	39	52
Debtors / Average Daily Sales	Days	74	80	46	50	68	71	54	61

Solution

You see, from the table it is clear that the performance of Firm D for the current year is better than the previous year. The return on operating has been increased by 1.75%. This is owing to the increase in the Margin (%) on Sale and Turnover of Operating Assets. If the current year's performance of Firm D is compared with that of Firm A and B, it will be seen that it is not attractive. Because the Margin (%) on Sale and Turnover of Operating Assets of Firms A and B is higher than that of D. There should not be any ground for higher satisfaction since there are much scope for increasing operational and managerial efficiency of the business. (Vide the performances of Firms A and B)

I think you have followed the above discussions. Is there any question?

☐ "Sir, are Published Accounts suitable for Interfirm Comparison?"

• Now you have put a very apt question. For this I would suggest you to go through the remarks, made by The Centre for Interfirm Comparison :

'Even though successive Companies Act made more and more data available about Limited Companies, published accounts cannot be used for proper Interfirm Comparisons :

So the reasons why it is not suitable for IFC are :

Are published accounts suitable for IFC?

(i) Firstly, Firms do not use the same accounting Convention and policies for measuring important quantities such as profit, assets, depreciation, operating cost etc.

(ii) Secondly, even the fullest set of accounts provide nothing like the minimum amount of information which a firm needs to compare its performance in detail. Only very few of the ratios which are provided in a proper IFC can be calculated from published accounts, and little or none of the supporting data is available which help to show why performances differ.

(iii) Thirdly, large companies tend to operate in different sectors of industry and their published accounts do not give separate figures for each of these.'

Please note that the above arguments advanced by the Centre should not be binding to all cases. Above, in other words, may be taken as 'adjusting areas' before introducing IFC based on published Annual Accounts. However, the information contained in the Published Accounts should be cut to size as circumstance dictated or should be tailored to fit each situation.

I think, you have followed the discussions made earlier. So, in my next lecture I shall be discussing with you about the Managerial Nexus in Cost Control.

Well, Good Night!

QUESTIONS

1. (a) "Uniform costing is a precondition of successful Interfirm Comparison." Explain.

(b) Following are the particulars about four companies which are supposed to follow uniform costing methods. From them calculate (in terms of percentages) the ratios : Profit/Capital Employed, Profit/Sales and Sales/Capital Employed for each firm for each year and draw an interfirm comparison with the help of the 'median' of each ratio in each year (the results may be shown in a table) :

Particulars of Firms (Rs. Lakhs)

Name of the Firms	Sales		Capital Employed		Profit	
	05-06	06-07	05-06	06-07	05-06	06-07
Orient Paper	1992	2211	2896	2804	116	123
Sree Gopal Paper	962	1001	713	789	67	99
Ballarpur Paper	717	833	897	949	84	94
Bengal Paper	637	668	763	783	30	4

[M.Com. (C.U.) Management Accounting]

2. Discuss the utility of Interfirm comparison in case of concerns which differ widely in size and methods of manufacture and sale. Outline the steps to be taken for introducing a scheme for Interfirm Comparison for a group of such concerns.

3. What is Interfirm Comparison? Discuss its advantages.

4. "It (IFC) is an instrument by which postmortem of business failure can be performed."—Discuss.

31

RESPONSIBILITY ACCOUNTING

● Good morning to you all.

☐ "Good morning Sir."

● Well, what will be discussed this morning?

☐ "Sir, you told us that Responsibility Accounting will be discussed."

● Before I am to discuss about it; first of all let us see what the term 'Responsibility' means!

You see, the term 'responsibility' means 'a state of being responsible'[1]; that is to say, 'person or thing for which one is responsible; duty, commitment, capacity for rational conduct.'

'You see, when the word 'Responsibility' is attached to the word 'Accounting', it attains a dimension—dimension as to 'reporting' on the costs at different management levels, which he or she is concerned with. This means that submission of report relates to those types of items for which he is entrusted with or delegated responsibility to control cost at his/her level.

Origin of the Concept

You see, larger the business, more removed the Proporietor or Chief Executive of any organisation from day to day business operations and control. To facilitate effective management control many large business organisations are found divided into different divisions and each division is assigned with certain time bound responsibility or responsibilities under the stewardship of each departmental manager. Each department, as stated above, is said to be Responsibility Centre. Needless to mention that number of Responsibility Centres depends upon the nature, size, status of the organisation as well as the *degree of delegation of authority*.

I think that you have followed my lecture. Is there any question(s)?

☐ "Sir, what is Responsibility Centre?"

● Your attention please!

You see, responsibility centre may be defined as :

Meaning of Responsibility Centre

A department or division of any organisation, under the stewardship of a manager, responsible for cost or revenue is said to be Responsibility Centre.

[1] Collin's *Gem English Dictionary,* New Edition, p. 458

Please note **Different Types of Responsibility Centres.**

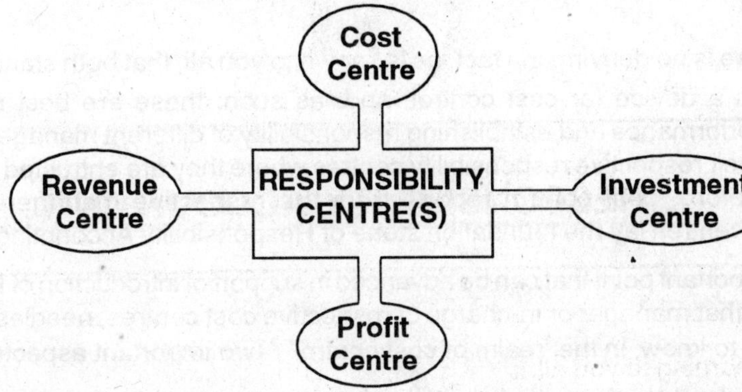

Please note different types of centres in details—

1. **Cost Centre :** Separate cost is designed and measured exclusively for particular object; such as equipment, function, designs, area or location. Here the steward of this centre such as manager, in-charge, foreman in case of factory, will be responsible for cost. That is to say, he/she will be accountable to higher authority relating to control of cost.

2. **Revenue Centre :** A centre concerned with raising revenue is considered Revenue Centre. For example sales departments, zones area.

3. **Profit Centre :** Profit centre consists of revenue and cost. Increasing revenue and reduction of cost or cost control may boost-up profitability of any organisation. A person in-charge of Profit Centre—he or she—may be manager. Financial Controller will be held responsible for decline in profitability. At the same time it should be ensured that the said in-charge be given free hand to fix up selling price and volume of production i.e., volume of output.

4. **Investment Centre :** It is the nerve centre of all responsibility centres—Cost Centre, Revenue Centre and Profit Centre; because it is the **end-desire** of all organisations that the return on investment should contribute to a greater extent to the organisation after meeting its cost of capital and cost of production. Therefore, person in-charge of Investment Centre—say Investment Centre's Manager—has to play a positive role with regard to its investment project(s). Needless to mention that the person in-change of Investment Centre would be held liable for not achieving desired level of returns on investment.

I feel that you all have understood the above discussions.

Is there any question please!

☐ "Sir, please explain the **Meaning of Responsibility Accounting**—who is the pioneer of the concept?"

• Well, there is no denying the fact, as is known to you all, that both standard cost and budget act as a device for cost control, and, as such, these are best measures for managerial performance and establishing responsibility of different managers or persons in-charge of their respective responsibility centres where they are entrusted with absolute control. Therefore, cost control reports from the respective managers of different responsibility centres lay the foundation stone of Responsibility Accounting.

Another important point that can be advanced in support of introduction of Responsibility Accounting is that manager or in-charge of respective cost centres, needless to mention, are supposed to know, in the 'realm of cost control',[2] two important aspects :

(i) What should be his or their cost; that is to say expectation of the top management regarding his or their job performance.

(ii) What is the actual cost(s) in reality; that is to say, actual performance regarding his or their job performance which are to be measured by top management.

You see, the former relates to budget function and the latter relates to accountability function.

Well you wanted me to let you know who is the pioneer of this concept?

Is it so?

☐ "Yes Sir."

• You see, it was Arthur Andersen & Co., a Certified Public Accountant firm, who made its first attempt for introduction of Responsibility Accounting with the main object of cost control. The said firm, as an advocacy of the Responsibility Accounting, prepared a report. A short extract from the report is given below[3] from where general concept and philosophy of Responsibility Accounting can be understood.

"This new approach to accounting and reporting is the development of an accounting system designed to control expenditures by directly relating the reporting of expenditures to the individuals in the company organisation who are responsible for their control. This system results in the preparation of accounting statements for all levels of management, designed primarily so that they can be effectively used by the operating people as a tool in controlling their operations and their costs.

This approach also makes possible the operation of a good budget system. No budget system is fully effective unless it is built around one basic philosophy—namely that each responsible individual in an organisation must feel that the budget is *his* budget and not something forced upon him which he might feel is unrealistic and unworkable. Unless the responsible individual does feel that it is *his* budget, he will only make a superficial attempt to live within it or use the information as a means of controlling his operations.

---

[2] Richard M. Lynch. "Accounting for Management : Planning and Control. McGraw Hill Company, International Student Edition, p. 242

[3] John A. Higgins, "Responsibility Accounting" The Arthur Andersen Chronicle, April 1952, Vol 2. no. 2 as appeared in Richard M. Lynch, op cit p. 242-243

Now if one will accept this philosophy in his approach to budgeting, one more step must be taken to complete the picture. One must put the reporting of expenditures (cost accounting) in phase with the budget performance responsibility which is another way of saying that expenditures must be reported on the basis of where they were incurred and who had responsibility for them. Hence comes the term *Responsibility Accounting*.

In effect, the system personalises the accounting statements by saying "Joe, this is what you originally budgeted and this is how you performed for the period with actual operations as compared against your budget." By definition it is a system of accounting which is *tailored to an organisation* so that costs are accumulated and reported by levels of responsibility within the organisation. Each supervisory area in the organisation is charged only with the cost for which it is responsible and over which it has control.

There are two major objectives of cost accounting in manufacturing companies : (1) cost control; (2) product cost. The cost systems of most companies meet the latter objective, but for the most part fall on their faces when it comes to the objective of real cost control. Practically, all of them have systems that emphasise the development of product cost instead of emphasising the controlling of costs at the centres where the costs are incurred. Under responsibility accounting it is possible to meet both of these objectives by first summarising cost on the basis of "who did it" and then reshuffling the deck, so to speak, or blending the costs to arrive at product cost. In effect what we are doing is putting the emphasis on the objective of cost control for the purposes of management reports but also arriving at the normal cost statements—but on a greatly de-emphasised basis."

Again, I am to bring to your attention that eight years after the publication of the excerpt of the report made by John A. Higgins, it was W.A. Dick who defined Reponsibility Accounting as :

"Essentially, responsibility accounting is a system whereby costs flow up the organisational lines and are accumulated and reported at the various levels of responsibility."

The philosophy behind this is that the best way to control cost is to delegate responsibility to individuals, define their responsibility, give them an idea of what constitutes effective performance of their job, and report back to them how they are going. If the latter step is to be accomplished, costs must be classified or segregated so that they can be summarised firstly on the basis of 'who did it' and then 'reshuffled' to arrive at conventional product or process costs." You please stand up; please tell me what is your problem.

☐ "Sir, I still cannot follow the definition of Responsibility Accounting'. Sir! give us your definition of Responsibility Accounting."

• Well, have a look here. Please jot down my definition on Responsibility Accounting.

Definition of Responsibility Accounting

Responsibility Accounting may be defined as a system or technique of recording of responsibilities of different personnels in charge of their respective responsibility centres, who are entrusted with controllable authority of his/her jurisdiction for performing job, by comparing 'Target-return' set up by Top Management for each cost centre with 'Actual return of different cost centres. It is one of the types of management information system which helps top management to take decision towards corrective measures. It may also be defined as Control Accounting—Cost Control.

I hope you have understood the said definition.

Is there any question?

☐ "Sir, for effective implementation of Responsibility Accounting what principles are to be adopted?"

● Well, you please stand up. What do you want to say?

☐ "Sir! I have one question .... I want to say something."

● What is that? Please tell me frankly.

☐ "Sir! I find certain relationship of Responsibility Accounting with that of Standard Costing. Because Target Return i.e., Standard Costs or Expenses, whatever sense it bears, are to be compared with Actual Return i.e., Actual Cost. I mean standard cost (SC) minus (–) Actual Cost. Result may be + Variance or – Variance, is it not similar to Standard Costing?"

● I am really very glad you have understood the concept of Responsibility Accounting. Your assumption is correct; you see, when administrative flavour is added to standard cost system, then it bears likeness of Responsibility Accounting. Thank you, my dear student.

Oh! yes, I have forgotten to answer your question. I am sorry. Is it about the effective implementation of Responsibility Accounting?

☐ "Yes Sir".

● Well, take down the notes on the principles or **requirement for effective implementation of Responsibility Accounting**.

Following are the few principles or requirements for effective implementation of Responsibility Accounting :

(i) Organisational structure of management should be based on sound footing. That is to say, clearly defined organisational structure with well-defined responsibility and delegation of authority.

(ii) Function of each level of Management from top to bottom should be clearly defined.

(iii) 'Target return' set up by the top management should be based on practical approach. In-charge(s) of cost centre(s) should be involved in the preparation of plan and policy.

(iv) Cost centre(s) should be inspected by the top management from time to time to ensure work-culture. This is because it may be easy to control cost, but it, sometimes, becomes difficult to control those people who control cost.[4]

(v) Reporting form should clearly indicate cost element under the control of in-charge of respective cost centre(s).

I hope that you all have understood the concept.

☐ "Yes Sir."

---

[4] Lecture delivered by Dr. B. K. Basu on the topic *"Cost Control"* at Eastern Coal Limited (ECL) Dishergarh, 1977

● Is there any question?

□ "Please enlighten about its advantages and disadvantages."

□ "Sir! Give us some problems on Responsibility Accounting. I mean Sir, practical problems."

● Well, regarding advantages of Responsibility Accounting I am to say the following. If you desire you can jot down the points of advantages :

Advantages of Responsibility Accounting

(i) It acts as a control device to boost up overall organisational efficiency.

(ii) Precision in the preparation of plan, policy and budget can be achieved through the result of different cost centres.

(iii) Deviation reports, from different cost centres, i.e., responsibility centres, resulting from difference between budgeted performance and actual performance, motivates managers or in-charge of different cost centres to strive towards perfection.

(iv) It gives much emphasis on the importance of decentralisation of authority which can ensure overall achievement of goal of the organisation through its effective control system.

(v) It may bring work-culture in different responsibility (cost) centres in particular and organisation as a whole if this system of accounting is taken as an effective tool for control measure.

(vi) It evaluates day to day performances of person(s) in-charge of different cost centre(s) through report on deviation. Thus it may be considered as an effective management information system.

I think you have followed my lecture. If you cannot understand, please be frank with me, I will discuss again.

□ "Sir, no problem to understand, but Sir ....."

● Yes, yes, what do you want to say?

□ "Sir, are there any disadvantages of Responsibility Accounting? If so, please throw us some light on the matter."

● Please note the disadvantages (limitations) of Responsibility Accounting :

Disadvantages of Responsibility Accounting

(i) It will fail to achieve its objectives if organisational structure of an enterprise does not clearly define *authority and responsibility* relationship.

(ii) Preparation of budget(s) or setting up of standard based on 'whim' and subjective consideration may spoil the spirit of this system.

(iii) Indifferent attitudes on the part of in-charge of responsibility centre(s), if there be any, may mar the objective of this system of accounting.

(iv) In the absence of effective strong management, its application will be confined to book of knowledge.

That is all on the topic of Responsibility Accounting.

Is there any question(s)?

☐ "Sir, give us some practical problems on Responsibility Accounting".

• Well, please note below a few worked-out problems :

Problem

A production department of XYZ Ltd. manufacturing organisation has furnished the following data for May 2006 :

Particulars	Budget	Actual
	Rs.	Rs.
Direct Materials	4,00,000	5,10,000
Direct Wages	2,50,000	3,25,000
Repairs and Maintenance (Rs 1,00,000 fixed)	2,00,000	2,20,000
Supervision (fixed)	1,00,000	1,10,000
Consumable Stores (variable)	75,000	95,000
Factory Rent (fixed)	50,000	50,000
Depreciation (fixed)	1,00,000	1,00,000
Tools (variable)	25,000	30,000
Power and Fuel (variable)	1,50,000	1,80,000
Administration (fixed)	2,50,000	2,65,000

The department has 50 identical machines. During May 2006, the budgeted and actual productions of the department are 10,000 and 12,500 units, respectively. However, if the department was closed and the machine production services were hired from outside, the cost of hiring the services of similar machines would be Rs 150 per unit.

(i) You are required to present reports showing the evaluation of the performance of the department based on the concept of

(a) Cost Centre

(b) Profit Centre, and

(c) Responsibility Centre.

(ii) It is felt that since the total budgeted cost of production per unit is greater than the cost of hired services, the possibility of closing down the department and use of hired services should be explored if the budgeted production cannot be increased in June 2006.

Assuming that the budgeted expenses and level of output planned for May 2006 will hold good for June 2006 also, calculate the volume of output required to justify the continuance of the department. **[Adapted from I.C.W.A., Final]**

Solution

(i) Statement showing evaluation of departmental performance according to different concepts :

(a) **Cost Centre Basis**

Particulars	**Budget**	**Allowed cost**	**Actual**
Output (in units)	10,000	12,500	12,500
	Rs.	Rs.	Rs.
Variable Costs			
Direct Materials	4,00,000	5,00,000	5,10,000
Direct Labour	2,50,000	3,12,500	3,25,000
Repairs and Maintenance	1,00,000	1,25,000	1,20,000
Consumable Stores	75,000	93,750	95,000
Tools	25,000	31,250	30,000
Power and Fuel	1,50,000	1,87,500	1,80,000
Total (A)	10,00,000	12,50,000	12,60,000
Fixed Costs			
Repairs and Maintenance	1,00,000	1,00,000	1,00,000
Supervision	1,00,000	1,00,000	1,10,000
Factory Rent	50,000	50,000	50,000
Depreciation	1,00,000	1,00,000	1,00,000
Administration	2,50,000	2,50,000	2,65,000
Total (B)	6,00,000	6,00,000	6,25,000
Grand Total (A + B)	16,00,000	18,50,000	18,85,000

Expenditure Variance = 18,50,000 – 18,85,000

= Rs. 35,000 (A)

Volume Variance $= \left(\dfrac{\text{Rs. } 6,00,000}{10,000} \times 12,500\right) - \text{Rs. } 6,00,000$

= Rs. 7,50,000 – Rs. 6,00,000

= Rs. 1,50,000 (F)

(b) **Profit Centre Basis**

Cost of production on hired machine

Particulars	**Amount**
	Rs.
Services (12,500 × 150)	18,75,000
Actual	18,85,000
Profit Variance	10,000 (A)

(c) **Responsibility Centre Basis**

Particulars	Budget	Actual	Variance
	Rs.	Rs.	Rs.
Controllable Costs			
Direct Materials	5,00,000	5,10,000	10,000 (A)
Direct Wages	3,12,500	3,25,000	12,500 (A)
Repairs and Maintenance	2,25,000	2,20,000	5,000 (F)
Consumable Stores	93,750	95,000	1,250 (A)
Tools	31,250	30,000	1,250 (F)
Power and Fuel	1,87,500	1,80,000	7,500 (F)
Supervision	1,00,000	1,10,000	10,000 (A)
Total	14,50,000	14,70,000	20,000 (A)
Non-controllable Costs			
Factory Rent	50,000	50,000	—
Depreciation	1,00,000	1,00,000	—
Administration	2,50,000	2,65,000	15,000 (A)
Total	4,00,000	4,15,000	15,000 (A)

(ii) Volume of output required to justify continuance of Department :

Variable cost of making own machine as per budget : $\frac{\text{Rs. } 10{,}00{,}000}{10{,}000 \text{ units}} = \text{Rs. } 100$

Variable cost of making, on hired services = Rs. 150

Saving, if manufactured on own machine = Rs. 50

Fixed Costs = Rs. 6,00,000

Hence, minimum number of units to justify the continuance of department is 12,000 units i.e., (6,00,000/50).

Problem

A company has 10 cars in operation. The budget for the transport department based on 25,000 km of run for a month is Rs. 87,500 out of which a sum of Rs. 25,000 is fixed. During the last month, the total kilometres run by all the 10 cars were 22,400 and the costs incurred were Rs. 83,150. The cost of hiring a car would have been Rs. 4 per km.

Evaluate the performance of the transport department on the basis of (a) Cost Centre, (b) Profit Centre. **[Adapted from I.C.W.A., Final]**

Solution

Particulars	Amount
	Rs.
Total budgeted expenditure	87,500
Less : Fixed Cost	25,000
	62,500
Variable cost per km $\left(\frac{\text{Rs. } 62{,}500}{25{,}000 \text{ km}}\right)$ = Rs. 2.50 per km	
Cost Centre Basis	
Allowed Cost : Variable 22,400 × Rs. 2.50	56,000
Fixed	25,000
	81,000
Actual Cost	83,150
Budget variance	2,150 (A)
Profit Centre Basis	
22,400 km × Rs. 4.00	89,600
Actual Expenditure	83,150
Profit Variance	6,450 (F)

QUESTIONS

1. What is Responsibility Accounting?
2. Briefly explain the terms Expense Centre, Profit Centre and Investment Centre.
3. Discuss the advantages and problems associated with the use of each of the following measures of divisional performance :

   (a) Return on Capital employed

   (b) Residual income.
4. Western division of a large multinational company has prepared the following forecast for 2006 :

	Rs.
Profit before depreciation	1,00,000
Depreciation	25,000
Net Current Assets at 1.1.2006	50,000
Net value of Fixed Assets on 1.1.2006	2,00,000
The company cost of capital is 10%	

The division is considering selling a fixed asset with a net book-value of Rs. 7,500 which, after depreciation of Rs. 600, generates a profit per annum of Rs. 3,000. The proceeds and a subsidy from head office would be used to purchase a new machine for Rs. 20,000 which would generate an annual profit of Rs. 6,000 after depreciation of Rs. 1,500.

Require :

(i) Assuming Western division does not sell and replace the machine, using the opening balance sheet values calculate :

—the division's return on investment

—the division's residual income.

(ii) If the machine is sold and replaced, calculate :

—the division's return on investment

—the division's residual income. **[Adapted from I.C.W.A. Final]**

5. A and B are two newly established divisions of SV Ltd. These two divisions operate as independent units. They have agreed to a 20% per annum charge for capital provided by SV Ltd. The budget for the two divisions are :

	Division (Rs. crores)	
	A	B
Initial investment	10	15
Expected net cash flow :		
First year	1.9	3.2
Years 2 to 8 (per annum)	2.9	4.2

In the first year of operation, A secured 5% increase in market share in sale of its products at the cost of B

Required :

(i) Evaluate the performance of the two divisions as envisaged in the budget using ROI and residual income bases.

(ii) Calculate the net profit of the two divisions for the first year of operation based on the achievement of market share increase of 5% for A with corresponding reduction in market share for B. **[Adapted from I.C.W.A., Final]**

6. A company engage 5 sales representatives who are provided with price lists to cater to five zones. Sales quota is fixed for each quarter and a commission of 4% on sales order booked is paid besides salary. Data for a quarter are :

(Rs. '000)

Sales Representatives	A	B	C	D	E
Standard cost of quota sales	1,895	1,425	2,030	1,650	1,750
Gross margin of mix variance	38 A	53 A	158 A	68 A	37 F
Selling Price variance	29 A	255 A	75 A	101 F	113 F
Sales volume variance	40 A	38 A	600 F	73 A	31 A
Commission earned	90	62	112	79	91

Note : A = Adverse, F = Favourable

Required :

(i) Determine the sales quota and actual contribution of each sales representative.

(ii) Rank them in order of their performance and state the basis of ranking.

[Adapted from I.C.W.A., Final]

7. X Ltd. has at the factory three Production Departments—Machine Shop, Fabrication, and Assembly—which are the responsibility of the Shop Superintendent. The Shop Superintendent along with Materials Manager, Planning Superintendent and Maintenance Engineer report to the Works Manager at the factory. The Office Administration, sales and publicity come under the Sales manager who along with the Works Manager, report to the Managing Director of the Company.

The data of a month's performance are from the books of the Company :

	Budget Rs.	Variance from Budget Rs.
Sale Commission	800	50 A
Raw Material & Components		
— Machine Shop	900	20 A
Publicity Expenses	1,100	100 A
Printing & Stationery	3,200	200 F
Travelling Expenses	4,000	200 A
Wages — Machine Shop	800	10 F
— Fabrication	600	20 A
— Assembly	720	10 A
Material — Assembly	760	40 A
— Fabrication	460	10 A
Utilities — Machine Shop	320	10 A
— Assembly	470	60 F
— Fabrication	560	30 F
— Maintenance	400	20 A
— Stores	210	40 F
— Planning	180	20 A
Shop Superintendent's Office		
— Salaries & Expenses	1,100	22 F
Depreciation — Factory	3,880	40 A
Works Manager's Office—Salaries & Admn.	3,810	40 A
General Office—Salaries & Admn.	4,270	30 A
Managing Director's Salary & Admn.	2,800	20 F

(A = Adverse, F = Favourable)

(i) Treating the Machine Shop, Fabrication and Assembly as Cost Centres, prepare Cost Sheets for each centre with the help of this additional information :

The Shop Superintendent devotes his time amongst Machine Shop, Fabrication and Assembly in the ratio 4 : 3 : 4. Other Factory Overheads are absorbed on the basis of Direct Labour in each Cost Centre.

Office Admn., Selling & Distribution Overheads are borne equally by the Cost Centres.

(ii) Treating the Machine Shop, Fabrication and Assembly as Responsibility Centres, prepare Responsibility Accounting Report for the Shop Superintendent.

[Adapted from C.A., Final]

32

PERFORMANCE EVALUATION

● Good morning to my dear students.

☐ "Good morning Sir."

● I want to hear from you any problems on any aspect of my previous lectures. Please be frank with me. I will discuss it again before I take up discussions on Performance Evaluation.

☐ "Thank you Sir. We have not faced any problem(s) regarding your previous lectures. You can proceed your discussion on Performance Evaluation."

● Well, you see, the dictionary meaning of the term 'Performance' is manner of functioning and the meaning of the term 'Evaluation' are assessment and appraisal.

The meaning of the said two terms 'Performance' and 'Appraisal' can focus the whole concept of Performance Evaluation. Here performance means functioning of any organisation or division of any entity. Therefore, Performance Evaluation means the assessment or appraisal of functioning of any organisation or division of any entity. A business is an entity, an artificial person or body, which has no soul to be damned and no body to be kicked. Needless to mention, business entity or an artificial person is being run by natural person(s) i.e., human being working at different levels of hierarchies i.e., divisions, units etc.

Meaning of Performance Evaluation

So, it is quite natural that performance or functioning of each division, unit etc. are to be evaluated by the top management. The impression of assessment of the functioning of respective divisions or units motivates the managers of the respective divisions to exert full efforts to achieve goal congruence of an organisation. Therefore, Performance Evaluation may be defined as an 'integral part' of Management Control System of an organisation.

Management Control

I think you have followed what I want to say in this regard.

☐ "Yes Sir, we have followed the importance of Performance Evaluation from your discussions".

● Thank you my dear students; I am delighted to see that you have grasped the concept of Performance Evaluation.

Now I would like to discuss the different performance measures that are used to measure the performance of managers of respective divisions of an organisation.

Performance Measures

Please take a look at the board :

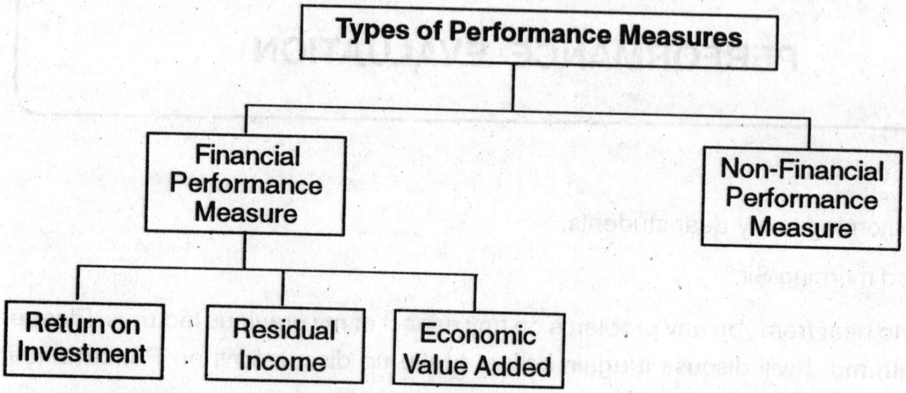

You see, Financial performance measures are based on financial performance information—both internal and external. For example, profitability, stock prices etc.

Non-financial performance measures are also based on non-financial information—both internal and external.

For example, customer satisfaction, number of new patents, developed, Govt. policy etc.

Now I will be discussing here financial performance measure.

1. Return on Investment (ROI)

You see, Return on Investment (ROI) is also known as Return on Capital Employed (ROCE).

Please note that Return on Capital (ROC) and ROCE or ROI—all are not the same. Because, Return on Capital (ROC) implies Return on Equity (ROE) whereas ROCE implies —

	Rs.
Equity Capital	**
Add : Reserve and Surplus	**
Net Worth	***
Add : Loan Capital ..... (Preference Share Capital + Debenture and Other Long Term Loans, if there be any)	**
Capital Employed (CE) or Investment (I)	****

Therefore ROI = ROCE

$$\text{ROCE or ROI} = \frac{\text{Profit or Income}}{\text{Capital Employed or Investment or Total Net Assets}} \times 100$$

I think you are following my lecture. Is there any question(s) from your side one?

☐ "Excuse me Sir, I have one question."

☐ "Sir, I have also one request."

• What is your question ? What is your request?

☐ "Sir, Is ROCE or ROI differ from Return on Total Net Assets"?

☐ "Sir, Please explain it with an example."

• Well, you see, ROCE or ROI does in no way differs from Total Net Asset; it means the same; only difference in the computation. I would like to show you that figure for ROCE or ROI will be the same as that of Total Net Assets. Please, take a look at the Board :

Balance Sheet of XYZ Co. Ltd.

Liabilities	Amount Rs.	Assets	Amount Rs.
Equity Share Capital of Rs. 10 each	1,00,000	Goodwill	25,000
Reserve and Surplus	50,000	Land & Building	1,25,000
6% Preference Share	50,000	Plant & Machinery	50,000
5% Debenture	50,000	Furniture & Fixture	25,000
Creditors	25,000	Stock	25,000
Bills Payable	25,000	Debtors	25,000
		Cash in Hand	25,000
	3,00,000		3,00,000

		Rs.
	Equity Share Capital	1,00,000
Add :	Reserve and Surplus	50,000
	Net Worth	1,50,000
Less :	Goodwill	25,000
	Tangible Net Worth	1,25,000
Add :	Loan Capital or Long Term Debt (Preference Share Capital and Debenture)	1,00,000
	Capital Employed or Investment	2,25,000 ***

Investment or Capital Employed is represented by Total Resources—which is similar to Investment or Capital Employed.

					Rs.
Tangible Fixed Assets					
	Land and Buildings				1,25,000
	Plant and Machinery				50,000
	Furniture & Fixture				25,000
					2,00,000
Add:	**Net Current Assets or Working Capital**				
i.e.	Total Current Assets	Rs.	75,000		
Less:	Total Current Liabilities	Rs.	50,000	Rs.	25,000
	Net Total Assets (Total Resources)			Rs.	2,25,000 ***

Concept of Return on Total Assets

You see from the above the figure Rs. 2,25,000 representing Capital Employed or Investment is equal to Rs. 2,25,000 representing Total Net Asset which may be termed as Total Resources. You can approach through any one of the above ways to find out Return on Capital Employed (ROCE) or Return on Investment (ROI) or Return on Total Resource. One important point to note is that return on equity capital may be expressed as Return on Equity (ROE).

I think you are following what I am discussing. Is there any question ?

☐ "Sir, please throw some light on the concept of return."

Real Meaning of Profit

● Well, you see, return means here fruits of the effort of the entrepreneur or the business entity. This fruit(s) implies profit which may be termed as entrepreneur's remuneration which represents excess of income over expenditure. You see, some authors assume income as profit; in that income (which is termed as profit) represents excess of revenue over expenses. Revenue here implies Sales.

Profit, i.e. Income, represents Net Profit or Net Income (i.e. excess of Income over Expenditure; or excess of revenue (Sales) over Expenses) which may be mixture of trading profit or income and non-trading profit or income.

You all know that the term trading represents operating and term non-trading represents non-operating.

It is important to note that performance of any division or unit of an organisation can be measured by drawing a relationship between two elements—(1) Profit or Income and (2) Investment (i.e. only Equity Capital and Capital Employed or Total Assets i.e. Total Net Assets or Total Tangible Assets minus Current Liabilities as decided by the Analyst or Performance Evaluator or Management).

You see, Income may be represented as Earning Before Interest and Tax (EBIT) or Earning After Interest and Tax (EAIT).

You see, I just narrated the relationship between two elements —

$$\frac{\text{Numerator}}{\text{Denominator}} \times 100$$

The Numerator is Profit or Income or EBIT whereas the Denominator is Equity (i.e. Equity Capital) and Capital Employed or Investment or Total Resources or Tangible Total Assets or Total Net Assets).

You, please stand up.

☐ "Me Sir?"

• Yes, yes, you. Why are you sleeping in the class? Are you feeling bored or tired?

☐ "Sir, your class is very exciting and interesting as well; I am not feeling bored but tired. Please give us a break for 10 (ten) minutes."

• Well, your request is granted . I will come back to the classroom after 15 minutes. Please be present. Don't miss your class. Thank you all...

• Are you all present in the class ?

☐ Yes Sir, kindly proceed for further discussion. We are refreshed.

• Well, I am discussing the subject again. Take a look at the Board.

Return on Equity Capital is known as Return on Equity (ROE)

$$= \frac{\text{Net Profit or Income}}{\text{Equity Capital}} \times 100$$

The above can be expressed as :

ROE = % Margin on Sale × Turnover of Equity Capital
(Profitability) (Effort)

By the by, I am to bring to your attention that White, Sondhi and Fried in their book titled "The Analysis and use of Financial Statement"[1] expressed ROE as :

$$\text{ROE} = \text{Profitability} \times \text{Activity} \times \text{Solvency}$$

$$= \frac{\text{Income}}{\text{Sales}} \times \frac{\text{Sales}}{\text{Assets}} \times \frac{\text{Assets}}{\text{Equity}}$$

I think you have followed ROE.

Now I would like to discuss ROI (Return on Investment). You see, ROE and ROI are not the same thing. I have pointed it earlier that there lies the difference between E and I. E is only Equity Capital. I represents the whole aspect i.e. E + Reserve and Surplus + Loan Capital i.e. Capital Employed.

[1] Whiley. Third Edition, p. 143

$$\left.\begin{array}{l}\text{Return on Investment (ROI)}\\ \text{or}\\ \text{Return on Capital Employed (ROCE)}\\ \text{or}\\ \text{Return on Total Net Assets}\end{array}\right\} = \frac{\text{Profit (Income)}}{\text{Investment or Capital Employed}} \times 100$$

Analysis of ROI or ROCE

Components of ROI or ROCE

$$1.\left\{\begin{array}{l}\textbf{\% Margin on Sale or Revenue}\\ = \dfrac{\text{Income or Profit}}{\text{Sales or Revenue}} \times 100\end{array}\right\} \times 2.\left\{\begin{array}{l}\textbf{Turnover of Investment or Capital Employed}\\ = \dfrac{\text{Revenue or Sales}}{\text{Investment or Capital Employed or Total Resources or Total Net Assets}}\end{array}\right\}$$

You see, the greatest advantage of ROI is that comparison among various organisations or divisions of the same industry or organisation can be made possible with ease.

Please note in this context that mere comparison of Income or Profit may not reflect the proper performance evalution of an organisation. A study on all ingredients of ROI or ROCE i.e. Profit, Sales and Investment is needed.

I am to caution you that do not get confused with the words Revenue and Income which many authors use in their book.

Consider Revenue as Sale; Income as Profit. It is to note in this context that ROI or ROA (Return on Total Net Assets) or ROCE or ROE is found to increase or decrease.

Reasons for increase in ROI etc. are—increase in sales, decreasing cost, controlling expenses, developing work culture among all levels of management including grass route level of the organisation, efficient management, proper handling of human resources.

Reasons for decrease in ROI, ROCE etc. are decrease in sales, increase in cost, excessive expenses, lack of work culture, inefficient management, improper handling and use of human resources etc.

☐ "Excuse me Sir, I have one question to ask."

• What is that ?

☐ "Sir, ROI or ROCE or ROE represents $\dfrac{\text{Profit or Income}}{\text{Capital Employed or ROI etc.}} \times 100$

The above is taken as accepted performance measure and as a comparable yardstick with other similar firm(s) or divisions(s) or unit(s). Sir, reported profit is represented by Cash + Debtors + Closing Stock; that is to say, profit is represented by realised as well as unrealised profit. Because, Closing Stock and debtors are unrealised portion of profit. My questions is does the result of Capital Employed i.e. ROI or ROC need be taken as actual income or profit under the situations of (i) non-realisation of a part of unrealised profit, and (ii) inflationary pressure?"

Scanning of Profit

● It is indeed, very interesting to see that you have gone deep in the subject.

You see, you are correct. The situations you have cited here really stand on the way to take decision with precision.

Besides the above, an insight into the matter would reveal the following :

True and Fair

You all know that ROI or ROCE, which is known to many as accounting or accrual accounting rate of return, is based on the relationship between two accounting measures —(i) Profit or Income, and (ii) Capital Employed or Investment. They cannot reflect a true and fair view of the trends of the business or organisation or division or unit, as the case may be.

An insight into the matter would reveal that accounting measure of profit or income reflects **current cost** whereas accounting measure of capital employed or investment represents **historical cost**. So, the relationship between current cost and historical cost may not be a realistic guide to the concept.

$$\text{ROCE or ROI} = \frac{\text{Profit or Income} \longrightarrow}{\text{Capital Employed or Investment} \longrightarrow} \times 100 \quad \frac{\text{Current Cost}}{\text{Historical Cost}} \times 100$$

So it is suggested that arriving at the judgement as to performance of any organisation, division or unit should be based on, besides ROCE or ROI, other performance measures — **Residual Income (RI)** and **Economic Value Added (EVA)**.

I think you are following my lecture.

☐ "Yes Sir, no problem in understanding your lecture. Sir, please explain the two concepts of measures of performance—RI and EVA."

● Well, I will discuss these concepts step by step. I have not completed my lecture on ROCE or ROI. I have something more to say. Please note the discussion very minutely.

Mechanism for Increase of ROI or ROCE

Well, note in this context that ROCE or ROI can be increased in the following manner :

(i) Effective use of capital or investment to increase sale, that is to say increase turnover of Investment or capital employed.

(ii) Increasing profit or income per rupee for sales or revenue.

(iii) Strengthening long term solvency position.

(iv) Proper handling of human resources which, in actual practice, boosts annual turnover of business, i.e. Sales.

(v) Judicious planning for capital structure.

(vi) Avoiding unnecessary expenses or expenditure and proper controlling of cost.

I am sure that you are following my lecture. If you desire that I should explain each and every aspect of the said point, I will discuss. I feel these points are very simple to understand on your part at your present level of knowledge.

Yes, you, please stand up. I feel that you want to say something. Please be frank. Don't hesitate to say anything. Please don't feel shy or fear me. One thing, please try to realise that I am your academic friend, not enemy. You all should further keep it in your mind that your success is my success.

☐ "Excuse me Sir ! I have followed your points on how ROCE or ROI can be increased; but Sir, please explain in details, though you have explained these earlier in a general way, points (i), (iv) and (v)."

● Regarding the point (i) **Effective use of capital or Investment,** I am to say that this aspect has a link with point (iv) **Proper Handling of Human Resources**. So, these two points here I am discussing together through a case study.

Case Study

A businessman came to me to know the reason of decline in ROCE or ROI. He told me "Being inspired by ensured profit on sale, i.e. margin on sale I started a business with my available fund (i.e. capital). Initially I got good result; but Sir! gradually my return on capital declines".

He furnished me his three consecutive years' information regarding percentage margin on Sales (% MS) and percentage return on Capital (% ROC). As he is a small business-man, his capital is treated here as Proprietary Capital :

	Years		
	I	**II**	**III**
% ROC	15%	12%	9%
% MS	3%	3%	3%

You see, I have already explaind that ROC is based on two products — % Margin on Sale (% MS) and Turnover of Capital (TC). As % MS is given i.e. 3%, it is clear from the said situation that turnover of capital decreased. Mere ensured percentage margin on sale does not ensure increase of % ROC. It is the sale frontier which is responsible for increase or decrease of capital turnover. So, efficiency of Investment or capital employed depends on the efficiency of human resources anddynamism on the part of top management. It is the human resource which rotates the annual turnover, i.e. Sales, of the business.

Reason for Decline of ROC or ROI

Now I am confident that you have followed my lecture.

☐ "Sir, I could not follow the reason for decline of % ROC of the case study. Please explain again".

● Well, look at the board :

$$\% \text{ ROC} \rightarrow \quad \frac{\text{Profit or Income}}{\text{Capital or Investment}} \times 100 = \text{Result in \%}$$

$$\% \text{ MS} \rightarrow \quad \frac{\text{Profit or Income}}{\text{Sales or Revenue}} \times 100 = \text{Result in \%}$$

$$\times \qquad \times$$

$$\text{Turnover of Capital} \rightarrow \quad \frac{\text{Sales or Revenue}}{\text{Capital or Investment}} \times 100 = \text{Result in Times}$$

So, as % ROC and % MS is given, there is no problem in finding out the result.

You see, ROC is the product of % MS and T.C. :

	I	II	III
% ROC	15%	12%	9%
% MS	3%	3%	3%
So, by dividing % ROC by % MS you can have T.C.	5 times	4 times	3 times

On enquiry I came to know that the proprietor stopped certain incentives such as free lunch, transport expenses of the salesmen.

Again, you see

% ROCE or ROI or ROC = % MS × TC

$$\% \text{ MS} = \frac{\text{Profit or Income}}{\text{Sales or Revenue}} \times 100$$

Profit or Income → Area of Financial Management or Planning for Profit.

Sales or Revenue → Area of Human Asset or Resource Management. It is the human being who rotate(s) capital or Investment. It may be assumed as operational aspect of Investment or Capital.

↓

X

$$\text{TC} = \frac{\text{Sales or Revenue}}{\text{Capital or Investment}} = \ldots \text{ Times}$$

Sales or Revenue → Area of Human Asset or Human Sales or Revenue Resource Management (Operational Investment or Capital or Asset)

Capital or Investment → Area of Financial Management or Investment Decision.

I hope that you have now realised that % ROC or ROCE etc. is the product of % Margin at Sales (%MS) and Turnover of Capital.

So in the above case study you are provided with two sets of information ROC and Margin on Sales (i.e. Net Profit Ratio); from this you are to find out other information :

	ROC (in %)	=	MS (in %)	×	TC ?
I year	15%	=	3%	×	5 times
II years	12%	=	3%	×	4 times
III years	9%	=	3%	×	3 times

So, the analysis of above reveals that there lies co-relation of % ROC and Turnover of Capital or Investment in a situation where profit margin on sale is fixed or ensured. Here the reason for decrease in ROC is the fall of turnover of capital.

So the main reason for decrease of TC, besides other aspects, is the lack of proper handling of human resources or living assets. It is the human being, as I already told you, who rotates capital or investment.

In actual practice it is revealed that offering incentive as good working condition, better remuneration of the employee, existence of work culture, effective management control, unbiased management attitude towards employees and other personnel—all these may result in increase in turnover of capital.

Human Resource in ROI or ROCE

This aspect of contribution of human asset towards sales promotion and earning income or profit was explained by me through a story in my lecture on 'Human Resource Accounting' delivered at the UGC-sponsored Advanced Level Summer Institute for Postgraduate Teachers held at University of Madras (1982) :

A gentleman had a pet dog. He sent the dog abroad for management education. After returning from abroad the dog asked his master (who was sitting by the side of a pond) "Sir ! what am I to do ?" The master said "What do you see here ?" The dog answered, "I see here a pond and paddy, lying on the yard". The master said, "Go to the pond and make your skin wet". Accordingly the dog wetted his body and returned to his master.

"What am I to do Sir", said the dog.

The master said, "Go round on the paddy, welter in the paddy and then shake your body".

For each round the dog collects 50 paisa worth of paddy on his body.

If the master can manage the dog to go round 10 (ten) times, the master would be able to collect paddy worth Rs. 5 (i.e. 50 paisa × 10 times).

But after the dog went round (welter) on the paddy 5 times, the dog refused to go round further on the ground that he does not accept 8.33 percent bonus offered by his master. He can move further provided 20 percent bonus is either paid or offered to him.

I feel that you want to say something which I realise from your face. Why do you hesitate?

☐ "Sir, after giving the example of dog in respect of bonus, you have said proper handling of human resource ....."

• Well, I understand your sentiment. In this regard I suggest, do go through a case law of Kingston Cotton Mill Company where Lord Justice Lopes remarked "Auditor is the watch-dog, not a blood-hound." Now I think that your sentiment is removed.

From the above it is clear that without proper motivation or handling of human resource with proper incentive, it is difficult to achieve desired level of profit or income.

I think, you have understood the deep-rooted cause for capital turnover.

Is there any questions from your side? Are you feeling tired?

☐ "Sir, it is very interesting indeed. The example you have given us is really worth remembering.

☐ Sir, if you don't mind, please give us a break for half an hour for lunch."

• Well, I will return to the class after 40 minutes...

☐ "Sir, we are all present in the class. Kindly enlighten us on the item (v) Judicious planning for capital structure."

• **Well, I would like to explain it with the help of a case study.**

Capital Leverage

You see, I already discussed in the Chapter on Leverage or Gearing of Capital structure that in a situation of high-geared capital structure (high-levered capital structure) the rate of return on equity capital (own capital) is high as compared to low-levered (low-geared capital sturcture).

You all know that high-geared (high-levered) capital structure denotes much dependence on loan capital which depicts under capitalisation; whereas low-levered (low-geared) capital structure exhibits too much dependence on own (equity) capital as compared to loan capital which reflects over-capitalisation. Here rate of return on equity or ordinary share capital (own capital) is low.

Please look at the board for the case study. This case study was drawn by me from field survey, nearly 15 years back.

Case Study

A businessman's family consists of 6 (six) members—himself, his wife, two married daughters and their two respective husbands A & B who are the two sons-in-law of the businessman. The businessman, tried to test. A and B to see which one is suitable for the business profession.

One day the father-in-law gave a proposal to A and B that if one can invest Rs. 50,000 return on own capital (suppose equity capital) is ensured for Rs. 10,000. One important point to note is that A is calm and quiet, intelligent and dynamic; whereas B is intelligent, sentimental and hot-tempered.

The planning for capital structure of A and B is given :

A

Balance Sheet

Liabilities	Amount Rs.	Assets	Amount Rs.
Own Capital (Suppose Equity Capital)	10,000	Necessary Assets to start the business	50,000
Father-in-law (Suppose 6% Preference Share Capital	30,000		
Loan from Mother-in-law (Suppose 5% debenture)	10,000		
	50,000		50,000

B

Balance Sheet

Liabilities	Amount Rs.	Assets	Amount Rs.
Own Capital (Suppose Equity Capital) [Money collection by selling his own ornaments and other domestic assets]	50,000	Necessary Assets to start the business	50,000
	50,000		50,000

Result of ROC (own capital) of A and B :

A Profit or Income after Debt Capital	B Profit or Income
$\frac{\text{Rs. } 10{,}000 \text{ (6\% of Rs. } 30{,}000 + \text{5\% of Rs. } 10{,}000)}{\text{Capital (own) Rs. } 10{,}000} \times 100$	$\frac{\text{Rs. } 10{,}000}{\text{Rs. } 50{,}000} \times 100$
$= \frac{\text{Rs. } 10{,}000 - (\text{Rs. } 1{,}800 + \text{Rs. } 500)}{\text{Rs. } 10{,}000} \times 100$	$= 20\%$
$= \frac{\text{Rs. } 77{,}000}{\text{Rs. } 10{,}000} \times 100 = 77\%$	

So, an analysis of the two situations reveals that as the rate of return on capital of A is much higher than the rate of return of capital B, A can face competitive market. Though capital structure of A appears to be risky, the same can be overcome by capitalising a part of the profit gradually to reach a stage of fair capitalisation, i.e. mixture of over- and under-capitalisation.

I think that you have followed my lecture. Is there any question(s) from your side.

☐ "Yes Sir, I have one question to ask.

Sir, the question which I am going to ask is of different nature although it has some relevance to the concept of ROC or ROI. I hesitate to ask."

• I told you earlier that don't feel shy. Please be frank with me. What is your question?

☐ "Sir, in a situation of unemployment problem many young persons are desirous to be self-employed by starting a business. But, Sir, lack of fund, i.e. capital, does not motivate them to take the venture. Sir, please throw some light on this aspect".

• Your question, indeed, is very interesting. I feel that one can overcome the problem of inadequate fund or capital. In this regard I would like to put forth a case study.

Before that, I want to say something about capital or fund.

You see, from my long-standing experience I realised that shortage of financial capital may be compensated by **Paradoxical Capital.**

☐ "Excuse me Sir, what is the meaning of the term Paradox and what constitutes Paradoxical Capital"?

• You see, the dictionary meaning of the term 'paradox' are 'seemingly absurd or contradictory though often true statement' (Pocket Oxford Dictionary); 'statement that seems self-contradictory but may be true (Collins Gem. English Dictionary)

Financial Capital ....
(whatever small
amount one has)

Add

Inspiration
+
Innovative approach
+
Patience for hard work
+
Mental strength
+
Firm determination
+
Definite clear objective
+
Managerial outlook

All this constitutes Paradoxical Capital

You see, the paradoxical capital may be interpreted as Compensatory Capital.

Now I would like to say that one can compete with others through the mix of Financial and Paradoxical Capital. This may be clear to you from the case study given here.

Case Study

All of you know about Rathayatra—Chariot Festival. It is the Hindu festival of Lord Juggernaut going in a chariot for a sea bath. During the festival days different fairs (mela) are being held in different places or localities. One of the attractions of the people visiting the fair(s) is pappad. People purchase pappad and eat.

You, why you have raised your hand? Would you like to say something ?

☐ "Yes Sir! What is pappad ?"

● You see, pappad is a kind of delicious thin saucer shaped fried bread, made of dal and powdered pulse.

Do you follow ? I am sorry that for practical taste of the pappad I cannot distribute the same in this classroom environment. If any occasion arises in the near future I will distribute pappad to you in a form of dividend.

☐ "Sir, what is Dividend ?"

● I thank you very much for your curiosity. It is not possible to discuss here. However, to quench your thirst for knowledge I would suggest you to go through my book "An Insight into Auditing—a multi-dimensional approach".

Well, coming to the discussion of the case study : how a person (say A) having negligible amount of capital armed with paradoxical capital can compete with a person (say B) having greater amount of capital.

Importance of Parodoxical Capital

On the first day of Chariot Festival, while coming to my residence from university, I saw a few young educated boys gossiping on the road, in front of my residence.

I asked them, why you are gossiping here. Have you no work to do ?

One of them who appeared to me an intelligent boy having courage and determination said, "Sir, We are unemployed. I searched for a job, but I could not find any job."

I said, then why you are gossiping on the road, why not in your house.

The boy answered, "So long I remain out of home I feel comfortable. Only for lunch and dinner I stayed home."

While talking with me I saw the boy weeping. I asked him what made him weep. I told him if you feel hurt from my talk I am sorry.

The boy answered "No Sir ! Not for you. Nobody talks with us as we are unemployed. We feel happy that you are an exception, at least you have enquired about us; you talked with us. I feel humilated when I found my father saying during my lunch hour that instead of spending money for my education, if the said amount of money was deposited (fixed) either in bank or post office, he could have earned at least some interest on the deposit."

Then I told him to do any business.

"Sir, I have no fund or capital for business" said the boy.

I told him you can sell pappad in the fair during Chariot Festival days; I will help you with petty amount of cash as your initial capital. I also instructed him for market survey to collect information of initial amount of capital to sale pappad to make a profit of Rs. 100. After his return from the market he reported to me that one of his known person (say B) has opened a shop of pappad and told him that if one can invest Rs. 500 (which amount was invested by B) the ensured profit is Rs. 100.

I gave him (suppose A) Rs. 100 as initial capital and asked him to compete with B and to make Rs. 100 profit. He answered me "It is not possible. I can't do that." Then I gave him tips how it is possible. Being inspired by my tips he earned Rs. 100 out of his borrowed investment Rs. 100. At end of the day he returned my money Rs. 100 and kept his profit Rs. 100 which he used as capital in future. Now he (A) is big business-man.

Take a look at the Board to see the mechanism.

Do you follow my lecture ?

☐ "It is really very exciting and thought-provoking. This incident of your life experience will act as paradoxical capital or compensatory capital. This will no doubt help us to write-off our frustration."

● Well take a look at the Board.

Performance Evaluation of B

Information in Brief :

B started business to sell pappad with Rs. 500 to earn ensured profit Rs. 100

Cash in Hand (Capital)	Purchase of Raw Pappad	Selling of Fried Pappad	Profit (Sale Price of Pappad Minus Purchase Price of Pappad)	Profit on Per Hundred Rupees of Purchase
↓	↓	↓	↓	↓
Rs. 500	Rs. 500	Rs. 600	Rs. 100	Rs. 20

$$\text{ROC} = \frac{\text{Profit or Income}}{\text{Capital or Investment}} \times 100 = \left(\frac{\text{Profit or Income}}{\text{Sales or Revenue}} \times 100\right) \times \frac{\text{Sales or Revenue}}{\text{Capital or Investment}}$$

$$= \frac{\text{Rs. } 100}{\text{Rs. } 500} \times 100 \qquad = \left(\frac{\text{Rs. } 100}{\text{Rs. } 600} \times 100\right) \times \frac{\text{Rs. } 600}{\text{Rs. } 500}$$

$$= 16.66666\% \times 1.2 \text{ times}$$

$$= 20\% \qquad = 19.999999 \text{ i.e. } 20\%$$

Performance Evaluation of A

Cash in Hand (Interest-free Borrowed Capital)	Purchase of of Raw Pappad for sale	Profit on Sale (on each Purchase)	Purchase Turnover (Desired Purchase Divided by Actual Purchase)	Selling Price for fried Pappad (on each Hundred Rupee Purchase)	Expected Sales Price for desired profit for Rs. 100 (Selling Price × Purchase Turnover (Rs. 120 × purchased Turn over 5)
↓	↓	↓	↓	↓	↓
Rs. 100	Rs. 100	Rs. 20	5 Times	Rs. 120	Rs. 600

$$\text{ROC} = \frac{\text{Profit or Income}}{\text{Capital (borrowed) or investment}} \times 100 = \left(\frac{\text{Profit or Income}}{\text{Sale or Revenue}} \times 100\right) \times \frac{\text{Sales or Revenue}}{\text{Capital (borrowed) or Investment}}$$

$$\text{ROC} = \%\ \text{Margin or Sale (\%MS)} \times \frac{\text{Sales or Revenue}}{\text{Capital (borrowed) or Investment}}$$

$$\frac{\text{Rs. }100}{\text{Rs. }100} \times 100 = \frac{\text{Rs. }20}{\text{Rs. }120} \times 100 \times \frac{\text{Rs. }600}{\text{Rs. }100}$$

$$\text{Rs. }100 = \frac{50}{3}\% \times 6 \text{ Times}$$

$$\text{Rs. }100 = \text{Rs. }16.66666 \times 6 \text{ Times}$$

$$\text{Rs. }100 = \text{Rs. }100$$

From the above it is clear that A had to work very hard; because he had to turnover his capital (which is Rs. 100) 6 times to compete with B whose capital turnover is 1.2 times. Here Paradoxical Capital helped him to reach his target profit.

I hope that you have followed the above discussion.

☐ "Excuse me Sir, I could not follow the above calculation."

• You see, it is very simple to understand. Please concentrate your attention on class discussion. Your attention please, Please direct your attention on the board.

Found in the following way :

$$\text{Turnover of Capital} = \frac{\text{Target Profit or Income}}{\%\ \text{Margin on Sale (M)}} = \text{............ Times}$$

$$= \frac{\text{Rs. }100}{\frac{50}{3}} = \frac{100}{1} \times \frac{3}{50} = 6 \text{ Times}$$

☐ "Yes Sir, I have followed now".

• Is there any question(s) from your side ?

☐ "I have one question to place before you Sir!"

• What is your question ?

☐ "Sir, What is Du Pont Method of Profitability Analysis ?"

• I have already discussed it earlier. You all know that two basic components or ingredients of ROE or ROC or ROI are % Margin on Sale or Revenue X Turnover of Capital or Investment.

$$\text{ROCE or ROE} = \left(\frac{\text{Profit or Income}}{\text{Sales or Revenue}} \times 100\right) \times \frac{\text{Sales or Revenue}}{\text{Capital or Investments}}$$

$$\qquad\qquad\downarrow\qquad\qquad\qquad\qquad\qquad\downarrow$$

$$\qquad\qquad\text{Area X}\qquad\qquad\qquad\qquad\text{Area Y}$$

Area X is concerned with increasing profit or income per rupee of sales or revenue.

Area Y is concerned with generating more sales or revenue by efficient, dynamic and judicious use of Investment or Capital or assets of the business.

The analysis of Area X i.e. MS (Margin on Sale) and Area Y i.e. turnover of capital or Investment or assets in called **Du Pont Method of Profitability Analysis**. This analysis is also named Du Pont Analysis because it was the Du Pont company of United States who was the initiator of the said profitability analysis.

Is it clear to you ?

☐ "Yes Sir."

☐ "Sir, Is ROC or ROI or ROCE method free from defects? Can decision as to performance of a division or an unit or of an organisation be taken on the basis of ROC or ROI ?"

• Well, your question is very interesting. Basically there lies no defects of ROC or ROI. It is taken as a first-hand impression or result to compare performance of one to another. If any defects are to be searched out, it lies with decision-making process.

For example, any decision taken by the Divisional Manager on the basis of result of ROC or ROI or ROA may not be acceptable by the top management from the point of view of overall goal congruence of a division or unit etc.

Did you follow what I have said?

☐ "No Sir, I could not follow. I think Sir, an example in this regard, will help me to understand."

• Take for an example, the present level of ROC or ROI or Return on Asset (ROA) of a division is 25%. The Divisional Manager has a proposal for investment of Rs. 50,000 which would generate 20% rate of return. The average cost of Capital is 15%.

The above investment proposal appears to be profitable to the top management because of the fact that its return is higher than the cost of capital. But the Divisional Management declined to accept the proposal, as it would reduce overall rate of return of the Division, which is 25%.

I think you have followed the concept. Are there any questions from you ?

☐ "Sir, besides ROI or ROC which you have discussed at length, are there any methods that should be taken into consideration while taking decision regarding performance of a division or an unit or of an organisation as a whole ?"

• Yes, those are Residual Income (RI) Method and Economic Value Added (EVA) Method. I will explain all these in my next class day after tomorrow...

☐ "Good morning, Sir."

● Good morning to you all.

Do you remember that today I will discuss on RI an EVA Method of performance evaluation ?

☐ "Yes Sir."

● Well, please listen to my lecture very carefully.

Residual Income (RI) Method

Residual Income (RI) is another measure for performance evaluation of a Department. It is the excess of income or profit over required rate of return on investment. That is to say, income or profit is desired to be, over and above, higher than imputed cost of capital investment. Note in this context that capital invested in the division(s) is subject to chargeable interest. Therefore, interest on the said capital invested is treated as cost. The basic philosophy behind the estimation of required rate of return lies in the concept of opportunity cost.

Analysis of RI Method

I hope that you have followed my lecture. Should I proceed for further discussions on this concept?

☐ "Excuse me Sir, I have a few questions to ask : (1) What is opportunity cost? (2) Is RI method substitute for ROC or ROI Method? (3) Does required rate of return include any interest on debt financing?"

● Well, regarding your first question :

You see, this concept I discussed in Part III of the book. However, for your ready reference I am to say, benefit or profit forgone (given up) for not availing other alternatives. That is to say foregone of profit (return) not for investing money in other alternative investment having similar risk.

Regarding your second question I am to say that RI is not substitute to ROC or ROI. RI is the alternative method to ROC or ROI for measuring divisional performance.

Regarding your third question please note that if there be any long term debt financing investment in the imputed cost of the Division, in that case Required Rate of Return must include the interest on debt financing.

I think you have followed the discussion so far. I am giving you an example. Please look at the board.

Example :

The Capital Structure of a Division, is assumed as follows :

	Rs.
Equity Capital	1,00,000
9% Debenture	50,000
	1,50,000

The opportunity cost to Equity Shareholders is 15%. In other words, they have forgone 15% rate of return by not investing elsewhere on equity share of similar risk.

Therefore, the required rate of return

$$15\% \times \frac{\text{Rs. } 1{,}00{,}000}{\text{Rs. } 1{,}50{,}000} + 9\% \times \frac{\text{Rs. } 50{,}000}{\text{Rs. } 1{,}50{,}000}$$

= 10% + 3% = 13%

If the operating income of this division is Rs. 25,000, the Residual Income (RI) would be

RI = Rs. 25,000 – (Rs. 150,000 X 13%)

= Rs. 25,000 – Rs. 19,500

= Rs. 5,500

Note in this context that RI Method is more acceptable in comparison to ROC or ROI Method of performance evaluation so far as goal congruence is concerned.

Now I would like to give you a flow chart covering all aspect of RI Method. Please look at the board :

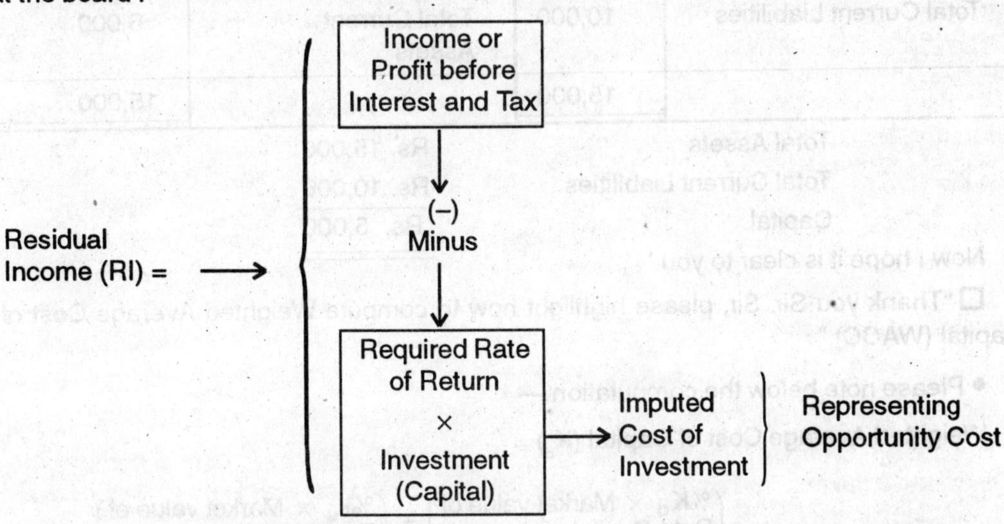

Economic Value Added (EVA)

Economic Value Added (EVA) is a very popular method of performance evaluation. It is more or less similar to RI Method of performance evaluation.

It is calculated by differentiating two figures :

Analysis of Economic Value Added

(1) Amount for After Tax Operating or Trading Income or Profit and (2) Multiplied Amount of two elements—(a) Weighted Average Cost of Capital (WACC), and (b) Capital or Investment.

$$\text{EVA} = \begin{pmatrix}\text{After Tax Operating}\\ \text{Income or Profit}\end{pmatrix} - \begin{pmatrix}\text{Weighted Average} \times \text{Capital or Investment}\\ \text{Cost of Capital}\\ \text{[WACC]}\end{pmatrix}$$

☐ "Excuse me Sir, I have some confusion as to Capital or Investment as you have shown above, because while at the University I have seen in one book that it is written as Total Assets – Current Liabilities. Is there any difference Sir?"

● Thank you for your query. Is it written like below :

$$\text{EVA} = \text{After tax operating income} - \left[\begin{array}{l}\text{Weighted Average} \\ \text{Cost of Capital}\end{array} \times \left(\begin{array}{l}\text{Total Current} \\ \text{Assets} - \text{Liabilities}\end{array}\right)\right]$$

☐ "Yes Sir."

● You see, it is all the same. Please look at the board. It is just a token example to make the concept clear.

Balance Sheet

Liabilities	Amount	Assets	Amount
	Rs.		Rs.
Capital	5,000	Total Fixed Assets	10,000
Total Current Liabilities	10,000	Total Current Assets	5,000
	15,000		15,000

Total Assets	Rs. 15,000
Total Current Liabilities	Rs. 10,000
Capital	Rs. 5,000

Now I hope it is clear to you.

☐ "Thank you Sir. Sir, please highlight how to compute Weighted Average Cost of Capital (WACC)."

● Please note below the computation —

Weighted Average Cost of Capital (K_o) =

$$\frac{\left(\%K_d \times \text{Market value of Debt Capital}\right) + \left(\%k_e \times \text{Market value of Equity Capital}\right)}{\text{Market value of Debt Capital (plus)} + \text{Market value of Equity Capital}}$$

For details I suggest to you through chapter 19 of this book.

Did you follow my lecture ?

☐ "Yes Sir. Thank you Sir."

● Now I think you have followed my lecture.

Is there any question?

☐ "Excuse me Sir, you have forgotten to discuss the non-financial aspect of performance appraisal."

• You see, I have not forgotten. I wanted to see whether you are bold enough to collect information from teacher(s). Because, most of the students feel shy to express their mind before the teachers; instead they pretend as if they understand the lecture. I am happy to see your alertness and keen interest in the subject.

Thank you.

Well, you see, a study on non-financial areas, as a measure of performance, forms an important considerations which rotates or whirls the wheels of different segments of financial performance of an organisation. It is important to note in this context that financial measures are long-term measures and, needless to mention that it is non-financial measures which affect financial measures in the future. It has been rightly observed by Horngren, Datar and Foster[1] that "the financial benefits of these long-run changes may not appear immediately in short-run earnings, but strong improvement in nonfinancial measures is an indicator of economic value creation in the future. For example, an increase in customer satisfaction, as measured by customer surveys and repeat purchases, is a signal of higher sales and income in the future".

Please note, non financial areas :

(i) constant watch on customer sentiments.

(ii) reviewing the organisational efficiency time-to-time.

(iii) effectiveness of human resource management.

(iv) developing work-culture among employees as well as management.

(v) just in time delivery of goods.

(vi) product guarantee

(vii) after sale service

(viii) innovation in product design.

(ix) market research for the expansion of marketing of product.

All the said points are self explanatory. So I don't like to discuss the same considering you all as matured listeners.

☐ "Thank you Sir, but Sir, I have one question to ask; what is Balanced Score Card"?

• Before I am to discuss on Balanced score card, I want to make you clear the two terms— (i) Balanced and (ii) Score Card.

You see the balanced indicates well proportionate and harmonious mix and the score card refers to report of performance. When the two terms are mixed together it attains a meaning which is greater than the break-up meaning of the two terms balanced and score card. You see to assess the short run and long run performance in a right report the Balance Score Card balances the application of financial and non financial performance measures in a well proportionate and harmonious manner. There is no denying the fact that the Balanced Score Card is a strategic management tool for measuring the performance of an organisation to attain its goal congruence.

[1] Horngren and others *"Cost Accounting : A Managerial Emphasis"* 11th Edition Prentice Hall of India.

Prof Dr. Robert Kaplan of Harvard Business School and Prof. David Norton coined this system as Balanced score card which gives a better perception regarding measuring stick in order to balance financial and nonfinancial perspectives. They highlighted four perspectives of performance measure, shown below :

Balanced Score Card

1. Financial

Economic Value Added (EVA),
Return on Investment,
Operating Income etc.

2. Non-financial

Customer

Market Share,
Customer satisfaction,
Complaints received from customer etc.

Internal Business Process Perspective

Number of new products or Services developed, Number of new patents developed, order processing time, time taken to replace defective products etc.

Learning and Growth

rate of employee turnover, information system availability employee participation to manage process, employee education and skill etc.

Problem

Following is the profit statement of three divisions of a company :

	Divisions		
	P (Rs. lakhs)	Q (Rs. lakhs)	R (Rs. lakhs)
Sales Revenues	4	8	8
Divisional Cost			
Variable Costs	1	2	2
Fixed Costs	1.4	2.2	2.2
Apportionment of Head Office Costs	0.4	1.8	1.8
Divisional Profits	1.2	2	2
Capital Employed (based on written down value of fixed assets)	4	10	20
ROCE (ROI)	30%	20%	10%

Required :

(i) From the view-point of controllability at divisional level critically review the profit statement and recalculate ROCE of Division Q and Division R.

(ii) Divisions Q and R are identical in every respect except the age of their operational Fixed Assets — R's being considerably more recent than Q's. Comment on the difference in ROCE of Q and R are represented above.

(iii) The capital employed based on original costs of fixed assets are Rs. 10 lakhs for P and Rs. 25 lakhs for Q. Compute ROCE and RI (Cost of Capital = 12%) for division of P and Q using appropriate data and give your comment on the result.

[C.U., M.Com.]

Solution

(i) **Profit Statement**

		Divisions Q (Rs.)		Divisions R (Rs.)
Sales Revenues		8,00,000		8,00,000
Less : Controllable Costs :				
Costs of Divisional Level :	Rs.			
Variable Costs	2,00,000		2,00,000	
Fixed Costs	2,20,000		2,20,000	
		4,20,000		4,20,000
Divisional profit at controllable cost		3,80,000		3,80,000
Capital Employed		10,00,000		20,00,000
ROCE (ROI)		38%		19%

(ii) The ROCE of division Q is double than the ROCE of division R. Though it is given in the problem that except age of operational fixed assets, both divisions are identical in all respect. The reasons for the differences is that because of inflation the cost price of recently purchased fixed assets is double than the earlier purchase by division Q. Though both have identical capacity Inflation adjusted capital employed will give more accurate measure of ROCE. Again, the difference may be due to the difference between their efficiency in the utilisation of capital.

	Divisions P Rs.	Divisions Q Rs.
Sales Revenues	4,00,000	8,00,000
Less : Controllable Cost at Divisional Level :		
Variable Costs	1,00,000	2,00,000
Fixed Costs	1,40,000	2,20,000
	2,40,000	4,20,000
(a) Divisional Profit	1,60,000	3,80,000
(b) Capital Employed	10,00,000	25,00,000
ROCE (ROI)	16%	15.2%
(c) Cost of Capital (12%)	1,20,000	3,00,000
ROI [(a) – (c)]	40,000	80,000

Based on ROCE, division P is slightly better than division Q. But if we consider RI, division Q's RI is double than division P's. Let us now consider head-office expenses —

	P Rs.	Q Rs.
Divisional Profit :	= 1,60,000 – 40,000	= 3,80,000 – 1,80,000
	= 1,20,000	= 2,00,000
	$= \frac{1,20,000 \times 100}{10,00,000}$	$= \frac{2,00,000 \times 100}{25,00,000}$
ROCE	= 12%	= 8%
RI (Divisional Profit minus Cost of Capital)	= (1,20,000 – 1,20,000) = Nil	= (2,00,000 – 3,00,000) = (–) 1,00,000

Division P is in a better position than division Q.

Problem

Calculate Return on Investment, Residual Income, and Economic Value Added from the information given :

Balance Sheet as on 31.03.2007

Liabilities	Amount	Assets	Amount
	Rs.		Rs.
Equity Share Capital	4,00,000	Fixed Assets	6,00,000
Reserve & Surplus	2,00,000	10% Investments	1,00,000
12% Debentures	2,00,000	Current Assets	3,00,000
Current Liabilities	2,10,000	Preliminary Expenses	10,000
	10,10,000		10,10,000

Further information :

i) Net profit after taxes for the year 2006-2007 : Rs. 1,20,000

ii) Rate of Income Tax — 40%

iii) Risk-free rate of return — 6%

iv) Average market rate of returns — 15%.

Solution

Investment in Net Assets :

Fixed Assets	=	Rs. 6,00,000	
10% Investments	=	Rs. 1,00,000	
Current Assets	=	Rs. 3,00,000	10,00,000
Less : Current Liabilities			2,10,000
			7,90,000

Net Profit after tax = Rs. 1,20,000

Rate of Tax = 40%

$$\therefore \text{ Net Profit before tax} = 1,20,000 \times \frac{100}{60} = \text{Rs. } 2,00,000$$

$$\therefore \text{ Return on Investment} = \frac{2,00,000}{7,90,000} \times 100 = 25.32\%$$

Calculation of required rate of return :

Return to equity shareholders may be measured by using Capital Assets Pricing Model According to CAPM required rate of return = Risk-free rate of return + (Market rate of return – risk-free rate of return) × beta coefficient.

= 6% + (15% – 6%) × 0.8
= 6% + 7.2%
= 13.2%

∴ Overall required rate of return

$$= 13.2 \times \frac{6,00,000}{8,00,000} + 12\% \times \frac{2,00,000}{8,00,000}$$

= 9.9% + 3%
= 12.9%

Income before interest and tax :

	Rs.
Income before tax	2,00,000
Add : Interest on Debenture	24,000
(2,00,000 X 12%)	2,24,000

∴ Residual Income = Rs. 2,24,000 – Rs. 7,90,000 × 12.9%
= Rs. 2,24,000 – Rs. 1,01,910
= Rs. 1,22,090

Economic Value Added (EVA) :

Calculation of Operating Profit after Tax :

	Rs.
Net Profit after Tax	1,20,000
Add : Interest in Debenture (net of tax)	14,400
2,00,000 × 12% × (1 – 0.4)	
	1,34,400

Cost of Capital (after Tax)

$$13.2 \times \frac{6}{8} + 12\% \,(1 - 0.4) \times \frac{2}{8}$$

$= 9.9\% + 1.8\%$

$= 11.7\%$

$\therefore$ EVA $= 1{,}34{,}400 - 7{,}90{,}000 \times 11.7\%$

$= 1{,}34{,}400 - 92{,}430$

$=$ Rs. 41,970

Problem

Division X and Y are both considering an outlay on new investment projects.

	Division X	Division Y
Investment outlay	Rs. 1,00,000	Rs. 1,00,000
Net return on new investment	Rs. 16,000	Rs. 11,000
Current ROI	18%	11%
Cost of Capital	13%	13%

Using ROI as the index state whether the project should be accepted or rejected? Will there by any change in the decision of the project is evaluated by using RI as an index for measuring performance? **[C.U., M.Com.]**

Solution

Particulars	Division X	Division Y
Current or existing ROI	18%	11%
ROI of new investment	$\frac{16{,}000}{1{,}00{,}000} \times 100$	$\frac{11{,}000}{1{,}00{,}000} \times 100$
	16%	11%

Using ROI as the index, Division Y should accept the project but Division X would reject the project, because ROI of new investment is lower than the current or existing ROI.

Using RI :	**Division X**	**Division Y**
	Rs.	Rs.
RI	$= 16{,}000 - 1{,}00{,}000 \times 13\%$	$= 11{,}000 - 1{,}00{,}000 \times 13\%$
	$= 16{,}000 - 13{,}000$	$= 11{,}000 - 13{,}000$
	$= 3{,}000$	$= -2{,}000$

RI from new investment of division X would be Rs. 3,000, where as, Division Y is negative. Therefore, project of Division X should be accepted while using RI method.

Problem

The following information relates to budgeted operation of Division 'K' of a manufacturing company.

	Rs.
Sales (50,000 units at Rs. 8)	4,00,000
Less : Variable Cost @ Rs. 6 p.a.	3,00,000
Contribution margin	1,00,000
Less : Fixed cost	75,000
Divisional Profit	25,000

The amount of divisional investment is Rs. 1,50,000 and the minimum desired rate of return on the investment is the cost of capital which is currently 20%.

Evaluate the performance of the division 'K' using RI as the index. The Divisional Manager has the opportunity to sell 10,000 units at Rs. 7.50 per unit variable cost would be the same as budgeted but fixed would increase by Rs. 5,000. Additional investment of Rs. 20,000 would also be required to meet the situation. If the manager accepts the special order, by how much and in what direction would his Residual Income Change? **[C.U., M.Com.]**

Calculation of Budgeted RI of Division K

	Rs.
Divisional Profit	25,000
Less : Cost of Capital (1,50,000 × 20%)	30,000
RI	(–) 5,000

Now, if the special proposal is accepted, then

Sales [50,000 + 10,000]	60,000 units
Selling price	Rs. 7.50 per unit
Variable cost	Rs. 6.00 per unit
Fixed Cost [75,000 + 5,000]	Rs. 80,000
Investment [Rs 1,50,00 + Rs. 20,000]	Rs. 1,70,000

The Actual RI after accepting Special proposal :

	Rs.
Sales [60,000 × Rs. 7.50]	4,50,000
Less : Variable Cost [60,000 × Rs. 6.00]	3,60,000
Contribution margin	90,000
Less : Fixed Cost	80,000
Divisional Profit	10,000

∴ RI = Rs. 10,000 – Rs. 1,70,000 × 20%

= Rs. 10,000 – Rs. 34,000

= (–) Rs. 24,000

∴ Change in residual income

= – 24,000 – (– 5,000)

= (–) 19,000

Therefore, the change is in negative direction.

Problem

Calculate Return on Investment, Residual Income and Economic Value Added from the information given below and comment on the results.

Income before depreciation, Interest and taxes	Rs. 1,95,000
Depreciation @ 10% on Tangible Fixed Assets	Rs. 30,000
10% Debt Capital	Rs. 1,50,000
Shareholders' Equity	Rs. 2,50,000
Current Assets	Rs. 2,00,000
Current Liabilities	Rs. 1,00,000
Rate of Tax	40%
Cost of Equity	14%
Current Market Value of 20,000 Equity shares of Rs. 10 each	Rs. 3,00,000

[C.U., M.Com.]

Solution

Calculation fo Net Operating Income before interest but after tax :

	Rs.
Income before depreciation, interest and taxes	1,95,000
Less: Depreciation	30,000
Earning before interest and tax (EBIT)	1,65,000
Less: Interest (1,50,000 × 10%)	15,000
	1,50,000
Less: Tax (1,50,000 × 40%)	60,000
	90,000
Add: Interest	15,000
Income before interest but after tax	1,05,000

Net operating assets or investment

= (Net Fixed Assets + Current Assets – Current Liabilities)

$= \text{Rs. } 30,000 \times \frac{90}{10} + \text{Rs. } 2,00,000 - \text{Rs. } 1,00,000$

= Rs. (2,70,000 + 2,00,000 – 1,00,000)

= Rs. 3,70,000

$$\therefore \text{Return on Investment} = \frac{\text{Earning before interest and tax} \times 100}{\text{Net operating assets}}$$

$$= \frac{\text{Rs. } 1,65,000 \times 100}{\text{Rs. } 3,70,000}$$

$$= 44.59\%$$

Residual Income = EBIT – (Net operating assets × cost of capital)

= Rs. 1,65,000 – (3,70,000 × 11.33%*)

= Rs. 1,65,000 – 41,921

= Rs. 1,23,079

* Weighted Average Cost of Capital taking market value of equity and debt as weights.

$K_o = K_e.W_e + K_d.W_d$

Where K_o = Cost of capital
K_e = Cost of equity
K_d = Cost of debt
W_e = Weight of equity
W_d = Weight of debt

$$K_o = 14\% \times \frac{3,00,000}{(3,00,000 + 1,50,000)} + 10\% (1 - t) \times \frac{1,50,000}{(3,00,000 + 1,50,000)}$$

$$= 14\% \times \frac{30}{45} + 10\% (1 - 0.4) \times \frac{15}{45}$$

$$= 9.33\% + 2\%$$

$$= 11.33\%$$

Economic Value Added (EVA) :

EVA = Net operating profit after tax – [Net operating assets × Weighted average Cost of Capital]

= Rs. 1,05,000 – [Rs. 3,70,000 × 11.33%]

= Rs. 1,05,000 – Rs. 41,921

= Rs. 63,079

QUESTIONS

1. Distinguish between Residual Income (RI) and Economic Value Added (EVA) as measures of financial performance.
2. Elucidate the concept of Economic Value Added (EVA).
3. Discuss the limitations of the traditional measures of ROCE. Do you think that some of the limitations of ROCE measure may be overcome by EVA measure. Justify your answer.
4. Make a comparative study of ROI and RI as tools of measurement of divisional performance.
5. What do you mean by divisional performance?What are the objectives of divisional performance measurement?
6. Discuss the effect of performance measurement on capital investment decisions.
7. Do you think that the use of return on investment as a performance measure lead to bad decisions? How do residual income and economic value added overcome this problem?
8. Residual Income and Return on Investment are commonly used measures of performance. However, they are frequently criticized for placing too great an emphasis on the achievement of short-term results, possibly damaging longer-term performance.

   You are required to discuss

   (a) the issues involved in the long-term : short-term conflict referred to in the above statement;

   (b) suggestions which have been made to reconcile this difference.

   [CIMA, Adapted]

9. The Dearden Company uses ROI to measure the the performance of its operating divisions. A summary of the annual reports from two divisions is shown below. The company's cost of capital is 12%.

	Division X	**Division Y**
Capital Investment	Rs. 4,800	8,000
Net Income	Rs. 960	Rs. 1,440
ROI	20%	18%

Required :

(i) Which division is more profitable?

(ii) At what cost of capital would both divisions be considered equally profitable?

(iii) What performance measurement procedure would more clearly show the relative profitability of the two divisions?

(iv) Suppose the manager of Division X were offered a one year project that would increase his investment base for that year by Rs. 1,000 and show a profit of Rs. 150. Would the manager accept this project if he were evaluated on his divisional ROI?

[C.U., M.Com]

10. X Ltd. has two divisions A and B. A new project is under consideration. This project can be intrusted to either A or B. The estimated annual costs and other date relevant for the project presented by the divisions are :

	A	B
	Rs.	Rs.
Variable Cost	40,000	50,000
Controllable divisional overheads	20,000	14,000
Allocation of general overheads	15,000	10,000
	75,000	74,000
Revenue	80,000	80,000
Gross value of total assets to be employed for the project	80,000	80,000
Value of assets less external liabilities (for the project)	50,000	40,000
The existing ROI of the divisions	30%	18%

Cost of capital of the company = 15%

(i) Compute ROI and RI for the new project for each division.

(ii) What would be the decisions as to acceptance of the project at divisional level based on ROI and RI and now the company's profit would be affected thereby?

[C.U., M.Com.]

11. Calculate Return on Investment, Residual Income and Economic Value Added from the information given below.

Balance Sheet as on 31.03.04

Liabilities	Amount	Assets	Amount
	Rs.		Rs.
Equity share capital	4,00,000	Fixed assets	6,00,000
Reserve and Surplus	2,00,000	10% Investments	1,00,000
12% Debentures	2,00,000	Current Assets	3,00,000
Current liabilities	2,10,000	Pre-piminary expenses	10,000
	10,10,000		10,10,000

Further information :

(i) Net profit after taxes for the year 2003-2004 — Rs. 1,20,000.

(ii) Rate of Income tax — 40%

(iii) Risk free rate of return — 6%

(iv) Average market rate of return — 15%

(v) Beta coefficient — 0.8

[C.U., M.Com.]

12. Consider the following information relating to A Ltd. and B Ltd.

	A Ltd.	B Ltd.
	Rs.	Rs.
Income (after Interest and taxes)	70,000	52,500
Shareholders' Equity	1,50,000	2,00,000
10% Debentures	2,00,000	—
Current Liabilities	50,000	40,000
Tax rate	30%	30%
Beta Co-efficient	0.8	0.6

Calculate ROI, and RI and briefly comment on the financial performance of the companies. (Assume risk-free rate of return as 6% and market rate of return as 15%). **[C.U., M.Com.]**

33

MANAGERIAL NEXUS IN COST CONTROL

☐ "Good evening Sir."

• Good evening.

What will be discussed now?

☐ "Sir, you promised to discuss Cost Control to day."

• Is it so?

Well, please note below.

Introduction

You see, Cost Control is an integral part of modern management thought. The existence of many variables arising from operational and communicational complexities of business, associated with decision-making process within the organisation has induced the top management to control the different activities of the business. This Cost Control is a continuous process through which the resources of an organisation and the factors of production of the business are used to the best maximum efficiency or utilisation without injuring the 'integrity of the capital structure' of the business for achieving higher productivity.

Do you follow my lecture?

☐ "Yes Sir, please Sir give us the definition of Cost Control."

• Well, please note that

Definition of Cost Control

Cost Control has been defined as 'the employment of management devices in the performance of any necessary operation so that pre-established objectives of quality, quantity and time may be attained at the lowest possible outlay for goods and services. Such devices include a bill of materials; instructions; standard of performance; competent supervision; cost limits on items and operations, and studies interim reports and decision based on these reports'. It follows that the main source of Cost Control is either Standard Costing or Budgetary Control. However, attempt has been made to improve Cost Control through Direct Costing System.

Following the proposition of Standard Costing and Budgetary Control, actual costs are compared with the standard or predetermined cost; accordingly the adverse variances can be scrutinised for corrective action. By doing so Cost Control can contribute much to increase profitability and productivity of an enterprise. In the context of planned economy in India where there are vast natural resources and great man-power, Cost Control has much to do in increasing productivity in each sector of accounting.

The basic philosophy of cost control concept will not be realised unless the environmental factors under which it operates or is likely to operate are studied properly or adjusted accordingly as circumstances necessitate. The environmental factors are social condition, 'economic change and consumers' behaviour' etc. Lack of proper understanding of the real concept of Cost Control may put the economy of an organisation into unstable condition, and lead to reduction of cost in the name of Cost Control. However, a close observation between Cost Control and Cost Reduction reveals that the former is concerned with predetermined standard, while, in the latter case, predetermined standard is not the proper criterion for assaying the operational efficiency.

I think, you have followed my lecture.

You see, some times students get confused with the two terms — Cost Reduction and Cost Control. This I came to know when many students put me question 'Sir Is Cost Reduction and Cost Control same? So I am duscussing it under the head Cost Reduction vs. Cost Control.

Cost Reduction vs Cost Control

Cost control and cost reduction are related concepts. The former aims at guiding and regulating by executive action the cost of operating an undertaking through standardisation, perfomance appraisal and corrective measure, the later is concerned with the potential economy which varies between wide extremes following the existing level of efficiency. Here standards are constantly challenged for their improvement. That is to say, under this method, standards become a subject matter of research for further standard. However, cost reduction indicates that high cost of production should be brought down at any cost. It should be noted in this connection that out of the many elements of profit, one of them is reduction of cost. That is why cost reduction plays an important role in management thinking and thus developing an organisational integrity. But the maintenance of an organisational integrity, which stands on the four pillars of management thought—Planning, Coordination, Motivation and Control—is not always possible through cost reduction techniques which do not follow any particular principles or standards. It follows the principles as circumstances dictate. Unlike cost reduction, which is used in a restricted sense in Cost Control, used in a broad sense, aims at reducing cost and increasing productivity, and this can avoid the adverse effects arising from Cost Reduction through its different scientific techniques viz. Standard Costing, Budgetary Control and Flexible Budget and Responsibility Accounting. As for an example—labour cost control does not mean the reduction of wages. Management should always benefit the workers through increased compensation and financial incentives if higher productivity and profitability are desired'. For that a clear understanding between the employer and the employee is required. Go slow tactics, strike, lock-out etc. are to be avoided as these are obstacles to Profitability and Productivity, and thereby put hindrances to the process of Cost Control.

Cost Reduction vs Cost Control

'Sometimes, indeed, cost control may lead you to increase in certain costs because this will produce a better overall result in terms of net profit for the business through higher sales, reduction of costs elsewhere or in some other direction'. Thus, unlike cost control system, cost reduction scheme does not give any opportunity under which cost increases. However, at the time when there are many adverse forces at work, it becomes very difficult on the part of the top management to arrive at any concrete management decisions regarding control of cost, because the terms 'control' possesses the characteristic of flexibility. Its application depends on the environment under which it is likely to operate. The technique of control varies widely from firm to firm or concern to concern because a particular technique which may be found suitable in a particular case may not be considered indispensable in other cases, that's why it sometimes becomes a vexed problem in management.

I think, it is now clear to you regarding Cost Control and Cost Reduction.

Is there any question from you?

☐ "Sir, we have followed your lecture. Sir, would you please enlighten us the managerial problems relating to Cost Control."

● I am very glad to see that you have taken much interest in this area.

You see, there is no doubt that the experiences of other concerns may provide tangible guide to other concerns but for that it should not be assumed that cent percent results of the other concerns will be realised in actual practice. If some result is to be obtained the experiences of other concerns are to be cut to size or the same are to be scrutinised for their proper application. For this, management information services are to be developed at all levels of management. It is a fact that decision-making would be more effective if the relevant data are communicated through report to the top management. Standard Costs and Budgets are the top management reports which are used as control device. However, standard and budgetary process help to exercise control at three points, namely the budget, appropriation and the expenditure. Whatever may be the points of control, it is a fact that control also helps better coordination. But it cannot be denied that deviation may be due to errors contained in the budget itself. These errors are mostly unforeseen. They are revealed after the sales and production budget or forecasts are prepared. This is due to the fact that different standards and budgets are based on the objective forecast based on the analysis of the past. A subjective approach in the preparation of standard cost and budget is welcome; and this subjective approach should be based on the past analysis, present judgement and intuition of the future. As for example, a standard or budget will produce an adverse result in actual practise if it does not take into account the rising prices in setting up a new preparation of the budgets. Cost of yesterday is not equal to the cost of today and cost of today will not be equal to the cost of tomorrow due to rising prices in the economy. Here time factor plays a dominant role in regulating cost control theory. Production, material and labour cost varies from time to time, place to place and person to person. For this the management and cost consultant should be well versed with the concept of 'time', 'place' and 'authority'; management should adopt a dynamic approach by introducing control budget 'system'. 'Controllable direct expenses in the budget are based upon foreman's estimates of expense for the coming period. Sometimes these estimates are too low. The cost department may know from past experience that some particular foreman is too optimistic on certain points. For this reason it will change the foreman's estimate to correspond to past experience and will include the adjusted figure in the normal expense budget'. Another problem which top management faces is the problem of Man-Management in cost control. This human relation is a problem area over which accounting impinges at many points, such as problem of integration of planning and control activities as well as problem of techniques etc.

Management Problem relating to Cost Control

In actual practice it becomes very difficult to control those people who affect cost. For this, motivation of the people can be developed. This can be done in three ways :

(i) Persuasion

(i) Monetary incentives—production bonus, profit bonus etc.

(iii) Administrative pressure for cost control.

This administrative pressure can be created through budgets which aim at cost control, for 'budgets are thought of as pressure device.' It becomes very difficult to create administrative pressure unless organisational structure is clearly defined and responsibility areas are properly located. For this, some training is necessary and a few concepts should be explained to those who administer cost. Mr. Dickey had rightly said in his book "Cost and Management" that 'It seems advisable to provide some specific training in human relations for those who administer cost control. An individual who had no training in accounting or in production techniques would seem an unlikely person to be put in charge of a budget. Since the aim of control devices is to influence the action of people, it seems equally important to include in the training of administrator's cost control programme some study of the art of influencing people.

Are you facing any problem?

☐ "No Sir, your lectures appear to us as a store of value; but Sir please say something on Cost Saving."

• Well, have a look on the Board where I am showing potential areas of leakage and Cost Saving.

Potential Areas of Leakage and Cost Saving

Areas of Cost Savings

(1) Material | **(2) Labour** | **(3) Time** | **(4) Organisation** | **(5) Method Study** | **(6) Production Design**

The above are the cost-saving areas. If the causes of excessive costs of the above factors are found out it would be possible on the part of the top management to take its decision accordingly. The causes are explained below chronologically :

1. **Material**
   (i) Excessive quantity of material
   (ii) Excessive material scrap
   (iii) Inefficient purchase of raw materials which are sometimes not in keeping with the requirement
   (iv) Lack of facilities for recovering byproduct
2. **Labour**
   (i) Failure to motivate man-power
   (ii) Failure to coordinate man-power
   (iii) Failure to control man-power
   (iv) Failure to study man, material and labour relationship

(v) Failure to employ efficient employees for higher production and productivity

(vi) Failure to detect social conditions and the impact of strikes and lockouts and go-slow tactics of the labourers

3. **Time**

(i) Failure to minimise time wastage

(ii) Failure to speed-up operation

(iii) Failure to run longer machine batches

(iv) Failure to increase effective working through overtime shift work

(v) Failure to implement proper planning for preventive maintenance—the introduction of this plan may stop idle machine hour

4. **Organisation**

(i) Failure to define adequately clear policy

(ii) Failure to introduce responsibility accounting in all levels and stages of production and management

(iii) Failure to motivate the employees and workers through persuasion, monetary incentives and administrative pressure

5. **Method Study**

(i) Failure to implement organisation and method study

(ii) Failure to layout the capital assets properly

(iii) Failure to implement adequate and planned maintenance

(iv) Failure to reduce excessive gap in idleness of machines

6. **Product design**

(i) Failure to realise that better product design is a defence against rising cost

(ii) Failure to examine the cost of product at the design stage

(iii) Failure to take into consideration the other aspects viz, handling, packing, storage, transports and, finally, marketability of the product.

● You please stand up.

☐ "Sir, am I?"

● No, you not, next to you, why you gentleman talking with each other?

☐ "Sir, I asked him what are the techniques of Cost Control."

● You see, I am here for your help, please direct your attention on the Board where I have shown what you want to know.

Techniques of Cost Control

Cost Control can be made more effective if the following techniques are introduced at all levels of management :

1. Work Study
2. Control Ratios
3. Cost Audit
4. Responsibility Accounting.

1. **Work Study :** It is one of the effective tools of Cost Control. It consists of Method Study and Work Measurement. It is concerned with steady and continuous check on the standard techniques and methods of work. Work Measurement provides a prefect basis for wage and labour control and implementation of incentive schemes; Method Study on the other hand is concerned with studying critically the existing and proposed method of study for their future improvement for both Product Design and Cost Control.

Objectives of Work Study are

(i) To conserve material, quality control and cost reduction.

(ii) To achieve and ensure the maximum effectiveness of skill for volume of work available to every individual and worker.

(iii) To show a direct path for the overall achievement of highest productivity of the enterprise.

As perfect standards are set for machine and labour under work study method, it becomes very easy to operate cost control. Because, cost control is concerned with predetermined cost. Method Study and Wrok Measurement guard the management against possible losses arising from lack of time and motion study.

2. **Control Ratios :** A number of ratios may be used as measure of cost control. These ratios can be measured with the predetermined ratios or these can be compared with the last year's performance and effective control measures can be suggested.

A. **Expense Ratios :** These ratios indicate the areas of excessive cost in relation to total sales.

(i) $\frac{\text{Factory Cost}}{\text{Sales}}$

(ii) $\frac{\text{Administration Cost}}{\text{Sales}}$

(iii) $\frac{\text{Research and Development Cost}}{\text{Sales}}$

(iv) $\frac{\text{Capital Expenditure}}{\text{Sales}}$

(v) $\frac{\text{Selling and Distribution Cost}}{\text{Sales}}$

B. **Efficiency Ratio :** The efficiency of producing a stated output can be found from this ratio :

$$\frac{\text{Allowed Hours}}{\text{Actual Hours for Actual Output}} \times 100$$

C. **Activity Ratio :** This ratio indicates the activity of the operation. It brings a relationship between the budgeted output and completed output.

$$\frac{\text{Allowed Hours}}{\text{Standard Hours for Budgeted Output}} \times 100$$

D. **Capacity Ratio :** This is termed as Volume Ratio. It brings a relationship between the actual hours worked and budgeted hours. This ratio indicates to what extent the available hours have been utilised :

$$\frac{\text{Actual Hours Worked}}{\text{Budgeted Hours}} \times 100$$

Functions of Cost Audit

3. **Cost Audit :** Of all the factors which accelerate the profit of the organisation, the most important is cost. Cost and its control plays a vital role towards the achievement of business philosophy. Verification of all costing figures and cost plans are the basis of cost audit. Cost Audit may be defined as 'The verification of Cost Accounts and a check on adherence to the Cost Accounting Plan'.

Major functions of Cost Audit may be summed up as :

(i) To vouch and verify cost accounts

(ii) To make a comparison between costing plan and actual performance

(iii) To facilitate internal control by pointing out the areas of exception. However, effective cost control mechanism does not only confine itself to the examination of cost accounts but also probe into the principles involved in the ascertainment of cost as well as technique. The differences between the ideas of what cost is and what cost should be, or should have been—these would lead the management consultant to make overall scrutiny of the following for the effective control of cost :

(a) Ascertainment and allocation of cost

(b) Distribution of overhead expense

(c) Valuation of closing stock

(d) Techniques involved in cost

(e) Correctness of cost accounts, statement, report and, finally, cost data.

Responsibility Accounting

4. **Responsibility Accounting :** It is a system of accounting whereby result of operating performance—which are subject to control—are reported at the various levels of management. 'Responsibility Accounting is a system whereby cost flows up the organisational lines and is accumulated and reported at the various levels of responsibility. The philosophy behind this is that the best way to control cost is to delegate responsibility to individuals define their responsibility, give them

an idea of what constitutes effective performance of their job and report back about how they are going. If the latter step is to be accomplished, costs must be classified or segregated so that they can be summarised firstly on the basis of 'who did it' and then 'reshuffled' to arrive at conventional product or process cost'. So the essence of Responsibility Accounting lies in the fact that after the identification of the responsibility areas, cost must be accounted as per specified area.

Well, in this respect I sugest you to go through chapter 31 of the book where I have discussed Responsibility Accounting in detail.

☐ "Excuse me Sir, please explain why Cost Control is necessary?"

● Please have a look on the Board.

Why Cost Control

The gist of the aforesaid discussions reveals that top management controls cost not only to earn more profit but also with a view :

Need for Cost Control

(i) To keep the 'integrity' of the capital of the business; thus to prevent 'capital erosion' arising out of non-control of cost and expenditure

(ii) To face competition in existing industry.

(iii) To social control of business through control of cost for production of quality and quantity goods for common people at a reduced price.

● I am glad to see that you have gone into the deep of the subject. That's why; you are putting different types of questions.

Is there any question from your side?

☐ "Sir, I have one question to ask but I feel for you that you are taking two class for about two hours."

● Well, are you feeling brave or tired.

☐ "No Sir."

● Then what is your question. You see if my students are not tired I am not tired you are my inspiration for my success. What is your question.

☐ "Sir, tell us something about the **Evaluation of the Concept of Cost Control**."

● Well, take down a note on it.

1. **Project Evaluation :** The term projects, progarmmes, plans etc. are apparently synonymous but they differ from each other if we go deeper into the matter. For correct evaluation we may divide plan into sector. This sector is project. Out of the many projects, which one would be more profitable and will have top priority? The problem of choice is the fundamental point of project evaluation. In order to choose one project which will receive early priority in relation to total resources, the management will have to find out the criteria—the basis on which selection will be made. This criterion is the Benefit Ratio :

Project Evaluation as an Approach to Cost Control

$$\text{Benefit Cost Ratio} = \frac{\text{Benefit}}{\text{Cost}}$$

Project Cost Rs. 2,338

	Rs.
(a) Value of benefit after operation	65,000
(b) Value of the benefit before operation	37,000
(c) Increase in the value of benefit (a – b)	28,000
(d) Associated Cost	8,000
Net Benefit (c – d)	20,000

$$\text{Benefit Cost Ratio} = \frac{\text{Benefit}}{\text{Cost}} = \frac{20{,}000}{2{,}338} = \text{Rs. } 8.55 \text{ (app.)}$$

A particular project will be welcome if the ratio is high and it will be rejected if the ratio shows a low figure. The relationship between benefit and cost will relieve management consultants from anxiety arising from initial increase in cost.

In modern management thinking on cost control, project evaluation includes :

(i) Search for Investment Opportunity

(ii) Search for Economic and Technical Study

(iii) Search for Market Research

(iv) Search for Cost-Volume-Profit Benefit

(v) Search for the calculation of financial tests of Investment Worth.

Concept of Value Analysis

2. **Value Analysis :** Value Analysis is a concept of saving cost from the point of view value. That is to say, it finds an alternative way to provide a function at lower cost without injuring the end performance or quality. 'At a certain factory, substitution of polythene (cheaper material) for stainless steel for a certain component brought down the overall cost of the product by nearly 7 percent. Similarly at another office, replacement of expensive quality of paper and envelops for internal use reduced the stationery costs by about 9 percent (again a cheaper material). However, at a foundry, the use of alloy steel (costlier material) instead of cast iron for a certain machinery component brought down the total cost of component by 4 percent, as the quality of alloy steel needed was much less than that of cast iron to meet the same function.' In a planned economy the need for such devices to cost conrol cannot be overstressed.

QUESTIONS

1. What is Cost Control? How it is related with the aspect of Management Decision?
2. Distinguish between Cost Control and Cost Reduction.
3. Explain the potential areas of Cost Leakages and Cost Savings.
4. Explain the following terms : (a) Responsibility Accounting, (b) Activity Ratio, (c) Capacity Ratio, (d) Project Evaluation, (e) Value Analysis.

34

ACCOUNTING CONTROL—INTERNAL, MANAGEMENT, COST AND APPRAISAL AUDIT

● Good afternoon to you all.

□ "Good afternoon Sir."

● Now I will discuss about Internal, Management and Cost Audit, separately, because these concepts are co-related and interlinked.

Need for Control in Business

You know that with the expansion of business, it becomes very difficult to coordinate all the departments under suitable footing. Because the proprietor of the business is removed far from the different affairs of the business because of the inherent and created complexities of the business. To overcome the adverse stages should be the ultimate object of the business. This is only possible if accounting control is applied in all the systems of business and process of management.

The accounting control can be subdivided into Financial, Management and Cost Audit. Sir John Morison, G. B. E., C.A., is of opinion that 'the longer the business and the more removed the proprietor is from day to day management details, the more important become the instruments of control. One of the instruments is Internal Audit.'

It should be noted in this context that a business is a continuous process. To keep this process of business running successfully, it is necessary that Accounting Control should be designed :

Principles of Accounting Control

(i) To keep high the integrity of the capital structure of the business

(ii) To keep running the future stability of the business

(iii) To keep the morale of the investor high.

However, Accounting Control can be explained as :

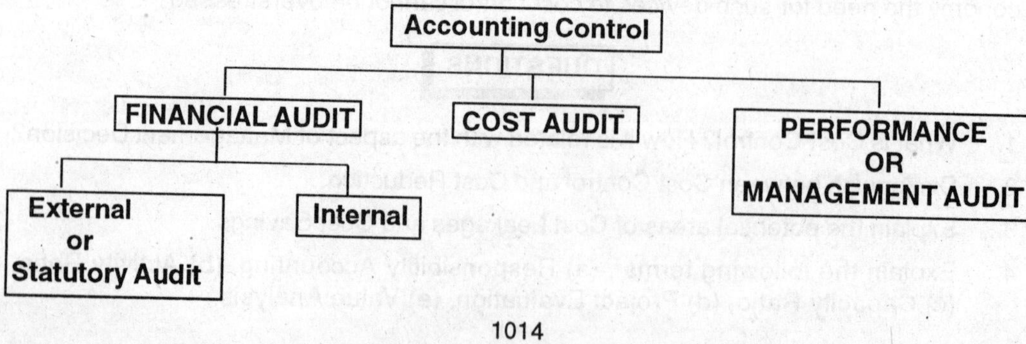

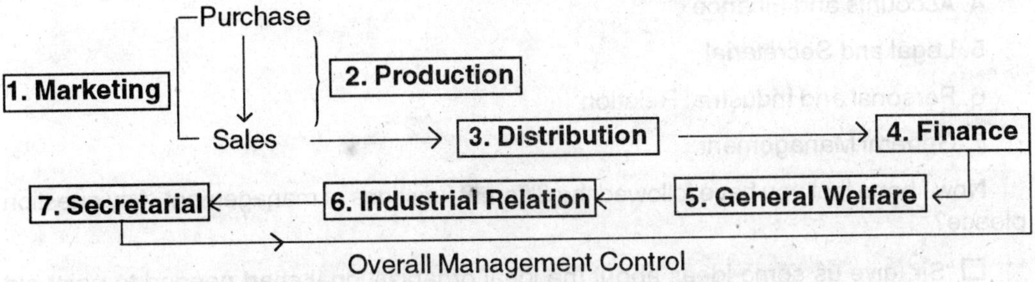

I think you have followed the stage of the evaluation of Management Audit.

☐ "No Sir, I cannot follow".

● Well, If you think over the affairs of the business, you will see that a business must have the following sides or wings :

Now, Management Audit indicates the overall supervision and control of the function of management. "Any management audit, therefore, to be effective, must check up on the organisation and effective working of each of these functions in turn. A clear understanding of organisation in relation to management responsibilities is of the greatest importance in management audit work."

Well, I think, you have understood the underlying philosophy behind Management Audit.

☐ "Yes Sir, but Sir ...."

● Yes, please be frank, what is your difficulty, tell me frankly.

☐ "Sir, what are the areas of business where Management Audit can play a vital role in assessing the performance?"

● Oh, but I have discussed all these areas earlier. The areas of management are :

Areas and Functions of Management

(i) Marketing
(ii) Production
(iii) Distribution
(iv) Finance
(v) General Welfare
(vi) Industrial Relation
(vii) Secretarial.

However, I would like to point out in this connection that The Institute of Industrial Administration recommended that the 'primary functions of management' should consist of :

1. Production
2. Distribution
3. Development

4. Accounts and Finance
5. Legal and Secretarial
6. Personal and Industrial Relation
7. General Management.

Now I hope that you have followed the different functions of management. Any question please?

☐ "Sir, give us some ideas about the ideal organisational chart needed to point out management responsibilities."

● Well, please note the chart :

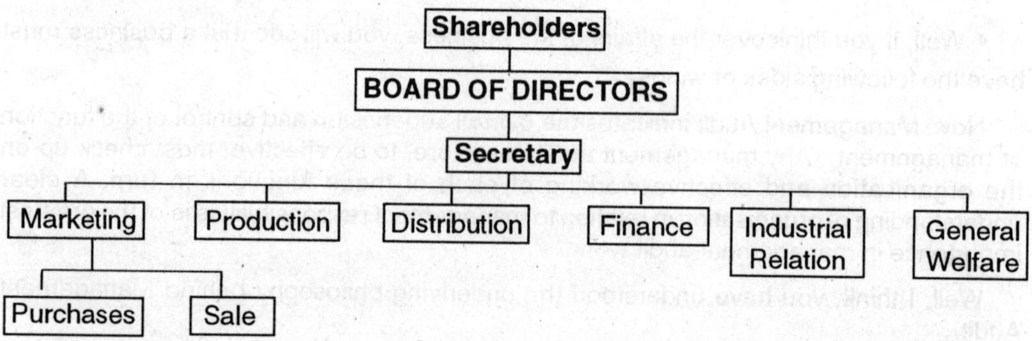

Now it becomes very difficult to achieve coordination and control among all departments of the business. Lack of proper coordination among the different departments of a business may bring loss. In this repsect the management auditors can play an important role.

Need for Management Audit

Because the management auditor acts as an coordinator the appointment of Management Auditor in the business does not indicate that the importance of the Secretary of the business is neglected, rather, it accelerates the progress of the business. That the Management Audit helps the business towards the achievement of higher profit and productivity was felt by Mr. T. G. Ross when he says 'An audit for management, on the other hand, may reveal a state of affairs which, though not at the moment causing a trading loss, may before long bring about that loss if steps are not taken to rectify what the management audit shows to be faulty. In other words, the management audit can prevent financial loss before it occurs, whilst the financial audit can only establish the fact that a loss has been made.'

☐ "Sir, is Management Audit a new idea?"

Origin of Management Audit

● Well, If you think about accounting evolution you will see that management audit is the third stage in the process of accounting evolution. That is to say, financial audit and cost audit are designed for the benefit of management needs. So the concept is not new but the manner in which it is implemented is definitely a new approach.

(1) Financial Audit → (2) Cost Audit → { (1) Financial Audit, (2) Cost Audit, (3) Performance Audit }

↑ Management Audit

↓

Appraisal Audit

Now I hope you have followed the whole discussion.

☐ "Sir, I shall be obliged if you please give us some idea about the Advantages and Functions of Management Audit."

• The functions of Management Audit can be summed up as :

Functions of Management Audit

1. To scrutinise and audit the different functions of management
2. To assess management efficiency
3. To review financial accounting and management control in light of management planning and decision
4. To verify the different stages of execution of policy and decision-making. 'At this point it should be emphasised once more that it certainly would not be a part of the management auditor's duties to challenge the general policy of the concern'. This is only to assist the top management to rectify their defects.

However, the functions and objects of Management Audit will be more clear to us if we consult the definition given by Professor B.K. Basu in his book "*An Insight into Auditing — a multidimensional approach*" :

Meaning of Management Audit

"The management audit may be defined as a comprehensive, constructive and appraisal and examination of organisational structure of a concern, its plan, objective, means of operation and use of physical facilities."

Advantages

Advantages of Management Audit

(i) It helps management in arriving at proper management decision.

(ii) It tries to bring a cordial relation between the top management and other departments of the company.

(iii) It provides a training ground for the young and busy executives.

(iv) It can check trading loss before it occurs by providing the top management adequate information needed for this purpose.

(v) As the management audit approaches its control through organisation chart, it brings a new system of accounting known as Responsibility Accounting which aids the management in arriving at its management decision.

I think you have followed my lecture. Any other point you would like to put to me?

☐ "Sir, Is there any fundamental difference between Management Audit and Internal Audit?"

• You see, apparently there is no fundamental difference between the two; since both are designed for the benefit of the management needs.

Difference between Management Audit and Internal Audit

Only difference is that the former keeps a constant watch on the overall performance of the company; while the latter keeps a constant watch 'on the system of internal check and the application of normal auditing method.'

Did you follow what I say?

☐ "Still Sir, I cannot understand the concept of overall performance of the company."

• Well, do you remember the different functions of management—marketing, production, distribution, finance and accounts etc.?

☐ "Yes Sir."

• Well, Management Audit controls overall the activities of the management. This indicates the overall performance of the business.

Did you follow?

☐ "Yes Sir."

• In my next part of lecture I would like to discuss in detail the concept of Cost Audit—a part of Management Audit.

Cost Audit

Meaning of Cost Audit

Now I would like to discuss about Cost Audit. I think you remember my last part of lecture where I classified accounting control under three heads—Financial Audit, Cost Audit, and Management Audit. It was also explained that Financial and Cost Audit are to be designed for the benefits of the management and business needs. However, it should be noted in this connection that every business must have some philosophy—as I explained earlier.

It should be noted in this connection that of all the factors which accelerate profit, the most important is cost. It plays a vital role towards the achievement of business philosophy. It regulates the whole process. Verification of all costing figures and cost plan is the basis of cost audit. However, cost audit may be defined as the verification of 'the correctness of accounts and of the adherence to the cost accounting plan'.

☐ "Sir, what are the functions of Cost Audit?"

• Well, I have already discussed the functions of cost audit in course of my lecture. The functions of cost audit may be summed up as :

Functions of Cost Audit

(i) To assist the top management in the formulation of policy

(ii) To vouch and verify cost accounts

(iii) To make a comparison costing plan with actual performance

(iv) To facilitate internal control by pointing out the areas of exception.

However, if you are interested to know about the procedure of Audit of Cost Accounts in actual practice, please consult Sec. 233B of The Companies Act, 1956, as amended in 1961.

I think you have followed what Cost Audit is.

Is there any question please?

☐ "Sir, would you kindly enlighten us about the concept of Appraisal Audit?"

• Appraisal Audit

Here I would like to give you a summary of my lecture on Appraisal Audit which I delivered at the First All India Summer Institute of Commerce held at the University of Calcutta.

The discussions on the topic was made on the following line of approach :

(1) Philosophy of Audit

(2) Appraisal of the concept 'True and Fair'

(3) Functions of Audit

(4) Extended Meaning of Audit

(5) Components of Appraisal Audit

(6) Role of the Auditor.

However, a summary of the lecture is given here for your study. Note it very carefully.

Philosophy of Audit

Philosophy of Audit

Though the work of the auditor may not be directly needed for the operation of the business, yet it is concerned with appraisal, interpretation analysis and valuation. For that it should not be assumed that the auditor is a professional 'appraisal analyst' or 'valuer'. However the auditor is under the statutory and/or moral obligation to protect or to look to the interest of various parties who are eager to know the 'state of affairs' of the business or firm. Therefore, he has to appraise and certify (i) 'Accuracy', and (ii) 'True and Fair' view of the financial statement as required by the law and generally accepted accounting principles and postulates. In fact, the modern concept of audit goes much beyond the statutory requirements.

Appraisal of the Concept 'True and Fair'

True and fair

'Fairness' of financial statements means : (a) Freedom from 'bias' and 'dishonesty' and (b) Completeness of information. 'Trueness' of financial statements means that the books of accounts are representative of the actual happenings of business.

The auditor should appraise 'true and fair' view in the light of the following conventions of accounting :

(i) Objectivity

(ii) Disclosure
(iii) Consistency
(iv) Materiality
(v) Conservatism.

Functions of Audit

Functions of Audit

Examination of books of accounts, with supporting vouchers and documents, in order to detect and prevent errors and fraud is the main function of auditing. As the nature and extent of work of the auditor is complicated and voluminous, it is not possible for him to make a complete and detailed examination of all records and documents. So he has to depend on the internal check system of the company or firm which he audits. Besides, in most of the cases, his examination is limited to a 'programme of test' or 'sample study' of accounting record which leaves the chances of a few errors and frauds remaining undetected. So this opinion regarding 'accuracy' and 'true and fair view', in most of the cases, is dependent on the system of internal check and 'programme of test' on which he has to depend. So, to have more 'precision' in his report, the auditor should appraise the system of internal check, avoid the strain of examining the inherent limitation of accounting process. And, moreover, to save time and cost of making an audit, the auditor, in most of the cases, has to depend on the Internal Audit Department of the business or firm. For that he should appraise the principles and purpose of the internal audit system of the firm.

Extended Meaning of Audit

Accounting Control

It has been stated earlier that the modern concept of audit goes much beyond the statutory requirements. So auditing can be defined as accounting control and it should be based on the concept of Environment Audit. That is to say, the audit work should entail rightness of expenditure incurred, appraisal of motives for the control of cost, etc.

Components of Appraisal Audit

Components of Audit

(i) Cost Audit
(ii) Management Audit
(iii) Operation Audit
(iv) Responsibility Audit
(v) Propriety Audit.

Role of Auditor

Role of Auditor

(i) To appraise the past accounting happenings and present system
(ii) To appraise the different inherent accounting leakage
(iii) To appraise the potentiality of future growth and operation of business.

I hope you have followed the discussions made earlier. Is there any question?

☐ "Yes Sir, I have two questions."

● What are your questions?

☐ "Sir, under the caption 'Function of Audit', you have used the words elements of audit, what are the elements of audit?"

• Well, note here the elements of Internal Audit :

ELEMENTS OF INTERNAL AUDIT

VERIFICATION | ANALYSIS | COMPLIANCE | APPRAISAL | REPORTING

Well, what is your other question?

☐ "Sir, what is Propriety Audit?"

• You see, the main aim of propriety audit is to analyse the rightness of management decision and to see that whether a particular cost or project ought to have been incurred or under taken or not. It questions the very basis of initiation of a cost project.

☐ "Excuse me Sir, please give us a title of a book from where we may get details of different concepts of auditing."

• Here I suggest you to go through a book titled "*An Insight into Auditing—A Multidimensional Approach*" written by Prof Dr. B. K. Basu.

QUESTIONS

1. What is Management Audit? What are its advantages?
2. What is Internal Audit? What are its components?
3. "The extended meaning of Audit is Accounting Control"—Explain.
4. What is Appraisal Audit? Explain its different aspects.
5. Write short notes on :

   (a) Cost Audit (b) Propriety Audit (c) Efficiency Audit (d) Responsibility Audit.

35

HOLDING COMPANY

☐ "Good evening Sir."

● Good evening.

Well, as per my previous talks with you, I would like to take up for discussion Holding Company.

☐ "Sir, is there any difference between Holding Company and Consolidated Accounts?"

● Yes, definitely there exist differences :

Holding company refers to a company which holds majority of equity shares of one or more companies (called subsidiary company(ies) or having power to appoint either directly or indirectly (i.e. through subsidiary) whole or majority of directors in the Board of Directors of those company(ies) and thus have control over those company(ies). On the other hand, Consolidated Accounts mean accounts of holding company and its subsidiary(ies) as a single entity in a consolidated form.

Did you follow?

☐ "Yes Sir."

● Now I will discuss about different aspects of Holding Company and Subsidiaries as well as different critical points for the solution of Consolidated Accounts.

Concept of Holding Company

You see, in day-to-day life we find trading concern. But in addition to trading function most of the companies are found in actual practice to invest a major portion of their share capital by purchasing shares of other company or companies which, under the situation, are termed as Subsidiary Company or Companies. Under the circumstances no direct trading operations are carried on. The main aim of investment in shares of subsidiaries is to enforce effective control in the management of the Subsidiary Companies. Well, you see, the Holding Company is known as "Parent" Company. I think you have followed.

☐ "Yes Sir."

Is there any question?

☐ "Sir, what are the factors which motivate the introduction of Holding Companies?"

• Well, please note that economies of scale of production, easier methods of raising of finance, elimination of expensive competition—all are factors which motivate towards the introduction of Holding Company.

□ "Sir, I have one question to place before you."

• Yes, you can speak frankly.

□ "Sir, is the identity of Subsidiary Companies lost because of the existence of controlling power of Holding Company?"

• No, definitely not. The Subsidiary Companies possess identity and entity of their own. And, as such, they maintain their separate Goodwill.

Do you follow?

□ "Yes Sir, but Sir..."

• Yes?

□ "Sir, what is the **legal definition of Subsidiary Company** and what are the procedures of presentation of accounts of Subsidary Companies by Holding Company?"

• Well, for that I refer you the Section 4 of the Companies Act, 1956, for definition and Section 212 to 214 of the Companies Act for Presentation of Accounts. However, I am placing before you the said sections for your ready reference. Please note :

Sec. 4. Meaning of 'holding company' and 'subsidiary'.

(1) For the purposes of this Act, a company shall, subject to the provisions of sub-section (3) be deemed to be a subsidiary of another if, but only if,—

(a) that other controls the composition of its Board of Directors; or

(b) that other —

(i) where the first mentioned company is an existing company in respect of which the holders of preference shares issued before the commencement of this Act have the same voting rights in all respects as the holders of equity shares, exercises or controls more than half of the total voting power of such company;

(ii) where the first mentioned company is any other company, holds more than half the nominal value of its equity share capital; or

(c) the first mentioned company is a subsidiary of any company which is that other's subsidiary.

Illustration

Company B is a subsidiary of Company A, and Company C is a subsidiary of Company B. Company C is a subsidiary of Company A, by virtue of clause (c) above. If Company D is a subsidiary of Company C, Company D will be a subsidiary of Company B and, consequently, also of Company A, by virtue of clause (c) above; and so on.

(2) For the purposes of sub-section (i) the composition of a company's Board of Directors shall be deemed to be controlled by another company if, but only if, that other company by the exercise of some powers exercisable by it at its discretion without the

consent or concurrence of any other person, can appoint or remove the holders of all or a majority of the directorships; but for the purposes of this provision that other company shall be deemed to have power to appoint to a directorship with respect to which any of the following conditions are satisfied, that is to say—

(a) that a person cannot be appointed thereto without the exercise in his favour by that other company of such a power as aforesaid;

(b) that a person's appointment thereto follows necessarily from his appointment as director, managing agent, secretaries and treasurers, or manager of, or to any other office of empolyment in, that other comopany; or

(c) that the directorship is held by an individual nominated by that other company or a subsdiary thereof.

(3) In determining whether one company is a subsidiary of another—

(a) any shares held or power exercisable by that other company in a fiduciary capacity shall be treated as not held or exercisable by it.

(b) subject to the provisions of clauses (c) and (d), any shares held or power exercisable—

(i) by any person as a nominee for that other company (except where that other is concerned only in a fiduciary capacity); or

(ii) by, or by a nominee for, a subsidiary of that other company, not being a subsidiary which is concerned only in a fiduciary capacity;

shall be treated as held or exercisable by that other company;

(c) any shares held or power exercisable by any person by virtue of the provisions of any debentures of the first mentioned company or of a trust deed for securing any issue of such debentures shall be disregarded;

(d) any shares held or power exercisable by, or by a nominee for, that other or its subsidiary (not being held or exercisable as mentioned in clause (c)) shall be treated as not held or exercisable by that other, if the ordinary business of that other or its subsidary, as the case may be, includes the lending of money and the shares are held or the power is exercisable as aforesaid by way of security for the purposes of a transaction entered in the ordinary course of that business.

(4) For the purpose of this Act a company shall be deemed to be the holding company of another if, but only if, that other is its subsidiary.

(5) In this section, the expression "company" includes any body corporate and the expression "equity share capital" has the same meaning as in sub-section (2) of Section 85.

(6) In the case of a body corporate which is incorporated in a country ouside India, a subsidiary or holding company of the body corporate under the law of such country shall be deemed to be a subsidiary or holding company of the body corporate within the meaning and for the purposes of this Act also, whether the requirements of this section are fulfilled or not.

(7) A private company, being a subsidiary of a body corporate incorporated outside India, which, if incorporated in India, would be a public company within the meaning of

this Act, shall be deemed for the purposes of this Act to be a subsidiary of a public company if the entire share capital in that private company is not held by that body corporate whether alone or together with one or more other bodies corporate incorporated outside India.

Sec. 212. "Balance Sheet of holding company to include certain particulars as to its subsidiaries — (1)There shall be attached to the balance sheet of a holding company having a subsidiary or subsidiaries at the end of the financial year as at which the holding company's balance sheet is made out, the following documents in respect of such subsidiary or of each subsidiary, as the case may be :

(a) a copy of the balance sheet of the subsidiary;

(b) a copy of its profit and loss account;

(c) a copy of the report of its Board of Directors;

(d) a copy of the report of its auditors;

(e) statement of the holding company's interest in the subsidiary as specified in sub-section (3);

(f) the statement referred to in sub-section (5), if any; and

(g) the report referred to in sub-section (6), if any.

(2) (a).The balance sheet referred to in clause (a) of sub-section (1) shall be made out in accordance with the requirements of this Act—

(i) as at the end of the financial year of the subsidiary, where such financial year coincides with the financial year of the holding company;

(ii) as at the end of the financial year of the subsidiary last before that of the holding company where the financial year of the subsidiary does not coincide with that of the holding company.

(b) The profit and loss account and the reports of the Board of Directors and of the auditors, referred to in clauses (b), (c) and (d) of subsection (1), shall be made out, in accordance with the requirements of this Act, for the financial year of the subsidiary referred to in clause (a).

(c) Where the financial year of the subsidiary does not coincide with that of the holding company, the financial year aforesaid of the subsidary shall not end on a day which precedes the day on which the holding company's financial year ends by more than six months.

(d) Where the financial year of a subsidiary is shorter in duration than that of its holding company, reference to the financial year of the subsidiary in clauses (a), (b) and (c) shall be construed as reference to two or more financial years of the subsidiary the duration of which, in the aggregate, is not less than the duration of the holding company's financial year.

(3) The statement referred to in clause (e) of sub-section (1) shall specify—

(a) the extent of the holding company's interest in subsidiary at the end of the financial year or of the last of the financial years of the subsidiary referred to in sub-section (2) :

(b) the net aggregate amount so far as it concerns members of the holding company and is not dealt with in the company's accounts, of the subsidiary's profits after deducting its losses, or vice versa—

(i) for the financial year or years of the subsidiary aforesaid; and

(ii) for the previous financial years of the subsidiary since it became the holding company's subsidiary.

(c) the net aggregate amount of the profits of the subsidiary after deducting its losses, or vice versa—

(i) for the financial year or years of the subsidiary aforesaid; and

(ii) for the previous financial years of the subsidiary since it became the holding company's subsidiary;

so far as those profits are dealt with, or provisions is made for those losses in the company's accounts.

(4) Clauses (b) and (c) of sub-section (3) shall apply only to profits and losses of the subsidiary which may properly be treated in the holding company's accounts as revenue profits or losses and the profits or losses attributable to any shares in a subsidiary for the time being held by the holding company or any other of its subsidiaries shall not (for that or any other purpose) be treated as aforesaid so far as they are profits or losses for the period before the date on or as from which the shares were acquired by the company or any of its subsidiaries, except that they may in a proper case be so treated where—

(a) the company is itself the subsidiary of another body corporate;

(b) the shares were acquired from that body corporate or a subsidiary of it;

and for the purposes of determining whether any profits or losses are to be treated as profits or losses for the said period, the profit or loss for any financial year of the subsidiary may, if it is not practicable to apportion it with reasonable accuracy by reference to the facts, be treated as accruing from day to day during that year and be apportioned accordingly.

(5) Where the financial year or years of a subsidiary referred to in sub-section (2) do not coincide with the financial year of the holding company, a statement containing information on the following matters shall also be attached to the balance sheet of the holding company—

(a) whether there has been any, and, if so, what change in the holding company's interest in the subsidiary between the end of the financial year or of the last of the financial years of the subsidiary and the end of the holding company's financial year;

(b) details of any material change which have occurred between the end of the financial year or of the last of the financial years of the subsidiary and the end of the holding company's financial year in respect of—

(i) the subsidiary's fixed assets;

(ii) its investments;

(iii) the moneys lent by it;

(iv) the money borrowed by it for any purpose other than that of meeting current liabilities.

(6) If, for any reason, the Board of Directors of the holding company is unable to obtain information on any of the matters required to be specified by sub-section (4), a report in writing to that effect shall be attached to the balance sheet of holding company.

(7) The documents referred to in clauses (e), (f) and (g) of sub-section (1) shall be signed by the persons by whom the balance sheet of the holding company is required to be signed.

(8) The Central Government may, on the application or with the consent of the Board of Directors of the company, direct that, in relation to any subsidiary, the provisions of this section shall not apply, or shall apply only to such extent as may be specified in the direction.

(9) If any such person, as is referred to in sub-section (6) of Section 209, fails to take all reasonable steps to comply with the provisions of this section, he shall, in respect of each offence, be punishable with imprisonment for a term which may extend to six months or with fine which may extend to one thousand rupees, or with both :

Provided that in any proceedings against a person in respect of an offence under this section, it shall be a defence to prove that a competent and reliable person was charged with the duty of seeing that the provisions of this section were complied with and was in a position to discharge that duty;

Provided further that no person shall be sentenced to imprisonment for any such offence unless it was committed wilfully.

(10) If any person not being a person referred to in sub-section (6) of Section 209, having been charged by the managing agent, secretaries and treasurers, managing director, manager or Board of Directors, as the case may be, with the duty of seeing that the provisions of this section are complied with, makes default in doing so, he shall, in respect of each offence, be punishable with imprisonment for a term which may extend to six months, or with fine which may extend to one thousand rupees, or with both :

Provided that no person shall be sentenced to imprisionment for any offence unless it was committed wilfully.

Sec. 213. Financial year of holding company and subsidiary—(1) Where it appears to the Central Government desirable for a holding company or a holding company's subsidiary to extend its financial year so that the subsidiary's fianancial year may end with that of the holding company, and for that purpose to postpone the submission of the relevant accounts to a general meeting, the Central Government may, on the application or with the consent of the Board of Directors of the company whose financial year is to be extended, direct that, in the case of that company, the submission of accounts to a general meeting, the holding of an annual general meeting or the making of an annual return shall not be required to be submitted, held or made, earlier than the dates specified in the direction notwithstanding anything to the contrary in this Act or in any other Act for the time being in force.

(2) The Central Government shall, on the application of the Board of Directors of a holding company or a holding company's subsidiary, exercise the powers conferred in that Government by sub-section (1) if it is necessary to do so, in order to secure that the end of the financial year of the subsidiary does not precede the end of the holding

company's financial year by more than six months, where that is not the case at the commencement of this Act, or at the date on which the relationship of holding company and subsidiary comes into existance where that date is later than the commencement of this Act.

Sec. 214. Rights of holding company's representatives and members (1) A holding company may by resolution, authorise representatives named in the resolution to inspect the books of account kept by any of its subsidiaries; and the books of accounts of any such subsidiary shall be open to inspection by those representatives at any time during business hours.

(2) The rights conferred by Section 235 upon members of a company may be exercised, in respect of any subsidiary, by members of the holding company as if they alone were members of the subsidiary'.

Now the course of study of Holding Company and its subsidiary in general, can be classified under two heads :

(A) **General Holding**

(B) **Chain Holding**

By General Holding I mean the acquisition of shares of one or more companies by the Holding Company. Please note that from the date of acquisition a company which is acquired by the Holding Company is known as Subsidiary to Holding Company.

For example, A Co. acquired the Shares of B company or both B Company and C Company Here B Company and C Company become the subsidiary of A Co.

Again, General Holding may be of two types :

(i) Acquisition of major part of shares of other company

(ii) Acquisition of all the shares of the other company.

Well, regarding Chain Holding I am to say that the question of chain holding arises when there are more than two companies within the group companies having holding subsidiary relationship.

For example, A company holds majority of shares with voting rights of both B company and C company. Here both B Company and C Company are subsidiary companies of A company. Again, suppose, X Ltd. holds majority of shares with voting rights of Y Ltd. and Y Ltd. holds majority of shares with voting rights of Z Ltd. Here X Ltd. is holding company of both Y Ltd. (Directly) and Z Ltd. (Indirectly) and Y Ltd. is holding company of Z Ltd.

A in B	X Ltd. in Y Ltd.
A in C	Y Ltd. in Z Ltd.
A in B & C	∴ X Ltd. in Y Ltd. and Z Ltd.

☐ "Sir, is it possible to have two holding companies of a same subsidiary company?"

• Yes, it is possible. As per Accounting Standard Interpretation (ASI) 24 issued by the Institute of Chartered Accountants of India a subsidiary company can have two holding companies. If one company controls the composition of the Board of Directors and the other company controls the same company's majority of voting power, then the situation of two holding companies of one subsidiary company is possible. In this situation both holding companies will prepare consolidated Financial statements with the same subsidiary company.

I think, you have followed the above discussion. Now I would like to take up certain points which are prerequisite to the workings of Consolidated Profit and Loss Account and Balance Sheet.

☐ Sir, what is **Consolidated Profit and Loss Account** and **Consolidated Balance Sheet**?

You see, Consolidated Profit and Loss Account means that all the items of Holding and Subsidiary Company are to be totalled and should be represented under the caption say, H Ltd. and S Ltd. Consolidated Profit and Loss Account for the year ended...

Please note that different points are to be taken into account or better to say, different adjustments are to be made before proceeding to the mechanism of Consolidated Profit and Loss Account. Similarly, while preparing the Consolidated Balance Sheet, all the assets and liabilities of Holding and Subsidiary are to be totalled except the share capital amount of the subsidiary company. Because the share capital of the subsidiary consist of two parts :

(a) Shares of the Holding Company; and

(b) Residual part of the Share Capital not acquired by the Holding Company. The residual part represents Minority Interest.

So instead of taking into account the share capital belonging to Minority Interest in the original share capital, Minority shareholders are presented in the liability side of the Balance Sheet with amount of their Share Capital including their proportion of Capital Profit and Revenue Profit.

However, a new item, say Goodwill may be included in the list of asset side of consolidated Balance Sheet—depending on the nature of the situation.

☐ "Excuse me Sir, what is Capital Profit and what is Revenue Profit in this context?"

● You see, suppose the business is acquired on 30.6.06. So before 30.6.06 all profits are Capital Profit and after 30.6.06 all profits are Revenue Profit.

Date of Acquisition

Pre-Acquisition Profit	↓	Post-Acquisition Profit
or		or
Capital Profit	→ 30.6.06 ←	Revenue Profit

You see, the above concepts are not enough. Certain matters are to be included and excluded in the list of Capital Profit before segregating the amount for Subsidiary and Minority Interest. There may be increase or decrease in the book value of any asset.

I think, you have followed. Are there any question?

☐ "Sir Please explain the different points which are to be taken into account while preparing Consolidated Balance Sheet."

☐ "Sir, kindly enlighten us about the machanism how Goodwill is ascertained in this context and capital profit and revenue profit are apportioned between Subsidiary Co. and Minority Share Holders."

● I will explain every point relating to Holding Company and subsidiary. Now please note the following points which may be termed "Keys to the Solution" of any problem.

Points to be considered for preparing Consolidated Balance Sheet :

1. Basis of Distribution

Suppose, Holding Company H. Ltd. acquire $\frac{3}{5}$th share of the Subsidiary Company S. Ltd.; better to say, the Holding Co. enjoys the right of $\frac{3}{5}$th shares of its subsidiary. Then the basis of division will be :

H Ltd. = $\frac{3}{5}$th

Minority Shareholders = $\frac{2}{5}$th.

Take for an example :

Balance Sheet

Liabilities	H. Ltd.	S. Ltd.	Assets	H. Ltd.	S. Ltd.
	Rs.	Rs.		Rs.	Rs.
Share Capital	2,00,000	50,000			
—Shares of 100			300 shares in		
each			S Ltd. at cost	65,000	

Here total Shares of S. Ltd. is $\left(\frac{\text{Rs. } 50,000}{\text{Rs. } 100}\right)$ = 500 shares and out of which 300 shares are controlled by the Holding Company. So Holding Company's proportion = $\frac{300}{500}$ = $\frac{3}{5}$th, Minority $(1 - \frac{3}{5}) = \frac{2}{5}$th

2. Capital Profit or Pre-acquisition Profit

All profits earned by the company up to the date of acquisition by the Holding Company may be termed Capital Profit. And profit arising from the revaluation of assets should be added, and any losses arising from devaluation of any asset may be deducted from the pre-acquisition profit. This can be expressed as :

General Reserve			***
Profit and Loss Account as on 1st January			***
Profit up to date of acquisition		***	
Less : Pref. Dividend (½ yr.) or for any period (depending on the siuation)		***	
Add : Increase in Value of Machinery			***
Book Value as on the date of acquisition	***		
Book Value	***		
Less : ½ Depreciation		***	
		***	
Increased Value of Machinery			***

Less :

Preliminary Expenses or any other item for writing off	***	
Reduction in the Value of any other Asset	***	***
Capital Profit		***

Suppose Capital Profit is Rs. 2,24,500

Here Holding Company's share of Capital Profit = $\frac{3}{5}$th of Rs. 2,24,500 = Rs. 1,34,700, assuming previous proportion.

Minority Shareholders proportion = $\frac{2}{5}$th of Rs. 2,24,500 = Rs. 89,800.

3. **Current Profit or Revenue Profit**

Profit after the date of acquisition	***
(after deducting Pref. Dividend, if any)	
Less : Depreciation @ % for the period ...	
Month on increased value of Assets	***
	***

Suppose current profit as per the above procedure is arrived at—Rs. 38,875. It will be divided between the Holding Company and Subsidiary Company in the following ways.

H. Ltd.	$\frac{3}{5}$th of Rs. 38,875 = Rs. 23,325
Minority Shareholders	$\frac{2}{5}$th of Rs. 38,875 = Rs. 15,550

4. **Goodwill/ Capital Reserve**

Amount paid for shares in Subsidiary Company		
or,		
Cost of Shares	***	
Less : Receipt of Interest if any	***	*** (x)
Less :		
Face Value of Shares	***	
Proportion of Capital Profit of the Holding Company	***	*** (y)
Goodwill/Capital Reserve		***

If x is greater than y, the difference figure (x – y) will represent the amount for Goodwill.

If y is greater than x, the difference figure (y – x) will represent the amount for Capital Reserve.

5. **Minority Shareholders' Interest**

Pref. Shareholder	***	
Add : Dividend for the Current Year	***	
Equity Shareholders		***
Proportion of Capital Profit		***
Proportion of Current Profit		***
Total Minority Interest		***

6. **Inter-Company Unrealised Profit**

The proportion of Holding Company's share in unrealised profit should be accounted for; and the Minority Shareholder in no case should be concerned with this aspect. The amount of unrealised profit must be deducted simultaneously from the current year's profit and from the value of stock.

However, as per Accounting Standard (AS) 21 on **"Consolidated Financial Statements"** the amount of unrealised profit should be deducted in full from both current year's profit and the value of unsold stock.

7. **Inter-Company Indebtedness or Balances**

The consideration included in the Debtors of the Holding Company is a debt due from Subsidiary Company, say Rs. 1,800, must be taken into account while preparing consolidated Balance Sheet. Please note that this sum must be deducted both from total Trade Debtor and Trade Creditor. I think you have followed? Is there any question?

☐ "Sir, does the same principle apply to Bills Accepted by one company and held by the other company?"

• Yes, the same applies to Bill.

☐ "Sir, is it true that bills discounted will continue to appear as a liability?"

• Yes, it is true, because the accepting company will have to pay to the outsider on its due date.

Well, regarding Debenture issued by one company and held by another it must be eliminated from the Investment, appearing on the Assets side, and, Debenture appearing on the liability side.

Do you follow? Is there any question?

☐ "Sir, please tell us about the treatment of Contingent Liability here."

• You see, Internal Contingent Liabilities, which mean the sum that may be paid to the Holding Company by the Subsidiary Company, or by the Holding Company to the Subsidiary Company should not be shown. As regards outsider contingent liabilities, I am to say that a footnote on the same should be given in the Consolidated Balance Sheet.

☐ "Sir, are there any other points worthy of noting?"

• You see, other minor and scattered points relating to the preparation of Consolidated Balance Sheet may be observed while working out a few complicated problems on Holding Company. Could you follow what I mean?

☐ "Yes Sir."

☐ "Thank you Sir, please work out few problems."

- Well, please note below a few worked out problems :

Problem

H Limited acquired the whole of the shares of S Limited on 1st July 2006 at Rs. 5,60,000. The Balance Sheets of H Ltd. and S Ltd. as at 31st December 2006 are given :

Balance Sheets of H Ltd. and S Ltd.

Liabilities	H Ltd.	S Ltd.	Assets	H Ltd.	S Ltd.
	Rs.	Rs.		Rs.	Rs.
Share Capital			Land and Building	5,15,000	1,50,000
Shares of Rs. 10 each	7,50,000	2,50,000	Plant and Machinery	1,50,000	1,35,500
General Reserve—			Investment	5,60,000	
as at 1st January 2006	4,75,000	10,000	Debtors	1,40,000	79,000
Profit and Loss A/c	4,00,000	1,80,000	Stock	1,70,000	1,01,000
Creditors	75,000	80,500	Cash at Bank	1,65,000	55,000
	17,00,000	5,20,500		17,00,000	5,20,500

Further Information

(a) Creditors of H Ltd. includes Rs. 30,000 for purchase from S Ltd. on which the latter company made a profit of Rs. 7,500.

(b) Stock of H Ltd. includes Rs. 15,000 stock at cost purchased from S Ltd.—part of Rs. 30,000 purchases (vide (a))

(c) Profit and Loss A/c includes Interim Dividend at the rate of 16% per annum from S Ltd.

Note : The Balance of Profit and Loss Account of S Ltd. at 1st January 2006 was Rs. 1,40,000.

Please note here that as all shares were held by the Holding Company, no question of Minority Shareholders will arise.

Solution

Statement of Capital Profit

	Rs.	Rs.
Profit and Loss in S Ltd. (opening) :		1,40,000
Add : Profit & Loss (Proportioned) i.e., up to 1.7.06		
(1,80,000 + 40,000 (Div.) – 1,40,000) × $\frac{6}{12}$ =	40,000	
Less : Dividend	40,000	Nil
Add : General Reserve in S Ltd.		10,000
		1,50,000

	Rs.
H Ltd.'s Share & Capital Profit (100%)	1,50,000
Add : Dividend out of Pre-acquisition Profit :	40,000
	1,90,000

Statement of Goodwill

	Rs.	Rs.
Cost of Share in S Ltd. held by H Ltd.		5,60,000
Less : Value of Shares in S Ltd.	2,50,000	
Add : Capital Profit	1,90,000	4,40,000
Goodwill		1,20,000

Statement of Revenue Profit

	Rs.
Profit in S Ltd. form 1.7.06 to 31.12.06 i.e., $80{,}000 \times \frac{6}{12}$	40,000

Consolidated P/L A/c

	Rs.	Rs.
Profit & Loss Account in H Ltd.	4,00,000	
Less : Dividend out of Pre-acquisition Profit	40,000	3,60,000
Add : Revenue Profit in S Ltd.		40,000
		4,00,000

	Rs.
Consolidated P/L A/c	4,00,000
Less : Unrealised Profit (7,500/2)	3,750
	3,96,250

Consolidated Balance Sheet of H Ltd. and its Subsidiary Company Ltd. as at 31.12.06

Liabilities	Amount	Amount	Assets	Amount	Amount
	Rs.	Rs.		Rs.	Rs.
Issued Capital-shares			Goodwill		1,20,000
of Rs. 50 each		7,50,000	Land & Building		
General Reserve		4,75,000	H Ltd.	5,15,000	
Consolidated P/L A/c		3,96,250	S Ltd.	1,50,000	6,65,000
Creditors			Plant & Machinery		
H Ltd.	75,000		H Ltd.	1,50,000	
S Ltd.	80,500		S Ltd.	1,35,500	
	1,55,500				2,85,500
Less : Internal Credit	30,000	1,25,500	Debtors		
			H Ltd.	1,40,000	
			S Ltd.	79,000	
				2,19,000	
			Less : Internal Debt	30,000	1,89,000

Liabilities	Amount	Amount	Assets	Amount	Amount
	Rs.	Rs.		Rs.	Rs.
			Stocks		
			H Ltd.	1,70,000	
			S Ltd.	1,01,000	
				2,71,000	
			Less : Unrealised Profit	3,750	2,67,250
			Cash at Bank		
			H Ltd.	1,65,000	
			S Ltd.	55,000	2,20,000
		17,46,750			17,46,750

Problem

From the Balance Sheets given below prepare a Consolidated Balance Sheet of Moti Ltd. and its subsidiary company, Chhoti Ltd. The interest of the minority shareholders of Chhoti Ltd. are to be shown as a separate item.

Balance Sheet of Moti Ltd.
as at 30.6.2006

Liabilities	Amount	Assets	Amount
	Rs.		Rs.
Share Capital :		Freehold Building at cost	72,000
Authorised and Issued		Plant & Machinery at cost	
12,000 shares of Rs. 10 each	1,20,000	(Rs. 40,000) *Less* : Depreciation	30,000
Trade Creditors	15,000	Shares in Chhoti Ltd. at cost	
General Reserve	25,000	2,000 shares of Rs. 10 each	25,000
Profit & Loss A/c	12,000	Stock at cost	18,000
		Trade Debtors	22,000
		Bank Balance	5,000
	1,72,000		1,72,000

Balance Sheet of Chhoti Ltd.
as at 30.6.2006

Liabilities	Amount	Assets	Amount
	Rs.		Rs.
Share Capital :		Leasehold Property at cost	
Authorised and Issued		(Rs. 30,000) *Less* : Depreciation	25,000
3,000 shares of Rs. 10 each	30,000	Plant & Machinery at cost	
Trade Creditors	5,000	(Rs. 15,000) *Less* : Depreciation	10,000
General Reserve	6,000	Stock at cost	3,000
Profit & Loss A/c	9,000	Trade Debtors	7,000
		Bank Balance	5,000
	50,000		50,000

At the date of acquisition by Moti Ltd. of its holding of 2,000 shares in Chhoti Ltd. the latter company had Undistributed Profits and Reserve amounting to Rs. 5000, none of which has been distributed since the date of acquisition. **[C.A. Final, Adapted]**

Solution

Statement of Capital Profit

	Rs.
Undistributed Profit and Reserve (i.e., Profit prior to acquisition)	5,000

	Rs.
Moti Ltd.'s Share of Capital Profit (5,000 × 2/3)	3,333
Minority's share of Capital (5,000 × 1/3)	1,667
	5,000

Goodwill Statement

		Rs.
Cost of Shares in Chhoti Ltd. held by Moti Ltd.		25,000
Less : Nominal Value of Shares in Chhoti Ltd. held by Moti Ltd.	20,000	
Add : Capital Profit	3,333	23,333
Goodwill		1,667

Statement of Revenue Profit and Reserve

	Rs.
Revenue Profit and Reserve in Chhoti Ltd. i.e., (9,000 + 6,000 – 5,000)	10,000

	Rs.
Moti Ltd.'s share of Revenue Profit & Reserve (10,000 × 2/3)	6,667
Minority's share of Revenue Profit & Reserve (10,000 × 1/3)	3,333
	10,000

Minority Interest

	Rs.
Value of Shares held by them	10,000
Add : Share of Capital Profit	1,667
Add : Share of Revenue Profit & Reserve	3,333
	15,000

Consolidated Profit and Loss and General Reserve

	Rs.
Profit and Loss in Moti Ltd.	12,000
Add : General Reserve in Moti Ltd.	25,000
Add : Revenue Profit and General Reserve	6,667
	43,667

Consolidated Balance Sheet of Moti Ltd.
and its subsidiary Co. Chhoti Ltd. at 30.6.2006

Liabilities		Amount	Assets		Amount
		Rs.			Rs.
Share Capital :			Goodwill		1,667
Authorised & Issued Capital			Freehold Building at Cost		72,000
Shares of Rs. 10 each		1,20,000	Leasehold Property at Cost		
Trade Creditors			(Rs. 30,000) *Less* : Depreciation		25,000
Moti Ltd.	15,000		Plant & Machinery		
Chhoti Ltd.	5,000	20,000	*Less* : Depreciation		
Consolidated P/L A/c and			Moti Ltd.	30,000	
General Reserve A/c		43,667	Chhoti Ltd.	10,000	40,000
Minority Interest		15,000	Stock at Cost		
			Moti Ltd.	18,000	
			Chhoti Ltd.	3,000	21,000
			Trade Debtors		
			Moti Ltd.	22,000	
			Chhoti Ltd.	7,000	29,000
			Bank Balance		
			Moti Ltd.	5,000	
			Chhoti Ltd.	5,000	10,000
		1,98,667			1,98,667

Problem

Following are the Balance Sheets of H Ltd. and S Ltd. as at December 31, 2006 :

Balance Sheet of H Ltd.

Liabilities	Amount	Assets	Amount
	Rs.		Rs.
Share Capital :		Goodwill	40,000
Sahres of Rs. 100 each	5,00,000	Fixed Assets	3,60,000
General Reserve		1,500 Shares in S Ltd. at cost	2,40,000
as at 1st January 2006	1,00,000	Stock	1,00,000
Profit and Loss A/c	1,40,000	Debtors	20,000
Bills Payable	—	Cash at Bank	60,000
Creditors	80,000		
	8,20,000		8,20,000

Balance Sheet of S Ltd.

Liabilities	Amount	Assets	Amount
	Rs.		Rs.
Share Capital :		Goodwill	30,000
Shares of Rs. 100 each	2,00,000	Fixed Assets	2,20,000
Profit and Loss A/c	90,000	Stocks	90,000
General Reserve (1st Jan. 2006)	60,000	Debtors	75,000
Bills Payable	40,000	Cash at Bank	25,000
Creditors	50,000		
	4,40,000		4,40,000

The Profit and Loss Account of S Ltd. showed a balance of Rs. 50,000 on 1st January, 2006. A dividend of 15 per cent was paid in October, 2006 for the year 2005. This dividend was credited by H Ltd. to its Profit and Loss A/c. H Ltd. acquired the shares on 1st July 2006. The Bills Payable of S Ltd. were all issued in favour of H. Ltd. which company got the Bills discounted. Included in the creditors of S Ltd. is Rs. 20,000 for goods supplied by H Ltd. Included in the stock of S Ltd. are goods of the value of Rs. 8,000 which were supplied by H Ltd. at a profit of $33\frac{1}{3}$% on cost.

Prepare Consolidated Balance Sheet of H Ltd. as at 31st December 2006.

[Adapted from C.A. Final]

Solution

Dividend due to the H Ltd.

$$2{,}00{,}000 \times \frac{15}{100} \times \frac{1{,}500}{2{,}000} = \text{Rs. } 22{,}500$$

Statement of Capital Profit :

		Rs.
Profit and Loss in S Ltd. (opening)		50,000
Add: Profit and Loss (proportionate) i.e., up to 1.7.06		
i.e., $[90{,}000 + 30{,}000 \text{ (Div.)} - 50{,}000] \times \frac{6}{12}$	35,000	
Less : Dividend	30,000	5,000
Add: General Reserve in S Ltd.		60,000
		1,15,000
	Rs.	Rs.
H Ltd.'s Share of Capital Profit $(1{,}15{,}000 \times \frac{3}{4})$	86,250	
Add: Dividend out of Pre-acquisition Profit	22,500	1,08,750
Minority's Share of Capital Profit $(1{,}15{,}000 \times \frac{1}{4})$		28,750

Statement of Capital Reserve :

	Rs.
Nominal Value of shares in S Ltd. held by H Ltd. (1,500 × 100)	1,50,000
Add : Share of Capital Profit	1,08,750
	2,58,750
Less : Cost of Shares in S Ltd. held by H Ltd.	2,40,000
	18,750

Combined Value of Goodwill as per Balance Sheet :

Balance Sheet

	Rs.	Rs.
Goodwill in H Ltd.	40,000	
Goodwill in S Ltd.	30,000	70,000
Less : Capital Reserve		18,750
		51,250

Statement of Revenue Profit :

	Rs.
Profit in S Ltd. from 1.6.06—31.12.06 i.e., 70,000 × $\frac{6}{12}$	35,000
	Rs.
H Ltd.'s Share of Revenue Profit (35,000 × $\frac{3}{4}$)	26,250
Minority's Revenue Profit (35,000 × $\frac{1}{4}$)	8,750
	35,000

Consolidated Profit and Loss as per Balance Sheet :

	Rs.	Rs.
Profit and Loss A/c in H Ltd.	1,40,000	
Less : Dividend out of Pre-acquisition Profit	22,500	1,17,500
Add : Revenue Profit in S Ltd.		26,250
		1,43,750
Less: Unrealised Profit * (8,000 × $\frac{1}{4}$)		2,000
		1,41,750

*As per AS21, unrealised profit should be deducted in full

Minority Interest

	Rs.
Value of Shares held by them (500 × Rs. 100)	50,000*
Add: Share of Capital Profit	28,750
Add: Share of Revenue Profit	8,750
	87,500

Consolidated Balance Sheet as at Dec. 31, 2006

Liabilities	Amount Rs.	Amount Rs.	Assets	Amount Rs.	Amount Rs.
Issue Capital :			Goodwill		51,250
Shares of Rs. 100 each		5,00,000	Fixed Assets :		
Consolidated P/L A/c		1,41,750	H Ltd.	3,60,000	
Consolidated General Reserve		1,00,000	S Ltd.	2,20,000	5,80,000
Creditors			Stocks :		
H Ltd.	80,000		H Ltd.	1,00,000	
S Ltd.	50,000		*Less* :		
	1,30,000		Unrealised Profit	2,000	
Less : Internal Credit	20,000	1,10,000		98,000	
Bills Payable		40,000,	*Add* : Stock of S Ltd.	90,000	1,88,000
Minority Interest		87,500	Debtors		
			H Ltd.	20,000	
			S Ltd.	75,000	
				95,000	
			Less : Internal Debt	20,000	75,000
			Cash at Bank :		
			H Ltd.	60,000	
			S Ltd.	25,000	85,000
		9,79,250			9,79,250

Note : Here it has been assumed that the Dividend has been paid fully out of Pre-acquisition Profit.

Problem

H Ltd. acquired controlling shares in S Ltd. as on 1st January 2006 when the latter company had Rs. 5,000 in General Reserve and Rs. 2,800 in Profit and Loss A/c. S Ltd. has decided to issue one bonus share for every four shares held out of pre-acquisition profit. Equity dividend of Rs. 1,500 was received by H Ltd. out of pre-acquisition profit and was credited to its Profit and Loss A/c.

Following is the Balance Sheet of both the companies as on 30.06.06 :

Liabilities	H Ltd.	S Ltd.	Assets	H Ltd.	S Ltd.
	Rs.	Rs.		Rs.	Rs.
Paid-up Share Capital			Goodwill	10,000	6,000
6% Preference Shares			Building	40,000	10,000
of Rs. 100 fully paid	20,000	10,000	Plant & Machinery	21,000	20,000
Equity Shares of			Stock	26,000	20,000
Rs. 10 each fully paid	1,00,000	20,000	Debtors	18,000	10,000
Reserves	6,000	6,000	Bills Receivable	6,000	2,000
Profit & Loss A/c	8,000	2,400	Advance to H Ltd.		2,400
5% Debentures	—	20,000	Investments in S Ltd.		
Loan from S Ltd.	2,000	—	60 of 6% Pref. Shares	5,600	
Sundry Creditors	18,000	12,000	1,500 Equity Shares	17,000	
Bills Payable	4,000	5,000	5% Debentures		
			(F.V. Rs. 10,000)	9,000	
			Bank	5,400	5,000
	1,58,000	75,400		1,58,000	75,400

Note :

(a) Bills Receivable of S Ltd. are all due from H Ltd.

(b) Stock of H Ltd. includes Rs. 1,200 stock purchased from S Ltd. on which S Ltd. made a profit at 20% on cost.

(c) An amount of Rs. 400 was sent by H Ltd. against Loan from S Ltd. but the same was not received by S Ltd.

(d) Dividend on Preference shares of S Ltd. was due for 6 months and Interest on Debentures remained due for whole year on 30.06.06.

Prepare a Consolidated Balance Sheet of H Ltd. as on 30.06.06.

[M.Com. C.U., Adapted]

Solution

Working Note :

(1) Proportion of Shareholding

H Ltd. : $\frac{1,500}{2,000} = \frac{3}{4}$th

Minority Shareholders : $\frac{500}{2,000} = \frac{1}{4}$th

(2) Calculation of Capital Profit

		Rs.
General Reserve on 1.1.06		5,000
Less : Issue of bonus share $\left[2{,}000 \times \frac{1}{4}\right] \times$ Rs.10		5,000
		Nil
Profit and Loss A/c		2,800
Less : Equity dividend $\left[1{,}500 \times \frac{4}{3}\right]$		2,000
		800

Share of H Ltd. : Rs. $800 \times \frac{3}{4}$ = Rs. 600

Share of Minority Shareholders = Rs. 200

(3) Calculation of Revenue Profit

		Rs.
General Reserve Rs. [6,000 − 5,000]		1,000
Profit and Loss A/c [2,400 − 800]		1,600
		2,600
Less : Pref. Dividend $\left[10{,}000 \times 6\% \times \frac{1}{2}\right]$	300	
arrear debenture interest [20,000 × 5%]	1,000	1,300
		1,300

Shares of H Ltd. : $1{,}300 \times \frac{3}{4}$ = Rs. 975

Share of minority shareholders : $1{,}300 \times \frac{1}{4}$ = Rs. 325

(4) Calculation of Goodwill/Capital Reserve

	Rs.	Rs.
Cost of Investment :		
Equity shares in S Ltd.	17,000	
Pref. shares in S Ltd.	5,600	
Debenture in S Ltd.	9,000	31,600
Less : Face value of Equity shares Rs. [1,500 × 10]	15,000	
Pref. shares Rs. [60 × 100]	6,000	
Debentures	10,000	
Share of capital profit	600	
Dividend out of pre-acquisition profit	1,500	
Bonus issue $\left[5{,}000 \times \frac{3}{4}\right]$	3,750	36,850
Capital Reserve		5,250

(5) Minority Interest

	Rs.
Face value of Equity Shares	5,000
Face value of Pref. Shares	4,000
Share of Capital Profit	200
Share of Revenue Profit	325
Arrear Pref. Dividend $\left[300 \times \frac{4}{10}\right]$	120
Bonus Shares $\left[5,000 \times \frac{1}{4}\right]$	1,250
	10,895

(6) Consolidated Profit and Loss A/c

		Rs.
Profit and Loss A/c balance of H Ltd.		8,000
Add : Share of Revenue Profit		975
Pref. Dividend		180
Debenture Interest		500
		9,655
Less : Unrealised Profit $\left[\text{Rs. } 1,200 \times \frac{20}{120}\right]$	200	
Dividend out of Capital Profit	1,500	1,700
		7,955

Consolidated Balance Sheet of H Ltd. and its subsidiary S Ltd. on 31.06.06

Liabilities	Amount	Amount	Assets	Amount	Amount
	Rs.	Rs.		Rs.	Rs.
Authorised Capital	?	?	Goodwill		
Issued & Subscribed			H Ltd.	10,000	
Capital :			S Ltd.	6,000	
6% Pref. Shares of				16,000	
Rs. 100 each		20,000	*Less* : Capital		
10,000 Equity Shares			Reserve	5,250	10,750
of Rs. 10 each		1,00,000	Building		
General Reserve		6,000	H Ltd.	40,000	
Profit & Loss A/c		7,955	S Ltd.	10,000	50,000

Liabilities	Amount	Amount	Assets	Amount	Amount
	Rs.	Rs.		Rs.	Rs.
5% Debentures		10,000	Plant & Machinery		
Minority Interest		10,895	H Ltd.	21,000	
S. Creditors			S Ltd.	20,000	41,000
H Ltd.	18,000		Stock		
S Ltd.	12,000	30,000	H Ltd.	26,000	
Bills Payable			S Ltd	20,000	
H Ltd.	4,000			46,000	
S Ltd.	5,000		*Less* : Unrealised		
	9,000		Profit	200	45,800
Less : Mutual holding	2,000	7,000	Debtors		
Outstanding Interest			H Ltd.	18,000	
on Debenture		500	S Ltd.	10,000	28,000
			Bills Receivable		
			H Ltd.	6,000	
			S Ltd.	2,000	
				8,000	
			Less : Mutual Holding	2,000	6,000
			Advance to H Ltd.	2,400	
			Less : Mutual Holding	2,400	Nil
			Bank		
			H Ltd.	5,400	
			S Ltd.	5,000	10,400
			Cash in transit		400
		1,92,350			1,92,350

Problem

The following are the Balance Sheets of A Ltd. and its subsidiary B Ltd. as on 30.11.2006 :

Liabilities	A Ltd.	B Ltd.	Assets	A Ltd.	B Ltd.
	Rs.	Rs.		Rs.	Rs.
Share Capital :			Land & Buildings	2,50,000	1,00,000
Authorised & Issued			Plant & Machinery		
Shares of Rs. 100 each			(at cost less Depre-		
fully paid	5,00,000	2,00,000	ciation)	1,60,000	50,000
General Reserve	1,00,000	—	Stock-in-trade	90,000	40,000

Liabilities	A Ltd.	B Ltd.	Assets	A Ltd.	B Ltd.
	Rs.	Rs.		Rs.	Rs.
Profit and Loss A/c	80,000	—	Sundry Debtors	60,000	30,000
5% Debentures	25,000	1,00,000	Investment : 1,500		
Sundry Creditors	50,000	45,000	Shares in B Ltd. at cost	1,20,000	
			Cash at Bank	75,000	25,000
			Profit and Loss A/c	—	1,00,000
	7,55,000	3,45,000		7,55,000	3,45,000

Prepare a Consolidated Balance Sheet as at 30th November, 2006 showing in detail necessary adjustments and taking into consideration the following information :

(a) A. Ltd acquired the Shares in B.Ltd on 1st June, 2006 when the latter's Profit and Loss Account showed a debit balance of Rs. 1,50,000.

(b) At the date of acquistion of the Shares, plant and machinery standing in B. Ltd. books at Rs. 24,000 was revalued at Rs. 20,000 but the new value was not incorporated in the books of B.Ltd. Between the date and 30th November 2006 depreciation amounting to 10% in all has been written-off on such plant and machinery.

(c) Sundry Creditors of B. Ltd on 30.11.06 included a sum of Rs.20,000 payable to A Ltd. for credit purchase of goods on which the latter company made a proft of 25% on cost. Half of the goods were still in stock on 30.11.06. **[M.Com. C.U., Adapted]**

Solution

Holding Company

Schedules I + II

		H.Co. $\frac{3}{4}$th	Minority Interest $\frac{1}{4}$th
	Rs.	Rs.	Rs.
Share Capital	2,00,000	1,50,000	50,000
Less : Capital Loss :			
Debit balance of Profit and Loss A/c at the date of Acquisition	1,50,000		
Loss on Revaluation of Plant and Machinery (24,000 – 20,000)	4,000	(–) 1,15,500	(–) 38,500
	1,54,000		
Intrinsic Value of Shares		34,500	
Cost of Shares		1,20,000	
Goodwill		85,500	

Schedule III

Statement of Profit and Loss A/c

	Rs.	Rs.	Rs.
Profit as per Balance of A Ltd.		80,000	
Loss as per Balance Sheet of B Ltd.	1,00,000		
Less : Pre-acquisition loss	1,50,000		
Profit for the Year	50,000		
Add : Depreciation on loss of Revalued Plant and Machinery (10% on 4,000)	400		
	50,400		
Less : $\frac{1}{4}$th Minority Interest	12,600		12,600
	37,800		
Less : Unrealised Profit on Stock $\left(10,000 \times \frac{25}{125}\right)$	2,000	35,800	
		1,15,800	
Minority Interest			24,100

Schedule IV

Statement of Plant and Machinery

		Rs.	Rs.
As per Balance Sheet	A Ltd.		1,60,000
As per Balance Sheet	B. Ltd.	50,000	
Loss on Revaluation		4,000	
		46,000	
Add : Depreciation		400	46,400
			2,06,400

Consolidated Balance Sheet of A Ltd. with its subsidiary B Ltd. as on 30.11.06

Liabilities	Amount	Amount	Assets	Amount	Amount
	Rs.	Rs.		Rs.	Rs.
Share Capital		5,00,000	**Fixed Assets**		
Reserve and Surplus			Goodwill (as per Sch. I)		85,500
General Reserve		1,00,000	Land and Building		
P/L/ (as per Schedule III)		1,15,800	A Ltd.	2,50,000	
Secured Loan			B Ltd.	1,00,000	3,50,000
5% Debenture			Plant and Machinery		
A Ltd.	25,000		(as per Schedule IV)		2,06,400
B Ltd.	1,00,000	1,25,000	**Current Assets**		
Current Liabilities and Provisions			A Ltd.	90,000	
			Less : Unrealised		
Creditors			Profit Sch. III	2,000	
A Ltd.	50,000			88,000	
B Ltd.	45,000		B Ltd.	40,000	1,28,000
	95,000		Sundry Debtors		
Less : Inter			A Ltd.	60,000	
Company transaction	20,000	75,000	B Ltd.	30,000	
Minority Interests		24,100		90,000	
			Less : Inter-Company		
			transaction	20,000	70,000
			Cash at Bank		
			A Ltd.	75,000	
			B Ltd.	25,000	1,00,000
		9,39,900			9,39,900

Problem

A Limited acquired 1,600 Ordinary Shares of B Ltd. of Rs. 100 each on 31st December 2006. The summarised Balance Sheet of A Ltd. and B Ltd. as on that date were :

Liabilities	A Ltd.	B Ltd.	Assets	A Ltd.	B Ltd.
	Rs.	Rs.		Rs.	Rs.
Capital					
5,000 Ordinary Shares			Land and Buildings	1,50,000	1,80,000
of Rs. 100 each	5,00,000		Plant and Machinery	2,40,000	1,09,400
2,000 Ordinary Shares			Investment in B Ltd.		
of Rs. 100 each		2,00,000	at cost	3,40,000	—
Capital Reserve	—	1,20,000	Stocks	1,20,000	36,000

Liabilities	A Ltd.	B Ltd.	Assets	A Ltd.	B Ltd.
	Rs.	Rs.		Rs.	Rs.
General Reserve	2,40,000	—	Sundry Debtors	44,000	40,000
Profit and Loss A/c	57,200	36,000	Bills Receivable		
Bank Overdraft	80,000	—	(including Rs 3,000		
Bills Payable (including			from B Ltd.)	15,800	—
Rs. 4,000 to A Ltd.)	—	8,400	Cash and Bank		
Creditors	47,100	9,000	Balance	14,500	8,000
	9,24,300	3,73,400		9,24,300	3,73,400

You are supplied the following information :

(1) B Ltd. had made a bonus issue on 31st December 2006 of one ordinary share for every two shares held by its shareholders. (Effect has yet to be given in the accounts for this issue.)

(2) The directors are advised that Land and Buildings of B Ltd. are undervalued by Rs. 20,000 and Plant and Machinery of B Ltd. over-valued by Rs. 10,000. These assets have to be adjusted accordingly.

(3) Sundry Creditors of A Ltd. include Rs. 12,000 due to B Ltd.

You are required to prepare the Consolidated Balance Sheet as at 31st December 2006 together with the adjustment Work Sheet. **[C.A. (India) Final, Adapted]**

Please go through the problem very minutely.

Now let me work out a few rough working, or, better to say, furnish, Working Sheets as to Goodwill or Capital Reserve, Capital Profit etc.

However, it should be noted in this connection that the business was acquired at the end of the year and not in the middle of the year. That is why here arises no question of post-acquisition profit; all are pre-acquisition or Capital Profit.

Solution

Goodwill

			Rs.
Cost of Shares Acquired			3,40,000
Less : Nominal Value of Shares			
(including Bonus Sahres)			
1,600 Shares of Rs. 100 each	1,60,000		
Bonus Shares (½ of 1,600 shares)			
i.e. 800 Shares of Rs. 100 each	80,000	2,40,000	
Capital Profit		52,800	2,92,800
Goodwill			47,200

☐ "Excuse me Sir, how is the figure for Capital Profit for Rs. 52,800 calculated?"

• We please note below :

Calculation of Capital Profit

		Rs.
General Reserve after Capitalisation of Bonus Shares		20,000
(General Reserve	Rs. 1,20,000	
Less : Capitalised	Rs. 1,00,000*	
	20,000)	
Net Increase in the Value of Assets Rs. (20,000 – 10,000)		10,000
Profit and Loss A/c		36,000
		66,000

H Ltd. $\frac{4}{5}$th of Rs. 66,000 = Rs. 52,800

S Ltd. $\frac{1}{5}$th of Rs. 66,000 = Rs. 13,200

* For 2 shares 1 Bonus Share (Ordinary) is issued

$2 = 1$

$1 = \frac{1}{2}$

$2{,}000 = \frac{1}{2} \times 2{,}000 = 1{,}000$ Bonus Shares @ Rs. 100 = Rs. 1,00,000

	Rs.	Rs.	Rs.
Land and Buildings			
A Ltd.		1,50,000	
B Ltd.	1,80,000		
Add : Increse on Revaluation	20,000	2,00,000	3,50,000
Plant and Machinery			
A Ltd.		2,40,000	
B Ltd.	1,09,400		
Less : Loss on Revaluation	10,000	99,400	3,39,400
Stock			
A Ltd.		1,20,000	
B Ltd.		36,000	1,56,000
Sundry Debtors			
A Ltd.			44,000
B Ltd.		40,000	
Less : Due by A Ltd.		12,000	28,000
			72,000

	Rs.	Rs.	Rs.
Bills Receivable			
A Ltd.	15,800		
Less : Due from B Ltd.	3,000		12,800
Cash and Bank Balances			
A Ltd.		14,500	
B Ltd.		8,000	22,500
Bills Payable			
B Ltd.		8,400	
Less : Bills Payable to			
A Ltd.	4,000		
Bills Receivable Discounted by A Ltd.	1,000	3,000	5,400
Creditors			
A Ltd.		47,100	
Less : Due to B Ltd.		12,000	35,100
B Ltd.			9,000
			44,100
Minority Interest			
Nominal Value Shares :			
400 Ordinary Shares of Rs. 100 each		40,000	
200 Bonus shares of Rs. 100 each		20,000	60,000
$\frac{1}{4}$th of Capital Profit			13,200
			73,200

Consolidated Balance Sheet of A Ltd. and B Ltd. as on 31.12.06

Liabilities	Amount Rs.	Assets	Amount Rs.
Capital		**Fixed Assets**	
Share Capital	5,00,000	Goodwill	47,200
Reserve and Surplus		Land and Buildings	3,50,000
General Reserve	2,40,000	Plant and Machinery	3,39,400
Profit and Loss A/c	57,200	**Current Assets**	
Current Liabilities		Stock	1,56,000
Bank Overdraft	80,000	Sundry Debtors	72,000
Bills Payable	5,400	Bills Receivable	12,800
Sundry Creditors	44,100	Cash and Bank	22,500
Minority Interest	73,200		
	9,99,900		9,99,900

Problem

H Ltd. acquired 2,000 Equity Shares of Rs. 100 each in S Ltd. as at 31.12.05. The summarised balance sheets of the two companies as at 31.12.06 were :

Liabilities	H Ltd.	S Ltd.	Assets	H Ltd.	S Ltd.
	Rs.	Rs.		Rs.	Rs.
Equity share capital			Fixed Assets	7,00,000	2,50,000
[Rs. 100 each]	8,00,000	2,50,000	Investment : 2,000		
General Reserve	3,00,000	50,000	Equity Shares of		
Profit & Loss A/c	1,00,000	2,00,000	Rs. 100 each in		
Creditors	2,00,000	50,000	S Ltd. at cost	3,00,000	—
			Current Assets	4,00,000	3,00,000
	14,00,000	5,50,000		14,00,000	5,50,000

S Ltd. had a credit balance of Rs. 50,000 in General Reserve and Rs. 20,000 in Profit and Loss A/c when H Ltd. acquired the shares.

S Ltd. issued bonus shares in the ratio of one for every five shares held out of profit earned during the year 2006. This is not shown in the above Balance Sheet of S Ltd.

Stock of S Ltd. includes goods purchased from H Ltd. for Rs. 60,000 which were invoiced by H Ltd. at a profit of 25% on cost.

Prepare a Consolidated Balance Sheet of H Ltd. and its subsidiary S Ltd. as at 31.12.06.

Solution

(i) Proportion of Holding

by H Ltd. $\frac{2,000}{2,500} = \frac{4}{5}$th

by Minority shareholders $\frac{500}{2,500} = \frac{1}{5}$th

(ii) Calculation of Capital Profit

	Rs.
General Reserve	50,000
Profit and Loss A/c	20,000
	70,000

Share of H Ltd. : Rs. 70,000 × $\frac{4}{5}$ = Rs. 56,000

Shares of Minority Shareholders : Rs. 70,000 × $\frac{1}{5}$ = Rs. 14,000

(iii) Calculation of Revenue Profit

	Rs.
Profit for the year 2006 [2,00,000 – 20,000]	1,80,000
Less : Issue of bonus shares [$2,500 \times \frac{1}{5} \times$ Rs. 100]	50,000
	1,30,000

Shares of H Ltd. Rs. $1,30,000 \times \frac{4}{5}$ = Rs. 1,04,000

Share of Minority Shareholders Rs. $1,30,000 \times \frac{1}{5}$ = Rs. 26,000

(iv) Calculation of Goodwill or Capital Reserve

Cost of Investment		3,00,000
Less : Paid-up value of shares [$2,000 \times 100$]	2,00,000	
Shares of Capital Profit	56,000	
Face value of bonus shares [$50,000 \times \frac{4}{5}$]	40,000	2,96,000
Goodwill		4,000

(v) Calculation of Minority Interest

Paid-up value of Equity Shares [$500 \times$ Rs. 100]	50,000
Add : Share of Capital Profit	14,000
Share of Revenue Profit	26,000
Bonus Shares [$50,000 \times \frac{1}{5}$]	10,000
	1,00,000

Consolidated Balance Sheet of H Ltd. and its subsidiary S Ltd. as on 31.12.06.

Liabilities	Amount Rs.	Amount Rs.	Assets	Amount Rs.	Amount Rs.
Authorised Capital	?	?	Goodwill		4,000
Issued and Subscribed Capital :			Fixed Assets :		
8,000 Equity Shares			H Ltd.	7,00,000	
of Rs. 100 each		8,00,000	S Ltd.	2,50,000	9,50,000
General Reserve		3,00,000	Current Assets :		
Profit & Loss A/c	1,00,000		H Ltd.	4,00,000	
Add : Share of Revenue Profit	1,04,000		S Ltd.	3,00,000	
	2,04,000			7,00,000	
Less : Unrealised Profit	12,000	1,92,000	*Less* : Unrealised Profit $[60,000 \times \frac{25}{125}]$	12,000	6,88,000
Minority Interest		1,00,000			
Creditors :					
H Ltd.	2,00,000				
S Ltd.	50,000	2,50,000			
		16,42,000			16,42,000

Problem

Following are the Balance Sheets of H Ltd. and S Ltd. as at 31st December 2006 :

Liabilities	H Ltd. Rs.	S Ltd. Rs.	Assets	H Ltd. Rs.	S Ltd. Rs.
Share Capital			Goodwill	40,000	30,000
(Shares of Rs. 100 each)	5,00,000	2,00,000	Land and Building	2,00,000	1,30,000
General Reserve on			Plant & Machinery	1,60,000	90,000
1st January 2006	1,00,000	60,000	Stock in Trade	1,00,000	90,000
Profit and Loss A/c	1,40,000	90,000	Debtors	20,000	75,000
Bills Payable	—	40,000	1,500 shares in		
Creditors	80,000	50,000	S Ltd. at cost	2,40,000	—
			Cash at Bank	60,000	25,000
	8,20,000	4,40,000		8,20,000	4,40,000

The Profit and Loss A/c of S Ltd. showed a credit balance of Rs. 50,000 on 1st January 2006. A dividend of 15% was paid in October 2006 for the year 2005. This dividend was credited to Profit and Loss A/c by H Ltd. H Ltd. acquired the sharés in S Ltd. on 1st July

2006. The bills payable of S Ltd. were all issued in favour of H Ltd. which company got the bill discounted.

Included in the creditors of S Ltd. is Rs. 20,000 for goods supplied by H Ltd. Included in the stock of S Ltd. are goods to the value of Rs. 8,000 which were supplied by H Ltd. at a profit of $33\frac{1}{3}$% on cost. In arriving at the value of the S Ltd. shares, the plant and machinery which then stood in the books at Rs. 1,00,000 was revalued at Rs. 1,50,000. The new value was not incorporated in the books. No change in these assets have been made since that date.

Prepare Consolidated Balance Sheet of H Ltd. as at 31st December 2006.

[C.A. Final Adapted]

Solution

		Rs.
Profit and Loss A/c of S Ltd. (Current Year Profit)		
Profit and Loss A/c as given		90,000
Less : Profit on 1st January 2006	50,000	
Less : Dividend for 2005 $\left(\frac{15}{100} \times 2,00,000\right)$	30,000	20,000
		70,000
Amount of Profit up to 1.7.06		35,000
(Preacquisition Profit $\frac{1}{2}$ of Rs. 70,000)		

$\frac{3}{4}$ of Rs. 35,000 = Rs. 26,250 (H Ltd.)

$\frac{1}{4}$ of Rs. 35,000 = Rs. 8,750 (Minority)

Capital Profit	
General Reserve 1.1.06	60,000
Profit and Loss A/c, Balance on 1.1.06	20,000
Profit (2006)	35,000
	1,15,000

H Ltd. $\frac{3}{4}$ of Rs. 1,15,000 = Rs. 86,250

S Ltd. $\frac{1}{4}$ of Rs. 1,15,000 = Rs. 28,750

Minority Interest	
500 Shares of Rs. 100 each	50,000
Shares of Capital Profit	28,750
Shares of Profit subsequent to 1st July 06	8,750
	87,500

	Rs.	Rs.
Cost of Control or Capital Reserve		
Amount paid for 1,500 shares in S Ltd.		2,40,000
Less : Dividend received for 2005 $\left(\frac{15}{100} \times 1,50,000 = 22,500\right)$		22,500
		2,17,500
Less : Face Value of Shares	1,50,000	
Capital Profit	86,250	2,36,250
Capital Reserve to be deducted from Goodwill		18,750
Combined Profit and Loss A/c for H Ltd. and S Ltd.		
Profit of H Ltd. as given	1,40,000	
Less : Dividend from S Ltd. for 2005 to be credited to investment in S Ltd.	22,500	1,17,500
Share of Profit of S Ltd.		26,250
		1,43,750
Less : Stock Reserve $\left(8,000 \times \frac{33\frac{1}{3}}{133\frac{1}{3}}\right)$		2,000
		1,41,750

Consolidated Balance Sheet of H Ltd. and its subsidiary S Ltd. as on 31.12.06

Liabilities	Amount	Amount	Assets	Amount	Amount
	Rs.	Rs.		Rs.	Rs.
Share Capital :			Goodwill :		
5,000 shares of			H Ltd.	40,000	
Rs. 100 each fully paid		5,00,000	S Ltd.	30,000	
General Reserve		1,00,000		70,000	
Profit and Loss A/c		1,41,750	*Less* : Capt. Res.	18,750	51,250
Bills Payable		40,000	Land and Building		
Sundry Creditors			H Ltd.	2,00,000	
H Ltd.	80,000		S Ltd.	1,30,000	3,30,000
S Ltd.	50,000		Plant and Machinery		
	1,30,000		H Ltd.	1,60,000	
Less : Inter-company			S Ltd.	90,000	2,50,000
Owing	20,000	1,10,000	Stock		
or			H Ltd.	1,00,000	
(*Less* : Due by			S Ltd.	90,000	
S Ltd. to H Ltd.)				1,90,000	
Minority Interest		87,500	*Less* : Stock		
			Reserve	2,000	1,88,000
			Debtors		
			H Ltd.	20,000	
			S Ltd.	75,000	
				95,000	
			Less : Inter-co.		
			owing (Due by		
			S Ltd. to H Ltd.)	20,000	75,000
			Cash at Bank		
			H Ltd.	60,000	
			S Ltd.	25,000	85,000
		9,79,250			9,79,250

Chain Holding

From the following three Balance Sheets as at 31st December 20 ....., prepare Consolidated Balance Sheet, as at that date :

A Ltd.

Liabilities	Amount	Amount	Assets	Amount	Amount
	Rs.	Rs.		Rs.	Rs.
Share Capital :			Fixed Assets		5,00,000
70,000 Shares of			Investment in		
Rs. 10 each		7,00,000	Subsidiaries		
Loan from B Ltd.		1,00,000	40,000 Shares in		
Current Liabilities		5,00,000	B Ltd. (at cost)	5,00,000	
Profit and Loss A/c		1,80,000	1,00,000 shares in		
			C Ltd. (at cost)	80,000	5,80,000
			Current Assets,		
			Loan and Advances		4,00,000
		14,80,000			14,80,000

B Ltd.

Liabilities	Amount	Amount	Assets	Amount	Amount
	Rs.	Rs.		Rs.	Rs.
Eq. Share Capital :			Fixed Assets		3,00,000
50,000 Shares of			Current Assets,		
Rs. 10 each		5,00,000	Loan and Advances		4,00,000
Current Liabilities		1,50,000			
Profit and Loss A/c :					
Pre-acquisition Profit	10,000				
Post-acquisition Profit	40,000	50,000			
		7,00,000			7,00,000

C Ltd.

Liabilities	Amount	Amount	Assets	Amount	Amount
	Rs.	Rs.		Rs.	Rs.
Eq. Share Capital :			Fixed Assets		1,50,000
10,000 Shares of			Investment :		
Rs. 10 each		1,00,000	50,000 Shares in		
Current Liabilities		1,75,000	B Ltd. (at cost)		60,000
Profit and Loss A/c :			Current Assets		
Post-acquisition Profit	90,000		Loan and Advances		1,40,000
Pre-acquisition Loss	15,000	75,000			
		3,50,000			3,50,000

[Adapted from C.A. Final]

Solution

B Ltd.

	Rs.
Share Capital of B. Ltd.	5,00,000
Capital Profit	10,000
	5,10,000

A Ltd. Share on B Ltd.

$\frac{40,000}{50,000} = \frac{4}{5}$th

$\frac{4}{5}$th of Rs. 5,00,000 Share Capital Rs. 4,00,000

$\frac{4}{5}$th of Rs. 10,000 of Capital Profit Rs. 8,000

	Rs.	Rs.
Cost of Investment		5,00,000
Less : Nominal value of Shares	4,00,000	
Capital Profit	8,000	4,08,000
Goodwill		92,000

C Ltd. Share on B Ltd.

$\frac{5,000}{50,000} = \frac{1}{10}$th

$\frac{1}{10}$th of Rs. 5,00,000	50,000	
$\frac{1}{10}$th of Rs. 10,000 Capital Profit	1,000	
Cost of Investment		60,000
Less : Nominal Value of Share	50,000	
Capital Profit	1,000	51,000
Goodwill		9,000

Total Goodwill :

B Ltd.	92,000
B Ltd. via C Ltd.	9,000
	1,01,000

A on C Ltd.	**Rs.**	**Rs.**
Share Capital	1,00,000	
Less : Loss on Acquisition (Pre-acquisition)	15,000	
	85,000	
Cost of Investment		80,000
Less : Nominal value of Shares	1,00,000	
Less : Loss on Acquisition	15,000	85,000
Capital Reserve		5,000

Minority Interest

$$1-\left(\frac{4}{5}+\frac{1}{10}\right)=1-\left(\frac{8+1}{10}\right)=1-\frac{9}{10}=\frac{1}{10}$$

	Rs.
$\frac{1}{10}$th of Share Capital Rs. 5,00,000	50,000
$\frac{1}{10}$th of Capital Profit Rs. 10,000	1,000
$\frac{1}{10}$th of Post-acquisition Profit Rs. 40,000	4,000
	55,000

No question of Minority in the investment of C Ltd. arises. Because, whole of the shares were acquired.

Consolidated Balance Sheet of A Ltd. and its subsidiaries B Ltd. and C Ltd. as on 31.12.20......

Liabilities	Amount	Amount	Assets	Amount	Amount
	Rs.	Rs.		Rs.	Rs.
Share Capital :			**Goodwill :**		
70,000 shares of			B Ltd.	92,000	
Rs. 10 each		7,00,000	B Ltd. via C Ltd.	9,000	
Minority Interest		55,000		1,01,000	
Current Liabilities			*Less* : Capital Resv.		
A Ltd.	5,00,000		C Ltd.	5,000	96,000
B Ltd.	1,50,000		**Fixed Assests :**		
C Ltd.	1,75,000	8,25,000	A Ltd.	5,00,000	
Profit and Loss A/c			B Ltd.	3,00,000	
Post-acquisition			C Ltd.	1,50,000	9,50,000

Liabilities	Amount	Amount	Assets		Amount	Amount
	Rs.	Rs.			Rs.	Rs.
A Ltd.	1,80,000		**Current Assets, Loan and Advance**			
B Ltd.'s Shares in B Ltd. ($\frac{4}{5}$ of 40,000)	32,000		A Ltd.		4,00,000	
A Ltd. shares in C Ltd. (100%)	90,000		B Ltd.	4,00,000		
A Ltd. shares in B Ltd. via C Ltd.	4,000	3,06,000	*Less* : Loan from B Ltd.	1,00,000	3,00,000	
(100% of $\frac{1}{10}$ × 40,000)			C Ltd.		1,40,000	8,40,000
$\frac{5,000}{50,000} = \frac{1}{10}$						
		18,86,000				18,86,000

Problem

On 1st January 2006 XYZ Ltd., a new company, raised its first Capital of Rs. 2,25,000 from the issue of 22,500 shares of Rs. 10 each at par, and on that date acquired the following shareholdings :

A Ltd. — 3,000 shares of Rs. 10 each fully paid, for Rs. 35,000

B Ltd. — 10,000 shares of Rs. 10 each, fully paid, for Rs. 72,000

C Ltd. — 8,000 shares of Rs. 10 each, fully paid for Rs. 92,000

Apart from these transactions and those detailed below, XYZ Ltd. neither paid nor received other monies during 2006.

Following are the condensed Balance Sheets of the subsidiary companies as on 31st December 2006 :

	A Ltd.	B Ltd.	C Ltd.
	Rs.	Rs.	Rs.
Goodwill	4,000	—	15,000
Freehold Property	18,000	41,000	50,000
Plant	16,000	30,000	12,000
Stock	11,000	32,000	21,000
Debtors	4,000	8,000	17,000
Cash at Bank	1,000	2,000	11,500
Profit and Loss Account	—	18,000	—
	54,000	1,31,000	1,26,500

	A Ltd.	B Ltd.	C Ltd.
	Rs.	Rs.	Rs.
Share Capital	40,000	1,20,000	1,00,000
4,000 Shares of Rs. 10 each, fully paid			
Reserve (as on 1st January 2006)	3,000	—	7,500
Profit and Loss Account	6,000	—	15,000
Creditors	5,000	11,000	4,000
	54,000	1,31,000	1,26,500

The following information is relevant :

(1) The Freehold property of C Ltd. is to be revalued at Rs. 65,000 as on 1st January 2006.

(2) Additional depreciation for the year 2006 of Rs. 3,000 on the Plant of B Ltd. is to be provided.

(3) The stock of A Ltd. as on 31st December 2006 has been undervalued by Rs. 2,000 and is to be adjusted.

(4) As on 31st December 2006, XYZ owed A Ltd. Rs. 3,000 and is owed Rs. 6,000 by B Ltd.; C Ltd. is owed Rs. 1,000 by A Ltd. and Rs. 2,000 by B Ltd.

(5) The balances on Profit and Loss Account as on 31st December 2005 were — A Ltd. Rs. 2,000 (credit); B Ltd. Rs. 12,000 (debit); C Ltd. Rs. 4,000 (credit). The credit balances of A Ltd. and C Ltd. were wholly distributed as dividend in March 2006.

(6) During 2006, A Ltd. and C Ltd. declared and paid interim dividends of 8% and 10%, respectively. No final dividends are to be provided.

You are required to prepare the Consolidated Balance Sheet of XYZ Ltd. and its subsidiary companies as on 31st December 2006.

Ignore Taxation. **[Adapted from C.A. (Eng.) Final]**

Consolidated Balance Sheet
XYZ Ltd. and its Subsidiary Companies A, B & C Ltd.
as on December 31st 2006

Liabilities	Amount	Amount	Assets	Amount	Amount
	Rs.	Rs.		Rs.	Rs.
Issued Share Capital :			**Fixed Assets :**		
22,500 shares of			Goodwill at cost	19,000	
Rs. 10 each, fully paid		2,25,000	*Less* : Attributable to		
Capital Reserve on			Holding Company and		
consolidation :			deducted from Capital		
Net excess of assets			Reserve per contra	15,000	4,000
(including book values			Freehold Property		1,24,000
of Goodwill)			Plant		55,000
attributable to Holding					1,83,000

Liabilities	Amount Rs.	Amount Rs.	Assets	Amount Rs.	Amount Rs.
Co. over cost of shares acquired	25,950		**Current Assets :**		
Less : Goodwill—proportion of book value attributable to Holding Company written-off	15,000	10,950	Stock	66,000	
Revenue Reserve :			Debtors	23,000	
Profit and Loss A/c		20,900	Bank Balance	52,600	1,41,600
Minority Interest (including Credit Balances on Profit and Loss A/c of Rs. 5,000)		56,750			
Current Liabilities :					
Creditors		11,000			
		3,24,600			3,24,600

WORKING

(1) **Cost of Control Account**

	A Ltd. Rs.	B Ltd. Rs.	C Ltd. Rs.		A Ltd. Rs.	B Ltd. Rs.	C Ltd. Rs.
Cost of Shares	35,000	72,000	92,000	Share capital	30,000	1,00,000	80,000
Less : Dividends paid out of pre-acquisition profits :				Freehold property—profit on revaluation—4/5ths of Rs. 15,000			12,000
3/4ths of Rs. 2,000	1,500			Pre-acquisition reserves :			
4/5ths of Rs. 4,000			3,200	3/4ths of Rs. 3,000	2,250		
				4/5ths of Rs. 7,500			6,000
	33,500	72,000	88,800	Balance, transferred to Capital Reserve Account	1,250		
Adjusted book value							
Pre-acquisition loss 5/6ths of Rs. 12,000		10,000					
Balances, transferred to Capital Reserve Account		18,000	9,200				
	33,500	1,00,000	98,000		33,500	1,00,000	98,000

(2)

Capital Reserve Account (Net)

Dr.	Amount		Cr. Amount
	Rs.		Rs.
Cost of Control—A Ltd.	1,250	Cost of Control—B Ltd.	18,000
Goodwill Account	15,000	Cost of Control—C Ltd.	9,200
Consolidated Balance Sheet—balance	10,950		
	27,200		27,200

(3)

Goodwill Account

Dr.	Amount		Cr. Amount
	Rs.		Rs.
As Per draft Balance Sheets :		Transfer to Capital Reserve	
A Ltd.	4,000	XYZ Ltd. shares :	
C Ltd.	15,000	A Ltd. 3/4ths of 4,000	3,000
		C Ltd.—4/5ths of 15,000	12,000
		Balance, carried forward (attributable to Minority Shareholders) .	4,000
	19,000		19,000

(4)

Minority Interests

	A Ltd.	B Ltd.	C Ltd.	
	Rs.	Rs.	Rs.	
Share Capital	10,000	20,000	20,000	
Reserves	750	—	1,500	
Profit on revaluation of Freehold Property			3,000	
Profit and Loss Account :				
1/4th of Rs. (6,000 + 2,000)	2,000			
1/6th of Rs. (18,000 + 3,000) Dr.		(3,500)		
1/5th of Rs. 15,000			3,000	
	12,750	16,500	27,500	= 56,750

(5) Profit and Loss Accounts

	XYZ Ltd.	A Ltd.	B Ltd.	C Ltd.
	Rs.	Rs.	Rs.	Rs.
Balances as per Trial Balance and working (6)	10,400	6,000	(18,000)	15,000
Profit on revaluation of Stock		2,000		
Depreciation of Plant			(3,000)	
	10,400	8,000	(21,000)	15,000
Deduct : Cost of Control—pre-acquisition loss—5/6th of Rs. 12,000			10,000	
			(11,000)	
Less : Minority Interest [vide working (4)]		2,000	(3,500)	3,000
	10,400	6,000	(7,500)	12,000
Consolidated Balance Sheet		Rs. 20,900		

(6) Abridged Balance Sheet— XYZ Ltd.

	Rs.	Rs.		Rs.	Rs.
Issued Share Capital		2,25,000	**Investments :**		
Profit and Loss —			Shares in A Ltd.	33,500	
Dividends received :			Shares in B Ltd.	72,000	
A Ltd.— 8 percent of			Shares in C Ltd.	88,800	1,94,300
Rs. 30,000	2,400		Debtors—B Ltd.		6,000
C Ltd.—10 percent			Balance at Bank		38,100
of Rs. 80,000	8,000	10,400			
Creditors—A Ltd.		3,000			
		2,38,400			2,38,400

(7) Elimination of Inter-Company Balances

	XYZ Ltd.	A Ltd.	B Ltd.	C Ltd.	Total
	Rs.	Rs.	Rs.	Rs.	Rs.
Debtors :					
B Ltd.	6,000			2,000	
A Ltd.				1,000	
XYZ Ltd.		3,000			
Inte-company	6,000	3,000		3,000	12,000
Outside	—	1,000	8,000	14,000	23,000
	6,000	4,000	8,000	17,000	35,000

	XYZ Ltd.	A Ltd.	B Ltd.	C Ltd.	Total
	Rs.	Rs.	Rs.	Rs.	Rs.
Creditors :					
A Ltd.	3,000				
C Ltd.		1,000	2,000		
XYZ Ltd.			6,000		
Inter-company :	3,000	1,000	8,000		12,000
Outside	—	4,000	3,000	4,000	11,000
	3,000	5,000	11,000	4,000	23,000

(8) Freehold Property

	Rs.	Rs.
A Ltd.		18,000
B Ltd.		41,000
C Ltd.	50,000	
Add : Increase in value	15,000	65,000
Consolidated Balance Sheet		1,24,000

(9) Plant

	Rs.	Rs.
A Ltd.		16,000
B Ltd.	30,000	
Less : Depreciation	3,000	27,000
C Ltd.		12,000
Consolidated Balance Sheet		55,000

(10) Stock

	Rs.	Rs.
A Ltd.	11,000	
Add : Increase in value	2,000	13,000
B Ltd.		32,000
C Ltd.		21,000
Consolidated Balance Sheet		66,000

(11) Bank

	Rs.	Rs.
A Ltd.		1,000
B Ltd.		2,000
C Ltd.		11,500
XYZ Ltd.		38,100
Consolidated Balance Sheet		52,600

Problem

The Balance Sheets of P Ltd. and Q Ltd. as on 31st March 2007 are given below :

Liabilities	P Ltd.	Q Ltd.	Assets	P Ltd.	Q Ltd.
	Rs.	Rs.		Rs.	Rs.
Share Capital :			Goodwill	1,26,000	46,000
Equity [Rs. 10 each)	1,80,000	1,00,000	Land & Building	95,000	47,000
14% Preference share	1,50,000	80,000	Plant & Machinery	45,000	50,400
Share Premium	36,000	—	Fixture	1,000	500
[Equity shares]			Govt. Securities	26,000	—
Reserve	26,000	30,000	9,000 Equity shares		
Profit & Loss A/c	71,000	25,200	in Q Ltd.	1,20,000	

Liabilities	P Ltd.	Q Ltd.	Assets	P Ltd.	Q Ltd.
	Rs.	Rs.		Rs.	Rs.
14% Debenture	40,000	50,000	2,000 Equity shares		
Creditores	19,000	34,800	in P Ltd.	—	24,000
			Stock	48,000	1,14,000
			Book Debts	55,000	35,000
			Cash	6,000	3,100
	5,22,000	3,20,000		5,22,000	3,20,000

Q Ltd. acquired the shares in P Ltd. on 1.4.2006 when it made a fresh issue of shares. P Ltd. acquired the shares in Q Ltd. on 1st October 2006.

Some of the figures on 1.4.2006 were :

	P Ltd.	Q Ltd.
	Rs.	Rs.
Reserve	26,000	30,000
Profit & Loss A/c	15,000 (Dr.)	8,000
Plant & Machinery	50,000	56,000

As on date of acquisition of control, P Ltd. valued the Plant & Machinery of Q Ltd. at Rs. 60,000. Creditors of P Ltd. include Rs. 15,000 due to Q Ltd. The stock of P Ltd. include goods of the value of Rs. 33,000 supplied by Q Ltd. at cost plus 10%.

Prepare consolidated balance sheet of the group as on 31.3.2007 taking into account the enhanced value of Plant and Machinery of Q Ltd. **[Adapted from C.A. Final]**

Solution

(1) Calculation of Proportion of Shareholdings

P Ltd. in Q Ltd : $\frac{9,000}{10,000} = \frac{9}{10}$th

Q Ltd. in P Ltd : $\frac{2,000}{18,000} = \frac{1}{9}$th

(2) Calculation of Profit up to 1st October 2006

	P Ltd.	Q Ltd.
Profit and Loss A/c balance on 31.03.07	71,000	25,200
Less : Profit and Loss A/c balance on 31.03.06	15,000 (Dr.)	8,000
	86,000	17,200
Less : Preference dividend for the year (1,50,000 × 14%), (80,000 × 14%)	21,000	11,200
	65,000	6,000
∴ Profit for 6 months up to 1st October 2006	32,500	3,000

(3) Calculation of Profit on Revaluation of Plant & Machinery

Depreciation up to 1st October 2006 of Plant and Machinery of Q Ltd.

$$\left[\text{Rs. } 56{,}000 - \text{Rs. } 50{,}400 \times \frac{1}{2}\right] = \text{Rs. } 2{,}800$$

	Rs.
Book Value of Plant and Machinery on 1.04.06	56,000
Depreciation up to 1.10.06	2,800
	53,200
Revalued figure of Plant and Machinery	60,000
Profit on revaluation	6,800

Additional depreciation $\left[\text{Rs } 6{,}800 \times 10\% \times \frac{1}{2}\right] = \text{Rs. } 340$

(4) Calculation of Capital Profit

	P Ltd. Rs.	Q Ltd. Rs.
Reserve	26,000	30,000
Profit and Loss A/c	15,000 (Dr.)	8,000
Profit up to 1.10.06	32,500	3,000
Profit on revaluation of Plant and Machinery	—	6,800
	43,500	47,800

Let Capital Profit of P Ltd. be X and Q Ltd. Y.

$\therefore \quad X = \text{Rs. } 43{,}500 + \frac{9}{10}(y)$

$y = \text{Rs. } 47{,}800 + \frac{1}{9}(x)$

or, $y = \text{Rs. } 47{,}800 + \frac{1}{9}\left[\text{Rs. } 43{,}500 + \frac{9}{10}y\right]$

$= \text{Rs. } 47{,}800 + \text{Rs. } 4{,}833 + \frac{1}{10}y$

or, $Y - \frac{1}{10}y = \text{Rs. } 52{,}633$

or, $\frac{9}{10}y = \text{Rs. } 52{,}633$

or, $y = \frac{\text{Rs. } 52{,}633 \times 10}{9} = \text{Rs. } 58{,}481$

Share of P Ltd. $\left(\text{Rs. } 58{,}481 \times \frac{9}{10}\right) = \text{Rs. } 52{,}633$

Minority Shareholders $\left(\text{Rs. } 58{,}481 \times \frac{1}{10}\right) = \text{Rs. } 5{,}848$

(5) Calculation of Revenue Profit

	P Ltd.	Q Ltd.
	Rs.	Rs.
Profit from 1st October 2006 to 31st March 2007	32,500	3,000
Less : Additional Depreciation	—	340
	32,500	2,660

Let Revenue Profit of P be p and Q be q.

$\therefore \quad p = \text{Rs. } 32{,}500 + \frac{9}{10}q$

$q = \text{Rs. } 2{,}660 + \frac{1}{9}p$

or, $q = \text{Rs. } 2{,}660 + \frac{1}{9}\left[\text{Rs. } 32{,}500 + \frac{9}{10}q\right]$

$= \text{Rs. } 2{,}660 + 3{,}611 + \frac{1}{10}q$

or, $q - \frac{1}{10}q = \text{Rs. } 6{,}271$

or, $\frac{9}{10}q = \text{Rs. } 6{,}271$

or, $q = \dfrac{\text{Rs. } 62{,}710}{9} = \text{Rs. } 6{,}968$

$\therefore$ Share of P Ltd. Rs. $6{,}968 \times \frac{9}{10} = \text{Rs. } 6{,}271$

Minority shareholders = Rs. $6{,}968 \times \frac{1}{10} = \text{Rs. } 697$

(6) Calculation of Capital Reserve

	Rs.	Rs.
Investment :		
P Ltd. in Q Ltd.	1,20,000	
Q Ltd. in P Ltd.	24,000	1,44,000
Less : Face Value of investment		
P Ltd. (9,000 × 10)	90,000	
Q Ltd. (2,000 × 10)	20,000	
Share of Capital Profit	52,633	1,62,633
Capital Reserve		18,633

(7) Minority Interest

Paid-up value of Equity Shares	10,000
Share of Capital Profit	5,848
Share of Revenue Profit	697
Paid-up value of Preference Shares	80,000
Dividend on preference Shares for the year (80,000 × 14%)	11,200
	1,07,745

(8) Calculation of Profit and Loss A/c balance for Consolidated Balance Sheet

			Rs.
Profit and Loss A/c balance after Preference Dividend :	P Ltd.		50,000
	Q Ltd.		14,000
			64,000
Add : Increase in value of P/M			6,800
			70,800
Less : Depreciation			340
			70,460
Add : Reserve of Q Ltd.			30,000
			1,00,460
Less : Minority Shareholders			
Capital Profit		5,848	
Revenue Profit		697	
Treated as Capital Profit		52,633	
Unrealised Profit $\left(33{,}000 \times \frac{10}{100}\right)$		3,000	62,178
			38,282

Consolidated Balance Sheet of P Ltd. and its subsidiary Q Ltd. on 31.03.07

Liabilities	Amount	Amount	Assets	Amount	Amount
	Rs.	Rs.		Rs.	Rs.
Authorised Capital	?	?	Goodwill P Ltd.	1,26,000	
Issued & Subscribed Capital			Q Ltd.	46,000	
				1,72,000	
18,000 Eq. Shares of			*Less* : Capital Reserve	18,633	1,53,367
Rs. 10 each	1,80,000		Land & Building		
Less : held by Q Ltd.	20,000	1,60,000	P Ltd.	95,000	
14% Pref. Shares		1,50,000	Q Ltd.	47,000	1,42,000
Share Premium		36,000	Plant & Machinery		
Reserve		26,000	P Ltd.	45,000	
Profit & Loss A/c			Q Ltd.	50,400	
[W.N.-8]		38,282		95,400	
14% Debenture		90,000	*Add* : Increase in value	6,800	
Minority Interest		1,07,745		1,02,200	
Creditors P Ltd.	19,000		*Less* : Additional		
Q Ltd.	34,800		Depreciation	340	1,01,860
	53,800		Fixture		
Less : Mutual Indebtedness			P Ltd.	1,000	
	15,000	38,800	Q Ltd.	500	1,500

Liabilities	Amount	Amount	Assets	Amount	Amount
	Rs.	Rs.		Rs.	Rs.
Outstanding Pref. Dividend		21,000	Govt. Securities		26,000
			Stock P Ltd.	48,000	
			Q Ltd.	1,14,000	
				1,62,000	
			Less : Unrealised Profit	3,000	1,59,000
			Book Debts		
			P Ltd.	55,000	
			Q Ltd.	35,000	
				90,000	
			Less : Mutual Indebtedness	15,000	75,000
			Cash P Ltd.	6,000	
			Q Ltd.	3,100	9,100
		6,67,827			6,67,827

Problem

Following is the Balance Sheet of X Ltd., Y Ltd. and Z Ltd. as on March 31, 2007.

Balance Sheet
as on March 31, 2007

	X Ltd.	Y Ltd.	Z Ltd.
	Rs.	Rs.	Rs.
Liabilities			
Equity shares of Rs. 10 each full paid	10,00,000	5,00,000	3,00,000
Profit and Loss A/c	6,00,000	3,00,000	1,00,000
10% Debentures of Rs. 100 each	5,00,000	3,00,000	—
Current Liabilities	3,00,000	4,00,000	3,00,000
	24,00,000	15,00,000	7,00,000
Assets			
Fixed Assets	12,00,000	6,00,000	4,00,000
Investment :			
30,000 Equity Shares in Y Ltd.	4,00,000	—	—
Equity Shares in Z Ltd.	50,000	2,20,000	—
2,000 Debentures in Y Ltd.	2,10,000	—	—
Current Assets	5,40,000	6,80,000	3,00,000
	24,00,000	15,00,000	7,00,000

Additional Information :

(i) X Ltd. acquired 10,000 equity shares of Y Ltd. on 1.4.2006, again 10,000 equity shares on 1.7.2006 and further 10,000 equity shares on 1.1.2007.

(ii) Profit and Loss Account balance of Y Ltd. stood at Rs. 60,000 on 1.4.2006. Y Ltd. has earned profit during the first three months, next six months and the last three months of the year in the ratio of 1:5:2.

(iii) X Ltd. acquired 5,000 shares in Z Ltd. on 1.4.2006.

(iv) Y Ltd. acquired 15,000 shares in Z Ltd. on 1.4.2006 and further 5,000 on 1.1.2007.

(v) Profit and Los account balance of Z Ltd. was Rs. 28,000 on 1.4.2006. Z Ltd. has earned profit evenly during the year.

(vi) Current assets of Y Ltd. include a stock of goods worth Rs. 1,10,000 purchased from X Ltd. at a cost plus 10%.

You are required to prepare a Consolidated Balance Sheet of X Ltd. as on 31.3.2007. **[C.U., M.Com.]**

Solution

X Ltd. becomes holding company of Y Ltd. on 1.1.2007 and Y Ltd. becomes holding company of Z Ltd. on 1.1.2007.

X Ltd.'s share of holding in Y Ltd. $= \frac{30,000}{50,000} = \frac{3}{5}$th

Minority holding in Y Ltd. $= \frac{20,000}{50,000} = \frac{2}{5}$th

Y Ltd.'s share of holding in Z Ltd. $= \frac{20,000}{30,000} = \frac{4}{6}$th

X Ltd.'s share of holding in Z Ltd. $= \frac{5,000}{30,000} = \frac{1}{6}$th

Minority holding in Z Ltd. $= \frac{5,000}{30,000} = \frac{1}{6}$th

Z Ltd. :

Calculation of Capital and Revenue Profit of Z Ltd. :

	Capital Profit Rs.	Revenue Profit Rs.
Profit and Loss Account balance on 1.4.06	28,000	—
Add : Profit uo to		
1.1.07 Rs. (1,00,000 – 28,000) $\times \frac{9}{12}$	54,000	
Profit for the remaining three months treated as		
Revenue profit Rs (1,00,000 – 28,000) $\times \frac{3}{12}$		18,000
	82,000	18,000

Share of Y Ltd. (7/6)	54,687	12,000
Share of X Ltd. (1/6)		
$\left[\text{Rs. } 82{,}000 \times \frac{1}{6} - \text{Rs. } 9{,}000\right]$	4,667	9,000
Share of X Ltd. in revenue Profit		
$\left[\text{Rs. } 18{,}000 \times \frac{1}{6}\right]$	—	3,000
		12,000
Share of minority shareholders (1/6)	13,666	3,000

Y Ltd. :

Calculation of Capital Profit and Revenue Profit

	Capital Profit	Revenue Profit
	Rs.	Rs.
Profit and Loss Account balance on 1.4.06	60,000	
Add : Profit up to 1.1.07		
First three months		
$\text{Rs. } (3{,}00{,}000 - 60{,}000) \times \frac{1}{8}$	30,000	
Second six months		
$\text{Rs. } (3{,}00{,}000 - 60{,}000) \times \frac{5}{8}$	1,50,000	
	2,40,000	
Add : Share in Z Ltd.	54,667	
	2,94,667	
Profit for the last three months		
$\text{Rs. } (3{,}00{,}000 - 60{,}000) \times \frac{2}{8}$		60,000
Add: Profit from Z Ltd.		12,000
		72,000

Share of X Ltd $\left(2{,}94{,}667 \times \frac{3}{5}\right)$ — 1,76,800

Share of minority shareholders—

$\left(2{,}94{,}667 \times \frac{2}{5}\right)$ — 1,17,867

Share of X Ltd. $\left(72{,}000 \times \frac{3}{5}\right)$ = Rs. 43,200

Share of minority sharholders $\left(72{,}000 \times \frac{2}{5}\right)$ = Rs. 28,800

Calculation of Goodwill/Capital Reserve

	Rs.	Rs.
Cost of Investment		
X Ltd. in Y Ltd.	4,00,000	
X Ltd. in Z Ltd.	50,000	
Y Ltd. in Z Ltd.	2,20,000	
2,000 Debentures in Y Ltd.	2,10,000	8,80,000
Less : Face Value of Investment :		
X Ltd. in Y Ltd.	3,00,000	
X Ltd. in Z Ltd.	50,000	
Y Ltd. in Z Ltd.	2,00,000	
Debentures	2,00,000	
Share of Capital Profit		
X Ltd. in Z Ltd.	4667	
X Ltd. in Y Ltd.	1,76,800	9,31,467
Capital Reserve		51,467

Calculation of Minority Interest

in Z Ltd. :		
Face value (5,000 × Rs. 10)	50,000	
Add : Share of Capital Profit	13,666	
Add : Share of revenu profit	3,000	66,666
in Y Ltd. :		
Face value (20,000 × Rs. 10)	2,00,000	
Add : Share of Capital profit	1,17,867	
Share of revenue profit	28,800	3,46,667
		4,13,333

Profit and Loss Account of X Ltd.

	Rs.
Balance on 31.03.07	6,00,000
Add: Share of revenue profit in Z Ltd.	12,000
Share of revenue profit in Y Ltd.	43,200
	6,55,200
Less: Unrealised profit $\left(1,10,000 \times \frac{10}{110}\right)$	10,000
	6,45,200

Consolidated Balance Sheet of X Ltd., Y Ltd. and Z Ltd. as on 31.03.07

Liabilities	Amount Rs.	Amount Rs.	Assets	Amount Rs.	Amount Rs.
Equity Shares of 10 each fully paid		10,00,000	Fixed Assets : X Ltd.	12,00,000	
Capital Reserve		51,467	Y Ltd.	6,00,000	
Profit and Loss A/c		6,45,200	Z Ltd.	4,00,000	22,00,000
10% Debentures of 100 each :			Current Assets :		
X Ltd.	5,00,000		X Ltd.	5,40,000	
Y Ltd.	3,00,000		Y Ltd.	6,80,000	
	8,00,000		Z Ltd.	3,00,000	
Less : Held by X Ltd.	2,00,000	6,00,000		15,20,000	
Minority Interest		4,13,333	*Less* : Unrealised profit	10,000	15,10,000
Current Liabilities :					
X Ltd.	3,00,000				
Y Ltd.	4,00,000				
Z Ltd.	3,00,000	10,00,000			
		37,10,000			37,10,000

QUESTIONS

1. On 1.1.2006 Beta Ltd. purchased 2,500 shares of Gamma Ltd. On 31.12.2006 Alpha Ltd. purchases from outside share-dealers (other than Beta Ltd.) 2,500 shares of Gamma Ltd. On the same date Alpha Ltd. purchased all the shares of Beta Ltd. The Balance Sheets of the three companies as at 31.12.2006 were :

	Alpha Ltd.	Beta Ltd.	Gamma Ltd.
	Rs.	Rs.	Rs.
Liabilities			
Share Capital (in shares of Rs. 10 each)	1,50,000	1,00,000	75,000
Profit and Loss A/c—1.1.2006	10,000	8,000	5,000
Profit for 2006	20,000	16,000	10,000
Creditors	15,000	10,000	9,000
	1,95,000	1,34,000	99,000
Assets			
Investments :			
in shares of Beta Ltd.	1,25,000	—	—
in shares of Gamma Ltd.	38,000	42,000	—
Sundry Assets	32,000	92,000	99,000
	1,95,000	1,34,000	99,000

Alpha Ltd.'s creditors include Rs. 4,000 due to Beta Ltd. and Gamma Ltd.'s Debtors include Rs. 2,000 due from Beta Ltd.

Prepare a Consolidated Balance Sheet as at 31st December 2006.

[C.A. Final, Adapted]

2. The following are the balance of X Ltd., Y Ltd. and Z Ltd. (before making the closing entries) as at 31st December 2006:

	X Ltd.	Y Ltd.	Z Ltd.
	Rs.	Rs.	Rs.
Credit			
Balance of Trading Account	1,54,900	98,500	54,000
Creditors	3,27,600	3,07,200	1,23,900
General Reserve	2,00,000	84,000	1,50,000
Sinking Fund for Leasehold (b/f)	40,000	7,500	—
Equity Share Capital (Rs. 10 each) (authorised and issued)	15,00,000	6,00,000	3,00,000
Preference Share Capital (6% cumulative of Rs. 10 each)	—	—	2,00,000
Profit and Loss A/c (Balance b/f)	51,700	63,000	31,500
Share Premium A/c	—	1,50,000	—
	22,74,200	13,10,200	8,59,400

Debit	Rs.	Rs.	Rs.
Bank Balance	48,400	40,200	16,500
Debtors	7,05,700	3,87,100	4,28,300
Directors' Fees	22,000	7,500	9,000
Interim Dividend (Equity)	60,000	—	12,000
Shares in Y Ltd. (at cost)	5,00,000	—	—
Shares in Z Ltd. (at cost)	—	5,00,000	—
Leasehold property (at cost)	1,05,000	52,500	—
Stock	—	—	12,000
Preference dividend for 2006 paid	8,33,100	3,22,900	3,81,600
	22,74,200	13,10,200	8,59,400
Rates of Proposed Dividend	6%	12%	5%

Y Ltd. was formed in 2006 and X Ltd. subscribed at Rs. 12.50 per share for two-third of its issued capital.

Y Ltd. acquired on 1st July 2006 the whole of the issued equity share capital of Z Ltd. ex 2006 interim dividend; no part of the Preference Capital was acquired.

All the companies carry on business as wholesalers, there being no intercompany transactions. The directors of both Y Ltd. and Z Ltd. are directors of X Ltd.

Provision is required for Leasehold Sinking Fund on the basis of 21 years' life. Each holding company takes credit for the proposed dividend receivable from its immediate subsidiary.

You are required to prepare (a) a Consolidated Profit and Loss A/c of X Ltd. for the year ended 31st December 2006, and (b) a Consolidated Balance Sheet of the group as at that date. **[C.A. Final, Adapted]**

3. Anthony & Co. Ltd. acquired 8,000 Equity Shares of Canning & Co. Ltd. on 1st January 2006.

The following are the Balance Sheets of the two campanies as at 31st December 2006 :

	Anthony & Co. Ltd. Rs.	Canning & Co. Ltd. Rs.
Liabilities		
Equity Shares of Rs. 100 each	20,00,000	10,00,000
General Reseve 1.1.06	4,00,000	2,00,000
Profit and Loss A/c 1.1.06	1,00,000	60,000
Profit for the year 2006	2,00,000	80,000
Sundry Creditors	1,00,000	1,00,000
Bills Payable	30,000	10,000
	28,30,000	14,50,000

Assets	Rs.	Rs.
Land and Buildings	5,00,000	3,00,000
Plant and Machinery	5,00,000	6,00,000
Stock	1,50,000	1,00,000
Sundry Debtors	1,00,000	1,20,000
Investment in Shares of Canning & Co. Ltd.	10,00,000	—
Bills Receivable	80,000	10,000
Cash and Bank Balances	5,00,000	3,20,000
	28,30,000	14,50,000

(1) Bills Receivable of Anthony & Co. Ltd. includes Rs. 10,000 accepted by Canning & Co. Ltd.

(2) Sundry Debtors of Anthony & Co. Ltd. include Rs. 50,000 due from Canning & Co. Ltd.

(3) Stock of Canning & Co. Ltd. includes goods purchased from Anthony & Co. Ltd. for Rs. 60,000 which were invoiced by Anthony & Co. Ltd. at a profit of 25% on Cost.

Prepare a Consolidated Balance Sheet of Anthony & Co. Ltd. and its subsidiary Canning & Co. Ltd. **[C.A. Final, Adapted]**

36

REPORTING

- Good morning to you all.

☐ "Good morning Sir."

- Now I would like to discuss Management Reporting. I think you remember my lectures on Budgets and Budgetary Control where I discussed business philosophy. I explained there that sources of profit are — (i) Increase of sale (ii) Elimination of unnecessary expenditures (iii) Reduction of cost and (iv) Increase in business efficiency. All these sources of profit are co-related. If a business wants to earn higher or good profit it should keep constant and close watch on all the sources mentioned earlier. A setback in any one of the sources will have its repercussion on the other sources too. It is not possible to integrate all these aspects under suitable footing unless some media to co-ordinate all these information are developed. Reporting acts as a 'media' which helps the management to take its decision accoridngly. It should be noted in this connection that the pattern of reporting can be studied under three heads :

Sources of Profit

Scope of Study

(a) Report about the past activities

(b) Report about the present condition

(c) Report about forecast.

That is to say, Sale Forecast, Production Forecast, Purchase Forecast etc.

Now the point : To is whom reporting should be made at all the levels of activities? When a reporting goes from down to up it may be termed as Informative Report; similarly, when the same moves from up to down it may be termed as Directive Report :

Directive Report ↓ ↑ Informative Report

It is not always possible and desirable that the system of reporting should follow stereotyped principles, rather it should follow the course of line depending on the circumstances of the cases. However, it should be noted in this context that presentation of report follows two directions —

(i) Horizontal, and

(ii) Vertical.

Accordingly, from direction point of view, Reporting System may be classified under **Horizontal Report** and **Vertical Report**. Top management report is an example of Vertical Report. Directive and Informative Reports can be concentrated under the Vertical type of report. Floor level management report may be considered as Horizontal Report.

The whole reporting system can be explained as :

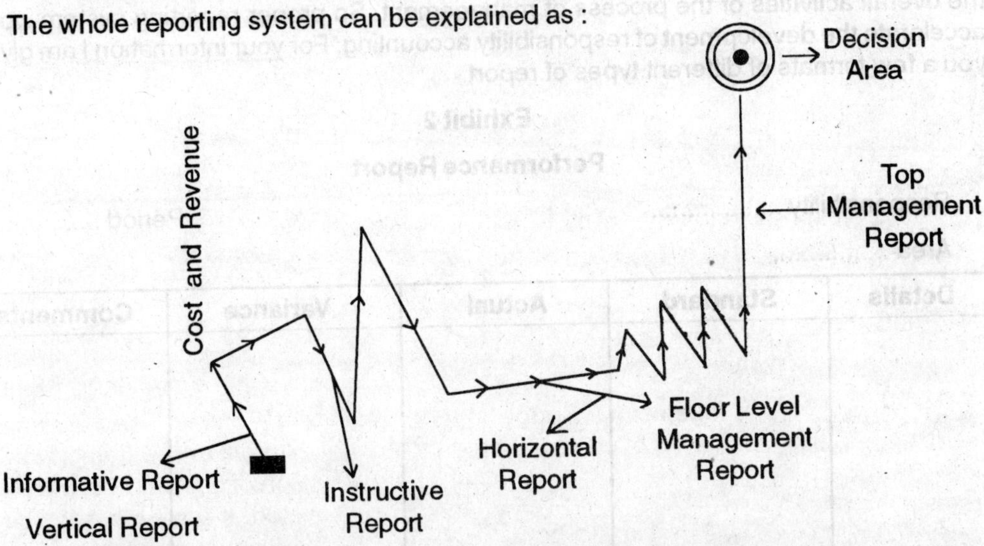

Pattern of Reporting

If the management services are to be improved, the lower level of management should be allowed to play a dynamic role. This will definitely help the top management to arrive at correct management decision. It is a fact that final management decision is to be taken by the top management. Now the point is, how can the lower level management assist the top management in arriving at the final decision? Besides the presentation of informative report which helps the top management in taking its final decision, the lower level management can assist the top management by way of Informative-cum-Suggesive Report. Take for an example, depending on the market research, in the frontier of sales carried out by the lower level of management, the top management produces a large quantity of goods; and suppose, a few days after, the market demand for the goods so produced falls—the loss arising from the overstock is not due to the wrong market research. It is the result of improper presentation of reporting system. The unforeseen losses could have been avoided if the market research report followed the principles of Informative-cum Suggestive Report.

Exhibit 1

Products	Past Records					Forecast		Suggestion
	1	2	3	4	5	Maxi.	Mini.	

It should be noted in this connection that proper reporting system relates the responsibilities of the persons who are working on their respective areas. It is a fact that proper reporting system would help the management to locate the 'area of responsibility'. If that be so it would assist the management to rectify only that area instead of scrutinising the overall activities of the process of management. So proper reporting system would accelerate the development of responsibility accounting. For your information I am giving you a few formats of different types of report.

Exhibit 2

Performance Report

Responsibility .... Period ....

Area ....

Details	Standard	Actual	Variance	Comments

Exhibit 3

Project Cost Report

Date .... Prepared by ....

Project Engineer ....

Suffix	Description	Appropriate Amount	Total Estimated Cost	Material Cost to date	Total	Physical % Complete
		Rs.	Rs.	Rs.	Rs.	

Reviewed with Project Engineer

....

Distribution

Date ....

(Source : National Association of Accountants — Accounting Practice Report 9)

Exhibit 4

Monthly Variance Report

	Actual	Better or Worse	Preformance %
	Rs.	Rs.	
Price Variance	***	***	%
Material Usage : Metal	***	(***)	%
Coating Materials	***	***	
Backing and Insulation	***	(***)	
Adhesive	***	(***)	
Total Material	***	***	
Direct Labour Costing	***	***	%
Indirect Assignment	***	(***)	
Down Time	***	(***)	
	***	***	%
Laminating	***	***	%
Indirect Assignment	***	***	
Down Time	***	***	
	***	***	%
Total Direct Labour	***	***	
Total Material and Direct Labour	***	***	%
Scrap			**% of Material and Direct Labour**
Natural		***	%
Spoiled Work		***	%
Total Scrap		***	%
Total Variances		***	Actual vs Planned

(Source : N.A.A. Bulletin)

Exhibit 5

Labour Efficiency Variance Report

Week Month ended ....20...............

Department	Actual Cost	Standard Cost	Variance
	Rs.	Rs.	Rs.

Exhibit 6

Direct Labour Hour Report

Dated ....

Departments	Total Direct Labour Hours	Direct Labour Hours	Productive Idle Direct Labour Hours	% of Hours Idle
A				
B				
C				
D				
Total				

Reasons for Idle Time :

Exhibit 7

Material Report

Excess Material Requisition

Date .... Dept. ....

Authorised by .... Received by ....

Quality	Code	Article	Price	Amount

Now I hope that you have understood the different forms of report. I shall be glad if you tell me frankly whether you have understood my previous lecture.

☐ "Yes Sir."

☐ "Sir, I shall be obliged if you kindly tell me **why management attaches too much importance on reporting system**."

● You see, management attaches too much imoportance because of :

(1) Controlling Current Operation

(2) Improving Efficiency

(3) Formulation of Policy and Decision-making.

Why Management Uses Report

It should be noted in this connection that the importance of reporting depends on the purpose for which it is designed. Because one report may be important and useful to a particular person or group of persons where it may be regarded as less important to the other group of persons. This does not necessarily indicate that one particular report is good or bad. That a report becomes good or bad depends on how the same has been designed to serve the purpose. However, the term 'reporting' should possess the characteristics of flexibility. Reporting should be adapted with all the changing condition of the business. Sound financial and other planning depends on the proper reporting of the different activities of the business. 'Management uses the reports to determine whether the execution of its work is proceeding according to plans and policies and to measure current performance against past experience and future objectives. The statement looks at backward reporting factual data to represent a correct picture of past events. It also looks onward, reporting past results as a guide to the future action of those responsible for the decisions on which the conduct of the organisation depends'. So it is clear that reporting should be designed to find out the total profit of the business and its relation with the other segments of the business. As already indicated earlier—the plans and policies of the business may come to a standstill and may collapsed if the plans and decisions are based on wrong report.

☐ "Sir, what should be the basis of report in order to eliminate the shortcomings arising therefrom?"

● Well, here, in this respect, I direct your attention to Mr. R. S. Laing's paper "Management Planning and Control", given at the Financial Executives Institute, Southern Area Conference, as appeared in "The Controller", May 1962. In this paper the basis of management report has been clearly defined :

(1) It must provide management, before a decision is made, with all the available data pertaining to the matter under review.

Basis of Management Report

(2) It must clearly define with repsect to the selected alternatives, the responsibility of each operating activity, and it must do so in sufficient detail so that actual results can be measured against the original plan and the responsibility for variances can be fixed.

(3) It must provide a reporting system to inform management of the progress of important programmes as to show up Variances in Time to permit corrective action.

I suppose you have understood the basis of Management Report.

☐ "Yes Sir."

☐ "Sir, what are the characteristics of a good report?"

● The characteristics of a good report are :

Characteristics of Good Report

(i) Simplicity

(ii) Promptness

(iii) Clarity and Brevity

(iv) Consistency, and finally,

(v) Cost.

☐ "Sir, in how many parts can report be classified?"

● Well, I have discussed all these parts while discussing the different formats of report. However, I am discussing the same in different ways :

Reporting

- **Marketing Report**
  - A Sales Control Report
  - Product-type Margin Contribution Report
  - Customer-type Margin Contribution Report
  - A Daily Sale and Margin Contribution Report
- **Cost Reporting**
  - Manufacturing Cost Report
  - Project Cost Report
- **Performance Reporting**
  - Labour Activity Report
  - Labour Efficiency Report
  - Employee Production Performance Report
  - Idle Machine Repot
  - Departmental Cost Summaries
- **Financial Reporting**
  - Profit and Loss Account
  - Balance Sheet

I think you have followd my lecture in above chart? Is there any question?

☐ "Sir, I have followed your lecture but I have one question to ask."

● What is your question?

☐ "Sir, what are different types of information that is, I mean, report are required for different hierarchy of management?"

● You see, it is the structure of the organisation which determine hierarchy of the management. For example in a small firm the hierarchy of management is sole proprietor or a group of persons (partners); incase of large scale organisation hierarchy of management are as follows :

1. Top level (Board of Directors, Chairman, Managing Directors, etc.)
2. Middle level (Different Departmental Managers, Zonal Managers, etc.)
3. Floor level (Foremen, Supervisor, Time keeper, Operative, etc.)

However, I am presenting here a flow chart of reporting to different hierarchy of management. It is important to note in this context that on the basis of different reports, prepared by the different persons serving at different levels of the organisation, top management generally arrive at the correct and final decision as well as also take the corrective measures to keep control over the different activities within the organisation.

Flow Chart of Reporting to Different Hierarchy of Management

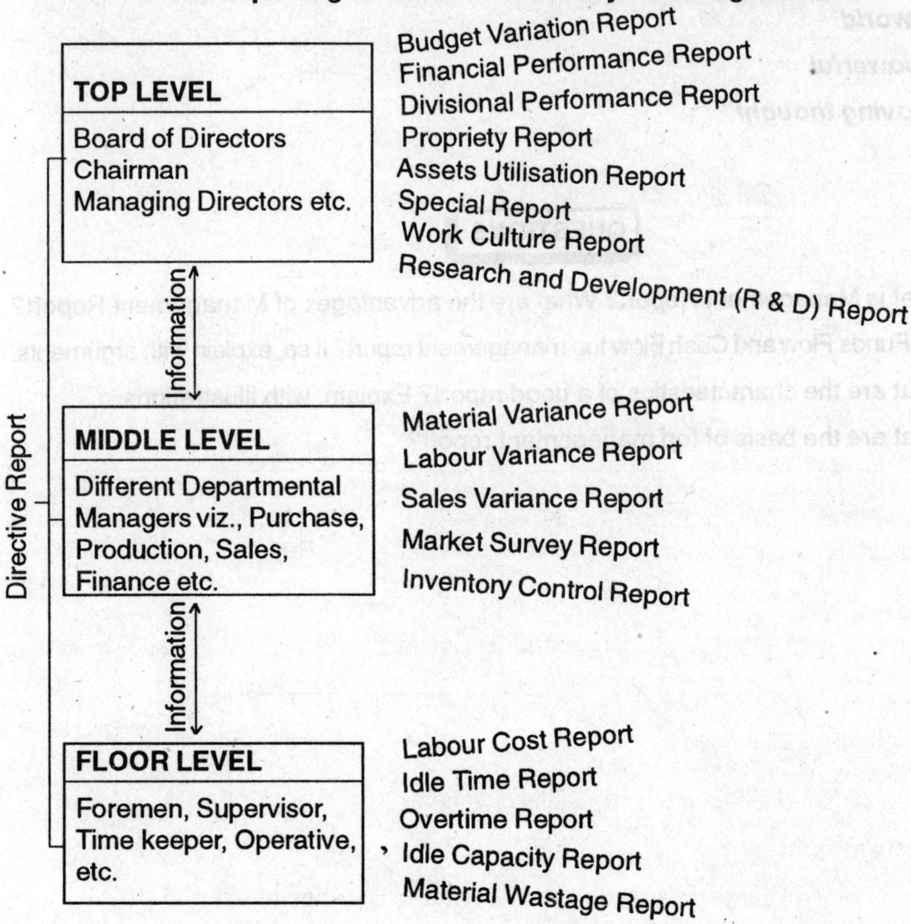

In the above chart you can have a view on transmission of different reports to the different hierarchy of management prepared at different levels within the same organisation. There is no denying the fact that the information contained in a report is vital for decision making process; it on the otherhand helps the management to pinpoint responsibility area of person entrusted for the same.

In totality the different reports are prepared at different levels of management responsible for their respective activities and it is transmitted to the different hierarchy of management to arrive at right decision at the right time for corrective measures.

Today, I conclude my lecture. I pray that all of you achieve success in life.

Goodbye to you all.

☐ "Sir, you will be remembered for your bright deliberation. You have made an abstruse subject very easy; we all will be benefitted.

Please Sir, give a message for us."

● Well, take down my message :

"There is no force

In the world

More powerful

Than loving thought".

Bye!

QUESTIONS

1. What is Management Report? What are the advantages of Management Report?
2. Are Funds Flow and Cash Flow top management report? If so, explain with arguments.
3. What are the characteristics of a good report? Explain, with illustrations.
4. What are the basis of top management report?

APPENDICES

APPENDIX 1

Present Value Tables

Table 1 : Present value of one rupee due at the end of *n* years @ *r*%

N	1%	2%	3%	4%	5%	6%	7%	8%	9%	10%
01	0.99010	0.98039	0.97007	0.96154	0.95238	0.94340	0.93458	0.92593	0.91743	0.90909
02	.98030	.96117	.94260	.92456	.90703	.89000	.87344	.85734	.84168	.82645
03	.97059	.94232	.91514	.88900	.86384	.83962	.81630	.79383	.77218	.75131
04	.96098	.92385	.88849	.85480	.82270	.79209	.76209	.73503	.70843	.68301
05	.95147	.90573	.86261	.82193	.78353	.74726	.71299	.68058	.64993	.62092
06	.94204	.88797	.83748	.79031	.74622	.70496	.66634	.63017	.59627	.56447
07	.93272	.87056	.81309	.75992	.71068	.66506	.62275	.58349	.54703	.51316
08	.92348	.85349	.78941	.73069	.67684	.62741	.58201	.54027	.50187	.46651
09	.91434	.83675	.76642	.70259	.64461	.59190	.54393	.50025	.46043	.42410
10	.90529	.82035	.74409	.67556	.61391	.55839	.50835	.46319	.42241	.38554
11	.89632	.80426	.72242	.64958	.58468	.52679	.47509	.42888	.38753	.35049
12	.88745	.78849	.70138	.62460	.55684	.49697	.44401	.39711	.35553	.31863
13	.87866	.77303	.68095	.60057	.53032	.46884	.41496	.36770	.32618	.28966
14	.86996	.75787	.66112	.57747	.50507	.44230	.38782	.34046	.29925	.26333
15	.86135	.74301	.64186	.55526	.48102	.41726	.36245	.31524	.27454	.23939
16	.85282	.72845	.62317	.53391	.45811	.39365	.33873	.29189	.25187	.21763
17	.84438	.71416	.60502	.51337	.43630	.37136	.31657	.27027	.23107	.19784
18	.83602	.70016	.58739	.49363	.41552	.35034	.29586	.25025	.21199	.17986
19	.82774	.68643	.57029	.47464	.39573	.33051	.27651	.23171	.19449	.16351
20	.81954	.67297	.55367	.45639	.37689	.31180	.25842	.21455	.17843	.14864
21	.81143	.65978	.53755	.43883	.35894	.29415	.24151	.19866	.16370	.13513
22	.80340	.64684	.52189	.42195	.34185	.27750	.22571	.18394	.15018	.13513
23	.79544	.63416	.50669	.40573	.32557	.26180	.21095	.17031	.13778	.11168
24	.78757	.62172	.49193	.39012	.31007	.24698	.19715	.15770	.12640	.10153
25	.77977	.60953	.47760	.37512	.29530	.23300	.18425	.14602	.11597	.09230

N	11%	12%	13%	14%	15%	16%	17%	18%	19%	20%
01	0.90090	0.89286	0.88496	0.86957	0.85470	0.86207	0.85470	0.84746	0.84034	0.83333
02	.81162	.79719	.78315	.76947	.75614	.74316	.73051	.71818	.70616	.69444
03	.73119	.71178	.69305	.67497	.65752	.64066	.62437	.60863	.59342	.57870
04	.65873	.63552	.61332	.59208	.57175	.55229	.53365	.51579	.49867	.48225
05	.59345	.56743	.54276	.51937	.49718	.47611	.45611	.43711	.41905	.40188
06	.53464	.50663	.48032	.45559	.43233	.41044	.38984	.37043	.35214	.33490
07	.48166	.45235	.42506	.39964	.37594	.35383	.33320	.31392	.29592	.27908
08	.43393	.40388	.37616	.35056	.32690	.30503	.28478	.26604	.24867	.23257
09	.39092	.36061	.33288	.30751	.28426	.26295	.24340	.22546	.20897	.19381
10	.35218	.32197	.29459	.26974	.24718	.22668	.20804	.19106	.17560	.16151
11	.31728	.28748	.26070	.23662	.21494	.19542	.17781	.16192	.14756	.13459
12	.28584	.25667	.23071	.20756	.18691	.16846	.15197	.13722	.12400	.11216
13	.25751	.22917	.20416	.18207	.16253	.14523	.12989	.11629	.10420	.09346
14	.23199	.20462	.18068	.15971	.14133	.12520	.11102	.09855	.08757	.07789
15	.20900	.18270	.15989	.14010	.12289	.10793	.09489	.08352	.07359	.06491
16	.18829	.16312	.14150	.12289	.10686	.09304	.08110	.07078	.06184	.05409
17	.16963	.14564	.112522	.10780	.09293	.08021	.06932	.05998	.05196	.04507
18	.15282	.13004	.11081	.09456	.08080	.06914	.05925	.05083	.04367	.03756
19	.13768	.11611	.09806	.08295	.07026	.05961	.05064	.04308	.03669	.03130
20	.12403	.10367	.08678	.07276	.06110	.05139	.04328	.03651	.03084	.02608
21	.11174	.09256	.07680	.06383	.05313	.04430	.03699	.03094	.02591	.02174
22	.10067	.08264	.06796	.05599	.04620	.03819	.03162	.02622	.02178	.01811
23	.09069	.07379	.06014	.04911	.04017	.03292	.02702	.02222	.01830	.01509
24	.08170	.06588	.05322	.04308	.03493	.02838	.02310	.01883	.01538	.01258
25	.07361	.05882	.04710	.03779	.03038	.02447	.01974	.01596	.01292	.01048

* *n* = number of years, *r* = rate of interest per annum

Present value of one rupee due at the end of *n* years @ @ *r*%

N	21%	22%	23%	24%	25%	26%	27%	28%	29%	30%
01	0.82645	0.81967	0.81301	0.80645	0.80000	0.79365	0.78740	0.78125	0.77519	0.76923
02	.68301	.67186	.66098	.65036	.64000	.62988	.62000	.61035	.60093	.59172
03	.56447	.55071	.53738	.52449	.51200	.49991	.48819	.47684	.46583	.45517
04	.46651	.45140	.43690	.42297	.40960	.39675	.38440	.37523	.36111	.35013
05	.38554	.37000	.35520	.34111	.32768	.31488	.30268	.29104	.27993	.26933
06	.31863	.30328	.28878	.27509	.26214	.24991	.23833	.22737	.21700	.20718
07	.26333	.24859	.23478	.22184	.20972	.19834	.18766	.17764	.16822	.15937
08	.21763	.20376	.19088	.17891	.16777	.15741	.14776	.13878	.13040	.12259
09	.17986	.16702	.15519	.14428	.13422	.12493	.11635	.10842	.10109	.09430
10	.14864	.13690	.12617	.11635	.10737	.09915	.09161	.08470	.07836	.07254
11	.12285	.11221	.10258	.9383	.8590	.07869	.07214	.06617	.06075	.05580
12	.10153	.09198	.08339	.07567	.06872	.06245	.05680	.05170	.04709	.04292
13	.08391	.07539	.06780	.06103	.05498	.04957	.04472	.04039	.03650	.03302
14	.06934	.06180	.05512	.04912	.04398	.03934	.03522	.03155	.02830	.02540
15	.05731	.05065	.04481	.03969	.03518	.03122	.02773	.02465	.02194	.01954
16	.04736	.04152	.03643	.03201	.02815	.02478	.02183	.01926	.01700	.01503
17	.03914	.03403	.02962	.02581	.02252	.01967	.01719	.01505	.01318	.01156
18	.03235	.02789	.02408	.02082	.01801	.01561	.01354	.01175	.01022	.00889
19	.02673	.02286	.01958	.01679	.01441	.01239	.01066	.00918	.00792	.0068
20	.02209	.01874	.01592	.01354	.01153	.00983	.00839	.00717	.00614	.0052
21	.01826	.01536	.01294	.01092	.00922	.00780	.00661	.00561	.00476	.00405
22	.01509	.01239	.01052	.00880	.00738	.00619	.00520	.00438	.00369	.00311
23	.01247	.01032	.00855	.00710	.00590	.00491	.00410	.00342	.00286	.00239
24	.01031	.00846	.00695	.00573	.00472	.00390	.00323	.00267	.00222	.00184
25	.00852	.00693	.00565	.00462	.00378	.00310	.00254	.00209	.00172	.00142

N	31%	32%	33%	34%	35%	36%	37%	38%	39%	40%
01	0.76336	0.75758	0.75188	0.74627	0.74040	0.73529	0.72993	0.72464	0.71942	0.71429
02	.58272	.57392	.56532	.55692	.54870	.54066	.53279	.52510	.51757	.51020
03	.44482	.43479	.42505	.41561	.40644	.39754	.38890	.38051	.37235	.36443
04	.33956	.32939	.31959	.31016	.30107	.29231	.28387	.27573	.26788	.26031
05	.25920	.24953	.24029	.23146	.22301	.21439	.20720	.19980	.19272	.18593
06	.19787	.18904	.18067	.17273	.16520	.15804	.15124	.14479	.13865	.13281
07	.15104	.14321	.13584	.12890	.12237	.11621	.11040	.10492	.09975	.09486
08	.11530	.10849	.10214	.09620	.09064	.08545	.08058	.07603	.07176	.06776
09	.08802	.08219	.07680	.07179	.06714	.06283	.05882	.05509	.05163	.04840
10	.06719	.06227	.05774	.05357	.04973	.04620	.04293	.03992	.03714	.03457
11	.05129	.04717	.04341	.03998	.03684	.03397	.03134	.02893	.02672	.02469
12	.03915	.03574	.03264	.02984	.02729	.02498	.02287	.02096	.01922	.01764
13	.02989	.02707	.02454	.02227	.02021	.01837	.01670	.01519	.01383	.01260
14	.02281	.02051	.01845	.01662	.01497	.01350	.01219	.01101	.00995	.00900
15	.01742	.01554	.01387	.01240	.01109	.00993	.00890	.00798	.00716	.00643
16	.01329	.01177	.01043	.00925	.00822	.00730	.00649	.00578	.00515	.00459
17	.01015	.00892	.00784	.00691	.00609	.00537	.00474	.00419	.00370	.00328
18	.00775	.00676	.00590	.00515	.00451	.00395	.00346	.00304	.00367	.00234
19	.00591	.00512	.00443	.00385	.00334	.00290	.00253	.00220	.00192	.00167
20	.00451	.00388	.00333	.00287	.00247	.00213	.00184	.00159	.00138	.00120
21	.00345	.00294	.00251	.00214	.00183	.00157	.00135	.00115	.00099	.00085
22	.00263	.00223	.00188	.00160	.00136	.00115	.00098	.00084	.00017	.00016
23	.00201	.00169	.00142	.00119	.00101	.00085	.00072	.00061	.00051	.00044
24	.00153	.00128	.00107	.00089	.00074	.00062	.00052	.00044	.00037	.00031
25	.00117	.00097	.00080	.00066	.00055	.00046	.00038	.00032	.00027	.00022

APPENDIX 2

Table 2 : Present value of one rupee due at the end of *n* years @ *r*%

N	1%	2%	3%	4%	5%	6%	7%	8%	9%	10%
01	0.9901	0.9804	0.9709	0.9615	0.9524	0.9434	0.9346	0.9259	0.9174	0.9091
02	1.9704	1.9416	1.9134	1.8861	1.8594	1.8334	1.8080	1.7833	1.7591	1.7355
03	2.9410	2.8838	2.8286	2.7751	2.7232	2.6730	2.6243	2.5771	2.5313	2.4868
04	3.9020	3.8077	3.6299	3.6299	3.5459	3.4651	3.3872	3.3121	3.2397	3.1699
05	4.8535	4.7134	4.5797	4.4518	4.3295	4.2123	4.1002	3.9927	3.8896	3.7908
06	5.7955	5.6014	5.4172	5.2421	5.0757	4.9173	4.7665	4.6229	4.4859	4.3553
07	6.7282	6.4720	6.2302	6.0020	5.7863	5.5824	5.3893	5.2064	5.0329	5.8684
08	7.6517	7.3254	7.0196	6.7327	6.4632	6.2098	5.9713	5.7466	5.5348	5.3349
09	8.5661	8.1622	7.7861	7.4353	7.1078	6.8017	6.5152	6.2469	6.9852	5.7590
10	9.4714	8.9825	8.5302	8.1109	7.7217	7.3601	7.0236	6.7101	6.4176	6.1446
11	10.3677	9.7868	9.2526	8.7604	8.3064	7.8868	7.4987	7.1389	6.8052	6.4951
12	11.2552	10.5753	9.9539	9.3850	8.8632	8.3838	7.9427	7.5361	7.1607	6.8137
13	12.1338	11.3483	10.6349	9.9856	9.3935	8.8527	8.3576	7.9038	7.4869	7.1034
14	13.0038	12.1062	11.2960	10.5631	9.8986	9.2950	8.7454	8.2442	7.7861	7.3667
15	13.8651	12.8492	11.9379	11.1183	10.3796	9.7122	9.1079	8.5595	8.0607	7.6061
16	14.7180	13.5777	12.5610	11.6522	10.8377	10.1059	9.4466	8.8514	8.3125	7.8237
17	15.5624	14.2918	13.1660	12.1656	11.2740	10.4772	9.7632	9.1216	9.5436	8.0215
18	16.3984	14.9920	13.7534	12.6592	11.6895	10.8276	10.0591	9.3719	8.7556	8.2014
19	17.2261	15.6784	14.3227	13.1339	12.0853	11.1581	10.3356	9.6036	8.9501	8.3649
20	18.0457	16.3514	14.8774	13.5903	12.4622	11.4699	10.5940	9.8181	9.1285	8.5136
21	18.8571	17.0111	15.4149	14.0291	12.8211	11.7640	10.8355	10.0168	9.2922	8.6487
22	19.6605	17.6580	15.9368	14.4511	13.1630	12.0416	11.0612	10.2007	9.4424	8.7715
23	20.4559	18.2921	16.4435	14.8568	13.4885	12.3033	11.2722	10.3710	9.5802	8.8832
24	21.2435	18.9139	16.9355	15.2496	13.7986	12.5503	11.4693	10.5287	9.7066	8.9847
25	22.0233	19.5234	17.4131	15.6220	14.0939	12.7833	11.6536	10.6748	9.2286	9.0770

N	11%	12%	13%	14%	15%	16%	17%	18%	19%	20%
01	0.9009	0.8929	0.8850	0.8772	0.8696	0.8621	0.8547	0.4875	0.8403	0.8333
02	1.7125	1.6901	1.6681	1.6467	1.6257	1.6052	1.5852	1.5656	1.5465	1.5278
03	2.4437	2.4018	2.3612	2.3216	2.2832	2.2459	2.2096	2.1743	2.1399	2.1065
04	3.1024	3.0373	2.9745	2.9137	2.8550	2.7982	2.7432	2.6901	2.6386	2.8557
05	3.6959	3.6048	3.5172	3.4331	3.3522	3.2743	3.1993	3.1272	3.0576	2.9906
06	4.2305	4.1114	3.9976	3.8887	3.7845	3.8647	3.5892	3.4976	3.4098	3.3255
07	4.7122	4.5638	4.4226	4.2883	4.1604	4.0386	3.9224	3.8115	3.7067	3.6046
08	5.1461	4.9676	4.7988	4.6389	4.4873	4.3463	4.2072	4.0776	3.9544	3.8372
09	5.5370	5.3282	5.1317	4.9464	4.7716	4.6065	4.4506	4.3030	4.1633	4.0310
10	5.8892	5.6502	5.4262	5.2161	5.0188	4.8332	4.6586	4.4941	4.3389	4.1925
11	6.2065	5.9377	5.6869	5.4527	5.2337	5.0286	4.8364	4.6560	4.4865	4.3271
12	6.4924	6.1944	5.9176	5.6603	5.4206	5.1971	4.9884	4.7932	4.6105	4.4392
13	6.7499	6.4235	6.1218	5.8424	5.5831	5.3423	5.1183	4.9095	4.7147	4.5327
14	6.9819	6.6282	6.3025	6.0021	5.7245	5.4675	5.2293	5.0081	4.8023	4.6106
15	7.1909	6.8109	6.4624	6.1422	5.8474	5.5755	5.3242	5.0916	4.8759	4.6755
16	7.3792	6.9740	6.7940	6.2659	5.9542	5.6685	5.4053	5.1624	4.9377	4.7296
17	7.5488	7.1196	6.2791	6.3724	6.0457	5.7487	5.4746	5.223	4.9897	4.7746
18	7.7046	7.2497	6.8399	6.4674	6.1280	5.8178	5.5339	5.2732	5.0333	4.8122
19	7.8393	7.3658	6.9380	6.5501	6.1982	5.8775	5.5845	5.3162	5.0700	5.8435
20	7.9633	7.4694	7.0248	6.6230	6.2693	5.9288	5.6278	5.3627	5.1009	4.8696
21	8.0751	7.5620	7.1016	6.8679	6.3125	5.9731	5.6648	5.3837	5.1268	4.8913
22	8.1757	7.6446	7.1695	6.7421	6.3587	6.0113	5.6964	5.4099	5.1486	5.9094
23	8.2664	7.1784	7.2297	6.7921	6.3988	6.0442	5.7234	5.4321	5.1668	4.9245
24	8.3481	7.7843	7.2829	6.8358	6.4338	6.0726	5.7465	5.4509	5.1822	4.9317
25	8.4217	7.8431	7.3300	6.8729	6.4641	6.0971	5.662	5.4669	5.1951	4.9476

Present value of one rupee due at the end of *n* years @ *r*%

N	21%	22%	23%	24%	25%	26%	27%	28%	29%	30%
01	0.8264	0.8197	0.8130	0.8065	0.8000	0.7937	0.7874	0.7813	0.7752	0.7692
02	1.5095	1.4915	1.4740	1.4568	1.4400	1.4235	1.4074	1.3916	1.3761	1.3609
03	2.0739	2.0422	2.0114	1.9813	1.9520	1.9234	1.8956	1.8684	1.8420	1.8161
04	2.5404	2.4936	2.4483	2.4043	2.3616	2.3202	2.2800	2.5320	2.4830	2.4356
05	2.9260	2.8636	2.8035	2.7454	2.6893	2.6351	2.5827	2.5320	2.4830	2.4356
06	3.2445	3.1669	3.0923	3.0205	2.9514	2.8850	2.8210	2.7594	2.7000	2.6427
07	3.5079	3.4155	3.3270	3.2423	3.1611	3.0833	3.0087	3.9370	2.8682	2.8021
08	3.7256	3.6193	3.5179	3.4212	3.3289	3.2407	3.1564	3.0758	2.9986	2.9247
09	3.9054	3.7863	3.6731	3.5655	3.4631	3.3657	3.2728	3.1842	3.0997	3.0190
10	4.0541	3.9232	3.7993	3.6819	3.5705	3.4648	3.3644	3.2689	3.1781	3.0915
11	4.1769	4.0354	3.9018	3.7757	3.6564	3.5435	3.4365	3.3351	3.2388	3.1473
12	4.2785	4.1274	3.9852	3.8514	3.7251	3.6060	3.4933	3.3351	3.2859	3.1903
13	4.3624	4.2028	4.0530	3.9124	3.7801	3.6555	3.6381	3.4272	3.3224	3.2233
14	4.4317	4.2646	4.1082	3.9616	3.8241	3.6949	3.5733	3.4587	3.3507	3.2487
15	4.4890	4.3152	4.1530	4.0013	3.8593	3.7261	3.6010	3.4834	3.3726	3.2682
16	4.5364	4.3567	4.1894	4.0333	3.8874	3.7509	3.6228	3.5026	3.3896	3.2832
17	4.5755	4.3908	4.2190	4.0591	3.9099	3.7705	3.6400	3.5177	3.4028	3.2948
18	4.6079	4.4187	4.2431	4.0799	3.9279	3.7861	3.6536	3.5294	3.4130	3.3037
19	4.6346	4.4415	4.2627	4.0967	3.9424	3.7985	3.6642	3.5386	3.4210	3.3105
20	4.6567	4.4603	4.2786	4.1103	3.9539	3.8083	3.6726	3.5458	3.4271	3.3158
21	4.6750	4.4756	4.2916	4.1212	3.9631	3.8161	3.6792	3.5514	3.4319	3.3198
22	4.6900	4.4882	4.3021	4.1300	3.9705	3.8223	3.6844	3.5558	3.4356	3.3230
23	4.7025	4.4985	4.3106	4.1371	3.9764	3.8273	3.6885	3.5592	3.4384	3.3254
24	4.7128	4.5070	4.3176	4.1428	3.9811	3.8312	3.6918	3.5619	3.4406	3.3272
25	4.7213	4.5139	4.3232	4.1474	3.9849	3.8342	3.6943	3.5640	3.4423	3.3286

N	31%	32%	33%	34%	35%	36%	37%	38%	39%	40%
01	0.6734	0.7576	0.7519	0.7463	0.7407	0.7353	0.7299	0.7246	0.7194	0.7143
02	1.3461	1.3315	1.3172	1.3032	1.2894	1.2760	1.2627	1.2497	1.2370	1.2245
03	1.7909	1.7663	1.7423	1.7188	1.6959	1.6735	1.6516	1.6302	1.6093	1.5889
04	2.1305	2.0957	2.0618	2.0290	1.9969	1.9658	1.9355	1.9060	1.8772	1.8492
05	2.3897	2.3452	2.3021	2.2602	2.2200	2.1807	2.1427	2.1058	2.0699	2.0352
06	2.5875	2.5342	2.4728	2.4331	2.3852	2.3388	2.2939	2.2506	2.2086	2.1680
07	2.7386	2.6775	2.6187	2.5620	2.5075	2.4550	2.4043	2.3555	2.3083	2.2628
08	2.8539	2.7860	2.7208	2.6582	2.5982	2.5404	2.4849	2.4315	2.3801	2.3306
09	2.9419	2.8681	2.7967	2.7300	2.6653	2.6033	2.5437	2.4866	2.4817	2.3790
10	3.0091	2.9304	2.8553	2.7836	2.7150	2.6475	2.5867	2.5265	2.4689	2.4136
11	3.0604	2.9776	2.8987	2.8236	2.7519	2.6834	2.6180	2.5555	2.4956	2.4383
12	3.0995	3.0133	2.9314	2.8534	2.7792	2.7084	2.6409	2.5764	2.5148	2.4559
13	3.1294	3.0404	2.9559	2.8757	2.7994	2.7268	2.6576	2.5916	2.5286	2.4685
14	3.1522	3.0609	2.9744	2.8923	2.8144	2.7403	2.6698	2.6026	2.5386	2.5775
15	3.1696	3.0764	2.9883	2.9047	2.8255	2.7502	2.6787	2.6106	2.5457	2.4839
16	3.1829	3.0882	3.9987	2.9140	2.8337	2.7575	2.6852	2.6164	2.5509	2.4885
17	3.1931	3.0971	3.0065	3.9209	2.8398	2.7629	2.6899	2.6206	2.5546	2.4918
18	3.2008	3.1039	3.0124	2.9260	2.8483	2.7668	2.6934	2.6263	2.5573	2.4941
19	3.2067	3.1090	3.0169	2.9299	2.8476	2.7697	2.6959	2.6258	2.5592	2.4958
20	3.2112	3.1129	3.0202	2.9327	2.8501	2.7718	2.6977	2.6274	2.5606	2.4970
21	3.2147	3.1158	3.0227	2.9349	2.8519	2.7734	2.6991	2.6285	2.5616	2.4979
22	3.2173	3.1180	3.0246	2.9365	2.8533	2.7746	2.7000	2.6294	2.5623	2.4985
23	3.2193	3.1197	3.0260	2.9377	2.8543	2.7754	2.7008	2.6300	2.5628	2.4989
24	3.2209	3.1210	3.0271	2.9386	2.8550	2.7760	2.7013	2.6304	2.5632	2.4992
25	3.2220	3.1220	3.0279	2.9392	2.8556	2.7765	2.7017	2.6307	2.5634	2.4994

BIBLIOGRAPHY

American Technical Society : Financial Management and Control.

Anthony : (i) Management Accounting — Principles.

(ii) Management Accounting — Test and Cases.

Basu : Accounting for Goodwill.

Batty : Management Accountancy.

Batty (Ed.) : Development in Management Accountancy.

Batty (Ed.) : Cost and Management Accountancy for Students.

Baxter (Ed.) : Studies in Accounting.

Bray : (i) Precision and Design in Accountancy.

(ii) Four Essays in Accounting Theory.

Bogen (Ed.) : Financial Hand Book,

Broad and Carmichael : A Guide to Management Accounting.

Bigg and Davies : Internal Auditing.

Briggs : Devaluation and Appreciation of Fixed Corporate Plant — From the Standpoint of Accounting.

Brown and Howard : Principles of Management Accountancy.

B. I. M. : (i) Application of Production Control.

(ii) Accounts for Management.

(iii) Interfirm Comparison.

Carroll : Overhead Cost Control.

Carsberg : Introduction to Management Accounting.

Carsberg and Edey : Modern Financial Management.

Chandra P. : Financial Management : Theory and Practice.

Chambers : Financial Management.

Creecy : Cost Accounting Simplified.

Currie : Financial Incentives.

Dickey : Cost Hand Book.

de Paula : Management Accounting in Practice.

Dobson : Management Information and Accounting.

Donnelly : Profit Through Cost Analysis and Direct Costing.

Evens-Hemming : Flexible Budgetary Control and Standard Costs.

Fisher : Cash Management.

Finney and Miller : (i) Principles of Accounting—Introductory

(ii) Principles of Accounting—Intermediate

(iii) Principles of Accounting—Advanced.

Foster : Understanding Financial Statements and Corporate Annual Reports.

Garbutt : Planning for Profit.

Gillespie : Standard and Direct Costing.

Gole : Accounting for Businessman.

Guthmann and Dougall : Corporate Financial Policy.

Gordon and Shillinglaw : Accounting : A Management Approach.

Harper : Management Accounting.

Harrell : Industrial Psychology.

Hadley (Editorial Staff) : Applied Bookkeeping.

Hadley : An Introduction to Business Acounting for Managers.

Horngren, Datar and Foster : Cost Accounting : A Managerial Emphasis.

House (Jr.) : Sensitivity Analysis in Making Capital Investment Decisions.

Howard : Principles of Auditing.

Holmes : Auditing — Principles and Procedure.

Irwin : Principles of Auditing.

Hunt and Others : Measuring the Cost of New Capital Funds.

I.C.W.A. (London) : (i) An Introduction to Budgetary Control, Standard Costing, Material and Production Control.
(ii) The Profitable use of Capital in Industry.
(iii) The Accountancy of changing Price Level.
(iv) A Report on Marginal Costing.

Irish : Current Development in Corporate Accounting.

ILO (Geneva) : How to Read a Balance Sheet.

Jaedicke and Sprouse : Accounting Flows : Income, Funds and Cash.

Johnson : Financial Management.

Jones : Guide to Company Balance-Sheet and Profit and Loss Accounts.

Jones and Trentin : Budgeting : Key to Planning and Control.

Keller and Ferrara : Management Accounting for Profit Control.

Lang : Cost Accountants' Hand Book.

Lerner : Managerial Finance.

Lipken and Others : Accountants' Hand Book of Formulas and Tables.

Lindsay and Sametz : Financial Management.

Littleton : Structure of Accounting Theory.

Lynch : Accounting for Management.

Marple : Towards a Basic Accounting Philosophy.

Matz and Others : Cost Accounting.

Mason : "Cash Flow" Analysis and the Funds Statement.

McFarland : Concepts for Management Accounting.

Mead : Corporation Finance.

Mikesell : Governmental Accounting.

Moonitz : The Entity Theory of Consolidated Statements.

Moore and Jaedicke : Managerial Accounting.

Most : Uniform Cost Accounting.

Murphy : Managerial Accounting.

Myer : Financial Statement Analysis.

N.A.A. : (i) Financial Analysis to Guide Capital Expenditure Decisions.

(ii) Financial Analysis Techniques for Equipment Replacement Decision.

(iii) The Analysis of Cost-Volume-Profit Analysis.

(iv) Return on Capital as a Guide to Management Decision.

(v) Cash Flow Analysis for Managerial Control.

(vi) Reports which Management Find Most Useful.

(vii) Development and Reporting Variances.

(viii) The Capital Expenditure Control Program.

(ix) Control of Maintenace Cost.

Newmaan and Logan : Business Policies and Central Management.

Paish : Business Finance.

Pandy I. M. : Financial Management.

Paton and Dixon : Essentials of Accounting.

Paton and Littleton : Corporate Accounting Standards.

Rauenstrauch and Villers : The Economics of Industrial Management.

Parkinson : (i) Acounting Ratios in Theory and Practice.

(ii) Ordinary Shares.

Pickles : Accountancy.

Roberts : Management Note Book.

Rose : (i) Top Management Accounting.

(ii) The Management Audit.

(iii) Higher Control in Management.

Rorem and Kerrigan : Accounting Method.

Roy : A Survey of Accounting Ideas.

Sarkar : Management Accountancy.

Savage and Small : Introduction to Managerial Economics.

Sengupta : (i) Accounting Theories.

(ii) Advanced Accounting.

Shome and Banerjee : Cost Audit Manual.

Sizer : An Insight into Management Accounting.

Smith : (i) Mangement Control Information.

(ii) The Effects of Taxation on Corporate Financial Policy.

Spicer and Pegler : Book-keeping and Accounts.

Stephan : Possibilities of the Use of Cost Accounting in Public Budget Making.

Sollenberger : Major Changes caused by the Implementation of A Management Information System.

Stigler : Capital and Rate of Return in Manufacturing Industries.

Souster : Integrated Cost and Financial Accounts.

Sur : (i) Principles of Corporate Finance.

(ii) Principles of Business Finance.

Sweeney : Stabilized Accounting.

Thomas : Readings in Cost Accounting and Control.

Tovey and de Paula : Balance Sheets.

Vickery : Principles and Practice of Book-keeping and Accounts.

Walker and Saugher : Financial Planning and Policy.

Welsch : Budgeting Profit Planning and Control.

Wilk : Accounting for Inflation.

Wheldon's : (i) Cost Accounting and Costing Methods.

(ii) Costing Simplified.

Wright : Discounted Cash Flow.

Woods : Accounting for Capital Construction, and Maintenance Expenditure.

Yorstons and Others : Advanced Accounting.

Zeyner : Cost Reduction in the Plant.

Journals and Other Publications :

Accountant.
Capital.
Finance and Society.
Indian Companies Act, 1956.
Management Accounting (N.A.A.)
The Chartered Accountant.
The Management Accountant (Kolkata and London).

INDEX

D

Some exciting gifts are up for grabs with this book!!

LECTURES ON MANAGEMENT ACCOUNTANCY

Professor Dr B. K. Basu

FREE Gifts Rs. 1000/-

DEAR READERS

By now you must have gone through this book in the entirety. So we invite your assessment on this title with absolute impartiality and candid observations. After all, we publishers blindly depend on your benchmarking. Friends, please fill up the open spaces below with CAPITAL LETTERS. You may add some extra sheets of paper if the space provided is not sufficient for you.

i. What are the important topics of your syllabus which are not adequately covered in this book?

ii. In which chapters and on what topics the treatment of the subject-matter by the author is not satisfactory and why?

iii. Have you come across the typos, factual inaccuracies, inconsistencies, and other forms of mistakes in the book? If yes, then please specify the mistakes and page numbers.

iv. Name top three books on the same subject, which, in your consideration, are better than this book. Could you provide some reasons?

Your 1st Preference: ....

Your 2nd Preference: ....

Your 3rd Preference: ....

v. Any suggestion to improve the quality of illustrations, diagrams etc.?

vi. How did you like the cover design? Any suggestions on colours?

vii. Suggestions for further improvement of production standard:

viii. Who recommended you this book:

☐ Teacher ☐ Friend ☐ Parents ☐ Bookseller ☐ Librarian

ix. Name of the person who has recommended:

Designation: ....

Address: ....

Phone No.: ....

e-mail: ....

x. Name and address of the bookseller from whom you have purchased this book:

....

....

....

xi. Name and address of the library where you would like to find the book:

....

....

xii. Name and address of your institution (Please mention the University or Board):

....

....

xiii. Your name, e-mail, and complete postal address:

....

....

....

xiv. A few other titles published by us that you would like to read:

....

....

The best assessment will be rewarded half-yearly. The award will be in the form of our publications, as decided by the Editorial and Marketing Operations Division, amounting to Rs. 1000/- (Rupees one thousand) only.

....

Please mail the filled up coupon at your earliest to :

Editorial & Marketing Operations Division

NEW CENTRAL BOOK AGENCY (P) LTD

8/1 Chintamoni Das Lane, Kolkata 700 009

West Bengal, INDIA

Ph. No.: 033 + 22418411, 22418573, 22419094

Fax: 033 + 22419573, 22413852

e-mail: ncbapvtltd@eth.net, ncba@cal2.vsnl.net.in

Website: www.centralgroup.com